Freedom of Information Law in China

Yong Tang

Freedom of Information Law in China

From Imperial Court Diaries to Open Government Information Regulations

palgrave
macmillan

Yong Tang
School of Communication and Media
College of Fine Arts
and Communication
Western Illinois University
Macomb, IL, USA

ISBN 978-981-96-7841-9 ISBN 978-981-96-7842-6 (eBook)
https://doi.org/10.1007/978-981-96-7842-6

This Palgrave Macmillan imprint is published by the registered company Springer Nature Singapore Pte Ltd.
The registered company address is: 152 Beach Road, #21-01/04 Gateway East, Singapore 189721, Singapore

This book is the result of the author's extensive research on Chinese freedom of information over many years. Over the past 16 years, the author has completed a PhD dissertation, presented numerous conference papers, and published nearly 10 journal articles. The doctoral thesis, along with the majority of these publications, focuses on China's national freedom of information law. In writing this book, the author reorganized and edited these materials to varying degrees. Some sections underwent substantial revisions, while others received only minor updates, depending on the relevance and validity of the original content. Certain parts of the text may resemble or replicate the original material, which has been included with the permission of the editors at Palgrave Macmillan. Each chapter clearly indicates the sources drawn from these previous works, in an effort to maintain transparency and avoid self-plagiarism.

Foreword

What is the role of law in an autocracy? Is law merely a mask to disguise the exercise of pure political power? A counterfeit ticket for admission to the community of nations? Or just another tool to suppress civil and human rights?

Law in People's Republic of China suffers from all these infirmities, and yet.... Law is essential for the economic development of its vast territory. For the stability of its enormous population. And for the supervision of its huge bureaucracy. Law may not rule in China, but not even an all-powerful Communist Party can rule without it.

And media law in particular? The Chinese government and Party exercise total control of the mass media. An army of censors patrols the internet. Reporters and editors routinely self-censor to stay within established boundaries (generally, the freedom to criticize anyone below you), or face arrest and imprisonment. Laws protecting journalists' right to report and the people's concomitant right to know have enjoyed periods of popularity in the PRC—especially in the 1980s, before the 1989 Tiananmen Square episode—but not today.

Except, perhaps, in one aspect of media law: the law providing journalists and all citizens the right of access to government-held information—within limits, of course. In China, where a culture of state secrecy evolved over millennia, freedom of information law is alive and reasonably well. That alone makes it a vital area of study.

Few scholars are as well positioned to undertake that study as Dr. Yong Tang, a veteran of the People's Daily, protégé of some of the finest media law scholars in the country, and professor of media law in both the U.S. and China. Dr. Tang's comprehensive survey of Chinese freedom of information law tackles four basic questions: How did China come to adopt access regulations in the first place? How do the Chinese regulations compare with international standards? What exemptions apply to limit access? And how did the Chinese media contribute to formulating those regulations?

Dr. Tang's analysis introduces the Western concept of transparency as it developed from the 18th to the 20th Century. He then takes the reader on an excursion through Chinese history, from before the Qin to the present day, tracing the evolution from secrecy to qualified transparency. A detailed analysis of contemporary access law follows, then an assessment of its application and effectiveness. Dr. Tang concludes with an appraisal of the role of news media in developing and implementing the law, enforcement or the lack thereof, and recommendations for reform. The book also includes a thorough bibliography and appendix of tables.

For those of us who have lived and worked in China, especially as teachers of journalism and law, this book is indispensable. On the subject of access to information, it is definitive. On the subject of law in China, it is revelatory.

Dr. Eric B. Easton
Professor of Law Emeritus
University of Baltimore School of Law
Baltimore, USA

Preface

Thousands of years ago, imperial court diaries were established to hold Chinese emperors accountable. It worked in a way that national free of information laws do for powerful government officials today. Under the imperial diary system, two highly educated officials shadowed the emperor daily and wrote quickly into a diary the emperor's actions and words. Their entries captured minute details, including when, where and for how long the monarch would sleep with his concubines. The raw materials from the diary served as the foundation for the officially sanctioned historical narrative, written by historians within the emperor's dynasty and the succeeding dynasty. Generations of scholars and scholar-officials across the country would then study the narrative and pass judgment on the emperor's governance and qualifications.

Imperial court diaries and remonstrators from the Censorate during the reign of Emperor Taizong of Tang Dynasty (626 AD–649 AD) inspired Sweden to create the world's first freedom of information law in 1766, known as the Freedom of the Press Act. The legislation established a legal right for Swedish citizens to access government-held documents and files. China then waited for 1,400 years for freedom of information to return to its hometown. In 2007, China enacted its first national freedom of information law, known as the Regulations of the People's Republic of China on Open Government Information. For the first time in the history of the People's Republic of China, ordinary citizens are given the right to apply for governmental information and challenge denials in court. The country has made remarkable progress in governmental transparency since the enforcement of the freedom of information law in 2008. Yet, a deeply ingrained culture of secrecy continues to shadow these advancements. This became evident during the global COVID-19 pandemic, when the country failed to disclose critical public health information proactively and reactively in 2020–2021, thus hindering efforts to contain the virus.

China's approach to freedom of information is a complex puzzle, rife with contradictions. As the world's second largest economy, a country with both authoritarian and libertarian traditions, a leader in digital communication and artificial intelligence, and home to one of the most censored media environments globally, China should never be ignored or simply delinked from. What it does at home and abroad in government transparency has profound international implications and consequences.

This book, authored by an American journalism professor and former journalist from China, offers an insider's perspective on China's political, legal, cultural, and media systems. Focusing particularly on China's freedom of information law, it guides readers through an immersive exploration of Chinese society, unraveling the complexities and nuances of its information freedoms, layer by layer.

Macomb, USA

Yong Tang

A Note on Citation Style

This book adopts the Bluebook system of citation because of the general writing inspired by Bluebook, because of the large amounts of details both in the footnotes and in the main text, and also because of the fact that Bluebook is a widely used legal citation system for legal research. However, Bluebook style is cumbersome for a lengthy English-language book that contains large volumes of Chinese-language materials (e.g., party directives, government reports, statutes, newspapers, journals, books). Hence, it is necessary, without harming the quality and integrity of the research, to modify the citation style to be more appropriate and reader-friendly for a work of this size and nature.

Bluebook style is used in this book for the text and footnotes with the following modifications: All statutes and court cases are italicized, no matter they are Chinese or foreign. No internal cross-references and short form citations such as Id, Supra, Infra and hereinafter are used. Names of journals and other periodicals are not abbreviated. Page/section numbers for newspaper and magazine articles and their corresponding hyperlinks are provided to the extent possible. URLs are provided for all the sources cited from the Internet. Working papers, conference papers, other nonperiodic materials (except reports, dissertations and theses), and website materials do not follow Bluebook style.

The Chicago Manual of Style is used for the bibliography. Page ranges of journal articles are provided to the extent possible and only starting pages are used when page ranges cannot be found. Short form citations are not used. Issue numbers of journal articles are provided to the extent possible. Section letters or numbers for newspaper articles are used whenever they can be found. URLs and corresponding access dates are provided to all cited sources that have clickable links.

Acknowledgments I began researching and writing for this book in 2009 when I studied at The Pennsylvania State University College of Communications as a doctoral student. My deepest gratitude, therefore, goes to my doctoral advisor, Dr. Martin Halstuk, who introduced me to the fascinating world of mass media law and policy. At the very beginning of my academic career when Pennsylvania State University College of Communications asked me to choose my area of concentration, I was hesitant about venturing into media law. The intimidating complexity of the Bluebook legal citation style guide, the dense legal documents, the abundance of footnotes in journal articles, the ubiquitous weird-sounding legal jargon, and the competitive job market for media law scholar made media law a daunting field-even for a native English speaker, let alone a foreign scholar whose first language is Chinese. Sitting in several media law classes taught by Professor Halstuk, I found myself immediately captivated by the legal issues surrounding mass communications. Media law, I realized, is full of drama and compelling stories! From that moment, I knew it was my passion. I thought to myself, "Media law is exactly what I want to pursue for my doctoral studies—and possibly for the rest of my career." I became Dr. Halstuk's mentee, embarking on a rewarding and enjoyable three-year journey with him in the Happy Valley (the nickname for the area surrounding Penn State University). Dr. Halstuk is a true role model of diligence and perseverance. The son of parents who survived Nazi death camps, he has an extraordinary background. Before entering academia, Dr. Halstuk spent many years as a reporter and editor for major U.S. newspapers. He completed his doctoral studies in his fifties, a testament to his determination. It was Dr. Halstuk who reignited my passion for media law. His deep knowledge of media law and international affairs, his sense of humor and optimism, his remarkable career and personal experiences, and his ability to simplify complex issues without distorting them are truly inspiring. I could not have completed my dissertation in three years without his unwavering dedication and unparalleled support.

A heartfelt thank you to Dr. Eric B. Easton, Professor of Law Emeritus at the University of Baltimore School of Law. As a media law scholar, I deeply admire his distinguished educational and professional credentials: a B.S. from Northwestern University, a J.D. from the University of Maryland, and a Ph.D. in journalism from the University of Maryland. With over two decades of experience as a professional journalist and publisher, he has also taught comparative media law in numerous countries and authored numerous books and articles on media law. Our professional friendship has flourished since we first met at an international conference many years ago. As the founding editor of Media Law and Ethics, Dr. Easton reviewed, edited, and published several of my articles on freedom of information and libel law in China. He consistently encouraged me to embark on book projects focused on Chinese media law. He also invited me to revise his Zoom lectures for his Chinese students at Shandong University Law School. When he retired, he recommended that I take up the mantle. Although I have never published a book in the United States, Dr. Easton's guidance and support have been invaluable. When I asked him to write a foreword for this book, he graciously agreed without hesitation.

I would like to extend another heartfelt thank-you to Dr. Doug Anderson and Dr. Kyu Ho Youm. Dr. Anderson, former dean of the Penn State College of Communications, and Dr. Youm, a distinguished media law scholar who spent many years at the University of Oregon, have both been instrumental in my journey. I consider them not only personal friends but also role models and peer mentors. Their unwavering inspiration and support have been a constant source of encouragement. I still vividly recall posing a photo with Dr. Anderson a few years ago on the campus of Arizona State University, each of us holding a book. Dr. Anderson had authored one, while Dr. Youm had written another, focused on press law in South Korea. Later, Dr. Anderson kindly sent me Dr. Youm's book as a gift, and I devoured it eagerly, like a person ravenous for knowledge. Today, it still occupies a place of honor on my bookshelf. In his writings and emails, Dr. Youm often emphasized that media law studies should move beyond a U.S.-centric focus and adopt a reverse perspective. His book and these insights on alternative viewpoints have been a tremendous source of inspiration for me as I work on my own media law projects.

I would like to express my heartfelt gratitude to all the remarkable individuals who have supported me throughout my doctoral studies and academic journey. These include Anthony Olorunisola, Ford Risley, Gretchen Casper, Mary Beth Oliver, Marie Hardin, John Nichols, Matt McAllister, Bu Zhong, Fuyuan Shen, Shyam Sundar, Matt Jackson, Amit Schejter, Patrick Parsons, Russell Frank, Curtis Chandler, Russell Eshleman, Betsy Hall, Debora Cheney, Robert Lawrence Kuhn, Mao Ye,

Dean C. Alexander, Hong Cheng, Mohammad A. Siddiqi, Amy Sanders, Ashwini Elango, and Hua Bai. I also extend my thanks to the editors, reviewers, and discussants from various conferences and journals who have contributed valuable insights along the way.

I am also deeply grateful to Yongzheng Wei, Zejin Yao, Weibing Xiao, Hanhua Zhou, Yanbin Lv, Jun Wang, Xiongshan Cai, Gang He, David Banisar, Jamie Horsley, and many other Chinese and international legal scholars, journalists, attorneys, and government officials, all of whom have inspired me in various ways. I would also like to express my heartfelt thanks to Chenyang Xie, Shanshan Wang, Jie Wu, Linda Liang, Jue Lin, Wentao Fu, Janet Tang, Jue Lin, and countless other Chinese friends who generously provided technological, logistical, and interview support. I was profoundly touched when Shanshan visited every major bookstore in Beijing to track down the out-of-print book I had requested. Similarly, whenever I struggled to find annual OGI work reports on the websites of certain Chinese government agencies, I could always rely on my friends back in China to assist me in locating the materials.

Finally, I would like to express my sincere gratitude to my parents, my wife, Catherine (Shuai) Zhao, and my son, George (Yeqiao) Tang. George, an undergraduate student at the University of Illinois Urbana-Champaign, carefully proofread the manuscript and caught quite a few subtle errors. Shuai assisted with entering data from numerous annual OGI work reports and took on much of the housework that I should have helped with. I faced many challenges during my childhood, but my parents instilled in me the invaluable lesson that self-reliance is key. Throughout my journey in the United States, my wife and son have been an unwavering source of support. Without their continued encouragement, the completion of this research project would not have been possible. It is with immense gratitude and a deep sense of accomplishment that I dedicate this book to them. Over the past 15 years, I have devoted an overwhelming amount of time to my doctoral studies at Penn State University and my scholarship and teaching at Western Illinois University. No matter where I work, I am always the last person to leave the office. As a result, I carry a deep sense of guilt for neglecting my responsibilities as a husband and father. Now, it is time for me to return home and spend some much-needed time with my family, to rest and reconnect.

I am deeply grateful to the many individuals who have supported this book project, though I recognize that it is impossible to thank each of them adequately here. My heartfelt appreciation goes to all those who accompanied me on this research journey. Although various individuals have reviewed the materials in this book to some extent, any remaining errors or shortcomings are solely my responsibility.

Competing Interests The author has no competing interests to declare that are relevant to the content of this manuscript.

Contents

About the Author

Dr. Yong Tang is a tenured full professor of mass communications and media law at Western Illinois University (WIU). He is the director of the journalism program in the School of Communication and Media and the author of four published journalistic books, and more than 20 academic conference papers and journal articles.

Dr. Tang's major areas of research are the First Amendment, freedom of information laws, media law and policy, international journalism, and international communications. Since 2011, Dr. Tang has presented more than 10 scholarly papers to various divisions of annual AEJMC, AEJMC Southeast Colloquium, ICA and NCA conventions, and elsewhere. He was an invited panelist at the 2014 AAS (Association for Asia Studies)-in-Asia Singapore Conference to discuss the impact of *New York Times. v. Sullivan* on Asian Countries. In 2016, he attended a Southwestern Law School symposium as an invited panelist to discuss the future of global freedom of information laws. In 2021, he was an invited speaker at the special forum "COVID-19 and the Role of Communication" organized by the International Law Institute and Potomac Institute for Policy Studies. His articles appear in many peer-reviewed journals, such as International Journal of Communication, Journal of Media Law and Ethics, Journal of Information Policy, Communication, Culture and Critique, Chinese Journal of Communication, and tripleC: Communication, Capitalism and Critique. Dr. Tang is an editorial member of *Communication*

Law and Policy, one of the top peer-reviewed journals for research in communication law and policy.

Since he came to WIU in August 2011, Professor Tang has taught a wide range of conceptual and skills courses such as mass communication law and ethics, mass communication research methods, international communication and foreign press, problems of contemporary mass communications, history of mass communications, magazine and newspaper feature writing, AP reporting and writing, and digital media skills for journalists and public relations professionals. During summer breaks and sabbatical leaves, Dr. Tang has taught media law at some prominent universities in China, such as China University of Political Science and Law, Southwestern University of Finance and Economics, Sichuan University, Xiamen University, and Hong Kong Baptist University.

He has received many awards and distinctions since his employment at WIU. Such awards and distinctions include COFAC (College of Fine Arts and Communication) Dean's Award for Excellence in Scholarly and Professional Activity (2017), COFAC Dean's Award for Excellence in Teaching (2016), Chinese Communication Association Outstanding Service Award (2015), Faces of Penn State (2013), Top 50 Journalism Professors by Journalismdegree.org (2012), AEJMC Top Faculty Paper Award (2012), and AEJMC Best Research Scholar-to-Scholar Presentation Award (2011).

Before joining U.S. academia, Tang had worked in Beijing, China, and Washington, D.C. for 15 years as an award-winning full-time journalist for China's leading newspaper, the *People's Daily*. During his time as an editor and reporter, Dr. Tang interviewed many prominent figures, including two Chinese presidents, one American president, four Ivy League university presidents, more than 10 Fortune 500 CEOs.

Dr. Tang holds a doctoral degree in mass communications law and policy from the Pennsylvania State University and another Ph.D. in international journalism from the Communication University of China. He received a master's degree in international affairs from the George Washington University. Dr. Tang attended China School of Journalism and received an undergradauate degree in international news editing and reporting. He graduated from Sichuan International Studies University with a bachelor's degree in English language and literature.

During his spare time at WIU, Dr. Tang loves writing classical Chinese poems and enjoys hiking with his family in Illinois and beyond.

List of Tables

CHAPTER 1

Introduction: Freedom of Information with Chinese Characteristics

Introduction

In the bone-chilling winter of 2020, Fuzheng Han, a muckraking lawyer in Hebei Province, applied for disclosure of COVID-19 related information held by various government agencies in Wuhan, Hubei Province, and Beijing, China.[1] Like everyone else in the world, the attorney

[1] Jiaxin Wang and Man Liu, *National Health Commission Denies a Lawyer's OGI Request for Daily Coronavirus Test Results on the Grounds of the Deliberative Privilege Exemption* [卫健委回复律师信息公开申请:疫情检测日报属过程性信息暂不公开], Southern Metropolis Daily, republished by Sohu News, March 28, 2020, https://www.sohu.com/a/383868171_161795 (accessed between February 21, 2025 and March 31, 2025).

This chapter is derived from the book author's doctoral dissertation that was successfully defended at The Pennsylvania State University in 2012. Portions of the text resemble or may replicate the original text from the unpublished PhD thesis and have been reproduced as such with the permission of Palgrave Macmillan editors. Yong Tang, "Chinese Freedom of Information: An Evaluation of the Legislative History, Rationales, Significance and Efficacy of Regulations of the People's Republic of China on Open Government Information" (2012) (unpublished Ph.D. diss., The Pennsylvania State University at University Park), *available at* https://etda.libraries.psu.edu/catalog/16287 (accessed between February 21, 2025 and March 31, 2025).

Y. Tang, *Freedom of Information Law in China*,
https://doi.org/10.1007/978-981-96-7842-6_1

was stunned by the widely publicized government's initial mismanagement of the COVID-19 epidemic and he was eager to know what had happened from early December 2019 to January 2020 in Wuhan—the ground zero of a global pandemic—and how various government agencies responded to the crisis there. Han's concerns were reasonable. Both Chinese and foreign media found that government efforts to conceal information, intentionally delay information disclosure, destroy evidence, and penalize whistleblowers did exist.[2] According to Caixin, the provincial health commission in Hubei Province began actively suppressing scientists' knowledge about the virus as early as January 1, 2020.[3]

[2] Chinese social media posts exposed some government cover-ups, but those posts have mostly disappeared from the Internet due to censorship from the authorities. *Caixin* and *People* are two rare examples of investigative journalism by Chinese legacy media during the pandemic. The two Beijing-based magazines published some reports on government suppression of information, but those articles are all deleted from the Internet. Therefore, the author has to cite from other sources that republished those articles. Foreign media reports on China's initial cover-up of the pandemic are numerous. Shawn Yuan, *Inside the Early Days of China's Coronavirus Cover-Up: The Dawn of a Pandemic—As Seen Through the News and Social Media Posts that Vanished from China's Internet*, Wired, San Francisco, California, May 1, 2020, *available at* https://www.wired.com/story/inside-the-early-days-of-chinas-coronavirus-coverup/ (accessed between February 21, 2025 and March 31, 2025); Jingqi Gong, *A Whistle Giver* [发哨子的人], PEOPLE, republished by Independent Chinese PEN Center, March 10, 2020, https://www.chinesepen.org/blog/archives/145003 (accessed between February 21, 2025 and March 31, 2025); Nick Paton Walsh, *The Wuhan Files*, CNN, December 1, 2020, https://www.cnn.com/2020/11/30/asia/wuhan-china-covid-intl/index.html (accessed between February 21, 2025 and March 31, 2025); Charlie Campbell and Amy Gunia, *China Says It's Beating Coronavirus. But Can We Believe Its Numbers?* TIME, April 1, 2020, https://time.com/5813628/china-coronavirus-statistics-wuhan/ (accessed between February 21, 2025 and March 31, 2025); Dake Kang, In Xi's China, even Internal Reports Fall Prey to Censorship, ASSOCIATED PRESS, October 31, 2022, https://apnews.com/article/health-china-beijing-covid-wuhan3c199e3fla084013ds18fc9e6061e775 (accessed between February 21, 2025 and March 31, 2025); Dali Yang, *Wuhan Officials Tried to Cover up Covid-19—and Sent It Careening Outward*, THE WASHINGTON POST, March 10, 2020, https://www.washingtonpost.com/politics/2020/03/10/wuhan-officials-tried-cover-up-covid-19-sent-it-careening-outward/ (accessed between February 21, 2025 and March 31, 2025).

[3] Shawn Yuan, *Inside the Early Days of China's Coronavirus Cover-Up: The Dawn of a Pandemic—As Seen Through the News and Social Media Posts that Vanished from China's Internet*, Wired, San Francisco, California, May 1, 2020, *available at* https://www.wired.com/story/inside-the-early-days-of-chinas-coronavirus-coverup/ (accessed between February 21, 2025 and March 31, 2025); Hui Xiao, Zhiming Bao and Yuwu Gao, *Zhongnan Hospital of Wuhan University in COVID-19 Pandemic: Doctors Fight from Beginning to End* [武汉疫情中的中南医院:他们打满全场], CAIXIN, May 3, 2020,

Within one month, Han sent out applications from his home to six different government agencies: Wuhan Municipal Health Commission, Wuhan Center for Disease Control and Prevention, Hubei Provincial Health Commission, Hubei Provincial Center for Disease Control and Prevention, National Health Commission, and Chinese Center for Disease Control and Prevention. Hubei Provincial Health Commission replied via phone that more time is needed for the agency to process the request. The National Health Commission in Beijing responded via mail that the information sought by Han was procedural and pre-decisional, thus not subject to disclosure. In an interview with a reporter from *Southern Metropolis Daily*, the legal professional said his requests were made according to the nation's 13-year-old freedom of information (FOI) law, *Regulations of the People's Republic of China on Open Government Information* (*OGI Regulations*), adding that, "Given the right to know what the government is doing and the right to hold government officials accountable, our citizens are entitled to apply for government-held information and officials should respond to societal concerns."[4]

In the sizzling summer of 2007, a prestigious Taiwanese businessperson planned to build a chemical plant in the city of Xiamen, Fujian, a prosperous coastal province in southeast China. Government authorities approved the plan, but construction was blocked by residents of the city, who feared that the plant would pollute the local environment.[5] The incident was unusual in the country because it was the first occasion local residents used cellular text messages and social media to mobilize the public by urging neighbors to "go out for a walk" (a Chinese euphemism

https://matters.town/a/vh2mam7fb4ic (accessed between February 21, 2025 and March 31, 2025).

[4] Jiaxin Wang and Man Liu, *National Health Commission Denies a Lawyer's OGI Request for Daily Coronavirus Test Results on the Grounds of the Deliberative Privilege Exemption* [卫健委回复律师信息公开申请:疫情检测日报属过程性信息暂不公开], Southern Metropolis Daily, republished by Sohu News, March 28, 2020, https://www.sohu.com/a/383868171_161795 (accessed between February 21, 2025 and March 31, 2025).

[5] *Chinese City Freezes Plans for Chemical Plant after Barrage of Complaints*, The New York Times, May 30, 2007, http://www.nytimes.com/2007/05/30/world/asia/30iht-pollution.1.5924588.html (accessed between February 21, 2025 and March 31, 2025).

for holding a peaceful demonstration) in front of the Xiamen City Hall.[6] In January 2009, China's Ministry of Environmental Protection decided to move the controversial factory to Zhangzhou, a neighboring city.[7]

Yongtong Su is a reporter from *Southern Weekend*, "China's most influential liberal newspaper,"[8] headquartered in the prosperous city of Guangzhou. On February 2, 2009, Su submitted a written request to the Ministry of Environmental Protection, citing the nation's fledging *OGI Regulations*. Su asked the agency to release the environmental impact assessment that approved the construction of the plant in Zhangzhou.[9] Sixteen days later, the journalist received a copy of the report from the agency.[10] Su's request was the 57th OGI request the Ministry of Environmental Protection received since the enactment of *OGI Regulations*.[11]

Such institutionalized government transparency was revolutionary in the People's Republic of China (PRC) until enactment, on April 5, 2007,

[6] Yue Yuan, *Xiamen PX Incident* [厦门PX事件], SANLIAN LIFE WEEKLY, September 27, 2007, http://news.sina.com.cn/c/2007-09-27/165713986641.shtml (accessed between February 21, 2025 and March 31, 2025); Andrew Jacobs, *Chinese Chemical Plant Site Moves After Outcry*, THE NEW YORK TIMES, January 14, 2009, http://www.nytimes.com/2009/01/15/world/asia/15fujian.html?scp=4&sq=px%20xiamen&st=cse (accessed between February 21, 2025 and March 31, 2025).

[7] Yongtong Su, *Exclusive: Zhangzhou PX Environmental Impact Assessment Approval Document* [独家披露:漳州PX环评批复书], SOUTHERN WEEKEND, February 22, 2009, http://www.infzm.com/content/24173 (accessed between February 21, 2025 and March 31, 2025).

[8] Elisabeth Rosenthal, *Under Pressure, Chinese Newspaper Pulls Exposé on a Charity*, THE NEW YORK TIMES, March 24, 2002, at para. 1, http://www.nytimes.com/2002/03/24/world/under-pressure-chinese-newspaper-pulls-expose-on-a-charity.html (accessed between February 21, 2025 and March 31, 2025).

[9] Yongtong Su, *Exclusive: Zhangzhou PX Environmental Impact Assessment Approval Document* [独家披露:漳州PX环评批复书], SOUTHERN WEEKEND, February 22, 2009, http://www.infzm.com/content/24173 (accessed between February 21, 2025 and March 31, 2025).

[10] Yongtong Su, *Exclusive: Zhangzhou PX Environmental Impact Assessment Approval Document* [独家披露:漳州PX环评批复书], SOUTHERN WEEKEND, February 22, 2009, http://www.infzm.com/content/24173 (accessed between February 21, 2025 and March 31, 2025).

[11] Yongtong Su, *Exclusive: Zhangzhou PX Environmental Impact Assessment Approval Document* [独家披露:漳州PX环评批复书], SOUTHERN WEEKEND, February 22, 2009, http://www.infzm.com/content/24173 (accessed between February 21, 2025 and March 31, 2025).

of the country's first nationwide[12] freedom of information law. The law, promulgated by the State Council, China's national cabinet, has granted the Chinese public an unprecedented legal right of access to government-held information.[13] Under the law, any Chinese citizen, legal person, or other organization may legally request governmental agencies' disclosure of records, reports, and other official documents, not otherwise exempted.[14] Also, under the law, the people's government and its departments at various levels are to disclose, proactively and promptly, certain categories of information without a specific request.

Internationally, the modern legal right of access to government-held information—specifically records, reports, and official documents encompass the concept of freedom of information (FOI). FOI, form of governmental transparency, is a Western concept, dating to 1766 when Sweden enacted the world's first FOI law, the *Freedom-of-Press and the Right-of-Access to Public Records Act*.[15] Applying the Freedom House "freedom

[12] Before the national FOI law was adopted, some provinces and cities in China had various forms of FOI provisions allowing limited public access to official records.

[13] Jamie P. Horsley, *China Adopts First Nationwide Open Government Information Regulations*, freedominfo.org, Washington, DC, May 9, 2007, *available at* http://www.freedominfo.org/2007/05/china-adopts-first-nationwide-open-government-information-regulations/ (accessed between February 21, 2025 and March 31, 2025).The Chinese FOI law was enacted in 2007 and revised in 2019. For the full text of the law in both Chinese and English, see *Chinese Law and Policy on Open Government Information*, Yale University Law School China Law Center, *available at* https://law.yale.edu/china-center/resources/open-government-information-china (accessed between February 21, 2025 and March 31, 2025).

[14] FOI laws around the world exclude certain categories of information. Typically, such exemptions include information that pertains to national security, personal privacy, law enforcement, business and trade secrets, and banking and financial records. The number of exemptions varies among the nations. A detailed explanation of Chinese FOI laws' exemptions and their uses appears in Chapter 6 of this book.

[15] An overview of the law is available on the website of the Swedish Ministry of Justice. *Public Access to Information and Secrecy: The Legislation in Brief*, the Ministry of Justice, Government Offices of Sweden, Stockholm, Sweden, *available at* https://www.government.se/contentassets/2ca7601373824c8395fc1f38516e6e03/public-access-to-information-and-secrecy.pdf (accessed between February 21, 2025 and March 31, 2025). An Australian journalism educator and FOI scholar, Stephen Lamble, found that the concept of freedom of information actually first evolved in China more than 1,000 years ago during the Tang Dynasty. According to his finding, Emperor Tai'-Zong (599 AD-649 AD) established an "Imperial Censorate," a powerful organization of a group of highly educated scholarly officials recorded governmental documents and activities and prepared to criticize the government, including the emperor. The information

in the world" methodology[16] to examine all the countries with FOI laws reveals that, of the approximately 111 countries adopting various forms of freedom of information laws as of 2017 (see Table 1.1), about 90 are democratic.[17] In other words, 11 authoritarian countries have FOI laws, and include Asian countries of China and Pakistan, African nations of Angola, Zimbabwe, and Rwanda, Middle East countries of Yemen and Jordan, and the former Soviet Union's member states of Russia, Uzbekistan, Azerbaijan, and Tajikistan. Among these 11 rare examples of authoritarian transparency, China ranks low, ahead of only Uzbekistan in the overall state protection of political rights and civil liberties (see Table 1.2).

China's low Freedom House score is not surprising. The Chinese government, according to other democracy-promoting organizations, has

policy of Tai'Zong inspired Anders Chydenius (1729 AD–1803 AD), born in Sotkamo, Sweden (in today's northeastern Finland). As a clergyman, Enlightenment philosopher, and great proponent of freedom of the press, he persuaded the Swedish government to adopt the *Freedom of Press Act* in 1766, the world's first Freedom of information legislation. Stephen Lamble, *Freedom of Information, a Finnish Clergyman's Gift to Democracy*, 97 Freedom of Information Review 2, 2–8 (2002).

[16] Freedom House is a Washington, D.C.-based NGO that studies and promotes human rights, political freedom, and democracy. Freedom House measures, annually, the quality of democracy or degree of authoritarianism for 194 countries from 1972 to the present. Each country is rated on a seven-point scale for both political rights and civil liberties, with 1 representing the freest and 7 the least free. Based on the scores, Freedom House determines if a country is "Free" (ratings average 1.0–2.5), "Partly Free" (3.0–5.0), or "Not Free" (5.5–7.0). According to Freedom House designations, "Free" countries are liberal democracies. "Partly Free" countries are electoral democracies. "Not Free" countries are nondemocratic or authoritarian. *Freedom in the World Research Methodology*, Freedom House, Washington, DC, *available at* https://freedomhouse.org/reports/freedom-world/freedom-world-research-methodology (accessed between February 21, 2025 and March 31, 2025).

[17] Democracy is a controversial term. Freedom House scores quantify a country's quality of democracy and/or authoritarianism. They ignore the variety of forms democracy may take. Obviously, democratic nations have different structures of government. For example, the United States has an executive branch under the president, a legislative branch under the Congress; the United Kingdom has an executive branch under the prime minister and a legislative branch in the form of Parliament; and the United Kingdom has a monarchy with no law-making powers. Meanwhile, Israel has an executive branch under the prime minster and a president who is little more than a figurehead, and a parliament known as the Knesset. Yet the United States, the United Kingdom, and Israel are all considered democracies because they all share certain characteristics, such as freedom of speech, freedom of the press, freedom of assembly, constitutionalism, the rule of law, and varying degrees of governmental transparency, among other criteria.

had consistent ratings of the least transparency in the world.[18] For an authoritarian communist regime such as China, long closed to the outside world prior to its reform and opening up efforts in 1979, the passage of *OGI Regulations* and the journey to governmental transparency have not been smooth or swift.

In the creation and implementation of the pro-democratic *OGI Regulations*, China is experiencing a profound schism in its deeply rooted historical, political, and social cultures. Plainly stated, a conflict exists between deeply embedded governmental secrecy and emerging governmental transparency. On one hand, Chinese citizens increasingly use *OGI Regulations* to access official records, and agencies at various levels are releasing, affirmatively, increasing amounts of key information. On the other hand, Chinese authorities continue to restrict, severely, dissemination of information held by the government despite enactment of the FOI law. For example, Shanghai, one of the most economically developed cities in China, is also at the forefront of promoting governmental transparency in the country.[19] From 2004, when Shanghai enacted its first OGI Rule, to 2008, filing of OGI lawsuits reached nearly 400 in this city. Of these 400 OGI lawsuits, only one plaintiff prevailed, 13 plaintiffs withdrew their lawsuits, and all the other plaintiffs lost their OGI litigations.[20]

[18] For example, according to Access to Information Index produced by the United Nations, Chinese government is rated among the least transparent in the world. The Information Access Index combines two annual surveys from two non-profit organizations (Transparency international and Freedom House) to measure key democratic components, which contribute to accessing and disseminating governmental information. Stephen A. Ronaghan, *Benchmarking E-Government: Assessing the United Nation's Member States* (report for United Nations Division for Public Economics and Public Administration, and American Society for Public Administration), New York, New York, May 2002, *available at* https://digitallibrary.un.org/record/3868821?ln=en&v=pdf (accessed between February 21, 2025 and March 31, 2025).

[19] The Shanghai municipal people's government is the first provincial government in China to adopt a local OGI rule, enacting *Provisions* of *Shanghai Municipality on Open Government Information in January 2004. Shanghai repealed the law in 2008 and enacted a new OGI rule.*

[20] Jian Bao, *Shanghai China: 400 OGI Cases Filed Within Four Years* [上海:四年400起政府信息公开 "民告官"居全国首位], PEOPLE'S DAILY, republished by China News Service, November 12, 2008, http://www.chinanews.com.cn/gn/news/2008/11-12/1446373.shtml (accessed between February 21, 2025 and March 31, 2025).

The possibility of FOI law in an authoritarian regime and the future viability of the law are among many issues requiring scholarly attention and many puzzles need solutions. This chapter begins an extended examination of China's political, media, and legal systems, purpose and significance of this research, definition of the study's scope, proposal of several relevant research questions, exploration of methodology, and a summary of the subsequent chapters.

Political, Media, and Legal Systems

A brief survey on China's political, media, and legal systems follows below in order to help readers better contextualize this book and understand the big environment where the concept and practice of government transparency in general and the freedom of information law in particular would germinate, take root, and grow into a tree.[21]

After 2,000 years of imperial dynasties ended in 1911, China established a republic that borrowed heavily from political systems of United States and many other Western democracies, but the young republic lasted for only 37 years (1912–1949).[22] During this short period of intellectual,

[21] For more detailed understanding of China's political, media and legal systems, see Xi Jinping, Xi Jinping: The Governance of China (2022); The Party Leads All: The Evolving Role of the Chinese Communist Party (Jacques deLisle and Guobin Yang, eds., 2022); The China Reader: The Reform Era (Orville Schell and David Shambaugh, eds., 1998); New Media for a New China (James F. Scotton and William A. Hachten, eds., 2010); Cheng Li, Chinese Politics in the Xi Jinping Era: Reassessing Collective Leadership (2016); David Shambaugh, China's Communist Party: Atrophy and Adaptation (2008); Benjamin L. Liebman, *Watchdog or Demagogue? The Media in the Chinese Legal System*, 105 Columbia Law Review 1 (2005, pp. 1–157); Benjamin L. Liebman, The *Media and the Courts: Towards Competitive Supervision?* 834 The China Quarterly 208 (2011, pp. 833–850); Perry Keller, *Privilege and Punishment: Press Governance in China*, 21 Cardozo Arts & Entertainment Law Journal 87 (2003); Weiguang Wu, *The Rationale of China's Media Regulation Policy in the Process of the Institutional Transformation*, 7 Notre Dame Journal of International & Comparative Law 1 (2017, pp. 64–114); Susan Trevaskes, *A Law Unto Itself: Chinese Communist Party Leadership and Yifa zhiguo in the Xi Era*, 44 Modern China 4 (2018, pp. 347–373).

[22] For example, Sun Yat-sen, the first president of Republic of China, studied for quite a few years in Honolulu, Hawaii before returning to China to topple the Qing dynasty. Sun also received a lot of financial support from his brother in Hawaii. He saw America basically as a model of success that China should learn from. David Gordon, *American*

cultural, and political revitalization, Chinese media institutions and courts had some degree of independence and professionalism. Many propaganda officials and journalists were either graduates from Missouri School of Journalism or alumni of college journalism programs in China that copied the Missouri model.[23] Judges, attorneys, and government officials with law degrees from major universities in China, United States, Europe, and Japan were common.[24] The Chinese government bureaucracy, divided into five branches, was relatively transparent.

When Mao Zedong and his communist comrades forced his major rival Chiang Kai-shek to flee to Taiwan and therefore won the civil war in 1949, they completely reshaped China's political system by, to some degree, copying and pasting Stalinism that characterized the Soviet Union's communism. The party-state controlled not only the government but also the military, the people's congress, news organizations, and courts. The Chinese bureaucracy made most decisions behind the closed doors and government transparency was nonexistent. Funded by the party or the government and staffed by party loyalists, news organizations were considered as a propaganda tool for the party/government to disseminate its policies and views on major issues of public concern. When needed, the party/government would ask news organizations to glorify or vilify whoever was regarded as the hero or enemy of the party. Holding the powerful and the rich accountable was a taboo in China's university journalism curriculum. Funded by the government and staffed by party loyalists, Chinese courts were considered as a law enforcement and justice administration tool for the party/government to penalize whoever deemed politically disloyal and dangerous. Mao's totalitarian rule reached its peak during the Cultural Revolution (1966–1976) when most

Influences on Sun Yat-sen, 16 Education about Asia 2 (special issue: US, Asia, and the World, 1620–1914) (fall 2011), *available at* https://www.asianstudies.org/publications/eaa/archives/american-influences-on-sun-yatsen/ (accessed between February 21, 2025 and March 31, 2025).

23 Yong Z. Volz and Chin-Chuan Lee, *American Pragmatism and Chinese Modernization: Importing the Missouri Model of Journalism Education to Modern China*, 31 Media Culture & Society 5 (2009, pp. 711–730).

24 Donghui Xie, *Justice Reform in Republic of China and Its Implications on Today* [民国时期的司法改革及其当下启示], 3 China Law Review [中国法律评论] (2016), *available at* http://sociologyol.ruc.edu.cn/shxyj/fzshx/flshx/697e781531fb4d61ba08496d1695db39.htm (accessed between February 21, 2025 and March 31, 2025).

of his revolutionary colleagues were purged, the Chinese bureaucracy was smashed, and he enjoyed absolute power over the party and the country.

After Mao died in 1976, one of leftovers of Mao's endless political purges Deng Xiaoping and his hand-picked policy followers began to take the helm of China and lead the country to an era of reform and opening up to the outside world (1978–2012). During this time period, China embarked on a dedicated and persistent experiment of political reform and economic liberalization characterized by establishing diplomatic ties with United States, learning from America and other Western democracies, intentionally limiting the power of the party, allowing the government to play a bigger role in decision-making, exerting less control over people's daily lives, encouraging citizen participation in public affairs, and privatizing inefficient state-owned enterprises. Although Deng and his followers' bold reform and opening up initiatives have not changed the fundamental structure of the party-state, they played a tremendous role in China's newly gained status as the world's No. 2 economy and at the same time prompted unprecedented protection of freedoms and civil liberties that average citizens rarely enjoyed in China's long history. With this backdrop of nationwide optimism and tolerance toward unorthodox ideas, Chinese news organizations experienced rapid commercialization and marketization since 1990s.[25] While still having to revolve around the orbit of the ruling party, news media outlets were allowed to repackage themselves as state-owned enterprises with a central goal of making profit from the market. Fulbright scholars were invited to China to teach college students on how to think, report, and write like Western journalists.[26] Investigative journalism was tolerated or even encouraged from time to time by reform-minded top leaders in the party.[27] Reform's

[25] For more about Chinese media's commercialization during the reform era, see YUEZHI ZHAO, MEDIA, MARKET, AND DEMOCRACY IN CHINA: BETWEEN THE PARTY LINE AND THE BOTTOM LINE (1998).

[26] The author of this book was taught in Beijing from 1993 to 1995 by two American Fulbright professors during his study at China School of Journalism.

[27] In a 1998 visit to China Central Television's newsroom in Beijing, the then-premier Zhu Rongji encouraged the Chinese media to act as the "watchdog of the government, mouthpiece of the masses, mirror and supervisor of the government, vanguard of reform (舆论监督, 群众喉舌,政府镜鉴,改革尖兵)." Jie Gui, *Reporters Should Go Wherever Tough Places: Inside Information about Premier Zhu Writing Inscription for CCTV Focus Report* [希望记者越是艰难的地方越要去——朱 镕基破例为《焦点访谈》题词内幕], CHINA YOUTH

momentum was running high not only in Chinese newsrooms but also in Chinese courtrooms. Judge professionalization and justice independence once again became hot-button issues among legal scholars, journalists, and intellectuals. Judges became better educated and lawyers had to be licensed via a rigorous national exam that is very similar to bar examinations in the United States. Even the China's top court was calling for an end of interference by party/government officials on justice independence.[28]

The reform and opening up initiative temporarily lost its momentum after the 1989 Tiananmen Square incident wherein the government used military forces to end the peaceful demonstrations organized by college students in Beijing who called for elimination of government corruption and greater democracy. The momentum was quickly resumed after Deng issued a stern warning against new leaders who just wanted to remain politically correct and was eager to adopt conservative policies. The momentum has finally lost its steam since Xi Jinping became general secretary of the Chinese Communist Party in 2012 and China's president in 2013. The emergence of Xi as the top leader of China has profound implications on the country's political, media, and legal systems. Under his leadership, power that used to be shared between the party and the government is increasingly in the hands of the party, with Xi and other Politburo Standing Committee members being at the highest echelon of power. Political loyalty, rather than professional expertise, once again becomes the golden standard when hiring or firing party and government officials at all levels. Media institutions and courts are not immune from this power redistribution and political conservatism. News organizations and courtrooms staffed by party loyalists begin to publicize their absolute loyalty shamelessly and ruthlessly to the party. Investigative journalism

DAILY, September 22, 2011, at sec. 11, https://zqb.cyol.com/html/2011-09/22/nw.D110000zgqnb_20110922_2-11.htm (accessed between February 21, 2025 and March 31, 2025). A *New Yorker* feature story vividly documented how far a Chinese editor can go in investigative journalism. Evan Osnos, *The Forbidden Zone: How Far can a Provocative Editor Go?* NEW YORKER, July 20, 2009, http://www.newyorker.com/reporting/2009/07/20/090720fa_fact_osnos (accessed between February 21, 2025 and March 31, 2025).

[28] Weihan Yang, *Supreme Court Research Institute Director Talks about Enhancing Justice Fairness and Credibility* [最高人民法院研究室主任谈加强公正司法提高公信力] XINHUA NEWS AGENCY, republished by Sina News, October 28, 2013, *available at* http://news.sina.com.cn/o/2013-10-28/215028554335.shtml accessed between February 21, 2025 and March 31, 2025).

dies down. Instrumental use of courts and selective compliance with laws become daily routine. Press freedom and justice independence become increasingly taboo subjects in university curriculum and public discourse. Many China watchers worry that a return to Mao's era is just a matter of time.[29]

Purpose and Significance

The major purpose of this book is examination, evaluation of the legal right of public access to government-held information in the People's Republic of China. Specifically, this research focuses on citizens' rights to access official documents gathered, created, and controlled by China's local (i.e., provinces, cities, counties, and towns) and national executive branches of government and various party organizations of the ruling Communist Party.

This research has particular significance at this time because the groundbreaking *OGI Regulations* have reached an opportune period for examination and evaluation. The year 2024 represents a sufficient length of time, since enactment of the Chinese freedom of information law in 2007 and enforcement of the law in 2008 to assess, meaningfully, the law's efficacy.

This study is further significant for four additional reasons: First, legal scholars, many government and non-government institutions, the United Nations, and other international organizations have long recognized freedom of information as an emerging fundamental human right.[30]

[29] Kevin Rudd, *The Return of Red China: Xi Jinping Brings Back Marxism*, FOREIGN AFFAIRS, November 9, 2022, https://www.foreignaffairs.com/china/return-red-china (accessed between February 21, 2025 and March 31, 2025); Peter Coy, *Xi Jinping is the Second Coming of Mao Zedong*, NEW YORK TIMES, October 7, 2022, https://www.nytimes.com/2022/10/07/opinion/xi-jinping-mao-zedong.html (accessed between February 21, 2025 and March 31, 2025).

[30] For detailed analysis of freedom of information from the human rights perspective, see Cheryl Ann Bishop, "Internationalizing the Right to Know: Conceptualizations of Access to Information in Human Rights Law" (2009) (unpublished Ph.D. diss., The University of North Carolina at Chapel Hill); K.M. SHRIVASTAVA, THE RIGHT TO INFORMATION: A GLOBAL PERSPECTIVE (2009); Cheryl Ann Bishop, *The United Nations and Access to Information as a Human Right*, paper presented at the annual meeting of the International Communication Association, Montreal, Quebec, Canada, May 22, 2008.

In 1946, the United Nations General Assembly stated in an early resolution: "Freedom of information is a fundamental human right and ... the touchstone of all freedoms to which the United Nations is consecrated."[31] Freedom from want is one of Four Freedoms articulated by former U.S. President Franklin Roosevelt and inspired the *1948 Universal Declaration of Human Rights*.[32] Freedom from want is not possible until freedom of information is available.[33] Article 19 of the *1948 Universal Declaration of Human Rights* (UDHR)[34] stated: "Everyone has the right to freedom of opinion and expression; this right includes freedom to hold opinions without interference and to *seek, receive* and impart information and ideas through any media and regardless of frontiers (emphasis added)."[35] Article 19 of the *1966 International Covenant on Civil and Political Rights* (ICCPR)[36] guarantees freedom of information

[31] Resolution 59(I), adopted by United Nations General Assembly, New York, 1946; TOBY MENDEL, FREEDOM OF INFORMATION AS AN INTERNATIONALLY PROTECTED HUMAN RIGHT, Article 19, London, at 1, *available at* http://www.article19.org/data/files/pdfs/publications/foi-as-an-international-right.pdf (accessed between February 21, 2025 and March 31, 2025).

[32] ELIZABETH BORGWARDT, A NEW DEAL FOR THE WORLD: AMERICA'S VISION FOR HUMAN RIGHTS (2005).

[33] Nobel Prize-winning economist, Amartya Sen, argued that freedom of information plays a key role in preventing famine. Amartya Sen, *Ingredients of Famine Analysis: Availability and Entitlements*, 96 QUARTERLY JOURNAL OF ECONOMICS 433 (1981).

[34] China signed and ratified the *1948 Universal Declaration of Human Rights* (UDHR) and promised to abide by its provisions including freedom of information. For discussions of Chinese human rights expert on the value of signing international covenants including UDHR, see *Human Rights Expert Highlights Significance of China's Signing 21 International Human Rights Covenants* [人权专家:中国加入21个国际人权公约的意义], SOHU, April 9, 2004, http://news.sohu.com/2004/04/09/87/news219788774.shtml (accessed between February 21, 2025 and March 31, 2025).

[35] Article 19, UDHR, adopted by the UN General Assembly on 10 December 1948, Resolution 217A (III), http://www.un.org/en/documents/udhr/ (accessed between February 21, 2025 and March 31, 2025).

[36] China signed and ratified the *1948 Universal Declaration of Human Rights* (UDHR) and promised to abide by its provisions including freedom of information. For discussions of Chinese human rights expert on the value of signing international covenants including UDHR, see *Human Rights Expert Highlights Significance of China's Signing 21 International Human Rights Covenants* [人权专家:中国加入21个国际人权公约的意义], SOHU, April 9, 2004, http://news.sohu.com/2004/04/09/87/news219788774.shtml (accessed between February 21, 2025 and March 31, 2025).

in terms very similar to those found at Article 19 of the UDHR.[37] Many other international organizations and documents, such as Organization of American States, Council of Europe, African Union, the Commonwealth, Inter-American Court of Human Rights, European Court of Human Rights, the 1992 Rio Declaration on Environment and Development, and the *UN 1998 Declaration on Human Rights Defenders*, have upheld similar rights to access information.[38] Abid Hussain, the UN Special Rapporteur on Freedom of Opinion and Expression, elaborated on freedom of information in his 1995 Report to the UN Commission on Human Rights: "Freedom will be bereft of all effectiveness if the people have no access to information. Access to information is basic to the democratic way of life. The tendency to withhold information from the people at large is therefore to be strongly checked."[39] The enactment of the Chinese FOI law is a significant advance for China's human rights protection. A thorough analysis of access to government-held information in China offers valuable lessons and recommendations useful to enhance governmental transparency and promote Chinese human rights.

Second, the evaluation of the Chinese FOI law may provide a mirror for other countries to identify flaws in their own FOI systems.[40] Third, this research is especially timely and relevant since China's emergence

[37] UN General Assembly Resolution 2200A (XXI) of 16 December 1966, in force on March 23, 1976, *available at* http://treaties.un.org/doc/Publication/UNTS/Volume%20999/volume-999-I-14668-English.pdf (accessed between February 21, 2025 and March 31, 2025).

[38] FREEDOM OF INFORMATION: A COMPARATIVE LEGAL SURVEY (Toby Mendel ed., 2nd edn, 2008).

[39] UN Doc. E/CN.4/1995/32, at para. 35; TOBY MENDEL, FREEDOM OF INFORMATION AS AN INTERNATIONALLY PROTECTED HUMAN RIGHT, Article 19, London, at 1, *available at* http://www.article19.org/data/files/pdfs/publications/foi-as-an-international-right.pdf (accessed between February 21, 2025 and March 31, 2025).

[40] Since *U.S. FOIA* is a model for other countries, some U.S. legal scholars may suppress the value of learning from other countries' FOI legislation. For example, the theory of legal transplants pays close attention to transplants' impact on the "recipient" country. However, some scholars argued that academics should avoid ignoring the impact of the legal transplanting process on the "donor" country. According to legal scholar, Frances Foster, legal transplants can "provide a mirror" for donor countries to "see flaws" in their systems and "new directions" for reform. Frances H. Foster, *American Trust Law in a Chinese Mirror*, 94 MINNESOTA LAW REVIEW 602, 607 (2010).

as the world's second most powerful economic engine.[41] The Chinese government is the largest single producer, collector, consumer, and disseminator of information in China. The government holds 80 percent of all information circulating in the country.[42] The state of transparency of such a large bureaucracy has not only direct and significant political and economic consequences for the Chinese people, but also for the rest of the world. Fourth, an understanding of China's current tendencies toward greater transparency and the implications of China's entry into the global community promoting freedom of information are significant. The implications are reflections of a global phenomenon as FOI laws proliferate since the fall of the Soviet Union.[43]

Research Scope

Use of the word "transparency" is wide but rarely well defined. In politics, transparency refers to enabling citizens to gather information of policies and behavior of governments.[44] In economics, the Working Group on

[41] David Barboza, *China Passes Japan as Second-Largest Economy*, The New York Times, August 15, 2010, http://www.nytimes.com/2010/08/16/business/global/16yuan.html (accessed between February 21, 2025 and March 31, 2025).

[42] Hanhua Zhou, *Open Government in China: Practice and Problems*, *in* The Right to Know: Transparency for an Open World 104 (Ann Florini & Joseph E. Stiglitz eds., 2007); Hanhua Zhou, *Basic Considerations in the Drafting of Regulations on the Openness of Government Information (Academic Draft)* [起草《政府信息公开条例》(专家建议稿)的基本考虑] 6 Chinese Journal of Law 57, 97 (2002). For additional examinations on how much information the Chinese government generates and controls, see Yunchuan Sun & Liubing Gao, *Environmental Management Research on Government Online Information Resources* [政府网上信息资源环境管理研究] 11 Journal of Library Science 13 (1999).

[43] The majority of countries with FOI legislation adopted FOI laws after the demise of the Soviet Union in 1991. For an overview of national freedom of information legislations, see David Banisar, Freedom of Information around the World 2006: A Global Survey of Access to Government Information Laws (report for Privacy International, London, United Kingdom, July 2006), *available at* http://www.freedominfo.org/documents/global_survey2006.pdf (accessed between February 21, 2025 and March 31, 2025).

[44] For example, there are many references to political transparency in the documents of the European Union, such as the Amsterdam Treaty. *The Treaty of Amsterdam*, Amsterdam, October 1997, *available at* https://www.cvce.eu/content/publication/1999/1/1/578ebb8e-d641-4650-b1e3-3b3a795e01c9/publishable_en.pdf (accessed between February 21, 2025 and March 31, 2025).

Transparency and Accountability of the Group of 22 defined transparency as "a process by which information about existing conditions, decisions and actions is made accessible, visible, and understandable."[45] In the security field, a United Nations group defined transparency as "involving systematic provision of information on specific aspects of activities in the military field under formal or informal international arrangements."[46]

For the purpose of this research, a broad definition is most useful. The book *The Right to Know: Transparency for an Open World* provides such a broad definition: transparency refers to "the degree to which information is available to outsiders that enables them to have informed voice in decisions and/or to access the decisions made by insiders."[47]

Narrowly speaking, access to official documents, reports, and records made or obtained by executive branches of government is commonly "freedom of information" (FOI).[48] FOI represents just one major category of governmental transparency; open government has several important components. Besides freedom of information, governmental transparency applies to ***meetings and facilities*** of governmental agencies. The public's right to attend official meetings falls under the rubric of "sunshine law."[49] In addition, governmental transparency pertains to judicial proceedings and records.[50] The people also have the right to

[45] INTERNATIONAL MONETARY FUND, REPORT OF THE WORKING GROUP ON TRANSPARENCY AND ACCOUNTABILITY, Washington D.C., October 1998, at p.v., *available at* http://www.imf.org/external/np/g22/taarep.pdf (accessed between February 21, 2025 and March 31, 2025).

[46] UNITED NATIONS, STUDY ON WAYS AND MEANS OF PROMOTING TRANSPARENCY IN INTERNATIONAL TRANSFERS OF CONVENTIONAL ARMS: REPORT OF THE SECRETARY-GENERAL (United Nations Experts Group, UN Document A/46/301, New York, New York, September 1991), at 22–23, *available at* https://front.un-arm.org/wp-content/uploads/assets/HomePage/ODAPublications/DisarmamentStudySeries/PDF/SS-24.pdf (accessed between February 21, 2025 and March 31, 2025).

[47] THE RIGHT TO KNOW: TRANSPARENCY FOR AN OPEN WORLD 5 (Ann Florini & Joseph E. Stiglitz eds., 2007).

[48] For instance, in the United States, enactment of *U.S. Freedom of Information Act* and similar state FOI laws guarantee the right of the public to access governmental information held by the executive branches of government.

[49] For example, in the United States, the federal *Government in the Sunshine Act* and similar state sunshine laws open federal and state governmental meetings and facilities to the public.

[50] For instance, in 1980, the U.S. Supreme Court ruled in *Richmond Newspapers v. Virginia* that the public and the press enjoy a constitutional right to attend a criminal

know the details of activities of legislative organs[51] and other entities that receive public funding.[52]

For the purposes of this book, a narrow definition of freedom of information is most useful. In other words, this research only examines transparency practices and legislations for Chinese administrative agencies and the Chinese Communist Party. This scope is reasonable because *OGI Regulations* apply to administrative agencies only and *OPA Regulations* apply to various levels of Communist Party organizations only.[53] Transparency practices and rules of other four branches of the

trial. In 1986, the U.S. Supreme Court fashioned the *Press-Enterprise* test, extending American people's access to other judicial proceedings and records. *Richmond Newspapers v. Virginia*, 448 U.S. 555 (1980); *Press-Enterprise v. Riverside Superior Court* 478 U.S. 1 (1986). Don R. Pember & Clay Calvert, Mass Media Law 458–459 (2013). However, statutory laws to guarantee judicial transparency are rare. Comparing with the legislative and executive branches of various levels of the U.S. government, the judicial branch, overall, tends to be less transparent. For detailed analysis of judicial transparency in the United States, see Katrina Hoch, "Judicial Transparency: Communication, Democracy and the United States Federal Judiciary" (2009) (unpublished Ph.D. diss., University of California, San Diego).

51 For example, U.S. Congress and state, and local legislatures are not subject to the FOI laws. Nevertheless, the U.S. House of Representatives, the U.S. Senate, and state and local legislatures enacted their own rules, opening a substantial portion of their proceedings and records to public inspection. *Access to Congress*, Citizen Media Law Project, Berkman Center for Internet & Society, Harvard University, *available at* http://www.citmedialaw.org/legal-guide/access-congress (accessed between February 21, 2025 and March 31, 2025).

52 For instance, most U.S. public universities such as University of California Berkeley (https://chancellor.berkeley.edu/faq/public-records) and Western Illinois University (https://www.wiu.edu/vpaps/university_relations/foia/) are subject to state open records laws because these institutions receive lots of funding from state governments and are considered, as a matter of law, as agencies subject to statutes for disclosure of public records. A small number of public universities in the United States are somewhat exempt from state open records laws because those colleges are state-related, such as the University of Pittsburgh, the Pennsylvania State University, and Temple University. These universities are only subject to limited provisions of Pennsylvania's Right-to-Know Law. Private universities and colleges in America are generally not subject to state open records laws. FAQ#29, About the Right-to-Know Law, Office of Open Records, *available at* https://www.openrecords.pa.gov/rtkl/about.cfm (accessed between February 21, 2025 and March 31, 2025).

53 *OPA Regulations*, namely *Regulations of the Chinese Communist Party on Open Party Affairs*, were passed in 2017 and widely regarded as the FOI law in the party. The details of this law will be discussed in Chapter 11 of this book. China had long experimented with disclosure of party affairs. For example, in 2010, the General Office of the CPC Central Committee issued an opinion on disclosure of party affairs at the grassroots level.

Chinese government,[54] such as the people's congress (*lifagongkai* 立法公开),[55] the court (*shenpangongkai* 审判公开),[56] the procuratorate

Establishment of the press secretary system exists for various levels of party committees. The party is conducting a nationwide experiment to guarantee the transparent exercise of power of county-level party committees. The Party School and other party organizations began to accept interview requests from foreign media. *Opinion of the General Office of the Chinese Communist Party Central Committee on Information Disclosure of Grassroots Party Organizations 2010* [关于党的基层组织实行党务公开的意见] Zhongbanfa (2010), No. 29, promulgated on September 15, 2010; Chunyu Hua, *Disclosure of Affairs of Chinese Communist Party: A Confident and Transparent Party Marks Its 90th Founding Anniversary* [中共党务公开 自信透明形象迎建党90周年] Xinhua News Agency, June 4, 2011, http://news.cjn.cn/gnxw/201106/t1371511.htm?fallback=1 (accessed between February 21, 2025 and March 31, 2025). Some Chinese scholars argued for greater disclosure of party affairs. For instance, one scholar insisted on greater disclosure of standard information of various levels of party organizations (e.g., party organization functions; party leaders' biographies and responsibilities; party's budget and financial accounting; audit of party organizations; use of party membership fees; operation of party-owned assets), and greater disclosure of information of the party's decision-making processes. Haibing Gu, *There Should Be Disclosure of Party Affairs* [应当有党务信息公开] 5 Journal of Cultural Criticism 76, 76–77 (2007).

54 Broadly speaking, each level of the Chinese government has six branches: the people's congress, the party, the people's government, the political consultative conference, the people's court, and the people's procuratorate. The six branches may not exist at all the village and township levels. Unlike the U.S. government in which none of the three branches is superior to the other two, the Chinese people's congress is the highest state organ at various levels of government. However, in practice, the Chinese Communist Party is more powerful than any of the other five.

55 China expended effort toward rendering its people's congress, at various levels, more transparent and accessible, although without legislating any relevant laws or regulations. For example, leading officials from the Shanghai Municipal People's Congress Standing Committee participate regularly in online chatting with citizens. On March 29, 2012, the live broadcast of a meeting held by the Henan Provincial People's Congress Standing Committee aroused media attention because it was the first of its kind. Yan Shi, *Valuable Experiment in Orderly Political Participation* [有序政治参与的有益尝试], People's Daily (republished on the website of National People's Congress), May 12, 2010, http://www.npc.gov.cn/zgrdw/npc///xinwen/rdlt/rdjs/2010-05/12/content_1572611.htm (accessed between February 21, 2025 and March 31, 2025); Rui Shuang, *Henan Provincial People's Congress Standing Committee Holds Meeting Live Broadcast by Internet* [河南省第十一届人大常委会会议首次实现网络直播], Xinhua News Agency (republished on the central Chinese government's official web portal), March 29, 2012, https://www.gov.cn/jrzg/2012-03/29/content_2102689.htm (accessed between February 21, 2025 and March 31, 2025).

56 China has attempted to establish a transparent, accessible, and efficient judiciary. According to the Supreme Court provisions, judicial information for litigation, trials, hearings, documents, and enforcement shall be accessible to the public except rare cases,

(*jianwugongkai* 检务公开),[57] and the political consultative conference (*zhengxiegongkai* 政协公开)[58] are beyond the scope of this book because these four branches are not subject to either *OGI Regulations or OPA Regulations*. Over the years, the Chinese have practiced opening governmental meetings to the public,[59] along with opening governmental

which involve civil or criminal litigations including state secrets, commercial secrets, and personal privacy, or non-disclosure is a stipulation of other laws and regulations. *Notice of the Supreme Court on Printing and Distributing Six Provisions on Transparent Judiciary and Several Provisions on Media Supervision of the Courts* [最高人民法院印发《关于司法公开的六项规定》和《关于人民法院接受新闻媒体舆论监督的若干规定》的通知] Fafa (2009), No. 58 (promulgated on December 8, 2009 and effective on December 8, 2009); *Several Provisions of The Supreme Court on Vigorously Enforcing the System of Public Trials* [最高人民法院关于严格执行公开审判制度的若干规定] Fafa (1999), No.3 (promulgated on March 8, 1999 and effective on March 8, 1999).

57 Procuratorate organs in China, somewhat similar to offices of American attorney generals, exercise the power of prosecution. China has attempted vigorously to establish a transparent, accessible, and efficient procuratorate system. According to the Supreme Procuratorate provisions, procuratorate information is available for disclosure to the public, except for relevant cases involving state secrets. *Decision of the Supreme Procuratorate on Enforcing Transparency at All Levels of Procuratorates* [关于在全国检察机关实行《检务公开》的决定] (promulgated on October 25, 1998 and effective on October 27, 1998); *Notice of the Supreme Procuratorate on Printing and Distributing the Opinion on Further Deepening the Disclosure of Procuratorate Information* [最高人民检察院关于印发《关于进一步深化人民检察院"检务公开"的意见》的通知] Gaojianfa (2006), No. 8 (promulgated on June 26, 2006 and effective on June 26, 2006).

58 Although the political consultative conference is not required by *OGI Regulations* to disclose information, various levels of political consultative conferences adopted rules for implementation for disclosing information. For example, the political consultative conference in Sinan County, Guizhou Province adopted rules for disclosure of information. The political consultative conference in Xuzhou City, Jiangsu Province formulated OGI Guide to facilitate disclosure of information. *Implementation Rules of Disclosure of Information Held by Sinan County Political Consultative Conference 2012* (adopted on May 26, 2012 and promulgated on June 15, 2012); *Guide on Disclosure of Information Held by Xuzhou Municipal Political Consultative Conference 2007* (promulgated on July 30, 2007).

59 Government meetings in China have never been systematically opened to the public. However, the party and the government traditionally allow certain privileged journalists to attend, regularly, key meetings. Leading officials from the Chinese bureaucracy assume that access to high-profile government meetings will inform journalists who can better propagandize the party's policies. For example, provincial bureau chiefs of Xinhua News Agency and *People's Daily* enjoy the privilege of regularly attending meetings held by standing committees of provincial party committees. Likewise, editors and publishers of Xinhua News Agency and the *People's Daily* regularly attended meetings of CPC Politburo before the reform era. For more information about journalistic privileges to attend certain governmental meetings, see *History and Development of Xinhua News Agency Heilongjiang Bureau* [新华通讯社在黑龙江省的分支机构的沿革和发展], XINHUA NEWS AGENCY,

facilities.[60] Likewise, such transparency practices are beyond the scope of this book because government meetings and facilities are not covered by the Chinese FOI law. Hong Kong, Taiwan, and Macao are parts of Chinese territories. Freedom of information codes, laws, and practices

January 10, 2013 (captured by Internet Archive Wayback Machine on March 21, 2015), retrieved from https://web.archive.org/web/20150510041641/http://hlj.xinhuanet.com/hljfs/2013-01/10/c_132092257.htm (noting that all Xinhua News Agency provincial bureau chiefs enjoy such privilege) (accessed between February 21, 2025 and March 31, 2025); Weiwei Fei, *Citizen-Based Approach Shall Be Adopted to Deal with Well-Being Issues* [抓民生, "群众主体是关键"], People's Daily, republished by Haixinews.com.cn, March 7, 2012 (captured by Internet Archive Wayback Machine on November 3, 2013), retrieved from https://web.archive.org/web/20131103083431/http://www.haixinews.com.cn/html/2012/zhongyangmeitikanhaixi_0307/3059.html (noting that the People's Daily Fujian Provincial bureau chief enjoys such privilege) (accessed between February 21, 2025 and March 31, 2025); Nengxi Wu, *Starting from Assessment of Joseph Stalin* [从评价斯大林说起], People's Daily Online, August 25, 2010 (captured by Internet Archive Wayback Machine on June 7, 2011), retrieved from https://web.archive.org/web/20110607235409/http://media.people.com.cn/GB/192301/192377/192680/201060/201062/12533386.html (noting that the Xinhua News Agency publisher and People's Daily editor in chief enjoyed such privilege) (accessed between February 21, 2025 and March 31, 2025); Liang Shen and Yunzi Wu, *People's Daily Editorials and Commentaries: Behind the Scene Stories* [探秘人民日报评论台前幕后] Southern Weekend, November 13, 2010, republished by Guancha.cn [观察者], July 26, 2013, *available at* https://www.guancha.cn/politics/2013_07_26_161344.shtml?web (noting that People's Daily publishers enjoyed such privilege) (accessed between February 21, 2025 and March 31, 2025).

[60] The Zhongnanhai, once briefly open to the public in the early 1980s, is central headquarters for the Communist Party of China and the State Council. The Great Hall of the People is meeting place of the National People's Congress, the Chinese parliament and is accessible to visitors during certain hours. In 2012, the Beijing people's government issued a notice encouraging government agencies, in Beijing, to allow tourists. Some dining halls of central agencies in Beijing are open to residents in nearby communities. These practices of opening government facilities to the public have no standardization or been written into law. Zhiyong Dai, *Government Facilities Should Not Be Off-Limits to the Public* [政府机关不是高墙深院], Southern Weekend, April 20, 2012, http://www.infzm.com/content/74411 (accessed between February 21, 2025 and March 31, 2025).

in Hong Kong,[61] Taiwan,[62] and Macao[63] are beyond the scope of this research, which focuses exclusively on the freedom of information movement in Mainland China because *OGI Regulations* and *OPA Regulations* do not have legal authority in the three special areas.[64]

Research Questions

In order to illuminate all previously mentioned issues, this book seeks to answer four general research questions:

1. **How did China, a country bereft of democratic political institutions and a democratic political culture of open government, adopt the Western concept of freedom of information? In other words, how have international experiences in FOI, and ancient**

[61] Hong Kong adopted *Code on Access to Information*. Unlike many FOI legislations in the world, the code is not law nor legislated by the Legislative Council of Hong Kong. Instead, the government of Hong Kong promulgated the code as an internal regulation affording minimal legal status. *Code on Access to Information* can be found on the Hong Kong government website, *available at* http://www.access.gov.hk/en/code.htm (accessed between February 21, 2025 and March 31, 2025). For analysis of legal status of the code, see Angharad Law, *Freedom of Information in Hong Kong*, the University of Hong Kong, Hong Kong, China, March 24, 2010, http://jmsc.hku.hk/2010/03/freedom-of-information-in-hong-kong/ (accessed between February 21, 2025 and March 31, 2025).

[62] Taiwan enacted *Freedom of Government Information Law* in 2005. The law passed the Legislative Yuan of the Taiwanese government (Republic of China). The legislation can be found in the Laws and Regulations Database of the Republic of China, *available at* https://law.moj.gov.tw/ENG/LawClass/LawAll.aspx?pcode=I0020026 (accessed between February 21, 2025 and March 31, 2025).

[63] Macao does not have any forms of freedom of information legislations. The city's Government Information Bureau (https://www.gcs.gov.mo/news/functions/en) aims to facilitate flow of information.

[64] According to the *Constitution of the People's Republic of China*, Macau and Hong Kong have special administrative regional status, which provides constitutional guarantees for implementing the policy of "one country, two systems" and the constitutional basis for enacting *Basic Law of the Macau Special Administrative Region* and *Basic Law of the Hong Kong Special Administrative Region*. The central government of China in Beijing, which controls the foreign affairs and defense of Macau and Hong Kong but otherwise grants the two regions "a high degree of autonomy," has no direct authority over the two Special Administrative Regions, although the two regions' autonomy is quickly eroding in recent years. The status of Taiwan remains controversial. Taiwan declined subjugation to the People's Republic of China and declined the granting of special administrative region status, similar to that granted Hong Kong and Macao.

Chinese philosophies and practices of transparency and secrecy influenced contemporary Chinese political leaders who played key roles in the adoption of the FOI law?

This question arises for two reasons: First, freedom of information closely relates to freedom of expression and the press. Liberal and electoral democracies, which protect freedom of expression and the press, easily nurture freedom of information. Consequently, most countries with freedom of information laws are democratic and have, more or less, traditions of access to official records.[65] China is a rare example of authoritarian transparency with a long history of maintaining confidentiality of official documents. In over 4,000 years of Chinese history, keeping official records hidden has been standard practice. An illuminating investigation would be to identify how and why the concept of freedom of information could take root in an authoritarian regime.

Second, the rationale for a country's efforts to move toward freedom of information is an important consideration. Specifically, identifying the political, economic, societal, legal, and cultural forces encouraging the creation of the FOI law is a crucial insight. For example, the Scandinavian countries such as Finland and Denmark adopted FOI laws early because of the influence of the Swedish FOI law and the strong liberal tradition in the area. Many new democracies like South Africa and South Korea adopted FOI laws because their political leaders, at the time, had strong commitment to democratic values and determination to sever ties with the countries' bitter authoritarian past.[66] Many emerging democracies in Central and Eastern Europe adopted FOI laws due to a desire to join the European Union.[67] In many long-established democracies like

[65] Among the more than 90 countries that have adopted various forms of freedom of information legislation, only 10 are nondemocratic. They are Asian countries of China and Pakistan, the African nations of Angola and Zimbabwe, the Middle East countries of Yemen and Jordan, and the former Soviet Union member states of Russia, Uzbekistan, Azerbaijan, and Tajikistan.

[66] John M. Ackerman & Irma E. Sandoval-Ballesteros, *The Global Explosion of Freedom of Information Laws*, 58 Administrative Law Review 85, 90–113 (2006).

[67] John M. Ackerman & Irma E. Sandoval-Ballesteros, *The Global Explosion of Freedom of Information Laws*, 58 Administrative Law Review 85, 90–122 (2006); David Goldberg, *Promoting Practical Access to Democracy: A Survey of Freedom of Information in Central and Eastern Europe*, edited by Sara Buchanan and Pauline Donaldson (report researched and written for Article 19), Article 19, London, United Kingdom,

Germany, the United Kingdom, and the United States, governmental agencies generally were reluctant to embrace access laws, but journalists, lawyers, and legislatures organized campaigns to fight for the creation of such laws.[68] Some developing countries, especially countries from Africa and Asia, joined the global FOI community to build favorable international images and to seek much-needed foreign investment.[69] What prompted the Chinese government to diverge from a long-established, traditional secretive approach to public access to information is the first issue for this research. Exploration, illumination, and discussion of the research question presented above are the focuses of Chapters 2, 3, 4, and 5.

2. **How does the statutory language of the Chinese FOI law (both *OGI Regulations 2007* and *OPA Regulations 2017*) align with international best practices? Given the statutory language of the law and the history of implementation since 2008, does the Chinese law qualify as a piece of effective freedom of information legislation?**

October 2002, at 3, *available at* http://www.article19.org/data/files/pdfs/publications/freedom-of-information-survey-of-central-and-e.pdf (accessed between February 21, 2025 and March 31, 2025) (stating that potential members of the Council of Europe were encouraged to see access to information as a fundamental right).

[68] John M. Ackerman & Irma E. Sandoval-Ballesteros, *The Global Explosion of Freedom of Information Laws*, 58 ADMINISTRATIVE LAW REVIEW 85, 90–114 (2006); Martin E. Halstuk & Bill F. Chamberlin, *The Freedom of Information Act 1966–2006: A Retrospective on the Rise Of Privacy Protection Over the Public Interest*, 11 COMMUNICATION LAW AND POLICY 511, 517 (2006).

[69] Many scholars have argued that a workable mechanism to ensure access to government information attracts more foreign direct investment. Abraham A. Azubuike, *Accessibility of Government Information as a Determinant of Inward Foreign Direct Investment in Africa*, paper presented at the 72nd IFLA (Internal Federation of Library Associations and Institutions) General Conference and Council, 20–24 August 2006, Seoul, South Korea, *available at* https://citeseerx.ist.psu.edu/document?repid=rep1&type=pdf&doi=e355c0ea7f586ad47416fe04bd6463213476ee6e (accessed between February 21, 2025 and March 31, 2025); *UJRC Convenes Three Training Workshops on Access to Information*, Al Urdun Al Jadid Research Center, March 2009, issue no.4, *available at* http://freedominfo.org/documents/Information%20is%20Right%20for%20all%20-%20Eng%202.pdf (accessed between February 21, 2025 and March 31, 2025).

China was later than the majority of FOI countries in adopting freedom of information legislation. China has had chances to borrow reformers' ideas of valuable aspects of international experiences. London-based FOI organization, Article 19, developed a model FOI law.[70] FOI scholar, Toby Mendel, formulated nine principles of ideal FOI laws: maximum disclosure, governments' obligation to publish proactively, promotion of open government, limited scope for exceptions, timely and fair processes for requests and independent review of any denied request, no excessive costs for access, open meetings, precedence for disclosure (all laws inconsistent with the principle of maximum disclosure require amendment or repeal), and protection for whistleblowers.[71] Prominent international FOI expert, David Banisar, identified international trends in development of global freedom of information laws.[72] He also thoroughly examined successes and failures of all national FOI laws.[73]

Legal scholar, Martin Halstuk, identified six characteristics of *effective* freedom of information laws: (1) All records are presumptively open, and disclosure is the standard; (2) exemptions to disclosure must be narrow and clear in the law's statutory language; (3) *any* person can request government-held records and documents for *any* purpose without the requirement of an explanation; (4) independent review, without cost to

[70] ARTICLE 19, A MODEL FREEDOM OF INFORMATION LAW, London, *available at* http://www.article19.org/data/files/pdfs/standards/modelfoilaw.pdf (accessed between February 21, 2025 and March 31, 2025).

[71] FREEDOM OF INFORMATION: A COMPARATIVE LEGAL SURVEY 23–36 (Toby Mendel ed., 2nd edn, 2008).

[72] David Banisar, *Freedom of Information International Trends and National Security*, paper presented at the Workshop on "Democratic and Parliamentary Oversight of Intelligence Services," held in Geneva 3rd–5th October 2002, organized by the Working Group on the Parliamentary Control of Armed Forces (PCAF) and the Working Group on Democratic Control of Internal Security Services (DCOIS) of the Geneva Center for the Democratic Control of Armed Forces, *available at* http://www.humanrightsinitiative.org/programs/ai/rti/articles/foia_intl_trends_and_nat_sec.pdf (accessed between February 21, 2025 and March 31, 2025).

[73] His global survey on all the national FOI laws was updated by April 2006. DAVID BANISAR, FREEDOM OF INFORMATION AROUND THE WORLD 2006: A GLOBAL SURVEY OF ACCESS TO GOVERNMENT INFORMATION LAWS (report for Privacy International, London, United Kingdom, July 2006), *available at* http://www.freedominfo.org/documents/global_survey2006.pdf (accessed between February 21, 2025 and March 31, 2025).

the requester should be available in those instances when the government rejects an FOI request; (5) an affirmative disclosure requirement, meaning that government agencies must publish on the Internet certain information without request, such as agencies' organizational plans, regulations, annual reports, statements of agencies' rules, policies, and instructions for using the FOIA. The rationale for affirmative disclosure is creating a guard against development of an agency's "secret law"—rules and regulations known to governmental officials but not the public; (6) copying fees for records should be reasonable and not exceeds the actual cost of production.[74]

The current research uses the latter six criteria to measure and analyze Chinese freedom of information law. The study also examines whether or not inspiration from international statutes inspired China. The study considers the reasons for China's embracing some international standards and rejecting global best FOI practices elsewhere. Based on the data gathered, this investigation considers enforcement of Chinese FOI law since 2008. Thus, Chapters 6, 7, 8, and 11 respond to the second set of research questions.

3. **What exemptions apply to Chinese government's internal working documents and journalistic internal reference materials under *OGI Regulations*? What is the impact of such exemptions on free flow of information in Chinese society?**

Internal working documents are a complicated subject for freedom of information jurisprudence. Many national FOI laws exempt such documents from disclosure. For example, under *U.S. FOIA*, two kinds of internal working documents have exemptions from disclosure. One is housekeeping practices in Exemption 2 of *U.S. FOIA*, and another is intra-agency and interagency memoranda and letters in Exemption 5 of *U.S. FOIA*.[75] Exemption 2 shields from disclosure risk-of-circumvention records and records of internal agencies' personnel rules and practices, like hiring and firing, work rules and discipline, and compensation and

[74] Martin E. Halstuk, *Freedom of Information*, *in* 5 INTERNATIONAL ENCYCLOPEDIA OF COMMUNICATION 1890, 1890–91 (Wolfgang Donsbach ed., 2008).

[75] 5 U.S.C. § 552((b) (2)(2006) and 5 U.S.C. § 552((b) (5)(2006).

benefits.[76] Exemption 5 shields three kinds of information from disclosure: working papers such as studies, reports, memoranda, and other sorts of documents prepared and circulated to assist official personnel's decisions or policies (the deliberative process privilege); conversations and materials between an agency and its attorneys (client-attorney privilege); communications between the president and key advisors (the executive privilege doctrine or the presidential communications privilege).[77] *OGI Regulations* do not explicitly exempt internal working documents from disclosure. This disclosure-friendly move seems indicating China's willingness to share internal working documents with the public. But in practice, Chinese government agencies have rejected many FOI requests on the ground that the files sought were internal working documents.

The issue on internal working documents is difficult, but a thornier issue concerns the journalistic internal reference. The internal reference system is the ruling party's method of controlling free flow of information in China. The system mandates major party news outlets to gather information for leading party and governmental officials. "Internal journalistic documents," delivered to party and government officials through special circulation channels, publish information of sensitive and controversial issues and events. Officials read those classified documents daily to gain appraisal of domestic and international events. Policy decisions are often the result of this reportage, analysis, and recommendations provided by journalists who author internal articles. Leaking internal journalistic documents to the public is a crime, and violators could be prosecuted. A preliminary search of databases revealed that no other countries in the world today have similar journalistic internal reference systems.

The existence of "internal journalistic documents" is a serious legal challenge for *OGI Regulations* and *OPA Regulations* because such documents contain large amounts of government-held and party-held information, most of which should have disclosure according to Chinese FOI law. Some Chinese bloggers are urging the government to abolish the internal reference system and turn "internal journalistic documents" into public periodicals. The mechanics of how internal working documents and journalistic internal references restrict flow of information are a topic hardly addressed by legal scholars. The topic is clearly worth exploring,

[76] Milner v. Department of the Navy, 131 S. Ct. 1259 (2011).

[77] Don. R. Pember & Clay Calvert, Mass Media Law 349–51 (2013).

and therefore, illuminating the third set of research questions is the focus of Chapter 9.

4. **What roles have Chinese journalists and news media outlets played in proposing, formulating, and publicizing *OGI Regulations*? What are the rationales for those roles? To what use have Chinese reporters and editors put FOI law for information access? What are the reasons for limited journalistic use of the law?**

OGI Regulations do not apply to the Chinese media specifically but have great implications for journalists' abilities to gather information. Access to government information is vital for the news media, as legal scholar, Vincent Blasi argued, without a right of access to governmental information, the press inevitably confronts enormous difficulties uncovering official misconduct.[78] Consequently, unsurprisingly, members of the news media in the United States and many other countries are always strong proponents of freedom of information legislation. For example, American reporters and editors were instrumental in making *U.S. FOIA* possible.[79] Once establishing legal right of access to government-held information by national FOI laws, American journalists and their colleagues in many other countries were among the first users of the laws. Muckrakers in many countries, especially in countries with strong protection for the press, have produced large quantities of news stories based on information obtained from FOI requests.[80]

The roles played by foreign journalists in proposing, formulating, and using the FOI laws may or may not be similar to Chinese colleagues.

[78] Vincent Blasi, *The Checking Value in First Amendment Theory*, 3 AMERICAN BAR FOUNDATION RESEARCH JOURNAL 521 (1977).

[79] Martin E. Halstuk & Bill F. Chamberlin, *The Freedom of Information Act 1966–2006: A Retrospective on the Rise Of Privacy Protection Over the Public Interest*, 11 COMMUNICATION LAW AND POLICY 511, 514–17 (2006) (finding that American news media led an influential campaign during and after the World War II to persuade Congress to enact a freedom of information law).

[80] EDUARDO BERTONI, FREEDOM OF INFORMATION, THREE HARMLESS WORDS? THE ROLE OF THE MEDIA AND ACCESS TO INFORMATION LAWS, report of Center for Studies on Freedom of Expression and Access to Information, Palermo University School of Law, Buenos Aires, Argentina, *available at* http://www.palermo.edu/cele/pdf/ATIandMedia.pdf (accessed between February 21, 2025 and March 31, 2025).

Equally, the roles of foreign reporters' exposing non-compliance of government agencies with the FOI requirements and similar roles by their Chinese counterparts remain cloudy. No easy clarity for these issues exists.

Today's Chinese mass media is in transition: On one hand, the media remains under the ruling party's tight control. Conversely, Chinese media is increasingly commercialized.[81] Many market-oriented metropolitan publications display aggressive investigative journalism, and such outlets could well advocate formulation of a freedom of information law. Enterprising journalists could advocate and use Chinese freedom of information law for details that may hold governmental officials accountable and expose irregularities in the enforcement of the law. Concerning reporters from traditional party news outlets, do they aspire to a right of access to government-held information? Do they cover FOI-related scandals and misconduct aggressively? If they use the law to access official documents, is the use similar to their colleagues from market-oriented, metropolitan, media outlets?[82] Especially revealing is examination of this fourth set of research questions regarding the role of Chinese news media in freedom of information, and this is the focus of Chapter 10.

Research Methodology

The principal methodology used in this book is legal research. In a commonly accepted definition, legal research involves "each step of a course of action that begins with an analysis of the facts of a problem and concludes with the application and communication of the results of the investigation."[83] Legal research usually involves: framing the issue,

[81] For more detailed discussions of the Chinese news media system after the death of Mao Zedong, see Yuezhi Zhao, Media, Market, and Democracy in China: Between the Party Line and the Bottom Line (1998); Junhao Hong, The Internationalization of Television in China: the Evolution of Ideology, Society and Media since the Reform (1998); Anne-Marie Brady, *Marketing Dictatorship: Propaganda and Thought Work in Contemporary China* (2008); Changing Media, Changing China (Susan L. Shirk, ed., 2010).

[82] Little research considers the role of Chinese journalists in the country's campaign for freedom of information. No scholars have systematically surveyed Chinese journalists on the topic. The study conducts qualitative interviews by email and telephone to examine the familiarity of Chinese journalists with *OGI Regulations*.

[83] J. Myron Jacobstein & Roy M. Mersky, Fundamentals of Legal Research 1 (8th ed., 2002).

locating primary sources (cases and statutes), locating secondary sources (law review articles and books), investigating relevant rules of legal and non-legal procedures, and determining the jurisprudential effects.[84] Legal research in this study includes:

- Examining the statutory language of *OGI Regulations and OPA Regulations.*
- Examining the statutory language of *U.S. FOIA* and its amendments.
- Reviewing the legislative history of *OGI Regulations* and *U.S. FOIA.*
- Analyzing pertinent OGI requests submitted by Chinese requesters for information held by governmental agencies at various levels.
- Analyzing pertinent OGI administrative reconsideration cases filed by Chinese information requesters for rectifying non-compliance with *OGI Regulations.*
- Analyzing pertinent OGI litigations filed by Chinese requesters to rectify non-compliance with *OGI Regulations.*
- Translating and interpreting Chinese-language legal documents, newspapers, magazines, and website articles, administrative reconsideration cases, court cases, and the party's and the people's government's directives on freedom of information.
- Examining Chinese-language official web portals that feature freedom of information content.
- Examining OGI-related governmental transparency laws and practices in China.
- Examining the use of open records law and other transparency-related laws, especially in the digital age.

Legal research resources used in the book include the HeinOnline database, Lexis-Nexis database, Google Scholar, Westlaw Campus, Westlaw China, *Beida Fabao*, China Judgement Online, Index to Legal Periodicals, China Academic Journals Database, China Core Newspapers Full-text Database, Internet Archive Wayback Machine, Google, Baidu, and other search engines. The research relies heavily on primary sources including in-depth interviews, party directives, governmental statutes and

[84] CHRISTINA L. KUNZ, DEBORAH A. SCHMEDEMANN, ANN L. BATESON, MATTHEW P. DOWNS & MEHMET KONAR-STEENBERG, THE PROCESS OF LEGAL RESEARCH 7 (2008).

other legal documents, and court cases. Also used in the research are secondary source materials, including books, newspaper and magazine articles, legal periodicals such as law journals and law reviews, mass communication journals, history and political science journals, and even Internet-only sources. In today's digital world, primary and secondary materials for legal research are easily accessible via well-designed searches of database services.[85] Thus, while expended time and energy identifies needed materials, more time and effort accrue to establishing relevant patterns and insights from the large quantities of available information of Chinese *OGI Regulations* and other relevant laws.

This book complements the legal research with interdisciplinary methods, specifically, qualitative historical research[86] to explore the events and public debates resulting in the legal structure of access to information in China. The study discusses the concept of freedom of information matured in the Western civilization and its transference to China. An examination provides details of the communication policies of the Chinese government evolved in the last four thousand years. In order to identify the true influences on the freedom of information laws, the research focuses primarily on legislative history, complemented by political and sociological history.

[85] Digital materials are easily accessible, but they come and go. This is especially true in China where major news websites such as the ones run by People's Daily and Xinhua News Agency have deleted a large number of articles published in the last 20 years. The author of this book found in February 2024 that many of the articles he published 20 years ago on the People's Daily website while he worked for the paper as a reporter were deleted and search engines can no longer find those articles. The author was told that he is among many (current and former) People's Daily journalists whose articles published on the newspaper's website have been blocked for viewing. The disappearance of articles from mainstream news websites makes it hard to trace the full history of FOI-related narratives and events that have been reported on in the past and also makes it hard to understand the evolution of the Chinese FOI law, its interpretation, and how information has been handled over time. For defunct Chinese-language web pages that are essential to understanding the Chinese FOI law, the author of this book uses the Internet Archive's Wayback Machine to bring them back to life. The Wayback Machine is also used to bring back to life some English-language materials.

[86] Scholars Charles Busha and Stephen Harter have detailed six steps for conducting historical research. It starts "from the recognition of a historical problem or the identification of a need for certain historical knowledge" and ends with "recording of conclusions in a meaningful narrative." CHARLES H. BUSHA & STEPHEN P. HARTER, RESEARCH METHODS IN LIBRARIANSHIP: TECHNIQUES AND INTERPRETATIONS 91 (1980).

Second, aspects of political economic research apply to the research. Commonly, political economic research involves methodology combining political science and economics to explore the qualitative effects of power on the well-being and the depth of knowledge of people.[87] By using political economic research methods, this study examines political and economic causes and effects from governmental transparency and secrecy.

Third, personal interviews with government officials, and email, telephone, and WeChat interviews with Chinese legal scholars and lawyers familiar with FOI issues, provide insight for the current research. Telephone and email interviews with editors and reporters from various kinds of media outlets across the country determine Chinese journalists' familiarity with *OGI Regulations*.[88] The author of this book compiles a dataset from hundreds of thousands of OGI annual work reports published by all the central and provincial government agencies (2008–2023) to examine enforcement of *OGI Regulations* since the 2008 institution of the law. The researcher also visits some Chinese government websites to personally experience the ease of access to official information. When examining the data regarding archives laws, state secrets laws and practices of secrecy and transparency of the Chinese government over the last several thousand years, the current researcher relies upon web-based e-text systems to search among large volumes of ancient Chinese historical classics such as *Records of the Grand Historian*, *Book of Han*, *Chronicle of Zuo,* and *Lv's Commentaries of History*.[89]

[87] VINCENT MOSCO, THE POLITICAL ECONOMY OF COMMUNICATIONS 2–9 (1996).

[88] Some sample questions asked during interviews with Chinese journalists include (1) "Do you know *OGI Regulations*?" (2) "Have you ever used *OGI Regulations* to access governmental documents?" (3) "If no, why?" (4) "If yes, how many times have you applied for information via filing OGI requests since 2008?" (5) "What kind of information are you requesting?" (6) "Are you requesting information as a citizen or as a journalist?" (7) "Have you ever obtained the information sought?" (8) "If yes, how do you usually use the information you obtained?" (9) "If no, have you ever tried administrative and/or judicial remedies?" (10) "Are you aware of any of your colleagues (in your newsroom or other media outlets) who have ever used the law for informational access?" (11) "Can you provide any suggestions, concerns, recommendations you may have for journalistic use of *OGI Regulations*?".

[89] Chinese historical classics are numerous. The current researcher first examines Chinese-language materials (e.g., newspapers, magazines, journals, online postings) to determine what kind of Chinese historical classics may contain information pertaining to mass communication policies of various Chinese governments. Then the researcher employs key words such as "secrecy" or "transparency" to search among the large

Although adopting an interdisciplinary approach in research is desirable, this study seeks to emphasize that legal analysis is the principal methodology. All the other methodologies, including historical research, political economic research and interviews are secondary. Overall, the book's discussion is in depth and lengthy, compared to a law review article in an academic journal, but appears similar to a law review article in structure and content.

Major Research Contributions

This research advances public understanding of Chinese freedom of information law, one of the most significant advancements of Chinese government toward greater transparency. This study differs significantly from existing literature, consequently contributing to existing scholarship.

The book

- Explains the influence of the Western concept of freedom of information inculcation in the Chinese authoritarian body politic and culture, which incorporated official secrecy as the norm throughout the nation's modern history.
- Investigates evolving official transparency and secrecy during China's civilization from the first dynasty to the PRC.
- Provides a detailed and comprehensive account of the legislative history of Chinese *OGI Regulations.*
- Examines, evaluates, and compares the statutory language of *OGI Regulations/OPA Regulations* and equivalent laws in the United States and other countries.
- Examines and evaluates the enforcement of *OGI Regulations*' proactive and reactive disclosure requirements by using data compiled from many sources.

volumes of classics. This searching work becomes easier because of the availability of the Chinese Text Project (http://ctext.org/) and some other bilingual web-based e-text systems such as the one on the website of the University of Virginia's Institute for Advanced Technology in the Humanities (http://www2.iath.virginia.edu/saxon/servlet/SaxonServlet?source=xwomen/texts/hanshu.xml&style=xwomen/xsl/dynaxml.xsl&chunk.id=d2.3&toc.depth=1&toc.id=0&doc.lang=bilingual). The current researcher also searches relevant Chinese texts on the website of guoxue.com (http://www.guoxue.com/), a site where one can search and locate numerous Chinese classics and ancient books.

- Assesses the Chinese FOI law's efficacy through an analysis of recent Chinese information requests, administrative reconsideration cases, and court cases.
- Examines the function of internal working documents and journalistic internal reference, as used by agencies and/or judges, to deny disclosure and the effect on people's legal right of access from these two exemptions that are not components of *OGI Regulations.*
- Discusses *OGI Regulations*' coinciding with the evolving paradigm of the Chinese news media. In other words, the study examines the role of Chinese journalists in formulating, publicizing, and using the law for access to information.
- Uses Freedom House scores that quantify the status of China's regime and press freedom to scrutinize a comparison of the Chinese government with more than 100 FOI countries.
- Combines legal research with other methodologies such as historiology, political economy, email and telephone interviews, qualitative data analyses, and experimental use of *OGI Regulations.*
- Proposes recommendations for China's policymakers and international stakeholders to improve official transparency in China and beyond.

Summary of Book Chapters

This book examines and evaluates the legal right of access to government-held information in the PRC. This research of Chinese freedom of information law includes 13 chapters. Chapter 1: *Introduction: Freedom of Information with Chinese Characteristics.* This chapter warms up readers by introducing and contextualizing the topic. After a brief survey on China's unique political, media, and legal systems that provides the fertile ground for the seeds of FOI to germinate, take root and grow, the chapter examines the research project's purpose and significance, research scope, research questions, research methodology, and major research contributions. It ends with summaries of all the chapters in the book.

Chapter 2: *Theoretical Applications and Literature Review.* This chapter examines all the major theories used in the book. Major theories providing philosophical and legal inspirations for freedom of information legislation are the freedom of expression theory, the right to know theory, the democratic political theory, and the checking value in First Amendment theory. The chapter examines reinterpretations of the right to know theory in the Chinese context. Discussion includes the four theories of the press and democratization theories and a review of existing literature pertaining to the Chinese FOI law. All relevant, major, scholarly articles, books, book chapters, conference papers, dissertations, theses, and other academic materials focusing on *OGI Regulations* have consideration to identify gaps in the academic literature.

Chapter 3: *Origins and Development of Freedom of Information Laws in the World.* The world's first freedom of information law emerged in Sweden in 1766. However, modern government transparency laws have roots in *U.S. FOIA* (1966), which inspired approximately 60 other nations' FOI laws. This chapter traces the origins of the concept of freedom of information, tracks the history and development of FOI laws around the world, identifies patterns and trends that may be reference points for the Chinese version of FOI legislation. This chapter examines the origins and milestones of *U.S. FOIA* in detail, its incomparable influence in the world, and the role of U.S. journalists in the formulation, revision, and use of the FOI law. This chapter also discusses how the law has been used as a model by U.S. state legislatures to craft open records laws of their own.

Chapter 4: *Secrecy and Transparency of the Chinese Government: A Historical Perspective.* Government secrecy, a Chinese practice for thousands of years, coexisted with practices of disclosure of information dating to the beginning of the Chinese civilization. This chapter examines both sides of the Chinese government's informational policies'—secrecy and transparency—evolution. Dynasties in Chinese history are numerous, and the scope of this research does not allow for thorough scrutiny of each dynasty. Thus, focus for review is on the government's informational policies in four major time periods: Pre-Qin China (2070 BC-221 BC), imperial China (221 BC-1911 AD), the Republic of China (1912–1949), and the People's Republic of China under the leadership of Mao Zedong (1949–1976). The study assesses the influence of ancient schools of thought such as Confucianism and Legalism on interpretation of the value of flow of information between the government and its subjects. The chapter analyzes the inspiration or discouragement of those schools of thought on subsequent rulers' thinking and practicing on governmental secrecy. Especially noteworthy is how information policies and practices of the Tang Dynasty inspired the world's first freedom of information law.

Chapter 5: *Legislative History of OGI Regulations and Rationales for the Rise of Chinese Freedom of Information.* This chapter provides an overview of the legislative background of various factors contributing to the final passage of *OGI Regulations*. Mao Zedong established a comprehensive information control system after assuming office in 1949. When Mao died in 1976 and Deng Xiaoping emerged as the paramount leader of China in 1978, the country began to liberalize its political and economic systems. As part of its efforts to reform and open to the outside world, China began to embrace, gradually, the concept of governmental transparency. This chapter examines three generation of Chinese leaders' (Deng Xiaoping, Jiang Zemin, and Hu Jintao) understanding of the value and necessity of governmental transparency and explores *OGI Regulations*' proposals, drafts, and adoption.

Chapter 6: *What the Law Promises: Analysis of Statutory Language of OGI Regulations.* This chapter provides an overview of the Chinese FOI law and its 2019 amendment by examining its statutory language in different categories necessary for freedom of information laws in a transparent government. The major categories covered are legal authority, legislative purpose, types of governmental bodies covered, identity of accessible information; identity of inquirers, fees for access, response time limits, exemptions, appeals and oversight, sanctions, affirmative publication, e-FOI, and whistleblowing.

Chapter 7: *What the Law Delivers: Implementation of OGI Regulations.* This chapter examines the enforcement of *OGI Regulations* during the last 16 years (2008–2023) in both proactive disclosure and reactive disclosure. The analysis of strengths and weaknesses of the enforcement of the law has a basis in data compiled by the author of this book from OGI-related court cases published by the China Supreme Court and annual OGI work reports published by all provincial and central government agencies. The chapter explores various factors contributing to strengths and problems.

Chapter 8: *Transparency of Public Enterprises and Institutions in China: A Freedom of Information Law Perspective.* This chapter examines a special category of entities that are subject to *OGI Regulations*: Public enterprises and public institutions. Similar to administrative agencies and entities authorized by law to perform the functions of administering public affairs, public institutions, and public enterprises have a legal obligation to disclose information both proactively and reactively. After examining the statutory language and enforcement of the Chinese FOI law with regard to public enterprises and institutions using a sample of 182 relevant lawsuits, this chapter finds a wide range of deficiencies in the law. Most strikingly, courts are reluctant to hold public enterprises and institutions accountable. Oversight government departments are even more so. Proposed solutions and theoretical implications are discussed.

Chapter 9: *Journalistic Internal Reference and Internal Working Documents: A Freedom of Information Law Perspective.* This chapter examines two kinds of official information exempt from disclosure requirements of *OGI Regulations*. One is journalistic internal reference; the other is working secrets or internal working documents. Both exemptions play significant roles in restricting the free flow of information between the Chinese government and citizens. This chapter argues that Chinese law reformers need to define relevant terms and narrow the scope of working secrets and internal working documents as an exemption. This chapter found that, although journalistic internal reports may expose some official corruption and misdeeds, the system faces many problems and challenges in today's legal, media, and political environment, therefore, gradual elimination of the practice of journalistic internal reports is desirable.

Chapter 10: *Journalistic Role in Chinese Freedom of Information.* This chapter examines the Chinese FOI law's compliance with the evolving paradigm of the Chinese news media. In many countries with freedom of information legislation, journalists executed important roles leading the campaign for greater access to government-held information and establishment of legal rights to access. Journalists in those countries are among the most active, enthusiastic, and successful users of, and commentators on, freedom of information laws. This chapter explores if Chinese journalism has played a similar role. In other words, the chapter attempts to investigate Chinese journalists' contributions to the drafting, publicizing, and enforcement of *OGI Regulations* and their use of the law to access government-held information for enhancing news gathering, reporting, producing, writing, and dissemination.

Chapter 11: *An Enforcement Blackhole: The Communist Party of China and Its Own Freedom of Information Law. OGI Regulations* do not apply to the Communist Party of China, but the party has its own transparency laws and guidelines. This chapter discusses the tentative Regulations of the Chinese Communist Party on Open Party Affairs (*OPA Regulations*), the party equivalent of OGI Regulations. Enacted in December 2017, *OPA Regulations* provide that the CCP Central Committee and various lower levels of party organizations shall proactively disclose certain types of information to party members and, in some circumstances, to the general public. The party's own FOI law does not allow party members and average citizens to apply for information held by party organizations at all levels. This chapter attempts to examine the statutory language of *OPA Regulations* and identify its dominant features and weaknesses. Using various databases and search engines, the chapter identifies a huge "enforcement blackhole." The analysis on the blackhole aims to shed light on how the party's FOI legislation has been implemented both proactively and reactively in the last several years.

Chapter 12: *Recommendations for Chinese Law Reformers and International Stakeholders.* This chapter includes a recapitulation of the book and provides recommendations and suggestions for reformers of Chinese law and international stakeholders to consider when revising *OGI Regulations* in the future and involving China on discussions of global governance. Additionally, the chapter discusses the limitations of the research and areas for future study.

Chapter 13: *Appendix (Tables).* This chapter contains all the tables used throughout the book, including the datasets compiled by the author from annual government OGI work reports (2008–2023) and OGI-related lawsuits (2014–2021). Chapter 1 has two tables. Chapter 6 has three tables. Chapter 7 contains 9 tables. Chapter 8 has only one table while Chapter 10 has five tables.

Back Matter: *Bibliography.* This section includes all the primary and secondary sources used in the book. All the OGI-related party and government directives, statutes, and reports, and bilateral and international treaties and documents are also included here.

CHAPTER 2

Theoretical Applications and Literature Review

Introduction

This chapter will examine all the major theories that apply to the current research. Major philosophical and legal inspirations for freedom of information legislation are the theories of freedom of expression, right to know, democratic politics, and checking value in the First Amendment. Considerations will also include four theories of the press and democratization. In addition, this chapter will review the existing literature pertaining to the Chinese freedom of information (FOI) law. The chapter will review major scholarly articles, books, book chapters, conference

This chapter is derived from the book author's doctoral dissertation that was successfully defended at The Pennsylvania State University in 2012. Portions of the text resemble or may replicate the original text from the unpublished Ph.D. thesis and have been reproduced as such with the permission of Palgrave Macmillan editors. Yong Tang, "Chinese Freedom of Information: An Evaluation of the Legislative History, Rationales, Significance and Efficacy of Regulations of the People's Republic of China on Open Government Information" (2012) (unpublished Ph.D. diss., The Pennsylvania State University at University Park), *available at* https://etda.libraries.psu.edu/catalog/16287 (accessed between February 21, 2025 and March 31, 2025).

Y. Tang, *Freedom of Information Law in China*,
https://doi.org/10.1007/978-981-96-7842-6_2

papers, theses, and other academic materials that focus on *OGI Regulations*. The discussion will include identification of the gaps in the academic literature.

Theoretical Framework

Freedom of Expression Theory

As the examination in Chapter 1 demonstrates, freedom of information is a loosely defined term with four interpretations. The first view maintains that freedom of information is the right of access to vital information, and it is a constituent of the right to free expression of opinions. For example, FOI scholar, Roberto Saba, argued that freedom of expression and opinion not only entail individuals' right to disseminate their thoughts to all kinds of people,[1] but also guarantee that users of information have access to all diverging views on a specific issue.[2] The United Nations adopted the same approach in preparing its human rights documents. Article 19 of the United Nations Universal Declaration of Human Rights states, "Everyone has the right to freedom of opinion and expression; this right includes freedom to hold opinions without interference and to *seek, receive* and impart information and ideas through any media and regardless of frontiers (emphasis added)."[3]

The second perspective asserts that freedom of information includes the right to information and freedom of expression. For example, FOI scholar, Ernesto Villanueva, insisted that "Right to Information" includes but goes beyond freedom of expression, and access to information consists of three elements: (1) the right to seek and receive information; (2) the right to inform; (3) the right to be informed.[4] Another FOI

[1] Roberto Saba, *An Individual's Right to Access Information in the Hands of the Government* [El derecho De la Persona a Acceder a la Informacion en Poder del Gobierno], 3 Comparative Media Law Journal [Derecho Comparado De La Informacion] 45 (January–June 2004).

[2] Roberto Saba, *An Individual's Right to Access Information in the Hands of the Government* [El derecho De la Persona a Acceder a la Informacion en Poder del Gobierno], 3 Comparative Media Law Journal [Derecho Comparado De La Informacion] 45 (January–June 2004).

[3] The *Universal Declaration of Human Rights*. Art. 19, *available at* http://www.un.org/en/documents/udhr/ (accessed between February 21, 2025 and March 31, 2025).

[4] *Ernesto Villanueva*, Right of Access to Public Information in Latin America: Introductory Studies and

scholar, Alasdair Roberts, also argued that information rights are essential constituents of basic rights for political participation, including but extending beyond the right of freedom of expression.[5]

The third view is that freedom of information and freedom of expression relate to each other but are separate civil rights. Neither is a component of the other. For example, FOI scholar, Mark Bovens, argued that similar to freedom of expression, freedom of information should be a civic right[6] and all FOI countries should include, in their constitutions, a universal right to information.[7]

The fourth view holds that freedom of information is the protection of freedom of expression on the Internet. Few FOI scholars hold this perspective, but many non-profit public interest organizations interpret freedom of information this way. For example, the Global Internet Freedom Consortium is an alliance of several leading organizations specializing in developing and deploying anti-censorship technologies for Internet users in oppressive regimes. The Consortium states on its website homepage, "There is no freedom without freedom of information. There is no freedom of information without Internet freedom."[8]

Despite the varying definitions of freedom of information, the intimate intertwining of freedom of information and freedom of expression is difficult to deny. Consequently, examination of the freedom of expression theory, which grounds freedom of information, is desirable.

COMPILATIONS *[DERECHO DE ACCESO A LA INFORMACIÓN PÚBLICA EN LATINO AMÉRICA: ESTUDIO INTRODUCTIORIA Y COMPILACION]* 17 (2003).

[5] Alasdair Roberts, *Structural Pluralism and the Right to Information*, 51 UNIVERSITY OF TORONTO LAW JOURNAL 262, 243–71 (2001) (noting that access rights are grounded in participation rights in addition to the freedom of expression).

[6] Mark Bovens, *Information Rights: Citizenship in the Information Society*, 10 JOURNAL OF POLITICAL PHILOSOPHY 317, 317–41 (2002) (discussing the necessity of adding FOI to the list of ancient civil rights).

[7] Mark Bovens, *Information Rights: Citizenship in the Information Society*, 10 JOURNAL OF POLITICAL PHILOSOPHY 317, 317–41 (2002) (discussing how access to information has become a social justice problem).

[8] *Background* ("There is no freedom without freedom of information. There is no freedom of information without Internet freedom"), Global Internet Freedom Consortium, *available at* http://www.internetfreedom.org/about (accessed between February 21, 2025 and March 31, 2025).

The concept of freedom of expression, a universally acknowledged civil right,[9] had its origins in ancient Greece and Rome.[10] The right to freedom of speech and expression emerged in the era of the European Enlightenment.[11] The free speech theory is a result of the primary advocacy and development of three "Johns" (John Milton, John Locke, and John Stuart Mill). John Milton (1608–1674), known for his strong opposition to the British government's licensing of printers and publishers for censorship, eloquently pleaded for freedom of expression and toleration of falsehood in his 1644 book *Areopagitica*: "Give me the liberty to know, to utter, and to argue freely according to conscience, above all liberties."[12] John Locke (1632–1704) followed John Milton in challenging suppression of freedom of speech. Locke argued for religious tolerance and believed that all people were equal and independent, and

[9] Freedom of speech is protected by the *International Covenant on Civil and Political Rights* that has 74 signatories and 174 parties as of June 2024. Article 19 of the covenant states clearly, "Everyone shall have the right to freedom of expression; this right shall include freedom to seek, receive and impart information and ideas of all kinds, regardless of frontiers, either orally, in writing or in print, in the form of art, or through any other media of his choice." International Covenant on Civil and Political Rights, adopted 16 December 1966 by United Nations General Assembly resolution 2200A (XXI), entry into force 23 March 1976 in accordance with Article 49, *available at* https://www.ohchr.org/en/instruments-mechanisms/instruments/international-covenant-civil-and-political-rights (accessed between February 21, 2025 and March 31, 2025).

[10] Kurt A. Raaflaub, Josiah Ober, Robert Wallace, Paul Cartledge, Cynthia Farrar, Origins of Democracy in Ancient Greece (2007); Laura Robinson, "Freedom of Speech in the Roman Republic" (1940) (unpublished Ph.D. diss., Johns Hopkins University).

[11] European Enlightenment is a European intellectual movement of the seventeenth and eighteenth centuries. Fundamental to the Enlightenment's philosophies were use and celebration of reason. By using reason, man understands the universe and improves the human condition. Rational humans pursue three major goals in their lives: Knowledge, freedom, and happiness. For more explanations about European Enlightenment, visit Britannica Online Encyclopedia, *available at* http://www.britannica.com/EBchecked/topic/188441/Enlightenment (accessed between February 21, 2025 and March 31, 2025).

[12] Christophe Tournu & Neil Forsyth, Milton, Rights and Liberties 37 (2007). For the full text of his book *Areopagitica*, see John Milton, Milton's Areopagitica; a Speech for the Liberty of Unlicensed Printing (1915).

everyone had a natural right to defend personal liberty.[13] John Stuart Mill (1806–1873) and other subsequent philosophers were more progressive than John Locke by arguing for more universal freedom of speech and toleration. Mill believed no progress would occur in science, law, or politics without free discussion of opinion. He published *On Liberty* in 1859, and it became a classic defense for the right to freedom of expression.[14] Mill argued that no fear should associate with the free expression of ideas. To the contrary, such expression should receive encouragement without regard even to truthfulness. Truth would excoriate falsehood in the process of allowing the airing of conflicting opinions.[15] He stated, "We can never be sure that the opinion we are endeavoring to stifle is a false opinion, and if we were sure, stifling it would be an evil still."[16]

The Right to Know Theory, Democratic Political Theory, and Checking Value in the First Amendment Theory

Freedom of expression and speech is a vital civil right; however, without the right of access to information, freedom of speech becomes meaningless. The right to access information determines how, why, and what individuals say about themselves and the world. This rationale led to the development of the right to know theory. According to this theory, individuals enjoy an unalienable right to obtain information, especially information of powerful institutions such as governmental agencies and

13 ALISTAIR E. MCGRATH, HISTORICAL THEOLOGY: AN INTRODUCTION TO THE HISTORY OF CHRISTIAN THOUGHT 214–215 (1998); JOHN LOCKE, THE TWO TREATISES OF GOVERNMENT (1824).

14 KAREN SANDERS, ETHICS AND JOURNALISM 66 (2003).

15 KAREN SANDERS, ETHICS AND JOURNALISM 67 (2003).

16 John Stuart Mill, *Chapter 2: Of the Liberty of Thought and Discussion*, *in* ON LIBERTY (1859).

important private entities.[17] Many scholars, such as Leonard Levy,[18] Daniel Hoffman,[19] Harold L. Cross,[20] Herbert Brucker,[21] Jerome Barron,[22] Alexander Meiklejohn,[23] Thomas Emerson,[24] and Anthony Lewis[25] advocated the right to know philosophies.

The term "right to know" first appeared in the 1787 speech of James Wilson, one of the Founding Fathers of the United States and a signer of the United States Declaration of Independence.[26] Harold L. Cross

[17] However, the right to know is not an unfettered right. As scholar Brian Richardson rightfully noted from the perspective of moral philosophy, the press would lose discretion in what to publish if individuals claim that they have an unfettered right to know all information. For example, if newspapers name a rape victim, it will cause unnecessary harm and damage a victim's moral right to privacy. In such case, naming the victim would be unethical despite the public's right to know. Brian Richardson, *The Public's Right to Know: A Dangerous Notion*, 19 JOURNAL OF MASS MEDIA ETHICS 46, 46–55 (2004).

[18] LEONARD W. LEVY, EMERGENCE OF A FREE PRESS (1985); LEONARD LEVY, ORIGINAL INTENT AND THE FRAMER'S CONSTITUTION (1988).

[19] DANIEL N. HOFFMAN, GOVERNMENT SECRECY AND THE FOUNDING FATHERS: A STUDY IN CONSTITUTIONAL CONTROLS (1981).

[20] HAROLD L. CROSS, THE PEOPLE'S RIGHT TO KNOW: LEGAL ACCESS TO PUBLIC RECORDS AND PROCEEDINGS (1953).

[21] HERBERT BRUCKER, FREEDOM OF INFORMATION (1949).

[22] Barron argued for a right of access to mass media. JEROME A. BARRON, FREEDOM OF THE PRESS FOR WHOM?: THE RIGHT OF ACCESS TO MASS MEDIA (1973).

[23] Meiklejohn argued eloquently for a constitutional right to know. ALEXANDER MEIKLEJOHN, FREE SPEECH AND ITS RELATION TO SELF-GOVERNMENT (1948); ALEXANDER MEIKLEJOHN, POLITICAL FREEDOM: THE CONSTITUTIONAL POWERS OF THE PEOPLE (1960); Alexander Meiklejohn, *The First Amendment is an Absolute*, 1961 SUPREME COURT REVIEW 245 (1961).

[24] Thomas I. Emerson, *Legal Foundations of the Right to Know*, 1976 WASHINGTON UNIVERSITY LAW QUARTERLY 1 (1976); THOMAS I. EMERSON, THE SYSTEM OF FREEDOM OF EXPRESSION (1970).

[25] Anthony Lewis, *A Public Right to Know about Public Institutions: The First Amendment as Sword*, 1980 SUPREME COURT REVIEW 1 (1980); Anthony Lewis, *The Right to Scrutinize Government: Toward a First Amendment Theory of Accountability*, 34 UNIVERSITY OF MIAMI LAW REVIEW 793 (1980).

[26] Brian Richardson, *The Public's Right to Know: A Dangerous Notion*, 19 JOURNAL OF MASS MEDIA Ethics 46, 46 (2004). As a delegate to the 1787 Federal Convention, James Wilson stated, "The people have a right to know what their Agents are doing or have done, and it should not be in the option of the Legislature to conceal their proceedings."

popularized the term as early as 1936.[27] Kent Cooper, then director of the Associated Press, used the term in a 1945 speech.[28] With the 1953 publication of the book *The People's Right to Know: Legal Access to Public Records and Proceedings,* Harold Cross further improved the popularity of the term. The term "right to know," initially used by journalists and professionals from media-related sectors, gradually became a popular term for people in general.[29] The environmental movement further popularized the term. Rachel Carson, a biologist and influential author of *Silent Spring*, said, "the obligation to endure gives us the right to know."[30]

The right to know theory grounds itself in well-established democratic political philosophies and gains additional legal support from the First Amendment theories. According to democratic political theory, citizens in democracies are governors of themselves; state's power belongs to the people, and the people elect officials to exercise the power on behalf of ordinary citizens. In order to fully participate in self-governance and render informed decisions for political candidates and their legislative responsibility, citizens should have full access to records and files held by the government, which does not retain ownership of those records and files: Governments are the custodians of those documents. The government-held documents belong to the people, who, as owners, naturally enjoy the right of examination. The access right creates an enabling

Madison Debates, the Avalon Project at Yale Law School, *available at* http://avalon.law.yale.edu/18th_century/debates_811.asp (accessed between February 21, 2025 and March 31, 2025).

[27] Kiyul Uhm, *The Founders and the Revolutionary Underpinning of the Concept of the Right to Know*, 85 JOURNALISM & MASS COMMUNICATION QUARTERLY 393, 405 (2008).

[28] KENT COOPER, THE RIGHT TO KNOW: AN EXPOSITION OF THE EVILS OF NEWS SUPPRESSION AND PROPAGANDA XII–XIII (1956) (claiming credit for coining the phrase "right to know" and defining it as a citizen's entitlement to "have access to news, fully and accurately presented").

[29] HERBERT N. FOERSTEL, FREEDOM OF INFORMATION AND THE RIGHT TO KNOW: THE ORIGINS AND APPLICATIONS OF THE FREEDOM OF INFORMATION ACT 14-18 (1999) (detailing the struggle U.S. journalists encountered during the 1950s in retrieving information from the government).

[30] Jonathan Norton Leonard, *Rachel Carson Dies of Cancer; "Silent Spring" Author Was 56*, THE NEW YORK TIMES, April 15, 1964, at para. 9, https://archive.nytimes.com/www.nytimes.com/books/97/10/05/reviews/carson-obit.html?_r=1 (accessed between February 21, 2025 and March 31, 2025); RACHEL CARSON, SILENT SPRING (1962).

environment for better governance, placing governmental secrecy as a breeding ground for corruption, inefficiency, distrust, and insecurity. A transparent government affords greater accountability because misconduct or transgressions become apparent if government documents and processes are visible for all to see.[31]

Democratic political theory, originating in Western Europe, is the development of many Enlightenment thinkers such as John Locke, Jean-Jacques Rousseau, and Charles-Louis de Secondat (Montesquieu).[32] John Locke argued that people surrender sovereignty to a government in order to receive or maintain social order through the rule of law. Legitimate state authority must derive from the consent of the governed. "Implicit in this arrangement is the concept of public access to government information, for without such information, consent would be uninformed."[33] Locke's thought deeply influenced the Framers of the U.S. Constitution.[34]

[31] Benjamin W. Cramer, "Freedom of Environmental Information in America" (August 2009) (unpublished Ph.D. diss., The Pennsylvania State University), 21.

[32] JOHN LOCKE, THE TWO TREATISES OF GOVERNMENT (1824). For in-depth discussions of the liberal democratic theory, see Derigan A. Silver, "National Security and Transparency: The Legal Frameworks and Factors Federal Courts Use to Balance Competing Democratic Values" (2009) (unpublished Ph.D. diss., The University of North Carolina at Chapel Hill), 6–23.

[33] Martin E. Halstuk, "Exploring the Future of Open Government in the Digital Age: A Reevaluation of the Significance of the Electronic Freedom of Information Act of 1996" (August 1999) (unpublished Ph.D. diss., University of Florida), 42.

[34] For example, Thomas Jefferson wrote in the Declaration of Independence (para. 2): "*[G]overnments are instituted among men, deriving their just powers from the consent of the governed.*" EDWARD CURRIER, THE POLITICAL TEXT BOOK 7 (2010). According to the Framers of the *United States Constitution*, "self-governing people should be well-informed about the workings of government to make intelligent political choices." Matthew D. Bunker, Sigman L Splichal, Bill F. Chamberlin & Linda M. Perry, *Access to Government-Held Information in the Computer Age: Applying Legal Doctrine to Emerging Technology*, 20 FLORIDA STATE UNIVERSITY LAW REVIEW 543, 545 (1992–1993). Other primary historical sources for theoretical support for public knowledge and self-government include the *Federalist Papers*, Thomas Paine's *Common Sense*, and the writings of Enlightenment philosophers who inspired the Founding Fathers. MARY E. WEBSTER, THE FEDERALIST PAPERS: IN MODERN LANGUAGE INDEXED FOR TODAY'S POLITICAL ISSUES (1999); THOMAS PAINE, COMMON SENSE (1986).

Democratic political theory further advanced in twentieth-century America by renowned philosopher and educator, Alexander Meiklejohn,[35] whose notability arises from efforts to link freedom of speech with democracy. For Meiklejohn, the free flow of information is vital for democracy, arguing that voters need full access to governmental operations and information in order to render well-informed decisions.[36] Meiklejohn wrote that "whatever truth may become available shall be placed at the disposal of all the citizens of the community"[37] in order for people to become their own governors. He said, "Public discussions of public issues, together with the spreading of information and opinion bearing on those issues, must have a freedom unabridged by our agents. Though they govern us, we, in a deeper sense, govern them. Over our governing, they have no power. Over their governing we have sovereign power."[38] Many other legal scholars, philosophers, and commentators have written extensively about the intertwined relationship between public access to information and democracy.[39]

[35] The basis for Meiklejohn's opinions on freedom of information was a unique absolutist view of freedom of speech as pertaining to political information and self-government. Alexander Meiklejohn, *The First Amendment Is an Absolute*, 1961 SUPREME COURT REVIEW 257 (1961).

[36] ALEXANDER MEIKLEJOHN, FREE SPEECH AND ITS RELATION TO SELF-GOVERNMENT 88 (1948); Alexander Meiklejohn, *The First Amendment Is an Absolute*, 1961 SUPREME COURT REVIEW 245 (1961). Meiklejohn's democratic self-rule theory, cited by renowned British media law scholar, Eric Barendt, is "probably the most attractive and certainly the most fashionable free speech theory in modern Western democracies." RANDAL MARLIN, PROPAGANDA AND THE ETHICS OF PERSUASION 226 (2002).

[37] *See* ALEXANDER MEKLEJOHN, FREE SPEECH AND ITS RELATION TO SELF-GOVERNMENT (1948).

[38] Alexander Meiklejohn, *The First Amendment Is an Absolute*, 1961 SUPREME COURT REVIEW 245, 257 (1961).

[39] JOHN RAWLS, A THEORY OF JUSTICE (1971); KARL R. POPPER, THE OPEN SOCIETY AND ITS ENEMIES (1971); HAROLD L. CROSS, THE PEOPLE'S RIGHT TO KNOW: LEGAL ACCESS TO PUBLIC RECORDS AND PROCEEDINGS (1953); ALEXANDER MEIKLEJOHN, FREE SPEECH AND ITS RELATION TO SELF-GOVERNMENT (1948). For additional scholarship on the same topic, see VINCENT BLASI, THE CHECKING VALUE IN FIRST AMENDMENT THEORY, 3 AMERICAN BAR FOUNDATION RESEARCH JOURNAL 523, 554–567 (1977); Thomas I Emerson, *Legal Foundations of the Right to Know*, 1956 WASHINGTON UNIVERSITY LAW QUARTERLY 1, 1(1976); Thomas I. Emerson, *Legal Foundations of the Right to Know*, 1976 WASHINGTON UNIVERSITY LAW QUARTERLY 1 (1976); THOMAS I. EMERSON, THE SYSTEM OF FREEDOM OF EXPRESSION (1970); Alexander Meiklejohn, T*he First Amendment Is an Absolute*, 1961 SUPREME COURT

The checking value in the First Amendment theory is the development of legal scholar, Vincent Blasi,[40] who argued that governmental officials have an inherent tendency to abuse their power. Thus, the responsibility accrues to the public to maintain vigilance over people with power. Blasi concluded that, given the complexity and size of modern governments, only an institutionalized media has resources and capacities to check the dangerous and harmful tendency of officials to abuse power.[41]

Blasi identified the value of news media to oversee government's power to justify the argument that news media deserve special constitutionally protected privileges in newsgathering. Such First Amendment-supported press privileges are still lacking in the United States.[42] Some scholars believed the Founding Fathers of the U.S. Constitution intended

REVIEW 245, 257 (1961); LEONARD W. LEVY, EMERGENCE OF A FREE PRESS (1985); DANIEL N. HOFFMAN, GOVERNMENT SECRECY AND THE FOUNDING FATHERS: A STUDY IN CONSTITUTIONAL CONTROLS (1981); HERBERT BRUCKER, FREEDOM OF INFORMATION (1949); JEROME A. BARRON, FREEDOM OF THE PRESS FOR WHOM?: THE RIGHT OF ACCESS TO MASS MEDIA (1973); Anthony Lewis, *A Public Right to Know about Public Institutions: The First Amendment as Sword*, 1980 SUPREME COURT REVIEW 1 (1980); Anthony Lewis, *The Right to Scrutinize Government: Toward a First Amendment Theory of Accountability*, 34 UNIVERSITY OF MIAMI LAW REVIEW 793 (1980).

[40] Vincent Blasi, *The Checking Value in First Amendment Theory*, 3 AMERICAN BAR FOUNDATION RESEARCH JOURNAL 523 (1977).

[41] Vincent Blasi, *The Checking Value in First Amendment Theory*, 3 AMERICAN BAR FOUNDATION RESEARCH JOURNAL 523 (1977).

[42] The *Freedom of Information Act* adopted in 1966 has granted anyone in the world an "enforceable legal right" to inspect documents or records held by the U.S. federal government. HAROLD L. CROSS, THE PEOPLE'S RIGHT TO KNOW: LEGAL ACCESS TO PUBLIC RECORDS AND PROCEEDINGS 197 (1953). However, the right is statutory, not constitutional. In the 1970s, the U.S. Supreme Court ruled in a series of related cases known as the "Prison Trio" that no constitutional right of access to governmental facilities including prisons exists. *Pell v. Procunier*, 417 U.S. 817 (1974); *Saxbe v. Washington Post*, 417 U.S. 843 (1974); *Houchins v. KQED*, 438 U.S. 1 (1978). These three cases served as a legal precedent denying the constitutional right of the general public's access to any kind of public institutions except criminal trials (*Richmond Newspapers v. Virginia (1980)* granted the public a right of access to criminal trials). In general, the First Amendment protection for newsgathering is poor in the United States. For example, reporters enjoy no special privileges in newsgathering. They may be liable for actions taken as a part of their newsgathering activities. They may be subject to arrest or suit on the grounds of trespass, fraud, and failure to obey lawful orders, or illegal taping and recording. DON. R. PEMBER & CLAY CALVERT, MASS MEDIA LAW 327–35 (2013).

the public's limited access, not specifically the press.[43] For example, FOI pioneer Harold Cross argued that the history of free speech and press "bars any notion that the men of 1791 intended to provide for freedom to disseminate such information but to deny freedom to acquire it."[44] Another prominent legal scholar, David O'Brien, provided a more comprehensive overview of a possible constitutional right to information for both individuals and the press in his seminal book, *The Public's Right to Know*.[45] Many other legal scholars and commentators have long argued that the people's right to information, especially the journalist's right to gather information, shall have protection under the First Amendment.[46] They contended that although laws grant limited access to information held by federal, state and local agencies in the United States, these laws are subject to change and modification by the U.S. Congress and the state legislatures. One potential solution to this tension between legislative efforts to provide access to information and subsequent legislative efforts to curtail access to that information is to recognize that individuals (e.g., citizens and journalists) have a constitutional right to information.[47]

[43] Kiyul Uhm, *The Founders and the Revolutionary Underpinning of the Concept of the Right to Know*, 85 JOURNALISM & MASS COMMUNICATION QUARTERLY 393, 397 (2008).

[44] HAROLD L. CROSS, THE PEOPLE'S RIGHT TO KNOW: LEGAL ACCESS TO PUBLIC RECORDS AND PROCEEDINGS 131–32 (1953).

[45] DAVID M. O'BRIEN, THE PUBLIC'S RIGHT TO KNOW: THE SUPREME COURT AND THE FIRST AMENDMENT (1981).

[46] Note, *The First Amendment Right to Gather State-Held Information*, 89 YALE LAW JOURNAL 923 (1980); Jeffrey J. Maciejewski & David T. Ozar, *Natural Law and the Right to Know in a Democracy*, 20 JOURNAL OF MASS MEDIA ETHICS 121 (2005); Christopher Meyers, *Justifying Journalistic Harms: Right to Know vs. Interest in Knowing*, 8 JOURNAL OF MASS MEDIA ETHICS 133, 136 (1993); Roy V. Leeper, *Richmond Newspapers, Inc. v. Virginia and the Emerging Right of Access*, 61 JOURNALISM QUARTERLY 615 (1984); Erik Ugland, *Demarcating a Right to Gather News: A Sequential Interpretation of the First Amendment*, 3 DUKE JOURNAL OF CONSTITUTIONAL LAW & PUBLIC POLICY 113 (2008); Candance Cummins Gauthier, *Right to Know, Press Freedom, Public Discourse*, 14 JOURNAL OF MASS MEDIA Ethics 197 (1999); Anthony Lewis, *Public Right to Know about Public Institutions: The First Amendment as Sword*, 1980 SUPREME COURT REVIEW 1, 1–25 (1980); Eric Freedman, *Freedom of Information and the First Amendment in a Bureaucratic Age*, 49 BROOKLYN LAW REVIEW 835, 835–55 (1983).

[47] Roy V. Leeper, *Richmond Newspapers, Inc. v. Virginia and the Emerging Right of Access*, 61 JOURNALISM QUARTERLY 615, 618–19 (1984); Phillip J. Cooper, *The Supreme Court, the First Amendment, and Freedom of Information*, 46 PUBLIC ADMINISTRATION REVIEW 622, 622 (1986).

More than 20 cases involving individual's First Amendment rights to information emerged in the United States in the last 80 years, with *Grosjean v. American Press* (1936) being the first and *Board of Education v. Pico* (1982) being the last.[48] The results are clearly discouraging, "[n]o party had ever even claimed a right to information as within the realm of their individual First Amendment rights."[49] *Richmond Newspapers v. Virginia* (1980) is a case in which the Supreme Court explicitly supported a constitutional right of the public to attend criminal trials.[50] This constitutional support for the right to know, however, was limited in scope because "the Supreme Court has never explicitly recognized this right outside of judicial proceedings" since after 1980.[51] As a result of lacking explicit and strong Supreme Court support, the efforts to conceptualize the right to know as a constitutional rather than statutory right have not succeeded.

However, the narrative is incomplete; scholars and journalists continue persuasive attempts to change the Supreme Court's course.[52] A change in direction of First Amendment jurisprudence is an expectation for the future, and despite the outcome, the theory for the value of a press brake

[48] All these cases address "either a broad enough right-to-information that individuals are almost certainly implicated" or "specifically refer to an individual's 'right-to-information.'" Katie Blevins, *The Constitutional Right-to-Information on the Individual Level: As Suggested by First Amendment Precedent in the Supreme Court,* paper accepted for presentation by the Communication Law and Policy Division of the AEJMC annual conference, Denver, Colorado, August 4–7, 2010, at 5.

[49] Katie Blevins, *The Constitutional Right-to-Information on the Individual Level: As Suggested by First Amendment Precedent in the Supreme Court,* paper accepted for presentation by the Communication Law and Policy Division of the AEJMC annual conference, Denver, Colorado, August 4–7, 2010, at 25.

[50] *Richmond Newspapers v. Virginia*, 448 U.S. 555 (1980). For a detailed legal analysis of *Richmond Newspapers v. Virginia* and other relevant cases and their implications on the right of the public and the press to access the U.S. court system, see Geoffrey Fattah, "'Strangers' in the Courtroom: An Examination of Access Theory and the Public's Right to Open Courts from Depasquale to Richmond" (May 2011) (unpublished master's thesis, The University of Utah).

[51] Don R. Pember & Clay Calvert, Mass Media Law 323 (18th ed., 2013).

[52] For example, legal scholars Roy Peled and Yoram Rabin have recently argued for a constitutional right to information. They contended that United States and many other democratic countries should incorporate right to know into their constitutions. Roy Peled & Yoram Rabin, *The Constitutional Right to Information*, 42 Columbia Human Rights Law Review 357, 357–401 (2011).

on governmental activity and relevant efforts to grant freedom of information the status of constitutionality continues to provide legal and moral support for FOI advocates in the United States and elsewhere. As Blasi identified, the right to know closely interrelates with the role of mass media to expose corrupt or incompetent officials who tend to hide their activities. Without a constitutional right to access governmental records or information, the news media encounters great difficulty conducting vigorous and unfettered investigations, leaving governmental misconduct or transgressions unidentified and unexposed.[53] The initial acquisition of information embodies the value of providing a check.[54]

The Concept of the Right to Know in the Chinese Context

Chinese scholarly literature first began to discuss the Western concept of a "right to know" in the early 1990s.[55] Even high-ranking political leaders sporadically mentioned, in public, the importance of the right to know. In a March 1999 article on villager self-rule, Chunyun Jiang, then vice chairperson of the National People's Congress Standing Committee, described a growing rural concept of a "right to information":

> Following the deepening of rural reform and development of the market economy, farmers' thinking, concepts, and value orientation have undergone profound changes. Their sense of democracy and their sense of participation in the management of economic and social affairs have constantly increased. And increasingly, they want to have the *right to information*, dialogue, and decision-making. They long for direct participation in making decisions on major affairs in the village and the management of village affairs (*emphasis added*).[56]

[53] Martin E. Halstuk, "Exploring the Future of Open Government in the Digital Age: A Reevaluation of the Significance of the Electronic Freedom of Information Act of 1996" (August 1999) (unpublished Ph.D. diss., University of Florida).

[54] Vincent Blasi, *The Checking Value in First Amendment Theory*, 3 AMERICAN BAR FOUNDATION RESEARCH JOURNAL 610 (1977).

[55] Jamie P. Horsley, *Toward a More Open China? in* THE RIGHT TO KNOW: TRANSPARENCY FOR AN OPEN WORLD 78 (Ann Florini & Joseph E. Stiglitz eds., 2007).

[56] Jamie P. Horsley, *Toward a More Open China? in* THE RIGHT TO KNOW: TRANSPARENCY FOR AN OPEN WORLD 59 (Ann Florini & Joseph E. Stiglitz eds., 2007); Cunyung Jiang, *Do well Matters of Primary Importance Which Allows 900 Million Peasants to Become Masters of Their Own Affairs* [把村民自治这件让九亿农民当家作主的大事办

Notably, the concept of the right to know was, generally, a politically sensitive topic in China throughout the 1990s and early 2000s because of a consensus among party hard-liners that freedom of information and expression contributed to the demise of the Soviet Union. Although Chunyun Jiang emphasized publicly the right to information, his comments were from the perspective of economic development rather than democratic values. In 2002, a retrospective television news program, "You Have the Right to Know," did not broadcast because of its sensitive and controversial nature.[57] Many conservative party and government leaders perceive freedom of information and the right to know to be unpleasant because the two terms so closely link to freedom of expression and the Soviet glasnost initiative. As Chinese FOI expert, Weibing Xiao, stated, "An overall negative impression of Gorbachev's glasnost reform highlighted political sensitivity to FOI and freedom of expression linkage, especially in the early stage of developing an FOI policy."[58]

In order to render the concept of the right to know politically acceptable, Chinese law reformers adopted an ambitious strategy. They delinked the Chinese concept of the right to know with freedom of expression and freedom of the press.[59] They argued for a people's right to know from the perspective of economic growth and informational development.[60] They relied on the democratic political theory to expound the rationale and viability of the Chinese version of the right to know. China is not

好], PEOPLE'S DAILY, republished on govopendata.com, March 3, 1999, https://cn.govopendata.com/renminribao/1999/3/3/10/#1146306 (accessed between February 21, 2025 and March 31, 2025).

[57] *News Probe* is a prominent China Central Television news program. Once Chinese audiences widely viewed its aggressive investigative journalism. 2002 marked the fifth anniversary of the program. The editors planned to produce a retrospective program to celebrate their achievement. When one leader glanced at the program title "You Have the Right to Know," he immediately cancelled the airing of the program and asked one editor, "Do you know why the former Soviet Union collapsed?" WEIBING XIAO, FREEDOM OF INFORMATION REFORM IN CHINA: INFORMATION FLOW ANALYSIS 145 (2011); Hanhua Zhou, *Legislative History of the OGI Regulations in China* [《政府信息公开条例》出台始末], 7 E-Government 15 (2008).

[58] WEIBING XIAO, FREEDOM OF INFORMATION REFORM IN CHINA: INFORMATION FLOW ANALYSIS 40 (2011).

[59] WEIBING XIAO, FREEDOM OF INFORMATION REFORM IN CHINA: INFORMATION FLOW ANALYSIS 43 (2011).

[60] WEIBING XIAO, FREEDOM OF INFORMATION REFORM IN CHINA: INFORMATION FLOW ANALYSIS 65 (2011).

a democracy, at least by Western standards. In order to bridge the gap between the Chinese concept of democracy and the Western one, Chinese law reformers found inspirations from the principle of the sovereignty of the people embodied in *Constitution of 1982*.

The right to know or information rights are not included in China's constitutional provisions. However, Chinese legal scholars argue that *Constitution of 1982* implies the right to know.[61] Prolific Yale law scholar Jamie P. Horsley further suggested, "certain [Chinese] constitutional principles do establish a legal basis for OGI and open governance."[62] For example, Article 2 of the *Constitution* stipulates the "foundational principle" that all power belongs to the people and that the people are to manage state affairs and economic, cultural, and social affairs through various channels and in various ways.[63] Article 3 provides that the people's congresses create and supervise all administrative, judicial, and procuratorial[64] organs of the state. The people elect, at different levels, the people's congresses, which are responsible to the people and subject to the people's supervision.[65] Article 27 requires state agencies and functionaries to maintain close ties to the people, heed their

[61] Weibing Xiao, Freedom of Information Reform in China: Information Flow Analysis 42 (2011); Hanhua Zhou, *Basic Considerations in Drafting of Regulations on the Openness of Government Information (Academic Draft)* [起草《政府信息公开条例》(专家建议稿)的基本考虑] 6 Chinese Journal of Law 57 (2002); Wei Zhu & Yanpin Teng, *From Concept to Fundamental Constitutional Rights: Several Legal Principles on Right to Know* [从观念到宪法基本权利—知情权的一般法理], 1 Journal of Hangzhou Teachers College (Social Sciences Edition) 103 (2005); Wei Zhu, *Government Information Publicity: Legislative Model and System Coordination* [政府信息公开:立法模式及制度协调], 1 Journal of Hangzhou Teachers College (Social Sciences Edition) 110 (2004); Jian Kang & Ling Fu, *Exploration of Legal Protection of Citizens' Right to Know* [公民知情权法律保障之探析], 32 Journal of Liaoning University (Philosophy and Social Sciences Edition) 124 (November 2004).

[62] Jamie P. Horsley, *Toward a More Open China?, in* The Right to Know: Transparency for an Open World 67 (Ann Florini & Joseph E. Stiglitz eds., 2007).

[63] *Constitution 1982.* Art. 2; Jamie P. Horsley, *Toward a More Open China? in* The Right to Know: Transparency for an Open World 67 (Ann Florini & Joseph E. Stiglitz eds., 2007).

[64] Procuratorial organs exercise the power of prosecution. They are elected by and report to the people's congress at the same level. Qian Sun, *Characteristics of China's Procuratorial System*, 2(2) Qiushi (April 2010).

[65] *Constitution 1982.* Art. 3.

opinions, and accept their supervision.[66] Article 41 grants citizens the right to criticize and make suggestions regarding government agencies and their functionaries. The relevant state organ shall, in a responsible manner, adjudicate citizens' complaints and charges against, or exposure to, violations of the law or derelictions of duty by any state organ or functionary.[67] These constitutional rights granted to the people have comprehensive protection only with the precondition that the people have the right to obtain adequate information regarding operations of the government. Without the people's right to know all aspects of governmental activities, the citizens are unable to exercise, fully and effectively, these constitutional rights.

According to Chinese reformers, freedom of information and the right to know are not alien to Chinese society. The assertions are that China has a long history of disclosing governmental information and *Constitution of 1982* supports the right to information and thus the concept becomes compatible with China's socialist political system. Chinese law reformers' assertion gained strength in late 2002 when the party and the central government fully endorsed the implementation of the *Constitution*.[68] Leading political operatives in China desired to elevate the status of the Constitution in order to implement the strategy of ruling the state by the rule of law. Although the *Constitution* is the supreme law of the country, it had a long history of disrespect, ignoring, or even trampling by a few powerful people. Hu Jintao stated in a speech commemorating the 20th anniversary of the adoption of the *Constitution*, "Implementation of the rule of law first and foremost requires full enforcement of the *Constitution*."[69] He reiterated the central role of the Constitution in a speech marking the 50th anniversary of the National People's Congress (NPC), stating, "[r]uling the state by the rule of law first needs ruling the state by the Constitution, [and] administration by law first requires administration

[66] *Constitution 1982*. Art. 27.

[67] *Constitution 1982*. Art. 41.

[68] Weibing Xiao, Freedom of Information Reform in China: Information Flow Analysis 42 (2011).

[69] Weibing Xiao, Freedom of Information Reform in China: Information Flow Analysis 42 (2011); Hu Jintao, *Fully Implementing the Constitution to Provide Legal Guarantees for Building a Well-Off Society in All Aspects* [宪法为建设小康社会提供法律保障], speech delivered at the 20th Anniversary of the Adoption of the Constitution, Beijing, December 4, 2002.

by the Constitution."[70] On December 26, 2002, the Central Politburo of the Communist Party invited constitutional scholars to give lectures on the Constitution.[71]

The Chinese law reformers' strategy clearly succeeded. Research of "the right to know" lost its status as taboo after 2002. Scholars began to mention the key phrase, "right to know," and attempted to include it in statutes via legislation.[72] Scholarly articles, media reports, and policy documents cited the term frequently.[73] The term, "the right to know," first appeared in an important Party document issued by the Fourth Plenum of the 16th Party Congress Central Committee in September 2004.[74] This document listed the right to know as one of the Chinese people's "four democratic rights."[75] According to the CCP, "four types of democracy" protect and permit the exercise of these four democratic

[70] WEIBING XIAO, FREEDOM OF INFORMATION REFORM IN CHINA: INFORMATION FLOW ANALYSIS 42 (2011); Hu Jintao, speech delivered at the 50th Anniversary of the National People's Congress [胡锦涛在纪念全国人大成立50周年大会上的讲话], Beijing, September 15, 2004.

[71] *Chinese Communist Party New Politburo Members Study Constitution together and Hu Jintao Delivers Speech* [新一届中共中央政治局集体学习 胡锦涛发表讲话] 中央政治局集体学法 胡锦涛强调领导干部要加强学习], CHINA NEWS SERVICE, December 26, 2002, https://www.chinanews.com.cn/2002-12-26/26/257773.html (accessed between February 21, 2025 and March 31, 2025).

[72] Wenjing Liu, *Approaching Democracy Through Transparency: A Comparative Law Study on Chinese Open Government Information*, 26 AMERICAN UNIVERSITY INTERNATIONAL LAW REVIEW 983 (2011).

[73] Jamie P. Horsley, *Toward a More Open China? in* THE RIGHT TO KNOW: TRANSPARENCY FOR AN OPEN WORLD 78 (Ann Florini & Joseph E. Stiglitz eds., 2007).

[74] *Decision by the Central Committee of the Chinese Communist Party on Strengthening the Construction of Party Governance Capability* [中共中央关于加强党的执政能力建设的决定] adopted by the Fourth Plenum of the 16th Party Congress Central Committee, Beijing, September 19, 2004.

[75] The party recognized the right to know one of four democratic rights Chinese citizens shall enjoy in a socialist democracy. The rights are the right to vote (*xuanjuquan* 选举权), the right to know (*zhiqingquan* 知情权), the right to participate (*canyuquan* 参与权), and the right to supervise (*jianduquan* 监督权). Later revision defined and formalized the four democratic rights as the right to know (*zhiqingquan* 知情权), the right to participate (*canyuquan* 参与权), freedom of expression (*biaodaquan* 表达权), and the right to supervise (*jianduquan* 监督权).

rights.[76] "Four democratic rights" and "four types of democracy" have frequent citation by major leaders attending important party meetings.[77] The white paper on human rights, issued in 2004 by the State Council Information Office, also listed the right to know as one of the civil and political rights China protects as part of its human rights program.[78]

[76] The four types of democracy are democratic elections (*minzhuxuanju* 民主选举), democratic decision-making (*minzhujuece* 民主决策), democratic management (*minzhuguanli* 民主管理), and democratic supervision (*minzhujiandu* 民主监督). Villagers' practices of self-rule inspired the four types of democracy in the 1980s and early 1990s. The term "four types of democracy" (*sidaminzhu* 四大民主) first appeared in a 1993 notice issued by the Ministry of Civil Affairs. Its first official use was in 1994 when the 10th National Convention on Civil Affairs was held. Formalization and standardization of the term occurred in the 1997 party report issued by the 15th National Congress of the Chinese Communist Party. The "four types of democracy" was later extended from villages to China's urban communities. For detailed analysis of how China has experimented grassroots democracy in urban communities, see Chow Bing Ngeow, "Democratic Development in China's Urban Communities" (January 2010) (unpublished Ph.D. diss., Northeastern University). For discussions of how Chinese scholars interpret the "four types of democracy," see Keping Yu, *Democracy in China: Challenge or Opportunity?* Harvard University, *available at* http://www.ash.harvard.edu/extension/ash/docs/democracyinchina.pdf (accessed between February 21, 2025 and March 31, 2025). For discussions about how the term was defined in the Chinese context, see *Democratic Elections, Democratic Decision-Making, Democratic Management, and Democratic Supervision* [民主选举、民主决策、民主管理、民主监督], PEOPLE'S DAILY ONLINE, June 5, 2013, http://qzlx.people.com.cn/n/2013/0605/c364582-21742507.html (accessed between February 21, 2025 and March 31, 2025). For an example of how Chinese political leaders used the term in official documents, see Jiang Zemin, *Hold High the Great Banner of Deng Xiaoping Theory for an All-round Advancement of the Cause of Building Socialism with Chinese Characteristics to the 21st Century* [高举邓小平理论伟大旗帜，把建设有中国特色社会主义事业全面推向二十一世纪], speech delivered at the 15th Party National Congress, Beijing, September 1997.

[77] Jiang Zemin, *Hold High the Great Banner of Deng Xiaoping Theory for an All-round Advancement of the Cause of Building Socialism with Chinese Characteristics to the 21st Century* [高举邓小平理论伟大旗帜, 把建设有中国特色社会主义事业全面推向二十一世纪], speech delivered at the 15th Party National Congress, Beijing, September 1997; Jiang Zemin, Build a Well-off Society in an All-Round Way and Create a New Situation in Building Socialism with Chinese Characteristics [全面建设小康社会，开创中国特色社会主义事业新局面], speech delivered at the 16th National Congress of the CPC, Beijing, November 2002; Hu Jintao, *Hold High the Great Banner of Socialism with Chinese Characteristics and Strive for New Victories in Budding a Moderately Prosperous Society in All Respects* [高举中国特色社会主义伟大旗帜 为夺取全面建设小康社会新胜利而奋斗], speech delivered at the 17th National Party Congress, Beijing, October 2007.

[78] White Paper on the Progress of Human Rights Cause in 2003 [2003年中国人权事业的进展], The State Council Information Office, published March 2004; Jamie P. Horsley,

Governmental resistance to the right to know, however, still existed, and at times, was overwhelming and tried to omit the key phrase, "the right to know," from appearing in the national OGI law. *Provisions of Guangzhou Municipality on Open Government Information 2003* were the first local OGI Rule that explicitly announced protection of "the right to know."[79] *The 2002 Academic Draft of OGI Regulations* also explicitly conferred to those requesting information "the right to know."[80] Unfortunately, the national *OGI Regulations* do not contain the right.

Although Chinese political leaders use the phrase "the right to know" frequently in public speeches and policy documents, the people' right to know clearly lacks statutory support as a result of the State Council's decision to redact the phrase from the text of *OGI Regulations,* and consequence of failing to include the right to know is extremely negative, placing requesters of information in an unfavorable position and governmental agencies in a more favorable position. Without explicit statutory and constitutional support for the right to know, citizens are more likely to confront informational non-disclosure and much less likely to seek administrative and judicial remedies for denied requests.

Although judges in China could not cite constitutional provisions as authority,[81] explicit constitutional support for the right to know is still crucial. Explicit support would more easily allow arguing for a more progressive and inspiring FOI law in the future. Support would also provide convincing constitutional rationales for the enactment of *Freedom of the Press Law* and any other relevant laws governing information. Some

Toward a More Open China?, in THE RIGHT TO KNOW: TRANSPARENCY FOR AN OPEN WORLD 78 (Ann Florini & Joseph E. Stiglitz eds., 2007).

79 *Provisions of Guangzhou Municipality on Open Government Information 2003.* Art. 1 (stating that the legislative purpose of the law is the protection of "the right to know").

80 *Academic Draft of OGI Regulations 2002.* Art.1. ACADEMIC DRAFT OF OGI REGULATIONS: DRAFT, EXPLANATION, RATIONALE AND LEGISLATIVE EXAMPLES 1 [政府信息公开条例专家建议稿-草案、说明、理由、立法例] (Hanhua Zhou ed., Chinese Legal Publishing House, 2003).

81 Bo Li, *What Is Constitutionalism?* 1 PERSPECTIVES (2000).

Chinese legal scholars[82] and National People's Congress deputies[83] argue that the right to know shall be explicitly written into the *Constitution*. Such advocacy is laudable, providing a basis for creating a comprehensive legal framework for a Chinese protection of the right to know. The best option is amending *Constitution of 1982* and *OGI Regulations*, at an opportune time, to reflect the Chinese people's aspirations for the right to know.

Four Theories of the Press

This book uses four theories of the press as a theoretical framework to conceptualize Chinese news media systems. Since publication in 1956, the four theories of the press are the bases for consistent critique and questioning by media scholars for a variety of reasons. Some scholars argued that the three authors' classifications of media systems in the world are lagging far behind the world reality and too simple.[84] Some scholars maintained that the authors of *Four Theories of the Press* misinterpreted Marxism and Leninism.[85] Some scholars contended that the

[82] Wei Zhu, *Government Information Publicity: Legislative Model and System Coordination* [政府信息公开:立法模式及制度协调], 1 JOURNAL OF HANGZHOU TEACHERS COLLEGE (SOCIAL SCIENCES EDITION) 112, 112–13 (2004); Jian Kang & Ling Fu, *Exploration of Legal Protection of Citizens' Right to Know* [公民知情权法律保障之探析], 32 JOURNAL OF LIAONING UNIVERSITY (PHILOSOPHY AND SOCIAL SCIENCES EDITION) 127 (November 2004); Xianggang Li, China's Constitution Shall Explicitly Include Right to Know [我国宪法应明确规定知情权], 2 SEEK TRUTH FROM FACTS (2006).

[83] Shaofeng Guo, *NPC Standing Committee Member Xu Xianming: The Right to Know and the Right to Supervise Shall Be Written into Constitution* [全国人大常委会委员徐显明:知情权监督权应入宪], BEIJING NEWS, republished on Phoenix News, December 11, 2008, https://news.ifeng.com/mainland/200812/1211_17_916562.shtml (accessed between February 21, 2025 and March 31, 2025).

[84] Jack M. McLeod & Jay G. Blumler, *The Macro-Social Level of Communication Science*, *in* HANDBOOK OF COMMUNICATION SCIENCE (Charles R. Berger & Steven H. Chaffee eds., 1989); JOHN LESLIE MARTIN & ARJU GROVER CHAUDHARY, COMPARATIVE MASS MEDIA SYSTEMS (1983); DENIS MCQUAIL, MASS COMMUNICATION THEORY: AN INTRODUCTION (1987).

[85] Haiming Liu, *Misunderstanding of Wilbur Lang Schramm's Soviet Communism Theory of Newspapers* [施拉姆在"报刊的苏联共产主义理论"论述中的误读] 5 JOURNAL OF HUNAN MASS MEDIA VOCATIONAL TECHNICAL COLLEGE 26 (2005). According to Liu, the Soviet Communist media theory neglected the differences among Marxism, Leninism, and Stalinism. Colin Sparks denounced the Soviet media theory as outdated and incorrect. For more details of his contention, see Colin Sparks, *Media Theory after the Fall*

four theories overemphasize state policies but afford insufficient attention to journalistic autonomy.[86] Some scholars insisted that the four theories rely on an outdated canon of political philosophy,[87] and some criticized the three authors for failure to be value-free despite appearance to the contrary.[88] Some scholars challenged the four theories for ignorance of non-western cultures, philosophies, and traditions,[89] while others developed new models in an attempt to replace or update the four theories of the press.[90] Despite all the criticism, *Four Theories of the Press*[91] remains a

of Communism, *in* DE-WESTERNIZING MEDIA STUDIES 35 (James Curran & Myung-Jin Park eds., 2000).

[86] Jennifer Ostini & Anthony Y. H. Ostini, *Beyond the Four Theories of the Press: A New Model of National Media Systems*, 5 MASS COMMUNICATION AND SOCIETY 41 (2002).

[87] John Merrill & John Nerone, *The Four Theories of the Press Four and a Half Decades Later: A Retrospective*, 3 JOURNALISM STUDIES 133 (2002).

[88] JOHN C. NERONE (ed.), LAST RIGHTS: REVISITING FOUR THEORIES OF THE PRESS 7 (1995).

[89] Betty H. Winfield, Takeya Mizuno & Christopher E Beaudion, *Confucianism, Collectivism and Constitutions: Press Systems in China and Japan*, 5 COMMUNICATION LAW AND POLICY 323 (2000).

[90] Jiafei Yin, *Beyond the Four Theories of the Press: A New Model for the Asian and the World Press*, 10 JOURNALISM & COMMUNICATION MONOGRAPHS 3 (2008); Jennifer Ostini & Anthony Y.H. Fung, *Beyond the Four Theories of the Press: A New Model of National Media Systems*, 5 MASS COMMUNICATION & SOCIETY 41 (2002); Ekaterina Ognianova, *The Transitional Media System of Post-Communist Bulgaria*, JOURNALISM AND MASS COMMUNICATION MONOGRAPHS 162 (1997); DANIEL C. HALLIN & PAOLO MANCINI, COMPARING MEDIA SYSTEMS: THREE MODELS OF MEDIA AND POLITICS (2004); CLIFFORD G. CHRISTIANS, THEODORE GLASSER and DENIS MCQUAIL, NORMATIVE THEORIES OF THE MEDIA: JOURNALISM IN DEMOCRATIC SOCIETIES (2009); WILLIAM A. HACHTEN & HARVA HACHTEN, THE WORLD NEWS PRISM: CHANGING MEDIA, CLASHING IDEOLOGIES (1987); William A Hachten, THE WORLD NEWS PRISM: CHANGING MEDIA OF INTERNATIONAL COMMUNICATION (1999); DENIS MCQUAIL, MASS COMMUNICATION THEORY: AN INTRODUCTION (1987); Terry Adams-Bloom & Johanna Cleary, *Staking a Claim for Social Responsibility: An Argument for Dual Responsibility Model*, 11 THE INTERNATIONAL JOURNAL ON MEDIA MANAGEMENT 1 (2009); J. HERBERT ALTSCHULL, AGENTS OF POWER: THE MEDIA AND PUBLIC POLICY (1995); ROBERT G. PICARD, THE PRESS AND THE DECLINE OF DEMOCRACY: THE DEMOCRATIC SOCIALIST RESPONSE IN PUBLIC POLICY (1985); Chengju Huang, *Transitional Media vs. Normative Theories: Schramm, Altschull, and China*, 53 JOURNAL OF COMMUNICATION 444 (2003).

[91] FRED S. SIEBERT, THEODORE PETERSON and WILBUR SCHRAMM, FOUR THEORIES OF THE PRESS: THE AUTHORITARIAN, LIBERTARIAN, SOCIAL RESPONSIBILITY AND SOVIET COMMUNIST CONCEPTS OF WHAT THE PRESS SHOULD BE AND DO (1956).

landmark study of national media systems.[92] Today this seminal research is a must-read book for journalism students in the United States and elsewhere because of its simplicity, clarity, and strong philosophical underpinnings.[93] The four theories are also a widely used resource for scholars as a foundational framework for examining media systems among nations.

Four Theories of the Press attempts to offer a general theoretical and philosophical framework to understand the roles and functions of mass communications in different societies. In this small book, Siebert, Peterson, and Schramm argued that, according to different relationships between the state and the press, the world media systems could consist of four models: authoritarian, libertarian, social responsibility, and Soviet/Communist.[94] As the oldest among the four models, the authoritarian theory developed in England during the sixteenth and seventeenth centuries, and its foundation is centuries of authoritarian political thought from Plato to Machiavelli.[95] Ownership of press organizations operating under this model can be either private or public.[96] The chief purpose of mass media is to support and advance the policies of the government for absolute power. Criticism of political machinery and officials in power is intolerable.

[92] James Curran & Myung-Jin Park, *Beyond Globalization Theory*, *in* DE-WESTERNIZING MEDIA STUDIES (James Curran & Myung-Jin Park eds., 2000); WILLIAM A HACHTEN, *THE WORLD NEWS PRISM: CHANGING MEDIA, CLASHING IDEOLOGIES* (1987); JOHN C. MERRILL, THE IMPERATIVE OF FREEDOM: A PHILOSOPHY OF JOURNALISTIC AUTONOMY (1974); JOHN C. MERRILL & RALPH L. LOWENSTEIN, MEDIA MESSAGES & MEN: NEW PERSPECTIVES IN COMMUNICATION (1971); JOHN C. MERRILL & S. JACK ODELL, PHILOSOPHY AND JOURNALISM (1983); WILLIAM L. RIVERS & WILBUR SCHRAMM, RESPONSIBILITY IN MASS COMMUNICATION (1969).

[93] *Four Theories of the Press* was required reading for journalism students including the author of this book who studied at the China School of Journalism in Beijing from 1993 to 1995.

[94] FRED S. SIEBERT, THEODORE PETERSON and WILBUR SCHRAMM, FOUR THEORIES OF THE PRESS: THE AUTHORITARIAN, LIBERTARIAN, SOCIAL RESPONSIBILITY AND SOVIET COMMUNIST CONCEPTS OF WHAT THE PRESS SHOULD BE AND DO (1956).

[95] According to authoritarian political thought, the state is superior to the individual. Without the state, individuals could not obtain happiness and civilization could not advance. Such thinking legitimizes state control of mass media.

[96] Newspapers in most authoritarian media systems are in private hands. The state usually owns television stations operating in such media systems.

Soviet Communist theory, an outgrowth of the authoritarian theory, arose from the political philosophies of Marx, Lenin, and Stalin.[97] Press organizations, in this model, are state-owned mouthpieces of the government and the Communist Party. The Soviet theory considers mass media outlets as "collective propagandists," "collective agitators," "collective organizers," and "instruments to be controlled by the state," "instruments of social change and social control," and "instruments of serious purpose."[98]

The libertarian theory, developed in England after 1688, employs liberalist political philosophies of John Milton, John Locke, John Stuart Mill, Thomas Jefferson, and many others.[99] Ownership of media organizations operating from the libertarian model is chiefly private. Mass media in this system are "information sources, entertainment providers, social knowledge creators, profit making machines, and most importantly the government's watchdog."[100]

The social responsibility theory is an outgrowth of the libertarian theory, with development and practice in the United States in the twentieth century. The theory maintains a skeptical view of humanity and suspicion of the marketplace of ideas.[101] Similar to mass media in libertarian systems, press organizations in the social responsibility model are private; publishers and journalists should assume moral responsibilities when informing the public. Unlike the libertarian theory that considers

[97] According to Marxist political thought, the press should not function as a fourth estate; instead, it is a part of the state apparatus. The Marxist notion of material and economic determinism legitimizes state ownership of mass communication facilities.

[98] FRED S. SIEBERT, THEODORE PETERSON and WILBUR SCHRAMM, FOUR THEORIES OF THE PRESS: THE AUTHORITARIAN, LIBERTARIAN, SOCIAL RESPONSIBILITY AND SOVIET COMMUNIST CONCEPTS OF WHAT THE PRESS SHOULD BE AND DO 116 (1956).

[99] According to liberalist political thought, the individual is superior to the state. Individuals have the willingness and capacity to make rational decisions and create knowledge. The state exists to serve the needs of individuals. Such thinking delegitimizes state control of mass media.

[100] Xi Chen, "The Dynamics of Chinese Media Practices and Regulation: Explanations and Interpretations" (August 2007) (unpublished Ph.D. diss., Virginia Polytechnic Institute and State University), at 39.

[101] As a central tenet of liberal democracy, the belief in the marketplace of ideas maintains that truth or best policies result from competition among a wide variety of ideas in free, transparent public discourse. However, in reality, as the media concentration and monopolization become increasingly evident in developed countries, the diversity of the opinions' market dwindles and adversely affects the people's right to know.

government to be the major opponent of liberty, governments operating in a social responsibility system are encouraged to play positive roles in maintaining the freedom of individuals and society.[102]

Four Theories of the Press in the Chinese Context

Under the Soviet communist media system described by Siebert, Peterson, and Schramm in their 1956 book,[103] the party-state completely monopolized Soviet communist media, using it instrumentally for propagating party policies, directives, and ideologies, agitation of the public, and organizing social movements and events. Without press revenues from advertising, the government subsidized the media and party propaganda officials faithfully exercised political control of media content. Criticism of the party and the government was intolerable. In the area of educating and training journalists, loyalty to the party and understanding Marxist journalism received emphasis. The Soviet communist media had one single purpose, and one voice for ideology and policy. Consequently, "a great deal of sameness about the content of Soviet media on any day" was the norm.[104] Soviet journalists had no legal access to government-held information and their reporting and interviewing activities had no legal protection.

When using the four theories of the press to examine communist media in pre-reform China, the current research finds striking similarities among the Chinese communist media and its Soviet counterpart for each of the eight categories: media ownership, media philosophy, funding sources, press censorship, watchdog role, journalism education, media content, and media laws. For example, the Soviet concept that the

[102] For more detailed examinations of the four theories of the press, see Xi Chen, "The Dynamics of Chinese Media Practices and Regulation: Explanations and Interpretations" (August 2007) (unpublished Ph.D. diss., Virginia Polytechnic Institute and State University).

[103] Fred S. Siebert, Theodore Peterson and Wilbur Schramm, Four Theories of the Press: The Authoritarian, Libertarian, Social Responsibility and Soviet Communist Concepts of What the Press Should Be and Do 105–46 (1956).

[104] Fred S. Siebert, Theodore Peterson and Wilbur Schramm, Four Theories of the Press: The Authoritarian, Libertarian, Social Responsibility and Soviet Communist Concepts of What the Press Should Be and Do 123 (1956).

mass media should act as the Communist Party's collective propagandists, agitators, and organizers was particularly "instrumental in shaping the Chinese Communist Party's journalism policy."[105] The only inconsistency between Soviet mass media and Mao's media system arises from the watchdog role. Mao established an internal journalistic reference system[106] to maintain surveillance of local officials; a similar system is absent in the former Soviet Union. However, the internal reference system generally failed to fulfill its watchdog role during Mao's rule. In summary, a reasonable conclusion is that Chinese mass media under Mao coincides, comfortably, with the Soviet Communist model.[107]

If the Soviet Communist model offers a similarly accurate picture of Chinese journalistic theories and practices during Mao Zedong's era, discovery of that similarity is more uncertain in the post-Mao era due to both consistencies and inconsistencies in the two media structures. As for consistency, the communist legacy lingers in the reform-era Chinese mass media. For example, like the Soviet communist media system, ownership of Chinese media during the reform era remains with the state.[108] All four generations of the leadership (Mao Zedong, Deng Xiaoping, Jiang Zemin, and Hu Jintao) consistently stressed the media's role as mouthpiece and the importance of positive propaganda.[109] Funding for

[105] Colin Sparks, *Media Theory after the Fall of European Communism: Why the Old Models from East and West Won't Do Any More? In* DE-WESTERNIZING MEDIA STUDIES (James Curran & Myung-jin Park eds., 2003).

[106] Under the journalistic internal reference system, mainstream party-run and government-run news media outlets in China gather intelligence for the party and the government. Journalists and publishers of internal journalistic periodicals cover controversial and sensitive news events and analysis. Leading officials at various levels read those periodicals carefully to keep themselves informed and make decisions accordingly. All the contents in the periodicals are protected as state secrets. Chapter 9 of this book examines the journalistic internal reference system.

[107] For a description of Chinese mass media during the pre-reform era, see ALAN P. L. LIU, COMMUNICATIONS AND NATIONAL INTEGRATION IN COMMUNIST CHINA (1971).

[108] YUEZHI ZHAO, MEDIA, MARKET, AND DEMOCRACY IN CHINA: BETWEEN THE PARTY LINE AND THE BOTTOM LINE (1998). The only exception might be the Internet. Private Internet companies such as Baidu, Sina, Tencent, Alibaba, and ByteDance dominate the Chinese Internet market due to the absence of powerful state-controlled Internet companies. Min Jiang, *Internet Companies in China: Dancing between the Party Line and the Bottom Line*, 47 ASIE VISIONS (2012).

[109] YUEZHI ZHAO, MEDIA, MARKET, AND DEMOCRACY IN CHINA: BETWEEN THE PARTY LINE AND THE BOTTOM LINE (1998); David Bandurski, *The Marxist View of*

major media outlets in China is governmental despite commercialization that began in the 1990s.[110] Censorship of media content is the continuing responsibility of propaganda officials at various levels,[111] and party loyalty is an emphasis in journalism education.[112] Direct criticism of the party and the government is intolerable but censors tolerate

Journalism (马克思主义新闻观), China Media Project, the University of Hong Kong, Hong Kong, China, July 5, 2007, *available at* https://chinamediaproject.org/2007/07/05/the-marxist-view-of-journalism-%E9%A9%AC%E5%85%8B%E6%80%9D%E4%B8%BB%E4%B9%89%E6%96%B0%E9%97%BB%E8%A7%82/ (accessed between February 21, 2025 and March 31, 2025).

110 Chengju Huang, *Transitional Media v. Normative Theories: Schramm, Altschull and China*, 53 Journal of Communication 444 (2003); Chin-Chuan Lee, Money, Power and Media: Communication Patterns and Bureaucratic Control in Cultural China (2000); Yuezhi Zhao, Media, Market, and Democracy in China: Between the Party Line and the Bottom Line (1998); Winfield Betty & Peng Zengjun, *Marketplace or Party Controls? Chinese Media in Transition*, 67 Gazette 255 (2005).

111 For example, Mainland China continues to block many foreign social networking websites including YouTube, X (previously Twitter), Meta (previously Facebook), Google, and Instagram, dubbing the blocking system, "the great firewall of China." Michael Bristow, *China's Internet Spin Doctors*, BBC, December 16, 2008, http://news.bbc.co.uk/2/hi/asia-pacific/7783640.stm (accessed between February 21, 2025 and March 31, 2025). The Central Propaganda Department and its provincial and local counterparts are still functional. They issue party directives and orders to prevent journalists from covering certain controversial issues and major public emergency incidents. Tingjun Wu & Changyong Xia, *History and Status Quo of Crisis Communication in China* [我国公共危机传播的历史回顾与现状分析], 6 Journal of Modern Communication 32 (2010).

112 Political indoctrination remains an important component of Chinese journalism education in colleges during the reform era. When studying at the China School of Journalism (1993–1995), the author of this book had to take courses such as Marxist journalism, world politics, and socialist market economy. Those Marxism-related and politics-related courses were mandatory. Those courses emphasized the virtue of party journalism. Similar courses continue to be mandatory for journalism college students in China today.

media content scapegoating foreign nationals for China's own social problems.[113] Propaganda continues to dominate the media content, despite expanded newspaper sections for entertainment and sports.[114]

Concerning inconsistencies, noticeable libertarian elements began to emerge in post-Mao Chinese media.[115] For instance, unlike the Soviet communist media system, most Chinese media outlets are no longer governmental institutions. Instead, they have become state-owned enterprises.[116] Chinese media, today, welcomes foreign and private investment, although with some preconditions.[117] In addition to role of mouthpiece,

[113] For example, researchers found that online racist expressions against Africans are basically tolerated in China. When explaining why government censors turn a blind eye on such offensive speech, Pfafman, Carpenter, and Tang said, "In a society where resistance to the government is highly restricted, stereotypical racial constructions provide a way of critiquing the government without personal consequences. Blaming Africans for China's social ills provides a way for netizens to express criticisms of the government without directly attacking the government." Tessa M. Pfafman, Christopher J. Carpenter and Yong Tang, *The Politics of Racism: Constructions of African Immigrants in China on ChinaSMACK*, 8 COMMUNICATION, CULTURE AND CRITIQUE 4, 551 (2015) [https://doi.org/10.1111/cccr.12098].

[114] As China specialist David Shambaugh noted, the propaganda system (including the Central Propaganda Department, the State Council Information Office, the Ministry of Information Industry, the Ministry of Culture, the State Administration of Radio, Film, and Television, the General Administration of Press and Publication, and many other relevant party and government apparatus) in China today "remains effective in controlling most of the information that reaches the Chinese public and officialdom." David Shambaugh, *China's Propaganda System: Institutions, Processes and Efficacy*, 57 THE CHINA JOURNAL 25, 25 (2007).

[115] The book *Changing Media, Changing China* documented those changes vividly and extensively. CHANGING MEDIA, CHANGING CHINA (Susan L. Shirk, ed., 2010).

[116] The party encourages acquisitions and mergers among different media companies in an attempt to build Western-like giant media conglomerates. The Zhejiang Daily Newspaper Group and the Guangzhou Daily Newspaper Group have become public companies after an initial public offering. The website of the *People's Daily* has become a public company as well. Xiang Liu, *Guangzhou Daily Newspaper Group Becomes Second Chinese Media Group Going for Initial Public Offering*, 广州日报社成第二家整体上市报业集团] ECONOMIC WEEKLY, republished by Sina News, April 10, 2012, http://news.sina.com.cn/m/2012-04-10/104124247401.shtml (accessed between February 21, 2025 and March 31, 2025); Zijing Wu, *Party-Controlled China Site Raises $222 Million In Enlarged IPO*, BLOOMBERG NEWS, Apr 19, 2012, http://www.bloomberg.com/news/2012-04-18/china-s-party-website-people-cn-seeks-18-ipo-premium.html (accessed between February 21, 2025 and March 31, 2025).

[117] Today, News Corporation, Viacom, Sony Pictures, and many other foreign media conglomerates have established joint ventures with Chinese media companies, although

Chinese media organizations are encouraged to disseminate information and transmit public opinion.[118] As state-owned enterprises, the majority of Chinese media companies have to be self-reliant to generate profit in order to survive and prosper in the market.[119] Political control of media content becomes increasingly haphazard for non-sensitive issues.[120] Investigative journalism is permissible and media outlets have adopted a greater watchdog role, although the space for editorial autonomy has been rapidly shrinking in recent years.[121] Western journalistic theories and

foreign media companies may not hold more than half of the shares, nor may they interfere with joint ventures' editorial content. Jiafei Yin, *Beyond the Four Theories of the Press: A New Model for the Asian and the World Press*, 10 JOURNALISM & COMMUNICATION MONOGRAPHS 3, 27 (2008).

[118] In fact, in addition to the traditional role of party propaganda, Chinese mass media, especially market-oriented metropolitan newspapers, have developed a competing paradigm of professional journalism. According to this new paradigm, news media in China are disseminators of information, watchdogs of government, and protectors of public interests. Zhongdang Pan & Joseph Man Chan, *Shifting Journalistic Paradigms: How China's Journalists Assess "Media Exemplars,"* 30 COMMUNICATION RESEARCH 649, 649–82 (2003).

[119] A governmental report, announced in 2003, eliminated subsidies to all newspapers in China, except for the *People's Daily* and other two CCP-affiliated publications, along with mandatory subscriptions to most party and government-run newspapers. *Print Media Reform Stops Mandatory Subscription*, PEOPLE'S DAILY, November 28, 2003, http://english.peopledaily.com.cn/200311/28/eng20031128_129230.shtml (accessed between February 21, 2025 and March 31, 2025).

[120] Even online discussions of sensitive issues like criticizing government policies and officials are not always censored today in China. For example, according to research finding by Gary King, director of Harvard University's Institute of Quantitative Social Science, Chinese social media censors today normally do not delete online posts criticizing the government and government leaders. What are censored are online postings calling for people to take collective actions (e.g., demonstrating or rioting somewhere, gathering together in large groups). Gary King, Jennifer Pan & Margaret Roberts, *How Censorship in China Allows Government Criticism but Silences Collective Expression*, AMERICAN POLITICAL SCIENCE REVIEW 107, 326–43 (May 2013), https://doi.org/10.1017/S0003055413000014, republished on the website of Harvard University, *available at* http://gking.harvard.edu/files/censored.pdf (accessed between February 21, 2025 and March 31, 2025); Gary King, *China's "Internet Police" Targets Collective Action*, NATIONAL PUBLIC RADIO, August 8, 2012, http://www.npr.org/2012/08/08/158448847/chinas-internet-police-targets-collective-action (accessed between February 21, 2025 and March 31, 2025).

[121] *Caijing* magazine, *China Youth Daily*'s Freezing Point, *Southern Weekend*, and many other news outlets have reputations in China for conducting aggressive investigative journalism. Editor of *Caijing* Hu Shuli earned the title of "the most dangerous woman in

practices have become an important component of Chinese journalism education.[122] Media content is increasingly diversified as propaganda, news, and entertainment coexist,[123] cultivation effects of party propaganda on Chinese TV audiences' world views and beliefs are dwindling in the world of digital media where foreign media content can be easily accessed via various platforms,[124] legal protection of journalists

China" for her role in breaking some high-profile financial scandals. David Barboza, *Most Dangerous in China: An Editor*, THE NEW YORK TIMES, April 18, 2005, http://www.nytimes.com/2005/04/17/business/worldbusiness/17iht-caijing.html (accessed between February 21, 2025 and March 31, 2025). In order to counter rampant corruption, some high-level governmental officials encouraged the press to become watchdogs. For example, former Premier Zhu Rongji praised a China Central Television news program as "a mirror and watchdog of the government and a supervisor of the government through public opinion." Jiafei Yin, *Beyond the Four Theories of the Press: A New Model for the Asian and the World Press*, 10 JOURNALISM & COMMUNICATION MONOGRAPHS 3, 25 (2008).

122 With Western research and theories of communications appeared in college curricula, Chinese journalism education during the reform era has attempted to combine political indoctrination with professional training. Anecdotal evidence arises from a graduate course of study at the China School of Journalism (1993–1995); courses included Marxist journalism, world politics, socialist market economy, journalism ethics, journalism history, news writing and editing, English news writing and interviewing, French, computer technology, marketing, advertising, Western press theories and practices, and journalistic photography. Two Fulbright-sponsored professors from American universities taught English news writing.

123 Mass media are becoming increasingly entertainment-oriented. In 2005, Hunan Satellite Television broadcast an American Idol-type talent contest. The contest became so popular that the government accused the program of being too "vulgar" and "rebellious." The program's full title was "The Mongolian Cow Sour Yogurt Super Girl Contest," and more than 400 million people in China in 2005 watched the broadcast, making it one of the most successful shows in Chinese television history. David Barboza, *Chinese Regulators Caution TV Talent Shows*, THE NEW YORK TIMES, March 21, 2006, http://www.nytimes.com/2006/03/21/technology/21iht-hunan.html (accessed between February 21, 2025 and March 31, 2025).

124 Yong Tang, Xue Dou & Mary Beth Oliver, "*Harmonious Middle Kingdom and Dangerous Beautiful Country?*" *Exploring Cultivation Effects of Domestic and U.S.-Made TV Programs on Chinese College Students*, 12 INTERNATIONAL JOURNAL OF COMMUNICATION 4421–4442 (2018).

is improving,[125] and legal protection of news products is improving as well.[126]

Given the theoretical and practical inconsistencies and consistencies, many scholars of media studies argued that the four theories of the press including the Soviet Communist model have become outdated and irrelevant when assessing the nature of Chinese media during the liberalizing reform. For instance, Hallin and Mancini argued that the four theories of the press are no longer useful and, "it is time to give it a decent burial and move on to the development of more sophisticated models based on real comparative analysis."[127] Chengju Huang insisted Soviet Communist theory "is significantly insufficient in conceptualizing the [post-Mao] Chinese case"[128] for four reasons: Post-Mao Chinese news media are multifunctional media entities; the reform era's relaxed media control; positive, instrumental use of media in post-Mao China; state socialism exemplified by Soviet Communist media conflicts with market socialism exemplified by post-Maoist media.[129]

To the contrary, arguably, the Soviet Communist model remains relevant and valid in today's Chinese context. Undeniably, Chinese media

[125] Journalists frequently encountered criticism, purges, torture, and incarceration during Mao's era. The reform era better protects legal rights of news reporting and publishing. A *Freedom of the Press Law*, proposed in the 1980s, died in its infancy after the 1989 incident. Open discussion of the law remerged in 2008 and then died out again. Xupei Sun, *Reflections on 30-Year-Long Legislative History of Press Law* [三十年新闻立法历程与思考], 2 Yan-Huang Historical Review (2012), republished by Aisixiang.com, February 10, 2012, https://www.aisixiang.com/data/49917.html (accessed between February 21, 2025 and March 31, 2025); Qing Hua, *Speed up Work on Legislation of Press Law according to Scientific Principle of Rule of Law and Effective Management* [科学、依法、有效管理 加快新闻领域立法工作], People's Daily, November 3, 2008, republished by Sohu News, November 4, 2008, https://news.sohu.com/20081104/n260419205.shtml (accessed between February 21, 2025 and March 31, 2025).

[126] For how news products are protected under the Chinese copyright law, see Yong Tang, *Journalistic Right in the "First Rough Draft of History": A Comparative Study of News Copyright in the United States and the People's Republic of China*, 6 Chinese Journal of Communication 1, 24–44 (2013).

[127] Colin Sparks, *Media Theory after the Fall of European Communism: Why the Old Models from East and West Won't Do Any More? In* De-Westernizing Media Studies (James Curran & Myung-jin Park eds., 2003).

[128] Chengju Huang, *Transitional Media vs. Normative Theories: Schramm, Altschull, and China*, 53 Journal of Communication 446 (2003).

[129] Chengju Huang, *Transitional Media vs. Normative Theories: Schramm, Altschull, and China*, 53 Journal of Communication 446–50 (2003).

entities are moving toward liberalization, commercialization, technological innovation, and professionalization. However, the power of such trends on regime change is actually an exaggeration. Above all, the fundamental relationship among the press, the party, and the government does not change at all. Despite the liberalizing trends, the party-state paradigm remains dominant over Chinese media in the reform era. Bruce Dickson, a prominent political science scholar of modern Chinese politics, stated:

> The commercialization of the media and the dissemination of new communication technology, especially the Internet and mobile phones, have weakened the party's control over the flow of information, but it is still able to limit the spread of unwanted news by blocking Internet sites, arresting journalists and editors, and closing down newspapers and magazines that stray too far from the party's guidelines.[130]

Given a lack of fundamental change in party-press relations in China, accumulating libertarian elements are insufficient to trigger a reclassification of Chinese media, especially when we think about the CCP's increasingly tight control of media in recent years. Of course, libertarian changes of Chinese media identified earlier are important to acknowledge, but they are evolutionary, not revolutionary. The party has created and encouraged all those changes. In other words, mass media in China today remain in the party's orbit, a socialist body with a capitalist face.

Actually, many media scholars agree that despite its limitations, the four theories of the press are useful for contemporary comparative media research. According to influential media scholar, Denis McQuail, the four theories proposed by Seibert and his colleagues provide a framework for understanding the relationship between media and society. All the new theories are modifications of the "four theories" by addition or subtraction.[131] Communication scholars, Junhao Hong and Jonathan Becker, suggested that the four theories' classifications of the media systems are

[130] Bruce J. Dickson, *The Future of the Chinese Communist Party: Strategies of Survival and Prospects for Change*, *in* CHARTING CHINA'S FUTURE: POLITICAL, SOCIAL, AND INTERNATIONAL DIMENSIONS 21 (Jae Ho Chung ed., 2006).

[131] DENIS MCQUAIL, MASS COMMUNICATION THEORY: AN INTRODUCTION (1987).

still very useful in interpreting media developments in post-communist countries.[132]

Democratization, News Media, and Transparency

Now it is time to examine democratization theories and discuss news media's contributions to governmental transparency, especially in authoritarian regimes. Political science scholars disagree on what constitutes democracy; however, they almost all agree that characterization of democracy includes the presence of at least one of three elements: competition of top leaders through fair, free, and periodic elections, participation of citizens who enjoy the freedom to vote and run for office, political rights, and civil liberties. According to democratization theories, in every wave of democratization, democracy supersedes authoritarian regimes, and some develop into consolidated democracies. Reverse waves occur when democracies collapse, and authoritarianism returns.[133]

Political scientists, Gasiorowski and Power, argued that more than 60 percent of new democracies collapse within 12 years of establishing a democracy. If a democracy survives for at least 12 years, then a safe assumption is that the regime has consolidated and becomes less likely to fail. This applies to new authoritarian regimes, as well.[134] China has

[132] Hong applied the four theories in his analysis of internationalization of Chinese television. For more details of his analysis, see JUNHAO HONG, THE INTERNATIONALIZATION OF TELEVISION IN CHINA: THE EVOLUTION OF IDEOLOGY, SOCIETY, AND MEDIA SINCE THE REFORM (1998). Becker applied the four theories in studying media in post-Cold War Russia. For more details of his study, see Jonathan Becker, *Lessons from Russia: A Neo-Authoritarian Media System*, 19 EUROPEAN JOURNAL OF COMMUNICATION 139, 139–63 (2004).

[133] For scholarly discussions of the basic concepts of authoritarianism, democracy, authoritarian consolidation and collapse, democratic consolidation and collapse, see SAMUEL P. HUNTINGTON, THE THIRD WAVE: DEMOCRATIZATION IN THE LATE TWENTIETH CENTURY (1991); Steven Levitsky & Lucan A. Way, *The Rise of Competitive Authoritarianism*, 13 JOURNAL OF DEMOCRACY 51, 51–65 (2002); Steven J. Hood, *The Myths of Asian-Style Democracy*, 38 ASIAN SURVEY 853, 853–66 (1998); Andreas Schedler, *What is Democratic Consolidation?* 9 JOURNAL OF DEMOCRACY 91, 91–207 (1998).

[134] Mark J. Gasiorowski & Timothy J. Power, *The Structural Determinants of Democratic Consolidation: Evidence from the Third World*, 31 COMPARATIVE POLITICAL STUDIES 740, 740–71 (December 1998).

passed the twelve-year rule; the PRC established itself as an authoritarian regime in 1949.

Scholars developed many measures to gauge the extent of a country's authoritarianism or democracy. Among them, five are authoritative and widely used: The Freedom House Scores,[135] the Vanhanen Polyarchy Dataset,[136] the Polity IV Dataset,[137] the Political Regime Change Dataset,[138] and the ACLP (Alvarez, Cheibub, Limongi, and Przeworski) Political Regime Classifications dataset.[139] All five measures consistently rate China as an authoritarian regime.

The role of news media in the democratization process has a long history of study.[140] Many political science scholars insist that news media guarantee governmental transparency, vital for democracy. According to Larry Diamond and Leonardo Morlino, transparency is an essential

135 *Freedom in the World Research Methodology*, Freedom House, Washington, DC, *available at* https://freedomhouse.org/reports/freedom-world/freedom-world-research-methodology (accessed between February 21, 2025 and March 31, 2025).

136 *Vanhanen Polyarchy Dataset*, *available at* https://xmarquez.github.io/democracyData/reference/vanhanen.html (accessed between February 21, 2025 and March 31, 2025); *Vanhanen's Index of Democracy*, the Peace Research Institute Oslo (PRIO), Oslo, Norway, *available at* https://www.prio.org/data/20 (accessed between February 21, 2025 and March 31, 2025 12/27/2011).

137 *The Polity IV Project*, the Center for Systemic Peace, Vienna, Virginia, *available at* http://www.systemicpeace.org/polity/polity4.htm (accessed between February 21, 2025 and March 31, 2025).

138 Mark J. Gasiorowski, *An Overview of the Political Regime Change Dataset*, 29 COMPARATIVE POLITICAL STUDIES 469, 469–83 (1996).

139 Mike Alvarez, JosJ Antonio Cheibub, Fernando Limongi and Adam Przeworski, *ACLP Political and Economic Database Codebook*, Pompeu Fabra University, Barcelona, Spain, December 1999, *available at* https://econ.upf.edu/~satorra/dades/ACLP_Codebook.PDF (accessed between February 21, 2025 and March 31, 2025); ADAM PRZEWORSKI, MICHAEL E. ALVAREZ, JOSE ANTONIO CHEIBUB AND FERNANDO LIMONGI, DEMOCRACY AND DEVELOPMENT: POLITICAL INSTITUTIONS AND WELL-BEING IN THE WORLD, 1950–1990 (2000).

140 For relevant literature, see DEMOCRATIZATION AND THE MEDIA (Vicky Randall ed., 1998); CHAPPELL H. LAWSON, BUILDING THE FOURTH ESTATE: DEMOCRATIZATION AND THE RISE OF A FREE PRESS IN MEXICO (2002); PETER GROSS, ENTANGLED EVOLUTIONS: MEDIA AND DEMOCRATIZATION IN EASTERN EUROPE (2002); YUEZHI ZHAO, MEDIA, MARKET, AND DEMOCRACY IN CHINA: BETWEEN THE PARTY LINE AND THE BOTTOM LINE (1998).

element of eight principal dimensions of democratic quality.[141] Many scholars believe that news media are instrumental for eliminating authoritarian regimes and installing democracies. For example, influential political scientist, Samuel Huntington, argued that snowballing effects are a factor contributing to the third wave of democratization.[142] In explanation for the effect in the third wave rather than the first two waves, he stated: "The reason is the tremendous expansion in global communications and transportation that occurred in the decades after World War II and particularly the blanketing of the world by television and communications satellites in the 1970s."[143]

Literature Review

Freedom of Information legislation is a regular topic of research in law journals. As of December 2012, a search of the HeinOnline database[144] revealed 727 English-language articles in law journals (in all disciplines) featuring "freedom of information" in their titles. Another HeinOnline search identified 19,562 English articles in law journals (in all disciplines) featuring "freedom of information" in their texts. As of March

[141] The eight different dimensions of democratic quality are: the rule of law, participation, competition, vertical accountability, horizontal accountability, respect for civil and political freedoms, the progressive implementation of greater political equality, and responsiveness. Larry Diamond & Leonardo Morlino, *The Quality of Democracy: An Overview*, 15 Journal of Democracy 21, 21–22 (2004).

[142] Samuel P. Huntington, The Third Wave: Democratization in the late Twentieth Century 100 (1991). Other factors are deepening crisis for the legitimacy of authoritarian systems, global economic prosperity in the 1960s, changes among churches from defenders of status quo to opponents of authoritarianism, European community membership expansion, U.S. promotion of human rights and democracy, and Gorbachev's dramatic policy changes in the U.S.S.R.

[143] Samuel P. Huntington, The Third Wave: Democratization in the late Twentieth Century 101 (1991).

[144] HeinOnline is one of the largest databases for legal research. For more information about the company, see *A Century of Serving the Library Community*, HeinOnline, Buffalo, New York, ***available at*** https://home.heinonline.org/about-us/ (accessed between February 21, 2025 and March 31, 2025).

31, 2025, a search of Legal Source[145] and Communication & Mass Media Complete[146] using the keyword "freedom of information" in the texts found 8,428 articles and 1,299 articles, respectively, in English-language and peer-reviewed academic journals. As of March 31, 2025, a search of the ProQuest Dissertations & Theses database[147] revealed 14,360 English-language dissertations and theses featuring "freedom of information" in their texts. Some books concern freedom of information and many Internet resources are available.[148] The presence of this large body of English-language academic literature dealing with freedom of

[145] Legal Source is another flagship database for legal research. For more information about the database, see *Full-Text Database Legal Source*, EBSCO, Ipswich, MA, ***available at*** https://www.ebsco.com/products/research-databases/legal-source (accessed between February 21, 2025 and March 31, 2025).

[146] Communication & Mass Media Complete is one of the largest databases in communication research. For more information about the database, see *Full-Text Database Communication & Mass Media Complete*, EBSCO, Ipswich, MA, ***available at*** https://www.ebsco.com/products/research-databases/communication-mass-media-complete (accessed between February 21, 2025 and March 31, 2025).

[147] ProQuest Dissertations & Theses is the world's largest database archiving PhD dissertations and master's theses.

[148] The comparative study, *Public Access to Government-Held Information*, needs to be updated. NORMAN MARSH (ED.), PUBLIC ACCESS TO GOVERNMENT-HELD INFORMATION (1987). For two important, contemporary surveys of Freedom of Information legislation, see DAVID BANISAR, FREEDOM OF INFORMATION AROUND THE WORLD 2006: A GLOBAL SURVEY OF ACCESS TO GOVERNMENT INFORMATION LAWS (report for Privacy International, London, United Kingdom, July 2006), ***available at*** http://www.freedominfo.org/documents/global_survey2006.pdf (accessed between February 21, 2025 and March 31, 2025) (investigating all the national freedom of information legislations in the world) and FREEDOM OF INFORMATION: A COMPARATIVE LEGAL SURVEY (Toby Mendel ed., 2nd edn, 2008) (exploring established global FOI standards). Additionally, several Internet sources publish relevant FOI cases and accounts of FOI activists: Article 19, http://www.article19.org (accessed between February 21, 2025 and March 31, 2025) (promoting FOI as a London-based international NGO); Freedominfo.org, http://www.freedominfo.org (accessed between February 21, 2025 and March 31, 2025) (providing online resources for freedom of information activists); Freedom of Information Advocates Network, http://www.foiadvocates.net (accessed between February 21, 2025 and March 31, 2025) (persuading countries without FOI legislation to move toward enactment); Open Society Institute Justice Initiative, http://www.justiceinitiative.org (accessed between February 21, 2025 and March 31, 2025) (involving in activities for human rights protection and access to information); Privacy International, http://www.privacyinternational.org (accessed between February 21, 2025 and March 31, 2025) (functioning as a watchdog on governments and corporations for surveillance and privacy invasions); Transparency International, http://www.transparency.org/ (accessed between February 21, 2025 and March 31, 2025) (combating global corporate and political corruption).

information indicates tremendous interest in this subject among Western scholars, and particularly for American freedom of information. A search of HeinOnline revealed 118 articles in law journals (in all disciplines) featuring "U.S. Freedom of information Act" in their texts. The overall legislative development in China has received significant scrutiny in the West. A search of the HeinOnline database revealed 101,179 articles in law journals (in all disciplines) featuring "China" in their texts and 5,393 articles featuring "China" in their titles.

In a sharp contrast, legal research into Chinese freedom of information is rare. A HeinOnline search yielded only one article containing "open government information regulations" in its footnote,[149] and only two articles containing "regulations on open government information" in their texts.[150] A similar search revealed only one article featuring "Chinese government transparency" in its text.[151] Another HeinOnline search identified zero articles in law journals (in all disciplines) featuring "Chinese freedom of information" in their texts. A search of the ProQuest Dissertations & Theses database revealed only one dissertation featuring "Chinese freedom of information" in its text.

A search of other databases[152] and the Internet yielded a small number of legal journal's articles, books, and other scholarly pieces focusing exclusively on Chinese *OGI Regulations*. Hanhua Zhou from the Chinese Academy of Social Sciences, a prolific legal scholar, researched Chinese governmental transparency laws and added personal involvement to creation of the Chinese FOI law. In a chapter of *The Right to Know:*

[149] Joel B.Eisen, *The New Energy Geopolitics? China, Renewable Energy, and the "Greentech Race,"* 86 CHICAGO-KENT LAW REVIEW 9, 33 (2011).

[150] Carl F. Minzner, *Riots and Cover-ups: Counterproductive Control of Local Agents in China*, 31 UNIVERSITY OF PENNSYLVANIA JOURNAL OF INTERNATIONAL LAW 115 (2009–2010). This article only briefly mentions the Chinese freedom of information law without any elaboration. *China's Efforts and Achievements in Promoting the Rule of Law*, *7 Chinese Journal of International Law* 513 (2008). This article is not the product of legal scholars, rather the Chinese government as an official whitepaper. The mention of Chinese *OGI Regulations* intended to publicize China's achievements in promoting the rule of law.

[151] "Chinese government transparency" appears only in the footnote of this article. Stephen O'Connor, *Global Internet Freedom Act: Can a Proactive United States' Internet Freedom Law Forestall China's One Internet, Two System Policy*, 2 INTERNATIONAL JOURNAL OF CIVIC SOCIETY LAW 30 (2004).

[152] Such databases are Google Scholar, Google Books, Westlaw, JSTOR, Communication and Mass Media Complete, and many others.

Transparency for an Open World, Hanhua Zhou discussed, from an insider's perspective, methods, and rationales for China's embarking on a path to governmental transparency. He concluded that the creation of the FOI law in China was elitist-driven.[153] In a Chinese-language journal article, Hanhua Zhou identified legal challenges facing Chinese FOI law and provided policy recommendations.[154]

Weibing Xiao, a scholar from Shanghai University of Political Science and Law, attempted to explain the rationales for China's freedom of information reform in several of his articles. He concluded that democratization is a key rationale for the rise of Chinese governmental transparency.[155] In his book *Freedom of Information Reform in China: Information Flow Analysis*, Weibing Xiao asserted that social, political, and legal factors should have central roles in facilitating the development of FOI in China.[156]

Ping Yin, another Chinese legal scholar, examined the contribution of the SARS crisis and other public health incidents to the formulation of the FOI law.[157] China specialist Changhua Wu investigated public access to environmental information in China before *OGI Regulations*

[153] Hanhua Zhou, *Open Government in China: Practice and Problems*, *in* THE RIGHT TO KNOW: TRANSPARENCY FOR AN OPEN WORLD (Ann Florini & Joseph E. Stiglitz eds., 2007).

[154] HanHua Zhou, *Some Problems and Policy Suggestions Concerning the Implementation of OGI Regulations* [政府信息公开条例》实施的问题与对策探讨], 7 CHINESE PUBLIC ADMINISTRATION 11 (2009).

[155] Weibing Xiao, *The Improved Information Environment As A Key Rationale for Freedom of Information Reform in China*, 15 JOURNAL OF INFORMATION POLITY (2010); Weibing Xiao, *China's Limited Push Model of FOI Legislation*, 27 GOVERNMENT INFORMATION QUARTERLY 346, 346–51 (2010); Weibing Xiao, *Democratization As A Rationale for Freedom of Information Reform in China*, working paper series of School of Economic Law, Shanghai University of Political Science and Law, available at Social Science Research Network (SSRN) website, November 9, 2010, *available at* https://papers.ssrn.com/sol3/papers.cfm?abstract_id=1706066 ((accessed between February 21, 2025 and March 31, 2025).

[156] WEIBING XIAO, FREEDOM OF INFORMATION REFORM IN CHINA: INFORMATION FLOW ANALYSIS (2011).

[157] Ping Yin, Chinese Government *Information Disclosure and Rule of Law: From SARS to Bird Flu*, 11 JOURNAL OF HEBEI LAW SCIENCE *146*, 146–49 (2004).

went into effect.[158] Two experts explored the same topic in 2010 and produced a lengthy report in which they provided recommendations for Chinese policymakers to improve access to environmental information.[159] In their Chinese-language journal articles, other Chinese scholars compared China's freedom of information law to similar laws of the United States and other Western nations.[160] Some Chinese-language theses and dissertations discussed the legal and conceptual framework needed to establish China's open government information mechanism and provided suggestions for law reformers to consider when proposing a FOI law.[161]

[158] Changhua Wu, *Improving the Legal and Policy Foundation for Public Access to Environmental Information in China*, 24 Temple Journal of Science, Technology & Environmental Law 291, 291–323 (2005).

[159] Sim Kok Eng Amy & Jing Hu, Access to Environmental Information in China: Evaluation of Local Compliance (report published both in Chinese and English as a final product of collaboration between Article 19 and The Center for Legal Assistance to Pollution Victims at China University of Political Science and Law, December 2010), *available at* https://www.article19.org/data/files/pdfs/reports/access-to-environmental-information-in-china-evaluation-of-local-compliance.pdf (accessed between February 21, 2025 and March 31, 2025).

[160] For relevant literature, see Silin Zheng, *Comparing U.S. Information Disclosure Laws with Its Chinese and Canadian Counterparts* [我国信息公开法与美国、加拿大关于信息公开条款的比较], *7* Archives of Hubei 14, 14–17 (2007); Fang Jiang & Yanhui Gao, *Freedom of information Act in the United States: A Comparison with Government Information Public Regulation in China* [美国 "情报自由法"浅析—兼与中国《政府信息公开条例》比较], Journal of Xi'an University of Electronics and Technology (Social Science Edition) 133, 133–36 (2008).

[161] Most of these theses and dissertations were completed prior to the promulgation of *OGI Regulations* in 2007. For an incomplete list of dissertations and theses that focus significantly on Chinese FOI, see Yong Wang, "Analysis of Open Government Information" [政府信息公开论] (April 2005) (unpublished Ph.D. diss., China University of Political Science and Law); Aijun Lin, "Legal Protection for the Right to Know: Insight of Journalism and Communication" [论知情权 的法律保障:新闻传播学的视角] (April 2007) (unpublished Ph.D. diss., Fudan University); Xiaoyang Yi, "Research on Legislation of Government Information Publicity" [政府信息公开的立法研究] (April 2003) (unpublished master's thesis, Xiangtan University); Yanjie Zhang, "Research on Legal System of Open Government Information from the Perspective of Information Exemption" [政府信息公开法律制度研究 —从豁免公开的角度] (March 2007) (unpublished master's thesis, China University of Political Science and Law); Dongmei Xiao, "Research on Public Access to Information Resources" [信息资源公共获取制度研究] (2007) (unpublished Ph.D. diss., Wuhan University); Jiandong Zhou, "The Studies on Open Government Information from the View of Public Field" [公共性视野下的政府信息公开研究] (March 2007) (unpublished Ph.D. diss., Shandong University).

Jamie P. Horsley from Yale University Law School is among the most productive Western scholars who focus on the Chinese government's transparency laws. Several of Horsley's articles concerning Chinese *OGI Regulations* examined the statutory language of the law and evaluated the law's efficacy.[162] In a chapter of *The Right to Know: Transparency for an Open World,* Horsley examined special considerations China adopted when preparing the FOI law.[163] Legal scholar, Jens. F. Reinertsen, examined the direction *OGI Regulations* followed according to international standards.[164] Other Western scholars conducted a survey among Chinese governmental officials and found that key issues surrounding implementation of *OGI Regulations* appear in many other countries.[165] FOI expert Paul Hubbard argued that Chinese governmental agencies at central and local levels are developing a wide range of OGI implementation models due to a lack of a strong legal contexts and clear directives for guidance.[166]

The pertinent literature reviewed above contributed to research of Chinese governmental transparency jurisprudence. However, ignoring the limitations of the existing literature is difficult. Most Chinese-language research projects regarding Chinese FOI are superficial, limited in scope,

162 Shili He [Jamie P. Horsley], *Some Thoughts on Typical Exemptions for Government Information Disclosure* [关于政府信息免予公开典型条款的几点思考] 3 POLITICS SCIENCE AND LAW 37 (2009); Jamie P. Horsley, *China Adopts First Nationwide Open Government Information Regulations*, freedominfo.org, Washington, DC, May 9, 2007, *available at* http://www.freedominfo.org/2007/05/china-adopts-first-nationwide-open-government-information-regulations/ (accessed between February 21, 2025 and March 31, 2025); Jamie P. Horsley, *Update on China's Open Government Information Regulations: Surprising Public Demand Yielding Some Positive Results*, Freedominfo.org, Washington, DC, April 23, 2010, *available at* http://www.freedominfo.org/2010/04/update-on-china-open-government-information-regulations/ (accessed between February 21, 2025 and March 31, 2025).

163 Jamie P. Horsley, *Toward a More Open China? in* THE RIGHT TO KNOW: TRANSPARENCY FOR AN OPEN WORLD (Ann Florini & Joseph E. Stiglitz eds., 2007).

164 Jens. F. Reinertsen, "Assessing Access to Information in China-Legal Development and International Standards" (November 2009) (unpublished master's thesis, China University of Political Science and Law).

165 Suzanne J. Piotrowski, Yahong Zhang, Wenxuan Yu & Weiwei Lin, *Key Issues for Implementation of the Chinese Open Government Information Regulations*, 69 PUBLIC ADMINISTRATION REVIEW S129, S129–S135 (December 2009).

166 Paul Hubbard, *China's Regulations on Open Government Information: Challenges of Nationwide Policy Implementation*, 4 OPEN GOVERNMENT (2008).

and lack in-depth analyses. In general, the quality of English-language scholarship is higher than that in Chinese, but none of the scholarship in English provided a detailed and comprehensive account of the legislative history of Chinese *OGI Regulations*. They have also failed to explain, convincingly, the avenue by which Western concepts of freedom of information insinuated into the Chinese, authoritarian body politic and culture, whose innate governmental secrecy represents the norm of the nation's modern history.[167]

Few of the scholarly articles or books in English are sufficiently comprehensive to cover a wide range of topics pertaining to the Chinese FOI. For example, none of Western FOI scholarship discussed, in detail, the evolution of the informational policy of the Chinese government over the last four thousand years, the influence of ancient schools of thought in relation to government transparency on contemporary Chinese governmental leaders, or the Chinese news media's contribution to formation of the FOI law, or Chinese reporters' use of the law to promote oversight of government. No scholars examined the enforcement of *OGI Regulations* by using fresh data gathered as recently as December 2023. No FOI scholars examined the relationship between journalistic internal documents and people's legal rights for access. Most scholars of Chinese government's transparency have no professional experiences in journalism

[167] For example, Chinese scholar Weibing Xiao argued that democratization is a key rationale for China's efforts to promote greater transparency. WEIBING XIAO, *Democratization as a Rationale for FOI Reform in China, in* FREEDOM OF INFORMATION REFORM IN CHINA: INFORMATION FLOW ANALYSIS 38–50 (2011). His argument seems not fully supportable because the Chinese FOI law is a means by which the central party and governmental authorities maintain legitimacy for the party. The adoption of the law is not a part of China's political liberalization. In other words, the law was possible not because Chinese leaders believed strongly in democratic values that are widely accepted in the Western world. The law was possible because of Chinese leaders' assumptions that the law could promote economic growth, informational development, corruption prevention, law-based administration, and crisis communication management. These are all goals set by the party within the framework of socialism with Chinese characteristics. For analysis of how public incidents like 2003 SARS episode prompted the Chinese government to improve their crisis communication, see Lidan Chen, *Open Information System and Crisis Communication in China*, 1 CHINESE JOURNAL OF COMMUNICATION 38, 38–54 (April 2008); Tingjun Wu & Changyong Xia, *History and Status Quo of Crisis Communication in China* [我国公共危机传播的历史回顾与现状分析], 6 JOURNAL OF MODERN COMMUNICATION 32 (2010).

or other media-related sectors.[168] Few scholars have comprehensively examined OGI-related access laws in China. Given the lack of scholarship for Chinese freedom of information, as evidenced by the literature reviewed above, and the lack of reverse perspectives in international and comparative media law research,[169] this book seeks to fill this gap.

Summary and Conclusion

This chapter examined all the major concepts and philosophies that contextualize the theoretical underpinnings of this book. The Western concept of freedom of information has a wide range of theoretical foundations: the theories of freedom of expression, right to know, democratic politics, and the First Amendment's value as a check on governmental activity. The freedom of expression theory argues for freedom of information from the perspective of truth and liberty. The right to know theory argues for freedom of information from the perspective of access rights. The democratic political theory argues for freedom of information from the perspective of democratic governance. The value of the First Amendment as a check on government theory argues for freedom of information from the perspective of institutionalized media. The four theories mentioned earlier operate in concert to provide solid philosophical, legal, and moral foundations for freedom of information.

The concept of freedom of information in the Chinese context lacks theoretical support from freedom of expression and checking value theories. Consistent with other research findings, this book finds that Chinese legal scholars who introduced the concept of "the right to know" to China disconnected the right to know from freedom of expression and freedom of the press for political reasons. They argued for the people's right to know from the perspective of the *Chinese Constitution* because the supreme law, like many other constitutions in the world, upholds

[168] This study represents legal research on media law. Consequently, highlighting the relationship between journalism and freedom of information is rational. On the other hand, many legal scholars consider FOI law as administrative rather than strictly media-related.

[169] Kyu Ho Youm and Amy Kristin Sanders, *International and Comparative Law as a Reverse Perspective on Communication Law*, 25 Communication Law & Policy 2, 103–112 (2020).

the sovereignty of the people, and thus, implies a right to access vital governmental information.

This chapter explored the four theories of the press and examined the applicability of the theories to the Chinese context. This study argues that the theories remain useful for understanding the evolution of the Chinese media system that plays an important role in promoting the flow of information in Chinese society. The chapter also investigates democratization theories and concludes that the freedom of information movement in China requires understanding from the framework of authoritarian transparency because China's ranking by all the major measures of democracy is one of authoritarianism.

This chapter thoroughly reviewed existing literature pertaining to the Chinese FOI law and concludes that the available, existing literature contributes to knowledge of freedom of information legislation in China. However, the existing literature, in general, lacks depth, scope, comprehensiveness, and ingenuity. Many important questions remain unanswered, and the gap in the academic literature regarding the Chinese freedom of information is vast. All subsequent chapters in this book attempt to fill this huge void.

CHAPTER 3

Origins and Development of Freedom of Information Laws in the World

Introduction

Inspired by the success of many national FOI laws, China inculcated international concepts when formulating *OGI Regulations*. This chapter will discuss the development of freedom of information legislation in Sweden, the United States, and many other countries in order to provide a reference point for the evolution of freedom of information in China. The chapter will trace the birth of the first freedom of information law in the world and see how the law's spirit was spreading to other parts of the world. This chapter will explore several patterns and trends emerging in the global expansion of freedom of information law.

This chapter is derived from the book author's doctoral dissertation that was successfully defended at The Pennsylvania State University in 2012. Portions of the text resemble or may replicate the original text from the unpublished PhD thesis and have been reproduced as such with the permission of Palgrave Macmillan editors. Yong Tang, "Chinese Freedom of Information: An Evaluation of the Legislative History, Rationales, Significance and Efficacy of Regulations of the People's Republic of China on Open Government Information" (2012) (unpublished Ph.D. diss., The Pennsylvania State University at University Park), *available at*†† https://etda.libraries.psu.edu/catalog/16287 (accessed between February 21, 2025 and March 31, 2025).

Y. Tang, *Freedom of Information Law in China*,
https://doi.org/10.1007/978-981-96-7842-6_3

The U.S. FOI law serves as the most influential example for many other countries and U.S. state legislatures to emulate. An overview of this law would provide an important international context to understand China's own FOI law. This chapter will examine the origins and milestones prior to enactment of *U.S. FOIA* in 1966 and investigate what roles American media professionals have played in formulating, amending, and using their federal freedom of information law. The emphasis on the role of U.S. journalists in FOI is an attempt to provide a reference for the examination of journalism's role in Chinese freedom of information, which will be examined in Chapter 10.

From Sweden to Sri Lanka: Global Expansion of Freedom of Information Laws

Governmental transparency has its roots in ancient Greece as well as in ancient China.[1] For example, Aristotle noted that the ideal state should not be too large in either size or population because "everyone [in the state] must know what is going on."[2] However, the modern concept of public access to governmental information originated during the European Enlightenment. In 1766, Sweden enacted the world's first freedom of information law, known as *Freedom-of-Press and the Right-of-Access to Public Records Act*.[3] According to the law, official documents were to be available immediately upon request, for no charge.[4] According to Swedish clergyman and congressman, Anders Chydenius, the principal sponsor of

[1] Chapter 4 of this book will discuss the roots of governmental transparency in the Chinese civilization.

[2] Herbert Brucker, Freedom of Information 10 (1949).

[3] An overview of the law is available on the website of the Swedish Ministry of Justice. *Public Access to Information and Secrecy: The Legislation in Brief*, the Ministry of Justice, Government Offices of Sweden, Stockholm, Sweden, *available at* https://www.government.se/contentassets/2ca7601373824c8395fc1f38516e6e03/public-access-to-information-and-secrecy.pdf (accessed between February 21, 2025 and March 31, 2025).

[4] David Banisar, Freedom of Information around the World 2006: A Global Survey of Access to Government Information Laws (report for Privacy International, London, United Kingdom, July 2006), *available at* http://www.freedominfo.org/documents/global_survey2006.pdf (accessed between February 21, 2025 and March 31, 2025).

the Swedish freedom of information law, Sweden's inspiration was the Chinese practice of governmental accountability and transparency.[5]

More than 20 years later, France and the Netherlands embraced similar principles of official transparency in their *Declaration of the Rights of Man*.[6] The South American country of Colombia followed suit. In 1888, Columbia enacted *Code of Political and Municipal Organization*, granting citizens the legal right to request documents held by agencies or in official archives.[7]

In 1966, 200 years after the Swedish FOI law's inception, the U.S. government adopted an FOI law, *Freedom of Information Act (FOIA)*. Since then, the American public and press have had an "enforceable legal right" to inspect documents or records held by the federal government.[8] The U.S. right to information law inspired many other nations to join the international freedom of information community, although some scholars believe using *U.S. FOIA* as a model is a mistake.[9]

[5] Some scholars argued that the concept of freedom of information actually first appeared in China more than 1,000 years ago during the Tang Dynasty. According to this argument, Emperor Tai'Zong (599–649 A.D.) established an "Imperial Censorate," a powerful organization of highly educated, scholarly officials recorded governmental documents and activities, and willingly criticized the government, including the emperor. The information policy of Tai'Zong inspired Anders Chydenius (1729–1803), born in Sotkamo, Sweden (today's northeastern Finland). He was a clergyman, Enlightenment philosopher, and great proponent of freedom of the press. He persuaded the Swedish government to adopt the Freedom of Press Act in 1766, the world's first Freedom of information legislation. Stephen Lamble, *Freedom of Information, a Finnish Clergyman's Gift to Democracy*, 97 FREEDOM OF INFORMATION REVIEW 2, 2–8 (2002).

[6] The *1789 French Declaration of the Rights of Man* called for access to information of governmental budgets. A similar declaration adopted in the Netherlands in 1795 stated that, "everyone has the right to concur in requiring, from each functionary of public administration, an account and justification on his conduct." DAVID BANISAR, FREEDOM OF INFORMATION AROUND THE WORLD 2006: A GLOBAL SURVEY OF ACCESS TO GOVERNMENT INFORMATION LAWS (report for Privacy International, London, United Kingdom, July 2006), at 18, *available at* http://www.freedominfo.org/documents/global_survey2006.pdf (accessed between February 21, 2025 and March 31, 2025).

[7] FREEDOM OF INFORMATION: A COMPARATIVE LEGAL SURVEY 22 (Toby Mendel ed., 2nd edn, 2008).

[8] HAROLD L. CROSS, THE PEOPLE'S RIGHT TO KNOW: Legal Access to Public Records and Proceedings 197 (1953). Cross was counsel to the American Society of Newspaper Editors and was a legal adviser to the subcommittees for the Government Operations Committee, which was responsible for drafting the *FOIA* legislation.

[9] Finland, Norway, Denmark, and the United States used the Swedish FOI system as a model. However, many more countries adopted the U.S. model. According to legal

In the 1970s and 1980s, many developed nations (Denmark, Norway, France, Australia, New Zealand, Canada, and Austria) adopted FOI laws. The global movement gathered momentum during the early 1990s when the Cold War ended and many communist countries in Central and Eastern Europe became new democracies. Although China arguably inspired the world's first FOI law and was "the model country of the freedom of the press"[10] more than 1,000 years ago, China is late in adopting FOI law of its own. Enactment of freedom of information legislation did not occur in China until 2007 when three other nations (Jordan, Nepal, and Kyrgyzstan) and a British overseas territory (Cayman Islands) joined the global FOI community in the same year. The momentum was strong in 2011 when Brazil, Malaysia, Nigeria, Niger, Mongolia, Tunisia, and El Salvador enacted FOI laws and in 2012 when Yemen adopted right to know legislation. The momentum has been robust since then, as three countries enacted the FOI laws in 2013 (Paraguay, Guyana, and Rwanda), four countries followed suit in 2014 (Ireland, Albania, Bhutan, and Maldives), four nations witnessed enactment of FOI legislations in 2016 (Argentina, Philippines, Tanzania, and Tunisia), and two national FOI legislations emerged in 2017 (Cyprus and Sri Lanka). No enactment of national FOI legislations has been reported since then.

Countries' tendencies toward freedom of information laws arise from the significant benefits: Less corruption, more freedom from hunger, healthier societies; cleaner environment; greater respect for human rights,

scholar, Stephen Lamble, using the U.S. FOI law as a model is a mistake because the U.S. law is not as progressive and inspiring as FOI laws in Sweden and many newly emerging democracies. Many countries that transplanted the American freedom of information system face a variety of implementation problems. Stephen Lamble, *United States FOI Laws Are a Poor Model for Statutes in Other Countries*, 106 FREEDOM OF INFORMATION REVIEW 51 (2003).

[10] Anders Chydenius, *Berattelse om chinesiska skrif-friheten, ofversatt af danskan* [A Report on the Freedom of the Press in China] (1766), *reprinted in* Stephen Lamble, *Freedom of Information, A Finnish Clergyman's Gift to Democracy*, 97 FREEDOM OF INFORMATION REVIEW 2, 3 (2002).

more respect for privacy, more secure societies; and more effective democracies, more accountability, and more public participation.[11] As of 2017, more than 100 countries enacted various forms of laws to protect people's right to access government-held records and documents. Among the more than 100 FOI countries, most are more developed. Since 1999, enactment of 73% of exiting FOI laws has occurred.

Noticeably, significant numbers of international or intergovernmental organizations are adopting FOI laws and policies to promote official transparency beyond the national level. For example, the United Nations Development Program (UNDP), the European Parliament, the Council of the European Union, the World Bank, and all four regional development banks[12] adopted informational disclosure policies.[13] Commenting on the positive aspects of proliferation of FOI legislation, Alasdair Roberts, author on government secrecy, said, "The burden was once on the proponents of access rights to make a case for transparency; today, the burden is on governments to make the case for secrecy."[14]

[11] ARITICLE19, FREEDOM OF INFORMATION TRAINING MANUAL FOR PUBLIC OFFICIALS (Article 19, London), at 17–19, *available at* https://www.ip-rs.si/fileadmin/user_upload/Pdf/Publikacije_ostalih_pooblascencev/Article_19__foitrainersmanual.pdf (accessed between February 21, 2025 and March 31, 2025).

[12] The four regional development banks are the Inter-American Development Bank, the African Development Bank Group, the Asian Development Bank, and the European Bank for Reconstruction and Development.

[13] FREEDOM OF INFORMATION: A COMPARATIVE LEGAL SURVEY 22–23 (Toby Mendel ed., 2nd edn, 2008).

[14] Alasdair Roberts, *Access to Government Information: An Overview of Issues* (first written for the Carter Center's Transparency for Growth Conference, Atlanta, Georgia, May 1999 and later compiled as a chapter in Laura Neuman (ed.)'s working paper Access to Information: A Key to Democracy, November 2002), the Carter Center, Alanta, Georgia, at 9, *available at* http://www.cartercenter.org/documents/1272.pdf (accessed between February 21, 2025 and March 31, 2025).

Patterns and Trends in Global Explosion of Freedom of Information

International FOI scholars identified four categories of FOI countries.[15] The first is historical pioneers who instituted FOI laws prior to the third wave of democratization in the 1980s (such as Sweden, Finland, Denmark, Norway, Canada, Australia, New Zealand, the United States, France, and Columbia).[16] FOI laws in these countries are not particularly progressive or innovative, but they have comparatively effective enforcement.[17] The second category of countries consists of those newly emerging democracies, recently freed from authoritarianism (Philippines, Spain, Portugal, South Korea, Thailand, South Africa, Mexico, and 22 former Soviet Union and Eastern Communist bloc countries). Their FOI laws tend to be very progressive and disclosure-friendly, at least in terms of statutory language, but enforcement commonly suffers from various internal and external influences.[18] The third category of countries represents wealthy, well-established democracies (Japan, Austria, Italy, Netherlands, Belgium, Iceland, Ireland, Israel, Greece, United Kingdom, Switzerland, Germany, and Liechtenstein). They are late in adopting

[15] John M. Ackerman & Irma E. Sandoval-Ballesteros, *The Global Explosion of Freedom of Information Laws*, 58 Administration Law Review 85, 115 (2006).

[16] John M. Ackerman & Irma E. Sandoval-Ballesteros, *The Global Explosion of Freedom of Information Laws*, 58 Administration Law Review 85, 109 (2006).

[17] John M. Ackerman & Irma E. Sandoval-Ballesteros, *The Global Explosion of Freedom of Information Laws*, 58 Administration Law Review 85, 110–12 (2006). In a ranking of quality of all the national FOI laws around the world, FOI laws in many of the first category countries, especially the older European laws, have poor scores. Fifteen of the bottom 20 FOI laws are from Europe. This ranking indicates that these old FOI laws are typically weak in scope, exceptions regimes, oversight and appeals mechanisms, and legal requirement for publicizing access to information. *World's First Rating of Right to Information: 89 Countries Ranked*, Access-info.org, 28 September 2011, https://www.access-info.org/2011-10-05/rti-rating/ (accessed between February 21, 2025 and March 31, 2025).

[18] John M. Ackerman & Irma E. Sandoval-Ballesteros, *The Global Explosion of Freedom of Information Laws*, 58 Administration Law Review 85, 112–13 (2006). According to a ranking of quality of all the national FOI laws around the world, new or transitional democracies tend to have stronger FOI laws than old democracies. The top 20 countries are almost all new democracies, and their FOI laws have an average age of just 5 years. *World's First Rating of Right to Information: 89 Countries Ranked*, Access-info.org, 28 September 2011, https://www.access-info.org/2011-10-05/rti-rating/ (accessed between February 21, 2025 and March 31, 2025).

FOI laws despite long democratic traditions. Their FOI laws are much less progressive and innovative than those adopted in emerging democratic countries.[19] The fourth category of countries is developing nations who indicate no transition toward democracy (Pakistan, Jamaica, Belize, Antigua and Barbuda, Peru, Panama, Dominican Republic, Angola, Zimbabwe, Uganda, and the Republic of Türkiye) and tend to have weaker FOI legislation.[20]

As for factors contributing to, and formulation of, FOI laws, FOI scholars, and organizations identified some key aspects. The first finding is that the level of economic development does not correlate with the presence or absence of FOI laws. Many wealthy countries and regions have no freedom of information laws (e.g., Singapore, Qatar, and Hong Kong). Conversely, many poor countries do not lack the legal right to know (e.g., Columbia and Ukraine). "Although economic growth may create some pressures in favor of freedom of information, the decisive factors with regard to whether a FOI law will be passed are political."[21]

[19] John M. Ackerman & Irma E. Sandoval-Ballesteros, *The Global Explosion of Freedom of Information Laws*, 58 ADMINISTRATION LAW REVIEW 85, 113–14 (2006). Countries in the third category have equally weak FOI laws as their counterparts in the first category, according to a ranking of quality of all the national FOI laws around the world. Austria is even rated at the bottom. *World's First Rating of Right to Information: 89 Countries Ranked*, Access-info.org, 28 September 2011, https://www.access-info.org/2011-10-05/rti-rating/ (accessed between February 21, 2025 and March 31, 2025).

[20] John M. Ackerman & Irma E. Sandoval-Ballesteros, *The Global Explosion of Freedom of Information Laws*, 58 ADMINISTRATION LAW REVIEW 85, 114 (2006).

[21] John M. Ackerman & Irma E. Sandoval-Ballesteros, *The Global Explosion of Freedom of Information Laws*, 58 ADMINISTRATION LAW REVIEW 85, 115 (2006).

The second finding is that civil society[22] and news media[23] play significant roles in adoption of FOI laws in many countries. The third finding concerns the presence or absence of constitutional provisions for the right to information. Some countries, such as the United States and Malta, only acknowledge freedom of information as a statutory right but decline to acknowledge a constitutional right.[24] Some countries, such as Venezuela and Kenya, have constitutional provisions for freedom of information but have not enacted relevant statutes. A growing number of countries have explicitly embraced both constitutional and statutory rights to access government-held information.[25]

[22] ANDREW PUDDEPHATT, EXPLORING THE ROLE OF CIVIL SOCIETY IN THE FORMULATION AND ADOPTION OF ACCESS TO INFORMATION LAWS: THE CASES OF BULGARIA, INDIA, MEXICO, SOUTH AFRICA, AND THE UNITED KINGDOM (Access to Information working paper series, World Bank Institute, Washington, D.C., 2009) (noting civil society's contribution to the adoption of access to information laws in five countries), *available at* https://documents.worldbank.org/en/publication/documents-reports/documentdetail/302751468044082294/pdf (accessed between February 21, 2025 and March 31, 2025).

[23] For example, after empirically examining the dataset of all FOI countries, FOI expert Jeannine Relly found that nations with strong news media rights tend to have greatest influence on global diffusion of freedom of information legislation. Jeannine E. Relly, *Freedom of Information Laws and Global Diffusion: Testing Rogers's Model*, 89 JOURNALISM & MASS COMMUNICATION QUARTERLY 431 (2012).

[24] In three cases *Pell v. Procunier*, 417 U.S. 817 (1974), *Saxbe v. Washington Post*, 417 U.S. 843 (1974), and *Houchins v. KQED*, 438 U.S. 1 (1978), the U.S. Supreme Court explicitly denied acknowledging the constitutional right of access to official facilities. These three cases become the legal precedent for denying the constitutional status of American people's right to know.

[25] For example, countries with explicit statutory and constitutional provisions on freedom of information are: Bulgaria (*1991 Constitution*, Article 41), Estonia (*1992 Constitution*, Article 44), Hungary (*1949 Constitution*, Article 61(1), Lithuania (*1992 Constitution*, Article 25(5)), Malawi (*1994 Constitution*, Article 37), Mexico (*1917 Constitution*, Article 6), the Philippines (*1987 Constitution*, Article III (7), Poland (*1997 Constitution*, Article 61), Romania (*Constitution of 1991*, Article 31), South Africa (*1996 Constitution*, Section 32), and Thailand (*2007 Constitution*, Section 56). Over 80 countries adopted a constitutional provision granting citizens a right to access government-held information. FREEDOM OF INFORMATION: A COMPARATIVE LEGAL SURVEY 21-22 (Toby Mendel ed., 2nd edn, 2008); DAVID BANISAR, FREEDOM OF INFORMATION AROUND THE WORLD 2006: A GLOBAL SURVEY OF ACCESS TO GOVERNMENT INFORMATION LAWS (report for Privacy International, London, United Kingdom, July 2006), *available at* http://www.freedominfo.org/documents/global_survey2006.pdf (accessed between February 21, 2025 and March 31, 2025).

The fourth finding concerning the global FOI movement involves two main types of actors who have roles contributing to creation of national FOI laws. The first group consists of international organizations, treaties, and conventions, many of which consider freedom of information to be a fundamental human right and either require or encourage member nations to adopt freedom of information laws. Such international actors include, but not limited to: the International Monetary Fund, the World Bank, the United Nations Convention Against Corruption, Article 19 with the Universal Declaration on Human Rights and the International Covenant on Civil and Political Rights, the UN Special Rapporteur on Freedom of Opinion and Expression, the United Nations Human Rights Committee, the 1992 Rio Declaration on Environment and Development, the UN Economic Commission on Europe (UNECE) Convention on Access to Environmental Information, the Council of Europe, the European Union,[26] the African Union Convention on Preventing and Combating Corruption, the Southern African Development Community (SADC) Protocol Against Corruption, the Organization of American States,[27] the Chapultepec Declaration, the Arab Charter on Human Rights, the Commonwealth, the Commonwealth of Independent States, the Asian Development Bank (ADB), and the Organization for Economic Cooperation and Development (OECD) Anti-Corruption Initiative for Asia–Pacific.[28] The second type

[26] Many Eastern and Central European countries adopted FOI legislations because they desired the status of membership of the European Union. Ellen M. Hampton, Freedom of Information in Post-Communist Countries: Case Studies of the Czech Republic, Croatia, and Bosnia and Herzegovina (April 2007) (unpublished master's thesis, The University of North Carolina at Chapel Hill) (on file with author), at 10–12; Jeannine E. Relly, *Freedom of Information Laws and Global Diffusion: Testing Rogers's Model*, 89 JOURNALISM & MASS COMMUNICATION QUARTERLY 431, 448 (2012).

[27] A large number of countries in the Americas region adopted FOI laws because of external pressure from the Organization of American States. Jeannine E. Relly, *Freedom of Information Laws and Global Diffusion: Testing Rogers's Model*, 89 JOURNALISM & MASS COMMUNICATION QUARTERLY 431, 448 (2012).

[28] DAVID BANISAR, FREEDOM OF INFORMATION AROUND THE WORLD 2006: A GLOBAL SURVEY OF ACCESS TO GOVERNMENT INFORMATION LAWS 8–16 (report for Privacy International, London, United Kingdom, July 2006), *available at* http://www.freedominfo.org/documents/global_survey2006.pdf (accessed between February 21, 2025 and March 31, 2025); John M. Ackerman & Irma E. Sandoval-Ballesteros, *The Global Explosion of Freedom of Information Laws*, 58 ADMINISTRATION LAW REVIEW 85, 115–22 (2006).

of international actors is non-governmental organizations (NGOs) and advocacy groups who track the development of freedom of information around the world and, assist formulation and/or improvement of FOI laws, and actively promote freedom of information in many parts of the world.[29] Such international actors include, but not limited to: the Open Society Institute,[30] Article19,[31] the Carter Center,[32] Transparency International,[33] the Access Initiative,[34] Privacy International,[35] Freedominfo.org,[36] and Right2INFO.org.[37]

History and Development of *U.S. FOIA*

To some, understanding the campaign for greater freedom of information in the United States is easy due to the country's democratic tradition. In fact, America's journey to freedom of information was long and not without obstacles. In the seventeenth and eighteenth centuries in England, people had no statutory or common law right to inspect public

[29] John M. Ackerman & Irma E. Sandoval-Ballesteros, *The Global Explosion of Freedom of Information Laws*, 58 Administrative Law Review 85, 121–22 (2006).

[30] The Open Society Institute, *available at* http://www.soros.org/ (accessed between February 21, 2025 and March 31, 2025).

[31] Article19, *available* at http://www.article19.org/ (accessed between February 21, 2025 and March 31, 2025).

[32] The Carter Center Global Access to Information Initiative (currently known as Rule of Law Program), *available at* https://www.cartercenter.org/peace/ati/index.html (accessed between February 21, 2025 and March 31, 2025).

[33] Transparency International, *available at* http://www.transparency.org/ (accessed between February 21, 2025 and March 31, 2025).

[34] The Access Initiative, *available at* http://www.accessinitiative.org/ (accessed between February 21, 2025 and March 31, 2025).

[35] Privacy International, *available at* https://www.privacyinternational.org/ (accessed between February 21, 2025 and March 31, 2025).

[36] Freedominfo.org, *available at* http://www.freedominfo.org/ (accessed between February 21, 2025 and March 31, 2025).

[37] Right2INFO.org was a website that provided an overview of international right to information laws. The website was launched in 2008 by the Open Society Justice Initiative. The website is no longer up accessible for unknown reasons. *The Right to Information: Good Law and Practice*, Right2info.org (captured by Internet Archive Wayback Machine on October 21, 2008), retrieved from https://web.archive.org/web/20081021053124/http://www.right2info.org/ (accessed between February 21, 2025 and March 31, 2025).

records or documents.[38] Reporters could not cover the activities of the House of Commons and the House of Lords. Fines or imprisonment were the consequences for violators for reports deemed seditious.[39] This legacy of British rule continued to American colonies whose officials disliked the idea of opening official activities to public inspection. Royal governor Sir William Berkeley of Virginia, in 1671, expressed strong resentment for the people's right to know in correspondence with English Lords and commissioners:

> ...I thank God, we have no free schools nor printing, and I hope we shall not have these hundred years. For learning has brought disobedience, and heresy, and sects into the world, and printing has divulged them, and libels against the government. God keep us from both![40]

In 1722, the royal governor of Pennsylvania, Sir William Keith, ordered printer and publisher, Andrew Bradford, not to print anything "relating to or concerning the affairs of this Government, or the government of any of the other of His Majesty's Colonies."[41]

The Constitutional Convention in Philadelphia held its deliberations in secret.[42] After ratification of the *U.S. Constitution* and the *Bill of Rights*, in 1787 and 1791, respectively, many prominent leaders of the republic

[38] Harold L. Cross, The People's Right to Know: Legal Access to Public Records and Proceedings 25 (1953).

[39] Herbert N. Foerstel, Freedom of Information and the Right to Know: The Origins and Applications of the Freedom of Information Act 1 (1999). Between 1476 and 1776, the British used the seditious libel laws to punish political dissent. According to the laws, anyone including members of the media could be convicted and face penalties of fine and/or a life imprisonment if the individual had seditious intent when publishing anything promoting hatred or ridicule against the sovereign, heirs, or successors, the government of the United Kingdom, the House of Parliament, or the administration of justice. Tom Crone, Philip Alberstat, Tom Cassels & Estelle Overs, Law and the Media 36 (2002).

[40] David M. Kennedy & Thomas A. Bailey, The American Spirit: United States History as Seen by Contemporaries, Volume I: to 1877 37 (2009).

[41] Press and Speech Freedom in America, 1619–1995: A Chronology 15–16 (Louis Edward Ingelhart ed., 1997).

[42] George Washington, the presiding officer of the Constitutional Convention, warned one delegate stiffly: "I am sorry to find that some one Member of this Body [Convention] has been so neglectful of the secrets of the Convention as to drop in the State House a copy of their proceedings." Daniel N. Hoffman, Government Secrecy and the Founding Fathers: A Study in Constitutional Controls 21 (1981).

still chose secrecy.[43] For example, the ratification vote of the Constitution in Philadelphia was secret and banned attendance of the public and the press at the Senate's proceedings until 1796.[44] Government secrecy was, in effect, legalized in 1789 when the Congress passed the Housekeeping Statute.[45] The statute said:

> The head of each department is authorized to prescribe regulations, for the government of his department, the conduct of its officers and clerks, the distribution and performance of its business, and the custody, *use and preservation* of the records, papers and property appertaining to it (emphasis added).[46]

Official agencies regularly cited the phrase, "use and preservation," to assert authority for rejecting disclosure of governmental information.[47] A leading advocate of freedom of information later condemned the Housekeeping Statute as "the fountainhead of secrecy" in administrative

[43] Martin E. Halstuk, *Policy of Secrecy-Pattern of Deception: What Federalist Leaders Thought about a Public Right to Know, 1794–98*, 7 COMMUNICATION LAW AND POLICY 51, 51–76 (2002).

[44] There is a controversy over the existence of the concept of the right to know during the founding period of the republic. For example, David O'Brien contended that the concept was merely "an abstract political right" for the Founding Fathers of the nation, not "the concrete rights embodied in the First Amendment." DAVID O'BRIEN, THE PUBLIC'S RIGHT TO KNOW: THE SUPREME COURT AND THE FIRST AMENDMENT 19 (1981). However, Kiyul Uhm argued that, despite repeated practices of governmental secrecy during the founding period of the republic, the concept of the people's right to know was "repeatedly articulated and underscored as one of the most important democratic principles." Kiyul Uhm, *The Founders and Revolutionary Underpinning of the Concept of the Right to Know*, 85 JOURNALISM & MASS COMMUNICATION QUARTERLY 393 (summer 2008). For example, James Wilson, one of the delegates to the Constitutional Convention, argued eloquently against governmental secrecy: "The people have a right to know what their Agents are doing or have done, and it should not be in the option of the Legislature to conceal their proceedings." Kiyul Uhm, *The Founders and Revolutionary Underpinning of the Concept of the Right to Know*, 85 JOURNALISM & MASS COMMUNICATION QUARTERLY 398 (summer 2008).

[45] 5 U.S.C. § 301 (1789) (previously codified as 5 U.S.C. § 22).

[46] 5 U.S.C. § 301 (emphasis added).

[47] HAROLD L. CROSS, THE PEOPLE'S RIGHT TO KNOW: LEGAL ACCESS TO PUBLIC RECORDS AND PROCEEDINGS 214–228 (1953); H.R. REP. 89–1497, at 2 (1966).

agencies,[48] and when the 1780 presidential campaign between Thomas Jefferson and Aaron Burr ended in a tie, the House vote to break the tie occurred behind closed doors.

During the eighteenth and early nineteenth centuries, the American news industry was largely partisan,[49] with the media either directly or indirectly subsidized by major political parties. The focus of newspapers was to publish harsh editorials and opinions, not news, rendering access to government-held information an insignificant concern for editors.

Understandably, the American Bar Association (ABA), not the news media, was among the first to criticize the secrecy of federal agencies.[50] A report of federal administrative agencies' law, published by the ABA in 1934, harshly criticized official secrecy.[51] In 1938, Roscoe Pound, chairman of the ABA's Special Committee on Administrative Law, attacked governmental secrecy as "administrative absolutism."[52]

Congress enacted the federal *Administrative Procedures Act* (APA) in 1946[53] to increase transparency; however, the statutory language was so poor[54] that the law provided the federal bureaucracy with numerous

[48] James S. Pope, *The Cult of Secrecy*, NIEMAN REPORTS, October 1951, at 9. James Pope was President of the American Society of Newspaper Editors in the 1950s.

[49] JAMES L. BAUGHMAN, THE FALL AND RISE OF PARTISAN JOURNALISM (Center for Journalism Ethics, School of Journalism & Mass Communication, University of Wisconsin-Madison, Madison, Wisconsin, April 20, 2011), *available at* http://ethics.journalism.wisc.edu/2011/04/20/the-fall-and-rise-of-partisan-journalism/ (accessed between February 21, 2025 and March 31, 2025).

[50] Erwin Griswold, *Government in Ignorance of the Law: A Plea for Better Publication of Executive Legislation*, 48 HARVARD LAW REVIEW 198, 198–200 (1934).

[51] Erwin Griswold, *Government in Ignorance of the Law: A Plea for Better Publication of Executive Legislation*, 48 HARVARD LAW REVIEW 198, 198–200 (1934).

[52] DANIEL PATRICK MOYNIHAN, SECRECY: THE AMERICAN EXPERIENCE 157 (1998).

[53] 5 U.S.C. § 1002 (1946).

[54] For example, APA Section 3 allowed agencies to hold documents "confidential for cause found," but without definition. The section also allowed the government to withhold any information "requiring secrecy in the public interest" but it failed to establish such a standard. It required information requesters to be "properly and directly concerned" with the information sought; agencies could thus deny access on the grounds of irrelevancy. The APA also failed to provide judicial remedies for non-compliance. 5 U.S.C. § 1002 (1946).

loopholes serving as "substantial statutory reasons not to release most requested information in its hands."[55]

In the 1950s, a coalition advocating a comprehensive law to promote governmental transparency emerged. Freedom of information advocates represented three primary interests: the media, bar associations and attorneys, and reform-minded members of Congress.[56]

Most media outlets ceased to be party organs in the early twentieth century and became market-oriented penny press newspapers instead.[57] Their focus was no longer publishing virulent editorials and opinions; instead, they considered their major responsibility to be supervising the activities of the government. Many muckraking journalists[58] exposed official misconduct and corruption through investigative journalism. Escalating official secrecy, following World War II, concerning primarily Cold War maneuvering, military readiness, and nuclear weapons research, outraged those reform-minded journalists and editors.

In order to facilitate reporting governmental activities, American reporters, editors, and publishers launched a highly organized political campaign for a statutory right to access official information.[59] Under

[55] Harvey L. Zuckman, Robert L. Corn-Revere, Robert M. Frieden & Charles H. Kennedy, 2 Modern Communications Law 168 (1999).

[56] Martin E. Halstuk & Bill F. Chamberlin, *The Freedom of Information Act 1966–2006: A Retrospective on the Rise of Privacy Protection Over the Public Interest*, 11 Communication Law and Policy 511, 517 (2006); Jacqueline Klosek, The Right to Know: Your Guide to Using and Defending Freedom of Information Law in the United States 13 (2009).

[57] Thomas C. Leonard, The Power of the Press: The Birth of American Political Reporting (Chapter 7) 193–221 (1986).

[58] For more information on the muckraker movement in American journalism history, see Fred James Cook, The Muckrakers (1972); Aileen Gallagher, Muckrakers: American Journalism during the Age of Reform (2006); Years of Conscience: The Muckrakers: An Anthology of Reform Journalism (Harvey Swados ed., 1962).

[59] For the international aspect of the freedom of information campaign after World War II, see Samuel Martin Lebovic, "Fighting for Free Information: American Democracy and the Problem of Press Freedom in a Totalitarian Age, 1920–1950" (August 2011) (unpublished Ph.D. diss., The University of Chicago), at 359–453.

the leadership of James Russell Wiggins,[60] James S. Pope,[61] Harold L. Cross,[62] and other leading media executives and attorneys, the American Society of Newspapers Editors (ASNE), the Society of Professional Journalists (SPJ), and the Associated Press Managing Editors (APME) brought the issue of officially controlled information to public's and government's attention. Each of these news professionals' organizations established a Freedom of Information committee.[63] The personal correspondence between James Russell Wiggins and his friends in the government and media industry "traces the development of the elements and structure of the 1966 law during the ten years before it's drafting in the late 1950s."[64] In his groundbreaking book *The People's Right to Know*,[65] Harold Cross advocated elimination of the federal APA of 1946[66] and the *1789 Housekeeping Statute*[67] because they represented two major, legal obstacles to a right for people to know of governments' activities. Enacting a piece of legislation on freedom of information could not have occurred without the help of journalists who had firsthand experiences for the need and difficulties in obtaining access to official information.

The legal establishment pushed open records legislation to obtain documents from federal agencies as a service for their clients. Attorneys often found requests for government-held information rejected without sufficient reason. It is clear that the freedom of information law was

[60] James Russell Wiggins was managing editor and then executive editor of *The Washington Post* from 1947 to 1968.

[61] James S. Pope was the first chairperson of American Society of National Editors' (ASNE) domestic Committee on Freedom of Information.

[62] Harold L. Cross was counsel for *New York Herald Tribune* and lecturer at Columbia University School of Journalism.

[63] Shannon E. Martin and Kamilla Benko, *Forming FOIA: The Influence of Editors and Publishers on the Freedom of Information Act*, 14 MEDIA HISTORY MONOGRAPHS 1 (2011–2012): 1–33.

[64] Shannon E. Martin and Kamilla Benko, *Forming FOIA: The Influence of Editors and Publishers on the Freedom of Information Act*, 14 MEDIA HISTORY MONOGRAPHS 1 (2011–2012): 1–33.

[65] HAROLD L. CROSS, THE PEOPLE'S RIGHT TO KNOW: LEGAL ACCESS TO PUBLIC RECORDS AND PROCEEDINGS (1953). The book has become the bible of the freedom of information movement.

[66] 5 U.S.C. § 1002 (1946).

[67] 5 U.S.C. § 301 (1789) (previously codified as 5 U.S.C. § 22).

the direct result of persistent lobbying from journalists and attorneys, however, reform-minded legislators on the Capitol Hill called the final shot.

Some members of the U.S. Congress involved themselves in the freedom of information movement due to disenchantment with administrative agencies' efforts to withhold public records from congressional inspection.[68] The Congressional movement for greater governmental transparency, led by U.S. Representative John Moss of California,[69] began in 1955.[70] Congress conducted more than 10 years of hearings before the *Freedom of Information Act* finally became law in 1966.[71]

According to *U.S. FOIA*, "any person" has the right to request release of documents or records held by the federal government; the statute does not require *FOIA* requesters to explain the purpose of the request,[72] and the burden of proof falls on the governmental agency to justify decisions to reject disclosure.[73] Official agencies must disclose all information

[68] Erwin Griswold, *Government in Ignorance of the Law: A Plea for Better Publication of Executive Legislation*, 48 HARVARD LAW REVIEW 198, 198–200 (1934). In fact, the conflict between Congress and the executive branch over the legislative branch's constitutional right to access executive materials began soon after the founding of the republic when George Washington refused to share with Congress the details of a trade pact with England Washington and later John Adams advocated. Archibald Cox, *Executive Privilege*, 122 UNIVERSITY OF PENNSYLVANIA LAW REVIEW 1383 (1974).

[69] Moss had personal experience of frustration when he requested administrative agency documents to verify Civil Service Commission claims that 2,800 federal employees were fired for "security reasons" and his request was flatly declined. DANIEL PATRICK MOYNIHAN, SECRECY: THE AMERICAN EXPERIENCE 172 (1998).

[70] In 1955, Moss was appointed the chair of the House Committee on Government Operations, a committee charged with amending the infamous *Housekeeping Statute* and the federal *Administrative Procedures Act*.

[71] JAMES T. O'REILLY, FEDERAL INFORMATION DISCLOSURE: PROCEDURES, FORMS AND THE LAW, 2–5 (1994).

[72] *NARA v. Favish*, 541 U.S. 157, 172 (2004).

[73] 255 U.S.C. § 552(a)(4)(B).

requested, exempting only nine categories of information.[74] The government also must disclose information affirmatively without a request being necessary.[75] If information requests are declined or not responded to in a timely manner, the requester has the option to appeal to the agency's officials.[76] Upon denial of the administrative appeal, the requester may appeal the decision in federal court.[77]

The U.S. news industry greeted adoption of *FOIA* positively and American journalists continued to encourage strengthening the freedom of information laws after 1966. Whether or not Carl Bernstein and Bob Woodward of *The Washington Post* used the *U.S. FOIA* themselves in their coverage of the Watergate scandal is unclear, but certainly the Watergate controversy brought officials' lack of transparency into public consciousness. After the Watergate scandal, as the muckraker movement reemerged in the form of watchdog journalism in the 1980s, the press felt that *U.S. FOIA was* not as effective as expected. In order to facilitate better access to official information, the U.S. Congress strengthened the *FOIA* of 1966 with a series of amendments.

The amendment of 1974 permitted federal district judges *in camera* inspection of top-secret classified information to verify the requested information's classification, established uniform search and copying fees among agencies,[78] imposed a limit of 10 working days for the original response and established the one-time 10-working-day extension for "unusual circumstances."[79] Congress amended *FOIA* for the second

[74] Nine categories of information are exempt from *U.S.* FOIA: National security matters; housekeeping materials (agency personnel rules and practices); materials exempted by other federal statutes; trade, commercial, or financial secrets; working papers/lawyer-client privileged materials; personal privacy files (personnel and medical files and similar files involving personal privacy); law enforcement records; financial institutions' materials, and geological and geophysical data.

[75] 5 U.S.C. § 552(a)(3) & §552(a)(4)(A) (2000). For example, organizational plans and federal agencies' regulations should be available in public reading rooms. Agencies must publish in the Federal Register and on the Internet frequently requested information and records.

[76] 5 U.S.C. § 552((a) (6)(A)(ii) (2006).

[77] S. REP. No. 110–59, at 10 (2007).

[78] THE *FOIA* GUIDE; 5 U.S.C. § 552 (1994), at 7.

[79] 5 U.S.C. § 552 (a) (6) (A) (i).

time in 1976 to restrict the discretion of agencies to withhold information.[80] In 1986, amendments to *FOIA*, *Freedom of Information Reform Act*,[81] provided Congressional approval for broader exemptions for law enforcement's informational protection, but reduced fees for freedom of information requests.[82] Significant amendments occurred in 1996 when Congress passed *Electronic Freedom of Information Act* (*EFOIA*),[83] which required governmental agencies to open records stored or saved in any formats, including electronic. Under the affirmative disclosure provision of the 1996 law, governmental agencies must use the Internet to disseminate commonly requested information of official activities.[84] The latest *FOIA* revisions occurred in 2007 when U.S. President George W. Bush signed *OPEN Government Act* and in 2016 when U.S. President Barack Obama signed *FOIA Improvement Act*.[85] The 2007 amendment established tracking numbers for each request made online,[86] compelled private-sector contractors to abide by the law's disclosure rules,[87] and ordered defendants who do not prevail in a *FOIA* lawsuit at the federal level to pay litigation costs.[88] The 2016 amendment codified the presumption of openness and required federal agencies to change how certain records and documents are made available for public inspection.[89]

[80] H.R. Rep. No. 880, 94th Cong., 2d Sess. pt. 1, 23, reprinted in 1976 U.S. Code Cong. & Ad. News 2204–05.

[81] 5 U.S.C. § 552 (b) (7).

[82] 5 U.S.C. §§ 552 (a) (4) (A) (i-vii).

[83] Pub. L. No. 104–231, 110 Stat. 3048, §§ 1–12 (1996) (amending various sections of 5 U.S.C. § 552).

[84] Pub. L. No. 104–231, 110 Stat. 3048, §§ 4, 10 & 11; H.R. Rep. No. 104–795, at 19–20. Commonly requested information includes agencies' annual reports, statements of agencies' rules and policies, agencies' adjudicative opinions, and *FOIA* handbooks. Before 1996, only the Federal Register was the required venue for publishing commonly requested information.

[85] Pub. L. No. 110–175 (2007). The acronym OPEN stands for Openness Promotes Effectiveness in our National (Government).

[86] Pub. L. No. 110–175, 121 Stat. 2524 (Section 7).

[87] Pub. L. No. 110–175 (Section 9).

[88] Pub. L. No. 110–175 (Section 4).

[89] Pub. L. No. 114–185 (2016).

Use of *U.S. FOIA* by American Journalists for Investigative Journalism

According to a UNESCO report, 123 countries and territories have enacted the right to information laws or similar provisions.[90] In many FOI countries, media professionals and organizations played a key role in the promotion and eventual enactment of access to information laws.[91] Once formulated, professionals in media sectors became among the most frequent users of the laws.[92]

America is a good case in point. Not surprisingly, American editors and reporters were not only among the first promoters of the freedom of information legislation, but also among the first users of the law. In the last five decades, American reporters produced a significant number of news stories based on information obtained through filing *FOIA* requests. Through the use of *FOIA*, journalists have played a key role in holding the government accountable, uncovering crimes, and significantly influencing American public policy. Some example exposés are:

- In 1981, *San Francisco Chronicle* acquired records via *FOIA* that revealed that during the 1950s and 1960s, the FBI agents covertly campaigned to fire University of California President Clark Kerr and conspired with the CIA director to pressure the California Board of Regents to force terminations of liberal professors.[93]
- In 1994, after a five-month investigation involving more than 150 interviews, 16 *FOIA* requests and nine governmental databases, *U.S.*

[90] *What You Need to Know about Access to Information*, UNESCO, September 26, 2022, *available at* https://www.unesco.org/en/articles/what-you-need-know-about-access-information (accessed between February 21, 2025 and March 31, 2025).

[91] Central and Eastern Europe is clearly one exception. "[T]hroughout the region media support for passage and implementation of access to information laws is spotty at best." The Right to Know: Transparency for an Open World 136 (Ann Florini & Joseph E. Stiglitz eds., 2007).

[92] Eduardo Bertoni, Freedom of Information, Three Harmless Words? The Role of the Media and Access to Information Laws (Center for Studies on Freedom of Expression and Access to Information, Palermo University School of Law, Buenos Aires, Argentina), *available at* http://www.palermo.edu/cele/pdf/ATIandMedia.pdf (accessed between February 21, 2025 and March 31, 2025).

[93] Martin E. Halstuk and Eric B. Easton, *Of Secrets and Spies: Strengthening the Public's Right to Know about the CIA*, 17 Standard Law and Policy Review 2 353 (2006).

News and World Report published a cover story portraying contamination of blood banks in America and found that risks to diseases through transfusion was far higher than people assumed.[94]

- In 1995, using documents obtained under the *FOIA*, *Deseret News* in Utah found that hundreds of U.S. sailors, in tests in the 1960s, suffered from cancer and other illnesses caused by exposure to warfare's chemical and biological agents, and denial of health and disability benefits to affected sailors. In 2002 the Pentagon officially acknowledged the existence of the tests.[95]
- In 2003, *The Philadelphia Inquirer* discovered from *FOIA* requests that federal citations for violations of pollution laws plummeted during 2002–2003 of the George W. Bush administration, dropping 35%, compared to the previous year.[96]
- In 2005, according to the Food and Drug Administration (FDA) reports released to the Associated Press under the *FOIA*, a new FDA-approved birth control patch demonstrated serious side effects. At least a dozen women died in 2004 from blood clots caused by using the patches.[97]
- In 2004 and 2005, *The Des Moines Register* in Iowa filed *FOIA* requests to the U.S. Justice Department, revealing a substantial overstatement of the recorded number of terrorism-related cases to justify demands for more funding and greater powers.[98]

[94] Richard J. Newman, Doug Podolsky & Penny Loeb, *Bad Blood*, 116 U.S. NEWS AND WORLD REPORT 25 (June 27, 1994), 68–78.

[95] Lee Davidson, *Sailors Exposed to Deadly Agents: Pentagon finally Concedes Dangers from 1960s Tests*, DESERT NEWS, May 24, 2002, https://www.deseret.com/2002/5/24/19656838/sailors-exposed-to-deadly-agents/ (accessed between February 21, 2025 and March 31, 2025).

[96] Martin E. Halstuk and Eric B. Easton, *Of Secrets and Spies: Strengthening the Public's Right to Know About the CIA*, 17 STANDARD LAW AND POLICY REVIEW 2 353 (2006).

[97] Brian Dakss, *Birth Control Patch Users Warned, FDA: It Puts Women at Higher Risk for Clots than Pill Does*, CBS/AP, November 11, 2005 (captured by Internet Archive Wayback Machine on November 24, 2005), retrieved from https://web.archive.org/web/20051124020740/http://www.cbsnews.com/stories/2005/11/11/earlyshow/health/health_news/main1037611.shtml (accessed between February 21, 2025 and March 31, 2025).

[98] Bert Dalmer, *Many of Bush Administration's Claimed "Terrorism" Arrests Are Misleading*, THE DES MOINES REGISTER, July 18, 2004; Bert Dalmer, *Creating "Terrorism" out of Misdemeanors*, THE DES MOINES REGISTER, May 16, 2005.

- In 2005, *USA Today* revealed, via *FOIA* requests, that the Bush administration paid prominent political commentator Armstrong Williams $240,000 to promote the No Child Left Behind Act.[99] Also discovered by *The Washington Post* through *FOIA* was propaganda at the U.S. Department of Agriculture which paid a writer to craft stories favorable to federal conservation programs.[100]
- In 2006, the Department of Defense released a complete list of all former and current detainees held at Guantanamo Bay Naval Base after the Associated Press sought such information through citing the *FOIA*.[101]
- In 2006, *Dayton Daily News* in Ohio obtained governmental documents via the *FOIA* requests which disclosed that the government largely ignored sexual assault charges brought by women in the military against enlistees and officers.[102]
- In 2006, the Associated Press filed *FOIA* requests with a dozen federal agencies, to examine the reasons and methods for issuing and collecting administrative penalties. The AP found uncollected fines and other payments of more than $35 billion.[103]
- From 2004 to 2007, *Sun-Sentinel* of Florida examined *FOIA*-released documents, obtained through requests and lawsuits, revealing Federal Emergency Management Agency's widespread disaster relief fraud after Hurricanes Frances and Katrina.[104]

[99] Greg Toppo, *Education Dept. Paid Commentator to Promote Law*, USA TODAY, January 7, 2005 (captured by Internet Archive Wayback Machine on April 8, 2005), retrieved from https://web.archive.org/web/20050408073305/http://www.usatoday.com/news/washington/2005-01-06-williams-whitehouse_x.htm (accessed between February 21, 2025 and March 31, 2025).

[100] JACQUELINE KLOSEK, THE RIGHT TO KNOW: YOUR GUIDE TO USING AND DEFENDING FREEDOM OF INFORMATION LAW IN THE UNITED STATES xvi–xvii (2009).

[101] Andrew Selsky, *Pentagon Releases Gitmo Detainees' Names*, THE WASHINGTON POST, May 15, 2006.

[102] Martin E. Halstuk and Eric B. Easton, *Of Secrets and Spies: Strengthening the Public's Right to Know about the CIA*, 17 STANDARD LAW AND POLICY REVIEW 2 353 (2006).

[103] Martha Mendoza & Christopher Sullivan, *Billions in Penalties for Wrongdoing Uncollected*, ASSOCIATED PRESS, republished by NBC News, March 18, 2006, https://www.nbcnews.com/id/wbna11877818 (accessed between February 21, 2025 and March 31, 2025).

[104] *Sun-Sentinel Investigation: FEMA*, SUN SENTINEL, November 23, 2004, https://www.sun-sentinel.com/2004/11/23/sun-sentinel-investigation-fema/ (accessed between February 21, 2025 and March 31, 2025); Sharon Rosenhause, *FEMA's Stumbles, Katrina*

- In 2008, apparently, military analysts on most U.S. cable television networks were Pentagon appointees directed to generate favorable news coverage of the Bush administration's wartime performance since September 11, 2001, according to 8,000 pages of email messages, transcripts, and records obtained by *The New York Times* after winning a lengthy FOI lawsuit against the Defense Department.[105]
- In 2010, from *The New York Times FOIA* request, the newspaper found that many immigrants died in detention centers, and officials attempted to hide evidence of mistreatment.[106]

This list is not exhaustive, and largely due to the drawbacks of the U.S. FOI system, American reporters' willingness to use *FOIA* to obtain information is declining. A study shows that reporters are no longer among the most active seekers of official information via *FOIA*.[107] The principal reasons for U.S. journalists not applying greater use of *Freedom of Information Act* are threefold: First, most reporters work with tight deadlines, but agencies usually fail to comply with *FOIA*'s time limits,[108] often

Controversy Lead the Sun-Sentinel on Dedicated Watchdog Campaign, Poynter, May 17, 2006, *available at* https://www.poynter.org/archive/2006/femas-stumbles-katrina-controversy-lead-the-sun-sentinel-on-dedicated-watchdog-campaign/ (accessed between February 21, 2025 and March 31, 2025).

[105] David Barstow, *Behind TV Analysts, Pentagon's Hidden Hand*, THE NEW YORK TIMES, April 20, 2008, http://www.nytimes.com/2008/04/20/us/20generals.html?pagewanted=1&_r=1 (accessed between February 21, 2025 and March 31, 2025).

[106] Nina Bernstein, *Officials Hid Truth of Immigrant Deaths in Jail*, THE NEW YORK TIMES, January 9, 2010, http://www.nytimes.com/2010/01/10/us/10detain.html (accessed between February 21, 2025 and March 31, 2025).

[107] SHANNON E. MARTIN, FREEDOM OF INFORMATION: THE NEWS THE MEDIA USE 78 (2008). The four official agencies sampled in this study are General Services Administration (GSA), Environmental Protection Agency (EPA), Department of Transportation and Department of Education. The survey, conducted during January to June 2001, revealed that corporations accounted for 910 requests, while media made only 119 requests. Individuals accounted for 373 queries; lawyers, 567; and nonprofits, 181.

[108] Under *U.S. FOIA*, The maximum response time limit is 30 working days. In other words, within 20 business days after accepting *FOIA* requests, official agencies must decide if the requested information should be released and immediately notify the requesters of their decisions. The clock of 20-day time limit starts on the day when requests are first received by agencies. In unusual circumstances, the time limits may be extended for up to 10 working days. 5 U.S.C. § 552((a) (6)(A)(i) (2006); Open Government Act of 2007, Pub. L. 110–175, §6, December 31, 2007, 121 Stat. 2524 (2007), codified at 5 U.S.C.

delaying responses to requests. The uncertainty and lengthiness required to resolve a *FOIA* lawsuit worsens the situation, and consequently, good stories often become old news by the time the reporters receive the information. According to a recent survey, more than two-thirds of U.S. health care reporters claim having stories held or left unpublished because the Food and Drug Administration (FDA) did not respond to *FOIA* requests in a timely manner.[109] Unsurprisingly then, the Associated Press criticized the federal *FOIA* as being "water torture. It's just drip, drip, drip. You wait and you wait, and you wait."[110] Some journalists complain that they never use *FOIA* because it is "cumbersome, unwieldy, and slow."[111] In order to meet a deadline, many American reporters have developed alternative methods for securing information withheld by an agency. For instance, reporters seek agencies' outsiders but those knowing something about the desired information and approving of publication.[112]

Second, government officials tend to deny waivers for reporters' fees. Under *FOIA*, representatives of the news media enjoy the privilege of paying reduced or even zero processing fees for their requests.[113] However, reporter Donald Goldberg, an investigator for two years for

A. § 552((a) (6)(A) (2006); 5 U.S.C. § 552((a) (6)(B)(i) (2006). Under exceptional circumstances, *FOIA* allows news media to receive expedited handling of their requests. 5 U.S.C. § 552(a)(6)(E)(v)(II) (2000) (mandating expedited processing when there is "urgency to inform the public concerning...Federal Government activity" and the request is made by "a person primarily engaged in disseminating information").

109 *FOIA Survey: FDA's Slow Response Means Stories Go Unpublished*, Association of Health Care Journalists, April 10, 2008, *available at* https://healthjournalism.org/blog/2008/04/foia-survey-fdas-slow-response-means-stories-go-unpublished/ (accessed between February 21, 2025 and March 31, 2025). The survey was conducted by graduate students from Northwestern University's Medill School of Journalism.

110 Martha Mendoza, *AP Review Finds Federal Government Missing Deadlines and Time Limits*, ASSOCIATED PRESS, March 13, 2006 (captured by Internet Archive Wayback Machine on May 15, 2006), retrieved from https://web.archive.org/web/20060515043200/http://www.ap.org/foi/foi_031306b.html (accessed between February 21, 2025 and March 31, 2025).

111 Jane E. Kirtley, *Legal Evolution of the Government News Media Relationship*, *in* THE INSTITUTIONS OF AMERICAN DEMOCRACY: THE PRESS 281 (Geneva Overholser & Kathleen Hall Jamieson eds., (2005).

112 Louis M. Kohlmeier, *The Journalist's Viewpoint*, 23 ADMINISTRATIVE LAW REVIEW 143,143 (1970–1971).

113 5 U.S.C. § 552(a)(4)(A)(ii)(II) (2000) ("[F]ees shall be limited to reasonable standard charges for document duplication when records are not sought for commercial use and the request is made by... a representative of the news media."). Ordinary commercial

a congressional subcommittee that oversees *FOIA* matters for all federal agencies, identified a different pattern. "It is their [federal agencies'] policy to deny fee waivers regardless of merit, and it is up to you [reporters] to get that decision overturned."[114] *FOIA* processing fees are usually prohibitive.[115] The financial burden of obtaining access to governmental documents is so high that many editors abandon *FOIA* requests and try something else.

Third, misinformation obtained through *FOIA* requests abound. For example, for U.S. reporters covering deaths of soldiers, *FOIA* can be a useful weapon since military records are accessible through the Department of Defense. However, the U.S. military often misreports the circumstances of soldiers' deaths.[116] The truth is difficult to ascertain, and in this scenario, reporters must combine constant skepticism with old-fashioned reporting. On the topic of soldiers' deaths, eyewitnesses are far better sources than the information accessed via *FOIA* requests.[117]

No matter how discouraged by the faulty FOI system, compared to counterparts in other countries, U.S. journalists still remain known for abilities to open official records using FOI requests and lawsuits. American journalists' penchant for a substantial role in formulating and strengthening *U.S. FOIA* arises from the long traditions of freedom of expression and freedom of the press. The vigorous use of the freedom of information laws by U.S. journalists has several explanatory factors. The right to access government-held records and documents is a long-established statutory right for American citizens, including members of the press. The media in the United States has an insatiable demand for official information because of an assumed watchdog role. American news organizations enjoy freedom to publish information obtained via *FOIA* requests and lawsuits from strong First Amendment protection. The awareness of the law among American reporters is generally high

requesters must pay fees related to document search and review in addition to copying costs. *See* 5 U.S.C. § 552(a)(4)(A)(ii)(I) (2000).

[114] James Popkin, *Running the New "Improved" FOIA Obstacle Course*, 28 Columbia Journalism Review 45, 45 (1989).

[115] James Popkin, *Running the New "Improved" FOIA Obstacle Course*, 28 Columbia Journalism Review 45, 45–48 (1989).

[116] Lauren Melcher, *The Fog of War?* 31 News Media & the Law 12 (2007).

[117] Lauren Melcher, *The Fog of War?* 31 News Media & the Law 12 (2007).

because journalism schools require undergraduate students to complete mass media law courses.[118]

Another reason for the frequent use of freedom of information laws among American journalists is unreserved support from editors and media attorneys that advise and represent news organizations on legal matters.[119] David Barstow, the investigative reporter for *The New York Times*, sued the government under the *FOIA* many times, and he has never lost.[120] Mark Pittman, an investigative reporter for Bloomberg News, filed an *FOIA* request with the Federal Reserve Board for information detailing the central bank's $2 trillion in assistance to collapsing financial firms. He sued the central bank for its failure to disclose information. The lawsuit continued after Pittman died in 2009 and Bloomberg

[118] Most undergraduate journalism and mass communication programs at American colleges and universities list mass media law courses, which include freedom of information laws, as mandatory, even when programs are small. For example, Western Illinois University has probably one of the smallest broadcasting and journalism programs in the country and it has assigned a professor to teach mass communication law and ethics all the time. That professor is the author of this book, who has been teaching media law in every single semester since 2011 when he was hired as an assistant professor. Professional organizations in journalism and mass communication keep encouraging U.S. journalism professors to teach freedom of information legal issues. According to Carnegie Media Law for Journalism Schools Task Force Suggestions developed in 2012, "Journalism programs should train and encourage students to utilize Freedom of Information laws and draft Freedom of Information requests. Students should be made aware of the National Freedom of Information Coalition and Reporters Committee for Freedom of the Press and the Student Press Law Center. Also, public universities and whether journalism program records are subject to FOI requests is unresolved and may vary depending upon state FOI law and individual situations." *Task Force Suggestions*, Carnegie Media Law for Journalism Schools, *availale at* https://jschoollegal.wordpress.com/task-force-suggestions/ (accessed between February 21, 2025 and March 31, 2025). Task Force Suggestions were distributed in hard copy to the author of this book and many other journalism professors who attended the annual convention of the Association for Education in Journalism and Mass Communication (AEJMC) in Chicago in August 2012.

[119] Hongqing Duan, *How Chinese Media Shall Push Forward Open Government Information* [中国媒体如何推进信息公开], 9 CHINA REFORM (2011) (captured by Internet Archive Wayback Machine on October 11, 2011), retrieved from https://web.archive.org/web/20111011013413/http://article.chinalawinfo.com/Article_Detail.asp?ArticleID=63344 (accessed between February 21, 2025 and March 31, 2025).

[120] David E. McCraw, *How I Got the Story: The Lawsuit behind The New York Times's Pulitzer-Winning Military Analyst Story*, COLUMBIA JOURNALISM REVIEW, April 29, 2009, *available at* http://www.cjr.org/campaign_desk/how_i_got_the_story_david_mccr.php?page=all (accessed between February 21, 2025 and March 31, 2025). David E. McCraw is vice president and assistant general counsel for The New York Times Company.

News ultimately won the litigation.[121] These are a few success stories representing many U.S. journalists' forcing government to be less secretive. These stories would not be possible without unreserved support from courageous and ambitious editors and media attorneys.

FOI litigation is costly, complex, and time-consuming. Confronting agencies in court is especially difficult for American mainstream news organizations that are struggling financially. American journalists willingly launch legal suits against agencies over FOI issues because some public interest groups provide legal assistance. America has many public interest groups or organizations devoted to assisting journalists with FOI legal issues. For example, Yale University Law School launched Media Freedom and Information Access Clinic (MFIA) in 2010.[122] A team of student practitioners from the MFIA program collaborates with *The New York Times* for FOI litigation, with the Yale students assisting the newspaper to win a FOI lawsuit, in November 2010. The litigation, filed against the U.S. Treasury Department for non-disclosure of information, concerned names of companies and individuals licensed by Treasury to conduct business with or in sanctioned nations like Iran and North Korea. Yale Law School covered all the litigation costs.[123] The MFIA

[121] Alan Feuer, *Battle Over the Bailout*, THE NEW YORK TIMES, February 12, 2010, http://www.nytimes.com/2010/02/14/nyregion/14fed.html?pagewanted=all (accessed between February 21, 2025 and March 31, 2025); Bob Ivry, *Fed Loses Bid for Review of Bailout Disclosure Ruling*, BLOOMBERG NEWS, August 23, 2010, http://www.bloomberg.com/news/2010-08-23/u-s-appeals-court-refuses-to-review-disclosure-ruling-on-fed-bailouts.html (accessed between February 21, 2025 and March 31, 2025); Bob Ivry, *Mark Pittman's Fed Legacy: "Maybe Tomorrow the Dog Will Talk,"* BLOOMBERG NEWS, November 27, 2011, http://www.bloomberg.com/news/2011-11-28/mark-pittman-s-fed-legacy-maybe-tomorrow-the-dog-will-talk-.html (accessed between February 21, 2025 and March 31, 2025).

[122] *Media Freedom and Information Access Clinic*, Law School, Yale University, New Haven, Connecticut, *available at* https://law.yale.edu/studying-law-yale/clinical-and-experiential-learning/our-clinics/media-freedom-and-information-access-clinic (accessed between February 21, 2025 and March 31, 2025).

[123] *MFIA and New York Times Win FOIA Case; Ruling Clarifies Law Surrounding Personal Privacy Exemption*, Yale University Law School, New Haven, Connecticut, November 11, 2010 (captured by Internet Archive Wayback Machine on November 25, 2011), retrieved from https://web.archive.org/web/20111125063954/http://www.law.yale.edu/news/12466.htm (accessed between February 21, 2025 and March 31, 2025); Jo Becker, *U.S. Approved Business with Blacklisted Nations*, THE NEW YORK TIMES, December 23, 2010, http://www.nytimes.com/2010/12/24/world/24sanctions.html?pagewanted=all (accessed between February 21, 2025 and March 31, 2025); *Court Sides*

students normally handle four to five similar FOI cases each semester.[124] The Digital Media Law Project at Harvard University provides free legal service to grassroots media and citizen-journalists.[125] The project has a team of 200 media attorneys who may represent citizen-journalists in FOI litigation and other legal confrontations.[126] Many public interest groups, focused on media and not affiliated with universities, have been useful for U.S. reporters who need legal assistance with FOI issues. The Media Law Resource Center,[127] Reporters Committee for Freedom of the Press,[128] Society of Professional Journalists,[129] National Press Club,[130]

with Clinics on Freedom of Information Act Exemptions, Yale University Law School, August 24, 2022, *available at* https://law.yale.edu/yls-today/news/court-sides-clinics-freedom-information-act-exemptions (accessed between February 21, 2025 and March 31, 2025).

124 Hongqing Duan, *How Chinese Media Shall Push Forward Open Government Information* [中国媒体如何推进信息公开], 9 China Reform (2011) (captured by Internet Archive Wayback Machine on October 11, 2011), retrieved from https://web.archive.org/web/20111011013413/http://article.chinalawinfo.com/Article_Detail.asp?ArticleID=63344 (accessed between February 21, 2025 and March 31, 2025).

125 The Digital Media Law Project, formerly the Citizen Media Law Project, was founded in 2007 by Harvard University researchers. It provides online journalism ventures and other digital media creators with free and reduced-fee legal service via a network of 250 law firms, law school clinics, in-house counsel, and individual lawyers throughout the United States. *Digital Media Law Project*, the Berkman Klein Center for Internet & Society, Harvard University, *available at* https://cyber.harvard.edu/research/dmlp (accessed between February 21, 2025 and March 31, 2025).

126 Hongqing Duan, *How Chinese Media Shall Push Forward Open Government Information* [中国媒体如何推进信息公开], 9 China Reform (2011) (captured by Internet Archive Wayback Machine on October 11, 2011), retrieved from https://web.archive.org/web/20111011013413/http://article.chinalawinfo.com/Article_Detail.asp?ArticleID=63344 (accessed between February 21, 2025 and March 31, 2025).

127 Media Law Resource Center (MLRC), *available at* http://www.medialaw.org/ (accessed between February 21, 2025 and March 31, 2025).

128 The Reporters Committee for Freedom of the Press, *available at* http://www.rcfp.org/ (accessed between February 21, 2025 and March 31, 2025).

129 Society of Professional Journalists, *available at* http://www.spj.org/ (accessed between February 21, 2025 and March 31, 2025).

130 National Press Club, *available at* http://press.org/ (accessed between February 21, 2025 and March 31, 2025).

The Freedom Forum,[131] and the Student Press Law Center[132] are all such non-profit organizations. Like university-affiliated public interest groups, they have a reputation for aiding reporters, at no cost, with issues pertaining to FOI, libel, privacy, and many others.

Many State Legislatures in America Used *U.S. FOIA* as a Model

All 50 U.S. states and the District of Columbia have some kind of open records laws.[133] This section examines states' open records laws' emulation of the federal *FOIA*.[134] The examination employs categories necessary for transparent government, as identified by international Freedom of information expert, David Banisar: Judicial enforcement and applicability to official entities, processes for disclosing information, fees for access and limits for time to respond, procedures for administrative and judicial relief, and conditions and exemptions.[135]

FOIA, despite its limitations, has long been a model for similar laws in many U.S. states. As media law scholars, Don Pember and Clay Calvert,

[131] The Freedom Forum, *available at* http://www.freedomforum.org/ (accessed between February 21, 2025 and March 31, 2025).

[132] The Student Press Law Center, *available at* https://splc.org (accessed between February 21, 2025 and March 31, 2025).

[133] These state open records laws are accessible through the following websites: The National Freedom of Information Coalition, https://www.nfoic.org/state-freedom-of-information-laws/ (accessed between February 21, 2025 and March 31, 2025); National Conference of State Legislatures, https://www.ncsl.org/cls/public-records-law-and-state-legislatures (accessed between February 21, 2025 and March 31, 2025); Digital Media Law Project of Harvard University, https://www.dmlp.org/legal-guide/access-records-from-state-governments (accessed between February 21, 2025 and March 31, 2025); The Reporters' Committee for Freedom of the Press, http://www.rcfp.org/ogg/ (accessed between February 21, 2025 and March 31, 2025).

[134] The subsequent comparison of various U.S. states' FOI laws with the federal open records law is the result of accessing a freedom of information database on the website of The Reporters' Committee for Freedom of the Press. *Open Government Guide*, The Reporters' Committee for Freedom of the Press, *available at* http://www.rcfp.org/ogg/ (accessed between February 21, 2025 and March 31, 2025).

[135] David Banisar, Freedom of Information around the World 2006: A Global Survey of Access to Government Information Laws (report for Privacy International, London, United Kingdom, July 2006), *available at* http://www.freedominfo.org/documents/global_survey2006.pdf (accessed between February 21, 2025 and March 31, 2025).

stated, "State open-records laws tend to mirror the federal law."[136] Almost half of the states now have laws that "closely model" the form adopted by Congress for crafting the Federal FOI law.[137]

Similar to *U.S. FOIA* that was drafted by U.S. Congress, all states' open records laws are enactments of legislative branches of states' governments. The right of access granted by *U.S. FOIA* is a statutory one, not a constitutional one. Most state laws, with a few exceptions,[138] followed this approach, providing information seekers only statutory rights to access government-held documents or records. Like the federal freedom of information law, which applies only to the executive branch of the federal government,[139] state open records statutes normally apply to records held by executive branches of state governments and exclude records of courts and legislatures.[140]

State open records laws, like their federal counterpart, compel state agencies and local governments' agencies to affirmatively disclose some information without the necessity of a request. Most state laws, like

[136] DON R. PEMBER & CLAY CALVERT, MASS MEDIA LAW 348 (2009–2010).

[137] ASSOCIATION OF METROPOLITAN WATER AGENCIES, STATE FOIA LAWS: A GUIDE TO PROTECTING SENSITIVE WATER SECURITY INFORMATION 2 (Washington, D.C., 2002), *available at* http://www.awwaneb.org/pdfs/securityprivacy.pdf (accessed between February 21, 2025 and March 31, 2025).

[138] In California, a right of public access to government "writings" appears in the state constitution. *See* DON R. PEMBER & CLAY CALVERT, MASS MEDIA LAW 344–345 (2009–2010). In Florida, the public's right of access to information held by the government is a fundamental constitutional right. BRECHNER CENTER FOR FREEDOM OF INFORMATION, FLORIDA'S GOVERNMENT IN THE SUNSHINE: A CITIZEN'S GUIDE, University of Florida, *2006, available at* https://original-ufdc.uflib.ufl.edu/UF00088828/00001/5x (accessed between February 21, 2025 and March 31, 2025). In Montana, the constitution provides not depriving a person of the opportunity to examine documents "except when the demand on an individual's privacy clearly exceeds the merits of public disclosure." Mont. Const. Ann. Art. II, § 9 (2001). ASSOCIATION OF METROPOLITAN WATER AGENCIES, STATE FOIA LAWS: A GUIDE TO PROTECTING SENSITIVE WATER SECURITY INFORMATION (Washington, D.C., 2002), *available at* http://www.awwaneb.org/pdfs/securityprivacy.pdf (accessed between February 21, 2025 and March 31, 2025).

[139] 5 U.S.C. § 552(f)(1) (2006).

[140] DON R. PEMBER & CLAY CALVERT, MASS MEDIA LAW 345 (2009–2010). There are many exceptions to this generalization. For example, records of legislative bodies and courts in the state of Arkansas and Connecticut are covered by their state freedom of information laws. Ark. Code. Ann. § 25-19-103(5)(A). Conn. Gen. Stat. § 1-200(1).

the federal statute, allow "any person"[141] the right to inspect public documents with no requirement that the information seeker explains the purpose of the request.[142] Only a few states require requestors of public records to be "citizens of the state."[143]

All state open records laws, like the federal equivalent, have policies for requesters' fees for processing state open records inquiries. Both federal and state laws mandate agencies' releasing documents or records in a timely manner. The specific amount of fees levied and limits to response times vary from state to state. All state laws provide either administrative or judicial relief to resolve a disputed freedom of information request.

Both *U.S. FOIA* and all states' freedom of information laws have exemption clauses that agencies or courts could use to justify withholding information. As with the federal law, most states assert that all records are presumptively open and then provide exceptions.[144] The number of exemptions varies among states,[145] and many states' exemptions do not follow the pattern of the federal Freedom of Information Act. However, all states' laws and the federal *FOIA* have some common or similar exemptions: information classified as confidential by another state or federal laws (Exemption 3 in *U.S. FOIA*), law enforcement and investigatory information (Exemption 7 in *U.S. FOIA*), trade secrets and commercial information (Exemption 4 in *U.S. FOIA*), preliminary departmental memoranda (working papers) (Exemption 5 in *U.S. FOIA*), and personal privacy information (Exemption 6 in *U.S FOIA*).[146]

141 Don R. Pember & Clay Calvert, Mass Media Law 345 (2009–2010); 5 U.S.C. § 552(a)(3)(A) (2006).

142 Don R. Pember & Clay Calvert, Mass Media Law 345 (2009–2010); NARA v. Favish, 541 U.S. 157, 172 (2004).

143 Such states include Alabama, Arkansas, Delaware, Georgia, New Hampshire, New Jersey, Tennessee, and Virginia. However, provisions barring non-residents from making public record requests may be no longer valid today after *Lee v. Minner* ruled that the restrictions on non-residents' rights to access public documents were unconstitutional. *Lee v. Minner*, 458 F. 3d 194 (3d Cir. 2006).

144 John D. Zelezny, Communications Law: Liberties, Restraints, and the Modern Media 259 (2010).

145 The Connecticut FOI law contains 21 specific exemptions. The *Virginia Freedom of Information Act* includes 100 specific exemptions. Florida's *Public Records Law* has 200 to 600 statutory exceptions.

146 5 U.S.C. § 552((b) (1–9) (2006); Don R. Pember & Clay Calvert, Mass Media Law 346 (2009–2010).

Some states follow the federal *FOIA* model so closely that statutory language in their exemptions is nearly identical. For example, *U.S. FOIA* exempts documents that are "personnel and medical files and similar files the disclosure of which would constitute a clearly unwarranted invasion of personal privacy."[147] The Connecticut Freedom of Information Act classifies as confidential records that are "personnel or medical files and similar files the disclosure of which would constitute an invasion of personal privacy."[148] According to the California Public Records Act, governmental agencies may justify withholding documents that are "personnel, medical or similar files, the disclosure of which would constitute an unwarranted invasion of personal privacy."[149]

The statutory languages used in the above-mentioned three personal privacy exemptions are so similar that any reasonable reader would have difficulty identifying subtle differences among them.

Summary and Conclusion

This chapter examined the origins and development of freedom of information laws from a global perspective. As of December 2024, more than 100 countries enacted various forms of laws to protect people's right to access government-held records and documents. The chapter explored the inception of the world's first FOI law, and the spreading of the concept of freedom of information throughout the world, including the United States and China.

This chapter examined four categories of countries with FOI statutes, as identified by other FOI scholars. The first is historical pioneers that passed FOI laws prior to the third wave of democratization in the 1980s. The second is newly emerging democracies that recently departed authoritarian rule. The third is wealthy and well-established democracies, and the last category is countries from the developing world. FOI laws in these four types of countries have different characteristics in terms of both statutory language and enforcement.

As for the contributor to formulation of FOI laws and the methods of formulation, apparently, four major patterns and trends appear: Economic

[147] 5 U.S.C. § 552((b) (6) (2006).

[148] Conn. Gen. Stat. § 1–210(b)(2).

[149] California Government Code §§ 6254 (C).

development has no direct cause-effect relationship with the presence or absence of FOI laws, and civil society's journalists and advocacy groups are instrumental in adoption of FOI laws in many countries. Many countries have constitutional provisions on the right to information, whereas some nations decline to embrace a constitutional right of access. International organizations such as the European Union and the Organization of American States, treaties, conventions, and non-governmental organizations (NGOs) played important roles in creation of many national FOI laws.

This chapter examined the origins and development of freedom of information laws in the United States. The detailed examination is necessary because *U.S. FOIA* is a model for many countries and provides a reference for Chinese FOI law. When Sweden embraced the world's first freedom of information legislation, Britain continued to enforce its infamous seditious libel laws. The *Housekeeping Statue of 1789* legalized governmental secrecy in the United States. The *Administrative Procedures Act (APA) of 1946* failed to increase official transparency, and after the World War II, especially in the 1950s, people from the legal establishment, the media, and Congress began to agitate for a legal right to obtain governmental information. Among the most prominent figures in the freedom of information movement were James Pope, Harold Cross, James Russell Wiggins, and John Moss. *U.S. FOIA* was signed into law reluctantly in 1966 by U.S. President Lyndon Johnson who set America on an unstoppable train ride of government transparency. Since then, several amendments to *FOIA* have been enacted to strengthen transparency in the federal government.

The chapter found that journalists in the United States are not only enthusiastic promoters of *U.S. FOIA* but also frequent users of the law. They have used information obtained via filing FOI requests to expose official scandals and hold the government accountable. Strong legal protection and ubiquitous legal assistance are among the major reasons for vigorous use of the FOI law in the country. However, many U.S. reporters avoid using *FOIA* today because requesting information via *FOIA* can be slow and costly. In addition, information obtained via FOI requests can be misleading.

This chapter also compared American state-level open records laws with the federal *FOIA* according to five categories: Judicial enforcement and applicability to official entities, processes for disclosing Information, fees for access and limit to response times, procedures for administrative and judicial relief, and conditions and exemptions. Despite major differences, states' open records laws and the federal open records law are strikingly similar. The *U.S. FOIA* and some states' open records laws use almost the same statutory language for exemption clauses. Such a striking similarity in legal wording is a strong testament to the fact that the federal *FOIA* is a measure for many American states in crafting open records laws of their own.

CHAPTER 4

Secrecy and Transparency of the Chinese Government: A Historical Perspective of Mass Communications

This chapter is derived from the book author's doctoral dissertation that was successfully defended at The Pennsylvania State University in 2012. The chapter is also derived from an article presented by the author of this book to the AEJMC 2012 annual conference in Chicago. Portions of the text resemble or may replicate the original text from the unpublished PhD thesis and the conference paper and have been reproduced as such with the permission of Palgrave Macmillan editors. Yong Tang, "Chinese Freedom of Information: An Evaluation of the Legislative History, Rationales, Significance and Efficacy of Regulations of the People's Republic of China on Open Government Information" (2012) (unpublished Ph.D. diss., The Pennsylvania State University at University Park), *available at* https://etda.libraries.psu.edu/catalog/16287 (accessed between February 21, 2025 and March 31, 2025); Yong Tang, *Secrecy and Transparency of the Chinese Government: A Historical Perspective*, paper accepted for presentation by the Law and Policy Division of the Association for Education in Journalism and Mass Communication annual convention, Chicago, Illinois, August 9–12, 2012 (winning Top Faculty Paper Award).

Y. Tang, *Freedom of Information Law in China*,
https://doi.org/10.1007/978-981-96-7842-6_4

Introduction

Many observers in Western countries view China's passage of the freedom of information legislation with perplexity and suspicion.[1] The puzzle is understandable given that China lacks strong democratic traditions, and governmental officials have practiced secrecy for thousands of years. Government secrecy, long embedded in Chinese society, included the widespread inclination of "reporting good, rather than bad news" (*baoxi bu baoyou* 报喜不报忧)[2] to deal with crises.[3] However, one should not ignore another side of the same coin. Chinese leaders, like many other rulers in the world, have long publicized at least portions of their government activities since ancient times. Current Chinese leaders borrowed the

[1] Rick Snell & Weibing Xiao, *Freedom of Information Returns to China*, 10 PUBLIC ADMINISTRATION TODAY 44 (2007).

[2] WEIBING XIAO, FREEDOM OF INFORMATION REFORM IN CHINA: INFORMATION FLOW ANALYSIS 28 (2011); ZHIHAO LOU, CHOICE OF THE PEOPLE AND FUTURE OF CHINA [人民的选择: 中国共产党与中国的前途] 129 (1991).

[3] WEIBING XIAO, FREEDOM OF INFORMATION REFORM IN CHINA: INFORMATION FLOW ANALYSIS 138 (2011). Li Hongzhang, the prime minister of the late Qing Dynasty, was an insightful observer and faithful practitioner of the tradition to suppress bad news. When he visited the United States in 1896, Li expressed his dissatisfaction with the Chinese newspapers in suppressing what was bad and spreading what was good. When U.S. reporters asked him if he would like to introduce the American and European newspaper system to China, Li said, "There are newspapers in China, but the Chinese editors, unfortunately, do not tell the truth. They do not, as your papers, tell 'the truth, the whole truth, and nothing but the truth.' The editors in China are great economizers of the truth; they tell only a part of it. ..." *Li on American Hatred*, THE NEW YORK TIMES, September 3, 1896, at 10, https://www.nytimes.com/1896/09/03/archives/li-on-american-hatred-chinese-laborers-he-says-have-higher-virtues.html (accessed between February 21, 2025 and March 31, 2025); Li himself, however, was not hesitant at all in suppressing bad news. In May 1896, Li visited Russia to attend the new emperor's coronation ceremony. Thousands of spectators were killed or injured in a crowd crush after the emperor left the ceremony. The crowd crush happened due to mass disorder on a square. Russia's prime minister was planning to report the tragedy to the emperor. Li persuaded him not to do so. Li said, according to his political experiences in China, reporting anything bad to the emperor would not be career-enhancing. Qingjun Jia, *Li Hongzhang's Chinese Political Experience Helps Russian Officials Escape Penalty for Crowd Crush* [李鸿章的"经验介绍"和沙俄朝臣的"啥事没有"], GUANGMING DAILY ONLINE, June 7, 2004, https://www.gmw.cn/02blqs/2004-06/07/content_76836.htm (accessed between February 21, 2025 and March 31, 2025).

idea of transparency not only from Western democracies[4] but also from their own ancient ancestors.[5] Of course, unlike leaders in modern democracies, ancient Chinese rulers employed a certain degree of governmental transparency, not for democratic governance, but for achieving effective and efficient autocracy.

This chapter will examine how both sides of governmental information management—secrecy and disclosure—have evolved in a long tradition of the Chinese civilization. Dynasties in Chinese history are numerous, and the scope of this book does not allow for a thorough scrutiny of each dynasty. Thus, the focus and review of government's informational or communication policies center on four major time periods: Pre-Qin China (2070 BC-221 BC), imperial China (221 BC-1912 AD), the Republic of China (1912 AD-1949 AD), and the People's Republic of China under the leadership of Mao Zedong (1949 AD-1976 AD). For pre-Qin China, this chapter will examine the Xia, Shang, and Zhou dynasties. For imperial China, the chapter will inspect the Qin, Han, Tang, Song, Ming, and Qing dynasties.

This division of time periods is rational because each time period involves different types of government. Slave owners ruled pre-Qin China; emperors ruled imperial China; the Kuomintang (KMT) Party, with an ideological commitment to introduce, gradually, full constitutional democracy, governed the Republic of China most of the time[6]; and Mao's China was under the control of communist revolutionaries who temporarily sided with the Soviet Union. All these various forms of government had different ruling ideologies, preached and practiced sometimes sharply divergent policies for handling governmental information.

[4] In an email interview with Yanbin Lü, a FOI scholar at China Academy of Social Sciences Institute of Law, Lü told the author of this book that he and his colleagues did extensive research on freedom of information systems in the United States, European countries, and Japan. They finally produced a draft of *OGI Regulations* (so called "Academic Draft") and submitted it to the State Council for leaders there to consider. He said that foreign legal experts on freedom of information laws also contributed to the making of *OGI Regulations* by offering their own comments to the State Council.

[5] The Chinese Communist Party advocates the policy of "making the past serve the present and foreign things serve China" [*guweijinyong yangweizhongyong*古为今用 洋为中用] in law making. FANGTONG LIU, SONGJIE HUANG & GEORGE F. MCLEAN, PHILOSOPHY AND MODERNIZATION IN CHINA 6 (1997).

[6] Yangsun Chou & Andrew J. Nathan, *Democratizing Transition in Taiwan*, 27ASIAN SURVEY 277, 284 (March 1987).

For each period considered in this book, assessment of governmental secrecy occurs by considering respective rulers' archiving official documents and records and the laws and codes enacted to guard state secrets and punish violators. Investigation of informational disclosure, if any, explores internal/within the bureaucracy and external/among common people, publicizing of governmental activities.

Governmental Informational Policy in Pre-Qin China

The Xia Dynasty (2070 BC-1600 BC) and the Shang Dynasty (1600 BC-1046 BC)

Chinese leaders began to realize the importance of storing government documents and maintain their secrecy since the Xia Dynasty, the first dynasty in China.[7] Xia monarchs appointed astronomers (*taishiling* 太史令) to collect and manage important government documents in secure and private places.[8]

Shang monarchs established China's first governmental archiving system, preserved in the form of scripts inscribed on oracle bones and containing large volumes of key governmental information.[9] Royal librarians (*shoucangshi* 守藏史) had responsibility for collecting and managing

[7] To date, no written records from the Xia Dynasty are available. However, written records about the dynasty are not rare.

[8] Gu Zhong was an astronomer during the reign of the last monarch of Xia. Zhong tried to persuade the ruler to practice benevolent governance, but he failed. During the petition, he let the king see all the archived governmental documents. He was so emotional that tears came streaming down his face. Seeing that his persuasion had no effect, Zhong finally defected to Shang and brought all Xia documents with him [夏太史令终古出其图法，执而泣之。夏桀迷惑，暴愈甚，太史令终古乃出奔如商]. The Gu Zhong story originally appears in *Lv's Commentaries of History,* an ancient Chinese classic compiled by Buwei Lv, the prime minister of the state of Qin. LV'S COMMENTARIES OF HISTORY [吕氏春秋] (Buwei Lv ed., Foreign Languages Press, 2010) (239 BC). For relevant scholarly article about the episode, see Wenying Liu, *An Evaluation of History of Chinese Archives* [中国档案事业发展史探析], 1 JOURNAL OF SICHUAN CULTURAL RELIC 66 (2002).

[9] Sharon Chien, *Historical Development of Library Education in China*, 20 THE JOURNAL OF LIBRARY HISTORY (1974–1987) 368 (1985); Wenying Liu, *An Evaluation of History of Chinese Archives* [中国档案事业发展史探析], 1 JOURNAL OF SICHUAN CULTURAL RELIC 66 (2002); Qingxin Gong, *Research on Origins of Chinese Government and University-Owned Archives* [中国档案、中国高校档案研究], 4 JOURNAL OF GUANZI 113 (2006); Shiping Xu, *An Overview of Ancient Preservation Technology Used*

these archives. Sacred ancestral temples, guarded 24 hours a day, 365 days a year, were the storehouses for important government documents and files and accessible only to an extremely limited number of people like kings and high officials.

During the two dynasties of Xia and Shang, no recorded instances of proactively disseminating government information exist, even among central and local bureaucrats. The two dynasties produced various forms of laws, but they were not made publicly available.[10] Rulers during this time believed that published laws had less power to deter undesirable activity than unpublished ones.

The Western Zhou Dynasty (1046 BC-771 BC) and the Eastern Zhou Dynasty (771 BC-256 BC)

The Zhou Dynasty continued the Shang tradition of archiving important records as engravings on animal bones, bronze wares, or bamboo slips.[11] During the Western Zhou period, the royal archival institution (*tianfu* 天府) archived all original copies of official documents and national treasures.[12] Royal librarians (*shoucangshishi* 守藏室史)[13] had responsibility

for Chinese Archives [中国古代档案保护技术概览], A08 JOURNAL OF ARCHIVES SCIENCE STUDY SUPPLEMENT 20, 20–21 (1996).

10 The law in the Xia Dynasty was *Yu Xing* [禹刑]. As a customary law, *Yu Xing* was unwritten and unpublished. The law in the Shang Dynasty was *Tang Xing* [汤刑]. *Tang Xing* was also unpublished. Yujun Feng, *Legal Culture in China: A Comparison to Western Law*, 15 NZACL YEARBOOK (2009).

11 Wenying Liu, An Evaluation of History of Chinese Archives [中国档案事业发展史探析], 1 JOURNAL OF SICHUAN CULTURAL RELIC 66 (2002).

12 Guodu Feng, *Archival Institutions in Ancient China* [我国古代档案馆], 3 JOURNAL OF ZHONGZHOU TODAY & YESTERDAY 19 (1997).

13 During the Western Zhou Dynasty, six government offices at the court of Zhou existed: Ministry of Heaven, Ministry of Earth, Ministry of Spring, Ministry of Summer, Ministry of Autumn, and Ministry of Winter. The keeper of imperial archival records was the 9th ranked official in the Ministry of Spring (Rites). Heiner Fruehauf, *The Science of Symbols Exploring a Forgotten Gateway to Chinese Medicine*, 69 JOURNAL OF CHINESE MEDICINE 23 (June 2002).

to oversee, properly, the maintenance and secrecy of all archived documents. Laozi, the legendary Taoist philosopher, was once such a keeper of archival records at the court of Zhou.[14]

As the Zhou bureaucracy grew in size, scope, and complexity, internal/organizational communication among central and local bureaucrats expanded rapidly. Consequently, kings of Zhou created a comprehensive system to ensure confidentiality. When administrators transmitted a confidential document, they wrote horizontally on three bundled bamboo-writing slips held together by a chord. Upon completion, each slip had only one-third of the whole document. Bureaucrats then separated the three slips and had each of them delivered in a sealed box by a different courier to the addressee. In so doing, officials had peace of mind that the addressee would not have the full document until he received all three slips. This methodology drastically reduced the likelihood of leaking government secrets.[15] As a standard practice, the Zhou kings authorized their prime ministers to handle all confidential government documents.

Unlike sovereigns in the Xia and Shang dynasties, supreme leaders in the Zhou Dynasty realized that governmental secrecy and certain degree of transparency could cooperate to increase stability and prosperity. Kings of this period created China's first postal system to facilitate freer flow of information within the bureaucracy. Courier stations, established along major routes of transportation across the empire, used labor, horses, carriages, and ships to deliver official documents on a regular basis. The prime minister was responsible for courier stations, and the Ministry of Military Affairs ensured secure transmission of urgent official documents. The establishment of this system allowed internal/organizational communication between the Zhou court and regional nobles.[16]

[14] Alan Chan, *Laozi*, Stanford Encyclopedia of Philosophy, first published on December 15, 2001; substantive revision on May 5, 2007, *available at* http://plato.stanford.edu/entries/laozi/ (accessed between February 21, 2025 and March 31, 2025).

[15] Ke Peng, *Study on Chinese Ancient Confidentiality Laws* [中国古代保密法律制度初探], 1 JOURNAL OF LIAONING POLICE ACADEMY 20 (2011); Zhuo Yuan, *Confidentiality of Ancient Chinese Official Documents* [管窥古代公文的保密制度] 02 × JOURNAL OF LANTAI WORLD 57 (2007).

[16] *Rites of Zhou*, one of four collections of ritual matters of the Zhou Dynasty, recorded the earliest Chinese courier stations. *Rites of Zhou* [周礼] (Xuan Qian, Xingqi Qian, Huabao Wang & Binghong Xie translated and annotated, 2001). For relevant literature, see Ying Zou, Postal System and Communication in Ancient China [中国古代邮驿制度与传播] 23 JOURNAL OF XIANNING COLLEGE 4, 99–102 (2003).

Zhou kings and regional warlords occasionally declassified certain official papers and announced directives in public decrees and government orders.[17] Governmental officials also wrote decrees or royal orders on wooden boards, bamboo slips, or silk tissues and hung them high in front of the palace gates for all to see.[18] These were the earliest recorded instances of the ancient Chinese government's systematically and proactively disclosing official information to the public.

The urgent issue was the degree of official information that should be kept secret and the amount appropriately shared with local officials and even the populace. This issue was hotly debated among philosophers from "Hundred Schools of Thought" that flourished from the Spring and Autumn Period (771 BC-476 BC) to the Warring States Period (475 BC-221 BC). During this era, the power of Zhou kings was in decline, regional warlords defied the court and called themselves kings

[17] Hailin Zhao, *Tianfu: National Archival Institution at Zhou Dynasty*, [周朝的国家档案馆——天府] 5 JOURNAL OF ARCHIVES (1985).

[18] Cited from *Rites of Zhou. Rites of Zhou* [周礼] (Xuan Qian, Xingqi Qian, Huabao Wang & Binghong Xie translated and annotated, 2001). For relevant literature, see Chunping Huang, *Information Dissemination Methods in Han Dynasty* [汉代信息发布手段探析], 18 (3) JOURNAL OF ZHEJIANG INSTITUTE OF MEDIA AND COMMUNICATIONS 7, 9 (June 2011).

as well.[19] Contentions among Confucianism,[20] Taoism,[21] Mohism,[22] and Legalism[23] are especially worth noting because these four ancient philosophies have profoundly influenced later generations of political leaders, including today's Chinese rulers.[24]

[19] Mark Edward Lewis, *The Spring and Autumn Period*, *in* THE CAMBRIDGE HISTORY OF ANCIENT CHINA: FROM THE ORIGINS OF CIVILIZATION TO 221 B.C (Michael Loewe & Edward L. Shaughnessy eds., 1999).

[20] Confucianism (*Rujia*; 儒家; "School of Scholars") was the dominant ideology of the Chinese government for all imperial dynasties except the Qin Dynasty. It emphasized the importance of moral virtues including altruism, righteousness, propriety, loyalty, and filial piety. For more information about Confucianism, see XINZHONG YAO, AN INTRODUCTION TO CONFUCIANISM (2000); RONNIE LITTLEJOHN, CONFUCIANISM: AN INTRODUCTION (2011).

[21] Taoism or Daoism (*Daojia*; 道家; "School of the Way") never became the dominant ideology of the imperial Chinese government except in the early Western Han Dynasty. It was a philosophy of ancient Chinese scholars at leisure or in retirement or political wilderness. It focused on individuals' living in harmony with the Tao, the essence and source of the natural and even the supernatural universe. For more information about Taoism, see ISABELLE ROBINET, TAOISM: GROWTH OF A RELIGION (1997); RUSSELL KIRKLAND, TAOISM: THE ENDURING TRADITION (2004); HOLMES WELCH, TAOISM: THE PARTING OF THE WAY (1966); JENNIFER OLDSTONE, TAOISM: ORIGINS, BELIEFS, PRACTICES, HOLY TEXTS, SACRED PLACES (2003).

[22] Mohism or Moism (*Mojia*; 墨家; "School of Mo") did not survive through the Qin Dynasty because of the ruling class suppression. It advocated universal love ("everyone is equal before heaven"), equality, nonaggression, frugality, and the use of experimental methods to discover the truth of nature. For more information about Mohism, see XING LU, *Conceptualization of Ming Bian: The School of Mohism*, *in* RHETORIC IN ANCIENT CHINA, FIFTH TO THIRD CENTURY, B.C.E.: A COMPARISON WITH CLASSICAL GREEK RHETORIC (1998).

[23] Legalism (*Fajia*; 法家; "School of Law") was the dominant ruling ideology of the Qin Dynasty. It held a cynical view of human nature and preached using severe penalties and high rewards to regiment society for the goal of strengthening the power of the states. For more information about Legalism, see WING-TSIT CHAN, *Legalism*, *in* A SOURCE BOOK IN CHINESE PHILOSOPHY 251–60 (1963); CHARLES O. HUCKER, CHINA'S IMPERIAL PAST: AN INTRODUCTION TO CHINESE HISTORY AND CULTURE 92–95 (1995).

[24] In addition to Confucianism, Taoism, Mohism, and Legalism, many other less well-known schools of thought flourished during the Spring and Autumn Period and the Warring States Period. For example, School of Naturalists (*Yin-Yangjia*阴阳家, "School of Yin-Yang"), Logicians (*Mingjia* 名家; "School of Names"), School of Diplomacy (*Zonghengjia* 纵横家, "School of Vertical and Horizontal Alliances"), Miscellaneous School (*Zajia* 杂家), School of "Minor-talks" (*Xiaoshuojia* 小说家), School of Agriculturalist (*Nongjia* 农家), School of the Military (*Bingjia* 兵家). An analysis of the relationship between freedom of information and those schools of thought is beyond the scope of this study.

Mencius, or Mengzi, refined Confucianism whose founder was Confucius, or Kongzi. Confucius and Mencius were among the first ancient Chinese philosophers who indirectly considered the subject of governmental information, and these two masters believed that individual rights were inferior to collective rights, thereby supporting the loyalty of the governed to the governor, as long as the latter is virtuous.[25] Based on this rationale, Confucius said, "The people may be made to follow a path of action, but they may not be made to understand it (*minkeshiyouzhi bukeshizhizhi* 民可使由之 不可使知之)."[26] In other words, Confucius suggested that the ruler should allow his people to obey rather than informing them or having knowledge. Confucius said that anyone working in the bureaucracy should speak and behave prudently to avoid accusation (*duowenqueyi shenyanqiyu zeguayou duojianquedai shenxingqiyu zeguahui yanguayou xingguahui luzaiqizhongyi* 多闻阙疑，慎言其余，则寡尤;多见阙殆,慎行其余,则寡悔。言寡尤,行寡悔,禄在其中矣).[27] When discussing the rationale for governors' always guarding against leaking information, Confucius stated:

> [W]hen disorder arises, it will be found that [ill-advised] speech was the stepping-stone to it. If a ruler does not keep secret [his deliberations with his minister], he will lose that minister. If a minister does not keep secret [his deliberations with his ruler], he will lose his life. If [important] matters

[25] CHU CHAI, THE SACRED BOOKS OF CONFUCIUS, AND OTHER CONFUCIAN CLASSICS (1965); LEONARD SHIHLIEN HSÜ, THE POLITICAL PHILOSOPHY OF CONFUCIANISM: AN INTERPRETATION OF THE SOCIAL AND POLITICAL IDEAS OF CONFUCIUS, HIS FORERUNNERS, AND HIS EARLY DISCIPLES (1975).

[26] This rendition is the most popular way of interpreting and translating this quote. However, conflicting interpretations abound due to the lack of a system of punctuation in ancient Chinese literature. For English translation of the original quote, refer to the Chinese Text Project, a web-based e-text system designed to present ancient Chinese texts, particularly those relating to Chinese philosophy, in a bilingual, well-structured and properly cross-referenced manner, making the most of the electronic medium to aid in the study and understanding of these texts, *available at* http://ctext.org/analects/tai-bo (accessed between February 21, 2025 and March 31, 2025). For the original Chinese text, see TAEKO BROOKS, THE ORIGINAL ANALECTS: SAYINGS OF CONFUCIUS AND HIS SUCCESSORS (1998).

[27] Cited from Guoxue.com, Beijing, China, *available at* http://www.guoxue.com/jinbu/13jing/lunyu/ly_002.htm (accessed between February 21, 2025 and March 31, 2025). For more relevant statements by Confucius, see Confucius, *The Analects* (David Hinton trans., Counterpoint Press, 1998).

in the germ are not kept secret, that will be injurious to their accomplishment. Therefore, the superior man is careful to maintain secrecy and does not allow himself to speak.[28]

Similar to Confucius and his disciples, Laozi, Zhuangzi, and their Taoist followers were opponents of governmental transparency, although probably to a lesser degree. Taoist philosophers argued for governors to avoid interfering with the governed. If people lack knowledge and desire, then they cannot act. If no action occurs, harmony remains. If rulers abolish knowledge and wisdom, people profit. If rulers use law to control a nation, the nation weakens. If rulers use nature to control a nation, the nation strengthens.[29] Laozi said, "The ancient followers of Tao did not use it to increase knowledge, but rather to preserve simplicity. People are difficult to govern when there is too much knowledge. Whoever rules a country by furthering knowledge is that nation's curse."[30] For Taoists, the best political communication is no communication at all.[31] Zhuangzi summarized his anti-transparency predilection in an eloquent statement:

Fish should not be taken from [the protection of] the deep waters;
the agencies for the profit of a state *should not be shown to men.*
But those sages [and their teachings] are the agencies for the
profit of the world and *should not be exhibited to it* (emphasis added).[32]

[28] Quoted from the Chinese Text Project, http://ctext.org/book-of-changes/xi-ci-shang/ens (accessed between February 21, 2025 and March 31, 2025). *The I Ching* or *Yi Jing*, also known as *the Classic of Changes, Book of Changes* and *Zhouyi*, is one of the oldest of the Chinese classic texts. For the full Chinese text of the Confucius statement, see CAROL K. ANTHONY & HANNA MOOG. I CHING: THE ORACLE OF THE COSMIC WAY (2002); JACK M. BALKIN, THE LAWS OF CHANGE: I CHING AND THE PHILOSOPHY OF LIFE (2002).

[29] For more similar statements by Taoists, see Chinese Text Project, http://ctext.org/daoism (accessed between February 21, 2025 and March 31, 2025).

[30] For more similar statements by Taoists, see Chinese Text Project, http://ctext.org/daoism (accessed between February 21, 2025 and March 31, 2025).

[31] Xiaoli Yu, *Study on Taoist Concept of Communication* [反传播还是愚民政策?, 试论道家的传播观], *97* JOURNAL OF FUYANG TEACHERS COLLEGE (Social Science) 1 (2004).

[32] Quoted from the Chinese Text Project, http://ctext.org/zhuangzi/cutting-open-satchels/ens (accessed between February 21, 2025 and March 31, 2025). CHUANG TZU, THE COMPLETE WORKS OF CHUANG TZU (Burton Watson, trans., Columbia University Press, 1968).

In a sharp contrast to Confucianism and Taoism, Mohism adopted a vastly different approach to politics and official information. Although Mozi, the founder of Mohism, did not explicitly discuss the issue of governmental transparency in his writings, he was arguably one of the most pro-democracy philosophers during his era.[33] Mozi was a robust supporter of selecting government officials (including the sovereign king) by virtue and merit rather than by heritage and family connections. He condemned the system of inherited governmental power. In a sharp contrast, none of his contemporary thinkers questioned the morality of primogeniture. When explaining the appointment of officials, Mozi stated bluntly:

> Thereupon Heaven wished to unify the standards in the world. he virtuous was selected and made emperor. Conscious of the insufficiency of his power alone to govern the empire, the emperor chose the next best [in virtue and wisdom] and honored them to be the three ministers. ... [T]he three ministers in turn divided the empire into feudal states and assigned them to feudal lords. ... [T]he feudal lord in turn selected his next best [in virtue and wisdom] and commissioned them ministers and secretaries. ... [T]he ministers and secretaries again selected their next best [in virtue and wisdom] and appointed them district heads and clan patriarchs.[34]

Mozi did not explicitly talk about the advantages and disadvantages of disclosing government information. However, from his people-based approach to governance, inferring that Mozi believed in the value of transparency is not difficult. An ideal government, according to the Mohism, is one in which constant, effective, and efficient sharing of information occurs between the governor and the governed. Otherwise, selecting the sovereign, other officeholders and the "next best in virtue

[33] As a scholar stated, "If Confucianism is the most influential school of thought with regard to Chinese culture and political systems, Mohism is the school most resembling Western logical, religious and ethical systems." Xing Lu, *conceptualization of ming bian: the school of mohism*, *in* RHETORIC IN ANCIENT CHINA, FIFTH TO THIRD CENTURY, B.C.E.: A COMPARISON WITH CLASSICAL GREEK RHETORIC 195–96 (1998).

[34] Quoted from the English translations of the Chinese Text Project, http://ctext.org/mozi/identification-with-the-superior-iii (accessed between February 21, 2025 and March 31, 2025). For more relevant information, see TZU MO, MO TZU: BASIC WRITINGS (Burto Watson trans., Columbia University Press, 1963).

and wisdom" is impossible.[35] According to Mozi, the management of an ideal government would naturally answer "the desires of the people"[36]; the success and failure of government policies becomes easily verifiable "by the senses of hearing and sight of the common people."[37]

Unlike Mohism, Legalism unequivocally embraced the value of disseminating information pertaining to laws and regulations. The legalist pioneer, Guan Zhong, once the prime minister of the Qi state, made the state much stronger. Guan stressed that potentates should often publicly worship mountains and pay respects to ancestral temples. Doing this would guarantee that the common people in the state follow the moral principles of propriety and piety.[38] As the prime minister of the Zheng state, Zichan did something more substantial and revolutionary than Guan in terms of governmental disclosure of information. In 536 BC, Zichan discarded the tradition of keeping laws secret, a cherished tradition of ancient Chinese monarchs for thousands of years. He engraved the full text of a criminal code on a bronze tripod vessel (*zhuxingding* 铸刑鼎) and made it public. This is the first, public statutory law in ancient China.[39]

[35] Quoted from the Chinese Text Project, http://ctext.org/mozi/identification-with-the-superior-iii (accessed between February 21, 2025 and March 31, 2025). For more relevant information, see TZU MO, MO TZU: BASIC WRITINGS (Burto Watson trans., Columbia University Press, 1963).

[36] Quoted from the Chinese Text Project, http://ctext.org/mozi/identification-with-the-superior-iii/ (accessed between February 21, 2025 and March 31, 2025). For more relevant information, see TZU MO, MO TZU: BASIC WRITINGS (Burto Watson trans., Columbia University Press, 1963).

[37] Quoted from the Chinese Text Project, http://ctext.org/mozi/anti-fatalism-i (accessed between February 21, 2025 and March 31, 2025). For more relevant literature, see TZU MO, MO TZU: BASIC WRITINGS (Burto Watson trans., Columbia University Press, 1963).

[38] Chi Zhang, *Preliminary Analysis of Legalist Communication Thought in Pre-Qin Period* [先秦法家传播思想述论], 21 (3) JOURNAL OF ANQING TEACHERS COLLEGE (SOCIAL SCIENCE EDITION) (2002).

[39] The story of Zichan making the first written law public appears in *Zuo Zhuan* or *The Chronicle of Zuo*, one of the earliest Chinese works of narrative history. For more information about how and why Zichan publicized his laws, see QIUMING ZUO, THE CHRONICLE OF ZUO (Dongrun Zhu, ed. 2007); QIUMING ZUO, *THE TSO CHUAN: SELECTIONS FROM CHINA'S OLDEST NARRATIVE HISTORY* (Burton Watson trans., Columbia University Press, 1989). For relevant literature about China's first public statutory law, see Chi Zhang, *Preliminary Analysis of Legalist Communication Thought in Pre-Qin Period* [先秦法家传播思想述论], 21 (3) JOURNAL OF ANQING TEACHERS

The noble class fiercely opposed the publication of the law, insisting that any mean person could now dispute with the judge, based on single terms or even a single Chinese character in the law. A political opponent in the government stated indignantly in a personal letter to Zichan:

> At first I considered you [as my model], but now I have ceased to do so. The ancient kings deliberated on [all the circumstances], and determined [on the punishment of crimes]; they did not make [general] laws of punishment, fearing lest it should give rise to a contentious spirit among the people... *When the people know what the exact laws are, they do not stand in awe of their superiors*. They also come to have a contentious spirit, and make their appeal to the express words, hoping peradventure to be successful in their argument. *They can no longer be managed* (emphasis added).[40]

Zichan confronted the opposition unwaveringly and responded, "I cannot accept your instructions, but I dare not forget your great kindness."[41] He reasoned that making the law public could ensure fairness and transparency of justice.[42] Zichan maintained a reputation for respecting public opinion. One day, someone proposed destroying all the village

COLLEGE (SOCIAL SCIENCE EDITION) (2002); AIJUN LIN, LEGAL PROTECTION FOR THE RIGHT TO KNOW [知情权的法律保障] 46–47 (2010); Yujun Feng, *Legal Culture in China: A Comparison to Western Law*, 15 NZACL YEARBOOK (2009).

[40] Quoted from the English translations of *Zuo Zhuan* by the Institute for Advanced Technology in the Humanities (IATH) at University of Virginia, http://www2.iath.virginia.edu/saxon/servlet/SaxonServlet?source=xwomen/texts/chunqiu.xml&style=xwomen/xsl/dynaxml.xsl&chunk.id=d2.16&toc.depth=1&toc.id=0&doc.lang=bilingual (accessed between February 21, 2025 and March 31, 2025). For more general information about the episode, see QIUMING ZUO, THE CHRONICLE OF ZUO (Dongrun Zhu, ed. 2007).

[41] Quoted from the English translations of *Zuo Zhuan* by the Institute for Advanced Technology in the Humanities (IATH) at University of Virginia, http://www2.iath.virginia.edu/saxon/servlet/SaxonServlet?source=xwomen/texts/chunqiu.xml&style=xwomen/xsl/dynaxml.xsl&chunk.id=d2.16&toc.depth=1&toc.id=0&doc.lang=bilingual (accessed between February 21, 2025 and March 31, 2025). For more general information about the episode, see QIUMING ZUO, THE CHRONICLE OF ZUO (Dongrun Zhu, ed. 2007).

[42] Chi Zhang, *Preliminary Analysis of Legalist Communication Thought in Pre-Qin Period* [先秦法家传播思想述论], 21 (3) JOURNAL OF ANQING TEACHERS COLLEGE (SOCIAL SCIENCE EDITION) (2002).

schools in the state of Zheng because many civilians gathered there to critique the conduct of the government.[43] Zichan responded:

> Why do so? If people retire morning and evening, and pass their judgment on the conduct of the government, as being good or bad, I will do what they approve of, and I will alter what they condemn;-they are my teachers. On what ground should we destroy [those schools]? I have heard that by loyal conduct and goodness enmity is diminished, but I have not heard that it can be prevented by acts of violence. It may indeed be hastily stayed for a while, but it continues like a stream that has been dammed up. If you make a great opening in the dam, there will be great injury done,-beyond our power to relieve. The best plan is to lead the water off by a small opening. [In this case] our best plan is to hear what is said and use it as a medicine.[44]

Zichan's notion of a transparent and accountable justice system and his close attention to public sentiment inspired one of his Legalist followers, Shang (Gongsun) Yang. As the prime minister of the State of Qin during the Warring States Period, Shang created a large variety of harsh laws and regulations. He believed strongly in the necessity and value of making those laws widely known.[45] When elaborating his overall strategy of making Qin strong, Shang stated openly:

> [T]here shall be no one among the government officials and people of the empire who does not know the law, and as the officials are clearly aware that the people know the laws and mandates, they

[43] DOMINIK DECLERCQ, WRITING AGAINST THE STATE: POLITICAL RHETORICS IN THIRD & FOURTH CENTURY CHINA 410–11 (1998).

[44] Quoted from the English translations of *Zuo Zhuan* by the Institute for Advanced Technology in the Humanities (IATH) at University of Virginia, http://www2.iath.virginia.edu/saxon/servlet/SaxonServlet?source=xwomen/texts/chunqiu.xml&style=xwomen/xsl/dynaxml.xsl&chunk.id=d2.15&toc.id=d2.15&doc.lang=bilingual (accessed between February 21, 2025 and March 31, 2025). For more general information about the episode, see QIUMING ZUO, THE CHRONICLE OF ZUO (Dongrun Zhu, ed. 2007).

[45] Shang Yang did not realize that he himself would become the victim of his government transparency. Shang fled to a small countryside hotel when the new king of Qin decided to kill him for revenge. When Shang begged the hotel owner to let him stay, the hotel owner declined because he knew doing so was against Shang's law to admit a guest without proper identification. QIAN SIMA, RECORDS OF THE GRAND HISTORIAN: SHANG YANG 68 (Burton Watson (Trans., Columbia University Press, 1993).

> dare not treat the people contrary to the law nor dare the people transgress the law, as they would come into conflict with the law officers.[46]

In order to warrant a legal system in which everybody knew all the laws, Shang Yang stressed that laws and rules should be made easy to understand. He said emphatically:

> [O]ne should not make laws so that only the intelligent can understand them, for the people are not all intelligent; and one should not make laws so that only the men of talent can understand them, for the people are not all talented. Therefore, did the sages, in creating laws, make them clear and easy to understand, and the terminology correct, so that stupid and wise without exception could understand them.[47]

Shang Yang believed that making laws transparent and public could have one big advantage: If the common people had basic knowledge about the laws, they would be able to identify the official who fails to follow proper procedures and then they could report him to his superiors for punishment. Official malfeasance would thus be curbed.[48]

Another Legalist, Han Fei, extended Shang Yang's promotion of legal transparency by asserting that laws were inherently transparent (*famoruxian* 法莫如显) and by defining law as a set of rules and guidelines that are created by the government, codified in books and

[46] Cited from the English translations of *The Book of Lord Shang* by the Chinese Text Project, http://ctext.org/shang-jun-shu/fixing-of-rights-and-duties (accessed between February 21, 2025 and March 31, 2025); For the print book, see YANG SHANG, THE BOOK OF LORD SHANG: A CLASSIC OF THE CHINESE SCHOOL OF LAW (Jan JuliusDuyvendak trans., The Lawbook Exchange, 2003) (260 BC).

[47] Cited from the English translations of *The Book of Lord Shang* by the Chinese Text Project, http://ctext.org/shang-jun-shu/fixing-of-rights-and-duties (accessed between February 21, 2025 and March 31, 2025). For the print book, see YANG SHANG, THE BOOK OF LORD SHANG: A CLASSIC OF THE CHINESE SCHOOL OF LAW (Jan JuliusDuyvendak trans., The Lawbook Exchange, 2003) (260 BC).

[48] Charles Sanft, *Law and Communication in Qin and Western Han China*, 53 JOURNAL OF THE ECONOMIC AND SOCIAL HISTORY OF THE ORIENT 679, 693 (2010).

documents, and made known to the ordinary people (*fazhe bianzhuzhi-tuji shezhiyuguanfu erbuzhiyubaixingzheye* 法者,编著之图籍,设之于官府,而布之于百姓者也).[49]

Legalism was the only ancient Chinese school of thought that unambiguously expressed the issue of disclosing governmental information. Legalists were stalwart proponents of judicial transparency; however, notably Legalism was highly restrictive toward disseminating information that was anti-Legalist.[50]

What is more important, Legalists drew clear boundaries for limits on official transparency. They supported wide advertisement of laws and regulations but resolutely supported secrecy for all other official matters. Han Fei, who deeply influenced Chinese emperors for many generations, regarded secrecy as a matter of life and death for rulers. Han argued that successful sovereigns were able to create an image of secrecy and mystery among his subjects and commoners (*shubuyuxian* 术不欲见).[51] When talking about how rulers should lead the country, Han stated straightforwardly:

> Therefore, the sovereign, when enforcing regulations, is as magnificent as heaven, and, when using men, *is as mysterious as the spirit*. For heaven cannot be confuted, and the spirit cannot be harassed by human beings. ...The lord of men has the duty of *devoting his attention to secrecy*. For this reason, when his delight is revealed, his conduct will be slighted; when his anger is revealed, his prestige will fall to the ground. The words of the intelligent sovereign, therefore, are blockaded in such wise that they are *not communicable* outwards

[49] Quoted from Difficulties III, *Hanfeizi*, the Chinese Text Project, https://ctext.org/hanfeizi/nan-san (accessed between February 21, 2025 and March 31, 2025). For the print book, see FEI TZU HAN, HAN FEI TZU: BASIC WRITINGS (Burton Watson trans., Columbia University Press, 1964).

[50] Chi Zhang, *Preliminary Analysis of Legalist Communication Thought in Pre-Qin Period* [先秦法家传播思想述论], 21 (3) JOURNAL OF ANQING TEACHERS COLLEGE (SOCIAL SCIENCE EDITION) (2002).

[51] Quoted from Difficulties III, Hanfeizi, the Chinese Text Project, https://ctext.org/hanfeizi/nan-san (accessed between February 21, 2025 and March 31, 2025). For the print book, see FEI TZU HAN, HAN FEI TZU: BASIC WRITINGS (Burton Watson trans., Columbia University Press, 1964). For the full text of Feizi Han's writings, see FEI TZU HAN, HAN FEI TZU: BASIC WRITINGS (Burton Watson trans., Columbia University Press, 1964).

and are kept in *such secrecy* that they are unknowable (emphasis added).[52]

Governmental Informational Policies in Imperial China

The Qin Dynasty (221 BC-206 BC)

The Qin Dynasty united China in 221 BC and created a centralized bureaucratic government. Qing Shi Huang, the first emperor in Chinese history, adopted Legalism as the official government philosophy and suppressed all other philosophic schools including Confucianism and Mohism by burying alive hundreds of non-Legalist scholars and burning books of non-Legalist philosophical viewpoints and intellectual subjects.[53]

Rulers in the Qin Dynasty made large volumes of laws and regulations and publicized[54] them (not surprisingly) through a "vertical information communication system,"[55] originating from the central level and extending to the prefecture and county levels. Such a communication system was possible through building roads connecting major cities across the country and linking with the capital Xianyang.[56] According to the laws at the time, archiving and managing all important official documents and records were *yushidaifu* (御史大夫), the vice minister who supervised

52 Quoted from the English translations of *Han Feizi* by the Institute for Advanced Technology in the Humanities (IATH) at University of Virginia, http://www2.iath.virginia.edu/saxon/servlet/SaxonServlet?source=xwomen/texts/hanfei.xml&style=xwomen/xsl/dynaxml.xsl&chunk.id=d2.48&toc.depth=1&toc.id=d2.20&doc.lang=bilingual (last accessed between February 21, 2025 and March 31, 2025). For the full text of Feizi Han's writings, see FEI TZU HAN, HAN FEI TZU: BASIC WRITINGS (Burton Watson trans., Columbia University Press, 1964).

53 1 THE CAMBRIDGE HISTORY OF CHINA: THE CH'IN AND HAN EMPIRES, 221 B.C. - A.D. 220 (Denis Crispin Twitchett, Michael Loewe & John King Fairbank eds., 1986).

54 For what motivated the rulers of the Qin Dynasty to publicize laws and how those legal codes were made known among the commoners, see Charles Sanft, *Law and Communication in Qin and Western Han China*, 53 JOURNAL OF THE ECONOMIC AND SOCIAL HISTORY OF THE ORIENT 679, 679–11 (2010).

55 Qinglin Li, "The Constitution and Narrative of Imperial Autocracy-on the Discourse and the Mode of Communication in Imperial China" [皇权专制的建构和叙事] (2006) (unpublished Ph.D. diss., the Communication University of China), at 44.

56 Ying Zou, *Postal System and Communication in Ancient China* [中国古代邮驿制度与传播], 23 JOURNAL OF XIANNING COLLEGE 4, 99 (2003).

all officials in the country.[57] Execution was the penalty for any individual, according to the Qin laws, who leaked classified official documents or other government secrets.

If ignoring publication of laws, then a safe conclusion is that a cloak of secrecy shrouded the whole empire. Two incidents illustrate the government's extreme clandestineness: The first concerns the Legalist promoter Li Si who, when young, was an ambitious minor functionary.

When Li became the influential prime minister of Qin, he enjoyed huge fanfare with his convoy whenever he was on inspection tours. One day when seeing Li's ostentatious convoy, the supreme leader Qin Shi Huang felt affronted and said something critical about the prime minister's pomposity. Secretly, reports conveyed the emperor's remarks to Li, and subsequently, when the supreme leader saw Li's convoy, it had become more modest and restrained. Qin Shi Huang realized his eunuchs[58] must have divulged the statements, and the sovereign launched an investigation that yielded no results. Finally, the ruthless ruler executed all the eunuchs who had been present on the day of his remarks.[59] By doing this, the monarch made sure that no one would dare to leak information again.

Another tragic incident of official secrecy changed the course of Chinese history. When Qin Shi Huang died suddenly on an inspection tour, the news remained secret for many days. Carts containing rotten fish prevented people from noticing the foul smell of the emperor's body, which was decomposing quickly in the summertime heat.[60] By delaying announcement of the death, Li Si and a few other high officials staged a successful coup d'état. They falsified the imperial decree, forced the eldest

[57] Wenying Liu, *An Evaluation of History of Chinese Archives* [中国档案事业发展史探析], 1 JOURNAL OF SICHUAN CULTURAL RELIC 66 (2002).

[58] Eunuchs were men who were castrated, usually as children, and used in many ancient Asian and Middle Eastern courts to help ensure their loyalty as servants, minor governmental functionaries, and as harem guards.

[59] QIAN SIM, RECORDS OF THE GRAND HISTORIAN: QIN DYNASTY (Burton Watson trans., Columbia University Press, 1993) (104 BC-91 BC).

[60] QIAN SIMA, THE FIRST EMPEROR: SELECTIONS FROM THE HISTORICAL RECORDS 15–20, 82, 99 (K. E. Brashier ed. Raymond Dawson trans., Oxford University Press, 2007) (104 BC-91 BC).

son of the emperor to commit suicide, and helped another son rise to the throne.[61]

The Han Dynasty (206 BC-220 AD)

The Qin Dynasty lasted no more than two decades. When Qin quickly collapsed, the replacement was the Han Dynasty. Since Legalism had a poor reputation in the Qin Dynasty for being excessively cruel and merciless, Han rulers adopted significantly revised imperial Confucianism[62] as the official state philosophy, as did most other successive dynasties. "Dismiss the hundred schools, revere only the Confucian (*bachubaijia duzunrushu* 罢黜百家 独尊儒术)," according to a Chinese proverb.[63] In reality, a combination of Confucian ideals in public life and Legalist principles in governance was the norm for Chinese emperors, which is called "Outside Confucian, Inside Legalist (*wairuneifa* 外儒内法)."[64]

As mentioned earlier, Confucius and his followers deemphasized the value of disseminating government information, and unsurprisingly, Han established a highly secretive government, which hoarded official documents in ancestral temples (*zongmiao* 宗庙). Those documents were carefully guarded by a government functionary responsible for the imperial library *(lantai lingshi* 兰台令史*)*.[65] Similar to documents, emperors'

[61] QIAN SIMA, THE FIRST EMPEROR: SELECTIONS FROM THE HISTORICAL RECORDS 15–20, 82, 99 (K. E. Brashier ed. Raymond Dawson trans., Oxford University Press, 2007) (104 BC-91 BC).

[62] The traditional Confucianism that flourished during the Zhou Dynasty was revised by the Han scholar Dong Zhongshu. Dong integrated Legalism, Moism, School of Yin-Yang, and many other philosophies into the new Confucianism. Robin R. Wang, *Dong Zhongshu's Transformation of "Yin-Yang" Theory and Contesting of Gender Identity*, 55 PHILOSOPHY EAST AND WEST 209, 209–31 (April 2005).

[63] XINZHONG YAO, AN INTRODUCTION TO CONFUCIANISM 83 (2000).

[64] Although Legalism ceased to be an independent school of thought since the Han Dynasty, it still played a major role in government. Legalist ideas merged with the mainstream Confucianism. Imperial rulers since the Han Dynasty used the Confucian exterior to unify people's minds and mediate the harsh Legalist regimentation of people's behavior. Some scholars termed this governing approach "externally Confucian, internally Legalist" [*wairuneifa rubiaofali* 外儒内法 儒表法里]. WIEBKE DENECKE, THE DYNAMICS OF MASTERS LITERATURE: EARLY CHINESE THOUGHT FROM CONFUCIUS TO HAN FEIZI (2011); XINZHONG YAO, AN INTRODUCTION TO CONFUCIANISM (2000).

[65] Wenying Liu, *An Evaluation of History of Chinese Archives* [中国档案事业发展史探析], 1 JOURNAL OF SICHUAN CULTURAL RELIC (2002); Qingxin Gong, *Research on*

health conditions were state secrets. Liu Bang, the first emperor of Han, died in his palace but the empress made no announcement until four days afterward. The delay was the consequence of a failed attempt to kill all the generals who helped Liu Bang's ascension to the throne.[66]

Leaking highly confidential official information like the death of an emperor was a felony. Violators and their family members could face execution. Even divulging less sensitive information could result in catastrophic consequences. During the reign of Emperor Yuan, a county magistrate Zhu Yun faced accusations of killing innocent people. The emperor heard the case in secret. The magistrate's friend, who was an assistant minister of justice at the court of Han, reported the accusation to Zhu before the emperor rendered a verdict. Following the minister's suggestion, the magistrate wrote a self-criticizing letter to the emperor to seek sympathy, resulting in the minister's arrest for leaking the "inside information (*xieloushengzhongyu* 漏泄省中语)."[67] In another development, Emperor Yuan planned to kill General of Chariots and Cavalry Zhang Anshi. In a private conversation, a royal instructor persuaded the emperor to stop the killing and the emperor agreed. The instructor's son made this conversation public while drinking with his father's political enemy and ultimately committed suicide for fear of punishment from leaking confidential information at the imperial court.[68]

Origins of Chinese Government and University-Owned Archives [中国档案、中国高校档案研究], 4 JOURNAL OF GUANZI 113 (2006); Shiping Xu, *An Overview of Ancient Preservation Technology Used for Chinese Archives* [中国古代档案保护技术概览], A08 JOURNAL OF ARCHIVES SCIENCE STUDY SUPPLEMENT (1996).

[66] Cited from *Records of the Grand Historian* [*siyuejiachen gaozubengchanglegong siribufasang* 四月甲辰 高祖崩长乐宫 四日不发丧]. For more relevant information about the incident, see QIAN SIMA, RECORDS OF THE GRAND HISTORIAN: HAN DYNASTY (Burton Watson trans., Columbia University Press, 1993) (104 BC-91 BC).

[67] Quoted from the Chinese Text Project, http://ctext.org/dictionary.pl?if=en&id=66715&remap=gb (accessed between February 21, 2025 and March 31, 2025). For more information about how government officials during Han Dynasty guarded state secrets, see GU BAN, BOOK OF HAN [汉书] (Shigu Yan Annotated, Zhonghua Press, 2000) (83 AD).

[68] Quoted from the Chinese Text Project, http://ctext.org/dictionary.pl?if=en&id=66836&remap=gb (accessed between February 21, 2025 and March 31, 2025). For more information about how government officials during Han Dynasty guarded state secrets, see GU BAN, BOOK OF HAN [汉书] (Shigu Yan Annotated, Zhonghua Press, 2000) (83 AD).

Since the court of Han penalized numerous officials for leaking state secrets, for self-protection, bureaucrats followed a set of precautionary measures. For example, officials in key decision-making positions always remained silent in public.[69] Functionaries preferred to write confidential messages under seal rather than convey oral messages, which they felt to be less secure. Administrators handling confidential matters would not conduct business at home nor would they allow family visits to their offices.

Government secrecy, however, did not eliminate internal communication among officials at various levels. On the contrary, the court of Han developed the internal communication system within the bureaucracy. Information flow among bureaucrats throughout the country was frequent and vibrant. Official documents constantly disseminated by couriers who occupied nearly 30,000 stage-houses built along major postal roads, running as long as 32,000 kilometers in total. The responsibility of one of the nine ministers at Han's court was the proper functioning of this gigantic communication system.[70]

External communication between the Han bureaucracy and commoners remained limited because Confucianism discouraged proactive disclosure of official activities and Legalism also convinced monarchs to practice secrecy. However, Han emperors followed the Legalist practice

[69] Kong Guang was a model official in guarding government secrets. As the Chief of Secretariat at the court of Emperor Cheng of Han Dynasty, Kong was the custodian of all confidential official information. However, whenever he visited his hometown and chatted with his family and relatives, Kong was sufficiently cautious and secretive to avoid a mention of his duties. Someone curious asked Kong what kinds of trees grew in the royal court in the capital, Chang'an. Kong did not respond to this inquiry; instead, he remained silent for a while and digressed to another subject. Yan Xia, *Government Secret Leaking and Protection in Ancient China* [古代官场的泄密与保密], 1 JOURNAL OF REPORTER'S NOTES (2011). The Kong Guang story appears in *Book of Han* [*muriguixiu xiongdiqiziyanyu zhongbujichaoshengzhengshi huowenguang wenshishengzhongshujiehemuye guangheibuying gengdayitayu qibuxierushi* 沐日归休,兄弟妻子燕语,终不及朝省政事。或问光:"温室省中树皆何木也?"光嘿不应,更答以它语,其不泄如是], quoted from the Chinese Text Project, http://ctext.org/han-shu/kuang-zhang-kong-ma-zhuan/ens (accessed between February 21, 2025 and March 31, 2025). For more information about this episode, see GU BAN, BOOK OF HAN [汉书] (Shigu Yan Annotated, Zhonghua Press, 2000) (83 AD).

[70] Ying Zou, *Postal System and Communication in Ancient China* [中国古代邮驿制度与传播], 23 JOURNAL OF XIANNING COLLEGE 4, 99 (2003).

of publicizing government orders, announcements, and laws.[71] Without the modern luxury of telephones, cables, newspapers, magazines, radio, television, and the Internet, Han governmental officials adopted four methods to ensure that newly announced royal orders and recently codified laws reached maximum exposure in the empire.[72]

The first method of information dissemination was *shubi* (书壁), meaning that writing down the information on buildings' walls in conspicuous places for everyone to see. The second approach *guabi* (挂壁) was copying official information onto wooden boards or silk and hanging these objects in highly visible places.[73]

Xuanjiang (宣讲) was another approach for disclosing information. Government officials would meet with people on the streets or conduct door-to-door outreach to ordinary people in an area. During the face-to-face encounter, the officers would announce, interpret, or even read word by word some government documents. Han's officials became

[71] Although Legalism ceased to be an independent school of thought since the Han Dynasty, it still played a major role in government. Legalist ideas merged with the mainstream Confucianism. Imperial rulers since the Han Dynasty used the Confucian exterior to unify people's minds and mediate the harsh Legalist regimentation of people's behavior. Some scholars termed this governing approach "externally Confucian, internally Legalist" [*wairuneifa rubiaofali* 外儒内法 儒表法里]. WIEBKE DENECKE, THE DYNAMICS OF MASTERS LITERATURE: EARLY CHINESE THOUGHT FROM CONFUCIUS TO HAN FEIZI (2011); XINZHONG YAO, AN INTRODUCTION TO CONFUCIANISM (2000).

[72] Chunping Huang, *Information Dissemination Methods in Han Dynasty* [汉代信息发布手段探析], 18 (3) JOURNAL OF ZHEJIANG INSTITUTE OF MEDIA AND COMMUNICATIONS 7, 7–11 (June 2011); Chunping Huang, *Release of News in Han Dynasty-Looked from the Aspect of Material of Bamboo Slips* [从出土简牍看汉帝国中央的信息发布], 4 JOURNAL OF JOURNALISM & COMMUNICATION (2006); Charles Sanft, *Law and Communication in Qin and Western Han China*, 53 JOURNAL OF THE ECONOMIC AND SOCIAL HISTORY OF THE ORIENT 679 (2010).

[73] Following the Zhou Dynasty tradition, Han rulers built watchtowers on either side of their palace gates and designated these buildings as places of public announcement. Public declarations and newly passed laws occupied noticeboards for the public to see. According to the law, in order to show respect for such an imperially designated area, people riding carriages should immediately dismount and walk, and pedestrians should walk by quickly [*cheguozhexia buguozhequ*车过者下 步过者趋]. Quoted and translated from Guoxue.com, http://www.guoxue123.com/shibu/0101/00hhsz/115.htm (accessed between February 21, 2025 and March 31, 2025). For more information about the use of palace gates as places of public announcements, see YE FAN, BOOK OF LATER HAN [后汉书] (Zhejiang Ancient Books Publishing House, 2000) (432 AD).

increasingly involved in the writing styles of documents.[74] The advantage of having an interpersonal communication between officials and their subjects was significant: Bureaucrats could explain governmental policies and have immediate feedback. The fourth method was *chuanyue* (传阅), meaning some public-intended official documents would neither be bundled nor sealed. They would be displayed in conspicuous places for all common people to read.[75]

The Tang Dynasty (618 AD-907 AD)

Both official secrecy and transparency developed in the Tang Dynasty, one of the most powerful dynasties in China's history. Rulers created a comprehensive and multifaceted system for dealing with official documents and archives, and laws on guarding state secrets became increasingly detailed and harsh. Conversely, the inception of the court gazette made possible wide sharing of official information among central and local government agencies.

Unlike rulers of the Qin and Han dynasties, those of the Tang Dynasty established a nationwide archival system. Regional and carefully preserved archived documents,[76] including documents of foreign intelligence, war expeditions, domestic rebellions, and other military and public security issues, were highly confidential.[77] According to the *Tang Code* (*Tanglv* 唐

[74] Shuya Wang, *Evolution of Writing Style of Official Documents from Pre-Qin to Han Dynasty* [试论先秦到汉代的公文文气演变], 2 JOURNAL OF DATA OF CULTURE AND EDUCATION 223 (June 2010).

[75] Chunping Huang, *Information Dissemination Methods in Han Dynasty* [汉代信息发布手段探析], 18 (3) JOURNAL OF ZHEJIANG INSTITUTE OF MEDIA AND COMMUNICATIONS 7, 7–11 (June 2011).

[76] Ruxia Fan, *Historical Characteristics of Archiving in Ancient China* [我国古代档案工作的历史特点], 1 JOURNAL OF FUJIAN NORMAL UNIVERSITY (SOCIAL SCIENCE EDITION) (2000); Qingxin Gong, *Research on Origins of Chinese Government and University-Owned Archives* [中国档案、中国高校档案研究], 4 JOURNAL OF GUANZI 113 (2006).

[77] Ruxia Fan, *Historical Characteristics of Archiving in Ancient China* [我国古代档案工作的历史特点], 1 JOURNAL OF FUJIAN NORMAL UNIVERSITY (SOCIAL SCIENCE EDITION) (2000); Qingxin Gong, *Research on Origins of Chinese Government and University-Owned Archives* [中国档案、中国高校档案研究], 4 JOURNAL OF GUANZI 113 (2006).

律),[78] anyone leaking such information could face a wide variety of penalties ranging from caning, demotion, deposition, imprisonment, hanging, decapitation, and family deportation, depending upon the severity of the crimes.[79] Anyone who stole and/or opened sealed documents without proper authorization would face similar penalties.

Restrictions on access to confidential information were common; however, the birth of "*dibao*" (邸报) or "*jinzouyuanzhuang*" (进奏院状), the first newspaper in China, in fact the world,[80] made information flow in the Tang bureaucracy smoother and more efficient. Officials from the Di (邸), liaison offices of local governments in the capital of Chang'an, gathered information from the court and various central agencies, then regularly compiled and published such information in a newspaper-like document. Officeholders in the capital and provincial commanders[81] received the periodicals through a highly developed postal system.[82]

[78] The *Tang Code* was a penal code combining Legalist and Confucian interpretations of law and became a model for later penal codes in China and other countries in East Asia. For more scholarly discussions of the *Tang Code*, see JACQUES GERNET, A HISTORY OF CHINESE CIVILIZATION 801 (1996); 1 THE TANG CODE: GENERAL PRINCIPLES (Wallace Johnson, trans., 1979).

[79] Zhuo Yuan, *Confidentiality of Ancient Chinese Official Documents* [管窥古代公文的保密制度] 02 × JOURNAL OF LANTAI WORLD 57, 57–58 (2007); Shusen Yang, *Secrets Guarding in Ancient China and Official Seal Management* [中国古代保密工作和印玺管理], 3 JOURNAL OF OFFICE ADMINISTRATION (2007).

[80] Two original copies of the Tang *Dibao* were discovered in 1900 in the Mogao Caves of Gansu Province. Some scholars argued that the first publication of *Dibao* was during the Han Dynasty, but no archeological evidence supports this contention. BARBARBA MITTLER, A NEWSPAPER FOR CHINA?: POWER, IDENTITY AND CHANGE IN SHANGHAI'S NEWS MEDIA, 1872–1912 177 (2004); Fen Zhao, *Comparing Official Gazettes with Short Reports in Ancient China* [中国古代官报与小报的比较], 3 JOURNAL OF YOUTH JOURNALIST (2010). Most Chinese scholars studying origins of Chinese newspapers maintained that categorizing the *Dibao* as one type of newspaper is appropriate. Hanqi Fang of Renmin University of China is one of them. HANQI FANG, A HISTORY OF CHINESE JOURNALISM [中国新闻事业通史] (1992). But a few other Chinese scholars such as Jitian Liao disagreed. Jitian Liao, I*s Dibao Ancient Newspaper? Reexamination of Evolution of Ancient Chinese Newspapers* [邸报是古代报纸吗? 中国古代报纸发展线索再梳理], 1 JOURNAL OF JOURNALISM & COMMUNICATION 12, 12–20 (2010).

[81] Lizi Liu, *Study of Dibao and Government Information Dissemination in Ancient China* [浅谈邸报与我国古代政务信息的公布], 7 JOURNAL OF LANTAI WORLD 49, 49–50 (2009).

[82] A Tang poem expressed efficiency of the Tang postal system: "One courier station after another, the courier horse runs like a shooting star. At dawn it departs in Xianyang. At dusk, it arrives in Long Mountain." [*yiyiguoyiyi yiqiruxingliu pingmingfaxianyang*

The newspaper focused on imperial activities and decrees, official policies, regulations, official promotions, demotions, and even military and political intelligence. Although the central government was not involved in the production and circulation of the publication, the *Dibao* was functionally the official court gazette and allowed no access to anyone outside the government.

Tang emperors further developed the system of imperial censorate, a supervisory central agency responsible for preventing corruption and malfeasance. The agency consisted of junior officials who excelled at national civil service examinations. Promotion was possible for them if they worked diligently or corrected governmental wrongs.[83] Those highly educated remonstrators' duties included identifying officials' misdeeds by constantly recording official decisions and correspondence and criticizing officials, even the emperors.[84] The imperial censorate system of Emperor Taizong of Tang (599 AD-649 AD) even inspired Anders Chydenius, a Swedish clergyman and a member of Swedish Parliament, to persuade the Swedish government to adopt the *Freedom of Press Act* in 1766, the world's first freedom of information legislation. In 1766, Mr. Chydenius published a book detailing how his inspiration for a law on freedom of information arose from the policies of Taizong. In the eyes of Chydenius, Taizong created checks and balances on governmental power by ensuring freedom of information.[85]

*mujilongshantou*一驿过一驿, 驿骑如星流。平明发咸阳,暮及陇山头] (Xianyang is more than 124 miles from Long Mountain). In 755 A.D., the general and regional commander An Lushan rebelled against the Tang Dynasty. Six days later, the court of Tang in Chang'an, 932 miles away from Fanyang where the rebellion began, received the report. This efficiency would not be possible without the help of the national courier system. Ying Zou, *Postal System and Communication in Ancient China* [中国古代邮驿制度与传播], 23 JOURNAL OF XIANNING COLLEGE 4, 100 (2003).

83 Actually, no censors received promotions to very high administrative ranks. Tang emperors feared that censors would be less critical of the government if they had high official status.

84 Charles O. Hucker, *The Traditional Chinese Censorate and the New Peking Regime*, XLV THE AMERICAN POLITICAL SCIENCE REVIEW 1041(1951); BAICHUAN TAO, THE CHINESE OMBUDSMAN AND CONTROL SYSTEM (1971); Cang-ze Hu, *The Change of the Supervisory System of the Tang Dynasty* [唐代监察体制的变革], 3 JOURNAL OF FUJIAN TEACHERS UNIVERSITY (PHILOSOPHY AND SOCIAL SCIENCES EDITION) (2001).

85 Stephen Lamble, *Freedom of information, a Finnish Clergyman's Gift to Democracy*, 97 FREEDOM OF INFORMATION REVIEW 2, 2–8 (February 2002); John M. Ackerman & Irma E. Sandoval-Ballesteros, *The Global Explosion of Freedom of Information Laws*,

The system of imperial court diaries (*qijuzhu* 起居注) during the peak of Tang Dynasty was probably even more inspiring than the imperial censorate system to Chydenius because the former was so similar to the concept and practices of a standard freedom of information law that we see today. In order to hold the emperor accountable, two writers of the imperial court diaries (both of them were righteous scholar-officials from Department of Imperial Secretariats or Department of Chancellors and later from Hanlin Academy) would go wherever the monarch goes and write down in diaries whatever the emperor did and spoke. Diaries were written on a daily basis to record a wide range of the emperor's activities, ranging from important meetings with his advisors, trips to ancestral temples for sacrifice offerings, inspection tours to faraway towns, to how he spent his leisure time including when and where he slept with which concubine for how long. Diary writers were allowed to sit or walk very close to the sovereign so the ruler could be seen and heard very clearly. Most importantly, the emperor was not allowed to see the contents of the diary, ensuring that the writers could perform their job duties without fear or favor. Emperor Taizong tried several times to access the diaries but was not successful. He said to the writer who was one of his beloved ministers: "If I did something bad or wrong, are you going to write it down in the diary?" The writer's answer was a definite YES. Taizong's worries were reasonable because he knew that imperial court diaries will be used by his ministers to write about veritable records (*huangdishilu* 皇帝实录) of him. Most importantly, court historians of the next dynasty would write a history book about his dynasty and lots of raw materials of that book would come from his dynasty's court diaries and veritable records. As soon as the book was written, it will be publicized by the succeeding dynasty to the maximum extent via various communication channels, and intellectuals across the country will read it as the official narrative of what had happened in the preceding dynasty.[86]

58 ADMINISTRATION LAW REVIEW 85 (2006); K. M. SHRIVASTAVA, THE RIGHT TO INFORMATION: A GLOBAL PERSPECTIVE 2–3 (2009).

[86] For detailed analysis of the imperial court diary system in ancient China, see BIN LI, COMMUNICATION, CIVILIZATION AND CHINA: DISCOVERING THE TANG DYNASTY (618–907) (2020); DENIS TWITCHETT, THE INNER PALACE DIARY (NEI CH'I-CHÜ CHU) (1986); Peng Zheng, *Evolution of Imperial Court Diaries During Tang and Song Dynasties: A Perspective of Imperial Power Abuse* [唐宋时期起居注的变迁—以皇权渗透为研究视角], SONG HISTORY RESEARCH COLLECTION 2 [宋史研究论丛] (2022), pp. 3–15; Moyupianpian, *What Did Imperial Court Diaries Do and Why Even Emperors Didn't Have the*

The imperial court diary system emerged in the Han Dynasty and was institutionalized in the Tang Dynasty. Emperor Taizong contributed to the development of the system, and he also damaged the system to some degree. He was finally able to see what was written in the court diary, although what he saw was hugely modified, with lots of negative and potentially offensive material being deleted by diary writers. By forcing his advisors to give him access to the court diaries, Taizong had created a dangerous precedent. Emperors after him in China all wanted to see the contents of the diaries. Although the diary system survived until the end of the Qing Dynasty in 1911, the system itself became increasingly ineffective in holding emperors accountable. The imperial censorate system was luckier. It was strengthened in the Tang Dynasty because Taizong was so willing to accept criticism from his advisors and he tried his best to protect his remonstrators. When one of his most important remonstrators Wei Zheng died, Taizong was so doleful that he cried and said to his ministers:

> With a bronze mirror, one can see whether he is properly dressed;
> with history as a mirror, one can understand the rise and fall of a nation;
> with men as a mirror, one can see the right from the wrong.
> Now I've lost my faithful mirror by the death of Wei Zheng.[87]

The differences between the information policy of Taizong and modern concept of freedom of information are significant. Taizong did not allow the public to access court diaries, veritable records, and other governmental documents. Nor did he feel an obligation to proactively disclose what his government was doing. Only a limited number of privileged officials had access to court diaries, veritable records, and other government-held records and documents. Regardless, the Tang government was arguably one of the most transparent in imperial China. Taizong's point of view on criticism from his subjects is still noteworthy from the perspective of free flow of information. The emperor knew that

Right to See Them ["起居注"是用来干什么的,为何连皇帝都无权拿来看], SOHU, January 15, 2019, https://www.sohu.com/a/289192159_209689 (accessed between February 21, 2025 and March 31, 2025).

[87] Quoted and translated from Guoxue.com, Beijing, China, *available at* http://www.guoxue.com/shibu/24shi/oldtangsu/jts_075.htm (accessed between February 21, 2025 and March 31, 2025). For more information about this episode, see *A Biography of Wei Zheng*, *in* OLD BOOK OF TANG [旧唐书] (Xu Liu ed., Zhonghua Press, 2002) (945 AD).

even the sovereign could be misguided or fooled by government secrecy. Subjects around him reported only good news of the country to him. That is why he tried to maintain access to people who opposed his policies and reported bad news occasionally. By doing this, Taizong became more informed and thus made more sound policies. Taizong's frustration with the death of remonstrators like Wei Zheng is understandable because his ability to access all kinds of information was weakened. Of course, he should be frustrated with his failure to control his own desire to see court diaries as well, as that failure contributed to decreased credibility and effectiveness of court diaries as a watchdog tool to check the monarch's power.

The Song Dynasty (960 AD-1279 AD)

Government agencies, at the central and local levels, continued to archive official documents and records in the Song Dynasty. The dynasty established, across the nation, 11 imperial libraries[88] with stack rooms filled with wooden shelves and cabinets (*jiageku* 架阁库) to preserve various archives.[89] Throughout the Song Dynasty, emperors defended the country from invasions of northern nomadic tribes. Official information regarding national security was highly protected state secrets. Officials who drafted royal decrees were often reminded of maintaining confidentiality, but enforcement was less rigorous than that of the Tang Dynasty. Many recorded cases detail officials' punishments for leaking military

[88] Shiping Xu, *An Overview of Ancient Preservation Technology Used for Chinese Archives* [中国古代档案保护技术概览], A08 JOURNAL OF ARCHIVES SCIENCE STUDY SUPPLEMENT (1996).

[89] Jinyu Wang, *Research on Central Archive of Southern Song Dynasty* [南宋六部架阁库研究], 6 JOURNAL OF ARCHIVES AND CONSTRUCTION (2001).

secrets or drafting official documents at home.[90] The haphazard enforcement of laws controlling state secrets could explain Song's frequent military setbacks when confronting northern invaders.

Internal communication between Song emperors, advisors, and local bureaucrats developed further, but more striking is the new height for external communication between the bureaucracy and common people during the same period. In addition to standardized mechanisms for information exchange established between emperors, major advisors, and local bureaucrats, several largely ignored communication channels are worthy of mention. First, Song emperors used the imperial lecture (*jingyan* 经筵) system to gather information from within the bureaucracy and beyond. Under the system, highly educated scholars, many of them were high-ranking officials, lectured, one-on-one, with the emperors in the royal palace, assisted rulers' better understanding of Confucian classics, and contributed to sound decisions.[91] The relaxed, informal, and private atmosphere of the lectures allowed emperors to gain information efficiently.

Second, the emperors in the Song Dynasty often used eunuchs[92] and other private groups to gather information. Eunuchs, with some exceptions, were generally more loyal to the emperors than officials and were less influenced by internal political struggles, thus affording the advantage of less prejudice and more disinterest in information gathering. By

[90] Two anecdotes illustrate the lax enforcement of laws regarding state secrets in the Song dynasty. Emperor Huizong of Song appointed Zen Bu as prime minister. Zen's brother, the imperial speechwriter, wrote the announcement. Zen's 9-year-old daughter overheard the news when she was playing at her uncle's house. She came home and said to her father, "Dad, you will be the prime minister tomorrow!" Criticism of an imperial official at the court of Emperor Shenzong of Song resulted in a loss of imperial trust from writing, at home, his memorial to impeach the prime minister, the brother's access to the document, and the brother's reporting the proposed impeachment to the minister. Records of both anecdotes first appear in Huizhulu [挥麈录], a popular Chinese historical text authored by Song Dynasty scholar, Mingqing Wang. For more information about these anecdotes, see MINGQING WANG, WAVING THE DUSTER [挥麈录] (2009).

[91] Chen Dong, *An Introduction of JingYan in Ancient China* [中国古代经筵概论], 1 QILU JOURNAL (2008); Huayu Wang, "A Study on the Emperors' Information Channels in Song Dynasty" [宋朝君主的信息渠道研究] (2008) (unpublished Ph.D. diss., Peking University).

[92] Eunuchs were men who were castrated, usually as children, and used in many ancient Asian and Middle Eastern courts to help ensure their loyalty as servants, minor governmental functionaries and as harem guards.

using eunuchs as "ears and eyes," Song emperors established an easily controlled and secret informational channel.[93]

Third, the growth of the court gazette enhanced the flow of official information. Starting with the Song Dynasty, the *Dibao* became the court's official gazette as the *Di*[94] became a part of the central government, and the appointment of its officials was direct from the court. The rough draft of the newspaper's reports went to high officials for review prior to printing, publication, and transmission. Restraints disallowed the court gazette to publish news items on major natural disasters, military secrets, imperial confidential matters, and memorials requiring clearance for publication.[95]

The Song *Dibao* lost the editorial independence enjoyed by its Tang predecessors, but the newspaper expanded its content to include not only news of the emperors and the central government but also of the regional and local governments.[96] The gazette, at the beginning, published and circulated bimonthly, gradually became a weekly or even daily publication. The paper's readership expanded rapidly, reaching not only officials above the prefectural (*zhoufu* 州府) level but also scholars who held no government positions.[97] Allowing scholars access to the official gazette was a remarkable advancement in terms of ensuring commoners' greater access to governmental information.

Fourth, "short reports" (*xiaobao* 小报) began to appear and profoundly influenced the way officials and the masses accessed official information. Short reports were newspapers similar to the court gazette; however, the two were sharply different in many ways: Short reports were private and unauthorized news sheets, owned by numerous businesses and the reports contained similar information, but rumors, government

[93] Huayu Wang, "A Study on the Emperors' Information Channels in Song Dynasty" [宋朝君主的信息渠道研究] (2008) (unpublished Ph.D. diss., Peking University).

[94] The *Di* was a liaison office of local governments in the capitals.

[95] Li Dong, *News Censorship in Song Dynasty* [浅析宋代新闻管制], 10 JOURNAL OF MAGNIFICENT WRITING 7, 11 (2010).

[96] Biao You, *Written Language Delivery Between Government and Locality of Song Dynasty* [宋代朝廷与地方之间的"文字"传递—围绕邸报及其相关问题而展开], 28(3) JOURNAL OF HEBEI UNIVERSITY (PHILOSOPHY AND SOCIAL SCIENCE EDITION) (2003).

[97] Lizi Liu, *Study of Dibao and Government Information Dissemination in Ancient China* [浅谈邸报与我国古代政务信息的公布], 7 JOURNAL OF LANTAI WORLD 49, 49–50 (2009).

secrets, and any information considered taboo for the official gazette also appeared. Short reports contained the court's news more rapidly than the gazette because the censorship process did not apply, and secret use of the official postal network was the channel for distribution. Officials and the public regularly read the publications.[98] Actually, people often read short reports first and then the court gazette second (*yixiaobaoweixian eryichaobaoweichang* 以小报为先, 而以朝报为常) in order to better understand the machinations of government. When reading official gazettes, court officials and county magistrates often exclaimed, "Oh! The short report on this has already arrived!".[99]

The Song government's authorities suppressed short reports as illegal and unauthentic publications because they interfered with the official sanctions of communications within the bureaucracy and between the center and the provinces. However, such publications survived and prospered in the capital and outlying areas due to the newsworthiness, timeliness, and unlimited supply of news sources. Some government officials leaked news for remuneration or to attack political enemies; some spies gained income from regularly gathering leaked reports from government offices.[100] Short reports, although shunned by rulers, provided Chinese people unprecedented opportunities to know if their "father-mother officials" (*fumuguan* 父母官)[101] were truly benevolent parental figures as portrayed in an ideal Confucian society.

[98] Fen Zhao, *Comparing Official Gazettes with Short Reports in Ancient China* [中国古代官报与小报的比较], 3 JOURNAL OF YOUTH JOURNALIST (2010); Hilde De Weerdt, *"Court Gazettes" and "Short Reports": Official Views and Unofficial Readings of Court News*, 27(2) JOURNAL OF CHINESE STUDIES 167 (2009); Dan Xie, Xiaotong Qi & Qingling Xiao, *Short Reports in Ancient China* [浅析中国古代小报], 2 JOURNAL OF MEDIA STUDIES (2008).

[99] Hilde De Weerdt, *"Court Gazettes" and "Short Reports": Official Views and Unofficial Readings of Court News*, 27(2) JOURNAL OF CHINESE STUDIES 167, 177 (2009).

[100] Hilde De Weerdt, *"Court Gazettes" and "Short Reports": Official Views and Unofficial Readings of Court News*, 27(2) JOURNAL OF CHINESE STUDIES 167, 167–200 (2009).

[101] According to Confucianism, filial piety should convert to loyalty for the emperor and his government. That is why traditional Chinese often called the emperor or even his officials as "fathers of all" or "father-mother officials." ROBERT G. WESSON, THE IMPERIAL ORDER 178 (1967).

The Ming Dynasty (1368 AD-1644 AD) and the Qing Dynasty (1644 AD-1912 AD)

Major leaders in the last two imperial dynasties continued to archive official records, installed security measures more stringent than in previous dynasties, to the extent of excluding most Ming and Qing officials from approved readers of those documents. For example, the imperial archival institution in the Ming Dynasty had such high security that "any official would not dare to gaze upon it."[102] The Grand Secretariat Archives (*neigedaku* 内阁大库) in the Forbidden City of the court of Qing, under vigilant protection, disallowed high-ranking Qing officials from seeing a word of the archives "during their lifetime(s)."[103]

Control of information flow during the Qing Dynasty was the most stringent.[104] Continuing the Legalist tradition, Qing laws used the harshest punishments for crimes that challenged the authority of the ruler and the state. Leaking state secrets, plotting against the state, spreading rumors were among those crimes, with execution being the punishment for anyone leaking military secrets. Officials of the royal court received 100 canings if they divulged non-confidential information, and beheaded if they leaked confidential information. The head of each agency was to personally open secret official documents, with delivery of intra-agency

[102] Ruxia Fan, *Historical Characteristics of Archiving in Ancient China* [我国古代档案工作的历史特点], 1 JOURNAL OF FUJIAN NORMAL UNIVERSITY (SOCIAL SCIENCE EDITION) (2000); MO LI, GU SHU POU TAN [孤树裒谈] (2002); Shiping Xu, *An Overview of Ancient Preservation Technology Used for Chinese Archives* [中国古代档案保护技术概览], A08 JOURNAL OF ARCHIVES SCIENCE STUDY SUPPLEMENT (1996); Qingxin Gong, *Research on Origins of Chinese Government and University-Owned Archives* [中国档案、中国高校档案研究], 4 JOURNAL OF GUANZI 113 (2006).

[103] Ruxia Fan, *Historical Characteristics of Archiving in Ancient China* [我国古代档案工作的历史特点], 1 JOURNAL OF FUJIAN NORMAL UNIVERSITY (SOCIAL SCIENCE EDITION) (2000); MO LI, GU SHU POU TAN [孤树裒谈] (2002); Shiping Xu, *An Overview of Ancient Preservation Technology Used for Chinese Archives* [中国古代档案保护技术概览], A08 JOURNAL OF ARCHIVES SCIENCE STUDY SUPPLEMENT (1996).

[104] Philip Kuhn, a prestigious Harvard-educated Western scholar on Chinese history, examined official control of information and its consequences in the late Qing Dynasty. PHILIP A. KUHN, SOULSTEALERS: THE CHINESE SORCERY SCARE OF 1768 (1990) (detailing mass hysteria of the late Qing dynasty caused by widespread fear among peasants, bureaucrats, and the emperor that sorcerers were able to steal people's souls and by lack of timely disclosure of credible governmental information).

files, sealed, then, unfolded, and archived, personally by the heads of involved agencies.[105]

Rulers in the Ming and Qing dynasties further consolidated their control of the official gazette-the *Dibao*. Unlike rulers of previous imperial dynasties, Ming and Qing emperors became the *Dibao*'s de facto editors-in-chief, reviewing and approving all its content prior to the publication.

If tighter control from the government countered freedom of information, some developments were encouraging. First, the system of imperial court diaries was suspended for a short period of time during the early Ming dynasty but quickly resumed. It continued to record, on a daily basis, what the emperors were doing and saying. One emperor of the Ming Dynasty had to change his mind about who should be the crown prince when he saw what the imperial diary wrote about his private life with his wife and concubines. The diary said very clearly when and where he had sex with a low-ranking palace housekeeper and when the woman delivered a baby boy. Knowing that he can no longer deny the boy as his biological son, the emperor had to reluctantly acknowledge the son as the next king of the country, despite the boy's low status.[106] Second, most copies of the official gazette had daily printing and circulation; social news emerged, making the paper timelier and fresher. Third, the court gazette reached the lowest-level officeholders during the Ming and Qing dynasties.[107] Fourth, another revolutionary form of mass media appeared to compete with the official court gazette and short reports: "metropolitan gazette" (*jingbao* 京报). As mentioned earlier, the court gazettes were government-run and thus legal; short reports were private businesses and thus illegal. The metropolitan gazettes were private but acknowledged by the government as alternative forms of the official gazettes.

[105] Shulei Sun, *Study of Official Documents in Qing Dynasty* [清代公文制度考略], 1 JOURNAL OF QINGHAI NORMAL UNIVERSITY (PHILOSOPHY AND SOCIAL SCIENCE EDITION) (2007); ZHENGYUAN FU, CHINA'S LEGALISTS: THE EARLIEST TOTALITARIANS AND THEIR ART OF RULING (1996).

[106] Moyupianpian, *What Did Imperial Court Diaries Do and Why Even Emperors Didn't Have the Right to See Them* ["起居注"是用来干什么的,为何连皇帝都无权拿来看], SOHU, January 15, 2019, https://www.sohu.com/a/289192159_209689 (accessed between February 21, 2025 and March 31, 2025).

[107] Lizi Liu, *Study of Dibao and Government Information Dissemination in Ancient China* [浅谈邸报与我国古代政务信息的公布], 7 JOURNAL OF LANTAI WORLD 49, 49–50 (2009).

The content of the metropolitan gazettes arose primarily from the court gazettes, but the former circulated, with permission, among political and scholarly elites and the public throughout the nation. As the metropolitan gazettes enjoyed more editorial independence than official organs, the papers clearly carried more newsworthy items and became increasingly popular. As a Western scholar on the origins of the Chinese press stated, the metropolitan gazettes were "very generally read and discussed by educated people in [Chinese] cities" during the late Qing Dynasty.[108] Even rural people read them to become informed. A Shānxī rural Confucian recorded in his diary that he read the metropolitan gazette at least five times in 1901 and 10 times in 1902.[109]

Governmental Informational Policy After Imperial China

The Republic of China (1912 AD-1949 AD)

Two thousand years of imperial rule came to a tragic end in 1912 as the regent, the Empress Longyu, announced abdication on behalf of the six-year-old child Emperor Puyi.[110] Sun Yat-sen, who was educated in Hawaii during his adolescent years, established the Republic of China (ROC) in 1912 and became its first temporary president. The country's chaos caused Sun's replacement, and after defeating regional warlords, in 1927, Chiang Kai-shek established the unified Nationalist Kuomintang (KMT) government, which collapsed in 1949 when Chiang lost a civil war to Mao Zedong and his communist comrades.

Various schools of thought reemerged and prospered for several decades immediately before and after the disintegration of the Qing

[108] S. WELLS WILLIAMS, 2 THE MIDDLE KINGDOM: A SURVEY OF THE GEOGRAPHY, GOVERNMENT, LITERATURE, SOCIAL LIFE, ARTS AND HISTORY OF THE CHINESE EMPIRE AND ITS INHABITANTS 420 (1883).

[109] The rural Confucian resident was Dapeng Liu (1857 AD-1942 AD), lived near Taiyuan in Shānxī, appropriately 900 miles from the Qing capital, Beijing. S. WELLS WILLIAMS, 2 THE MIDDLE KINGDOM: A SURVEY OF THE GEOGRAPHY, GOVERNMENT, LITERATURE, SOCIAL LIFE, ARTS AND HISTORY OF THE CHINESE EMPIRE AND ITS INHABITANTS (1883).

[110] EVELYN SAKAKIDA RAWSKI, THE LAST EMPERORS: A SOCIAL HISTORY OF QING IMPERIAL INSTITUTIONS 136 (2001); PAUL JOHN BAILEY, CHINA IN THE TWENTIETH CENTURY 14 (2001).

Dynasty, including the value of long-lost Mohism.[111] The Western concepts of freedom, democracy, and Christianity, introduced to China, inspired intellectual richness at the time,[112] leading to Sun Yat-sen's creation of a government combining Western democratic ideals and traditional Chinese spirit.[113] According to the *Provisional Constitution*, the sovereignty of the republic belonged to the people and Chinese citizens enjoyed freedoms, including freedoms of speech, composition, and publication.[114] It was the first time that China codified such freedoms and its significance should not be deemphasized although, in reality, China had yet to fully achieve those freedoms.

In order to avoid trampling on these freedoms, Sun advocated Three Principles of the People[115] and envisioned a five-power constitution, which created an accountable government with five independent and equally important branches (*yuan* 院): legislative branch, executive branch, judicial branch, examination branch, and control branch.[116]

[111] XIPING YANG, NEW INSPIRATIONS FROM MOHISM (CHAPTER I) [墨学新悟] (第一章) (2012).

[112] Fu Yan (1854–1921) translated the following Western classics into Chinese: Thomas Henry Huxley's *Evolution and Ethics* (1896), John Stuart Mill's *On Liberty* (1899), Adam Smith's *Wealth of Nations* (1900), Spencer's *Study of Sociology* (1903), and Montesquieu's *The Spirit of the Laws* (1905). Qichao Liang (1873–1929) translated and commented on the works of Hobbes, Rousseau, Locke, and Hume. THOMAS HENRY HUXLEY, EVOLUTION AND ETHICS AND OTHER ESSAYS (1896); HERBERT SPENCER, THE STUDY OF SOCIOLOGY (1873); ADAM SMITH, AN INQUIRY INTO THE NATURE AND CAUSES OF THE WEALTH OF NATIONS (Edwin Cannan ed., 1977); MONTESQUIE, CHARLES DE SECONDAT, THE SPIRIT OF THE LAWS (David Wallace Carrithers, ed., 1977); Pengcheng Lu, *Historical Review of Concept of Freedom of Speech, Freedom of the Press and Freedom of Information in Modern China* [言论自由、出版自由与新闻自由概念传入中国的历史考察] 6 CHINA MEDIA REPORT OVERSEAS 20 (2010).

[113] WILLIAM L. TUNG, THE POLITICAL INSTITUTIONS OF MODERN CHINA 26 (1968); TUAN-SHÊNG CHÌEN, THE GOVERNMENT & POLITICS OF CHINA 1912–1949 70 (1970).

[114] *The Provisional Constitution of the Republic of China*, 6 THE AMERICAN JOURNAL OF INTERNATIONAL LAW 149 (1912).

[115] Three Principles of the People are nationalism (*minzuzhuyi*民族主义), democracy (*minquanzhuyi* 民权主义), and people's livelihood (*minshengzhuyi*民生主义).

[116] The examination branch and the control branch are absent in most Western democracies. The examination branch's responsibility was administering civil service examinations. The control branch authorized monitoring public officials and recommended impeachment or other corrective measures for miscreant officeholders. Sun Yat-sen, *Fundamentals*

As the Qing Dynasty collapsed and the new democratic republic emerged, governmental power declined to its lowest while civil liberties rose to its height. Unsurprisingly, "[t]he years...from 1912 to 1927, marked perhaps the period of greatest freedom in 20th-century China."[117] Chiang Kai-shek and his Kuomintang Party (KMT), to some degree, continued Sun's democratic ideals.

The Republic of China continued to attend, scrupulously, to archiving and preserving official documents and records, as did imperial rulers. However, frequent civil wars and sudden changes of regime made archival preservation a daunting task. Officials sold the Qing Dynasty archives for profit, and some valuable documents were like wastepaper.[118] This lack of respected value was partially due to the trend of decreased harshness of laws for guarding state secrets. The death penalty applied only to leaking significant military secrets, but laws punishing the press publishing state secrets emerged.[119]

The Republic of China promoted remarkable growth of newspaper businesses, both state-run and private. The modern press replaced court gazettes, short reports, and metropolitan gazettes. Unlike other Leninist parties in the world, The Chiang-led Kuomintang party had an ideological commitment to full constitutional democracy.[120] Furthermore, the government was weak both politically and militarily, leading to haphazard and erratic enforcement of press censorship laws. Lin Yutang (1895 AD-1976 AD), a well-known Chinese writer and social commentator, once

of National Reconstruction, *in* 2 SOURCES OF WORLD HISTORY 281–285 (Mark A. Kishlansky ed., 1995); ALAN LAWRANCE, CHINA SINCE 1919: REVOLUTION AND REFORM: A SOURCEBOOK 23 (2004).

117 Yu Hua, *Fear of Dragons*, THE NEW YORK TIMES, October 7, 2011, http://www.nytimes.com/2011/10/08/opinion/08iht-edyu08.html (accessed between February 21, 2025 and March 31, 2025).

118 DANIEL LEESE, MAO CULT: RHETORIC AND RITUAL IN CHINA'S CULTURAL REVOLUTION IX (2011).

119 Qun Zhang, *Development of Secrets Protection Laws in Late Qing Dynasty and Republic of China* [清末和民国时期保密法律发展概略], Baomi.org, Beijing, China, January 29, 2012 (captured by Internet Archive Wayback Machine on October 31, 2012), retrieved from https://web.archive.org/web/20121031191752/http://www.baomi.org/bmyw_info.php?optionid=31&auto_id=1256 (accessed between February 21, 2025 and March 31, 2025).

120 Yangsun Chou & Andrew J. Nathan, *Democratizing Transition in Taiwan*, 27 ASIAN SURVEY 277 (March 1987).

observed, "The anarchy of Chinese [ROC] censorship is shown in its lack of system, coordination and consistency. News suppressed in one city may be passed in another. The deletion of news often depends on the whims and vagaries of the individual censors."[121] Many prominent private publications like *Impartial Daily (dagongbao 大公报)*[122] consistently covered official activities and were highly critical of Chiang and his government. Fortunately, the Kuomintang-controlled arena continued to allow such publications to circulate.[123] During World War II, the Western concept of freedom of the press transmitted to China.[124] Governmental press officers coveted and revered foreign correspondents based in the wartime capital city of Chongqing.[125]

Similar to any society, not many ROC officials preferred governmental transparency, and the government did not sponsor freedom of information laws during its rule in Mainland China.[126] However, the republic's bureaucracy, as a whole, attempted to enhance governmental transparency because of the short-term need to publicize policies and mobilize public support against communism, and because of the long-term commitment to constitutional democracy. Partially achieving this

[121] YUTANG LIN, A HISTORY OF THE PRESS AND PUBLIC OPINION IN CHINA 177 (1936).

[122] *Dagong bao* was known for investigative journalism and it was a recipient of the 1941 foreign press award from the University of Missouri School of Journalism. MAKING JOURNALISTS: DIVERSE MODELS, GLOBAL ISSUES 111 (Huge de Burgh ed., 2005); L. Sophia Wang, *The Independent Press and Authoritarian Regimes: The Case of the Dagong bao in Republican China*, 67 PACIFIC AFFAIRS 216 (Summer 1994).

[123] JAY TAYLOR, THE GENERALISSIMO: CHIANG KAI-SHEK AND THE STRUGGLE FOR MODERN CHINA 103–104 (2009).

[124] Pengcheng Lu, *Historical Review of Concept of Freedom of Speech, Freedom of the Press and Freedom of Information in Modern China* [言论自由、出版自由与新闻自由概念传入中国的历史考察] 6 CHINA MEDIA REPORT OVERSEAS 20 (2010).

[125] Chonghua Li, *How Did Nationalist Government Treat Foreign Journalists in Temporary Capital* [国民政府对陪都外国记者的态度], 2 JOURNAL OF ZHEJIANG NORMAL UNIVERSITY (SOCIAL SCIENCES) 77 (2006); Feng Dun & Ting Zhao, *Wartime Management of Foreign Journalists by Chongqing Nationalist Government During War Against Japanese Aggression* [抗战时期重庆国民政府对外国记者的 管理刍议], 10 SOUTHEAST COMMUNICATION 83 (2010).

[126] In 2005, the Republic of China (Taiwan) adopted its first freedom of information law, known as *Freedom of Government Information Law*. The law protects the people's right to know, understand, trust, and oversee public affairs and establishes procedures for citizens to request access to governmental information. *Freedom of Government Information Law 2005* (The Republic of China, Taiwan).

goal was allowance of some degree of editorial independence to the press for covering and reporting official activities. Consequently, citizens had unprecedented access to governmental information, and the provincial Shānxī government was even more disclosure-friendly than many other provincial bureaucracies. The Shānxī government established rooms across the province, some staffed by officials to assist the illiterate, for reading newspapers in many towns and villages.[127] A Western scholar vividly portrayed how ROC local officials used mass media to disseminate official information to ordinary citizens:

> In 1919 the *Shanxi Daily News* ... published an account by one of its readers who had visited some remote villages and had been impressed at how well informed the villagers were about recent government policies and reforms. He explained that the villagers now understood that certain traditional customs were wrong, because when they were resting, enlightened village leaders or schoolteachers often hold a copy of this newspaper in their hands and read it aloud and explain it.[128]

The People's Republic of China (1949 AD-1976 AD)

When Mao Zedong and his revolutionary comrades exiled Chiang Kai-Shek to Taiwan and founded the People's Republic of China (PRC) in 1949, communist leaders began to establish a system to control, tightly, official information. They embraced the traditional Legalist approach of totalitarianism for social control[129] and also adopted the characteristic of the former Soviet Union's complete secrecy.[130]

[127] Henrietta Harrison, *Newspapers and Nationalism in Rural China, 1890–1929*, 166 PAST & PRESENT 181, 202 (2000).

[128] Henrietta Harrison, *Newspapers and Nationalism in Rural China, 1890–1929*, 166 PAST & PRESENT 181, 181 (2000).

[129] Mao Zedong removed Confucianism as old thought and replaced it with socialism and Marxism. He often claimed that he was a Legalist and identified himself with the emperor Qin. GUCHENG LI, A GLOSSARY OF POLITICAL TERMS OF THE PEOPLE'S REPUBLIC OF CHINA 346 (1995).

[130] The highly restrictive information policy of the former Soviet Union did not end until the last Soviet Union President, Mikhail Gorbachev, assumed office in the 1980s. Jiwen Deng, *Information Dissemination of the Former Soviet Union from the Point of View*

Communist leaders long recognized the importance of archiving government documents and maintaining them as classified. In 1950, the new communist government issued orders protecting archives from "plundering and profiteering and to prevent betrayal of state secrets."[131] One year later, *Provisional Rules for Managing Public Documents* came into effect.[132] In 1954, establishment of the State Archives Bureau (*guojiadang'anju* 国家档案局) gained responsibility for nationwide archival matters and assumed regulation of both party and governmental archives. In 1956, Henan Province established the country's first provincial archive and three years later the Central Archives opened in Beijing. By 1966, among 32 provinces and autonomous regions, 28 had established archives.[133] Renowned Western scholar of Chinese politics, Andrew Nathan, noted:

> [T]he Chinese Communist Party obsessively collects its own documents and with equal obsessiveness keeps them secret. National-level Party and state civilian archives reaching back to the early history of the Communist movement and up to the recent past are kept by the Central Archives ... Local government archives, military archives, and archives of the pre-1949 Nationalist regime are held elsewhere. Drafts and originals of official telegrams, reports, decisions, meeting minutes, and the like are sent to the archives ... after having been kept in their original units for a number of years ... [T]he archives were off-limits, except in rare cases, to high-ranking Party officials.[134]

During Mao's rule, archiving the government's documents became permanent, indicating that unalterable status as classified. Mao and his advisors not only denied the people's right to access governmental

of the Media: A Brief History [传媒视野下前苏联的信息发布:一个简史], 5 (2) JOURNAL OF CENTRAL SOUTH UNIVERSITY OF FORESTRY AND TECHNOLOGY (SOCIAL SCIENCES) 11, 11–13 (April 2011).

131 William W. Moss, *Dang'an: Contemporary Chinese Archives*, 145 THE CHINA QUARTERLY 112, 113 (March 1996).

132 William W. Moss, *Dang'an: Contemporary Chinese Archives*, 145 THE CHINA QUARTERLY 112, 113 (March 1996).

133 William W. Moss, *Dang'an: Contemporary Chinese Archives*, 145 THE CHINA QUARTERLY 112, 115 (March 1996).

134 WENQIAN GAO, ZHOU ENLAI: THE LAST PERFECT REVOLUTIONARY ix-x (2008).

archives but also classified any information considered potentially inappropriate for the public. Leaking such information incurred severe penalties. In 1951, the PRC promulgated *Provisional Act on Guarding State Secrets*, which was so vague that almost all information, not officially made public, could be "state secrets."[135] *People's Daily* republished the law in 1980 to reiterate authority and the law did not expire until replaced in 1989 by *Law on Guarding State Secrets*.

Under Mao's leadership, most private media that flourished in the pre-1949 Republic of China era disappeared.[136] All the news media outlets became governmental institutions, with each having its corresponding administrative rank.[137] The role of mass media was to propagandize government policies and gather intelligence for the party.[138] Editors subverting the party line were eliminated.[139] Any journalists promulgating or disseminating criticism of the conduct of government became pariahs, rightists, and encountered persecution, imprisonment, torture, and even death. Mao, first in 1957, advocated a news reporting principle of "the news, old news or no news" (*xinwen jiuwen buwen* 新闻 旧闻 不闻).[140] The principle means that certain categories of information should be timely released whereas postponement, or deliberate ignoring applies

[135] SHAO-CHUAN LENG & HUNGDAH CHIU, CRIMINAL JUSTICE IN POST-MAO CHINA: ANALYSIS AND DOCUMENTS 182 (1985).

[136] Since 1953, only four privately owned newspapers were left in China, but all lost their independence status. They were all staffed with Communists or pro-Communists. Franklin W. Houn, *Chinese Communist Control of the Press*, 22 THE PUBLIC OPINION QUARTERLY 438 (1958–1959).

[137] For example, *People's Daily* and Xinhua News Agency are the two news organizations having the most senior administrative rank. Publishers and editors-in-chief of these two media outlets enjoy political status as governmental ministers. Newspapers with lower administrative rank were not allowed to criticize party and government officials with higher administrative rank.

[138] YUEZHI ZHAO, MEDIA, MARKET, AND DEMOCRACY IN CHINA: BETWEEN THE PARTY LINE AND THE BOTTOM LINE (1998).

[139] Changjiang Fan, a famed journalist for the prestigious *Impartial Daily (Dagong bao)* that prospered in the pre-1949 Nationalist era, was the publisher of *People's Daily*. Tuo Deng was the editor-in-chief of the *People's Daily*. Both were purged by Mao and committed suicide during the Cultural Revolution.

[140] MAO ZEDONG, SELECTED WORKS OF MAO ZEDONG ON JOURNALISM [毛泽东新闻工作文选] 193 (1983).

to other categories of official information. The government followed the Mao principle for reporting many crises until the early 2000s.[141]

Citizens could not obtain meaningful official information from the mass media due to heavy-handed governmental suppression of press freedom. Constant political indoctrination and Mao's call for continuous political campaigns was the staple of the media. According to Amartya Sen, a Nobel Prize laureate in economics, lack of freedom of information played a major role in the deaths of tens of millions of Chinese people from starvation during the great famine from 1959 to 1962.[142]

Fortunately, at least government officials' access to information was not completely absent. Communist bureaucrats at various levels relied on the internal reference system to know what was really happening in the country and elsewhere. The system, created in the 1930s when Chinese communists were still fighting guerilla wars against the ruling KMT military forces, was highly innovative but costly. Any information (e.g., governmental infighting, official corruption, social scandals, and major natural disasters, rural and urban unrest) deemed too sensitive for the public to see appeared in separately published internal reports[143]

[141] For example, The Tonghai earthquake in 1970 killed 15,621 civilians, however, the death toll was not publicized until January 2000. Yi Lei, *Three Earthquakes during the Cultural Revolution* [“文革”中的三次地震], ECONOMIC OBSERVER ONLINE, June 10, 2008, https://www.eeo.com.cn/observer/special/2008/06/10/102682.shtml (accessed between February 21, 2025 and March 31, 2025). The Tangshan earthquake in 1976 killed 240,000 people and severely injured 160,000. However, the Chinese public did not know this information until November 23, 1979 when *People's Daily* published those numbers. Xuejiang Xu, *Death Toll of Tangshan Earthquake: More Than 240,000* [唐山地震死亡24万多人], PEOPLE'S DAILY, November 23, 1979, at 4.

[142] Amartya Sen was awarded the Nobel Prize in 1998. He links food supply and famine with freedom of information. He argued that the Chinese famine of 1959 to 1962 and other major famines in the developing world occurred because of a lack of a free press and the absence of democratic practices. Famines cannot occur in a democracy because the free press and opposition parties disclose information that contributes greatly to famine prevention. Amartya Sen, *Development: Which Way Now?*, 93 THE ECONOMIC JOURNAL 745, 759 (1983); Amartya Sen, *Food and Freedom*, *in* A WORLD TO MAKE: DEVELOPMENT IN PERSPECTIVE (Francis X. Sutton ed., 1990); LORNA STEFANICK, CONTROLLING KNOWLEDGE: FREEDOM OF INFORMATION AND PRIVACY PROTECTION IN A NETWORKED WORLD 77 (2011).

[143] *Cancao Xiaoxi* (Reference News) was such an internal report. Created in 1931 by the Xinhua News Agency, *Cancao Xiaoxi* symbolizes the beginning of the internal reference system in China. Today, *Cancao Xiaoxi* is no longer an internal report, instead, it has become a regular newspaper with a circulation of over 2 million, far exceeding any other newspaper in the country. Xinmin Zhang, *Cancao Xiaoxi: From*

by official media outlets and sent exclusively to party and governmental leaders at various levels.[144] Central and local agencies published similar internal periodicals on a regular basis.[145] Political and government leaders relied heavily on this system to gather information and make decisions.

Government secrecy culminated during the Cultural Revolution (1966 AD-1976 AD).[146] During these ten tumultuous years, the only freedom of information the ordinary Chinese enjoyed was reading Mao's Little Red Book (*hongbaoshu* 红宝书)[147] and posting big-character posters

Internal Report to Newspaper Accessible to All [《参考消息》:从"内部刊物"到公开发行], PHOENIX TV, November 15, 2007, https://news.ifeng.com/history/3/200710/1019_337_264646.shtml (accessed between February 21, 2025 and March 31, 2025).

[144] Both Chinese and foreign media have covered the journalistic internal reference system. Ruoqiao Liang, "*For Whose Eyes Only?*," GLOBAL TIMES, August 24, 2010, https://www.globaltimes.cn/content/566822.shtml (accessed between February 21, 2025 and March 31, 2025). Nicholas D. Kristof, *The Real News in China Comes out in Restricted Periodicals*, THE NEW YORK TIMES, September 24, 1991, http://www.nytimes.com/1991/09/24/world/the-real-news-in-china-comes-out-in-restricted-periodicals.html (accessed between February 21, 2025 and March 31, 2025). *Chinese Whispers: Not Believing What They Read in the Papers, China's Leaders Commission Their Own*," THE ECONOMIST, June 17, 2010, https://www.economist.com/asia/2010/06/17/chinese-whispers (accessed between February 21, 2025 and March 31, 2025). Dake Wang, *In Xi's China, even Internal Reports Fall Prey to Censorship*, ASSOCIATED PRESS, October 31, 2022, https://apnews.com/article/health-china-beijing-covid-wuhan-3c199e3f1a084013da18fc9e6061e775 (accessed between February 21, 2025 and March 31, 2025).

[145] Chinese Party and governmental agencies continue to publish internal documents today. For example, The Chinese Communist Party (CCP) Central Propaganda Department publishes *Propaganda Trend* (*Xuanchuan dongtai* 宣传动态) on a weekly basis. YUEZHI ZHAO, MEDIA, MARKET, AND DEMOCRACY IN CHINA: BETWEEN THE PARTY LINE AND THE BOTTOM LINE 20 (1998). The Central Organization Department issues *Party Construction Research Internal Reference* (*Dangjian yanjiu neican* 党建研究内参), which is accessible online only to subscribers who are party and government leaders above county level. Each institute at the China Academy of Social Sciences, a prestigious official think tank, produces various types of internal reference materials (*neican*). DECISION-MAKING IN DENG'S CHINA: PERSPECTIVES FROM INSIDERS 114 (Carol Lee Hamrin & Suisheng Zhao eds., 1995). Even some large public libraries in China publish internal reference materials on a regular basis. For example, the Sun Yat-Sen Library of Guangdong Province issues *Decision-Making Neican* intended for political elites in the Gudangdong area.

[146] In order to create a classless society and regain lost authority, Mao launched the Cultural Revolution. Mao destroyed the bureaucratic machine and purged the majority of comrades who once fought with him against Chiang Kai-shek.

[147] The book consists of quotations from Chairman Mao Zedong. During the Cultural Revolution, nearly every Chinese citizen carried a copy of this book, making it the bible of

(*dazibao* 大字报).[148] During Mao's final years, even well-connected officials lost the opportunity to see Mao in person and remained ignorant of the government's direction.[149] Nearly 16 hours passed before the news of Mao's death became public.[150]

Summary and Conclusion

This chapter examined the development of Chinese governmental secrecy and transparency beginning with the Xia Dynasty and ending in 1976 when Mao Zedong died, a span of over 4,000 years. Five aspects are worthy of note after the detailed examination of communication and/or informational policies in Chinese history:

First, like the two sides of the same coin, both secrecy and transparency were necessary means for controlling official information. Almost all ancient governments in the world believed both in the power of

the nation. XING LU, RHETORIC OF THE CHINESE CULTURAL REVOLUTION: THE IMPACT ON CHINESE THOUGHT, CULTURE AND COMMUNICATION 66 (2004).

148 Big-character posters are wall-mounted newspapers and pamphlets used by Chinese citizens during the Cultural Revolution to voice political dissent. According to Article 13 of the *1975 Constitution*, citizens had the right to write big-character posters. JOHN DOWNING, RADICAL MEDIA: REBELLIOUS COMMUNICATION AND SOCIAL MOVEMENTS 171 (2001); WOEI LIEN CHONG, CHINA'S GREAT PROLETARIAN CULTURAL REVOLUTION: MASTER NARRATIVES AND POST-MAO COUNTERNARRATIVES 108 (2002); Hua Sheng, *Perspective on Free Speech in China: Big Character Posters in China: A Historical Survey*, 4 THE JOURNAL OF ASIA LAW 234 (Spring 1990). *Constitution 1975*. Art. 13.

149 Mao died in 1976. He was so ill during his final years that he was unable to attend high-level party and governmental meetings. Yuanxin Mao, Mao's nephew, became the formal liaison between Mao and the Politburo of the Chinese Communist Party in 1975. Yuanxin Mao had considerable power for a short period of time because no other officials had access to Mao. RICHARD BAUM, BURYING MAO: CHINESE POLITICS IN THE AGE OF DENG XIAOPING 34 (1996); LAWRENCE SULLIVAN, HISTORICAL DICTIONARY OF THE CHINESE COMMUNIST PARTY 174 (2011); FREDERICK C. TEIWES & WARREN SUN, THE END OF THE MAOIST ERA: CHINESE POLITICS DURING THE TWILIGHT OF THE CULTURAL REVOLUTION, 1972–1976 399 (2008).

150 Mao died at 12:10 a.m., September 9, 1976, and China National Radio announced his death at 4 p.m. the same day. In the 1970s, radio was the most efficient way to disseminate information in China. Zhenquan Yang, B*ehind-the-Scene Story about Public Broadcasting Mao Zedong's Death (One)* [毛泽东主席逝世公开广播的背后(上)],8 INTERNATIONAL COMMUNICATIONS 52, 52–55 (2006); Zhenquan Yang, *Behind-the-Scene Story about Public Broadcasting Mao Zedong's Death* (TWO) [毛泽东主席逝世公开广播的背后(下)], 9 INTERNATIONAL COMMUNICATIONS (2006).

behind-the-scenes politics[151] and a certain degree of government disclosure. China was no exception. In Chinese history, no form of government characterized a complete informational blackout. Likewise, no form of government allowed total disclosure of official information.

The Xia and Shang dynasties initiated secrecy for official documents. No instances record official transparency during this period. The likelihood is that practices of disclosure of official information were just too old to be recorded at the dawn, more than 4,000 years ago, of the Chinese civilization. All subsequent rulers after the Xia and Shang dynasties, ranging from the Zhou Dynasty to Mao's communist regime, restricted the free flow of information, and at the same time publicized certain categories of information. Different rulers in different periods, regardless of the nature of the form of government, tended to have diverging views and predilections toward openness and secrecy, thus leading to varying degrees of transparency. However, any differences in policies were matters of degree, not kind.

Second, divergent ruling philosophies and political theories led to sharply different informational policies. The hundred schools of thought that flourished in the Zhou Dynasty significantly impacted Chinese rulers in terms of crafting informational policy. Mohism had the greatest potential of helping establish a transparent government, but its democratic nature led resentment and suppression by early rulers. The philosophy reemerged in the early years of the Republic of China. In conjunction with Western democratic ideals, Mohism played a role in making the ROC government more transparent. Legalists were strong advocates of government transparency, but they only allowed dissemination of laws and regulations among commoners. Confucianism disagreed with governmental openness and Taoism was a philosophy reserved for officials experiencing leisure, retirement, or political ostracism. Legalism became dominant in some Warring States and the Qin Dynasty's rulers created the precedent for publicizing written laws. When Confucianism modified and incorporated Legalism and became the ruling ideology of imperial dynasties from the Han Dynasty to the Qing Dynasty, emperors and officials practiced official secrecy but at the same time allowed very limited sharing of a category of information with the public: laws and regulations.

[151] Even in the ancient United Kingdom, the birthplace of modern democracy, the king and his top advisors discussed all the major issues of the state in a small and private chamber, the original meaning of the English word "cabinet.".

Mao's rule relegated Chinese freedom of information to a new low by combining Legalism, Socialism, Marxism, and the former Soviet Union's penchant for secretive politics.

Third, ranking Chinese governments of different time periods in terms of governmental transparency is difficult, but a safe conclusion is that, overall, governmental openness in China had an upward trajectory, with some peaks and depressions. The first peak for governmental transparency was during the Zhou Dynasty due to the proliferation of practices for publicizing written laws and relatively greater freedom of expression enjoyed by commoners. The second peak occurred in the Tang and Song dynasties when rulers and common citizens used newspapers (the court gazettes or short reports) to disseminate governmental information. People had greater access to official information in the Tang and Song dynasties also because emperors and their prime ministers shared power, thus allowing greater flow of information between the sovereigns and their subjects.[152] The Republic of China witnessed a third ascent of governmental openness when private news outlets rigorously covered official activities. The Qing Dynasty and Mao's China, without doubt, represent the deepest descents in terms of governmental transparency.[153] During these two periods, both suppression of individual liberties and concentration of power in the hands of paramount leaders reached new heights.

Fourth, imperial China developed an extraordinary self-enclosed communication system to sustain its huge bureaucracy. The Chinese saying, "the sky is high, the emperor is far away," (*tiangaohuangdiyuan* 天高皇帝远) reveals the challenge of controlling local officials in ancient

[152] Prime ministers in the Tang and Song dynasties had significant power. Elimination of the office of prime minster occurred after the Yuan Dynasty, allowing emperors to consolidate power. INSTITUTE FOR ADVANCED CHINESE STUDIES, 9 CHINESE CULTURE (1968); CRAIG A. LOCKARD, B SOCIETIES, NETWORKS, AND TRANSITIONS: A GLOBAL HISTORY 286 (2010); GEORGE FUSUN LING, CHINA DEVELOPING: CULTURAL IDENTITY OF EMERGING SOCIETIES 37 (2008).

[153] Philip Kuhn, a prestigious Harvard-educated Western scholar on the Chinese history, examined the extent of government secrecy in the late Qing Dynasty and its severe consequences. PHILIP A. KUHN, SOULSTEALERS: THE CHINESE SORCERY SCARE OF 1768 (1990) (chronicling mass hysteria of the late Qing dynasty caused by lack of governmental information disclosure and widespread fear among peasants, bureaucrats, and the emperor that sorcerers were able to steal people's souls).

China, given the empire's incredible geographic size and large population. In order to broadcast the voice of the central government to every corner of the country, emperors granted advisors and local officials certain freedom of information that common people did not enjoy. Governmental officials, despite their locations, the capitals or remote places, regularly received official gazettes and other official documents through the postal courier system. Depending upon their administrative ranks, they had the privilege of accessing: Activities and speeches of the leaders (e.g., emperors, warlords), imperial orders and governmental decisions, policies, laws, regulations, official appointments, promotions, demotions, compliments, disciplinary actions, memorials to the throne, working plans of central and local governments, recommendations, and remonstrance from local officials.[154] The developed communication system contributed to the Chinese empire's longevity.[155] However, this communication system excluded most common people. Information affirmatively and proactively disclosed to the public was little and carefully selected.[156] Governors only disclosed information that they wanted the public to know; anything else became a state secret since the authority to determine the classification of information rested solely with the governors. As a Chinese communication scholar stated, "The communication history of imperial China is a history of communication suppression."[157]

Fifth, with the help of technology, pre-modern and modern mass media played an important role in propagating Chinese governmental information. Ancient Chinese rulers used many innovative methods to

[154] Lizi Liu, *Study of Dibao and Government Information Dissemination in Ancient China* [浅谈邸报与我国古代政务信息的公布] 7 JOURNAL OF LANTAI WORLD 49, 49–50 (2009).

[155] A widely accepted notion is that the publication of *Acta Diurna* (Daily Public Record), the official gazette of the Roman Empire, contributed to the empire's ability to rule a vast empire. The Roman Empire collapsed partially due to overextended lines of communication. NORMAN F. CANTOR, THE CIVILIZATION OF THE MIDDLE AGES: A COMPLETELY REVISED AND EXPANDED EDITION OF MEDIEVAL HISTORY 41 (1994); KEVIN WILLIAMS, READ ALL ABOUT IT!: A HISTORY OF THE BRITISH NEWSPAPER 26 (2010).

[156] Lizi Liu, *Study of Dibao and Government Information Dissemination in Ancient China* [浅谈邸报与我国古代政务信息的公布] 7 JOURNAL OF LANTAI WORLD 49, 49-50 (2009).

[157] Qinglin Li, "The Constitution and Narrative of Imperial Autocracy-on the Discourse and the Mode of Communication in Imperial China" [皇权专制的建构和叙事] (2006) (Ph.D. diss., the Communication University of China), at 106.

enable information to reach as many commoners as possible. The inception of the court gazette in the Tang Dynasty allowed unprecedented ease for bureaucratic internal communication. Short reports that emerged in the Song Dynasty and independent private media that flourished in the Republic of China changed even the communication dynamics. These media outlets challenged official versions and interpretations of social events and greatly enhanced common people's capability to access governmental information.

As discussed previously, Mao's era brought governmental suppression of transparency to an unprecedented depth. Soon after his death and the downfall of the Gang of Four,[158] Deng Xiaoping came to power and became the supreme leader of the Chinese Communist Party and the state. Deng adopted the fundamental policy of reform and opening up to the outside world in 1978. Economic reform was high on the agenda. The party was also determined to set socialist democracy and rule of law as its goal due to painful experiences of most purged top leaders during the Cultural Revolution.[159] Deng valued the development of government information resources to facilitate economic modernization.[160] He also started to reestablish the legal system that was severely damaged during Mao's rule. This policy change paved the way for subsequent administrative law reform that began in the 1980s and 1990s.[161] Jiang Zemin and Hu Jintao, the core leaders of the third and fourth generation of the

158 The Gang of Four consisted of Jiang Qing, Mao's last wife and her close associates Zhang Chunqiao, Yao Wenyuan, and Wang Hongwen. During the Cultural Revolution, they all became powerful members in the Party. Mao used the Gang of Four to purge his political opponents. BILL BRUGGER, CHINA SINCE THE "GANG OF FOUR" (1980).

159 Deng Xiaoping himself was a victim of Mao Zedong's ruthlessness and lawlessness. Deng was purged three times by Mao, and Deng's first son was crippled by the Red Guards and became a paraplegic. Vital differences existed between Deng and Mao in their views of socialist democracy despite that both believed in the unquestionable ruling status of the Communist Party. Mao paid lip service to socialist democracy most of the time whereas Deng intended to implement socialist democracy and the rule of law to prevent the chaos of the Cultural Revolution from occurring again.

160 DAVID S. G. GOODMAN, DENG XIAOPING AND THE CHINESE REVOLUTION: A POLITICAL BIOGRAPHY (1994); THE RIGHT TO KNOW: TRANSPARENCY FOR AN OPEN WORLD 63 (Ann Florini & Joseph E. Stiglitz eds., 2007).

161 For example, in 1998, the National People's Congress adopted *Organic Law on Villagers Committees*. The law requires village committees to proactively disclose financial information at least once every six months. This marked the beginning of the village-level open governance in China. Hanhua Zhou, *Open Government in China: Practice*

party, continued Deng's work.[162] All of these initiatives have provided strong political commitment to transparency, probably creating the fourth peak in government transparency in China's history. The ambitious experiment finally crystallized in 2007 in the country's first national freedom of information law-*Regulations of the People's Republic of China on Open Government Information* (*OGI Regulations*).

and Problems, *in* THE RIGHT TO KNOW: TRANSPARENCY FOR AN OPEN WORLD 59 (Ann Florini & Joseph E. Stiglitz eds., 2007). *Organic Law on Villagers Committees 1998.*

[162] Jiang Zemin, *Hold High the Great Banner of Deng Xiaoping Theory for an All-round Advancement of the Cause of Building Socialism with Chinese Characteristics to the 21st Century* [高举邓小平理论伟大旗帜, 把建设有中国特色社会主义事业全面推向二十一世纪], speech delivered at the 15th Party National Congress, Beijing, 12 September 1997; Hu Jintao, *Hold High the Great Banner of Socialism with Chinese Characteristics and Strive for New Victories in Budding a Moderately Prosperous Society in All Respects* [高举中国特色社会主义伟大旗帜 为夺取全面建设小康社会新胜利而奋斗], speech delivered at the 17th National Party Congress, Beijing, October 2007.

CHAPTER 5

Legislative History of *OGI Regulations* and Rationales for the Rise of Chinese Freedom of Information

Introduction

Mao Zedong established a comprehensive information control system after assuming office in 1949. Mao died in 1976, a purge of the Gang of Four[1] occurred one month later. Within two years, when Deng Xiaoping emerged as supreme leader of China, the country began a long

[1] The Gang of Four consisted of Jiang Qing, Mao's last wife and her close associates Zhang Chunqiao Zhang, Yao Wenyuan, and Wang Hongwen. During the Cultural Revolution, they all became powerful members in the Party. Mao used the Gang of Four to purge his political opponents. Bill Brugger, China Since the "Gang of Four" (1980).

This chapter is derived from the book author's doctoral dissertation that was successfully defended at The Pennsylvania State University in 2012. Portions of the text resemble or may replicate the original text from the unpublished PhD thesis and have been reproduced as such with the permission of Palgrave Macmillan editors. Yong Tang, "Chinese Freedom of Information: An Evaluation of the Legislative History, Rationales, Significance and Efficacy of Regulations of the People's Republic of China on Open Government Information" (2012) (unpublished Ph.D. diss., The Pennsylvania State University at University Park), *available at* https://etda.libraries.psu.edu/catalog/16287 (accessed between February 21, 2025 and March 31, 2025).

Y. Tang, *Freedom of Information Law in China*,
https://doi.org/10.1007/978-981-96-7842-6_5

journey toward socialist democracy and the rule of law.[2] As a part of efforts to reform and openness to the outside world, post-Mao China began to embrace, gradually, the concept of greater official transparency. This chapter will provide an overview of the legislative background of *Regulations of the People's Republic of China on Open Government Information (OGI Regulations)* and explore the influence of various factors' contributing to final passage of the OGI legislation in 2007.

Proactive Disclosure at Village Level[3]: Open Village Affairs (OVA)

For freedom of information in the international community, standard practice supports publicizing government-held information in two main ways. The first is reactive disclosure (*yi shenqinggongkai* 依申请公开) by which individual citizens file requests for the information and wait for approval or rejection. The second is proactive disclosure (*zhudonggongkai* 主动公开) by which public bodies disclose information, voluntarily, according to their own initiatives, without a prior request.[4]

The Chinese movement toward greater official transparency began in the form of proactive disclosure of information held by governmental

[2] Deng Xiaoping himself was a victim of Mao Zedong's ruthlessness and lawlessness. Deng was purged three times by Mao and Deng's first son, crippled by the Red Guards, became a paraplegic. Vital differences existed between Deng and Mao in their views of socialist democracy despite both believing in the unquestionable ruling status of the party. Mao paid lip service to socialist democracy most of the time, whereas Deng intended to implement socialist democracy and the rule of law to prevent the chaos of the Cultural Revolution from recurring.

[3] China has six practical (de facto) levels of central and local government: the central, province, prefecture, county, township, and village. Practically, the village is the lowest level of government. Officially, the township is the lowest level of government. For each level of government, normally excluding village and township, the government has six branches (*liutao banzi* 六套班子): the party, the government, the people's congress, the court, the procuratorate, and the political consultative conference. In order to avoid confusion, notably, *OGI Regulations* only cover the government, not any other branches.

[4] Helen Darbishire, *Proactive Transparency: The Future of the Right to Information? A Review of Standards, Challenges, and Opportunities* (World Bank Institute Governance Working Paper Series), World Bank, Washington, DC, 2010, https://documents1.worldbank.org/curated/en/100521468339595607/pdf/565980WP0Box351roactiveTransparency.pdf (accessed between February 21, 2025 and March 31, 2025).

units in the rural areas where Deng Xiaoping initiated his national economic reform. This bottom-up approach to transparency promotion is contrary to common assumptions that higher educational and socio-economic status of citizens leads to greater aspirations and higher capacities for the free flow of information. However, the approach seems suitable to the Chinese political environment. Given the sensitivity and complexity of the issue, political reforms (including governmental transparency) implementation in China has been gradual, cautious, and incremental. If political reforms originated in large cities and at the central level, insurmountable resistance from powerful interest groups would ensue. Once such reforms failed, social turmoil would likely result. Political reforms, originating in rural areas and at local levels, provided a solid foundation for similar reforms to germinate in higher levels of government. Even if such local level political reforms failed, unbearable political and social consequences for the whole nation would be unlikely.

In the late 1970s and early 1980s, dismantling of rural communes[5] began. Villagers organized committees as governing institutions to manage public properties and agricultural production. Villagers directly elected all committee members, and some committees introduced the practice of "open village affairs" (OVA, *cunwugongkai* 村务公开) by periodically publicizing the village's budgets and expenditures.[6] Similar OVA practices later extended to all villages in the country. In 1982, the *Chinese Constitution* included this system of autonomy.[7]

The OVA program became institutionalized, and according to *Organic Law of Villager Committees* with a pilot trial in 1987 and fully adopted

[5] Mao Zedong founded the people's communes in 1958. Mao did this to promote small-scale production of steel in order to compete with Britain and the United States. Communal dining characterized communes, which banned private cooking. Governmentally sanctioned communes exercised tremendous power over distribution and management of all rural resources.

[6] The author of this book was born in the 1970s and grew up in a village in Sichuan Province until he left for college at the age of 18. As a teenager and college student returning home for winter/summer vacations, he personally witnessed many practices of OVA. For example, he attended village committee meetings several times with his mother and saw in person how the village committee announced budgets and expenditures, and how villagers questioned their leaders ferociously about the truthfulness of the financial information disclosed.

[7] *Constitution of the People's Republic of China 1982*. Art. 111; Hanhua Zhou, *Open Government in China: Practice and Problems*, *in* THE RIGHT TO KNOW: TRANSPARENCY FOR AN OPEN WORLD 93 (Ann Florini & Joseph E. Stiglitz eds., 2007).

in 1998 by the National People's Congress, village committees were to follow "the system of open administration of village affairs" by publicizing, every six months, information concerning various aspects of village governance.[8] Information obligatory for committees to disclose range from revenues, expenditures, property status, debts, financial claims, and village leaders' official contractual performances, family planning, disaster relief, and land expropriation.[9]

The success of the OVA initiatives attracted the attention of the party and the central government, which held many meetings[10] and issued a series of notices and documents[11] to enhance transparency in the countryside. OVA oversight teams (*cunwugongkaijianduxiaozu* 村务公开监督小组) established in 2004 for villages throughout the country oversaw

[8] *Organic Law of the Villager Committees 1998. Art. 22.* The law, amended in 2010, contains a revision that increases the rigor of the disclosure standard. According to the revised law, "information concerning general matters shall be disclosed at least once every quarter; financial receipts and expenditures shall be disclosed at least once every month if collective financial transactions are frequent; and significant matters involving the interests of villagers shall be disclosed at any time when they occur." *Organic Law of the Villager Committees 1998* (amended in 2010). Art. 30.

[9] Hanhua Zhou, *Open Government in China: Practice and Problems*, *in* THE RIGHT TO KNOW: TRANSPARENCY FOR AN OPEN WORLD 95 (Ann Florini & Joseph E. Stiglitz eds., 2007).

[10] For example, the National Conference on the Construction of Grassroots Organizations in Rural Areas [全国农村基层组织建设工作会议] convened in 1994; the Ministry of Civil Affairs' meeting in 1995 shared among meeting participants experiences from villagers' autonomy [全国村民自治工作经验交流会]; the Central Commission for Discipline Inspection of the Chinese Community Party and the Ministry of Supervision held a forum in Tianjin in 1997 to discuss villages' open affairs [*cunwu gongkai gongzuo zuotanhui* 村务公开工作座谈会].

[11] In October 1994, the General Office of the Chinese Communist Party Central Committee issued *Notice on Enhancing the Construction of Grassroots Organizations in the Rural Areas* [中共中央办公厅关于加强农村基层组织建设的通知]. In April 1998, the General Office of the Chinese Communist Party Central Committee and the General Office of the State Council issued *Notice on Universalizing the System of Open Village Affairs and Democratic Administration in the Rural Areas* [中共中央办公厅、国务院办公厅关于在农村普遍实行村务公开和民主管理制度的通知]. In October 1998, the Third Plenary Session of the 15th National Congress of the Chinese Communist Party adopted *Decisions on Some Major Issues in the Agricultural and Rural Works* [中共中央关于农业和农村工作若干重大问题的决定]. In June 2004, the General Office of the Chinese Communist Party Central Committee and the General Office of the State Council issued *Opinions on Perfecting and Improving the System of Openness and Democratic Administration of Village Affairs* [《中共中央办公厅、国务院办公厅关于健全和完善村务公开和民主管理制度的意见》].

implementation of the OVA system.[12] Team members, elected, have some expertise in finance and accounting. Elections exclude village cadres, spouses, and lineal relatives. Oversight teams examined whether or not information disclosed is "complete and real,"[13] and the expectation is for performance of duties in an "impartial and honest" manner.[14]

After nearly 30 years of virtually complete informational blackout from the government under Mao's rule, Chinese farmers began, in the 1980s, to enjoy unprecedented freedom of information due to frequent and proactive disclosure of information by village committees. The OVA system became so popular that many villagers called it the "Sunshine Project."[15] Opening village affairs to public scrutiny appears trivial on the surface because a wealth of information in the cabinets, safes, and document files of the whole Chinese bureaucracy above the village level still remained inaccessible to the public at the time. However, the importance of village transparency is apparent: The establishment of the OVA system is modern China's first step toward greater government transparency. Jamie P. Horsley, a prolific Yale University scholar of Chinese freedom of information, stated that open village affairs in China "marked

[12] Oversight teams were made possible as a result of the party and government decision. In June 2004, the General Office of the Chinese Communist Party Central Committee and the General Office of the State Council issued a legally binding document. In this document, the party and the government require villages to set up supervision teams to make sure the open village affairs system is implemented effectively. Opinions on Perfecting and Improving the System of Openness and Democratic Administration of Village Affairs [《中共中央办公厅、国务院办公厅关于健全和完善村务公开和民主管理制度的意见》] issued in June 2004.

[13] *Opinions of the General Office of the Chinese Communist Party Central Committee and the General Office of the State Council on Perfecting and Improving the System of Openness and Democratic Administration of Village Affairs* [《中共中央办公厅、国务院办公厅关于健全和完善村务公开和民主管理制度的意见》] issued in June 2004.

[14] *Opinions of the General Office of the Chinese Communist Party Central Committee and the General Office of the State Council on Perfecting and Improving the System of Openness and Democratic Administration of Village Affairs* [《中共中央办公厅、国务院办公厅关于健全和完善村务公开和民主管理制度的意见》] issued in June 2004.

[15] MY COUNTRY'S EXPERIENCE WITH AND CONSIDERATION OF OPEN GOVERNMENT AFFAIRS [我国政府公开的实践与探索] 83 (Hanhua Zhou ed., China Law Publishers, 2003).

a significant advance in the institutionalization of open governance at the village level."[16]

Proactive Disclosure at Township Level: Openness in Governmental Affairs (OGA)

The practices of "open village affairs" (OVA) formally extended from the village level to the township level in December 2000 when the party and the State Council issued *Notice on Promoting Openness in Government Affairs around All Government Agencies at the Township Level*,[17] The "open village affairs" program was subsequently renamed the "openness in government affairs" (OGA, *zhengwugongkai* 政务公开) program. Similar to the "open village affairs" program, the OGA program required township governments to disclose fully to the public all the information vital to the interests of towns' residents.[18] Some exceptions remained: Information of charges for entertainment and traveling expenses, information of rewards and punishments to cadres, and information about whether a township's leading cadres were uncorrupted, honest, and self-disciplined, represented the exemptions to disclosures to the public, but township leaders and their staff must have access to the information.[19] Publication of information occurred through notice billboards, meetings, radio, television, handbooks, and electronic touch screens.[20] Established

[16] Jamie P. Horsley, *Toward a More Open China?*, *in* The Right to Know: Transparency for an Open World 59 (Ann Florini & Joseph E. Stiglitz eds., 2007).

[17] *Notice of the General Office of the Chinese Communist Party Central Committee and the General Office of the State Council on Promoting Openness in Government Affairs around All Government Agencies at the Township Level* [中共中央办公厅、国务院办公厅关于在全国乡镇政权机关全面推行政务公开制度的通知], issued December 2000.

[18] *Notice of the General Office of the Chinese Communist Party Central Committee and the General Office of the State Council on Promoting Openness in Government Affairs around All Government Agencies at the Township Level* [中共中央办公厅、国务院办公厅关于在全国乡镇政权机关全面推行政务公开制度的通知] issued December 2000.

[19] *Notice of the General Office of the Chinese Communist Party Central Committee and the General Office of the State Council on Promoting Openness in Government Affairs around All Government Agencies at the Township Level* [中共中央办公厅、国务院办公厅关于在全国乡镇政权机关全面推行政务公开制度的通知] issued December 2000.

[20] *Notice of the General Office of the Chinese Communist Party Central Committee and the General Office of the State Council on Promoting Openness in Government Affairs around All Government Agencies at the Township Level* [中共中央办公厅、国务院办公厅关于在全国乡镇政权机关全面推行政务公开制度的通知] issued December 2000.

oversight teams scrutinized the township's OGA program for operation and effectiveness.[21] The *Notice* even encouraged news media to report townships' OGA programs. People were free to have programs' irregularities exposed by journalists.[22]

Proactive Disclosure Above Township Level: Openness in Governmental Affairs (OGA)

Responding to the party and the central government,[23] governmental agencies extended the practices of "openness in governmental affairs" program from the township level to higher-level, county governments (*xian* 县) and county-level city governments (*xianjishi* 县级市).[24]

21 *Notice of the General Office of the Chinese Communist Party Central Committee and the General Office of the State Council on Promoting Openness in Government Affairs around All Government Agencies at the Township Level* [中共中央办公厅、国务院办公厅关于在全国乡镇政权机关全面推行政务公开制度的通知] issued December 2000.

22 *Notice of the General Office of the Chinese Communist Party Central Committee and the General Office of the State Council on Promoting Openness in Government Affairs around All Government Agencies at Township Level* [中共中央办公厅、国务院办公厅关于在全国乡镇政权机关全面推行政务公开制度的通知] issued December 2000.

23 In the *Notice on Promoting Openness in Government Affairs around All Government Agencies at the Township Level* issued in 2000, the party and the State Council mandated governments above township-level to prepare for implementation of a similar "openness in governmental affairs" program.

24 According to a 2015 news reports, Mainland China has more than 2800 county-level administrative regions, including counties and county-level cities. Liang Chen, *Beijing Summons Thousands of County-Level Officials to Learn the art of Ruling*, Global Times, January 26, 2015, https://www.globaltimes.cn/content/904046.shtml (accessed between February 21, 2025 and March 31, 2025). In 1988, the Gaocheng County in Hebei Province became the first county-level government to disclose administrative rules and decisions as a gesture of accepting the public's supervision. However, similar practices of open government affairs at the county-level were sporadic throughout the 1980s and the 1990s. Institutionalization of practices did not occur until after 2000 upon issuance of the notice on township governmental transparency. Openness in Governmental Affairs [政务公开] 7 (The General Office of the Central Commission for Discipline Inspection, ed., Beijing Fangzheng Press, 2004).

Provinces (*sheng* 省),[25] autonomous regions (*zizhiqu* 自治区),[26] municipalities directly under the central government (*zhixiashi* 直辖市),[27] and central governmental ministries (*guojiabuwei* 国家部委)[28] followed suit.

For example, many ministries, such as the General Office of the State Council in 2002,[29] the National Auditing Office in 2003,[30] the Ministry

[25] Provinces total 23, including Taiwan, *available at* http://english.www.gov.cn/archive/china_abc/2014/08/27/content_281474983873401.htm (accessed between February 21, 2025 and March 31, 2025).

[26] Mainland China has five autonomous regions (Xinjiang, Tibet, Inner Mongolia, Ningxia and Guangxi), *available at* http://english.www.gov.cn/archive/china_abc/2014/08/27/content_281474983873401.htm (accessed between February 21, 2025 and March 31, 2025).

[27] Four municipalities are directly beneath the central government (Beijing, Shanghai, Tianjin, and Chongqing). These four big cities have provincial-level governments, available at http://english.www.gov.cn/archive/china_abc/2014/08/27/content_281474983873401.htm (accessed between February 21, 2025 and March 31, 2025).

[28] The State Council under the leadership of Prime Minister Li Qiang consists of 26 ministries and commissions, such as the Ministry of Foreign Affairs, the Ministry of Finance, the Ministry of Agriculture, and the Ministry of Public Security. For organizational structure of the State Council, visit https://www.gov.cn/gwyzzjg/zuzhi/ (accessed between February 21, 2025 and March 31, 2025) and https://english.www.gov.cn/archive/chinaabc/201911/22/content_WS5ed77233c6d0b3f0e9499854.html (accessed between February 21, 2025 and March 31, 2025).

[29] Beginning in 2002, the General Office of the State Council provided free copies of Gazettes of the State Council to all branches of government above township-level and democratic parties. Songyan Zhu, *Analysis of and Thoughts on Current Situation of FOI in China*, 3 Journal of Expanding Horizons 31 (2003). The Gazette contains almost all the Chinese laws, regulations, and executive orders published later than 1999. Currently anyone in the world can access the website (https://english.www.gov.cn/archive/statecouncilgazette/) for the Gazette of the State Council. The U.S. equivalent of the Gazette of the State Council is the *Federal Register*, the official journal of the federal government of the United States, published daily, since the 1930s, with proposed rules and final rules of federal agencies.

[30] In 2003, the National Auditing Office decided to open all auditing reports and investigation reports to the public by 2007. Previously, almost all auditing reports were secret, submitted only to the State Council and the NPC. *Auditing Reports to Be Opened*, People's Daily Online, July 05, 2003, http://english.peopledaily.com.cn/200307/05/eng20030705_119503.shtml (accessed between February 21, 2025 and March 31, 2025).

of Commerce in 2003,[31] the Ministry of Transportation,[32] and the Ministry of Foreign Affairs (MFA) in 2004, adopted OGA practices in the 2000s. The establishment of the OGA program at the MFA is most noteworthy. As one of the most secretive governmental agencies in China, the MFA has become more transparent since 2004 by boldly declassifying huge volumes of diplomatic documents.[33] The declassified archives "disclose many unknown stories for the first time to the public."[34]

[31] *Notice of the Ministry of Commerce on Issuing the "Interim Measures of the Ministry of Commerce for Making Administrative Affairs Known to the Public"* [商务部关于印发《商务部政务公开暂行办法》的通知] No. 444 (2003).

[32] *Notice of the Ministry of Transportation on Printing the Interim Rules on Openness in Government Affairs* [《关于印发《交通部机关政务公开规定（试行）》的通知》] No. 58 (2004).

[33] In 2004, the MFA declassified diplomatic archives from between 1949 and 1955. In 2006, it declassified archives from between 1956 and 1960. In 2008, it opened archives from between 1961 and 1965; one-third of these documents once had top-secret classifications. The MFA opened 81,487 classified documents to public inspection by the end of 2011. The transparency movement didn't lose its momentum until 2013. Tingying Zheng, *Declassified Diplomatic Documents Show that Dalai Lama Stole and Sold Gold, Silver and Jewelry when Exiled from Tibet* [中国外交部解密档案显示达赖流亡时盗卖金银财宝] YOUTH REFERENCE NEWS, republished on Sina News, January 13, 2009, http://news.sina.com.cn/c/2009-01-13/145817035599.shtml (accessed between February 21, 2025 and March 31, 2025); *Annual OGI Work Report of the Ministry of Foreign Affairs (2011)* [外交部 2011 年政府信息公开工作年度报告], the Ministry of Foreign Affairs, Beijing, China, March 30, 2012, *available at* https://www.mfa.gov.cn/web/wjb_673085/zfxxgk_674865/zfxxgknb/201203/t20120330_9277415.shtml (accessed between February 21, 2025 and March 31, 2025); Patrick Boehler, *China's Foreign Ministry Curtails Access to Declassified Historic Archives*, SOUTH CHINA MORNING POST, August 9, 2013, https://www.scmp.com/news/china-insider/article/1295456/chinas-diplomats-curtail-access-their-historic-archives (accessed between February 21, 2025 and March 31, 2025).

[34] *China further Declassifies Diplomatic Files*, PEOPLE'S DAILY ONLINE, May 13, 2006, (captured by Internet Archive Wayback Machine on November 5, 2007), retrieved from https://web.archive.org/web/20071105100800/http://english.peopledaily.com.cn/200605/13/eng20060513_265380.html (accessed between February 21, 2025 and March 31, 2025).

Similar to the State Council's ministries, provincial governments in Fujian,[35] Guangdong,[36] and many other provinces scrambled to open their files to public inspection after 2000. Major cities, like Harbin, Taiyuan and Shenzhen, also institutionalized OGA practices.[37] Thirty-one provincial governments, 36 ministerial agencies, and 15 sub-provincial cities (*fushengjichengshi* 副省级城市) adopted OGA rules or regulations, according to a 2006 investigation.[38]

Proactive and Reactive Disclosure at City and Provincial Levels: From OGA to OGI

Inspired by the accomplishments of the OGA program, the State Council joined the Chinese Communist Party's Central Committee to issue *Opinions on Further Promoting Openness in Government Affairs* in 2005,[39] the

[35] *Interim Rule of Fujian Province on Openness in Government Affairs* [《福建省政务公开暂行办法》] No. 70 (2001). Fujian was the first province to institutionalize the OGA practices at provincial level. Xi Jinping, China's incumbent president and secretary general of the Communist Party, signed the Rule in 2001 when he was the governor of Fujian Province.

[36] *Guangdong Provincial Regulations on Making Government Administration Open* [《广东省政务公开条例》] passed on July 29, 2005 and came into effect on October 1, 2005. Guangdong was the first province to elevate the status of OVA rules to OVA regulations. In China, provincial people's congresses have the authority to enact local regulations, which have a higher legal standing than administrative rules.

[37] All these three cities adopted its *Openness in Government Affairs Rules* in 2003.

[38] Yajie Li & Qin Zhang, *Thirty-One Provincial Governments Adopted Rules on Openness in Government Affairs* [目前全国31个省（自治区、直辖市）政府建立政务公开管理制度] Xinhua News Agency, December 10, 2006 (captured by Internet Archive Wayback Machine on December 12, 2006), retrieved from https://web.archive.org/web/20061212054433/http://news.xinhuanet.com/politics/2006-12/10/content_5463416.htm (accessed between February 21, 2025 and March 31, 2025).

[39] *Opinions of the General Office of the Chinese Communist Party Central Committee and the General Office of the State Council on Further Promoting Openness in Government Affairs* [《中共中央办公厅国务院办公厅关于进一步推行政务公开的意见》] No. 12 (2005) of the General Office of the Chinese Communist Party Central Committee.

year of extending the OGA proactive disclosure practices to all levels of government.[40] The Opinions *are* significant for four reasons:

First, the *Opinions* required government agencies to further enhance the proactive disclosure of information and establish a system of "reactive disclosure of information."[41] From open village affairs (OVA) in the 1980s to openness in governmental affairs (OGA) in the early 2000s, the sphere of Chinese freedom of information was incomplete because programs relied solely on proactive disclosure of information. The term, "reactive disclosure," initially introduced in 2005, had explicit mention in the policy document of the Chinese Communist Party, indicating that freedom of information in China would soon be wide-ranging.

Second, the *Opinions* sought the relevant parties to expedite formulation of *Open Government Information (OGI) Regulations* and encouraged local governments to adopt interim OGI Rules.[42] This demonstrated the central government's determination to enhance practices of governmental transparency and use reactive disclosure to supplement proactive dissemination.

Third, the policy directive required agencies to disclose all types of information held, with the only exceptions being state secrets, trade secrets, or individual privacy.[43] Fourth, the *Opinions* mandated agencies at all levels to establish offices to lead and execute OGI initiatives.[44]

[40] *Opinions of the General Office of the Chinese Communist Party Central Committee and the General Office of the State Council on Further Promoting Openness in Government Affairs* [《中共中央办公厅国务院办公厅关于进一步推行政务公开的意见》] No. 12 (2005) of the General Office of the Chinese Communist Party Central Committee.

[41] *Opinions of the General Office of the Chinese Communist Party Central Committee and the General Office of the State Council on Further Promoting Openness in Government Affairs* [《中共中央办公厅国务院办公厅关于进一步推行政务公开的意见》] No. 12 (2005) of the General Office of the Chinese Communist Party Central Committee.

[42] *Opinions of the General Office of the Chinese Communist Party Central Committee and the General Office of the State Council on Further Promoting Openness in Government Affairs* [《中共中央办公厅国务院办公厅关于进一步推行政务公开的意见》] No. 12 (2005) of the General Office of the Chinese Communist Party Central Committee.

[43] *Opinions of the General Office of the Chinese Communist Party Central Committee and the General Office of the State Council on Further Promoting Openness in Government Affairs* [《中共中央办公厅国务院办公厅关于进一步推行政务公开的意见》] No. 12 (2005) of the General Office of the Chinese Communist Party Central Committee.

[44] *Opinions of the General Office of the Chinese Communist Party Central Committee and the General Office of the State Council on Further Promoting Openness in Government*

Boosted by the *Opinions* and invigorated by the achievements of the OGA program, in 2002, Chinese local governments began to experiment with OGI-related legislation or rulemaking. Among the 49 comparatively larger cities[45] in China, in November 2002, Guangzhou was the first city to initiate OGI legislation.[46] By the end of 2006, 17 comparatively larger cities had adopted OGI Rules.[47] Many provincial governments expressed the same eagerness for construction of OGI rules, and among 31 provincial governments in Mainland China, Shanghai published the first provincial-level OGI legislation in 2004.[48] Twelve governments at the province level had adopted OGI Rules by the end of 2006.[49] Unlike the local OGA rules that required governmental agencies to disseminate, only proactively, information, the city and provincial-level OGI rules compelled relevant administrative agencies to engage in proactively divulging information but also to release information upon request from individuals or organizations. These local OGI provisions all established "two fundamental novel ideas: that Chinese government agencies have an *obligation* to disseminate, on their own initiatives and disclose upon request most of the information that they hold, and that Chinese citizens have a *right* to access such information."[50] The OGI Rules passed

Affairs [《中共中央办公厅国务院办公厅关于进一步推行政务公开的意见》] No. 12 (2005) of the General Office of the Chinese Communist Party Central Committee.

45 A comparatively larger city in China refers to a city where a provincial or autonomous regional people's government is located or where a special economic zone is located, or a city approved as such by the State Council. According to Article 73 of *Legislation Law 2000*, a comparatively larger city has the authority to enact local rules, whose legal status is weaker than the *Constitution*, the law, and the regulations. *Legislation Law 2000*. Art. 73.

46 *Guangzhou Municipal Provisions on Open Government Information* [《广州市政府信息公开规定》] issued November 6, 2002, and effective January 1, 2003.

47 Weibing Xiao, Freedom of Information Reform in China: Information Flow Analysis 73 (2011).

48 *Provisions of Shanghai Municipality on Open Government Information* (promulgated on January 20, 2004, and nullified by *Provisions of Shanghai Municipality on Open Government Inform*ation on April 28, 2008).

49 Those 12 provincial governments are Beijing, Hebei, Liaoning, Jilin, Helongjiang, Shanghai, Jiangsu, Hubei, Guangdong, Hainan, Chongqing, and Shanxi. Weibing Xiao, Freedom of Information Reform in China: Information Flow Analysis 75 (2011).

50 Jamie P. Horsley, *Toward a More Open China?*, *in* The Right to Know: Transparency for an Open World 71 (Ann Florini & Joseph E. Stiglitz eds., 2007).

by city and provincial governments provided the central government with "the most comprehensive framework" to use as a reference and basis for drafting national OGI legislation.[51]

Proactive and Reactive Disclosure at the National Level: From OGA to OGI

Ultimately, the OGI legislation was extended from city and provincial levels to the national level because the success of proactive and reactive disclosure of government-held information at the sub-national level provided Chinese OGI reformers with valuable lessons and experiences for drafting the national OGI legislation. The party provided important political and policy guidance for creating nationwide OGI legislation[52]; whereas, the National People's Congress (NPC) and the State Council had direct involvement in formulation of national *OGI Regulations*.

Failed Legislative Endeavor at the NPC

Despite both the NPC's and State Council's involvement, the law-making activities of these two powerful organizations generated sharply different

[51] Jamie P. Horsley, *Shanghai Advances the Cause of Open Government Information in China*, freedominfo.org, Washington, DC, April 20, 2004, *available at* http://www.freedominfo.org/2004/04/shanghai-advances-the-cause-of-open-government-information-in-china/ (accessed between February 21, 2025 and March 31, 2025).

[52] Since 2004, leaders from the party-affiliated national anti-corruption or supervisory agencies, such as the Central Commission for Discipline Inspection (CCDI) and the Leading Group on National Openness in Government Affairs (LGNOGA) reiterated the need to accelerate legislation of *OGI Regulations*. For example, Yong He, deputy director of CCDI and director of LGNOGA, emphasized the importance of *OGI Regulations* on several occasions. Yong He, speech delivered at the Second Meeting of the Leading Group on National Openness in Government Affairs [何勇同志在全国政务公开领导小组第二次会议上的讲话], Beijing, 29 April 2004; Yong He, *The Leading Group on National Openness in Government Affairs Answered the Questions from Journalists about Notice on Further Promoting Openness in Government Affairs* [全国政务公开领导小组有关负责人就《中共中央办公厅 国务院办公厅关于进一步推行政务公开的意见》的颁布答记者问] press release, 27 April 2005; Yong He, speech delivered at the Sixth Meeting of the Leading Group on National Openness in Government Affairs [何勇同志在全国政务公开领导小组第六次会议上的讲话], Beijing, 31 March 2006; Yong He, speech delivered at the Seventh Meeting of the Leading Group on National Openness in Government Affairs [何勇同志在全国政务公开领导小组第七次会议上的讲话], Beijing, 21 March 2007.

outcomes. Many NPC deputies advocated OGI law, arguing that the OGI law would resolve problems that "local OGI rules failed to tackle."[53] Li Li, a deputy of the NPC, submitted a proposal to the First Session of the 10th National People's Congress in 2003, petitioning the NPC to enact a national OGI law.[54] Li said that many local OGI rules exempt disclosing state secrets; however, no rules clearly defined state secrets. Consequently, a national OGI law needed to standardize local OGI legislation activities and "avoid confusion."[55] Li was just one of many NPC deputies submitting proposals to the NPC for enactment of a national OGI law. NPC Deputies submitted such proposals seven times between 2002 and 2009.[56]

[53] Local OGI Rules became less effective because many other conflicting regulations and laws had higher legal standing than OGI Rules. Zhuobin Liao & Xiaozhen Cheng, *Focus on Legislative Proposals of the Chinese People's Political Consultative Conference and the National People's Congres: Citizens can Sue Government Agencies for Non-Disclosure of Information* [聚焦两会之提案议案 信息不公开市民可起诉] *INFORMATION TIMES*, March 4, 2003, at A3, republished on China.com.cn (captured by Internet Archive Wayback Machine on June 24, 2003), retrieved from https://web.archive.org/web/20030624004653/http://www.china.com.cn/chinese/law/285943.htm (accessed between February 21, 2025 and March 31, 2025).

[54] Zhuobin Liao & Xiaozhen Cheng, *Focus on Legislative Proposals of the Chinese People's Political Consultative Conference and the National People's Congres: Citizens can Sue Government Agencies for Non-Disclosure of Information* [聚焦两会之提案议案 信息不公开市民可起诉] *INFORMATION TIMES*, March 4, 2003, at A3, republished on China.com.cn (captured by Internet Archive Wayback Machine on June 24, 2003), retrieved from https://web.archive.org/web/20030624004653/http://www.china.com.cn/chinese/law/285943.htm (accessed between February 21, 2025 and March 31, 2025).

[55] Zhuobin Liao & Xiaozhen Cheng, *Focus on Legislative Proposals of the Chinese People's Political Consultative Conference and the National People's Congres: Citizens can Sue Government Agencies for Non-Disclosure of Information* [聚焦两会之提案议案 信息不公开市民可起诉] *INFORMATION TIMES*, March 4, 2003, at A3, republished on China.com.cn (captured by Internet Archive Wayback Machine on June 24, 2003), retrieved from https://web.archive.org/web/20030624004653/http://www.china.com.cn/chinese/law/285943.htm (accessed between February 21, 2025 and March 31, 2025).

[56] WEIBING XIAO, FREEDOM OF INFORMATION REFORM IN CHINA: INFORMATION FLOW ANALYSIS 76 (2011).

In 2003, the Standing Committee of the 10th NPC listed OGI law in the "secondary priority category" of its five-year legislative plan (2003–2008).[57] However, since this plan lacked enactment, the NPC decided to postpone indefinitely the legislation of OGI law and allow the State Council to draft *OGI Regulations* first. The explanation for the NPC's tabling the OGI law from the Internal and Judicial Affairs Committee of the NPC, in 2004, was that the State Council was drafting *OGI Regulations*, and that enactment of OGI law would not occur until after gathering "practical experiences" from implementation of *OGI Regulations*.[58] Despite the postponement of formulation of the OGI law, the NPC stressed that "it is highly necessary" to adopt OGI law in the future in order to hold government agencies accountable and safeguard the public's rights to know (*zhiqingquan* 知情权), participate (*canyuquan* 参与权), and supervise (*jianduquan* 监督权).[59]

The OGI legislative attempt at the NPC failed for several key reasons. First, introducing laws directly without following prior regulatory processes did not coincide with previous Chinese law-making practices. In China, lawmakers usually formulate administrative regulations and wait several years to identify problems associated with implementation. Only then can upgrading administrative regulations to administrative laws occur. Second, the NPC legislators may have felt insecurity for possible political and social implications of a national OGI law. Provincial OGI practices indicate that local OGI legislation did not undermine

[57] Weibing Xiao, Freedom of Information Reform in China: Information Flow Analysis 76 (2011). According to legal scholar, Weibing Xiao, the five-year legislative plan of the Standing Committee of the 10th National People's Congress classified bills and amendments into two categories. Bills and amendments of first priority should undergo review in the 10th National People's Congress. Bills and amendments representing secondary priority required research and drafting. Whether or not and when review of second priority bills and amendments would occur remained undetermined.

[58] *Report on the Review Results of the Proposals from the Deputies of the Second Plenary Session of the 10th National People's Congress by the Internal and Judicial Affairs Committee of the National People's Congress* [全国人大内务司法委员会关于第四届全国人民代表大会第二次会议主席团交付审议的代表提出的议案审议结果的报告], Beijing, October 2004.

[59] *Report on the Review Results of the Proposals from the Deputies of the Second Plenary Session of the 10th National People's Congress by the Internal and Judicial Affairs Committee of the National People's Congress* [全国人大内务司法委员会关于第四届全国人民代表大会第二次会议主席团交付审议的代表提出的议案审议结果的报告], Beijing, October 2004.

national security, privacy, trade secrets, and other key social interests,[60] but most legislators, in 2004, remained uncertain of political and social consequences that enactment of a national OGI law would entail.

Long-Delayed Legislative Attempt in the State Council

The legislative effort of the State Council to relax government information control began in the late 1990s. In 1997, the National Administration for the Protection of State Secrets recognized a need to revise *the Law on Guarding State Secrets*, adopted in 1988. The law, increasingly and overly restrictive of disclosing governmental information,[61] had a scope so expansive that finding a Chinese document labeled "absolutely secret" in American university libraries was easy, due to the impossibility of the Chinese government maintaining so many secrets.[62] The Administration leaders invited the Law Institute of the Chinese Academy of Social Science (CASS)[63] to assume responsibility for revision of the law. Legal scholar, Hanhua Zhou, and his CASS colleagues began research of OGI under the guise of the neutral-sounding program, "Exploitation, Use and Management of Government Information Resources."[64] Zhou

60 *Explanation Memorandum of the Draft of OGI Regulations 2002* [政府信息公开条例 (草案) 起草说明], The State Council Informatization Office, Beijing, 2002, at 13.

61 Wei Zhang, *Initial Purpose of the Legislation Was to Create a Mechanism to Push Reform: View of CASS Scholar Zhou Hanhua on OGI Regulations* [立法初衷就是要建立一种改革倒逼机制: 中国社科院研究员周汉华谈政府信息公开条例], Legal Daily, republished by Sohu News, May 3, 2011, http://news.sohu.com/20110503/n280474900.shtml (accessed between February 21, 2025 and March 31, 2025).

62 Jasper Becker, *Comrade Jiang Zemin Does Indeed Seem a Proper Choice*, 23 London Review of Books 10, May 24, 2001, at 12, *available at* http://www.lrb.co.uk/v23/n10/jasper-becker/comrade-jiang-zemin-does-indeed-seem-a-proper-choice (accessed between February 21, 2025 and March 31, 2025).

63 The Chinese Academy of Social Sciences (CASS), *available at* http://casseng.cssn.cn/sky_about/aboutcass/ (accessed between February 21, 2025 and March 31, 2025). CASS is one of the most prestigious official think tanks of the Chinese government. According to the CASS website, the CASS is the highest academic research organization in the fields of philosophy and social sciences as well as a national center for comprehensive studies in China.

64 Wei Zhang, *Initial Purpose of the Legislation Was to Create a Mechanism to Push Reform: View of CASS Scholar Zhou Hanhua on OGI Regulations* [立法初衷就是要建立一种改革倒逼机制: 中国社科院研究员周汉华谈政府信息公开条例], Legal Daily, republished by Sohu News, May 3, 2011, http://news.sohu.com/20110503/n280474900.shtml (accessed between February 21, 2025 and March 31, 2025).

created this ruse because OGI remained a politically sensitive topic in China at that time.[65] OGI was politically unacceptable to the Chinese authorities at the time, a reaction to the failure of Glasnost in the Soviet Union and the close link between freedom of information and freedom of expression.[66] Authorities had good reason to fear freedom of information. As Western scholars observed, "Access to government information and freedom of expression are intimately linked. In order to form opinions that are worthy of being expressed, individuals must have access to relevant government information."[67]

Largely due to their experiences researching OGI, the Leading Group of National Informatization (LGNI) (*guojiaxinxihualingdaoxiaozu* 国家信息化领导小组) and the State Council Informatization Office (SCIO) (*guowuyuanxinxihuagongzuobangongshi* 国务院信息化工作办公室) chose Hanhua Zhou and his CASS colleagues, in May 2002, to draft *OGI Regulations*.[68] The LGNI and the SCIO, two leading agencies consisting of many leaders in the party, the State Council, and the military, received the task of establishing the Chinese e-government.[69] The two agencies, supported by the policy document, *Guidance on Building E-Government*,[70] promoted OGI from the perspective of responding to their assigned task.[71]

[65] Zhou recalled that he refused the invitation from the National Administration for the Protection of State Secrets at first because of the sensitivity of the task. However, an Administration leader finally persuaded Zhou into taking up the task of law revision. HANHUA ZHOU, GOVERNMENT GOVERNANCE AND ADMINISTRATIVE LAW (PREFACE) [政府监管与行政法 (序言)] (2007).

[66] Many party elders felt uncomfortable with extravagant levels of freedom of expression enjoyed by people during the Cultural Revolution.

[67] John M. Ackerman & Irma E. Sandoval-Ballesteros, *The Global Explosion of Freedom of Information Laws,* 58 ADMINISTRATIVE LAW REVIEW. 85, 88 (2006).

[68] *Explanation Memorandum of the Draft of OGI Regulations 2002* [政府信息公开条例 (草案) 起草说明], The State Council Informatization Office, Beijing, 2002, at 23.

[69] The LGNI was created in 1999 and reorganized in 2001. The LGNI is headed by Chinese primers. As the administrative arm of the LGNI, the SCIO, founded in 2001, merged with the Ministry of Industry and Information Technology in 2008.

[70] *Notice on Forwarding LGNI Guidance on the Establishment of E-Government* [关于转发《国家信息化领导小组关于我国电子政务建设指导意见》的通知] No. 17 [2002] of the General Office of the Chinese Communist Party Central Committee.

[71] *Explanation Memorandum of the Draft of OGI Regulations 2002* [政府信息公开条例 (草案) 起草说明], The State Council Informatization Office, Beijing, 2002, at 23.

The completed academic draft of *OGI Regulations* (scholarly version for comment),[72] submitted to the SCIO in August 2002,[73] solicited comments and suggestions from experts and government officials. The SCIO revised the draft and, in December 2002, submitted it to the State Council Legislative Affairs Office, the ministerial-level administrative agency within the State Council that assists the Premier with legal advice for legislating administrative laws.[74]

However, the State Council Legislative Affairs Office declined to include, immediately, the generation of *OGI Regulations* in its five-year legislative plan because local OGI rule-making activities, begun in 2002, had not yet provided sufficient practical experiences for the State Council to use for national level OGI legislation; in 2002, the State Council Legislative Affairs Office had "little passion" for enacting *OGI Regulations*.[75]

The situation improved in 2004 when *OGI Regulations* gained listing in the "third priority category" of the legislative plan of the State Council,

[72] In an email interview with Yanbin Lv, a scholar at the CASS Institute of Law and Hanhua Zhou's colleague, Lv expressed that he and his CASS colleagues extensively researched freedom of information legislation in the United States, European countries, and Japan. They produced a draft of *OGI Regulations* for submission to the State Council. Foreign legal experts of OGI legislation received invitations from the State Council to comment and suggest additions. This draft, proposed by experts and academics, remains without official publication; however, a book published in August 2003 contains the text. ACADEMIC DRAFT OF OGI REGULATIONS: DRAFT, EXPLANATION, RATIONALE AND LEGISLATIVE EXAMPLES [政府信息公开条例专家建议稿-草案、说明、理由、立法例] (Hanhua Zhou ed., Chinese Legal Publishing House, 2003).

[73] *Explanation Memorandum of the Draft of OGI Regulations 2002* [政府信息公开条例（草案）起草说明], The State Council Informatization Office, Beijing, 2002, at 23.

[74] *Explanation Memorandum of the Draft of OGI Regulations 2002* [政府信息公开条例（草案）起草说明], The State Council Informatization Office, Beijing, 2002, at 24; Hanhua Zhou, *Legislative History of OGI Regulations in China* [政府信息公开条例]出台始末], 7 E-GOVERNMENT *17* (2008).

[75] WEIBING XIAO, FREEDOM OF INFORMATION REFORM IN CHINA: INFORMATION FLOW ANALYSIS 77 (2011).

indicating a requirement for more research.[76] The status of the proposed *OGI Regulations* did not change in 2005.[77]

As OGI legislations at the city and provincial levels developed in 2006, the central government recognized the timeliness of considering national OGI legislation. In early 2006, Hu Jintao, in a meeting of the Chinese Communist Party Central Politburo, stressed the need to accelerate governmental action.[78] In that same year, the State Council finally listed drafting of *OGI Regulations* in the "first priority category" of its legislative plan, indicating approval of the law within that year.[79] However, the approval did not occur until 2007 when the State Council adopted *OGI Regulations*, in principle, on January 17, and approved the revision on April 5, after further revision, published the final text on April 24.[80] *OGI Regulations* came into force on May 1, 2008, after nearly

[76] Ming Tu, *Behind-the-Scene Proponent of OGI Regulations* [政府信息公开条例的背后推手], PHOENIX TV, republished by reformdata.org, March 21, 2007, http://www.reformdata.org/2007/0321/15413.shtml (accessed between February 21, 2025 and March 31, 2025).

[77] Ming Tu, *Behind-the-Scene Proponent of OGI Regulations* [政府信息公开条例的背后推手], PHOENIX TV, republished by reformdata.org, March 21, 2007, http://www.reformdata.org/2007/0321/15413.shtml (accessed between February 21, 2025 and March 31, 2025).

[78] Ming Tu, *Behind-the-Scene Proponent of OGI Regulations* [政府信息公开条例的背后推手], PHOENIX TV, republished by reformdata.org, March 21, 2007, http://www.reformdata.org/2007/0321/15413.shtml (accessed between February 21, 2025 and March 31, 2025).

[79] Xiaofang Feng, *OGI Regulations Listed on Legislative Plan and Could Be Adopted by the End of 2006* [《政府信息公开条例》入立法计划 有望年内出台], XINHUA NEWS AGENCY, republished on the official website of the State Council of the People's Republic of China, March 17, 2006, http://www.gov.cn/jrzg/2006/0317/content_229647.htm (accessed between February 21, 2025 and March 31, 2025).

[80] Jamie P. Horsle, *China Adopts First Nationwide Open Government Information Regulations*, Freedominfo.org, para. 37, *available at* https://www.freedominfo.org/2007/05/china-adopts-first-nationwide-open-government-information-regulations/ (accessed between February 21, 2025 and March 31, 2025) (noting "an unusually long gap between approval and promulgation"); *New Rules Issued to Require Government Transparency*, CHINA DAILY, April 24, 2007, http://www.chinadaily.com.cn/china/2007-04/24/content_858745.htm (accessed between February 21, 2025 and March 31, 2025); *Landmark Decree to Encourage Government Transparency*, CHINA DAILY, April 24, 2007, http://www.chinadaily.com.cn/china/2007-04/24/content_857930.htm (accessed between February 21, 2025 and March 31, 2025); *China Announces New Measures to Promote Openness*, VOICE OF AMERICA, April 24, 2007, https://www.voanews.com/a/a-13-2007-04-24-voa9/337433.html (accessed between February 21, 2025

30 years of incremental and uneven progress toward greater governmental transparency. China finally broke a millennium-long tradition of governmental secrecy and joined the global community with freedom of information.

Rationales for the Rise of Freedom of Information in China

The reasons for the Chinese move toward greater governmental transparency are multifold with both foreign and domestic factors contributing. Among all the external factors, competition for the 29th International Summer Olympic Games is a short-term and superficial one. *OGI Regulations* became effective on May 1, 2008, just three months before the Olympics in Beijing. For China to be selected to host the Olympics, an event long hoped for by Chinese people, the Chinese government needed greater transparency to garner a favorable international image. Pressure and influence from the United States and the World Trade Organization (WTO),[81] however, was a prominent and long-lasting encouragement for China's transparent governance and final adoption of *OGI Regulations*.

Transparency Pressure from the United States and the WTO

China embraced the strategy of reform and engaging the outside world in 1978. One year later, the country established diplomatic relations with its long estranged ideological rival, the United States. The economic and trade exchanges between these two powers soon burgeoned. In the 1980s, the United States began its bilateral investment treaty (BIT) negotiations with China as part of a move to encourage foreign countries, including China, to adopt market-oriented domestic policies that

and March 31, 2025); Anthony Kuhn, *China Moves Toward Release of Classified Data*, National Public Radio, April 24, 2007, http://www.npr.org/templates/story/story.php?storyId=9803236 (accessed between February 21, 2025 and March 31, 2025).

[81] Wenjing Liu, *Approaching Democracy Through Transparency: A Comparative Law Study on Chinese Open Government Information*, 26 American University International Law Review 983, 989 (noting that WTO principle of transparency played a major role in the reform of Chinese administrative law and that the China Law Center of Yale Law School helped draft *Guangzhou Municipal Measures on Public Participation in Formulating Rules* in 2005).

treat private investment in "an open, transparent, and non-discriminatory way."[82] The negotiations ceased in 1989 as a result of the Tiananmen Square Incident. Negotiations did not resume until 2008.[83]

Although BIT negotiations were not smooth, the United States achieved progress for encouraging China toward greater transparency after a history of obscure trade rules and opaque administrative procedures. In 1992, the United States signed a market access agreement with China. The first article of this document concerns transparency:

> The Chinese Government will publish *[on] a regular and prompt basis* all laws, regulations, rules, decrees, administrative guidance and policies… only laws, regulations, rules, decrees, administrative guidance, and policies that are published and readily available to other governments and foreign traders will be enforced… Any publication…shall include the effective date of these measures… and provide a contact point within each authority from which relevant information can be obtained…The Chinese Government will designate an official journal dedicated to the publication of the items referred to in this Article and all such items will be published in this journal. The Chinese Government will publish this journal *on a regular basis* and make copies of the issues of this journal *readily available* to domestic and foreign nationals. (emphasis added)[84]

In order to promote closer economic and trade ties with the United States and other countries and resume, as soon as possible, China's status as a contracting party to the General Agreement on Tariffs and Trade (GATT, later replaced by the WTO), Chinese leaders' commitment to

[82] U.S. bilateral investment treaty (BIT) program, The Office of United States Trade Representative, *available at* http://www.ustr.gov/trade-agreements/bilateral-investment-treaties (accessed between February 21, 2025 and March 31, 2025).

[83] Benjamin A. Shobert, *US Inches a BIT Closer to China*, The Asia Times, May 5, 2010 (captured by Internet Archive Wayback Machine on May 8, 2010), retrieved from https://web.archive.org/web/20100508203418/http://www.atimes.com/atimes/China_Business/LE05Cb01.html (accessed between February 21, 2025 and March 31, 2025).

[84] *Memorandum of Understanding Between the Government of the United States of America and the Government of People's Republic of China Concerning Market Access* [《中华人民共和国政府和美利坚合众国政府关于市场准入的谅解备忘录] signed October 10, 1992.

transparency was serious. In March 1992, the State Council issued a directive to publish all national foreign trade and investment laws, regulations, and policies.[85]

China's entry into the World Trade Organization (WTO) in December 2001, and according to its basic dictates, required the country's trade-related rules and procedures to be transparent. Aligning with WTO rules reached between China and other member countries, China should publish trade-related laws, regulations, and other relevant measures and allow wide access before enforcing them; China should also designate an "official journal" to publish relevant legal and policy documents; China should provide an opportunity for people to comment before implementing trade measures; China should establish one or more "inquiry points" to allow inquirers to obtain information within a designated time frame.[86]

China's leaders and reformers "take these accession agreements seriously."[87] They consistently cited WTO's officially documented obligations to promote greater governmental transparency.[88] For example, Chinese government agencies at all levels conducted a nationwide review of all the trade-related laws, regulations, and practices to revise and nullify normative documents countering the WTO's spirit of transparency. The coastal province of Fujian was at the forefront of this movement toward greater government transparency. Prior to China's accession to the WTO in 2001, the province amended or abolished all trade-related

85 *Notice on Reaffirming the Provisions on Formulation and Publication of Nationally Applicable Foreign Trade and Investment-Related Laws, Regulations, and Policies* [国务院办公厅关于重申制定、发布全国性对外经贸法规、政策有关规定的通知] issued by the General Office of the State Council, March 26, 1992.

86 Jamie P. Horsley, *Toward a More Open China?*, *in* THE RIGHT TO KNOW: TRANSPARENCY FOR AN OPEN WORLD 62 (Ann Florini & Joseph E. Stiglitz eds., 2007); Hanhua Zhou, *Basic Considerations in Drafting of Regulations on the Openness of Government Information (Academic Draft)* [起草《政府信息公开条例》(专家建议稿)的基本考虑] 6 CHINESE JOURNAL OF LAW 57 (2002).

87 Jamie P. Horsley, *Toward a More Open China?*, *in* THE RIGHT TO KNOW: TRANSPARENCY FOR AN OPEN WORLD 62 (Ann Florini & Joseph E. Stiglitz eds., 2007).

88 Jamie P. Horsley, *Toward a More Open China?*, *in* THE RIGHT TO KNOW: TRANSPARENCY FOR AN OPEN WORLD 62 (Ann Florini & Joseph E. Stiglitz eds., 2007).

rules, regulations, and normative documents inconsistent with the WTO's transparency obligations.[89]

Ten years after China's accession to the WTO, many leaders and experts spoke highly of the WTO's encouraging China to greater government transparency. Zhenyu Sun, the first ambassador of China to the WTO and the president of China WTO Research Society, observed that the WTO played "an enormous role" for China's transparency in legislative processes.[90]

Andrew L Stoler, Deputy Director-General of the WTO from November 1999 to October 2002, noted that China's entry into the WTO improved transparency of Chinese policies. He asked one journalist, "Do you know that foreign trade statistics in China were once state secrets?"[91]

Eagerness to compete in face-lifting global events like the Olympic Games, increasing pressure from the United States and other developed countries to meet transparency obligations as a precondition for enhancing economic and trade relations, among other external factors, contributed to a gradual rise of freedom of information in China. The main motivations underlying Chinese *OGI Regulations*, however, are largely domestic and internal.

Among all domestic factors that contributed to the rise of freedom of information in China, economic growth and anti-corruption efforts are worthy of mention. Many academics, both Chinese and foreign, view

[89] *Notice of the Fujian Provincial People's Government on Printing and Distributing the Fujian Province's Working Plan to Handle Challenges Related to Accession into World Trade Organization* [福建省人民政府关于印发福建省应对加入世贸组织行动计划纲要的通知] issued by the Fujian Provincial People's Government [Gazette of Fujian Provincial People's Government, minzheng 2001, No. 175], *available at* http://zfgb.fj.gov.cn/929 (accessed between February 21, 2025 and March 31, 2025).

[90] *Expert Says that External Pressure from WTO Compelled China to Reform Internally* [专家谈入世十年: 外部压力倒逼国内改革], YANGCHENG EVENING NEWS, republished by *China News Service*, December 5, 2011, https://www.chinanews.com.cn/cj/2011/12-05/3509402.shtml (accessed between February 21, 2025 and March 31, 2025).

[91] Wei Chen, *WTO Official Exclaims that WTO Has Made China More Transparent and Foreign Trade Statistics Are No Longer State Secrets* [WTO 官员叹中国入世后政策透明: 此前外贸数字都是机密], XINHUA NEWS AGENCY, republished by Phoenix TV, November 20, 2011 (captured by Internet Archive Wayback Machine on November 23, 2011), retrieved from https://web.archive.org/web/20111123041456/http://finance.ifeng.com/news/macro/20111120/5101852.shtml (accessed between February 21, 2025 and March 31, 2025).

these two factors to be key driving forces for adoption of freedom of information legislation in many countries including China.[92] Perhaps, these two forces are overly emphasized. Weibing Xiao, one of the most cited scholars in this book, argued that the aforementioned two factors "should be accorded important but secondary role in FOI reform, as they only have a limited and indirect influence on relaxing Chinese information environment."[93]

Four other factors, as Xiao and many other FOI scholars noted, are largely ignored or discounted in the literature. Actually, these four factors deserve more scholarly attention: reform-minded top leaders' political commitment, legal reform for limiting governmental power and enhancing transparency, improved capacity for disseminating governmental information, and changes in societal and media environments.[94]

Political Commitment from Reform-Minded Top Leaders

Post-Maoist China began the experiment of transparency in villages. The reason for the movement's gathering momentum to expand transparency in all levels of Chinese government is mostly political. The experiment would have failed, at the beginning without unswerving political commitment from Chinese political leaders moving toward socialist democracy and rule of law.

[92] Alasdair Roberts, Blacked Out: Government Secrecy in the Information Age 110 (2006); Zhengqun Zhao, *Discussion of Anti-Corruption through Openness in Government Affairs* [以政务公开反腐败论要] 6 Theory and Modernization 54 (2001); Freedom of Information: A Comparative Legal Survey (Toby Mendel ed., 2nd edn, 2008); Jamie P. Horsley, *Toward a More Open China?, in* The Right to Know: Transparency for an Open World (Ann Florini & Joseph E. Stiglitz eds., 2007); Hanhua Zhou, *Open Government in China: Practice and Problems*, *in* The Right to Know: Transparency for an Open World (Ann Florini & Joseph E. Stiglitz eds., 2007); Colin Darch & Peter G. Underwood, Freedom of Information and the Developing World: The Citizen, the State and Models of Openness 13–15 (2009); Thomas S. Blanton, *Openness Revolution: The Rise of a Global Movement for Freedom of Information*, 1 Development Dialogue 16 (2002).

[93] Weibing Xiao, Freedom of Information Reform in China: Information Flow Analysis 17 (2011). For Xiao's discussion of these two factors, see Chapter 6 of this book: Reassessment of Economic Growth and Anti-Corruption Efforts as Rationales for FOI Reform in China.

[94] Weibing Xiao, Freedom of Information Reform in China: Information Flow Analysis (2011).

Scholars may argue that freedom of information's concept has deep roots in liberal democratic traditions, thus incompatible with China's Marxist-Leninist political system. Gorbachev's 1980s Glasnost failure may further confirm incompatibility.

However, Chinese political leaders feel no strong need to borrow Western democratic principles to support their argument for a law-based, open society. They have particular rationales for greater governmental transparency. First, China, as discussed in Chapter 4, accumulated significant experiences for both governmental transparency and secrecy after several thousand years of civilization. Many practices and ideals for government openness in ancient China could be revived and used for today's new China.

Second, Chinese political leaders gained determination to gradually build a socialist democracy and rule of law after surviving the ruthless and destructive Cultural Revolution (1966–1976).[95] Four democratic means of developing socialist democracy: democratic elections, decision-making, management, and supervision (*minzhuxuanju minzhujuece minzhuguanli minzhujiandu* 民主选举 民主决策 民主管理 民主监督)[96] safeguard four democratic rights of Chinese citizens: the right to know, vote, participate, and supervise (*zhiqingquan xuanjuquan canyuquan jianduquan* 知情权、选举权、参与权、监督权).[97] Lack of transparency would eviscerate the four democratic means and the four democratic rights.

Third, Chinese political leaders found ideological support from leading Marxists that support transparency and freedom of information. Karl

[95] DENG XIAOPING, 2 SELECTED WORKS OF DENG XIAOPING 168 (2nd ed., 1994).

[96] Jiang Zemin, *Build a Well-off Society in an All-Round Way and Create a New Situation in Building Socialism with Chinese Characteristics* [全面建设小康社会，开创中国特色社会主义事业新局面], speech delivered at the 16th National Congress of the Chinese Communist Party, Beijing, November 2002; Eleventh Five-Year Plan Outline of the People's Republic of China for National Economy and Social Development [中华人民共和国国民经济和社会发展第十一个五年规划纲要], Beijing, March 2006.

[97] Eleventh Five-Year Plan Outline of the People's Republic of China for National Economy and Social Development [中华人民共和国国民经济和社会发展第十一个五年规划纲要], Beijing, March 2006.

Marx,[98] Friedrich Engels,[99] and Vladimir Lenin[100] recognized the value and necessity of transparency for building communism and socialism. Mao Zedong supported transparency, although he basically failed to follow his own policy after 1949.[101] Zhou Enlai, the first premier of China, was an advocate of governmental transparency and said that the masses should be informed of any changes in policy to allow the party's gaining understanding and support.[102]

[98] Marx stressed the importance of openness when he discussed the experiences of the Paris Commune. He said, "[T]he Commune did not pretend to infallibility…It published its doings and sayings; it initiated the public into all its shortcomings." KARL MARX & FRIEDRICH ENGELS, 22 MARX AND ENGELS COLLECTED WORKS 340 (1986).

[99] Engels stressed the importance of openness when he discussed the conflict between the right to privacy and public affairs. He said, "Privacy should be protected according to law. However, when privacy associates with the most important public interest, privacy is no longer privacy. Instead, it becomes a part of politics and should unavoidably be covered by the press." Sibei Zhu, *Officials Should Not Be Considered Freak When They Become Disclosure Friendly* [应剔除"一公开就异类"思维], XINMIN EVENING NEWS, republished by Economic Daily Online, February 29, 2012, http://views.ce.cn/view/ent/201202/29/t20120229_23113736.shtml (accessed between February 21, 2025 and March 31, 2025).

[100] Lenin said that "Everyone will probably agree that 'the broad democratic principle' presupposes the following two conditions: first, *full publicity* and secondly, election to all offices. It would be absurd to speak of democracy without publicity, moreover, without a publicity that is not limited to the membership of the organization. We call the German Socialist Party a democratic organization because *all its activities are carried out publicly; even its party congresses are held in public. But no one would call an organization democratic that is hidden from everyone but its members by a veil of secrecy* [emphasis added]." V LENIN, 5 LENIN COLLECTED WORKS 477 (1961).

[101] Mao relied on the Mass Line to support transparency. The Mass Line is a leadership method developed by Mao. According to the method, ideas arose "from the masses" and then ideas turn into policies. The policies should return "to the masses" for comment and criticism to allow adjustment. In 1948, Mao directed governmental officials to change their secretive styles to inform the public of land reform policies in order to gain support and implement policies. However, he became increasingly secretive after assuming office in 1949. The Mass Line remains an adoption of the Chinese Communist Party today. MAO ZEDONG, 4 COLLECTED WORKS OF MAO ZEDONG 1318–1319 (2nd edn., 1961). WEIBING XIAO, FREEDOM OF INFORMATION REFORM IN CHINA: INFORMATION FLOW ANALYSIS 41–42 (2011).

[102] WEIBING XIAO, FREEDOM OF INFORMATION REFORM IN CHINA: INFORMATION FLOW ANALYSIS 42 (2011); ENLAI ZHOU, SELECTED WORKS OF ENLAI ZHOU 301 (1984). In 1956, Zhou said, "The Iron Curtain will not be on our side." Enlai Zhou, Speech on the Current International Situation and Our Foreign Policy at the Third Session of the First National People's Congress [在一届人大三次会议上关于目前国际形势、我国外交政策的发言], Beijing, June 1957.

When explaining why Chinese leaders are not afraid of government transparency, FOI scholar Weibing Xiao said, "Leading Marxists' support of transparency suggested that [Chinese] reformers would not make any serious political mistakes if they undertook transparency reform."[103] Post-Mao Chinese political leaders thus embarked on a campaign for greater governmental transparency despite the topic's sensitivity. Deng Xiaoping, the core leader of the Chinese Communist Party's second generation,[104] embraced enthusiastically the concept of an "information society" in the 1980s.[105] Although Deng's original intent of publicizing the "information society" was to achieve the party's goal of modernizing the country, economically, application to governmental transparency is undeniable.

Zhao Ziyang, Deng's hand-picked successor for party leadership in the 1980s, was a strong proponent of transparent government. In his report to the 13th National Party Congress in 1987, Zhao exhorted leading agencies to improve the openness of activities and allow people's familiarity and discussion of important matters.[106]

Although Deng dismissed Zhao due to the Tiananmen Square Incident in 1989 and China lost momentum for political reform since, Zhao's successor, Jiang Zemin, continued progress toward transparency.[107] Jiang first introduced the concept of open government when reporting to the 15th National Party Congress in 1997[108] and stressed the need to implement further a system of open government in 2002 in a report to the 16th

[103] WEIBING XIAO, FREEDOM OF INFORMATION REFORM IN CHINA: INFORMATION FLOW ANALYSIS 42 (2011).

[104] Mao Zedong is widely considered as the core leader of the Chinese Communist Party's first generation.

[105] Jamie P. Horsley, *Toward a More Open China?*, *in* THE RIGHT TO KNOW: TRANSPARENCY FOR AN OPEN WORLD 63 (Ann Florini & Joseph E. Stiglitz eds., 2007). In 1984, Deng's inscription "develop information resources, serve four modernizations [*kaifaxinxiziyuan fuwusihuajianshe* 开发信息资源, 服务四化建设]" was published on the front page of *Economic Information Daily*, a major Chinese newspaper in Beijing affiliated with Xinhua News Agency. *Chronicle of Events*, ECONOMIC INFORMATION DAILY, http://www.jjckb.cn/wyj/2020aboutus03.html (accessed between February 21, 2025 and March 31, 2025).

[106] Zhao Ziyang, *Take Strides along the Road to Socialism with Chinese Characteristics* [沿着有中国特色的社会主义道路前进], speech delivered at the 13th National Party Congress, Beijing, October 1987.

[107] Jiang has been officially referred to as the core leader of the party's third generation.

[108] Jiang Zemin, *Hold High the Great Banner of Deng Xiaoping Theory for an All-round Advancement of the Cause of Building Socialism with Chinese Characteristics to the*

National Party Congress.[109] From Deng to Jiang, clearly, open governmental information was no longer a technological and economic issue. Jiang moved closer to establishment of a nationwide disclosure system.[110]

Hu Jintao and Wen Jiabao[111] openly acknowledged the values of establishing a transparent government. In March 2004, during the NPC annual meeting in Beijing, Wen advocated a system of "open government information" to enhance the transparency of governmental operations.[112] In 2007, Hu emphasized importance of official transparency in a report to the 17th National Party Congress.[113] Hu affirmed the party's and the

21st Century [高举邓小平理论伟大旗帜, 把建设有中国特色社会主义事业全面推向 二十一世纪], speech delivered at the 15th National Party Congress, Beijing, September 1997.

[109] In this report, Jiang stated, "The departments handling affairs of immediate concern to the people should carry out *an open administrative system* to make sure what they do is fair, just and *open* (emphasis added)." Jiang Zemin, Report to the 16th National Party Congress, Beijing, November 2002.

[110] Both Deng and Jiang approved of using foreign media to publicize the party and official policies on various issues. Apparently, Jiang was even more willing and skillful in dealing with foreign journalists, exemplified by the 1986, 85-minute interview with CBS's Mike Wallace, and another 3-hour 57-minute interview in August 2000 with the same journalist, during which Jiang answered all the 88 hostile questions. *A Leader with Unmatched Wisdom-Deng Xiaoping in the Eye of Oriana Fallaci*, CHINA DAILY, July 29, 2021, https://www.chinadaily.com.cn/a/202107/29/WS615c4c8ea310cdd39bc6d299.html (accessed between February 21, 2025 and March 31, 2025); Yan Shi, Xiaojia Zhu, Xiaohan Shi & Shu Wang, *Behind-the-Scene Story about CBS Journalist Wallace's Interview with Jiang Zemin* [华莱士采访江泽民内幕], SOUTHERN METROPOLIS DAILY, republished by Wenxuecity on April 13, 2012, *available at* https://www.wenxuecity.com/news/2012/04/13/1723950.html (accessed between February 21, 2025 and March 31, 2025).

[111] Hu was the incumbent Chinese president and Wen the incumbent premier. Unlike Mao, Deng, and Jiang, Hu has never had official reference as "core leader" of the "Fourth Generation." The subtle change of the term indicates a trend toward more collective leadership at the top.

[112] Wen Jiabao, Report on the Work of the Government to the National People's Congress, Beijing, March 2004.

[113] Hu Jintao, *Hold High the Great Banner of Socialism with Chinese Characteristics and Strive for New Victories in Building a Moderately Prosperous Society in All Aspects* [高举中国特色社会主义伟大旗帜为夺取全面建设小康社会新胜利而奋斗], speech delivered at the 17th National Party Congress, Beijing, October 2007.

government's guaranteeing "the people's rights to be informed, to participate, to be heard, and to oversee" and explicitly observed "power must be exercised in the sunshine to ensure that it is exercised correctly."[114]

Legal Reform for Limiting Government Power and Enhancing Transparency

Consistent with prior studies by FOI scholars such as Weibing Xiao, the author of this book believes that legal reform for limiting government power and enhancing transparency has paved the way for the final enactment of China's first national FOI law.[115]

After the Cultural Revolution (1966–1976) ended, Chinese political leaders, including Deng, realized the lawless situation in the country was dangerous and rebuilding the shattered legal system was vital.[116] Deng, Jiang, and Hu, three generations of Chinese communist leadership, followed the policy of gradually establishing a socialist legal system with Chinese characteristics. By the end of August 2011, China had enacted 240 laws including the current Constitution, 706 administrative regulations, and over 8600 local regulations.[117] Among all those laws and regulations, many have provisions limiting governments' powers. Over 80 laws and administrative regulations include provisions stipulating the obligation of official agencies' greater transparency,[118] and implementation of those laws has relaxed the restrictive, secretive Chinese informational

[114] Hu Jintao, *Hold High the Great Banner of Socialism with Chinese Characteristics and Strive for New Victories in Building a Moderately Prosperous Society in All Aspects* [高举中国特色社会主义伟大旗帜为夺取全面建设小康社会新胜利而奋斗], speech delivered at the 17th National Party Congress, Beijing, October 2007.

[115] Weibing Xiao, *Law-Based Administration a Rationale for FOI Reform in China* (Chapter 5), Freedom of Information Reform in China: Information Flow Analysis 51–59 (2011).

[116] Deng Xiaoping, 2 Selected Works of Deng Xiaoping *147* (2nd ed., 1994); *The White Paper on China's Efforts and Achievements in Promoting the Rule of Law* [中国的法治建设]白皮书], *The* State Council Information Office, Beijing, 28 February 2008.

[117] The *White Paper on the Socialist System of Laws with Chinese Characteristics* [中国特色社会主义法律体系白皮书], The State Council Information Office, Beijing, 27 October 2011.

[118] *Explanation of the State Council Legislative Affairs Office on Draft OGI Regulations* [国务院法制办关于《中华人民共和国政府信息公开条例（草案)》的说明] No. 244078, Beijing, 2006.

environment, thereby creating an atmosphere conducive to the rise of freedom of information.[119]

In 1982, adoption of the *Chinese Constitution*[120] was a landmark event for the movement toward greater governmental transparency because the supreme law in the land limits many aspects of governments' powers and implies the people's right to know. The *Constitution* states that all the power in China belongs to the people,[121] all state agencies, political parties, and public organizations must abide by the *Constitution* and the law, and all actions in violation of the *Constitution* or other laws require investigation.[122] All government agencies and officials must accept supervision of the people.[123] Without the people's right to know, the people cannot gain insight into operations of government activities or supervise agencies and officials.

The subsequent five amendments to the *1982 Constitution* further enhanced the rule of law and greater transparency. The 1988 amendment protects lawful rights and interests of the private sector of the economy,[124] thus encouraging more people to create private enterprises. Increased economic freedom leads to people's increased need for information from the government. According to the 1993 amendment, the state no longer follows a planned economy, instead, it strives for a socialist market economy.[125] This new emphasis on the role of the market allows

[119] For how administrative law reforms contributes to the rise of freedom of information in China, see WEIBING XIAO, FREEDOM OF INFORMATION REFORM IN CHINA: INFORMATION FLOW ANALYSIS 51–59 (2011).

[120] *Constitution of the People's Republic of China* (adopted on December 4, 1982), *available at* https://english.www.gov.cn/archive/lawsregulations/201911/20/content_WS5ed8856ec6d0b3f0e9499913.html (accessed between February 21, 2025 and March 31, 2025). The 1982 Constitution has been amended five times so far: in 1988, 1993, 1999, 2004 and 2018. There are three previous versions of the constitution, including those of 1954, 1975 and 1978, which were all repealed.

[121] *Constitution 1982*, Chap. 1, Art. 2.

[122] *Constitution 1982*, Chap. 1, Art. 5.

[123] *Constitution 1982*, Chap. 1, Art. 27.

[124] *Amendment to the Constitution of the People's Republic of China* (adopted on April 12, 1988), *available at* http://hrlibrary.umn.edu/research/China-amend.html (accessed between February 21, 2025 and March 31, 2025).

[125] *Amendment to the Constitution of the People's Republic of China* (adopted at the First Session of the Eighth National People's Congress and promulgated for implementation by the announcement of the National People's Congress on March 29, 1993), *available at*

expansion of transparency because a market-based economy is conditional on free flow of information. The 1999 amendment states that governing the country and building socialism must be from the rule of law.[126] This revision laid a solid constitutional foundation for nurturing all transparency-related laws and regulations in China. The 2004 amendment states that lawful private property is inviolable, the state shall compensate for expropriation, and the state must respect human rights.[127] The 2018 amendment emphasizes the socialist rule of law and orders all government officials to make a public oath of allegiance to the Constitution when taking office.[128] In general, these constitutional amendments furthered China's move to the rule by law.

Administrative laws and regulations, adopted or revised since the 1980s and were consistent with the spirit of the *Constitution*, promoted law-based administration.[129] In general, adoptions or revisions limited the

http://hrlibrary.umn.edu/research/China-1993amend.html (accessed between February 21, 2025 and March 31, 2025).

126 *Amendment to the Constitution of the People's Republic of China* (adopted at the Second Session of the Ninth National People's Congress and promulgated for implementation by the announcement of the National People's Congress on March 15, 1999), *available at* http://hrlibrary.umn.edu/research/China-amend99.html (accessed between February 21, 2025 and March 31, 2025).

127 *Amendment to the Constitution of the People's Republic of China* (adopted at the Second Session of the Tenth National People's Congress and promulgated for implementation by the announcement of the National People's Congress on March 14, 2004), *available at* http://hrlibrary.umn.edu/research/China-amend04.html (accessed between February 21, 2025 and March 31, 2025).

128 *Amendment to the Constitution of the People's Republic of China* (adopted at the First Session of the Thirteenth National People's Congress and promulgated for implementation by the announcement of the National People's Congress on March 11, 2018), *available at* https://www.loc.gov/item/global-legal-monitor/2018-05-18/china-2018-constitutional-amendment-adopted/ (accessed between February 21, 2025 and March 31, 2025).

129 Major administrative laws and regulations adopted or revised since the 1980s are *Civil Procedure Law 1982*, *Organic Law of the State Council 1982*, *Archives Law 1988*, *Law on Guarding State Secrets 1989*, *Administrative Litigation Law 1989*, *State Compensation Law 1994*, *Audit Law 1995*, *Administrative Penalty Law 1996*, *Administrative Supervision Law 1997*, *Administrative Reconsideration Law 1999*, *Administrative Permission Law 2003*, *Regulations on Preparedness for and Response to Emergent Public Hazards 2003*, *Law on Prevention and Care of Infectious Diseases 2004*, *Civil Servants Law 2005*, *Emergency Response Law 2007*, and *Open Government Information Regulations 2007*.

power of the government and made administrative procedures and decisions less arbitrary and opaque, thus facilitating the flow of information between government, the civil society, and citizens.

Archives Law 1988 is a good example. According to the revised *Archives Law*[130] and *Provisions for the Implementation of the Archives Law*,[131] records in the Chinese state archives created prior to 1949 have become publicly accessible as of 1999. Archives created after 1949 become "open to society" 30 years after their dates of origin. Economic, scientific, technological, and cultural archives are accessible at any time.[132] Various media, including newspapers, radio, television, and the Internet, are to disseminate information concerning opened archives.[133] Any Chinese citizens with proper identity cards and even foreign nationals with proper authorization from relevant archival agencies have the right to inspect opened archives.[134] The adoption and revision of *Archives Law* allowed the Chinese public unprecedented access to millions of government records and documents, previously sealed indefinitely in ancient China and the pre-Deng communist regime.

The progression of laws for guarding state secrets is another valuable case. As discussed in Chapter 4, rulers of ancient China frequently used similar laws to deter and criminalize leaking classified information. During the Mao's rein (1949–1976), any information from the government could gain listing as a state secret because the definition of state secrets in the *1951 Interim Regulations on Guarding State Secrets* was

[130] *Archives Law* was adopted by the National People's Congress in 1988 and revised in 1996.

[131] The State Administration of Archives adopted *Provisions for the Implementation of the Archives Law* in 1990, revised in 1999.

[132] Archives Law 1996, Article 19; *Provisions for the Implementation of Archives Law 1996*, Art. 20.

[133] *Provisions for the Implementation of Archives Law*, Art. 23.

[134] *Implementation Measures for Archives Law of the People's Republic of China*, The State Archives Bureau Order No. 1 (effective 19 November 1990); *Procedures to Open Records at Every Level to the Public*, the State Archives Bureau Order No. 2 (effective 26 December 1991); T*rial Procedures for Foreign Organizations and Individuals to Use Chinese Archives*, the State Archives Bureau Order No. 3 (effective 1 July 1992). William W. Moss, *Dang'an: Contemporary Chinese Archives*, 145 The China Quarterly 112, 116 (March 1996).

exceedingly expansive.[135] The scope of state secrets finally narrowed from 17 categories of information in *Interim Regulations* to seven in *Law on Guarding State Secrets 1989*, which classified information into three categories of escalating sensitivity: "confidential," "secret," and "top secret,"[136] with each category having a correspondingly higher degree of protection.[137]

As the law for protecting classified information showed subtle signs of relaxing informational control in the late 1980s, unsurprisingly, China announced declassifying new national laws as secret.[138] Previously, issuing all regulations approved by the State Council was "in documents with red characters designating them as restricted."[139] As mentioned earlier, in the late 1990s, the National Administration of Protecting State Secrets invited Huanhua Zhou to participate in the revision of the law, thus establishing a link between freedom of information legislation and state secrecy laws.[140]

In September 2005, the National Administration of Protecting State Secrets boldly announced that China would no longer classify death tolls from natural disasters as state secrets.[141] This move, prompted by the issuance of a notice from the Ministry of Civil Affairs,[142] facilitated distribution of crisis information. In April 2010, the National People's

135 Repeal of *1951 Interim Regulations on Guarding State Secrets* occurred in 1989 with the adoption of *Law on Guarding State Secrets*. *Interim Regulations* enumerated 17 categories of information as state secrets including the states' expenditures and budgets.

136 *Law on Guarding State Secrets 1989*. Art. 9.

137 *Law on Guarding State Secrets 1989*. Art. 18 and Art. 27.

138 Nicholas D. Kristof, *What's the Law in China? It's No Secret (Finally)*, THE NEW YORK TIMES, November 20, 1988, http://www.nytimes.com/1988/11/20/world/what-s-the-law-in-china-it-s-no-secret-finally.html?scp=2&sq=China+internal+periodicals&st=nyt (accessed between February 21, 2025 and March 31, 2025).

139 Nicholas D. Kristof, *What's the Law in China? It's No Secret (Finally)*, THE NEW YORK TIMES, November 20, 1988, http://www.nytimes.com/1988/11/20/world/what-s-the-law-in-china-it-s-no-secret-finally.html?scp=2&sq=China+internal+periodicals&st=nyt (accessed between February 21, 2025 and March 31, 2025).

140 HANHUA ZHOU, GOVERNMENT GOVERNANCE AND ADMINISTRATIVE LAW [政府监管与行政法] (2007).

141 Joseph Kahn, *China's State Secrets Agency Will Guard One Less: Death Tolls*, THE NEW YORK TIMES, September 13, 2005, http://www.nytimes.com/2005/09/13/international/asia/13china.html (accessed between February 21, 2025 and March 31, 2025).

142 *Notice on Declassifying Death Tolls from Natural Disasters and the Related Information* No 116 [2005] of the Ministry of Civil Affairs.

Congress approved the newly amended law, *Law on Guarding State Secrets*, whose revisions narrowed the definition of "state secrets" and increased the administrative rank of governmental departments having authority to classify information as state secrets.[143] More importantly, the newly revised law states that classified information should not be forever inaccessible. Declassification of a secret should be automatic once the term for guarding it expires.[144] Publication of the draft, appearing in 2012, of *Rules for the Implementation of the Law Guarding State Secrets* clarifies nine kinds of state secrets and standardizes the procedure for classifying certain official information as state secrets.[145] All these amendments are clear, significant steps toward greater flow of information in China.

Other legal reforming initiatives dealing with health crisis are reflections of increasing willingness of government agencies and officials to share information with the people. In 2003, the State Council introduced *Regulations on Preparedness for and Response to Emergent Public Health Hazards*[146] to cope with the outbreak of SARS.[147] *Regulations* required all levels of agencies to disclose relevant health crisis information in a "timely, accurate, and comprehensive" manner.[148] China modified *Law on the Prevention and Cure of Infectious Diseases* in 2004, adding SARS to the second class of infectious diseases requiring health agencies at

[143] Huizi Li & Zhuo Cheng, *China Narrows Definition of "State Secrets" to Boost Government Transparency*, XINHUA NEWS AGENCY, April 29, 2010 (captured by Internet Archive Wayback Machine on May 3, 2010), retrieved from https://web.archive.org/web/20100503144515/http://news.xinhuanet.com/english2010/china/2010-04/29/c_13272939.htm (accessed between February 21, 2025 and March 31, 2025).

[144] *Law on Guarding State Secrets 1989, Art. 15*, revised and adopted by the National People's Congress in 2010. According to the revision, "top secrets [绝密]" shall remain sealed no more than 30 years, "secrets [机密]" shall be classified no more than 20 years, "confidential information [秘密]" shall be closed no more than 10 years.

[145] Yunshi Lin, *China Plans to Specify Nine Kinds of State Secrets* [中国拟明确界定国家秘密的九种类型], CAIXIN, May 15, 2012, http://china.caixin.com/2012-05-15/100390469.html (accessed between February 21, 2025 and March 31, 2025).

[146] *Regulations on Preparedness for and Response to Emergent Public Health Hazards 2003.*

[147] SARS is abbreviation of Severe Acute Respiratory Syndrome, a viral respiratory disease in humans.

[148] *Regulations on Preparedness for and Response to Emergent Public Health Hazards 2003.* Art. 25.

all levels to disclose regularly epidemic information.[149] Three years later, China enacted the more ambitious *Emergency Response Law*, compelling government agencies at all levels to report emergency information to higher levels of government and the general public in a "unified, accurate and timely" manner.[150] According to the draft of the *Emergency Response Law*, news organizations that publish emergency information without proper authorization and/or release fraudulent emergency information incur fines if the reports lead to serious consequences. Fearing that local officials might use provisions to cover-up emergency incidents, legislators removed the provisions from the law.[151]

In order to promote further administrative law reform, the State Council published, in 2004, *the Implementation Outline for Pushing Forward Administration by Law in an All-Round Way*.[152] *Implementation Outline* states, in a manner reminiscent of the statutory language of *OGI Regulations*, adopted three years later:

> Administrative agencies must disseminate any information with the only exception of information concerning state secrets, commercial secrets and personal privacy. The citizens have the right to examine government information that is disclosed. Administrative agencies shall provide convenient conditions for such public inspection.[153]

These legal reform initiatives dramatically increased the flow of information from the government to society in China, thus creating a more favorable environment for consolidation of OGI legislation.[154]

[149] *Prevention and Cure of Infectious Diseases Law 1989*. Art. 38.

[150] *Emergency Response Law 2007*. Art. 53.

[151] Junchang Zhang, *Evolution of Chinese Policies, Laws and Regulations on News Coverage of Emergency Incidents* [中国媒体报道突发事件政策法律法规之变迁], 5 TV RESEARCH 33 (2009).

[152] *Implementation Outline for Pushing Forward Administration by Law in An All-Round Way* [全面推进依法行政实施纲要] issued by the General Office of the State Council, March 22, 2004.

[153] *Implementation Outline for Pushing Forward Administration by Law in An All-Round Way* [全面推进依法行政实施纲要] issued by the General Office of the State Council, March 22, 2004.

[154] For more detailed analysis of how administrative law reforms contributes to the rise of freedom of information in China, see WEIBING XIAO, FREEDOM OF INFORMATION REFORM IN CHINA: INFORMATION FLOW ANALYSIS 51–59 (2011).

Improved Government Information Dissemination Capacity

The improved capacity of the government in the early 2000s to disseminate information is another factor worthy of attention. The progress of the e-government program, especially the creation of official and social media websites for official agencies and functionaries at various levels, and the establishment of the system for governmental spokespersons contributed to enhancing China's capacity to share information, not only among officials at different levels but also between the bureaucracy and Chinese citizens.

Nations throughout the world embrace electronic government (e-government),[155] and China is no exception. China initiated a program of e-government in the early 1980s, followed by implementation of 12 "Golden Projects" ranging from "Golden Cards" (to create unified banking systems) to "Golden Tax" (to curb tax evasion)[156] in the 1990s. In 1998, creation of the Ministry of Information Industry further promoted e-governance, and in the late 1990s and early 2000s, establishing the Leading Group of National Informatization and the State Council Informatization Office led to policy formulation and implementation of e-government programs. This "e-government" program finally created a Chinese governmental Intranet enabling agencies and

[155] According to the World Bank, e-government has been defined as "government-owned or operated systems of information and communications technologies (ICTs) that transform relations with citizens, the private sector and/or other government agencies so as to promote citizen empowerment, improve service delivery, strengthen accountability, increase transparency, or improve government efficiency." Roberto Panzardi, Carlos Calcopietro, and Enrique Fanta Ivanovic, *New-Economy Sector Study: Electronic Government and Governance: Lessons from Argentina*, the World Bank, Washington, DC, July 2002, at 2, *available at* http://documents.worldbank.org/curated/en/527061468769894044 (accessed between February 21, 2025 and March 31, 2025). According to the United Nations, "[e]-governance is the public sector's use of the most innovative information and communication technologies, like the [I]nternet, to deliver to all citizens improved services, reliable information and greater knowledge in order to facilitate access to the governing process and encourage deeper citizen participation." Stephen A. Ronaghan, *Benchmarking E-Government: Assessing the United Nation's Member States* (report for United Nations Division for Public Economics and Public Administration, and American Society for Public Administration), New York, New York, May 2002, at 54, *available at* https://digitallibrary.un.org/record/3868821?ln=en&v=pdf (accessed between February 21, 2025 and March 31, 2025).

[156] Randolph Kluver, *The Architecture of Control: A Chinese Strategy for E-Governance*, 25 Journal of Public Policy 75 (2005).

officials at various levels and different localities to share information efficiently.[157] As a part of the e-government effort, government agencies and even party organizations ranging from the central, provincial, city levels to the county and even township levels launched official websites to increase information flow between the bureaucracy and citizens.[158] The Government Internet Project, which began in 1999, prompted the action.[159] The number of Chinese government websites grew rapidly. Most ministry-level agencies have websites.[160] The central government launched its official web portal in late 2005.[161]

[157] *Highlights of Development of Chinese E-Government: From September 2002 to September 2003* [2002.9–2003.9 中国电子政务大事记], China.com.cn, Beijing, China, February 6, 2004 (captured by Internet Archive Wayback Machine on May 12, 2004), retrieved from https://web.archive.org/web/20040512225649/http://www.china.com.cn/chinese/zhuanti/dzzwbg/492027.htm (accessed between February 21, 2025 and March 31, 2025); Baoling Li, *On the Barriers to the Development of E-Government in China*, in proceedings of the 7th International Conference on Electronic Commerce, Xi'an, China, August 2005, at 549–52. Despite its impressive strides in recent years, China was still underdeveloped in e-government construction in the 2000s. According to a United Nations 2002 survey, China's e-government index was 1.04, indicating that its e-government capacity is still "minimal" in (four levels of development: "high," "medium," "minimal," and "deficit"). Stephen A. Ronaghan, *Benchmarking E-Government: Assessing the United Nation's Member States* (report for United Nations Division for Public Economics and Public Administration, and American Society for Public Administration), New York, New York, May 2002, at 7 and 52, *available at* https://digitallibrary.un.org/record/3868821?ln=en&v=pdf (accessed between February 21, 2025 and March 31, 2025).

[158] The party is lagging far the government in the creation of official websites. Some central level party organizations launched official web portals, such as the Central Commission for Discipline Inspection (https://www.ccdi.gov.cn) and the International Liaison Department (https://www.idcpc.org.cn/english2023/zlbjj/jgsz/). However, most central party agencies (e.g., the Chinese Communist Party Central Committee, the Central Propaganda Department, the Central Organization Department) are still invisible on the World Wide Web. Party committees at provincial, city, county, and township levels either have no official websites or share the same websites with their corresponding governmental agencies.

[159] Hanhua Zhou, *Open Government in China: Practice and Problems, in* THE RIGHT TO KNOW: TRANSPARENCY FOR AN OPEN WORLD 100 (Ann Florini & Joseph E. Stiglitz eds., 2007).

[160] Most ministries and commissions under the State Council have launched their official websites, with a few exceptions such as the Ministry of State Security.

[161] Xinhua News Agency, the Chinese equivalent of the Associated Press, created the website for the central government of China. The web portal is accessible at http://english.gov.cn/. *Operation of Chinese Central Government Website Draws*

Some Chinese agencies and officials are sufficiently open-minded toward dissemination of information that even technologically savvy, Internet-oriented youth would have admiration. Since the early 2000s, agencies and officeholders began creating governmental online forums, blogs, and micro-blogs to facilitate exchanging information between the public and the government. The Department of Public Security in Hebei Province was the first administrative agency in Mainland China to create an official blog.[162] In 2006, Yong Fu, the mayor of Lingao County, Hainan Province, became the first blogger among government officials in China when he created an account, with his true identity and cell phone number, on a popular Chinese social networking site.[163]

Online, governmental forums provide "fascinating spaces for politically active citizens to engage in public discourses."[164] Similarly, the use of social media has enhanced the ability of officials' and citizens' sharing timely information engagingly.

Establishment of press conferences and a system of official spokespersons added another layer of mechanism for timely distribution of public

Worldwide Attention [中国政府网开通吸引世界目光], XINHUA NEWS AGENCY, January 4, 2006 (captured by Internet Archive Wayback Machine on January 12, 2006), retrieved from https://web.archive.org/web/20060112022617/http://news.xinhuanet.com/politics/2006-01/04/content_4005174.htm (accessed between February 21, 2025 and March 31, 2025).

162 Min Wang, *Analysis of China's Government-Run Blogs* [我国政府博客现状分析], PEOPLE'S DAILY ONLINE, May 10, 2007 (captured by Internet Archive Wayback Machine on May 13, 2007), retrieved from https://web.archive.org/web/20070513051417/http://media.people.com.cn/GB/22114/44110/75857/5714324.html (accessed between February 21, 2025 and March 31, 2025). Originally titled the "Public Security Blog," this government-run social media website was created in 2005 and renamed to "First Blog in Public Security of China." [中国第一公安博客], *available at* http://blog.sina.com.cn/gongan (accessed between February 21, 2025 and March 31, 2025).

163 Min Wang, *Analysis of China's Government-Run Blogs* [我国政府博客现状分析], PEOPLE'S DAILY ONLINE, May 10, 2007 (captured by Internet Archive Wayback Machine on May 13, 2007), retrieved from https://web.archive.org/web/20070513051417/http://media.people.com.cn/GB/22114/44110/75857/5714324.html (accessed between February 21, 2025 and March 31, 2025).

164 Min Jiang, "Civic Interactions with Chinese Government Networks: Information Technology, Institutions, and Agency" (2007) (unpublished Ph.D. diss., Purdue University), at xiv.

information. Press spokespersons are common in Western liberal democracies[165]; China began experimenting with a similar system in 1983 when the press officer from the Ministry of Foreign Affairs made his first public appearance.[166]

The work made sluggish progress until 2003 when the SARS crisis created a public relations disaster for the government.[167] Since then, many central and provincial agencies established positions for spokespersons. The arrangements extended to agencies at various levels in 2004.[168] The structure strengthened in 2005 when the State Council, with more than 70 ministry-level agencies and commissions, 27 provinces, and autonomous regions, established specific positions for press secretaries.[169] Spokespersons received frequent training for conducting press

165 The author of this book was a Washington-based correspondent reporting and writing for the *People's Daily* of China from 2004 to 2007. One important responsibility was to attend, regularly, press conferences organized by spokespersons from various U.S. administrative and legislative agencies including the White House, the Department of Defense, the State Department, and the Capitol Hill.

166 Mingde Li, *Commentary on Research of Press Spokespersons System* [新闻发言人制度研究述评], 5 SHANGHAI JOURNALISM REVIEW (2006); Huiqing Niu, *Review of Current Problems of China's Government Press Secretaries* [中国政府新闻发言人现存问题剖析], PEOPLE'S DAILY ONLINE, May 25, 2007 (captured by Internet Archive Wayback Machine on June 18, 2013), retrieved from https://web.archive.org/web/20130618135256/http://media.people.com.cn/GB/22114/84301/84308/5778820.html (accessed between February 21, 2025 and March 31, 2025).

167 Mingde Li, *Commentary on Research of Press Spokespersons System* [新闻发言人制度研究述评], 5 SHANGHAI JOURNALISM REVIEW (2006); Huiqing Niu, *Review of Current Problems of China's Government Press Secretaries* [中国政府新闻发言人现存问题剖析], PEOPLE'S DAILY ONLINE, May 25, 2007 (captured by Internet Archive Wayback Machine on June 18, 2013), retrieved from https://web.archive.org/web/20130618135256/http://media.people.com.cn/GB/22114/84301/84308/5778820.html (accessed between February 21, 2025 and March 31, 2025).

168 Mingde Li, *Commentary on Research of Press Spokespersons System* [新闻发言人制度研究述评], 5 SHANGHAI JOURNALISM REVIEW (2006); Huiqing Niu, *Review of Current Problems of China's Government Press Secretaries* [中国政府新闻发言人现存问题剖析], PEOPLE'S DAILY ONLINE, May 25, 2007 (captured by Internet Archive Wayback Machine on June 18, 2013), retrieved from https://web.archive.org/web/20130618135256/http://media.people.com.cn/GB/22114/84301/84308/5778820.html (accessed between February 21, 2025 and March 31, 2025).

169 Mingde Li, *Commentary on Research of Press Spokespersons System* [新闻发言人制度研究述评], 5 SHANGHAI JOURNALISM REVIEW (2006); Huiqing Niu, *Review of Current Problems of China's Government Press Secretaries* [中国政府新闻发言人现存问题剖析], PEOPLE'S DAILY ONLINE, May 25, 2007 (captured by Internet Archive

conferences and dealing with Chinese and foreign journalists.[170] The director of the State Council Information Office, the agency responsible for training and guiding government public relations professionals, contended that government-appointed press secretaries should play a vital role in handling emergencies.[171]

The availability and expertise of press secretaries for various administrative agencies[172] enhanced the willingness and capability of the government to disclose information to the public and augmented the government's willingness to national *OGI Regulations*.[173]

Wayback Machine on June 18, 2013), retrieved from https://web.archive.org/web/20130618135256/http://media.people.com.cn/GB/22114/84301/84308/5778820.html (accessed between February 21, 2025 and March 31, 2025).

[170] Official training of government press secretaries began in 2003 when the State Council Information Office launched the first nationwide workshop on government spokespersons. Jie Gui, *Press Release System Pushes Public Governance to Greater Transparency* [新闻发布制度推动公共治理走向透明], CHINA YOUTH DAILY, September 15, 2012, https://zqb.cyol.com/html/2012-09/15/nw.D110000zgqnb_20120915_4-03.htm (accessed between February 21, 2025 and March 31, 2025).

[171] Jie Gui, *Press Release System Pushes Public Governance to Greater Transparency* [新闻发布制度推动公共治理走向透明], CHINA YOUTH DAILY, September 15, 2012, https://zqb.cyol.com/html/2012-09/15/nw.D110000zgqnb_20120915_4-03.htm (accessed between February 21, 2025 and March 31, 2025).

[172] The Communist Party is establishing a similar system that applies to various levels of party committees and party organizations. Wang Chen, *Vigorously Push Forward Construction of System of Party Committee Press Secretaries* [积极推进党委新闻发言人制度建设], QIUSHI, October 16, 2010 (captured by Internet Archive Wayback Machine on October 20, 2010), retrieved from https://web.archive.org/web/20101020221143/http://www.qstheory.cn/zxdk/2010/201020/201010/t20101012_52116.htm (accessed between February 21, 2025 and March 31, 2025). The party's move to establish such a system began in 2000. By the end of 2009, eight party organizations under the Chinese Communist Party Central Committee established the system of spokespersons: Central Commission for Discipline Inspection, Organization Department, United Front Work Department, International Department, Party History Research Center, Party Literature Research Center, Taiwan Affairs Office and Central Archives. Yongtong Su & Jing Ju, *Press Secretaries of Party Committees Share Party Information with Citizens* [党委新闻发言人: 与人民共享"党务信息"] SOUTHERN WEEKEND, January 14, 2010, http://www.infzm.com/content/40253 (accessed between February 21, 2025 and March 31, 2025).

[173] For more discussion on how the establishment of governmental press secretary system contributes to the rise of freedom of information in China, see WEIBING XIAO, *The Improved Information Environment as a Rationale for FOI Reform in China (chapter 3)*, FREEDOM OF INFORMATION REFORM IN CHINA: INFORMATION FLOW ANALYSIS 27–37 (2011).

Changed Societal and Media Environment

Consistent with prior studies by FOI scholars such as Weibing Xiao, the author of this book finds that the changed social and media conditions has created a favorable environment for freedom of information seeds to germinate and take root in China.[174]

China experienced profound changes in its social and media environments since the late 1990s and early 2000s. As China entered the social, conflict-prone period, information of major social crises is abundant. The spread of crisis information among citizens is unprecedentedly easy and rapid since the new media allows any Chinese individual with access to the Internet to produce and distribute information, globally, with just a click of the mouse. The new scenario presented a threat to social stability and challenged the legitimacy of the party and the government. The changed societal and media environments[175] prompted the Chinese government to abandon its old-fashioned, restrictive, and secretive management of information and embrace a new mode of proactive disclosure. As FOI scholar Weibing Xiao noted, this tremendous change gave OGI reform "a workable foothold in the Chinese information environment."[176]

The Chinese bureaucracy had long been comfortable with restricting free flow of crisis information due to political,[177] philosophical and

[174] WEIBING XIAO, *The Improved Information Environment as a Rationale for FOI Reform in China (chapter 3)*, FREEDOM OF INFORMATION REFORM IN CHINA: INFORMATION FLOW ANALYSIS 27–37 (2011).

[175] Communication scholar Yuezhi Zhao documented in her two books, in great detail and depth, the change of Chinese media and communication environments during the post-Mao reform era. YUEZHI ZHAO, COMMUNICATION IN CHINA: POLITICAL ECONOMY, POWER, AND CONFLICT (2008); YUEZHI ZHAO, MEDIA, MARKET, AND DEMOCRACY IN CHINA: BETWEEN THE PARTY LINE AND THE BOTTOM LINE (1998).

[176] WEIBING XIAO, FREEDOM OF INFORMATION REFORM IN CHINA: INFORMATION FLOW ANALYSIS 28 (2011).

[177] Chinese officials tend to report only good news about his area to their supervisors but are reluctant to report bad news, fearing that they may lose their positions or create a negative impression on their supervisor's minds (*baoxi bu baoyou* 报喜不报忧). *Vigorously Fight Against Unhealthy Practices of Reporting Good News Only* [坚决纠正报喜不报忧的不良风气], PEOPLE'S DAILY, September 10, 2001, at 1 (captured by Internet Archive Wayback Machine on December 15, 2002), https://web.archive.org/web/20021215170730/http://www.people.com.cn/GB/guandian/26/20010910/555626.html (accessed between February 21, 2025 and March 31, 2025).

cultural,[178] technological,[179] psychological,[180] or economic factors.[181] The Chinese information environment became less and less restrictive after 1978 when the country adopted the fundamental policy of reform and engagement with the outside world. Economic liberalization, initiated by Deng Xiaoping and his communist colleagues, created greater need and freedom for information exchange among citizens. The flow of crisis information between the government and the society, however, remained limited for two major reasons:

[178] As discussed in Chapter 4, both Confucianism and Taoism persuade officials to handle information in a secretive and reactive manner. Although Legalism embraces disclosure of laws and regulations, its attitude toward free flow of information is even more restrictive than Confucianism and Taoism with regard to any other category of information. Despite long suppression by rulers, Mohism has the greatest potential for developing avocation for governmental transparency.

[179] In China, the lack of effective technological tools to disseminate information as quickly as possible and as widely as possible has long hampered dissemination of information. Traditional media, such as notice boards, court gazettes, short reports, and newspapers contributed to the flow of information in ancient China, but the speed and scope of distribution was primitive by modern and contemporary standards. In addition, the cost of censoring traditional media content was low.

[180] Chinese officials tend to view the masses as individuals who have low mental capacities and could be easily agitated. Officials argued that the masses, informed of crises, would panic causing destabilization. Concealing crises' information could restrain public panic. Linda Chen & Junín Chen, *On Impediments to Information Flow During Crisis of Songhuajiang River Contamination* [松花江水污染事件中信息流障碍分析], 6 JOURNAL OF PRESS CIRCLES 21 (2005); Dalin Sheng, *It Is Encouraging to Find that Government Is No Longer Covering up Sensitive Events* [喜见对敏感事件不再捂盖子], QILU EVENING NEWS, republished by Phoenix TV, November 19, 2008, https://news.ifeng.com/opinion/200811/1119_23_884599.shtml (accessed between February 21, 2025 and March 31, 2025).

[181] Nobel Prize-winning economist Joseph E. Stiglitz argued for the necessity of freedom of information in political life from the perspective of information economics. He contended an inherent tendency in all governmental power, democratic or nondemocratic, to practice secrecy because asymmetry or imperfection of information provides ample opportunities for incumbents to pursue careers and deter political rivalry. Consequently, the United States and the United Kingdom, the two most transparent governments in the world, continue to maintain many secrets that should have disclosure. Joseph E. Stiglitz, *On Liberty, the Right to Know, and Public Discourse: The Role of Transparency in Public Life*, Oxford Amnesty Lecture, Oxford, UK, January 27,1999, *available at* http://documents.worldbank.org/curated/en/436941546609601734 (accessed between February 21, 2025 and March 31, 2025); THE RIGHT TO KNOW: TRANSPARENCY FOR AN OPEN WORLD vii–viii (Ann Florini & Joseph E. Stiglitz eds., 2007).

First, social conflicts began to emerge in the 1980s and 1990s as the Chinese people began a monumental social transformation from communism to economic capitalism.[182] However, most people, in general, were happy with economic reform and openness, and thus optimistic for the future.[183] The scarcity of social crises during these 20 years was insufficient to promote widespread distribution of crisis information.

Second, the government was willing and capable of restricting informational flow in the pre-Internet age by controlling and censoring traditional media outlets. Under Mao's rule, China established a Communist press system[184] extending from the central level to the county level. News media became a component of the party and governmental institutions, and censors at all levels attended closely to the operations of the media to assure non-disclosure of inappropriate content.[185] As media became increasingly commercialized in the 1990s, control of the press relaxed to some degree.[186] However, the media's role of party and government spokesperson remains unchanged. In such a restrictive environment for media, government officials and news media gatekeepers[187]

[182] The 1989 Tiananmen Square Incident was one such social conflict. It is widely believed that most student demonstrators did not want to overthrow the Chinese Communist Party. They just wanted the party to engage in meaningful political reforms to deal with corruption and social injustice.

[183] Many popular songs produced in the 1980s in Mainland China indicated a strong sense of optimism and hope, reflecting, in part, the collective mood of the Chinese.

[184] FRED S. SIEBERT, THEODORE PETERSON & WILBUR SCHRAMM, FOUR THEORIES OF THE PRESS: THE AUTHORITARIAN, LIBERTARIAN, SOCIAL RESPONSIBILITY AND SOVIET COMMUNIST CONCEPTS OF WHAT THE PRESS SHOULD BE AND DO (1956).

[185] YUEZHI ZHAO, MEDIA, MARKET, AND DEMOCRACY IN CHINA: BETWEEN THE PARTY LINE AND THE BOTTOM LINE (1998).

[186] Chengju Huang, *Transitional Media v. Normative Theories: Schramm, Altschull and China*, 53 JOURNAL OF COMMUNICATION 444 (2003); CHIN-CHUAN LEE, MONEY, POWER AND MEDIA: COMMUNICATION PATTERNS AND BUREAUCRATIC CONTROL IN CULTURAL CHINA (2000); YUEZHI ZHAO, MEDIA, MARKET, AND DEMOCRACY IN CHINA: BETWEEN THE PARTY LINE AND THE BOTTOM LINE (1998); Winfield Betty & Peng Zengjun, *Marketplace or Party Controls? Chinese Media in Transition*, 67 GAZETTE 255 (2005).

[187] Gatekeepers are professional editors, reporters, and other opinion leaders involved in filtering news and opinion in the process of dissemination. David Manning White, *The "Gate Keeper:" A Case Study in the Selection of News*, 27 JOURNALISM QUARTERLY 383, 383–91 (1950); Karine Barzilai-Nahon, *Gatekeeping: A Critical Review*, 43 ANNUAL REVIEW OF INFORMATION SCIENCE AND TECHNOLOGY *433*, 433–78 (2009).

easily suppressed distribution of crisis or controversial information by downplaying newsworthy items or simply ignoring them.

The social and media environment, however, changed considerably in the early 2000s, when information of official misconduct and corruption, food and drug safety concerns, public health problems, environmental pollution, and clashes among residents, developers and local governments in land disputes flooded the media. Social unrest rose for complex reasons[188]: "Mass incidents," including riots, strikes, demonstrations, and protests, increased from 8700 in 1993 to 74,000 in 2004.[189] "Public order disturbances"[190] rose in 2005 by 6.6% over 2004, reaching

[188] The party often ascribes the rise of social unrest in China to massive social and economic transformations over the last several decades. For example, the party often touts a dubious theory that social conflicts may surface in large numbers when per capita GDP enters the $1000–$3000 range. China's per capita GDP surpassed $1000 in 2003 and reached $1714 in 2005. *CPC Plenum to Discuss Social Harmony*, CHINA DAILY, October 8, 2006, http://www.chinadaily.com.cn/china/2006-10/08/content_703052.htm (accessed between February 21, 2025 and March 31, 2025). Some domestic and foreign observers, however, maintain that governance flaws at the heart of the Chinese state are the breeding ground for social unrest. Jianrong Yu, *Use Constitution to Hold Bottom Line of Social Stability* [让宪法成为社会稳定的底线], speech delivered at the Beijing Lawyers Association, Falvjie [法律界], Beijing, China, February 21, 2010 (captured by Internet Archive Wayback Machine on March 2, 2010), retrieved from https://web.archive.org/web/20100302202616/http://news.mylegist.com/1607/2010-02-21/21030.html (accessed between February 21, 2025 and March 31, 2025); Liping Sun, *Precise Assessment of Social Conflicts* [准确定位社会矛盾], EEO [经济观察网], December 17, 2007, http://www.eeo.com.cn/observer/special/2007/12/17/89477.shtml (accessed between February 21, 2025 and March 31, 2025); Carl Minzner, *Social Instability in China: Causes, Consequences, and Implications* (report of Center for Strategic and International Studies), Washington, DC, June 12, 2005 (captured by Internet Archive Wayback Machine on September 10, 2009), retrieved from https://web.archive.org/web/20090910132629/http://csis.org/files/media/csis/events/061205_mizner_abstract.pdf (accessed between February 21, 2025 and March 31, 2025).

[189] Murray Scot Tanner, *China Rethinks Unrest*, 27 THE WASHINGTON QUARTERLY 138, 138–40 (Summer 2004); Edward Cody, *China Growing More Wary over Rash of Protests: Cell Phones, Internet Spread the Word, Magnify Fallout*, THE WASHINGTON POST, August 10, 2005, https://www.washingtonpost.com/archive/politics/2005/08/10/china-grows-more-wary-over-rash-of-protests/7e21a4f4-45e3-4a6f-928b-9294c98339f4/ (accessed between February 21, 2025 and March 31, 2025).

[190] Chinese authorities use two different terms ("mass incidents" and "public order disturbances") to describe social unrest. This approach complicates direct comparisons between them.

87,000 incidents.[191] As one American academic noted, "By the early 21st century, social unrest had become a normal feature of Chinese society."[192] The avalanche of social unrest provided sufficient fodder for distribution of information of crises, rumors, or unverified explanations.[193]

Complicating the situation were the party's and the government's increasing sense of restraint for their abilities to control the changing media, which attempted to report social crises. First, the traditional media became increasingly independent during the post-Mao reform era as they strove to survive and prosper in the news market. Chinese traditional party-run or government-run media, such as the China Central Television and *People's Daily* played an expanding role as watchdog of the government.[194] Many prominent market-oriented media outlets, such as *Caijing*

[191] Joseph Kahn, *Pace and Scope of Protest in China Accelerated in '05*, THE NEW YORK TIMES, January 20, 2006, http://www.nytimes.com/2006/01/20/international/asia/20china.html?_r=0 (accessed between February 21, 2025 and March 31, 2025).

[192] Thomas Bernstein, *Unrest in Rural China: A 2003 Assessment*, Escholarship.org, working paper for Center for the Study of Democracy, University of California Irvine, August 1, 2004, at 1, *available at* http://escholarship.org/uc/item/1318d3rx (accessed between February 21, 2025 and March 31, 2025).

[193] According to Peterson and Gist, rumor means "an unverified account or explanation of events, circulating from person to person and pertaining to an object, event or issue of public concern." Warren A. Peterson & Noel P. Gist, *Rumor and Public Opinion*, 57 THE AMERICAN JOURNAL OF SOCIOLOGY 159 (1951).

[194] Former Chinese Premier Zhu Rongji praised a China Central Television news program as "a mirror and watchdog of the government and a supervisor of the government through public opinion." Jiafei Yin, *Beyond the Four Theories of the Press: A New Model for the Asian and the World Press*, 10 JOURNALISM & COMMUNICATION MONOGRAPHS 3, 25 (2008); *People's Daily* was successful in uncovering the 2001 scandal of the concealment of mining water leakage which killed 81 coal miners in Nandan County, Guangxi Province. The leadership in Nandan County and the coal owners decided to hide the catastrophe. The journalists of *People's Daily* based in Guangxi exposed the disaster. The major players in this scandal received severe punishments, including execution of the party secretary of Nandan County. This is the first major human-caused disaster gaining exposure by journalists in the People's Republic of China. Xinghang Huang, Wenbin Fei & Jian Huang, *Former Nandan County Party Secretary Ruizhong Wan Blames Himself as Disloyal and Unfilial before Being Executed* [南丹原县委书记万瑞忠临行刑前自责"不忠不孝 "], PEOPLE'S COURT DAILY, February 21, 2004, at 4, republished by China News Service on February 23, 2004, https://www.chinanews.com.cn/n/2004-02-23/26/405057.html (accessed between February 21, 2025 and March 31, 2025); Shengfeng Zheng, *Inspirations from Exposing Nandan Coal Disaster Concealment* [南丹矿难的成功揭露留给人们的启示] 9 JOURNALISTIC FRONT (2003).

and *Caixin* magazines,[195] the *China Youth Daily*'s Freezing Point,[196] and *Southern Weekend*[197] have reputations, in China, for aggressive investigative journalism. Shuli Hu, former editor of *Caijing*, earned the title of "the most dangerous woman in China" for her role in publicizing high-profile financial scandals.[198] Internal reports[199] also frequently expose problems throughout the country, indict corrupt officials, and criticize official misconduct.[200] A newly established Internal Reference News

[195] *Caijing*'s driving mission is to have an "independent standpoint, exclusive coverage and unique perspective." Here is *Caijing*'s official website: http://magazine.caijing.com.cn (accessed between February 21, 2025 and March 31, 2025); *Caixin* is even more independent than *Caijing*, as the former was created by a group of editors and reporters from the latter. Here is *Caxin*'s official website: https://www.caixinglobal.com (accessed between February 21, 2025 and March 31, 2025).

[196] *China Youth Daily's* Freezing Point is a very popular news column known for its aggressiveness and candidness in reporting significant social issues. Here is its official website: http://zqb.cyol.com/node/node_6443.htm (accessed between February 21, 2025 and March 31, 2025).

[197] The *Southern Weekend's* official website: http://www.infzm.com/ (accessed between February 21, 2025 and March 31, 2025).

[198] David Barboza, *Most Dangerous in China: An Editor*, THE NEW YORK TIMES, April 18, 2005. http://www.nytimes.com/2005/04/17/business/worldbusiness/17iht-caijing.html (accessed between February 21, 2025 and March 31, 2025).

[199] Party and government leaders enjoy exclusive access to internal reports that cover sensitive subjects regularly. Traditional party and governmental mainstream news organizations publish these confidential periodicals on a regular basis. These confidential publications often have large volumes of crisis information. The journalistic internal reports will be examined in depth in Chapter 9.

[200] For examples of exposure and discipline of corrupt officials during China's reform era by internal reports, see *Garbage Collectors Take away Two-Million-Yuan Deposit Book Mistakenly Abandoned by Corrupt Official's Wife* [男子收废品收走纪委书记巨款存折], CHINA WEEKLY, republished by Phoenix TV, May 6, 2009, https://news.ifeng.com/society/1/200905/0506_343_1142568.shtml (accessed between February 21, 2025 and March 31, 2025); Ruoqiao Liang, *For Whose Eyes Only?* GLOBAL TIMES, August 24, 2010, https://www.globaltimes.cn/content/566822.shtml (accessed between February 21, 2025 and March 31, 2025); *China Cover-up Official Executed*, BBC NEWS, February 20, 2004, http://news.bbc.co.uk/2/hi/asia-pacific/3507067.stm (accessed between February 21, 2025 and March 31, 2025); *Xinhua Neican Exposes Black Whistle in Chinese Football* [新华社内参捅破中国足坛的"黑哨"坚冰], NEW DAILY [每日新报], January 8, 2002, republished by China.com (captured by Internet Archive Wayback Machine on November 9, 2002), retrieved from https://web.archive.org/web/20021109210646/http://www.china.com.cn/chinese/SPORT-c/94580.htm (accessed between February 21, 2025 and March 31, 2025); *Chinese Football Fans Riot over Penalty*, BBC NEWS, March 25, 2002, http://news.bbc.co.uk/2/hi/asia-pacific/1892421.stm (accessed

Department of *People's Daily* plans to compete aggressively with Xinhua News Agency in quality and quantity of internal reports. All changes in the traditional media facilitated dissemination of crisis or controversial information that many officials prefer to remain permanently sealed.

Another equally important development for media that hampered the government's ability to restrict the flow of information is the expansion of the Internet and citizen journalism. As China enters the twenty-first century, the country has been gaining parity with many technologically developed countries for construction and use of the Internet. By December 31, 2009, the number of Chinese Internet users reached 384 million and penetration of the Internet reached 28.9%.[201] China's Internet population grew rapidly and reached 513 million people at the end of 2011, among them nearly 257 million are frequent users of social networking sites.[202] By June 2024, the number of Internet users in China reached nearly 1.1 billion and Internet penetration rate reached 78%.[203] In the meantime, increasing numbers of Chinese, urban or rural, are subscribers of resources provided by mobile phones. These users in China represent a record of 1.03 billion at the end of April 2012, and 159 million are users of terminals based on third-generation technologies, indicating that access to the Internet with cell phones is convenient and common.[204]

between February 21, 2025 and March 31, 2025); Yanhui Chen, *Demystify Neican* [内参揭秘], PHOENIX WEEKLY 14 (2005): 35–39.

201 Limin Chen, *Internet Users Hit 384 Million*, CHINA DAILY, January 16, 2010, https://www.chinadaily.com.cn/bizchina/////2010-01/16/content_9330234.htm#:~:text=Updated:%202010%2D01%2D16,Internet%20only%20through%20mobile%20phones (accessed between February 21, 2025 and March 31).

202 *China's Massive Web Audience Turns to Social, Mobile, Video*, eMarketer, New York, New York, March 6, 2012 (captured by Internet Archive Wayback Machine on March 8, 2012), retrieved from https://web.archive.org/web/20120308210132/http://www.emarketer.com/Article.aspx?R=1008882 (accessed between February 21, 2025 and March 31, 2025).

203 *The 54 Statistical Report on China's Internet Development*, China Internet Network Information Center, Beijing, China, *available at* https://www.cnnic.com.cn/IDR/ReportDownloads/202411/P020241101318428715781.pdf (accessed between February 21, 2025 and March 31, 2025).

204 *China's Mobile Phone Users Hit 1b*, CHINA DAILY, May 24, 2012, http://www.chinadaily.com.cn/business/2012-05/24/content_15374280.htm (accessed between February 21, 2025 and March 31, 2025).

New media allows the flow of information among media, citizens, and the civil society extremely easy and inexpensive. Any Chinese citizen can become a citizen-journalist by distributing information globally, thereby eroding the traditional media's ability to establish an agenda.[205] The publisher of *People's Daily* warned the elite, traditional media in China of the danger of "becoming marginalized" in the era of microblogging.[206] The warning is not an exaggeration. For example, during the 2008 Sichuan earthquake, a cell phone recorded the first live video; its posting on the Internet by a university student occurred within 10 minutes of the quake and eight minutes prior to the official announcement.[207] Professional journalists use the Internet as a platform to publish sensitive articles, unacceptable to traditional media.[208]

In the meantime, new media created a disproportionately high cost and difficulty for government officials to control the flow of information. China currently has one of the most filtered and censored Internet environments,[209] but Internet censorship "cannot keep up with the spread

[205] Agenda setting describes a powerful influence of the media for influencing what and how people think. Max McCombs and Donald Shaw, in a study on the 1968 presidential election, formally developed the agenda-setting theory. Maxwell E. McCombs & Donald L. Shaw, *The Agenda-Setting Function of Mass Media*, 36 PUBLIC OPINION QUARTERLY 2 (1972).

[206] Yannong Zhang, *Full Text of People's Daily Publisher Yannong Zhang's Speech to Kick off His Paper's College Campus Tour* [人民日报校园行活动启动 社长张研农演讲全文], PEOPLE'S DAILY ONLINE, November 23, 2009 (captured by Internet Archive Wayback Machine on November 27, 2009), retrieved from https://web.archive.org/web/20091127204920/http://media.people.com.cn/GB/120837/10433201.html (accessed between February 21, 2025 and March 31, 2025); *Li Wang, People's Daily Publisher Says that "Microblog Queen" Yao Chen Is Our Competitor* [人民日报社长: "微博女王"姚晨是我们的"对手"], PHOENIX TV, April 29, 2012, http://culture.ifeng.com/1/detail_2012_04/29/14235106_0.shtml (accessed between February 21, 2025 and March 31, 2025).

[207] The video, first posted to Tudou, similar to YouTube, had roughly 1.8 million hits and international media groups, such as CNN forwarded the recording.

[208] *People's Daily* published its articles exposing the Nandan coalmine disaster first on its digital edition (People's Daily Online) when the print edition's report was premature. Huaxin Zhu, Jiangchun Hu & Wentao Sun, *Analysis Report on Public Opinions on the Internet in China in 2007* [2007 中国互联网舆情分析报告], 2 JOURNAL OF TODAY'S MASS MEDIA 31 (2008).

[209] Although Chinese citizens have domestic social networking sites, such as Weibo, Tudou, and QQ, many foreign social networking websites, including YouTube, X (previously Twitter), Facebook, and Instagram are unavailable in Mainland China, and China filters or removes much sensitive Internet content. The blocking system is dubbed

of information,"[210] and produces an environment that is "increasingly difficult for the government to regulate what information is accessed."[211] Some officials confessed, "We can prevent one journalist from reporting bad news, but we cannot prevent all journalists from doing so; or even if we can require all journalists not to report bad news, we are still incapable of asking all citizens not to expose it."[212]

The Severe Acute Respiratory Syndrome (SARS)[213] incident in 2003 provides a good example to illustrate the severe consequences of delaying proactive disclosure of official information in the Internet age. The mysterious SARS flu first appeared in Guangdong Province and rapidly spread to other areas. However, government restrictions disallowed traditional media from reporting this epidemic at the time of the crisis.[214] Instead, censors instructed reports to cover, heavily, the Iraq War.[215] Knowing that obtaining reliable information of the flu from the traditional media and the government was unlikely, Chinese citizens began using cell phones to forward text messages about the epidemic.[216] They also used the

"the great firewall of China." Michael Bristow, *China's Internet Spin Doctors*, BBC, December 16, 2008, http://news.bbc.co.uk/2/hi/asia-pacific/7783640.stm (accessed between February 21, 2025 and March 31, 2025); *Internet Filtering in China in 2004–2005: A Country Study*, OpenNet Initiative, Harvard University, Cambridge, Massachusetts, April 13, 2005, *available at* http://cyber.law.harvard.edu/publications/2005/Internet_Filtering_in_China_in_2004_2005 (accessed between February 21, 2025 and March 31, 2025). For political implications of Internet use and censorship in China, see Xiaoru Wang, "Behind the Great Firewall: The Internet and Democratization in China" (2009) (unpublished Ph.D. diss., The University of Michigan).

210 John Gittings, The Changing Face of China: From Mao to Market 8–9 (2006).

211 John Gittings, The Changing Face of China: From Mao to Market 8–9 (2006).

212 Huaxin Zhu, Jiangchun Hu & Wentao Sun, *Analysis Report on Public Opinions on the Internet in China in 2007* [2007 中国互联网舆情分析报告], 2 Journal of Today's Mass Media 31(2008).

213 The SARS crisis occurred in China between November 2002 and August 2003, infecting 5,327 individuals and causing 349 fatalities.

214 Local Chinese governments maintained secrecy for the spread of the SARS virus and imposed a news blackout.

215 Mu Qiao, *Communication Effects and Political Impact of SMS Messages* [手机短信的传播效果与政治影响], 4 Journal of Contemporary Communications 76 (2008).

216 According to the Guangdong Mobile Communication Co., Ltd., 40 million text messages transmitted on February 8, 2003, with an increase of one million the next day,

Internet, landline telephones, and word of mouth to seek and disseminate relevant information.[217]

Although the SARS virus is highly contagious, it is not lethal and preventable. However, people were unaware because traditional news sources and the government failed to distribute such information. Rumors circulated and flooded the Internet.[218] Some rumors speculated that the flu was a large-scale biological and chemical attack.[219] Soon people throughout the country panicked and rushed to purchase masks, medicines, and all sorts of necessities. Beijing witnessed a mass exodus of migrant workers and students,[220] creating a state of national chaos.[221]

The Chinese authorities lacked the power to contain international media; eventually *Time* magazine carried a story detailing a letter from a courageous military doctor in Beijing. In the letter, the doctor exposed

and five million on 10 February. Most of these text messages related to the outbreak of the SARS flu. Guoqiang Yun & Pin Lv, *Relationship Between Media and Government: Taking Example of SARS Incident* [以 SARS 疫情为例看传媒与政府的关系] 14 21ST CENTURY (2003).

217 Dahong Min, *Chinese Internet amid SARS Crisis* [“非典” (SARS) 危机中的中国互联网], *People's Daily Online*, November 22, 2004 (captured by Internet Archive Wayback Machine on January 18, 2005), retrieved from https://web.archive.org/web/20050118080030/http://www.people.com.cn/GB/14677/40628/3003430.html (accessed between February 21, 2025 and March 31, 2025).

218 Allport and Postman argued that the quantity of rumors in circulation depends on two factors: the importance of the news and the ambiguity of the evidence. GORDON W. ALLPORT & LEO J. POSTMAN, THE PSYCHOLOGY OF RUMOR 34 (1947).

219 Guoqiang Yun & Pin Lv, *Relationship Between Media and Government: Taking Example of SARS Incident* [以 SARS 疫情为例看传媒与政府的关系] 14 21ST CENTURY (2003).

220 Xiangyuan Sun, *Information Disclosure: Double-Edged Sword, Taking SARS Coverage As Example* [从 SARS 报道看信息公开的“双刃剑”作用] 29 JOURNAL OF HUNAN UNIVERSITY OF ARTS AND SCIENCE (SOCIAL SCIENCE EDITION) 5 50 (September 2004).

221 Dahong Min, *Chinese Internet amid SARS Crisis* [“非典” (SARS) 危机中的中国互联网], *People's Daily Online*, November 22, 2004 (captured by Internet Archive Wayback Machine on January 18, 2005), retrieved from https://web.archive.org/web/20050118080030/http://www.people.com.cn/GB/14677/40628/3003430.html (accessed between February 21, 2025 and March 31, 2025); Guoqiang Yun & Pin Lv, *Relationship Between Media and Government: Taking Example of SARS Incident* [以 SARS 疫情为例看传媒与政府的关系] 14 21ST CENTURY (2003); Ying Zhu and Yi Liu, *From SARS to H1N1 Flu: Evolution of China's Government Information Disclosure* [从“非典”到“甲型 H1N1 流感”—中国政府信息公开的变迁] SOUTHEAST COMMUNICATION 61 (9) (2009): 66.

the Ministry of Health's concealment of the SARS situation.[222] The heroic actions of this whistleblower prompted an immediate international outcry. Western media described China as "not only an autocratic authority, but also an outdated communist country" that attempted to hide the truth "from its people as well as the outside world."[223]

Fearing that a global epidemic might be spiraling beyond control, the Chinese central government responded several months after the emergence of the SARS crisis by dismissing the minister of the Health Ministry and the mayor of Beijing for concealment of information of SARS patients.[224] On April 23, 2003, the government required officials at all levels to "report information on SARS accurately, honestly, and in a timely manner."[225] The traditional media ultimately covered the crisis vigorously, and the public's panic gradually subsided.[226]

After the SARS incident, the Chinese government accelerated establishment of the OGI system.[227] The SARS crisis, just like the COVID-19 crisis that swept China 17 years later, offered China's leaders a valuable lesson that governmental information needs proactive release in a timely manner in the event of crises in the changed media environment.[228] A late

[222] Susan Jakes, *Beijing's SARS Attack*, TIME, April 8, 2003, https://content.time.com/time/subscriber/article/0,33009,441615,00.html (accessed between February 21, 2025 and March 31, 2025).

[223] Chia-ju Lin, *A Textual Analysis of the Coverage of SARS and the Image of China*, 8 ASIAN SOCIAL SCIENCE 49 (March 2012).

[224] Ling Lan, *Open Government and Transparency Policy: China's Experience with SARS*, 6 INTERNATIONAL PUBLIC MANAGEMENT REVIEW 63 (2005).

[225] Ling Lan, *Open Government and Transparency Policy: China's Experience with SARS*, 6 INTERNATIONAL PUBLIC MANAGEMENT REVIEW 63 (2005).

[226] For a detailed description of governmental and media cover-up of the SARS incident and analysis of how SARS-like public incidents prompted the Chinese government to improve its crisis communication, see Lidan Chen, *Open Information System and Crisis Communication in China*, 1 CHINESE JOURNAL OF COMMUNICATION 38, 38–54 (April 2008).

[227] Ping Yin, *Chinese Government Information Disclosure and Rule of Law: From SARS to Bird Flu*, 11 JOURNAL OF HEBEI LAW SCIENCE 146, 146–49 (2004).

[228] Large-scale health crises or public emergencies do not necessarily lead to public panic and social disintegration if governmental authorities react with timeliness and proactivity, disclose information quickly, and allow media to report crises fully. Such policies underscore the United States' maintaining social stability in 2001 when terrorists attacked the World Trade Center and the Pentagon, and in 2009 when the mysterious swine flu swept through the country.

or delayed disclosure of information results in spreading rumors, endangerment of social stability, eroding trust in government authorities, and shattered international image.[229]

Summary and Conclusion

This chapter examined the gradual and incremental legislative process of national *OGI Regulations*, and exposed movement toward governmental transparency in China beginning in rural areas (OVA) and slowly expanding to higher levels of government in the form of OGA and OGI. Experiences from transparent practices at local and provincial levels provided a firm foundation for shaping national legislation.

The chapter also explored the rationales for the rise of freedom of information in China. Consistent with other research findings, this study finds that China's entry into the WTO and pressure from the United States, its largest trading partner, are major external factors encouraging China toward greater transparency. China's competition for participation in global events is a short-term transparency-enhancing element easily ignored.

The chapter argued that internal and domestic factors are much more important than external ones for realizing freedom of information legislation. OGI reform in China did not lose momentum during the reform era (1978–2012) because of strong and consistent commitment from reform-minded top political leaders. OGI legislation is a component of China's overall legal reform. Rule of law-oriented administrative reform offered statutory and constitutional support for reformers to draft OGI legislation. The adoption and/or amendment of transparency-related laws and regulations created a beneficial legal environment for the inception of OGI legislation.

Consistent with prior research, this chapter also found another transparency-enhancing factor worthy of discussion: Improving the government's capacity to distribute information. By establishing official websites, online forums, and engaging in social networking, the Chinese government, at various levels, increased its technological ability to release

[229] For in-depth analysis of how changed media and information environment in China contributes to the rise of freedom of information in China, see WEIBING XIAO, FREEDOM OF INFORMATION REFORM IN CHINA: INFORMATION FLOW ANALYSIS 27–37 (2011).

information. By adopting systems for press conferences and the mechanism for press secretaries, governmental agencies enhanced their capacities to deal with delivery of information and communication with foreign and domestic journalists.

Last but not least, the changed social and informational environment in the early 2000s, as examined by many legal scholars, stimulated the Chinese government to become more transparent and proactive when dealing with crises. Frequent occurrences of social unrest/crises and the delayed and reactive disclosure of information allowed rumors to foment in the online and offline worlds. Citizen-journalists (they can be any citizens with an Internet-accessible computer) spread facts and rumors to every corner of the world with a click of the mouse. This chain reaction created a severe threat to social stability and denigrated the party's and the government's legitimacy. The Chinese government had no choice but to abandon the old-fashioned reactive and secretive approach to managing information, practiced for thousands of years. After disposing the old approach, Chinese bureaucrats began to embrace a new proactive disclosure of information. The change of attitude among government officials laid a solid foundation for the emergence of OGI legislation.

Chinese FOI scholar, Weibing Xiao, argued that democratization is a key rationale for China's efforts to promote greater transparency.[230] The analysis presented in this chapter indicates that his argument is insightful but not fully valid because the Chinese FOI law is a means, which the central party and governmental authorities use to maintain the ruling party's legitimacy. The adoption of *OGI Regulations* and relevant transparency laws and regulations is not a component of China's political liberalization. In other words, the FOI law became possible, not because of Chinese leaders' strong beliefs in democratic values widely accepted in the Western world, but rather, freedom of information legislation became reality because Chinese reformers successfully convinced political leaders of the benefits of FOI law to economic growth, informationization development, corruption prevention, law-based administration, and crisis management. These are all goals of the party within the framework of characteristically Chinese socialism.

[230] Weibing Xiao, *Democratization as a Rationale for FOI Reform in China (Chapter 4)*, Freedom of Information Reform in China: Information Flow Analysis 38–50 (2011).

CHAPTER 6

What the Law Promises: Analysis of Statutory Language of *OGI Regulations*

As part of the author's doctoral dissertation that was successfully defended at The Pennsylvania State University in 2012, this chapter was later revised and presented at the AEJMC Southeast Colloquium in 2013 and then published in *Journal of Information Policy* in 2014. The author of this book retains copyright of this journal article. Certain parts of the text in this chapter may resemble or replicate the original material, which has been included with the permission of the editors at Palgrave Macmillan. Yong Tang, "Chinese Freedom of Information: An Evaluation of the Legislative History, Rationales, Significance and Efficacy of Regulations of the People's Republic of China on Open Government Information" (2012) (unpublished Ph.D. diss., The Pennsylvania State University at University Park), *available at* https://etda.libraries.psu.edu/catalog/16287 (accessed between February 21, 2025 and March 31, 2025); Yong Tang, *"Feeling for Rocks while Crossing the River": Analysis of The Statutory Language of China's First Freedom of Information Law*, paper accepted for presentation by the annual AEJMC (Association for Education in Journalism and Mass Communication) Southeast Colloquium convention, University of South Florida, Tampa, Florida, February 28–March 2, 2013; Yong Tang, *Feeling for Rocks while Crossing the River: Analysis of the Statutory Language of China's First Freedom of Information Law*, 4 JOURNAL OF INFORMATION POLICY 342–376 (2014).

Y. Tang, *Freedom of Information Law in China*,
https://doi.org/10.1007/978-981-96-7842-6_6

Introduction

This chapter will provide a detailed analysis of statutory language of 2007 *OGI Regulations*[1] in the light of the Academic Draft of the law,[2] relevant legal interpretations,[3] and its 2019 amendment.[4] China has three forms of legally binding statutory interpretations. One is legislative interpretation issued by the National People's Congress and its Standing Committee; another is administrative interpretation issued by the State Council, and the third is judicial interpretation promulgated

[1] *OGI Regulations 2007* (amended in 2019).

[2] Hanhua Zhou and other legal scholars in China developed and submitted the *Academic Draft of OGI Regulations 2002* to the State Council. The State Council used the *Academic Draft* as a basis for the drafting *OGI Regulations*. Academic Draft of OGI Regulations: Draft, Explanation, Rationale and Legislative Examples [政府信息公开条例专家建议稿-草案、说明、理由、立法例] (Hanhua Zhou ed., Chinese Legal Publishing House, 2003). Prior to 2007, normally drafts of Chinese laws and regulations were not published. *Academic Draft of OGI Regulations 2002* is a rare exception, published in 2003 in a book edited by Hanhua Zhou. From 2007, the State Council required publication of draft versions of laws and regulations and sought public comment and opinion. *Interim Rules of the State Council Legislative Affairs on Publicizing Drafts of Laws and Regulations for Public Comment* [国务院法制办公室法律法规草案公开征求意见暂行办法] effective date: March 29, 2007.

[3] *Notice of the General Office of the State Council on Preparing the Implementation of the OGI Regulations*[国务院办公厅关于做好施行《中华人民共和国政府信息公开条例》准备工作的通知] General Office of the State Council, Guo Ban Fa [2007] No. 54, effective date: August 4, 2007; *Opinions of the General Office of the State Council on Several Issues Concerning the Enforcement of the Regulations of the People's Republic of China on the Disclosure of Government Information* [国务院办公厅关于施行《中华人民共和国政府信息公开条例》若干问 题的意见] General Office of the State Council, Guo Ban Fa [2008] No. 36, effective date: April 29, 2008; *Opinions of the State Council General Office on Doing a Good Job of Disclosing Government Information on Request* [国务院办公厅关于做好政府信息依申请公开工作的意见] Guo Ban Fa [2010] No. 5, effective date: January 12, 2010; *Provisions of the Supreme People's Court on Issues concerning Trying Administrative Cases of Government Information Disclosure* [最高人民法院关于审理政府信息公开行政案件若干问题的规定] Fa Shi [2011] No. 17, effective date: August 13, 2011.

[4] *OGI Regulations 2007* was revised in 2019 and took effect on May 15, 2019. When revising the law, the State Council expanded its content from 38 to 56 articles. The Chinese-language amendment can be found on the Chinese central government's official web portal, *available at* https://www.gov.cn/zhengce/content/2019-04/15/content_5382991.htm (accessed between February 21, 2025 and March 31, 2025). The English-language amendment can be found on the website of Yale University Law School China Center, *available at* https://law.yale.edu/sites/default/files/area/center/china/2022-9-5_jph_rev_ogir.pdf (accessed between February 21, 2025 and March 31, 2025).

by the Supreme People's Court. Of the three, judicial interpretation has the weakest legal significance; however, judicial interpretation is increasingly important for judges in China for rendering legal decisions.[5] This chapter will examine statutory language of judicial and administrative interpretations relative to *OGI Regulations*.

The bases for the method for the analysis of statutory language is nine common features of global FOI laws, as identified by international FOI expert, David Banisar: types of governmental bodies covered, accessibility, identity of those allowed access, exemptions, appeals and oversight, sanctions, affirmative publication, e-FOI, and accusations of malfeasance.[6] The chapter will identify additional common features of world FOI laws and discusses relationship with *OGI Regulations*: legal authority, legislative purpose, fees for access, and limits to response times.

The chapter will examine *OGI Regulations* and relevant interpretations regarding these categories and comparison of Chinese law with those of the United States and other countries. This section will explain the reasons for Chinese law reformers embracing some United States and global standards and rejecting others. The discussion will include the strengths and weaknesses of OGI legislation. Choosing *U.S. FOIA* for comparison is because it "has probably been the most influential [FOI] law"[7] and provides "a model for an effective public records statue."[8]

[5] Li Wei, *Comment: Judicial Interpretation in China*, 5 WILLAMETTE JOURNAL OF INTERNATIONAL LAW AND DISPUTE RESOLUTION 87 (1997); Ronald Colin Keith & Zhiqiu Lin, *Judicial Interpretation of China's Supreme People's Court as "Secondary Law" with Special Reference to Criminal law*, 23 CHINA INFORMATION 223, 223–55 (2009).

[6] DAVID BANISAR, FREEDOM OF INFORMATION AROUND THE WORLD 2006: A GLOBAL SURVEY OF ACCESS TO GOVERNMENT INFORMATION LAWS 20–26 (report for Privacy International, London, United Kingdom, July 2006), *available at* http://www.freedominfo.org/documents/global_survey2006.pdf (accessed between February 21, 2025 and March 31, 2025).

[7] DAVID BANISAR, FREEDOM OF INFORMATION AROUND THE WORLD 2006: A GLOBAL SURVEY OF ACCESS TO GOVERNMENT INFORMATION LAWS 20 (report for Privacy International, London, United Kingdom, July 2006), *available at* http://www.freedominfo.org/documents/global_survey2006.pdf (accessed between February 21, 2025 and March 31, 2025).

[8] Martin E. Halstuk, *Freedom of information*, *in* 5 THE INTERNATIONAL ENCYCLOPEDIA OF COMMUNICATION 1890 (Wolfgang Donsbach ed., 2008).

Legal Authority and Standing of *OGI Regulations*

Both the National People's Congress (NPC) and the State Council accepted formulation of OGI legislation for their legislative agenda; however, the NPC effort failed to produce the OGI law. The State Council, China's cabinet, finally promulgated *OGI Regulations*. Under the Chinese legislative system, the State Council has certain powers to formulate administrative regulations, such as *OGI Regulations*; noticeably such regulations are less powerful than laws framed by the NPC and its Standing Committee.[9]

OGI law has advantages compared to *OGI Regulations*, principally, creation of new and enforceable access rights and imposition of criminal sanctions for violations of disclosure requirements.[10] China adopted numerous laws that either promote or limit access to information. In order to avoid seriously undermining OGI law with hundreds of conflicting statutes, the NPC could assign precedence to OGI law[11] over other laws, thereby permitting governmental agencies to use exemptions to OGI law as the sole reason for withholding information, similar to

[9] According to *Legislation Law 2000*, the *Constitution*, adopted and amended by the National People's Congress, enjoys the highest level of legal authority. An act or law, adopted and amended by the National People's Congress or the standing committee of the National People's Congress, represents the second level of legal authority. Regulations, divided into administrative regulations, local regulations, autonomous regulations and separate regulations, represent the third level of legal authority. This third tier of laws is from the State Council or local people's congresses and cannot override a law. *OGI Regulations* are administrative regulations, adopted by the State Council. Administrative rules represent the fourth level of legal authority, and are actions of state organs, provincial governments, or governments in comparatively larger cities. Many local OGI Rules are of the fourth level. *Legislation Law 2000*. Art. 78, 79, 80, 81, 82.

[10] Academic Draft of OGI Regulations: Draft, Explanation, Rationale and Legislative Examples [政府信息公开条例专家建议稿-草案、说明、理由、立法例] 18 (Hanhua Zhou ed., Chinese Legal Publishing House, 2003); Mingjie Zhang, *Open Government: Research on OGI Laws* [开放的政府-政府信息公开法律制度研究] *218* (2003).

[11] The State Council cannot allow *OGI Regulations* to have precedence over laws because administrative regulations have lower legal standing than laws.

other countries.[12] In addition, most countries with FOI legislation such as the United States and Sweden, enacted FOI laws, not FOI Regulations.[13]

The reasons China ultimately adopted *OGI Regulations* instead of OGI law are threefold. First, the State Council has the authority to formulate administrative regulations as long as the regulations do not impinge on the people's congress, the court, and the procuratorate. Second, legislating regulations requires less time and effort than enacting laws. Third, the lawmaking process of *OGI Regulations* is consistent with standard legislative practices in China: The State Council formulates a regulation, and the NPC enacts a corresponding law when the NPC considers timing to be opportune, after gaining sufficient lessons and practical experience from implemented regulation.[14]

Chinese OGI reformers' legislative considerations do make sense in the Chinese context; however, ignoring the drawbacks of *OGI Regulations* resulting from its low legal authority is unwise. Currently China has enacted many official information-related laws, such as *Law on Guarding State Secrets*, *Archives Law*, *Criminal Law*, *Statistics Law*, and *Emergency Response Law*. Many clauses in those laws are incompatible with requirements for establishing an open government. Due to weak legal standing, *OGI Regulations* do not supersede all those relevant laws when conflicts arise.[15] Consequently, the daunting task of amending relevant laws needs to occur first to assure that *Regulations* operate correctly.

[12] David Banisar, Effective Open Government: Improving Public Access to Government Information 14 (report for Organization for Economic Co-operation and Development, Paris, France), May 29, 2012, *available at* https://papers.ssrn.com/sol3/papers.cfm?abstract_id=2069870# (accessed between February 21, 2025 and March 31, 2025).

[13] Hanhua Zhou, *Basic Considerations in Drafting of Regulations on the Openness of Government Information (Academic Draft)* [起草《政府信息公开条例》(专家建议稿)的基本考虑] 6 Chinese Journal of Law 57 (2002).

[14] Hanhua Zhou, *Basic Considerations in Drafting of Regulations on the Openness of Government Information (Academic Draft)* [起草《政府信息公开条例》(专家建议稿)的基本考虑] 6 Chinese Journal of Law 57 (2002).

[15] One of the major principles of freedom of information legislation advocated by Article 19 states that the law for freedom of information should take precedence, and "laws inconsistent with the principle of maximum disclosure require amendment or repeal." Article 19, the Public's Right to Know: Principles on Freedom of Information Legislation 10 (London, June 1999), *available at* http://www.article19.org/data/files/pdfs/standards/righttoknow.pdf (accessed between February 21, 2025 and March 31, 2025).

Legislative Purpose and Principle of *OGI Regulations*

In stating the legislative purpose and principle, *Academic Draft 2002*, *OGI Regulations 2007* and *OGI Regulations 2019* provide, respectively:

> These Regulations are formulated according to the Constitution in order to ensure the protection of the public's exercise of *the right to know* and of public participation in the management of state and social affairs, promotion of the flow of government information, and supervision of government agencies in the exercise of their powers in accordance with the law...[d]isclosure of government information is *the principle*, while exemption is *the exception*. (emphasis added)[16]

> These Regulations are formulated in order to ensure that citizens, legal persons and other organizations legally obtain government information, to enhance the transparency of the government work to facilitate the exercise of administrative functions in accordance with the law and to give full play to government information in serving the people in production, daily living and social economic activities.[17]

> In order to ensure that citizens, legal persons and other organizations obtain government information in accordance with the law, enhance transparency of the work of government, promote administration in accordance with the law, and bring into full play the role of government information in serving the people's production and livelihood and their economic and social activities, these Regulations are hereby formulated.[18]

The differences between *Academic Draft* and *OGI Regulations* are significant. Some Chinese local OGI Rules adopted the principle of presumptive disclosure.[19] The progressiveness of local OGI experimenters

[16] *Academic Draft of OGI Regulations 2002*. Art. 1 and Art. 2. Academic Draft of OGI Regulations: Draft, Explanation, Rationale and Legislative Examples [政府信息公开条例专家建议稿-草案、说明、理由、立法例] 1 (Hanhua Zhou ed., Chinese Legal Publishing House, 2003).

[17] *OGI Regulations 2007*. Art. 1.

[18] *OGI Regulations 2019*. Art. 1.

[19] OGI Rules in Hebei, Hubei, Jiangsu and Liaoning Provinces provided for the principle of presumptive disclosure. Weibing Xiao, Freedom of Information Reform in China: Information Flow Analysis 88, 171 (2011).

inspired Chinese scholars, and OGI academics believed that governmental agencies would have too much discretion to deny disclosure if the law did not include provisions for presumption of disclosure and the right to know.[20] Thus, the *Academic Draft* clearly adopts the widely accepted principle of maximum disclosure[21] and explicitly confers requesters a statutory right of access to governmental information. Contrarily, *OGI Regulations 2007* omitted the maximum disclosure principle and at best only implied a right of access.[22] This significant omission indicated the State Council's reluctance to embrace, explicitly, the right to know.[23]

OGI Regulations 2007's ambiguity in mandating the right to know created problems for subsequent implementation of the law. As legal scholar, Jamie P. Horsley, said, "The overall impression is that the *OGI*

[20] Hanhua Zhou, *Basic Considerations in Drafting of Regulations on the Openness of Government Information (Academic Draft)* [起草《政府信息公开条例》(专家建议稿)的基本考虑] 6 CHINESE JOURNAL OF LAW 57 (2002).

[21] Principle One of Article 19 designates maximum disclosure as the primary principle of freedom of information legislation. ARTICLE 19, THE PUBLIC'S RIGHT TO KNOW: PRINCIPLES ON RIGHT TO INFORMATION LEGISLATION (London, United Kingdom, 2006), *available at* http://www.article19.org/data/files/pdfs/standards/righttoknow.pdf (accessed between February 21, 2025 and March 31, 2025). Article 19, founded in 1987, is a London-based human rights organization with a specific mandate and focus on the defense and promotion of freedom of expression and freedom of information, worldwide. The organization's name originates from Article 19 of the Universal Declaration of Human Rights.

[22] In the process of revising local OGI Rules and the *Academic Draft*, the State Council decided to be less progressive with *OGI Regulations 2007* than that represented by Chinese OGI scholars, local OGI experimenters and international standards. In a sharp contrast, decades of U.S. House and Senate legislative reports and U.S. Supreme Court decisions early establish a presumption of disclosure, despite the FOIA's statutory language not explicitly stating that disclosure is the overriding principle and non-disclosure is an exception. H.R. REP. No. 110-45, at 2 (2007); *Department of Air Force v. Rose*, 425 U.S. 352, 361 (1976).

[23] The name of the FOI law in China reflects this reluctance. The *U.S. Freedom of Information Act* emphasizes the right of "any person" to access governmental information. Contrarily, *Regulations on Open Government Information* suggest that official agencies "open" information by using their administrative powers. Wenjing Liu, *Approaching Democracy Through Transparency: A Comparative Law Study on Chinese Open* Government Information, 26 AMERICAN UNIVERSITY INTERNATIONAL LAW REVIEW 983, 998 (2011).

Regulations [2007] favor non-disclosure as the default."[24] Given that the *Constitution 1982* also fails to mention explicitly the right to know,[25] the enforcement of this controversial civil right became problematic in China.

The failure of *OGI Regulations 2007* to embrace the principle of maximum disclosure created implementation obstacles as well. Although Premier Wen,[26] other senior governmental officials,[27] and the media[28] frequently stressed the implied maximum disclosure principle in the FOI law, all announcements and media fanfare carried no legal weight and could not override the absence of presumptive disclosure in the law. The result was that, whenever a conflict between disclosure and non-disclosure arose in OGI cases, governmental officials and courts would have the latitude, even encouragement to err toward secrecy.

[24] Jamie P. Horsley, *China Adopts First Nationwide Open Government Information Regulations*, freedominfo.org, Washington, DC, May 9, 2007, at para 14, *available at* http://www.freedominfo.org/2007/05/china-adopts-first-nationwide-open-government-information-regulations/ (accessed between February 21, 2025 and March 31, 2025).

[25] Academic Draft of OGI Regulations: Draft, Explanation, Rationale and Legislative Examples [政府信息公开条例专家建议稿-草案、说明、理由、立法例] 16 (Hanhua Zhou ed., Chinese Legal Publishing House, 2003).

[26] Wen Jiabao, *Seriously Adhere to the Spirits of the 17th National Congress of the CPC to Promote Vigorously the Work of Incorruptibility Construction and Anti-Corruption* [认真贯彻党的十七大精神大力推进廉政建设和反腐败工作], 9 Qiushi [求是] 6 (2008):5-10; Wen Jiabao, *Let Power Be Exercised in the Sunshine* [让权力在阳光下运行], *Qiushi* 8 (2012).

[27] For example, during an *OGI Regulations* press conference in 2007, Qiong Zhang, the deputy director of the State Council Legislative Affairs Office, said, "Disclosure is the principle and nondisclosure is the exception," rendering *OGI Regulations* as implications, not guarantees. *State Council Legislative Affairs Office Deputy Director Meets the Press* [国务院法制办副主任就《政府信息公开条例》答记者问], Xinhua News Agency, republished by Phoenix TV, April 24, 2007, https://news.ifeng.com/mainland/200704/0424_17_108239.shtml (accessed between February 21, 2025 and March 31, 2025).

[28] A Google search of articles published in major Chinese-language news portals indicates that the news media consider the principle of maximum disclosure as embedded in *OGI Regulations*. A *People's Daily* commentary even took the principle of presumptive disclosure as its title. Jianfeng Bai, *Disclosure of Governmental Information Is the Principle While Nondisclosure Is an Exception* [政府信息公开是原则， 不公开是例外], People's Daily, April 30, 2008 (captured by Internet Archive Wayback Machine on May 11, 2008), retrieved from https://web.archive.org/web/20080511072252/http://opinion.people.com.cn/GB/7182797.html (accessed between February 21, 2025 and March 31, 2025).

This significant flaw of *OGI Regulations 2007* was discussed and somewhat remedied in 2019 when the law was revised. Article 5 of *OGI Regulations 2019* says clearly: "When disclosing government information, administrative organs should uphold disclosure as the norm and non-disclosure as the exception, and abide by the principles of justice, fairness, and convenience to the people."[29] In addition to codifying the presumption of disclosure of government information, *OGI Regulations 2019* provide in Article 13 that all government information must be disclosed, except the information specified by the Regulations that may be withheld from disclosure.[30] It appears the Chinese FOI law has made remarkable improvement in its 2019 amendment in terms of making a stronger statement about the presumption of disclosure, although both Article 5 and Article 13 could have been incorporated into Article 1.

Types of Bodies Covered by *OGI Regulations*

Under both *OGI Regulations 2007 and OGI Regulations 2019*, three types of government entities are subject to mandatory information disclosure. The first is administrative agency (*xingzheng jiguan* 行政机关), which has no definition in law.[31] In order to avoid confusion, some basic understanding of the Chinese government, the largest bureaucracy in the world, is necessary. China has six practical (de facto) levels of central and local government: central, province, prefecture, county, township, and village.[32] Broadly speaking, each level of government

[29] *OGI Regulations 2019*. Art.5.

[30] *OGI Regulations 2019*. Art. 13.

[31] In an email interview with the author of this book, Yanbin Lv, a Chinese Academy of Social Sciences legal scholar, stressed that *OGI Regulations* do not define "administrative agency" because (1) *Regulations* were promulgated by the State Council, automatically indicating that the law only applies to the executive branch of the government; (2) when defining "governmental information," the State Council is equating "government" with "administrative agency." Also, village committees are not subject to *OGI Regulations* because they are not a form of government but grassroots self-governing mass organizations. According to *Organic Law of the Village Committees 1998* (村民委员会组织法), such organizations also have obligations to disclose information (financial information in particular) to villagers on a regular basis.

[32] Practically speaking, village is the lowest level of government. But officially, township is the lowest level of government. Villages are within townships, townships are within counties, counties are within cities, cities are within prefectures, and provinces include all five. For China's administrative division system and names of provinces,

has six branches: the people's congress, the party, the people's government, the political consultative conference, the people's court, and the people's procuratorate.[33] *OGI Regulations* apply only to one of these six branches: the people's government.[34] Given the complexity and size of the Chinese bureaucracy, obtaining an accurate number of administrative agencies under all levels of the people's government is daunting.[35] Such administrative agencies are numerous.

The second type of government entity covered by *OGI Regulations* is an organization authorized by laws or regulations to manage

autonomous regions and municipalities, see http://www.china.org.cn/english/feature/38436.htm (accessed between February 21, 2025 and March 31, 2025).

[33] The six branches may not all exist at village and township levels. According to *Constitution 1982*, the people's congress at various levels is the highest state organ at various levels of government. In practice, the Chinese Communist Party is more powerful than any of the other five.

[34] The people's government runs from the central level to the township level. The State Council is the people's government at the central level. *OGI Regulations* apply to central level government and its administrative agencies, such as the State Council http://www.gov.cn/, the Ministry of Public Security http://www.mps.gov.cn/n16/index.html, the Ministry of Finance http://www.mof.gov.cn, the Ministry of Education http://www.moe.gov.cn/ and the Ministry of Foreign Affairs https://www.mfa.gov.cn/eng/. Click the sites below https://english.www.gov.cn/archive/chinaabc/201911/22/content_WS5ed77233c6d0b3f0e9499854.html and https://www.gov.cn/gwyzzjg/zuzhi/ to see the organizational structure of the State Council. Provincial-level governments and their administrative agencies, subject to *OGI Regulations*, are many, for example, Jiangsu Provincial People's Government https://en.jiangsu.gov.cn and Jiangsu Provincial Department of Public Security https://gat.jiangsu.gov.cn. County-level governmental agencies covered by *OGI Regulations* are numerous, for example, the people's government of Jixi County in Anhui Province https://www.cnjx.gov.cn and the people's government of Dayi County in Sichuan Province https://www.day.gov.cn. Examples of township-level agencies subject to *OGI Regulations* are numerous too. One example is the Dalingshan Township People's Government in Guangdong Province http://www.dg.gov.cn/dalingshan/index.html) (all the websites in this footnote were accessed between February 21, 2025 and March 31, 2025).

[35] Under the State Council http://english.peopledaily.com.cn/data/organs/statecouncil.shtml, 28 ministries and commissions are subject to disclosure requirements of *OGI Regulations*. China has, officially, 34 provincial-level people's governments, over 300 prefecture-level people's governments, nearly 3000 county-level people's governments, and over 40,000 township-level people's governments. *OGI Regulations* cover all of these governmental bodies. For a detailed analysis of China's modern political system, see Michael F. Martin, *Understanding China's Political System*, Congressional Research Service, Washington, DC, April 14, 2010, *available at* http://www.fas.org/sgp/crs/row/R41007.pdf (accessed between February 21, 2025 and March 31, 2025).

public affairs.[36] *OGI Regulations* do not define such organizations, but according to *Administrative Permission Law 2003* and *Civil Servants Law 2005*, such organizations are quasi-administrative. They are not administrative in themselves, but governmental sponsorship permits their fulfilling obligations for public affairs management. Examples of such organizations are China Securities Regulatory Commission, China Insurance Regulatory Commission, China Certification and Accreditation Administration.[37]

The third type of entities subject to disclosure requirements of *OGI Regulations* are public enterprises and public institutions engaging in sectors "closely related to the interests of the people," such as education, medical treatment and health care, family planning, water supply, electricity supply, gas supply, heating supply, environmental protection and public transportation.[38] Largely due to this provision, all public colleges and universities,[39] public hospitals and clinical institutions,[40] public utilities companies,[41] environmental protection-related public institutions,[42]

[36] *OGI Regulations 2007*. Art. 36.

[37] Similar organizations in the United States include Fannie Mae and Freddie Mac and other independent regulatory agencies such as the Federal Communications Commission, the Federal Trade Commission, and the United States Securities and Exchange Commission.

[38] *OGI Regulations 2007*. Art. 37.

[39] Colleges and universities shall follow the *Information Disclosure Implementation Rules of Colleges and Universities 2010* formulated by the Ministry of Education according to *OGI Regulations. Information Disclosure Implementation Rules of Colleges and Universities 2010* [高等学校信息公开办法] Jiaoyubu Ling [2010] No. 29, effective date: September 1, 2010.

[40] Hospitals, clinical institutions and health care centers shall follow the *Information Disclosure Rules of Health Institutions (Exposure Draft) 2009* formulated by the Ministry of Health in accordance with OGI Regulations. *Information Disclosure Rules of Health Institutions (Exposure Draft) 2009* [医疗卫生机构信息公开实施办法 (征求意见稿)] the General Office of the Ministry of Health, publication date: August 24, 2009.

[41] Public utilities companies shall follow the *Information Disclosure Implementation Rules of Public Utilities Institutions such as Water, Gas, Heating Supply Companies 2008* formulated by the Ministry of Housing and Urban–Rural Development according to OGI Regulations. *Information Disclosure Implementation Rules of Public Utilities Institutions such as Water, Gas, Heating Supply Companies 2008* [供水、供气、供热等公用事业单位信息公开实施办法] Jiancheng [2008] No. 213, effective date: October 12, 2008.

[42] Public sectors' undertakings for environmental protection shall follow the *Interim Rules of Information Disclosure Implementation for Public Institutions on Environmental Protection 2010* formulated by the Ministry of Environmental Protection in accordance

and public transportation companies[43] in China are subject to *OGI Regulations*. Given the large number of public enterprises and institutions, the number of organizations complying with *OGI Regulations* exceeds many countries' national FOI laws.[44]

Countries with freedom of information laws represent four categories in terms of types of bodies regulated[45]: The first category includes countries in which only the executive branch of the government is subject to information disclosure[46]; the second category are those in which all executive, judicial, and legislative organs are subject to disclosure requirements[47]; the third category countries are those in which all three branches of government and quasi-government organizations are subject to the law[48]; the fourth category are those countries in which all three branches of government, quasi-government organizations and private entities must comply with disclosure requirements.[49]

with OGI Regulations. *Interim Rules of Information Disclosure Implementation for Public Institutions on Environmental Protection 2010* [《环境保护公共事业单位信息公开实施办法(试行)》] Huanfa [2010] No. 82, effective date: October 1, 2010.

43 Public transportation companies shall follow the *Guiding Opinion on Information Disclosure of Public Transportation Entities 2008* formulated by the Ministry of Transport according to the OGI Regulations. *Guiding Opinion on Information Disclosure of Public Transportation Entities 2008* [《交通运输公共企事业单位信息公开指导意见》] Jiaobanfa [2008] No. 350, effective date: October 8, 2008.

44 Chapter 8 of this book will discuss transparency of public enterprises and institutions in China from a freedom of information law perspective.

45 Hanhua Zhou, *Basic Considerations in Drafting of Regulations on the Openness of Government Information (Academic Draft)* [起草《政府信息公开条例》(专家建议稿)的基本考虑] 6 Chinese Journal of Law 57 (2002).

46 USA and Japan fall into this category. US. FOI laws at the federal and state levels apply to only the executive branch of the Government. 5 U.S.C. § 552(f)(1) (2006). The FOI statutes do not apply to records held by congresses, the courts, private individuals or private companies, including private entities under federal contracts. U.S. Department of Justice, Freedom of Information Act Guide & Privacy Act Overview 31–36 (May 2004). However, it is important to note that U.S. constitutional law and common law precedents mandate transparency obligations of U.S. judicial and legislative organs.

47 The European Union falls into this category.

48 New Zealand falls into this category.

49 South Africa falls into this category. In South Africa, the *Promotion of Access to Information Act* allows individuals to demand information from both public and private entities. A few countries have adopted this approach. Richard Calland, *Prizing Open the Profit-Making World*, *in* The Right to Know: Transparency for an Open World 214–42 (Ann Florini & Joseph E. Stiglitz eds., 2007).

Globally, most countries fall into the first category.[50] Countries as progressive as South Africa toward freedom of information are few. China does not fall into any of the four categories, since a comparison indicates China's law seems more disclosure-friendly than its counterparts in the first category in terms of variety of bodies covered. China's approach to subject quasi-government organizations, public enterprises, and educational and medical institutions to disclosure requirements renders its policy more aggressive. However, China's inability to encompass the other five branches of the government, especially the party, into compliance of *OGI Regulations* is significantly negative.[51]

As the only ruling party of the country, the Chinese Communist Party[52] is the leading decision-maker on virtually all the major issues, and the party formulates the most important policies concerning various aspects of Chinese society. Understandably, the party generates, stores and obtains a wealth of documents and records of vital importance to the Chinese public. Although the party is not a governing body recognized by the *Constitution 1982*,[53] control of "all state apparatuses and of the

[50] David Banisar, Freedom of Information around the World 2006: A Global Survey of Access to Government Information Laws 20 (report for Privacy International, London, United Kingdom, July 2006), *available at* http://www.freedominfo.org/documents/global_survey2006.pdf (accessed between February 21, 2025 and March 31, 2025).

[51] This negativity was reduced in 2017 when the tentative *Regulations of the Chinese Communist Party on Open Party Affairs* (*OPA Regulations*) were adopted. *OPA Regulations* are very similar to *OGI Regulations* in terms of disclosure of official information.

[52] Almost in parallel with the people's government, the party is a huge bureaucratic hierarchy with party committees ranging from the central level to the village level. Party secretaries, appointed by higher-level party committees, head the lower-level committees. Party secretaries at various levels are normally more powerful and influential than their counterparts in the corresponding people's government.

[53] Interestingly, the *Constitution 1982* rarely mentions the Chinese Communist Party. The Preamble to the *Constitution* states that "under the leadership of the Communist Party of China and the guidance of Marxism-Leninism and Mao Zedong Thought, the Chinese people of all nationalities will continue to adhere to the people's democratic dictatorship and follow the socialist road..." However, the *Constitution* does not state the method for implementing this leadership role in the country's political structure, nor does it specifically define the relationship of the party to the legislative, executive, and judicial branches of the government.

legislative process"[54] secures the party's position as the "supreme political authority and power" in China.[55] Given the influence and prestige of the ruling party, disappointingly, *OGI Regulations* are not applicable to records and documents held by numerous powerful party organizations.[56]

What Is Accessible Under *OGI Regulations*

Internationally, two approaches describe the materials accessible under the FOI law. One is the use of the term "information" while the other uses terms such as "records," "files," and "documents." Most FOI laws,[57] especially newer ones, prefer the former for its expansiveness.[58]

[54] Ralph H. Folsom, John H. Minan and Lee Ann Otto, Law and Politics in the People's Republic of China in a nutshell 76–77 (1992).

[55] Ralph H. Folsom, John H. Minan and Lee Ann Otto, Law and Politics in the People's Republic of China in a nutshell 76–77 (1992).

[56] *OGI Regulations* are unable to subject the party to its disclosure requirements due to the regulation's low legal status and authority. As an administrative regulation, it can only compel administrative agencies under the people's government to comply with the transparency requirements. The party, the courts, and the people's congress are beyond the scope of administrative regulations. The tentative *Regulations of the Chinese Communist Party on Open Party Affairs* (*OPA Regulations*) were adopted in December 2017 and it is the party's FOI law. According to the law, CCP Central Committee and various lower levels of party organizations shall proactively disclose certain types of information to party members and, in some circumstances, to the general public. Chapter 11 of this book will examine the law in detail. For the law's Chinese-language version, see https://www.gov.cn/zhengce/2017-12/25/content_5250271.htm (accessed between February 21, 2025 and March 31, 2025). For the law's English-language translation, see https://law.yale.edu/sites/default/files/china-law-documents/horsley_eng._open_party_affairs_regulations.pdf (accessed between February 21, 2025 and March 31, 2025).

[57] The following laws use the term "information": the *U.S. FOIA* and many state FOI laws (USA); the *Freedom of Information Act* (Australia); the *Access to Information Act* (Canada); The *Right to Information Act* (India); the *Freedom of Information Law* (Israel); the *Promotion of Access to Information Act* (South Africa); The *Act on Disclosure of Information by Public Agencies* (South Korea).

[58] Hanhua Zhou, *Basic Considerations in Drafting of Regulations on the Openness of Government Information (Academic Draft)* [起草《政府信息公开条例》(专家建议稿)的基本考虑] 6 Chinese Journal of Law 57, 58 (2002); David Banisar, Freedom of Information around the World 2006: A Global Survey of Access to Government Information Laws 22 (report for Privacy International, London, United Kingdom, July 2006), *available at* http://www.freedominfo.org/documents/global_survey2006.pdf (accessed between February 21, 2025 and March 31, 2025).

In keeping with international standards, *OGI Regulations* use "information" to describe accessible materials and defines government information as "information prepared or obtained by an administrative organ in the process of exercising its duties and recorded and preserved in a certain form."[59]

The statutory language "recorded and preserved in a certain form" is sufficiently expansive to include all medium of all types, electronic or non-electronic. This approach aligns with international practice; however, problems arise because governmental officials try to orally transmit information (such as in a meeting) to avoid the obligation for disclosure. This is a challenge facing many FOI countries.

OGI Regulations 2007 do not stipulate if individuals' access to information requires governmental agencies to produce, collect, summarize, and analyze the material. In narrowing the scope of information accessible under the Chinese FOI law, the State Council, the Supreme Court and *OGI Regulations 2019* clarified that the information sought shall be in existence already and acquiring the information requested would not entail extra effort.[60] The State Council further limits the scope of accessible information by stating, in *OGI Regulations 2019* and one of its legally binding documents, that procedural information used for research and internal management are off-limits to requesters.[61]

The State Council clarifies whether or not official information transferred to archives or archival administrations is accessible by specifying that *OGI Regulations* do not apply.[62] The Supreme Court supports the

[59] *OGI Regulations 2007*. Art. 2.

[60] *Opinions of the State Council General Office on Doing a Good Job of Disclosing Government Information on Request* [国务院办公厅关于做好政府信息依申请公开工作的意见] Guo Ban Fa [2010] No. 5, effective date: January 12, 2010; *Provisions of the Supreme People's Court on Issues concerning Trying Administrative Cases of Government Information Disclosure* [最高人民法院关于审理政府信息公开行政案件若干问题的规定] Fa Shi [2011] No. 17, effective date: August 13, 2011; *OGI Regulations 2019*. Art. 38.

[61] *OGI Regulations 2019*. Art. 16; *Opinions of the State Council General Office on Doing a Good Job of Disclosing Government Information on Request* [国务院办公厅关于做好政府信息依申请公开工作的意见] Guo Ban Fa [2010] No. 5, effective date: January 12, 2010.

[62] *Opinions of the General Office of the State Council on Several Issues Concerning the Enforcement of Regulations of the People's Republic of China on the Disclosure of Government Information*[国务院办公厅关于施行《中华人民共和国政府信息公开条例》若干问 题的意见] General Office of the State Council, Guo Ban Fa [2008] No. 36, effective date: April 29, 2008.

exception by holding that *OGI Regulations* apply if governmental information represents content in a defendant's archives, and *OGI Regulations* do not apply if national archives at all levels have received official material.[63] According to *Archives Law 1988*, government documents transfer to archival institutions after a certain period. Once documents become archives, their designation is "sealed" and disclosure to the public may not occur for an extended time. The administrative and judicial interpretations concerning archived information may prompt agencies to expedite, unduly, the process of archiving sensitive information.

Affirmative Publication of Governmental Information

Similar to FOI laws in other countries, *OGI Regulations* mandate a duty for agencies to release, actively and proactively, certain categories of information. What differentiates China's *OGI Regulations* from other FOI laws is that the former "include broader requirements for proactive disclosure than FOI laws elsewhere."[64]

OGI Regulations 2007 contain a general clause, with four criteria, any one of which is sufficient to satisfy the mandate:

1. Information involving the vital interests of citizens, legal persons, or other organizations;
2. Information that needs wide dissemination or involves a situation that requires participation of the public;
3. Information pertaining to establishment, functions, working procedures, and the like concerning an official agency, or
4. Other information that should have proactive publication in accordance with laws, regulations, and relevant rules.[65]

[63] Article 7, *Provisions of the Supreme People's Court on Issues Concerning Trying Administrative Cases of Government Information Disclosure* [最高人民法院关于审理政府信息公开行政案件若干问题的规定] Fa Shi [2011] No. 17, effective date: August 13, 2011.

[64] Weibing Xiao, Freedom of Information Reform in China: Information Flow Analysis 82 (2011).

[65] *OGI Regulations 2007*. Art. 9.

This general clause in *OGI Regulations 2007* "sets broad standards" for governmental agencies to justify proactive disclosure of governmental information.[66] In addition to the inclusion of basic criteria for proactive disclosure, *OGI Regulations 2007* establish "minimum standards" by listing in three types of important information requiring proactive disclosure for governments at different levels.[67] Article 10 enumerates 11 categories of key information that governmental agencies at or above the county level shall affirmatively disclose.[68] Article 11 lists four categories stressing additional information that governmental agencies at the county level shall disclose.[69] Article 12 enumerates eight types of key information agencies at the village and township level shall publicize.[70] Once, publicizing officials' salaries and other personal assets was a proposal from some experts as key information; however, the Academic Draft and official version of the law did not include this proposal.[71] *OGI Regulations 2019*

[66] WEIBING XIAO, FREEDOM OF INFORMATION REFORM IN CHINA: INFORMATION FLOW ANALYSIS 84 (2011).

[67] WEIBING XIAO, FREEDOM OF INFORMATION REFORM IN CHINA: INFORMATION FLOW ANALYSIS 83 (2011).

[68] *OGI Regulations 2007*. Art. 10. Article 10 emphasizes the publicizing of administrative regulations, rules, and regulatory documents; national economic and social development plans; statistical information, budgets and expenses; centralized procurement projects, administrative licensing, major construction projects, public health, environmental protection, and food, drug safety and product quality.

[69] *OGI Regulations 2007*. Art. 11. Article 11 mandates the publicizing of information on urban and rural construction, social and public welfare construction, land requisition or expropriation, house demolition and compensation, emergency rescue, disaster relief, subsidy funds, and assistance to low-income families.

[70] *OGI Regulations 2007*. Art. 12. Article 12 provides the publicizing of key governmental information concerning implementation of national rural policies, use of state funds, land use plans, land requisition or expropriation, house demolition and compensation, emergency rescue and disaster relief, assistance to low-income families, township or village enterprises, and family planning.

[71] A Sina.com survey shows that 77.5% Chinese citizens anticipate disclosure of public officials' personal assets and salaries in accordance with *OGI Regulations*, but this requirement does not appear in either the Academic Draft or final version of the law. Yuchuan Mo was one Chinese reformer who drafted *OGI Regulations*. He is a law professor at the prestigious Renmin University of China. Mo explained that, in drafting *OGI Regulations*, legal academics and experts once considered writing disclosure of public officials' personal assets and salaries into the law. They changed their position because of pressure from the party and governmental officials. Xuyang Sun, *First OGI Lawsuit Stalled in Chenzhou* [政府信息公开第一案僵持郴州], BEIJING NEWS, republished by Sina

continues to be comprehensive and thorough in terms of what information should be proactively disclosed. The revised FOI law covers virtually all the governmental information that needs affirmative dissemination under *OGI Regulations 2007* and further expands the scope of information that must be proactively disclosed to include the basis, requirements, and procedures for imposing administrative penalties.[72]

In order to ensure compliance with proactive disclosure requirements, *OGI Regulations* devised legal methods and procedures.[73] First, *Regulations* compel governmental agencies to disseminate information via various communication channels such as official gazettes and websites, press conferences, and other mass media.[74] Second, the Chinese government requires agencies to provide all proactively disclosed information to national archives, public libraries, and created facilities such as public reading rooms and electronic monitors.[75]

Third, *OGI Regulations* require agencies to compile, publish, and update OGI guides and inventories to facilitate easy access to proactively

Finance, May 13, 2008, https://finance.sina.cn/sa/2008-05-13/detail-ikftpnny1555957.d.html?from=wap (accessed between February 21, 2025 and March 31, 2025).

[72] *OGI Regulations 2019*. Art. 20.

[73] WEIBING XIAO, FREEDOM OF INFORMATION REFORM IN CHINA: INFORMATION FLOW ANALYSIS 84–85 (2011).

[74] *OGI Regulations 2007*, Art. 15; *OGI Regulations 2019*, Art. 23. Both Article 15 and Article 23 mandate agencies proactively disclose governmental information through official gazettes, governmental websites, press conferences, newspapers and periodicals, radio or television broadcasting, or any other means easily accessible to the public.

[75] *OGI Regulations 2007*, Art. 16; *OGI Regulations 2019*, Art. 25. Both Article 16 and Article 25 require agencies to provide proactively disclosed information to national archives and public libraries in a timely manner and establish facilities in those locations to allow easy access to the information. The articles also compel agencies to establish public reading rooms, material distribution venues, information bulletin boards, and electronic monitors to facilitate dissemination of official information.

disclosed information.[76] Fourth, an established consultation and coordination mechanism among agencies ensures that involved administrative organs disclose information in an accurate and consistent manner.[77]

Fifth, *OGI Regulations* establish a time limit for affirmatively disseminating official information; this aspect is absent from *U.S. FOIA* and many other countries' FOI legislation. *Regulations* require proactive publication of disclosed information within 20 working days after its formulation or modification.[78] Sixth, Chinese citizens may file complaints to the next higher-level agency or supervisory agency when a certain agency fails to perform its obligation of proactively publicizing information.[79] Last, imposition of administrative sanctions occurs for agencies and relevant officials who fail to perform the obligation of disclosing information or updating OGI guides and inventories on a timely basis.[80]

In a sharp contrast with the *Academic Draft* and many other countries' FOI laws such as *U.S. FOIA*,[81] *OGI Regulations 2007* and its 2019 amendment offer a very comprehensive and detailed list of information for proactive dissemination.[82] Various legal measures ensure compliance by official agencies mandated to disclose proactively. The emphasis on official, proactive disclosure is rational in the Chinese context. First, in the Chinese political culture, which has, for years through Confucianism, cultivated common people's respect for governmental agencies and officials, reactive disclosure of information may imply an antagonistic challenge to governmental authority.

[76] *OGI Regulations 2007*, Art. 19; *OGI Regulations 2019*, Art. 12. Both Article 19 and Article 12 require agencies to formulate and publish OGI guidelines and OGI indexes. The OGI guidelines include classification and arrangement systems, methods for obtaining official information, contact information for governmental agencies responsible for the OGI activities. The OGI inventory includes an index of information, title, summary and date of generation.

[77] *OGI Regulations 2007*, Art. 7; *OGI Regulations 2019*, Art. 11.

[78] *OGI Regulations 2007*, Art.18; *OGI Regulations 2019*, Art. 26.

[79] *OGI Regulations 2007*, Art. 33; *OGI Regulations 2019*, Art. 51.

[80] *OGI Regulations 2007*, Art. 35; *OGI Regulations 2019*, Art. 52 and Art. 53.

[81] 5 U.S.C. § 552(a)(3) & §552(a)(4)(A) (2000).

[82] The *Academic Draft* lists seven categories of information for proactive disclosure by governmental agencies at all levels. Academic Draft of OGI Regulations: Draft, Explanation, Rationale and Legislative Examples [政府信息公开条例专家建议稿-草案、说明、理由、立法例] 3 (Hanhua Zhou ed., Chinese Legal Publishing House, 2003).

Second, the approach to details and comprehensiveness of proactive disclosure enables agencies and officials in China to adapt to OGI compliance more easily. Attention to OGI is new for many agencies and officials. A detailed list of information requiring proactive disclosure serves as a practical guide for OGI officials in initial compliance and enables identification of material to disclose. Third, establishment of official websites and the system of spokespersons has enhanced the capacity of official agencies in China to disseminate, proactively, information. Fourth, proactive disclosure of information is beneficial to governmental agencies: "It can reduce the administrative burden of answering routine requests."[83] In a legally binding document used to interpret *OGI Regulations*, the State Council clearly reiterates official agencies' responsibility to improve proactive disclosure of information to allow reduction of administrative costs and improve administrative efficiency.[84]

Who Can Ask for Disclosure of Governmental Information

In addition to the obligation of proactively publicizing governmental information, governmental agencies in China have a mandate to release information upon request. *OGI Regulations* provide that "citizens, legal persons or other organizations" may file OGI applications with relevant governmental agencies.[85] If information applicants have difficulties reading, hearing, or seeing, administrative agencies must provide necessary assistance.[86] *Regulations* also grant individuals the right to correct

[83] David Banisar, Freedom of Information around the World 2006: A Global Survey of Access to Government Information Laws 25 (report for Privacy International, London, United Kingdom, July 2006), *available at* http://www.freedominfo.org/documents/global_survey2006.pdf (accessed between February 21, 2025 and March 31, 2025).

[84] *Opinions of the State Council General Office on Doing a Good Job of Disclosing Government Information on Request* [国务院办公厅关于做好政府信息依申请公开工作的意见] Guo Ban Fa [2010] No. 5, effective date: January 12, 2010.

[85] *OGI Regulations 2007*, Art. 13; *OGI Regulations 2019*, Art. 27.

[86] *OGI Regulations 2007*, Art. 28; *OGI Regulations 2019*, Art. 43.

personal information held by any administrative agency.[87] Most importantly, *OGI Regulations 2007* provide a special needs test, stipulating that the information requested be relevant to requesters' special needs including "production, livelihood and scientific research"[88] while *OGI Regulations 2019* noticeably eliminated that test.

The State Council and the Supreme Court clarified the special needs test respectively in 2008 and 2011:

> Where an applicant applies for the disclosure of governmental information *irrelevant to his/her special needs*, including production, livelihood and scientific research needs, the administrative organ concerned is not required to provide such information. (emphasis added)[89]

> Under any of the following circumstances, where a defendant has performed the obligation of legal notification or explaining the reason, the people's court shall dismiss the plaintiff's claims:...The plaintiff fails to reasonably explain that the application for acquiring government information is based on *its special production, life and scientific research demands*, and the defendant refuses to provide the information for this reason. (emphasis added)[90]

> Where the defendant refuses to provide government information on the grounds that the information is *irrelevant to the applicant's special demands for production, life and scientific research*, the people's court may require

[87] *OGI Regulations 2007*, Art. 25. *OGI Regulations 2019*, Art. 41. The law requires governmental agencies to correct personal information if individuals have evidence showing that certain personal information is not accurate and file an application for correction.

[88] *OGI Regulations 2007*. Art. 13.

[89] *Opinions of the General Office of the State Council on Several Issues Concerning the Enforcement of the Regulations of the People's Republic of China on Open Government Information* [国务院办公厅关于施行《中华人民共和国政府信息公开条例》若干问 题的意见] General Office of the State Council, Guo Ban Fa [2008] No. 36, effective: April 29, 2008.

[90] Article 12, *Provisions of the Supreme People's Court on Issues concerning Trying Administrative Cases of Government Information Disclosure* [最高人民法院关于审理政府信息公开行政案件若干问题的规定] Fa Shi [2011] No. 17, effective: August 13, 2011.

> the plaintiff to make explanation on the special demands. (emphasis added)[91]

OGI Regulations align with international standards for mandating the legal obligation of administrative organs for both proactive and reactive disclosure of governmental information. The requirement that assist illiterate and disabled applicants is also encouraging, given the large number of Chinese people with those disabilities. Regarding applicants' eligibility for information and the special needs test, *Regulations 2007* retreated significantly from the *Academic Draft* and indicated the Chinese government's unwillingness many years ago to accept standards widely embraced by most FOI countries including the United States. *OGI Regulations 2019* corrected that mistake.

The *Academic Draft* entitles all natural persons (thus covering foreign citizens), legal persons, and other organizations to non-exempt, official information.[92] The *Draft* does not provide a special needs test. Both moves indicate adoption of international best practices allowing anyone to exercise the access right, whether or not they have any grounds or legal interest.[93] *U.S. FOIA*[94] and most FOI laws in the world accept the liberal standard. Some countries, such as Finland specifically allow for "anonymous requests" to ensure that no discrimination against requestors

[91] Article 5, *Provisions of the Supreme People's Court on Issues concerning Trying Administrative Cases of Government Information Disclosure* [最高人民法院关于审理政府信息公开行政案件若干问题的规定] Fa Shi [2011] No. 17, effective: August 13, 2011.

[92] *Academic Draft of OGI Regulations 2002.* Art. 2. ACADEMIC DRAFT OF OGI REGULATIONS: DRAFT, EXPLANATION, RATIONALE AND LEGISLATIVE EXAMPLES [政府信息公开条例专家建议稿-草案、说明、理由、立法例] 1 (Hanhua Zhou ed., Chinese Legal Publishing House, 2003).

[93] OPEN SOCIETY JUSTICE INITIATIVE, TRANSPARENCY & SILENCE: A SURVEY OF ACCESS TO INFORMATION LAWS AND PRACTICES IN 14 COUNTRIES (Justice in Action Series, New York, New York, September 2006), https://www.justiceinitiative.org/uploads/016719b6-115e-40b8-ad00-00d24b1e3f71/transparency_20060928.pdf (accessed between February 21, 2025 and March 31, 2025); Venkat Iyer, *Freedom of Information: Principles for Legislation*, 28 MEDIA ASIA 1, 17-22 (May 2016), https://doi.org/10.1080/01296612.2001.11726629.

[94] *U.S. FOIA* allows "any person," regardless of his or her citizenship, residency or legal interest, to ask for governmental information. 5 U.S.C. § 552(a)(3)(A) (2006). U.S. FOIA requesters are not required to explain the purpose of the request. NARA v. Favish, 541 U.S. 157, 172 (2004).

occurs.[95] China's temporary failure to allow ***any person*** to apply for information for ***any purpose*** indicated the government's limited tolerance for reactive disclosure of information, and constrained individuals, such as foreigners[96] and citizens without special needs,[97] from obtaining information from the Chinese government. The elimination of the special needs test is a big step in the right direction.

Governmental Response Time Limits and Application Fees for Access

Similar to *U.S. FOIA*[98] and other FOI laws in the world, the Chinese freedom of information law requires agencies' timely response to information requests.

Under *OGI Regulations*, governmental agencies must immediately reply after receiving an application for disclosure of certain information if possible.[99] If an immediate reply is not possible, administrative

[95] David Banisar, Freedom of Information around the World 2006: A Global Survey of Access to Government Information Laws 22 (report for Privacy International, London, United Kingdom, July 2006), ***available at*** http://www.freedominfo.org/documents/global_survey2006.pdf (accessed between February 21, 2025 and March 31, 2025).

[96] Qiong Zhang, the deputy director of the State Council Legislative Affairs Office, assisted formulation of *OGI Regulations*. Zhang stated during a press conference in 2007 that foreign citizens and foreign organizations should apply for governmental information in accordance with the principle of reciprocity in international laws. He did not elaborate on this point and the practical effect of his statement remains uncertain. ***State Council Legislative Affairs Office Deputy Director Meets the Press*** [国务院法制办副主任就《政府信息公开条例》答记者问], Xinhua News Agency, republished by Phoenix TV, April 24, 2007, https://news.ifeng.com/mainland/200704/0424_17_108239.shtml (accessed between February 21, 2025 and March 31, 2025).

[97] Some information requesters may find difficulty justifying special needs, although the special needs test is rather expansive. In addition, governmental agencies and courts may rule in favor of non-disclosure on the grounds that applicants fail to satisfy the special needs test.

[98] The maximum governmental response time limits according to *U.S. FOIA* are 30 working days. First, U.S federal governmental agencies must notify information requesters of their decisions within 20 days after accepting the *FOIA* requests. 5 U.S.C. § 552((a) (6)(A)(i) (2006). Second, additional 10 working days shall apply if the situation warrants. 5 U.S.C. § 552((a) (6)(B)(i) (2006).

[99] *OGI Regulations 2007*, Art. 24; *OGI Regulations 2019*, Art. 33.

organs must reply within 15 working days after receiving the application.[100] The maximum extension, if needed, is not to exceed 15 working days; notification of the extension is necessary.[101] *OGI Regulations 2019* extended replying time. Under the revised law, government agencies have 20 business days to respond and can have another 20 business days if needed.[102]

Similar to *U.S. FOIA*[103] and many other FOI laws, *OGI Regulations* authorize governmental agencies to levy a fee to reduce administrative burdens and prevent repeated applications, while simultaneously imposing fees' limits.

According to *OGI Regulations 2007*, when providing information upon request, administrative agencies may not charge any other fees except the fees to cover the cost of searching, photocopying, and mailing the requested information.[104] *OGI Regulations 2019* is obviously more generous to information applicants than the original FOI law. The revised law says clearly that agencies should handle OGI requests without charge and they may charge information processing fees only when such requests are made on a scale or at a frequency that is "manifestly unreasonable."[105] Under *OGI Regulations 2007*, administrative agencies may not receive remuneration from selling government information and this provision was eliminated in 2019 amendment.[106]

OGI Regulations 2007 differs sharply from *Academic Draft of OGI Regulations 2002*, *OGI Regulations 2019*, *U.S. FOIA* and many other FOI laws for standards on fees' reductions or exemptions. Although the 2007 FOI law did not define income criteria for fee reduction or exemption, a financial hardship test did apply, indicating an applicant with

[100] *OGI Regulations 2007*. Art. 24.

[101] *OGI Regulations 2007*. Art. 24.

[102] *OGI Regulations 2019*. Art. 33.

[103] Under the *U.S. FOIA*, requestors are required to pay certain fees and fees are limited to "reasonable standard charges" for document search, duplication, and review. 5 U.S.C. § 552((a) (4)(A)(ii)(I) (2006). Fees are only for governmental agencies to recover the "direct costs" of search, duplication or review. 5 U.S.C. § 552((a) (4)(A)(iv) (2006).

[104] *OGI Regulations 2007*. Art. 27.

[105] *OGI Regulations 2019*. Art. 42.

[106] *OGI Regulations 2007*. Art. 27.

financial difficulties could apply for a reduction or exemption.[107] *OGI Regulations 2019* eliminated the financial hardship test because applicants do not have to pay for fees any more. The public interest test does not appear in the new law probably because of the same reason. In addition to the financial hardship test, *Academic Draft* adopts a public interest test, meaning that fees reduced or waived are appropriate if disclosure of information is "in the public interest."[108]

Chinese scholars, who formulated the *Academic Draft*, clearly gained inspiration from the public interest test used by many other FOI laws including *U.S. FOIA*. Under *U.S. FOIA*, reduction or exemption from application fees may occur if agencies believe disclosure is "in the public interest." In other words, satisfaction of the public interest test occurs when dissemination "is likely to contribute significantly to public understanding of the operations of the government."[109] By using the public interest test, many professional and freelance journalists[110] in the United States gain information at no cost or lowered cost.

Given that applicants may still have to pay for OGI requests if their requests are too often and/or documents they are asking for are too big, the economic hardship test used by *OGI Regulations 2007* should be retained in *OGI Regulations 2019*. The test is sensible in the Chinese context because China remains poor in terms of per capita income of citizens.[111] The use of this test encourages people of low socio-economic status to request information. Unlike wealthy residents who have widespread social and personal connections for obtaining information, poor people in China face an informational divide and *OGI*

[107] *OGI Regulations 2007*. Art. 28.

[108] *Academic Draft of OGI Regulations 2002*. Art. 18. ACADEMIC DRAFT OF OGI REGULATIONS: DRAFT, EXPLANATION, RATIONALE AND LEGISLATIVE EXAMPLES [政府信息公开条例专家建议稿-草案、说明、理由、立法例] 7 (Hanhua Zhou ed., Chinese Legal Publishing House, 2003).

[109] 5 U.S.C. § 552((a) (4)(A)(iii) (2006).

[110] In the United States, "independent journalists" are allowed to apply for *FOIA* fee waiver although they "lack an institutional affiliation with a recognized news media entity." S. REP. No. 110-59, at 6 (2007).

[111] According to the International Monetary Fund data, China's GDP (PPP) per capita in 2011 was $8382 and ranked 92 among 183 countries and regions in the world. According to the World Bank data, China's GDP (PPP) per capita in 2010 was $7599 and ranked at 96 among 181 countries and regions in the world. China's corresponding GDP (nominal) per capita and rankings were even lower than its PPP equivalents.

Regulations may be the only tool available for seeking information from the government.

Further, exploring the reasons for, and consequences of a lack of a public interest test in the Chinese FOI law with regard to fees is worthwhile. China's refusal to accept the public interest test might have explanation from: First, China seeks reduction of financial burdens on agencies. Second, law crafters may have difficulty defining the public interest. Third, journalists' requests for information could easily pass the public interest test due to the nature of mass media and journalism.[112] Establishing the public interest test would encourage news organizations and journalists to apply for governmental information because they would knowingly receive preferential treatment for fees. However, China shuns special considering treatment for journalists regarding fees. In short, at this stage, the government's disinclination is to encourage journalists' non-prominent roles when using *OGI Regulations* due to political sensitivity toward freedom of the press.[113]

Governmental Information Exempt from Disclosure

Exemptions are probably among the most important and most controversial clauses of FOI laws. *Academic Draft of OGI Regulations 2002* lists seven categories of information exempted from disclosure: state secrets, information specifically exempted from disclosure in other statutes, internal personnel rules and affairs, commercial secrets, personal

[112] News media, electronic or non-electronic, enable wide distribution of information, thus contributing to public understanding of governmental activities.

[113] Chinese officials attempt to downplay the role/right of journalists in reactive disclosure of information. No officials link the freedom of information with freedom of speech and press. Qiong Zhang, the deputy director of the State Council Legislative Affairs Office, digressed and answered evasively when a *Wall Street Journal* reporter, attending an OGI press conference in Beijing in 2007, asked about the right of journalists in OGI deliberations. The journalist asked, "The right of journalists is not placed prominently in *OGI Regulations*. What rights do journalists enjoy under *OGI Regulations*?" Zhang prevaricated, "Government agencies and news organizations shall publicize government information in accordance with the laws." *State Council Legislative Affairs Office Deputy Director Meets the Press* [国务院法制办副主任就《政府信息公开条例》答记者问], Xinhua News Agency, republished by Phoenix TV, April 24, 2007, https://news.ifeng.com/mainland/200704/0424_17_108239.shtml (accessed between February 21, 2025 and March 31, 2025).

privacy, procedural information used for decision-making, and criminal law enforcement.[114] The *Draft* conforms generally to international practices[115] represented by *U.S. FOIA*.[116]

However, officials in the State Council declined to accept exemptions formulated by legal scholars. Instead, they configured another version of exemptions, ostensibly more limited than many similar FOI laws in the world. In establishing a basic principle for guiding agencies to disclose information, Article 8 of *OGI Regulations 2007* and Article 14 of *OGI Regulations 2019* provide that governmental agencies may not disclose information that may endanger "state security (*guojiaanquan* 国家安全), public security (*gonggonganquan* 公共安全), economic security (*jingjianquan* 经济安全), and social stability (*shehuiwending* 社会稳定)."[117]

Article 23 of *OGI Regulations 2007* and Article 15 of *OGI Regulations 2019* further stipulate non-disclosure of information involving commercial secrets (*shangyemimi* 商业秘密) or personal privacy (*gerenyinsi* 个人隐私) if agencies believe that such action would harm legitimate rights and interests of a third party.[118] The new FOI law has tremendously enlarged the scope of information that may be withheld from disclosure to include the following: (1) Information prohibited by laws and regulations from disclosure. (2) Internal affairs information, including information on personnel management, logistical management, and internal

[114] Article 19, *Academic Draft of OGI Regulations 2002*. ACADEMIC DRAFT OF OGI REGULATIONS: DRAFT, EXPLANATION, RATIONALE AND LEGISLATIVE EXAMPLES [政府信息公开条例专家建议稿-草案、说明、理由、立法例] 7–8 (Hanhua Zhou ed., Chinese Legal Publishing House, 2003).

[115] DAVID BANISAR, FREEDOM OF INFORMATION AROUND THE WORLD 2006: A GLOBAL SURVEY OF ACCESS TO GOVERNMENT INFORMATION LAWS 22 (report for Privacy International, London, United Kingdom, July 2006), *available at* http://www.freedominfo.org/documents/global_survey2006.pdf (accessed between February 21, 2025 and March 31, 2025).

[116] The *U.S. FOIA* has nine categories of exemptions. The exemptions cover information in the categories: national security, agency personnel rules and practices, information specifically exempted from disclosure by other statutes, trade, commercial or financial secrets interagency or intraagency memorandums or letters; personnel and medical files and similar files involving personal privacy, law enforcement information, information concerning financial institutions, and geological and geophysical information. 5 U.S.C. § 552((b) (1–9) (2006).

[117] *OGI Regulations 2007*, Art. 8; *OGI Regulations 2019*, Art. 14.

[118] *OGI Regulations 2007*, Art. 23; *OGI Regulations 2019*, Art. 15.

work flows. (3) In-process information such as deliberative records, pre-decisional drafts, consultation letters, and reports requesting instructions. (4) Administrative law enforcement case files. (5) Information that cannot be handled through segregation. (6) Information that needs summarization, assembly, reproduction or statistical analysis by agencies. (7) Information that is sought in the form of OGI requests but is actually for the purpose of consulting or filing petitions, accusations or complaints.[119] The first four categories of information mentioned here are new exemptions that are absent from *OGI Regulations 2007* and somewhat similar to Exemption 2, Exemption 3, Exemption 5 and Exemption 7 in *U.S. FOIA*.[120]

In order to ensure compliance with exemption requirements, Article 14 of *OGI Regulations 2007* requires agencies to establish a "confidentiality review" mechanism.[121] Any information that governmental agencies planning to disclose, proactively or reactively, require review by the mechanism to ensure disclosure does not involve state secrets, commercial secrets, and personal privacy.[122] For whatever reason, such review mechanism does not appear in *OGI Regulations 2019*.

Problems with Chinese OGI exemptions are evident. First, most exemptions from OGI and other relevant laws[123] do not have clear, narrow, definitions as requested by international best practices "to avoid

[119] *OGI Regulations 2019*, Art. 14, Art. 16, Art. 37, Art. 38, Art. 39.

[120] Exemption 2 (Housekeeping Practices) protects American federal government agencies from burden of producing records about trivial agency workings that are of no public interest and safeguards predominantly internal documents whose disclosure might significantly risk circumvention of a legal requirement. Exemption 3 (Statutory Exemption) covers matters specifically exempted from disclosure by statute. Exemption 5 (Working Papers/Correspondence) shields pre-decisional and deliberative working papers and protects communications between an agency and its attorney. Exemption 7 (Law Enforcement) covers records compiled for law enforcement purposes, whose disclosure would: (a) Interfere with enforcement proceedings, (b) Deprive a person of a right to fair trial, (c) Constitute an unwarranted invasion of personal privacy, (d) Disclose the identity of confidential sources, (e) Disclose law enforcement techniques that might risk circumvention of the law, or (f) Endanger the life or physical safety of any individual. 5 U.S.C. § 552((b) (2, 3, 5, 7) (2006).

[121] *OGI Regulations 2007*. Art. 14.

[122] *OGI Regulations 2007*. Art. 14.

[123] *Archives Law 1988* is a good example. This law, formulated to strengthen the management of historical records in various forms, keeps archives from the public as a rule, and disclosure archives is an exception, which conflicts with *OGI Regulations*. Once

including material which does not harm the legitimate interest."[124] Although state secrets, defined in Article 9 of *Law on Guarding State Secrets 1988*[125] and amended in 2010 and narrows the scope of state secrets,[126] the definition still remains too vague and broad. Although state and working secrets appear in *Public Servants Law 2005*, no definition exists at all.[127] While Article 10 of *Anti-trust Law 1993* defines commercial secrets,[128] clarity for "whether or not this definition will be widened to include information in governmental procurements and other contracts to which the government is a party" is absent.[129] *OGI Regulations* and any other relevant laws, regulations, and legal interpretations

governmental information transfers to the archives, the chances of release to the public is low except when the declassification date expires.

124 ARTICLE 19, THE PUBLIC'S RIGHT TO KNOW: PRINCIPLES ON FREEDOM OF INFORMATION LEGISLATION 6 (London, June 1999), *available at* http://www.article19.org/data/files/pdfs/standards/righttoknow.pdf (accessed between February 21, 2025 and March 31, 2025).

125 *Law on Guarding State Secrets 1988*. Art. 9. The 1988 law stipulates information concerning major state policies and decisions, armed forces, and diplomatic events, national economic and social development, science and technology, and acts safeguarding national security and criminal investigation, among other items, are state secrets. The scope of the law tends to be too broad. Under the law, a governmental agency may deem most of its official information as state secrets.

126 Huizi Li & Zhuo Cheng, *China Narrows Definition of "State Secrets" to Boost Government Transparency*, XINHUA NEWS AGENCY, April 29, 2010 (captured by Internet Archive Wayback Machine on May 3, 2010), retrieved from https://web.archive.org/web/20100503144515/http://news.xinhuanet.com/english2010/china/2010-04/29/c_13272939.htm (accessed between February 21, 2025 and March 31, 2025).

127 *Civil Servants Law 2005*, created to improve China's civil servant system, defines officials' rights and responsibilities. Under *Civil Servants Law 2005*, officials have legal obligations to maintain secrets of the state and secrets relating to occupational responsibilities. The law does not define these secrets. Agencies could use *Civil Servants Law 2005* to create an exemption for releasing information that *OGI Regulations* require disclosure.

128 Commercial or trade secrets refer to any technology information or businesses' operational information which unknown to the public, can cause economic benefits to the obligee, has practical utility, and about which the obligee has adopted secret-keeping measures. *Anti-trust Law 1993*. Art. 10.

129 WEIBING XIAO, FREEDOM OF INFORMATION REFORM IN CHINA: INFORMATION FLOW ANALYSIS 87 (2011).

do not define terms such as state security, public security, economic security, social stability[130] and personal privacy.[131] They are all legitimate state interests but their specific meanings are elusive.[132] The gravity of social instability in today's China warrants an exemption for disclosing information, which may endanger social stability.[133] However, the lack of

[130] China is among the few countries that exempt from disclosure information that agencies believe publicizing may endanger social stability. Chinese political leaders regarded social stability as a prerequisite for reform and development since the late 1970s. They stated that "Stability is of overriding importance" and "Nothing can be achieved without stability." DENG XIAOPING, 3 SELECTED WORKS OF DENG XIAOPING 364 [邓小平文选第三卷] (2nd ed. 1994); Jiang Zemin, *Hold High the Great Banner of Deng Xiaoping Theory for an All-round Advancement of the Cause of Building Socialism with Chinese Characteristics to the 21st Century* [高举邓小平理论伟大旗帜, 把建设有中国特色社会主义事业全面推向 二十一世纪], speech delivered at the 15th National Party Congress, Beijing, September 1997; Hu Jintao, *Hold High the Great Banner of Socialism with Chinese Characteristics and Strive for New Victories in Building a Moderately Prosperous Society in All Aspects* [高举中国特色社会主义伟大旗帜为夺取全面建设小康社会新胜利而奋斗], speech delivered at the 17th National Party Congress, Beijing, October 2007.

[131] In China, the concept of individual privacy is still without legal status, and no laws exclusively apply to protection of personal information. As Jamie Horsley said, all those legal issues concerning personal privacy "are not yet addressed comprehensively in Chinese law." Jamie P. Horsley, *China Adopts First Nationwide Open Government Information Regulations*, Freedominfo.org, at para.13, http://www.freedominfo.org/2007/05/china-adopts-first-nationwide-open-government-information-regulations/ (accessed between February 21, 2025 and March 31, 2025); Lei Zheng, *Enacting and Implementing Open Government Information Regulations in China: Motivations and Barriers*, paper presented at the First International Conference on Theory and Practice of Electronic Governance, Macao, December 10–13, 2007.

[132] Guangyu Li, the deputy director of the Administrative Tribunal of the Supreme Court, responsible for drafting the judicial interpretation of *OGI Regulations*, affirmed trying to explain terms like state security, public security, economic security and social stability in the judicial interpretation, but he failed. Talking to a *China Youth Daily* journalist, Li said, "The whole world is struggling to solve this problem [*zheshiyigeshijiexingdenanti* 这是一个世界性的难题]!" Junxiu Wang & Pengjie Zhang, *Supreme Court Official Says Half of OGI-Related Lawsuitss Are Dismissed* [官员称: 半数信息公开诉讼案被法院拒之门外], CHINA YOUTH DAILY, republished by Global Times, November 27, 2011, at para.11, https://china.huanqiu.com/article/9CaKrnJthcb (accessed between February 21, 2025 and March 31, 2025).

[133] Social unrest is rising rapidly in China. According to the data from the China Ministry of Public Security, incidents of social unrest in China were climbing from 8700 cases in 1993 to 58,000 cases in 2003. The nationwide "white paper protests" in 2022 against COVID-19 lockdowns is a more recent example. Albert Keidel, *The Economic Basis for Social Unrest in China*, a Carnegie Endowment for International Peace paper presented for The Third European-American Dialogue on China, The George Washington University, Washington, DC, May 26–27, 2005

clearly drawn definitions of those terms provides governmental agencies and courts too much discretion for denying disclosure. Basically, agencies may use those ambiguous terms to withhold most information they do not want to release.[134] This reason is one explanation for judicial interpretation of the *OGI Regulations'* maintaining those terms in its draft but deleted them from the final version.[135]

Second, China's *OGI Regulations* fail to include a "substantial harm test" as required by many FOI laws around the world.[136] In order to justify exempting certain categories of information, agencies must show that disclosure of the information would cause substantial or significant

(captured by Internet Archive Wayback Machine on August 18, 2005), retrieved from https://web.archive.org/web/20050818215841/http://www.carnegieendowment.org/files/keidel_social_unrest.pdf (accessed between February 21, 2025 and March 31, 2025). Amy Chang Chien and Chang Che, *Memes, Puns and Blank Sheets of Paper: China's Creative Acts of Protest*, THE NEW YORK TIMES, November 28, 2022, https://www.nytimes.com/2022/11/28/world/asia/china-protests-blank-sheets.html (accessed between February 21, 2025 and March 31, 2025). Largely due to the seriousness of social instability, many officials in China have strong senses of crisis and urgency. When discussing in a private conversation social unrest, instability and necessity of further political reform and increased openness, an official confided to the author of this book, "The Chinese people are facing the most dangerous and critical moment ever in history, just like what the national anthem announces, 'China has reached the brink of national collapse!'" Face-to-face and one-on-one interview, June 2009.

[134] Mingan Jiang, the director of the *Constitution* and Administrative Law Research Center at Peking University, contended that statutory language in the *OGI Regulations* such as state security, public security, economic security, and social stability may provide agencies with a laundry basket. Whenever they want to reject disclosure of any information, they may dump that information in the laundry basket. Yijun Wang, *State Secrets Become Excuse for Nondisclosure*? [拒绝公开信息, "国家秘密"成挡箭牌?], CHINA YOUTH DAILY, December 12, 2009, http://article.cyol.com/home/zqb/content/2009-12/02/content_2963336.htm (accessed between February 21, 2025 and March 31, 2025).

[135] Baocheng Chen, *Judicial Interpretation on OGI Regulations Deleted "Three Security and One Stability"* [最高法公布《关于审理政府信息公开行政案件若干问题的规定》,"三安全一稳定信息不公开"被删], SOUTHERN METROPOLIS DAILY, republished by Aoyi News [奥一新闻], August 15, 2011, at AA11 (captured by Internet Archive Wayback Machine on September 23, 2011), retrieved from https://web.archive.org/web/20110923120823/http://gcontent.oeeee.com/0/3f/03f5446139179452/Blog/ea0/4e2a0b.html (accessed between February 21, 2025 and March 31, 2025).

[136] ARTICLE 19, THE PUBLIC'S RIGHT TO KNOW: PRINCIPLES ON FREEDOM OF INFORMATION LEGISLATION 6 (London, United Kingdom, June 1999), *available at* http://www.article19.org/data/files/pdfs/standards/righttoknow.pdf (accessed between February 21, 2025 and March 31, 2025); WEIBING XIAO, FREEDOM OF INFORMATION REFORM IN CHINA: INFORMATION FLOW ANALYSIS 87 (2011).

harm to certain legitimate interests, such as national security, trade secrets, and personal privacy. A low degree of harm is insufficient to trigger sealing information. In keeping with this substantial harm test, Article 8 of *OGI Regulations 2007* and Article 14 of *OGI Regulations 2019* should have the following revision:

> Disclosure of government information by administrative organs shall not endanger state security, public security, economic security and social stability.[137]
>
> Government information determined in accordance with law to be state secrets, government information prohibited by laws and administrative regulations from being disclosed, and government information that might endanger national security, public security, economic security, or social stability after disclosure shall not be disclosed.[138]
>
> Government information determined in accordance with law to be state secrets, government information prohibited by laws and administrative regulations from being disclosed, and government information that might *substantially or significantly* endanger national security, public security, economic security, or social stability after disclosure shall not be disclosed. (emphasis added)[139]

Third, as a FOI scholar noted, China's *OGI Regulations* fail to include a public interest test that applies to all exemptions.[140] Many national FOI laws provide that the public interest test shall apply to all exemptions despite authorities' and oversight bodies' believing disclosure of information may cause substantial or significant harm to a legitimate aim. Officials and courts must balance interests for withholding information against public interest for disclosure.[141] Releasing information occurs

[137] *OGI Regulations 2007*. Art. 8.

[138] *OGI Regulations 2019*. Art. 14.

[139] *OGI Regulations 2019*. Art. 14 (proposed by the author of this book).

[140] WEIBING XIAO, FREEDOM OF INFORMATION REFORM IN CHINA: INFORMATION FLOW ANALYSIS 87 (2011).

[141] DAVID BANISAR, FREEDOM OF INFORMATION AROUND THE WORLD 2006: A GLOBAL SURVEY OF ACCESS TO GOVERNMENT INFORMATION LAWS 23 (report for Privacy International, London, United Kingdom, July 2006), *available at* http://www.freedominfo.org/documents/global_survey2006.pdf (accessed between February 21, 2025

when "[t]he public benefit in disclosure of the information outweighs any harm that may be caused by doing so."[142] In China, the public interest test is inapplicable to exemptions of state secrets. Under both *OGI Regulations 2007* and *OGI Regulations 2019*, the public interest test applies only to commercial secrets and privacy.[143]

Fourth, unlike many FOI laws that provide discretionary rather than mandatory exemptions,[144] the *OGI Regulations* provide mandatory exemptions (with the only exception of commercial secrets and privacy), indicating that the Chinese government prohibits agencies from disclosing any exemption under *OGI Regulations*.[145] Governmental agencies and officials responsible for disclosure of exempted information could receive punishment.[146] Fifth, unlike most FOI laws requiring that

and March 31, 2025); ARTICLE 19, THE PUBLIC'S RIGHT TO KNOW: PRINCIPLES ON FREEDOM OF INFORMATION LEGISLATION 6 (London, United Kingdom, June 1999), *available at* http://www.article19.org/data/files/pdfs/standards/righttoknow.pdf (accessed between February 21, 2025 and March 31, 2025).

142 DAVID BANISAR, EFFECTIVE OPEN GOVERNMENT: IMPROVING PUBLIC ACCESS TO GOVERNMENT INFORMATION 15 (report for Organization for Economic Co-operation and Development, Paris, France), May 29, 2012, *available at* https://papers.ssrn.com/sol3/papers.cfm?abstract_id=2069870# (accessed between February 21, 2025 and March 31, 2025).

143 *OGI Regulations 2007*, Art.14; *OGI Regulations 2019*, Art. 15. Both articles provide that governmental agencies may still publicize governmental information involving commercial secrets and personal privacy without the consent of the third parties if agencies believe that non-disclosure may result in significant injury on the public interests. In explaining Article 14 of *OGI Regulations 2007*, Qiong Zhang, deputy director of the Legislative Affairs Office of the State Council that presided at the drafting of *OGI Regulations*, stated that information concerning major economic crimes, business frauds, and sex crimes fall into this category. *State Council Legislative Affairs Office Deputy Director Meets the Press* [国务院法制办副主任就《政府信息公开条例》答记者问], XINHUA NEWS AGENCY, republished by Phoenix TV, April 24, 2007, https://news.ifeng.com/mainland/200704/0424_17_108239.shtml (accessed between February 21, 2025 and March 31, 2025).

144 For example, the nine exemptions under *U.S. FOIA* are discretionary, not mandatory.

145 WEIBING XIAO, FREEDOM OF INFORMATION REFORM IN CHINA: INFORMATION FLOW ANALYSIS 87 (2011).

146 *OGI Regulations 2007*. Art. 35. The subparagraph (5) of Article 35 provides that corrections shall be made, and disciplinary penalty or criminal liability shall be imposed on governmental agencies and the officer in charge of publicizing of governmental information that should not be publicized. Similar provision cannot be found in *OGI Regulations 2019*.

"[o]nce the reason for exemption has passed, the information should be made available,"[147] *OGI Regulations* set exemptions for an indeterminate duration. The five problems regarding exemptions seriously constrain the ability and willingness of agencies and oversight bodies to disclose information. The drawbacks also severely limit the capacity of applicants to acquire information held or generated by administrative organs.[148]

Appeals Process and Oversight Bodies

Under *OGI Regulations*, the General Office of the State Council and corresponding general offices of local people's government at or above the county level or their designated departments are responsible for promoting, guiding, coordinating, and supervising OGI in their respective administrative areas.[149] The people's government at various levels and their departments are to establish OGI offices responsible for handling day-to-day OGI operations, maintaining and updating official information, formulating OGI guidelines, compiling OGI indexes and OGI annual reports, and examining information that will be disclosed.[150] Production of the OGI annual activity report for the prior year by administrative organs at all levels must occur before January 31 of each year and its publication must occur before March 31 of each year.[151] The report includes information on both proactive disclosure and reactive disclosure, information on requests for administrative reconsideration and OGI

[147] For instance, the FOI exemptions only apply for 12 years in Mexico. David Banisar, Effective Open Government: Improving Public Access to Government Information 14 (report for Organization for Economic Co-operation and Development, Paris, France), May 29, 2012, *available at* https://papers.ssrn.com/sol3/papers.cfm?abstract_id=2069870# (accessed between February 21, 2025 and March 31, 2025).

[148] In an email interview with Yanbin Lv, a legal scholar at the Chinese Academy of Social Sciences Institute of Law, he acknowledged to the author of this book that poorly designed exemptions are a big flaw in *OGI Regulations*.

[149] *OGI Regulations 2007*, Art. 3; *OGI Regulations 2019*, Art. 3.

[150] *OGI Regulations 2007*, Art. 4; *OGI Regulations 2019*, Art. 4.

[151] *OGI Regulations 2019*. Art. 49. *OGI Regulations 2007* provide a firm deadline for publication of annual OGI reports but does not say anything about when those reports should be completed. *OGI Regulations 2007*. Art. 31.

lawsuits, major problems, self-evaluations, social appraisals and accountability results.[152] *OGI Regulations 2007*, *OGI Regulations 2019* and one of the State Council interpretations, without details, oblige all levels of the peoples' government to establish systems for OGI activities' evaluation, a public comment and review, and accountability.[153]

In order to ensure that an administrative organ fulfills obligations to publicize, proactively, information according to the law, the Chinese government allows citizens to report problems to the government body at the next higher level, the supervisory body, or the general office of the people's government at the corresponding level. The agency that receives the report must investigate and resolve the issue.[154]

In order to ensure that administrative organs fulfill their obligations for disclosing information upon request, *OGI Regulations* provide that citizens, legal persons, or other organizations may apply for administrative reconsideration or file an administrative lawsuit if they believe a specific administrative action has infringed upon their lawful rights and interests.[155] When interpreting an OGI administrative lawsuit, the Supreme Court clarified that burden of proof is the defendant's (government agency's) responsibility,[156] indicating Chinese government's adoption of international standards for FOI litigations.[157]

[152] *OGI Regulations 2019*, Art. 50; *OGI Regulations 2007*, Art. 32.

[153] *OGI Regulations 2007*, Art. 29; *OGI Regulations 2019*, Art. 46. *Opinions of the General Office of the State Council on Several Issues Concerning the Enforcement of the Regulations of the People's Republic of China on the Disclosure of Government Information* [国务院办公厅关于施行《中华人民共和国政府信息公开条例》若干问 题的意见] General Office of the State Council, Guo Ban Fa [2008] No. 36, effective date: April 29, 2008.

[154] *OGI Regulations 2007*, Art. 33; *OGI Regulations 2019*, Art. 51; *Opinions of the General Office of the State Council on Several Issues Concerning the Enforcement of the Regulations of the People's Republic of China on the Disclosure of Government Information* [国务院办公厅关于施行《中华人民共和国政府信息公开条例》若干问 题的意见] General Office of the State Council, Guo Ban Fa [2008] No. 36, effective date: April 29, 2008.

[155] *OGI Regulations 2007*, Art. 33; *OGI Regulations 2019*, Art. 51.

[156] Article 5, *Provisions of the Supreme People's Court on Issues concerning Trying Administrative Cases of Government Information Disclosure* [最高人民法院关于审理政府信息公开行政案件若干问题的规定] Fa Shi [2011] No. 17, effective date: August 13, 2011.

[157] The United States is one of many countries that oblige agencies to accept the burden of proof in FOI lawsuits, because the agency must demonstrate full discharge of *FOIA* obligations. *Department of Justice v. Tax Analysts*, 492 U.S. 136,142 n.3 (1989)

Most FOI laws have three appeals and oversight mechanisms: an internal review (administrative reconsideration), an external review (review by an independent information commission or ombudsman) and the court review.[158] The internal review can be inexpensive and rapid, but it tends to uphold FOI denials.[159] The court review is independent and can make binding decisions, but it is expensive and time-consuming. Judges are usually deferential to agencies and most court judges lack the expertise needed for systematic FOI investigations.[160] The external review tends to uphold disclosure. Agencies usually accept the non-binding decisions.[161] Therefore, FOI experts consider the external review, "the most effective system of oversight."[162]

The three oversight mechanisms in *U.S. FOIA* are valuable examples: When fully or partially denied a U.S. FOIA request, the requestor

(ruling that "the burden is on the agency to demonstrate, not the requester to disprove, that the materials sought...have not been improperly withheld").

158 DAVID BANISAR, EFFECTIVE OPEN GOVERNMENT: IMPROVING PUBLIC ACCESS TO GOVERNMENT INFORMATION 16 (report for Organization for Economic Co-operation and Development, Paris, France), May 29, 2012, *available at* https://papers.ssrn.com/sol3/papers.cfm?abstract_id=2069870# (accessed between February 21, 2025 and March 31, 2025).

159 DAVID BANISAR, EFFECTIVE OPEN GOVERNMENT: IMPROVING PUBLIC ACCESS TO GOVERNMENT INFORMATION 16 (report for Organization for Economic Co-operation and Development, Paris, France), May 29, 2012, *available at* https://papers.ssrn.com/sol3/papers.cfm?abstract_id=2069870# (accessed between February 21, 2025 and March 31, 2025).

160 DAVID BANISAR, EFFECTIVE OPEN GOVERNMENT: IMPROVING PUBLIC ACCESS TO GOVERNMENT INFORMATION 17 (report for Organization for Economic Co-operation and Development, Paris, France), May 29, 2012, *available at* https://papers.ssrn.com/sol3/papers.cfm?abstract_id=2069870# (accessed between February 21, 2025 and March 31, 2025).

161 DAVID BANISAR, EFFECTIVE OPEN GOVERNMENT: IMPROVING PUBLIC ACCESS TO GOVERNMENT INFORMATION 16 (report for Organization for Economic Co-operation and Development, Paris, France), May 29, 2012, *available at* https://papers.ssrn.com/sol3/papers.cfm?abstract_id=2069870# (accessed between February 21, 2025 and March 31, 2025).

162 DAVID BANISAR, FREEDOM OF INFORMATION AROUND THE WORLD 2006: A GLOBAL SURVEY OF ACCESS TO GOVERNMENT INFORMATION LAWS 23 (report for Privacy International, London, United Kingdom, July 2006), *available at* http://www.freedominfo.org/documents/global_survey2006.pdf (accessed between February 21, 2025 and March 31, 2025).

can apply for an internal review appealing the decision.[163] Requestors may also appeal when governmental agencies reject requests due to "no records," deny requests for fee waivers or expedited processing.[164] The *FOIA* requester center of each agency reports the appeal to the *FOIA* Public Liaison. If the dispute reaches no resolution, the Chief *FOIA* Officer of each agency receives notifications, and may extend to the Attorney General of the United States.[165] After exhausting the internal review processes,[166] the complainant may embark upon an external review, a court review, or an appeal to the Office of Governmental Information Services,[167] a federal agency nicknamed "the Federal FOIA ombudsman"[168] that mediates disputes between persons making FOIA requests and agencies. An appeal to the federal court system is possible.[169]

Chinese legal scholars who formulated the *Academic Draft of OGI Regulations 2002* borrowed heavily from the international practice of appeals and oversight. In addition to the administrative review system and the judicial remedy, the *Draft* provides establishment of an independent information commission consisting of prestigious experts[170] and chief information officers[171] from official agencies above the county level

163 S. REP. No. 110-59, at 10 (2007).

164 *DOJ FOIA Regulations*, 28 C.F.R. § 16.6(c) (2008).

165 *Open Government Act of 2007*, Pub. L. 110–175, §10, December 31, 2007, 121 Stat. 2524 (2007), codified at 5 U.S.C. A. § 552(h-l) (2006).

166 A U.S. FOI requester must exhaust his/her "administrative remedies" before appealing to the court. 5 U.S.C. § 552(a)(6)(C)(i) (2006).

167 The Office of Governmental Information Services https://www.archives.gov/ogis, created within the National Archives and Records Administration, is the *OPEN Government Act of 2007*'s amendment to the *Freedom of Information Act* (5 U.S.C. § 552). The Congress created this independent agency to help defray rising costs of *FOIA* litigation. S. REP. No. 110-59, at 2, 7 (2007).

168 H.R. REP. No. 110-45, at 4 (2007). *About OGIS*, the Federal *FOIA* ombudsman, https://www.archives.gov/ogis (accessed between February 21, 2025 and March 31, 2025).

169 S. REP. No. 110-59, at 10 (2007).

170 Article 27, *Academic Draft of OGI Regulations 2002.* ACADEMIC DRAFT OF OGI REGULATIONS: DRAFT, EXPLANATION, RATIONALE AND LEGISLATIVE EXAMPLES [政府信息公开条例专家建议稿-草案、说明、理由、立法例] 10–11 (Hanhua Zhou ed., Chinese Legal Publishing House, 2003).

171 Article 25, *Academic Draft of OGI Regulations 2002.* Article 25 provides the establishment of the chief information officer and the CIO office for governmental agencies at various levels. ACADEMIC DRAFT OF OGI REGULATIONS: DRAFT, EXPLANATION,

in the people's government.[172] All commission members are part-time, and the commission has the power to request documents from relevant official bodies for investigative purposes,[173] can render non-binding decisions for disputes between requesters and agencies.[174] The commission may recommend administrative penalty to punish officials violating *OGI Regulations*.[175]

In revising the *Academic Draft*, however, the State Council Legislative Affairs Office rejected the proposal establishing the independent OGI information commission and the office of chief information officer.[176]

Rationale and Legislative Examples [政府信息公开条例专家建议稿-草案、说明、理由、立法例] 9 (Hanhua Zhou ed., Chinese Legal Publishing House, 2003).

172 Article 27, *Academic Draft of OGI Regulations 2002*. Article 27 provides for more than one third of information commission members to be academics. Academic Draft of OGI Regulations: Draft, Explanation, Rationale and Legislative Examples [政府信息公开条例专家建议稿-草案、说明、理由、立法例] 10 (Hanhua Zhou ed., Chinese Legal Publishing House, 2003).

173 Article 32, *Academic Draft of OGI Regulations 2002*. Academic Draft of OGI Regulations: Draft, Explanation, Rationale and Legislative Examples [政府信息公开条例专家建议稿-草案、说明、理由、立法例] 12 (Hanhua Zhou ed., Chinese Legal Publishing House, 2003).

174 Article 31, *Academic Draft of OGI Regulations 2002*. Academic Draft of OGI Regulations: Draft, Explanation, Rationale and Legislative Examples [政府信息公开条例专家建议稿-草案、说明、理由、立法例] 11 (Hanhua Zhou ed., Chinese Legal Publishing House, 2003).

175 Article 33, *Academic Draft of OGI Regulations 2002*. Academic Draft of OGI Regulations: Draft, Explanation, Rationale and Legislative Examples [政府信息公开条例专家建议稿-草案、说明、理由、立法例] 12 (Hanhua Zhou ed., Chinese Legal Publishing House, 2003).

176 The CASS legal scholar, Hanhua Zhou, was among experts drafting *Academic Draft of OGI Regulations 2002*. Zhou speculated that the State Council jettisoned the idea of OGI information commissions and chief information officers because the proposal is too ambitious for *OGI Regulations*. Only laws passed by the National People's Congress have the power to handle issues like configuring agencies and personnel arrangements. Ming Tu, *Behind-the-Scene Proponent of OGI Regulations* [政府信息公开条例的背后推手], Phoenix TV, republished by reformdata.org, March 21, 2007, http://www.reformdata.org/2007/0321/15413.shtml (accessed between February 21, 2025 and March 31, 2025). The idea of creating the chief information officer (CIO) system was clearly inspired by practices of many other FOI countries including the United States. For detailed analysis of the CIO system in the United States, see Charles R McClure & John Carlo Bertot, *The Chief Information Officer (CIO): Assessing Its Impact*, 17 Government Information Quarterly 7, 7–12 (2000).

The consequences of this rejection are grave. China has lost an opportunity to embrace international standards in FOI oversight. The lack of an independent body to mediate OGI disputes casts doubt on the effective implementation of the law.

However, an encouraging aspect in appeal and oversight under the Chinese law is present: the lower threshold for filing an OGI lawsuit in China. Under standard administrative procedures, exhausting internal appeals is necessary before seeking external review and judicial remedy.[177] But Chinese applicants for information may resort to judicial review without exhausting administrative review.[178] Apparently, the Chinese government, wittingly or unwittingly, encouraged use of judicial remedies. This attitude is rational in the Chinese context because litigation expenses in China are relatively low.[179] Furthermore, the Chinese people's preoccupation has long been resolution of disputes outside court because of cultural and societal proclivities.[180] *OGI Regulations'* framers have good reason to believe that most requesters of information would

[177] The United States is such an example. A *U.S. FOIA* requester must exhaust "administrative remedies" before appealing to the court. 5 U.S.C. § 552(a)(6)(C)(i) (2006).

[178] Article 33 of *OGI Regulations* provides that individuals and organizations may apply for administrative reconsideration or file an administrative lawsuit. The law does not specify which review (administrative or judicial) should be first.

[179] Steven C. Bennett is a partner in the New York City offices of Jones Day. He specializes in international litigation. When talking about the price of lawsuits in China, Bennett said, "The cost of litigation usually is lower since litigation in China is a relatively fast process with few documents and no discovery." Steven C. Bennett, *Litigation in China: Ten Things You Must Know*, posted on the Corporate Counsel Business Journal website, October 1, 2008, at 26, *available at* https://ccbjournal.com/articles/litigation-china-ten-things-you-must-know (accessed between February 21, 2025 and March 31, 2025). The costs of litigation are much higher in the United States and many other countries. The rising cost of litigation is one of the most serious crises facing the legal profession in the United States. Leonard S. Janofsky, *A.B.A. Attacks Delay and the High Cost of Litigation*, 65 AMERICAN BAR ASSOCIATION JOURNAL 1323 (1979); Leonard S. Janofsky, *Facing the Crises of Court Costs and Delay-Initiatives for the Bar*, 7B LEADER 22 (1981–1982).

[180] The reluctance of Chinese people to sue is rooted in traditional Chinese culture. Confucianism, Taoism and Buddhism all play a role in this regard. Deeply influenced by the thought of harmony and unity, officials in ancient China are required to discourage litigation. People are guided to detest litigation and pursue settlement of disputes by consultation. This social ethos contributes to the popularity of "*he shi lao*," elders acting as mediators or facilitators to resolve conflicts arising from family, community and inter-village disputes. Xiaofeng Wu, *Understanding of Criminal Reconciliation in*

not avoid administrative reconsideration and thus flood courts with OGI cases.

Sanctions on Public Authorities and Employees

Similar to other FOI laws in the world, *OGI Regulations* include provisions for imposing sanctions on public authorities and employees for violating the law. Accordingly, if an administrative organ fails to establish the OGI system or violates any provisions of *OGI Regulations*, the administrative organ at the next higher level shall order corrective measures.[181] If the circumstances are serious, imposition of administrative disciplinary measures[182] on the principally responsible person(s) are possible.[183] Most importantly, administrative sanctions[184] and criminal penalties may accrue

Ancient China, 5 Frontiers of Law in China 1 91, 95–96 (2010); Dennis Sing-Wing Wong, "RJ in Mainland China," in *Restorative Justice for Juveniles in Hong Kong: Reflections of a Practitioner*, paper from "Building a Global Alliance for Restorative Practices and Family Empowerment, Part 3," the IIRP's Sixth International Conference on Conferencing, Circles and other Restorative Practices, March 3–5, 2005, Penrith, New South Wales, Australia, *available at* https://www.iirp.edu/news/restorative-justice-for-juveniles-in-hong-kong-reflections-of-a-practitioner (accessed between February 21, 2025 and March 31, 2025).

[181] *OGI Regulations 2007*. Art. 34; *OGI Regulations 2019*. Art. 52, Art. 53. Under the 2007 FOI law, supervisory organs can also order corrective measures. The 2019 law eliminates supervisory organs as an option. Supervisory organs a part of the people's government in China. They exercise supervision over state administrative organs, governmental functionaries, and other personnel appointed by state administrative organs. *Administrative Supervision Law 1997*, Article 2. Supervisory organs run from the central level to the county level. The central level supervisory organ is the Ministry of Supervision (dissolved and merged into the National Supervisory Commission in 2018. The commission shares offices and staff with the CCP's Central Commission for Discipline Inspection).

[182] There are six kinds of administrative disciplinary measures: warning, record of a demerit, record of a serious demerit, demotion, removal from office, and discharge from public employment. *Administrative Supervision Law 1997*. Art. 24; *Law on Public Servants 2005*. Art.56.

[183] *OGI Regulations 2007*. Art. 34; *OGI Regulations 2019*. Art. 52, Art. 53.

[184] There are six kinds of administrative disciplinary measures: warning, record of a demerit, record of a serious demerit, demotion, removal from office, and discharge from public employment. *Administrative Supervision Law 1997*. Art. 24; *Law on Public Servants* 2005. Art. 56.

to official agencies, agencies' leaders who are responsible for OGI activities and relevant employees if they violate provisions of *OGI Regulations 2007* and have engaged in:

1. Failure to fulfill, in accordance with the law, open government information obligations;
2. Failure to timely update the contents of government information that has been disclosed, the guide to open government information and the catalogue of open government information;
3. Collecting fees in violation of provisions;
4. Providing governmental information as a paid service through other organizations or individuals;
5. Disclosing government information that should not be disclosed, and
6. Other actions that violate the provisions of these Regulations.[185]

Likewise, the 2019 *OGI Regulations* amendment imposes criminal penalties on government officials who have engaged in:

1. Failure to fulfill, in accordance with the law, open government information functions;
2. Failure to timely update the contents of government information that has been disclosed, the guide to open government information and the catalogue of open government information;
3. Other actions that violate the provisions of these Regulations.[186]

In many aspects, *OGI Regulations* are consistent with international standards for sanctions on governmental agencies and officials. The sanctions indicate the Chinese government's desire for agencies at various levels to appreciate the seriousness of penalties on non-compliance. More encouraging is the elimination of sub-paragraph (5) of Article 35 of *OGI Regulation 2007* from the 2019 revised law. This clause would penalize Chinese officials for disclosing, even in good faith, information

[185] *OGI Regulations 2007*. Art. 35.

[186] *OGI Regulations 2019*. Art. 53.

not subject to disclosure.[187] This clause, if retained in the 2019 amendment, would strengthen the culture of secrecy in the Chinese bureaucracy because "officials may be excessively cautious about requests for information…to avoid any personal risk."[188] A weakness in the Chinese FOI law sanctions is that *OGI Regulations* fail to include provisions for administrative organs to provide compensation for harms incurred from OGI violations.[189]

E-FOI and Whistleblowing

As the world enters the digital age, disseminating and accessing information becomes increasingly efficient, convenient and effective. Many national FOI laws prescribe an agency's duties to publicize information on websites[190] and provide requestors with a mechanism to apply for information using electronic mail or web-based forms.[191] However, the digital divide prevents people from accessing electronic information. Older people tend to avoid using electronic devices. Consequently,

[187] *OGI Regulations 2007*. Art. 35.

[188] Article 19, The Public's Right to Know: Principles on Freedom of Information Legislation 10 (London, United Kingdom, June 1999), *available at* http://www.article19.org/data/files/pdfs/standards/righttoknow.pdf (accessed between February 21, 2025 and March 31, 2025).

[189] Article 37 of *Academic Draft of OGI Regulations 2002* does provide that applicants for information and third parties receive compensation in accordance with *Law on State Compensation 1994*. Academic Draft of OGI Regulations: Draft, Explanation, Rationale and Legislative Examples [政府信息公开条例专家建议稿-草案、说明、理由、立法例] 12 (Hanhua Zhou ed., Chinese Legal Publishing House, 2003). *U.S. FOIA* also provides a compensation mechanism. Once the *FOIA* requestor/plaintiff substantially prevails in a case, the federal district court can order the administrative agency to disclose information and pay for reasonable legal fees and other litigation costs. 5 U.S.C. § 552((a)(4)(E) (2006); 5 U.S.C. § 552((a) (4)(B) (2006) and 5 U.S.C. § 552((a) (4)(E) (2006).

[190] David Banisar, Freedom of Information around the World 2006: A Global Survey of Access to Government Information Laws 25 (report for Privacy International, London, United Kingdom, July 2006), *available at* http://www.freedominfo.org/documents/global_survey2006.pdf (accessed between February 21, 2025 and March 31, 2025).

[191] David Banisar, Freedom of Information around the World 2006: A Global Survey of Access to Government Information Laws 26 (report for Privacy International, London, United Kingdom, July 2006), *available at* http://www.freedominfo.org/documents/global_survey2006.pdf (accessed between February 21, 2025 and March 31, 2025).

most FOI laws require governmental agencies to prepare documents and records in both electronic and physical forms.[192]

The Chinese law coincides with international standards by providing that administrative organs proactively disclose information by means of governmental websites.[193] International best practices include stipulation for filing requests in written form (including digital and electronic forms).[194]

Similar to the United States and many other countries, China encourages governmental agencies to establish public reading rooms and other facilities to allow access to both electronic and physical copies of documents and records.[195]

China's full embrace of e-FOI is in stark contrast to a flat refusal to protect whistleblowers from retaliation. A whistleblower is an individual (usually a government or company employee) who discloses an

[192] David Banisar, Effective Open Government: Improving Public Access to Government Information 27 (report for Organization for Economic Co-operation and Development, Paris, France), May 29, 2012, *available at* https://papers.ssrn.com/sol3/papers.cfm?abstract_id=2069870# (accessed between February 21, 2025 and March 31, 2025).

[193] *OGI Regulations 2007*, Art. 15; *OGI Regulations 2019*, Art. 23. In a legally binding document, the State Council stresses that agencies consider governmental websites as priority platforms to disseminate information. Agencies are to establish OGI columns and OGI opinion boxes on their websites. *Notice of the General Office of the State Council on Preparing the Implementation of OGI Regulations* [国务院办公厅关于做好施行《中华人民共和国政府信息公开条例》准备工作的通知] General Office of the State Council, Guo Ban Fa [2007] No. 54, effective date: August 4, 2007.

[194] *OGI Regulations 2007*, Art. 20; *OGI Regulations 2019*, Art. 29. In an administrative interpretation, the State Council emphasized the use of governmental websites to promptly disclose information and the use of online inquiry functions to process requests. *Opinions of the General Office of the State Council on Several Issues Concerning the Enforcement of the Regulations of the People's Republic of China on the Disclosure of Government Information* [国务院办公厅关于施行《中华人民共和国政府信息公开条例》若干问 题的意见] General Office of the State Council, Guo Ban Fa [2008] No. 36, effective date: April 29, 2008.

[195] *OGI Regulations 2007*, Art. 16; *OGI Regulations 2019*, Art. 25. The 2007 law provides that the people's governments at all levels shall establish official information reading places in the state archives and public libraries and install appropriate facilities and equipment for the convenience of citizens, legal persons, and other organizations to obtain governmental information. Administrative organs may, as needed, establish places and facilities such as public reading rooms, materials request stations, information bulletin boards, and electronic information screens, to disclose official information. The 2019 amendment has similar provisions.

alleged wrongdoing[196] in organizations such as governmental departments and companies. Article 19, a London-based organization advancing global freedom of information, lists protection for whistleblowers who frequently face reprisals from people in power, as the ninth principle of freedom of information legislation.[197] Article 19 argued that whistleblowers must be protected from any legal, administrative or employment-related penalties as long as they "acted in good faith" and had evidence to support their belief that the information was "substantially true."[198]

The Article 19 principle, widely accepted by the international FOI community, includes over 30 countries, which adopted specific whistleblower protections in FOI laws.[199] The *Freedom of Press Act* in Sweden is a typical example of an FOI law insulating whistleblowers from reprisal. Under the Act, criticizing the actions of official bodies anonymously is a "fundamental right" of public servants.[200] The United States does not have whistleblower protection in FOI laws; however, other relevant laws

[196] Wrongdoing includes "the commission of a criminal offense, failure to comply with a legal obligation, a miscarriage of justice, corruption or dishonesty, or serious maladministration regarding a public body. It also includes a serious threat to health, safety or the environment, whether linked to individual wrongdoing or not." ARTICLE 19, THE PUBLIC'S RIGHT TO KNOW: PRINCIPLES ON FREEDOM OF INFORMATION LEGISLATION 10 (London, United Kingdom, June 1999), *available at* http://www.article19.org/data/files/pdfs/standards/righttoknow.pdf (accessed between February 21, 2025 and March 31, 2025).

[197] ARTICLE 19, THE PUBLIC'S RIGHT TO KNOW: PRINCIPLES ON FREEDOM OF INFORMATION LEGISLATION 10 (London, United Kingdom, 2016), *available at* http://www.article19.org/data/files/pdfs/standards/righttoknow.pdf (accessed between February 21, 2025 and March 31, 2025).

[198] ARTICLE 19, THE PUBLIC'S RIGHT TO KNOW: PRINCIPLES ON FREEDOM OF INFORMATION LEGISLATION 11 (London, United Kingdom, 2016), *available at* http://www.article19.org/data/files/pdfs/standards/righttoknow.pdf (accessed between February 21, 2025 and March 31, 2025).

[199] DAVID BANISAR, FREEDOM OF INFORMATION AROUND THE WORLD 2006: A GLOBAL SURVEY OF ACCESS TO GOVERNMENT INFORMATION LAWS 26 (report for Privacy International, London, United Kingdom, July 2006), *available at* http://www.freedominfo.org/documents/global_survey2006.pdf (accessed between February 21, 2025 and March 31, 2025).

[200] DAVID BANISAR, FREEDOM OF INFORMATION AROUND THE WORLD 2006: A GLOBAL SURVEY OF ACCESS TO GOVERNMENT INFORMATION LAWS 26 (report for Privacy International, London, United Kingdom, July 2006), *available at* http://www.freedominfo.org/documents/global_survey2006.pdf (accessed between February 21, 2025 and March 31, 2025).

include protections.[201] Australia has no whistleblowing component in its FOI laws; however, separate whistleblowing protection legislations were introduced at state and territory levels.[202]

China has no whistleblower protection in any laws including *OGI Regulations*. Even the progressive *Academic Draft of OGI Regulations* does not mention whistleblower protection. Perhaps, drawing a lesson from the Cultural Revolution, the Chinese government today seems uncomfortable with mobilizing common people to counter corruption in public and private entities. Social stability concerns are another major obstacle for the whistleblower legislation; however, contending never enacting a whistleblower law in China is premature.

Increasing numbers of people in China today are aware of the importance of whistleblower legislation. Without such a law, the chances for disclosure of negative activities by official agencies and private entities would severely decrease. When discussing resolutions for widespread contaminated food scandals and abuse of power by government agencies and state-owned enterprises, a prestigious economist,[203] a member of

[201] The *Whistleblower Protection Act of 1989* provides statutory protections for U.S. federal employees who engage in whistleblowing. *The Whistleblower Protection Act: An Overview*, Congressional Research Service, Washington, DC, March 12, 2007, http://www.fas.org/sgp/crs/natsec/RL33918.pdf (accessed between February 21, 2025 and March 31, 2025); David Banisar, Freedom of Information around the World 2006: A Global Survey of Access to Government Information Laws 26 (report for Privacy International, London, United Kingdom, July 2006), *available at* http://www.freedominfo.org/documents/global_survey2006.pdf (accessed between February 21, 2025 and March 31, 2025).

[202] John McMillan (Commonwealth Ombudsman of Australia), *Freedom of Information and Whistleblower Legislation: An Australian Perspective*, paper delivered to the 9th Asian Ombudsman Association Conference, Hong Kong, 30 November 2005, *available at* https://www.ombudsman.gov.au/__data/assets/pdf_file/0021/34437/30-November-2005-Freedom-of-information-and-whistleblower-legislation-an-Australian-perspective.pdf (accessed between February 21, 2025 and March 31, 2025).

[203] Xianping Lang, *Campaigns Do Not Work for Managing Economy* [治理经济不能靠"运动"], Jrj.com [金融界], Beijing, China, May 16, 2012 (captured by Internet Archive Wayback Machine on May 19, 2012), retrieved from https://web.archive.org/web/20120519092855/http://finance.jrj.com.cn/opinion/2012/05/16091613139548-1.shtml (accessed between February 21, 2025 and March 31, 2025). As one of the most influential economists in China, Xianping Lang works for the Chinese University of Hong Kong as Chair Professor of Finance. Lang holds a doctoral degree from the Wharton School of Business, the University of Pennsylvania. Lang himself was the whistleblower in corporate scandals in China.

the NPC Standing Committee,[204] a citizen blogger,[205] a State Council guidance opinion issued in 2019[206] and a legal scholar[207] all suggested consideration of whistleblower protection law in China.

Summary and Conclusion

This chapter examined the statutory language of *OGI Regulations 2007*, *OGI Regulations 2019* and relevant legal interpretations. Comparing the Chinese law with other national FOI laws, such as *U.S. FOIA* and international best practices, this chapter identified strengths and weakness of *OGI Regulations* in areas widely recognized as necessary for most FOI legislation: legal standing, legislative purpose, types of bodies covered, accessible materials; affirmative publication; qualification for inquirer, fees for access and response time limits, exemptions, appeals and oversight, sanctions, e-FOI, and whistleblowing.

Overall, the Chinese FOI law has made remarkable improvements when it was revised in 2019, as shown in the Global Right to Information Rating. The total score of *OGI Regulations*, after lingering around 70 points for quite a few years starting in 2011, jumped suddenly to 75 points in 2021 on a scale of 0–150 points (the higher the score, the better) and has been there since then (see Table 6.1).[208] The new law

[204] Hui Ma, *Food Safety Inspection Team Served Tainted Fruit, NPC Member Recommends Whistleblowing Protection* [食品安全检查组遇问题水果招待 委员建议监督放权于民], 21st Century Business Herald, June 30, 2011.

[205] Jiayu Zhang, "Whistleblowers and Proper Functioning of Society" [吹哨人与社会良性运转], in Spicy World-A Note of Social Observation by a young man from Mainland China [麻辣人世间-一个大陆青年的社会观察笔记], Xiuwei Publishing House[秀威出版], Taibei, Taiwan, April 2011.

[206] *State Council of China Talks about Whistleblower Law for the First Time, Proposing High Rewards and Rigorous Protections for Whistleblowers* [国务院首提企业"吹哨人"制度: 重奖、严格保护内部"告密者"], The Paper [澎湃新闻], September 23, 2019, https://m.thepaper.cn/baijiahao_4503267 (accessed between February 21, 2025 and March 31, 2025).

[207] Jianguo Xu, *Enact China's Own Whistleblower Protection Law: Inspirations from European Union's Legislative Experience* [徐国建: 制定一部中国的"吹哨人"保护法-欧盟立法的启示], Shanghai University of Political Science and Law, February 10, 2020, *available at* https://www.shupl.edu.cn/2020/0217/c1170a73457/page.htm (accessed between February 21, 2025 and March 31, 2025).

[208] Since 2011, the Rating has begun to comparatively assess the strength of legal frameworks for the right to information from around the world. The rating does

has codified the presumption of disclosure of government information, expanded the scope of information for proactive disclosure, eliminated the special needs test, clarified information not to be disclosed, extended replying time to OGI requests, and removed penalty on officials for improper disclosure of information.[209] However, *OGI Regulations*, on the whole, are still weak in reactive disclosure of information.

Many factors significantly constrain OGI requesters' abilities to apply for information, not proactively disclosed. The law's exemptions are not clearly and narrowly defined and fails to include a substantial harm test and nor apply a public interest test to all exemptions. *Regulations* provide mandatory rather than discretionary exceptions. The law is equivocal in establishing a statutory right of access. *OGI Regulations* fail to take precedence over other laws and thus are unable to supersede conflicting laws. The law fails to establish an independent oversight body. Documents and records held or generated by the ruling Communist Party of China are covered by a law similar to *OGI Regulations*, but reactive disclosure is not permissible. The Chinese FOI law does not protect whistleblowers from retaliation. All these factors contribute to decreased willingness and capacity of governmental officials to disclose information upon request and contribute to strengthened belief among requesters that governmental information is off-limits to the common people.

OGI Regulations are strongly proactive for disclosure of information, with a very detailed list of information for which agencies have the initiative to release. In order to ensure compliance with proactive disclosure, the law provides various legal measures, such as requiring agencies to publicize information via governmental websites and press conferences, sending information to national archives and public libraries, creating public reading rooms and other facilities easily accessible to the general public, and formulating OGI guides, OGI catalogues and OGI

not measure quality of FOI law implementation. It only measures quality of the FOI legislations in seven different categories: Right of access, scope, requesting procedures, exceptions and refusals, appeals, sanctions and protections, and promotional measures. *Methodology*, Global Right to Information Rating, *available at* https://www.rti-rating.org/methodology/ (accessed between February 21, 2025 and March 31, 2025).

209 Laney Zhang, *China: Open Government Regulations Revised*, Library of Congress, Washington, DC, September 10, 2019, *available at* https://www.loc.gov/item/global-legal-monitor/2019-09-10/china-open-government-regulations-revised/ (accessed between February 21, 2025 and March 31, 2025).

annual reports. Administrative organs must proactively disclose information within a specified time, a practice rare in other FOI countries. In order to show the seriousness of the law, *OGI Regulations* provide sanctions for agencies and responsible officials who fail to fulfill their duty of proactively disclosing information. Another striking feature of the law is that the obligations of proactive disclosure of information do not only extend to governmental agencies at all levels but also apply to all quasi-governmental agencies at corresponding levels, all public enterprises and institutions across the country.

The emphasis of the Chinese government on proactive disclosure rather than reactive dissemination[210] is sensible in the Chinese context because disclosing information on governmental agencies' own initiative may be more effective than reactive disclosure for "prompting officials to abandon their longstanding secretive and reactive informational management approach, proven outdated in the expanded Chinese informational environment."[211] The prominence of proactive disclosure in FOI laws is also rational in the global context. In recent years, a growing global consensus of FOI practices shows that affirmative disclosure is gradually replacing reactive disclosure.[212] FOI scholars,[213] FOI practitioners,[214]

[210] This finding is consistent with prior research conducted by many FOI scholars. For example, FOI expert Weibing Xiao concluded that push model (proactive disclosure), not pull model (reactive disclosure), characterizes China's current FOI system. Weibing Xiao, *China's Limited Push Model of FOI Legislation*, 27 Government Information Quarterly 346, 346-51 (2010); Weibing Xiao, Freedom of Information Reform in China: Information Flow Analysis 80-88 (2011).

[211] Weibing Xiao, Freedom of Information Reform in China: Information Flow Analysis 82 (2011).

[212] Weibing Xiao, Freedom of Information Reform in China: Information Flow Analysis 80 (2011).

[213] Rick Snell, *Opening up the Mindset Is Key to Change*, The Canberra Times, November 4, 2008, at 10–11.

[214] Andrea Neill (Assistant Information Commissioner of Canada), *Liberating Information Shifting from Reactive to Proactive Disclosure*, speech delivered at the conference of the Association sur l'accès et la protection de l'information (AAPI), Quebec, Canada, April 20, 2010 (captured by Internet Archive Wayback Machine on May 13, 2013), retrieved from https://web.archive.org/web/20130513211539/http://www.oic-ci.gc.ca/eng/med-roo-sal-med_speeches-discours_2010_3.aspx (accessed between February 21, 2025 and March 31, 2025).

international organizations,[215] and governments across the globe,[216] call for the shift because the traditional reactive mode of disclosing information has proven to be inefficient, costly, and often confrontational.

In totality, the system of proactive disclosure of information in China is far from perfect. Undeniably, the system of proactive disclosure is better designed than the access request regimen from the perspective of statutory language. However, many factors that debilitate reactive disclosure also hinder proactive disclosure. For instance, poorly defined exemptions may lead officials to withhold, improperly, information. The reason is simple: The law forces officials to err for safety in order to avoid personal risk. Without doubt, a large amount of governmental information that should have proactive disclosure will remain sealed.

Legal scholar, Martin Halstuk, identified six common characteristics of effective FOI laws: (1) Disclosure should be the standard and non-disclosure the exception; (2) any person is entitled to information for any purpose; (3) exemptions must be clearly and narrowly drawn; (4) independent review should be available; (5) governmental agencies are required to publish certain information affirmatively, and (6) request fees should be reasonable.[217] In light of the criteria, it is safe to conclude that

[215] Helen Darbishire, *Proactive Transparency: The Future of the Right to Information? A Review of Standards, Challenges, and Opportunities* (World Bank Institute Governance Working Paper Series), World Bank, Washington, DC, 2010, https://documents1.worldbank.org/curated/en/100521468339595607/pdf/565980WP0Box351roactiveTransparency.pdf (accessed between February 21, 2025 and March 31, 2025).

[216] The United States revised its FOI legislation in 1996 to accommodate the information age, thus paving the way for more aggressive electronic disclosure of information in a proactive manner. On May 21, 2009, the U.S. Government launched the website http://www.data.gov/ with the purpose of providing direct public access to machine-readable datasets generated by the Executive Branch of the U.S. Federal Government. On January 21, 2010, the British government launched a similar website http://data.gov.uk/ that allows governmental agencies the potential to disseminate, proactively, information in a user-friendly way. On June 18, 2009, the world's first treaty on access to information, the *Council of Europe Convention on Access to Official Documents*, containing provisions for proactive disclosure, became available for signature. *Council of Europe Convention on Access to Official Documents*, Council of Europe Treaty Series No. 205, Council of Europe, Strasbourg Cedex, France, *available at* http://conventions.coe.int/Treaty/en/Treaties/html/205.htm (accessed between February 21, 2025 and March 31, 2025).

[217] Martin E. Halstuk, *Freedom of information*, *in* 5 The International Encyclopedia of Communication 1890, 1890–91 (Wolfgang Donsbach ed., 2008).

OGI Regulations 2007 are barely effective because four of the six above-mentioned criteria remain unmet[218] and *OGI Regulations 2019* are way better because four of the six criteria are met.[219] If we look at the Global Right to Information Rating developed by AccessInfo Europe and Centre for Law and Democracy, we will know why we need to be cautiously optimistic. China, similar to the United States, has experienced a tremendous decline in the national FOI rankings. From 2011 to 2024, despite the country's climbing FOI scores, China's FOI law ranking has dropped dramatically from 55th to 90th whereas USA has slipped 45 places to rank 82nd in 2024 (see Tables 6.1 and 6.2).

China could have embraced a better-designed FOI law if top leaders desired. The *Academic Draft* is very progressive and adopts many practices proven successful by many other national FOI laws. Nonetheless, the Chinese government substantially revised the *Academic Draft* and discarded many such practices. No officials have explained the considerations behind the government's choice, but reasons are not obscure. Under the current Chinese political and economic environment, many leaders believe that *OGI Regulations*, if too progressive and aggressive, would cause unpredictable social instability and even turmoil. The current versions of *OGI Regulations* represent what most people in power, reform-minded or conservative, are willing to accept. The progress made by the 2019 FOI law that revised *OGI Regulations 2007* in many significant aspects is such a good example of incremental approach in contemporary Chinese lawmaking.

The incremental, gradual, experimental approach to lawmaking is evident not only in the legislative process of *OGI Regulations* but also in the enactment of many other laws and regulations in China. Above all, such an approach characterizes the post-Mao Chinese political and economic reform masterminded by Deng Xiaoping. Ping Jiang was a professor of China University of Political Science and Law and a leading scholar in the field of Chinese civil laws. He argued that progress offset

[218] *OGI Regulations 2007* obviously meet the No. 5 criterion ("governmental agencies are required by the law to publish certain information affirmatively") and the No. 6 criterion ("request fees should be reasonable").

[219] *OGI Regulations 2019* obviously meet the No. 1 criterion ("disclosure should be the standard and nondisclosure the exception"), the No. 2 criterion ("any person is entitled to information for any purpose"), the No. 5 criterion ("governmental agencies are required to publish certain information affirmatively") and the No. 6 criterion ("request fees should be reasonable").

by setbacks has been the theme for legal reform in China over the past 30 years (1978–2008).[220] Even foreign legal scholars are cognizant of the incremental nature of China's lawmaking. An observer of China's law reforms noted that China's rule of law remains an evolving, "two-steps-forward, one-step-back dance."[221] Another famous Chinese saying, "feeling for rocks while crossing the river," characterizes the gradual evolution of Chinese law.

For OGI lawmakers in China, striking a subtle balance between international standards and Chinese characteristics is always a challenge. Some scholars accuse *OGI Regulations* of being too reluctant to embrace international standards[222]; others believe such a cautious and incremental approach is necessary for gradual reform, and too rapid change would very likely result in unfathomable and tremendous risks for the country.[223] The "founding fathers" of the Chinese FOIA side with the latter.

220 Wei Wang, *Jiang Ping: Rule of Law Progressing in China*, China.org.cn [中国网], Beijing China, October 31, 2008, http://www.china.org.cn/china/reform-opening-up/2008-10/31/content_16697241.htm (accessed between February 21, 2025 and March 31, 2025).

221 Rebecca Weiner, *Chinese Justice: The Fiction, The Facts, The Favoritism*, 14 YALE JOURNAL OF LAW AND THE HUMANITIES 225 (Winter 2002).

222 Jens. F. Reinertsen, "Assessing Access to Information in China-Legal Development and International Standards" (November 2009) (unpublished master's thesis, China University of Political Science and Law).

223 Doug Guthrie, Associate Professor of Sociology at New York University, contended that the incremental nature of Chinese legal reform is understandable because the construction of a workable legal system is hard work. Training of lawyers and change of culture all require time and effort. Doug Guthrie, *The Quiet Revolution: The Emergence of Capitalism*, 25 HARVARD INTERNATIONAL REVIEW 48 (2003); Jamie P. Horsley, a scholar at Yale Law School China Law Center, has also acknowledged the value of incremental progress in rule of law in China. Jamie P. Horsley, "Rule of Law in China: Incremental Progress," in *The China Balance Sheet in 2007 and Beyond* 93 (C. Fred Bergsten, N. Lardy, B. Gill & D. Mitchell eds., 2007), a joint project by Center for Strategic and International Studies and the Peterson Institute for International Economics, Washington, DC, *available at* https://www.csis.org/programs/freeman-chair-china-studies/past-projects/china-balance-sheet/papers (accessed between February 21, 2025 and March 31, 2025).

CHAPTER 7

What the Law Delivers: Implementation of *OGI Regulations*

As part of the author's doctoral dissertation that was successfully defended at The Pennsylvania State University in 2012, this chapter was later revised and presented to the ICA annual conference in 2016. The manuscript was then published in *Journal of Media Law and Policy* in 2020. The author of this book retains copyright of this journal article. Certain parts of the text in this chapter may resemble or replicate the original material, which has been included with the permission of the editors at Palgrave Macmillan. Yong Tang, "Chinese Freedom of Information: An Evaluation of the Legislative History, Rationales, Significance and Efficacy of Regulations of the People's Republic of China on Open Government Information" (2012) (unpublished Ph.D. diss., The Pennsylvania State University at University Park), *available at* https://etda.libraries.psu.edu/catalog/16287/ (accessed between February 21, 2025 and March 31, 2025); Yong Tang, *Merely Window Dressing? Accomplishments and Challenges in Enforcing China's First Freedom of Information Law*, paper accepted for presentation by the annual ICA (International Communication Association) convention, Fukuoka, Japan, June 9–13, 2016; Yong Tang, *Merely Window Dressing or Substantial Authoritarian Transparency? Twelve Years of Enforcing China's Version of Freedom of Information Law*, 8 JOURNAL OF MEDIA LAW AND ETHICS 2: 68–97 (Fall/Winter 2020).

Y. Tang, *Freedom of Information Law in China*,
https://doi.org/10.1007/978-981-96-7842-6_7

Introduction

In response to a grave public health crisis that swept China in 2003, Chinese government passed *Open Government Information Regulations* (*OGI Regulations*) in 2007.[1] Under the country's first freedom of information (FOI) law that went into effect in 2008 and was amended in 2019, government agencies, for the first time in Chinese history, have legal obligations to proactively and reactively disseminate information held by them. Although the law was influenced by American and European freedom of information legislation,[2] many Western observers view China's passage of the FOI legislation with perplexity and suspicion. They insist that FOI law can only survive and thrive in constitutional democracies. They predict that the law is likely to fail or at best serve merely as window dressing for the ruling Chinese Communist Party.[3] As the COVID-19 was spreading around the world like wildfire in 2020,[4]

[1] *OGI Regulations 2007. OGI Regulations Amendment 2019.* The Chinese government has never systemtically published official English translations of its laws and regulations. For the full text of *OGI Regulations* (both in Chinse and English), see *Chinese Law and Policy on Open Government Information*, Open Government Information in China, Yale University Law School China Center, New Haven, Connecticut, *available at* https://law.yale.edu/china-center/resources/open-government-information-china (accessed between February 21, 2025 and March 31, 2025).

[2] Hanhua Zhou, *Basic Considerations in Drafting of Open Government Information Regulations (Academic Version)*, 6 Chinese Journal Of Law 57 (2002).

[3] Rick Snell & Weibing Xiao, *Freedom of Information Returns to China*, 10 Public Administration Today 44 (2007); Lei Zheng, *Enacting and Implementing Open Government Information Regulations in China: Motivations and Barriers*, in proceedings of the 1st International Conference on Theory and Practice of Electronic Governance, Macao, China, December 10–13 2007, at 117–20; David Caragliano, *China's Transparency Reform: Is It for Real?* The Atlantic, November 6, 2012, https://www.theatlantic.com/international/archive/2012/11/chinas-transparency-reform-is-it-for-real/264609/ (accessed between February 21, 2025 and March 31, 2025).

[4] As of August 4, 2020, 18,387,725 people in the world have been infected with the novel coronavirus and 696,586 people globally have died of the virus. *Coronavirus Resources Center*, Johns Hopkins University, Baltimore, Maryland (JHU has stopped collecting data as of March 10, 2023), *available at* https://coronavirus.jhu.edu (accessed between February 21, 2025 and March 31, 2025).

numerous Western media reports believe that it was lack of government transparency and initial cover-up that caused the early coronavirus outbreak in Wuhan, China.[5]

The purpose of this chapter is to examine implementation and enforcement of *OGI Regulations* in the last 16 years (2008–2023) to see if the law has been effectively enforced or just an act of showmanship, as many Western scholars believe, and news editors suggest. A database search finds some English-language scholarly materials on China's FOI law.[6] Few Western researchers, however, have examined how well *OGI Regulations* have been enforced and what improvements can be made. This research seeks to fill this gap. Government agencies in Taiwan, Hong Kong and Macao are excluded from consideration as *OGI Regulations* do not apply to governments in the breakaway province and two special administrative regions.

[5] *Coronavirus: What Did China Do about Early Outbreak?* BBC News, June 9, 2020, https://www.bbc.com/news/world-52573137 (accessed between February 21, 2025 and March 31, 2025); *China Didn't Warn Public of Likely Pandemic for 6 Key Days*, Associated Press, April 15, 2020, https://apnews.com/article/virus-outbreak-health-ap-top-news-international-news-china-clamps-down-68a9e1b91de4ffc166acd6012d82c2f9 (accessed between February 21, 2025 and March 31, 2025); Nick Wadhams and Jennifer Jacobs, *China Concealed Extent of Virus Outbreak, U.S. Intelligence Says*, Bloomberg News, April 1, 2020, https://www.bloomberg.com/news/articles/2020-04-01/china-concealed-extent-of-virus-outbreak-u-s-intelligence-says (accessed between February 21, 2025 and March 31, 2025); Josh Rogin, *Bill Gates Is Wrong. China's Coronavirus Coverup Is Not a "Distraction,"* The Washington Post, April 30, 2020, https://www.washingtonpost.com/opinions/global-opinions/bill-gates-is-wrong-chinas-coronavirus-coverup-is-not-a-distraction/2020/04/30/080c6986-8b11-11ea-9dfd-990f9dcc71fc_story.html (accessed between February 21, 2025 and March 31, 2025); Nicholas Kristof, *Coronavirus Spreads, and the World Pays for China's.*

Dictatorship, The New York Times, January 29, 2020, https://www.nytimes.com/2020/01/29/opinion/coronavirus-china-government.html?searchResultPosition=6 (accessed between February 21, 2025 and March 31, 2025

[6] Hanhua Zhou, *Open Government in China: Practice and Problems*, in The Right To Know: Transparency For An Open World, ed. Ann Florini and Joseph E. Stiglitz (2007); Weibing Xiao, Freedom Of Information Reform In China: Information Flow Analysis (2011); Changhua Wu, *Improving the Legal and Policy Foundation for Public Access to Environmental Information in China*, 24 Temple Journal Of Science, Technology And Environmental Law 291 (2005); Suzanne J. Piotrowski, Yahong Zhang, Wenxuan Yu and Weiwei Lin, *Key Issues for Implementation of the Chinese Open Government Information Regulations*, 69 Public Administration Review (2009); Paul Hubbard, *China's Regulations on Open Government Information: Challenges of Nationwide Policy Implementation*, 4 Open Government Journal (2008).

This chapter relies upon annual OGI work reports published by various levels of Chinese government agencies from 2008 to 2023 and OGI-related court cases compiled by the author of this book from China Judgements Online, the largest collection of judgments and decisions from Chinese courts. As for annual OGI reports, they were all downloaded by the author from official websites of corresponding governmental agencies. Based on the reports, the study produced four tables that reflect the total number of informational items proactively and reactively released by government agencies across the country in the last 16 years. Many research findings are drawn from these tables. The tables cover all levels of the people's government of China, from central, to provincial to county and township levels, because the data released by provincial people's governments are aggregate (see Tables 7.1–7.4). A total number of 540 sample OGI-related court cases were examined, and a table was produced to demonstrate when and where a decision (by an administrative agency, superior agency, trial court, appellate court and retrial court) was made on what grounds (see Table 7.9). Four additional tables in this chapter are based on data provided by the World Bank and Transparency International, a Berlin-based non-profit organization focusing on fighting global corruption and promoting governmental transparency. These four additional tables are included in the study with the intent to show whether more than a decade of enforcement of China's FOI law leads to lesser corruption and greater transparency in the government (see Tables 7.5–7.8).

The data in the first four tables (Tables 1–4) should be undertaken with caution due to four reasons. First, all the numbers do not arise from independent sources; instead, the data is from annual reports of OGI activities produced by official agencies. The numbers compiled from annual reports of OGI activities of central and provincial-level agencies (2008–2023) indicate that roughly 57.87% of OGI requests accepted by government agencies at all levels gained approval (see Table 7.3). The OGI request approval rate provided by research organizations and news media such as the China Academy of Social Science, Peking University, *Southern Weekend*, and *Southern Metropolis Daily* seems far lower. Those relatively independent sources obtained the approval rate by sending staff to apply for information under the guise of ordinary requesters. Those rates are likely more reliable.[7] On the contrary, officials at various levels might be tempted to gloss over their transparency failures by improving their numbers because their performance evaluations relate to OGI activities.

Second, a significant amount of information is not provided by agencies in their OGI annual reports for whatever reasons, so numbers drawn from those reports are just a rough estimate of quantity of government information disclosure. Third, agencies may also make good-faith mistakes in reporting their activities for various reasons.[8] Lastly, interpretation of annual reports of OGI activities may be prone to error due to ambiguity or vagueness in the wording of the materials involved.

Despite all the shortcomings of the data presented in these four tables, the author of this book believes that the datasets are useable because no other alternative dataset is as comprehensive and longitudinal as the data provided by the Chinese government at various levels. The government data are valuable in that they provide researchers a bird's-eye view of all Chinese OGI activities occurring at central and local levels from 2008 to 2023, unlike other datasets which at best offer sporadic, short-range and anecdotal evidence of OGI activities in China. The aggregate data

[7] Hongqing Duan, *How Chinese Media Shall Push Forward Open Government Information*, 9 China Reform (2011); Xing Wang, *Journalistic OGI Applications for PM2.5 Data Yield 32% of Response Rate* [记者申请PM2.5信息公开 31省区市10个答复], Southern Metropolis Daily, republished by ChinaTransparency.org, January 11, 2012, at AA33 (captured by Internet Archive Wayback Machine on February 19, 2022), retrieved from https://web.archive.org/web/20220219172530/http://www.ogichina.org/article/180/12880.html (accessed between February 21, 2025 and March 31, 2025); Mingyan Wei & Shaofeng Guo, *OGI Regulations Still Encounter Implementation Bottlenecks Four Years After Its Enactment* [信息公开条例实施4年仍遭执行难], Beijing News, May 15, 2012, http://www.bjnews.com.cn/news/2012/05/15/199113.html (accessed between February 21, 2025 and March 31, 2025).

[8] It was found that the two annual OGI work reports published by the Ministry of Human Resources and Social Security in 2009 and 2010 were identical. The annual OGI work reports published by the Dongguan Municipal Bureau of Statistics in Guangdong Province from 2008 to 2010 were also similar in every detail. Both agencies have corrected this error. Baocheng Chen, *Ministry of Human Resources and Social Security Publishes Same Annual OGI Work Reports in Two Years* [人社部官网信息公开年报被指两年一字不差], Southern Metropolis Daily, March 29, 2011, at AA17, republished by Sina News, http://news.sina.com.cn/c/p/2011-03-29/062622198498.shtml (accessed between February 21, 2025 and March 31, 2025); Weihua Chen, *Dongguan Statistics Bureau Publishes Almost Duplicate Annual OGI Work Reports in Three Years* [东莞统计局信息公开工作报告 三年几乎一字未改] Beijing Times, April 3, 2011, at AA03, republished by CNTV, http://news.cntv.cn/map/20110403/100240.shtml (accessed between February 21, 2025 and March 31, 2025).

are valuable also in that researchers can find problems and trends that government officials may wish to hide.

Implementation of Proactive Disclosure in China

When *OGI Regulations* became effective in May 2008, governmental agencies throughout the country began releasing information according to the "affirmative disclosure" provision of the law.

A Large Variety of Communication Channels

This study finds that governmental agencies throughout China affirmatively disseminate information through a variety of communications platforms, such as official websites[9] and gazettes,[10] OGI access facilities,[11] press conferences,[12] "Government's Sunshine Hotlines,"[13] social

[9] Visiting websites of all provincial-level governments, most ministries, and commissions within the State Council, this study finds that governmental websites have become the most important platforms for distributing information. Apparently, most governmental websites investigated have special OGI columns, leaders' mailboxes, and chatroom capabilities. Chinese citizens can electronically search proactively disclosed information. The author of this book found most annual OGI work reports from those websites. Some work reports are not downloadable from his office computer in America for unknown reasons, and the author had to ask for help from his friends back in China. Without exceptions, a copy of the needed report will be quickly available to the author.

[10] In order to ensure maximum distribution of governmental gazettes, official agencies at various levels provide free electronic access to users. Websites' visitors can search gazettes easily. Relevant organizations and OGI access centers receive free and hard copies of gazettes.

[11] OGI access facilities exist throughout the country. Normally, governmental service centers, state and local archival institutions, and public libraries are their locations. Anyone can use these facilities to access proactively publicized information maintained in digital and physical forms.

[12] For example, governmental agencies at various levels in Sichuan Province conducted 1,660 press conferences in 2011. In the same year, the Ministry of Foreign Affairs held 133 press conferences.

[13] "Government's Sunshine Hotlines" enable leaders of various agencies to appear on radio shows to chat, live, with listeners. Jointly established between radio stations and agencies, the Hotlines have wide acceptance for proactively disseminating official information of greatest concern to ordinary people.

networking sites and social media,[14] media interviews,[15] OGI annual reports and guides,[16] declassified archives,[17] OGI publications, and other OGI publicity activities.[18]

Wealth of Information Proactively Disseminated

The ministries, commissions and other organizations directly controlled by the State Council disclosed a total of 30,060,562 items containing official information in the years running from 2008 to 2023, making an average of roughly 1.88 million informational items available to the general public per year (see Table 7.1). Proactive disclosure reached its peak in 2009 when 7,132,207 informational items were released by various government agencies in the central level. The release of standard governmental information and information generated or obtained prior to May 2008, contributed to the explosive growth in the number of informational items openly available. After 2009, the volume of official information proactively released annually by central agencies declined and fluctuated until reaching its nadir in 2020 when only 37,715 pieces of governmental information were released. The number started to climb again in 2021 and peaked in 2023 with 2,229,283 informational items

[14] Government's websites, online forums, and blogs are popular among officials. Even more popular is microblogging and WeChat. While China blocks X (previously Twitter), agencies and officials at various levels use Twitter-like microblogging sites (Weibo) to disseminate information. WeChat, or Weixin as it is known in China, is definitely the most powerful mobile app in China today. Vast amount of government agencies across the country use their WeChat public accounts to reach ordinary citizens.

[15] Many OGI annual reports list the number of media interviews officials arranged with journalists in the corresponding year. In general, many officials in China are increasingly willing to accept interview requests from journalists of their own country.

[16] Most agencies from central to township levels publish OGI annual reports, OGI guides, and OGI indexes in order to facilitate the people's access to proactively released information.

[17] Before enforcement of *OGI Regulations* in 2008, many official archives scheduled for declassification under *Archives Law 1988* remained sealed. Since enactment of *Regulations*, agencies have become increasingly progressive in opening archives to the public.

[18] Many agencies often publish OGI leaflets and OGI whitepapers. They also arrange OGI Publicity Week or OGI Publicity Month to enhance public awareness of the law. During the publicity weeks or months, during OGI forums and training sessions, ordinary citizens receive invitations to attend many publicity activities.

were disclosed in that year. Agencies, ranging from provincial to township levels, affirmatively publicized an approximate total of 3,281,314,326 items from 2008 to 2023 (see Table 7.2). On average, government agencies at provincial level and below released 205 million pieces of information annually. The number of information items disclosed affirmatively by these agencies saw steady growth in the years running from 2008 to 2018. A sharp decline, however, was recorded in 2019 when only 22 million items of information were disseminated proactively by these agencies. A tremendous uptick was recorded in 2020 with 674,915,614 informational items were released in that year and the volume peaked in 2023 when 905,397,836 informational items were made public.

In sum, the Chinese government, at all levels, affirmatively released a total of 3,311,374,888 items of governmental information from 2008 to 2023 (see Table 7.3). Provincial and local government agencies released information 109 times as much as their central counterparts did. This is understandable from the Chinese context, because of the much smaller size of central agencies than their provincial and local equivalents, and the relative detachment of central agencies from ordinary people's daily lives. The sharp decrease in 2019 in the number of informational items disclosed by agencies at all levels was probably because a new State Council-recommended OGI report template began to be widely used in that year and the template narrowed the scope of government information suitable for proactive disclosure. Government information involving administrative licensing, administrative enforcement and administrative penalty was added to the annual reports, contributing to significant increases in proactive disclosure since 2020.

Categories of Information Publicized

Documents and records affirmatively disclosed by various levels of Chinese administrative organs in the last 16 years covered a large variety of areas and represented four categories: The first category constituted standard information involving activities of various government agencies and government leaders, agencies' structures, functions, and working procedures required by proactive provisions of *OGI Regulations*. The second category of information that official agencies vigorously and proactively disclosed was information on rulemaking or decision-making, which expects public participation or at least familiarity.[19] The third category of information widely disclosed, affirmatively, were government-held records and files involving money collected and spent by public agencies. The last category of official information disseminated affirmatively involved human-caused and/or natural disasters or anything bad for agencies.[20]

Reasons for Relatively Effective Implementation of Proactive Disclosure

It seems flagrant violations of *OGI Regulations* in terms of proactive disclosure of the first two categories of government information are on the decline. This book finds that the gap between the promises of *OGI Regulations* and delivery in practice in terms of proactive disclosure of such standard official information is clearly not as wide as many Western FOI scholars might expect. Many reasons exist for relatively effective implementation of proactive disclosure in China. Some major ones are: First, the Chinese government has accumulated thousands of years of experiences in proactive disclosure. Second, the design of *OGI Regulations* places a strong emphasis on proactive disclosure. Third, leaders from the party and the central government have played a key role in ensuring effective implementation of proactive disclosure. Fourth, international FOI practices prove that the existence of a central body that "coordinates FOI policy within government"[21] is crucial for successful implementation of FOI law and the General Office of the State Council and general offices of the people's government at various levels are such central bodies. Fifth, improved professional civil service contributes to effective enforcement of proactive disclosure.[22] Last, rights activists, legal

[19] *OGI Regulations (passed in 2007 and revised in 2019)*, Art.19 (2019) and Art.20 (2019); WEIBING XIAO, FREEDOM OF INFORMATION REFORM IN CHINA: INFORMATION FLOW ANALYSIS 99 (2011).

[20] WEIBING XIAO, FREEDOM OF INFORMATION REFORM IN CHINA: INFORMATION FLOW ANALYSIS 97–98 (2011).

[21] DAVID BANISAR, EFFECTIVE OPEN GOVERNMENT: IMPROVING PUBLIC ACCESS TO. GOVERNMENT INFORMATION 19 (report for Organization for Economic Co-operation and Development, Paris, France), May 29, 2012, *available at* https://papers.ssrn.com/sol3/papers.cfm?abstract_id=2069870# (accessed between February 21, 2025 and March 31, 2025).

[22] WEIBING XIAO, FREEDOM OF INFORMATION REFORM IN CHINA: INFORMATION FLOW ANALYSIS 96–97 (2011).

professionals, and interested citizens have played a role in redressing agencies' non-compliance with proactive disclosure requirements in China.[23] For example, Jie Cheng, a law professor, filed an OGI request to the State Earthquake Administration on June 13, 2008 for a seismic intensity distribution map just one month after a major earthquake struck Sichuan Province and killed nearly 90,000 people. Thanks to the pressure from citizens and media, the map became freely accessible to the public on August 29, 2008.[24]

Problems for Enforcement of Proactive Disclosure Requirements

The previous discussion indicates that the gap between the promises of *OGI Regulations* and delivery in practice in terms of proactive disclosure is relatively narrow. Nonetheless, the enforcement of proactive disclosure requirements of *OGI Regulations* is far from perfect. For some agencies, especially those at the central level ones,[25] even standard information such as OGI annual reports and normative documents do not have proactive publication. For instance, despite persistent efforts to search on the Internet, governmental websites, and Chinese legal databases, locating 2008 OGI annual reports for provincial people's governments in Ningxia, Guizhou and Hebei is impossible, and the same is true for reports for some ministerial-level agencies including State Administration for Religious Affairs, Government Offices Administration of the State

[23] Weibing Xiao, Freedom Of Information Reform In China: Information Flow Analysis 102–03(2011).

[24] Hujun Li, *Tsinghua Academic Requests Information on Seismic Intensity Distribution* [清华学者申请公开汶川地震烈度信息], Caijing, June 13, 2008, https://china.caixin.com/2008-06-13/100059101.html (accessed between February 21, 2025 and March 31, 2025); Hujun Li, *State Earthquake Administration Officially Releases Wenchuan Earthquake Intensity Distribution Map* [中国地震局正式公布汶川地震烈度分布图], Caixin, September 1, 2008, https://china.caixin.com/2008-09-01/100059432.html (accessed between February 21, 2025 and March 31, 2025).

[25] China Administrative Transparency Annual Watch (2010–2011), an investigative report compiled by Peking University, found that agencies under the State Council are far below provincial agencies in effectiveness for implementing *OGI Regulations*. Aini Mi, *Annual Watch Says that County-Level Government Agencies Are Weakest in Opening Government Information* [报告称县级政府信息公开最薄弱], Oriental Outlook Weekly, republished by Sina News, November 21, 2011, http://news.sina.com.cn/c/sd/2011-11-21/140623499862.shtml (accessed between February 21, 2025 and March 31, 2025).

Council and National Bureau of Corruption Prevention. In 2011, journalists, researchers, and interested citizens vainly attempted to uncover *Implementation Rules of the Ministry of Railways on Open Government Information*, a document that should have had proactive disclosure.[26]

These flagrant violations of *OGI Regulations* in terms of proactive disclosure of standard official information are isolated cases in China and becoming less and less common over time. What deserves serious attention are the prevalent problems, of varying degrees, at various levels of government.

First, as the primary and foremost platform for proactively distributing information, governmental websites need improvement in order to render them more efficient and user-friendly. A nationwide survey conducted by the Chinese Academy of Social Sciences (CASS) in late 2009, regarding official websites of 43 larger cities, found that "more than half" of cities' websites surveyed are substandard.[27] A similar CASS survey in 2010 included 59 ministries and commissions under the State Council and found many government websites inoperative.[28] In June 2012, a similar random survey of official websites revealed that the quality of governmental websites improved over the previous three years; however, problems persist. For example, many websites run slowly; many OGI columns are either unclickable or unsearchable; OGI information is too scattered on websites; contact information, such as telephone numbers and email addresses are incorrect or outdated; many OGI inquires via

[26] Doudou Ye, *Ministry of Railways, How Hard Is Its Open Government Information?* [铁道部，信息公开有多难?], CAIXIN, September 29, 2011, http://china.caixin.com/2011-09-29/100310845.html (accessed between February 21, 2025 and March 31, 2025). Discovering this document on the official website required nearly one year of search. The Ministry of Railway was later dissolved and replaced by the National Railway Administration. *The Implementation Rules of the National Railway Administration on Open Government Information* [国家铁路局政府信息公开实施办法] (effective date: May 15, 2019), https://www.nra.gov.cn/xxgk/gkzd/201905/t20190529_337076.shtml (accessed between February 21, 2025 and March 31, 2025).

[27] Yijun Wang, *Chinese Academy of Social Sciences Survey Finds that More Than Half of Chinese City Government Websites Substandard* [社科院调研发现逾半数城市政府网站"不及格"], CHINA YOUTH DAILY, republished by China News Service, February 22, 2010, http://www.chinanews.com.cn/gn/news/2010/02-22/2130014.shtml (accessed between February 21, 2025 and March 31, 2025).

[28] Yanbin Lv, *Review Third Anniversary of Implementation of OGI Regulations* [政府信息公开条例实施三周年检讨], 5 CHINA REFORM (2011).

telephone or email receive no timely responses or go completely unanswered; updates to released information are not timely.[29] The National Library of China launched a coordinated platform govinfo.nlc.gov.cn/ on which users can search for official information of official agencies, nationwide.[30] However, the platform seems unreliable and hardly user-friendly; access to website remain unfruitful despite the book author's repeated logon efforts.

Second, county-level governmental bodies are weakest for opening official information for public inspection. The reasons for the poor performance of county-level administrative agencies for proactive disclosure are fivefold: China's OGI work is basically policy-driven, but counties are where party and governmental policies have their weakest impact; counties usually do not have scholars and media organizations who often play a positive role in promoting governmental transparency; county residents have a desire to know official information but are unaware of the right to know; many county governments believe that releasing information of public emergencies or major incidents are likely to generate more severe incidents; many county-level governmental leaders, coming from other localities and having limited residence, have difficulty communicating with local residents.[31]

Third, proactive disclosure of crisis information or negative activities of official agencies continue to encounter many obstacles when officials fear that disclosure of such information would likely bring them embarrassment, shame, demotion or even loss of their jobs. Although large amounts of crisis information have had proactive release since May 2008, as evidenced by previous discussions in the book, the release of

[29] A few official websites remained in a dormant state for several months and even up to two years. Yanbin Lv, *Review Third Anniversary of Implementation of OGI Regulations* [政府信息公开条例实施三周年检讨], 5 CHINA REFORM (2011).

[30] Yi Liao, *National Library of China Creates Nation's First Coordinated Platform for Distributing Government Information* [国家图书馆建立我国首个"政府信息整合服务平台"], XINHUA NEWS AGENCY, republished by Gov.cn, April 30, 2009, https://www.gov.cn/jrzg/2009-04/30/content_1301142.htm (accessed between February 21, 2025 and March 31, 2025).

[31] Aini Mi, *Annual Watch Says that County-Level Government Agencies Are Weakest in Opening Government Information* [报告称县级政府信息公开最薄弱], ORIENTAL OUTLOOK WEEKLY, republished by Sina News, November 21, 2011, http://news.sina.com.cn/c/sd/2011-11-21/140623499862.shtml (accessed between February 21, 2025 and March 31, 2025).

potentially negative information remains without guarantee. Concealment of negative information is very likely if responsible agencies have reputations for maintaining secrets, as exemplified by the Wenzhou train collision in Zhejiang Province[32]; if involved companies provide significant sources for revenue to government, as demonstrated in the tainted milk scandal in Hebei Province.[33] Suppression of information flow may be

[32] The Ministry of Railways has consistently ranked among the least transparent central agencies. Thus, understanding criticism of its handling of the Wenzhou train collision as a public relations disaster is not difficult. On July 23, 2011, two high-speed trains collided in the suburbs of Wenzhou, Zhejiang Province, killing 40 people and injuring 192. The alleged cover-up of the crash and the arrogant performance of its spokesman Yongping Wang gained wide circulation. Baocheng Chen, *Only 20 Percent of Agencies Under the State Council Get Passing Grade in Transparency* [国务院机构仅二成透明度及格], SOUTHERN METROPOLIS DAILY, September 29, 2011, at AA30 (captured by Internet Archive Wayback Machine on October 1, 2011), retrieved from https://web.archive.org/web/20111001200910/http://gcontent.oeeee.com/0/3f/03f5446139179452/Blog/8f0/20cf31.html (accessed between February 21, 2025 and March 31, 2025); Tania Branigan, *Chinese Anger over Alleged Cover-up of High-Speed Rail Crash: Authorities Accused of Muzzling Media Coverage after Crash in Zhejiang Province Kills at least 38 People and Injures 192*, THE GUARDIAN, July 25, 2011, http://www.guardian.co.uk/world/2011/jul/25/chinese-rail-crash-cover-up-claims (accessed between February 21, 2025 and March 31, 2025); David Bandurski, *History of High-Speed Propaganda Tells All*, China Media Project, The University of Hong Kong, Hong Kong, China, July 25, 2011 (captured by Internet Archive Wayback Machine on August 27, 2011), retrieved from https://web.archive.org/web/20110827052438/http://cmp.hku.hk/2011/07/25/14036/ (accessed between February 21, 2025 and March 31, 2025).

[33] Sanlu, based in the city of Shijiazhuang, Hebei Province, was China's number one dairy company. In September 2008, findings showed adulteration of Sanlu's infant formula with the industrial chemical melamine. The company was one of the major sources of revenue for the city government; thus, understanding the city government's collusion with the company to conceal the milk contamination scandal is not difficult. The one-month-long concealment led to catastrophic consequences. The tainted milk powder continued to be sold. China reported an estimated 300,000 victims. Six infants died from kidney failure and thousands of babies hospitalized. People involved paid huge prices for non-disclosure of the scandal. The company announced bankruptcy. The company's former chairwoman received a sentence of life imprisonment. Thirty-two officials received punishment for mismanagement of the scandal. Lei Li, *Changing Functions of Local Governments and Lessons from Sanlu Tainted Milk Scandal* [地方政府职能转变与三鹿奶粉事件的教训], Sina Finance, Beijing, China, January 12, 2009, *available at* http://finance.sina.com.cn/china/hgjj/20090112/17335750186.shtml (accessed between February 21, 2025 and March 31, 2025); Duan Wang, *Tainted Milk Victims Take Fight to Hong Kong*, CAIXIN, May 6, 2010, https://www.caixinglobal.com/2010-05-06/tainted-milk-victims-take-fight-to-hong-kong-101018319.html (accessed between February 21, 2025 and March 31, 2025); *Shijiazhuang City Government Spokesperson: We Have Undeniable*

likely if avoiding domestic and international panic becomes the paramount concern of the government as evidenced by China's failure to alert the public, timely, of a pending COVID-19 epidemic in late 2019 and early 2020,[34] if economic or political scandals embroil high-ranking officials such as the Wang Lijun incident in Chongqing,[35] if arrests of human

Responsibility for Sanlu Milk Contamination Incident [石家庄政府新闻发言人:三鹿奶粉事件我们有不可推卸的责任], China Central Television, September 30, 2008, http://news.cctv.com/xwlb/20080930/101980.shtml (accessed between February 21, 2025 and March 31, 2025).

[34] According to the Chinese FOI law, government agencies must emphasize proactive disclosure of government information involving public health, and disclosure must be timely and accurate. *OGI Regulations (passed in 2007 and revised in 2019)*, Art. 20 (2019) and Art. 6 (2019). At the very beginning of the global COVID-19 pandemic, however, National Health Commission, Hubei Provincial Health Commission, and Wuhan Health Commission all failed to tell the world, affirmatively, what was going on in Wuhan, the original epicenter of the coronavirus outbreak. Dali L. Yang, *Wuhan Officials Tried to Cover up Covid-19 —* and *Sent It Careening Outward*, The Washington Post, March 10, 2020, https://www.washingtonpost.com/politics/2020/03/10/wuhan-officials-tried-cover-up-covid-19-sent-it-careening-outward/ (accessed between February 21, 2025 and March 31, 2025*); China Didn't Warn Public of Likely Pandemic for 6 Key Days*, Associated Press, April 15, 2020, https://apnews.com/article/virus-outbreak-health-ap-top-news-international-news-china-clamps-down-68a9e1b91de4ffc166acd601 2d82c2f9 (accessed between February 21, 2025 and March 31, 2025).

[35] Chongqing city's government and the central government's proactive disclosure of information of the Wang Lijun incident have gained wide criticism for inadequacy. The secretive approach is understandable because of the level of officials involved and the political sensitivity of the subject. On February 6, 2012, Wang Lijun, former director of Chongqing Public Security Bureau and then-vice mayor of Chongqing, fled to the nearby United States Consulate in Chengdu in an attempt to seek refuge from his supervisor, Bo Xilai, the Chongqing party secretary and the member of China's powerful Politburo. Wang stayed in the Consulate for one day and was transported to Beijing for investigation. Both Bo and Wang were removed from their posts. In August 2012, Bo's wife was given suspended death sentence for the murder of a British businessman. Wang was convicted with defection, abuse of power and bribe-taking. Bo was expelled from the party and parliament and then sentenced to life imprisonment. The Wang Lijun incident is the most serious political scandal for the party and the government since the 1989 Tiananmen Square incident. Given the sensitivity of the incident, relevant agencies have released little information. Some agencies spread rumors to hide the truth. For example, on February 8, 2012, the Chongqing municipal government announced on its official Weibo that Wang was receiving "vacation-style medical treatment." Lack of official information leads to spreading wild rumors on the Internet. Some rumors alleged sounds of gunshots in Beijing and military vehicles on the streets of the capital. Allegations of a coup d'état led by Bo and Zhou Yongkang, Bo's strongest supporter in the Politburo Standing Committee, proved to be false. *Chongqing Vice Mayor Wang Lijun Is Receiving Vacation-Style Treatment* [重庆市副市长王立军正接受休假式治

rights activists and political dissidents occur, as represented by the jailing of Xiaobo Liu, Weiwei Ai, and Guangcheng Chen.[36] Wide reports claim that authorities hire armies of Internet policemen to "amend or delete

疗], Xinhua News Agency, February 8, 2012 (captured by Internet Archive Wayback Machine on February 11, 2012), retrieved from https://web.archive.org/web/20120211005933/http://news.xinhuanet.com/local/2012-02/08/c_122672681.htm (accessed between February 21, 2025 and March 31, 2025); *A Collection of Media Reports on the Wang Lijun Incident* [媒体报道王立军薄熙来事件始末], 21cn.com, Guangzhou, China, May 22, 2012 (captured by Internet Archive Wayback Machine on May 25, 2012), retrieved from https://web.archive.org/web/20120525121116/http://news.21cn.com/today/topic/2012/05/22/11937242.shtml (accessed between February 21, 2025 and March 31, 2025); *China's Bo Xilai Implicated in Wife's Crime - State Media*, BBC, September 19, 2012, http://www.bbc.co.uk/news/world-asia-china-19645314 (accessed between February 21, 2025 and March 31, 2025).

36 Xiaobo Liu, detained in 2008 and arrested in 2009, was the result of reported association with the Charter 08 manifesto, a document calling for the realization of constitutional democracy in China. Liu, tried on the charges of inciting subversion of state power, received a sentence of 11 years' imprisonment. He was awarded the 2010 Nobel Peace Prize. Chinese contemporary artist, Weiwei Ai, known for vocal criticism of the Chinese government was detained in April 2011 for allegations of economic crimes (tax evasions). Ai was released on bail two months later and the bail was lifted in June 2012. Blind from an early age and self-taught in law, Guangcheng Chen's well-known moniker is "barefoot lawyer" who exposes alleged abuses in official family planning policy in Chinese rural areas. In 2006, Chen was sentenced to four years and three months in prison. After serving his full sentence, and upon release in 2010, he remained under house arrest. On April 22, 2012, Chen escaped his house arrest and fled to the U.S. Embassy in Beijing. After negotiations with the Chinese government, the U.S. government granted Chen a visa, allowing him to be a visiting scholar at the New York University. The Chinese government has released very little information regarding the cases involving Liu, Ai and Chen. Most state-run media organizations shy from covering them.

content considered unproductive of 'harmony.'"[37] Hired "50-cent bloggers" create online content favorable toward party and official policies.[38] These examples illustrate Chinese limits to proactive disclosure.

The Implementation of Reactive Disclosure in China

Since the enforcement of *OGI Regulations* in May 2008, citizens, legal persons, and other organizations throughout the country have begun to exercise the legal right of access to government-held information via submitting OGI requests. The interest in applying for governmental information via reactive disclosure provisions of the law was generally high.

For example, within the first two months after *OGI Regulations* went into effect, the Beijing municipal government received 520 disclosure applications.[39] In 2008, Jilin Province received 45,992 OGI filings.[40] People and organizations were not hesitant to seek administrative and judicial remedies upon denial of OGI petitions. For instance, in 2008, the superior administrative agencies in Shanghai received requests for reconsideration of 683 denied inquiries, and 258 denied OGI requests seeking judicial relief came before court in the same city. In the same year, 118 OGI requests, rejected by agencies in Jilin Province, were transferred

[37] John Keane, *The China Labyrinth*, The New York Times, February 14, 2012, at para. 22–23, http://www.nytimes.com/2012/02/15/opinion/the-china-labyrinth.html?ref=china (accessed between February 21, 2025 and March 31, 2025).

[38] "Fifty Cent Bloggers" or "Fifty Cent Party" is a nickname for Internet commentators reportedly hired by provincial and local authorities in China to spin bad news and influence public opinion. Internet commentators receive basic monthly wages from the government. In addition to that, they reportedly receive RMB 50 cents for each post they generate, giving rise to the moniker, "Fifty Cents Party." Nan Wu, *Chinese Bloggers on the History and Influence of the "Fifty Cent Party,"* The Digital Times, May 15, 2008, http://chinadigitaltimes.net/2008/05/chinese-bloggers-on-the-history-and-influence-of-the-fifty-cent-party/ (accessed between February 21, 2025 and March 31, 2025).

[39] Yongtong Su and Muzi Cai, *Initial Enforcement of OGI Regulations Faces Obstacles* [实施信息公开新法遭遇开头难], Southern Weekend, July 10, 2008, http://www.infzm.com/content/14378 (accessed between February 21, 2025 and March 31, 2025).

[40] Huazhou Han, *Some Problems and Policy Suggestions Concerning the Implementation of OGI Regulations*, 7 Chinese Public Administration 11 (2009).

to superior administrative agencies for reconsideration, and 34 similarly rejected requests sought judicial relief.[41]

This chapter identifies various trends and patterns that dominate the landscape of reactive disclosure in the 16-year span when the FOI law has witnessed enforcement in China. These trends and patterns emerge when the study examined data involving governmental agencies processing OGI requests, administrative organs handling reconsideration of information request denials, courts handling OGI litigations, geographic and bureaucratic imbalance in the use of reactive disclosure, and military and national security agencies that are still in the dark.

Governmental Agencies Processing OGI Requests

According to the data gathered from various OGI annual reports published from 2008 to 2023, the ministries, commissions, and other organizations under the State Council received a total number of 401,247 requests in the last 16 years (2008–2023), registering an average of 25,077 requests per year (see Table 7.1). With a few exceptions, there was a steady growth in the number of OGI petitions made and received and the number reached its peak in 2015 when 142,217 requests were recorded. Agencies at provincial, prefecture, city, county, and township levels received approximately 5,597,231 applications in the years running from 2008 to 2023, registering an average of 349,826 submissions on a yearly basis (see Table 7.2). The number of OGI requests made to these agencies grew from 132,266 in 2008 to 415,955 in 2017, declined to 375,820 in 2019, and then climbed to 646,962 in 2023. In sum, the Chinese agencies at all levels received 5,998,478 applications for disclosure of government-held documents and files within the 16-year time span since institution of *OGI Regulations* in 2008 (see Table 7.3). Major findings concerning administrative agencies handling OGI requests are:

1. Most requests were accepted for processing.

Apparently, most OGI requests gained acceptance for processing. Some requests remained unprocessed, either ignored by the receiving agencies

[41] Huazhou Han, *Some Problems and Policy Suggestions Concerning the Implementation of OGI Regulations*, 7 CHINESE PUBLIC ADMINISTRATION 11 (2009).

or marked as invalid applications for procedural reasons (e.g., the request format was inappropriate, addressed to the incorrect agency). According to the data for this study, central governmental agencies received 401,247 OGI requests from 2008 to 2023. Among all these requests received, 392,813 gained acceptance for processing, an acceptance rate of 97.89% (see Table 7.1). In the same 16-year period, provincial and lower-level agencies received a total of 5,597,231 OGI requests, among which 5,416,487 were acceptable as valid applications, with an acceptance rate of 96.77% (see Table 7.2). Although the acceptance rates were high, they were far from perfect. Under *OGI Regulations*, official agencies are to accept and process all requests, so, ideally the acceptance rate should be 100%. This requirement is clearly not enforced to the extent desired by the law, and thus ignoring or rejecting OGI requests even before acceptance is disturbing.

2. The majority of OGI requests submitted to provincial and local agencies gained approval.

Irritation is the result upon rejection of OGI requests even before acceptance for processing, but the procedures of the lengthy OGI request-submission and relief-seeking process are surprisingly encouraging. The data show that the majority of OGI requests accepted at provincial and local levels in China gained approval by corresponding agencies while approval rate for OGI requests at the central level is much lower. According to gathered statistics, of all the OGI requests accepted for processing in the years running from 2008 to 2023 by ministries, commissions and other organizations of the State Council, 8.19%, 15.73%, 5.29%, 6.45%, 11.93%, 11.88%, 37.68%, 77.17%, 30.93%, 29.73%, 23.24%, 28.65%, 27.84%, 10.32%, 21.29%, and 27.58% gained acceptance respectively for each year, registering an average approval rate of 40.95% (see Table 7.1). On the contrary, the approval rate for the OGI requests processed by provincial and local agencies was 63% for 2008, 64.44% for 2009, 63.49% for 2010, 64.94% for 2011, 80.38% for 2012, 72.32% for 2013, 62.60% for 2014, 67.71% for 2015, 65.12% for 2016, 60.90% for 2017, 53.89% for 2018, 54.33% for 2019, 52.46% for 2020, 49.18% for 2021, 51.83% for 2022, and 48.74% for 2023, with an average approval rate of 59.10% (see Table 7.2). In sum, the Chinese bureaucracy at all levels approved 57.87% of OGI requests it had processed in the 16-year period from 2008 to 2023 (see Table 7.3).

The relatively high approval rate for OGI requests especially at provincial and local levels is significant for official attention because the majority of OGI applications submitted, received, and accepted for processing in the country were for provincial and local agencies. As an indicator of effectiveness of reactive disclosure, the surprisingly high approval rate at provincial and local levels seems contradicting, to some degree, Western scholars' prophecies that the FOI system fails in authoritarian regimes like China.

However, caution is necessary when considering the common occurrence of agencies' consenting to applicants' disclosure requests for three reasons: First, the approval rates are based upon calculations from annual OGI work reports produced by various levels of administrative agencies with vested interest in OGI activities, not from independent sources that often produce much lower rates of approving OGI requests. According to personal assessment of Zejin Yao, a famed professor of media law in China, the average OGI request approval rate stands at around 30%,[42] far below 57.87% indicated above. Second, the rates represent a relatively short period of time (2008–2023). A different outcome would be possible if the data had represented a much longer time span. Third, most of the information sought by applicants did not involve issues of public interest/concern. Instead, requested documents and records were closely related to the immediate interests of requesters. FOI scholar Weibing Xiao identified several major categories for information Chinese citizens sought via OGI requests since 2008: State-owned enterprises' privatization and restructuring, house demolition, and land use, all of which aids determining violations of individuals' interests.[43] According to Xiao, other areas for inquiries include: Pending criminal and civil cases and other personal legal matters, official agencies' processing business transactions, historical records for matters, such as housing takeovers prior

[42] WeChat interview with Zejin Yao (December 2024). Yao is director of the Communication Law Research Center at China University of Political Science and Law. He is executive associate dean of the university's Guangming School of Journalism and Communication.

[43] WEIBING XIAO, FREEDOM OF INFORMATION REFORM IN CHINA: INFORMATION FLOW ANALYSIS II (2011).

to and during the Cultural Revolution, and personnel files for claiming government-funded benefits.[44]

When releasing these types of information, government officials have few concerns for any impact on their careers. The approval rate would precipitately drop if most information sought had involved the welfare or well-being of the general public, such as information pertaining to environmental pollution and public health crisis, financial records of high-ranking officials, and files about government corruption and officials' embezzlement. Release of such information would likely cause civil unrests, mass protests and resentment toward the ruling party.

3. Approval rates among governmental agencies were sharply uneven.

As identified in previous discussion, the average percentage of requests approved by agencies at provincial and lower levels (59.10%) is relatively high, with Beijing and Shanghai being two exceptions. As two provincial-level cities, Beijing (40.51%) and Shanghai (39.54%) recorded far lower approval rate than other provincial equivalents from 2012 to 2023. This finding is consistent with a previous study based on 245 annual OGI activity reports from 2008 to 2010.[45] The difference in approval ratings between central and local agencies may have an explanation from the perspective of the special needs test.

Prior to *OGI Regulations*' amendment in 2019, the applicant had to provide evidence to prove existence of a special need for daily productivity, livelihood, or scientific research to substantiate the request.[46] Normally, the information sought via OGI requests submitted to provincial and lower-level official agencies are related more closely to citizens' daily productivity and livelihoods than information pursued via OGI requests to central level agencies. Information requests sent to provincial and lower-level governmental bodies are thus more likely to satisfy the special needs test. Ironically enough, in the last 16 years, official agencies at

[44] Weibing Xiao, Freedom Of Information Reform In China: Information Flow Analysis 119 (2011).

[45] Ming Xiao, *Analysis of State of Operation of OGI System According to 245 Annual OGI Work Reports from 2008 to 2010*, 10 Law Science Monthly (2011).

[46] *OGI Regulations (passed in 2007 and revised in 2019)*, Art. 13 (2007). The special needs test was abolished when *OGI Regulations* were revised in April 2019. The revised law went into effect in May 2019.

various levels in Beijing and Shanghai were more likely to deny disclosure requests than other provincial-level government entities because, on average, information sought in these two large cities had greater difficulty meeting the special needs test. In socially and economically developed areas, like Beijing and Shanghai, where a more mature civil society exists, people are more likely to apply for information of public interest.[47]

4. Many OGI requests were denied on non-legal grounds.

Although the majority of OGI applications submitted from 2008 to 2023 to provincial and lower-level agencies gained approval in China, a small number of requests were denied by agencies either on substantive/legal grounds[48] or on non-legal/procedural grounds.[49] According to annual OGI reports, at the central government's level, the total number of OGI denials on non-legal grounds was 101 for 2008, 837 for 2009, 665 for 2010, 1,006 for 2011, 935 for 2012, 987 for 2013, 2,618 for 2014, 10,338 for 2015, 12,639 for 2016, 8,759 for 2017, 8,545 for 2018,

[47] Ming Xiao, *Analysis of State of Operation of OGI System According to 245 Annual OGI Work Reports from 2008 to 2010*, 10 Law Science Monthly (2011).

[48] This study identifies denied OGI requests as "denied on substantive/legal grounds" in the tables when agencies' decisions assert: (a) requested information involves state secrets; (b) requested information involves commercial secrets; (c) requested information involves personal privacy; (d) requested information involves commercial secrets or personal privacy and the third party involved did not consent to disclosure; (e) requested information might harm state security, public security, economic security, or social stability if disclosed; (f) requested information appears in internal documents; (g) requested information is internal management information or procedural information; (h) requested information needs summarization, assembly, or reproduction; (i) requested information is irrelevant to the applicant's special needs; (j) information sought are files and documents involving administrative law enforcement; k) any other legal reasons specified by laws and regulations.

[49] This study identifies denied OGI requests as "denied on non-legal/procedural grounds" in the tables when agencies' decisions assert: (a) requested governmental information does not exist; (b) requested information is not in the possession of the agency which received the request; (c) the request is ambiguous and fails to conform to required format; (d) requested information is not official information; (e) requested information has been transferred to archival institutions; (f) requested information is the subject of repeated requests; (g) information sought are easily available publications; (h) the OGI annual reports do not specify grounds for agencies' denying requests; (i) government agency asks for correction or additional information; (j) government agency asks information to be sought through other means; k) any other non-legal reasons.

10,963 for 2019, 9,737 for 2020, 39,593 for 2021, 13,696 for 2022, and 9,682 for 2023 (see Table 7.1). At the provincial and lower levels, the number of OGI requests rejected for non-legal reasons was 6,741 for 2008, 14,368 for 2009, 15,463 for 2010, 22,363 for 2011, 28,915 for 2012, 29,137 for 2013, 75,185 for 2014, 81,170 for 2015, 96,926 for 2016, 121,947 for 2017, 116,719 for 2018, 145,511 for 2019, 150,232 for 2020, 198,456 for 2021, 191,359 for 2022, and 278,196 for 2023 (see Table 7.2). In sum, the people's government at all levels rejected a total of 1,703,789 OGI requests for non-legal reasons in the 16-year period (see Table 7.3), creating an upward trend with 6,842 rejections in 2008 and 287,878 rejections in 2023. The numbers listed indicate a continuous increase of OGI rejections for non-legal reasons.

Agencies have designed a variety of non-legal strategies to reject OGI requests. Since rejections are for non-legal reasons, the requirements of *OGI Regulations* allow bypassing. For example, as FOI scholar, Weibing Xiao, observed, official bodies set many unreasonable obstacles for access.[50] Some agencies require the applicants to provide file numbers of the documents sought.[51] Some administrative organs compel requesters to use government-provided application forms.[52] Some agencies ask for personal signatures on application forms.[53] Some agencies order the applicants to submit copies of their identifying documents in certain formats and even authenticity verification of those documents is

[50] Weibing Xiao, Freedom Of Information Reform In China: Information Flow Analysis iii (2011).

[51] A government agency in Beijing rejected Fuxiang Zhu's OGI request for this reason. Zongzhi He, Sijing Wang & Ran Huang, *FOI Still Has a Long Way to Go* [政府信息公开:还有一段路要走], 21St Century Business Herald, republished by Sina Finance, July 8, 2008, http://finance.sina.com.cn/china/hgjj/20080708/02595065285.shtml (accessed between February 21, 2025 and March 31, 2025).

[52] In May 2008, Beijing lawyer, Jinsong Hao, submitted an OGI request to the State Forestry Administration in Beijing. The administration rejected the application because he did not use the form designated by the agency. Kulei An, *Skills of Jinsong Hao* [郝劲松的技术活], Southern People Weekly 20 (2008): 64.

[53] Yanbin Lv, *Review Third Anniversary of Implementation of OGI Regulations*, 5 China Reform (2011).

needed.[54] Some agencies prohibit OGI requesters from photocopying the documents sought.[55] Some agencies keep applicants from submitting applications online.[56] Many governmental bodies deny requests for information on the grounds that the information sought does not exist or is

[54] Yanbin Lv, *Review Third Anniversary of Implementation of OGI Regulations*, 5 CHINA REFORM (2011). In December 2011, a journalist from the *Southern Metropolis Daily* submitted an OGI application to the Hubei Provincial Bureau of Environmental Protection for surveillance data concerning PM2.5. The agency required a scanned copy of the applicant's photo ID by telefax and refused to accept a photo ID having certain formats. Xing Wang, *Journalistic OGI Applications for PM2.5 Data Yield 32% of Response Rate* [记者申请PM2.5信息公开 31省区市10个答复], SOUTHERN METROPOLIS DAILY, republished by ChinaTransparency.org, January 11, 2012, at AA33 (captured by Internet Archive Wayback Machine on February 19, 2022), retrieved from https://web.archive.org/web/20220219172530/http://www.ogichina.org/article/180/12880.html (accessed between February 21, 2025 and March 31, 2025).

[55] In November 2007, Linxing Xu and Yulai Yuan submitted an OGI request to the Shanghai Municipal Environmental Protection Bureau. The Bureau accepted the request but informed the applicants that the information sought was only accessible for reading or transcription by hand in the Bureau office. Although this incident occurred before enactment of *OGI Regulations*, similar incidents continued after institution of the law. For example, in 2012, Wei County Civil Affairs Bureau in Hebei Province asked an applicant to visit the agency office to examine, personally, the requested document, but without allowing him to photocopy it. Junxiu Wang, *Lawyer Discusses Various Strange Phenomena Regarding FOI* [一律师披露政府信息公开之怪现状], CHINA YOUTH DAILY, May 10, 2008, at 3,
http://zqb.cyol.com/content/2008-05/10/content_2175261.htm (accessed between February 21, 2025 and March 31, 2025); Jing Wei, *Journalist Sues Wei County Civil Affairs Bureau in Hebei Province for Non-Compliance of OGI Regulations* [媒体人诉河北蔚县民政局不公开低保名单], ChinaTransparency.org, Beijing, China, May 17, 2012 (captured by Internet Archive Wayback Machine on February 19, 2022), retrieved from.
https://web.archive.org/web/20220219074641/http://www.ogichina.org/article/180/13954.html (accessed between February 21, 2025 and March 31, 2025).

[56] In December 2011, a journalist from the *Southern Metropolis Daily* submitted an online OGI application to the official website of the Shānxī Provincial Bureau of Environmental Protection for the surveillance data concerning PM2.5. Unfortunately, the website declined to accept the electronic application. Xing Wang, *Journalistic OGI Applications for PM2.5 Data Yield 32% of Response Rate* [记者申请PM2.5信息公开 31省区市10个答复], SOUTHERN METROPOLIS DAILY, republished by ChinaTransparency.org, January 11, 2012, at AA33 (captured by Internet Archive Wayback Machine on February 19, 2022), retrieved from https://web.archive.org/web/20220219172530/http://www.ogichina.org/article/180/12880.html (accessed between February 21, 2025 and March 31, 2025).

not governmental information.[57] Some agencies archive the information sought immediately after receiving information requests.[58]

5. Increasingly OGI requests were denied on legal grounds.

Many OGI requests received rejection for legal reasons in the last 16 years. According to the gathered data from annual OGI reports, at the central level of government, the number of OGI denials for legal reasons was 27 in 2008, 51 in 2009, 185 in 2010, 64 in 2011, 136 in 2012, 91 in 2013, 357 in 2014, 18,516 in 2015, 1,530 in 2016, 2,127 in 2017, 10,972 in 2018, 2,126 in 2019, 1,305 in 2020, 2,269 in 2021, 1,571 in 2022, and 1,468 in 2023 (see Table 7.1). At provincial and lower levels, the number of OGI requests rejected for legal reasons was 1,853 in 2008, 2,530 in 2009, 2,470 in 2010, 4,306 in 2011, 4,091 in 2012, 2,995 in 2013, 9,831 in 2014, 33,740 in 2015, 21,600 in 2016, 27,277 in 2017, 26,650 in 2018, 22,871 in 2019, 21,696 in 2020, 22,460 in 2021, 28,451 in 2022, and 35,982 in 2023 (see Table 7.2). In sum, the people's government, at all levels, rejected a total of 311,598 OGI requests for legal reasons from 2008 to 2023 (see Table 7.3). The numbers listed above indicate some fluctuations in different years but overall, there was

[57] Jinsong Hao, a muckraking attorney in Beijing, lodged separate OGI applications in October 2008 to the Taiyuan Railway Public Security Bureau, the Shanghai Zhabei District People's Government, the Shanghai Public Security Department and the Shanghai Zhabei District Public Security Bureau for information of the criminal case of Jia Yang, a jobless youth executed in November 2008 for murdering six Shanghai police officers and injuring many others. All four agencies denied releasing the information sought, arguing that the information did not comply with *OGI Regulations*' definition. *Famous Lawyer Jinsong Hao Requests Information Disclosure on Jia Yang Case* [知名律师郝劲松申请杨佳案信息公开], HSW.cn [华商网], Xi'an, China, October 20, 2008 (captured by Internet Archive Wayback Machine on March 15, 2016), retrieved from https://web.archive.org/web/20160315202433/http://news.jcrb.com/lvshi/200810/t20081020_84260.html (accessed between February 21, 2025 and March 31, 2025); Zhuwang Jiao, *Shanghai Police Authority Responds to Jinsong Hao who Requested Information Disclosure on Jia Yang Case* [上海警方对郝劲松就杨佳案申请信息公开进行答复], HSW.cn [华商网], Xi'an, China, November 13, 2008 (captured by Internet Archive Wayback Machine on May 22, 2009), retrieved from.

https://web.archive.org/web/20090522212730/http://www.hsw.cn/news/2008-11/13/content_10403312.htm (accessed between February 21, 2025 and March 31, 2025).

[58] Weibing Xiao, Freedom Of Information Reform In China: Information Flow Analysis 107 (2011).

clearly a steady increase in OGI applications denied by official agencies for reasons specified in *OGI Regulations 2007 and OGI Regulations 2019*, and other relevant laws and regulations.

Official agencies have used a variety of legal strategies to block information access. In an effort to avoid compliance with *OGI Regulations*, agencies try to limit the coverage of the law such as excluding the General Office of the State Council from the reactive disclosure obligations,[59] require purpose for access requests,[60] force applicants to document their special needs for the information sought and promise not to abuse special needs data,[61] limit the scope of governmental information,[62] and use

[59] Although the major responsibility of the General Office of the State Council is drafting, examining, verifying and circulating official documents, and should hold official information for public access, the General Office still issued a notice providing that it will not process directly any OGI requests filed to it by any citizens, legal persons or other organizations. *Opinions of the General Office of the State Council on Several Issues Concerning the Enforcement of Regulations of the People's Republic of China on the Disclosure of Government Information*, General Office of the State Council, Guo Ban Fa [2008] No. 36, effective date: April 29, 2008; WEIBING XIAO, FREEDOM OF INFORMATION REFORM IN CHINA: INFORMATION FLOW ANALYSIS 105–111 (2011).

[60] A survey conducted by the Chinese Academy of Social Sciences in 2010 showed that 48.8 percent of the 48 larger cities and 59.3 percent of the 59 official agencies under the State Council require information requesters to indicate and substantiate the purpose of applications. Failure to specify a purpose resulted in many rejections. Yanbin Lv, *Review Third Anniversary of Implementation of OGI Regulations*, 5 CHINA REFORM (2011).

[61] In December 2011, a journalist from *Southern Metropolis Daily* submitted an online OGI application to the Guangdong Provincial Bureau of Environmental Protection for the surveillance data concerning PM2.5. As a part of the online submission requirements, the agency website asked the applicant to document special needs for the surveillance data. The website also asked the applicant to sign an agreement to use the information "legally and reasonably." Xing Wang, *Journalistic OGI Applications for PM2.5 Data Yield 32% of Response Rate* [记者申请PM2.5信息公开 31省区市10个答复], SOUTHERN METROPOLIS DAILY, republished by ChinaTransparency.org, January 11, 2012, at AA33 (captured by Internet Archive Wayback Machine on February 19, 2022), retrieved from https://web.archive.org/web/20220219172530/http://www.ogichina.org/article/180/12880.html (accessed between February 21, 2025 and March 31, 2025). The special needs test was eliminated from *OGI Regulations* when the law was revised in 2019.

[62] According to legal scholar, Weibing Xiao, limiting the scope of Chinese governmental information is possible by many methods. First, agencies restrict the scope of information by adopting their own OGI Rules. Second, agencies exclude information involving functions of criminal enforcement or prosecution. Third, agencies narrowed the scope of official information to information generated or obtained after enactment of *OGI Regulations*. Fourth, agencies interpreted the definition of official information literally. WEIBING

statutory and non-statutory exemptions to control access.[63] Government agencies continued to use those strategies in March 2020, when the National Health Commission (NHC) rejected a lawyer's OGI application for information about how COVID-19 started in Wuhan, China, why the outbreak was initially out of control there, what three teams of NHC public health experts found out in Wuhan, what Chinese Center for Disease Control and Prevention suggested for outbreak control, and why daily release of epidemic information in the city stopped for a while. When explaining the rejections, the commission reasoned that what the applicant requested were all pre-decisional materials written as part of the decision-making process in government agencies, citing the newly added deliberative privilege exemption in *OGI Regulations*.[64]

6. Most OGI request denials were made for non-legal reasons.

Apparently, although the Chinese government seems less and less willing to reject requests for disclosure of information, a disturbing pattern is emerging for Chinese governmental bodies. Governmental agencies around the world normally base denials to FOI requests on legal grounds. China is clearly an exception.

Xiao, Freedom Of Information Reform In China: Information Flow Analysis 106–107 (2011).

[63] One example of statutory and non-statutory exemptions is internal working documents. According to legal scholar, Weibing Xiao, agencies have used two broad and vague exemptions delineated in *OGI Regulations* to refuse access. First, before the deliberative privilege was added to *OGI Regulations* in 2019, many agencies added an exemption through a deliberative process to their OGI Rules, thus broadening the exemptions found in *OGI Regulations*. Second, some agencies interpreted the exemption for state secrets broadly to include information barely sensitive. Some agencies interpreted the exemption of trade secrets to include information on governments' procurement and other contracts to which the government is a party. Governmental bodies also used the privacy exemption to deny releasing information already disclosed. Weibing Xiao, Freedom Of Information Reform In China: Information Flow Analysis 108–110 (2011). *OGI Regulations (passed in 2007 and revised in 2019)*, Art.16 (2019).

[64] Jiaxin Wang and Man Liu, *National Health Commission Denies a Lawyer's OGI Request for Daily Coronavirus Test Results on the Grounds of the Deliberative Privilege Exemption* [卫健委回复律师信息公开申请:疫情检测日报属过程性信息暂不公开], Southern Metropolis Daily, republished by Sohu News, March 28, 2020, https://www.sohu.com/a/383868171_161795 (accessed between February 21, 2025 and March 31, 2025). The deliberative privilege exemption was added to *OGI Regulations* in 2019. *OGI Regulations (passed in 2007 and revised in 2019)*, Art. 16 (2019).

The tables for this study show that, from 2008 to 2023, most OGI requests denied by Chinese government agencies were denied not on substantive or legal grounds, but on non-legal or procedural grounds. According to the data (see Table 7.3), in 2008, the Chinese government, at all levels, rejected 6,842 OGI applications on non-legal grounds. In the same year, it denied 1,880 applications on legal grounds. The more frequent use of non-legal reasons was also present in 2009, accounting for 15,205 OGI applications' rejection for non-legal reasons and 2,581 applications' rejection for legal reasons. In 2010 and 2011, the Chinese government denied 16,128 and 23,369 OGI requests, respectively, by citing non-legal reasons whereas it rejected 2,655 and 4,370 applications, respectively, in those two years for legal reasons.

The same pattern continued in the following years. In 2012, government agencies across the country rejected 29,850 requests on non-legal grounds while rejecting 4,227 requests for legal reasons. In 2013, 30,124 non-legal denials were made whereas only 3,086 applications were rejected for legal reasons. In 2014, non-legal reasons were cited when rejecting 77,803 applications and 10,188 denials were made out of legal considerations in the same year. In 2015, 91,508 requests were rejected by agencies on non-legal grounds and in the same year 52,256 requests were rejected on legal grounds. In 2016, government agencies used non-legal reasons to deny 109,565 requests and they used legal reasons to deny 23,130 requests. In 2017, the total number of requests rejected on non-legal grounds was 130,706 whereas the total number of requests denied on legal grounds was 29,404. In 2018, governments withheld 125,264 pieces of information, citing non-legal reasons, and they withheld 37,622 pieces of information, citing *OGI Regulations* and relevant laws. In 2019, agencies across the country rejected 156,474 OGI requests, citing procedural rationales. In the same year, 24,997 OGI requests were denied on legal grounds. In 2020, only 23,001 OGI requests were denied on legal grounds while 159,969 OGI requests were rejected on non-legal grounds. In 2021, 24,729 requests were denied for legal reasons while 238,049 applications were rejected for non-legal reasons. In 2022, Chinese government agencies at all levels rejected 30,022 requests on the basis of legality and rejected 205,055 applications for reasons that had nothing to do with the OGI law. In 2023, the Chinese government at all levels denied 37,450 OGI requests on legal grounds and at the same time rejected 287,878 OGI applications for non-legal reasons. Of all the 2,015,387 OGI requests denied in the 16-year period by all levels of the Chinese government from 2008 to 2023, 84.54% of denials were for non-legal reasons and only 15.46% of denials were for legal reasons.

The explanation for the much more frequent use of non-legal or procedural reasons to justify denial of OGI applications for access arises from the significant discretionary power of governmental agencies in China. The lack of clear-cut legal rules contributes to willful determination of whether or not non-legal reasons cited by agencies are valid. The abusive use of non-legal grounds for denying OGI access is troubling. First, many non-legal reasons cited to support non-disclosure are clearly unreasonable. Second, OGI requesters whose rejections had non-legal bases have difficulty pursuing administrative and judicial remedies. Even if the applicants file for administrative reconsideration or institute court action against an agency, the chance of having a decision overturned is slim.[65]

Governmental Agencies Handling Reconsideration of Information Request Denials

Under *OGI Regulations*, applicants for information have three legal mechanisms to rectify non-disclosure of official information. First, they may report the non-disclosure to a superior agency or agency in charge of OGI activities for corrections. Second, if denied OGI requests, applicants may appeal decisions to the administrative agencies for reconsideration. Third, they may file OGI lawsuits to seek judicial remedy.[66] This study does not examine enforcement of the first mechanism due to lack of relevant data.

Cases for OGI administrative reconsideration in China are many. The Chinese government at all levels received 554 OGI appeals for administrative reconsideration in 2008, 1,843 cases in 2009, 1,532 similar cases in 2010, 2,228 cases in 2011, 1,456 cases in 2012, 2,729 cases in 2013, 10,814 cases in 2014, 20,230 cases in 2015, 20,310 cases in 2016, 20,524 cases in 2017, 18,162 cases in 2018, 18,611 cases in 2019, 17,310 cases in 2020, 28,138 cases in 2021, 19,798 cases

[65] Ming Xiao, *Analysis of State of Operation of OGI System According to 245 Annual OGI Work Reports from 2008 to 2010*, 10 Law Science Monthly (2011).

[66] *OGI Regulations (passed in 2007 and revised in 2019)*, Art. 33 (2007) and Art. 51 (2019).

in 2022, and 25,629 cases in 2023 for OGI administrative reconsideration (see Table 7.3). In total, during the 16-year period from 2008 to 2023, 209,868 cases applied for administrative reconsideration of an agency's decision for requests for access submitted to all central and local governmental agencies. The increasing numbers of applications for administrative reconsideration for OGI decisions indicate a growing consciousness of legal rights among Chinese citizens.

1. Reconsideration rulings included a small number of administrative decisions in favor of disclosure.

From 2008 to 2023, government agencies across the country ruled in favor of disclosure only for a small number of OGI cases filed for administrative reconsideration. Of the 10,430 cases received in the 16-year period by agencies for administrative reconsideration at the central level, only 394 cases gained favorable rulings for OGI applicants (see Table 7.1), registering a shockingly low disclosure rate of 3.78%. Likewise, of the 199,438 cases for administrative reconsideration at provincial and lower levels during the same period, only 32,269 cases gained favorable rulings for information requesters (see Table 7.2), meaning that only 16.18% of OGI requests were approved in the process of administrative reconsideration. In sum, the Chinese agencies for administrative reconsideration at all levels only approved disclosure of information for 15.56% of cases they have received in the last 16 years (see Table 7.3).

For information requesters, cases winning administrative reconsideration were very rare. Yaofang Xu and 67 other villagers in Zhejiang Province were among those lucky citizens. The villagers were unhappy with the decisions of the local government to expropriate their land without providing appropriate compensation. They lodged an application with the Yuyao municipal government on May 26, 2008, seeking detailed information of the land transfer. The Yuyao government asked the petitioners to provide additional identifying documentation and informed them to bring the case to the local land resources bureau.[67] Disappointed with the official strategy of shifting the responsibility, the

[67] Junxiu Wang, *Sixty-Eight Villagers of Yu Yao, Zhejiang Province Successfully Force Municipal Government to Change Its Original Non-Disclosure OGI Decision* [浙江余姚68名村民信息公开案告赢市政府], CHINA YOUTH DAILY, republished by China News Service, October 10, 2008,

villagers appealed to the higher level, Ningbo municipal government on July 4, 2008 for administrative reconsideration. Three months later, the Ningbo government overruled the original administrative decision. The lower-level Yuyao government received orders to release the requested information within 30 days of the decision.[68] A resident in the city of Tangshan, Hebei Province also used administrative reconsideration to force two agencies to change their original non-disclosure decisions.[69]

2. Most administrative reconsideration rulings or determinations favored non-disclosure.

According to the data (see Tables 7.1–7.3), agencies for administrative reconsideration in China upheld most original administrative decisions. Of the 10,430 and 199,438 OGI cases received in the last 16 years by agencies for administrative reconsideration, at the central level and local levels, 96.22% and 83.82%, respectively, resulted in rulings favoring

http://www.chinanews.com.cn/sh/news/2008/10-10/1407244.shtml (accessed between February 21, 2025 and March 31, 2025).

[68] Junxiu Wang, *Sixty-Eight Villagers of Yu Yao, Zhejiang Province Successfully Force Municipal Government to Change Its Original Non-Disclosure OGI Decision* [浙江余姚68名村民信息公开案告赢市政府], China Youth Daily, republished by China News Service, October 10, 2008,
http://www.chinanews.com.cn/sh/news/2008/10-10/1407244.shtml (accessed between February 21, 2025 and March 31, 2025).

[69] On February 25 and March 1, 2012, the Hebei resident filed an application to Tangshan Land and Resources Bureau and Tangshan Lunan District Development and Reform Bureau for official documents that approved demolition of her house. Both applications did not receive responses within legally designated 15 working days. On March 22 and March 28, 2012, the resident, Lan Xie (pseudonym), petitioned Hebei Province Land and Resources Bureau and Hebei Province Development and Reform Commission for reconsideration. In May 2012, two agencies for administrative reconsideration issued separate decisions, ruling that specific administrative actions of the two local agencies not releasing the information within the legal time limit were illegal. Hongmei Du, *After Two Consecutive Victories in Administrative Reconsideration, House Demolition Documents Are Finally Released* [行政复议两连胜,拆迁文件终获公开], Wqsheng.com, Beijing Shengyun Law Firm, Beijing, China, June 1, 2012,
https://web.archive.org/web/20220219110320/http://www.wqsheng.com/template/T_Content/wapindex.aspx?nodeid=23&itemid=1293 (accessed between February 21, 2025 and March 31, 2025).

non-disclosure. In sum, the Chinese agencies for administrative reconsideration at all levels rejected disclosure of information for 84.44% of cases they received.

In addition to rejecting requests for access in the rulings, agencies for administrative reconsideration in China used other strategies to create de facto denials of disclosure.[70] Of the 209,868 cases for administrative reconsideration at various levels received in the 16-year period, 52,880 cases received no final rulings (indicated as "Other" in the tables), many of which resulted in de facto denials of disclosure (see Table 7.3). Shuhuai Chen, in the city of Shenzhen, Guangdong Province, faced de facto denial of disclosure when he challenged an original administrative decision via administrative reconsideration. The Guangdong Provincial Land and Resources Bureau rejected Chen's request for information concerning a project to create farmland.[71] He received no response from the Ministry of Land and Resources after reporting the denial and requesting administrative reconsideration.[72]

3. Administrative reconsideration for rectifying non-disclosure was basically ineffective.

The above analysis substantiates the international consensus that administrative reconsideration is not effective for rectifying agencies' non-compliance with legal requirements for reactive disclosure. As FOI

[70] Denials of disclosure listed in the tables as "Other" were counted as de facto denials as long as administrative reconsideration agencies did not rule formally, but the situations fell into the following categories: (a) the requester's complaint was received but not accepted; (b) the case was pending for an extended period of time; (c) the case was closed but the ruling from the agency for reconsideration is not available. According to *Administrative Reconsideration Law 1999*, officials responsible for cases of administrative reconsideration incur administrative penalties if they fail to make decisions in the legally designated time limit and if they fail to give justifiable reasons for not considering and dismissing cases. However, despite existence of the law, delayed decisions are many. The same is true for rejection of cases and dismissal complaints without sufficient reasons.

[71] Weibing Xiao, Freedom Of Information Reform In China: Information Flow Analysis 112–113 (2011).

[72] Weibing Xiao, Freedom Of Information Reform In China: Information Flow Analysis 112–113 (2011). Although the case occurred in 2007, similar de facto denials of disclosure of information by agencies for administrative reconsideration were far from disappearing since enforcement of *OGI Regulations* in 2008.

scholars, David Banisar and Rick Snell, observed, administrative reconsideration as an internal review mechanism in the FOI legislation "tends to uphold the [FOI] denials and is used more by departments for delaying releases than enhancing access."[73] Around the world, internal review upholds more than 75% of original decisions.[74] China clearly has similar rates in this regard.

The global trend that administrative review is becoming increasingly ineffective for rectifying FOI non-disclosure is not difficult to comprehend. Both governmental agencies making initial decisions and the corresponding superior agencies making decisions for reconsideration are different components of the same bureaucracy, unlike independent information commissions or ombudsman widely adopted in many FOI countries. Neither can agencies always resist the natural tendency to withhold information. In addition, officeholders normally do not wish to embarrass their bureaucratic colleagues. Accordingly, when handling FOI complaints, expecting agencies for administrative reconsideration to truly act with independent oversight is unrealistic.

However, notably, Chinese leaders are aware of the problems and are attempting to improve effectiveness of administrative reconsideration. In September 2008, the State Council began a pilot project for developing committees for administrative reconsideration in eight provinces and special municipalities to process applications.[75] Consisting of experts, scholars, and governmental officials, the expectation is that committees establish "a more centralized, professional and impartial administrative reconsideration mechanism.[76] As of 2011, 19 provinces

[73] David Banisar, Effective Open Government: Improving Public Access To. Government Information 16 (report for Organization for Economic Co-operation and Development, Paris, France), May 29, 2012, *available at* https://papers.ssrn.com/sol3/papers.cfm?abstract_id=2069870# (accessed between February 21, 2025 and March 31, 2025).

[74] Rick Snell, *Administrative Compliance-Evaluating the Effectiveness of Freedom of Information*, 93 Freedom of Information Review. 28 (2001).

[75] Weibing Xiao, Freedom of Information Reform In China: Information Flow Analysis 101 (2011); *Notice on the Pilot Project for Developing the Administrative Reconsideration Committees in Several Provinces and Special Municipalities*, No. 71 [2008] of the Legislative Affairs Office of the State Council.

[76] Weibing Xiao, Freedom Of Information Reform In China: Information Flow Analysis 101 (2011).

established committees for administrative reconsideration.[77] Apparently, at the present stage, those pilot committees only handle significant, complex, and confusing cases covering a wide range of areas including cases for requests to access information. According to a 2023 amendment to a national law on administrative reconsideration, all government agencies above the county level in China should establish a committee consisting of government officials, experts and scholars and the committee should advise the agency on important and complex cases. It's clear that the pilot program has been expanded into a full-scale nationwide endeavor, with professionalization being the new focus.[78] However, evaluating the effectiveness of committees' handling OGI complaints is beyond the scope of this research.

Courts Handling OGI Litigations

Under *OGI Regulations*, applicants for information may bring governmental agencies to court for judicial relief when denied request according to OGI. OGI lawsuits in China are many. According to the data compiled from annual OGI work reports, Chinese courts throughout the country received a total of 305 OGI cases in 2008, 573 OGI cases in 2009, 1,025 OGI-related cases in 2010, 1,532 OGI cases in 2011, 1,050 cases in 2012, 1,039 OGI cases in 2013, 6,191 lawsuits in 2014, 13,081 cases in 2015, 16,467 cases in 2016, 15,795 cases in 2017, 17,147 cases in 2018, 18,322 OGI cases in 2019, 15,764 in 2020, 17,927 in 2021, 15,722 in 2022, and 18,915 in 2023, signifying an overall steady growth in the number of OGI lawsuits filed in the 16-year period. In sum, between May 2008 when the Chinese FOI law started to be implemented and December 2023 when the most recent annual OGI report datasets are available for this book, Chinese courts made decisions about a total of 159,806 OGI complaints filed by requesters for judicial review (see

[77] Yang Zhang & Changchun Cai, *Administrative Reconsideration Committees Are Established across 108 Government Agencies in 19 Provinces to Ensure Impartiality* [19省份108单位设行政复议委员会 杜绝官官相护], People's Daily, republished by China News Service, March 28, 2012, http://www.chinanews.com/fz/2012/03-28/3779138.shtml (accessed between February 21, 2025 and March 31, 2025).

[78] *Administrative Reconsideration Law of the People's Republic of China* [中华人民共和国行政复议法], Xinhua News Agency, republished by web portal of the State Council, September 1, 2023, https://www.gov.cn/yaowen/liebiao/202309/content_6901584.htm (accessed between February 21, 2025 and March 31, 2025).

Table 7.3). The increasing number of OGI litigations reflect growing familiarity of Chinese citizens with *OGI Regulations* and people's eagerness to use law to pry open Chinese bureaucracy for information vital to their daily lives.

1. A small number of cases granted access to information.

The datasets show that Chinese courts ruled in favor of complainants only in a very small number of OGI cases from 2008 to 2023. The number is small but praiseworthy, as Jamie Horsley, a leading scholar on China's freedom of information law, said, "Although many of those victories simply ordered the government to issue or reconsider its response, they were significant in the Chinese context because the courts were willing to rule against the government, a phenomenon that is becoming more commonplace."[79]

According to annual OGI reports, out of 159,806 OGI cases filed with Chinese courts in the last 16 years, only 13,458 gained rulings in favor of disclosure, with a rate of 8.42% disclosure-friendly cases (see Table 7.3). Specifically, in 2008, for the entire country, 305 OGI cases gained judicial review, and none ended with plaintiffs prevailing; of the 573 OGI cases in court in 2009 throughout the country, 1.92% ended in favor of plaintiffs; for all of China, 1,025 OGI cases had judicial review in 2010 with 3.41% favoring plaintiffs and in 2011, 1,532 OGI cases heard by courts resulted in only 5.29% having findings that favored plaintiffs. The percentage of cases in which courts ruled in favor of disclosure for the subsequent years are: 10.95 for 2012, 6.93 for 2013, 14.22 for 2014, 10.92 for 2015, 8.59 for 2016, 8.16 for 2017, 8.12 for 2018, 8.46 for 2019, 8.72 for 2020, 7.17 for 2021, 7.70 for 2022, and 7.77 for 2023 (see Table 7.3). An analysis of the data from court cases published on the website of China Judgment Online reveals an equally low approval rate of the judiciary for disclosure. Out of 540 sample OGI-related court cases tried from 2014

[79] Jamie Horsley, *Open Government Developments in China: Implications for US Businesses*, CHINA BUSINESS REVIEW, para.33–36, republished by US-China Business Council, Washington, DC, July 1, 2019, *available at.*

https://www.chinabusinessreview.com/open-government-developments-in-china-implications-for-us-businesses/ (accessed between February 21, 2025 and March 31, 2025). Jamie Horsley is a visiting fellow at the Brookings Institution and works at Yale Law School as a senior fellow.

to 2021, only 32 cases ruled in favor of disclosure at both trial courts and appellate courts, yielding a disclosure approval rate of 5.93% (see Table 7.9).

The chance of prevailing in OGI lawsuits was so slim for information requesters that achieving judges' support in OGI complaints became a matter of pure luck. Hunan Province resident, Yan Li, was fortunate because he defeated the government in court for the defendant's failure to respond in time to the plaintiff's OGI request.[80] The legal victory of Hubei resident, Jian'guo Xu, was far more significant. In October 2008, just five months after *OGI Regulations* became effective, Xu defeated a powerful governmental agency in an OGI lawsuit in a local court, indicating progressive potential for the court system in China to become more independent. This lawsuit is the first in the country's history in which an OGI case had public airing through regular court procedures and in which the plaintiff prevailed.[81] Another fortunate petitioner was the Shitou Dyestuff Company, a dye-making corporation in Shanghai. Among the 400 OGI complaints filed to courts from 2004 to 2008 in Shanghai,[82] this company's litigation was the only one in which the plaintiff prevailed.[83] Kai Li was more fortunate than the previous three plaintiffs. He won the litigation despite the fact that the information sought did not originate with the governmental agency.[84]

2. Majority of lawsuits' rulings denied access to information.

According to the data gleaned from various government annual OGI reports (see Table 7.3), the majority of courts' rulings in China from 2008 to 2023 upheld administrative decisions. Of 305 OGI litigations received by Chinese courts in 2008, 8 cases' rulings favored non-disclosure. Of 573 OGI litigations received in 2009, Chinese courts

[80] *Yan Li v. Jiyuan Municipal Bureau of Housing and Urban–Rural Construction (2010), Beida Fabao.*

[81] *Jian'guo Xu v. Huangzhou District Transportation Bureau (2008), Beida Fabao.*

[82] *The Shanghai Municipality OGI Provision* became enforceable in 2004 whereas the National *OGI Regulations* became enforceable in 2008.

[83] *Shitou Dyestuff Company v. Shanghai Science and Technology Commission (2008), Beida Fabao.*

[84] *Kai Li v. Sichuan Provincial Bureau of Education (2009), Beida Fabao.*

rejected 224 for non-disclosure. This indicates the rates of denying disclosure in 2008 and 2009 were not too high, but clearly, many OGI lawsuits in these two years ended with no rulings but de facto denials of disclosure. Of 1,025 OGI litigations received by Chinese courts in 2010, 760 lawsuits gained rejection for non-disclosure. Of 1,532 OGI litigations in 2011, Chinese courts rejected 1211 for non-disclosure. The percentage of lawsuits in which courts ruled in favor of non-disclosure for the years running from 2012 to 2023 are: 86.76 for 2012, 91.53 for 2013, 65.38 for 2014, 59.45 for 2015, 62.03 for 2016, 62.87 for 2017, 66.36 for 2018, 58.36 for 2019, 58.62 for 2020, 59.48 for 2021, 55.90 for 2022, and 53.49 for 2023. In sum, Chinese courts throughout the country ruled against disclosure of information for 60.22% of cases they received from 2008 to 2023. An analysis of the data from court cases published on the website of China Judgment Online reveals a far lower rate of the judiciary for non-disclosure. Out of 540 sample OGI-related court cases tried from 2014 to 2021, 148 cases denied, in whole, disclosure of the requested information at both trial and appellate courts, yielding a rejection rate of 27.41% (see Table 7.9).

3. Some OGI litigations resulted in neither granting nor denying access.

The situation for information access becomes more uncertain when considering OGI litigation that neither granted nor denied access, indicated as "court decisions (other)" in the tables (see Tables 7.1–7.3). In addition to the judicial rulings, either supporting or denying disclosure, a large number of "uncertain situations" remain in which the requester's complaint did not receive acceptance, or remains in litigation, or the closed case did not appear in OGI annual reports with details of the ruling. Many of these "uncertain situations" involve de facto denials of access to information.

For example, the fact of non-acceptance of plaintiffs' claims often indicates rejection of OGI complains prior to entering the judicial process. Guangyu Li, the deputy director of the administrative tribunal of the

Supreme Court, said that more than one third of OGI plaintiffs in China failed to have complaints accepted by courts.[85]

According to the data, from 2008 to 2023, 912 cases of legal disputes regarding OGI requests submitted to central governmental agencies could have categorization as "other" or "uncertain situations," constituting 25.49% of total filings against central agencies (see Table 7.1). Likewise, within the same period, 49,204 cases of legal disputes regarding OGI requests submitted to provincial and lower-level agencies populate the category of "other" or "uncertain situations," constituting 31.50% of total litigations filed against local agencies (see Table 7.2). In sum, in the 16-year period, 31.36% of OGI litigation actions filed against various levels of Chinese government agencies ended up with neither disclosure of information nor non-disclosure of information (see Table 7.3). Among such lawsuits, many constituted de facto denials for disclosure.

4. Information access was denied by courts for substantive and procedural reasons.

Similar to official agencies, courts in China rejected disclosure of information for both substantive and procedural reasons. The substantive reasons often cited by courts for denial were that the information sought concerns state secrets, commercial secrets, personal privacy, or endangerment of state security, public security, economic security, and social stability, thereby exempting the information from disclosure.[86] As legal scholar, Weibing Xiao, argued, courts in China use strategies of limiting

[85] Guangyu Li, *Deputy Director of Supreme Court Administrative Tribunal Guangyu Li Talks about Stories Behind Judicial Interpretation of OGI Regulations at 48th Rule of Law Forum* [最高人民法院行政审判庭副庭长李广宇做客第四十八期法治政府论坛 政府信息公开司法解释的台前幕后], Institute of Rule of Law, China University of Political Science and Law, Beijing, China, November 23, 2011, *available at* http://fzzfyjy.cupl.edu.cn/info/1223/4323.htm (accessed between February 21, 2025 and March 31, 2025).

[86] State secrets, commercial secrets, personal privacy, state security, public security, economic security, and social stability all seem vital interests that warrant protection but none of those interests are clearly defined. Courts use those ill-defined terms to deny access. For example, the exemption for commercial secrets is often the basis for denying access to information. See *Yousheng Lu v. Shanghai Municipal Bureau of Industry and Commerce (2009), Beida Fabao*; *Bingting Wang v. Shanghai Hongkou District People's Government (2009), Beida Fabao.*

the scope of administrative lawsuits,[87] imposing unreasonable burden of proof on plaintiffs,[88] and rejecting OGI lawsuits on the grounds that the requester has no legal interest in the information.[89]

As the Judicial Interpretation of *OGI Regulations* became effective in August 2011,[90] those strategies no longer apply in the Chinese judicial system, since the interpretation provides that OGI lawsuits are within the scope of administrative lawsuits, OGI refusals are within the scope of administrative cases, information sought is within the scope of administrative lawsuits, requesters have legal interests in the information, and official agencies carry the predominant burden of proof.[91] However,

[87] According to Weibing Xiao, limiting the scope of administrative lawsuits employed three avenues: First, courts rejected an OGI lawsuit for the reason that it does not fall within the scope of administrative lawsuits. Second, courts held that an OGI refusal has no real impact on the complainant's right and duty, and places it outside the scope of administrative cases. Third, courts rejection of an FOI legal action can be on the basis that information is outside the scope of administrative lawsuits. WEIBING XIAO, FREEDOM OF INFORMATION REFORM IN CHINA: INFORMATION FLOW ANALYSIS 113-14 (2011).

[88] FOI scholar Weibing Xiao said, "Courts have used the ambiguity of burden of proof to dismiss [OGI] legal actions, especially when reviewing [OGI] decisions in which officials claim that the information sought does not exist. Such claims create difficulties for courts, which must decide whether plaintiffs or defendants bear the burden of proof, and to what degree." WEIBING XIAO, FREEDOM OF INFORMATION REFORM IN CHINA: INFORMATION FLOW ANALYSIS 117 (2011).

[89] According to legal scholar, Weibing Xiao, under the Supreme Court's explanation of *Administrative Litigation Law 1989*, individuals, entitled to file an administrative lawsuit, are those who have a legal interest in administrative actions. This sets a limit on the qualification of a plaintiff. The *Supreme Court's Explanation on Several Questions Related to Implementation of the Administrative Litigation Law* (1989), Art. 12. WEIBING XIAO, FREEDOM OF INFORMATION REFORM IN CHINA: INFORMATION FLOW ANALYSIS 116-117 (2011).

[90] *Provisions of the Supreme People's Court on Issues Concerning Trying Administrative Cases of Government Information Disclosure* [Fa Shi [2011] No.17, effective date: August 13, 2011.

[91] *Provisions of the Supreme People's Court on Issues Concerning Trying Administrative Cases of Government Information Disclosure* [Fa Shi [2011] No.17, effective date: August 13, 2011; Xianming Zhang, *Supreme Court of China Issues Judicial Interpretation of OGI Regulations, Providing Courts with Guidance on OGI-Related Lawsuits* [最高人民法院颁布司法解释 全面规范审理政府信息公开行政案件有关问题], PEOPLE'S COURT DAILY, republished by the Supreme Court of China website, August 15, 2011 (captured by Internet Archive Wayback Machine on February 19, 2022), retrieved from https://web.archive.org/web/20220219074628/https://www.court.gov.cn/zixun-xiangqing-3024.html (accessed between February 21, 2025 and March 31, 2025).

courts retain the ability to rule in favor of officials for other substantive reasons.

As FOI expert Weibing Xiao observed, courts could literally explain the definition of official information[92] and examine purposes for access requests[93] in order to deny disclosure. Courts can also deny access to information on the ground that information sought is internal[94] or procedural.[95]

Procedural reasons are often used by Chinese courts to deny disclosure. Given that annual OGI work reports do not contain information about on what grounds courts deny disclosure, the author of this book read judicial opinions from 540 sample OGI-related court cases tried from 2014 to 2021 and found massive use of procedural reasons by trial courts to reject OGI applications. Out of these 540 court cases, 93 cases denied

92 Weibing Xiao found that Chinese courts could adopt a mechanical interpretation of the definition of governmental information to block access to information. For example, information compiled, rather than generated or acquired by a government agency, is not subject to disclosure; oral information is an exclusion for disclosure; information irrelevant to the exercise of official responsibilities is an exclusion for disclosure. WEIBING XIAO, FREEDOM OF INFORMATION REFORM IN CHINA: INFORMATION FLOW ANALYSIS 116 (2011). *See also Qiuqin Xu v. Shanghai Pudong District Construction and Transportation Commission (2009), Beida Fabao.*

93 Weibing Xiao argued that Chinese courts used the special purpose test to reject OGI legal actions with the rationale that examining the requester's purpose in OGI applications could prevent abusive use of rights to access. WEIBING XIAO, FREEDOM OF INFORMATION REFORM IN CHINA: INFORMATION FLOW ANALYSIS 116 (2011). As the special needs test was removed from *OGI Regulations* when the law was revised in 2019, courts can no longer use this test to deny access.

94 *Jia Lei v. Shanghai Jing'an District People's Government (2010), Beida Fabao.* As internal information is explicitly listed as an exemption in *OGI Regulations 2019*, Chinese courts today can use it as a substantive/legal reason to deny disclosure.

95 *Ronghua Zhang*, et al. *v. Zhengzhou Huiji District Human Resources and Social Security Bureau (2010), Beida Fabao.* As procedural information is explicitly listed as an exemption in *OGI Regulations 2019*, Chinese courts today can use it as a substantive/legal reason to deny disclosure.

disclosure for NI,[96] 55 cases denied disclosure for NL,[97] 4 cases denied disclosure for NG.[98] In total, in an average of 28.15% of sampled court cases, procedural reasons were cited by courts to support judicial decisions in favor of official agencies. Appellate courts, on the other hand, did a much better job by denying disclosure for procedural reasons in only 7.59% of sampled lawsuits (see Table 7.9). For example, judges ruled in favor of Shandong Normal University at both trial court and appellate court, reasoning that the document sought "is the subject of repeated requests" and the requested file has already been reactively disclosed."[99]

As legal scholar, Weibing Xiao observed, Chinese courts rejected OGI lawsuits by arguing that the requester sent a case to an incorrect jurisdiction[100] or by postponing acceptance.[101] The cases of six law

[96] NI is the code used by the author of this book to create Table 7-9. A "NI" designation means court judges cite the following reasons to support verdicts in favor of non-disclosure: Request is ambiguous and fails to conform to required application format/channel. Request is in essence consulting or filing petitions, accusations or complaints in disguise of applying for governmental information via OGI Regulations. Request contains too many applications. There is no proof of the request being sent by the applicant and/or being received by the entity. Some required application information is missing. The applicant is asking for information that is hard to share for whatever reason. Therefore, the applicant should examine the information in person at a designated government facility.

[97] NL is the code used by the author of this book to create Table 7-9. A "NL" designation means court judges cite the following reasons to support verdicts in favor of non-disclosure: Requested information is the subject of repeated requests, or the sought information is already proactively/reactively disclosed. The applicant intends to overwhelm courts by producing a massive number of OGI lawsuits.

[98] NG is the code used by the author of this book to create Table 7-9. A "NG" designation means court judges cite the following reasons to support verdicts in favor of non-disclosure: Requested information does not exist. Requested information cannot be found.

[99] *Li Mingliang v. Shandong Normal University* [李明亮诉山东师范大学信息公开案] (Shandong Province Ji'nan City Intermediate Court, March 29, 2019). https://wenshu.court.gov.cn/ (registration needed for access) (accessed between February 21, 2025 and March 31, 2025). As *OGI Regulations* were revised in 2019, repeated requests today will be considered by courts as a substantive legal reason to deny disclosure. They are no longer a procedure reason.

[100] Weibing Xiao, Freedom Of Information Reform In China: Information Flow Analysis 115 (2011).

[101] Weibing Xiao, Freedom Of Information Reform In China: Information Flow Analysis 115–116 (2011).

professors,[102] five retired workers[103] and six villagers in Hunan Province are examples of such denials.[104] Courts once denied requests for access to information using reason that the information could not be determined and the plaintiff failed to provide additional materials to specify the information pursued.[105] Chinese courts rejected plaintiffs' petitions simply due to information's being non-governmental, and the courts did not provide any rationales for the decisions.[106]

5. Effectiveness of judicial review in rectifying non-disclosure is questionable.

The previous analyses substantiate the international consensus that judicial review is not effective for rectifying non-compliance of official agencies with legal requirements of reactive disclosure according to freedom of information laws. As international FOI expert, David Banisar, observed, courts are not the most effective mechanisms to ensure governmental compliance with the FOI laws because judicial systems "have significant negative aspects," like being too expensive, time-consuming, deferential to agencies, and having no expertise with practices of agencies like informational commissions or FOI ombudsmen.[107]

The court system confronts additional obstacles in the Chinese context. Under the current Chinese judicial system, the Communist Party, the people's government, the people's congress, and many influential individuals are capable of exerting significant and undue influence on judges.

[102] *Five Xiangtan University Professors v. Hunan Province Xiangtan Municipal Government (2008), Beida Fabao.*

[103] *Five Retired Workers v. Rucheng People's Government (2008), Beida Fabao.*

[104] *Jianqiu Zhang*, et al. *v. Henan Province Chaling County Finance Bureau (2008), Beida Fabao.*

[105] *Zhang*, et al. *v. Shanghai Bureau of Planning, Land and Resources (2010), Beida Fabao; Wang v. Shanghai Municipal Bureau of Human Resources and Social Security (2011), Beida Fabao.*

[106] *Bao v. Shanghai Yangpu District Bureau of Housing (2010), Beida Fabao.*

[107] David Banisar, Effective Open Government: Improving Public Access To.

Government Information 17 (report for Organization for Economic Co-operation and Development, Paris, France), May 29, 2012, *available at* https://papers.ssrn.com/sol3/papers.cfm?abstract_id=2069870# (accessed between February 21, 2025 and March 31, 2025).

Given the fear of possible retribution from officials and other influential stakeholders, most courts are unwilling to accept cases involving official information. Retribution can be withholding political appointments or cutting budgets for courts that show too much independence. For these reasons, courts are reluctant to hear OGI cases. Despite accepting those cases, few judges are willing to render decisions unfavorable to official agencies.[108]

Geographic and Agency Imbalance in the Use of Reactive Disclosure

Before concluding the analysis on the status of the Chinese FOI system for reactive disclosure, it is worthwhile to discuss the geographic and agency imbalance in reactive disclosure.

The geographic imbalance in terms of the number of OGI requests received by official agencies is astonishing. According to the data gathered from annual OGI reports for this study (see Table 7.4), Guangdong Province received the largest number of OGI requests (477,303) among all provinces and other provincial-level regions/cities from 2008 to 2023, having an average number of 29,831 requests submitted per year. In a sharp contrast, Xinjiang Autonomous Region received the smallest number of OGI requests (9,323) during the same period, recording an average of 583 requests per year.

The agency imbalance in terms of the number of OGI requests received and OGI reconsideration cases and litigations filed against different levels of governmental agencies is equally startling. According to the data (see Tables 7.1–7.3), from 2008 to 2023, cabinet-level central agencies received a total number of 401,247 OGI requests; findings for 10,430 OGI reconsideration cases and 3,578 OGI litigations against cabinet-level central governmental agencies under the direct authority of the State Council occurred. By comparison, the use of reactive disclosure was far more prevalent at the lower levels of the Chinese bureaucratic hierarchy. Within the same time period, provincial and lower-level governmental agencies received filings for 5,597,231 OGI applications, 199,438 OGI reconsideration cases, and 156,228 OGI litigations against administrative agencies in provincial to the township levels.

[108] Many Chinese judges refuse to work in the administrative divisions of the courts "because of the politically sensitive nature of the cases." RANDALL PEERENBOOM, CHINA'S LONG MARCH TOWARD RULE OF LAW 399 (2002).

The striking imbalance between central agencies and their provincial/ local counterparts shows that, contrary to expectations among officials for abuse or overuse of *OGI Regulations*, in some regions and at some levels of the bureaucracy, use of the law is actually never or superficial. The reasons are at least threefold: First, a lack of understanding of the freedom of information law among some Chinese citizens forces them to believe that initiating OGI requests, reporting complaints to superior agencies for reconsideration, and suing official agencies for access to information are to be avoided at all cost. Citizens simply do not want to confront powerful officials. Many Chinese officials are hostile to OGI applicants. Officials often consider the information requester to be someone finding fault with the government. Some officials thus do not like people who request information, file administrative reconsideration complaints, or lawsuits. The low awareness of *OGI Regulations* and reluctance to exercise the right of access among many ordinary citizens contribute to the neglected state of the law in some regions.

Second, the low use of reactive disclosure at the central level is attributable to the fact that the public has much less interest in information made or obtained by central governmental agencies because most of that information has nothing to do with ordinary citizens' daily lives and immediate interests. Third, economic development does play a role in promoting government transparency.[109] In the last 16 years, on average, wealthier and more developed provinces, cities and regions such as Guangdong, Beijing, Jiangsu, Shanghai, Shandong and Zhejiang saw far more OGI requests, far more cases for administrative reconsideration, and far more OGI-related lawsuits than poorer areas such as Xinjiang, Xizang, Ningxia, Hebei, Gansu, Qinghai and Guizhou (see Table 7.4). Actually, this finding is consistent with widely held assumptions among Western

[109] Xixin Wang, director of Peking University Center for Public Participation Studies and Supports, may disagree. He argued that the geographical imbalance in the implementation of *OGI Regulations* has nothing to do with economic development. Instead, it depends upon local leaders' truly valuing governmental transparency. Mingyan Wei and Shaofeng Guo, *OGI Regulations Still Encounter Implementation Bottlenecks Four Years After Its Enactment* [信息公开条例实施4年仍遭执行难], BEIJING NEWS, May 15, 2012, http://www.bjnews.com.cn/news/2012/05/15/199113.html (accessed between February 21, 2025 and March 31, 2025).

scholars that higher levels of socio-economic development promote freedom of information.[110]

Lack of Proactive and Reactive Disclosure by National Defense and State Security Agencies

Both the Ministry of National Defense[111] and the Ministry of State Security are subject to *OGI Regulations*. However, both agencies have shown little to no willingness to comply with the proactive and reactive requirements for disclosure. The Ministry of National Defense has created an official website,[112] proactively released certain kinds of information regarding the Chinese military, and established spokesperson system to deal with Chinese and foreign journalists.[113] This ministry trained an initial team of military communicators whose jobs include assisting foreign audiences' understanding of the Chinese military.[114]

Unlike other cabinet-level executive departments in the State Council, the Ministry of National Defense has no OGI sections on its official website. Since 2008, the agency has not released any OGI annual activities' reports; no system exists to allow requesters to apply for information

110 Research conducted by Western scholars found that the financial strength of a city's government in China determines the quality of the city's environmental transparency. In explaining the correlation, the scholars observed, "Establishing the institutions to collect, organize, and disseminate information is costly and remains a low priority for cash-strapped local governments." Peter Lorentzen, Pierre Landry & John Yasuda, *Transparent Authoritarianism? An Analysis of Political and Economic Barriers to Greater Government Transparency in China,* paper accepted for presentation by the American Political Science Association annual meeting, Washington, D.C., September 4, 2010, at 1.

111 Unlike the U.S. Department of Defense and many similar agencies in the world, the Chinese Ministry of National Defense has no power to mobilize and command the armed forces. The power is in the hands of the ruling Communist Party.

112 The Ministry of National Defense, *available at* http://www.mod.gov.cn/ (accessed between February 21, 2025 and March 31, 2025).

113 Peng Wang, *Military Spokespersons Show off Chinese Military's Openness and Confidence* [军事新闻发言人制度展示我军开放与自信], CHINA YOUTH DAILY, November 29, 2013, http://zqb.cyol.com/html/2013-11/29/nw.D110000zgqnb_20131129_2-10.htm (accessed between February 21, 2025 and March 31, 2025).

114 Jie Zheng, *All Branches of Chinese Military Train First Team of Experts in Foreign Publicity* [中国军队培训首批外宣团队 覆盖全军各军兵种], ORIENTAL MORNING POST, republished by Sina News, March 23, 2009, http://mil.news.sina.com.cn/2009-03-23/0825546181.html (accessed between February 21, 2025 and March 31, 2025).

held by the agency. The Ministry of State Security is even more secretive, lacks an official website, has released no annual OGI activities' reports, and established no system to disclose information, proactively and reactively. When talking about the mysterious agency, a *South China Morning Post* article said, "Intelligence agencies are by nature secretive, but China's MSS [Ministry of State Security] seems to operate under a heavier veil of secrecy than most—unlike the CIA or MI6, it does not have an official website, any publicly listed contacts or spokesmen or women."[115]

Understandably, national defense and state security agencies are more secretive than other less sensitive official departments. This does not mean, however, that these agencies should be given blanket authority to deny disclosure of information. Certainly, not all information created or obtained by the Ministry of National Defense and the Ministry of State Security coincides with state secrets. According to law, any national defense and security information, not exempt from *OGI Regulations*, should have prompt release. Otherwise, no accountability accrues to national defense officers and national security officials. These two agencies need to exert stronger commitment to the Chinese people's right to know.

More Transparency Does Not Translate into Less Corruption

This chapter examined the implementation and enforcement of *OGI Regulations* in the last 16 years (2008–2023) in terms of both proactive and reactive disclosure of governmental information in China.

It appears Chinese government has successfully established a system of proactively disclosing standard official information since 2008. Four kinds of official records and files, from less sensitive ones to more sensitive ones, have had affirmative dissemination by agencies from central to township levels throughout the country from 2008 to 2023 via a large variety of communication channels such as official websites, press conferences, and facilities for OGI access. Various levels of agencies compiled OGI guides,

[115] Nectar Gan, *What Do We Actually Know about China's Mysterious Spy Agency?* South China Morning Post, December 22, 2018, https://www.scmp.com/news/china/politics/article/2179179/what-do-we-actually-know-about-chinas-mysterious-spy-agency (accessed between February 21, 2025 and March 31, 2025).

OGI indexes, and OGI annual activities' reports that facilitated proactive disclosure of information. It is reasonable to conclude that the Chinese government has been successful in enforcing the requirements for proactive disclosure requirements according to *OGI Regulations* when it comes to disclosure of information that is standard, routine and uncontroversial.

As for implementation of requirements for reactive disclosure, this chapter found that most OGI applications processed by official agencies at various levels have gained approval from 2008 to 2023. This is a significant achievement for the Chinese government because the Chinese FOI law is weak in statutory language for reactive disclosure of information, although this achievement should be viewed with caution due to the limitations of the data gathered from annual OGI work reports.

In liberal democracies, reduction of government secrecy often leads to less corruption and stronger accountability/governance. In order to find out if similar correlation exits in authoritarian contexts such as China's, the study examined datasets compiled from China's ratings from 2008 to 2023 in Corruption Perception Index (see Table 7.5),[116] Control of

[116] The compiled table is according to the Corruption Perceptions Index provided by Transparency International. Since 1995, Transparency International publishes the Corruption Perceptions Index (CPI). As "the most widely used indicator of corruption worldwide," the index ranks countries annually by perceived levels of public sector-corruption determined by expert assessments and opinion surveys. The index generally defines corruption as "the misuse of public power for private benefit." The CPI ranks 180 countries and territories on a scale from 0 (highly corrupt) to 100 (very clean). *Corruption Perceptions Index*, Transparency International, Berlin, http://www.transparency.org/research/cpi/overview (accessed between February 21, 2025 and March 31, 2025).

Corruption Governance Metric (see Table 7.6),[117] Government Effectiveness Index (see Table 7.7),[118] and Transparency of Government Policymaking Index (see Table 7.8).[119] An analysis of those ratings indicates that the Chinese government has not made remarkable progress in accountability/governance since 2008 when *OGI Regulations* came into force. In some years, the country's bureaucracy became even more corrupt and less accountable than in previous years.

Unlike liberal democracies where transparency promotes accountability, it is clear that China fails to translate its hard-earned authoritarian transparency into greater accountability and better governance. With introduction and enforcement of an unprecedented freedom of information law over a decade to ensure greater transparency, China remains one of the most corrupt countries in the world. This finding is consistent with

[117] The datasets are compiled from the World Bank-sponsored Worldwide Governance Indicators (WGI) project. *Worldwide Governance Indicators*, World Bank Group, Washington, DC, *available at* https://www.worldbank.org/en/publication/worldwide-governance-indicators (accessed between February 21, 2025 and March 31, 2025). The WGI cover over 200 countries and territories, measuring six dimensions of governance starting in 1996 and ending in 2018. Control of Corruption, one of WGI's indicators, captures perceptions of the extent to which public power is exercised for private gain, including both small and big forms of corruption, as well as control of the state by elites and private interests. Governance Score (2.5 to +2.5) is an estimate of quality of governance measured on a scale from approximately 2.5 to +2.5. Higher values correspond to better governance. Percentile Rank (0–100) indicates rank of country among all the countries in the world. 0 corresponds to lowest rank and 100 corresponds to highest rank.

[118] Government Effectiveness is an indicator developed by the World Bank to estimate perceptions of the quality of public services, the quality of the civil service and the degree of its independence from political pressures, the quality of policy formulation and implementation, and the credibility of the government's commitment to such policies. Higher scores correspond to more government effectiveness. Percentile Rank (0–100) indicates rank of country among all the countries in the world. "0" corresponds to lowest rank and "100" corresponds to highest rank. The dataset is compiled from the World Bank website. *Worldwide Governance Indicators*, 2024 Update, World Bank, Washington, DC, *available at*.

https://www.worldbank.org/en/publication/worldwide-governance-indicators (accessed between February 21, 2025 and March 31, 2025).

[119] The number "1" means least transparent and "7" indicates most transparent. The higher the percentile rank, the less transparency. This dataset covered 151 countries in the world from 2007 to 2017. The dataset is compiled from the World Bank website. *Transparency of Government Policymaking, 1–7 (best)*, World Bank, Washington, DC, *available at* https://prosperitydata360.worldbank.org/en/indicator/WEF+GCIHH+EOSQ049 (accessed between February 21, 2025 and March 31, 2025).

prior studies, as a Harvard University scholar said in his study on China's disclosure of environmental information, "[T]he relationship between transparency and accountability is not straightforward in the Chinese context. Contrary to popular expectations, increased transparency has not mapped directly onto improved accountability."[120]

Summary and Conclusion

After analyzing annual OGI work reports published in the last 16 years (2008 to 2023) by the Chinese government at all levels and examining 540 sample OGI-related lawsuits (2014 to 2021), this chapter identified a wide range of enforcement problems that hinder people from having more meaningful access to governmental information.

Government information is most likely to be withheld when it involves public interest and its disclosure may bring officials embarrassment, shame, demotion or even dismissal, as exemplified in various levels' Chinese government agencies' initial mismanagement and cover-up of the novel coronavirus crisis in Wuhan, Hubei Province. The denial of OGI requests prior to processing is unacceptably frustrating. Approval rates for OGI requests among different official agencies are sharply uneven. The use of administrative and judicial remedies displays geographic and bureaucratic imbalance. The percentage of OGI requests in which disclosure of information was denied by agencies and courts for non-legal or procedural reasons is exceedingly high. Courts and government agencies can make non-disclosure decisions for reasons not mentioned in *OGI Regulations* and relevant laws, thus bypassing the FOI legislation. Agencies for administrative reconsideration and courts are basically ineffective in correcting agencies' disclosure-unfriendly decisions and ensuring freer flow of information. The Ministry of National Defense and the Ministry of State Security are faltering in proactively and reactively releasing information. Both agencies are operating in virtually complete darkness.

Despite these egregious shortcomings, the Chinese government has established foundational freedom of information platforms, and its enforcement of proactive and reactive disclosure requirements under the

[120] Yeling Tan, *Transparency Without Democracy: The Unexpected Effects of China's Environmental Disclosure Policy*, 27 Governance: An International Journal Of Policy, Administration, And Institutions 23 (2014), https://doi.org/10.1111/gove.12018 (accessed between February 21, 2025 and March 31, 2025).

law seems more forceful than many Western observers expected. Since 2009, various levels of Chinese government agencies have consistently published annual OGI reports detailing how much government-held information was disclosed proactively and reactively in prior years via a multitude of communication channels. *OGI Regulations* have many inherent problems in statutory language, allowing very limited access to information. Given the law's inadequate promises, its actual delivery is surprising and encouraging.

Overall, China deserves recognition for its determination and accomplishments in freedom of information. Unlike many countries, including even democratic ones, such as the United States in which the federal *Freedom of Information Act* "was weak and rarely used" after initial enactment in 1966,[121] China has had prolific use of *OGI Regulations* since 2008 despite the country having a deeply embedded culture of secrecy. The system established for proactive disclosure has become routinely deployed for most official agencies. Citizens, legal persons, and other organizations have actively sought official information via filing OGI requests. Most OGI requests gained approval. It is particularly significant in that all these accomplishments have been achieved in a decade when the country has abandoned liberalization and democratization and instead become more repressive and authoritarian. Jamie Horsley, long-time observer of China's freedom of information movement, said in a 2019 article, "The People's Republic of China continues to modernize the Chinese regulatory state through its open government project, even as the Chinese Communist Party (CCP) asserts comprehensive leadership and tightens political and social controls under General Secretary Xi Jinping."[122]

When looking ahead, Chinese decision makers must keep three things in mind. First, think about how to address problems discussed in the study. If resolutions to those problems do not have serious vetting, the role of the freedom of information law in eradicating governmental

[121] Robert Freeman, *Thirty Years of FOIL*, 11 GOVERNMENT, LAW & POLICY JOURNAL 4 (2009).

[122] Jamie Horsley, *Open Government Developments in China: Implications for US Businesses*, CHINA BUSINESS REVIEW, para.33–36, US-China Business Council, Washington, DC, July 1, 2019, *available at* https://www.chinabusinessreview.com/open-government-developments-in-china-implications-for-us-businesses/ (accessed between February 21, 2025 and March 31, 2025). Jamie Horsley is a visiting fellow at the Brookings Institution and works at Yale Law School as a senior fellow.

corruption and encouraging democratic participation in decision-making will have significant limits.

Second, think about how to translate greater transparency into better governance. Unlike liberal democracies, where enactment of freedom of information (FOI) laws often leads to reduction of government secrecy, less corruption and stronger accountability, various rankings mentioned in this chapter indicate that China fails to translate its hard-earned authoritarian transparency into accountability and better governance. Despite over a decade of rigorous enforcement of freedom of information law, China remains one of the most corrupt countries in the world.

Third, think about how to strengthen the FOI law that applies to the Chinese Communist Party. Discussed in previous chapters, OGI regulations do not apply to the party. In 2017, the party adopted a transparency code. Similar to *OGI Regulations*, the code requires "the CCP Central Committee—and other party organizations at all levels, including the anti-graft body that has led a wide-ranging anti-corruption campaign—to disclose certain information to party members and, in some circumstances, to the general public."[123] Unlike *OGI Regulations*, the code does not embrace reactive disclosure. Given that the party bureaucracy is far more secretive than government bureaucracy in China, it will be much harder to enforce the code than *OGI Regulations*. How this code has been enforced will be discussed in Chapter 11.

[123] Jamie P. Horsley, *The Chinese Communist Party's Experiment with Transparency: Unpacking the CCP's New Regulations on "Open Party Affairs*, THE DIPLOMAT, para.10–15, February 1, 2018, *available at* https://thediplomat.com/2018/02/the-chinese-communist-partys-experiment-with-transparency/ (accessed between February 21, 2025 and March 31, 2025).

CHAPTER 8

Transparency of Public Enterprises and Institutions in China: A Freedom of Information Law Perspective

Introduction

According to Resolution 59 of the United Nations General Assembly and Article 19 of the Universal Declaration of Human Rights, freedom of information is a fundamental human right.[1] Likewise, many international

[1] *Joint Statement on Freedom of Expression as a Driver of All Other Human Rights on the Occasion of the World Press Freedom Day 2023*, United Nations Educational, Scientific and Cultural Organization, Paris, France, May 2, 2023, *available at* https://www.unesco.org/en/days/press-freedom-2023/joint-statement#:~:text=At%20its%20very%20first%20session,the%20United%20Nations%20is%20consecrated.%E2%80%9D (accessed between February 21, 2025 and March 31, 2025); *Universal Declaration of Human Rights*, United Nations, New York, *available at* https://www.un.org/en/about-us/universal-declaration-of-human-rights (accessed between February 21, 2025 and March 31, 2025).

This chapter is derived from a 2024 AEJMC conference paper presented by the author of this book. Portions of the text in the chapter resemble or may replicate the original text from the paper and have been reproduced as such with the permission of Palgrave Macmillan editors. Yong Tang, *Transparency of Public Enterprises and Institutions in China: A Freedom of Information Law Perspective*, paper accepted for presentation by the annual AEJMC (Association for Education in Journalism and Mass Communication) convention, Philadelphia, Pennsylvania, August 8–11, 2024.

Y. Tang, *Freedom of Information Law in China*,
https://doi.org/10.1007/978-981-96-7842-6_8

organizations have long recognized access to information as a cornerstone human right that all other rights of human beings depend upon.[2] However, even a long-time Western observer of China's human rights in general and freedom of information in particular will find the following lawsuits both intriguing and puzzling:

A farmer in Shandong Province sued State Grid Shandong Province Electric Power Company for failing to disclose information pertaining to technological standards of electricity supply. After losing the lawsuit in a trial court, the plaintiff appealed to an intermediate court in 2016 and finally prevailed. The appellate court's verdict reasoned that technological standard of electricity supply, to an electricity company, is disclosable information under China's national freedom of information law, namely *Regulations of the People's Republic of China on Open Government Information* (*OGI Regulations*).[3]

Peking Union Medical College Hospital, found in 1921 by Rockefeller Foundation, is one of the most prestigious hospitals in Beijing and China today. The health institution was sued in 2015 for failing to disclose its pharmacy information to an applicant. Both the trial court and appellate court ruled against the plaintiff, reasoning that public institutions such as the hospital sued here are proper defendants in administrative litigation, therefore, alleged infringement by the defendant can be reviewed in courts, but the information sought by the plaintiff was not created by the defendant in the process of providing medical and health services to the public.[4]

[2] For detailed analysis of freedom of information from the human rights perspective, see Cheryl Ann Bishop, "Internationalizing the Right to Know: Conceptualizations of Access to Information in Human Rights Law" (2009) (unpublished Ph.D. diss., The University of North Carolina at Chapel Hill); K.M. SHRIVASTAVA, THE RIGHT TO INFORMATION: A GLOBAL PERSPECTIVE (2009); Cheryl Ann Bishop, *The United Nations and Access to Information as a Human Right*, paper presented at the annual meeting of the International Communication Association, Montreal, Quebec, Canada, May 22, 2008.

[3] *Wang Zhenbao v. State Grid Shandong Province Electric Power Company* [王振宝诉国网山东省电力公司信息公开案] (Shandong Province Ji'nan City Intermediate Court, March 8, 2016). https://wenshu.court.gov.cn/ (registration needed for access) (accessed between February 21, 2025 and March 31, 2025).

[4] *Xia Xin v. Peking Union Medical College Hospital* [夏欣诉中国医学科学院北京协和医院信息公开案] (Beijing City No.2 Intermediate Court, May 18, 2015). https://wenshu.court.gov.cn/ (registration needed for access) (accessed between February 21, 2025 and March 31, 2025).

State Grid Nanjing Power Supply Company was sued in 2016 for failing to release information sought by residents of an upscale apartment in Nanjing, Jiangsu Province. When ruling against the defendant, the court said that although the company was neither an administrative organ nor an organization authorized by law to manage public affairs, it should still be distinguished from an ordinary enterprise. The court ruled that the company provides electricity services to the public, was undoubtedly closely related to the people's interests and therefore should be subject to administrative litigation regarding its open information activities.[5]

A port management company in Wenzhou, Zhejiang Province was sued for refusing to disclose its construction of port berths. The appellate court ruled in 2017 that such information is related to the infrastructure projects carried out by a public enterprise for the provision of public services, thus qualifying as disclosable public service information.[6]

A drainage company in Beijing was sued for refusing to disclose information involving the laying of an underground sewage pipe. The appellate court ruled in 2018 that such information is related to the infrastructure projects carried out by a public enterprise for the provision of public services, thus qualifying as public service information.[7]

A customer of a local branch of China Mobile in Jiangsu Province sued the company for non-disclosure of text messages of another customer. The appellate court ruled in 2016 against the plaintiff, concluding that the information sought was private and should be legally protected from being released to any third parties, therefore, the non-disclosure decision made by the defendant was not violating *OGI Regulations*.[8]

[5] *Homeowner Association of Nanjing Fengshang International Apartment v. State Grid. Nanjing Power Supply Company* [南京市锋尚国际公寓住宅小区业主委员会诉国网江苏省电力公司南京供电公司信息公开案] (Jiangsu Province Nanjing Railway Transport Trial Court, July 27, 2016). https://wenshu.court.gov.cn/ (registration needed for access) (accessed between February 21, 2025 and March 31, 2025).

[6] *Yan Xiantong v. Wenzhou Port Group Corporation* [颜贤童诉温州港集团有限公司信息公开案] (Zhejiang Province Wenzhou City Intermediate Court, March 14, 2017). https://wenshu.court.gov.cn/ (registration needed for access) (accessed between February 21, 2025 and March 31, 2025).

[7] *You Hanrui v. Beijing Drainage Group* [尤瀚睿诉北京城市排水集团有限责任公司信息公开案] (Beijing City No. 2 Intermediate Court, May 14, 2018). https://wenshu.court.gov.cn/ (registration needed for access) (accessed between February 21, 2025 and March 31, 2025).

[8] Wang Dejun v. China Mobile Hai'an Branch [王德军诉中国移动通信集团江苏有限公司海安分公司信息公开案] (Jiangsu Province Nantong City Intermediate Court, March 4,

OGI Regulations, widely regarded as China's first national freedom of information law, apply to two categories of entities: Administrative agencies and entities authorized by law to perform the functions of administering public affairs. What is unknown to many Western observers of China's media law development is that the law also applies to another category of entities: Public enterprises and institutions.

Adopted in 2007, *OGI Regulations* provide the following:

> Disclosing information that is made or obtained in the course of providing public services by ***public enterprises and institutions*** that are closely related to the people's interests...shall be done with reference to these Regulations (emphasis added).[9]

Amended in 2019, *OGI Regulations* provide the following:

> Disclosing information that is made or obtained in the course of providing public services to society by ***public enterprises and institutions*** that are closely related to the people's interests...shall be done with reference to relevant laws, regulations and the provisions of the relevant departments in charge or institutions of the State Council... (emphasis added).[10]

To some media law scholars and observers, subjecting non-government entities (e.g., public enterprises and institutions) to the same disclosure standards required for government entities is rarely seen in the world of freedom of information laws. The seemingly novel approach of the

2016). https://wenshu.court.gov.cn/ (registration needed for access) (accessed between February 21, 2025 and March 31, 2025).

[9] *Regulations of the People's Republic of China on Open Government Information*, enacted on April 5, 2007, effective May 1, 2008. Art. 37, *available at* https://law.yale.edu/sites/default/files/documents/pdf/china/ogi_regulations_eng_jph_rev_9-11.pdf (English translation) (accessed between February 21, 2025 and March 31, 2025) and https://law.yale.edu/sites/default/files/documents/pdf/Intellectual_Life/CL-OGI-Regs-Chinese%281%29.pdf (Chinese version) (accessed between February 21, 2025 and March 31, 2025).

[10] *Regulations of the People's Republic of China on Open Government Information*, revised on April 3, 2019, and effective May 15, 2019. Art.55, *available at* https://law.yale.edu/sites/default/files/area/center/china/2022-9-5_jph_rev_ogir.pdf (English translation) (accessed between February 21, 2025 and March 31, 2025) and https://law.yale.edu/sites/default/files/area/center/china/2019-4_ch_revsd_ogi_regulations.pdf (Chinese version) (accessed between February 21, 2025 and March 31, 2025).

Chinese law has drawn Chinese and Western scholars' attention but relevant scholarship is sparse.[11] This chapter will examine the statutory language of *OGI Regulations* with regard to public enterprises and institutions, the provisions of the Supreme Court on relevant lawsuits,[12] the implementation measures passed by the State Council,[13] the implementation measures passed by various ministries on disclosure of information held by various public enterprises and institutions such as universities and colleges,[14] hospitals, family planning institutions and other medical

[11] For relevant English-language literature, see Chun Peng, *Beyond Government Transparency in China? The Challenges to Open Public Enterprises and Institutions*, 16 UNIVERSITY OF PENNSYLVANIA ASIAN LAW REVIEW 214 (2021) (evaluating poor performance of Chinese public Enterprises and Institutions in transparency and proposing some solutions); Paula Hubbard & Xiao Weibing, *Open Government Information in Chinese State-owned Enterprises*, 22 I/S: A JOURNAL OF LAW AND POLICY FOR THE INFORMATION SOCIETY 57 (2017) (discussing the haphazard implementation of China's open government information law with respect to its state-owned enterprises). The Chinese-language scholarship on this issue is also quite scanty.

[12] The Provisions of the Supreme Court on Several Issues Involving OGI Regulations-Related Lawsuits [最高人民法院关于审理政府信息公开行政案件若干问题的规定] (effective on August 13, 2011), *available at* http://gongbao.court.gov.cn/Details/61bd00a77cc0e399c4302b230aff84.html (accessed between February 21, 2025 and March 31, 2025).

[13] Implementation Measures of the State Council for Formulating Information Disclosure Provision Regarding Public Enterprises and Institutions [国务院办公厅《公共企事业单位信息公开规定制定办法》](effective on January 1, 2021), *available at* https://www.chinalawtranslate.com/en/public-enterprise-institution-ogi/ (English translation) (accessed between February 21, 2025 and March 31, 2025) and https://www.gov.cn/zhengce/content/2020-12/21/content_5571847.htm (Chinese version) (accessed between February 21, 2025 and March 31, 2025).

[14] The Implementation Measures of the Ministry of Education on Disclosure of Information Held by Universities and Colleges [教育部《高等学校信息公开办法》](effective on September 1, 2010), *available at* https://www.gov.cn/flfg/2010-05/11/content_1603696.htm (accessed between February 21, 2025 and March 31, 2025).

care institutions,[15] water supply, gas supply and heating supply companies and institutions,[16] electricity supply companies and institutions,[17]

[15] The Implementation Measures of the Ministry of Health on Disclosure of Information Held by Hospitals and Other Medical Care Institutions [卫生部《医疗卫生服务单位信息公开管理办法》(试行)](effective on August 1, 2010), *available at* https://www.gov.cn/gongbao/content/2010/content_1730705.htm (accessed between February 21, 2025 and March 31, 2025); The Implementation Measures of the National Health Commission, the National Administration of Traditional Chinese Medicine and the National Administration of Disease Control and Prevention on Disclosure of Information Held by Hospitals and Other Health Care Providers [国家卫生健康委、国家中医药局和国家疾控局《医疗卫生机构信息公开管理办法》(effective on February 1, 2022), *available at* https://www.gov.cn/zhengce/zhengceku/2022-01/05/content_5666487.htm (accessed between February 21, 2025 and March 31, 2025); The Implementation Measures of the National Population and Family Planning Commission on Disclosure of Information Held by Population and Family Planning Service Providers [国家人口计生委《人口和计划生育技术服务机构信息公开办法》](试行)(effective on February 3, 2009), *available at* http://www.nhc.gov.cn/zwgkzt/pzcyj/201310/b5d98f82992b47a2955c52d057723eb6.shtml (accessed between February 21, 2025 and March 31, 2025); The Implementation Measures of the National Population and Family Planning Commission on Disclosure of Information (for Trial Implementation) [人口计生委《政府信息公开规定(试行)](effective on May 20, 2008), *available at* http://www.nhc.gov.cn/zwgk/wtwj/201305/4d9d6793bb1a4b22b151244ee00faed3.shtml (accessed between February 21, 2025 and March 31, 2025).

[16] The Implementation Measures of the Ministry of Housing and Urban-Rural Development on Disclosure of Information Held By Water Supply, Gas Supply and Heating Supply Companies [住房和城乡建设部《供水、供气、供热等公共企事业单位信息公开实施办法》](effective on February 1, 2022), *available at* https://www.gov.cn/zhengce/zhengceku/2022-01/12/content_5667816.htm (accessed between February 21, 2025 and March 31, 2025).

[17] The Implementation Measures of the National Energy Administration on Disclosure of Information Held By Electricity Supply Companies [国家能源局《供电企业信息公开实施办法》](effective on November 23, 2021), *available at* https://www.gov.cn/zhengce/zhengceku/2021-12/08/content_5659272.htm (accessed between February 21, 2025 and March 31, 2025).

environmental protection companies and institutions,[18] and public transportation companies and institutions.[19] After identifying patterns of problems and inconsistencies in the statutory language of various legislations mentioned above, the chapter will explore how the legislations have been implemented since 2008 to hold public enterprises and institutions accountable. In particular, the chapter will explore how public enterprises and institutions release information proactively, how they manage OGI requests, how appeals and administrative reconsiderations are handled, how court judges review lawsuits and make judicial decisions. In the conclusion section, major weaknesses will be discussed and suggestions for solutions will be proposed.

David Banisar, an internationally acclaimed freedom of information law expert, finds nine common features of global freedom of information laws: Types of governmental bodies covered, accessibility, identity of those allowed access, exemptions, appeals and oversight, sanctions, affirmative publication, e-FOI, and accusations of malfeasance.[20] This chapter will use some of those common features to examine the Chinese FOI law with regard to public enterprises and institutions. Additional common

[18] The Implementation Measures of the State Environmental Protection Administration on Disclosure of Environmental Information [国家环境保护总局《环境信息公开办法》(试行)](effective on May 1, 2008), *available at* https://www.gov.cn/flfg/2007-04/20/content_589673.htm (accessed between February 21, 2025 and March 31, 2025); The Implementation Measures of the Ministry of Ecology and Environment on Disclosure of Information Held by Public Environmental Protection Institutions [生态环境部《环境保护公共事业单位信息公开实施办法(试行)](effective on October 1, 2010), *available at* https://www.mee.gov.cn/gkml/hbb/bwj/201007/t20100727_192655.htm (accessed between February 21, 2025 and March 31, 2025); The Implementation Measures of the Ministry of Environmental Protection on Disclosure of Information Held by Environmental Protection Enterprises and Institutions [环境保护部《企业事业单位环境信息公开办法》] (effective on January 1, 2015), *available at* https://www.gov.cn/gongbao/content/2015/content_2838171.htm (accessed between February 21, 2025 and March 31, 2025).

[19] The Implementation Measures of the Ministry of Transport on Disclosure of Information Held by Public Transportation Enterprises [交通运输部《公共交通企业信息公开规定》](effective on April 1, 2022), *available at*.
https://www.gov.cn/gongbao/content/2022/content_5692858.htm (accessed between February 21, 2025 and March 31, 2025).

[20] David Banisar, Freedom Of Information Around The World 2006: A Global Survey Of Access To Government Information Laws 20–26 (report for Privacy International, London, United Kingdom, July 2006), *available at* http://www.freedominfo.org/documents/global_survey2006.pdf (accessed between February 21, 2025 and March 31, 2025).

features of world freedom of information laws such as legal authority and legislative purpose will also be investigated.

Legal Authority and Standing

According to *Legislation Law 2000,* there are four tiers of Chinese laws: The *Constitution,* adopted and amended by the National People's Congress, enjoys the highest level of legal authority. An act or law, adopted and amended by the National People's Congress or the standing committee of the National People's Congress, represents the second level of legal authority. Regulations, divided into administrative regulations, local regulations, autonomous regulations and separate regulations, represent the third level of legal authority. This third tier of laws is from the State Council or local people's congresses and cannot override a law. Administrative rules represent the fourth level of legal authority, and are actions of state organs, provincial governments, or governments in comparatively larger cities.[21]

OGI Regulations are administrative regulations enacted by the State Council, representing the third tier of Chinese law. The OGI implementation measures passed by the State Council and various central government ministries/administrations are administrative rules, representing the fourth tier of Chinese law. Since *OGI Regulations* have only one article related to public enterprises and institutions,[22] most legal authority for requirements of public enterprises and institutions to be transparent comes from the fourth tier of Chinese law. This creates a weaker legal basis for them to comply with *OGI Regulations*.

What makes things worse is the exact wording of the law. Both Article 37 of the *2007 OGI Regulations* and Article 55 of the 2019 amendment made clear that information disclosure by public enterprises and institutions "shall be done *with reference to* these Regulations" instead of "shall be done *according to* these Regulations."[23] The statutory language of the OGI Regulations demonstrates that public enterprises and institutions are only encouraged or advised to adhere to the legal requirements of *OGI*

[21] *Legislation Law 2000*. Art. 78, 79, 80, 81, 82, *available at* https://www.gov.cn/xinwen/2023-03/14/content_5746569.htm (accessed between February 21, 2025 and March 31, 2025).

[22] *OGI Regulations 2007*. Art. 37; *OGI Regulations Amendment 2019*. Art. 55.

[23] *OGI Regulations 2007*. Art. 37. *OGI Regulations Amendment 2019*. Art. 55.

Regulations, unlike administrative agencies and authorized entities that must comply with the law.

Legislative Purpose and Principle

In stating the legislative purpose and principle, the State Council OGI Implementation Measures provide the following:

> In order to establish and improve the information disclosure system of public enterprises and institutions, further promote the information disclosure of public enterprises and institutions, strengthen the supervision and management of public enterprises and institutions, improve the service level of public enterprises and institutions, better protect the vital interests of the people, and help optimize the business environment, these Measures are hereby formulated in accordance with the relevant stipulations of the Regulations of the People's Republic of China on Open Government Information.[24]

Unlike *OGI Regulations*, which are reluctant to explicitly embrace the concept of the people's right to know in its statutory language, the OGI implementation measures adopted by the State Council seem willing to adopt such a concept. With that being said, the State Council implementation measures embrace the public's right to know only half-heartedly. The Chinese Constitution embraces both elective democracy (via the people's congress system) and participatory democracy (through various channels and in various ways). It should have become the constitutional basis for the OGI Regulations and State Council OGI Implementation Measures. Unfortunately, both the legislations fail to address the constitutional perspective on open public enterprises and institutions. Instead, lawmakers explain the rationales of the law more from a business management and economic growth perspective.

[24] Implementation Measures of the State Council for Formulating Information Disclosure Provision Regarding Public Enterprises and Institutions [国务院办公厅《公共企事业单位信息公开规定制定办法》](effective on January 1, 2021), ***available at*** https://www.chinalawtranslate.com/en/public-enterprise-institution-ogi/ (English translation) (accessed between February 21, 2025 and March 31, 2025); https://www.gov.cn/zhengce/content/2020-12/21/content_5571847.htm (Chinese version (accessed between February 21, 2025 and March 31, 2025).

Types of Bodies Covered

According to *OGI Regulations* and *State Council OGI Implementation Measures*, types of bodies covered under the national freedom of information law in China range from public enterprises to public institutions. Public enterprises are among more than 150,000 state-owned enterprises (SEOs).[25] The 1.26 million public institutions are all fully or partly funded by the government and include all public schools, universities, clinics, hospitals, libraries, performing groups, research institutes and media organizations.[26]

Not all the public enterprises and public institutions have to comply with the legal requirements of *OGI Regulations*. According to the State Council measures, Only the following entities have a legal obligation for information disclosure: "[P]ublic enterprises and institutions that have a dominant market position, have a relatively strong public nature, and are directly related to the people's physical health and safety, or public enterprises and institutions that have prominent information asymmetries with service targets and require a focus on strengthened regulation."[27]

Although the FOI law fails to give a clear definition of the term "public enterprises and institutions," it does enumerate a long list of entities that carry the legal burden of information disclosure: Universities and colleges, hospitals, family planning institutions and other medical care institutions, water supply, gas supply and heating supply companies and institutions, electricity supply companies and institutions, environmental protection companies and institutions, and public transportation companies and institutions.

[25] Tianyu Wang, *Explainer: Why Does China Have So Many State-Owned Enterprises*, China Global Television Network, June 14, 2021, https://news.cgtn.com/news/2021-06-14/Explainer-Why-China-has-so-many-state-owned-enterprises-115vt8ntcZ2/index.html (accessed between February 21, 2025 and March 31, 2025).

[26] *Redefining Public Institutions*, Beijing Review, republished by China.org.cn, May 23, 2012, *available at* http://www.china.org.cn/opinion/2012-05/23/content_25450895.htm (accessed between February 21, 2025 and March 31, 2025).

[27] Implementation Measures of the State Council for Formulating Information Disclosure Provision Regarding Public Enterprises and Institutions [国务院办公厅《公共企事业单位信息公开规定制定办法》] (effective on January 1, 2021) (Art.4), *available at* https://www.chinalawtranslate.com/en/public-enterprise-institution-ogi/ (English translation) (accessed between February 21, 2025 and March 31, 2025); https://www.gov.cn/zhengce/content/2020-12/21/content_5571847.htm (Chinese version) (accessed between February 21, 2025 and March 31, 2025).

Colleges and universities: As of 2022, China has 3,013 universities and colleges. More than 75% of universities and colleges are funded by the government and they enroll 80 percent of students in the country.[28] Unlike the United States where most prestigious universities are private, China is a country where most prestigious colleges are public.

Hospitals, family planning institutions and other medical care institutions: As of 2022, China has 37,000 hospitals and 32% of them are public.[29] Although the percentage of public hospitals seems low, nationwide they admit 84% of patients.[30]

Water supply, gas supply, heating supply and electricity supply companies and institutions: Chinese cities have numerous state-owned utility companies focusing on providing water, gas, heating, electricity services to tens of millions of their customers. Some utility companies are among the world's largest corporations. For example, the State Grid Corporation of China is the largest utility company in the world. As of 2022, State Grid is the world's third largest company overall by revenue, behind only Walmart and Saudi Aramco.[31]

Public transportation companies and institutions: It is hard to even do a rough estimate on the total number of public transportation companies and institutions in China. Numerous state-owned companies focus on providing their urban and rural customers with public transportation services. Tens of millions of people move in and out of the country daily by riding on busses, trolley busses, taxis, subways, highways, railways, ferries, and airplanes.

28 *Report in 2022 on National Development in Education* [2022年全国教育事业发展统计公报], the Ministry of Education, Beijing, China, *available at* http://www.moe.gov.cn/jyb_sjzl/sjzl_fztjgb/202307/t20230705_1067278.html (accessed between February 21, 2025 and March 31, 2025).

29 *Health and Physical Education in 2022* [2022年卫生健康和体育], the National Bureau of Statistics, Beijing, China, *available at* https://www.gov.cn/guoqing/2023-03/10/content_5745876.htm (accessed between February 21, 2025 and March 31, 2025).

30 *National Bureau of Statistics: Health Institutions Nationwide Admit 8.4 Billion Patients in 2022* [国家统计局:2022年医疗卫生机构总诊疗人次数达84亿人次], Sohu, Beijing, China, March 2, 2023, https://www.sohu.com/a/648495618_121118853 (accessed between February 21, 2025 and March 31, 2025).

31 *Fortune Global 500*, FORTUNE MAGAZINE, *available at* https://fortune.com/ranking/global500/ (accessed between February 21, 2025 and March 31, 2025).

Public companies and institutions that work on environmental protection: Numerous state-owned enterprises specialize in water treatment, waste incineration, hazardous waste storage, utilization and disposal, urban sanitation, environment protection equipment manufacturing, and other environmental protection services. According to a study, 185 publicly traded environmental protection companies in China, many of which are state-owned enterprises, generated total revenue of $59 billion in 2020.[32]

What Information Is Accessible

According to the Chinese FOI law and relevant implementation measures, public enterprises and institutions should disclose information that is produced and/or obtained in the process of providing public services. The State Council measures list the following information as disclosable:

> (1) Service information closely related to the daily production and livelihood of the people.
> (2) Information that has a relatively great impact on the business environment.
> (3) Information directly related to the vital interests of service targets.
> (4) Information related to production safety and consumers' personal and property safety.
> (5) Information of high concern to public opinion and that reflects more issues.
> (6) Other important information that shall be disclosed.[33]

[32] Ruichi Yi, *Most Comprehensive Survey: Revenues of 198 Publicly-Traded Environmental Protection Companies in 2020* [最全盘点!涉198家!环保上市公司2020年业绩大榜], China Shuiwang [中国水网], Beijing, China, May 31, 2021, *available at* https://www.h2o-china.com/news/324142.html (accessed between February 21, 2025 and March 31, 2025).

[33] Implementation Measures of the State Council for Formulating Information Disclosure Provision Regarding Public Enterprises and Institutions [国务院办公厅《公共企事业单位信息公开规定制定办法》](effective on January 1, 2021 (Art. 7) https://www.chinalawtranslate.com/en/public-enterprise-institution-ogi/ (English translation) (accessed between February 21, 2025 and March 31, 2025); https://www.gov.cn/zhengce/content/2020-12/21/content_5571847.htm (Chinese version) (accessed between February 21, 2025 and March 31, 2025).

Like *OGI Regulations* and *State Council OGI Implementation Measures*, the implementation measures of various central government agencies (e.g., ministries and administrations) enumerate long lists of information that should be proactively released without requests being necessary. But after a close reading of the full texts of those measures, this chapter identified two major weaknesses of those measures regarding what information is accessible:

First, the measures adopted by central government agencies are, in general, less progressive and transparency-friendly than the State Council measures. Most information on the lists of affirmative disclosure is about daily operations of public enterprises and institutions, such as basic company facts, contact information, standard procedures and policies, organizational structures, and leadership profiles.

Second, the measures adopted by central government agencies tend to prioritize disclosure of information regarding achievements and accomplishments. Very few measures prioritize disclosure of information involving potential problems and mismanagement and information regarding how money is earned and spent by public enterprises and institutions. No measures mention anything about disclosure of information involving salaries and personal assets of leaders from those public enterprises and institutions. This shortcoming is not surprising at all, given that *OGI Regulations* fail to say anything about the disclosure of personal assets.

Affirmative and Reactive Disclosure of Information

The State Council OGI Implementation Measures and measures adopted by various central government agencies all mandate a legal duty for eligible public enterprises and institutions to release, timely and proactively, certain categories of information.

In order to ensure public enterprises and institutions' compliance with proactive disclosure requirements, the implementation measures by the State Council and various central government agencies provide various methods and procedures for disclosure. First, public enterprises and institutions are required to compile catalogues listing information to be disclosed. Disclosure of information on the catalogues should be proposed, verified, approved and disseminated. Second, public enterprises and institutions are compelled to disseminate information via various traditional and new communication channels such as company websites, annual reports, campus media, meeting minutes, public libraries, information bulletin boards, press conferences, news outlets, and smartphone apps.

The implementation measures provide that public enterprises and institutions should affirmatively disclose information in a timely manner, but none of them specify a clear-cut time limit for disclosure, which differs sharply from *OGI Regulations* that establish a time limit of 20 working days since the creation of the information for affirmative dissemination.[34]

Can Chinese citizens apply for disclosure of information held by public enterprises and institutions? It depends upon when the application is made. Reactive disclosure of information held by public enterprises and institutions had definitely been permissible during the time span from May 2008 to May 2019. After *OGI Regulations* were revised in May 2019, the role of reactive disclosure becomes more uncertain as the following paragraph was added to the law:

> If the public enterprises and institutions...fail to disclose the information...citizens, legal persons or other organizations may appeal to the relevant departments in charge or organizations and offices, and the department or organization of office that accepts the appeal should investigate and handle it in a timely manner and notify the appellant of the result of the handling.[35]

The role of reactive disclosure was further reduced when the implementation measures regarding disclosure of information held by public enterprises and institutions was adopted by the State Council in December 2020 and went into effect in January 2021. The State Council measures provide the following:

[34] *OGI Regulations 2007* (amended in 2019). Art. 26.

[35] Regulations of the People's Republic of China on Open Government Information, revised April 3, 2019, and effective May 15, 2019. Art.55. *Open Government Information in China*, Yale University Law School China Center, New Haven, Connecticut, *available at* https://law.yale.edu/sites/default/files/area/center/china/2022-9-5_jph_rev_ogir.pdf (English translation) (accessed between February 21, 2025 and March 31, 2025) and https://law.yale.edu/sites/default/files/area/center/china/2019-4_ch_revsd_ogi_regulations.pdf (Chinese version) (accessed between February 21, 2025 and March 31, 2025).

> The method of information disclosure by public enterprises and institutions shall mainly be proactive disclosure and, *in principle, disclosure on request shall not be adopted*. Where public enterprise and institution information disclosure provisions do provide for disclosure on request, such matters as the deadline for handling, processing methods, and supervision and relief channels shall be specified to ensure that the procedures for disclosure on request are operable (emphasis added).[36]

A huge mess has hence been created today regarding the legal status of "disclosure upon request" since the enactment of the above State Council measures. Some implementation measures created by central government agencies still allow reactive disclosure because they were adopted prior to 2021 and have not been amended to reflect the principle of the State Council measures. Some central government agency measures no longer permit any information applications. Some other central government agency measures stand in the middle, meaning that people are still allowed to apply for information, but they can no longer sue public enterprises and institutions for non-disclosure. The only remedy for non-disclosure is to appeal to an oversight government agency.

The special needs test was removed from the Chinese FOI law when the legislation was revised in 2019, meaning that information requesters no longer need to demonstrate what they intend to seek is relevant to their special needs of personal production, livelihood and scientific research. Some OGI implementation measures regarding disclosure of information held by public enterprises and institutions still require applicants to demonstrate a special need, ignoring the remarkable change in the FOI law. The Ministry of Education implementation measures are among such legislations and have not revised to reflect the change.[37]

[36] Implementation Measures of the State Council for Formulating Information Disclosure Provision Regarding Public Enterprises and Institutions [国务院办公厅《公共企事业单位信息公开规定制定办法》](effective on January 1, 2021 (Art. 5), *available at* https://www.chinalawtranslate.com/en/public-enterprise-institution-ogi/ (English translation) (accessed between February 21, 2025 and March 31, 2025) and https://www.gov.cn/zhengce/content/2020-12/21/content_5571847.htm (Chinese version) (accessed between February 21, 2025 and March 31, 2025).

[37] The Implementation Measures of the Ministry of Education on Disclosure of Information Held by Universities and Colleges [教育部《高等学校信息公开办法》](effective on September 1, 2010) (Art. 9), *available at* https://www.gov.cn/flfg/2010-05/11/content_1603696.htm (accessed between February 21, 2025 and March 31, 2025).

What Information Is Exempt from Disclosure

OGI Regulations exempt from disclosure information involving state security, public security, economic security, social stability, commercial secrets and personal privacy.[38] In that spirit, the State Council implementation measures provide the following:

> Public enterprise and institution information disclosure provisions shall properly handle the relationship between information disclosure and other important interests such as state secrets, public security, industrial security, commercial secrets and personal information protection, and pay attention to distinguishing information disclosure from business inquiry services.[39]

Exemptions mentioned above can be seen in all the implementation measures adopted by various central government agencies. Problems with those exemptions are even more obvious in the context of public enterprises and institutions. What is state security, public security, industrial security, economic security, social stability, commercial secrets, and personal privacy? None of the terms listed here are defined in China's *FOIA* and other relevant laws and regulations. Such relevant laws and regulations include *Law on Guarding State Secrets 1988*, *Civil Servants Law 2005*, *Counter-Espionage Law 2014*, *National Security Law 2015*, *Cybersecurity Law 2016*, and *National Intelligence Law 2017*. After a close reading of those laws and regulations, the author of this book is unable to find even minimally sufficient definitions of those terms. Lack of definitions of those confusing terms create huge potential for public enterprises and institutions to avoid disseminating information that could cause them any political or legal troubles.

In fact, since Xi Jinping came to power in 2013, China has begun to pay more attention to national security even in the world of business.

[38] *OGI Regulations 2007*. Art. 8. Art. 23. When being amended in 2019, *OGI Regulations* added internal working documents and pre-decisional information as additional exemptions.

[39] Implementation Measures of the State Council for Formulating Information Disclosure Provision Regarding Public Enterprises and Institutions [国务院办公厅《公共企事业单位信息公开规定制定办法》](effective on January 1, 2021 (Art. 11), *available at* https://www.chinalawtranslate.com/en/public-enterprise-institution-ogi/ (English translation) (accessed between February 21, 2025 and March 31, 2025) and https://www.gov.cn/zhengce/content/2020-12/21/content_5571847.htm (Chinese version) (accessed between February 21, 2025 and March 31, 2025).

In 2014, he clearly identified 16 types of security in his "comprehensive national security" campaign. They include political security, territorial security, military security, economic security, cultural security, societal security, technological security, cyber security, ecological security, resource security, nuclear security, security of overseas interests, biosecurity, space security, polar security and deep-sea security. After examining the intent and ramifications of the newly defined national security strategy of China, two China watchers in Europe said in a study report, "Xi has made national security into a core component of party ideology, a state doctrine that permeates all aspects of China's governance."[40] Another China expert said recently to CNN, "Everything in Xi's PRC is national security and there is an intensifying focus on better coordinating security and development, with the security side winning out over the economics side it appears."[41]

The "security first" paradigm in state governance and Xi's enchantment with the securitization of everything probably explains in part why the exemption clauses in some of the implementation measures contain so many words ending with "security."[42] This paradigm change in state governance will definitely have negative impact on the process of law-making and law enforcement. It will leave enforcement of the measures to the whims of people from public enterprises and institutions. In a political climate of prioritizing security over everything else, public enterprises and institutions would err on the side of caution when they perform the balancing act of meeting the legal requirements of proactive dissemination while also pondering potential political and security risks of disclosure.

[40] Katja Drinhausen and Helena Legarda, *"Comprehensive National Security" Unleashed: How Xi's Approach Shapes China's Policies at Home and Abroad*, The Mercator Institute for China Studies (MERICS), Berlin, Germany, September 15, 2022, *available at* https://www.merics.org/en/report/comprehensive-national-security-unleashed-how-xis-approach-shapes-chinas-policies-home-and (accessed between February 21, 2025 and March 31, 2025).

[41] Nectar Gan, *Xi Jinping Tells China's National Security Chiefs to Prepare for "Worst Case" Scenarios*, CNN, June 1, 2023, https://www.cnn.com/2023/05/31/china/china-xi-national-security-meeting-intl-hnk/index.html (accessed between February 21, 2025 and March 31, 2025).

[42] The word "security" is used 18 times in the implementation measures of the Ministry of Transport. The Implementation Measures of the Ministry of Transport on Disclosure of Information Held by Public Transportation Enterprises [交通运输部《公共交通企业信息公开规定》] (effective on April 1, 2022), *available at.*

https://www.gov.cn/gongbao/content/2022/content_5692858.htm (accessed between February 21, 2025 and March 31, 2025).

Administrative and Judicial Remedies

Prior to the 2019 amendment of *OGI Regulations 2007*, citizens aggrieved by non-disclosure decisions made by public enterprises and institutions may pursue three different options: First, they can appeal to the relevant supervisory administrative departments. Second, apply for administrative reconsideration of the decisions. Third, bring public enterprises and institutions to court for judicial relief. When *OGI Regulations* were revised in 2019, administrative reconsideration and administrative litigation, the two previous remedies, are almost no longer available. The only remedy available is appeal. The applicant can do nothing more as soon as his/her appeal to the supervisory or oversight government agency is denied. The role of administrative reconsideration and administrative lawsuits involving public enterprises and institutions was further eroded in 2020 when the State Council implementation measures were passed to include the following paragraph: "The method of supervising public enterprise and institution information disclosure shall be mainly through appeals to the departments in charge at all levels, and in principle shall not include applying for administrative reconsideration or filing administrative litigation."[43]

Like the implementation measures adopted by the State Council and various central government agencies, the Supreme Court is also not supportive of using administrative litigation to pry open secrecy of public enterprises and institutions. According to a Supreme Court interpretation that came into force in 2011, public enterprises and institutions cannot be sued for violations of *OGI Regulations*.[44]

[43] The State Council Implementation Measures for Formulating Information Disclosure Provision Regarding Public Enterprises and Institutions [国务院办公厅《公共企事业单位信息公开规定制定办法》](effective on January 1, 2021 (Art. 8), *available at* https://www.chinalawtranslate.com/en/public-enterprise-institution-ogi/ (English translation) (accessed between February 21, 2025 and March 31, 2025) and https://www.gov.cn/zhengce/content/2020-12/21/content_5571847.htm (Chinese version) (accessed between February 21, 2025 and March 31, 2025).

[44] The Provisions of the Supreme Court on Several Issues Involving OGI Regulations-Related Lawsuits [最高人民法院关于审理政府信息公开行政案件若干问题的规定](effective on August 13, 2011), *available at* http://gongbao.court.gov.cn/Details/61bd00a77cc0e399c4302b230aff84.html (accessed between February 21, 2025 and March 31, 2025).

Sanctions on Officials for Violations

OGI Regulations include detailed provisions for imposing sanctions on public authorities and employees for violating the law.[45] Administrative sanctions,[46] civil and criminal penalties may accrue to official agencies, agencies' leaders who are responsible for OGI activities and relevant employees if they violate provisions of *OGI Regulations*.

Likewise, according to various implementation measures, penalty can be imposed on public enterprises and institutions that fail to comply with the legal requirements of the FOI law. However, the implementation measures are not clear about supervision and accountability. Article 9 of the State Council measures is the only provision that mandates accountability on the part of public enterprises and institutions that violate the law:

> Public enterprise and institution information disclosure provisions shall include special responsibility clauses, and implementing responsibility shall be strengthened by means of circulating notices of criticism, ordering correction of the situation, and administrative punishments.[47]

The law does not say anything about what would constitute "administrative punishments." It does not say anything either about how the investigation will proceed and what administrative penalties could apply to what violations. We can only assume that the following punishments would be imposed in the event of a violation according to the Administrative Punishments Law: (1) Warnings and circulating a notice of criticism; (2) Fines and confiscation of illegal proceeds or property; (3) Suspending or revoking a license and reduction of qualification levels;

[45] *OGI Regulations 2007*. Art. 34. The 2019 amendment has similar provisions.

[46] There are six kinds of administrative disciplinary measures: warning, record of a demerit, record of a serious demerit, demotion, removal from office and discharge from public employment. *Administrative Supervision Law 1997*. Art.24; *Civil Servants Law* 2005. Art.56.

[47] The State Council Implementation Measures for Formulating Information Disclosure Provision Regarding Public Enterprises and Institutions [国务院办公厅《公共企事业单位信息公开规定制定办法》](effective on January 1, 2021 (Art.9), *available at* https://www.chinalawtranslate.com/en/public-enterprise-institution-ogi/ (English translation) (accessed between February 21, 2025 and March 31, 2025) and https://www.gov.cn/zhengce/content/2020-12/21/content_5571847.htm (Chinese version) (accessed between February 21, 2025 and March 31, 2025).

(4) Ordering the suspension of production or business, and punishments of restricting the development of production and operational activities, ordering business closure and restricting employment; (5) Administrative detention; (6) Other administrative punishments provided by Laws and Regulations.[48]

Enforcement of Transparency Law Holding Public Enterprises and Institutions Accountable

1. Proactive Disclosure

This chapter will now examine how Chinese public enterprises and institutions are complying with the proactive disclosure provision of the FOI law. This project examined Tsing Hua University and Peking University to see how the two most prestigious colleges in China are complying with the proactive disclosure requirements of *OGI Regulations* and if a mechanism for reactive disclosure has been established. It was found that both universities have maintained a website where all OGI-related information can be found easily. Such information includes relevant legislations, annual OGI reports, annual budgets and final accounts, leadership profiles, OGI guidelines, and procedures for complaints and appeals. Anyone can download a form from the website and use it to apply for information that is not proactively released.[49] This finding contradicts sharply with another scholar who argued that none of the most prestigious universities in China disclosed their annual budget information to the public.[50]

[48] Administrative Punishments Law of People's Republic of China [中华人民共和国行政处罚法] (effective on July 15, 2021) (Art.9), *available at* http://www.xinhuanet.com/politics/2021-01/23/c_1127015256.htm (accessed between February 21, 2025 and March 31, 2025).

[49] *OGI Website*, Tsinghua University, Beijing, China, *available at* https://www.tsinghua.edu.cn/zjqh/xxgk1.htm (accessed between February 21, 2025 and March 31, 2025); *OGI Website*, Peking University, Beijing, China, *available at* https://xxgk.pku.edu.cn/ (accessed between February 21, 2025 and March 31, 2025).

[50] Chun Peng, *Beyond Government Transparency in China? The Challenges to Open Public Enterprises and Institutions*, 16 University Of Pennsylvania Asian Law Review 224–225 (2021).

A similar survey was done to explore how Peking Union Medical College Hospital and West China Hospital of Sichuan University are disclosing information. It was found that the two preeminent health institutions provide some OGI-related information on their websites. The former hospital publishes information such as its own OGI implementation measures, bidding notices, annual budgets, and final accounts. The latter hospital publicizes such information as its basic facts, relevant OGI statutes, prices for different medical services, and press releases. Unlike the former hospital that allows downloads of a form for information requests, the latter hospital does not publish an OGI request form although contact information for processing information requests is listed on its website.[51]

Nanjing Water Group Corporation and Shenyang Water Group Corporation are two large-scale public enterprises that deal with city water supply and wastewater treatment. The OGI website of the Nanjing-based company features quarterly, half-yearly, and annual OGI reports and surprisingly lists salaries of its leading officers. OGI-related information involving all its subsidiary companies can be found from there as well. The Shenyang-based company has a similar but much less detailed website where visitors can find the following OGI information: Leadership profiles, organizational charts, hiring announcements, and annual total revenues.[52] This finding is inconsistent with another scholar who examined water companies for 31 provinces in China and did not find one single company that published its annual OGI report.[53]

However, a major flaw of the Nanjing-based water company is that its official website has anti-hacking protection which may deny access requests from visitors whose IP addresses are outside of China. The

[51] *OGI Website*, Peking Union Medical College Hospital, Beijing, China, *available at* http://www.cams.ac.cn/xxgk/xxgkzd/index.htm (accessed between February 21, 2025 and March 31, 2025); *OGI Website*, West China Hospital of Sichuan University, Chengdu, China, *available at* https://www.wchscu.cn/xxgk.html (accessed between February 21, 2025 and March 31, 2025).

[52] *OGI Website*, Nanjing Water Group Corporation, Nanjing, China, *available at* https://www.jlwater.com/portalSection/10000165 (accessed between February 21, 2025 and March 31, 2025); *OGI Website*, Shenyang Water Group Corporation, Shenyang, China, available at https://www.syswgw.com/swgk?id=39 (accessed between February 21, 2025 and March 31, 2025).

[53] Chun Peng, *Beyond Government Transparency in China? The Challenges to Open Public Enterprises and Institutions*, 16 University Of Pennsylvania Asian Law Review 224 (2021).

author of this book experienced similar obstacles when trying to access from the United States some government websites in China. Most of the time, my friends in China can easily access those websites while I was not so lucky no matter how hard I tried from my office or home computer in America. This double standard in website accessibility is a not a real legal problem for government agencies in China because foreign citizens have no legal right of access to government information in China, whereas in the United States foreign citizens do have legal right of access to documents held by the federal government as *FOIA* allows anyone in the world to access information held by federal agencies. Therefore, the hypothetical scenario below is understandable: A resident in South Korea may successfully sue U.S. Department of Commerce for his inability to access the agency's official website from his Soul home computer, but he is very unlikely to prevail in a similar lawsuit in China.

State Grid Corporation of China Beijing Branch and China Datang Corporation are two leading public enterprises that provide electricity services to their customers. The former company's OGI website features a wide variety of information ranging from proactively disseminated items, OGI guidelines, annual OGI reports to information involving subsidiary electricity supply companies and environmental protection.[54] The following information can be found on the OGI website of the latter company: Company implementation measures, personnel changes, salary and compensations of its leading officers. What makes China Datang Corporation stand out from other public enterprises is that its OGI implementation measures describe in detail how OGI information should be released proactively and upon request.[55]

China Everbright Environment Corporation is a leading public enterprise dealing with environmental protection. It does have an OGI website,

[54] *OGI Website*, State Grid Corporation of China Beijing Branch, Beijing, China, ***available at*** http://www.bj.sgcc.com.cn/ (accessed between February 21, 2025 and March 31, 2025).

[55] *OGI Website*, China Datang Corporation, Beijing, China, ***available at*** https://www.china-cdt.com/dtwz/xxgk/jbxx/A024006001Gone1.html (accessed between February 21, 2025 and March 31, 2025).

but nothing can be found from there.[56] Another environmental protection business giant, Beijing Capital Group Corporation, has an OGI website too, but disclosure of information is equally lacking in scope and breadth except for publishing the executive-level managers' salaries on an annual basis.[57]

China State Railway Group and Beijing Public Transport Corporation are two leading public enterprises in the field of public transportation. The former company does not have a website at all that focuses exclusively on OGI. Instead, it publishes some company information on a webpage called "For Your Services."[58] The latter company's disclosure of information is equally superficial and haphazard, as its OGI website only features the company's historical statistical data and press releases.[59]

2. Administrative Remedy

Supported by the Supreme Court of China, China Judgements Online (*zhongguocaipanwenshuwang* 中国裁判文书网) offers the largest collection of judgments and decisions from all levels of Chinese courts.[60] A search by the author of this book on the database using the Chinese-language keywords "公共企事业单位" (meaning "public enterprises and institutions") and "信息公开"(meaning "information disclosure") resulted in a sample of 182 lawsuits where public enterprises and institutions were sued by citizens and legal persons for alleged violations of *OGI Regulations* (*see Table 8–1*).

[56] *OGI Website*, China Everbright Environment Corporation, Hong Kong, China, *available at* https://www.cebenvironment.com/sc/env_man/infodisclosure.php (accessed between February 21, 2025 and March 31, 2025).

[57] *OGI Website*, Beijing Capital Group Corporation, Beijing, China, *available at* https://www.bjcapital.com/html1/folder/2112/4503-1.htm (accessed between February 21, 2025 and March 31, 2025).

[58] *For Your Services*, China State Railway Group Corporation, Beijing, China, *available at* http://www.china-railway.com.cn/wnfw/ (accessed between February 21, 2025 and March 31, 2025).

[59] *OGI Website*, Beijing Public Transport Corporation, Beijing, China, *available at* https://www.bjbus.com/home/fun_information.php?uSec=00000186&uSub=00000186 (accessed between February 21, 2025 and March 31, 2025).

[60] China Judgements Online [中国裁判文书网], *available at* https://wenshu.court.gov.cn (accessed between February 21, 2025 and March 31, 2025).

Out of the 182 lawsuits mentioned above, 169 lawsuits did not involve oversight departments of public enterprises and institutions at all in the process of information applicants seeking administrative and judicial relief. In other words, when their information requests were denied, 93 percent of citizens and legal persons would bring the involved public enterprises and institutions directly to court without bothering to ask for administrative reconsideration or file complaints to oversight departments. Among the remaining 13 lawsuits in which information requesters did turn to oversight departments for administrative relief, 12 lawsuits emerged because oversight departments ruled against disclosure.

The numbers above demonstrate that the mechanism of using oversight departments to hold public enterprises and institutions accountable has rarely been used by information applicants, although *OGI Regulations* and various OGI Implementation Rules strongly recommend this mechanism.[61] This finding is more or less consistent with legal scholar Chun Peng, who believed that oversight departments have not paid much attention to these laws and regulations.[62] When evaluating effectiveness of oversight departments, Peng said, "To date, no oversight department has ever carried out any assessment of public enterprises and institutions'

[61] Article 37 of the 2007 OGI Regulations provides that oversight departments should formulate specific measures for open public enterprises and institutions. Article 35 of the law authorizes superior administrative organs to correct and punish subordinate agencies' violations of the law. Article 19 of the 2008 State Council Opinions on Several Issues Concerning the Implementation of the OGI Regulations mandate oversight departments to establish specific measures for open public enterprises and institutions. The 2008 Guiding Opinions on Open Information Work of Public Enterprises and Institutions in the Transportation Sector [交通运输公共企事业单位信息公开指导意见] compel relevant oversight departments to institute telephone helplines or online channels to accept public complaints. Article 8 of the 2020 State Council General Office Measures force oversight departments at all levels to create a special work system for promptly handling complaints concerning information disclosure by public enterprises and institutions. Article 9 of the law urges oversight departments to establish special responsibility clauses and improve enforcement against violations.

[62] Chun Peng, *Beyond Government Transparency in China? The Challenges to Open Public Enterprises and Institutions*, 16 University Of Pennsylvania Asian Law Review 214, 230 (2021).

transparency record and there has not been a single incident where officials get sanctioned for violating open public enterprises and institutions obligations."[63]

3. Judicial Remedy

After examining 182 lawsuits decided by Chinese courts between 2014 and 2021 (*see Table 8–1*), this chapter found that court judges were reluctant to allow implicated information to be released by public enterprises and institutions with reference to *OGI Regulations*, however, in general, Chinese courts did a better job of holding public enterprises and institutions accountable than Chinese oversight departments. At the trial court level, 28 percent of sample cases resulted in the plaintiffs winning the litigation. At the appellate court level, 20 percent of sample cases resulted in the plaintiffs winning the litigation. At the retrial court level, 1 percent of sample cases resulted in the plaintiffs winning the litigation (only 18 cases reached higher courts for retrial). This finding is more or less consistent with another legal scholar who examined 108 cases decided by Chinese prefectural and provincial courts between 2011 and 2018. He found that 24 percent of sample OGI related cases involving public enterprises and institutions resulted in the plaintiffs winning the litigation.[64]

In the 182 cases mentioned above, public enterprises and institutions approved disclosure of information in nine cases, denied disclosure of information in 46 cases, simply ignored the requests sent to them in 126 cases, and the outcome of one case is unknown, generating an approval rate of 4.95 percent for disclosure. Out of 182 sample cases, oversight departments approved disclosure in one case, denied disclosure in 11 cases, were skipped by information applicants in 170 cases, creating an approval rate of 0.55 percent for disclosure. In 182 lawsuits, trial court judges ruled in favor of disclosure in 54 cases, ruled against disclosure in 127 cases, and one case's trial court outcome is unknown, registering an approval rate of 2.97 percent for disclosure. In total, appellate court

[63] Chun Peng, *Beyond Government Transparency in China? The Challenges to Open Public Enterprises and Institutions*, 16 UNIVERSITY OF PENNSYLVANIA ASIAN LAW REVIEW 214, 229 (2021).

[64] Chun Peng, *Beyond Government Transparency in China? The Challenges to Open Public Enterprises and Institutions*, 16 UNIVERSITY OF PENNSYLVANIA ASIAN LAW REVIEW 214, 231–232 (2021).

judges ruled in favor of disclosure in 38 cases, ruled against disclosure in 104 cases, and one case's appellate court outcome is unknown (39 cases did not reach the appellate courts), generating an approval rate of 2.09 percent for disclosure. In sum, retrial court judges ruled in favor of disclosure in three cases and ruled against disclosure in 15 cases (164 cases did not reach the retrial courts), witnessing an approval rate of 1.65 percent for disclosure (*see Table 8–1*).

Public enterprises and institutions used the following rationales most frequently to justify disclosure: The organization is a public enterprise or institution implied by *OGI Regulations* and relevant laws. The requested information is not exempt from disclosure and should be disclosed according to *OGI Regulations* and/or relevant laws. The requested information is in the hands of the organization. When they rejected information requests, public enterprises and institutions used the following most often to justify non-disclosure decisions: Requested information does not exist. Requested information is not official information (*see Table 8–1*).

Noticeably, oversight departments were not used by information applicants most of the time. When complaints were filed to oversight departments, those departments used the following rationales most frequently to support the non-disclosure decisions of public enterprises and institutions: Information is not in the possession of the organization which received the request, and the applicant should look for the information elsewhere. The organization is neither an administrative agency nor an empowered organization, thus not subject to administrative reconsideration (*see Table 8–1*).

Court judges used the following rationales most frequently to support their verdicts in favor of disclosure: The organization is a public enterprise or institution explicitly provided in *OGI Regulations* and relevant laws. The organization failed to fulfill its legal obligation of reviewing the information request, deciding laws to apply and what decision to make, and notifying the applicant of the decision. The organization failed to cite proper laws when making the non-disclosure determination (*see Table 8–1*).

Court judges used the following rationales most frequently to support their verdicts against disclosure: Requested information is not created by the organization in the process of performing its duties that may involve public interests. Requested information is not official information. The organization is not a public enterprise or institution, thus not subject to *OGI Regulations* and relevant laws. The organization is not a public enterprise or institution, thus not subject to administrative reconsideration and administrative litigation. The organization is neither an administrative agency nor an empowered organization, thus not subject to administrative litigation. The organization is neither an administrative agency nor an empowered organization, thus not subject to *OGI Regulations* (*see Table 8–1*).

Court judges often ruled against disclosure of information even though the involved public enterprises or institutions were proper defendants, and they should disclose information with reference to *OGI Regulations*. Judges often cited the following scenarios as reasons for making verdicts that favor non-disclosure: The information sought has already been disclosed upon request (either verbally or in writing). The petitioner has failed to prove that the information sought is held or produced by the organization. The organization has not received the application. The organization has already replied to the information request. The information does not exist. The information needs summarization, assembly, reproduction, or statistical analysis. The information is internal and has nothing to do with public service. The information sought does not qualify as disclosable governmental information defined in the OGI Regulations and implementation measures. The information sought is irrelevant to the applicant's special needs. Whether the public enterprise/institution should disclose the requested information or not should be determined by itself, not by courts. The organization does not have the sought information, and it should be obtained from elsewhere. The organization does not know how to disclose the requested information due to lack of implementation measures by the oversight agency in the State Council. The applicant should have appealed to an oversight organization for information instead of bringing the public enterprise/institution to court. The oversight agency in the State Council has not created binding rules regarding disclosure of information held by the subordinate public enterprise/institution (*see Table 8–1*).

The analysis of the 182 sample lawsuits mentioned above clearly demonstrates that judicial relief is not quite an effective remedy for information applicants who want to pry open files of public enterprises and institutions. However, courts are far more effective than oversight departments in helping citizens get what they want. As one legal scholar said, "Nonetheless, on the whole, it is the courts, not the oversight departments that have taken the lead in promoting transparent public enterprises and institutions in China during the first decade of enforcement of the 2008 OGI Regulations."[65]

4. Sanctions for Violations

Since *OGI Regulations* came into force in 2008, media reports about how public bodies have enforced the law abound. Newspapers, TV and radio programs, magazines, and popular news portals in China published and broadcast numerous news stories containing the keywords "OGI Regulations." Most stories were quite positive and demonstrated the party and government's ability to enhance transparency using the FOI law. Some stories were negative and showed how government officials were irresponsive to OGI requests, how they were sued and even lost the lawsuits. Publications such as *Southwestern Weekend, Caijing* and *Southern Metropolis Daily* were among the Chinese news organizations that were at the forefront of media coverage of misconduct and irregularities by government officials. This chapter decides to use leading search engines and media databases to examine if any public enterprises and institutions were sanctioned for violations of *OGI Regulations* and relevant OGI implementation measures.

Google is the most popular search engine in the world while Baidu is the most popular search engine in China. A search of Google and Baidu using the Chinese-language keywords "中国公共企事业单位信息公开" and its English translation "information disclosure of public enterprises and institutions in China" has yielded something unusual. All the articles found from the search results were about *OGI Regulations* and various OGI implementation rules with regard to public enterprises and institutions. Not a single news article even tangentially touched upon the subject of how public enterprises and institutions are complying with the FOI law, not to mention news articles about penalties imposed on public enterprises and institutions.

[65] Chun Peng, *Beyond Government Transparency in China? The Challenges to Open Public Enterprises and Institutions*, 16 University Of Pennsylvania Asian Law Review 214, 238 (2021).

China Core Newspapers Full-text Database is a database that contains newspaper articles of approximately 1,000 publicly issued newspapers from mainland China.[66] A database search using the Chinese-language keywords "中国公共企事业单位信息公开" (meaning "information disclosure of public enterprises and institutions in China") has yielded similar results. The search is unable to find any Chinese-language news stories that reported on how sanctions were imposed on public enterprises and institutions that fail to comply with *OGI Regulations*.

Three possible scenarios may explain why this project cannot find any media reports about public enterprises and institutions that were held accountable for their violations of the Chinese FOI law: First, no public enterprises and institutions were penalized, therefore the media has no stories to report on. If that is the case, then it will be consistent with the finding of another scholar who said, "there has not been a single incident where officials get sanctioned for violating open public enterprises and institutions obligations."[67] Second, some public enterprises and institutions were penalized but the media did not report on them. Given that Chinese media outlets today are increasingly submissive, it is likely for them to avoid any stories that could cast the Chinese bureaucracy in a negative light. Third, some public enterprises and institutions were penalized, and the media did report on them, but those stories were quickly deleted for whatever reasons, therefore, they no longer appear in the search results.

Theoretical Implications

The concept and practice of freedom of information began to emerge in Sweden when the country created the world's first freedom of information law in 1766. As one of the earliest countries to enter the world club of freedom of information legislations, United States has become a model for many other countries including some developing countries and even authoritarian regimes. When journalists, attorneys, legal scholars,

[66] The database can be accessed from here: https://oversea.cnki.net/kns?dbcode=CCND (accessed between February 21, 2025 and March 31, 2025). It is part of the China National Knowledge Infrastructure (CNKI) database.

[67] Chun Peng, *Beyond Government Transparency in China? The Challenges to Open Public Enterprises and Institutions*, 16 University Of Pennsylvania Asian Law Review 214, 229 (2021).

and government officials created a movement in their own countries to embrace a constitutional or statutory right of access to governmental information, they cited a wide variety of theories and philosophical/moral thoughts to justify what they tried to accomplish. Such theories and underpinnings ranged from theories of freedom of expression, right to know, democratic politics, and checking value in the First Amendment to the four theories of the press and the theory of democratization. All these theories had its origins in ancient Greece and Rome and were later advocated/expanded/reinterpreted by more modern thinkers such as three "Johns" (John Milton, John Locke, and John Stuart Mill).[68]

When the right to know and other relevant theories were imported from Western democracies to China in the early 1990s, the term "right to know" was still a political taboo. Although one of the founders of the world's first freedom of information law claimed that the Swedish legislation was inspired by what the Tang dynasty emperors did to make the imperial rule more accountable,[69] the concept of opening government documents and files for public inspection was still a foreign one to most Chinese citizens, political leaders, businesspeople and even the intelligentsia. In order to make the term politically acceptable and compatible with China's socialist political system, Chinese law reformers "delinked the Chinese concept of the right to know with freedom of expression and freedom of the press. They argued for a people's right to know from the perspective of economic growth and informational development."[70]

Thanks to the term "right to know" losing its political sensitivity, the movement to embrace freedom of information gained its momentum in

[68] For a discussion of theoretical and philosophical foundations of freedom of information legislations, see Yong Tang, "Chinese Freedom of Information: An Evaluation of the Legislative History, Rationales, Significance and Efficacy of Regulations of the People's Republic of China on Open Government Information" (2012) (unpublished Ph.D. diss., The Pennsylvania State University at University Park), 39–76.

[69] Anders Chydenius, *Berattelse om chinesiska skrif-friheten, ofversatt af danskan* [A Report on the Freedom of the Press in China] (1766), reprinted in Stephen Lamble, *Freedom of Information, A Finnish Clergyman's Gift to Democracy*, 97 FREEDOM OF INFORMATION REVIEW 2, 3 (2002).

[70] Yong Tang, "Chinese Freedom of Information: An Evaluation of the Legislative History, Rationales, Significance and Efficacy of Regulations of the People's Republic of China on Open Government Information" (2012) (unpublished Ph.D. diss., The Pennsylvania State University at University Park), 54; HANHUA ZHOU, GOVERNMENT GOVERNANCE AND ADMINISTRATIVE LAW (PREFACE) [政府监管与行政法(序言)] (2007).

China, finally paving the way for the final passage of *OGI Regulations* in 2007 and *OPA Regulations* in 2017.[71] However, there is a tradeoff. *OGI Regulations* were born with limitations in both statutory language and enforcement due to the low priority placed by the Chinese government on freedom of expression and freedom of the press. All the weaknesses of the OGI Regulations with regard to public enterprises and institutions mentioned above have something to do with this delinking strategy.

Summary and Conclusion

Enacted in 2007, Open Government Information (OGI) Regulations are China's freedom of information law. This chapter examined the statutory language of *OGI Regulations*, the Supreme Court interpretations, and a few OGI implementation measures with regard to public enterprises and institutions. The chapter also examined how public enterprises and institutions have released information affirmatively and reactively, using a sample of 182 lawsuits involving public institutions and public enterprises.

In general, the OGI regime regarding disclosure of information held by public enterprises and institutions in China has low legal authority. All the legislations are at the third and fourth tier of Chinese law. The use of the words "with reference to the OGI Regulations" rather than "according to the OGI Regulations" to describe the applicability of the FOI law to public enterprises and institutions makes the situation even worse. When stating legislative purpose and principle, the OGI regime fails to address a constitutional need for a more democratic society where people are allowed to exercise the right to know what is going on in numerous state-owned companies and institutions. Instead, subjecting public enterprises and institutions to transparency standards that government agencies must follow is more intended by the Chinese government to create an environment where state-owned corporations can be better managed, supervised, and more profit-making.

[71] *OPA Regulations*, namely *Tentative Regulations of the Chinese Communist Party on Open Party Affairs*, were adopted in December 2017 and widely considered as the FOI law within the party. For the Chinese-language OPA Regulations, see https://www.gov.cn/zhengce/2017-12/25/content_5250271.htm (accessed between February 21, 2025 and March 31, 2025). For the English-language translation of the law, see https://law.yale.edu/sites/default/files/china-law-documents/horsley_eng._open_party_affairs_regulations.pdf (accessed between February 21, 2025 and March 31, 2025).

In terms of types of bodies covered under *OGI Regulations*, the law numerates an extensive list of "public enterprises and institutions," but fails to define the term. The transparency obligations of these entities have changed tremendously. Under *OGI Regulations 2007*, public enterprises and institutions were treated like administrative organs/authorized organizations. Like the latter, the former had a legal obligation to both proactively and affirmatively release information. Citizens can appeal, apply for administrative reconsideration, or bring administrative litigations against public enterprises and institutions if they desire so. However, the 2019 amendment to China's *FOIA has* changed all of this arrangement. Under the revised law, public enterprises and institutions have fewer transparency obligations than administrative organs and empowered organizations. They are discouraged to handle reactive disclosure. Therefore, citizens can hardly resort to administration reconsideration or administrative lawsuits for remedies. They are advised by the law to appeal to oversight departments in the government for decisions made by public enterprises and institutions. When public enterprises and institutions face lawsuits for violations of *OGI Regulations*, these lawsuits are likely to be dismissed because court judges do not consider public enterprises and institutions as proper defendants.

According to Chun Peng, a Chinese legal scholar, Chinese government made such a drastic change in the revised FOI law out of four considerations: First, public enterprises and institutions do not qualify as administrative subjects and thus are immune from administrative litigation. Second, oversight departments in the people's government are in a far better position than the judiciary to settle grievances and scrutinize public enterprises and institutions for transparency violations. Third, public enterprises and institutions are more like listed companies and charitable organizations, therefore transparency obligations for the former should look more like the latter. Fourth, to some Chinese lawmakers, subjecting non-government organizations to the 2007 OGI Regulations "deviated from the mainstream in the world."[72]

Contrary to what Chinese lawmakers may assume, internationally, private entities that receive government funding are like government agencies and therefore must shoulder similar transparency obligations.

[72] Chun Peng, *Beyond Government Transparency in China? The Challenges to Open Public Enterprises and Institutions*, 16 University Of Pennsylvania Asian Law Review 214, 223 (2021).

After examining the 2017 Global Right to Information Rating, Peng found that among the 108 countries surveyed, "only 26 have a transparency law that completely excludes application to private entities performing public functions or receiving public funds."[73] Therefore, subjecting non-governmental entities performing public functions and/or receiving public funds is an international standard.

The FOI regime with regard to public enterprises and institutions strongly favors affirmative disclosure, but no time limit has been set for when the information should start being released without a request being necessary. Affirmative disclosure of public enterprises and institutions is, in general, haphazard in real life. In comparison, substantial progress has been made in the area of proactive disclosure for administrative agencies at various levels of the Chinese government.[74]

When it comes to disclosure of information held by public institutions and public enterprises, the Chinese FOI law does not completely abolish reactive disclosure, and it strongly favors the use of oversight departments to handle complaints from citizens and legal persons whose applications are rejected by public enterprises and institutions. Unfortunately, such a mechanism has been rarely used in real life. When citizens and legal persons face information request rejections, they will tend to bypass the oversight departments and directly bring the involved public enterprises and institutions to court. However, courts are not an effective channel either. Most of the time, court judges will side with public enterprises and institutions, citing various reasons for their endorsement of non-disclosure. Even when judges side with information requesters, often times, courts will not order the information to be disclosed. Instead, they will merely order the involved public enterprises and institutions to reexamine the situation and let them decide by themselves if the information at issue should be released or not.

So far, no public enterprises and institutions have ever been punished for their failure to comply with *OGI Regulations* and various implementation rules. Zero sanctions against OGI violators cast doubt on the

[73] Chun Peng, *Beyond Government Transparency in China? The Challenges to Open Public Enterprises and Institutions*, 16 UNIVERSITY OF PENNSYLVANIA ASIAN LAW REVIEW 214, 241–242 (2021).

[74] See Yong Tang, *Merely Window Dressing or Substantial Authoritarian Transparency? Twelve Years of Enforcing China's Version of Freedom of Information Law*, 8 (2) JOURNAL OF MEDIA LAW AND ETHICS 68–101 (2020).

seriousness of the Chinese government's commitment to greater transparency in the world of Chinse economy and business. As the nation becomes increasingly willing to restrict flow of information and intolerant toward economic transparency and political liberalization, the chance seems remote that public enterprises and institutions will be more harshly scrutinized to better protect a fundamental human right of Chinese people. With problems in mind, this chapter attempts to propose the following solutions for people who can and want to turn the tide:

1. Revise *OGI Regulations* to ensure China will adopt an international standard in FOI: Non-government entities that receive government funding should comply with the freedom of information laws. In this spirit, Article 55 of the 2019 amendment to *OGI Regulations* can be revised as such:

   Disclosing information that is made or obtained in the course of providing public services to society by public enterprises and institutions that are closely related to the people's interests such as education, health, water, power, gas, heating, environmental protection, and public transportation shall be done *according to* relevant laws, regulations and the provisions of the relevant departments in charge or institutions of the State Council. The national department in charge of open government information work may formulate special regulations according to actual requirements (italicized portion added by the author of this book to replace "with reference to").

   If the public enterprises and institutions specified in the preceding paragraph fail to disclose the information produced or obtained in the process of providing public services to society in accordance with the relevant laws, regulations and the provisions of the relevant departments in charge or organizations and offices of the State Council, citizens, legal persons or other organizations may appeal to the relevant departments in charge or organizations and offices, and the department or organization of office that accepts the appeal should investigate and handle it in a timely manner and notify the appellant of the result of the handling. *Citizens, legal persons or other organizations may also sue public enterprises and institutions for judicial relief* (italicized portion added by the author of this book).
2. Revise the Supreme Court provision to ensure that public enterprises and institutions will be acknowledged clearly as proper

defendants in administrative lawsuits, just like how the provision treats government agencies and empowered organizations in similar lawsuits.

3. Revise the State Council implementation measures and various implementation measures passed by central and local government agencies to reflect the proposed change mentioned in 1 and 2.
4. Revise all the relevant laws to make sure there are no conflicts or inconsistencies between *OGI Regulations* and implementations rules with regard to public enterprises and institutions. For example, the special needs test was removed from *OGI Regulations* in the 2019 amendment. Implementation measures should be revised accordingly to ensure citizens and legal persons will not be asked to demonstrate special needs when they apply for disclosure of information.
5. Drastically reduce the number of rationales (especially those procedural reasons) that public enterprises and institutions, oversight government departments and courts can use to deny disclosure.

CHAPTER 9

Journalistic Internal Reference and Internal Working Documents: A Freedom of Information Law Perspective

As part of the author's doctoral dissertation that was successfully defended at The Pennsylvania State University in 2012, this chapter was later revised and presented to the AEJMC Southeast Colloquium annual convention in 2013. The conference paper was then revised and published in *Journal of Information Policy* in 2017. The author of this book retains copyright of this journal article. Certain parts of the text in the chapter may resemble or replicate the original material, which has been included with the permission of the editors at Palgrave Macmillan. Yong Tang, "Chinese Freedom of Information: An Evaluation of the Legislative History, Rationales, Significance and Efficacy of Regulations of the People's Republic of China on Open Government Information" (2012) (unpublished Ph.D. diss., The Pennsylvania State University at University Park), *available at* https://etda.libraries.psu.edu/catalog/16287/ (accessed between February 21, 2025 and March 31, 2025; Yong Tang, *Journalistic Internal Reference: Exemption from China's Freedom of Information Law*, paper accepted for presentation by the AEJMC (Association for Education in Journalism and Mass Communication) Southeast Colloquium annual conference, University of South Florida, Tampa, Florida, February 28-March 2, 2013; Yong Tang, *For Whose Eyes Only? China's Journalistic Internal Reference System and Its Legal and Political Implications*, 7 JOURNAL OF INFORMATION POLICY 1–37 (2017).

Y. Tang, *Freedom of Information Law in China*,
https://doi.org/10.1007/978-981-96-7842-6_9

Introduction

This chapter will examine two special categories of governmental information that has tremendous freedom of information law implications: Journalistic internal reference and internal working documents. Both played a significant role in restricting free flow of information between the Chinese government and citizens, thus creating lots of legal and political problems that need to be addressed soon.

This chapter will examine the specifics of how internal working documents or working secrets are exempt from disclosure under many national FOI laws, the handling of internal working documents according to *OGI Regulations*, relevant rules, and legal interpretations, and the Chinese agencies' shielding information from disclosure using the loophole in the law.

The internal reference system[1] in China is unique; and *Law on Guarding State Secrets 1988* generally shields from public view three kinds of materials: internal periodicals published by news outlets on sensitive subjects and sent exclusively to party and governmental leaders; internal periodicals published by party organizations, governmental agencies, and other non-media entities[2]; internal movies and internal literature.[3] This

[1] This chapter uses internal reference, internal publication, internal periodical, inner-circulated reference material, internal report, *neibu cankao* and *neican* interchangeably.

[2] The Chinese party and governmental agencies at various levels regularly publish internal periodicals. For example, The Chinese Communist Party (CCP) Central Propaganda Department publishes *Propaganda Trend* (*Xuanchuan dongtai*) weekly. The CCP Central Organization Department issues *Party Construction Research* Internal Reference (*Dangjian yanjiu neican*). Each institute at the China Academy of Social Sciences, a prestigious official think tank, produces various types of internal reference materials. Some large libraries in China publish internal reference materials for leading officials. For example, Sun Yat-Sen Library of Guangdong Province issues *Decision-making Neican* intended for political elites in Guangdong. Yuezhi Zhao, Media, Market, And Democracy In China: Between The Party Line And The Bottom Line 20 (1998); David Shambaugh, China's Communist Party: Atrophy And Adaptation (2008); Decision-Making In Deng's China: Perspectives From Insiders 114 (Carol Lee Hamrin & Suisheng Zhao (eds., 1995); the Sun Yat-Sen Library Internal Reference Online Subscription, *available at* http://www.zslib.com.cn/jingtaiyemian/taigangao/jcnc.html (accessed between February 21, 2025 and March 31, 2025).

[3] Most internal films and internal literature were foreign films and books internally circulated only among the Chinese political elite during Mao Zedong's era. Some erotic Chinese classics, like *Prayer Mat Flesh and Jin Ping Mei* (also known as *The Golden*

study will examine media-produced internal reference materials only. Internal reference materials generated by party and governmental agencies and non-media entities are beyond the scope of this research, despite deserving academic attention and examination. Internal movies and literature are also beyond the scope of this research because they have little relevance, and this book ignores them because they have gradually faded into oblivion since China's adopting policies of reform and openness to the outside world in the late 1970s.

As one method for controlling the free flow of information, the government's internal reference system of Chinese news media is influential, but also mysterious. Guoguang Wu, a former *People's Daily* commentator, recalled a warning in his first journalism class at Peking University, "an important part of a Chinese reporter's job was to write internal articles that the public never sees."[4] Xingdou Hu, a social science professor at the Beijing Institute of Technology, confirmed that journalistic internal references "are the most important way for [Chinese] party and governmental officials to learn about bad news."[5] When discussing the roles of internal publications and regular newspapers, Western scholars observed that, these two kinds of publications are "twin pillars" of the broader propaganda and political system of China.[6] The unique role of

Lotus), once classified as internal materials were accessible only to a small number of people in China. Paul Theroux is the author of many Western train travel classics such as *The Great Railway Bazaar*, *The Old Patagonian Express* and *Riding the Iron Rooster: By Train through China*. He provided extensive details of the classification of foreign books as internal reference materials by the Chinese government. George Orwell's novel *1984* was a victim of many such foreign books during the reign of Mao Zedong. Lei Cao & Xiu Su, *Mysterious Internal Movies during the Cultural Revolution* [文革中神秘的 "内参片"] 8 JOURNAL OF MEMORIES AND ARCHIVES (2010); PAUL THEROUX, RIDING THE IRON ROOSTER: BY TRAIN THROUGH CHINA (2006).

[4] Nicholas D. Kristof, *The Real News in China Comes out in Restricted Periodicals*, THE NEW YORK TIMES, September 24, 1991, http://www.nytimes.com/1991/09/24/world/the-real-news-in-china-comes-out-in-restricted-periodicals.html (accessed between February 21, 2025 and March 31, 2025).

[5] Mark Magnier, *Rosy Reports from Underlings Leave Chinese Leaders in the Dark: Workers are Conditioned to Give Bosses only Good News, Letting Problems such as SARS Get out of Control*, THE LOS ANGELES TIMES, February 16, 2004, http://articles.latimes.com/2004/feb/16/world/fg-info16 (accessed between February 21, 2025 and March 31, 2025).

[6] Ching-chang Hsiao & Timothy Cheek, *Open and Closed Media: External and Internal Newspapers in the Propaganda System*, *in* DECISION-MAKING IN DENG'S CHINA: PERSPECTIVES FROM INSIDERS 86 (Carol Lee Hamrin & Suisheng Zhao eds., 1995).

journalistic internal reference in Chinese society has aroused the intense interest of Western media. *The New York Times* once reported:

> The Chinese sometimes complain that the one place
> where news is never found is in the newspapers. So
> perhaps it is not surprising that officials are so fond
> of a special breed of publications bearing the warning,
> "Internal Periodical-Guard Carefully."[7]

Most ordinary Chinese citizens consider internal reference to be something even more magical. They firmly believe that their voices would be heard, and their problems instantly resolved as soon as their grievances appear in journalistic internal periodicals. As such, the mass production of fake internal reference materials used to be a thriving industry in Beijing.[8] Some Chinese petitioners even contacted correspondents of the foreign media in Beijing and asked to have their complaints and grievances forwarded to relevant Chinese officials, assuming that Western media publish similar internal reference periodicals.[9]

This chapter will examine historical origins of the journalistic internal reference system in China, preparation of internal reference materials by journalists, publication by news organizations, and distribution to leading political and governmental officials for review. The chapter will also investigate legal privileges granted to internal reference materials, scrutinize the roles the journalistic internal reference system plays in communication processes of the party and the government. The chapter will consider the challenges of the system and its emerging trends and analyze government agencies' using the system to obscure their activities.

[7] Nicholas D. Kristof, *The Real News in China Comes out in Restricted Periodicals*, THE NEW YORK TIMES, September 24, 1991, http://www.nytimes.com/1991/09/24/world/the-real-news-in-china-comes-out-in-restricted-periodicals.html (accessed between February 21, 2025 and March 31, 2025).

[8] Tailing Zhang, *Fake Newsrooms Write Fake Journalistic Internal Reference for Desperate Petitioners* [假编辑部收千元为上访者写内参], BEIJING NEWS, republished by Sina Finance, August 2, 2010, https://finance.sina.cn/sa/2010-08-02/detail-ikftpnny0176483.d.html?from=wap (accessed between February 21, 2025 and March 31, 2025).

[9] Susan Jakes, *The Time Magazine Office of Letters and Visits*, TIME, January 23, 2007, http://china.blogs.time.com/2007/01/23/the_time_magazine_office_of_le/ (accessed between February 21, 2025 and March 31, 2025).

The study of journalistic internal reference from the perspective of freedom of information is significant. A number of English-language, scholarly articles and books, to varying degrees, relate to the internal reference system in China.[10] Legal scholar, Benjamin Liebman, improved Western understanding of the Chinese system of journalistic internal reference through research of Chinese laws and media.[11] However, the research focused only on the legal implications of internal references when nationwide FOI law was still nonexistent in China. Communications scholars, Jennifer Grant, Huai Yan, and Suisheng Zhao are Western researchers who produced articles exclusively focusing on the role of internal reference in China. However, Jennifer Grant published studies nearly 40 years ago and the other two scholars published their research more than 30 years ago.[12] In the last 30 years, China's media and mass communication landscape has changed rapidly with the rise of digital

[10] For relevant English-language scholarly articles and books covering the subject of Chinese internal reports to various degrees, see Benjamin L. Liebman, *Watchdog or Demagogue? The Media in the Chinese Legal System,* 105 COLUMBIA LAW REVIEW 1 (January 2005); Chin-fu Hung, *The Politics of Cyber Participation in the PRC: The Implications of Contingency for the Awareness of Citizens' Rights*, 42 ISSUES & STUDIES 137, 139 (December 2006); Ching-chang Hsiao & Timothy Cheek, *Open and Closed Media: External and Internal Newspapers in the Propaganda System, in* DECISION-MAKING IN DENG'S CHINA: PERSPECTIVES FROM INSIDERS (Carol Lee Hamrin & Suisheng Zhao eds., 1995); DANIEL C. LYNCH, AFTER THE PROPAGANDA STATE: MEDIA, POLITICS, AND "THOUGHT WORK" IN REFORMED CHINA 270 (1999); INVESTIGATIVE JOURNALISM IN CHINA: EIGHT CASES IN CHINESE WATCHDOG JOURNALISM 121 (David Bandurski & Martin Hala eds., 2010); THE MAKING OF CHINESE FOREIGN AND SECURITY POLICY IN THE ERA OF REFORM, 1978–2000 53–54 (David M. Lampton (ed., 2001); Huai Yan & Suisheng Zhao, *Notes on China's Confidential Documents*, 2 JOURNAL OF CONTEMPORARY CHINA 75 (1993); Jennifer Grant, *Internal Reporting by Investigative Journalists in China and Its Influence on Government Policy*, 41 INTERNATIONAL COMMUNICATION GAZETTE 53 (1988); Judy Polumbaum, *Professionalism in China's Press Corps, in* CHINESE DEMOCRACY AND THE CRISIS OF 1989: CHINESE AND AMERICAN REFLECTIONS 299 (ROGER V. DES FORGES, NING LUO & YEN-BO WU eds., 1993); YUEZHI ZHAO, COMMUNICATION IN CHINA: POLITICAL ECONOMY, POWER, AND CONFLICT (2008).

[11] Benjamin L. Liebman, *Watchdog or Demagogue? The Media in the Chinese Legal System,* 105 COLUMBIA LAW REVIEW 1 (January 2005).

[12] Jennifer Grant, *Internal Reporting by Investigative Journalists in China and Its Influence on Government Policy*, 41 INTERNATIONAL COMMUNICATION GAZETTE 53 (1988); Huai Yan & Suisheng Zhao, *Notes on China's Confidential Documents*, 2 JOURNAL OF CONTEMPORARY CHINA 75 (1993).

media and social media. China's legal landscape has changed tremendously as well with the advent of FOI law and other newly passed laws pertaining to flow of information. As a whole, research of journalistic internal reference in Western academia is generally lacking in depth, scope, freshness and comprehensiveness. Few have discussed how the system was established and how it works. Chinese-language scholarly publications on internal reference abound,[13] but database searches indicate that none of the articles examined the internal reference system from a FOI perspective. This chapter aims to fill some of those gaps.

Due to sensitivity of journalistic internal references, obtaining copies of internal reference materials is both difficult and illegal. As such, the author of this book relies heavily on Chinese-language articles retrieved from China Academic Journals (CAJ) Database and firsthand experience of a former Chinese journalist. Published in Chinese newspapers and magazines, many Chinese-language articles relate vivid stories of writing internal reference (*neican* 内参), leaders' reviews, and *neicans*' influence on official decision-making. Such stories became public either because authors had long retired as journalists, or because the government declassified the material. Additionally, some articles are instructions intended for young journalists to improve their reporting and writing skills in *neican*. In truth, the publications are extremely useful primary sources. Several interviews with Chinese journalists provided current information concerning the internal reference system. Secondary sources, such as academic journal articles, also provide insight, although they are not voluminous when compared to primary sources. This study uses only declassified internal reference materials.

Journalistic Internal Reference First Emerged in the 1930s

Establishment of the journalistic internal reference system occurred in the 1930s when Chinese communists were guerrilla forces, and Chiang Kai-shek was the legitimate ruler of China. The Chinese Communist Party

[13] Jie Shang, "Research on Mechanism of China's Journalistic Internal Reference" [中国新闻内参机制分析] (2008) (unpublished master's thesis, Henan University); Qiuping Cheng and Jian Peng, *Communication Analysis of Internal Reference*, Press Outpost 6, 41 (2005).

(CCP) broke Chiang's military encirclement and created a Soviet-style regime in Ruijin, Jiangxi Province.[14]

The CCP created two distinct communication systems in Ruijin. One is the "top-down" mode of communication which disseminated officially sanctioned information "from the leadership to the general public" via regular publications. Another was the "bottom-up" mode of communication, in which information accumulated at grass roots levels moved "upwards into the bureaucratic hierarchy" via internal reference.[15]

Reference News (*Cankao Xiaoxi*) is the first journalistic, internal periodical in modern Chinese history. Today, *Reference News* is no longer an internal publication; instead, it is China's leading newspaper with a daily circulation of 3.2 million.[16] However, at the newspaper's founding in 1931 by Xinhua News Agency, the intent for *Reference News* was not general readers but communist leaders above a certain level. Xinhua selected articles from the world's major news agencies and journals and translated them into Chinese.[17] "This practice of news organizations' providing intelligence for high-level Party leaders continues today."[18]

No country in the world today has a journalistic internal reference system except China. In democratic countries, officials enjoy no more right of access to information than ordinary voters. They "learn about international events first from CNN, not from internal sources."[19] Even in authoritarian regimes including communist ones, leaders in the government usually do not oblige reporters to gather intelligence for them. The inspiration for Chinese communists to create such a unique system is a worthy topic.

[14] Tony Saich & Benjamin Yang, The Rise To Power Of The Chinese Communist Party: Documents And Analysis 509 (1996).

[15] Chin-fu Hung, *The Politics of Cyber Participation in the PRC: The Implications of Contingency for the Awareness of Citizens' Rights,* 42 Issues & Studies 137, 139 (December 2006).

[16] *Reference News*, China Media Guide, Danwei.org, August 9, 2008 (captured by Internet Archive Wayback Machine on May 6, 2009), retrieved from https://web.archive.org/web/20090506073529/http://www.danwei.org/media_guide/newspapers/reference_news.php (accessed between February 21, 2025 and March 31, 2025).

[17] Jörg Rudolph, Cankao-Xiaoxi: Foreign News In The Propaganda System Of The People's Republic Of China (1984).

[18] Yuezhi Zhao, Media, Market, And Democracy In China: Between The Party Line And The Bottom Line 15 (1998).

[19] Changing Media, Changing China 8 (Susan L. Shirk, ed., 2010).

Historical Origins of Journalistic Internal Reference

The system of journalistic internal reference is not unique to Chinese history. The former Soviet Union used a similar system to gather information for party and government leaders.[20] Bulgarian journalists served the government as intelligence agents when the country was under communist rule.[21] Communist Poland had an elaborate system of internal bulletins that were prepared by the Polish Press Agency and Polish Radio and read exclusively by party and government leaders.[22] It was widely believed that China imported its internal reference system from the Soviet Union. Some scholars maintain that inspiration for Chinese journalists was Soviet colleagues' publication of hidden reference materials for leading government officials. For example, historian of Chinese journalism, Stephen Mackinnon, stated in one study, "the wholesale importation into the PRC in the 1950s of the Soviet practice of 'internal' (*neibu*) publications [is] a uniquely diabolical method of combining censorship and propaganda in media control."[23] Another scholar of Chinese communication, Anne Brady, said that the dual role of Chinese mass media propagandizing party positions and policies and preparing internal reports for the party was established "under the influence of the Soviet Union."[24]

However, Mackinnon did not provide compelling evidence to support the claim. The result of a database search by the author of this book

[20] Lilita Dzirkals, Thane Gustafson and A. Ross Johnson, *The Media and Intra-Elite Communication in the USSR*, Rand Report (September 1982, R.2869): 34–35, *available at* https://www.rand.org/pubs/reports/R2869.html (accessed between February 21, 2025 and March 31, 2025).

[21] Ekaterina Ognianova, *The Transitional Media System of Post-Communist Bulgaria*, Journalism And Mass Communication Monographs 162 (1997): 1.

[22] Jane Leftwich Curry, *The Media and Intra-Elite Communication in Poland: The Role of "Special Bulletins,"* Rand Report (December 1980, N-1514/4), *available at* https://www.rand.org/pubs/notes/N1514z4.html (accessed between February 21, 2025 and March 31, 2025).

[23] Stephen R. Mackinnon, *Toward a History of the Chinese Press in the Republican Period*, 23 Modern China 3, 15 (1997).

[24] Anne-Marie Brady, *Marketing Dictatorship: Propaganda And Thought Work In Contemporary China* (2008), 12; Chinese Communist Party Central Propaganda Department Office, ED. *Party Propaganda Work Documents 1949–1993 Volume One* (1994), 65.

fails to establish convincing support for the argument,[25] and contrary to Mackinnon, the CCP created the internal reference system in the 1930s, not the 1950s.

To determine if China imported the journalistic internal reference system from the Soviet Union requires additional research. The task is beyond the scope of this book. Despite Mackinnon's possibly correct assertion, seeking additional factors to explain adoption of journalistic internal reference in China is worthwhile. Rationally, one source is Chinese communists' obtaining inspiration from the country's long history.[26] Media law scholar, Benjamin Liebman, specifically observed:

> The development of such alternative sources of information to inform Party leadership of developments at the local level was not a complete innovation. During imperial times, China's emperors relied on complex systems of communication, including secret reporting concerning local conditions or popular opinion, to keep themselves informed.[27]

The origins of the Chinese journalistic internal reference probably trace back more than 1,000 years to publication of the world's first newspaper, *dibao (*邸报) during the Tang Dynasty.[28] *Dibao* was an internal publication circulated only among officials throughout the country. D*i* officials

[25] Fang Zuo is the founding editor of *Southern Weekend*. According to Zuo, in the 1950s, Chinese media copied the model of *Pravda*, which was the official newspaper of the Soviet Communist Party until 1991. Learning from *Pravda*, most Chinese newspapers, at that time, created "mass work departments" (*qungongbu* 群工部) to deal with letters to editors. The media published some letters while other letters may have had review by governmental officials, arguably, a precursor of internal reference. Bing Hong, *A Newspaperman Who Never Feels Anxious: Interview with Fang Zuo, Founding Editor of Southern Weekend* [《从容不迫的办报人:南方周末》创始人左方访谈], Sohu Media, October 31, 2003, https://media.news.sohu.com/74/76/news215027674.shtml (accessed between February 21, 2025 and March 31, 2025).

[26] Silas H.L. Wu, Communication And Imperial Control In China: Evolution Of The Palace Memorial System, 1693–1735 (1970).

[27] Benjamin L. Liebman, *Watchdog or Demagogue? The Media in the Chinese Legal System*, 105 Columbia Law Review 1, 16 (January 2005).

[28] Some scholars disagree about when the publication originated. They argue that *Dibao* first appeared in the Han Dynasty, which preceded the Tang Dynasty. Barbara Mittler, A Newspaper For CHINA? Power, Identity, And Change In Shanghai's News Media 1872–1912 (2004).

who were "in charge of liaison between the court and regional administrations,"[29] authored the articles for the regularly printed and circulated publication, which covered emperors' activities, imperial rules and orders, official policies, promotions, demotions, and much other official information. Throughout subsequent dynasties, internal publications like *dibao* circulated among officials to keep them well informed.[30]

For better understanding of events in their empires, Chinese emperors often employed human intelligence to complement internal publications. For example, the Kangxi Emperor (1654–1722) of the Qing Dynasty secretly sent agents to gather important and confidential information.[31] The information returned to Kangxi in envelopes that only Kangxi had the right to unseal. Later discoveries unmasked the grandfather of Xueqing Cao, author of the Chinese classic novel, *Dream of the Red Chambers*, as Kangxi's secret intelligence gatherer.[32] Internal publications and human intelligence employed by rulers in ancient China probably inspired Chinese communists' creation of their internal reference system. Future research may gather more evidence to support this assumption.

Journalistic Internal Reference Materials' Publication and Circulation

The journalistic internal reference system established by Chinese communists in Ruijin, Jiangxi Province was small and primitive. Communist leaders had an opportunity to upgrade that system after 1949, the year when Mao Zedong and his comrades exiled Chiang Kai-shek to Taiwan and established the People's Republic of China.

Based on the Soviet media system, Chinese communist leaders created a unique media system, in which all media organizations are extensions of the party and governmental apparatus, each having an individual administrative rank. For example, the Chinese Communist Party (CCP)

[29] Barbara Mittler, A Newspaper For China? Power, Identity, And Change In Shanghai's News Media 1872–1912 177 (2004).

[30] Shaoyuan Wanyan, *Neican in Ancient Chinese Governments* [古代官府的"内参"], 1 Digest (2007).

[31] Zhao Xiao, *Kangxi Emperor Used Secret Spies to Investigate Public Opinion* [康熙借密探察民情], 2 Happiness (2009).

[32] Zhao Xiao, *Kangxi Emperor Used Secret Spies to Investigate Public Opinion* [康熙借密探察民情], 2 Happiness (2009).

Central Committee has an official organ, *People's Daily*, with a ministerial rank. The State Council, China's national cabinet, controls Xinhua News Agency, also at the ministerial level, China Central Television (CCTV) and China National Radio (CNR) both of vice-ministerial level.[33] Despite affiliation with the party or the government, the CCP Central Propaganda Department censors those news organizations, and a member of the CCP Politburo Standing Committee supervises.

The three major, national news organizations, *People's Daily*, Xinhua News Agency and China Media Group (parent company of CCTV and CNR) occupy the top slot in the media hierarchy in China. In addition to the ruling party and the government, non-Communist parties in China also have official media.[34] The party's organizations for the masses, such as the All-China Workers Federation and the Chinese Communist Youth League have official publications. This media structure is "more or less reproduced" at the provincial, municipal, and county levels with decreased complexity.[35] Typically, a province, a city (or prefecture district) or a county[36] has a party news organ, a radio station, and a television station. The party's media affiliates with the party committee. The radio station and the television station affiliate with the government. All need to report to the local CCP propaganda departments according to their corresponding administrative ranks. For example, supervision of *Sichuan Daily* occurs by the Sichuan Provincial CCP Committee Propaganda Department, while *Chengdu Daily* reports to the Chengdu City CCP Committee Propaganda Department.

[33] CCTV, CNR and CRI (China Radio International) later merged in 2018 to form a new state-owned broadcasting giant, China Media Group or Voice of China. *China to Merge State Media Broadcasting Giants*, China Global Television Network, March 21, 2018, https://america.cgtn.com/2018/03/21/china-to-merge-state-media-broadcasting-giants (accessed between February 21, 2025 and March 31, 2025).

[34] There are eight registered minor parties under the Chinese Communist Party direction: Revolutionary Committee of the Kuomintang, China Democratic League, China Democratic National Construction Association, China Association for Promoting Democracy, Chinese Peasants' and Workers' Democratic Party, China Zhi Gong Party, Jiusan Society, and Taiwan Democratic Self-Government League.

[35] Yuezhi Zhao, Media, Market, And Democracy In China: Between The Party Line And The Bottom Line 16–18 (1998).

[36] The county level media outlets are at the lowest level of the media hierarchy in China. Xiaoling Zhang, *Seeking Effective Public Space: Chinese Media at the Local Level*, 5 China: An International Journal 55 (March 2007).

According to four theories of the press,[37] news media in communist countries have roles as organizers, agitators, and propagandists for the ruling Communist Party. Applied to the Chinese context, interpretation of these roles identifies the "mouth and tongue" (*houshe* 喉舌) of the party and the government. However, news media in China fulfill an additional important function, the "ear and eye" (*ermu* 耳目) of the party-state bureaucracy. As communication scholar, Jennifer Grant observed, "The gathering and reporting of intelligence on domestic affairs to the government is central to the importance of the position of the Chinese investigative journalist within contemporary Chinese society."[38] Such dual functions of journalists apply to all mainstream news media organizations in China regardless of administrative rank or political prestige. However, in practice, traditional party and government-run news outlets such as the Xinhua news agency, *People's Daily* and CCTV prepare most internal reports; commercialized media "rarely, if ever, prepare internal reports."[39] Among traditional party and official news outlets, Xinhua News Agency is the largest and most influential producer of internally circulated news-related materials.[40]

No clear-cut standards exist for what could appear in internal reports. Usually, people assigned to write for *neican* are professionally capable and politically loyal, investigative journalists. Their training includes recognition of news appropriate for public release and those for internal references. In general, any information deemed too sensitive for the public but too important for officials to ignore become journalistic internal references. Such information includes, but is not limited to local corruption, official misconduct, social unrest, major natural disasters, and public health incidents. Central and local policy experiments considered by officials too premature for publicizing also appear in internal periodicals.

[37] Fred S. Siebert, Theodore Peterson and Wilbur Schramm, Four Theories Of The Press: The Authoritarian, Libertarian, Social Responsibility And Soviet Communist Concepts Of What The Press Should Be and Do (1956).

[38] Jennifer Grant, *Internal Reporting by Investigative Journalists in China and Its Influence on Government Policy*, 41 International Communication Gazette 53, 54 (1988).

[39] Benjamin L. Liebman, *Watchdog or Demagogue? The Media in the Chinese Legal System*, 105 Columbia Law Review 1, 23 (January 2005).

[40] Yanhui Chen, *Demystify Neican* [内参揭秘], Phoenix Weekly 14 (2005): 35–39.

Journalists normally write internal references for their own employers; however, exceptions occur. Internal publications sometimes print, or reprint articles provided by contributing journalists. For example, the internal publication of *People's Daily* once carried a report of an irrigation project fraud and the report was authored by Qinrong Gao, a journalist in Shanxi Province.[41] *People's Daily* or Xinhua reprinted many articles from *Hebei Daily's* internal reports.[42]

Depending on the publication or program, internal reports, usually magazine-like, appear either on a regular schedule or only when issues of special importance arise.[43] The administrative rank of the news organization and other factors determine recipients of internal publications based on party and officials' levels. For example, internal reports from *People's Daily*, CCTV and Xinhua News agency have general circulation to the party's central level and state leaders. Internal reports from provincial party papers and electronic media generally circulate to provincial-level leaders. News media affiliated with municipal party committees prepare internal reports circulated to municipal leaders. The sensitivity of the issue involved, and the degree of confidentiality are also determining factors.[44]

[41] Yefengchui [野风吹], *Lack of Aggressive Media Outlets Leads to Prevalence of Fake Reporters* [假记者猖獗背后是真媒体缺位], Sohu, Beijing, China, December 15, 2006, *available at* https://star.news.sohu.com/20061215/n247060757.shtml (accessed between February 21, 2025 and March 31, 2025); *CPC Central Committee Pays High Attention to Qinrong Gao's Suffering, Causing His Surprising Retrial Likely* [打假记者高勤荣案重大转折:中央高度关注,或将迎来再审], Jingpingtai [鲸平台], Shanghai, China, April 18, 2023, *available at* https://www.jingpt.com/article/c7141726-bfcf-4998-8b05-d31ce8978dfb (accessed between February 21, 2025 and March 31, 2025).

[42] Benjamin L. Liebman, *Watchdog or Demagogue? The Media in the Chinese Legal System*, 105 Columbia Law Review 1, 23 (January 2005).

[43] Benjamin L. Liebman, *Watchdog or Demagogue? The Media in the Chinese Legal System*, 105 Columbia Law Review 1, 22 (January 2005). Some investigative programs on CCTV prepare internal reports in the form of video stories. However, radio stations and some local television stations prepare internal reports, most often in written form. Benjamin L. Liebman, *Watchdog or Demagogue? The Media in the Chinese Legal System*, 105 Columbia Law Review 1, 23 (January 2005).

[44] For example, Xinhua News Agency publishes a wide range of internal reports with each circulated to different leadership ranks. Supplemental Final Proof of Domestic Trends (*Guonei Dongtai Qingyang Fuye*) circulates only among members of the CCP Politburo standing committee and members of the Politburo. Final Proof of Domestic Trends (*Guonei Dongtai Qingyang) and* Reference Materials Proof (*Cankao Ziliao Qingyang*) are only for leaders at provincial (*sheng*) and ministerial (*bu*) levels. Internal Reference (*Neibu Cankao*) circulates among party and officials at prefecture (*di/shi*) and bureau (*si/ju*) levels

Unlike most regular newspapers and magazines circulated by the state-run postal offices or private circulation companies, journalistic internal reference materials use secure and confidential channels for delivery.[45] When leading party and government officials receive internal reports, they read them carefully. Actually, the first thing many CCP and governmental leaders do in the morning is read internal reports prepared by Xinhua.[46] Officials write their opinions in the margins of the internal publications if warranted. Having written suggestions, recommendations, or instructions, officials immediately forward copies of the annotated reports to lower-level officials responsible for the issue.[47] Often, prompt investigation of exposed problems ensues.

Legal Implications: Privileges of Journalistic Internal Reference

Compared to regular publications, internal reference materials in China enjoy special legal privileges. All internal materials have protection from *Law on Guarding State Secrets 1988*.[48] Information included in internally

and above. Selected Compilation of Internal References (*Neican Xuanbian*) is only for leaders at county, division (*xian/tuan*), and section (*ke/ying*) levels. The accepted standard is that the smaller number of leaders having access to internal reports, the more sensitive and important the internally circulated information becomes. Yanhui Chen, *Demystify Neican* [内参揭秘], Phoenix Weekly 14 (2005): 35–39.

[45] An informative example of the delivery of internal reference materials to officials is: "[t]he classified channel for internal reports includes a system of couriers-in Beijing; they once included a corps of motorcyclists in black uniforms with special vehicle number plates that allowed them to drive directly from the *People's Daily* office into the Zhongnanhai compound. In Shanghai, a special vehicle carried a sealed box of internal reports daily from the *Wenhui Daily* [headquarters] to the airport; in Beijing the plane was met by a similar set of couriers, who drove the materials direct to Politburo offices. These reports are delivered to a special classified communications office within the Central Committees' [CCP] General Office." Ching-chang Hsiao & Timothy Cheek, *Open and Closed Media: External and Internal Newspapers in the Propaganda System*, *in* Decision-Making In Deng's China: Perspectives From Insiders 82 (Carol Lee Hamrin & Suisheng Zhao eds., 1995).

[46] Yanhui Chen, *Demystify Neican* [内参揭秘], Phoenix Weekly 14 (2005): 35–39.

[47] Yibo Bo, a former senior leader in the Chinese Communist Party, had the habit of reading *neican* very carefully and writing voluminous opinions in the margins of *neican* articles. Zhenguo Yan, *Review Comments in Memory of Bo Lao* [重温批示 追忆薄老], 9 Hundred Year Tide (2009).

[48] *Law on Guarding State Secrets 1988* (amended in 2010 and 2024).

circulated publications represent three categories: top secret (*juemi* 绝密), highly secret (*jimi* 机密), and secret (*mimi* 秘密).[49] Divulging of top-secret information results in extremely serious harm to state security and national interests; divulging highly secret information causes serious harm to state security and national interests, and exposing secret information causes harm to state security and national interests.[50] Internal journalistic information dubbed, "top secret," has protection for a maximum of 30 years, beginning on the date of creation. Internal materials designated, "highly secret," are classified for 20 years, and internal reference materials designated, "secret" are prohibited from public view for up to 10 years.[51] A state secret automatically loses its classification when the proscribed time for guarding it expires.[52]

Under *Law on Guarding State Secrets 1988*, anyone violating the provisions of this state secrecy law receives punishment; if the violation constitutes a crime, prosecution of the individual for criminal responsibility ensues.[53] An example is Shanghai lawyer, Enchong Zheng, arrested and sentenced to three years in prison in a 2003, high-profile case for allegedly telefaxing a Xinhua internal reference article[54] to a non-profit

[49] *Law on Guarding State Secrets 1988* (amended in 2010 and 2024). Art. 14.

[50] *Law on Guarding State Secrets 1988* (amended in 2010 and 2024). Art. 14.

[51] *Law on Guarding State Secrets 1988* (amended in 2010 and 2024). Art. 20.

[52] *Law on Guarding State Secrets 1988* (amended in 2010 and 2024). Art. 24.

[53] *Law on Guarding State Secrets 1988* (amended in 2010 and 2024). Art. 57. Art. 62.

[54] On April 30, 2003, Xinhua journalist, Tingjun Huang, published an article in one of the Xinhua internal reference publications. The article concerned forced housing demolition incident in which a journalist on the spot was besieged. On May 28, 2003, the lawyer, Enchong Zheng, telefaxed a copy of the article to Human Rights in China, a non-profit organization based in New York. Zheng left a note on the copy of the article: "Xinhua internal reference, please cite." Both the Shanghai Administration for the Protection of State Secrets and the National Administration for the Protection of State Secrets certified that the transmitted article was, indeed, "secret" (*mimi*) and protected by *Law on Guarding State Secrets 1988*. He Deng, *How Did Lawyer Enchong Zheng Divulge State Secrets?* [律师郑恩宠是如何泄露国家秘密的?], BUND PICTORIAL, republished by People's Daily Online, November 6, 2003 (captured by Internet Archive Wayback Machine on January 6, 2004), retrieved from https://web.archive.org/web/20040106195750/http://unn.people.com.cn/GB/14748/2172850.html (accessed between February 21, 2025 and March 31, 2025).

human rights organization in the United States.[55] The Shanghai Second Intermediate Court ruled that Zheng violated the *Law on Guarding State Secrets* by leaking the protected journalistic internal reference to an overseas organization.[56]

Given the serious legal repercussions for violating the law on state secrets, even reporters who write *neican* articles must be very cautious. They cannot disclose the internal reference materials to anyone without appropriate, prior authorization from relevant official bodies. Even repeating the *neican* content, orally, to a third party constitutes leaking state secrets. Having written a *neican* article, the reporter must submit the original to his supervisor and remove the article from the computer or whatever generating medium. Reauthorization is necessary if the reporter needs to review the article, and photocopying is forbidden. A former veteran journalist of an official Chinese news organization observed, "When publishable news is upgraded as secrets and placed under self-regulation, public discourse becomes effectively controlled by the officials."[57]

However, the state secrets protection law does not always entail forceful enforcement. Reporters who leaked classified internal materials avoid punishment if the consequences of releasing the secrets are minimal, if wrongdoers are powerful, if act has authorization, or if the situation is a combination of these factors. Lin Xia is an example: As the incumbent deputy editor-in-chief of Xinhua News Agency, Xia revealed many shocking and unknown stories from internal reference publications in May 2010 when he lectured at Tianjin Foreign Studies University.[58]

[55] Edward Cody, *China Uses Heavy Hand Even with Its Gadflies*, THE WASHINGTON POST, April 9, 2008, http://www.washingtonpost.com/wp-dyn/content/article/2008/04/08/AR2008040803274.html?sid=ST2008040801507 (accessed between February 21, 2025 and March 31, 2025).

[56] INVESTIGATIVE JOURNALISM IN CHINA: EIGHT CASES IN CHINESE WATCHDOG JOURNALISM 144 (David Bandurski & Martin Hala eds., 2010).

[57] Yanhui Chen, *Demystify Neican* [内参揭秘], PHOENIX WEEKLY 14 (2005): 35–39.

[58] Xiao Qiang, *Xia Lin, Xinhua Deputy Chief Editor, Reveals Secret Details of Old News Stories*, CHINA DIGITAL TIMES, June 1, 2010, http://chinadigitaltimes.net/2010/06/xia-lin-%E5%A4%8F%E6%9E%97-xinhua-deputy-chief-editor-reveals-secret-details-of-old-news-stories/ (accessed between February 21, 2025 and March 31, 2025); *Chinese Whispers: Not Believing What They Read in the Papers, China's Leaders Commission Their Own*, THE ECONOMIST, June 17, 2010, https://www.economist.com/asia/2010/06/17/chinese-whispers (accessed between February 21, 2025 and March 31, 2025).

According to Xia, Liwei Yang, the first man sent into space by the Chinese space program, emerged from the Shenzhou spacecraft cabin with his face covered in fresh blood. In order to make him look better before television cameras, "Workers had cleaned blood from Mr. Yang's face before closing and reopening the capsule..."[59] Xia also disclosed that Xinhua purposefully discounted the seriousness of the ethnic riots that erupted in Xinjiang in July 2009 in order to avoid escalation of the conflict.[60] However, after reading the unadulterated internal report from Xinhua, Chinese President Hu Jintao shortened his overseas trip and returned home to deal with the crisis.[61]

Xia's biographical information on the Xinhua website after the incident clearly shows no punishment for Xia's aggressive leaking classified information carried in Xinhua internal reference publications.[62] The government's gesture, ignoring Xia's breech of regulations might lead to an interpretation indicating the party' and the government's gradual relaxing restrictions on internal reference materials to allow public accessibility and to declassify less sensitive information in a timelier manner.

In addition to the law protecting journalistic internal materials as state secrets, another legal privilege of the internal reference system concerns libel. In 1998, the Supreme Court issued a judicial interpretation of defamation, stating that, unlike other forms of news reporting, internal reports produced by reporters and intended for political leaders are

[59] Andrew Jacobs, *In Leaked Lecture, Details of China's News Cleanups*, The New York Times, June 3, 2010, http://www.nytimes.com/2010/06/04/world/asia/04china.html (accessed between February 21, 2025 and March 31, 2025).

[60] Andrew Jacobs, *In Leaked Lecture, Details of China's News Cleanups*, The New York Times, June 3, 2010, http://www.nytimes.com/2010/06/04/world/asia/04china.html (accessed between February 21, 2025 and March 31, 2025).

[61] Andrew Jacobs, *In Leaked Lecture, Details of China's News Cleanups*, The New York Times, June 3, 2010, http://www.nytimes.com/2010/06/04/world/asia/04china.html (accessed between February 21, 2025 and March 31, 2025).

[62] Agencies in China normally remove officials' biographical information from official websites upon investigations of officials or their dismissals. The Xinhua website shows that Xia remained Xinhua's deputy editor-in-chief after the incident. *Biography of Lin Xia* [夏林简介], Xinhua News Agency, 2000–2003 (captured by Internet Archive Wayback Machine on February 14, 2003), retrieved from https://web.archive.org/web/20030214211854/http://www.xinhuanet.com/xhsjj/ling_xl.htm (accessed between February 21, 2025 and March 31, 2025).

"immune from liability for defamation."[63] This protection is significant for journalists writing internal reports, first, because most internal reports are critical and prone to accusations of defamation, and second, given time constraints, journalists usually do not have sufficient evidence to fully support reports' claims. The legal interpretation, prompted by a high-profile 1989 case in Sichuan Province, involved Haideng, a famous monk at Shaoling Temple in Henan Province, who sued a *Sichuan Daily* reporter for libel and failed on the grounds that the allegedly libelous article appeared in a Xinhua internal periodical. Ultimately, Haideng won the case on other grounds.[64]

Reporters have no concerns for libel suits when preparing internal reports for the party's or governmental leaders. However, caution is advisable when quoting from internal reports. The CCP Central Propaganda Department and the State Administration of Press and Publication issued a joint notice in 1998, prohibiting all news organizations in China from quoting Xinhua internal reference materials for regular publications.[65] Requirements insist news organizations file written applications to Xinhua for declassification when seeking to publish any information from Xinhua internal references.[66] With this legal restriction, news media intending to cite or publish internal reference materials must weigh many variables. The relative position of a news organization in the official media hierarchy is one. "While a national level newspaper might opt to use a provincial level *neican*-not lightly, to be sure-a provincial newspaper would be tempting fate to do so."[67]

[63] Benjamin L. Liebman, *Watchdog or Demagogue? The Media in the Chinese Legal System*, 105 Columbia Journalism Review 1, 102 (January 2005).

[64] Xudong Yi, *Account on Haideng v. Yongxiang Jing* [舌剑唇枪辩海灯-范应莲诉敬永祥"侵害海灯法师名誉权"一案始末] 10 Journalism Review (1993).

[65] *Notice of the CCP Central Propaganda Department and the State Administration of Press and Publication on Prohibiting Regular Open Publications from Citing Xinhua Internal Reference Materials* [关于不得在出版物上公开引用发表新华社内参涉密信息的通知] *Xinchulian* [1998] No.10, promulgated in April 30, 1998.

[66] *Notice of the Chinese Communist Party Central Propaganda Department and the State Administration of Press and Publication on Prohibiting Regular Open Publications from Citing Xinhua Internal Reference Materials* [关于不得在出版物上公开引用发表新华社内参涉密信息的通知] Xinchulian [1998] No.10, promulgated in April 30, 1998.

[67] Investigative Journalism In China: Eight Cases In Chinese Watchdog Journalism 144 (David Bandurski & Martin Hala eds., 2010).

Legal Implications: Government Agencies and Courts May Use National Security Exemption to Withhold Information from Journalistic Internal Reference

Scholars may argue that China's journalistic internal reference system and the propaganda system as a whole constitute breach of "freedom of speech, the press, assembly, association, procession and demonstration" stipulated in the country's 1982 Constitution.[68] It is true that internal reference system has trampled upon people's freedom of speech and of the press in many ways. Given that the existence of constitutional review in China is still controversial,[69] however, this chapter will not focus on constitutionality of the internal reference system. Instead, the chapter will mainly examine the conflict between the system and China's first FOI law.

China enacted *OGI Regulations* in 2007, as the first nationwide legislation for FOI and as a statutory obligation for agencies to disclose information, proactively. The law also allows any citizen, any legal person, and any other organization in China to apply for the disclosure of government-held information. Upon rejection of an OGI application by governmental agencies, the requester has the right to pursue administrative and judicial remedies.[70]

China's entry into the global FOI community indicates strongly that China seeks to establish a more open, accessible, and transparent government. Although the FOI law does not include statutory language expressly supporting people's access rights, the law itself sends a strong signal to the world that the party is serious about people's right to know. Such a right, although an American concept, has been repeatedly emphasized by various mainstream publications, party documents, and directives.[71] The internal reference system, however, clearly counters

[68] *Chinese Constitution 1982* (amended April 1988, March 1993, March 1999, March 2004 and March 2018). Art. 35.

[69] Guobin Zhu, *Constitutional Review in China: An Unaccomplished Project or a Mirage?* 43 Suffolk University Law Review 3 (May 25, 2010): 625–653.

[70] *OGI Regulations 2007* (amended in 2019).

[71] Harold L. Cross, The People's Right To Know: Legal Access To Public Records And Proceedings (1953); Lidan Chen, *The 17th Party Congress Report Supports an Open Information Policy* [十七大报告展现开放的信息政策], Changzhou Zugong, Changzhou CCP Committee Organization Department, Changzhou, China,

the concept of governmental transparency and people's right to know. It poses significant public relations and legal challenges to the party who is determined, at least rhetorically, to move toward rule of law instead of rule of man. The practice of classifying newsworthy information as state secrets is definitely not a public relations success story for the party.

Disclosure of government information becomes difficult because of the existence of China's journalistic internal reference system. Under the current media system, news organizations gather a large volume of information about government activities. A big portion of that information is printed or broadcast for public consumption because that portion is about positive stories, and the party wants everyone to see them. Unfortunately, most information that concerns government misconduct, human-caused disasters, or scandals goes to journalistic internal reference. In other words, media organizations compile a big slice of the information pie for exclusive consumption of party and government officials only. The people's right to know is thus harmed. When government agencies receive journalistic internal reference materials from news organizations, those materials become government-held records and files. Government agencies would not proactively disseminate those records because those records are state secrets, thus enjoying exemption from *OGI Regulations*. Government units would not reactively release those records for the same reason. It is clear that the people's right to know is thus harmed again.

Previous studies have found that government agencies in China already used working secrets/internal working documents as a reason to shield official information from disclosure when they were asked to release such documents.[72] It is highly likely that agencies may shield journalistic internal reference materials from public view in the same manner, given the vagueness of the term "state secrets" in Chinese laws and the widespread non-disclosure mentality among FOI stakeholders such as court judges and officials in charge of OGI affairs. So far, this book

December 14, 2007, https://zg.changzhou.gov.cn/content/suitable/show?id=4772&catid=2206 (accessed between February 21, 2025 and March 31, 2025).

[72] FOI scholar Weixing Xiao, in a study of freedom of information in China, found that agencies once rejected OGI requests because those petitions for instructions, research reports, leading officials' views, meeting minutes, and information on the processes of individual petitions are working secrets/internal working documents. WEIBING XIAO, *FREEDOM OF INFORMATION REFORM IN CHINA: INFORMATION FLOW ANALYSIS* 108–109 (2011).

project has not identified any media reports about government agencies proactively releasing information from journalistic internal reference. Likewise, this study has not found a single case in which government agencies released journalistic internal reference materials upon request. Indeed, the study has found that no one in China has submitted OGI requests for information from internal reference publications, classified or declassified. If such an application occurs in the future, it is highly likely that agencies and courts may use the state secrets exemption in *OGI Regulations* to withhold information.

The second issue that is hard to tackle is the legal status of news organizations under China's current FOI law. Under the law, entities with responsibilities fulfilling administrative obligations and/or managing public affairs have an obligation to release information. Some public enterprises and institutions have a similar legal obligation for disclosure.[73] News organizations as institutions directly under the party, the court, the procuratorate, the people's congress, and the political consultative conference (e.g., People's Daily and People's Court Daily) do not have an obligation to follow *OGI Regulations* because their supervisors are not official agencies defined by law. Some news organizations directly under the authority of the people's government, however, may have an obligation to follow *OGI Regulations* like governmental agencies because they are still government-run entities having various kinds of responsibilities, including fulfilling administrative obligations and/or managing public affairs.

Unlike private news media in Western countries, most traditional news media in China are institutions affiliated with the party's and state's bureaucracies, and all have corresponding administrative ranks. The party and the government have an ambitious plan to reshape the media landscape by delinking most party-run or government-run news organizations from their original supervisors and restructuring them into market-oriented, state-owned, Western-style media conglomerates. However, the basic media management structure remains unchanged today due to

[73] Article 54 and Article 55 of OGI Regulations 2019 provide that *OGI Regulations* apply to organizations authorized by laws or regulations to exercise functions for managing public affairs, and also apply to public enterprises and institutions that have a close bearing on people's daily lives. *OGI Regulations 2019*. Art. 54 and Art. 55; Article 36 and Article 37 of OGI Regulations 2007 have similar provisions. OGI Regulations 2007. Art. 36 and Art. 37.

the sensitivity and complexity of reform.[74] For example, Xinhua News Agency, the largest producer of internal reference materials in China, is still an institution directly under the State Council. There are many other institutions directly under the State Council.[75] Most of these institutions are mandated by the State Council to follow *OGI Regulations*.[76] Why should Xinhua News Agency become an exception? More importantly, Xinhua should shoulder some disclosure obligations also because it can be considered as a public media institution that has a close bearing on Chinese people's daily lives. Its transparency obligation under *OGI Regulations* also comes from the fact that it is an empowered entity with authority to manage all the foreign news services in China.

One blogger affirmed the need of disclosure of Xinhua internal reference materials to the public similar to any other official information identified by *OGI Regulations*.[77] The blogger's view is valid, at least from

[74] Shaoxiang Shang, *Reform of Press and Publication Industry and Ensuing Challenges* [新闻出版业改革及面临的问题], PEOPLE'S DAILY ONLINE, January 21, 2009 (captured by Internet Archive Wayback Machine on November 16, 2009), retrieved from https://web.archive.org/web/20091116083155/http://media.people.com.cn/GB/22114/52789/143863/8709400.html (accessed between February 21, 2025 and March 31, 2025).

[75] They are Chinese Academy of Sciences, Chinese Academy of Social Sciences, Chinese Academy of Engineering, Development Research Center of the State Council, China National School of Administration, China Earthquake Administration, China Meteorological Administration, China Banking Regulatory Commission, China Securities Regulatory Commission, China Insurance Regulatory Commission, State Electricity Regulatory Commission, National Council for Social Security Fund, National Natural Science Foundation, Taiwan Affairs Office of the State Council, Information Office of the State Council, and State Archives Administration. For organizational structure of the State Council, visit https://www.gov.cn/gwyzzjg/zuzhi/ (accessed between February 21, 2025 and March 31, 2025) and https://english.www.gov.cn/archive/chinaabc/201911/22/content_WS5ed77233c6d0b3f0e9499854.html (accessed between February 21, 2025 and March 31, 2025).

[76] For example, China Securities Regulatory Commission has promulgated rules to release information under *OGI Regulations. Guidelines Regarding Information Disclosure of China Securities Regulatory Commission* [中国证监会政府信息公开指南], China Securities Regulatory Commission, Beijing, China, *available at* http://www.csrc.gov.cn/csrc/c100033/zfxxgk_zdgk.shtml (accessed between February 21, 2025 and March 31, 2025).

[77] Yihailongmoshiniandeng [衣海弄墨十年灯], *Internal Reference Materials Written by Reporters from Xinhua News Agency Shall Be Disclosed as Open Government Information* [新华社内参也应属于公开的政府信息之列], Tianya Forum [天涯论坛], Haikou, China, July 23, 2009, *available at* https://tianya.my/thread/0/12504535/1.html (accessed between February 21, 2025 and March 31, 2025).

the perspective of Xinhua's special status. As the country's official news agency, authorized by the State Council to supervise and certify information gathering and dissemination of foreign news agencies in China,[78] Xinhua News Agency could be regarded not only as a public institution under Article 55 of the revised OGI Regulations but also a quasi-official agency having responsibility for disclosing information under Article 54 of the revised OGI Regulations.[79]

Although China Central Television, China National Radio, and China Radio International merged in 2018 to form one single entity-China Media Group,[80] they face similar legal challenges regarding whether they are governmental agencies that are subject to *OGI Regulations*. These three electronic media giants remain institutions directly controlled by the National Radio and Television Administration.[81] Compared to Xinhua, whether these three electronic media giants are OGI-designated quasi-agencies authorized by law to manage public affairs[82] or OGI-stipulated public institutions providing basic public services[83] is less certain due to a lack of definitions for "public affairs" and "public services." An expansive interpretation of the public affairs and public services clauses in *OGI Regulations*[84] would likely include CCTV, China National Radio, and

[78] Measures for Administration of Release of News and Information by Foreign News Agencies [外国通讯社在中国境内发布新闻信息管理办法] (promulgated on September 10, 2006 by Xinhua News Agency) (effective on September 10, 2006).

[79] Articles 55 and 54 provide that *OGI Regulations* apply to opening official information activities of public enterprises and institutions and organizations authorized by laws or regulations to exercise functions for managing public affairs. *OGI Regulations 2007* (amended in 2019). Art. 54. Art. 55.

[80] CCTV, CNR and CRI merged in 2018 to form a new state-owned broadcasting giant, China Media Group or Voice of China. *China to Merge State Media Broadcasting Giants*, CHINA GLOBAL TELEVISION NETWORK, March 21, 2018, https://america.cgtn.com/2018/03/21/china-to-merge-state-media-broadcasting-giants (accessed between February 21, 2025 and March 31, 2025).

[81] The National Radio and Television Administration, Beijing, China, *available at* https://www.nrta.gov.cn/ (accessed between February 21, 2025 and March 31, 2025).

[82] *OGI Regulations 2007* (amended in 2019). Art. 54.

[83] Article 55 of the revised FOI law provides that *OGI Regulations* apply to public institutions and public enterprises that provide public services closely related to the people's interests. *OGI Regulations 2007* (amended in 2019). Art. 55.

[84] *OGI Regulations 2007* (amended in 2019), Art. 54. Art. 55.

China Radio International as empowered organizations or public institutions/enterprises having a legal obligation to publicize information made or obtained in the process of performing their duties. A similar legal analysis is possible to examine the applicability of *OGI Regulations* to news organizations at provincial and local levels. If it is finally decided that news organizations really have a legal obligation to be more transparent under the requirements of *OGI Regulations*, no one could answer what kind of information they should release. News organizations would say that journalistic internal reference materials are definitely off-limits to the public because they are "state secrets."

The third issue that deserves attention is giving writers of journalistic internal reference materials immunity from defamation lawsuits[85] and prohibiting such materials from being cited or republished for public consumption.[86] The immunity from defamation charges seems media-friendly at first glance because various studies find that reporters in China lose defamation cases most of the time.[87] This legal privilege, however, may create unfairness in enforcement of libel law for journalists whose assignments are for regular reporting and journalists whose assignments are for internal reporting. People may question why the latter deserves more legal protection than the former. The current system of prohibiting journalists from quoting and/or republishing internal journalistic reference materials for public consumption is also problematic. This policy deprives journalists of the opportunity to have their work consumed

[85] Mei Han, *Interpretation and Applicability of Answers of the Supreme People's Court about Several Issues Concerning Reputation-Related Lawsuits* [《最高人民法院关于审理名誉权案件若干问题的解答》的理解与适用], posted on the website of the National People's Congress, Beijing, China, *available at* http://www.npc.gov.cn/zgrdw/huiyi/lfzt/qqzrfca/2008-12/21/content_1462861.htm (accessed between February 21, 2025 and March 31, 2025); Benjamin L. Liebman, *Watchdog or Demagogue? The Media in the Chinese Legal System*, 105 Columbia Law Review 1, 102 (January 2005).

[86] The Notice of the Chinese Communist Party Central Propaganda Department and the State. Administration of Press and Publication on Prohibiting Regular Open Publications from Citing Xinhua Internal Reference Materials, Xinchulian (1998), No. 10, promulgated April 30, 1998.

[87] For how likely journalists in China prevail in defamation lawsuits, see Yong Tang, *Defaming Officials and Celebrities: Evolution of Libel Law and the Sullivan Impact in China*, paper accepted for presentation by the annual ICA (International Communication Association) convention, San Diego, California, May 25–29, 2017; Yong Tang, *Defaming Officials and Celebrities: Evolution of Libel Law and the Sullivan Impact in China*, 7 Journal Of Media Law And Ethics ½, 41–67 (Spring 2019).

by more people. This policy also penalizes news organizations that use internal reference materials to report on sensitive and controversial issues and events for public readership. The general public becomes the last victim because their right to know what is going on locally, nationally, or even internationally has been harmed as a result of their consuming media content lacking depth, freshness, and context that materials from internal reports could add to regular reports. Working together with the state secret laws, the journalistic internal reference policy aims to restrict freer flow of information.

Although most of the issues mentioned previously have not yet been tested because of the lack of administrative cases, court cases, and other developments, those issues are real and significant. Eventually, law and media reformers will have to think about how to address them. As of December 2023, no government agencies in China have proactively disclosed information from journalistic internal reference.[88] Likewise, as of December 2021, no submitted OGI requests for information included applications for classified or declassified internal reference publications.[89] For processes of individual petitions for working secrets/internal working documents,[90] the author of this book found a similar pattern. If such an application occurs in the future, agencies may use the state secrets exemption in OGI Regulations to withhold information.

"Watchdog" Role of Journalistic Internal References in Chinese Politics

The contribution of the internal reference system to China's political process is largely ignored in Western academia. To Western scholars and China observers, positive stories of official activities frequently occupy front pages of regular Chinese newspapers and constantly fill prime-time television hours. The scenario creates the impression that China does not have aggressive Western-style investigative journalism.

[88] The result was based on the author's analysis of all annual OGI work reports published by all levels of Chinese government from 2008 to 2023.

[89] The result was based on the author's analysis of judicial opinions of 540 OGI-related court cases tried from 2014 to 2021.

[90] Weibing Xiao, Freedom Of Information In China: Information Flow Analysis 108–109 (2011).

The impression is misguided. China has two channels for investigative journalism. One is the visible side of Chinese journalism that everyone in the country can watch, hear, and read. Although it is highly restricted, investigative journalism originated in China in the late 1970s and reached its peak in the mid-1990s and declined in 2003. Media outlets, whether state-run or market-oriented, occasionally expose government scandals and bring them to attention of millions of Chinese readers/viewers. *Caixin*'s in-depth coverage of Zhou Yongkang and his falling from grace epitomizes the most recent effort of Chinese journalists in investigative journalism.[91] Another channel for investigative journalism is the internal reference system, the invisible side of Chinese journalism.[92] The greater latitude for internal references' covering newsworthy and sensitive events, issues, and people has contributed to the vibrancy of investigative journalism, albeit accessible to a limited population in China. Internal reports frequently expose problems and corrupt officials from across the country, criticize official misconduct, and voice the suffering and grievances of ordinary people.

To many media and party leaders, the journalistic internal reference system serves the party and government as a watchdog. For example, the 2007 arrest of Zhiye Wang, the deputy party secretary of Zhengzhou City in Henan Province, was made possible by a Xinhua internal report exposing his corruption.[93] The 2004 execution of Zhongrui Wan, the

[91] Haiyan Wang and Francis L. F. Lee, *Research on Chinese Investigative Journalism, 1978–2013: A Critical Review*, 14 CHINA REVIEW 2 (Special Issue: Doing Sinology in Former Socialist States) (Fall 2014): 215–51; Jingrong Tong and Colin Sparks, Investigative Journalism in China Today, 10 JOURNALISM STUDIES 3 (2009): 337–52; DAVID BANDURSKI MARTIN HALA, EDS. INVESTIGATIVE JOURNALISM IN CHINA: EIGHT CASES IN CHINESE WATCHDOG JOURNALISM (2010); Haitao Xie, Ning Yu, Xin He, Jieqi Luo, Kaixi Huang, and Duan Wang, *Zhou Family Legacy: Thick Blood, Fat Profits*, CAIXIN MAGAZINE, August 22, 2014, http://english.caixin.com/2014-08-22/100720251.html (accessed between February 21, 2025 and March 31, 2025).

[92] Haiyan Wang and Francis L. F. Lee, *Research on Chinese Investigative Journalism, 1978–2013: A Critical Review*, 14 CHINA REVIEW 2 (Special Issue: Doing Sinology in Former Socialist States) (Fall 2014): 215–51; Jingrong Tong and Colin Sparks, Investigative Journalism in China Today, 10 JOURNALISM STUDIES 3 (2009): 337–52; DAVID BANDURSKI MARTIN HALA, EDS. INVESTIGATIVE JOURNALISM IN CHINA: EIGHT CASES IN CHINESE WATCHDOG JOURNALISM (2010).

[93] *Garbage Collectors Take away Two-Million-Yuan Deposit Book Mistakenly Abandoned by Corrupt Official's Wife* [男子收废品收走纪委书记巨款存折], CHINA WEEKLY, republished by Phoenix TV, May 6, 2009, https://news.ifeng.com/society/1/200905/0506_343_1142568.shtml (accessed between February 21, 2025 and March 31, 2025).

party secretary of Nandan County in Guangxi Province, resulted from covering up a major mine incident and employing thugs to threaten journalists attempting to report the incident. Two reporters from *People's Daily* exposed the wrongdoing in internal reports.[94] Internal reference contributed to the strengthened *Production Safety Law*, passed six months later.[95] Examples of such "watchdog journalism" are numerous.[96]

The list of Western-style investigative journalism could go on and on. It is important to note, however, that such "watchdog journalism" differs sharply from "watchdog journalism" in the West. In Western democracies such as the United States, the press serves as the public's watchdog

[94] Ruoqiao Liang, *For Whose Eyes Only?* GLOBAL TIMES, August 24, 2010, https://www.globaltimes.cn/content/566822.shtml (accessed between February 21, 2025 and March 31, 2025); *China Cover-up Official Executed*, BBC NEWS, February 20, 2004, http://news.bbc.co.uk/2/hi/asia-pacific/3507067.stm (accessed between February 21, 2025 and March 31, 2025).

[95] Ruoqiao Liang, *For Whose Eyes Only?* GLOBAL TIMES, August 24, 2010, https://www.globaltimes.cn/content/566822.shtml (accessed between February 21, 2025 and March 31, 2025).

[96] Such examples include but are not limited to the following: Xinhua internal references once exposed corrupt referees in Chinese football. They also exposed Qinghai Provincial Higher People's Court judges in 1985 for shielding a murderer. The imprisonment of Junfeng Bai, the deputy party secretary of Zhanjiang City in Guangdong Province in the late 1970s, followed the internal report to his supervisor from *Nanfang Daily*, detailing Bai's willful misconduct, rape, and corruption. A Xinhua journalist described in his 1978 internal report articles the shocking poverty in Yan'an, a Shanxi city that once served as the capital of Chinese communists. Zhigang Sun, a 27-year-old graphic designer, detained in March 2003 by Guangzhou police, died from torture due to mistaken identification as one of the "three withouts"—a person without identification papers, without a normal residence permit, and without proof of income. Xinhua internal periodicals, sent to leaders, covered the Zhigang Sun incident. In June 2003, the infamous *Regulations on Custody and Repatriation of Homeless Beggars 1982* were repealed. *Xinhua Neican Exposes Black Whistle in Chinese Football* [新华社内参捅破中国足坛的 "黑哨"坚冰], NEW DAILY [每日新报], January 8, 2002, republished by China.com (captured by Internet Archive Wayback Machine on November 9, 2002), retrieved from https://web.archive.org/web/20021109210646/http://www.china.com.cn/chinese/SPORT-c/94580.htm (accessed between February 21, 2025 and March 31, 2025); *Chinese Football Fans Riot over Penalty*, BBC NEWS, March 25, 2002, http://news.bbc.co.uk/2/hi/asia-pacific/1892421.stm (accessed between February 21, 2025 and March 31, 2025); Quanshi Deng, *A Big Case Alarming Deng Xiaoping* [惊动邓小平的一桩大案], YAN-HUANG HISTORICAL REVIEW 12 (2004): 14–17; Ruoqiao Liang, *For Whose Eyes Only?* GLOBAL TIMES, August 24, 2010, https://www.globaltimes.cn/content/566822.shtml (accessed between February 21, 2025 and March 31, 2025); Bingshen Jia, *A Truth-Seeking Warrior: Note on Famous Xinhua Journalist Senling Feng* [追求真理的战士(下)-记新华社著名记者冯森龄], JOURNALISM KNOWLEDGE 2 (1998): 10–14.

on the government. It "barks" to inform the public about government wrongdoing when it sees something wrong in the government. China implements a media system under the so-called authoritarian regime that is different than liberal democratic countries. The roles of Chinese media and journalists are thus different than those of Anglo-American journalists. In China, the function of the internal reference system is not only to act as a watchdog for the public but to act as a watchdog for the party and government. The journalistic internal reference system is meant to serve the senior CCP and government leaders in their policy-making and governance, provide information and advice, and enhance the legitimacy of the party. The system is not designed to make senior party and government leaders look bad. News organizations "bark" all the time to inform the public about government accomplishments, but most of the time, bury the bones of trouble they dig up in internal reference reports that *only* certain levels of party and government officials are entitled to see.

One cannot expect such an internal watchdog to "bark" when it learns about wrongdoings by "tigers" or high-ranking officials. Normally, no journalist would dare to use internal reports to expose bad things made by officials above provincial/ministerial levels unless authorized by people at the pinnacle of the bureaucracy. Misconduct by officials at the very pinnacle of the Chinese political hierarchy would definitely be taboo for internal reports. Expecting *neican* to break a scandal of a similar magnitude to Watergate is a futile exercise in China.[97]

Another area almost untouchable by internal reports is the People's Liberation Army (PLA). The military plays an extremely important role in Chinese politics. Without the full support of soldiers, the party would have difficulty maintaining power and protecting national security/defense.[98] The party, at times, would willingly ignore misdeeds despite

[97] China's journalism often receives ridicule from the public as "only targeting flies" (low-ranking officials and low-level corruption) and "dead tigers" (high-level corruption that the state has already determined to eliminate) but rarely "unrestrained tigers" (high-ranking corrupt officials still in power). This finding applies to regular publications and also to internal publications, although to a lesser degree for the latter. Haiqing Yu, Media And Cultural Transformation In China (2009), 94–95.

[98] David M. Finkelstein And Kristen Gunness, Eds. Civil-Military Relations In Today's China: Swimming In A New Sea (2006).

knowing that military corruption was no less rampant than in civil governments.[99] The civilian authorities just "don't dare to use the media, civil or military, as a watchdog to monitor the PLA the way they do over local governments."[100] It looks like things are changing as the new leadership of the party takes the reins. As many high-ranking military leaders have been arrested and charged with corruption since Xi Jinping and his colleagues launched the massive anti-corruption campaign in the military, it would be interesting to see what kind of role internal reports played in bringing down those military officials.

Journalists drafting internal reports can exert influence on political and governmental leaders, but reporters are vulnerable to manipulation of those leaders. In China, journalistic internal reference production is a part of the internal intelligence gathering and analysis system of the Communist Party-state. The very practice of producing and submitting internal references by journalists (and at times others with some other official capacity) is an exercise of the political power. Journalists who produce such internal reports via means analogous to investigative journalism often have the explicit backing or acquiescence of, or even instruction from, higher ranking officials. At least in the first 30 years of the PRC, producing internal references and persecuting journalists who produced such reports have both been parts of the internal political power struggle. This is another fundamental difference from investigative journalism in the West.

For example, during the Cultural Revolution, a large number of ***neican*** reporters were investigated and even jailed after they were considered espousing Mao's political rivals.[101] Among such journalists were Gongran Xia, who was the director of the Xinhua Internal Reference Department, and Feng Jin, who was an influential *People's Daily* journalist. Xia was purged for writing "politically incorrect" internal reports and standing

99 Mark Magnier, *China's Leaders Take Aim at Military Corruption*, THE LOS ANGELES TIMES, January 17, 2007, https://www.latimes.com/archives/la-xpm-2007-jan-17-fg-china17-story.html (accessed between February 21, 2025 and March 31, 2025); James Mulvenon, *So Crooked They Have to Screw Their Pants On: New Trends in Chinese Military Corruption*, CHINA LEADERSHIP MONITOR 19 (2006).

100 SUSAN L. SHIRK, ED. CHANGING MEDIA, CHANGING CHINA (2011), 31–32.

101 YUEZHI ZHAO, MEDIA, MARKET, AND DEMOCRACY IN CHINA: BETWEEN THE PARTY LINE AND THE BOTTOM LINE (1998), 30.

with Liu Shaoqi, a top leader Mao wanted to purge.[102] After arrest, Jin received a sentence of five years in prison for writing three internal reports exposing the dark side of Chinese air forces and Central Cultural Revolution Small Group.[103] The power struggle between Deng Xiaoping and his political opponents Hu Yaobang and Zhao Ziyang in the late 1980s student demonstrations in China's major cities also led to the downfall of several prestigious *neican* journalists. Editors at *World Economic Herald* in Shanghai were purged in 1989 for its support of student demonstrators, although its internal report once went directly to Deng Xiaoping and other senior party leaders.[104] Binyan Liu, a *People's Daily* journalist who once sent internal reports personally to the then CCP General Secretary, Hu Yaobang, was also purged and died in exile in the United States.[105]

"Think-Tank" Role of Journalistic Internal References in Chinese Politics

In addition to the "internal watchdog" role that media and party leaders are proud of, another role in which *neican* reporters in China take pride is advising the party and government on a wide range of political, economic, social, and other issues to help the state make more informed decisions. Cases exemplifying such "think tank" role are numerous. In four internal reports, a *People's Daily* journalist, Yunshan Lian, recommended creation of a special economic zone in Shenzhen, which is adjacent to Hong Kong. The reports prompted Deng Xiaoping to create

[102] Gongran Xia and Xiaomei Xia, *Cultural Revolution Transformed Me* [“文革”对我的洗礼], Observation And Reflection 4 (2002): 10–14.

[103] Feng Jin, *My Experience of Writing Neican as a People's Daily Journalist* [我在《人民日报》写内参的经历], Yan-Huang Historical Review 10 (2005), republished by Difangwenge.org, August 18, 2017, *available at* https://difangwenge.org/forum.php?mod=viewthread&tid=15199 (accessed between February 21, 2025 and March 31, 2025).

[104] Xiaoqin Guo, State And Society In China's Democratic Transition: Confucianism, Leninism, And Economic Development (2003), 69.

[105] Jennifer Grant, *Internal Reporting by Investigative Journalists in China and Its Influence on Government Policy*, 41 International Communication Gazette 1 (1988): 53–65, 62. For Binyan Liu's life and death, see David Barboza, *Liu Binyan, a Fierce Insider Critic of China, Dies at 80*, The New York Times, December 6, 2005, http://www.nytimes.com/2005/12/06/international/asia/06liu.html?_r=1 (accessed between February 21, 2025 and March 31, 2025).

the Shenzhen Special Economic Zone in 1980.[106] The resumption of Gaokao, the National College Entrance Examination in China, was made possible when a *People's Daily* journalist sent a *neican* article to Deng Xiaoping in 1977 when the Cultural Revolution just ended.[107] Some Xinhua *neican* articles saved the life of Jinrun Chen, one of the most famous Mathematicians in China, and helped the party adjust its policy toward intellectuals.[108] Internal reports helped the party establish the farmer household responsibility system in China's countryside in the early 1980s.[109] Zhongguancun, China's Silicon Valley, was created as a result of recommendations from *neican* articles.[110] The infamous agriculture taxation was completely abolished in 2006 after several *neican* articles reported the death of many poor farmers who were forced by violence to pay tax.[111] On the 100th day of the 2010 World Expo in Shanghai, Xinhua reporters filed 101 internal reference reports to leaders.

[106] Yun Su, *Internal Reports on Massive Exodus of Shenzhen Residents to Hong Kong in 1960s* [六十年代深圳大逃亡期间一份用生命写出的内参], CENTURY 5 (1994): 4–7.

[107] Huanchun Yu, *One Neican Article Repudiates "Two Estimations"* [一份内参推翻"两个估计"] YAN-HUANG HISTORICAL REVIEW 8 (2004);Zhongyuan Cheng, Zhenghua Li & Jincai Zhang, *Elimination of "Two Estimations" and Resumption of National College Entrance Exam* [推倒 "两个估计"与恢复高考], CHINA READING WEEKLY, June 21, 2017, http://epaper.gmw.cn/zhdsb/html/2017-06/21/nw.D110000zhdsb_20170621_1-05.htm (accessed between February 21, 2025 and March 31, 2025). "Two Estimations" was the theoretical basis for suspending the national college entrance exam system. The argument was made by the Gang of Four, claiming that education in China has been controlled by the bourgeoisie and most Chinese intellectuals have a bourgeois worldview. Huan Huang, *Memories of Yang Mu on Writing Neican to Repudiate "Two Estimations"* [穆扬回忆高考恢复:写内参揭发"两个估计"], China.com.cn, Beijing, China, republished by Reformdata.org, May 29, 2007, *available at* http://www.reformdata.org/2007/0529/13908.shtml (accessed between February 21, 2025 and March 31, 2025).

[108] Mai'nan Gu, *Looking for Mathematician Jinrun Chen* [寻访数学家陈景润], YAN-HUANG HISTORICAL REVIEW 8 (2007): 58–61.

[109] Xunlei Xu, *Review on Bid Farewell to Hunger* [读《告别饥饿》],], YAN-HUANG HISTORICAL REVIEW 11 (2009); Gongran Xia and Xiaomei Xia, *How Neican Covers Farmer Household Responsibility System* [内参反映"包产到户"的前前后后], OBSERVATION AND REFLECTION 1 (2002): 10–14.

[110] Junsheng Xia, *How Zhongguancun Came into Birth* [中关村高新技术产业区的由来],], YAN-HUANG HISTORICAL REVIEW 7 (2009).

[111] Yanhui Chen, *Demystify Neican* [内参揭秘], PHOENIX WEEKLY 14 (2005): 35–39.

A veteran Xinhua reporter said proudly, "We are like a think tank for the government."[112]

Producing internal references for policy-making is not limited to journalists. Today, it has become a basis for the proliferation of various Chinese research centers/institutes that are competing to be "think tanks." Their work performance is evaluated on whether their references receive favorable written comments from officials of higher up. By 2014, just one year after Xi Jinping unveiled a plan to create "think tanks with Chinese characteristics," China had become a country with the second largest number of think tanks in the world, second only to the United States.[113] Among those hundreds of thousands of think tanks are ones affiliated with major news media organizations, such as *People's Daily*, Xinhua News Agency, *Guangming Daily* and *Caixin*.[114] The media think tanks' major goal is to advise the party and government on various issues relating to media, propaganda, and communication. If we say that, in the past, the phrase "think tank" was just a figure of speech for media's role, then today it is no longer a literary term, at least for the Chinese media. The media has become a think tank for the Chinese bureaucracy, at least judging from what the media often claims.

Someone may argue that Chinese journalists authoring internal reports contribute to the political policy-making process, similar to the role enjoyed by think tanks in the West. Intelligence gathered by journalists may indicate that a policy implemented in the past was inappropriate, thereby influencing political leaders to abolish the policy. Internal reports might expose "inadequacies and flaws" within a policy and convince policymakers to reform or revise the policy. Journalists drafting internal

[112] Ruoqiao Liang, *For Whose Eyes Only?* GLOBAL TIMES, August 24, 2010, https://www.globaltimes.cn/content/566822.shtml (accessed between February 21, 2025 and March 31, 2025).

[113] Ziyi Meng and Yuan Ye, *China's Think Tanks: One Hundred Schools of Thought Contend, at Least Seemly* [中国智库:看上去的百家争鸣?], FINANCIAL TIMES CHINESE, September 24, 2015, https://wap.ftchinese.com/story/001063806?archive (accessed between February 21, 2025 and March 31, 2025).

[114] Lili Wang, Chinese *Think Tanks Affiliated with Media Organizations: Positioning and Growth Paths* [中国媒体智库的定位与发展路径], THE PRESS 2 [新闻战线] (2018), *available at* http://paper.people.com.cn/xwzx/html/2018-02/01/content_1840129.htm (accessed between February 21, 2025 and March 31, 2025).

reports might raise questions or issues previously unconsidered by decision makers, leading to formulation of new policies.[115]

The reason that the party and the government in China designate journalists as unofficial advisors for governmental policy-making is fourfold: first, journalists have advantages in collecting information. They travel widely and have a wide range of contacts. They have easy access to high-level leaders and prestigious scholars, but at the same time, they can converse with ordinary people without restraint. Second, investigative reporters are usually insightful and accustomed to meeting deadlines, so their reports are usually fresh and timely. Third, decision makers can combine internal reports with information acquired through routine bureaucratic channels to better understand a situation. Last, internal reports provided by news organizations are especially valuable when regular communication channels within the bureaucracy are blocked "for bureaucratic and political reasons."[116]

With all of this being said, the so-called "think tank" role has huge problems. First, advising the government like think tanks is an inappropriate role for newspapers, TV stations, and other mass media outlets. News media organizations are not think tanks at all. "Jack of all trades and master of none" is something encouraged in journalism. Journalists thus cannot compete with think tanks in terms of depth of thought and feasibility of policy recommendations because think tank scholars normally have Ph.D. degrees, many years of academic experiences, and expertise on specific areas or issues. Most importantly, think tank scholars in the West often have much experience working in the government so they know exactly what kind of policy recommendation would most likely be accepted by the administration. The best think tanks in America and other developed countries are often independent from government and receive funding from private donors. Their independence enables them to formulate unbiased and more effective policy recommendations. Journalists and news organizations in China have none of these qualities.

[115] Jennifer Grant, *Internal Reporting by Investigative Journalists in China and Its Influence on Government Policy*, 41 International Communication Gazette 57 (1988).

[116] Jennifer Grant, *Internal Reporting by Investigative Journalists in China and Its Influence on Government Policy*, 41 International Communication Gazette 61 (1988).

Second, even if the think tank role is legitimate, media organizations could do a better job of helping the party and government if they were to publish or broadcast internal reports, because the general public would not know that the party and government is doing something great if problems are exposed and solved secretly.

Third, criticizing and advising officials behind closed doors but remaining silent when controversial and newsworthy events happen creates unfavorable impressions among readers and viewers. The public would perceive news media organizations as being deceitful and having no real concern for the masses. This perception crisis would happen as soon as internal reports are publicized when the national security protection term expires.

Fourth, internal reports will accomplish nothing if the supreme leader in the party/government refuses to accept recommendations proposed by such reports. Although Mao Zedong received a significant number of fake reports from local officials glorifying the achievements of the Great Leap Forward Movement in 1958, Mao actually knew, clearly, the gravity of the economic situation of the whole country at that time. Mao had sufficient information about the real economic situation from daily journalistic internal references he had received from various leading media organizations[117]; however, he did not modify the disastrous economic policies those reports suggested. The same thing happened to top political leaders in China a few years ago when they refused to revise their COVID-19 policy even after they knew what was truly going on in the pandemic via Xinhua News Agency internal reports.[118]

[117] Ching-chang Hsiao & Timothy Cheek, *Open and Closed Media: External and Internal Newspapers in the Propaganda System*, *in* DECISION-MAKING IN DENG'S CHINA: PERSPECTIVES FROM INSIDERS 82 (Carol Lee Hamrin & Suisheng Zhao eds., 1995).

[118] Dake Wang, *In Xi's China, even Internal Reports Fall Prey to Censorship*, ASSOCIATED PRESS, October 31, 2022, https://apnews.com/article/health-china-beijing-covid-wuhan-3c199e3f1a084013da18fc9e6061e775 (accessed between February 21, 2025 and March 31, 2025).

Internet and Market-Oriented Media Reform Are Disincentives for Journalistic Internal Reference

Another challenge that the journalistic internal reference system is facing now is the increasing pervasiveness of the Internet in all aspects of Chinese people's daily lives. Compared to traditional media, the Internet enjoys clear advantages for gathering, producing, and delivering information to the widest audiences possible. For instance, in a recent 10-year span, internal reports of *Liberation Daily*, official newspaper of the CCP Shanghai Committee, are coming less and less from contributing writers and have to rely increasingly upon staff writers. The percentage of contributing articles dropped from 30 percent to 5 percent. Most contributing writers no longer send articles to *Liberation Daily Internal Report*; instead, contributors submit stories on the Internet for timely publication and greater social impact.[119]

Market-oriented media reforms have also created financial, reputational, and other disincentives for journalistic internal reference. Chinese media organizations are becoming increasingly commercial in recent years,[120] and as a result, market-oriented media outlets have proliferated in China. Many media outlets such as the *Caijing* magazine in Beijing and the newspaper *Southern Weekend* in Guangzhou are metropolitan magazines and newspapers[121] that receive no funding from the government and survive independently. In order to gain credibility and compete successfully in the market, market-oriented media entities are more eager than traditional party and government news organizations in airing and publishing sensitive and controversial news stories. Perhaps the parent newspapers[122] may require their affiliated media outlets to write *neican* in some cases, but generally, those market-oriented publications "rarely,

119 Lingying Wang, *Examination of Internal Reference Orientation in the Internet Age* [网络时代的内参取向探析], 9 Shanghai Journalism Review 81 (2010).

120 Yuezhi Zhao, Media, Market, And Democracy In China: Between The Party Line And The Bottom Line 52–71 (1998).

121 Yuezhi Zhao, Communication In China: Political Economy, Power, And Conflict (2008).

122 In China, most market-oriented metropolitan newspapers and magazines are affiliated with party newspapers.

if ever, prepare internal reports."[123] This situation contributes to many news stories appearing on front pages of metropolitan publications. In the past, those stories would have appeared on desks of high-ranking officials in the form of journalistic internal reference.

The party's traditional news outlets prepare most internal reports for leaders, confronting the pressure of commercialization. Most of the party's traditional news organizations face reduced subsidies from the government.[124] In order to gain credibility, and increase circulation and adverting revenues, even traditional party-run media outlets tended to publish more stories that would otherwise have been printed in internal periodicals in the past.

Commercialization also contributes to the decreasing number of staff reporters willing to be unknown or unsung heroes. If the byline of an investigative journalist appears frequently on the front pages of a prestigious, regular publication, fame ensues among tens of millions of readers. However, even if the byline appears on the front page of an internal publication with the same frequency, no notoriety results outside the realm of political and governmental leaders. For this reason, some reporters prefer writing for regular publications than for internal ones. Binyan Liu, the renowned former journalist of the *People's Daily*, expressed such disenchantment with internal reports in a semi-fictional story, "The Inside News of the Newspaper."[125]

[123] Benjamin L. Liebman, *Watchdog or Demagogue? The Media in the Chinese Legal System*, 105 COLUMBIA LAW REVIEW 1 (January 2005), 23.

[124] China announced in 2003 that they were ending subsidies to all newspapers in the country, except some major ones like the *People's Daily*. The announcement directed all publications to suspend ties to official departments and cease mandatory subscriptions. Jiafei Yin, *Beyond Four Theories of the Press: A New Model for the Asian and the World Press*, 10 *JOURNALISM & COMMUNICATIONS MONOGRAPHS* 1 (Spring 2008): 3–62.

[125] In that piece, Liu described vividly a young journalist's dissatisfaction with internal reports. "For a long time now, her reports had been classified as inside information. They were typed, printed, and distributed to the offices concerned, or used as reference materials for guest authors writing articles." Jennifer Grant, *Internal Reporting by Investigative Journalists in China and Its Influence on Government Policy*, 41 INTERNATIONAL COMMUNICATION GAZETTE 53, 58–59 (1988).

Journalistic Internal Reference: Breeding Ground for Corruption

The journalistic internal reference system was designed, at least partially, by Chinese leaders to catch corruption. The system itself, however, is becoming a breeding ground for corruption. This is because the power of deciding what appears in public media and what appears in journalistic internal reference is too huge and the potential for abuse of such power is tremendous. Normally, it is up to journalists and their news organizations to decide what goes where, with constant guidance from party and government censors. Since no clear-cut standards exist for what could appear in internal reports, anyone who has the duty of gatekeeping could classify reports on a newsworthy event as secrets as long as he or she desires. People are thus motivated to use the power of classifying news to seek personal gains.

It is thus not surprising for some journalists to write for internal publications with ulterior motives. Some reporters threaten to write negative pieces and internal reference materials to obtain "publicity fees" from businesses.[126] Some journalists promise to write positive pieces for officials who want to be covered in internal reference materials because appearing in a positive internal reference story is an effective way for local officials to get attention of top leaders. No matter what, producing journalistic internal reference is becoming a huge power that is largely left unchecked. The mass production of fake internal reference materials used to be a thriving industry in Beijing.[127] Kui Feng, a young journalist from the *People's Daily* bureau in Liaoning Province, was arrested and jailed for accepting bribes from a corrupt mayor of Shenyang City. After taking the bribes, Feng submitted two internally circulated articles to central leaders in Beijing to whitewash the official.[128] Some Xinhua journalists

[126] Yuezhi Zhao, Media, Market, And Democracy In China: Between The Party Line And The Bottom Line 79 (1998).

[127] Tailing Zhang, *Fake Newsrooms Write Fake Journalistic Internal Reference for Desperate Petitioners* [假编辑部收千元为上访者写内参], Beijing News, republished by Sina Finance, August 2, 2010, https://finance.sina.cn/sa/2010-08-02/detail-ikftpnny0176483.d.html?from=wap (accessed between February 21, 2025 and March 31, 2025).

[128] Weixin Jin and Xudong Zhou, *Deputy Mayor Xiangdong Ma's Wife Buys over Officials and Journalists* [马向东老婆贿倒官员记者], Beijing Youth Daily, republished by People's Daily Online, March 26, 2002 (captured by Internet Archive Wayback

were expelled for using the power of *neican* to extort a local coalmine owner in Shanxi Province. The mine exploded due to negligent security. After accepting payoffs in cash and gold ingots from mine owners, the Xinhua journalists remained silent on the accident. Ironically enough, a reporter from *China Youth Daily* exposed this journalistic scandal in his internal reference articles that caught the attention of a CCP politburo member.[129] Those incidents are just a tip of iceberg, reaffirming the eternal truth that any power corrupts if it is left in the dark without public oversight.

Journalistic Internal Reference Is Expanding Despite Criticism

Given the shortcomings and drawbacks, some scholars and National People's Congress deputies argue for abolishing journalistic internal reference and accessibility of newsworthy items for everyone. For example, Jiang Zhan, a media law scholar and former professor of Beijing Foreign Studies University Department of Journalism and Communication, argued that internal reference is "an information vehicle for a small, privileged class. They are like *Dibao* in ancient times, and they are not standard news in modern society. Internal reference materials are only suitable for an agrarian society or in a time of war…solving social issues should depend on a free flow of information."[130]

Communications scholar, Yuezhi Zhao, attacked the internal reference system from the perspective of participatory democracy or informed citizenry. Due to limitations on regular news coverage of the government's decision-making process and classified status of internal reference reports carrying information relevant to policy-making, "Citizens are systematically excluded from vital information that would enable them

Machine on April 14, 2002), retrieved from https://web.archive.org/web/20020414005701/http://www.people.com.cn/GB/shizheng/19/20020326/694898.html (accessed between February 21, 2025 and March 31, 2025).

129 Investigative Journalism In China: Eight Cases In Chinese Watchdog Journalism 121 (David Bandurski & Martin Hala eds., 2010).

130 Yanhui Chen, *Demystify Neican* [内参揭秘], Phoenix Weekly 14 (2005): 35–39; Ruoqiao Liang, "*For Whose Eyes Only*?" Global Times, August 24, 2010. https://www.globaltimes.cn/content/566822.shtml (accessed between February 21, 2025 and March 31, 2025).

to participate in policy-making."[131] Shunxing Huang, the member of the seventh NPC Standing Committee, refused to grant an interview to a journalist who promised that the conversation would be published in internal reference publications. He said to the reporter, "I am a people's congress deputy. The people are above anyone else. External reference is more important than internal reference!"[132]

Most ordinary Chinese citizens seem disenchanted with the practice of classifying newsworthy information as internal reference. Some bloggers argue that internal reference is an information privilege enjoyed by the political elite and abolishment should occur immediately because the system deprives Chinese citizens of the right to know. The enforcement of *OGI Regulations* renders the abolishment of journalistic internal reference an even more urgent and necessary task. A blogger stated that the public ought to have access to Xinhua internal reference materials like any other official information according to *OGI Regulations*.[133]

However, not all scholars or journalists agree with the abolishing journalistic internal reference. Guoming Yu, professor of Renmin University of China, contended that "internal reference system might be abolished in the future. However, at the moment, eliminating internal reports is intolerable for China's political system."[134] Yu explained that disclosing all internal publication materials to the public without any restriction would

[131] Yuezhi Zhao, Media, Market, And Democracy In China: Between The Party Line And The Bottom Line 30 (1998).

[132] Dong Ding, *Shunxing Huang, a Scientist Who Does Not Yield to Political Pressure Easily* [水土不服的黄顺兴], 163 History Reference [文史资料选辑] 22 (2010), excerpted by People's Daily Online, April 14, 2011 (captured by Internet Archive Wayback Machine on March 4, 2016), retrieved from https://web.archive.org/web/20160304090638/http://history.people.com.cn/GB/198819/207809/14391587.html (accessed between February 21, 2025 and March 31, 2025).

[133] Yihailongmoshiniandeng [衣海弄墨十年灯], *Internal Reference Materials Written by Reporters from Xinhua News Agency Shall Be Disclosed as Open Government Information* [新华社内参也应属于公开的政府信息之列], Tianya Forum [天涯论坛], Haikou, China, July 23, 2009, *available at* https://tianya.my/thread/0/12504535/1.html (accessed between February 21, 2025 and March 31, 2025).

[134] Yanhui Chen, *Demystify Neican* [内参揭秘], Phoenix Weekly 14 (2005): 35–39; Ruoqiao Liang, "*For Whose Eyes Only*?" Global Times, August 24, 2010. https://www.globaltimes.cn/content/566822.shtml (accessed between February 21, 2025 and March 31, 2025).

cause "enormous societal conflict."[135] Xinhua editor Lin Xia maintains a similar attitude by citing ethnic rioting in Xinjiang in July 2009 as an example. He said that if Xinhua reported the riots to the fullest extent, that "would have only further inflamed the conflict" and caused more serious human and economic damages.[136]

Despite the criticism and system's shortcomings, party and governmental officials in China continue to rely heavily on the internal reference system for the near future. Perhaps, the influence of journalistic internal reference will increase in coming years. Statistics support the rise of Chinese journalistic internal reference in the digital age.

According to Xinhua data compiled to measure the impact of its activities, at the party's five-year congress in 2007, Xinhua issued more than twice as many internal reports as for the 2002 event.[137] In 2003, the number of comments written by leaders in the margins of *Reference Materials Proof* rose by 88 percent, compared with the year before. Chinese President Hu Jintao wrote six.[138] *Reference Proofs (Supplementary Sheets)*, published more than three times as many reports in 2003 as in 2002.[139] In 2007, Xinhua's yearbook reported a 15 percent growth in the number of *Proofs of Domestic Trends* (A Digest of Online Public Sentiment) and

[135] Yanhui Chen, *Demystify Neican* [内参揭秘], PHOENIX WEEKLY 14 (2005): 35–39; Ruoqiao Liang, "*For Whose Eyes Only*?" GLOBAL TIMES, August 24, 2010. https://www.globaltimes.cn/content/566822.shtml (accessed between February 21, 2025 and March 31, 2025).

[136] Xiao Qiang, *Xia Lin, Xinhua Deputy Chief Editor, Reveals Secret Details of Old News Stories*, CHINA DIGITAL TIMES, June 1, 2010, http://chinadigitaltimes.net/2010/06/xia-lin-%E5%A4%8F%E6%9E%97-xinhua-deputy-chief-editor-reveals-secret-details-of-old-news-stories/ (accessed between February 21, 2025 and March 31, 2025).

[137] *Chinese Whispers: Not Believing What They Read in the Papers, China's Leaders Commission Their Own*, THE ECONOMIST, June 17, 2010, https://www.economist.com/asia/2010/06/17/chinese-whispers (accessed between February 21, 2025 and March 31, 2025).

[138] *Chinese Whispers: Not Believing What They Read in the Papers, China's Leaders Commission Their Own*, THE ECONOMIST, June 17, 2010, https://www.economist.com/asia/2010/06/17/chinese-whispers (accessed between February 21, 2025 and March 31, 2025).

[139] *Chinese Whispers: Not Believing What They Read in the Papers, China's Leaders Commission Their Own*, THE ECONOMIST, June 17, 2010, https://www.economist.com/asia/2010/06/17/chinese-whispers (accessed between February 21, 2025 and March 31, 2025).

a 50 percent increase in leaders' comments on them.[140] *People's Daily* is planning to compete aggressively with Xinhua in quality and quantity of internal reports. One indication of the competition is the creation of the Internal Reference News Department in 2008 by *People's Daily*. Fifteen editors and reporters work exclusively for production and dissemination of internal reports.[141]

The growth of journalistic internal reference is unsurprising because Chinese party and governmental leaders view journalistic internal reference as an indispensable source of information. Ambitious investigative journalists who are politically reliable and professionally insightful are authors of internal reference materials, and sensitive and controversial materials transmit directly to central and local leaders without filtering or delay. Many problems and conflicts have quiet resolution without incurring negative publicity.[142] In addition, CCP and government officials can compare journalistic internal reference with the similar information gathered through bureaucratic channels to discover inconsistencies and possible prevaricators in the communication process.

Working Secrets are Exempt in Many National FOI Laws

After examining journalistic internal reference and its legal implications in the context of freedom of information legislation, now it is time to talk about working secrets/internal working documents.

Working secrets in the Chinese context are the equivalent of "internal working documents" widely exempt in many national FOI laws. In the

140 *Chinese Whispers: Not Believing What They Read in the Papers, China's Leaders Commission Their Own*, The Economist, June 17, 2010, https://www.economist.com/asia/2010/06/17/chinese-whispers (accessed between February 21, 2025 and March 31, 2025).

141 Ruoqiao Liang, "*For Whose Eyes Only?*," Global Times, August 24, 2010. https://www.globaltimes.cn/content/566822.shtml (accessed between February 21, 2025 and March 31, 2025). *Roster of Editors and Reporters at People's Daily* [人民日报采编部门人员名单], People's Daily Online, February 16, 2007 (captured by Internet Archive Wayback Machine on February 24, 2007), retrieved from https://web.archive.org/web/20070224143536/http://media.people.com.cn/GB/5406002.html (accessed between February 21, 2025 and March 31, 2025).

142 Lingying Wang, *Examination of Internal Reference Orientation in the Internet Age* [网络时代的内参取向探析], 9 Shanghai Journalism Review 81 (2010).

United States, for example, *U.S. FOIA* identifies two kinds of internal working documents that are exempt from disclosure. One is housekeeping practices in Exemption 2 of the U.S. *FOIA* and the other is intra-agency and interagency memoranda and letters identified in Exemption 5.[143] Exemption 2 shields from disclosure risk-of-circumvention records and records of internal agency personnel rules and practices like hiring, dismissal, work rules, discipline, compensation, and benefits.[144] Exemption 5 shields three kinds of information from disclosure: working papers such as studies, reports, memoranda, and other sorts of documents prepared and circulated to assist official decisions or policies (deliberative process privilege); conversations and materials between an agency and its attorneys (client-attorney privilege), and communication between the president and key advisors (executive privilege doctrine or presidential communications privilege).[145] Most information in Exemptions 2 and 5 of *U.S. FOIA* coincides with the Chinese context of working secrets.

Internal working documents are exempt in *U.S. FOIA* and many other national FOI laws for several reasons. Official records of employees' work schedules, coffee break rules, sick leave policies, and personal parking assignments are trivial administrative matters and have no basis for genuine public interest. The release of public records of pre-decisional and deliberative communications could inhibit frankness and candor in future pre-decisional communications. The disclosure of information of deliberations of policy alternatives could lead to confusion and harm the integrity of the decision-making process.[146] Communications between an attorney and a client are inviolately private. However, the internal working documents exemption is not absolute. In order to prevent agencies from abusing this exemption, many national FOI laws impose restrictions on scope. For example, in *U.S. FOIA,* the deliberative process privilege is not absolute. The privilege does not protect purely factual information related to the process of policy development from being disclosed. Disclosure of factual information generated in the decision-making process must

[143] 5 U.S.C. § 552((b) (2) (2006) and 5 U.S.C. § 552((b) (5) (2006).

[144] *Milner v. Department of the Navy*, 131 S. Ct. 1259 (2011).

[145] Don. R. Pember & Clay Calvert, Mass Media Law 349–351 (2013).

[146] Yingping Zhu, *Analysis of Disclosure of Internal and Preparatory Government Information* [行政机关内部准备性行为的信息公开问题探析] 3 Studies In Law And Business 69 (2010).

occur unless such information is inextricable from protected information regarding an agency's decision.[147]

Working Secrets Inconsistencies in Chinese OGI Legislation

The term "working secrets" appears in *Law on Public Servants 2005*,[148] *Public Procurators Law 1995*,[149] *Judges Law 1995*,[150] administrative rules,[151] and local rules.[152] Despite the frequent use of the term, the definition of "working secrets" is vague. In practice, working secrets are

[147] Yingping Zhu, *Analysis of Disclosure of Internal and Preparatory Government Information* [行政机关内部准备性行为的信息公开问题探析] 3 Studies In Law And Business 69 (2010); Comparison Of Foreign Freedom Of Information Systems 59 [外国政府信息公开制度比较] (Hanhua Zhou ed., China Legal Publishing House, 2003).

[148] The law mandates public servants' responsibility to perform the duties of guarding state secrets and working secrets. The law also prohibits public servants from disclosing state secrets and working secrets. *Law on Public Servants 2005*. Art.12. Art. 53.

[149] The law provides that public procurators maintain state secrets and procuratorial working secrets. According to the law, public procurators who score outstanding achievement for protecting state secrets and procuratorial working secrets receive rewards and those divulging state secrets or procuratorial working secrets receive punishment. *Public Procurators Law 1995*. Art. 8. Art. 31. Art. 33.

[150] The law provides that judges maintain state secrets and judicial working secrets. According to the law, judges who excel in guarding state secrets and judicial working secrets receive rewards, and those who divulged state secrets and judicial working secrets receive punishment. *Judges Law 1995*. Art. 7. Art. 30. Art. 32.

[151] For example, *Rules of Determining the Scope of State Secrets in Auditing 1995* provide that working secrets regarding auditing are matters that are not state secrets but inappropriate for public inspection and unavailable for disclosure without proper prior authorization. *Rules of Determining the Scope of State Secrets in Personnel Management 1989* provides that working secrets in personnel work that are not state secrets but inappropriate for public inspection are unavailable to the public without authorization. Twenty-three administrative rules determine the scope of state secrets and provide for protection of working secrets. *Rules of Determining the Scope of State Secrets in Auditing 1995*. Art. 5; *Rules of Determining the Scope of State Secrets in Personnel Management 1989*. Art.3.

[152] For example, *Guangzhou Provision on Guarding Working Secrets 2001*, the first local rule of its kind, provides that working secrets involve matters whose sensitivity does not reach the level of state secrets but remains prohibited for public inspection. *Guangzhou Provision on Guarding Working Secrets 2001*. Art. 2.

loosely defined as internal working documents that cover a wide range of information but are insufficiently sensitive to classify as state secrets.

Whether or not working secrets or internal working documents shall have exemptions in *OGI Regulations* has engendered significant debate in China since drafting the initial FOI law. Most Chinese legal reformers object to the proposal of writing "working secrets" into *OGI Regulations* as an exemption because the term has no boundaries and may apply to any information that is not designated a state secret.[153] However, some scholars argued that internal working documents, such as requests for instructions, research reports, leading officials' views, and minutes need exclusion from disclosure, and shielding such documents from disclosure is standardized international practice.[154]

Among the seven exemptions in the *Academic Draft of OGI Regulations* formulated by legal scholars in 2002, two concern internal working documents. Exemption 3 states that matters of no public interest and matters that relate purely to internal agency's personnel rules are not subject to disclosure.[155] Exemption 6 states that pre-decisional and deliberative information generated in interagencies' or intra-agencies' policy discussions are exempt from disclosure if such disclosure may prejudice the integrity of the decision-making process and cause public confusion.[156]

The State Council officials, who approved the final statutory language of *OGI Regulations*, rejected legal scholars' recommendations for exempting internal working documents from disclosure. Finally, *OGI*

[153] WEIBING XIAO, FREEDOM OF INFORMATION REFORM IN CHINA: INFORMATION FLOW ANALYSIS 108 (2011); Mo Chen, *Key of OGI Regulations Is to Make OGI Legal Obligation of Government* [条例的要害是把信息公开变成政府的法定义务], 21ST CENTURY BUSINESS HERALD, republished by Sina Finance, April 26, 2007, http://finance.sina.com.cn/g/20070426/09223543933.shtml (accessed between February 21, 2025 and March 31, 2025).

[154] Hua Liu, *On Several Legal Issues Concerning Government Information Disclosure* [论政府信息公开的若干法律问题] 6 POLITICS SCIENCE AND LAW 70 (2008); COMPARISON OF FOREIGN FREEDOM OF INFORMATION SYSTEMS [外国政府信息公开制度比较] (Hanhua Zhou ed., China Legal Publishing House, 2003).

[155] ACADEMIC DRAFT OF OGI REGULATIONS: DRAFT, EXPLANATION, RATIONALE AND LEGISLATIVE EXAMPLES 8 [政府信息公开条例专家建议稿-草案、说明、理由、立法例] (Hanhua Zhou ed., Chinese Legal Publishing House, 2003).

[156] ACADEMIC DRAFT OF OGI REGULATIONS: DRAFT, EXPLANATION, RATIONALE AND LEGISLATIVE EXAMPLES 8 [政府信息公开条例专家建议稿-草案、说明、理由、立法例] (Hanhua Zhou ed., Chinese Legal Publishing House, 2003).

Regulations 2007 provide no provisions to clarify if working secrets or internal working documents are exempt from disclosure. The ministries, commissions and departments under the State Council followed this approach. None of the rules for implementation of *OGI Regulations* formulated by those central agencies have provisions for this issue.[157] Some local governments' OGI rules for implementation provide that internal working documents are exempt from disclosure but provide no restrictions to limit the scope of that exemption.[158]

In an administrative interpretation, the State Council provides that internal working documents are exempt from disclosure.[159] According to the interpretation, shielding from disclosure requirements of *OGI Regulations* remains for information generated or obtained from routine management of internal agencies and procedural information still under deliberation, investigation, and review.[160] Following the State Council's approach, the Supreme Court included procedural documents and other internal working documents in the exemptions when drafting the judicial interpretation of *OGI Regulations*.[161] Ultimately, the Supreme Court

[157] For example, both *Information Disclosure Implementation Rules of the Ministry of Housing and Urban–Rural Construction 2009* and *Information Disclosure Implementation Rules of Colleges and Universities 2010* fail to specify if pre-decisional and deliberative official information is exempt from disclosure. I*nformation Disclosure Implementation Rules of the Ministry of Housing and Urban–Rural Construction 2009*[住房和城乡建设部政府信息公开实施办法] Jianban [2009] No.145, effective date: August 31, 2009; *Information Disclosure Implementation Rules of Colleges and Universities 2010* [高等学校信息公开办法] Jiaoyubu Ling [2010] No.29, effective date: September 1, 2010.

[158] For example, *Provisions of Shanghai Municipality on Openness of Government Information 2008* provides that official, pre-decisional and deliberative information is exempt from disclosure because the disclosure of such information may harm state security, public security, economic security, or social stability. *Provisions* do not impose any restrictions on the scope of the exemption. *Provisions of Shanghai Municipality on Openness of Government Information 2008* [上海市政府信息公开规定] effective date: May 1, 2008, revised in December 2010.

[159] *Opinions of the State Council General Office on Doing a Good Job of Disclosing Government Information on Request* [国务院办公厅关于做好政府信息依申请公开工作的意见] Guo Ban Fa [2010] No. 5, effective date: January 12, 2010.

[160] *Opinions of the State Council General Office on Doing a Good Job of Disclosing Government Information on Request* [国务院办公厅关于做好政府信息依申请公开工作的意见] Guo Ban Fa [2010] No. 5, effective date: January 12, 2010.

[161] *Exposure Draft of Provisions of the Supreme People's Court on Issues concerning Trying Administrative Cases of Government Information Disclosure* [最高人民法院关于审理政府信息公开行政案件若干问题的规定(征求意见稿)] promulgated in November 2, 2009.Art.11.

removed that provision from the final version of the judicial interpretation of *OGI Regulations* due to strong opposition from the public and some legal scholars.[162] Those petitions for instructions,[163] research reports,[164]

[162] *Provisions of the Supreme People's Court on Issues concerning Trying Administrative Cases of Government Information Disclosure* [最高人民法院关于审理政府信息公开行政案件若干问题的规定] Fa Shi [2011] No.17, effective date: August 13, 2011. Xianming Zhang, *Supreme Court of China Issues Judicial Interpretation of OGI Regulations, Providing Courts with Guidance on OGI-Related Lawsuits* [最高人民法院颁布司法解释全面规范审理政府信息公开行政案件有关问题], PEOPLE'S COURT DAILY, republished by the Supreme Court of China website, August 15, 2011 (captured by Internet Archive Wayback Machine on February 19, 2022), retrieved from https://web.archive.org/web/20220219074628/https://www.court.gov.cn/zixun-xiangqing-3024.html (accessed between February 21, 2025 and March 31, 2025).

[163] For example, Lianmian Kang and 25 other citizens lodged an OGI application in 2007 to Guangzhou Municipal Bureau of Labor and Social Security. The agency refused their request, and the local court upheld the denial. Both the agency and the court determined that the information sought fell into the category of internal affairs because it was a letter sent by the agency to the Ministry of Labor to request instructions for the criteria used to count dismissed employees' total working years. This case predated *OGI Regulations*' enforcement. Noticeably, the use of requests for instructions as grounds to deny access continues after May 2008. For example, on June 11, 2008, Yulai Yuan submitted an OGI request to the Anhui provincial people's government for a letter sent by the agency for law and policy instructions concerning establishment of developmental zones and industrial parks. The agency denied the application, asserting that the information sought was pre-decisional information used to assist the agency's handling an administrative reconsideration case. Yuan sued the agency in a local court later. WEIBING XIAO, FREEDOM OF INFORMATION REFORM IN CHINA: INFORMATION FLOW ANALYSIS 108 (2011); Jie Lin & Xiangyang Sun, *Twenty Six Guangzhou Citizens Bring Guangzhou Labor Bureau to Court* [26名市民状告广州市劳保局], CHINA YOUTH DAILY, January 7, 2008, http://zqb.cyol.com/content/2008-01/07/content_2022076.htm (accessed between February 21, 2025 and March 31, 2025); Xudong Qin, *Anhui Provincial People's Government Is Tried at an Administrative Court for Possible Violations of OGI Regulations* [信息公开行政诉讼案开庭安徽省政府成被告], CAIJING, October 9, 2008 (captured by Internet Archive Wayback Machine on October 10, 2008), retrieved from https://web.archive.org/web/20081010211853/http://www.caijing.com.cn/2008-10-09/110018705.html (accessed between February 21, 2025 and March 31, 2025).

[164] In the early morning of May 4, 2008, Youjian Huang, Baisong Deng and three other retired workers in Hunan Province filed an OGI application to the Rucheng County people's government for a research report made by the agency concerning restructure of the Rucheng County Water Supply Company. The agency immediately rejected the application on the ground that the research report was an internal working document used only to assist leaders' decisions. The next day, the requesters sued the agency for failure to disclosure information. WEIBING XIAO, FREEDOM OF INFORMATION REFORM IN CHINA: INFORMATION FLOW ANALYSIS 109 (2011); Wenming Zhao, *First OGI Lawsuit: Retired Workers Take Government to Court for Its Failure to Disclose Information* [政府

leading officials' views,[165] meeting minutes,[166] and information on the processes of individual petitions[167] are internal working documents.

A big change happened in 2019 when OGI Regulations were revised. Internal, procedural and pre-decisional information is explicitly exempt from disclosure.[168] Article 16 provides the following:

> Administrative organs may decline to disclose internal affairs information, including information on personnel management, logistical management, and internal work flows.

信息公开条例第一案:退休职工告政府信息不公开], LEGAL DAILY, republished by Xinhua News Agency, May 6, 2008 (captured by Internet Archive Wayback Machine on May 9, 2008), retrieved from https://web.archive.org/web/20080509015423/http://news.xinhuanet.com/legal/2008-05/06/content_8112790.htm (accessed between February 21, 2025 and March 31, 2025).

165 WEIBING XIAO, FREEDOM OF INFORMATION REFORM IN CHINA: INFORMATION FLOW ANALYSIS 109 (2011); Lei Zhao and Yongtong Su, *Many Doubts about Government Information Disclosure* [政府信息疑点仍多], SOUTHERN WEEKEND, May 8, 2008, http://www.infzm.com/content/11911/ (accessed between February 21, 2025 and March 31, 2025).

166 In July 2008, Wu and three other retired workers from a county transportation company in Shandong Province submitted an OGI application to the county people's government for minutes of a 2006 meeting. The agency declined the request on the grounds that minutes are not official information. Administrative organs generally reject similar requests for meeting minutes. According to legal scholar, Weibing Xiao, the reluctance of agencies to release meeting minutes may gain explanation from the danger of exposing "inconsistencies in government officials' arguments." WEIBING XIAO, FREEDOM OF INFORMATION REFORM IN CHINA: INFORMATION FLOW ANALYSIS 109 (2011); Lei Zhao and Yongtong Su, *Many Doubts about Government Information Disclosure* [政府信息疑点仍多], SOUTHERN WEEKEND, May 8, 2008, http://www.infzm.com/content/11911/ (accessed between February 21, 2025 and March 31, 2025).

167 In October 2008, four companies, two National People's Congress deputies and seven experts submitted an OGI request to The General Administration of Quality Supervision, Inspection and Quarantine for disclosure of the investigation report concerning the quality of rolling mills produced and sold by the Zhengzhou Top Rolling Company. However, the agency rejected the request on the ground that the report was issued to "respond to petitions for internal research." WEIBING XIAO, FREEDOM OF INFORMATION REFORM IN CHINA: INFORMATION FLOW ANALYSIS 109 (2011); Quan Cheng, *General Administration of Quality Supervision, Inspection and Quarantine Is Embroiled in OGI Scandal [质检总局深陷信息公开门]*, Sina Finance, November 5, 2008, https://m.cj.sina.cn/page/aHR0cDovL2ZpbmFuY2Uuc2luYS5jb20uY24vZy8yMDA4MTEwNS8wNTI0NTQ2ODgxNC5zaHRtbA?from=redirect (accessed between February 21, 2025 and March 31, 2025).

168 *OGI Regulations 2007* (amended in 2019). Art. 16.

> Administrative organs may decline to disclose in-process type information such as deliberative records, pre-decisional drafts, consultation letters, and reports requesting instructions formed in the course of performing their administrative management functions, as well as administrative law enforcement case file information. Where laws, regulations or rules stipulate that the above-mentioned information should be disclosed, those provisions shall be followed.[169]

As discussed earlier, many international FOI law are exempting working secrets or internal working documents from disclosure and the revised Chinese FOI law is clearly embracing the international standard. However, the Chinese FOI amendment fails to comply with another international standard: Define terms whenever possible. When adding internal working documents to the list of OGI exemptions, the State Council did not define terms such as "internal affairs information" and "in-process type information," thus failing to impose restrictions on the scope of this newly added exemption. Chinese agencies and courts can therefore use this loophole to abusively deny disclosure. FOI scholar Weixing Xiao, in a study of freedom of information in China, found a disturbing pattern that agencies often rejected OGI requests on the grounds that those petitions for instructions, research reports, leading officials' views, meeting minutes, and information on the processes of individual petitions are working secrets/internal working documents.[170] After examining 540 sample OGI-related court cases tried from 2014 to 2021, the author of this book found a similar pattern. Out of 540 cases, administrative agencies denied disclosure in 29 cases, oversight agencies denied disclosure in 7 cases, trial courts denied disclosure in 25 cases, appellate courts denied disclosure in 19 cases, and all denials were made due to the argument that the information sought was internal, procedural or pre-decisional (see *Table 7–9*). In none of those cases, judicial opinions clearly and adequately explained why and how the requested information would qualify as information from internal working documents. Given that the internal documents/working secrets exemption was added to *OGI Regulations* just a few years ago, it is highly likely to see an explosive use of this exemption to reject applications in the near future.

[169] *OGI Regulations 2007* (amended in 2019). Art. 16.

[170] Weibing Xiao, Freedom Of Information Reform In China: Information Flow Analysis 108–109 (2011).

Summary and Conclusion

This chapter examined two special categories of governmental information that has tremendous freedom of information law implications: Journalistic internal reference and working secrets. Working secrets or internal working documents are exempt, by statute, from disclosure in many FOI countries including the United States. In a sharp contrast, *OGI Regulations 2007* have no provisions regarding exemptions for internal working documents or working secrets. The 2019 amendment includes internal working documents as a new exemption but fails to limit the scope of the exemption. Agencies and courts in China have used the loopholes of the FOI regime to reject access to requests for instructions, research reports, leading officials' views, meeting minutes, and information on the process of individual petitions, and many other similar informational items. In order to ensure both maximum disclosure of information and proper functioning of administrative activities, Chinese law reformers need to define relevant terms and narrow the scope of working secrets and internal working documents as an exemption.

This chapter also examined the journalistic internal reference system in China and its legal and political implications with a particular focus on conflicts, inconsistencies, and discrepancies between this special kind of information privilege and relevant laws such as *OGI Regulations*, state secrets laws, libel laws, and relevant party policies and directives. The journalistic internal reference system, established by Chinese communists in the 1930s, incorporates influences from journalism in the Soviet Union with probably ancient Chinese practices of publishing certain categories of government information in internally circulated newspaper-like publications. Today, journalists from mainstream party and official media outlets in China prepare most internal reference materials. Journalistic internal reference materials cover a wide range of topics and issues. Most importantly, they cover sensitive and controversial issues, such as official misconduct and corruption, that most regular publications would not dare to expose. The intent is that internal reference documents are beyond the public's purview and transmit exclusively to leading political and governmental officials at various levels.

The chapter found that, although journalistic internal reports may expose some official corruption and misdeeds, the system faces many problems and challenges in today's legal, media, and political environment. The concept and practice of sealing newsworthy information for government leaders' consumption only run counter to the presumption of government openness embodied in China's FOI law.[171] Government agencies and courts have already used working secrets/internal working documents to shield official information from disclosure.[172] We still don't know how government agencies and courts are going to handle cases involving request of journalistic internal reference because this study has not found actual cases involving request of journalistic internal reference under OGI. Given the vagueness and expansiveness of the term "state secrets" in both the FOI law and the secret secrets law, and the presumption of non-openness widely adopted by agencies and courts in China when coming to OGI affairs, it is highly likely that agencies and courts will shield journalistic internal reference materials from public view in the same manner as they do for working secrets/internal working documents. Justification for such rejection would be according to the grounds that the information sought coincides with the state secret exemption in *OGI Regulations*. Of course, in the future, it will be interesting to see how government agencies and courts in China will respond when they face such actual cases.

This study also found that the current law prohibiting reporters from quoting journalistic internal reference materials is problematic, as it restricts freer flow of information about important social issues and events. The law giving journalistic internal reference immunity from defamation lawsuits creates potential unfairness in enforcement of libel law, as we could generate two different classes of journalists, one with immunity and another without immunity. The argument that journalistic internal reference plays the role of watchdogs and think tanks is far-fetched as well. Internal reference does not have the power to hold top leaders accountable and is not well equipped to advise the government effectively like Western-style think tanks. The rise of Internet and social media and market-oriented media reforms are also discouraging journalists from pursuing careers in internal reference. Last but not least, journalistic internal reference is becoming a source of corruption. All these factors

[171] The revised FOI law provides that disclosure is the norm and nondisclosure the exception. In practice, however, nondisclosure is the norm. *OGI Regulations 2007* (amended in 2019). Art. 5.

[172] Weibing Xiao, Freedom Of Information Reform In China: Information Flow Analysis 108–109 (2011).

mentioned earlier contribute to tarnished party and government image and decreased credibility of media.

One may wonder if the journalistic internal reference system should continue. Someone may propose keeping the journalistic internal reference with decreased quantity and improved quality. In other words, people may argue that the scope for internally circulated materials should be narrowed down. There should be a clear-cut standard for what comes into limited-circulation publications and what becomes the subject of public coverage. The standard would allow and also force news organizations to determine more fairly what news should be accessible to all and what news should be restricted to a few. Only truly secret information should have classification as internal reference. Such a proposal is undesirable because it does not solve the fundamental problems. It is hard to create and enforce such a standard. The standard would leave room for corruption. A reasonable assumption for ordinary citizens is that a wealth of data in journalistic internal reference does not comprise state secrets. Instead, most information represents newsworthy stories comprehensible by the public.

Some Chinese communication scholars recommend that the party eliminate the journalistic internal reference system completely, whereas other scholars argue for the system's continued viability.[173] Given all the problems associated with the journalistic internal reference system discussed in this chapter, this study proposes gradual elimination of the practice of journalistic internal reports. Saying goodbye to journalistic internal reports may not be acceptable to some political elites at this point, but doing so would be a great blessing in the long term for the media, the party, the government, the public, and the whole country. Above all, sunshine is the best disinfectant. A few arguments can be made to support the ending of journalistic internal reports.

First, Chinese history repeatedly proves that freer flow of information benefits not only the governed but also the governor. The Qin dynasty was among the most short-lived dynasties partly because the emperors

[173] For example, media scholars Jiang Zhan and Yuezhi Zhao agree with elimination of the system while anther media scholar Guoming Yu disagrees. Yanhui Chen, *Demystify Neican* [内参揭秘], Phoenix Weekly 14 (2005): 35–39; Ruoqiao Liang, *For Whose Eyes Only?* Global Times, August 24, 2010, https://www.globaltimes.cn/content/566822.shtml (accessed between February 21, 2025 and March 31, 2025).

were too ruthless in restricting what people could talk and write.[174] On the contrary, the Tang and Song dynasties were among the most politically stable, economically prosperous, and culturally rich dynasties partly because the rulers were more tolerant toward criticism and commoners enjoyed greater freedom of expression/information.

Second, according to Article 19 of the Universal Declaration of Human Rights, "[e]veryone has the right to freedom of opinion and expression; this right includes freedom to hold opinions without interference and to seek, receive and impart information and ideas through any media and regardless of frontiers."[175] The practice of classifying newsworthy information as state secrets clearly infringes on people's rights to receive and disseminate information. Getting rid of the nearly century-long journalistic internal reference tradition would demonstrate China's firm commitment to promote and protect freedom of expression, a fundamental human right acknowledged and upheld by the United Nations.

Third, the CCP is trying to create a cleaner, more transparent and accountable party/government and more credible media organizations. Gradually eliminating journalistic internal reports and allowing more classified news to be published for everyone to see would in some ways help the party achieve this goal. If the CCP allows news organizations to publish materials that would otherwise end up appearing in internal reports, the state-run media would instantly become more popular in the eyes of readers and viewers. This would earn the Chinese media credibility, something the party always wants its media apparatus to have in face of severe competition from Western media conglomerates. At the same time, the party's anti-corruption campaign would become more effective because of the participation of the media and public. This is exactly what the Central Commission for Discipline Inspection (CCDI) is doing. Its official website publishes so many high-profile corruption cases in such a timely, authoritative, and detailed manner that it has become one of the

[174] According to *Records of the Grand Historian*, under the Qin dynasty law, anyone who criticized the emperor or the government would see his or her entire family exterminated. Likewise, anyone who participated in public conversations with others would face execution in public [史记・高祖本纪 22:"诽谤者族,偶语者弃市"], quoted from the Chinese Text Project, ***available at*** https://ctext.org/shiji/gao-zu-ben-ji#n4918 (accessed between February 21, 2025 and March 31, 2025).

[175] *The Universal Declaration of Human Rights*. Art. 19.

most visited websites in China.[176] In many ways, the CCDI website is making journalistic internal reference obsolete and irrelevant.

Some people may fear that allowing the media to publish so much bad news would create social instability or even chaos. This kind of fear is unwarranted. Since Xi Jinping took office in 2012 as the party's general secretary, Chinese media organizations have exposed all kinds of high-level corruption and official misdeeds with vivid details (of course with prior party approval).[177] No massive social chaos is happening as a result of massive media exposure of corruption. On the contrary, Xi and his Communist Party are gaining increasing public support from home and abroad. A Harvard Kennedy School study indicates that Xi is becoming the world's most popular leader.[178] A Pew Research Center survey shows that 95 percent of Chinese citizens report being pleased with Xi's leadership.[179] Indeed, the party's image has improved greatly partly because of efforts to publicize Xi's anti-corruption campaigns. Such achievements would be unthinkable for the party if all corruption cases had been sealed for journalistic internal reports only.

Fourth, when journalistic internal reference disappears from history, other forms of internal reference will continue to stay. Like previously mentioned, in addition to internal reports prepared by journalists, party organizations, governmental agencies, and other non-media entities

[176] *Chinese Government Launches Anti-Corruption Mobile App*, CHINA GLOBAL TELEVISION NETWORK, January 1, 2015, https://america.cgtn.com/2015/01/01/chinese-government-launches-anti-corruption-mobile-app (accessed between February 21, 2025 and March 31, 2025).

[177] The *Caixin* magazine is a good example. The publication, led by aggressive editor Hu Shuli, has covered high-ranking corruption with timeliness, authoritativeness, and vivid details. Before Xi Jinping took office as China's number one leader, such materials would be taboo for any domestic media or probably publishable for journalistic internal reference only. Here is the website of the magazine: http://english.caixin.com (accessed between February 21, 2025 and March 31, 2025).

[178] Dexter Roberts, *Xi Jinping Is the World's Most Popular Leader, Says Survey*, BLOOMBERG NEWS, December 18, 2014, http://www.bloomberg.com/bw/articles/2014-12-18/xi-jinping-wins-the-popularity-conest (accessed between February 21, 2025 and March 31, 2025).

[179] Wall Street Journal China Real Time Report, *How Does the World See Xi Jinping? Pew Offers a Report Card*, THE WALL STREET JOURNAL, July 15, 2014, http://blogs.wsj.com/chinarealtime/2014/07/15/pew-report-finds-many-worried-about-war-unimpressed-by-xi-jinping/ (accessed between February 21, 2025 and March 31, 2025).

produce internally circulated journals dealing with sensitive and controversial issues and events. The disappearance of journalistic internal reports would not make party and government leaders less informed if they read those non-journalistic internal reports carefully and if they follow news diligently.

One must see, however, that journalistic internal reports will continue to be viable and needed in China's political system in the near future. The reasons are at least threefold. First, journalistic internal reports are timely and fresh. Internal reports by news organizations are often produced quickly and sent to leaders quickly. This is very important for leaders who want to find and solve problems before it is too late. Second, media organizations have a unique position in the party-state structure. Although they are a part of the party-state apparatus, just like any other party and government entity such as the Department of Agriculture, the Department of Transportation, and the Department of Propaganda, media entities often do not have a stake in an area/region's development/prosperity and are thus more likely to provide senior leaders with unfiltered versions of facts and events. When communication channels in the bureaucracy are cut off for political or other reasons, internal reports from news media organizations would become vital sources of information for senior leaders.

Third, the fate of journalistic internal reference would be gloomy if China were to move toward more political liberalization. This is clearly not the case. Many Western media reports and scholars believe that Chinese politics is becoming increasingly conservative.[180] This does not bode well for the dismantlement of the journalistic internal reference system. The party's new emphasis on the concept of "party control of media" or "the media's Party nature" (*meitixingdang* 媒体姓党)[181]

[180] *China's Strongman Rule Sets a Test for the West: President Xi Challenges Notion that Prosperity Leads to Liberalism*, Financial Times, October 30, 2016, https://www.ft.com/content/76c27ac6-9c5b-11e6-a6e4-8b8e77dd083a (accessed between February 21, 2025 and March 31, 2025); Willy Lam, *The Maoist Revival and the Conservative Turn in Chinese Politics*." China Perspectives, no. 2012/2 (2012): 5–15, https://chinaperspectives.revues.org/5851?file=1 (accessed between February 21, 2025 and March 31, 2025).

[181] *China's Xi Underscores CPC's Leadership in News Reporting*, Xinhua News Agency, February 19, 2016 (captured by Internet Archive Wayback Machine on February 20, 2016), retrieved from https://web.archive.org/web/20160220102128/http://news.xinhuanet.com/english/2016-02/19/c_135114305.htm (accessed between February 21, 2025 and March 31, 2025); Shaozhe Wang, *Op-ed: Accusations Saying China Will Tighten*

seems to be contrary to the Western expectation that the information will go freer, and the government will be more open and transparent. Given the current situation in China, the possibility and feasibility of the Chinese government getting rid of the journalistic reference system and reforming the media system to align with the FOI law is slim. Various initiatives led by the CCP indicate that the country is trying hard to revitalize the journalistic internal reference system despite its declining influence and flaws discussed in previous sections of this chapter. The *People's Daily* created its Internal Reports Department more than a decade ago.[182] Xinhua News Agency has increased quantity of its internal reports.[183] When visiting Xinhua headquarters in Beijing in February 2016, Chinese President Xi Jinping said to journalists, "[Journalistic] internal reports are very important. I attached great importance to them when I worked as a local and provincial leader. I have attached greater importance to them when I came to work in Beijing as a central leader. Keep up your good work!"[184]

Media Control Are Groundless, PEOPLE'S DAILY ONLINE, February 24, 2016, http://en.people.cn/n3/2016/0224/c98649-9020663.html (accessed between February 21, 2025 and March 31, 2025).

182 *Roster of Editors and Reporters at People's Daily* [人民日报采编部门人员名单], People's Daily Online, February 16, 2007 (captured by Internet Archive Wayback Machine on February 24, 2007), retrieved from https://web.archive.org/web/20070224143536/http://media.people.com.cn/GB/5406002.html (accessed between February 21, 2025 and March 31, 2025).

183 According to Xinhua statistics compiled to measure the impact of its works, at the Party's five-yearly congress in 2007, Xinhua issued more than twice as many *neican* reports as it had at the 2002 event. In 2003, the number of comments written by leaders in the margins of *Reference Materials Proof* rose by 88 percent compared with the year before. Six were written by the then Chinese President Hu Jintao. *Reference Proofs* (Supplementary Sheets) published more than three times as many reports in 2003 as in 2002. In 2007, Xinhua's yearbook reported a 15 percent growth in the number of *Proofs of Domestic Trends* (A Digest of Online Public Sentiment) and a 50 percent increase in leaders' comments on them. *Chinese Whispers: Not Believing What They Read in the Papers, China's Leaders Commission Their Own*, THE ECONOMIST, June 17, 2010, https://www.economist.com/asia/2010/06/17/chinese-whispers (accessed between February 21, 2025 and March 31, 2025).

184 Xiaoguang Huo and Bin Li, *General Secretary Xi Jinping Chairs News and Public Opinion Work Conference and Visits People's Daily, Xinhua News Agency and China Central Television* [习近平总书记主持召开党的新闻舆论工作座谈会并到人民日报社、新华社、中央电视台调研侧记], XINHUA NEWS AGENCY, February 20, 2016, http://news.xinhuanet.com/politics/2016-02/20/c_1118106530.htm (accessed between February 21, 2025 and March 31, 2025).

CHAPTER 10

"Laws Are a Big Bell…It Will Never Ring Itself:" Journalistic Role in China's First Freedom of Information Law

As part of the author's doctoral dissertation that was successfully defended at The Pennsylvania State University in 2012, this chapter was later revised and presented to the ICA (International Communication Association) annual convention in 2013. The conference paper was then revised and published in *Journal of Media Law and Ethics* in 2016. The author of this book retain copyright of this journal article. Certain parts of the text in the chapter may resemble or replicate the original material, which has been included with the permission of the editors at Palgrave Macmillan. Yong Tang, "Chinese Freedom of Information: An Evaluation of the Legislative History, Rationales, Significance and Efficacy of Regulations of the People's Republic of China on Open Government Information" (2012) (unpublished Ph.D. diss., The Pennsylvania State University at University Park), *available at* https://etda.libraries.psu.edu/catalog/16287/ (accessed between February 21, 2025 and March 31, 2025); Yong Tang, *Journalistic Role in Chinese Freedom of Information*, paper accepted for presentation by the ICA (International Communication Association) annual convention, London, United Kingdom, June 17–21, 2013; Yong Tang, *"Laws Are A Big Bell…It Will Never Ring Itself!" Journalistic Role in China's First Freedom of Information Law*, 5 JOURNAL OF MEDIA LAW AND ETHICS 3–4: 77–105 (2016).

Y. Tang, *Freedom of Information Law in China*,
https://doi.org/10.1007/978-981-96-7842-6_10

Introduction

As of 2017, at least 111 countries and regions have various forms of freedom of information (FOI) laws.[1] In many FOI countries, media professionals (e.g., reporters, editors and executives) and news media outlets have played a key role in the promotion and eventual enactment of access to information laws. Once formulated, professionals in media sectors become among the most frequent users of the laws.[2] For example, the United States is where journalists have contributed enormously to the formulation, amendment and use of *Freedom of Information Act*.[3]

China joined the global FOI club in 2007 when the country adopted Regulations of the People's Republic of China on Open Government Information (*OGI Regulations)* and made the law effective one year later.[4] Like all FOI laws in the world, China's first nationwide FOI law aims to create a more transparent government. It compels all levels of administrative agencies to proactively publicize government-held documents and files if they are not exempted and reactively releases government-held documents and files if they are not publicly available

[1] *Statement by European RTI Community on the world's First Official Access to Information Day*, Access Info Europe, Madrid, Spain, September 28, 2016, *available at* https://www.access-info.org/2016-09-28/statement-by-european-rti-community-on-the-worlds-first-official-access-to-information-day/ (accessed between February 21, 2025 and March 31, 2025); *By Country*, Global Right to Information Rating (produced by Access Info Europe and Centre for Law and Democracy), *available at* http://www.rti-rating.org/country-data/ (accessed between February 21, 2025 and March 31, 2025).

[2] Eduardo Bertoni, *Freedom of Information, Three Harmless Words? The Role of the Media and Access to Information Laws*, Center for Studies on Freedom of Expression and Access to Information at the Palermo University School of Law, Buenos Aires, Argentina, originally published by the World Bank Institute in Spanish, *available at* http://www.palermo.edu/cele/pdf/ATIandMedia.pdf (accessed between February 21, 2025 and March 31, 2025).

[3] Shannon E. Martin and Kamilla Benko, *Forming FOIA: The Influence of Editors and Publishers on the Freedom of Information Act*, 14 Media History Monographs 1 (2011–2012): 1–33.

[4] The 2007 national FOI law was revised in 2019. For the full text of the law and its amendment in both Chinese and English, see *Chinese Law and Policy on Open Government Information*, Open Government Information in China, Yale University Law School Paul Tsai China Center, New Haven, Connecticut, *available at* https://law.yale.edu/china-center/resources/open-government-information-china (accessed between February 21, 2025 and March 31, 2025).

but demanded by people for disclosure. People have the right to sue government agencies for judicial relief if their OGI requests are rejected. According to the law, such right is given to all legal persons, other organizations and citizens including journalists. The purpose of this chapter is to explore Chinese journalism's methods of and contributions to drafting, publicizing and enforcement of the FOI law. This project is significant. Research materials about Chinese FOI law abound,[5] but little research considers the role of Chinese journalists in the country's campaign for freedom of information.[6] Legal scholar Yang Guo explored journalistic use of the *OGI Regulations* from 2011 to 2013.[7] FOI scholar Weibing Xiao examined how journalists, legal professionals, rights activists and ordinary citizens have used *OGI Regulations* for information access.[8] However, few scholars including Guo and Xiao have systematically and comprehensively surveyed the role of Chinese journalists in the country's journey to government transparency and FOI law. This study aims to fill that gap.

As for methodology, this study employs legal research supported by information gathered through Internet searches, database searches and

[5] See HANHUA ZHOU, "*Open Government in China: Practice and Problems*," in THE RIGHT TO KNOW: TRANSPARENCY FOR AN OPEN WORLD, ed. Ann Florini and Joseph E. Stiglitz (New York: Columbia University Press, 2007); WEIBING XIAO, FREEDOM OF INFORMATION REFORM IN CHINA: INFORMATION FLOW ANALYSIS (New York: Routledge, 2011); Changhua Wu, *Improving the Legal and Policy Foundation for Public Access to Environmental Information in China*, TEMPLE JOURNAL OF SCIENCE, TECHNOLOGY & ENVIRONMENTAL LAW 24 (2005), 291–323; Suzanne J. Piotrowski, Yahong Zhang, Wenxuan Yu and Weiwei Lin, *Key Issues for Implementation of the Chinese Open Government Information Regulations*, PUBLIC ADMINISTRATION REVIEW 69 (1) (2009); Paul Hubbard, *China's Regulations on Open Government Information: Challenges of Nationwide Policy Implementation*, OPEN GOVERNMENT JOURNAL 4 (2008); Renu Rana, *China's Information Disclosure Initiative: Assessing the Reforms*, 51 CHINA REPORT 2 (2015) 129–143; *State Administration of Cultural Heritage Freedom of Information Annual Work Report for 2013*, 48 CHINESE LAW AND GOVERNMENT 3 (2016) 230–233; Guosong Shao, Jiayin Lu and Ye Hao, Assessing China's Media Reform, 40 Asian Perspective (2016) 27–50.

[6] This conclusion is based on search results of various databases including Communication & Mass Media Complete, Westlaw Campus and Google Scholar.

[7] Yang Guo, *An Investigation into Journalistic Use of OGI Regulations* [新闻记者对《政府信息公开条例》使用情况的调查], 1 SOUTHEAST COMMUNICATION (2016), 73–75.

[8] WEIBING XIAO, FREEDOM OF INFORMATION REFORM IN CHINA: INFORMATION FLOW ANALYSIS 120 (2011).

interviews with a group of conveniently sampled Chinese journalists.[9] In order to find media reports about Chinese reporters involved in the FOI law in various capacities, Baidu and Chinese-language Google searches were conducted by using key words "journalist (*jizhe* 记者)" and "government information disclosure (*zhengfuxinxigongkai* 政府信息公开)." Also examined was the list of OGI-related court cases from various sources. Searched databases were China Academic Journal Database, Beida Fabao and Westlaw China.

In June and July 2012, contact with journalists in China via email and telephone queried journalists' and news media outlets' involvement in drafting FOI law and their use of *OGI Regulations* since 2008 to access official information. Journalists from the following media outlets participated in the interviews: *People's Daily*, Xinhua News Agency, China Central Television, *Caijing, Southern Weekend, China Economic Times, Oriental Morning Post, Southern Metropolis Daily, Hebei Daily Newspaper Group,* Hebei Television, *Hebei News Network,* China News Service Hebei Bureau, *Yanzhao Metropolis Daily, Yanzhao Metropolis Daily Online Edition, Shijiazhuang Daily,* Shijiazhuang Television, *Yanzhao Evening News, Hebei Farmers News, Hebei Youth Daily, Hebei Legal Daily,* and Sichuan Bazhong City Television. The journalists were asked to answer the following four questions: "Do you know OGI Regulations?" "Do you and/or your news organization get involved in the legislative process of the law?" "Have you ever requested government-held documents via OGI Regulations?" "Have you ever sued government agencies for non-disclosure?" Although participants are definitely a convenience sample for the population of Chinese professional journalists, their employers represent a wide range of Chinese media, from print media to electronic media, from traditional party organs to market-oriented metropolitan newspapers, from news agencies to newspapers, periodicals, radio and television broadcasters, from central and national media to local media. Some journalists responded and offered details for use of OGI Regulations by their colleagues. Some journalists responded but demurred, claiming inappropriateness for involvement in this kind of research. Some journalists

[9] All journalists surveyed are reporters/editors with press cards issued by the State Administration of Press, Publication, Radio, Film and Television of the People's Republic of China. When talking about Chinese journalists, this chapter refer to licensed reporters and editors affiliated with state-run or party-run news media outlets. Freelancers and citizen journalists are not included in this study.

did not respond at all despite persistent email and telephone inquiries. The names of the journalists contacted do not appear here due to the sensitivity of the interviews.

Are Chinese journalists filing more OGI requests since 2012? Are they suing more government agencies for non-disclosure since 2012? In order to find the answer, in February 2017, this study tried to contact those participating journalists again for follow-up interviews, but the efforts yielded no results for various reasons. As a remedy, this study did searches on the official websites of most news organizations mentioned above by using the keywords "government information disclosure (*zhengfu xinxi gongkai* 政府信息公开)" and "journalist (*jizhe* 记者)." The purpose of the searches is to locate possible news stories showing that journalists and/or news organizations requested government information via OGI. Various legal databases were searched to look for any possible lawsuits in which journalists sued government agencies for non-disclosure.

Section I of this chapter will discuss whether or not Chinese journalists contributed to formulation of *OGI Regulations* and the nature of those contributions. Section II will investigate Chinese journalists' coverage and publicizing the freedom of information movement and the reasons for vigorous and extensive media coverage of a plethora of issues pertaining to *OGI Regulations*. More importantly, Section III will assess Chinese journalists' use of *OGI Regulations* to obtain official information for the purposes of newsgathering and reporting and how they are bringing agencies to court for judicial remedies. Section IV will explore various reasons for the limited journalistic use of *OGI Regulations* in China.

Role of Chinese Journalists in Formulating *OGI Regulations*

Investigative journalism enables the people's right to know events, procedures and policies of government and that right is a guarantee of freedom of information legislation. A reasonable expectation is, therefore, journalists' advocacy for establishing FOI laws. However, this study finds that, unlike their American colleagues, Chinese journalists are excluded from the entire Chinese legislative process for *OGI Regulations*. According to *Legislation Law* passed in 2000, the State Council has the power to formulate administrative regulations in accordance with the Constitution and laws.[10] In drafting administrative regulations, opinions from relevant agencies, organizations, and citizens were to be heeded, and relevant forums, seminars, and hearings held.[11] However, a database search and interviews with journalists show that, in drafting *OGI Regulations*, Chinese law reformers did not listen to opinions from journalists and news media. No Chinese reporters or editors participated actively in the formulation of the law, nor did leading professional organizations[12] participate in the process. *OGI Regulations* were elite-driven, proposed, drafted, and formulated entirely by officials and a small number of leading legal scholars.[13]

Chinese editors and reporters were absent in the formulation of the freedom of information laws, which is rare in many other countries. In Western countries, freedom of expression and freedom of information are intertwined with each other. Both concepts spring from the same fountain of liberal philosophical and political thoughts advanced by thinkers such as three "Johns" (John Milton, John Locke, and John Stuart Mill).[14] Hence it is not surprising to see journalists actively engage in pushing FOI laws. In China, however, political and academic elites treat freedom of information and freedom of expression as different animals. Freedom of information research was politically sensitive in China in the late 1990s, and many leading hard-liners in the party and the government believed that the Glasnost reform in the Soviet Union in the late 1980s contributed to the deterioration of that communist empire. These officials asserted that a similar nationwide transparency reform in China would

[10] *Legislation Law 2000*. Art. 56.

[11] *Legislation Law 2000*. Art. 58.

[12] All China Journalists' Association, China Media Culture Promotion Association, China Newspaper Association, China Radio and TV Association, and China Internet Association are prominent industrial organizations in journalism and media in China.

[13] Similar practices of closed-door legislation are numerous in China despite enactment of Legislative Law mandating more public participation in the legislative process. See DINGJIAN CAI & CHENGUANG WANG, CHINA'S JOURNEY TOWARD THE RULE OF LAW: LEGAL REFORM, 1978–2008 85 (2010).

[14] See JOHN MILTON, AREOPAGITICA: A SPEECH FOR THE LIBERTY OF UNLICENSED PRINTING (1915); JOHN LOCKE, THE TWO TREATISES OF GOVERNMENT (1824); JOHN STUART MILL, Chapter II: Of the Liberty of Thought and Discussion, in ON LIBERTY (1859).

lead to the same catastrophic consequences.[15] In addition, legal infeasibility and political inappropriateness would occur if linking freedom of information with freedom of expression because of "the lack of Freedom of the Press Act and an authoritative interpretation of freedom of expression laid down in Article 35 of the Constitution."[16] Chinese reformers thus adopted a strategy of linking OGI legislation with economic growth and informationization development.[17] This strategy, as FOI scholar Weibing Xiao asserted, decreased political sensitivity toward FOI research and "allowed the idea of FOI to be openly discussed in China."[18] However, this strategy created a misguided impression of journalism' disassociation with *OGI Regulations*, thus marginalizing journalists' roles promoting OGI legislation.

Role of Chinese Journalists in Covering and Publicizing *OGI Regulations*

Chinese journalists had marginal roles in formulation of *OGI Regulations*, but reporters have been instrumental in ensuring effective enforcement of the law. Their reporting on non-compliance with the law has created significant pressures from public opinion on agencies and forced corrections. The vigorous coverage on a wide range of issues and events related to governmental transparency contributed to wider public awareness of the law. A random Baidu and Google search shows that the Chinese print media published large volumes of news stories and commentaries regarding open official information since adoption of *OGI Regulations* in 2007. OGI-related stories and critiques appeared frequently on airwaves and the Internet portals. *Southern Weekend* is an example; as "China's

[15] Weibing Xiao, Freedom of Information Reform in China: Information Flow Analysis 40 (2011).

[16] Weibing Xiao, Freedom of Information Reform in China: Information Flow Analysis 43 (2011).

[17] Weibing Xiao, Freedom of Information Reform in China: Information Flow Analysis 65 (2011).

[18] Weibing Xiao, Freedom of Information Reform in China: Information Flow Analysis 41 (2011).

most influential liberal newspaper,"[19] the weekly publication, from May 1, 2008 to April 30, 2010, printed 129 articles concerning OGI matters.[20] During that time, 58% of the weekly's total coverage was in-depth investigative reporting (35 articles), and commentaries (40 articles) devoted to OGI.[21]

Legal professionals are allies of journalists for covering and publicizing *OGI Regulations*. Apparently, legal professionals are the most frequent requesters of governmental information under *OGI Regulations*.[22] Attorneys in China normally do not rely on *OGI Regulations* to obtain information for their cases; instead, they rely heavily on personal connections in government to obtain needed documents. The government discourages lawyers from becoming involved in OGI litigation[23]; however, increasing number of lawyers, law academics, and students actively use OGI legislation to access official information that is primarily in the public interest.[24] Many lawyers' involvements in OGI requests and litigations are not for commercial gains but for educational purposes.[25]

[19] Elisabeth Rosenthal, *Under Pressure, Chinese Newspaper Pulls Exposé on a Charity*, The New York Times, March 24, 2002, http://www.nytimes.com/2002/03/24/world/under-pressure-chinese-newspaper-pulls-expose-on-a-charity.html (accessed between February 21, 2025 and March 31, 2025).

[20] Lin Yu and Jun Guo, *Examination of Coverage by Southern Weekend on OGI Matters* [《南方周末》政府信息公开问题报道分析], Journal of Youth Journalist 16 (2010): 77.

[21] Lin Yu and Jun Guo, *Examination of Coverage by Southern Weekend on OGI Matters* [《南方周末》政府信息公开问题报道分析] Journal of Youth Journalist 16 (2010): 77.

[22] Weibing Xiao, Freedom of Information Reform in China: Information Flow Analysis 120 (2011); Yang Guo, *An Investigation into Journalistic Use of OGI Regulations* [新闻记者对《政府信息公开条例》使用情况的调查], 1 Southeast Communication 73–75 (2016).

[23] During a February 2012 telephone interview with the author of this book, a Beijing lawyer said that internal policies circulated among lawyers in Beijing instructed them to avoid OGI litigation. The interviewee studied at The Pennsylvania State University Law School as a visiting scholar and doctoral candidate.

[24] Weibing Xiao, Freedom of Information Reform in China: Information Flow Analysis 120 (2011).

[25] Xixin Wang and two of his colleagues at Peking University Law School applied for information concerning the toll charges at the Beijing Capital Airport Express Way. Five law professors from Xiangtan University in Hunan Province submitted OGI requests for information of the toll charges in the city of Xiangtan. Xiangtan University professors sued the agency for non-disclosure. Both requests' intent was

These legal actions gain wide coverage from local and national media because of their newsworthiness. Publicity is possible because legal professionals and journalists successfully collaborated for the common goal of enhancing public awareness of OGI legislation.

Constant media exposure of *OGI Regulations* promoted the public's understanding of the law and the concept of the right to know. According to a Peking University survey conducted prior to the May 2008 enforcement of *OGI Regulations*, China's young Internet users, aged from 10 to 45, knew little about freedom of information. Among 197 respondents, 124 claimed unawareness of the promulgation, 145 admitted unfamiliarity with the key provisions in the law, and 127 said that they did not know that many other countries had adopted freedom of information laws.[26] Apparently, subsequent research to update the data is nonexistent. However, given that the Chinese media inundated citizens with constant details of OGI matters during the last nine years (2008–2017), a safe assumption is the level of public awareness would be significantly higher for the same survey in 2017.[27]

to educate the public on OGI issues, not for making money. Shuming Li & Weihong Lv, *Three Professors from Beijing University Watch Closely on Tolls of Beijing Airport Expressway* [北大三教授 "盯上"首都机场高速路], PROCURATORIAL DAILY, June 18, 2008 (captured by Internet Archive Wayback Machine on June 21, 2008), retrieved from https://web.archive.org/web/20080621223627/http://news.xinhuanet.com/legal/2008-06/18/content_8389725.htm (accessed between February 21, 2025 and March 31, 2025); Wenjie Liu, *Five Doctoral Candidates from Hunan's Xiangtan University Sue Government for Refusing to Release Information about Administrative Fees* [湖南湘潭大学五博士状告政府 要求公开收费信息], XINHUA NEWS AGENCY, June 6, 2008 (captured by Internet Archive Wayback Machine on June 8, 2008), retrieved from https://web.archive.org/web/20080608093817/http://news.xinhuanet.com/legal/2008-06/06/content_8319893.htm (accessed between February 21, 2025 and March 31, 2025). WEIBING XIAO, FREEDOM OF INFORMATION REFORM IN CHINA: INFORMATION FLOW ANALYSIS 120 (2011).

[26] Maosheng Lai and Hui Yan, *Survey on Public Awareness of OGI Regulations* [我国《政府信息公开条例》的 "公众认知度"调查], 5 DIGITAL LIBRARY FORUM [数字图书馆论坛] 10–13 (2008): 42.

[27] Most information applicants are not highly educated professionals such as doctors, journalists, professors, or accountants (lawyers are an exception). Instead, the majority of OGI requesters in China are ordinary urban residents, workers, farmers, college students, NGO employees, rights activists, and many other people of low socio-economic status. This demographic pattern indicates that *OGI Regulations* have had wide publicity throughout Chinese society.

As examined earlier, Chinese journalists enjoyed relative freedom for exposing non-compliance of government agencies with FOI law because freedom of information was no longer a politically sensitive topic in China under the leadership of Hu Jintao and Wen Jiabao. In addition, Central party and governmental leaders publicly announced full support for the media's role for covering irregularities and scandals related to official transparency.[28]

Another factor, equally important but widely ignored, could also help explain the freedom granted to Chinese journalists who write about OGI matters. The factor relates to the nature of China's political system. According to typology generated by political scientist, Barbara Geddes, the world's governments include three types of authoritarian regimes: single-party regimes such as China, military regimes such as Thailand after 2014 and Myanmar before 2015, and personalist/dictatorship regimes such as North Korea.[29] A theory, advanced and empirically tested by political scholar, Bogdan Popescu, argued that these three regime types allow for varying degrees of press freedom. Single party regimes normally have the freest press (comparatively speaking), personalist/dictatorship regimes have the least free media, and military regimes stand between the two.[30] The theory explains that single-party regimes are relatively more transparent and inclusive than the other two non-democratic regime

[28] Then-Premier Wen Jiabao stressed the role of watchdog for journalism in correcting official wrongs in administration in his speech at the National Meeting on Law-based Administration in 2010. Wen emphasized at the Fifth State Council Working Meeting on Anti-Corruption in 2012 that the government creates conditions for citizens to supervise officeholders. Wen Jiabao, *Speech Delivered by Chinese Primer Wenjia Bao at National Meeting on Law-Based Administration* [温家宝在全国依法行政工作会议上的讲话], PEOPLE'S DAILY, September 20, 2010 (captured by Internet Archive Wayback Machine on September 23, 2010), retrieved from https://web.archive.org/web/20100923193404/http://politics.people.com.cn/GB/101380/12772650.html (accessed between February 21, 2025 and March 31, 2025); *Wen Jiabao: Advance Open Government Information and Create Conditions for Citizens to Hold Government Accountable* [温家宝:推进政务公开 创造条件让群众监督政府], Gov.cn, the State Council of the People's Republic of China, Beijing, China, March 26, 2012, https://www.gov.cn/ldhd/2012-03/26/content_2100430.htm (accessed between February 21, 2025 and March 31, 2025).

[29] BARBARA GEDDES, AUTHORITARIAN BREAKDOWN: EMPIRICAL TEST OF A GAME THEORETIC ARGUMENT (1999); BARBARA GEDDES, PARADIGMS AND SAND CASTLES: THEORY BUILDING AND RESEARCH DESIGN IN COMPARATIVE POLITICS (2003).

[30] Bogdan G. Popescu, *Press Freedom in Non-Democratic Regimes*, paper prepared for delivery at the ECPR (European Consortium for Political Research) Graduate Conference, Dublin City University, Dublin, Ireland, August 30-September 1, 2010, 1 and 22.

types, thus allowing for the greatest level of press freedom among the three. The personalist/dictatorship regimes, characterized by the most severe censorship, are the result of political insulation surrounding the ruling clique. Military regimes need no censorship because journalists resort to self-censorship due to the presence of military as a "symbol of coercive power."[31] The vibrancy in coverage of *OGI Regulations* by Chinese journalists attests to the validity of this theory.

Role of Chinese Journalists as OGI Requesters of Governmental Information

Chinese media reported on official transparency vigorously, but their aggressive use of *OGI Regulations* to access governmental information remains a question, and the response is, for practical purposes, in the negative. After media interviews, database searches, and Internet searches, the results indicate that, as of December 2024, only a very small number of Chinese journalists used *OGI Regulations* to request official information. This is consistent with a prior study showing that among various kinds of OGI requestors, journalists are the least active.[32] A list, in chronological order from 2006 to 2017, details Chinese media professionals' requests:

Pin Ma is a reporter for *Jiefang Daily*, the official newspaper of the Shanghai Committee of the Communist Party of China. In April 2006, Ma twice attempted to interview officials from the Shanghai Municipal Urban Planning Bureau for information needed for a news story. Ma applied, in the name of a citizen, to the agency for the same information on April 23, 2006, two years after enactment of *Provisions* of *Shanghai*

[31] Bogdan G. Popescu, *Press Freedom in Non-Democratic Regimes*, paper prepared for delivery at the ECPR (European Consortium for Political Research) Graduate Conference, Dublin City University, Dublin, Ireland, August 30-September 1, 2010, 1 and 22.

[32] An analysis of four major categories of Chinese OGI requestors (lawyers, citizens, college students and journalists) applying from 2011 to 2013 for government-held information indicates that lawyers are the most active (52% of information requests were made by attorneys), journalists are the least active (7%), citizens (22%) and college students (19%) stand in the middle. Yang Guo, *An Investigation into Journalistic Use of OGI Regulations* [新闻记者对《政府信息公开条例》使用情况的调查], 1 SOUTHEAST COMMUNICATION (2016): 73–75.

Municipality on Open Government Information.[33] On May 18, 2006, Ma sued the agency for failure to release the information under Shanghai OGI Provisions. The Shanghai Huangpu District Court accepted the lawsuit, and Ma became the first Chinese reporter to sue the government under local OGI provisions. However, Ma withdrew the litigation on June 2, 2006, due to pressure from various parties.[34] The national and local media except *Jiefang Daily* covered the episode extensively.

On April 8, 2008, *Press Digest*[35] editor, Ping Ma, submitted an OGI application to the Shanghai Municipal Urban Planning Bureau for the same information requested in 2006 while working as a *Jiefang Daily* reporter. The request coincided with the new *Provisions of Shanghai Municipality on Open Government Information.*[36] Considering the released information to be self-contradictory, Ma sued the agency for a second time, but the court declined to accept his complaint. On July 8, 2008, the editor sent a request to the National Development and Reform Commission for the same information. The agency redirected the query to the Shanghai Municipal Development and Reform Commission for the information.[37] Ma's newspaper and the other publications in the Jiefang

[33] Implementation of local OGI rules occurred before enactment of the nationwide *OGI Regulations* in 2007. Shanghai enacted *Provisions* of *Shanghai Municipality on Open Government Information in January 2004. The Provisions were repealed and replaced by a new OGI rule in 2008.*

[34] Hongqing Duan, *Pin Ma: One Single Person Fights Lonely and Publicly Against Government Violations of OGI Regulations* [马骋:一个人的信息公开战争], Caixin blog, April 24, 2015, *available at* https://duanhongqing.blog.caixin.com/archives/84413?originReferrer=caixinsearch_pc (accessed between February 21, 2025 and March 31, 2025); Dequan Zhu, *Unanswered Questions about First OGI Litigation Involving a Journalist* ["政府侵犯新闻采访权第一案"悬疑] DAZHONG NEWSPAPER GROUP ONLINE, August 23, 2006 (captured by Internet Archive Wayback Machine on January 5, 2011), retrieved from https://web.archive.org/web/20110105051846/http://qnjz.dzwww.com/zk/200608/t20060801_1680429.htm (accessed between February 21, 2025 and March 31, 2025).

[35] *Press Digest* (*baokan wenzhai*报刊文摘) is a popular newspaper of the Jiefang Daily Newspaper Group in Shanghai.

[36] *Provisions of Shanghai Municipality on Open Government Information* (promulgated on April 28, 2008 by the Shanghai municipal people's government (order No.2) (effective date: May 1, 2008) (amended on December 20, 2010) (order No.52).

[37] Hongqing Duan, *Pin Ma: One Single Person Fights Lonely and Publicly Against Government Violations of OGI Regulations* [马骋:一个人的信息公开战争], Caixin blog, April 24, 2015, *available at* https://duanhongqing.blog.caixin.com/archives/84413?originReferrer=caixinsearch_pc (accessed between February 21, 2025 and March 31, 2025).

Daily Newspaper Group did not cover the application and the ensuing attempt to seek judicial remedy.

Ling Su and her colleagues at the influential *Southern Weekend* experimented with submitting OGI requests after enforcement of *OGI Regulations* in May 2008. The OGI requests, filed with 25 Bureaus of Land and Resources in 21 cities, sought relevant real estate information. Only four agencies approved disclosure that otherwise should have had proactive dissemination, thereby creating an approval rate of only 16%.[38] The results of the experiment appeared in the newspaper to illustrate the difficulty citizens have using *OGI Regulations* for accessing information.

On February 2, 2009, *Southern Weekend* reporter, Yongtong Su, made written request to the Ministry of Environmental Protection for an environmental impact assessment that approved construction of the PX chemical plant in the Chinese coastal city of Zhangzhou, Fujian Province. The newspaper covered its reporter's OGI request in an attempt to follow-up the PX plant controversy, widely reported by Chinese media at that time.[39]

On March 8, 2010, 163.com auto editor, Wenjun Liu, submitted and publicized an OGI request, in the name of an ordinary citizen, with General Administration of Quality Supervision, Inspection and Quarantine for information concerning the total number of people killed or injured in traffic accidents in the nation due to alleged malfunctioning auto parts. Also included in the request was the number of complaints filed by Chinese purchasers against Toyota over the years and the agency's investigation and resolutions for those complaints. Liu filed the application based on a sense of obligation to inform the public of the safety of Toyota vehicles in China, after the 2009–2011 global recall of Toyota vehicles.[40]

[38] Ling Su, *Reporter Personally Experiences Non-Disclosure of Government Information* [记者亲历 "信息不公开"], SOUTHERN WEEKEND, July 10, 2008, http://www.infzm.com/content/14380 (accessed between February 21, 2025 and March 31, 2025).

[39] Sixteen days after submission of the request, Yongtong Su received a copy of the report from the ministry. Yongtong Su, *Exclusive: Zhangzhou PX Environmental Impact Assessment Approval Document* [独家披露:漳州PX环评批复书], SOUTHERN WEEKEND, February 22, 2009, http://www.infzm.com/content/24173 (accessed between February 21, 2025 and March 31, 2025).

[40] The agency accepted Liu's application immediately. On April 28, 2010, the agency responded that both the number of people affected by defective auto parts and the number of auto complaints do not fall into the category of official information

On May 20, 2010, *Southern Weekend* journalists lodged OGI applications with bureaus of environmental protection in 31 major Chinese cities[41] for information concerning enterprises penalized from January 2010 to May 2010 for violating environmental laws and regulations, and information for justifying the penalties. The experimental use of *OGI Regulations* appeared prominently in the newspaper to demonstrate the difficulty with obtaining official information via the OGI platform.[42]

On July 11, 2010, *Beijing News* journalist, Bo Chen, submitted an OGI request with the Beijing Municipal Traffic Law Enforcement General Team, in the name of a Chinese citizen, for information of the number of unlicensed taxis in Beijing and the total fines levied against those illegal cabs over the years. The reporter sought to expose police officers who

released according to *OGI Regulations*. As for the investigation and resolution of the complaints, the agency directed the applicant to the agency's website for relevant information. Liu did not appeal for administrative reconsideration to rectify non-disclosure. Nor did he sue the agency. He did post the agency's official response letter on a personal blog. Dong Dong, *General Administration of Quality Supervision, Inspection and Quarantine Accepts First OGI Request for Information Concerning Toyota Recall Incident* [国家质检总局受理第一例丰田召回信息公开申请], Netease Auto, March 9, 2010 (captured by Internet Archive Wayback Machine on March 15, 2010), retrieved from https://web.archive.org/web/20100315042928/http://auto.163.com/10/0309/13/61BC5KAL000816HJ.html (accessed between February 21, 2025 and March 31, 2025).

[41] Cities with "Major Chinese Cities" designations include four municipalities directly under the State Council, five capital cities in autonomous regions, and 22 provincial capital cities.

[42] Submission of OGI applications to Lhasa and Haikou fails due to technical reasons. The newspaper successfully sent the applications to the environmental protection agencies in 29 cities by telefax from the publication's Guangzhou office. Among the 29 cities, 14% approved disclosure of the information requested; 14% denied the request; 27% responded that they had proactively released the information requested; 45% did not respond at all. Four cities (Xining, Tianjin, Guiyang, and Hangzhou) rejected the request for different reasons. Xining held that compilation of the information was incomplete. Tianjin maintained that the information sought was pre-decisional and deliberative and disclosure may endanger state security, public security, economic security, and social stability. Guiyang insisted that the information sought involved commercial secrets, personal privacy, and the third party did not consent to disclosure. Hangzhou required the newspaper to provide a photocopy of its certificate of business registration and documents certifying its status as legal person. Duanduan Yuan and Nan Xu, *Why Is Environmental Information Disclosure So Hard? Story of 29 OGI Request Forms* [环境信息公开咋这么难 29份信息公开申请表的遭遇], Southern Weekend, June 23, 2010, https://www.infzm.com/contents/46698 (accessed between February 21, 2025 and March 31, 2025).

willfully fined taxi drivers. The whole application process appeared in the newspaper as a series of articles about unlicensed taxis.[43]

In August 2010, *Press Digest* editor, Ping Ma, submitted an OGI application to the Shanghai Public Security Bureau Xuhui Branch. The request was for documents and records detailing certain types of public security cases received by the branch from March 1, 2006 to December 31, 2009. All those public security cases involved incidents of beating and slightly injuring innocent individuals and represented public security cases closed without adjudication and wrongdoers receiving administrative penalties.[44] Dissatisfied with the agency's responses,[45] Ma sued the agency, asking a

[43] The agency rejected on August 4, 2010 the request for disclosure of total amount of fines and total number of penalized unlicensed cabs, ruling that the applicant failed to satisfy the special needs test in *OGI Regulations*. In other words, the information sought was irrelevant to special needs of the journalist's production, livelihood and scientific research. The journalist did not resort to administrative appeal and judicial review to rectify non-disclosure.Bo Chen, *Officials Respond to Allegations of "Bargaining for Reduced Fines Levied Against Unlicensed Cabs* [官方回应 "黑车罚款还价"], THE BEIJING NEWS, republished by Sina News, August 5, 2010, https://news.sina.com.cn/o/2010-08-05/090317917524s.shtml (accessed between February 21, 2025 and March 31, 2025).

[44] On February 2, 2010, a traffic accident involved Ma's parking and a collision with a Passat sedan. Ma, beaten and slightly injured by the angry driver of the Passat, reported the beating to the Shanghai Public Security Bureau Xuhui Branch. The agency imposed no penalties against the Passat driver. Ma sought the information to determine if the agency enforced administrative penalties laws fairly. Shuming Li, *Shanghai Resident Questions Fairness of Being Beaten Without Compensation* [上海市民追问"打了白打"], PROCURATORIAL DAILY, November 3, 2010, (captured by Internet Archive Wayback Machine on April 13, 2021), retrieved from https://web.archive.org/web/20210413034001/http://news.jcrb.com/jxsw/201011/t20101103_461426.html (accessed between February 21, 2025 and March 31, 2025).

[45] Upon request from the branch, Ma rewrote the request into seven separate applications. On September 9, 2010, the agency responded that legal documents concerning public security cases, which imposed administrative penalties on wrongdoers, did not exist because the agency did not create or obtain them. On September 16, 2010, the agency responded again that it had received, from March 2006 to December 2009, a total of 14,404 public security cases, which recorded innocent persons' beatings and slight injuries. Shuming Li, *Shanghai Resident Questions Fairness of Being Beaten Without Compensation* [上海市民追问"打了白打"], PROCURATORIAL DAILY, November 3, 2010, (captured by Internet Archive Wayback Machine on April 13, 2021), retrieved from https://web.archive.org/web/20210413034001/http://news.jcrb.com/jxsw/201011/t20101103_461426.html (accessed between February 21, 2025 and March 31, 2025).

local court to rule in favor of the disclosure of the information.[46] Neither Ma's newspaper nor other newspapers in the Jiefang Daily Newspaper Group covered the application and the ensuing litigation.

In December 2010, *Southern Weekend* reporter, He Huang, published a story about the controversial genetically modified rice (GMR). In the story the journalist mentioned that he submitted an OGI application to the Grain Administration of Fujian Province for a copy of an administrative order that temporarily banned sale of GMR in the province. The agency did not respond at all to the request.[47]

In July 2011, *Southern Metropolis Daily* reporter, Baocheng Chen,[48] working outside official duties, sent an OGI request, in the name of a Chinese citizen, to the Ministry of Railways for the full list of victims who died in the Wenzhou train collision.[49] The agency confirmed receipt of the application. Whether the agency responded or not is unknown, and the newspaper did not publicize the application, but the application did appear on the reporter's personal Twitter-like microblogging site.

In December 2011, Xing Wang, a journalist from *Southern Metropolis Daily* in Guangzhou, submitted OGI applications in the name of a

[46] Shuming Li, *Shanghai Resident Questions Fairness of Being Beaten Without Compensation* [上海市民追问"打了白打"], Procuratorial Daily, November 3, 2010, (captured by Internet Archive Wayback Machine on April 13, 2021), retrieved from https://web.archive.org/web/20210413034001/http://news.jcrb.com/jxsw/201011/t20101103_461426.html (accessed between February 21, 2025 and March 31, 2025).

[47] He Huang, *Genetically Modified Rice: Fujian Province Suspends Ban on GMR* [转基因大米:福建 "叫停通知"被叫停], Southern Weekend, republished by QQ News, December 20, 2010 (captured by Internet Archive Wayback Machine on December 8, 2022), retrieved from https://web.archive.org/web/20221208051823/http://news.qq.com/a/20101220/001341.htm (accessed between February 21, 2025 and March 31, 2025).

[48] Yu Wu, *Citizens Are Calling for Special Investigation into 723 Train Crash* [民间呼吁启动"7·23动车事故"特别调查], DW News, July 26, 2011, https://www.dw.com/zh/%E6%B0%91%E9%97%B4%E5%91%BC%E5%90%81%E5%90%AF%E5%8A%A8723%E5%8A%A8%E8%BD%A6%E4%BA%8B%E6%95%85%E7%89%B9%E5%88%AB%E8%B0%83%E6%9F%A5/a-15265997 (accessed between February 21, 2025 and March 31, 2025).

[49] More than 40 people died on July 23, 2011, when two high-speed trains collided on a viaduct in the suburbs of Wenzhou, Zhejiang Province. Ian Johnson, *Train Wreck in China Heightens Unease on Safety Standards*, The New York Times, July 24, 2011, http://www.nytimes.com/2011/07/25/world/asia/25train.html (accessed between February 21, 2025 and March 31, 2025).

Chinese citizen. The applications, forwarded to 32 environmental protection agencies at the central and provincial levels, requested surveillance data regarding PM2.5[50] and ozone density. Among all the environmental protection agencies involved, only one released partial data.[51] The newspaper published the application process.

On April 1, 2012, Fuqiang Gao, an editor of *Rural Women*[52] in Beijing, sent an OGI request to the Wei County Civil Affairs Bureau in Hebei Province for a list of low-income rural families who receive monthly cash assistance.[53] The agency responded on May 9, 2012 that Gao could visit the agency to personally examine the document; but prohibited photocopying the document or removing a photocopied file.[54] Gao sued

[50] PM2.5 is a term for particles less than 2.5 μm in diameter. Arguably, PM2.5 particles pose the greatest risk to health among all types of particles in the air. They can penetrate deeply into human lungs because of their small size. China has decided to monitor PM2.5 pollution since 2011. *Frequent Questions*, Area Designations for the 2012 Annual Fine Particle (PM2.5) Standard, United States Environmental Protection Agency, Washington, DC, *available at* https://www3.epa.gov/pmdesignations/2012standards/faq.htm (accessed between February 21, 2025 and March 31, 2025); Kai Guo, *China Decides to Accept PM2.5*, THE GLOBAL TIMES, December 23, 2011, http://www.globaltimes.cn/content/689657.shtml (accessed between February 21, 2025 and March 31, 2025).

[51] Submission of applications to 12 provincial-level agencies failed due to technical reasons, submission of 20 applications was successful. As of January 10, 2012, the reporter received responses from the Ministry of Environmental Protection and 10 other relevant agencies at the provincial level. The response rate was 55%. Among all 11 agencies that responded, only the Shanghai Municipal Bureau of Environmental Protection released the average density data for PM 2.5. Xing Wang, *Journalistic OGI Applications for PM2.5 Data Yield 32% of Response Rate* [记者申请PM2.5信息公开 31省区市10个答复], SOUTHERN METROPOLIS DAILY, republished by ChinaTransparency.org, January 11, 2012, at AA33 (captured by Internet Archive Wayback Machine on February 19, 2022), retrieved from https://web.archive.org/web/20220219172530/http://www.ogichina.org/article/180/12880.html (accessed between February 21, 2025 and March 31, 2025).

[52] *Rural Women* is a magazine affiliated with *China Women Daily* in Beijing.

[53] The editor sought information to verify a rumor that some rural families in the county are not eligible for cash assistance, and they are on the subsidy's roles due to favoritism. Jing Wei, *Journalist Sues Wei County Civil Affairs Bureau in Hebei Province for Non-Compliance of OGI Regulations* [媒体人诉河北蔚县民政局不公开低保名单], ChinaTransparency.org, Beijing, China, May 17, 2012 (captured by Internet Archive Wayback Machine on February 19, 2022), retrieved from https://web.archive.org/web/20220219074641/http://www.ogichina.org/article/180/13954.html (accessed between February 21, 2025 and March 31, 2025).

[54] Jing Wei, *Journalist Sues Wei County Civil Affairs Bureau in Hebei Province for Non-Compliance of OGI Regulations* [媒体人诉河北蔚县民政局不公开低保名单],

the agency for its failure to comply with *OGI Regulations* on May 10, 2012.[55] Neither Gao's magazine nor the periodical's parent company, *China Women Daily* covered the application and the ensuing lawsuit.

From 2008 to 2012, *Caijing* journalists lodged three to four OGI requests with various government agencies in China. The prestigious financial news magazine has a reputation in China for investigative journalism. Its journalists once applied to the State Council Information Office for the official schedule for restructuring the website of *People's Daily* and converting the website into a publicly traded company. The agency denied the request on the grounds that the information sought has an exemption from disclosure.[56] *Caijing* did not cover the OGI applications of its journalists.[57]

This study finds that no reporters in China filed OGI requests after 2012. After 2012, none of Chinese journalists sued any government agencies for denied access to governmental information. The result is according to recent Internet searches, database search, interviews with Chinese journalists, and reading of FOI requests and OGI-related court cases found on China Judgements Online.[58] The result is also based on another dataset, compiled by the author of this book according to annual reports of OGI activities (2008–2023) published by all central agencies and all provincial people's governments (see Table 7.3).

The data mentioned above speaks volumes about the level of journalistic use of OGI to pry open government files and documents. From

ChinaTransparency.org, Beijing, China, May 17, 2012 (captured by Internet Archive Wayback Machine on February 19, 2022), retrieved from https://web.archive.org/web/20220219074641/http://www.ogichina.org/article/180/13954.html (accessed between February 21, 2025 and March 31, 2025).

[55] Article 40 of *OGI Regulations* provides that official agencies shall provide the requested information in the form required by the applicant. *OGI Regulations 2007* (amended in 2019). Art. 40.

[56] *Caijing* and other media entities did not publicize those OGI applications. The information is the result of a September 11, 2011 telephone interview with the magazine's managing editor, Gang He.

[57] No relevant stories could be found by using key words to search on the website of *Caijing* magazine, http://www.caijing.com.cn/ (accessed between February 21, 2025 and March 31, 2025).

[58] China Judgements Online is a website that offers the largest collection of judgments and decisions from Chinese courts. It is supported and maintained by the Supreme People's Court of China. https://wenshu.court.gov.cn (accessed between February 21, 2025 and March 31, 2025).

May 2008 to December 2011, reporters and editors originated a total of 84 OGI requests in China. During the same period, Chinese citizens, legal persons, and other organizations made a total of 996,469 OGI requests. This indicates that the percentage of journalist-filed OGI requests is extremely low. The same period recorded a total of 6157 administrative reconsideration cases and 3435 OGI litigations in China. However, from May 2008 to December 2011, journalists in China filed zero administrative appeals and only one OGI lawsuit. The situation is not far better even if viewed with a much longer period. Within the 10 years beginning in 2002[59] and ending in July 2012, journalists were plaintiffs in only four recorded OGI litigations. The first litigation occurred in 2006, ending with withdrawal of the case.[60] The second occurred in 2008 and ended with the court dismissing the complaint.[61] The third[62] in 2010 and the fourth[63] in 2012 remain pending litigations. Filing of all four litigations are in the names of Chinese citizens, and currently almost no filings of OGI lawsuits represent interests of journalists or media

[59] In November 2002, the Guangzhou municipal people's government promulgated China's first local OGI rule. *Provisions of the Guangzhou Municipal Open Government Information* (promulgated on November 6, 2002) (effective on January 1, 2003).

[60] Dequan Zhu, *Unanswered Questions about First OGI Litigation Involving a Journalist* ["政府侵犯新闻采访权第一案"悬疑] DAZHONG NEWSPAPER GROUP ONLINE, August 23, 2006 (captured by Internet Archive Wayback Machine on January 5, 2011), retrieved from https://web.archive.org/web/20110105051846/http://qnjz.dzwww.com/zk/200608/t20060801_1680429.htm (accessed between February 21, 2025 and March 31, 2025).

[61] Hongqing Duan, *Pin Ma: One Single Person Fights Lonely and Publicly Against Government Violations of OGI Regulations* [马骋:一个人的信息公开战争], Caixin blog, April 24, 2015, *available at* https://duanhongqing.blog.caixin.com/archives/84413?originReferrer=caixinsearch_pc (accessed between February 21, 2025 and March 31, 2025);

[62] Shuming Li, *Shanghai Resident Questions Fairness of Being Beaten Without Compensation* [上海市民追问"打了白打"], PROCURATORIAL DAILY, November 3, 2010, (captured by Internet Archive Wayback Machine on April 13, 2021), retrieved from https://web.archive.org/web/20210413034001/http://news.jcrb.com/jxsw/201011/t20101103_461426.html (accessed between February 21, 2025 and March 31, 2025).

[63] Jing Wei, *Journalist Sues Wei County Civil Affairs Bureau in Hebei Province for Non-Compliance of OGI Regulations* [媒体人诉河北蔚县民政局不公开低保名单], ChinaTransparency.org, Beijing, China, May 17, 2012 (captured by Internet Archive Wayback Machine on February 19, 2022), retrieved from https://web.archive.org/web/20220219074641/http://www.ogichina.org/article/180/13954.html (accessed between February 21, 2025 and March 31, 2025).

outlets. In addition, unlike American journalists who use FOI requests to produce award-winning investigative reports, all current use of the freedom of information law in China by journalists focus on official agencies' enforcement of the law. Media exposure of non-compliance of the law itself is important; however, more significant is media exposure of official mismanagement, scandals, and corruptions found through examination of large volumes of governmental documents and records obtained via OGI requests.

Reasons for Limited Use of *OGI Regulations* by Chinese Journalists to Access Governmental Information

In the United States and many other Western countries, freedoms of information laws are very important reporting and research tools for reporters. Johan Lidberg, an Australian FOI scholar, said, "The most frequent, experienced, and at times frustrated, users of FOI are journalists and media organizations. It can be argued that FOI needs journalists to realize its potential as a political accountability tool and journalists need FOI to fulfill their role[s] as the fourth estate, scrutinizing societal power in general and political power in particular."[64]

The anecdotal examples mentioned above, however, demonstrate that, Chinese journalists are far less passionate than their Western colleagues about using FOI laws as a newsgathering, reporting and research tool. From May 2008 when China's *FOIA* was enforced across the country, Chinese reporters and editors did occasionally use *OGI Regulations* to obtain documents from the government. While some reporters and editors resorted to actions in court for non-disclosure, such Chinese journalists were too few. Compared with lawyers, college students and citizens, Chinese journalists are the least active users of government documents obtained through OGI requests. The use of administrative and judicial reviews for rectifying non-compliance with *OGI Regulations* is even more uncommon among Chinese journalists.

A migrant worker in Beijing said to a *Caixin* journalist, "Laws are a big bell made by a country. If you don't ring it, it will never ring

[64] Johan Lidberg, "Keeping the Bastards Honest-The Promise and Practice of Freedom of Information Legislation" (2006) (unpublished Ph.D. diss., Murdoch University), 12.

itself!"[65] Sixin Wang, a media law professor from the Communication University of China in Beijing, said in an interview with *The Wall Street Journal* that *OGI Regulations* could be a "sword" for Chinese journalists.[66] It is worthwhile to ask why Chinese editors and reporters do not ring the "bell" harder. It is also worthwhile to ask why Chinese editors and reporters do not use the "sword" more frequently. The reasons for the insufficient use of the *OGI Regulations* by news media outlets to access information are multifold.

First, the FOI law in China, before it was revised in 2019, required information seekers to prove that the documents sought are for special needs of the applicants' production, livelihood and scientific research. Journalists often find it hard to meet this "special needs test" and government agencies often use the argument "the information sought was irrelevant to your special needs."[67] Second, many government officials and employees are often cautious with reporters. Reporters often find that they can get the information through OGI more easily if they hide their professional affiliations.[68] Third, *OGI Regulations* have been enforceable for 16 years, and many reporters are still not fully aware of the law's magnitude, especially among journalists from local media and underdeveloped regions.[69] Fourth, obtaining official information via the lengthy

[65] Hongqing Duan, *How Chinese Media Shall Push Forward Open Government Information* [中国媒体如何推进信息公开], 9 CHINA REFORM (2011) (captured by Internet Archive Wayback Machine on October 11, 2011), retrieved from https://web.archive.org/web/20111011013413/http://article.chinalawinfo.com/Article_Detail.asp?ArticleID=63344 (accessed between February 21, 2025 and March 31, 2025).

[66] Geoffrey A. Fowler and Juying Qin, *China Pushes Openness: First Order: Unveil Rules Dictating Transparency*, THE WALL STREET JOURNAL, February 28, 2007, http://online.wsj.com/article/SB117260663002921026.html (accessed between February 21, 2025 and March 31, 2025).

[67] *OGI Regulations 2007* (amended in 2019). Art. 13.

[68] Xing Wang, *Is It Hard to Interview Government Officials? Much Easier If You Don't Say You Are a Reporter* [采访政府难?别说你是记者就容易了], Guancha.cn [观察者], Shanghai, China, July 12, 2014, *available at* https://www.guancha.cn/WangXing?web (accessed between February 21, 2025 and March 31, 2025).

[69] Email and telephone interviews from June 2012 to July 2012 to measure Chinese journalists' use of *OGI Regulations* showed that most reporters from national media in Guangzhou, Beijing, and Shanghai have familiarity with *OGI Regulations* whereas many reporters from local media in Hubei and Sichuan Provinces have no familiarity.

process of filing OGI requests is time-consuming, and consequently, ill-suited for reporters with restrictive deadlines.[70] Another factor that limits journalistic use of *OGI Regulations* is the low percentage of OGI requests approved by official agencies[71] and the remote possibility of succeeding in OGI litigation.[72] The prospect of failure in obtaining the materials

[70] Gang He, managing editor of a prestigious financial publication known for investigative journalism in China, stated in a September 11, 2011 telephone interview that his journalists have occasionally used *OGI Regulations*. But most of his reporters prefer to obtain official information from other sources because the OGI approach is too slow.

[71] Annual reports of OGI activities of central and provincial-level agencies (2008–2023) indicate that the majority of OGI requests submitted to provincial and local agencies gained approval. However, those numbers deserve cautious interpretation because the raw data arises from official agencies, not from independent sources. The OGI request approval rate provided by research organizations and news media such as the *China Academy of Social Science*, Peking University, *Southern Weekend*, and *Southern Metropolis Daily* is far lower. Those independent sources obtained the approval rate by sending staff to apply for information under the guise of ordinary requesters. Those rates are likely more reliable. For example, the China Academy of Social Sciences conducted an OGI application experiment in 2010 and found that the OGI request approval rate was 6.7% for central agencies and 4.6% for local agencies. Peking University Center for Public Participation Studies and Supports has not released any approval rates, but its staff reportedly faced frequent complaints when applying for information from all agencies. *Southern Weekend* conducted an OGI application experiment in 2010 and found that the approval rate was 41%. The *Southern Metropolis* Daily experiment in 2011 found that the corresponding rate was 5%. The approval rate may be even lower if requesters are journalists. Governmental agencies may reject disclosure, claiming that the journalists failed to satisfy the special needs test or argue that the materials sought might be used for sensationalism. Hongqing Duan, *How Chinese Media Shall Push Forward Open Government Information* [中国媒体如何推进信息公开], 9 China Reform (2011) (captured by Internet Archive Wayback Machine on October 11, 2011), retrieved from https://web.archive.org/web/20111011013413/http://article.chinalawinfo.com/Article_Detail.asp?ArticleID=63344 (accessed between February 21, 2025 and March 31, 2025); Xing Wang, *Journalistic OGI Applications for PM2.5 Data Yield 32% of Response Rate* [记者申请PM2.5信息公开 31省区市10个答复], Southern Metropolis Daily, republished by ChinaTransparency.org, January 11, 2012, at AA33 (captured by Internet Archive Wayback Machine on February 19, 2022), retrieved from https://web.archive.org/web/20220219172530/http://www.ogichina.org/article/180/12880.html (accessed between February 21, 2025 and March 31, 2025); Mingyan Wei and Shaofeng Guo, *OGI Regulations Still Encounter Implementation Bottlenecks Four Years After Its Enactment* [信息公开条例实施4年仍遭执行难], Beijing News, May 15, 2012, http://www.bjnews.com.cn/news/2012/05/15/199113.html (accessed between February 21, 2025 and March 31, 2025).

[72] Judicial review is normally ineffective for rectifying non-disclosure of information. The chance of winning OGI litigation is even slimmer if the plaintiffs are journalists. Zhengjun Zhao, an ordinary citizen in Zhengzhou City, Henan Province, filed 12 OGI lawsuits since May 2008 when upon enforcement of *OGI Regulations*. His success rate

sought convinces journalists that the information request is useless. Lack of support from newsrooms and media attorneys also contributes to the reluctance of journalists to use the law for access to information.[73]

The limited use of *OGI Regulations* to access information may also have an explanation from the changing prototype of the Chinese news media. As a newly emerging model that directly challenges the dominance of party journalism, professional journalism has created favorable conditions for the use of *OGI Regulations*. However, breathing space available to professional journalism remains limited in China. As Chinese media are moving toward liberalization, commercialization, industrialization, technological innovation, and professionalism since the 1980s, professional journalism has emerged as a new paradigm and a direct competitor to the dominant party journalism model.[74] Market-oriented metropolitan newspapers exemplify professional journalism whereas party organs exemplify party journalism. The two journalistic models sharply embrace different journalistic values and practices. Since they are much less censored than

was high: nearly 60%. Among the 12 litigations he filed, he won 7, lost 2, and withdrew 3. Zhao is fortunate, unlike most reporters, such as *Jiefang Daily* journalist, Pin Ma. As mentioned earlier in this chapter, Ma filed several OGI litigations and won none. Changrong Qu, F*rom Zero to 60%: Citizen Zhengjun Zhao's Journey to Protect His Right to Know* [从0到60%:公民赵正军的 "公开"维权路], PEOPLE'S DAILY, May 5, 2009.

[73] Pin Ma is a good case in point. The ambitious *Jiefang Daily* journalist applied for governmental information several times and brought agencies to court several times. Unfortunately, his persistent use of *OGI Regulations* was not career enhancing. His newspaper did not publish any articles to support his applications. To the contrary, his newspaper persuaded him to withdraw the 2006 lawsuit because of pressure the publication received from powerful party and official censors. The newspaper demoted him, transferred him from *Jiefang Daily* to another much less prominent sister newspaper, *Press Digest*. His newspaper also rejected his application for a senior professional title. The situation for Ma would improve if he could obtain free legal assistance from media attorneys and public interest organizations, similar to American colleagues. Unfortunately, media attorneys in China are scarce; public interest groups specializing in providing free-of-charge legal services to media organizations do not exist in China. Hongqing Duan, *How Chinese Media Shall Push Forward Open Government Information* [中国媒体如何推进信息公开], 9 CHINA REFORM (2011) (captured by Internet Archive Wayback Machine on October 11, 2011), retrieved from https://web.archive.org/web/20111011013413/http://article.chinalawinfo.com/Article_Detail.asp?ArticleID=63344 (accessed between February 21, 2025 and March 31, 2025).

[74] Zhongdang Pan and Joseph Man Chan, "Assessing Media Exemplars and Shifting Journalistic Paradigms: A Survey Study of China's Journalists," paper presented at the annual meeting of International Communication Association, San Diego, CA, May 23, 2003, 1–54.

party organs, metropolitan dailies have greater involvement in investigative journalism, thus creating a need for information obtained through filing OGI requests. Both media interviews and careful examination of OGI articles published by Chinese media confirm this speculation. Most media outlets that have used *OGI Regulations* since 2002 are metropolitan publications. But the problem is that many metropolitan dailies are either permanently closed or in tremendous financial strain in the era of mobile communication characterized by ubiquitous smartphones. Nonetheless, metropolitan newspapers are still at the forefront of using the freedom of information law. A People's Daily journalist disclosed no need for journalists at his newspaper to apply for information via OGI requests because information released through official meetings and websites is sufficient. He admitted that the information released through these two channels is far from sufficient for market-oriented metropolitan newspapers.[75]

One of the more important reasons for media's limited use of *OGI Regulations* for information access, however, is the lack of stronger legal protection for Chinese journalists' right to gather and publish news. A journalist would not seek information via OGI requests in the first place, knowing in advance of the application that the censors would consider the information inappropriate for public view.

The Chinese journey to freedom of expression and freedom of the press is clearly less smooth than the journey to its freedom of information law. Modern Chinese media originated in the early 1900s after the Qing Dynasty collapsed. Enactment of the *Publishing Act* occurred in 1930, amended in 1937, and followed by *Press Act* in 1943.[76] Chiang Kai-shek and his Kuomintang regime used both laws to suppress freedom of expression and the press, however, with lackluster enforcement.[77] After Mao Zedong and his communist comrades created the People's Republic

[75] The journalist, together with other reporters and editors across the country, participated in in-depth interviews with the author of this book on journalistic use of *OGI Regulations*. The interviews were conducted via email and telephone. The interviews lasted from June 2012 to November 2012. All interviewees requested anonymity due to the sensitive nature of the topic.

[76] Xiaowei Song, *Research on Legislative History of Chinese Press Shall Value Tradition* [新闻立法史研究须重传统], CHINESE SOCIAL SCIENCES TODAY, May 30, 2012, at B02.

[77] YUTANG LIN, A HISTORY OF THE PRESS AND PUBLIC OPINION IN CHINA 177 (1936).

of China, Chinese political elite included concepts of freedom of expression and the press into the 1954 Constitution.[78] The same aspirations appear in the subsequent 1975 Constitution,[79] 1978 Constitution,[80] and 1982 Constitution.[81] Under Mao's leadership, the twin freedoms of expression and the press never reached practice, since the party established a Soviet Union-like media system characterized by complete party control.[82] During the Cultural Revolution (1966–1976), the Constitution became a worthless piece of paper. The Constitution failed to protect Chinese President Liu Shaoqi from illegal imprisonment, torture,

[78] Article 87 of the 1954 Constitution proclaimed that "[c]itizens of the People's Republic of China enjoy freedom of speech, freedom of the press, freedom of assembly, freedom of association, freedom of procession and freedom of demonstration. To ensure that citizens can enjoy these freedoms, the state provides the necessary material facilities." The Chinese Constitution 1954 (adopted in 1954 and repealed by 1975 Constitution), *available at* https://ecommons.cornell.edu/server/api/core/bitstreams/f7bbb8b4-822c-467e-b51c-430e44430e4d/content (accessed between February 21, 2025 and March 31, 2025).

[79] Article 28 of the 1975 Constitution provided that "Citizens enjoy freedom of speech, correspondence, the press, assembly, association, procession, demonstration and the freedom to strike, and enjoy freedom to believe in religion and freedom not to believe in religion and to propagate atheism." The Chinese Constitution 1975 (adopted in 1975 and repealed by 1978 Constitution), *available at* https://china.usc.edu/sites/default/files/article/attachments/peoples-republic-of-china-constitution-1975.pdf (accessed between February 21, 2025 and March 31, 2025).

[80] Article 45 of the 1978 Constitution provided that "Citizens enjoy freedom of speech, correspondence, the press, assembly, association, procession, demonstration and the freedom to strike, and have the right to speak out freely, air their views fully, hold great debates and write big-character posters." The Chinese Constitution 1978 (adopted in 1978 and repealed by the 1982 Constitution), *available at* https://china.usc.edu/sites/default/files/article/attachments/peoples-republic-of-china-constitution-1978.pdf (accessed between February 21, 2025 and March 31, 2025).

[81] The 1982 Constitution is the fourth and last constitution of China. Article 35 of the 1982 Constitution provides that "Citizens of the People's Republic of China enjoy freedom of speech, of the press, of assembly, of association, of procession and of demonstration." The Chinese Constitution 1982 (adopted in 1982 and amended in 1988, 1993, 1999, 2004 and 2018), *available at* https://china.usc.edu/node/20328 (accessed between February 21, 2025 and March 31, 2025).

[82] FRED S. SIEBERT, THEODORE PETERSON and WILBUR SCHRAMM, FOUR THEORIES OF THE PRESS: THE AUTHORITARIAN, LIBERTARIAN, SOCIAL RESPONSIBILITY AND SOVIET COMMUNIST CONCEPTS OF WHAT THE PRESS SHOULD BE AND DO 105–146 (1956).

and death.[83] Many reporters, purged by the authorities for being rightists, investigated and imprisoned without the due process of the law,[84] committed suicide.[85]

Legal protections for journalists became stronger after Mao died and Deng Xiaoping emerged as the top leader of the country in the late 1970s. As a part of Deng's effort to reestablish a legal system severely damaged by Mao, journalists in China began reflecting on the lessons of the Cultural Revolution and the experiences of the rule of law in journalism in Western countries. Journalists, scholars, and the National People's Congress (NPC) deputies began proposing the enactment of the *Freedom of the Press Law* in the early 1980s. In 1980, many articles advocating greater rule of law in journalism appeared in leading periodicals.[86] Since the common notion was that judges could not cite constitutional

[83] On the eve of the Cultural Revolution when Red Guards physically attacked Liu Shaoqi, Liu produced a copy of the Constitution and said angrily with the document in his hand, "I am the president! I am protected under the Constitution." But he was still tortured to death. JIAQI YAN and GAO GAO, TURBULENT DECADE: A HISTORY OF THE CULTURAL REVOLUTION 156 (1996).

[84] YUEZHI ZHAO, MEDIA, MARKET, AND DEMOCRACY IN CHINA: BETWEEN THE PARTY LINE AND THE BOTTOM LINE 30 (1998).

[85] Two top journalists who committed suicide during the Cultural Revolution were Deng Tuo and Fan Changjiang. Deng was founding editor of *People's Daily*. Fan once served as publisher of *People's Daily* and Xinhua News Agency. Both killed themselves for being criticized and purged by Mao. TIMOTHY CHEEK, PROPAGANDA AND CULTURE IN MAO'S CHINA: DENG TUO AND THE INTELLIGENTSIA (1997). Jianguang Guo, *He Stays at Northwestern Corner of China Forever: Famous Journalist Fan Changjiang's Last Days of His Life in Luzhuang* [永远的 "西北角"——新闻巨擘范长江在芦庄的最后岁月], THE PAPER, March 30, 2021, https://m.thepaper.cn/baijiahao_11960039 (accessed between February 21, 2025 and March 31, 2025).

[86] Xupei Sun, *Reflections on 30-Year-Long Legislative History of Press Law* [三十年新闻立法历程与思考], 2 YAN-HUANG HISTORICAL REVIEW [炎黄春秋] (2012), republished by Aisixiang.com, February 10, 2012, https://www.aisixiang.com/data/49917.html (accessed between February 21, 2025 and March 31, 2025); Hong Shen, *Sun Xupei: China Is Missing Best Opportunity to Enact Press Law* [中国错过了新闻法出台的最佳时机], THE NEW YORK TIME CHINESE, June 28, 2013, https://cn.nytimes.com/china/20130628/cc28pressfreedom/ (accessed between February 21, 2025 and March 31, 2025);

Hong Shen, *Sun Xupei: Telling the Truth is Harder than Finding the Truth in China* [在中国表达真理比发现真理还难], THE NEW YORK TIME CHINESE, June 29, 2013, https://cn.nytimes.com/china/20130629/cc29pressfreedom/ (accessed between February 21, 2025 and March 31, 2025).

provisions an authority in China,[87] *Freedom of the Press Law* would be vital for translating democratic ideals in Article 35 of the 1982 Constitution into reality. The law would also allow judicial remedy for violations of journalists' legal rights.

In 1983, some NPC deputies[88] submitted proposals to the first session of the sixth National People's Congress, calling on the NPC to "legislate the Freedom of the Press Law of the People's Republic of China when the opportunities are ripe."[89] In January 1984, The Central Propaganda Department of the Chinese Communist Party issued a report for instructions on the drafting of the *Press Law*. The CPC Secretariat and the Chairperson of the NPC Standing Committee soon approved the report.[90] In May 1984, the Press Law Research Institute, established in Beijing under the auspices of the NPC and the Chinese Academy of Social Sciences, produced a draft of the *Freedom of the Press Law* in 1985. In 1986, Shanghai produced a local version of the press law known as *Provisions of the Shanghai Municipality on Journalism Work*. In 1987, the Administration of Press and Publication,[91] created in Beijing, authored another draft of the *Freedom of the Press Law*, which appeared in early 1989.[92]

Among the three drafts of the *Freedom of the Press Law,* the draft produced by the Press Law Research Institute is the most comprehensive and progressive for guaranteeing journalistic rights. The draft, after three revisions, was completed in 1988. Article 1 of the third version provides that freedom of the press means the right of the citizens to publish and

[87] Bo Li, *What Is Constitutionalism?* 1 PERSPECTIVES (2000).

[88] Many NPC deputies were journalists.

[89] Xupei Sun, *Reflections on 30-Year-Long Legislative History of Press Law* [三十年新闻立法历程与思考], 2 YAN-HUANG HISTORICAL REVIEW (2012), para. 4–5.

[90] Xupei Sun, *Reflections on 30-Year-Long Legislative History of Press Law* [三十年新闻立法历程与思考], 2 YAN-HUANG HISTORICAL REVIEW (2012).

[91] The Administration of Press and Publication is a vice-ministerial-level administrative agency directly under the supervision of the State Council. It is responsible for regulating and distributing news, print and Internet publications in China. Renamed the General Administration of Press and Publication in 2001, its upgraded administrative rank became ministerial-level. The agency was then renamed in 2013 as State Administration of Press, Publication, Radio, Film, and Television. The agency was renamed again in 2018 as National Radio and Television Administration.

[92] Xupei Sun, *Reflections on 30-Year-Long Legislative History of Press Law* [三十年新闻立法历程与思考], 2 YAN-HUANG HISTORICAL REVIEW (2012).

obtain news via news media and the right of citizens to enjoy and exercise freedom of expression and publication. Article 7 provides that citizens and social organizations enjoy the right to criticize the government and public officials. Article 8 provides that the state may not engage in any forms of censoring the content of news media, except when the country is in a state of national emergency/general mobilization. Article 12 provides that citizens' groups and natural persons may establish newspapers and periodicals. Article 22 provides that news media can make editorial judgments, independently, without the need for approval from any individual or organization outside the news organization. News gathered by the journalist may arrive at a news organization without undue interception. Individuals or organizations may not obstruct, threaten, persecute, or endanger journalists who are fulfilling their professional duties.[93] Aspirations for greater editorial autonomy were evident and even shocking to some conservative leaders in the CCP, given that most media organizations in China are components of the party and government, and each has its corresponding administrative rank. A party directive that was issued in 1953 and followed by media organizations as a cannon prohibits reporters from openly criticizing party committees and official departments with which the news organizations have affiliations.[94]

[93] All the key provisions of the draft of the law appear in an article written by Hu Jiwei, former editor-in-chief and publisher of *People's Daily* and one of the leading writers of the law. Jiwei Hu, *Hardships and Misfortunes in Formulation of First Press Law in People's Republic of China (1–8)* [制定中国第一部新闻法的艰辛与厄运1-8], Xys.org [新语丝], *available at* http://www.xys.org/xys/ebooks/others/history/contemporary/hujiwei/ (accessed between February 21, 2025 and March 31, 2025).

[94] In 1953, the Chinese Communist Party Central Committee Department of Propaganda issued a notice providing that party papers shall not openly criticize same-rank party committees. This party directive is still enforced today despite criticism from scholars and journalists. Ming Jing, *Origins of the Party Directive that "Party Papers Shall Not Criticize Same-Level Party Committees,"* ["党报不得批评同级党委"指示的来历] 7 YAN-HUANG HISTORICAL REVIEW (2008); Xiaotian Tang, *New Thoughts on the Party Directive that "Party Papers Shall Not Criticize Same-Level Party Committees,"* ["党报不得批评同级党委"规定之新认识] 15 JOURNAL OF YOUTH JOURNALIST 63 (2009); Shaozhang Li, *Questioning the Party Directive that "Party Papers Shall Not Criticize Same-Level Party Committees,"*["党报不得批评同级党委"质疑] 9 BAOKAN YEWU TANSUO (2009); Bifeng Jing & Zhishuang Su, *Revisiting the Party Directive that "Party Papers Shall Not Criticize Same-Level Party Committees,"* ["党报不得批评同级党委"再认识] 7 YOUTH JOURNALIST (2011).

Although conservative hard-liners in the party strongly opposed to the passage of the *Press Law*,[95] Zhao Ziyang[96] and many reform-minded leaders supported the idea of *Freedom of the Press Law*. However, coincidentally, the 1989 Tiananmen Square incident occurred unexpectedly, just when the three drafts of *Freedom of the Press Law* were ready for submission to the State Council and the NPC Standing Committee for review. The gunshots fired on the Tiananmen Square in the early morning of June 4, 1989 not only killed student demonstrators but also destroyed *Freedom of the Press Law* at its infancy.

Since the 1989 Tiananmen Square incident, legislation of *Freedom of the Press Law* has stalled. Although *Freedom of the Press Law* appears in the legislative plan's agenda of the eighth National People's Congress Standing Committee, the lawmaking process lost momentum.[97] In March 1998, 33 NPC deputies submitted a proposal to the NPC, calling on the speedy formulation of *Freedom of the Press Law*. In December 1998, The Chairperson of the NPC Standing Committee, Li Peng, said during an interview, that China would formulate a press law that is consistent

95 Some high-ranking officials in the party strongly opposed enactment of the *Freedom of the Press Law*. They argued that the Press Act led to the breakdown of many regimes such as Chiang Kai-shek's rule in Mainland China, the Soviet Union and many Eastern European countries. They also argued that the *Freedom of the Press Law* would displace various propaganda departments. Jiwei Hu, *Hardships and Misfortunes in Formulation of First Press Law in People's Republic of China (1–8)* [制定中国第一部新闻法的艰辛与厄运1-8], Xys.org [新语丝], *available at* http://www.xys.org/xys/ebooks/others/history/contemporary/hujiwei/ (accessed between February 21, 2025 and March 31, 2025).

96 As the party general secretary in the late 1980s, Zhao was very supportive of political reform including greater rule of law in journalism. One day during the Spring Festival in 1989, Zhao invited one of the leading framers of the *Press Law* to his office. The two discussed formulation of *Freedom of the Press Law* for a whole morning. Jiwei Hu, *Hardships and Misfortunes in Formulation of First Press Law in People's Republic of China (1–8)* [制定中国第一部新闻法的艰辛与厄运1-8], Xys.org [新语丝], *available at* http://www.xys.org/xys/ebooks/others/history/contemporary/hujiwei/ (accessed between February 21, 2025 and March 31, 2025).

97 Xupei Sun, *Reflections on 30-Year-Long Legislative History of Press Law* [三十年新闻立法历程与思考], 2 YAN-HUANG HISTORICAL REVIEW (2012); Jin Zhao, *Why Is Press Freedom Law Still a Dream in China?* [《新闻法》为何至今悬而未立?], THE YOUTH JOURNALIST, republished by People's Daily Online, February 12, 2009 (captured by Internet Archive Wayback Machine on February 19, 2009), retrieved from https://web.archive.org/web/20090219221025/http://media.people.com.cn/GB/22114/42328/145310/8792516.html (accessed between February 21, 2025 and March 31, 2025); Lu Keng, *Press Control in "New China" and "Old China,"* in CHIN-CHUAN LEE (ed.), MEDIA'S CHINA, CHINA'S MEDIA 147–162 (1994).

with Chinese national conditions. Beginning in 2003, NPC deputies have submitted proposals for the establishment of *Freedom of the Press Law* almost every year.[98] In 2008, *People's Daily* published an article urging relevant agencies to speed up their work on formulating the long-delayed *Freedom of the Press Law*.[99] Despite all these efforts, no indications exist that such a progressive law on press freedom will become a reality in the near future.

Limitations to press freedom in China are due to a lack of *Freedom of the Press Law*. Then how is China ranked against other countries in terms of press freedom? Several measures are available to quantify a country's press freedom.[100] Freedom House press freedom score is a widely used

[98] Hong Shen, *Sun Xupei: China Is Missing Best Opportunity to Enact Press Law* [中国错过了新闻法出台的最佳时机], The New York Time Chinese, June 28, 2013, https://cn.nytimes.com/china/20130628/cc28pressfreedom/ (accessed between February 21, 2025 and March 31, 2025); Hong Shen, *Sun Xupei: Telling the Truth is Harder than Finding the Truth in China* [在中国表达真理比发现真理还难], The New York Times Chinese, June 29, 2013, https://cn.nytimes.com/china/20130629/cc29pressfreedom/ (accessed between February 21, 2025 and March 31, 2025).

[99] Qing Hua, *Speed up Work on Legislation of Press Law according to Scientific Principle of Rule of Law and Effective Management* [科学、依法、有效管理 加快新闻领域立法工作], People's Daily, November 3, 2008, republished by Sohu News, November 4, 2008, https://news.sohu.com/20081104/n260419205.shtml (accessed between February 21, 2025 and March 31, 2025).

[100] Measures developed by the Committee to Protect Journalists, Reporters Without Borders, International Research and Exchanges Board, and Freedom House are four major indicators of global press freedom. Committee to Protect Journalists quantifies a country's press freedom by identifying the number of reporters killed, imprisoned, exiled, or missing in a certain year. *Explore CPJ's Database of Attacks on the Press*, Committee to Protect Journalists, New York, *available at* https://cpj.org/data/location/ (accessed between February 21, 2025 and March 31, 2025). The Reporters Without Borders Press Freedom Index ranks a country's press freedom by incorporating the number of violations directly affecting journalists, frequent users of the Internet and news media, and the level of self-censorship and financial pressures on news organizations. *World Press Freedom Index*, Reporters Without Borders, Paris, France, *available at* https://rsf.org/en/index (accessed between February 21, 2025 and March 31, 2025). The IREX (International Research and Exchanges Board) Media Sustainability Index ranks a country's press freedom by quantifying the ability of media to play its vital role as the "fourth estate." Measurement of the ability is an assessment of five objectives that shape a media system: freedom of speech, professional journalism, and plurality of news, business management, and supporting institutions. *Media Sustainability Index (MSI)*, International Research and Exchanges Board, Washington, DC, *available at* https://www.mediasustainabilityindex.org/ (accessed between February 21, 2025 and March 31, 2025) and *Media Sustainability Index: Archived Reports*, International Research and Exchanges

indicator of press freedom because it is the "most comprehensive data on global media freedom available."[101] Freedom House press freedom scores have constantly ranked the United States (see Table 10.1) as one of the most "free" countries in terms of press freedom and rated China as one of the least free. The scores for China's press freedom (see Table 10.2) is so low that it trails closely behind North Korea (see Table 10.3) and Cuba (see Table 10.4), two communist regimes widely considered in the West as highly authoritarian.[102] Among almost all non-democratic regimes with freedom of information laws, China again ranks at the bottom in terms

Board, Washington, DC, *available at* https://www.irex.org/media-sustainability-index-archived-reports (accessed between February 21, 2025 and March 31, 2025). Freedom of the Press rankings by Freedom House quantifies a country's press freedom annually by measuring the legal environment, political environment and economic environment in which media system operate. *Freedom of the Press Research Methodology*, Freedom House, Washington, DC, *available at* https://freedomhouse.org/freedom-press-research-methodology (accessed between February 21, 2025 and March 31, 2025) and Freedom of the Press, Publication Archives, Freedom House, Washington, DC, *available at* https://freedomhouse.org/reports/publication-archives (accessed between February 21, 2025 and March 31, 2025).

[101] According to the Freedom House press freedom rankings, countries receive scores from 0 (best) to 100 (worst) on the basis of a set of 23 methodological questions, divided into three subcategories: legal environment, political influences, and economic pressure. For each question, a lower number of points coincides with a freer situation, while a higher number of points represents a less free environment. *Freedom of the Press Research Methodology*, Freedom House, Washington, DC, *available at* https://freedomhouse.org/freedom-press-research-methodology (accessed between February 21, 2025 and March 31, 2025) and Freedom of the Press, Publication Archives, Freedom House, Washington, DC, *available at* https://freedomhouse.org/reports/publication-archives (accessed between February 21, 2025 and March 31, 2025).

[102] Under the ranking system by Freedom House, the degree to which each country permits the free flow of news and information determines the classification of its media as Free, Partly Free, or Not Free. Countries scoring 0 to 30 have Free media; 31 to 60, Partly Free media; and 61 to 100, Not Free media. Freedom House began to compile press freedom scores in 1980, with scores compiled annually. The four tables (Tables 10.1–10.4) list press freedom scores for 2008 to 2017 because the Chinese *OGI Regulations* have had enforcement only since 2008. Also including all the years in the tables is infeasible. *Freedom of the Press Research Methodology*, Freedom House, Washington, DC, *available at* https://freedomhouse.org/freedom-press-research-methodology (accessed between February 21, 2025 and March 31, 2025) and Freedom of the Press, Publication Archives, Freedom House, Washington, DC, *available at* https://freedomhouse.org/reports/publication-archives (accessed between February 21, 2025 and March 31, 2025).

of each country's press freedom for the year of enactment of the freedom of information legislation (see Table 10.5).

Although Freedom House scores seem unable to capture the subtle change in a country's media freedom on a yearly basis, they do reflect, in some way, the worrisome status of journalists' rights in China. Largely due to the country's failure to enact *Freedom of the Press Law*, the Chinese government has the discretion to use party directives and rules to suppress the freedom of the media in news reporting.[103] Propaganda departments at various levels of the party bureaucracy formulate and enforce those directive and rules.[104] Since those directives and rules are vague, censors from propaganda departments enjoy wide latitude for restricting the flow of any information they dislike.[105]

[103] Xupei Sun, *Reflections on 30-Year-Long Legislative History of Press Law* [三十年新闻立法历程与思考], 2 Yan-Huang Historical Review (2012).

[104] The Central Propaganda Department formulates many party rules and directives. For example, in July 1987, the Central Propaganda Department, CPC Foreign Propaganda Small Leading Group and Xinhua News Agency issued a joint opinion, which provides that news media adhere to the principle of being conducive to social stability, stable economic development, smooth operation of reform, and open to publishing articles on sensitive social issues and major public emergencies or incidents. All the important numbers and key facts about those issues and incidents are to remain unpublished until verified and approved by relevant official agencies. In January 1989, the Central Propaganda Department issued a notice, which provided that news media ask for instructions from the State Council leading officials before journalists report on major emergencies or incidents. Normally, only news media outlets at the central level may report on those emergencies or incidents. Xinhua News Agency has exclusive right to cover those emergencies or incidents whenever the situation warrants. In August 1994, the General Office of the CPC Central Committee and the General Office of the State Council issued another notice, which reaffirms the spirit of the January 1989 notice. In addition, the new notice provides that the CCP Office of Foreign Propaganda coordinate foreign audience-intended news coverage of emergency incidents. Xinhua News Agency is the only domestic news organization that can report on those incidents. Other news media outlets are not to report those incidents without proper prior authorization from relevant official agencies. From the middle of the 1990s to the present, party and governmental censors have changed their methods of circulating orders and directives. Similar orders and directives are no longer printed and circulated in party and official documents and files. Instead, most such orders and directives transmit through telephone calls or small internal meetings. News media normally receive a few telephone calls from party and governmental propaganda officials for instructions for reports' contents. Tingjun Wu and Changyong Xia, *History and Status Quo of Crisis Communication in China* [我国公共危机传播的历史回顾与现状分析], 6 Journal of Modern Communication 32 (2010).

[105] *People's Daily* published, in 2005, an interview with an American writer and investment banker. Editors' enthusiasm for this interview caused its prominent placement in the

A common notion is that China is "cautiously but resolutely" on the road to media freedom.[106] The reality, however, is something opposite. Various movements in the Chinese media law environment indicate that legal protection for professional and citizen journalism is becoming weaker and weaker in recent years. In 2013, The Supreme Court criminalizes online defamation by stating that anyone posting defamatory comments online may face up to three years in prison, probation or deprivation of political rights if such statements are clicked and viewed more than 5000 times, or reposted/retweeted more than 500 times.[107] In 2015, China adopted a new national security law that the country will use to defend its sovereignty and security and "maintain political security and social stability."[108] In 2016, the country passed a cyber security

paper and they planned an award for the reporter in recognition of his outstanding work. However, one official from the Central Propaganda Department News Reading and Evaluation Small Group was highly critical of this article. He wrote a letter to the Department head and forwarded the letter to *People's Daily* for censure. After the investigation, the newspaper editors insisted that the Propaganda Department was inappropriately concerned and declined to punish the author. Instead, they ordered the copy editor to pay ¥50RMB (worthy of $6.85) as a small and symbolic gesture of penalty. This incident reflects that the severity of punishment imposed by the party on politically incorrect journalists is on the decline. However, the incident also exposes the truth that party directives and rules on journalism are normally vague and overly broad. They can be interpreted from many perspectives. Even senior editors in party organs may not easily distinguish what is publishable from what is off limits. Perry Link, a famous scholar of modern Chinese literature and politics, described the vagueness of the censorship machine as an effective strategy for deterrence. Perry Link, *China: The Anaconda in the Chandelier*, NEW YORK REVIEW OF BOOKS, April 11, 2002, http://www.nybooks.com/articles/15258 (accessed between February 21, 2025 and March 31, 2025).

106 *China's Road of Free Information Flow Cautious but Resolute*, PEOPLE'S DAILY ONLINE, November 8, 2007, para. 1 (captured by Internet Archive Wayback Machine on June 29, 2018), retrieved from https://web.archive.org/web/20180629050930/http://en.people.cn/90001/90782/6299198.html (accessed between February 21, 2025 and March 31, 2025).

107 *Interpretation of Supreme People's Court and Supreme People's Procuratorate on Several Issues Regarding Applicable Law in Cases of Using Information Networks to Commit Defamation and Other Such Crimes* [最高人民法院、最高人民检察院关于办理利用信息网络实施诽谤等刑事案件适用法律若干问题的解释], Beijing, China [issued on September 6, 2013 and took effect on September 10, 2013].

108 *National Security Law of People's Republic of China* [中华人民共和国国家安全法], Beijing, China [adopted on July 1, 2015]; *China Adopts National Security Law*, CHINA DAILY, July 1, 2015, http://www.chinadaily.com.cn/china/2015-07/01/content_21150783.htm (accessed between February 21, 2025 and March 31, 2025).

law that aims to "safeguard sovereignty on cyber space, national security and the rights of citizens."[109] In 2017, China's first unified code of civil law added a clause providing that anyone who defames communist heroes and revolutionary martyrs will face civil liability.[110] In recent years, many high-profile detainees have appeared on national TV, making forced confessions even before arrest or conviction.[111] All these laws and developments may have potential chilling effect on journalism.

Given the current status of media freedom in China, the continuing current state of languidness among journalists in China in terms of using *OGI Regulations* for quality news reporting and writing, would not be surprising. Above all, journalists would not seek information via filing OGI requests knowing in advance, through the slightest indication, that the information pursued would not appear in print.

[109] *Cyber Security Law of People's Republic of China* [中华人民共和国网络安全法], Beijing, China [adopted on November 7, 2016]; *China Adopts Law on Cyber Security*, PEOPLE'S DAILY, November 7, 2016, http://en.people.cn/n3/2016/1107/c90000-9138132.html (accessed between February 21, 2025 and March 31, 2025).

[110] Xiaosong Zhang and Zhengguang Luo, *Code of Civil Law Draft Rules See 126 Revisions and Anyone Who Defames Communist Heroes And Revolutionary Martyrs Will Face Civil Liability* [民法总则草案作126处修改 抹黑英雄烈士将被追责], GLOBAL TIMES, March 13, 2017, http://lianghui.huanqiu.com/2017/roll/2017-03/10298234.html (accessed between February 21, 2025 and March 31, 2025); *China Lawmakers Add Defaming Party Heroes to Civil Code Offences*, REUTERS, March 12, 2017, https://www.reuters.com/article/world/china-lawmakers-add-defaming-party-heroes-to-civil-code-offences-idUSKBN16K0AF/ (accessed between February 21, 2025 and March 31, 2025).

[111] Tania Branigan, *Televised Confessions on State-Run TV Consolidate China's Social Control*, THE GUARDIAN, August 11, 2014, https://www.theguardian.com/world/2014/aug/11/televised-confessions-state-tv-china-social-control (accessed between February 21, 2025 and March 31, 2025); Steven Jiang, *Trial By Media? Confessions Go Prime Time in China*, CNN, January 26, 2016, http://www.cnn.com/2016/01/26/asia/china-television-confessions/ (accessed between February 21, 2025 and March 31, 2025); Jonathan Kaiman, *China Airs "Confession" by Swedish Rights Worker; Critics Charge Coercion*, THE LOS ANGELES TIMES, January 20, 2016, http://www.latimes.com/world/asia/la-chinese-held-swedish-rights-activist-20160120-story.html (accessed between February 21, 2025 and March 31, 2025); Russell Lynch, *A Chinese Journalist Has Appeared on State Television "Confessing" to Causing the Stock Market Chaos: Journalist and Brokers Admit Trading Abuses After Two-Month Share Slump*, THE INDEPENDENT, August 31, 2015, http://www.independent.co.uk/news/business/news/a-chinese-journalist-has-appeared-on-state-television-confessing-to-causing-the-stock-market-chaos-10480041.html (accessed between February 21, 2025 and March 31, 2025).

Summary and Conclusion

Relying upon various databases, search engines, annual OGI work reports, media reports and interviews with reporters and lawyers in China, this chapter examined the role of journalists in China's first freedom of information law. Unlike American journalists who have played a pivotal role in proposing, formulating, and using freedom of information legislation for news reporting, Chinese journalists have not involved in the recommendation and formulation of *OGI Regulations*. Chinese law reformers delinked freedom of information from freedom of expression and the press and convinced top leaders that promoting freedom of information would contribute greatly to economic growth and development of informationization. This strategy, although rendering freedom of information research politically acceptable in the late 1990s, marginalized the role of journalists in the drafting of the law.

This chapter also found that Chinese editors and reporters played a much more prominent role in covering and publicizing *OGI Regulations* in the early years of the law's enforcement. Constant media coverage of *OGI Regulations* has promoted the public's understanding of the law and the level of public consciousness of the concept of the right to know. Vibrant media exposure of non-compliance of *OGI Regulations* creates significant pressure on administrative organs that ignore legal obligations to exercise power transparently. Freedom of information is no longer a politically sensitive topic, which leads journalists in China to cover official transparency issues and vigorously expose irregularities.

This chapter found that Chinese journalists are among the least active users of the FOI law for news reporting. They file OGI requests to obtain government-held files and documents. They do bring government agencies to court for legal remedies when their information requests are fully or partially rejected. However, on average, they do so rarely, which is in sharp contrast to their Western colleagues. When explaining the limited use of *OGI Regulations* by reporters in China, Yongzheng Wei, China's most prominent media law expert, said that *OGI Regulations* play a very insignificant role in Chinese journalists' newsgathering activities. "It is unnecessary for China's party-run media outlets or journalists to apply for government information via OGI platforms or through judicial means."[112] The true reason reporters shy away from the open records

[112] WeChat interviews with Yongzheng Wei (June 2020 and December 2024).

law may lie elsewhere. After all, *OGI Regulations* are widely considered in China as a piece of administrative law, not as a legislation to protect people's right to know. When viewed as a law used by reporters to protect people's right to know, *OGI Regulations* would suddenly become sensitive. Journalistic use of the FOI law is not career enhancing at all in China. A reporter from *Jiefang Daily* was reassigned to a role completely unrelated to journalism simply because of his use of the Chinese FOI law to apply for government information and bring government agencies to court. Therefore, when writing a Chinese-language textbook on media law for college students in journalism, Wei avoided discussing *OGI Regulations* too much in the book.[113] Another Chinese legal scholar, Zejin Yao, shared a similar sentiment, "As professionals dealing with information gathering and dissemination, very few journalists are successful when obtaining information via OGI requests, substantially compromising the effectiveness of the law's enforcement."[114]

One additional reason for Chinese journalists' limited use of the FOI law is the law itself demanding reporters to meet a special needs test before the test was eliminated in 2019. A more fundamental rationale is the lack of stronger legal protections for press freedom. Freedom House scores show that China is one of the least free countries in terms of press freedom, attributable to many factors. One of the most important is the lack of *Freedom of the Press Law*. Although Chinese reformers expended great effort to formulate a law to protect the rights of journalists to gather

[113] When teaching mass communication law and ethics at Western Illinois University, the author of this book dedicates one week to covering open records laws and open meetings laws. The textbook, *Mass Media Law*, is regularly updated by its authors and includes an entire chapter focused on the constitutional, statutory, and common law rights of access to government records, meetings, and facilities. In contrast, college journalism education in Mainland China regarding FOI (Freedom of Information) and access to information appears less thorough and more inconsistent. As the author of one of the most widely used Chinese media law textbooks, Yongzheng Wei did not address FOI in earlier editions of the book, which makes sense, given that the Chinese FOI law had not yet been established. The most recent edition, published in 2022, briefly mentions *OGI Regulations* and its amendment in Chapter 1 (Constitutional Principles), but the book omits detailed coverage of the law. DON R. PEMBER AND CLAY CALVERT, MASS MEDIA LAW (2013); YONGZHENG WEI AND LINA ZHOU, THE LAW OF JOURNALISM AND MASS COMMUNICATION IN CHINA [新闻传播法教程] (2022) (7TH EDITION).

[114] WeChat interview with Zejin Yao (December 2024). Yao is director of the Communication Law Research Center at China University of Political Science and Law. He is executive associate dean of the university's Guangming School of Journalism and Communication.

and publish news, the law died in its infancy amid political upheavals in the late 1980s. Without stronger legal protection, meaningful journalism encounters heavy suppression from censors in propaganda departments at various levels. This chapter concludes that lack of stronger legal protections for press freedom contributes substantially to the limited use of *OGI Regulations* among Chinese journalists.

It is encouraging to see the elimination of the special needs test in the 2019 OGI Regulations amendment, and more work needs to be done. FOI lawmakers must make sure that journalists receive preferential treatment in OGI requests such as fee waivers and expedited services. Journalism schools in China should offer media law courses and include FOI as a part of course offerings.[115] News organizations should encourage journalists to attend OGI workshops. The top legislature must speed up drafting laws and regulations that expand protection on freedom of expression and the press enshrined in the Chinese constitution.

Freedom of information law is a vital tool by which the Chinese public will learn what the government is up to. Most Chinese citizens, however, will not file an OGI request throughout their lives. They expect the news media to pry open government files and dig up some dirt. In light of these considerations, Chinese journalists and news organizations should use *OGI Regulations* more vigorously and sue government agencies more fearlessly if officials choose to seal documents without a good reason.

115 When teaching mass communication law and ethics at Western Illinois University, the author of this book dedicates one week to covering open records laws and open meetings laws. The textbook, *Mass Media Law*, is regularly updated by its authors and includes an entire chapter focused on the constitutional, statutory, and common law rights of access to government records, meetings, and facilities. In contrast, college journalism education in Mainland China regarding FOI (Freedom of Information) and access to information appears less thorough and more inconsistent. As the author of one of the most widely used Chinese media law textbooks, media law scholar Yongzheng Wei did not address FOI in earlier editions of the book, which makes sense, given that the Chinese FOI law had not yet been established. The most recent edition, published in 2022, briefly mentions *OGI Regulations* and its amendment in Chapter 1 (Constitutional Principles), but the book omits detailed coverage of the law. DON R. PEMBER AND CLAY CALVERT, MASS MEDIA LAW (2013); YONGZHENG WEI AND LINA ZHOU, THE LAW OF JOURNALISM AND MASS COMMUNICATION IN CHINA [新闻传播法教程] (2022) (7TH EDITION).

CHAPTER 11

An "Enforcement Black Hole": The Chinese Communist Party and Its Own Freedom of Information Law

Introduction

According to Resolution 59 of the United Nations General Assembly and Article 19 of the Universal Declaration of Human Rights, freedom of information is a fundamental human right.[1] Likewise, many legal scholars

[1] *Joint Statement on Freedom of Expression as a Driver of All Other Human Rights on the Occasion of the World Press Freedom Day 2023*, United Nations Educational, Scientific and Cultural Organization, Paris, France, July 4, 2023, ***available at*** https://www.unesco.org/en/days/press-freedom-2023/joint-statement#:~:text=At%20its%20very%20first%20session,the%20United%20Nations%20is%20consecrated.%E2%80%9D (accessed between February 21, 2025 and March 31, 2025); *Universal Declaration of Human Rights*, United Nations, New York, ***available at*** https://www.un.org/en/about-us/universal-declaration-of-human-rights#:~:text=Article%2019,media%20and%20regardless%20of%20frontiers (accessed between February 21, 2025 and March 31, 2025).

This chapter is derived from the book author's conference paper presented at the National Communication Association annual conference in 2014. Portions of the text resemble or may replicate the original text from the paper and have been reproduced as such with the permission of Palgrave Macmillan editors. Yong Tang, *An Enforcement "Black Hole"—The Chinese Communist Party and Its Own Freedom of Information Law*, paper accepted for presentation by the NCA (National Communication Association) annual convention, New Orleans, Louisiana, November 21–24, 2024.

Y. Tang, *Freedom of Information Law in China*,
https://doi.org/10.1007/978-981-96-7842-6_11

and non-government organizations have long recognized access to information as a cornerstone human right that all other rights of human beings depend upon.[2] Therefore, when the Open Government Information (OGI) Regulations, China's first national freedom of information (FOI) law, was adopted in 2007 and came into force in 2008, China's revolutionary entry into the world FOI club was regarded by some media law scholars as a remarkable step toward better human rights protection.[3] However, this law has one big drawback: It applies to the executive branch of the Chinese government only and does not apply to the Chinese Communist Party (CCP), the ruling party of China that holds the vast majority of the country's most important government information.

The limited scope of the Chinese FOI law does not mean the party has no legal transparency obligations to comply with. Among the constantly amended Party Constitution[4] and many intraparty regulations that have been passed by the party in recent years are the tentative Regulations of the CCP on Open Party Affairs (*OPA Regulations*).[5] Adopted in December 2017, *OPA Regulations* provide that the CCP Central

[2] For detailed analysis of freedom of information from the human rights perspective, see Cheryl Ann Bishop, "Internationalizing the Right to Know: Conceptualizations of Access to Information in Human Rights Law" (2009) (unpublished Ph.D. diss., The University of North Carolina at Chapel Hill); K.M. SHRIVASTAVA, THE RIGHT TO INFORMATION: A GLOBAL PERSPECTIVE (2009); Cheryl Ann Bishop, *The United Nations and Access to Information as a Human Right*, paper accepted for presentation by the ICA (International Communication Association) annual convention, Montreal, Quebec, Canada, May 22, 2008.

[3] See Yong Tang, "Chinese Freedom of Information: An Evaluation of the Legislative History, Rationales, Significance and Efficacy of Regulations of the People's Republic of China on Open Government Information" (2012) (unpublished Ph.D. diss., The Pennsylvania State University at University Park), 10–13.

[4] The Party Constitution, also known as the Party Charter, is widely considered as the most important intra-party regulation for the CCP. It has been amended or even rewritten nearly 20 times since its enactment in 1922. *Full Text of Constitution of Communist Party of China*, the State Council of the People's Republic of China, Beijing, China, *available at* http://english.www.gov.cn/news/topnews/202210/26/content_WS635921cdc6d0a757729e1cd4.html (accessed between February 21, 2025 and March 31, 2025).

[5] For the Chinese-language Regulations of the CCP on Open Party Affairs (*OPA Regulations*), see https://www.gov.cn/zhengce/2017-12/25/content_5250271.htm (accessed between February 21, 2025 and March 31, 2025). For the English-language translation of the law, see https://law.yale.edu/sites/default/files/china-law-documents/horsley_eng._open_party_affairs_regulations.pdf (accessed between February 21, 2025 and March 31, 2025).

Committee and various lower levels of party organizations shall proactively disclose certain types of information to party members and, in some circumstances, to the general public.

The enactment of the Communist Party's FOI law has drawn Chinese media and Western scholars' attention.[6] This chapter attempts to examine the statutory language of *OPA Regulations* (the party equivalent of *OGI Regulations*) and identify its dominant features and weaknesses. Using various databases and search engines, the chapter also aims to shed light on how information disclosable under the party's freedom of information law has been releaseded both proactively and reactively in the last seven years (2017–2024).

David Banisar, an internationally acclaimed freedom of information law expert, finds nine common features of global freedom of information laws: Types of governmental bodies covered, accessibility, identity of those allowed access, exemptions, appeals and oversight, sanctions, affirmative publication, e-FOI, and accusations of malfeasance.[7] This chapter will use some of those common features to examine *OPA Regulations*. Additional common features of world freedom of information laws such as legal authority and legislative purpose will also be explored.

Legal Authority and Standing

According to *Legislation Law 2000,* under the Chinese political and legal system, there are four tiers of laws: The Constitution enjoys the highest level of legal authority. An act or law, adopted and amended

[6] For example, the leading English-language publication in China, *China Daily*, published an article from Xinhua News Agency to recognize the enactment. *CPC Unveils Regulation to Promote Transparency in Party Affairs*, CHINA DAILY, December 25, 2017, http://global.chinadaily.com.cn/a/201712/25/WS5a410271a31008cf16da35a0.html (accessed between February 21, 2025 and March 31, 2025). Jamie Horsley, a Yale University scholar on China's government transparency issues, published a commentary on the website of the Brookings Institution to explain the party's FOI law. Jamie Horsley, *The Chinese Communist Party's Experiment with Transparency*, Brookings Institution, Washington, DC, February 8, 2018, ***available at*** https://www.brookings.edu/articles/the-chinese-communist-partys-experiment-with-transparency/ (accessed between February 21, 2025, and March 31, 2025).

[7] David Banisar, Freedom of Information around the World 2006: A Global Survey of Access to Government Information Laws 20–26 (report for Privacy International, London, United Kingdom, July 2006), ***available at*** http://www.freedominfo.org/documents/global_survey2006.pdf (accessed between February 21, 2025, and March 31, 2025).

by the National People's Congress or the standing committee of the National People's Congress, represents the second level of legal authority. Regulations, divided into administrative regulations, local regulations, autonomous regulations, and separate regulations, represent the third level of legal authority. This third tier of laws is from the State Council or local people's congresses and cannot override a law. Administrative rules represent the fourth level of legal authority, and are actions of state organs, provincial governments, or governments in comparatively larger cities.[8]

It is clear that *OGI Regulations* are administrative regulations enacted by the State Council, representing the third tier of Chinese law. However, *Legislation Law* says nothing about the legal authority and standing of the intraparty regulations. In fact, the law mentions the word "the party" in just one single sentence in one single place: "Legislation shall adhere to the leadership of the Communist Party of China."[9]

Although the legal standing of *OPA Regulations* is unclear, it does not mean the law is not legally binding or has no legal authority. In fact, *OPA Regulations* and many other intraparty regulations that have been formulated in the last decade are widely considered as "soft laws" or "laws within the party." They are as powerful as laws and sometimes even more powerful than the latter. As a legal scholar from the Chinese University of Hong Kong noted, "Intraparty regulations are a set of CCP's internal rules, which for the most part govern Party members' conduct and the institutional relations between various Party organs…[I]ntraparty regulations operate as the brains and the nerve system of the 90-million-member CCP, enabling the Party leadership to control the body and limbs of this vast organization."[10] Intraparty regulations are also used by plaintiffs and defendants to advance their legal arguments. Furthermore, court judges often use intraparty regulations to support their reasoning when

[8] *Legislation Law 2000*. Art. 78, 79, 80, 81, 82, *available at* https://www.gov.cn/xinwen/2023-03/14/content_5746569.htm (accessed between February 21, 2025, and March 31, 2025).

[9] *Legislation Law 2000*. Art. 3, *available at* https://www.gov.cn/xinwen/2023-03/14/content_5746569.htm (accessed between February 21, 2025 and March 31, 2025).

[10] Samuli Seppanen, Interrogating *Illiberalism Through Chinese Communist Party Regulations*, 52 Cornell International Law Journal 2 (2019) 267, 271.

they make judicial decisions.[11] The party has intensified intraparty regulations' role in the party-state system since Xi Jinping became the new leader of China. As the party leads on everything, "the boundary between intraparty regulations and state laws is becoming increasingly blurred."[12]

Legislative Purpose and Principle

In stating the legislative purpose and principle, *OPA Regulations* provide the following:

> These Regulations are formulated based on the Constitution of the Communist Party of China in order to carry out and implement the spirit of the 19th National Party Congress, promote the deep development of comprehensive and strict control over Party governance, strengthen and standardize open party affairs work, develop intraparty democracy, strengthen intraparty supervision, make the many party members better understand and participate in intra- party affairs, mobilize and organize the people to carry out and implement well the Party's theories, lines, principles and policies, and improve the Party's governing ability and leadership level.[13]

Like *OGI Regulations* that are reluctant to explicitly embrace the concept of the people's right to know, *OPA Regulations* fail to adopt the widely used FOI principle of presumptive and maximum disclosure.[14] It appears the party considers *OPA Regulations* more as an instrument

[11] Fan Yang, *The Role of CPC Regulations in Chinese Judicial Decisions*, 19 China Review 2 (May 2019), 69–98.

[12] Jiang Feng, *Party Regulations and State Laws in China: A Disappearing Boundary and Growing Tensions*, 51 Chinese Law & Government (5–6) 260 (2019).

[13] *OPA Regulations 2017*. Art. 1. *The Regulations of the Communist Party of China on Open Party Affairs (For Trial Implementation)* (translation by Jamie P. Horsley), Yale University Law School China Law Center, New Haven, Connecticut, *available at* https://law.yale.edu/sites/default/files/china-law-documents/horsley_eng._open_party_affairs_regulations.pdf (accessed between February 21, 2025 and March 31, 2025).

[14] Article 19 designates maximum disclosure as the primary principle of freedom of information legislation. Article 19, *The Public's Right to Know: Principles on Right to Information Legislation*, at 4 (London, United Kingdom, 2016), *available at* http://www.article19.org/data/files/pdfs/standards/righttoknow.pdf (accessed between February 21, 2025 and March 31, 2025). Article 19, founded in 1987, is a London-based human rights organization with a specific mandate and focus on the defense and promotion of

to broadcast positive data, optimize propaganda, and garner support for the party than as a tool to hold various levels of powerful party officials accountable. Such conservative legislative intent does not bode well for the implementation of the law. Party officials will be encouraged to hide negative information that should otherwise be disclosed.

Types of Bodies Covered

Under *OPA Regulations*, the following types of party organizations are subject to mandatory information disclosure: Central party organizations, local party organizations, primary-level party organizations, party discipline inspections organs, party work organs, and other party organizations.[15] When meeting the press not long after the enactment of *OPA Regulations*, an official from the General Office of the CCP said the above organizations can be grouped into three different categories: 1. Central party organizations, local party organizations, primary-level party organizations; 2. party discipline inspections organs; 3. party work organs, party committee dispatched organs, institutions directly affiliated with party committees, and party groups. These three categories basically cover all levels of party organizations. “No party organizations are left untouched.”[16]

What the official said about the types of bodies covered by the Chinese Communist Party’s *FOIA* is exceedingly significant and inspiring for people who want to see a more transparent China, given the large number of party organizations in China and the vast amount of power they hold. China has six practical (de facto) levels of central and local party-state bureaucracy. Power and decisions flow from the top level to the

freedom of expression and freedom of information, worldwide. The organization’s name originates from Article 19 of the Universal Declaration of Human Rights.

[15] *OPA Regulations 2017*. Art. 3.

[16] *Open Party Affairs to Ensure Proper Exercise of Power, Official from General Office of CCP Answers Reporters’ Questions about OPA Regulations* [推进党务公开 让权力在阳光下运行 ——中央办公厅有关负责人就《中国共产党党务公开条例(试行)》答记者问], Xinhua News Agency, December 25, 2017, http://www.xinhuanet.com/politics/2017-12/25/c_1122164925.htm (accessed between February 21, 2025 and March 31, 2025).

bottom. Those six levels of bureaucracy are: Central, province, prefecture, county, township, and village.[17] Broadly speaking, each level of the Chinese bureaucracy has six branches: the people's congress, the party, the people's government, the political consultative conference,[18] the people's court, and the people's procuratorate.[19] According to *Constitution 1982*, the people's congress at various levels represents the legislative branch of state power and is the highest state organ at various levels of government. In practice, however, the party is always more powerful than any of the other five at each level.

Almost in parallel with the people's government, the party is a huge bureaucratic hierarchy with party committees ranging from the central level to the village level. Party secretaries, appointed by higher-level party committees, head the lower-level committees. Party secretaries at various levels are normally more powerful and influential than their counterparts in the corresponding people's government. After all, most leaders from the other five branches are appointed by the party. For example, Sichuan provincial party secretaries are more powerful than governors of Sichuan Provincial People's Government. Likewise, mayors of Bazhong Municipal People's Government are not influential as secretaries of the Bazhong Municipal Party Committee.

As the only ruling party of the country, the Chinese Communist Party is the leading decision-maker on virtually all the major issues facing the country, and the party formulates the most important policies concerning various aspects of Chinese society. Understandably, the party generates, stores, and obtains a wealth of documents and records of vital importance to the Chinese public. Although the party is not a governing

[17] Practically speaking, village is the lowest level of bureaucratic system. But officially, township is the lowest level of Chinese bureaucracy. Villages are within townships, townships are within counties, counties are within cities, cities are within prefectures, and provinces include all five.

[18] The political consultative conference is a political advisory organ whose members can propose laws and policies to party authorities, yet with no legislative power of its own. It often consists of party and government officials in semi-retirement.

[19] The procuratorate is a public prosecutor in charge of conducting investigations of criminal cases and prosecuting criminal defendants. The agency also has power to issue legally binding judicial interpretations and review rulings made by local procuratorates and the lower people's courts. It is somewhat similar to attorney generals or prosecutors in the United States.

body recognized by the *Constitution 1982*,[20] control of "all state apparatuses and of the legislative process"[21] secures the party's position as the "supreme political authority and power" in China.[22] Given the influence and prestige of the ruling party in China, it is thrilling to see ALL party organizations, even including the Central Committee and the Politburo Standing Committee, are subject to *OPA Regulations*.

What Information Is Accessible

According to *OPA Regulations*, party organizations should, in general, disclose information regarding "party organizations' implementation of the Party's basic theories, basic line and basic strategies, their leadership over economic and social development, their implementation of the responsibility to comprehensively and strictly govern the Party and strengthen party building, and their functions and institutional structure."[23]

According to the CCP's FOI law, party organizations at the central, local, and primary levels have different priorities for disclosure. Central party organizations shall disclose information about party theories, lines, principles, and policies, major decisions made by the CCP and the state, speeches, and instructions by General Secretary Xi Jinping, important meetings and activities of the Central Committee, appointment and removal of officials by the Central Committee.[24]

According to the Regulations, local party organizations should disclose information regarding how they study and implement decisions made

[20] Interestingly, *Constitution 1982* rarely mentions the Chinese Communist Party. The Preamble to the *Constitution* states that "under the leadership of the Communist Party of China and the guidance of Marxism-Leninism and Mao Zedong Thought, the Chinese people of all nationalities will continue to adhere to the people's democratic dictatorship and follow the socialist road..." However, the *Constitution* does not state the method for implementing this leadership role in the country's political structure, nor does it specifically define the relationship of the party to the legislative, executive, and judicial branches of the government.

[21] Ralph H. Folsom, John H. Minan and Lee Ann Otto, Law and Politics in the People's Republic of China in a nutshell 76–77 (1992).

[22] Ralph H. Folsom, John H. Minan and Lee Ann Otto, Law and Politics in the People's Republic of China in a nutshell 76–77 (1992).

[23] *OPA Regulations 2017*. Art. 7.

[24] *OPA Regulations 2017*. Art. 9.

by the Central Committee, how they formulate major policies and make major decisions, how they respond to major emergencies, how they build and govern themselves, and how they appoint and dismiss important officials.[25]

According to the law, information that primary-level party organizations should disclose appears more detailed and comprehensive. Such information includes how they study and implement decisions made by the Central Committee and higher-level party organizations, how they plan and execute key tasks, how they recruit, educate, train, and evaluate party members, how they collect, use, and manage party membership dues, and how they conduct elections, develop party cells, hold party meetings, protect party members' rights, and discipline party members who violate party regulations.[26]

Notably, *OPA Regulations* specifically talks about the information disclosure obligations of the party's discipline inspection organs. The Central Commission for Discipline Inspection, along with provincial and lower-level anti-corruption organizations within the party, must publicize information about how they study and implement important policies and major decisions made by the Central Committee, how they uphold the Party Constitution, how they investigate and penalize party members and leading cadres for serious dereliction of duty and misconduct, and how they investigate and dismiss party members and leading cadres for serious violations of discipline or even crimes.[27]

A close reading of the full text of *OPA Regulations* demonstrates that the list of party information available for disclosure under the law is very detailed and wide-ranging. It covers virtually all aspects of information involving party organizations. If implemented forcefully, the Regulations can be a powerful tool for the party to deepen transparency and clean itself. With this being said, it is necessary to point out some weaknesses. First, the statutory language of the law is rather vague and full of party jargon. The vagueness can be used by party officials in charge of open party affairs to deliberately deny disclosure. Second, it appears the party mainly wants to use its own version of the FOI law to publicize and glorify its policies and accomplishments. It's why most information required for

[25] *OPA Regulations 2017*. Art. 10.

[26] *OPA Regulations 2017*. Art. 11.

[27] *OPA Regulations 2017*. Art. 12.

disclosure is information that the party wants its members and even the general public to see or hear. For information disclosure of which has potential for problems, the party is still cautious. For example, for many years, people have called for personal assets of various levels of party leaders to be shared with party members or even the public. Unfortunately, the law clearly ignores such pleas as it fails to say anything about disclosure of personal assets. Third, it is very unusual for Chinese law makers to include an individual's name in a piece of law or party regulations when the name is not affiliated with a guiding theory/thought in the party. It was true even during the reign of Mao Zedong (1949–1976). *OPA Regulations*, however, break with precedent as the law mentions "Xi Jinping" six times in the body of the text.[28] This extraordinary move signifies Xi Jinping's efforts to consolidate his status as the core leader of the CCP in every field including the world of law making. The move makes *OPA Regulations* sound less formal, official, and authoritative, paving the way for a future when the law may succumb to the political whim of a top leader.

Affirmative Publication of CCP Information

Unlike *OGI Regulations*, *OPA Regulations* do not mandate a duty for party organizations to reactively release information or disclose information upon request. Therefore, it is impossible for people or organizations to apply for disclosure of party-related information. Likewise, neither party members nor the general public have the right to sue party organizations for non-compliance.

However, *OPA Regulations* do mandate a political and even legal duty for party organizations to release, timely and proactively, certain categories of information, which is similar to *OGI Regulations* and FOI laws in other countries.

In order to ensure compliance with proactive disclosure requirements, *OPA Regulations* provide various methods and procedures for disclosure. First, party organizations at various levels should compile catalogues listing information to be disclosed. Disclosure of information on the catalogues should be proposed, verified, approved, and implemented

[28] *OPA Regulations* mention "Comrade Xi Jinping" four times, "Secretary General Xi Jinping" one time, and "Xi Jinping Thought on Socialism with Chinese Characteristics for a New Era" one time.

according to open party affairs plans. Second, the law compels party organizations to disseminate information via various communication channels such as meetings, reports, websites, press conferences, party committee spokespersons, news outlets (party-run media in particular), and possibly any OGI disclosure platforms affiliated with people's governments.[29]

OPA Regulations provide that party organizations should disclose information in a timely manner, but do not specify a clear-cut time limit for disclosure, which differs sharply from *OGI Regulations* that establish a time limit of 20 working days for affirmatively disseminating official information.[30]

Disclosure of Party-Related Information to Whom

According to *OPA Regulations*, party-related information should be disclosed to either party members or the general public, depending upon how such information is connected or relevant to a particular audience. The scope of openness increases as the number of people and party organizations involved gets bigger and bigger.

There are four levels of openness: Level 1 (lowest degree of openness): Disclosure is limited to particular party organizations, party members, and nonmembers. Level 2 (intermediate degree of openness): Disclosure is expanded to target respective regions, departments, and units. Level 3 (high degree of openness): Disclosure is further expanded to include all the 100 million members of the Communist Party. Level 4 (highest degree of openness): Disclosure is maximized to reach the general public (including all the Chinese population of 1.4 billion).[31]

The regulations do explain that the importance of issues involved determine the degree of openness. For example, it says, "Party affairs concerning leadership of economic and social development and involving

[29] *OPA Regulations 2017*. Art. 14, 15, 16, 17.

[30] *OPA Regulations 2017*. Art.15. *OGI Regulations 2007*. Art.18.

[31] *OPA Regulations 2017*. Art. 8.

the production and livelihood of the people shall be publicly disclosed...- Party affairs involving major issues concerning party building or the obligations and rights of party members and that require the general understanding of and compliance and implementation by all party members shall be disclosed to the entire Party."[32]

Unlike *OGI Regulations* specifying that governmental information that is not exempt from disclosure should be released to the general public, *OPA Regulations* adopt a much more complex, nuanced, and thus confusing approach in terms of scope of openness. Plus, the statutory language of the law is so vague that determining what information deserves which level of disclosure becomes nearly impossible even for a seasoned party official. When creating implementation rules, party organizations at various levels need to iron out those challenges. Otherwise, the party's FOI law would be rarely used.

What Information Is Exempt from Disclosure

All transparency laws have exemptions and *OPA Regulations* are not an exception. Like *OGI Regulations* that exempt from disclosure information involving state security, public security, economic security, social stability, commercial secrets, and personal privacy,[33] *OPA Regulations* explicitly provide the following:

> Open party affairs may not endanger political security, especially regime security and institutional security, as well as economic security, military security, cultural security, societal security, homeland security and national security.[34]

Problems with the party's FOI exemptions are obvious. What is political security? What is regime security? What is institutional security? What is economic security? What is military security? What is cultural security? What is societal security? What is homeland security? What is national security? Their meanings are so elusive, and they are so hard to define. No wonder the whole room burst into laughter when the author of this book talked about those exemptions during his podium presentation

[32] *OPA Regulations 2017*. Art. 8.

[33] *OGI Regulations 2007*. Art. 8, 23.

[34] *OPA Regulations 2017*. Art. 7.

to the annual National Communication Association conference in New Orleans in November 2024 and a PowerPoint slide showed all the exemptions ending with the word "security." None of the terms listed here are defined in *OPA Regulations*. They are not clearly defined in other laws and regulations either. Such relevant laws and regulations include *Law on Guarding State Secrets 1988*, *Civil Servants Law 2005*, *Open Government Information Regulations 2007*, *Counter-Espionage Law 2014*, *National Security Law 2015*, *Cybersecurity Law 2016*, and *National Intelligence Law 2017*. After a close reading of those laws and regulations, the author of this book is unable to find even minimally sufficient definitions of those terms. Those terms are probably made internationally hard to define. Lack of definitions of those confusing terms create huge potential for party officials to willfully deny disclosure.

In fact, since Xi Jinping came to power in 2012 and 2013, China has begun to pay more attention to national security. In 2014, he clearly identified 16 types of security in his "comprehensive national security" campaign. They include political security, territorial security, military security, economic security, cultural security, societal security, technological security, cyber security, ecological security, resource security, nuclear security, security of overseas interests, biosecurity, space security, polar security, and deep-sea security. After examining the intent and ramifications of the newly defined national security strategy of China, two China watchers in Europe said in a study report, "Xi has made national security into a core component of party ideology, a state doctrine that permeates all aspects of China's governance."[35] Another China expert in the United States said recently to CNN, "Everything in Xi's PRC is national security and there is an intensifying focus on better coordinating security and development, with the security side winning out over the economics side it appears."[36] The "security first" paradigm in state governance and Xi's enchantment

[35] Katja Drinhausen and Helena Legarda, "*Comprehensive National Security*" *Unleashed: How Xi's Approach Shapes China's Policies at Home and Abroad*, the Mercator Institute for China Studies (MERICS), Berlin, Germany, September 15, 2022, *available at* https://www.merics.org/en/report/comprehensive-national-security-unleashed-how-xis-approach-shapes-chinas-policies-home-and (accessed between February 21, 2025 and March 31, 2025).

[36] Nectar Gan, *Xi Jinping Tells China's National Security Chiefs to Prepare for "Worst Case" Scenarios*, CNN, June 1, 2023, https://www.cnn.com/2023/05/31/china/china-xi-national-security-meeting-intl-hnk/index.html (accessed between February 21, 2025 and March 31, 2025).

with the securitization of everything explains why the exemption clause in *OPA Regulations* contains so many words ending with "security." This paradigm shift in state governance will have a negative impact on the process of lawmaking and law enforcement. It will leave enforcement of *OPA Regulations* to the whims of various levels of party officials. In a political climate of prioritizing security over everything else, party bureaucrats at various levels would err on the side of caution when they perform the balancing act of meeting the legal requirements of proactive dissemination while also pondering potential political and security risks of disclosure.

Sanctions on Officials in Charge of Open Party Affairs

Party organizations at various levels should annually report their OPA work to party members and nonmembers in their jurisdictions. That's the time for scrutiny. But *OPA Regulations* are very vague on what penalty would happen to party officials who fail to comply with the legal requirements of the law.

OGI Regulations include detailed provisions for imposing sanctions on public authorities and employees for violating the FOI law.[37] Administrative sanctions,[38] civil and criminal penalties may accrue to official agencies, agencies' leaders who are responsible for OGI activities and relevant employees if they violate provisions of *OGI Regulations*. Unlike *OGI Regulations*, *OPA Regulations* are not clear about supervision and accountability. Article 23 of the law is the only provision that mandates accountability on the part of party organizations, party members, and party leaders who violate the law. It provides the following:

> When a violation of the provisions of these Regulations causes adverse consequences, relevant party organizations, party members and leading

[37] *OGI Regulations 2007*. Article 34.

[38] There are six kinds of administrative disciplinary measures: warning, record of a demerit, record of a serious demerit, demotion, removal from office and discharge from public employment. *Administrative Supervision Law 1997*. Art.24; *Civil Servants Law 2006*. Art.56.

cadres and staff should be investigated for accountability in accordance with [intra-party] regulations and discipline.[39]

The law does not say anything about what would constitute "adverse consequences." It does not say anything either about how the investigation will proceed and what penalties could emerge. It can be only assumed that party members who break the party's FOI law will not face civil or criminal lawsuits. Instead, they may face the following consequences imposed by various party organizations: Warnings, serious warnings, removal from internal party positions, party probation, and expulsion from the party.[40] Party organizations that seriously violate *OPA Regulations* may be restructured or disbanded.[41] In the following section on enforcement, this chapter will explore if such sanctions have ever happened in China.

"Enforcement Black Hole"

Since *OGI Regulations* went into effect in 2007, media reports about how the law was enforced abound. Newspapers, TV and radio programs, magazines, and popular news portals in China were flooded with news stories containing the keywords "OGI Regulations." Unsurprisingly, most stories were quite positive and demonstrated the party and government's ability to enhance transparency using the law. Some stories were negative and showed how government officials were irresponsive to OGI requests, how they were sued, and even lost the lawsuits. *Southwestern Weekend, Caijing,* and *Southern Metropolis Daily* were among the Chinese news organizations that were at the forefront of media coverage of misconduct and irregularities by government officials. If nothing changes, this time Chinese media will publish or broadcast some stories about *OPA Regulations*. This chapter will use leading search engines and media databases to examine if any relevant media reports about the CCP's FOI law have ever been published or broadcast. From there, the study will see how the law on paper and the law in practice differ.

[39] *OPA Regulations 2017*. Art. 23.

[40] *Party Disciplinary Regulations 2003*. Amended in 2015, 2018 and 2023. Art. 7.

[41] *Party Disciplinary Regulations 2003*. Amended in 2015, 2018 and 2023. Art. 8.

Google is the most popular search engine in the world. As of March 31, 2025, a Google search using the Chinese keyword "中国共产党党务公开条例" and its English translation "Chinese Communist Party Regulations on Open Party Affairs" has yielded something unusual. The Chinese-language articles found in all the 15 pages of the Google search results and the English-language articles found in all the 22 pages of the Google search results were about what provisions *OPA Regulations* have, how officials, scholars, and media commentators interpret the law, which local party organizations were studying the law, and which party organizations have published OPA implementation rules.[42] Not a single news article even tangentially touched upon the subject of how *OPA Regulations* have been enforced since its enactment in 2017.

Baidu is the most popular search engine in China. As of March 31, 2025, a Baidu search using the Chinese-language keyword "中国共产党党务公开条例" and its English translation "Chinese Communist Party Regulations on Open Party Affairs" has yielded similar results. An analysis of the 31 pages of the Chinese-language search results and the 21 pages of the English-language search results finds zero news stories that reported on the topic of how enforcement of *OPA Regulations* has been accomplished.

China Core Newspapers Full-text Database is a database that contains newspaper articles of approximately 1,000 publicly issued newspapers

[42] For example, the Chongqing Municipal Party Committee, the Party Committee of Jiangsu Province, the Party Committee of Heilongjiang Province, and the Party Committee of Peking University all created their own rules regarding how to implement *OPA Regulations* in their areas. *The Chongqing Municipal Party Committee Publishes Its OPA Implementation Rules* [中共重庆市委印发《重庆市实施〈中国共产党党务公开条例(试行)〉办法》], Hualongwang [华龙网], May 7, 2018, *available at* http://cq.cqnews.net/html/2018-05/07/content_44265299.htm (accessed between February 21, 2025 and March 31, 2025); *The Party Committee of Jiangsu Province Publishes Its OPA Implementation Rules* [中共江苏省委关于贯彻《中国共产党党务公开条例(试行)》实施细则], Xinhua Daily, republished by People's Daily Online, July 31, 2018, *available at* http://cpc.people.com.cn/n1/2018/0731/c64387-30180003.html (accessed between February 21, 2025 and March 31, 2025); *The Party Committee of Heilongjiang Province Publishes Its OPA Implementation Rules* [黑龙江省贯彻《中国共产党党务公开条例(试行)》实施细则], Heilongjiang Daily, April 16, 2018, http://epaper.hljnews.cn/hljrb/20180416/347421.html (accessed between February 21, 2025 and March 31, 2025); *Note on Publication of the OPA Implementation Rules by the Party Committee of Peking University* [关于印发《北京大学党务公开实施办法》的通知], Peking University, Beijing, China, May 18, 2021, *available at* https://xxgk.pku.edu.cn/docs/20210518152610022473.pdf (accessed between February 21, 2025 and March 31, 2025).

from mainland China.[43] A search of the database using the Chinese-language keyword "中国共产党党务公开条例(试行)" has yielded results that are similar to Google and Baidu. As of March 31, 2025, the search has found a total number of 8 newspaper articles containing the keyword and all of them were published after 2017, but none of them reported on the topic of how *OPA Regulations* have been enforced.[44] A search of the database using the Chinese-language keyword "党务公开" has yielded similar results. As of March 31, 2025, the search has found a total number of 487 newspaper articles containing the keyword, of which 34 were published after 2017, but none of those articles discussed the enforcement or implementation of *OPA Regulations*.[45]

A close reading of OPA implementation rules enacted by party committees of the provincial-level city of Chongqing, Jiangsu Province, Heilongjiang Province, and Peking University[46] shows that those rules

43 China Core Newspapers Full-text Database, *available at* https://oversea.cnki.net/kns?dbcode=CCND (accessed between February 21, 2025 and March 31, 2025). It is part of the China National Knowledge Infrastructure (CNKI) database.

44 The database allows keyword searches of newspaper articles on its homepage. Available search results include article summaries, publication years and newspaper titles. Database users must pay to log into the site, view and download the full text of each article. For search results, see https://oversea.cnki.net/kns/DefaultResult/Index?dbcode=CCND&kw=%E2%80%9C%E4%B8%AD%E5%9B%BD%E5%85%B1%E4%BA%A7%E5%85%9A%E5%85%9A%E5%8A%A1%E5%85%AC%E5%BC%80%E6%9D%A1%E4%BE%8B%E2%80%9D&korder=SU (accessed between February 21, 2025 and March 31, 2025).

45 The database allows keyword searches of newspaper articles on its homepage. Available search results include article summaries, publication years and newspaper titles. Database users must pay to log into the site, view and download the full text of each article. For search results, see https://oversea.cnki.net/kns/DefaultResult/Index?dbcode=CCND&kw=%E2%80%9C%E5%85%9A%E5%8A%A1%E5%85%AC%E5%BC%80%E2%80%9D&korder=SU (accessed between February 21, 2025 and March 31, 2025).

46 *The Chongqing Municipal Party Committee Publishes Its OPA Implementation Rules* [中共重庆市委印发《重庆市实施〈中国共产党党务公开条例(试行)〉办法》], Hualongwang [华龙网], May 7, 2018, *available at* http://cq.cqnews.net/html/2018-05/07/content_44265299.htm (accessed between February 21, 2025 and March 31, 2025); *The Party Committee of Jiangsu Province Publishes Its OPA Implementation Rules* [中共江苏省委关于贯彻《中国共产党党务公开条例(试行)》实施细则], XINHUA DAILY, republished by People's Daily Online, July 31, 2018, *available at* http://cpc.people.com.cn/n1/2018/0731/c64387-30180003.html (accessed between February 21, 2025 and March 31, 2025); *The Party Committee of Heilongjiang Province Publishes Its OPA Implementation Rules* [黑龙江省贯彻《中国共产党党务公开条例(试行)》实施细则], HEILONGJIANG DAILY, April 16, 2018, http://epaper.hljnews.cn/hljrb/20180416/347421.html (accessed between February 21, 2025 and March 31, 2025); *Note on*

are strikingly similar to *OPA Regulations*. They are too general and do not make implementation of the law any easier.

According to *OPA Regulations*, some party-related information should be publicized only within the party and some other information should be disclosed to the general public. Therefore, it is understandable to see no media reports on information that is shared only among party members. However, it is surprising and even shocking to see no media reports on information that is shared among the general public. Three possible scenarios may explain the puzzle: First, *OPA Regulations* have not been implemented at all. In the last seven years (2017–2024), party organizations at all levels could have been busy creating their implementation rules. Before they are done with this task, they don't want to release any information to anyone. Second, party organizations did release some information to party members but not to the general public. Releasing information to people outside the party would entail greater political risks. Third, party-related information was released vigorously to both party members and the general public and violators of *OPA Regulations* have been penalized. However, the media did not report on them. Given that Chinese media outlets today are becoming increasingly conservative and cautious when it comes to enterprise journalism, it is likely for them to avoid any topics that could cast the party in a negative light.

Theoretical Implications

The current OPA legislation is for trial implementation only. Therefore, the law will be revised at some point in the future. But the author of this book is not optimistic about the possibility of the law's major weaknesses being addressed in its amendment. The current political environment is not favorable to government transparency. The theoretical foundations of the Chinese freedom of information movement also hinders the law's potential from being utilized. This chapter will now discuss theoretical origins, limitations, and implications of the Chinese FOI adventure.

Publication of the OPA Implementation Rules by the Party Committee of Peking University [关于印发《北京大学党务公开实施办法》的通知], Peking University, Beijing, China, May 18, 2021, *available at* https://xxgk.pku.edu.cn/docs/20210518152610022473.pdf (accessed between February 21, 2025 and March 31, 2025).

The concept and practice of freedom of information began to emerge in Sweden when the country created the world's first freedom of information law in 1766. As one of the earliest countries to enter the world club of freedom of information legislations, United States has become a model for many other countries including some developing countries and even authoritarian regimes. When journalists, attorneys, legal scholars, and government officials created a movement in their own countries to embrace a constitutional or statutory right of access to governmental information, they cited a wide variety of theories and philosophical/moral thoughts to justify moving toward greater government transparency. Such theories and underpinnings ranged from theories of freedom of expression, right to know, democratic politics, and checking value in the First Amendment to the four theories of the press and the theory of democratization. All these theories had its origins in ancient Greece and Rome and were later advocated/expanded/reinterpreted by more modern thinkers such as three "Johns" (John Milton, John Locke, and John Stuart Mill).[47]

When the right to know and other relevant theories were imported from Western democracies to China in the early 1990s, the term "right to know" was still a political taboo. Although one of the founders of the world's first freedom of information law said that the Swedish FOI law was inspired by what the Tang Dynasty emperors did to make the imperial rule more accountable,[48] the concept of opening government documents and files for public inspection was still a foreign one to most Chinese citizens, political leaders, businesspeople, and even the intelligentsia. In order to make the term politically acceptable and compatible with China's socialist political system, Chinese law reformers "delinked the Chinese concept of the right to know with freedom of expression and freedom of

[47] For a discussion of theoretical and philosophical foundations of freedom of information legislations, see Yong Tang, "Chinese Freedom of Information: An Evaluation of the Legislative History, Rationales, Significance and Efficacy of Regulations of the People's Republic of China on Open Government Information" (2012) (unpublished Ph.D. diss., The Pennsylvania State University at University Park) (Chapter 2), 39–76.

[48] Anders Chydenius, *Berattelse om chinesiska skrif-friheten, ofversatt af danskan* [A Report on the Freedom of the Press in China] (1766), reprinted in Stephen Lamble, *Freedom of Information, A Finnish Clergyman's Gift to Democracy*, 97 FREEDOM OF INFORMATION REVIEW 2, 3 (2002).

the press. They argued for a people's right to know from the perspective of economic growth and informational development."[49]

Thanks to the term "right to know" losing its political sensitivity, the movement to embrace freedom of information gained its momentum in China, finally paving the way for the final passage of *OGI Regulations* in 2007 and *OPA Regulations* in 2017. However, there is a tradeoff. *OPA Regulations* were born with limitations in both statutory language and enforcement due to the low priority placed by the Chinese government on freedom of expression and freedom of the press. All the weaknesses of the law mentioned above have something to do with this delinking strategy.

Summary and Conclusion

The CCP has a long history of opening the complex Chinese bureaucracy to the outside world. The oldest form of government transparency took the shape of "opening village affairs" that began in 1980s. Some village governments adopted the practice of proactively releasing information to villagers. In 1998, *Organic Law of the Villagers Committees of the People's Republic of China* mandates that all the village-level governments have a legal obligation to open their files and documents for public inspection.[50] In 2007, *OGI Regulations* were adopted. The legal obligation of open government affairs was expanded from the village level to the highest level. In 2017, the 19th National Party Congress reaffirmed its commitment to party transparency and then *OPA Regulations* were adopted in the same year.

The CCP's efforts to promote transparency go beyond the people's government and the party. The court system and legislative bodies are also covered. The CCP has asked all the courts in China to open their trials, publicize their decisions, disseminate enforcement actions, and create a judicial information database where people can find large volumes of

[49] Yong Tang, "Chinese Freedom of Information: An Evaluation of the Legislative History, Rationales, Significance and Efficacy of Regulations of the People's Republic of China on Open Government Information" (2012) (unpublished Ph.D. dissertation, The Pennsylvania State University at University Park), 54.

[50] *Organic Law of the Villagers Committee 1998* (amended in 2010). Art. 30.

searchable court decisions.[51] The CCP has also asked the nation's top legislative body, the National People's Congress to publish all the draft laws, and encourage input from the general public and experts.

The Open Party Affairs Regulations are a commendable step toward greater transparency and enhanced human right protection in China. China's government, in its broadest sense of the word, is made up of the CCP, the people's government, the people's court, the people's congress, the military, the political consultative conference and the people's procuratorate. The CCP is the most important and powerful part of this huge bureaucratic machine. It is the nerve center of the Chinese bureaucracy. For the first time in the history of PRC, party members of the CCP and even the general public who are not CCP members are given the chance to know more about what the most important part of their government is doing on a daily basis through information released via *OPA Regulations*. In a time when the party is tightening information flow, it is encouraging to see China's transparency journey continue uninterrupted. As Jamie Horsley, a Yale University scholar known for studying China's transparency laws, said, "The 'Open Party Regulations' institutionalize the CCP's call for making party affairs more transparent...Its passage also signals the CCP's continued—albeit cautious—support for using transparency to modernize the Chinese governance system."[52]

However, it is worthwhile to scrutinize here more closely the weaknesses of the law and its implementation "black hole" to avoid leading readers of this chapter to get overly optimistic about China's transparency governance. In terms of statutory language and implementation, below are some big flaws that "lawmakers" within the CCP may want to consider fixing when they are asked to revise the law in the future.

First, the OPA exemptions strongly favor non-disclosure. Legal scholar, Martin Halstuk, identified six common characteristics of effective FOI

[51] China Judgements Online [中国裁判文书网], Supreme Court of China, Beijing, China, *available at* https://wenshu.court.gov.cn (accessed between February 21, 2025 and March 31, 2025). Unlike the United States where public access to judicial information is constitutionally and/or statutorily protected but a single database for all the court records does not exist, China has prided itself for maintaining this database where anyone in the world can view almost all the court judgements in China.

[52] Jamie Horsley, *The Chinese Communist Party's Experiment with Transparency*, Brookings Institution, Washington, DC, February 8, 2018, *available at* https://www.brookings.edu/articles/the-chinese-communist-partys-experiment-with-transparency/ (accessed between February 21, 2025 and March 31, 2025).

laws: (1) Disclosure should be the standard and non-disclosure the exception; (2) any person is entitled to information for any purpose; (3) exemptions must be clearly and narrowly drawn; (4) independent review should be available; (5) governmental agencies are required to publish certain information affirmatively, and (6) request fees should be reasonable.[53] In light of the criteria, it is safe to conclude that the *OPA Regulations* are weak in terms of exemptions. None of the exemptions in *OPA Regulations* are clearly or narrowly defined. Exemptions are written in such a way as to intentionally encourage non-disclosure.

Second, the reactive disclosure provision is completely absent in the law. According to international FOI standard practices, people have a legal right to compel government agencies to release information that government agencies do not want to release affirmatively. If government agencies do not approve the requests, the officials may be sued by requestors. If government agencies do not prevail in the lawsuits, they will still have to release the information requested. *OPA Regulations* are definitely not following this international precedent or standard practice. The law does not say anything about the rights of CCP members to apply for information and sue in case of non-disclosure. The law does not say anything either about the rights of non-CCP members to apply for such information and sue for judicially enforced disclosure. Therefore, if party organizations withhold some information someone may want to look at, he or she has nowhere to seek help. They cannot appeal. They cannot sue either.

Third, the poorly drafted clause on sanctions make the law appear toothless. Unlike *OGI Regulations* that include detailed provisions for imposing sanctions on leaders and employees from administrative agencies for violating the law, *OPA Regulations* have very little information about what penalties will happen to party officials who violate the law. The law does not define "serious consequences" that would justify an investigation. The law does not tell us how an investigation would go and what penalties would emerge, either political, administrative, civil, criminal, or otherwise.

Fourth, an enforcement "black hole" makes people wonder if the CCP has really started vigorously enforcing *OPA Regulations*. An examination of Chinese media reports on the OPA enforcement using search engines

[53] Martin E. Halstuk, *Freedom of information*, *in* 5 THE INTERNATIONAL ENCYCLOPEDIA OF COMMUNICATION 1890, 1890–91 (Wolfgang Donsbach ed., 2008).

and databases demonstrates that there is a "black hole" in the world of enforcement of the law. For whatever reason, relevant media reports cannot be found, and they all appear vanishing into a "black hole." Therefore, any media law scholar who has interest in China's freedom of information cannot help asking the following questions: In the last seven years (2017–2024), how many party officials in China were investigated for possible violations of the law? After the investigations, how many of them were given warnings and serious warnings by party committees? How many of them were removed from internal party positions and even expulsed from the party? How many of them were placed on probation for a period of time? How many party organizations were restructured or even disbanded due to serious violations of the party's FOI law? How many items of party-related information have been disclosed to members of the CCP? How many items of party-related information have been disclosed to nonmembers? Why do the party-run media outlets refuse to publish or broadcast any stories about how *OPA Regulations* have been enforced? What percentage of information released is positive and what percentage of information released is negative? How did the party organization at various levels comply with the law when the COVID-19 pandemic hit China and the whole world?

CHAPTER 12

Recommendations for Chinese Law Reformers and International FOI Stakeholders

Introduction

This chapter will conclude an extensive exploration and summarize all the major points covered in the previous chapters of the book, identify major research findings, provide suggestions and recommendations for Chinese law reformers and international stakeholders, and reiterate contributions to the existing literature. The chapter will also acknowledge the research's limitations and suggest possible directions for future research on the Chinese freedom of information.

This chapter is derived from the book author's doctoral dissertation that was successfully defended at The Pennsylvania State University in 2012. Portions of the text resemble or may replicate the original text from the unpublished PhD thesis and have been reproduced as such with the permission of Palgrave Macmillan editors. Yong Tang, "Chinese Freedom of Information: An Evaluation of the Legislative History, Rationales, Significance and Efficacy of Regulations of the People's Republic of China on Open Government Information" (2012) (unpublished Ph.D. diss., The Pennsylvania State University at University Park), *available at* https://etda.libraries.psu.edu/catalog/16287/ (accessed between February 21, 2025 and March 31, 2025).

Y. Tang, *Freedom of Information Law in China*,
https://doi.org/10.1007/978-981-96-7842-6_12

Recapitulation of Research

Chapter 1 introduces the topic: the legal right of access to government-held information in the People's Republic of China. The explanation includes the rationale for the topic, the significance of the subject, the scope of the research, and the methodologies employed. The chapter lists several relevant research questions that the study addresses and summarizes the key points of the subsequent chapters.

Chapter 2 examines all the major theories that form legal and theoretical frameworks for this study. The theories considered are the freedom of expression theory, the right to know theory, democratic political theory, the checking value of First Amendment theory, four theories of the press, and democratization theories. Consideration of the first four theories represents the broad base of Western concepts of freedom of information. Examination of the four theories of the press is useful to conceptualize Chinese mass media that plays a key role in either promoting or stifling the free flow of information. The democratization theories examined provide strong theoretical rationales and convincing empirical data to quantify China as an authoritarian regime that began to emulate Western democracies in the late 1970s with frequent setbacks. A thorough literature review identified significant gaps in existing literature regarding Chinese freedom of information.

Chapter 3 considers the origins and development of freedom of information laws from a global perspective. The chapter examines the genesis of the world's first FOI law, China's influence on the inception, and the spread of the concept of freedom of information to more than 100 countries. The discussion identifies four categories of FOI countries and four major patterns and trends in the worldwide expansion of FOI laws. Specifically, the rise of freedom of information in the United States represents the baseline example that other countries followed. The chapter inspects how U.S. journalists and other sectors had worked together in making the country's federal freedom of information law possible.

Chapter 4 traces the historical development of over 4000 years of governmental secrecy and transparency in China, beginning with the Xia Dynasty and ending in 1976 when the paramount leader Mao Zedong died. The chapter examines the influence of ancient Chinese schools of thought, such as Confucianism and Legalism for providing philosophical and ideological rationales for governmental secrecy and transparency. Of particular significance is the introduction to the centuries-old concept and practice of using imperial court diaries to make Chinese government transparent and hold Chinese emperors more accountable.

Chapter 5 thoroughly examines the gradual and incremental legislative movement toward the final passage of Chinese *OGI Regulations* in 2007. The transparency movement began in rural areas in the early 1980s when Deng Xiaoping was the supreme leader of the country. The movement accelerated in the 1990s and the early 2000s under the subsequent party leadership of Zhao Ziyang, Jiang Zemin, and Hu Jintao. The chapter also explores the rationales for the rise of freedom of information in China.

Chapter 6 analyses the statutory language of *OGI Regulations 2007* and its 2019 amendment, comparing the Chinese FOI law with international best practices and other relevant Chinese legal documents. The chapter evaluates the scope and efficacy of *OGI Regulations* in areas widely recognized as necessary for most FOI legislation: legal standing, legislative purpose, types of organizations and agencies covered, identification of accessible information, affirmative publication, identity requirements for inquirers, fees for access, time limits for responses, exemptions, appeals and oversight, sanctions, E-FOI, and whistle blowing.

Chapter 7 examines implementation and enforcement of *OGI Regulations* in terms of both proactive and reactive disclosure of governmental information in China. Based on the data gathered from annual reports of OGI activities published by the Chinese government (2008–2023), 540 sample OGI-related lawsuits compiled from China Judgements Online (2014 to 2021), and alternative data provided by think tanks, universities and news media outlets, the investigation reveals major strengths and weaknesses of proactive disclosure and reactive disclosure, and the reasons for those characteristics.

Chapter 8 examines the statutory language of *OGI Regulations*, the Supreme Court interpretations, and a few OGI implementation measures with regard to public enterprises and public institutions. The chapter also examines how public enterprises and institutions have released information affirmatively and reactively, using a sample of 182 lawsuits involving public institutions and public enterprises. The chapter finds a wide range of deficiencies in both statutory language and enforcement of the law. Most importantly, both oversight government departments and courts are unwilling to hold public enterprises and institutions accountable when OGI applications are willfully rejected.

Chapter 9 examines two types of official information that are, for all theoretical and practical purposes, exempt from the disclosure requirements of *OGI Regulations*: internal working documents and journalistic internal reference. Administrative organs in China used internal working documents to shield official information from disclosure and they are now more likely to do so after internal working documents were written explicitly into *OGI Regulations* as an exemption. Likewise, agencies may use journalistic internal reference as a reason to reject a request for disclosure. The chapter examines the journalistic internal reference exemption's abilities, although yet to be written into *OGI Regulations*, to restrict, significantly, the flow of information.

Chapter 10 explores the relationship between the FOI law and Chinese news media. The discussion considers if journalists in China participated in formulation of the FOI law and how Chinese editors and reporters have publicized the FOI law and exposed agencies' non-compliance. Most importantly, the research examines if, how, and why Chinese journalists have used *OGI Regulations* to access information for news reporting.

Chapter 11 discusses the tentative Regulations of the Chinese Communist Party on Open Party Affairs (*OPA Regulations*), the party's equivalent of OGI Regulations. Enacted in December 2017, *OPA Regulations* provide that the CCP Central Committee and various lower levels of party organizations shall proactively release disclosable information to party members and even non-members. The chapter examines the statutory language of *OPA Regulations* and identify its dominant features and weaknesses, including an absence of reactive disclosure requirements in the provisions. Using various databases and search engines, the chapter identifies a huge "enforcement black hole." The analysis on the "black hole" demonstrates that the party's FOI legislation has probably never been implemented in the last several years.

Major Research Findings

After extensive research on the topic of Chinese freedom of information, this book has found that, by comparison, the Western concept of the right to know intimately entwines with philosophies of freedom of expression and freedom of the press. China has a long history of practices of disclosure of governmental information, as exemplified by imperial court diaries, however, the modern concept of the right to know had long been absent in this country. The Western concept of the right to know, introduced to China in the 1990s, underwent modification by Chinese legal scholars and law reformers in an attempt to create compatibility with the unique Chinese political conditions and cultural traditions. The modification omitted the original ties of the right to know to freedom of expression and the press, and instead, highlighted relationship between the right to know and the sovereignty of the people, a principle of the Chinese Constitution. Chinese legal scholars and law reformers argue that the right to know contributes greatly to economic growth and E-governance of the country, thus advancing the general welfare of the Chinese people. Although the term "the right to know (*zhiqingquan* 知情权)" does not appear in the final text of *OGI Regulations*, scholarly and media discussions of the concept have become politically acceptable. The above finding is consistent with prior studies conducted by Weibing Xiao and other FOI scholars in China.

This study has found that the four theories of the press remain useful tools for conceptualizing the changing paradigm of the Chinese news media. Despite the Chinese media system's movement toward liberalization, commercialization, technological innovation, and professionalization since the late 1980s and early 1990s, the fundamental relationship between the press, the party, and the state remains unchanged in the post-Mao reform era. The Chinese press, in general, are still extensions of the party and the government. Such a relationship constitutes the basis for the instrumental use of the media by the Chinese bureaucracy to either facilitate or stifle flow of information.

This research project has also found that Chinese rulers from the Xia Dynasty to the PRC, under the leadership of Chinese communists, held diverging views and predilections toward openness and secrecy, regardless of the nature of government. Further, these findings explain, at least partially, the varying degrees of official transparency during China's long history. Hundred schools of thought, flourishing during the Zhou Dynasty, influenced subsequent Chinese rulers, including today' leaders, in terms of their crafting particular policies toward dissemination of information. Mohism embraces transparency, but most rulers suppressed Mohism because of its democratic nature. Legalism advocates disclosure of imperial orders, directives, laws, regulations, and other legal codes but objects to disclosure of any other information concerning the conduct of the government. As the ruling ideology of most imperial dynasties in China, Confucianism does not agree with official openness at all. Taoism basically embraces anti-communication. Taoists have limited influence on official policies of information because Taoism applies mostly to officials at leisure, in retirement, or politically ostracized.

The book has identified four peak periods of Chinese official transparency. The first peak occurred during the Zhou Dynasty through the practices of proliferating publicized, written laws, and allowing relative greater freedom of expression enjoyed by common people. The second peak occurred in the Tang and Song Dynasties when rulers and ordinary citizens used newspapers (the court gazettes or short reports) to disseminate official information. Greater public access to governmental information in the Tang and especially Song dynasties was possible also because emperors and prime ministers in these two dynasties shared power. Emperors had no absolute power. They had to consult with their prime ministers on major issues before making decisions. Transfer of official documents between emperors and prime ministers were thus frequent. Additionally, imperial court diaries and imperial censors played a significant role in holding Tang and Song emperors more accountable. Through recording daily activities of the emperor and publicizing them, imperial diaries served as a deterrent to any monarch who wants to create an image of benevolence, integrity, and competence, much like what FOI laws would do today to government officials. These checks and balances in the political system allowed greater information flow between the sovereigns and their subjects.[1] The Republic of China represents the third peak of official openness when private news outlets covered governmental activities rigorously. The fourth peak had arguably occurred during the post-Mao communist China (1979-present). The movement toward greater government transparency emerged in the 1980s when Deng Xiaoping was the paramount leader and culminated in the 2000s when Hu Jintao and Wen Jiabao carried on the torch of transparency and formulated the country's first freedom of information law. Two lows of official transparency are noticeable: The Qing Dynasty and Mao's China were among the most restrictive regimes in terms of disclosure of information. The bureaucracies in the Qing Dynasty and the pre-reform PRC

[1] The Qin Dynasty established the position of prime minister. The prime minister gradually became a check in the ruling power of emperors. The Ming Dynasty finally abolished the office of prime minister. For a more detailed discussion of power competition between emperors and their prime ministers in imperial China, see Wm. Theodore De Bary, *The "Constitutional Tradition" in China*, 9 THE JOURNAL OF CHINESE LAW 7 (1995).

were highly secretive through the state's suppression of mass media and absolute power of its supreme leaders.

This book has found that ancient China developed an extraordinary self-enclosed communication system to sustain its huge bureaucracy. The flow of information among emperors, high-ranking advisors and local bureaucrats was frequent and efficient even by modern standards. Such a developed communication system contributed to the longevity of the Chinese empire. Of course, this communication system excluded most common people. However, pre-modern mass media played a significant role in publicizing official information inside and outside of the bureaucracy in ancient China. Chinese rulers used many innovative methods to allow information to reach as many common people as possible. The inception of the court gazette in the Tang Dynasty facilitated and fostered better communication within the bureaucracy. Short reports that emerged in the Song Dynasty and independent private media that flourished in the Republic of China changed the rules. These two methods challenged official interpretation of social events and greatly enhanced the people's knowledge of the government's activities.

This research, consistent with many other research findings, has found that the entire OGI legislative process in China was elite-driven and policy-driven. The movement toward final passage of the FOI law in China began in the early 1980s in rural areas and slowly expanded to higher levels of government. Experiences from practices of open government at local and provincial levels provided a firm foundation for shaping national legislation. However, despite grassroots-level experiments, political and academic elites dominated the legislative process. While some prominent legal academics advised political leaders for the formulation of the FOI law, the majority of civil society (journalists, lawyers, professors, students, NGOs, rights activists, ordinary citizens) played no key roles in drafting the Chinese FOI law. This elite-driven process contrasts sharply with many other FOI countries where the civil society contributed significantly to the formulation of the laws.

This book has identified two major external factors and at least five internal determinants that made the passage of the FOI law in China possible. China's entry into the World Trade Organization and pressure from the United States, its largest trading partner, are the two major external factors influencing China's transition toward greater transparency. The five internal determinants, some of which were examined by other scholars, are: the political leaders' unswerving commitments to enhance transparency; administrative law reform that offered statutory and constitutional support for reformers drafting OGI legislation; the improved capacity for government to distribute information; the changed social and informational environments in the early 2000s that stimulated the Chinese government to become more transparent and proactive in dealing with crises; and reduced political sensitivity of OGI reform made possible by law reformers who convinced top leaders that an FOI law would contribute significantly to China's economic growth, E-governance, and prevention of corruption.

FOI scholar Weibing Xiao conducted an insightful examination of some of these internal factors in his research of Chinese FOI law reform and he argued that democratization, among other factors, is a key rationale for China's efforts to promote greater transparency.[2] This research contends that "democratization" is not the goal of the Chinese government in advocating greater transparency, if the term is used in the Western sense of the word to indicate the transition from an authoritarian regime to a full democracy or semi-democracy or a more democratic political regime. This research argues that the adoption of *OGI Regulations* and relevant transparency laws and regulations is not a component of Chinese democratization. In other words, the FOI law is possible not from Chinese leaders' strong beliefs in democratic values that are widely accepted in the Western world. Freedom of information legislation emerged in China because law reformers successfully persuaded the political leaders that a FOI law would not cause unbearable social turmoil. On the contrary, the law would benefit economic growth, E-governance, corruption prevention, law-based administration, and crisis communication management. These are all goals set by the party within the socialist framework characteristic of China. The ultimate goal of promoting transparency is to help maintain legitimacy and ruling status of the party.

After examining statutory language of *OGI Regulations* and other relevant legal documents, this research project has found that China has embraced many international best practices in its FOI law and even go beyond international standards in some regards but at the same time tends to be conservative in many key aspects of the law. For example, *OGI Regulations* are strongly proactive for disclosure and includes a

[2] Weibing Xiao, Freedom of Information Reform in China: Information Flow Analysis (2011).

comprehensive list of information that agencies are to disclose, affirmatively, without requiring a request. *OGI Regulations* also establish time limits, not found in the United States and many other countries' FOI legislations, for affirmatively disseminating official information. The scope of non-government entities covered by *OGI Regulations* is more expansive than many FOI laws of other nations. All public colleges and universities, public hospitals and clinical institutions, public utilities companies, environmental protection-related public institutions, and public transportation companies are subject to the requirements of *OGI Regulations.* Most importantly, the Chinese Communist Party is now subject to its own FOI law, thus creating tremendous potential for making the world's largest, most influential but extremely secretive political party more transparent and accountable.

However, this book has found that *OGI Regulations* and *OPA Regulations* are generally weak regarding reactive disclosure. The internationally adopted principle of a presumption of disclosure was absent in *OGI Regulations 2007*. Although the principle was finally added to the law in 2019, it should have been given a more prominent placement in the provisions. The exemption clauses in *OGI Regulations* and the exemption clauses in *OPA Regulations* are among the most restrictive in the world. Many crucial terms such as state security, public security, economic security, political security, cultural security, homeland security, social stability, commercial secrets, and personal privacy are vague or not defined. The Chinese FOI law subjects only two parts of the Chinese bureaucracy, the people's government and the Communist Party, to requirements of disclosure. Other branches of the party-state bureaucracy such as the legislature, the judiciary, the procuratorate, the military, and the political consultative conference are not subject to the law although they hold large volumes of information that the public has a right to know. China could have embraced a stronger and more effective FOI law if the lawmakers were more willing to listen to Chinese legal scholars' recommendations. The half-heartedness of the government in promoting greater transparency reflects the gradual and incremental nature of China's political reform. Political leaders fear that a more progressive FOI law would encounter more resistance from people in power and lead to social chaos and instability.

Overall, *OGI Regulations 2007* were lacking effectiveness in terms of its statutory language, although some improvements were accomplished when the law was amended in 2019. Given the law's limited promise for transparency, government agencies at various levels are surprisingly compliant. This research project has found that the people's government, at various levels, proactively disclosed information required by the provisions of *OGI Regulations*, after enforcement in May 2008. Overall, the people's government has been successful in establishing the FOI platforms and enforcing proactive disclosure requirements under *OGI Regulations*. Data collected from agency annual reports of OGI activities (2008–2023) show that most OGI applications processed by Chinese agencies, at various levels, have gained approval during this time span. This is a significant achievement for the Chinese government because *OGI Regulations* are weak in statutory language for disclosure of information upon request.

In the meantime, considering the quality of enforcement of affirmative and reactive disclosure requirements requires caution because of the limitations of data released by the government and unavailability of sufficient data from independent sources. Furthermore, most official information sought from 2008 to 2023 did not involve the public interest and was thus less sensitive. This factor might also inflate the actual compliance of agencies with requirements of *OGI Regulations*.

This research project has also found some additional significant problems in the enforcement of *OGI Regulations and OPA Regulations*. Generally, administrative reconsideration and judicial review are ineffective for rectifying non-compliance with *OGI Regulations*. Administrative agencies, superior administrative agencies that review non-disclosure decisions for administrative reconsideration, and courts normally take stand in favor of withholding information on procedural/non-statutory grounds rather than legal/statutory grounds. In other words, they tend to reject information disclosure requests for reasons not listed in *OGI Regulations* and other relevant laws. These practices are especially troubling because they make it harder for requesters to seek any administrative or judicial remedies for requests denied on non-statutory grounds. In addition, another notable loophole is that disclosure of governmental information held by military and national security agencies (the Ministry of National Defense and the Ministry of State Security) are lacking, despite both agencies' being subject to *OGI Regulations*. This book project has found an "enforcement black hole" for *OPA Regulations*, meaning that the CCP's FOI law has probably witnessed no enforcement at all since its implementation in 2017. A similar "sanctions black hole" was identified by this book for public enterprises and public institutions, meaning that no individuals from those entities have ever been reportedly penalized for their failure to comply with transparency requirements of *OGI Regulations*.

This book has also found that laws regulating journalistic internal reference and internal working documents are problematic. *OGI Regulations 2007* had no provisions for whether or not internal working documents should be exempt from disclosure, and those documents were added to the law as a new exemption in 2019, but the law fails to limit the scope of the exemption. It is a significant omission, given that all the exemptions in the Chinese FOI law are mandatory rather than discretionary. *OGI Regulations* have no provisions for whether or not journalistic internal reference should be exempt. Agency officials and court judges have abusively used internal working documents as shields for disclosing information. Likewise, agencies and courts may use journalistic internal reference in the future as a reason to deny disclosure.

Another major finding of this research project concerns journalistic contributions to the proposal, formulation, passage, publicizing, and use of *OGI Regulations*. Unlike many foreign journalists who played pivotal roles for proposing, formulating, and using freedom of information legislation, this book has found that Chinese journalists did not play a role in recommending and formulating *OGI Regulations*. However, it is encouraging that Chinese editors and reporters played prominent roles in covering and publicizing *OGI Regulations* in the early years of the law's enforcement. Widespread media exposure of non-compliance with OGI *Regulations* created significant pressure on administrative organs that flatly ignored legal obligations to exercise power openly. Detailed examination of media content and personal interviews with insiders show that Chinese journalists have not systemically and vigorously used *OGI Regulations* to obtain official information. One reason, among others, for journalists' limited use of the FOI law is a lack of strong legal protections for press freedom.

Major Suggestions and Recommendations

The findings and relevant analyses in the previous chapters give rise to some suggestions and recommendations. In order to realize the principle of maximum disclosure and at the same time protect certain legitimate categories of information from undue dissemination for effective administration, Chinese FOI reformers should adopt a wide variety of legal and policy remedies. The principal proposed remedies that could make China's FOI system more efficient and effective include:

(1) Amend the statutory language of *OGI Regulations* and *OPA Regulations* at the appropriate opportunity. When revising the current FOI law regime, Chinese law reformers should abolish old, ineffective provisions and add new, progressive provisions. It was encouraging to see the elimination of the special needs test in the 2019 amendment of *OGI Regulations*. It was even more thrilling to see the addition of the principle of maximum disclosure to the OGI amendment. When revising *OGI Regulations* again in the future, China may wish to do the following: A. Cite the Chinese Constitution and use the term "fulfilling people's right to know" to explain the rationale and purpose of the law. B. Define all the exemptions, narrow down their scope, add a "substantial harm test" to all the exemptions and a "public interest test" to the national security exemption,[3] make all the exemptions (except national security) discretionary rather than mandatory.[4] C. Encourage professional journalists, citizen-journalists, and public interest groups to apply for information disclosure of which would contribute to debate on public issues.[5] D. Strengthen transparency requirements of public enterprises and public institutions and treat them just like administrative agencies and empowered organizations under *OGI Regulations*. E. Add a provision protecting whistleblowers who report in good-faith OGI-related wrongdoings and violations of *OGI Regulations*. F. Grant the legal right of access to governmental information to foreign citizens whose countries

[3] The substantia harm test means that in order to justify exempting certain categories of information, agencies must show that the disclosure of the information would cause substantial or significant harm to certain legitimate interests, such as national security, trade secrets, and personal privacy. Low degree of harm is insufficient to trigger decisions to seal information. The public interest test means that information should still be released if sufficient evidence exists to prove that public interest from disclosure outweighs harm to national security, trade secrets, personal privacy, and other legitimate interests.

[4] Discretionary exemptions mean that Chinese officials will have protection from sanctions if they disclose, in good faith, information that is not subject to disclosure.

[5] Requesters who ask for governmental information with the intent for widest dissemination can be given application fee waivers, expedited delivery of requested information and other privileges.

reciprocate China on FOI issues. When revising *OPA Regulations* in the future, China may wish to add reactive disclosure and learn from *OGI Regulations* as much as possible.

(2) Strive for a rule of law-based administration and establishment of a relatively independent and impartial judicial branch. For example, reformers may wish to persuade the Ministry of National Defense and the Ministry of State Security that disclosure of non-sensitive information held by these two secretive agencies enhances administrative efficiency and accountability. China may wish to prohibit administrative agencies, administrative reconsideration agencies, and courts from denying disclosure of information for procedural or non-legal reasons. China may wish to create the position of Chief Information Officer at each appropriate administrative agency to supervise, coordinate, and centralize OGI activities. Also desirable is the creation of an independent organization, such as an OGI information commission or ombudsman to mediate OGI disputes. The organization may consist of governmental officials, chief information officers, journalists, and OGI legal scholars. All members should be part-time.

(3) Determine how to deal with governmental information contained in "journalistic internal reference" and "internal working documents." Journalistic internal reference itself creates lots of legal, political, and social problems, and short-term solutions are to include "journalistic internal reference" in the Chinese FOI law as an exemption and clearly narrow the scope of this exemption. At the same time, China may consider reducing the number of journalistic internal reference publications and ensure that journalistic internal reference materials contain only information that is sensitive enough to be designated as state secrets. All of these proposals, however, are short-term solutions. Gradual elimination of journalistic internal references should be considered as a long-term plan. Given that internal working documents were added to OGI *Regulations* in 2019 as a new exemption, writers of a new amendment in the future should think about how to narrow the scope of this exemption in clearly stated language.

(4) Engage in a wide variety of lawmaking activities to make sure the Constitution and all the other FOI-related laws and regulations could provide a nurturing legal environment for the FOI law to grow and become truly effective. For example, formulate *OGI Law*

to replace *OGI Regulations* when the opportunity is appropriate to enhance its legal standing; amend *Constitution 1982* and explicitly enshrine the key phrase "the right to know" in the amended document as a foundational constitutional principle; amend existing laws relating to FOI[6] to make sure that disclosure takes precedence whenever there is a conflict between *OGI Law* and other laws; draft access laws that apply to the people's congress, the courts, the procuratorate, the political consultative conference[7]; access laws applying to the military should have consideration as well; develop a set of FOI-related transparency laws, such as *Privacy Protection Law and Personal Information and Data Protection Law*,[8] *Public Servants' Personal Assets Disclosure Law*, *Freedom of the Press Law*, and Chinese sunshine laws entitling citizens to attend important party and government meetings and access official facilities.

In addition to the aforementioned principal remedies, the Chinese government may also wish to do the following: (1) Strengthen FOI training for leading officials at various levels because full support from leading party and governmental officials is a key component for successful enforcement of *OGI Regulations* in China. Party schools and other cadres' training institutions should have FOI as a mandatory course. (2) Ensure that all Chinese undergraduate and graduate students with majors in journalism, public relations, or mass communications complete at least one mass media law course. The mass media law course should provide an overview of Chinese FOI law, other laws, regulations, and codes relevant to journalism and mass communications in China. This changed curriculum would enhance FOI awareness of prospective Chinese journalists and other professional communicators. (3) Promote civic education among pre-college Chinese students. Effective civic education would

[6] Such laws include but are not limited to: *Law on Guarding State Secrets*, *Archives Law*, *Emergency Response Law*, *Public Servants Law*, *Administrative Litigation Law*, *Criminal Law*, and *Statistics Law*.

[7] These four branches of the government control a wealth of information probably less important than documents and records held by the Chinese people's government and the Chinese Communist Party. Like the party and the government, these "big four" should be accountable too.

[8] Such a law was enacted in 2021 but still fails to define privacy. *Personal Information Protection Law 2021* (adopted August 20, 2021, effective November 1, 2021).

cultivate a political culture that is conducive to the emergence of a civil society and realization of rule of law. (4) Strengthen collaboration between China and other FOI countries. Officials, journalists, lawyers, professors, NGOs, and other FOI stakeholders from different countries would benefit from regular exchanges of lessons and experiences from various issues concerning FOI. Such exchanges could be institutionalized.

China is a civil law country, not a common law country. Legal precedents have limited judicial value. In this regard, formulating a strong and functional statute is crucial, and amending laws to reflect the changing social realities is also vital. However, lawmaking cannot be successful if it happens during times of rigorous resistance The CCP and the Chinese people's government may wish to consider this book's recommendations at opportune times. In China, changes require political wisdom to determine appropriate timing. Chinese law reformers have shown sufficient political willpower for rendering FOI politically acceptable. Good reasons exist to believe that reformers would succeed again in moving China toward greater governmental transparency in the coming years.

China failed miserably to disclose, both proactively and reactively, relevant public health information at the very beginning of the COVID-19 global pandemic. The global village has paid a high price for a single villager's failure.[9] It is a good example to demonstrate that a single country's failure to comply with its own FOI law has worldwide implications and global consequences. International FOI stakeholders should work together to develop a global mechanism to incentivize good behavior in government transparency and penalize ruthless violations of national FOI laws. They may wish to do the following: 1. Redesign the Global

[9] According to World Health Organization estimates, about 14.9 million people died from the COVID-19 globally in 2020–21. Prabhat Jha, Patrick E Brown & Rashid Ansumana, *Counting the Global COVID-19 Dead*, 399 THE LANCET 10339 (2022), 1937–1938, published at the same time on the journal's website, May 21, 2022, *available at* https://www.thelancet.com/journals/lancet/article/PIIS0140-6736(22)00845-5/fulltext (accessed between February 21, 2025 and March 31, 2025). According to estimates from two Harvard scholars, United States alone has lost $16 trillion, or approximately 90% of its annual gross domestic product from the COVID-19 pandemic. David M Cutler and Lawrence H Summers, *The COVID-19 Pandemic and the $16 Trillion Virus*, 324 THE JOURNAL OF THE AMERICAN MEDICAL ASSOCIATION 15, 1495–1496 (2020), published at the same on the website of JAMA Network, October 12, 2020, *available at* https://jamanetwork.com/journals/jama/fullarticle/2771764 (accessed between February 21, 2025 and March 31, 2025).

Right to Information Rating to make it a more accurate and encompassing indicator of a national freedom of information law's effectiveness in both statutory language and enforcement. For example, the rating should measure not only reactive disclosure but also proactive disclosure, and the ranking should reflect not only the quality of the national FOI laws but also the quality of the laws' enforcement. Publish the ratings annually and publicize the ratings as rigorously as possible. 2. Pressure countries without FOI legislations to join the FOI club as soon as possible. 3. International mechanisms such as the United Nations, World Bank, International Monetary Fund, World Trade Organization, World Health Organizations, and European Union should consider FOI and government transparency as a factor when determining whether or not to give countries memberships or member-only privileges. Bilateral and multilateral trade negotiations may include FOI. 4. Penalize countries with records of willfully violating FOI laws that cause significant financial and human cost. 5. Create an annual FOI Summit where world leaders, FOI scholars, journalists, government officials, attorneys, court judges, and other FOI stakeholders will meet to discuss how to enhance global governance via international FOI collaboration.

Research Limitations and Directions for Future Research

This research made a substantial and innovative contribution to the existing FOI literature. It explains, in great detail and depth, how official transparency and secrecy has evolved during China's civilization and how the Western concept of freedom of information was accepted and modified in the Chinese context to adapt to Chinese conditions. The research analysis, based on large amount of qualitative and quantitative data concerning legislative process, statutory language and enforcement of China's first nationwide freedom of information law, shows convincingly why a freedom of information law could become possible in an authoritarian regime with no strong civil society and rule of law. The research also explains why, despite all the shortcomings of *OGI Regulations* and widely held Western assumption that FOI law in nondemocratic countries are used merely for democratic window dressing, the Chinese FOI law can be surprisingly vibrant and resilient at times. Overall, this research contributes enhanced understanding of intricacies of authoritarian transparency.

The research has its limitations. First, the original plan considered inviting ordinary Chinese citizens, governmental officials, and journalists to participate in an online survey, whose purpose was to gather quantitative data for statistical analysis examining the perceptions and use of Chinese FOI law. However, time constraints and other logistical problems prevented conducting the survey. Plans also included exploration of the relationship among different types of authoritarian regimes and degrees of press freedom. The goal was to establish additional statistical support for the theory that among the three types of authoritarian regimes (military regimes, single-party regimes, and personalist/dictatorship regimes), single-party regimes allow for the greatest level of press freedom. That theory, in combinations with the four theories of the press, was to conceptualize the Chinese news media system. The intended statistical analysis was to be running cross-sectional, time-series, linear regression using the SPSS computer program. While all datasets are complete, cleaned, and verified, the statistical analysis is incomplete due to time constraints and other logistical problems. The quantitative research has value as a potential contribution to understanding the Chinese FOI law. This aspect of the research is worthy of future consideration.

Second, a planned comparison of *OGI Regulations* with the FOI laws in an authoritarian country, an Eastern European newly democratic country, and an East Asian country where Confucianism has a strong presence, is not possible due to time constraints and the scope of this research project. These comparisons may be topics for future study. When comparing the Chinese FOI law with the similar law in an authoritarian country (Zimbabwe would be a good choice[10]), investigating the differences in passage and enforcement of FOI laws in the two authoritarian countries would be illuminating. When comparing China's FOI law with the equivalent legislation from an Eastern European country (Hungary would be a choice[11]), a valuable inquiry would be analyzing one communist country and another former communist country for their

[10] Zimbabwe adopted the *Access to Information and Privacy Protection Act* (AIPPA) in 2002. The *AIPPA* is similar to many other FOI laws around the world in FOI rights and procedures for access. Unfortunately, the government of Zimbabwe has used the law to suppress freedom of expression and the press.

[11] As a new democracy with communist history, Hungary passed the *Act on the Protection of Personal Data and Public Access to Data of Public Interest* in 1992 and the *Act on the Freedom of Information by Electronic Means* in 2005. The Hungarian FOI law covers all three branches of government and incorporates the privacy law.

differing creations and implementations of FOI laws. When comparing *OGI Regulations* with the FOI law in an East Asian country with a strong Confucianism tradition (e.g., South Korea[12]), the differences between two Confucian countries for the promises and practices of access laws would be a valuable addition. Investigating these three international FOI models (authoritarian model, communist model, and Confucianism model) would be invaluable.

Third, philosophies and practices of official transparency and accountability in ancient China inspired the world's first FOI law. This study examined perspectives of traditional Chinese philosophies in relation to governmental secrecy and transparency. Many questions remain unanswered due to time constraints and the scope of this study. For example, in the discussions of the information policies of various dynasties and governments, the current research does not address the reasons specific information policies or official actions did or did not occur. For instance, Tang emperor Taizong did not allow access to documents except for privileged officials. Some writers of short reports in the Song Dynasty received punishment; others did not. Analysis of the rationales for openness or secrecy would provide a clearer understanding of the progression of Chinese information policies. In addition, hundred schools of thought that flourished in the Zhou Dynasty cover a wide range of Chinese philosophies, and Mohism, Taoism, Legalism, and Confucianism, some other philosophies such as School of Diplomacy and School of the Military, to varying degrees, introduce many issues on governmental information. The School of the Military emphasized that rulers should develop good information sources inside enemies' countries to understand the enemies fully and win wars.[13] Further investigation should examine philosophical foundations of imperial court diaries and the Censorate and consider the influences of ancient Chinese philosophies on Chinese rulers' handling official information.

Last, original plans included devoting a chapter to predicting future development of the freedom of information movement in China. This plan did not reach realization due to time constraints and the scope of this study. Perhaps, investigation of these predictions can occur after

[12] South Korea passed the *Act on Disclosure of Information by Public Agencies* in 1996 and the law went into effect in January 1998.

[13] SUN TZU, THE ART OF WAR 230 (Lionel Giles trans., El Paso Norte Press) (2009).

the Chinese FOI law matures and the future of China becomes more certain. Governmental transparency is a component of China's political reform, which involves too many uncertainties. As for the outcome of Chinese political reform and the future of the CCP, many China specialists in the West have outlined a range of possible scenarios.[14] For example, Bruce Dickson, a prominent political scientist, speculated four scenarios; according to their likelihood they are: continued CCP (Chinese Communist Party) rule, unconsolidated democracy or illiberal democracy, successful democratization, and military regime.[15] An interesting speculation would involve applying the status of freedom of information in China to each scenario. Arguably, the first scenario (continued CCP rule) is the most likely prospect for China during the next twenty years, so the near future entails movement of freedom of information in China within the orbit of the party. International observers should continue to watch the party's unique defining of freedom of information.

Summary and Conclusion

This chapter provides a recapitulation of key points covered in the previous chapters, discusses the major research findings, offers suggestions and recommendations for Chinese FOI law reformers and international FOI stakeholders, highlights major research contributions, acknowledges limitations, and suggests several possible directions for future research of the Chinese freedom of information.

Where does China stand in terms of quality of FOI law and effectiveness of enforcement? Some scholars produced incomplete rankings and China was not included.[16] Two non-profit organizations, Access

[14] Those China specialists include but are not limited to: Robert Scalapino of the University of California, Berkeley; Richard Baum of the University of California, Los Angeles; the Stanford University professor Andrew Walder; the Harvard University professor Tony Saich; the George Washington University professor Bruce Dickson; the Brookings Institution scholar Cheng Li and the George Washington University professor David Shambaugh. David Shambaugh, China's Communist Party: Atrophy and Adaptation 170–81(2008).

[15] Bruce J. Dickson, *The Future of the Chinese Communist Party: Strategies of Survival and Prospects for Change*, *in* Charting China's Future: Political, Social, and International Dimensions 40, 40–46 (Jae Ho Chung ed., 2006).

[16] For example, Australian FOI scholar Johan Lidberg produced a tentative FOI Index to rank Sweden, Australia, the USA, Thailand and South Africa in term of gap between

Info Europe, and The Centre for Law and Democracy,[17] announced in September 2012 the world's most comprehensive FOI rating that included all the 93 countries with access to information legislations.[18] Countries are evaluated in seven categories (see Table 6.3) and then assigned a total score out of maximum 150 points.

Judging from China's rankings in different years (see Table 6.1), anyone can see clearly that China is lagging far behind many FOI countries in terms of the effectiveness of the law. However, Chinese law reformers do not need to be overly pessimistic because the rating has two major shortcomings. One is that the ranking does not take proactive disclosure into consideration. Second is that the rating does not evaluate how effectively a country's FOI law is enforced in practice, instead, it assesses only the law itself. Despite all the aforementioned drawbacks of *OGI Regulations* in this chapter, the Chinese FOI law regime is strong in proactive disclosure of information and *OGI Regulations* are, overall, vigorously used and forcefully implemented in the last 16 years (2008–2023), especially if party and governmental leaders prioritize OGI or information sought is not sensitive. China would definitely have a

the FOI legislation promise and the practice; two British FOI experts Robert Hazell and Ben Worthy developed a number of measures to compare the FOI law in the United Kingdom with similar laws in Australia, New Zealand, Canada, and Ireland. Johan Lidberg, *The International Freedom of Information Index: A Watchdog of Transparency in Practice*, 30 NORDICOM REVIEW 167 (2009); Johan Lidberg, *Beyond the Freedom of Information Index: An Audit of FOI Reform*, paper presented at the Media and Global Divides Conference in Stockholm, Sweden, July 20–25, 2008; Robert Hazell & Ben Worthy, *Assessing the Performance of Freedom of Information*, 27 GOVERNMENT INFORMATION QUARTERLY 352 (2010).

[17] AccessInfo Europe (http://www.access-info.org/) is a Madrid-based Spanish human rights organization devoted to promotion and protection of the right of access to information in Europe and globally. The Centre for Law and Democracy is a Halifax-based Canadian non-profit organization aimed at promoting fundamental human rights. For unknown reasons, its website http://www.law-democracy.org/ is no longer up and running. The author of this book is unsure if the disappearance of its website is temporary or permanent. *What We Do*, The Centre for Law and Democracy, Halifax, Nova Scotia, Canada (captured by Internet Archive Wayback Machine on October 16, 2010), retrieved from https://web.archive.org/web/20110125175850/http://www.law-democracy.org/?page_id=110 (accessed between February 21, 2025 and March 31, 2025).

[18] The FOI or RTI (Right to Information) Rating was initially announced in September 2011 and 89 countries with FOI laws were ranked. It is the first time for AccessInfo Europe and Centre for Law and Democracy to update the rating. The most recent rating was published in 2024 to cover more than 100 countries.

much better rating if the rating had adopted a different methodology incorporating both proactive disclosure and enforcement of the law.

Further, China could find relief from the fact that a large number of democracies were rated poorly by Access Info Europe and The Centre for Law and Democracy. Of the bottom 10 FOI countries/regions in 2012, most are democratic ones.[19] The 2011–2024 rankings for United States (see Table 6.2), and the 2012 rankings for well-established constitutional democracies such as the United States, Canada, Switzerland, France, and Demark[20] are particularly embarrassing for people who believe that long democratic traditions would give a free pass to effective freedom of information law.

No matter how to interpret the FOI ratings,[21] one thing is certain: China's progress is commendable for the government's achievements, during the last 40 years, for gradually and incrementally changing traditionally secretive bureaucratic activities into more open actions.[22] Jamie Horsley, a long-time observer of China's FOI development and one of the most cited Western legal scholars in this book, often carries a tone of optimism in her OGI-related and OPA-related commentaries. Zejin Yao,

[19] The following are such countries/regions and their corresponding ratings: Austria, 93; Liechtenstein, 92; Greece, 91; Germany, 89; Italy, 87; Taiwan, 84; Belgium, 85. *Historical Data on Country RTI Rating Scores*, Global Right to Information Rating, a joint project by AccessInfo Europe and the Centre for Law and Democracy, *available at* https://www.rti-rating.org/historical/ (accessed between February 21, 2025 and March 31, 2025).

[20] The following are such countries and their respective ratings: United States, 39; Canada, 55; Switzerland, 66; France, 68; Denmark, 78. *Historical Data on Country RTI Rating Scores*, Global Right to Information Rating, a joint project by AccessInfo Europe and the Centre for Law and Democracy, *available at* https://www.rti-rating.org/historical/ (accessed between February 21, 2025 and March 31, 2025).

[21] Any ranking is prone to controversy due to the methodology used and complexity of issues involved.

[22] Easy availability of financial records on private corporations and their major shareholders to a foreign journalist is a testament to this remarkable change. According to a New York Times correspondent who requested and successfully obtained financial records from the State Administration for Industry and Commerce and its local branches, seeking financial records in China is not as hard as someone in the West may expect. "[C]orporate and financial information [in China] is often readily available to the public." David Barboza, *Obtaining Financial Records in China*, The New York Times, October 26, 2012, para. 1–2, http://www.nytimes.com/2012/10/27/business/global/obtaining-financial-records-in-china.html?ref=world&_r=0 (accessed between February 21, 2025 and March 31, 2025).

a media law scholar from Mainland China, also said, despite *OGI Regulations'* various flaws, overall, he is pleased about the "tremendous role" the Chinese FOI regime has played in promoting and enhancing four democratic rights of Chinese citizens.[23] Of course, more transparency is necessary; the Chinese government clearly has a lot more to do to uncover powerful officials' activities for public scrutiny.

One may interpret China from many perspectives. The country boasts over 4,000 years of uninterrupted civilization and more than 1,000 years ago inspired the world's first freedom of information law. The country invented the world's first printing machine and the first piece of paper, the universal medium for carrying and recording information and knowledge. The country suffered from the Western domination and humiliation for nearly 100 years due to a closed-door policy, and the path to greater freedom of information began in 1978 with the country's policies of reform and openness to the outside world. Since then, Chinese citizens have gained increasing access to information vital to their lives.

Today, China has become one of the most powerful nations on earth, politically, economically, militarily, and culturally.[24] As the world's second most populous country enjoys unprecedented prosperity, it also faces unprecedented political, economic, social, and environmental challenges. Among all the laws People's Republic of China enacted in the last 70 years, freedom of information legislation has the greatest potential

[23] WeChat interview with Zejin Yao (December 2024). Yao is director of the Communication Law Research Center at China University of Political Science and Law. He is executive associate dean of the university's Guangming School of Journalism and Communication. The four democratic rights are four rights recognized within the legal framework of Chinese socialist system. The party recognized the right to know one of four democratic rights Chinese citizens shall enjoy in a socialist democracy. The rights are the right to vote (*xuanjuquan*选举权), the right to know (*zhiqingquan* 知情权), the right to participate (*canyuquan* 参与权), and the right to supervise (*jianduquan* 监督权). Later revision defined and formalized the four democratic rights as the right to know (*zhiqingquan* 知情权), the right to participate (*canyuquan* 参与权), freedom of expression (*biaodaquan* 表达权), and the right to supervise (*jianduqua*n 监督权). The four rights have never appeared in the statutory language of the Chinese FOI law.

[24] The awarding of the 2012 Nobel Prize in Literature to an author with Chinese citizenship is a most recent testament to China's cultural strength. In evaluating the significance of China's winning the prize, a *New Yorker* writer said, "Achieving it was always seen as a referendum on China's cultural development." Evan Osnos, *Mo Yan and China's "Nobel Complex,"* NEW YORKER, October 11, 2012, http://www.newyorker.com/online/blogs/books/2012/10/mo-yan-and-chinas-nobel-complex.html (accessed between February 21, 2025, and March 31, 2025).

for successfully addressing those challenges. Witnessing the maturity of Chinese FOI law is potentially illuminating and rewarding.[25] China's successes and setbacks in freedom of information will continue to provide significant inspirations for the rest of the world.

[25] Yanbin Lv is a legal scholar at the Chinese Academy of Social Sciences and an expert familiar with *OGI Regulations*. In an email interview with the author of this book, he said that the National People's Congress is likely to legislate *OGI Law* to replace *OGI Regulations*, but he is not sure when that will happen.

CHAPTER 13

Appendix

See Tables 1.1, 1.2, 6.1, 6.2, 6.3, 7.1, 7.2, 7.3, 7.4, 7.5, 7.6, 7.7, 7.8, 7.9, 8.1, 10.1, 10.2, 10.3, 10.4, and 10.5

Table 1.1 Chronology of FOI Laws in the World[1]

Year	*Country*
1766	Sweden
1888	Columbia
1951	Finland

(continued)

[1] Based on the data from international FOI legal scholars such as David Banisar, John M. Ackerman, Irma E. Sandoval-Ballesteros, and Roger Vleugels, the author of this book constructed this table. The table was also based on the data provided by some non-profit FOI entities such as the Open Society Justice Initiative. The table was updated to include all the countries that joined the global freedom of information community from 1766 to 2017. A total number of 111 countries/regions (including Taiwan) are included in the table. The year in the table refers to when the respective legislative organ or any other relevant branch of the government passed the freedom of information law or regulation. Countries with FOI-related laws but without FOI laws are not included in the table. Countries that have constitutional provisions to protect freedom of information but no specific legislations to guarantee this right are not included in the table. David Banisar, Freedom of Information around the World 2006: A Global Survey of Access to Government Information Laws (report for Privacy International, London, United Kingdom, July 2006), *available at* http://www.freedominfo.org/documents/global_survey2006.pdf (accessed between February 21, 2025 and

Y. Tang, *Freedom of Information Law in China*,
https://doi.org/10.1007/978-981-96-7842-6_13

Table 1.1 (continued)

Year	*Country*
1966	United States
1970	Denmark
1970	Norway
1978	France
1982	Australia
1982	New Zealand
1983	Canada
1987	Austria
1987	Denmark (repealed the 1970 Act)
1990	Italy
1991	Netherlands
1992	Hungary
1992	Ukraine
1992	Spain
1993	Portugal
1994	Belize
1994	Belgium
1996	Iceland
1996	Lithuania
1996	South Korea
1997	Thailand
1997	Ireland
1998	Israel
1998	Latvia
1999	Czech Republic
1999	Albania
1999	Georgia
1999	Greece
1999	Japan
1999	Liechtenstein
1999	Trinidad and Tobago
2000	South Africa
2000	United Kingdom
2000	Bosnia and Herzegovina
2000	Bulgaria
2000	Lithuania

(continued)

March 31, 2025); John M. Ackerman & Irma E. Sandoval-Ballesteros, *The Global Explosion of Freedom of Information Laws*, 58 ADMINISTRATIVE LAW REVIEW 85 (2006); *Freedom of Information*, Open Society Foundations, New York, http://www.soros.org/topics/freedom-information (accessed between February 21, 2025 and March 31, 2025).

Table 1.1 (continued)

Year	*Country*
2000	Moldova
2000	Slovakia
2000	Estonia
2001	Poland
2001	Romania
2002	Panama
2002	Pakistan
2002	Mexico
2002	Jamaica
2002	Peru
2002	Tajikistan
2002	Uzbekistan
2002	Zimbabwe
2002	Angola
2003	Croatia
2003	Argentina
2003	Kosovo
2003	Armenia
2003	Slovenia
2003	Türkiye
2004	Dominican Republic
2004	Serbia
2004	Switzerland
2004	Ecuador
2005	India
2005	Uganda
2005	Germany
2005	Antigua & Barbuda
2005	Azerbaijan
2005	Montenegro
2005	Republic of China (Taiwan)
2006	Macedonia
2006	Honduras
2007	Jordan
2007	**People's Republic of China**
2007	Nepal
2007	Kyrgyzstan
2007	Cayman Islands
2007	Nicaragua
2008	Chile
2008	Uruguay
2008	Indonesia

(continued)

Table 1.1 (continued)

Year	*Country*
2008	Ethiopia
2008	Guatemala
2008	Cook Islands
2008	Malta
2008	Iran
2009	Bangladesh
2009	Russia
2010	Liberia
2010	Guinea
2010	Bermuda
2011	Brazil
2011	Malaysia
2011	Nigeria
2011	Niger
2011	Mongolia
2011	Tunisia
2011	El Salvador
2012	Yemen
2013	Paraguay
2013	Guyana
2013	Rwanda
2014	Ireland (repealed the 1997 Act)
2014	Albania
2014	Bhutan
2014	Maldives
2016	Argentina
2016	Philippines
2016	Tanzania
2016	Tunisia
2017	Cyprus
2017	Sri Lanka

Table 1.2 Freedom House Scores of the 11 Authoritarian Countries with FOI Laws[2]

Country	*Political rights in the year of 2012*	*Civil liberties in the year of 2012*	*Freedom status in the year of 2012*
Angola	6	5	Not free
Azerbaijan	6	5	Not free
China	7	**6**	Not free
Ethiopia	6	6	Not free
Jordan	6	5	Not free
Russia	6	5	Not free
Tajikistan	6	5	Not free
Uzbekistan	7	7	Not free
Yemen	6	6	Not free
Zimbabwe	6	6	Not free
Rwanda	6	5	Not free

Table 6.1 Global Right to Information Rating for China (2011–2024)[3]

Year	*Total score out of 150 points*	*Ranking among all the countries with FOI laws*
2011	72	55
2012	72	62
2013	72	64
2014	70	72
2015	NA	NA
2016	70	80

(continued)

[2] The table was based on the data from Freedom House. *Comparative and Historical Data*, Freedom in the World, Freedom House, Washington, DC, *available at* https://freedomhouse.org/reports/publication-archives (accessed between February 21, 2025 and March 31, 2025).

[3] The dataset in this table came from the Global Right to Information Rating produced by two non-profit organizations AccessInfo Europe and Centre for Law and Democracy. Since 2011, the Rating has begun to comparatively assess the strength of legal frameworks for the right to information from around the world. The rating does not measure quality of FOI law implementation. It only measures quality of the FOI legislations in seven different categories: Right of access, scope, requesting procedures, exceptions and refusals, appeals, sanctions and protections, and promotional measures. For research methodology of the rating, see *Methodology*, Global Right to Information Rating, *available at* https://www.rti-rating.org/methodology/ (accessed between February 21, 2025, and March 31, 2025). For longitudinal country data involving China, see *Historical Data on Country RTI Rating Scores*, Global Right to Infromation Rating, *available at* https://www.rti-rating.org/historical/ (accessed between February 21, 2025 and March 31, 2025).

Table 6.1 (continued)

Year	*Total score out of 150 points*	*Ranking among all the countries with FOI laws*
2017	73	77
2018	73	84
2019	73	87
2020	70	97
2021	75	87
2022	75	89
2023	75	90
2024	75	90

Table 6.2 Global Right to Information Rating for USA (2011–2024)[4]

Year	*Total score out of 150 points*	*Ranking among all the countries with FOI laws*
2011	89	37
2012	89	39
2013	89	42
2014	89	46
2015	NA	NA
2016	83	55
2017	83	57
2018	83	69
2019	83	72
2020	83	72
2021	83	72
2022	83	74
2023	83	76

(continued)

[4] The dataset in this table came from the Global Right to Information Rating produced by two non-profit organizations AccessInfo Europe and Centre for Law and Democracy. Since 2011, the Rating has begun to comparatively assess the strength of legal frameworks for the right to information from around the world. The rating does not measure quality of FOI law implementation. It only measures quality of the FOI legislations in seven different categories: Right of access, scope, requesting procedures, exceptions and refusals, appeals, sanctions and protections, and promotional measures. For research methodology of the rating, see *Methodology*, Global Right to Information Rating, *available at* https://www.rti-rating.org/methodology/ (accessed between February 21, 2025 and March 31, 2025). For longitudinal country data involving the United States, see *Historical Data on Country RTI Rating Scores*, Global Right to Infromation Rating, *available at* https://www.rti-rating.org/historical/ (accessed between February 21, 2025 and March 31, 2025).

Table 6.2 (continued)

Year	*Total score out of 150 points*	*Ranking among all the countries with FOI laws*
2024	78	82

Table 6.3 Global Right to Information Rating Seven Categories of FOI Effectiveness[5]

Section	Max Points
1. Right of Access	6
2. Scope	30
3. Requesting Procedures	30
4. Exceptions and Refusals	30
5. Appeals	30
6. Sanctions and Protections	8
7. Promotional Measures	16
Total score	**150**

[5] According to the rating, countries with FOI laws are evaluated in seven categories and then assigned a total score out of maximum 150 points. The table is copied and pasted from the Global Right to Information Rating website. *RTI Rating Methodology*, Global Right to Information Rating, para. 5, *available at* https://www.rti-rating.org/wp-content/uploads/2021/01/Indicators.final_.pdf (accessed between February 21, 2025 and March 31, 2025).

Table 7.1 Information Disclosure of All Central Government Agencies (2008–2023)[6]

Year	Proactive disclosure	OGI requests received	OGI requests processed	OGI requests approved	OGI requests denied on legal grounds	OGI requests denied on non-legal grounds	Administrative reconsideration decisions in favor of disclosure	Administrative reconsideration decisions against disclosure	Administrative reconsideration decisions (other)	Court decisions in favor of disclosure	Court decisions against disclosure	Court decisions (other)
2008	400,228	4,830	4,822	395	27	101	0	8	9	0	0	0
2009	7, 132, 207	9,884	9,844	1,548	51	837	2	14	50	0	1	1
2010	1, 570, 090	10, 078	9,983	528	185	665	17	52	92	0	1	13
2011	2, 969, 187	10, 964	10,939	706	64	1,006	6	129	205	0	0	18
2012	2, 033, 628	9,284	8,985	1,072	136	935	6	60	83	0	1	2
2013	1, 130, 813	12, 218	11,978	1,423	91	987	11	343	10	0	24	0
2014	1, 982, 784	11,464	11,177	4,212	357	2,618	4	184	20	0	6	2
2015	1, 543, 218	142, 217	141,984	109,567	18,516	10,338	32	102	11	1	73	16
2016	2, 544, 879	24, 464	22,601	6,991	1,530	12,639	56	237	51	15	174	34
2017	1, 998, 660	19, 276	17,748	5,277	2,127	8,759	12	383	0	14	443	28
2018	711, 692	27, 993	27,636	6,423	10,972	8,545	52	486	18	33	375	25

(continued)

[6] The table was created by the author of this book. The dataset in the table came from annual OGI work reports published by various central government agencies in China.

Table 7.1 (continued)

Year	*Proactive disclosure*	*OGI requests received*	*OGI requests processed*	*OGI requests approved*	*OGI requests denied on legal grounds*	*OGI requests denied on non-legal grounds*	*Administrative reconsideration decisions in favor of disclosure*	*Administrative reconsideration decisions against disclosure*	*Administrative reconsideration decisions (other)*	*Court decisions in favor of disclosure*	*Court decisions against disclosure*	*Court decisions (other)*
2019	499, 832	19, 018	18,344	5,255	2,126	10,963	70	361	241	6	371	267
2020	37, 715	16, 247	15,302	4,260	1,305	9,737	43	230	139	8	199	67
2021	1, 876, 868	47, 487	46,677	4,815	2,269	39,593	19	2,840	1,357	2	275	181
2022	1, 399, 478	19, 917	19,397	4,130	1,571	13,696	30	1,130	134	1	238	124
2023	2, 229, 283	15, 906	15,396	4,246	1,468	9,682	34	907	150	3	402	134
Total	30, 060, 562	401, 247	392,813	160,848	42,795	131,101	394	7,466	2,570	83	2,583	912

Table 7.2 Information Disclosure of All Provincial Government Agencies (2008–2023)[7]

Year	*Proactive disclosure*	*OGI requests received*	*OGI requests processed*	*OGI requests approved*	*OGI requests denied on legal grounds*	*OGI requests denied on non-legal grounds*
2008	10,028,780	132,266	129,063	81,315	1,853	6,741
2009	24,874,766	393,716	387,033	249,385	2,530	14,368
2010	31,256,156	219,162	213,769	135,723	2,470	15,463
2011	30, 999, 281	215,569	208,809	135,602	4,306	22,363
2012	43, 614, 687	248,675	239,694	192,659	4,091	28,915
2013	56,639,557	232,842	211,372	152,864	2,995	29,137
2014	52,079,895	305,812	302,006	189,054	9,831	75,185
2015	55,933,078	400,600	380,394	257,554	33,740	81,170
2016	64,266,784	397,501	367,967	239,625	21,600	96,926
2017	70,012,632	415,955	405,430	246,891	27,277	121,947
2018	71,258,396	338,423	332,638	179,269	26,650	116,719
2019	22,784,128	375,820	368,655	200,273	22,871	145,511
2020	674,915,614	366,685	357,691	187,639	21,696	150,232
2021	552, 162,580	445,018	433,018	212,973	22,460	198,456
2022	615,090,156	462,225	452,074	234,301	28,451	191,359
2023	905,397,836	646,962	626,874	305,562	35,982	278,196
Total	3,281,314,326	5,597,231	5,416,487	3,200,689	268,803	1,572,688

Year	*Administrative reconsideration decisions in favor of disclosure*	*Administrative reconsideration decisions against disclosure*	*Administrtive reconsideration decisions (Other)*	*Court decisions in favor of disclosure*	*Court decisions against disclosure*	*Court decisions (other)*
2008	48	444	45	0	8	297
2009	231	757	789	11	223	337
2010	61	675	635	35	759	217
2011	86	636	1,166	81	1,211	222
2012	103	1,165	39	115	910	22
2013	204	2,086	75	72	927	16
2014	1,154	7,427	2,025	731	3,356	1,047
2015	2,424	14,130	3,531	1,427	7,704	3,860
2016	2,935	11,993	5,038	1,399	10,041	4,804
2017	3,106	11,888	5,135	1,275	9,488	4,547

(continued)

[7] The table was created by the author of this book. The dataset in the table came from annual OGI work reports published by various provincial government agencies in China.

Table 7.2 (continued)

Year	*Administrative reconsideration decisions in favor of disclosure*	*Administrative reconsideration decisions against disclosure*	*Administrtive reconsideration decisions (Other)*	*Court decisions in favor of disclosure*	*Court decisions against disclosure*	*Court decisions (other)*
2018	2,476	10,828	4,302	1,360	11,004	4,350
2019	3,185	9,756	4,998	1,544	10,322	5,812
2020	3,125	9,221	4,552	1,366	9,042	5,082
2021	3,880	14,568	5,474	1,283	10,387	5,799
2022	3,807	9,505	5,192	1,210	8,551	5,598
2023	5,444	11,780	7,314	1,466	9,716	7,194
Total	32,269	116,859	50,310	13,375	93,649	49,204

Table 7.3 Information Disclosure of All Government Agencies (2008–2023)[8]

Year	*Proactive disclosure*	*OGI requests received*	*OGI requests processed*	*OGI requests approved*	*OGI requests denied on legal grounds*	*OGI requests denied on non-legal grounds*
2008	10,429,008	137,096	133,885	81,710	1,880	6,842
2009	32,006,973	403,600	396,877	250,933	2,581	1,5,205
2010	32,826,246	229,240	223,752	136,251	2,655	16,128
2011	33,968,468	226,533	219,748	136,308	4,370	23,369
2012	45,648,315	257,959	248,679	193,731	4,227	29,850
2013	57,770,370	245,060	223,350	154,287	3,086	30,124
2014	54,062,679	317,276	313,183	193,266	10,188	77,803
2015	57,476,296	542,817	522,378	367,121	52,256	91,508
2016	66,811,663	421,965	390,568	246,616	23,130	109,565
2017	72,011,292	435,231	423,178	252,168	29,404	130,706
2018	71,970,088	366,416	360,274	185,692	37,622	125,264
2019	23,283,960	394,838	386,999	205,528	24,997	156,474
2020	674,953,329	382,932	372,993	191,899	23,001	159,969
2021	554,039,448	492,505	479,695	217,788	24,729	238,049
2022	616,489,634	482,142	471,471	238,431	30,022	205,055
2023	907,627,119	662,868	642,270	309,808	37,450	287,878

(continued)

[8] The table was created by the author of this book. The dataset in the table came from annual OGI work reports published by various central government agencies and provincial government agencies in China.

Table 7.3 (continued)

Year	*Proactive disclosure*	*OGI requests received*	*OGI requests processed*	*OGI requests approved*	*OGI requests denied on legal grounds*	*OGI requests denied on non-legal grounds*
Total	3,311,374,888	5,998,478	5,809,300	3,361,537	311,598	1,703,789

Year	*Administrative reconsideration decisions in favor of disclosure*	*Administrative reconsideration decisions against disclosure*	*Administrative reconsideration decisions (other)*	*Court decisions in favor of disclosure*	*Court decisions against disclosure*	*Court decisions (other)*
2008	48	452	54	0	8	297
2009	233	771	839	11	224	338
2010	78	727	727	35	760	230
2011	92	765	1,371	81	1,211	240
2012	109	1,225	122	115	911	24
2013	215	2,429	85	72	951	16
2014	1,158	7,611	2,045	731	3,362	1,049
2015	2,456	14,232	3,542	1,428	7,777	3,876
2016	2,991	12,230	5,089	1,414	10,215	4,838
2017	3,118	12,271	5,135	1,289	9,931	4,575
2018	2,528	11,314	4,320	1,393	11,379	4,375
2019	3,255	10,117	5,239	1,550	10,693	6,079
2020	3,168	9,451	4,691	1,374	9,241	5,149
2021	3,899	17,408	6,831	1,285	10,662	5,980
2022	3,837	10,635	5,326	1,211	8,789	5,722
2023	5,478	12,687	7,464	1,469	10,118	7,328
Total	32,663	124,325	52,880	13,458	96,232	50,116

Table 7.4 Total OGI Requests Received by Provincial Government Agencies (2008–2023)[9]

Provinces	*2008*	*2009*	*2010*	*2011*	*2012*	*2013*	*2014*	*2015*	*2016*	*2017*	*2018*	*2019*	*2020*	*2021*	*2022*	*2023*	*Total*
Anhui	279	7,934	9,389	10,409	2,236	4,110	7,013	9,205	8,564	9,035	11,428	11,064	9,669	11,605	13,571	18,190	143,701
Beijing	3,631	6,889	6,996	12,544	17,017	17,509	36,670	32,271	34,200	37,499	36,065	35,286	38,194	68,258	36,398	45,580	465,007
Chongqing	1,000	1,100	1,100	1,300	93	218	948	763	632	9,834	7,896	7,671	5,931	5,646	6,548	10,415	61,095
Fujian	0	4,878	3,209	2,938	2,897	4,519	5,874	7,930	9,473	9,108	8,386	9,295	8,573	10,605	11,853	11,990	111,528
Gansu	616	1,236	21,649	5,094	3,502	3,741	3,712	1,823	2,071	2,365	2,333	4,644	2,339	3,951	3,774	4,665	67,515
Guangdong	10	31	85	73	158	93	208	69,361	45,104	42,364	52,971	44,754	49,033	47,496	53,101	72,461	477,303
Guangxi	0	11,079	8,642	6,270	1,998	1,498	3,024	4,724	3,151	3,797	3,873	4,366	4,405	5,278	7,566	9,644	79,315
Guizhou	0	5,776	4,267	11,961	16,590	7,880	6,943	5,556	5,319	3,860	4,487	4,384	3,577	5,306	7,051	9,607	102,564
Hainan	0	2,995	7,417	3,092	1,105	74	268	1,135	992	1,315	1,594	2,908	2,944	2,520	3,408	3,777	35,544
Hebei	0	732	703	1,463	979	1,350	1,718	6,156	5,230	0	0	8,428	10,163	14,449	16,266	21,182	88,819
Heilongjian[g]	214	758	1,436	8,453	6,842	3,567	18,441	6,495	21,489	5,964	5,250	5,737	6,189	7,669	8,402	9,700	116,606
Henan	15,749	83,054	16,991	28,167	18,411	20,131	20,613	18,342	18,441	20,962	23,623	22,059	20,273	20,207	23,834	54,331	425,188
Hubei	3,867	21	367	317	4,312	15,755	12,155	9,294	9,792	12,472	10,121	9,378	8,197	12,436	16,556	22,143	147,183
Hunan	21	117	21	551	6,638	0	10,760	7,953	9,048	0	0	16,570	10,516	9,853	11,583	19,916	103,547
Mongolia	0	1,291	375	521	246	831	1,007	1,452	1,359	1,190	1,485	158	2,428	3,228	4,043	6,559	26,173
Jiangsu	29	50	76	79	103	19,616	31,909	30,846	29,410	32,224	31,127	31,418	31,291	42,510	46,594	64,103	391,385
Jiangxi	1,957	3,031	854	1,192	1,307	2,183	1,579	1,784	2,315	2,681	2,931	3,089	4,303	5,259	5,348	8,973	48,786
Jilin	45,992	99,318	17,352	16,533	14,403	21,096	26,284	31,176	68,047	71,250	3,804	3,169	3,460	6,686	5,417	8,304	442,291
Liaoning	27	1,198	1,157	256	3,271	4,049	4,588	5,023	6,484	11,718	11,849	6,665	6,175	7,429	11,484	17,589	98,962
Ningxia	0	3,824	30	4,000	2,031	2,257	13,617	680	886	1,608	750	1,257	5,580	3,505	2,342	3,790	46,157
Qinghai	0	9,858	8,311	7,303	5,696	3,148	1,041	1,111	671	435	387	643	701	760	1,108	1,422	42,595
Shandong	16,368	25,097	12,262	30,156	31,077	1,032	21,289	15,079	18,097	21,194	3,409	25,785	29,975	36,714	40,441	54,604	382,579
Shanghai	9,388	11,773	12,006	19,758	18,945	19,170	24,204	32,724	47,451	42,404	31,425	32,006	30,530	30,201	26,775	36,525	425,285
Shaanxi	380	3,972	4,672	4,527	3,627	3,302	5,261	7,066	8,126	6,526	10,832	11,372	9,831	14,932	17,256	23,001	134,683
Shanxi	5,751	23,810	15,895	14,175	8,437	2,344	2,021	1,432	1,151	1,695	2,365	2,963	3,062	4,341	4,946	6,181	100,569
Sichuan	7,395	11,169	6,210	3,553	7,092	6,624	9,553	10,288	12,534	15,498	17,846	19,863	16,607	21,320	22,144	34,124	221,820

(continued)

[9] The table was created by the author of this book. The dataset in the table came from annual OGI work reports published by various provincial government agencies in China.

Table 7.4 (continued)

Provinces	*2008*	*2009*	*2010*	*2011*	*2012*	*2013*	*2014*	*2015*	*2016*	*2017*	*2018*	*2019*	*2020*	*2021*	*2022*	*2023*	*Total*
Tianjin	1,020	2,270	1,562	3,129	3,726	5,146	0	0	0	13,044	14,819	16,185	17,494	14,680	16,911	21,070	131,056
Xinjiang	2	3	12	6	41	49	92	0	768	1,154	616	26	1,012	1,484	1,294	2,764	9,323
Xizang	62	2,184	769	284	31,418	22,070	1,724	1,430	0	202	520	1,245	68	317	525	470	63,288
Yunnan	17,955	22,618	23,314	12,498	26,213	29,534	10,029	11,351	2,542	2,582	3,605	2,775	3,559	7,304	7,162	8,146	191,187
Zhejiang	553	45,650	32,033	4,967	8,264	9,946	23,267	68,150	24,154	31,975	32,626	30,657	27,010	28,275	37,349	47,817	452,693

Table 7.5 China's Corruption Perception Index (2008–2023)[10]

Year	*CPI score*	*Country rank*
2023	42/100	76/180
2022	45/100	65/180
2021	45/100	66/180
2020	42/100	78/180
2019	41/100	80/198
2018	39/100	87/198
2017	41/100	77/198
2016	40/100	79/198
2015	37/100	83/198
2014	36/100	100/198
2013	40/100	80/198
2012	39/100	80/198
2011	3.6/10	75/183
2010	3.5/10	78/178
2009	3.6/10	79/180
2008	3.6/10	72/180

[10] The compiled table is according to the Corruption Perceptions Index provided by Transparency International. Since 1995, Transparency International publishes the Corruption Perceptions Index (CPI). As "the most widely used global corruption ranking in the world," the index ranks countries annually by perceived levels of public sector-corruption determined by expert assessments and opinion surveys. The index generally defines corruption as "the abuse of entrusted power for private gain." The CPI ranks 180 countries and territories on a scale from 0 (highly corrupt) to 100 (very clean). *The CPI Explained*, Transparency International, Berlin, Germany, para.2-3, *available at* https://www.transparency.org/en/cpi/2024 (accessed between February 21, 2025 and March 31, 2025); *Corruption Perceptions Index*, Transparency International, Berlin, Germany, *available at* http://www.transparency.org/research/cpi/overview (accessed between February 21, 2025 and March 31, 2025); *What Is Corruption?* Transparency International, Berlin, Germany, para.2-3, *available at* https://www.transparency.org/en/what-is-corruption (accessed between February 21, 2025 and March 31, 2025).

Table 7.6 Control of Corruption Governance Metric for China (2008–2018)[11]

Year	*Governance (−2.5 to +2.5)*	*Percentile rank (0–100)*
2018	−0.27	45.67
2017	−0.27	46.63
2016	−0.25	49.04
2015	−0.28	48.08
2014	−0.34	45.67
2013	−0.36	44.55
2012	−0.44	40.28
2011	−0.51	37.91
2010	−0.56	33.33
2009	−0.51	36.84
2008	−0.52	36.41

Table 7.7 Government Effectiveness Index for China (2008–2018)[12]

Year	*Score*	*Percentile rank*
2018	0.48	69.71

(continued)

[11] The datasets are compiled from the World Bank-sponsored Worldwide Governance Indicators (WGI) project. *Worldwide Governance Indicators*, World Bank Group, Washington, DC, *available at* https://www.worldbank.org/en/publication/worldwide-governance-indicators (accessed between February 21, 2025, and March 31, 2025). The WGI cover over 200 countries and territories, measuring six dimensions of governance starting in 1996 and ending in 2018. Control of Corruption, one of WGI's indicators, captures perceptions of the extent to which public power is exercised for private gain, including both small and big forms of corruption, as well as control of the state by elites and private interests. Governance Score (−2.5 to +2.5) is an estimate of quality of governance measured on a scale from approximately −2.5 to +2.5. Higher values correspond to better governance. Percentile Rank (0–100) indicates rank of country among all the countries in the world. 0 corresponds to lowest rank and 100 corresponds to highest rank.

[12] Government Effectiveness is an indicator developed by the World Bank to estimate perceptions of the quality of public services, the quality of the civil service and the degree of its independence from political pressures, the quality of policy formulation and implementation, and the credibility of the government's commitment to such policies. Higher scores correspond to more government effectiveness. Percentile Rank (0–100) indicates rank of country among all the countries in the world. "0" corresponds to lowest rank and "100" corresponds to highest rank. *Worldwide Governance Indicators*, World Bank, Washington, DC, *available at* https://www.worldbank.org/en/publication/worldwide-governance-indicators (accessed between February 21, 2025 and March 31, 2025).

Table 7.7 (continued)

Year	*Score*	*Percentile rank*
2017	0.42	67.79
2016	0.35	66.83
2015	0.41	68.27
2014	0.32	64.90
2013	0	55.45
2012	0.02	57.82
2011	0.09	58.29
2010	0.09	57.89
2009	0.09	57.89
2008	0.15	58.74

Table 7.8 Transparency of Government Policymaking Index for China (2008–2017)[13]

Year	*Score*	*Percentile rank*
2017	4.48	45
2016	4.58	40
2015	4.52	36
2014	4.49	33
2013	4.42	46
2012	4.48	51
2011	4.73	41
2010	4.76	38
2009	4.82	32
2008	4.49	46

[13] The number "1" means least transparent and "7" indicates most transparent. The higher the percentile rank, the less transparency. This dataset covered 151 countries in the world from 2007 to 2017. The dataset is compiled from the World Bank website. *Transparency of Government Policymaking, 1-7 (Best),* World Bank, Washington, DC, *available at* https://prosperitydata360.worldbank.org/en/indicator/WEF+GCIHH+EOSQ049 (accessed between February 21, 2025, and March 31, 2025).

Table 7.9 Chinese Government Agencies and Other Entities Sued for Non-Disclosure of Information (2014–2021)[14]

Case citation	*Year/city and province of original jurisdiction*	*Decision and rationale of Chinese entities receiving OGI requests*	*Decision and rationale of oversight department for administrative reconsideration*	*Decision and rationale of primary or trial court*	*Decision and rationale of intermediate or appellate court*	*Decision and rationale of high or supreme court for retrial*
Han Suhua v. Zhenzhou Orphanage	2020 Zhenzhou Henan	4 NS	2 NO	2 NO	2 NO	5
Yongfa Security Equipment Factory v. Changzhou City Institute for Product Quality Supervision and Testing	2018 Changzhou Jiangsu	4 NS	2 NO	2 NM NO	2 NM NO	5
Chen Daxue and Wu Changling v. Rui'an City Office for Immigrant Resettlement	2017 Rui'an Zhejiang	3 DC DG DH NB NH	5	2 NB NH NN	2 NB NH	5
Chenhong v. State Grid Changshu City Electricity Supply Company	2017 Zhangjiagang Jiangsu	4 NS	5	1 DA DF DG DH	1 DA DE DI	5

(continued)

[14] The table was created by the author of this book. The dataset in the table came from OGI-related judicial opinions published on the China Supreme Court's website, China Judgements Online [中国裁判文书网]. *China Judgements Online* [中国裁判文书网], China Supreme Court, Beijing, China, *available at* https://wenshu.court.gov.cn (accessed between February 21, 2025 and March 31, 2025).

Table 7.9 (continued)

Case citation	*Year/city and province of original jurisdiction*	*Decision and rationale of Chinese entities receiving OGI requests*	*Decision and rationale of oversight department for administrative reconsideration*	*Decision and rationale of primary or trial court*	*Decision and rationale of intermediate or appellate court*	*Decision and rationale of high or supreme court for retrial*
Zhang Zongfa v. State Grid Changshu City Electricity Supply Company	2016 Zhangjiagang Jiangsu	4 NS	5	1 DA DF DI	1 DA DE DF DI	5
Liu Shuiping v. State Grid Zhongmou County Electricity Supply Company	2017 Zhengzhou Henan	4 NS	5	2 NB NF NJ NN	2 NB NF NJ NN	2 NB NF NJ NN
Yang Jiandong v. State Grid Changshu City Electricity Supply Company	2016 Zhangjiagang Jiangsu	4 NS	5	1 DA DK	1 DA DE DK	5
Bi Yongyuan v. State Grid Changshu City Electricity Supply Company	2016 Zhangjiagang Jiangsu	4 NS	5	1 DA DK	1 DA DE DI DK	5
Wang Zhenbao v. State Grid Shandong Province Electric Power Company	2015 Ji'nan Shandong	4 NS	5	2 NP NQ	1 DA DK	5
Wang Zhenbao v. State Grid Shandong Province Electric Power Company	2016 Ji'nan Shandong	4 NS	5	2 NL	1 DA DK	5
Wang Zhenbao v. State Grid Shandong Province Electric Power Company	2018 Ji'nan Shandong	4 NS	5	2 NB NN	2 NB NN	5

(continued)

Table 7.9 (continued)

Case citation	*Year/city and province of original jurisdiction*	*Decision and rationale of Chinese entities receiving OGI requests*	*Decision and rationale of oversight department for administrative reconsideration*	*Decision and rationale of primary or trial court*	*Decision and rationale of intermediate or appellate court*	*Decision and rationale of high or supreme court for retrial*
Liang Chaotang v. State Grid Shandong Province Electric Power Company	2020 Ji'nan Shandong	4 NS	5	2 NN NP	5	5
Liang Chaotang v. State Grid Liaocheng City Electricity Supply Company	2020 Liaocheng Shandong	2 NA ND	5	2 NB NF NN	2 NB NF NN	5
Wang Zheliang v. State Grid Changshu City Electricity Supply Company	2016 Zhangjiagang Jiangsu	4 NS	5	1 DA DK	1 DA DE DK	5
Chenhong v. Jiangsu Changshu Sino French Water Company	2017 Zhangjiagang Jiangsu	4 NS	5	1 DA	1 DA DE	5
Shao Mingliang v. Jiangsu Changshu Sino French Water Company	2016 Zhangjiagang Jiangsu	4 NS	5	1 DA DK	1 DA DE DK	5
Bi Yongyuan v. Jiangsu Changshu Sino French Water Company	2016 Zhangjiagang Jiangsu	4 NS	5	1 DA DK	1 DA DE DK	5
Wang Zheliang v. Jiangsu Changshu Sino French Water Company	2016 Zhangjiagang Jiangsu	4 NS	5	1 DA DK	1 DA DE DK	5

(continued)

Table 7.9 (continued)

Case citation	*Year/city and province of original jurisdiction*	*Decision and rationale of Chinese entities receiving OGI requests*	*Decision and rationale of oversight department for administrative reconsideration*	*Decision and rationale of primary or trial court*	*Decision and rationale of intermediate or appellate court*	*Decision and rationale of high or supreme court for retrial*
Zhang Zongfa v. Jiangsu Changshu Sino French Water Company	2016 Zhangjiagang Jiangsu	4 NS	5	1 DA DK	1 DA DE DK	5
Yang Jiandong v. Jiangsu Changshu Sino French Water Company	2016 Zhangjiagang Jiangsu	4 NS	5	1 DA DK	1 DA DE DK	5
Qiu Ailing v. Fuzhou City Water Supply Company	2021 Fuzhou Fujian	2 NL	5	2 NL NN	5	5
Chen Yuejun v. Tianjin Bus Company	2018 Tianjin Tianjin	4 NS	5	1 DA DF	5	5
Chen Yuejun v. Tianjin Metro	2015 Tianjin Tianjin	4 NS	5	2 NR	2 NR	5
Luo Siwen v. Guizhou Power Grid Guiyang Station	2017 Guiyang Guizhou	4 NS	5	1 DA DF DI	5	5
Xing Wenyuan v. State Grid Beijing Electric Power Company	2019 Beijing Beijing	4 NS	5	1 DA	3 DA NG NH NI NL	3 DA NG

(continued)

Table 7.9 (continued)

Case citation	*Year/city and province of original jurisdiction*	*Decision and rationale of Chinese entities receiving OGI requests*	*Decision and rationale of oversight department for administrative reconsideration*	*Decision and rationale of primary or trial court*	*Decision and rationale of intermediate or appellate court*	*Decision and rationale of high or supreme court for retrial*
Xing Wenyuan v. State Grid Beijing Electric Power Company	2018 Beijing Beijing	4 NS	5	1 DA DK	1 DA DK	5
Shao Mingliang v. State Grid Changshu Power Supply Company	2017 Zhangjiagang Jiangsu	4 NS	5	1 DA DF DI	1 DA DE DF DI	5
Ding Zipeng v. State Grid Zaozhuang Power Supply Company	2019 Zaozhuang Shandong	3 DJ NQ	5	2 NE NL NN	5	5
Ding Ruibing v. Haimen City Radio and TV Station	2017 Rugao Jiangsu	4 NS	5	2 ND NN	2 ND NN	5
Fang Jinhua v. China Telecom Suqian Branch	2014 Suqian Jiangsu	4 NQ	5	2 NH NN	2 NG NN	5
Yan Hongjun v. China Mobile Dongguan Branch	2017 Dongquan Guangdong	4 NS	5	1 DB DE DF DH	1 DB DE DF DH	5
Sun Yangbing v. China Mobile Shenzhen Branch	2014 Shenzhen Guangdong	4 NS	5	1 DB DE DF DH	1 DB DE DF DH	5

(continued)

Table 7.9 (continued)

Case citation	*Year/city and province of original jurisdiction*	*Decision and rationale of Chinese entities receiving OGI requests*	*Decision and rationale of oversight department for administrative reconsideration*	*Decision and rationale of primary or trial court*	*Decision and rationale of intermediate or appellate court*	*Decision and rationale of high or supreme court for retrial*
Residents' Committee of Jiuduyangguang Community v. Zhaozhou Electric Power Supply Company	2018 Daqing Heilongjiang	4 NS	2 NJ	1 DA DF	5	5
Zhong Weixi v. Juye County Service Center for Coal Industry	2020 Juye County Shandong	2 NH	5	2 NH	2 NH NM	5
Feng Genqing v. Taizhou City Jiaojiang District Bureau for Housing and Urban-Rural Development	2019 Taizhou Zhejiang	2 NG	5	1 DB DG DH	5	5
Liu Shuping v. China Post Zhongmou County Branch	2017 Xinzheng Henan	4 NS	5	2 NJ NN	2 NJ NN	5
Liu Shuping v. China Post Zhongmou County Branch	2017 Xinzheng Henan	4 NS	5	2 NJ	2 NJ	5
Liu Shuping v. State Grid Zhongmou County Branch	2016 Xinzheng Henan	4 NS	5	2 NJ NN	2 NJ NN	5
Liu Aijun v. Zhengzhou Preschool Education College	2016 Zhengzhou Henan	4 NS	5	1 DA	1 DA	5
Liu Aijun v. Beijing No. 6 Hospital	2016 Beijing Beijing	4 NS	5	2 NN	2 NN	5

(continued)

Table 7.9 (continued)

Case citation	*Year/city and province of original jurisdiction*	*Decision and rationale of Chinese entities receiving OGI requests*	*Decision and rationale of oversight department for administrative reconsideration*	*Decision and rationale of primary or trial court*	*Decision and rationale of intermediate or appellate court*	*Decision and rationale of high or supreme court for retrial*
Liu Hong v. Beijing Dongcheng District No. 1 Center for Public Housing and Land Management	2014 Beijing Beijing	3 DB DG NS	5	2 NN	2 NN	5
Bao Guoqing v. Guangzhou No. 1 Bus Company	2015 Guangzhou Guangdong	2 NH	5	1 DA	2 NN	5
You Hanrui v. Beijing Drainage Group	2018 Beijing Beijing	4 NS	5	6 DA DK	6 DA DK	5
Zhuo Liangbing v. Taizhou City Jiaojiang District Bureau for Housing and Urban-Rural Development	2019 Taizhou Zhejiang	2 NG NM	5	1 DB DL	5	5
Homeowner Association of Nanjing Fengshang International Apartment v. State Grid Nanjing Power Supply Company	2016 Nanjing Jiangsu	4 NS	5	1 DA DE DK	5	5
Lu Jing v. Taizhou City Jiaojiang District Bureau for Housing and Urban-Rural Development	2019 Taizhou Zhejiang	2 NG NM	5	1 DB DL	5	5
Zhang Jianguo v. Stage Grid Zhuzhou Power Supply Company	2018 Zhuzhou Hunan	4 NS	5	2 NM	5	5

(continued)

Table 7.9 (continued)

Case citation	*Year/city and province of original jurisdiction*	*Decision and rationale of Chinese entities receiving OGI requests*	*Decision and rationale of oversight department for administrative reconsideration*	*Decision and rationale of primary or trial court*	*Decision and rationale of intermediate or appellate court*	*Decision and rationale of high or supreme court for retrial*
Qu Zhe v. Shenyang Office of Work Capacity Evaluations and Rehabilitation Management	2018 Shenyang Liaoning	3 DB DH NG	5	2 NN	5	5
Qu Wenheng v. Shenyang Office of Work Capacity Evaluations and Rehabilitation Management	2018 Shenyang Liaoning	3 DB DH NG	5	2 NN	5	5
Ma Juncai v. Xi'an Daxing District Commission for Comprehensive Urban Redevelopment and Management	2018 Xi'an Shaanxi	2 NG	5	2 NG NJ NN	5	5
Lv Haili v. China United Network Communication Group Jiyuan Branch	2018 Mengzhou Henan	4 NS	5	1 DB DK	5	5
Lin Fei v. China United Network Communication Group Yanbian Branch	2014 Yanji Jilin	4 NS	5	2 NG NN	2 NG NN	5
Zhou Yong v. The First Affiliated Hospital of Zhengzhou University	2018 Zhengzhou Henan	4 NS	5	1 DA DK	5	5
Zhou Jianguo v. State Grid Changshu Power Supply Company	2017 Zhangjiagang Jiangsu	4 NS	5	1 DA DK	1 DA DE DI DK	5

(continued)

Table 7.9 (continued)

Case citation	*Year/city and province of original jurisdiction*	*Decision and rationale of Chinese entities receiving OGI requests*	*Decision and rationale of oversight department for administrative reconsideration*	*Decision and rationale of primary or trial court*	*Decision and rationale of intermediate or appellate court*	*Decision and rationale of high or supreme court for retrial*
Zhou Jianguo v. Jiangsu Changshu Sino French Water Company	2016 Zhangjiagang Jiangsu	4 NS	5	1 DA DK	1 DA DE DK	5
Tang Libo v. Jiangsu Changshu Sino French Water Company	2016 Zhangjiagang Jiangsu	4 NS	5	1 DA DK	1 DA DE DK	5
Yu Wufang v. Wuhan Land Consolidation and Banking Center	2014 Wuhan Hubei	2 NJ NM NP NQ	5	2 NB NJ NN	2 NB NJ NN	5
Yang Zhengquan v. State Grid Shandong Electric Power Company and State Grid Feicheng City Electricity Supply Company	2017 Tai'an Shandong	4 NS	5	1 DA DK	1 DA DK	5
Hengfeng County Xuhai Renewable Resources Company v. State Grid Hengfeng County Electricity Supply Company	2019 Shangrao Jiangxi	2 NJ NM NQ	5	1 DA DK	2 NE NN	2 NE NG NN
Xia Xin v. Peking Union Medical College Hospital	2015 Beijing Beijing	2 ND NN	5	2 NB ND NJ NN	2 NB ND NJ NN	5

(continued)

Table 7.9 (continued)

Case citation	*Year/city and province of original jurisdiction*	*Decision and rationale of Chinese entities receiving OGI requests*	*Decision and rationale of oversight department for administrative reconsideration*	*Decision and rationale of primary or trial court*	*Decision and rationale of intermediate or appellate court*	*Decision and rationale of high or supreme court for retrial*
Xia Xin v. Peking Union Medical College Hospital	2014 Beijing Beijing	2 NA	5	2 NE NN	2 NE NN	5
Yao Tushan v. Quzhou Land Banking Center	2016 Quzhou Zhejiang	4 NS	5	2 NM NQ	2 NB NF	5
Sun Baomei v. Beijing Xicheng District Center for Public Housing and Land Management	2017 Beijing Beijing	2 NJ	2 NJ	2 NN	2 NJ NN	5
Jiang Aiming, et al. v. State Grid Corporation of China	2016 Beijing Beijing	4 NS	2 NO NQ	2 NB NO	2 NN NO	5
Sun Qingjun v. State Grid Zhenjiang Electricity Supply Company	2015 Zhenjiang Jiangsu	2 NF NG	5	1 DA DK	1 DA DK	1 DA DK
Sun Qingjun v. Jiangsu Province Zhenjiang City Transportation Management Office	2019 Zhenjiang Jiangsu	2 ND	5	2 NN	2 NN NP	5
Sun Yangbing v. China Mobile Anhui Branch	2018 Hefei Anhui	4 NS	5	2 NN	5	5
Sun Yangbing v. China Mobile Anhui Branch	2019 Hefei Anhui	4 NS	5	2 NP NQ	2 NF NL	5
Sun Yangbing v. China Mobile Shenzhen Branch	2015 Shenzhen Guangdong	2 NJ	5	2 NJ	2 NJ NN	5

(continued)

Table 7.9 (continued)

Case citation	*Year/city and province of original jurisdiction*	*Decision and rationale of Chinese entities receiving OGI requests*	*Decision and rationale of oversight department for administrative reconsideration*	*Decision and rationale of primary or trial court*	*Decision and rationale of intermediate or appellate court*	*Decision and rationale of high or supreme court for retrial*
Song Wenchao v.Changsha Kaifu District Public Works Bureau	2018 Changsha Hunan	4 NS	5	2 NN	5	5
Long Taiping v. State Grid Yuanjiang Electricity Supply Company	2016 Yuanjiang Hunan	4 NS	5	2 NN	2 NN	5
Guo Junmei v. Shenzhen City Management Center for Public hospitals	2015 Shenzhen Guangdong	2 NH	5	1 DA DK	1 DA DK	5
Cui Xunzhang v. Ji'nan City Huaiyin District Bureau for Housing Security and Property Management	2018 Ji'nan Shandong	2 NG	5	2 NG	2 NG NN	5
Liao Chuanshang v. Hongjiang City Center for Tourism Development Affairs	2019 Huaihua Hunan	2 NB NJ NL	5	3 DB DH NB NJ NL	5	5
Liao Guoqing v.Huainan City Construction Investment Corporation	2016 Huainan Anhui	4 NS	5	2 NP	2 NP	5
Zhang Shiyan v. Suzhou University	2016 Nanjing Jiangsu	3 DN NA NB	2 NO	2 NO	2 NO	5

(continued)

Table 7.9 (continued)

Case citation	*Year/city and province of original jurisdiction*	*Decision and rationale of Chinese entities receiving OGI requests*	*Decision and rationale of oversight department for administrative reconsideration*	*Decision and rationale of primary or trial court*	*Decision and rationale of intermediate or appellate court*	*Decision and rationale of high or supreme court for retrial*
Zhang Lilei v. Langfang City Qingquan Water Supply Company	2018 Langfang Hebei	4 NS	5	1 DA DE DK	5	5
Xu Chunmiao v. State Grid Zhoushan City Electricity Supply Company	2018 Zhoushan Zhejiang	3 DN NS	2 NB NI	2 NB NI	2 NB NI	5
Zeng Qinghua v. China Mobile Shenzhen Branch	2017 Shenzhen Guangdong	2 NJ NL	5	2 NJ	2 NJ NN	5
Zeng Qinghua v. China Mobile Jiangxi Branch	2018 Nanchang Jiangxi	4 NS	5	2 NB NN	2 NB NM	2 NJ
Cheng Wenyi v. China Mobile Ezhou Branch	2016 Ezhou Hubei	2 NG NH NI NL	5	3 DB DK ND NG NI NL	3 DB DK ND NG NI NL	5
Li Kangnian v. Guangzhou Medical University	2014 Guangzhou Guangdong	2 NR	5	2 NP	1 DA	5
Li Kangnian v. Guangzhou Medical University	2015 Guangzhou Guangdong	2 NR	5	2 NB ND NJ NN	2 NB ND NJ NN	2 ND

(continued)

Table 7.9 (continued)

Case citation	*Year/city and province of original jurisdiction*	*Decision and rationale of Chinese entities receiving OGI requests*	*Decision and rationale of oversight department for administrative reconsideration*	*Decision and rationale of primary or trial court*	*Decision and rationale of intermediate or appellate court*	*Decision and rationale of high or supreme court for retrial*
Li Kangnian v. Guangzhou Medical University	2017 Guangzhou Guangdong	2 NR	5	2 NB NJ	2 NG	5
Guo Junmei v. Shenzhen Public Hospital Management Center	2015 Shenzhen Guangdong	2 NH	5	1 DA DK	1 DA DK	5
Jia Youbao v. Communication University of China	2018 Beijing Beijing	4 NS	5	1 DA DK	5	5
Bai Yan v. Renmin University of China	2018 Beijing Beijing	3 DN NA NL NH	5	3 DA DG DK NE NN	5	5
Wang Wujun v. China Mobile Tangyin Branch	2018 Anyang Henan	4 NS	5	2 NF NN	1 DB DF DK	5
Yang Jianping v. China Mobile Huizhou Branch	2017 Huizhou Guangdong	7	5	2 NN	2 NN	5
Ke Yuehui v. China Telecom Guangdong Branch	2015 Guangzhou Guangdong	4 NS	5	1 DB DK	1 DB DK	5
Wang Dejun v. China Mobile Hai'an Branch	2015 Nantong Jiangsu	4 NS	5	2 NA NN	2 NA NN	5

(continued)

Table 7.9 (continued)

Case citation	*Year/city and province of original jurisdiction*	*Decision and rationale of Chinese entities receiving OGI requests*	*Decision and rationale of oversight department for administrative reconsideration*	*Decision and rationale of primary or trial court*	*Decision and rationale of intermediate or appellate court*	*Decision and rationale of high or supreme court for retrial*
Yan Xiantong v. Wenzhou Port Group Corporation	2016 Wenzhou Zhejiang	4 NS	2 NS	1 DA DK	1 DA DK	5
Liu Zhongfeng v. Tsinghua University	2016 Beijing Beijing	2 NB NJ	5	1 DA DK	1 DA DK	5
Li Jinghai v. Wafangdian City Social Security Center for Government Agencies and Institutions	2018 Zhuanghe Liaoning	4 NS	5	1 DB DK	5	5
Yang Yang v. Zhuzhou City Public Transportation Company	2018 Zhuzhou Hunan	2 NA ND NN	5	1 DA DG	5	5
Li Zhengxiang v. Taihe County Shayinghe National Wetland Park Management Bureau	2018 Fuyang Anhui	4 NS	5	1 DA DK	5	5
Li Hanhe v. Hunan Province Information Center for Land and Resources	2017 Changsha Hunan	4 NS	5	2 NM	2 NM	5
Ma Zhenjun v. Xichuan County Dashiqiao Township Elementary and Junior High School	2017 Nanyang Henan	4 NS	5	1 DA DK	1 DA DK	5

(continued)

Table 7.9 (continued)

Case citation	*Year/city and province of original jurisdiction*	*Decision and rationale of Chinese entities receiving OGI requests*	*Decision and rationale of oversight department for administrative reconsideration*	*Decision and rationale of primary or trial court*	*Decision and rationale of intermediate or appellate court*	*Decision and rationale of high or supreme court for retrial*
Nanyang Zhenghe Information Consulting Company v. Xichuan County Dashiqiao Township Elementary and Junior High School	2017 Nanyang Henan	4 NS	5	1 DA DK	1 DA DK	5
Man Guipeng v. Linghai City Service Center for Urban and Rural Development	2019 Linghai Liaoning	4 NS	2 NH	2 NH	2 NH NM	5
Wang Jinyang v. Yancheng Xinyang Economic Zone Administration Committee	2015 Yancheng Jiangsu	4 NS	5	2 NM	1 DB DK	5
Li Zhiguo v. Changsha City Furong District Office for Land Acquisition and Property Demolition	2019 Changsha Hunan	2 NM	1 DN	1 DB DK	1 DB DK	5
Pan Guomin, et al. v. Chengde City Shuangfengsi Reservoir Construction Management Bureau	2017 Chengde Hebei	4 NS	5	1 DB DK	1 DB DK	5
Jiao Qihong v. Hefei High-tech Industrial Development Zone Management Council for Baiyan Science and Technology Park	2018 Hefei Anhui	4 NS	5	1 DB DK	5	5

(continued)

Table 7.9 (continued)

Case citation	*Year/city and province of original jurisdiction*	*Decision and rationale of Chinese entities receiving OGI requests*	*Decision and rationale of oversight department for administrative reconsideration*	*Decision and rationale of primary or trial court*	*Decision and rationale of intermediate or appellate court*	*Decision and rationale of high or supreme court for retrial*
Sanhe Tongxin Cement Products Company v. State Grid Jibei Electric Power Company	2019 Beijing Beijing	4 NS	5	2 NB NN	2 NB NN	5
Wang Wei v. China Mobile Shaanxi Branch	2015 Xi'an Shaanxi	4 NS	5	2 NM NP NQ	5	5
Cheng Yuejun v. China Mobile Communications Corporation	2015 Beijing Beijing	4 NS	5	2 NM NP	2 NB NM NP	5
Yin Yanting v. China University of Political Science and Law	2020 Beijing Beijing	3 DA DG NA ND NN	2 NS	2 NM NP NQ	2 NN	5
Li Mingliang v. Shandong Normal University	2018 Ji'nan Shandong	2 NL	5	2 NL NN	2 NL NN	5
Liu Ping v. Tsinghua University	2017 Beijing Beijing	2 NG NH	5	2 NN	2 NN	5
Rao Sixia v. Chongqing City Construction Investment Group Corporation	2018 Chongqing Chongqing	4 NS	5	2 NM NP	2 NM NP	5

(continued)

Table 7.9 (continued)

Case citation	*Year/city and province of original jurisdiction*	*Decision and rationale of Chinese entities receiving OGI requests*	*Decision and rationale of oversight department for administrative reconsideration*	*Decision and rationale of primary or trial court*	*Decision and rationale of intermediate or appellate court*	*Decision and rationale of high or supreme court for retrial*
Rao Sixia v. China State Railway Group Company	2017 Beijing Beijing	4 NS	5	2 NM NP	2 NM NP	5
Rao Sixia v. Chongqing-Guiyang Railway Company	2018 Chongqing Chongqing	4 NS	5	2 NM NP NQ	2 NM NP NQ	5
Shanghai New Wenhui Law Firm v. Zhejiang Province Monitoring Center for Press, Publication, Radio and Television	2018 Hangzhou Zhejiang	4 NS	5	2 NM NP NQ	5	5
Jia Youbao v. China Telecommunications Corporation Beijing Branch	2017 Beijing Beijing	4 NS	5	2 NP	2 NB NP	2 NB NN
Yu Shaoli v. Beijing City Yanqing District Heating Supply Station	2017 Beijing Beijing	2 NJ	5	2 NJ	2 NE	5
Hongyilong Investment Management Company v. National Small and Medium Enterprise Stock Transfer System	2017 Beijing Beijing	4 NS	5	2 NJ NM	2 NM NP NQ	2 NM NP NQ
Yang Jinzhu v. China State Railway Group Company	2016 Beijing Beijing	4 NS	5	1 DA DK	2 NM NP NQ	5

(continued)

Table 7.9 (continued)

Case citation	*Year/city and province of original jurisdiction*	*Decision and rationale of Chinese entities receiving OGI requests*	*Decision and rationale of oversight department for administrative reconsideration*	*Decision and rationale of primary or trial court*	*Decision and rationale of intermediate or appellate court*	*Decision and rationale of high or supreme court for retrial*
Ni Yulan v. Beijing Xicheng District Center for Public Housing and Land Management	2019 Beijing Beijing	4 NS	5	2 NN	2 NN	5
Ni Jinke v. Yuyao City Association for Science and Technology	2015 Yuyao Zhejiang	4 NS	5	2 NM NP NQ	2 NM NP NQ	5
Fu Wenrong v. State Grid Yiwu Electricity Supply Company	2016 Yiwu Zhejiang	4 NS	5	2 NB NN	2 NB NN	5
Liu Shuxiang v. Dalian City Emergency Medical Service	2019 Dalian Liaoning	4 NS	5	2 NP	2 NB NN NP	5
Shi Huifeng v. Zhejiang University	2019 Hangzhou Zhejiang	4 NS	5	2 NB NN	2 NB NN	5
Ye Lijuan v. Zhejiang Province Jiande City Notary Office	2018 Jiande Zhejiang	2 NJ NM NP NQ	5	2 NJ NM NP NQ	5	5
Song Qichen v. Shandong Province Tai'an City Daiyue Notary Office	2018 Tai'an Shandong	2 NJ	5	2 NM NP NQ	2 NM NP NQ	5

(continued)

Table 7.9 (continued)

Case citation	*Year/city and province of original jurisdiction*	*Decision and rationale of Chinese entities receiving OGI requests*	*Decision and rationale of oversight department for administrative reconsideration*	*Decision and rationale of primary or trial court*	*Decision and rationale of intermediate or appellate court*	*Decision and rationale of high or supreme court for retrial*
Tang Yanjun v. Beijing City Dongcheng District Center for Public Security and Forensic Science Services	2015 Beijing Beijing	4 NS	5	2 NJ NM NP NQ	5	5
Sun Longxiang v. Beijing Xingchuang Investment Company	2015 Beijing Beijing	4 NS	5	2 NM NP NQ	2 NB NN	5
Guangzhou Famous Store Management Company v. Guangdong Airport Authority	2016 Guangzhou Guangdong	4 NS	5	2 NB NM	2 NB NM	2 NB NN
Lujiang County Jufulou Restaurant v. China Mobile Lujiang Branch and China Mobile Anhui Branch	2019 Hefei Anhui	4 NS	5	2 NP NQ	2 NP NQ	5
Zhang Qiang v. South China University of Technology	2017 Guangzhou Guangdong	2 ND	5	2 NB NN	5	5
Zhang Jinzhu v. Beijing Shijingshan District Environmental Sanitation Service Center	2018 Beijing Beijing	4 NS	5	2 NB NJ	2 NB NJ	5
Xu Shanlang v. Nanjing Medical University	2020 Nanjing Jiangsu	2 NA	5	2 NB NJ NN	2 NB NJ NN	5

(continued)

Table 7.9 (continued)

Case citation	*Year/city and province of original jurisdiction*	*Decision and rationale of Chinese entities receiving OGI requests*	*Decision and rationale of oversight department for administrative reconsideration*	*Decision and rationale of primary or trial court*	*Decision and rationale of intermediate or appellate court*	*Decision and rationale of high or supreme court for retrial*
Xu Bin v. Tianjin Binhai New Area Xiangluowan Public Utilities Company	2015 Tianjin Tianjin	2 NH	5	2 NH NN	2 NB NN	2 NB NN
Dai Wei v. Ji'nan City Huaiyin District Housing Acquisition Service Center	2017 Ji'nan Shandong	4 NS	5	2 NM NP NQ	2 NM NP NQ	1 DB DK
Bai Yan v. National Education Examinations Authority	2018 Beijing Beijing	4 NS	2 NG NH	1 DA DK	2 NR	5
Zeng Lingxin v. China Telecom Yancheng Branch	2017 Yancheng Jiangsu	4 NS	5	2 NB	2 NB	5
Yang Xianhua v. China Telecom Changsha Branch	2018 Changsha Hunan	4 NS	5	2 NN	2 NJ	5
Li Junkun v. Zhejiang University	2017 Hangzhou Zhejiang	2 NB	5	2 NB NN	5	5
Li Shuanglin v. China Railway Beijing Group Company	2016 Beijing Beijing	4 NS	5	2 ND NJ	2 NB NN	5
Li Jinghai v. Wafangdian City Public Housing Management Office	2018 Zhuanghe Liaoning	4 NS	5	2 NB ND NJ NM	2 NM NP NQ	5

(continued)

Table 7.9 (continued)

Case citation	*Year/city and province of original jurisdiction*	*Decision and rationale of Chinese entities receiving OGI requests*	*Decision and rationale of oversight department for administrative reconsideration*	*Decision and rationale of primary or trial court*	*Decision and rationale of intermediate or appellate court*	*Decision and rationale of high or supreme court for retrial*
Li Xiuzhen v. Beijing Xuanfang Investment Management Group Company	2020 Beijing Beijing	2 NG	5	2 NM	2 NM	5
Yang Ou v. Suzhou Lawyers Association	2019 Suzhou Jiangsu	4 NS	5	2 NM NP NQ	2 NJ NM NP NQ	5
Tang Jinghua, et al. v. Fuzhou Land Development Center	2015 Fuzhou Fujian	4 NS	5	2 NI NM	5	5
Chen Ce and Chen Ruidi v. Wenzhou City Lucheng District Center for Urban Village Redevelopment	2020 Yueqing Zhejiang	4 NS	5	1 DB DK	2 NM NP NQ	5
Wen Hongjun and Fan Lingling v. Zhengzhou City Huiji District Financial Development Corporation	2020 Zhengzhou Henan	4 NS	5	2 NM NP NQ	2 NN NP NQ	5
Wang Guohai, Zhang Chunxiang and Wang Lin v. Hangzhou Land Banking Center	2015 Hangzhou Zhejiang	2 NG	5	2 NM NP NQ	5	5
Wang Jiaxin, et al. v. Qingdao-Ji'nan High-Speed Railway Company	2017 Ji'nan Shandong	4 NS	5	2 NM NP NQ	2 NM NP NQ	5

(continued)

Table 7.9 (continued)

Case citation	*Year/city and province of original jurisdiction*	*Decision and rationale of Chinese entities receiving OGI requests*	*Decision and rationale of oversight department for administrative reconsideration*	*Decision and rationale of primary or trial court*	*Decision and rationale of intermediate or appellate court*	*Decision and rationale of high or supreme court for retrial*
Wang Qiang v. Wenzhou Daily Media Group	2019 Wenzhou Zhejiang	4 NS	5	2 NB NJ NM	2 NN NP NQ	5
Wang Zhongxiang v. Tianjin Taida Cogeneration Company	2017 Tianjin Tianjin	2 NN	5	2 NN	2 NB NN	5
Wang Jiangli v. Beijing Xingchuang Investment Company	2015 Beijing Beijing	4 NS	5	2 NM NP NQ	2 NB NN	5
Wang Ronghua v. Feidong County No.4 People's Hospital	2020 Hefei Anhui	4 NS	5	2 NN	2 NJ NN	5
Wenda Kindergarten v. Heilongjiang Center for Disease Control and Prevention	2018 Harbin Heilongjiang	4 NS	5	2 NR	5	5
Hu Yukun v. Peking University	2018 Beijing Beijing	2 ND	5	2 ND	2 NB NJ NP NQ	5
Geng Liping v. Tangshan City Center for Municipal Engineering and Environmental Sanitation	2020 Tangshan Hebei	2 NN	5	2 NP	2 NP	5

(continued)

Table 7.9 (continued)

Case citation	*Year/city and province of original jurisdiction*	*Decision and rationale of Chinese entities receiving OGI requests*	*Decision and rationale of oversight department for administrative reconsideration*	*Decision and rationale of primary or trial court*	*Decision and rationale of intermediate or appellate court*	*Decision and rationale of high or supreme court for retrial*
Geng Chaochao v. Hangzhou Xiaoshan Environment Group Company	2020 Hangzhou Zhejiang	2 NJ	5	2 NJ NN	2 NN	5
Cai Xiaoming v. China Mobile Changsha Branch	2014 Changsha Hunan	4 NS	5	2 NP	5	5
Yuan Tie v. Capital Iron and Steel Corporation	2016 Beijing Beijing	4 NS	5	2 NM NP NQ	5	5
Gu Fengxiao v. Beijing Xingchuang Investment Company	2015 Beijing Beijing	4 NS	5	2 NM NP NQ	2 NB NN	5
Ma Li v. Fuwai Huazhong Cardiovascular Hospital	2020 Zhengzhou Henan	4 NS	5	2 NN	5	5
Gu Ming v. China Mobile Suqian Branch	2020 Suqian Jiangsu	4 NS	5	2 NN	2 NN	5
Wu Zaimei v. Pingxiang Hospital of Traditional Chinese Medicine	2017 Pingxiang Jiangxi	2 NL	5	2 NJ NM NQ	2 NJ NM NQ	5
Zheng Mingjie v. China Internet Network Information Center	2018 Beijing Beijing	4 NS	5	2 NM NP NQ	2 NM NP NQ	2 NM NP NQ

(continued)

Table 7.9 (continued)

Case citation	*Year/city and province of original jurisdiction*	*Decision and rationale of Chinese entities receiving OGI requests*	*Decision and rationale of oversight department for administrative reconsideration*	*Decision and rationale of primary or trial court*	*Decision and rationale of intermediate or appellate court*	*Decision and rationale of high or supreme court for retrial*
Guo Bing v. China State Railway Group Company	2018 Beijing Beijing	2 NJ	5	2 NN NP NQ	2 NN	2 NN
Guo Zheng v. Cangzhou Sports Management Center	2020 Cangzhou Hebei	4 NS	5	2 NP NQ	1 DB DK	5
Yang Shifeng v. Guangxi Working Fitness Assessment Committee	2019 Nanning Guangxi	4 NS	5	2 NP NQ	2 NM NP NQ	5
Chen Shiqing v. Gutian County Party School	2015 Ningde Fujian	4 NS	5	2 ND NP NQ	2 NJ NM NP NQ	5
Chen Shiqing v. Fujian Province Party School	2015 Fuzhou Fujian	4 NS	5	2 NP NQ	2 NP NQ	5
Chen Yuejun v. China United Network Communication Group	2015 Beijing Beijing	4 NS	5	2 NP	2 NB NN	5
Chen Hua v. Nanjing University of Information Science and Technology	2020 Nanjing Jiangsu	4 NS	5	2 NN	2 NJ NN NP	5

(continued)

Table 7.9 (continued)

Case citation	*Year/city and province of original jurisdiction*	*Decision and rationale of Chinese entities receiving OGI requests*	*Decision and rationale of oversight department for administrative reconsideration*	*Decision and rationale of primary or trial court*	*Decision and rationale of intermediate or appellate court*	*Decision and rationale of high or supreme court for retrial*
Chen Lin v. Jianghan University	2019 Wuhan Hubei	4 NS	5	2 NN NP NQ	2 NN NP NQ	2 NN NP NQ
Jia Youbao v. Beijing Mass Transit Railway Operation Corporation	2019 Beijing Beijing	4 NS	5	2 NM NP	2 NM NP	5
Jia Youbao v. Great Wall Broadband Network Service Corporation Qingdao Branch	2018 Qingdao Shandong	4 NS	5	2 NN	2 NN	5
Jia Youbao v. China Mobile Qingdao Branch	2017 Qingdao Shandong	4 NS	5	2 NN	2 NN	2 NN
Jia Youbao v. China United Network Communication Group Qingdao Branch	2017 Qingdao Shandong	4 NS	5	2 NB NN	2 NB NN	2 NB NN
Jia Youbao v. China United Network Communication Group Beijing Branch	2018 Beijing Beijing	4 NS	5	2 NB NN	2 NF	5
Jia Youbao v. Shandong Broadcast & TV Network Company	2017 Ji'nan Shandong	4 NS	5	2 NP	2 NP	2 NP
Jia Youbao v. Beijing Xianglong Bus Passenger Transport Company	2019 Beijing Beijing	4 NS	5	2 NM NP NQ	2 NM NP NQ	5

(continued)

Table 7.9 (continued)

Case citation	*Year/city and province of original jurisdiction*	*Decision and rationale of Chinese entities receiving OGI requests*	*Decision and rationale of oversight department for administrative reconsideration*	*Decision and rationale of primary or trial court*	*Decision and rationale of intermediate or appellate court*	*Decision and rationale of high or supreme court for retrial*
Jia Youbao v. Beijing Municipal Administration & Communication Car Company	2019 Beijing Beijing	4 NS	5	2 NM NP NQ	2 NF NL	5
Jia Youbao v. Beijing Xiaoju Technology Company	2018 Beijing Beijing	4 NS	5	2 NM	2 NM	2 NM
Jia Youbao v. Beijing Public Transport Corporation	2019 Beijing Beijing	2 NR	5	2 NR	5	5
Jia Youbao v. China State Railway Group Company	2018 Beijing Beijing	4 NS	5	2 NN	2 NN	2 NN
Jia Youbao v. China Postal Express & Logistics Corporation	2018 Beijing Beijing	4 NS	5	2 NN	2 NF NN	5
Wan Yun v. Jiangxi Provincial People's Government	2020 Nanchang Jiangxi	2 NG NH NL	5	2 NG NH NL	5	5
Ürümqi Haida Breeding Company v. Ürümqi City Tianshan District People's Government	2017 Ürümqi Xinjiang	2 NG NH	5	6 DC DK	5	5
Fu Tianxi, et al. v. Honghu Municipal People's Government	2018 Jingzhou Hubei	4 NH NL	5	6 DC DK	5	5

(continued)

Table 7.9 (continued)

Case citation	*Year/city and province of original jurisdiction*	*Decision and rationale of Chinese entities receiving OGI requests*	*Decision and rationale of oversight department for administrative reconsideration*	*Decision and rationale of primary or trial court*	*Decision and rationale of intermediate or appellate court*	*Decision and rationale of high or supreme court for retrial*
Dai Zongming v. Yichang Municipal People's Government and Hubei Provincial People's Government	2019 Yichang Hubei	2 NH NG	2 NH NG	2 NH NG	5	5
Ren Heguo v. Chongqing Municipal People's Government	2021 Chongqing Chongqing	2 NJ NL	5	2 NJ NL	5	5
Ren Yuanyuan v. Qingjian County People's Government	2019 Yulin Shaanxi	4 NL	5	1 DC DK	5	5
Wu Zhongren v. Zhijin County People's Government	2020 Bijie Guizhou	2 NJ	5	6 DC DK	5	5
He Gailan v. Xi'an Municipal People's Government and Shaanxi Provincial People's Government	2019 Xi'an Shaanxi	2 NA	2 NI	6 DK DL	5	5
He Yurui v. Nanyang City Wolong District People's Government	2021 Nanyang Henan	2 NE NG NL	5	1 DM	5	5
He Yufu v. Jilin City Fengman District People's Government	2018 Jilin Jilin	2 NA	5	1 DC DG DI	5	5

(continued)

Table 7.9 (continued)

Case citation	*Year/city and province of original jurisdiction*	*Decision and rationale of Chinese entities receiving OGI requests*	*Decision and rationale of oversight department for administrative reconsideration*	*Decision and rationale of primary or trial court*	*Decision and rationale of intermediate or appellate court*	*Decision and rationale of high or supreme court for retrial*
He Xiuqing, et al. v. Nanchong Municipal People's Government and Sichuan Provincial People's Government	2019 Nanchong Sichuan	2 NG NH NL	2 NG NH NL	2 NG NH NL	5	5
Gong Chengyuan v. Urumqi Municipal People's Government	2021 Urumqi Xinjiang	2 NI	5	2 NI	5	5
Long Derui v. Yunnan Province Baoshan Municipal People's Government and Yunnan Provincial People's Government	2021 Baoshan Yunnan	2 NH	2 NH	2 NH	5	5
Yu Yi v. Henan Province Zhengzhou City Erqi District People's Government	2016 Zhengzhou Henan	2 NI	5	2 NI	2 NI	6 DK
Yu Hongli v. Chongqing City Jiulongpo District People's Government	2018 Chongqing Chongqing	2 NB NJ	5	2 NB NJ	5	5
Huang Longyuan v. Zunyi County People's Government	2015 Zunyi Guizhou	2 NL	5	2 NL	2 NL	5
Dang Xiulan, et al. v. Liulin County People's Government	2020 Jinzhong Shanxi	2 NA NI	5	6 DC DL	5	5

(continued)

Table 7.9 (continued)

Case citation	*Year/city and province of original jurisdiction*	*Decision and rationale of Chinese entities receiving OGI requests*	*Decision and rationale of oversight department for administrative reconsideration*	*Decision and rationale of primary or trial court*	*Decision and rationale of intermediate or appellate court*	*Decision and rationale of high or supreme court for retrial*
Ran Shufang v. Fengjie County People's Government and Chongqing Municipal People's Government	2018 Chongqing Chongqing	2 NH	2 NS	2 NH	5	5
Feng Yongjun v. Shantai County Development and Reform Bureau	2020 Jiangyou Sichuan	3 DC NE	5	2 NE	2 NE	5
Feng Haijun v. Changsha City Wangcheng District People's Government and Changsha Municipal People's Government	2018 Changsha Hunan	1 DC DH	2 NL	2 NL	2 NL	5
Feng Ruiyang v. Zhongxiang Municipal People's Government	2018 Jingmen Hubei	3 DC NI NJ	5	3 DC DI DK	5	5
Liu Yun, et al. v. Anshan Municipal People's Government	2019 Anshan Liaoning	2 NH NL	5	2 NH NL	5	5
Liu Daiqiang v. Chongqing Municipal People's Government	2016 Chongqing Chongqing	3 DC DH NA ND NH	5	3 DC DH NA ND NH	3 DC DH DI	5
Liu Jiankun v. Emeishan Municipal People's Government	2020 Leshan Sichuan	4	5	1 DK	5	5

(continued)

Table 7.9 (continued)

Case citation	*Year/city and province of original jurisdiction*	*Decision and rationale of Chinese entities receiving OGI requests*	*Decision and rationale of oversight department for administrative reconsideration*	*Decision and rationale of primary or trial court*	*Decision and rationale of intermediate or appellate court*	*Decision and rationale of high or supreme court for retrial*
Liu Kaizhen v. Ministry of Natural Resources	2019 Beijing Beijing	2 NG	2 NG	1 DM	5	5
Huang Qunlin v. Miluo Municipal People's Government	2020 Yueyang Hunan	2 NH NI	5	2 NH NL	5	5
Liu Xian v. Shanghai City Hongkou District Bureau of Housing Security and Management	2019 Shanghai Shanghai	1 DC	5	1 DC	1 DC	5
Huang Yu v. Changsha Municipal People's Government	2014 Changsha Hunan	2 ND NJ	2 NS	2 NF NJ	1 DK	5
Liu Dejun v. Shifang Municipal People's Government	2017 Deyang Sichuan	2 NL	5	2 NL	6 DC DG	5
Liu Huiqing v. Dongtai Municipal People's Government	2020 Yancheng Jiangsu	2 NH	5	2 NH	5	5
Liu Xiaoyun v. Xinyu Municipal People's Government	2019 Nanchang Jiangxi	2 NH	5	2 NH	5	5
Liu Zhenghua v. Yanjin County People's Government and Zhaotong Municipal People's Government	2019 Zhaotong Yunnan	2 NL	2 NL	2 NL	5	5
Liu Xianguang v. Nanzhao County People's Government	2019 Nanyang Henan	2 NE	2 NS	2 NG		5

(continued)

Table 7.9 (continued)

Case citation	*Year/city and province of original jurisdiction*	*Decision and rationale of Chinese entities receiving OGI requests*	*Decision and rationale of oversight department for administrative reconsideration*	*Decision and rationale of primary or trial court*	*Decision and rationale of intermediate or appellate court*	*Decision and rationale of high or supreme court for retrial*
Liu Yuxin v. Harbin Municipal People's Government	2018 Daqing Heilongjiang	2 NL	5	6 NR	5	5
Liu Rongmei v. Yuan'an County People's Government	2018 Yichang Hubei	2 NI	5	2 NI	5	5
Liu Peng v. Shayang County People's Government	2018 Jingmen Hubei	2 NI	5	2 NB NH NJ	2 NB NI NL	2 NI NL
Nanjing Zhang Gangning Piano Manufacturing Company v. Nanjing City Yuhuatai District People's Government	2017 Nanjing Jiangsu	2 NH NI	5	6 DC DK	5	5
Nanjing Taishan Educational Service Management Company v. Nanjing Municipal People's Government	2020 Nanjing Jiangsu	2 NA	5	2 NA	5	5
Nan Zhongxi, et al. v. Huangling County People's Government and Yan'an Municipal People's Government	2018 Tongchuan Shaanxi	4	4	6	5	5
Lu Zhiming v. Yueyang City Yunxi District People's Government	2021 Yueyang Hunan	2 NG NI	5	2 NG	5	5

(continued)

Table 7.9 (continued)

Case citation	*Year/city and province of original jurisdiction*	*Decision and rationale of Chinese entities receiving OGI requests*	*Decision and rationale of oversight department for administrative reconsideration*	*Decision and rationale of primary or trial court*	*Decision and rationale of intermediate or appellate court*	*Decision and rationale of high or supreme court for retrial*
Huang Wanbi v. Chongqing City Ba'nan District People's Government	2019 Chongqing Chongqing	2 NH	5	2 NH	5	5
Wei Shaolin v. Henan Provincial People's Government	2017 Zhengzhou Henan	3 DC NH	3 DC NH	3 DC NH	5	5
Chen Fengjiao v. Xingyang Municipal People's Government	2018 Zhengzhou Henan	2 NI	5	2 NI	5	5
Lu Xiuzhen v. Hui'an County People's Government	2019 Xiamen Fujian	2 NG NI	5	1 DH	5	5
Shi Chunlin v. Yilan County People's Government	2021 Ha'erbin Heilongjiang	2 NA NG NI NJ	5	6 DF DG	5	5
Lv Yanqin v. Gaoyi County People's Government	2020 Shijiazhuang Hebei	2 NI	5	6 DH DK	5	5
Wu Yuankai v. Guizhou Provincial People's Government [	2019 Guiyang Guizhou	1 DM	1 DM	1 DM	5	5
Wu Hefa v. Qiannan Buyi and Miao Autonomous Prefecture People's Government	2019 Duyun Guizhou	2 NH	2 NH	2 NH	2 NH	5

(continued)

Table 7.9 (continued)

Case citation	*Year/city and province of original jurisdiction*	*Decision and rationale of Chinese entities receiving OGI requests*	*Decision and rationale of oversight department for administrative reconsideration*	*Decision and rationale of primary or trial court*	*Decision and rationale of intermediate or appellate court*	*Decision and rationale of high or supreme court for retrial*
Wu Sijuan, et al. v. Zhejiang Provincial People's Government	2020 Hangzhou Zhejiang	2 ND NG NI NL	5	2 ND NG NI NL	5	5
Wu Guoxing v. Kaili Municipal People's Government	2017 Kaili Guizhou	4	5	2 NL	2 NL	5
Wu Zhou v. Yancheng City Tinghu District People's Government and Yancheng Municipal People's Government	2020 Yancheng Jiangsu	2 NJ	2 NJ	2 NJ	5	5
Zhou Xin'ai v. Beijing Municipal People's Government	2018 Beijing Beijing	2 NH NL	2 NH NL	2 NH NI	5	5
Xia Guixian v. Jiangxi Provincial People's Government	2019 Nanchang Jiangxi	2 NE NH	5	2 NH	5	5
Xia Maogen v. Jiangxi Provincial People's Government	2019 Nanchang Jiangxi	2 NH NL	5	2 NH	5	5
Jiang Yuelin v. Shulan Municipal People's Government	2019 Jilin Jilin	2 NE NH NL	5	2 NF NL	5	5
Sun Lan v. Yancheng Municipal People's Government	2019 Yancheng Jiangsu	2 NI	5	2 NI	5	5

(continued)

Table 7.9 (continued)

Case citation	*Year/city and province of original jurisdiction*	*Decision and rationale of Chinese entities receiving OGI requests*	*Decision and rationale of oversight department for administrative reconsideration*	*Decision and rationale of primary or trial court*	*Decision and rationale of intermediate or appellate court*	*Decision and rationale of high or supreme court for retrial*
Sun Jinya v. Yancheng Municipal People's Government	2019 Yancheng Jiangsu	2 NH NI	5	2 NH NI	5	5
Song Kuihua v. Shenyang City Yuhong District People's Government	2018 Shenyang Liaoning	2 NF	5	1 DC DG DI	5	5
Ju Xianying, et al. v. Pei County People's Government	2019 Xuzhou Jiangsu	4 NI	5	6 DK	5	5
Cui Xunzhang v. Ji'nan City Huaiyin District People's Government	2017 Ji'nan Shandong	4	2 NO	2 NO	1 DB DD	5
Wu Yuda v. Ministry of Transport	2019 Beijing Beijing	2 NI	5	2 ND NI	5	5
Liao Xingguo v. Chongqing City Ba'nan District People's Government	2019 Chongqing Chongqing	2 NI	5	2 NI	5	5
Liao Haijun v. Anhua County People's Government and Yiyang Municipal People's Government	2019 Yiyang Hunan	2 NA NF NG NH NL	3 DN NS	2 NR	5	5
Zhang Yuangui v. Chongqing City Yongchuan District People's Government	2020 Chongqing Chongqing	3 DN NG	5	6 DL	5	5

(continued)

Table 7.9 (continued)

Case citation	*Year/city and province of original jurisdiction*	*Decision and rationale of Chinese entities receiving OGI requests*	*Decision and rationale of oversight department for administrative reconsideration*	*Decision and rationale of primary or trial court*	*Decision and rationale of intermediate or appellate court*	*Decision and rationale of high or supreme court for retrial*
Zhang Hua v. Hunan Provincial People's Government	2015 Changsha Hunan	2 NI	2 NS	2 NR	2 NI	5
Zhang Jiying v. Tianjin City Xiqing District People's Government	2018 Tianjin Tianjin	2 NG NH	5	2 NG NH	5	5
Zhang Yuxiang v. Changsha City Yuelu District People's Government and Changsha Municipal People's Government	2015 Changsha Hunan	2 NH	2 NH	2 NH	6 DC DH	5
Zhang Zongqing v. Tianjin City Xiqing District People's Government	2018 Tianjin Tianjin	2 NH	5	2 NH	5	5
Zhang Zhiyun v. Jiangsu Province Department of Natural Resources and Jiangsu Provincial People's Government	2020 Nanjing Jiangsu	3 DN NG NH	2 NS	2 NG NH	5	5
Zhang Zhihua v. Shifang Municipal People's Government	2017 Deyang Sichuan	2 NL	5	2 NL	6 DG DK	5
Zhang Shuanjun v. Mianchi County People's Government	2018 Sanmenxia Henan	2 NH	5	2 NH	5	5
Zhang Zheng v. Mian County People's Government	2018 Hanzhong Shaanxi	4	5	6 DC DK	5	5

(continued)

Table 7.9 (continued)

Case citation	*Year/city and province of original jurisdiction*	*Decision and rationale of Chinese entities receiving OGI requests*	*Decision and rationale of oversight department for administrative reconsideration*	*Decision and rationale of primary or trial court*	*Decision and rationale of intermediate or appellate court*	*Decision and rationale of high or supreme court for retrial*
Zhang Xujiang v. Hanzhong City Nanzheng District People's Government	2021 Hanzhong Shaanxi	4	5	6 DC DK	5	5
Zhang Mingwang v. Guangshan County People's Government	2020 Xinyang Henan	2 NA NE NH NL	5	6 DC DK	5	5
Zhang Meixiang v. Haiyang Municipal People's Government	2019 Yantai Shandong	2 NE NH	5	7 DC DK	5	5
Zhang Xiuchun v. Mianyang City Anzhou District People's Government and Mianyang Municipal People's Government	2017 Mianyang Sichuan	2 NJ NH	2 NJ NH	2 NJ NH	5	5
Zhang Weiyan v. Liaoyuan Municipal People's Government	2019 Liaoyuan Jilin	4	5	2 NE NL	5	5
Peng Yihe v. Guiyang Municipal People's Government and Guizhou Provincial People's Government	2020 Guiyang Guizhou	2 NH	2 NH	2 NH	5	5
Xu Xianliu, et al. v. Taizhou City Gaogang District People's Government	2021 Taizhou Jiangsu	2 NG	5	2 NG NH	5	5

(continued)

Table 7.9 (continued)

Case citation	*Year/city and province of original jurisdiction*	*Decision and rationale of Chinese entities receiving OGI requests*	*Decision and rationale of oversight department for administrative reconsideration*	*Decision and rationale of primary or trial court*	*Decision and rationale of intermediate or appellate court*	*Decision and rationale of high or supreme court for retrial*
Xu Guangyue v. Chongqing City Nan'an District People's Government	2019 Chongqing Chongqing	2 NJ	5	6 DH	5	5
Xu Jiaxiu v. Guiyang Municipal People's Government	2016 Guizhou Guiyang	4	6	2 NH	2 NH	5
Xu Gen v. Chongqing City Jiulongpo District People's Government	2020 Chongqing Chongqing	2 NF NH NI NL	5	2 NH	5	5
Xu Zehui v. Yuan'an County People's Government	2019 Yichang Hubei	2 NF NH	5	2 NF NH	5	5
Xu Hongyuan v. Chengdu City Shuangliu District People's Government and Chengdu Municipal People's Government	2015 Chengdu Sichuan	2 NH	2 NH	2 NH	2 NH	5
Xu Yunxiang v. Xuchang Municipal People's Government	2020 Xuchang Henan	2 NH	6	6	5	5
Cheng Xinwu v. Xuyong County People's Government	2020 Luzhou Sichuan	4	6	6	5	5
Liu Qinfeng and Yao Baohua v. Changzhou City Zhonglou District People's Government	2017 Changzhou Jiangsu	2 NI NJ	5	2 NH	5	5

(continued)

Table 7.9 (continued)

Case citation	*Year/city and province of original jurisdiction*	*Decision and rationale of Chinese entities receiving OGI requests*	*Decision and rationale of oversight department for administrative reconsideration*	*Decision and rationale of primary or trial court*	*Decision and rationale of intermediate or appellate court*	*Decision and rationale of high or supreme court for retrial*
Qi De'an v. Xi'an City Baqiao District People's Government	2020 Xi'an Shaanxi	2 NS	5	6	5	5
Fang Wei v. Wuchang Municipal People's Government	2018 Harbin Heilongjiang	4 NL	5	6	5	5
Li Juan v. Anshan Municipal People's Government	2020 Anshan Liaoning	2 NH	5	2 NH	5	5
Fang Shumei v. Yantai City Fushan District People's Government	2019 Yantai Shandong	2 NL	5	7	5	5
Wen Hao, et al. v. Sanya Municipal People's Government	2020 Haikou Hainan	2 NH	5	1 DC DH DK	5	5
Fang Yuzhen v. Yichang Municipal People's Government	2019 Yichang Hubei	2 NJ	5	2 NJ	5	5
Li Guoli v. Tangshan Municipal People's Government	2019 Tangshan Hebei	4	6	2 NG	5	5
Ming Jing and Lin Ming v. Chongqing Municipal People's Government	2019 Chongqing Chongqing	2 NH	5	2 NH	5	5
Zhu Yuangang v. Guangyuan City Lizhou District People's Government	2017 Guangyuan Sichuan	2 NI NH NL	5	6	5	5

(continued)

Table 7.9 (continued)

Case citation	*Year/city and province of original jurisdiction*	*Decision and rationale of Chinese entities receiving OGI requests*	*Decision and rationale of oversight department for administrative reconsideration*	*Decision and rationale of primary or trial court*	*Decision and rationale of intermediate or appellate court*	*Decision and rationale of high or supreme court for retrial*
Li Sihua v. Jiangxi Provincial People's Government	2019 Nanchang Jiangxi	2 NH	5	2 NH	5	5
Li Yuzhen v. Guizhou Provincial People's Government	2019 Guiyang Guizhou	3 NE	2 NE	2 NE	5	5
Li Kunming v. Chongqing City Ba'nan District People's Government	2020 Chongqing Chongqing	2 NH	5	2 NH	5	5
Li Fengping v. Mohe Municipal People's Government	2021 Daxing'anling Prefecture Heilongjiang	4	5	6	5	5
Yang Zaiyun v. Guizhou Provincial People's Government	2019 Guiyang Guizhou	3 NE	2 NE	2 NE	5	5
Li Wenwen v. Guizhou Provincial People's Government	2018 Guiyang Guizhou	2 NL NH	2 NL NH	2 NL NH	5	5
Hu Zhengli v. Guizhou Provincial People's Government	2019 Guiyang Guizhou	3 NE	2 NE	2 NE	5	5
Yang Dezhi v. Guizhou Provincial People's Government	2019 Guiyang Guizhou	3 NE	2 NE	2 NE	5	5
Yang Maohe v. Guizhou Provincial People's Government	2019 Guiyang Guizhou	3 NE	2 NE	2 NE	5	5

(continued)

Table 7.9 (continued)

Case citation	*Year/city and province of original jurisdiction*	*Decision and rationale of Chinese entities receiving OGI requests*	*Decision and rationale of oversight department for administrative reconsideration*	*Decision and rationale of primary or trial court*	*Decision and rationale of intermediate or appellate court*	*Decision and rationale of high or supreme court for retrial*
Yang Enwen v. Guizhou Provincial People's Government	2018 Guiyang Guizhou	2 NG	2 NG	2 NG	5	5
Yang Chaogui v. Guizhou Provincial People's Government	2019 Guiyang Guizhou	3 NE	2 NE	2 NE	5	5
Wei Mingxian v. Guizhou Provincial People's Government	2019 Guiyang Guizhou	7	7	7	5	5
Wang Zuyu v. Guizhou Provincial People's Government	2017 Guiyang Guizhou	2 NH	5	2 NH	5	5
Shi Weiyue v. Guizhou Provincial People's Government	2018 Guiyang Guizhou	2 NG	2 NG	2 NG	5	5
Mo Congxiang v. Guizhou Provincial People's Government	2019 Guiyang Guizhou	3 NE	2 NE	2 NE	5	5
Luo Jinju v. Guizhou Provincial People's Government	2019 Guiyang Guizhou	3 NE	2 NE	2 NE	5	5
Han Linghua v. Xuchang Municipal People's Government	2020 Xuchang Henan	2 NH	2 NH	6	5	5
Zeng Xianru v. Xinjiang Uygur Autonomous Region People's Government	2019 Urumqi Xinjiang	2 NH	5	2 NH NL	5	5

(continued)

Table 7.9 (continued)

Case citation	*Year/city and province of original jurisdiction*	*Decision and rationale of Chinese entities receiving OGI requests*	*Decision and rationale of oversight department for administrative reconsideration*	*Decision and rationale of primary or trial court*	*Decision and rationale of intermediate or appellate court*	*Decision and rationale of high or supreme court for retrial*
Wang Ran v. Beijing Municipal People's Government	2018 Beijing Beijing	2 ND	2 ND	2 ND	5	5
Gao Fuyun and Yun Zhonghe v. Inner Mongolia Autonomous Region People's Government	2018 Hohhot Inner Mongolia Autonomous Region	2 NH	5	2 NH	5	5
Yan Weiguo v. Shandong Provincial People's Government	2019 Ji'nan Shandong	2 NJ	2 NJ	2 NJ	5	5
Hu Zhengqun v. Guizhou Provincial People's Government	2019 Guiyang Guizhou	3 NE	2 NE	2 NE	5	5
Luo Zhongjing v. Guizhou Provincial People's Government	2018 Guiyang Guizhou	2 NG NH	5	2 NG NH	5	5
Guo Zijun, et al. v. Shandong Provincial People's Government	2016 Ji'nan Shandong	2 NH	5	2 NH	6	5
Bai Jintao v. Shanxi Provincial People's Government	2016 Taiyuan Shanxi	2 NH	5	2 NH	2 NF	5
Luo Shuqiang and Luo Shuli v. Hebei Provincial People's Government	2019 Shijiazhuang Hebei	2 NG	5	2 NG	5	5
Xu Zhuoyun v. Jiangxi Provincial People's Government	2018 Nanchang Jiangxi	2 NG	5	2 NG	5	5

(continued)

Table 7.9 (continued)

Case citation	*Year/city and province of original jurisdiction*	*Decision and rationale of Chinese entities receiving OGI requests*	*Decision and rationale of oversight department for administrative reconsideration*	*Decision and rationale of primary or trial court*	*Decision and rationale of intermediate or appellate court*	*Decision and rationale of high or supreme court for retrial*
Xu Zhuoyun v. Nanchang Municipal People's Government	2019 Nanchang Jiangxi	2 NH NI	5	2 NH NI	5	5
Gao Yongchen v. Tangshan Municipal People's Government	2018 Tangshan Hebei	2 NG	5	2 NG	5	5
Gu Hongru v. Wen County People's Government	2019 Jiaozuo Henan	2 NJ	5	2 NI	5	5
Lei Yingsu v. Chongqing Municipal People's Government	2018 Chongqing Chongqing	2 NH	5	2 NH	5	5
Fang Hong v. Nan'ning City Qingxiu District People's Government	2017 Nan'ning Guangxi	2 NG	2 NG	2 NG	5	5
Zheng Junhai v. Pingdingshan Municipal People's Government	2018 Luohe Henan	2 NI	5	6	5	5
Li Sihua v. Xinyu Municipal People's Government	2019 Nanchang Jiangxi	2 NH	5	2 NH	5	5
Kuang Tianfang v. Suining Municipal People's Government	2018 Suining Sichuan	1 DN	5	2 NH	5	5
Chao Chunfu v. Tianjin City Baodi District People's Government	2019 Tianjin Tianjin	2 NH NG	5	2 NH NG	5	5

(continued)

Table 7.9 (continued)

Case citation	*Year/city and province of original jurisdiction*	*Decision and rationale of Chinese entities receiving OGI requests*	*Decision and rationale of oversight department for administrative reconsideration*	*Decision and rationale of primary or trial court*	*Decision and rationale of intermediate or appellate court*	*Decision and rationale of high or supreme court for retrial*
Ju Hongqin v. Weihai Municipal People's Government	2017 Weihai Shandong	2 NI	5	2 NI	5	5
Li Zhongmin v. Xinhua County People's Government	2019 Loudi Hunan	4	5	6	5	5
Li Wuguo v. Linxiang Municipal People's Government	2020 Yueyang Hunan	2 NF NL	5	2 NA NL	5	5
Lei Xiangda v. Shuicheng County People's Government	2018 Liupanshui Guizhou	2 NG	1 DN	6	5	5
Pan Jun v. Yichang Municipal People's Government	2017 Yichang Hubei	2 NR	2 NR	2 NR	5	5
Du Yongzhong v. Wensu County People's Government	2021 Aksu Xinjiang	2 NH	5	1 DC DK	5	5
Yang Yaquan v. Wuchuan Municipal People's Government	2018 Zhanjiang Guangdong	4	5	6	5	5
Li Xueyu v. Guiyang County People's Government	2020 Chenzhou Hunan	4	5	1 DK	5	5
Yang Guoan v. Xiangcheng Municipal People's Government	2018 Zhoukou Henan	4	5	1 DK	5	5

(continued)

Table 7.9 (continued)

Case citation	*Year/city and province of original jurisdiction*	*Decision and rationale of Chinese entities receiving OGI requests*	*Decision and rationale of oversight department for administrative reconsideration*	*Decision and rationale of primary or trial court*	*Decision and rationale of intermediate or appellate court*	*Decision and rationale of high or supreme court for retrial*
Hu Weijuan v. Jiangxi Provincial People's Government	2018 Nanchang Jiangxi	2 ND NL	5	2 ND NL	5	5
Chen Xinrong v. Ningdu County People's Government	2020 Ganzhou Jiangxi	4	5	2 NH	5	5
Guo Meirong v. Xuchang Municipal People's Government	2020 Xuchang Henan	2 NH	5	6	5	5
Yang Lianzhao v. Wuyang County People's Government	2019 Luohe Henan	4	5	6	5	5
Yang Xiaochun v. Dongtai Municipal People's Government	2019 Yancheng Jiangsu	2 NG	2 NG	2 NH	5	5
Li You v. Chongqing City Ba'nan District People's Government	2020 Chongqing Chongqing	2 NG	5	2 NG	5	5
Zheng Guoyong v. Longyan Municipal People's Government	2017 Sanming Fujian	2 NH	5	2 NH NI	5	5
Li Ruiling v. Xingyang Municipal People's Government	2020 Zhengzhou Henan	2 NI	5	2 NI	5	5
Xie Meimei v. Guiyang Municipal People's Government	2016 Guiyang Guizhou	2 NH	5	2 NH	2 NH	5

(continued)

Table 7.9 (continued)

Case citation	*Year/city and province of original jurisdiction*	*Decision and rationale of Chinese entities receiving OGI requests*	*Decision and rationale of oversight department for administrative reconsideration*	*Decision and rationale of primary or trial court*	*Decision and rationale of intermediate or appellate court*	*Decision and rationale of high or supreme court for retrial*
Xie Qing v. Guiyang Municipal People's Government	2016 Guiyang Guizhou	2 NH	5	2 NH	2 NH	5
Li Weiping v. Chongqing City Yongchuan District People's Government	2019 Chongqing Chongqing	2 NI	5	2 NI	5	5
Dong Jianshe v. Qingzhou Municipal People's Government	2019 Weifang Shandong	2 NH	5	6	5	5
Li Shuai v. Tianjin City Xiqing District People's Government	2018 Tianjin Tianjin	2 NH	5	2 NH	5	5
Wang Leying v. Yichang Municipal People's Government	2019 Yichang Hubei	2 NJ	5	2 NJ	5	5
Gui Kangjie v. Hubei Province Xiaochang County People's Government	2019 Xiaogan Hubei	2 NH	5	2 NH	5	5
Jia Longzhou v. Xi'an City Lintong District People's Government	2018 Xi'an Shaanxi	2 NH	5	6	5	5
Chen Jiafa, et al. v. Dafang County People's Government	2018 Bijie Guizhou	4	5	6	5	5
Xie Zhaohui v. Chongqing Municipal People's Government	2020 Chongqing Chongqing	2 NG	5	2 NG	5	5

(continued)

Table 7.9 (continued)

Case citation	*Year/city and province of original jurisdiction*	*Decision and rationale of Chinese entities receiving OGI requests*	*Decision and rationale of oversight department for administrative reconsideration*	*Decision and rationale of primary or trial court*	*Decision and rationale of intermediate or appellate court*	*Decision and rationale of high or supreme court for retrial*
Lin Ming v. Chongqing City Ba'nan District People's Government	2019 Chongqing Chongqing	1 DC DH	5	2 NL	5	5
Wang Juan v. Xi'an Municipal People's Government	2020 Xi'an Shaanxi	2 NG	5	6	5	5
Pan Xiaoling v. Tonglu County People's Government	2019 Hangzhou Zhejiang	2 NH	6	6	5	5
Qin Dayou v. Jianshi County People's Government	2019 Enshi Hubei	4	5	2 NL	5	5
Ma Junling v. Harbin City Hulan District People's Government	2020 Harbin Heilongjiang	1 DN	5	2 NG	5	5
Han Xiangjun, et al. v. Gushi County People's Government	2020 Xinyang Henan	2 NG NJ	2 NG NJ	2 NG NJ	5	5
Huo Weidi v. Jimsar County People's Government	2021 Changji Xinjiang	3 DN NS	5	1 DC DG DH	5	5
Xie Rujing, et al. v. Zhuhai City Jinwan District People's Government	2018 Zhuhai Guangdong	2 NH NL	5	2 NH NL	5	5
Wang Yongjie v. Zhengzhou City Zhongyuan District People's Government	2019 Zhengzhou Henan	2 NH	5	2 NE NG NH	5	5

(continued)

Table 7.9 (continued)

Case citation	*Year/city and province of original jurisdiction*	*Decision and rationale of Chinese entities receiving OGI requests*	*Decision and rationale of oversight department for administrative reconsideration*	*Decision and rationale of primary or trial court*	*Decision and rationale of intermediate or appellate court*	*Decision and rationale of high or supreme court for retrial*
Cheng Ansheng v. Shenqiu County People's Government	2019 Zhoukou Henan	4	5	6	5	5
Jiang Xinqiao v. Mohe Municipal People's Government	2018 Mohe Heilongjiang	2 NH	5	3 DC DG NG NH	5	5
Wang Daohong v. Hefei City Shushan District People's Government	2018 Hefei Anhui	2 NH	5	6	5	5
Wang Xinmei v. Yueyang Municipal People's Government	2020 Yueyang Hunan	2 NH	5	2 NH	5	5
Chen Qiyu v. Shangrao County People's Government and Shangrao Municipal People's Government	2018 Shangrao Jiangxi	2 NH	2 NH	6	5	5
Niu Congquan v. Zhengzhou City Zhongyuan District People's Government	2019 Zhengzhou Henan	2 NH	5	2 NE NH NL	6	5
Zhu Yanli v. Tenchong Municipal People's Government and Baoshan Municipal People's Government	2019 Baoshan Yunnan	2 ND NE NH NJ	2 ND NE	2 ND NE NH	5	5

(continued)

Table 7.9 (continued)

Case citation	*Year/city and province of original jurisdiction*	*Decision and rationale of Chinese entities receiving OGI requests*	*Decision and rationale of oversight department for administrative reconsideration*	*Decision and rationale of primary or trial court*	*Decision and rationale of intermediate or appellate court*	*Decision and rationale of high or supreme court for retrial*
Wang Shicui v. Duyun Municipal People's Government	2018 Duyun Guizhou	4	5	6	5	5
Chen Zhenbang v. Changsha City Furong District People's Government	2016 Changsha Hunan	2 NH NL	5	2 NH NL	1 DI DK	5
Lin Lan v. Chengdu City Jinjiang District People's Government	2015 Chengdu Sichuan	2 NG NH NL	5	2 NG NH NL	2 NG NH NL	5
Geng Jiafeng v. Huantai County People's Government	2018 Zibo Shandong	2 NH	5	6 DH	2 NS	2 NH
Ruan Chengjun v. Fenggang County People's Government and Zunyi Municipal People's Government	2019 Zunyi Guizhou	3 NH	2 NH	6	5	5
Luo Sujun v. Zhengzhou City Guancheng Hui Ethnicity District People's Government	2020 Zhengzhou Henan	2 NH	5	2 NH	5	5
Wang Shuhua v. Zunhua Municipal People's Government	2020 Tangshan Hebei	2 NL	5	6	5	5
Xiao Xianhuai, et al. v. Shangyou County People's Government	2019 Ganzhou Jiangxi	4	1	2 NL	5	5

(continued)

Table 7.9 (continued)

Case citation	*Year/city and province of original jurisdiction*	*Decision and rationale of Chinese entities receiving OGI requests*	*Decision and rationale of oversight department for administrative reconsideration*	*Decision and rationale of primary or trial court*	*Decision and rationale of intermediate or appellate court*	*Decision and rationale of high or supreme court for retrial*
Tian Ning v. Xi'an City Weiyang District People's Government	2018 Xi'an Shaanxi	2 NJ	5	6	5	5
Shen Fengqing v. Yangzhou Municipal Health Commission	2017 Yangzhou Jiangsu	4	5	2 ND	2 ND	2 ND
Wang Xiang and Li Liqiong v. Maguan County People's Government	2019 Maguan Yunnan	4	5	1 DG	5	5
Fan Qigang v. Haining Municipal People's Government	2020 Jiaxing Zhejiang	3 NH	5	2 NH	5	5
Wang Yan and Hu Jianying v. Anyue County People's Government	2018 Ziyang Sichuan	2 NH	5	1 DG	5	5
Bai Guangming v. Urumqi City Saybagh District People's Government	2018 Urumqi Xinjiang	4	5	6	5	5
Li Buyun v. Yancheng City Tinghu District People's Government and Yancheng Municipal People's Government	2020 Yancheng Jiangsu	2 ND	2 ND	2 ND	5	5
Tao Wei v. Fu'ning County People's Government and Yancheng Municipal People's Government	2020 Yancheng Jiangsu	2 NH	2 NH	2 NH	5	5

(continued)

Table 7.9 (continued)

Case citation	*Year/city and province of original jurisdiction*	*Decision and rationale of Chinese entities receiving OGI requests*	*Decision and rationale of oversight department for administrative reconsideration*	*Decision and rationale of primary or trial court*	*Decision and rationale of intermediate or appellate court*	*Decision and rationale of high or supreme court for retrial*
Wang Qingning v. Xianning Municipal People's Government and Hubei Provincial People's Government	2020 Xianning Hubei	4	6	2 NL	5	5
Tian Xiaohua and Luo Mingfang v. Anyue County People's Government and Ziyang Municipal People's Government	2018 Ziyang Sichuan	2 NG	2 NG	2 NR	5	5
Yang Jinzhu v. Yancheng Municipal People's Government and Jiangsu Provincial People's Government	2020 Yancheng Jiangsu	2 NL	2 NL	2 NL	5	5
Yang Jinzhu v. Wuxi City Liangxi District People's Government and Wuxi Municipal People's Government	2020 Wuxi Jiangsu	2 NG	2 NG	2 NG	5	5
Mao Zhifan v. Changchun City Kuancheng District People's Government and Changchun Municipal People's Government	2020 Changchun Jilin	2 NG	2 NG	2 NG	5	5

(continued)

Table 7.9 (continued)

Case citation	*Year/city and province of original jurisdiction*	*Decision and rationale of Chinese entities receiving OGI requests*	*Decision and rationale of oversight department for administrative reconsideration*	*Decision and rationale of primary or trial court*	*Decision and rationale of intermediate or appellate court*	*Decision and rationale of high or supreme court for retrial*
Zhu Pingguo v. Yichang City Xiling District People's Government and Yichang Municipal People's Government	2020 Yichang Hubei	2 NH	2 NH	2 NH	5	5
Li Mingbo v. Nanjing City Jiang Bei New District Taxation Department, Jiangsu Provincial Tax Service, State Taxation Administration	2019 Nanjing Jiangsu	4 NJ	5	6	5	5
Ou Hongyu and Li Fei v. Xichong County People's Government	2019 Nanchong Sichuan	4 NJ	5	2 NJ	5	5
Mei Guiying v. Changzhou Municipal People's Government and Jiangsu Provincial People's Government	2020 Nanjing Jiangsu	2 NG	2 NG	2 NG	5	5
Chen Huagang v. Yichang City Xiling District People's Government and Yichang Municipal People's Government	2020 Yichang Hubei	2 NH NI	2 NH NI NJ	2 NH NI NJ	5	5
Zhao Shuiyun and Shi Pengwen v. Quwo County People's Government and Linfen Municipal People's Government	2018 Yuncheng Shanxi	2 ND NH	2 ND NH	6	5	5

(continued)

Table 7.9 (continued)

Case citation	*Year/city and province of original jurisdiction*	*Decision and rationale of Chinese entities receiving OGI requests*	*Decision and rationale of oversight department for administrative reconsideration*	*Decision and rationale of primary or trial court*	*Decision and rationale of intermediate or appellate court*	*Decision and rationale of high or supreme court for retrial*
Chen Yudan v. Shanghai City Chongming District Urban Planning and Natural Resources Bureau	2019 Shanghai Shanghai	2 NI	5	2 NI	2 NI	5
Xie Zhi v. Guiyang Municipal People's Government	2016 Guiyang Guizhou	2 NH	5	2 NH	2 NH	5
Wu Baoshan v. Yongqing County People's Government	2018 Yongqing Hebei	2 NH	5	2 NH	2 NH	5
Wang Yonghua v. Tianquan County People's Government	2017 Ya'an Sichuan	2 NH	5	2 NH	2 NH	5
Jin Min v. Xingyi Municipal People's Government	2019 Xingyi Guizhou	2 NA ND	5	2 ND	2 ND	5
Li Xiaoxia v. Hukou County Public Security Bureau	2020 Jiujiang Jiangxi	2 NA NG	5	2 NA NG	2 NA NG	5
Li Hong v. Zhengzhou City Zhongyuan District People's Government	2015 Zhengzhou Henan	2 NH NK	5	2 NK	1 DH DK	5
Wang Qingdou, et al. v. Weng'an County People's Government	2018 Duyun Guizhou	2 NG	6	2 ND	1 DI	5
Pan Gangju v. Guizhou Provincial Department of Natural Resources	2019 Guiyang Guizhou	2 NH	2 NH	2 NH	2 NH	5

(continued)

Table 7.9 (continued)

Case citation	*Year/city and province of original jurisdiction*	*Decision and rationale of Chinese entities receiving OGI requests*	*Decision and rationale of oversight department for administrative reconsideration*	*Decision and rationale of primary or trial court*	*Decision and rationale of intermediate or appellate court*	*Decision and rationale of high or supreme court for retrial*
Zeng Huiyuan v. Guiyang City Yunyan District People's Government	2016 Guiyang Guizhou	2 NH	5	6	2 NH	5
Zhong Jiazi v. Jiangsu Provincial Department of Civil Affairs and Ministry of Civil Affairs	2020 Nanjing Jiangsu	3 NG NL	2 NG NL	2 NG NL	5	5
Jiangsu Yongda Pharmaceutical Company v. Yancheng Municipal People's Government	2019 Yancheng Jiangsu	1	5	2 NL	5	5
Jiangxi Haojing Rice Industry Limited Company v. Suichuan County People's Government and Ji'an Municipal People's Government	2018 Ji'an Jiangxi	2 NF	2 NF	2 NF	5	5
Yu Ping v. Nanjing City Liuhe District People's Government and Nanjing Municipal People's Government	2020 Nanjing Jiangsu	2 NG NH	2 NG NH	2 NG NH	5	5
Wang Huizhong v. Dongtai Municipal People's Government and Yancheng Municipal People's Government	2019 Yancheng Jiangsu	2 NI	2 NI	2 NI	5	5

(continued)

Table 7.9 (continued)

Case citation	*Year/city and province of original jurisdiction*	*Decision and rationale of Chinese entities receiving OGI requests*	*Decision and rationale of oversight department for administrative reconsideration*	*Decision and rationale of primary or trial court*	*Decision and rationale of intermediate or appellate court*	*Decision and rationale of high or supreme court for retrial*
Zhao Fuqian and Zhao Longsheng v. Xiuwen County People's Government	2014 Guiyang Guizhou	2 NA NH	5	2 NA NH	2 NA NH	5
Yan Qiaoying v. Taiyuan Municipal People's Government	2016 Yangquan Shaanxi	4	4	6	6	5
Bai Yan v. Gansu Provincial Department of Public Security and Gansu Provincial People's Government	2019 Lanzhou Gansu	3 NH	2 NH	2 NH	2 NH	5
Chen Jianguo, et al. v. Fuzhou City Jin'an District People's Government and Fuzhou Municipal People's Government	2015 Fuzhou Fujian	2 NG NH	2 NG NH	2 NG NH	2 NG NH	5
Zheng Wangjie v. Xinzheng Municipal People's Government	2016 Zhengzhou Henan	2 NH	5	6	6	5
Xie Changlin v. Guiyang Municipal People's Government	2016 Guiyang Guizhou	2 NH	5	2 NH	2 NH	5
Pu Qingrong v. Chengdu City Wuhou District Municipal People's Government	2018 Chengdu Sichuan	2 NG	2 NG	2 NG	2 NG	5

(continued)

Table 7.9 (continued)

Case citation	*Year/city and province of original jurisdiction*	*Decision and rationale of Chinese entities receiving OGI requests*	*Decision and rationale of oversight department for administrative reconsideration*	*Decision and rationale of primary or trial court*	*Decision and rationale of intermediate or appellate court*	*Decision and rationale of high or supreme court for retrial*
Mo Congxiang v. Qiannan Buyi and Miao Autonomous Prefecture Municipal People's Government	2019 Duyun Guizhou	2 NH	2 NH	2 NH	2 NH	5
Nie Cheng'an v. Chuxiong Municipal People's Government	2016 Chuxiong Yunnan	4	5	6	6	5
Zhu Yanli v. Tengchong Municipal Public Security Bureau	2019 Tengchong Yunnan	2 ND NL	2 ND NL	2 ND NL	2 ND NL	5
Li Yunping v. Kunming City Xishan District People's Government	2015 Kunming Yunnan	3 NG	5	6	6	5
Li Yuzhen v. Qiannan Buyi and Miao Autonomous Prefecture Municipal People's Government	2019 Duyun Guizhou	2 NH	2 NH	2 NH	2 NH	5
Yang Dezhi v. Qiannan Buyi and Miao Autonomous Prefecture Municipal People's Government	2019 Duyun Guizhou	2 NH	2 NH	2 NH	2 NH	5
Yang Dehai v. Qiannan Buyi and Miao Autonomous Prefecture Municipal People's Government	2019 Duyun Guizhou	2 NH	2 NH	2 NH	2 NH	5

(continued)

Table 7.9 (continued)

Case citation	*Year/city and province of original jurisdiction*	*Decision and rationale of Chinese entities receiving OGI requests*	*Decision and rationale of oversight department for administrative reconsideration*	*Decision and rationale of primary or trial court*	*Decision and rationale of intermediate or appellate court*	*Decision and rationale of high or supreme court for retrial*
Yang Jun v. Tu Autonomous County of Huzhu People's Government	2020 Haidong Qinghai	2 NF NH NL	5	2 NA NF NH NL	1 DC DG DK DL	5
Li Suzhen, et al. v. Henan Province Luoyang Municipal People's Government	2017 Luoyang Henan	2 NH	2 NH	2 NH	1 DC DH	1 DC DH
Ding Shujuan v. Nanchang City Xihu District People's Government	2015 Nanchang Jiangxi	2 NL	5	2 NL	2 NL	5
Shanghai Tairui Property Development Corporation v. Shanghai City Jing'an District People's Government and Shanghai Municipal People's Government	2017 Shanghai Shanghai	2 NI	2 NI	2 NE NI	5	5
CITIC Land Corporation v. Shangli County Bureau of Natural Resources and Planning	2020 Pingxiang Jiangxi	3 NS	5	2 NI	5	5
Wulian County Bus Company v. Wulian County People's Government	2020 Rizhao Shandong	2 NS	5	2 NR	5	5
Fu Ailian v. Beijing Municipal Commission of Planning and Natural Resources	2020 Tongzhou Beijing	2 NG	5	2 NJ	5	5

(continued)

Table 7.9 (continued)

Case citation	*Year/city and province of original jurisdiction*	*Decision and rationale of Chinese entities receiving OGI requests*	*Decision and rationale of oversight department for administrative reconsideration*	*Decision and rationale of primary or trial court*	*Decision and rationale of intermediate or appellate court*	*Decision and rationale of high or supreme court for retrial*
He Dan v. Ningxia Hui Autonomous Region Health and Family Planning Commission	2018 Yinchuan Ningxia	4	5	2 NI	5	5
Tong Lihui v. Development and Reform Commission of Hunan Province	2019 Changsha Hunan	2 NI	5	2 NI	5	5
Fu Shuqing v. Chongqing City Changshou District Public Security Bureau	2019 Chongqing Chongqing	2 NL	5	2 NL	5	5
Feng Huina v. Sichuan Provincial People's Government	2019 Chengdu Sichuan	2 NA NJ	5	2 NA NJ	5	5
Feng Yan v. Mianyang Municipal Bureau of Public Security	20201 Mianyang Sichuan	2 ND	5	2 NF	2 ND NF	5
Feng Wen v. Beijing City Xicheng District People's Government	2019 Beijing Beijing	2 ND NG	5	2 NE	5	5
Liu Shuping v. Henan Province Zhengzhou City Zhengdong New District People's Government	2019 Zhengzhou Henan	2 ND	5	2 ND	2 ND	2 ND
Liu Xingyuan v. Tangshan Municipal People's Government	2018 Tangshan Hebei	2 NL	5	2 NJ	5	5

(continued)

Table 7.9 (continued)

Case citation	*Year/city and province of original jurisdiction*	*Decision and rationale of Chinese entities receiving OGI requests*	*Decision and rationale of oversight department for administrative reconsideration*	*Decision and rationale of primary or trial court*	*Decision and rationale of intermediate or appellate court*	*Decision and rationale of high or supreme court for retrial*
Huang Jinlan v. Jiangsu Province Nanjing Municipal Bureau of Public Security Gulou Branch	2019 Nanjing Jiangsu	2 NI NJ	5	2 NI NJ	2 NI NJ	2 NI NJ
Huang Shengkun v. Liancheng County People's Government	2019 Liancheng County Fujian	2 NF NI	5	2 NF NI	5	5
Huang Zhengfeng and Liu Xiaodi v. Nanjing City Traffic Transport Bureau	2017 Nanjing Jiangsu	2 NK NL	5	2 NI	5	5
Ye Lijuan v. Jiande Municipal People's Government	2019 Hangzhou Zhejiang	2 ND NG	5	2 NI	5	5
Xiao Gui v. Huarong County People's Government	2020 Yueyang Hunan	2 NE	5	2 NI	5	5
Liu Cuihua v. Renshou County Public Security Bureau	2019 Meishan Sichuan	2 NL	5	2 NI	5	5
Liu Yonghong, et al. v. Chongqing City Shapingba District People's Government	2020 Chongqing Chongqing	2 NE	5	2 NE	5	5
Sun Jiayang v. Shenyang Municipal People's Government	2017 Shenyang Liaoning	2 NH NK	5	2 NB NJ	5	5
Zhao Guanghai v. Chongqing Municipal People's Government	2017 Chongqing Chongqing	2 NI	5	2 NI	5	5

(continued)

Table 7.9 (continued)

Case citation	*Year/city and province of original jurisdiction*	*Decision and rationale of Chinese entities receiving OGI requests*	*Decision and rationale of oversight department for administrative reconsideration*	*Decision and rationale of primary or trial court*	*Decision and rationale of intermediate or appellate court*	*Decision and rationale of high or supreme court for retrial*
Chen Zhong v. Qidong Municipal People's Government	2018 Nantong Jiangsu	2 NH NL NQ	5	2 NJ	5	5
Liu Defa v. Ye County Bureau of Civil Affairs	2019 Wugang Henan	4	5	2 NE	5	5
Liu Minying, et al. v. Chengdu Municipal People's Government	2014 Chengdu Sichuan	2 NH	5	2 NH	1 DM	5
Liu Chunhua v. Ordos Municipal Bureau of Supervision	2017 Ordos Inner Mongolia Autonomous Region	4	5	2 NJ	5	5
Liu Jiang v.The Ministry of Public Security	2021 Beijing Beijing	2 NI	5	2 NI	5	5
Liu Yanmei v. Baoqing County People's Government	2017 Shuangyashan Heilongjiang	4	5	2 NJ	5	5
Kuang Meimei v. Anyang Municipal Bureau of Public Security Yindu Branch	2017 Anyang Henan	2 NA NJ NE	5	2 NI	5	5
Qian Cuoliang v. Dongyang City Geshan Township People's Government	2018 Dongyang Zhejiang	4	5	2 NI	5	5

(continued)

Table 7.9 (continued)

Case citation	*Year/city and province of original jurisdiction*	*Decision and rationale of Chinese entities receiving OGI requests*	*Decision and rationale of oversight department for administrative reconsideration*	*Decision and rationale of primary or trial court*	*Decision and rationale of intermediate or appellate court*	*Decision and rationale of high or supreme court for retrial*
Wu Wengui v. Chengdu Municipal People's Government and Sichuan Provincial People's Government	2019 Chengdu Sichuan	2 NH NI	2 NH NI	2 NI	5	5
Sun Yujian v. China Ministry of Justice	2014 Beijing Beijing	2 NH NJ NL	2 NH NJ NL	2 NJ NL	5	5
Sun Yujian v. Dalian Municipal People's Government	2018 Dalian Liaoning	2 NH	5	2 NE NI	5	5
Xue Zhaohui v. Jiangsu Provincial Department of Public Security and China Ministry of Public Security	2019 Beijing Beijing	2 NI	2 NI	2 NI	5	5
Li Bangjun v. China Ministry of Public Security	2020 Beijing Beijing	2 ND	2 ND	2 ND NI	5	5
Meng Haixia v. Jiangsu Provincial Department of Public Security	2015 Nanjing Jiangsu	4 NF NJ	5	2 NJ	5	5
Song Chunyou v. Beijing City Haidian District People's Government	2015 Beijing Beijing	2 NI	5	2 NI	5	5
Song Weizhong v. Beijing Municipal Department of Public Security Changping Branch	2020 Beijing Beijing	2 NJ	5	2 NJ	5	5

(continued)

Table 7.9 (continued)

Case citation	*Year/city and province of original jurisdiction*	*Decision and rationale of Chinese entities receiving OGI requests*	*Decision and rationale of oversight department for administrative reconsideration*	*Decision and rationale of primary or trial court*	*Decision and rationale of intermediate or appellate court*	*Decision and rationale of high or supreme court for retrial*
Zhang Guoshun v. Queshan County People's Government	2018 Zhumadian Henan	2 NI	5	2 NI	5	5
Shi Huiqing v. Fuzhou Municipal People's Government	2020 Fuzhou Fujian	2 NI	5	2 NI	5	5
Chen Qiwu v. Beijing City Chaoyang District People's Government	2019 Beijing Beijing	2 NJ	5	2 NJ	5	5
Shaanxi Dazheng Electric Group Company v. Xi'an City Yanta District People's Government	2016 Xi'an Shaanxi	2 NH	5	2 NH	2 NH	5
Gao Yanhua v. Beijing City Xicheng District People's Government	2019 Beijing Beijing	2 ND NG	5	2 NE	5	5
Zhou Yang v. Wuhan City Jiang'an District People's Government and Wuhan Municipal People's Government	2018 Wuhan Hubei	2 NG	2 NG	2 NJ	5	5
Xianyang Taixi Chemical Fertilizer Company v. Xianyang Municipal Department of Finance	2017 Xianyang Shaanxi	2 NJ	5	2 NF	5	5
Tang Lizhen v. Health Commission of Guilin Municipal People's Government	2019 Guilin Guangxi	2 NH	2 NH	2 NJ	2 NJ	5

(continued)

Table 7.9 (continued)

Case citation	*Year/city and province of original jurisdiction*	*Decision and rationale of Chinese entities receiving OGI requests*	*Decision and rationale of oversight department for administrative reconsideration*	*Decision and rationale of primary or trial court*	*Decision and rationale of intermediate or appellate court*	*Decision and rationale of high or supreme court for retrial*
Tang Moumou v. Changsha City Furong District Bureau of Urban Management and Law Enforcement and Changsha City Furong District People's Government	2018 Changsha Hunan	2 NJ	5	2 NI	5	5
Tianjin Changtian Law Firm v. Tianjin City Hedong District Department of Taxation	2019 Tianjin Tianjin	2 NJ NL	5	2 NI	5	5
Yao Baohua v. Changzhou City Housing and Urban-Rural Development Bureau	2019 Changzhou Jiangsu	2 NH NI	5	2 NH NI	5	5
Jiang Yumin v. Changzhou City Zhonglou District People's Government	2014 Changzhou Jiangsu	2 NG	5	2 NG	5	5
Kong Lingjie v. Zhengzhou City Jinshui District People's Government	2016 Zhengzhou Henan	2 NE	5	2 NE	5	5
Xu Congdong v. China Ministry of Public Security	2018 Beijing Beijing	2 NJ	2 NJ	2 NJ	5	5
Zhang Tao v. Fujian Provincial People's Government	2015 Fuzhou Fujian	2 NH	5	2 NI NJ	5	5

(continued)

Table 7.9 (continued)

Case citation	*Year/city and province of original jurisdiction*	*Decision and rationale of Chinese entities receiving OGI requests*	*Decision and rationale of oversight department for administrative reconsideration*	*Decision and rationale of primary or trial court*	*Decision and rationale of intermediate or appellate court*	*Decision and rationale of high or supreme court for retrial*
Zheng Yuexiang v. Xiamen Municipal People's Government	2017 Zhangzhou Fujian	2 NF NI	5	2 NF NI	5	5
Ma Yunqing, et al. v. China Ministry of Public Security	2019 Beijing Beijing	4	5	2 NJ	5	5
Hu Dongsheng v. Beijing Municipal Department of Public Security	2019 Beijing Beijing	2 ND NG	2 ND NG	2 NJ	5	5
Gao Lichun v. Suzhou City National High-Tech Industrial Development Zone Development and Reform Commission and Suzhou City Huqiu District People's Government	2018 Suzhou Jiangsu	2 NI	2 NI	2 NI	5	5
Song Shuping v. Beijing City Xicheng District People's Government	2019 Beijing Beijing	2 ND NG	5	2 NE	5	5
Hongyilong Investment Management Company v. China Securities Regulatory Commission Xiamen Branch	2017 Xiamen Fujian	2 ND	5	2 ND	5	5
Yue Zhiqiang v. Tieling Municipal Bureau of Public Security	2019 Changtu Liaoning	2 NH NI	5	2 NH NI	5	5
Cui Dongmei v. Zhengzhou City Huiji District People's Government	2017 Zhengzhou Henan	2 NI NG	5	2 NI NG	5	5

(continued)

Table 7.9 (continued)

Case citation	*Year/city and province of original jurisdiction*	*Decision and rationale of Chinese entities receiving OGI requests*	*Decision and rationale of oversight department for administrative reconsideration*	*Decision and rationale of primary or trial court*	*Decision and rationale of intermediate or appellate court*	*Decision and rationale of high or supreme court for retrial*
Zuo Qizhong v. Chongqing City Changshou District Bureau of Public Security	2017 Chongqing Chongqing	2 NL	5	2 NI	5	5
Ma Junliu v. Beijing City Haidian District Bureau of Public Security	2020 Beijing Beijing	2 NA	5	2 NJ	5	5
Zhang Xihua v. Tangshan City Lu'nan District People's Government	2017 Tangshan Hebei	4	5	2 NI NJ	5	5
Xu Xiuwen v. Hanshan County People's Government	2018 Maanshan Anhui	1	2 NI	2 NI	5	5
Mo Congxiang v. Duyun Municipal People's Government	2020 Duyun Guizhou	1	5	2 NJ NP NQ	5	5
Zhang Daxue v. Shijiazhuang City Qiaoxi District People's Government	2018 Shijiazhuang Hebei	2 NG	5	2 NF	5	5
Chen Jiaonan v. Changzhou City Benniu Township People's Government	2019 Changzhou Jiangsu	2 NG	5	2 NI NJ	5	5
Cao Lishu v. Chongqing City Rongchang District People's Government	2017 Chongqing Chongqing	2 NI	5	2 NI	5	5
Chen Fagao v. Feidong County Bureau of Finance	2017 Feidong Anhui	2 NI	5	2 NI	5	5

(continued)

Table 7.9 (continued)

Case citation	*Year/city and province of original jurisdiction*	*Decision and rationale of Chinese entities receiving OGI requests*	*Decision and rationale of oversight department for administrative reconsideration*	*Decision and rationale of primary or trial court*	*Decision and rationale of intermediate or appellate court*	*Decision and rationale of high or supreme court for retrial*
Chen Qingguo, et al. v. Yiwu Municipal People's Government	2017 Yiwu Zhejiang	2 NG NJ	2 NG NJ	2 NI NJ	5	5
Fang Jifeng v. Beijing City Xicheng District People's Government	2019 Beijing Beijing	2 ND NG	5	2 NE	5	5
Li Hong v. Anhui Provincial People's Government	2014 Hefei Anhui	4	5	2 NJ	2 NE NI	5
Li Chengbao v. Beijing Municipal People's Government	2018 Beijing Beijing	2 NH NJ	5	2 NJ	5	5
Zhang Yicai v. Beijing City Miyun District Bureau of Public Security and Beijing Municipal Bureau of Public Security	2019 Beijing Beijing	2 NJ	2 NJ	2 NJ	5	5
Zhang Xiongwei v. Shanghai City Hongkou District People's Government	2017 Shanghai Shanghai	2 NI	5	2 NI	5	5
Xing Chunming v. Rongcheng Municipal Bureau of Public Security	2019 Rongcheng Shandong	4 NJ	5	2 NJ	5	5
Lu Zuoyu v. Beijing City Chaoyang District Bureau of Public Security	2019 Beijing Beijing	2 NJ	5	2 NJ	5	5
Zhao Lichun v. Xiamen Municipal Bureau of Public Security	2018 Xiamen Fujian	2 NS	2 NS	2 NF NL	2 NJ	5

(continued)

Table 7.9 (continued)

Case citation	*Year/city and province of original jurisdiction*	*Decision and rationale of Chinese entities receiving OGI requests*	*Decision and rationale of oversight department for administrative reconsideration*	*Decision and rationale of primary or trial court*	*Decision and rationale of intermediate or appellate court*	*Decision and rationale of high or supreme court for retrial*
Zhang Zhicheng v. Tianjian City Heping District Bureau of Public Security and Tianjin Municipal Bureau of Public Security	2018 Tianjin Tianjin	2 NI	2 NS	2 NJ	5	5
Peng Houchang v. Chengdu City Wenjiang District Bureau of Public Security	2018 Chengdu Sichuan	2 NI	2 NI	2 NL	2 NF NL	5
Xu Qipeng, et al. v. Qingdao Municipal Bureau of Public Security Traffic Police Unit	2018 Qingdao Shandong	2 NI	5	2 NF NI NJ NL	5	5
Xu Shuang v. Liaoyang City Baita District Bureau of Public Security	2018 Dengta Liaoning	2 NI	5	2 NI	5	5
Yang Wei v. Xiangtan Municipal Bureau of Public Security	2020 Xiangtan Hunan	2 NI	5	2 NI	5	5
Wei Taifang v. Chengdu Municipal Bureau of Public Security and Sichuan Provincial Bureau of Public Security	2018 Chengdu Chengdu	2 NJ	2 NJ	2 NJ	2 NJ	5
Qin Mingkang v. Gaoyou Municipal Bureau of Public Security	2020 Yangzhou Jiangsu	2 NE NJ	5	2 NI	5	5

(continued)

Table 7.9 (continued)

Case citation	*Year/city and province of original jurisdiction*	*Decision and rationale of Chinese entities receiving OGI requests*	*Decision and rationale of oversight department for administrative reconsideration*	*Decision and rationale of primary or trial court*	*Decision and rationale of intermediate or appellate court*	*Decision and rationale of high or supreme court for retrial*
Hu Xiuhua v. Beijing City Fengtai District Bureau of Public Security	2021 Beijing Beijing	2 ND	5	2 NJ	5	5
Zuo Dengfeng v. Tongling City Yi'an District Bureau of Natural Resources and Planning	2023 Tongling Anhui	4	5	2 NI	5	5
Tian Shuwu v. Tianjin City Jinghai District Bureau of Public Security Firefighting Unit	2018 Tianjin Tianjin	2 NG	5	2 NG NI	5	5
Wang Juan v. Beijing Municipal Bureau of Public Security	2017 Beijing Beijing	2 ND NJ	5	2 ND NJ	5	5
Yang Jin v. Chongqing City Yuzhong District Bureau of Public Security	2020 Chongqing Chongqing	2 NG	5	2 NI NJ	2 NI NJ	5
Du Laixing v. Nan'an Municipal Bureau of Public Security and Quanzhou Municipal Bureau of Public Security	2017 Quanzhou Fujian	2 NA NF NJ	2 NA NF NJ	2 NA NF NJ	5	5
Chen Kaiquan and Gao Longxiang v. Meishan City Dongpo District Chongli Township People's Government	2018 Meishan Sichuan	2 NH NI NL	5	2 NI	5	5

(continued)

Table 7.9 (continued)

Case citation	*Year/city and province of original jurisdiction*	*Decision and rationale of Chinese entities receiving OGI requests*	*Decision and rationale of oversight department for administrative reconsideration*	*Decision and rationale of primary or trial court*	*Decision and rationale of intermediate or appellate court*	*Decision and rationale of high or supreme court for retrial*
Deng Xiulan v. Chengdu Municipal People's Government	2014 Chengdu Chengdu	4	5	2 NS	1 DC DK	5
Zhu Yanli v. Tengchong Municipal People's Government	2020 Baoshan Yunnan	2 NH	5	2 ND	5	5
Yuan Wubing v. Qidong Municipal Bureau of Civil Affairs	2017 Haimen Jiangsu	2 NI	5	2 NI	5	5
Xu Wenyan v. Sheyang County Bureau of Planning	2018 Jianhu Jiangsu	4	5	2 NI	5	5
Hua Wenmao v. Beijing City Tongzhou District People's Government	2014 Beijing Beijing	2 NH	5	2 NL	5	5
Qian Meiying v. Changzhou Municipal Commission for Development and Reform	2019 Changzhou Jiangsu	2 NH	5	2 NL	5	5
Shen Gongming v. Shanghai Municipal People's Government	2020 Shanghai Shanghai	2 NI	2 NI	2 NL NO NP NQ	5	5
Wang Mufa v. Huian County People's Government	2019 Xiamen Fujian	1	2 NR	2 NJ	5	5
Zhang Jinfeng v. Huinan County Fumin Zhen People's Government	2018 Huinan Jilin	2 NI	5	2 NI	5	5

(continued)

Table 7.9 (continued)

Case citation	*Year/city and province of original jurisdiction*	*Decision and rationale of Chinese entities receiving OGI requests*	*Decision and rationale of oversight department for administrative reconsideration*	*Decision and rationale of primary or trial court*	*Decision and rationale of intermediate or appellate court*	*Decision and rationale of high or supreme court for retrial*
Xu Baoyuan v. China Ministry of Commerce	2019 Beijing Beijing	2 NL NI	5	2 NI	5	5
Zhu Guohong v. Wuxi Municipal Bureau of Land and Resources	2018 Wuxi Jiangsu	2 NL	5	2 NL	5	5
Yuan Fujiao v. Beijing City Xicheng District Bureau of Public Security and Beijing City Xicheng District People's Government	2019 Beijing Beijing	2 NJ	2 NJ	2 NJ	5	5
Zhao Rui v. Hanzhong City Hantai District Bureau of Transportation	2018 Hanzhong Shaanxi	2 NL	5	2 NH	5	5
Tian Ye v. Liaoning Provincial Commission for Development and Reform	2018 Shenyang Liaoning	2 NS	2 NI NR	2 NR	5	5
Fu Guangyi v. Beihai City Haicheng District People's Government	2017 Beihai Guangxi	4	5	2 NR	5	5
Bi Yanhai v. Gu County People's Government	2016 Linfen Shanxi	4	5	2 NR	5	5
Wang Guoji v. Baoji City Jintai District People's Government	2021 Baoji Shaanxi	2 NJ	5	2 NR	5	5
Zhao Jihua v. Shanghai City Jing'an District People's Government	2017 Shanghai Shanghai	2 NL	5	2 NI	5	5

(continued)

Table 7.9 (continued)

Case citation	*Year/city and province of original jurisdiction*	*Decision and rationale of Chinese entities receiving OGI requests*	*Decision and rationale of oversight department for administrative reconsideration*	*Decision and rationale of primary or trial court*	*Decision and rationale of intermediate or appellate court*	*Decision and rationale of high or supreme court for retrial*
Zhao Jihua v. Shanghai City Jing'an District Bureau of Affordable Housing and Shanghai City Jing'an District People's Government	2017 Shanghai Shanghai	2 NI	2 NI	2 NI	5	5
Li Simo v. Chongqing City Shapingba District People's Government	2020 Chongqing Chongqing	2 NE	5	2 NE	5	5
Wang Shuai v. Wenshui County Xicheng Township People's Government	2020 Fenyang Shanxi	2 NH	5	2 NH NL	5	5
Xie Xiaofeng v. Harbin City Xiangfang District People's Government	2016 Harbin Heilongjiang	4	5	2 NR	5	5
Wang Yuting v. Shanghai Municipal People's Government	2018 Shanghai Shanghai	2 NS	2 NF NL	2 NI	2 NI	5
Hu Guiqin v. Chongqing City Yubei District People's Government and Chongqing Municipal People's Government	2018 Chongqing Chongqing	2 NA	2 NA	2 NE	2 NE	5
Zhao Liang v. Hunan Provincial Department of Environmental Protection	2015 Changsha Hunan	2 NF	5	2 NR	2 NR	5
Wang Wensheng v. Xiamen Municipal Bureau of Market Supervision	2019 Xiamen Fujian	2 NI NL	5	2 NI	5	5

(continued)

Table 7.9 (continued)

Case citation	*Year/city and province of original jurisdiction*	*Decision and rationale of Chinese entities receiving OGI requests*	*Decision and rationale of oversight department for administrative reconsideration*	*Decision and rationale of primary or trial court*	*Decision and rationale of intermediate or appellate court*	*Decision and rationale of high or supreme court for retrial*
Xu Zhuoyun v. Nanchang Municipal Bureau of Urban and Rural Planning	2018 Nanchang Jiangxi	2 NI	5	2 NI	5	5
Li Wanzheng v. Zunhua Municipal People's Government	2019 Tangshan Hebei	2 NJ	5	2 NJ	5	5
Zhao Donghua v. Yibin Municipal People's Government	2019 Yibin Sichuan	2 NI	5	2 NI	5	5
Xu Liya v. Henan Provincial Bureau of Natural Resources	2020 Zhengzhou Henan	2 NH	2 NH	2 NI	5	5
Fan Renyuan v. Changzhou Municipal Archival Institution and Changzhou Municipal People's Government	2020 Changzhou Jiangsu	2 NI	2 NS	2 NR	5	5
Xiong Shiwei, et al. v. Chongqing City Shapingba District People's Government	2020 Chongqing Chongqing	2 NE	5	2 NE	5	5
Fang Wenping v. Shanghai City Jiading District Bureau of Affordable Housing and Shanghai Municipal Bureau of Affordable Housing	2020 Shanghai Shanghai	2 NL	2 NL	2 NH NL	5	5
Li Zhongwen v. Fujian Provincial People's Government	2019 Fuzhou Fujian	2 NE NI	2 NE NI	2 NI	5	5

(continued)

Table 7.9 (continued)

Case citation	*Year/city and province of original jurisdiction*	*Decision and rationale of Chinese entities receiving OGI requests*	*Decision and rationale of oversight department for administrative reconsideration*	*Decision and rationale of primary or trial court*	*Decision and rationale of intermediate or appellate court*	*Decision and rationale of high or supreme court for retrial*
Chen Weizhi v. Henan Provincial Administration of Culture and Tourism	2020 Zhengzhou Henan	2 NI NL	5	2 NR	5	5
Wang Yanling v. Xinxiang Municipal Bureau of Finance	2020 Xinxiang Henan	2 NS	5	2 NR	5	5
Qin Yun'e v. Qidong Municipal Bureau of Affordable Housing and Urban-Rural Development	2020 Nantong Jiangsu	2 NL	5	2 NL	5	5
Lu Lanfa v. Shanghai City Pudong New Area Bureau of Planning and Natural Resources and Shanghai Municipal Bureau of Planning and Natural Resources	2020 Shanghai Shanghai	2 NJ	2 NJ	2 NJ	5	5
Ju Bangyu v. Harbin City Pingfang District Bureau of Economic Development	2018 Harbin Heilongjiang	4	5	2 NR	5	5
Guo Wenchun v. Ningxia Hui Autonomous Region Commission for Health and Family Planning	2018 Yinchuan Ningxia	2 NG NI	5	2 NI	5	5
Zhang Guoping v. Shanghai City Minxin District Commission for Development and Reform	2018 Shanghai Shanghai	2 NH	2 NL	2 NF NL	2 NF NL	5

(continued)

Table 7.9 (continued)

Case citation	*Year/city and province of original jurisdiction*	*Decision and rationale of Chinese entities receiving OGI requests*	*Decision and rationale of oversight department for administrative reconsideration*	*Decision and rationale of primary or trial court*	*Decision and rationale of intermediate or appellate court*	*Decision and rationale of high or supreme court for retrial*
Luo Zhanghua v. Chengdu City Jinjiang District People's Government and Chengdu Municipal People's Government	2020 Chengdu Sichuan	2 NS	2 NS	2 NL	5	5
Luo Wenbin v. Chengdu City Jinjiang District People's Government and Chengdu Municipal People's Government	2020 Chengdu Sichuan	2 NS	2 NS	2 NL	5	5
Cao Linlin v. Anhui Provincial Bureau of Finance and China Ministry of Finance	2020 Hefei Anhui	2 NH	2 NH	2 NI	5	5
Mengzi Hongfeng Chemical Company v. Mengzi Municipal Bureau of Education	2019 Mengzi Yunnan	2 NF	5	2 NF	5	5
Hangzhou Huayuan Hotel v. Hangzhou City Xiacheng District People's Government	2020 Hangzhou Zhejiang	2 NG NH	2 NI	2 NI	5	5
Chen Chuanbing v. Fujian Provincial People's Government and Fuzhou Municipal People's Government	2017 Fuzhou Fujian	2 NE	2 NE	2 NE	5	5

(continued)

Table 7.9 (continued)

Case citation	*Year/city and province of original jurisdiction*	*Decision and rationale of Chinese entities receiving OGI requests*	*Decision and rationale of oversight department for administrative reconsideration*	*Decision and rationale of primary or trial court*	*Decision and rationale of intermediate or appellate court*	*Decision and rationale of high or supreme court for retrial*
Xue Mingyuan v. Sichuan Provincial Bureau of Land and Resources and China Ministry of Land and Resources	2017 Chengdu Sichuan	2 NI	2 NI	2 NI	5	5
Li Shu'an v. Henan Provincial Administration for Market Regulation and China State Administration for Market Regulation	2020 Zhengzhou Henan	2 NJ	2 NJ	2 NI	5	5
Zeng Yuzhong v. Jintang County Bureau of Development and Reform and Chengdu Municipal Commission for Development and Reform	2018 Pengzhou Sichuan	2 NI	2 NR	2 NI	5	5
Zhang Hongxin v. Shandong Province Laixi Municipal People's Government and Shandong Province Qingdao Municipal People's Government	2018 Jinan Shandong	2 NG NI	2 NG NI	2 NG NI	2 NG NI	2 NG NI
Han Junxue v. Linzhou Municipal Bureau of Public Security	2017 Anyang Henan	4	5	2 NJ	2 NJ	2 NJ

(continued)

Table 7.9 (continued)

Case citation	*Year/city and province of original jurisdiction*	*Decision and rationale of Chinese entities receiving OGI requests*	*Decision and rationale of oversight department for administrative reconsideration*	*Decision and rationale of primary or trial court*	*Decision and rationale of intermediate or appellate court*	*Decision and rationale of high or supreme court for retrial*
Wang Minghui v. Jilin Provincial Prison for Women and Jilin Provincial Prison Administration Agency	2020 Changchun Jilin	2 NG	2 NG	2 ND	2 ND	5
Peng Xiongli v. Chengdu Municipal Bureau of Local Taxation and Sichuan Provincial Bureau of Local Taxation	2018 Chengdu Sichuan	2 NH NI NL	2 NS	2 NH NI NL	2 NF NH	5
Peng Xiongli v. State Taxation Administration Chongzhou Municipal Branch and State Taxation Administration Chengdu Municipal Branch	2018 Chengdu Sichuan	2 NG	2 NG	2 NF NL	2 NF	5
Zheng Xinming, et al. v. Fuzhou Municipal Bureau of Natural Resources and Planning and Fuzhou Municipal People's Government	2020 Fuzhou Fujian	2 NJ	2 NS	2 NI	5	5
Zou Huinan v.State-Owned Assets Supervision and Administration Commission of the State Council	2015 Beijing Beijing	2 NG	4	2 NR	5	5

(continued)

Table 7.9 (continued)

Case citation	*Year/city and province of original jurisdiction*	*Decision and rationale of Chinese entities receiving OGI requests*	*Decision and rationale of oversight department for administrative reconsideration*	*Decision and rationale of primary or trial court*	*Decision and rationale of intermediate or appellate court*	*Decision and rationale of high or supreme court for retrial*
E Yanping v. Benxi City Pingshan District People's Government and Benxi Municipal People's Government	2016 Benxi Liaoning	4	2 NS	2 NF	5	5
Zhuhai Special Economic Zone White Lotus Industrial Development Corporation v. Zhuhai Municipal Bureau of Land and Resources	2016 Zhuhai Guangdong	2 NJ	5	2 NE NI	2 NE NG NI	5
Yang Moumou v. Guangzhou City Huadu District People's Government and Guangzhou Municipal People's Government	2018 Guangzhou Guangdong	2 NH	2 NH	2 NI	5	5
Zhang Aihong and Kang Yuqiu v. Hengshui Municipal Center of Land Banking	2019 Hengshui Hebei	2 NQ	5	2 NP NQ	2 NP NQ	5
Zhang Baozhen, et al. v. Luoyang National High and New Technology Industries Development Zone Management Commission	2020 Luoyang Henan	2 NS	5	2 NJ	2 ND	5
Qiu Haifeng v. Haikou City Qiongshan District People's Government	2019 Haikou Hainan	2 NS	5	2 NI	2 NI	5

(continued)

Table 7.9 (continued)

Case citation	*Year/city and province of original jurisdiction*	*Decision and rationale of Chinese entities receiving OGI requests*	*Decision and rationale of oversight department for administrative reconsideration*	*Decision and rationale of primary or trial court*	*Decision and rationale of intermediate or appellate court*	*Decision and rationale of high or supreme court for retrial*
Li Shuhua and Peng Shujun v. Zigong City Ziliujing District People's Government and Zigong Municipal People's Government	2020 Zigong Sichuan	2 NG	2 NG	2 NJ	5	5
Li Anlin v. Henan Provincial Health Commission and Henan Provincial People's Government	2020 Zhengzhou Henan	2 NG	2 NG	2 NI	5	5
Peng Longmei v. Guizhou Province Suiyang County People's Government	2016 Zunyi Guizhou	2 NI	5	2 NI	2 NI NR	5
Jiang Yifei, et al. v. Guilin Municipal Bureau of Ecological and Environmental Protection	2020 Guilin Guangxi	2 NL	5	1 DN	1 DM	1 DM
Shi Lianyou, et al. v. Jilin Province Dunhua Municipal People's Government	2017 Yanji Jilin	4	5	2 NR	2 NE	2 NE NI
Tang Liangwei, et al. v. Fuzhou Municipal Land Development Center	2018 Fuzhou Fujian	2 NH	5	2 NH	2 NH	2 NH

Table 8.1 Public Enterprises and Institutions Sued for Non-Disclosure of Information (2014–2021)[15]

Case citation	*Year/city and province of original jurisdiction*	*Decision and rationale of public enterprise or Institution*	*Decision and rationale of oversight department*	*Decision and rationale of primary or trial court*	*Decision and rationale of intermediate or appellate court*	*Decision and rationale of high or supreme court for retrial*
Han Suhua v. Zhenzhou Orphanage	2020 Zhenzhou Henan	4 NS	2 NO	2 NO	2 NO	5
Yongfa Security Equipment Factory v. Changzhou City Institute for Product Quality Supervision and Testing	2018 Changzhou Jiangsu	4 NS	2 NO	2 NM NO	2 NM NO	5
Chen Daxue and Wu Changling v. Rui'an City Office for Immigrant Resettlement	2017 Rui'an Zhejiang	3 DC DG DH NB NH	5	2 NB NH NN	2 NB NH	5
Chenhong v. State Grid Changshu City Electricity Supply Company	2017 Zhangjiagang Jiangsu	4 NS	5	1 DA DF DG DH	1 DA DE DI	5
Zhang Zongfa v. State Grid Changshu City Electricity Supply Company	2016 Zhangjiagang Jiangsu	4 NS	5	1 DA DF DI	1 DA DE DF DI	5

(continued)

15 The table was created by the author of this book. The dataset in the table came from OGI-related judicial opinions published on the China Supreme Court's website, China Judgements Online [中国裁判文书网]. *China Judgements Online* [中国裁判文书网], China Supreme Court, Beijing, China, *available at* https://wenshu.court.gov.cn (accessed between February 21, 2025, and March 31, 2025).

Table 8.1 (continued)

Case citation	*Year/city and province of original jurisdiction*	*Decision and rationale of public enterprise or Institution*	*Decision and rationale of oversight department*	*Decision and rationale of primary or trial court*	*Decision and rationale of intermediate or appellate court*	*Decision and rationale of high or supreme court for retrial*
Liu Shuiping v. State Grid Zhongmou County Electricity Supply Company	2017 Zhengzhou Henan	4 NS	5	2 NB NF NJ NN	2 NB NF NJ NN	2 NB NF NJ NN
Yang Jiandong v. State Grid Changshu City Electricity Supply Company	2016 Zhangjiagang Jiangsu	4 NS	5	1 DA DK	1 DA DE DK	5
Bi Yongyuan v. State Grid Changshu City Electricity Supply Company	2016 Zhangjiagang Jiangsu	4 NS	5	1 DA DK	1 DA DE DI DK	5
Wang Zhenbao v. State Grid Shandong Province Electric Power Company	2015 Ji'nan Shandong	4 NS	5	2 NP NQ	1 DA DK	5
Wang Zhenbao v. State Grid Shandong Province Electric Power Company	2016 Ji'nan Shandong	4 NS	5	2 NL	1 DA DK	5
Wang Zhenbao v. State Grid Shandong Province Electric Power Company	2018 Ji'nan Shandong	4 NS	5	2 NB NN	2 NB NN	5
Liang Chaotang v. State Grid Shandong Province Electric Power Company	2020 Ji'nan Shandong	4 NS	5	2 NN NP	5	5
Liang Chaotang v. State Grid Liaocheng City Electricity Supply Company	2020 Liaocheng Shandong	2 NA ND	5	2 NB NF NN	2 NB NF NN	5

(continued)

Table 8.1 (continued)

Case citation	*Year/city and province of original jurisdiction*	*Decision and rationale of public enterprise or Institution*	*Decision and rationale of oversight department*	*Decision and rationale of primary or trial court*	*Decision and rationale of intermediate or appellate court*	*Decision and rationale of high or supreme court for retrial*
Wang Zheliang v. State Grid Changshu City Electricity Supply Company	2016 Zhangjiagang Jiangsu	4 NS	5	1 DA DK	1 DA DE DK	5
Chenhong v. Jiangsu Changshu Sino French Water Company	2017 Zhangjiagang Jiangsu	4 NS	5	1 DA	1 DA DE	5
Shao Mingliang v. Jiangsu Changshu Sino French Water Company	2016 Zhangjiagang Jiangsu	4 NS	5	1 DA DK	1 DA DE DK	5
Bi Yongyuan v. Jiangsu Changshu Sino French Water Company	2016 Zhangjiagang Jiangsu	4 NS	5	1 DA DK	1 DA DE DK	5
Wang Zheliang v. Jiangsu Changshu Sino French Water Company	2016 Zhangjiagang Jiangsu	4 NS	5	1 DA DK	1 DA DE DK	5
Zhang Zongfa v. Jiangsu Changshu Sino French Water Company	2016 Zhangjiagang Jiangsu	4 NS	5	1 DA DK	1 DA DE DK	5
Yang Jiandong v. Jiangsu Changshu Sino French Water Company	2016 Zhangjiagang Jiangsu	4 NS	5	1 DA DK	1 DA DE DK	5
Qiu Ailing v. Fuzhou City Water Supply Company	2021 Fuzhou Fujian	2 NL	5	2 NL NN	5	5

(continued)

Table 8.1 (continued)

Case citation	*Year/city and province of original jurisdiction*	*Decision and rationale of public enterprise or Institution*	*Decision and rationale of oversight department*	*Decision and rationale of primary or trial court*	*Decision and rationale of intermediate or appellate court*	*Decision and rationale of high or supreme court for retrial*
Chen Yuejun v. Tianjin Bus Company	2018 Tianjin Tianjin	4 NS	5	1 DA DF	5	5
Chen Yuejun v. Tianjin Metro	2015 Tianjin Tianjin	4 NS	5	2 NR	2 NR	5
Luo Siwen v. Guizhou Power Grid Guiyang Station	2017 Guiyang Guizhou	4 NS	5	1 DA DF DI	5	5
Xing Wenyuan v. State Grid Beijing Electric Power Company	2019 Beijing Beijing	4 NS	5	1 DA	3 DA NG NH NI NL	3 DA NG
Xing Wenyuan v. State Grid Beijing Electric Power Company	2018 Beijing Beijing	4 NS	5	1 DA DK	1 DA DK	5
Shao Mingliang v. State Grid Changshu Power Supply Company	2017 Zhangjiagang Jiangsu	4 NS	5	1 DA DF DI	1 DA DE DF DI	5
Ding Zipeng v. State Grid Zaozhuang Power Supply Company	2019 Zaozhuang Shandong	3 DJ NQ	5	2 NE NL NN	5	5
Ding Ruibing v. Haimen City Radio and TV Station	2017 Rugao Jiangsu	4 NS	5	2 ND NN	2 ND NN	5

(continued)

Table 8.1 (continued)

Case citation	*Year/city and province of original jurisdiction*	*Decision and rationale of public enterprise or Institution*	*Decision and rationale of oversight department*	*Decision and rationale of primary or trial court*	*Decision and rationale of intermediate or appellate court*	*Decision and rationale of high or supreme court for retrial*
Fang Jinhua v. China Telecom Suqian Branch	2014 Suqian Jiangsu	4 NQ	5	2 NH NN	2 NG NN	5
Yan Hongjun v. China Mobile Dongguan Branch	2017 Dongquan Guangdong	4 NS	5	1 DB DE DF DH	1 DB DE DF DH	5
Sun Yangbing v. China Mobile Shenzhen Branch	2014 Shenzhen Guangdong	4 NS	5	1 DB DE DF DH	1 DB DE DF DH	5
Residents' Committee of Jiuduyangguang Community v. Zhaozhou Electric Power Supply Company	2018 Daqing Heilongjiang	4 NS	2 NJ	1 DA DF	5	5
Zhong Weixi v. Juye County Service Center for Coal Industry	2020 Juye County Shandong	2 NH	5	2 NH	2 NH NM	5
Feng Genqing v. Taizhou City Jiaojiang District Bureau for Housing and Urban-Rural Development	2019 Taizhou Zhejiang	2 NG	5	1 DB DG DH	5	5
Liu Shuping v. China Post Zhongmou County Branch	2017 Xinzheng Henan	4 NS	5	2 NJ NN	2 NJ NN	5
Liu Shuping v. China Post Zhongmou County Branch	2017 Xinzheng Henan	4 NS	5	2 NJ	2 NJ	5

(continued)

Table 8.1 (continued)

Case citation	*Year/city and province of original jurisdiction*	*Decision and rationale of public enterprise or Institution*	*Decision and rationale of oversight department*	*Decision and rationale of primary or trial court*	*Decision and rationale of intermediate or appellate court*	*Decision and rationale of high or supreme court for retrial*
Liu Shuping v. State Grid Zhongmou County Branch	2016 Xinzheng Henan	4 NS	5	2 NJ NN	2 NJ NN	5
Liu Aijun v. Zhengzhou Preschool Education College	2016 Zhengzhou Henan	4 NS	5	1 DA	1 DA	5
Liu Aijun v. Beijing No. 6 Hospital	2016 Beijing Beijing	4 NS	5	2 NN	2 NN	5
Liu Hong v. Beijing Dongcheng District No. 1 Center for Public Housing and Land Management	2014 Beijing Beijing	3 DB DG NS	5	2 NN	2 NN	5
Bao Guoqing v. Guangzhou No. 1 Bus Company	2015 Guangzhou Guangdong	2 NH	5	1 DA	2 NN	5
You Hanrui v. Beijing Drainage Group	2018 Beijing Beijing	4 NS	5	6 DA DK	6 DA DK	5
Zhuo Liangbing v. Taizhou City Jiaojiang District Bureau for Housing and Urban-Rural Development	2019 Taizhou Zhejiang	2 NG NM	5	1 DB DL	5	5
Homeowner Association of Nanjing Fengshang International Apartment v. State Grid Nanjing Power Supply Company	2016 Nanjing Jiangsu	4 NS	5	1 DA DE DK	5	5
Lu Jing v. Taizhou City Jiaojiang District Bureau for Housing and Urban-Rural Development	2019 Taizhou Zhejiang	2 NG NM	5	1 DB DL	5	5

(continued)

Table 8.1 (continued)

Case citation	*Year/city and province of original jurisdiction*	*Decision and rationale of public enterprise or Institution*	*Decision and rationale of oversight department*	*Decision and rationale of primary or trial court*	*Decision and rationale of intermediate or appellate court*	*Decision and rationale of high or supreme court for retrial*
Zhang Jianguo v. Stage Grid Zhuzhou Power Supply Company	2018 Zhuzhou Hunan	4 NS	5	2 NM	5	5
Qu Zhe v. Shenyang Office of Work Capacity Evaluations and Rehabilitation Management	2018 Shenyang Liaoning	3 DB DH NG	5	2 NN	5	5
Qu Wenheng v. Shenyang Office of Work Capacity Evaluations and Rehabilitation Management	2018 Shenyang Liaoning	3 DB DH NG	5	2 NN	5	5
Ma Juncai v. Xi'an Daxing District Commission for Comprehensive Urban Redevelopment and Management	2018 Xi'an Shaanxi	2 NG	5	2 NG NJ NN	5	5
Lv Haili v. China United Network Communication Group Jiyuan Branch	2018 Mengzhou Henan	4 NS	5	1 DB DK	5	5
Lin Fei v. China United Network Communication Group Yanbian Branch	2014 Yanji Jilin	4 NS	5	2 NG NN	2 NG NN	5
Zhou Yong v. The First Affiliated Hospital of Zhengzhou University	2018 Zhengzhou Henan	4 NS	5	1 DA DK	5	5
Zhou Jianguo v. State Grid Changshu Power Supply Company	2017 Zhangjiagang Jiangsu	4 NS	5	1 DA DK	1 DA DE DI DK	5

(continued)

Table 8.1 (continued)

Case citation	*Year/city and province of original jurisdiction*	*Decision and rationale of public enterprise or Institution*	*Decision and rationale of oversight department*	*Decision and rationale of primary or trial court*	*Decision and rationale of intermediate or appellate court*	*Decision and rationale of high or supreme court for retrial*
Zhou Jianguo v. Jiangsu Changshu Sino French Water Company	2016 Zhangjiagang Jiangsu	4 NS	5	1 DA DK	1 DA DE DK	5
Tang Libo v. Jiangsu Changshu Sino French Water Company	2016 Zhangjiagang Jiangsu	4 NS	5	1 DA DK	1 DA DE DK	5
Yu Wufang v. Wuhan Land Consolidation and Banking Center	2014 Wuhan Hubei	2 NJ NM NP NQ	5	2 NB NJ NN	2 NB NJ NN	5
Yang Zhengquan v. State Grid Shandong Electric Power Company and State Grid Feicheng City Electricity Supply Company	2017 Tai'an Shandong	4 NS	5	1 DA DK	1 DA DK	5
Hengfeng County Xuhai Renewable Resources Company v. State Grid Hengfeng County Electricity Supply Company	2019 Shangrao Jiangxi	2 NJ NM NQ	5	1 DA DK	2 NE NN	2 NE NG NN
Xia Xin v. Peking Union Medical College Hospital	2015 Beijing Beijing	2 ND NN	5	2 NB ND NJ NN	2 NB ND NJ NN	5
Xia Xin v. Peking Union Medical College Hospital	2014 Beijing Beijing	2 NA	5	2 NE NN	2 NE NN	5

(continued)

Table 8.1 (continued)

Case citation	*Year/city and province of original jurisdiction*	*Decision and rationale of public enterprise or Institution*	*Decision and rationale of oversight department*	*Decision and rationale of primary or trial court*	*Decision and rationale of intermediate or appellate court*	*Decision and rationale of high or supreme court for retrial*
Yao Tushan v. Quzhou Land Banking Center	2016 Quzhou Zhejiang	4 NS	5	2 NM NQ	2 NB NF	5
Sun Baomei v. Beijing Xicheng District Center for Public Housing and Land Management	2017 Beijing Beijing	2 NJ	2 NJ	2 NN	2 NJ NN	5
Jiang Aiming, et al. v. State Grid Corporation of China	2016 Beijing Beijing	4 NS	2 NO NQ	2 NB NO	2 NN NO	5
Sun Qingjun v. State Grid Zhenjiang Electricity Supply Company	2015 Zhenjiang Jiangsu	2 NF NG	5	1 DA DK	1 DA DK	1 DA DK
Sun Qingjun v. Jiangsu Province Zhenjiang City Transportation Management Office	2019 Zhenjiang Jiangsu	2 ND	5	2 NN	2 NN NP	5
Sun Yangbing v. China Mobile Anhui Branch	2018 Hefei Anhui	4 NS	5	2 NN	5	5
Sun Yangbing v. China Mobile Anhui Branch	2019 Hefei Anhui	4 NS	5	2 NP NQ	2 NF NL	5
Sun Yangbing v. China Mobile Shenzhen Branch	2015 Shenzhen Guangdong	2 NJ	5	2 NJ	2 NJ NN	5
Song Wenchao v.Changsha Kaifu District Public Works Bureau	2018 Changsha Hunan	4 NS	5	2 NN	5	5

(continued)

Table 8.1 (continued)

Case citation	*Year/city and province of original jurisdiction*	*Decision and rationale of public enterprise or Institution*	*Decision and rationale of oversight department*	*Decision and rationale of primary or trial court*	*Decision and rationale of intermediate or appellate court*	*Decision and rationale of high or supreme court for retrial*
Long Taiping v. State Grid Yuanjiang Electricity Supply Company	2016 Yuanjiang Hunan	4 NS	5	2 NN	2 NN	5
Guo Junmei v. Shenzhen City Management Center for Public hospitals	2015 Shenzhen Guangdong	2 NH	5	1 DA DK	1 DA DK	5
Cui Xunzhang v. Ji'nan City Huaiyin District Bureau for Housing Security and Property Management	2018 Ji'nan Shandong	2 NG	5	2 NG	2 NG NN	5
Liao Chuanshang v. Hongjiang City Center for Tourism Development Affairs	2019 Huaihua Hunan	2 NB NJ NL	5	3 DB DH NB NJ NL	5	5
Liao Guoqing v.Huainan City Construction Investment Corporation	2016 Huainan Anhui	4 NS	5	2 NP	2 NP	5
Zhang Shiyan v. Suzhou University	2016 Nanjing Jiangsu	3 DN NA NB	2 NO	2 NO	2 NO	5
Zhang Lilei v. Langfang City Qingquan Water Supply Company	2018 Langfang Hebei	4 NS	5	1 DA DE DK	5	5
Xu Chunmiao v. State Grid Zhoushan City Electricity Supply Company	2018 Zhoushan Zhejiang	3 DN NS	2 NB NI	2 NB NI	2 NB NI	5

(continued)

Table 8.1 (continued)

Case citation	*Year/city and province of original jurisdiction*	*Decision and rationale of public enterprise or Institution*	*Decision and rationale of oversight department*	*Decision and rationale of primary or trial court*	*Decision and rationale of intermediate or appellate court*	*Decision and rationale of high or supreme court for retrial*
Zeng Qinghua v. China Mobile Shenzhen Branch	2017 Shenzhen Guangdong	2 NJ NL	5	2 NJ	2 NJ NN	5
Zeng Qinghua v. China Mobile Jiangxi Branch	2018 Nanchang Jiangxi	4 NS	5	2 NB NN	2 NB NM	2 NJ
Cheng Wenyi v. China Mobile Ezhou Branch	2016 Ezhou Hubei	2 NG NH NI NL	5	3 DB DK ND NG NI NL	3 DB DK ND NG NI NL	5
Li Kangnian v. Guangzhou Medical University	2014 Guangzhou Guangdong	2 NR	5	2 NP	1 DA	5
Li Kangnian v. Guangzhou Medical University	2015 Guangzhou Guangdong	2 NR	5	2 NB ND NJ NN	2 NB ND NJ NN	2 ND
Li Kangnian v. Guangzhou Medical University	2017 Guangzhou Guangdong	2 NR	5	2 NB NJ	2 NG	5
Guo Junmei v. Shenzhen Public Hospital Management Center	2015 Shenzhen Guangdong	2 NH	5	1 DA DK	1 DA DK	5
Jia Youbao v. Communication University of China	2018 Beijing Beijing	4 NS	5	1 DA DK	5	5

(continued)

Table 8.1 (continued)

Case citation	*Year/city and province of original jurisdiction*	*Decision and rationale of public enterprise or Institution*	*Decision and rationale of oversight department*	*Decision and rationale of primary or trial court*	*Decision and rationale of intermediate or appellate court*	*Decision and rationale of high or supreme court for retrial*
Bai Yan v. Renmin University of China	2018 Beijing Beijing	3 DN NA NL NH	5	3 DA DG DK NE NN	5	5
Wang Wujun v. China Mobile Tangyin Branch	2018 Anyang Henan	4 NS	5	2 NF NN	1 DB DF DK	5
Yang Jianping v. China Mobile Huizhou Branch	2017 Huizhou Guangdong	7	5	2 NN	2 NN	5
Ke Yuehui v. China Telecom Guangdong Branch	2015 Guangzhou Guangdong	4 NS	5	1 DB DK	1 DB DK	5
Wang Dejun v. China Mobile Hai'an Branch	2015 Nantong Jiangsu	4 NS	5	2 NA NN	2 NA NN	5
Yan Xiantong v. Wenzhou Port Group Corporation	2016 Wenzhou Zhejiang	4 NS	2 NS	1 DA DK	1 DA DK	5
Liu Zhongfeng v. Tsinghua University	2016 Beijing Beijing	2 NB NJ	5	1 DA DK	1 DA DK	5
Li Jinghai v. Wafangdian City Social Security Center for Government Agencies and Institutions	2018 Zhuanghe Liaoning	4 NS	5	1 DB DK	5	5

(continued)

Table 8.1 (continued)

Case citation	*Year/city and province of original jurisdiction*	*Decision and rationale of public enterprise or Institution*	*Decision and rationale of oversight department*	*Decision and rationale of primary or trial court*	*Decision and rationale of intermediate or appellate court*	*Decision and rationale of high or supreme court for retrial*
Yang Yang v. Zhuzhou City Public Transportation Company	2018 Zhuzhou Hunan	2 NA ND NN	5	1 DA DG	5	5
Li Zhengxiang v. Taihe County Shayinghe National Wetland Park Management Bureau	2018 Fuyang Anhui	4 NS	5	1 DA DK	5	5
Li Hanhe v. Hunan Province Information Center for Land and Resources	2017 Changsha Hunan	4 NS	5	2 NM	2 NM	5
Ma Zhenjun v. Xichuan County Dashiqiao Township Elementary and Junior High School	2017 Nanyang Henan	4 NS	5	1 DA DK	1 DA DK	5
Nanyang Zhenghe Information Consulting Company v. Xichuan County Dashiqiao Township Elementary and Junior High School	2017 Nanyang Henan	4 NS	5	1 DA DK	1 DA DK	5
Man Guipeng v. Linghai City Service Center for Urban and Rural Development	2019 Linghai Liaoning	4 NS	2 NH	2 NH	2 NH NM	5
Wang Jinyang v. Yancheng Xinyang Economic Zone Administration Committee	2015 Yancheng Jiangsu	4 NS	5	2 NM	1 DB DK	5
Li Zhiguo v. Changsha City Furong District Office for Land Acquisition and Property Demolition	2019 Changsha Hunan	2 NM	1 DN	1 DB DK	1 DB DK	5

(continued)

Table 8.1 (continued)

Case citation	*Year/city and province of original jurisdiction*	*Decision and rationale of public enterprise or Institution*	*Decision and rationale of oversight department*	*Decision and rationale of primary or trial court*	*Decision and rationale of intermediate or appellate court*	*Decision and rationale of high or supreme court for retrial*
Pan Guomin, et al. v. Chengde City Shuangfengsi Reservoir Construction Management Bureau	2017 Chengde Hebei	4 NS	5	1 DB DK	1 DB DK	5
Jiao Qihong v. Hefei High-tech Industrial Development Zone Management Council for Baiyan Science and Technology Park	2018 Hefei Anhui	4 NS	5	1 DB DK	5	5
Sanhe Tongxin Cement Products Company v. State Grid Jibei Electric Power Company	2019 Beijing Beijing	4 NS	5	2 NB NN	2 NB NN	5
Wang Wei v. China Mobile Shaanxi Branch	2015 Xi'an Shaanxi	4 NS	5	2 NM NP NQ	5	5
Cheng Yuejun v. China Mobile Communications Corporation	2015 Beijing Beijing	4 NS	5	2 NM NP	2 NB NM NP	5
Yin Yanting v. China University of Political Science and Law	2020 Beijing Beijing	3 DA DG NA ND NN	2 NS	2 NM NP NQ	2 NN	5
Li Mingliang v. Shandong Normal University	2018 Ji'nan Shandong	2 NL	5	2 NL NN	2 NL NN	5

(continued)

Table 8.1 (continued)

Case citation	*Year/city and province of original jurisdiction*	*Decision and rationale of public enterprise or Institution*	*Decision and rationale of oversight department*	*Decision and rationale of primary or trial court*	*Decision and rationale of intermediate or appellate court*	*Decision and rationale of high or supreme court for retrial*
Liu Ping v. Tsinghua University	2017 Beijing Beijing	2 NG NH	5	2 NN	2 NN	5
Rao Sixia v. Chongqing City Construction Investment Group Corporation	2018 Chongqing Chongqing	4 NS	5	2 NM NP	2 NM NP	5
Rao Sixia v. China State Railway Group Company	2017 Beijing Beijing	4 NS	5	2 NM NP	2 NM NP	5
Rao Sixia v. Chongqing-Guiyang Railway Company	2018 Chongqing Chongqing	4 NS	5	2 NM NP NQ	2 NM NP NQ	5
Shanghai New Wenhui Law Firm v. Zhejiang Province Monitoring Center for Press, Publication, Radio and Television	2018 Hangzhou Zhejiang	4 NS	5	2 NM NP NQ	5	5
Jia Youbao v. China Telecommunications Corporation Beijing Branch	2017 Beijing Beijing	4 NS	5	2 NP	2 NB NP	2 NB NN
Yu Shaoli v. Beijing City Yanqing District Heating Supply Station	2017 Beijing Beijing	2 NJ	5	2 NJ	2 NE	5
Hongyilong Investment Management Company v. National Small and Medium Enterprise Stock Transfer System	2017 Beijing Beijing	4 NS	5	2 NJ NM	2 NM NP NQ	2 NM NP NQ

(continued)

Table 8.1 (continued)

Case citation	*Year/city and province of original jurisdiction*	*Decision and rationale of public enterprise or Institution*	*Decision and rationale of oversight department*	*Decision and rationale of primary or trial court*	*Decision and rationale of intermediate or appellate court*	*Decision and rationale of high or supreme court for retrial*
Yang Jinzhu v. China State Railway Group Company	2016 Beijing Beijing	4 NS	5	1 DA DK	2 NM NP NQ	5
Ni Yulan v. Beijing Xicheng District Center for Public Housing and Land Management	2019 Beijing Beijing	4 NS	5	2 NN	2 NN	5
Ni Jinke v. Yuyao City Association for Science and Technology	2015 Yuyao Zhejiang	4 NS	5	2 NM NP NQ	2 NM NP NQ	5
Fu Wenrong v. State Grid Yiwu Electricity Supply Company	2016 Yiwu Zhejiang	4 NS	5	2 NB NN	2 NB NN	5
Liu Shuxiang v. Dalian City Emergency Medical Service	2019 Dalian Liaoning	4 NS	5	2 NP	2 NB NN NP	5
Shi Huifeng v. Zhejiang University	2019 Hangzhou Zhejiang	4 NS	5	2 NB NN	2 NB NN	5
Ye Lijuan v. Zhejiang Province Jiande City Notary Office	2018 Jiande Zhejiang	2 NJ NM NP NQ	5	2 NJ NM NP NQ	5	5
Song Qichen v. Shandong Province Tai'an City Daiyue Notary Office	2018 Tai'an Shandong	2 NJ	5	2 NM NP NQ	2 NM NP NQ	5

(continued)

Table 8.1 (continued)

Case citation	*Year/city and province of original jurisdiction*	*Decision and rationale of public enterprise or Institution*	*Decision and rationale of oversight department*	*Decision and rationale of primary or trial court*	*Decision and rationale of intermediate or appellate court*	*Decision and rationale of high or supreme court for retrial*
Tang Yanjun v. Beijing City Dongcheng District Center for Public Security and Forensic Science Services	2015 Beijing Beijing	4 NS	5	2 NJ NM NP NQ	5	5
Sun Longxiang v. Beijing Xingchuang Investment Company	2015 Beijing Beijing	4 NS	5	2 NM NP NQ	2 NB NN	5
Guangzhou Famous Store Management Company v. Guangdong Airport Authority	2016 Guangzhou Guangdong	4 NS	5	2 NB NM	2 NB NM	2 NB NN
Lujiang County Jufulou Restaurant v. China Mobile Lujiang Branch and China Mobile Anhui Branch	2019 Hefei Anhui	4 NS	5	2 NP NQ	2 NP NQ	5
Zhang Qiang v. South China University of Technology	2017 Guangzhou Guangdong	2 ND	5	2 NB NN	5	5
Zhang Jinzhu v. Beijing Shijingshan District Environmental Sanitation Service Center	2018 Beijing Beijing	4 NS	5	2 NB NJ	2 NB NJ	5
Xu Shanlang v. Nanjing Medical University	2020 Nanjing Jiangsu	2 NA	5	2 NB NJ NN	2 NB NJ NN	5
Xu Bin v. Tianjin Binhai New Area Xiangluowan Public Utilities Company	2015 Tianjin Tianjin	2 NH	5	2 NH NN	2 NB NN	2 NB NN

(continued)

Table 8.1 (continued)

Case citation	*Year/city and province of original jurisdiction*	*Decision and rationale of public enterprise or Institution*	*Decision and rationale of oversight department*	*Decision and rationale of primary or trial court*	*Decision and rationale of intermediate or appellate court*	*Decision and rationale of high or supreme court for retrial*
Dai Wei v. Ji'nan City Huaiyin District Housing Acquisition Service Center	2017 Ji'nan Shandong	4 NS	5	2 NM NP NQ	2 NM NP NQ	1 DB DK
Bai Yan v. National Education Examinations Authority	2018 Beijing Beijing	4 NS	2 NG NH	1 DA DK	2 NR	5
Zeng Lingxin v. China Telecom Yancheng Branch	2017 Yancheng Jiangsu	4 NS	5	2 NB	2 NB	5
Yang Xianhua v. China Telecom Changsha Branch	2018 Changsha Hunan	4 NS	5	2 NN	2 NJ	5
Li Junkun v. Zhejiang University	2017 Hangzhou Zhejiang	2 NB	5	2 NB NN	5	5
Li Shuanglin v. China Railway Beijing Group Company	2016 Beijing Beijing	4 NS	5	2 ND NJ	2 NB NN	5
Li Jinghai v. Wafangdian City Public Housing Management Office	2018 Zhuanghe Liaoning	4 NS	5	2 NB ND NJ NM	2 NM NP NQ	5
Li Xiuzhen v. Beijing Xuanfang Investment Management Group Company	2020 Beijing Beijing	2 NG	5	2 NM	2 NM	5

(continued)

Table 8.1 (continued)

Case citation	*Year/city and province of original jurisdiction*	*Decision and rationale of public enterprise or Institution*	*Decision and rationale of oversight department*	*Decision and rationale of primary or trial court*	*Decision and rationale of intermediate or appellate court*	*Decision and rationale of high or supreme court for retrial*
Yang Ou v. Suzhou Lawyers Association	2019 Suzhou Jiangsu	4 NS	5	2 NM NP NQ	2 NJ NM NP NQ	5
Tang Jinghua, et al. v. Fuzhou Land Development Center	2015 Fuzhou Fujian	4 NS	5	2 NI NM	5	5
Chen Ce and Chen Ruidi v. Wenzhou City Lucheng District Center for Urban Village Redevelopment	2020 Yueqing Zhejiang	4 NS	5	1 DB DK	2 NM NP NQ	5
Wen Hongjun and Fan Lingling v. Zhengzhou City Huiji District Financial Development Corporation	2020 Zhengzhou Henan	4 NS	5	2 NM NP NQ	2 NN NP NQ	5
Wang Guohai, Zhang Chunxiang and Wang Lin v. Hangzhou Land Banking Center	2015 Hangzhou Zhejiang	2 NG	5	2 NM NP NQ	5	5
Wang Jiaxin, et al. v. Qingdao-Ji'nan High-Speed Railway Company	2017 Ji'nan Shandong	4 NS	5	2 NM NP NQ	2 NM NP NQ	5
Wang Qiang v. Wenzhou Daily Media Group	2019 Wenzhou Zhejiang	4 NS	5	2 NB NJ NM	2 NN NP NQ	5
Wang Zhongxiang v. Tianjin Taida Cogeneration Company	2017 Tianjin Tianjin	2 NN	5	2 NN	2 NB NN	5

(continued)

Table 8.1 (continued)

Case citation	*Year/city and province of original jurisdiction*	*Decision and rationale of public enterprise or Institution*	*Decision and rationale of oversight department*	*Decision and rationale of primary or trial court*	*Decision and rationale of intermediate or appellate court*	*Decision and rationale of high or supreme court for retrial*
Wang Jiangli v. Beijing Xingchuang Investment Company	2015 Beijing Beijing	4 NS	5	2 NM NP NQ	2 NB NN	5
Wang Ronghua v. Feidong County No.4 People's Hospital	2020 Hefei Anhui	4 NS	5	2 NN	2 NJ NN	5
Wenda Kindergarten v. Heilongjiang Center for Disease Control and Prevention	2018 Harbin Heilongjiang	4 NS	5	2 NR	5	5
Hu Yukun v. Peking University	2018 Beijing Beijing	2 ND	5	2 ND	2 NB NJ NP NQ	5
Geng Liping v. Tangshan City Center for Municipal Engineering and Environmental Sanitation	2020 Tangshan Hebei	2 NN	5	2 NP	2 NP	5
Geng Chaochao v. Hangzhou Xiaoshan Environment Group Company	2020 Hangzhou Zhejiang	2 NJ	5	2 NJ NN	2 NN	5
Cai Xiaoming v. China Mobile Changsha Branch	2014 Changsha Hunan	4 NS	5	2 NP	5	5
Yuan Tie v. Capital Iron and Steel Corporation	2016 Beijing Beijing	4 NS	5	2 NM NP NQ	5	5

(continued)

Table 8.1 (continued)

Case citation	*Year/city and province of original jurisdiction*	*Decision and rationale of public enterprise or Institution*	*Decision and rationale of oversight department*	*Decision and rationale of primary or trial court*	*Decision and rationale of intermediate or appellate court*	*Decision and rationale of high or supreme court for retrial*
Gu Fengxiao v. Beijing Xingchuang Investment Company	2015 Beijing Beijing	4 NS	5	2 NM NP NQ	2 NB NN	5
Ma Li v. Fuwai Huazhong Cardiovascular Hospital	2020 Zhengzhou Henan	4 NS	5	2 NN	5	5
Gu Ming v. China Mobile Suqian Branch	2020 Suqian Jiangsu	4 NS	5	2 NN	2 NN	5
Wu Zaimei v. Pingxiang Hospital of Traditional Chinese Medicine	2017 Pingxiang Jiangxi	2 NL	5	2 NJ NM NQ	2 NJ NM NQ	5
Zheng Mingjie v. China Internet Network Information Center	2018 Beijing Beijing	4 NS	5	2 NM NP NQ	2 NM NP NQ	5
Guo Bing v. China State Railway Group Company	2018 Beijing Beijing	2 NJ	5	2 NN NP NQ	2 NN	2 NN
Guo Zheng v. Cangzhou Sports Management Center	2020 Cangzhou Hebei	4 NS	5	2 NP NQ	1 DB DK	5
Yang Shifeng v. Guangxi Working Fitness Assessment Committee	2019 Nanning Guangxi	4 NS	5	2 NP NQ	2 NM NP NQ	5

(continued)

Table 8.1 (continued)

Case citation	*Year/city and province of original jurisdiction*	*Decision and rationale of public enterprise or Institution*	*Decision and rationale of oversight department*	*Decision and rationale of primary or trial court*	*Decision and rationale of intermediate or appellate court*	*Decision and rationale of high or supreme court for retrial*
Chen Shiqing v. Gutian County Party School	2015 Ningde Fujian	4 NS	5	2 ND NP NQ	2 NJ NM NP NQ	5
Chen Shiqing v. Fujian Province Party School	2015 Fuzhou Fujian	4 NS	5	2 NP NQ	2 NP NQ	5
Chen Yuejun v. China United Network Communication Group	2015 Beijing Beijing	4 NS	5	2 NP	2 NB NN	5
Chen Hua v. Nanjing University of Information Science and Technology	2020 Nanjing Jiangsu	4 NS	5	2 NN	2 NJ NN NP	5
Chen Lin v. Jianghan University	2019 Wuhan Hubei	4 NS	5	2 NN NP NQ	2 NN NP NQ	2 NN NP NQ
Jia Youbao v. Beijing Mass Transit Railway Operation Corporation	2019 Beijing Beijing	4 NS	5	2 NM NP	2 NM NP	5
Jia Youbao v. Great Wall Broadband Network Service Corporation Qingdao Branch	2018 Qingdao Shandong	4 NS	5	2 NN	2 NN	5
Jia Youbao v. China Mobile Qingdao Branch	2017 Qingdao Shandong	4 NS	5	2 NN	2 NN	2 NN
Jia Youbao v. China United Network Communication Group Qingdao Branch	2017 Qingdao Shandong	4 NS	5	2 NB NN	2 NB NN	2 NB NN

(continued)

Table 8.1 (continued)

Case citation	*Year/city and province of original jurisdiction*	*Decision and rationale of public enterprise or Institution*	*Decision and rationale of oversight department*	*Decision and rationale of primary or trial court*	*Decision and rationale of intermediate or appellate court*	*Decision and rationale of high or supreme court for retrial*
Jia Youbao v. China United Network Communication Group Beijing Branch	2018 Beijing Beijing	4 NS	5	2 NB NN	2 NF	5
Jia Youbao v. Shandong Broadcast & TV Network Company	2017 Ji'nan Shandong	4 NS	5	2 NP	2 NP	2 NP
Jia Youbao v. Beijing Xianglong Bus Passenger Transport Company	2019 Beijing Beijing	4 NS	5	2 NM NP NQ	2 NM NP NQ	5
Jia Youbao v. Beijing Municipal Administration & Communication Car Company	2019 Beijing Beijing	4 NS	5	2 NM NP NQ	2 NF NL	5
Jia Youbao v. Beijing Xiaoju Technology Company	2018 Beijing Beijing	4 NS	5	2 NM	2 NM	2 NM
Jia Youbao v. Beijing Public Transport Corporation	2019 Beijing Beijing	2 NR	5	2 NR	5	5
Jia Youbao v. China State Railway Group Company	2018 Beijing Beijing	4 NS	5	2 NN	2 NN	2 NN
Jia Youbao v. China Postal Express & Logistics Corporation	2018 Beijing Beijing	4 NS	5	2 NN	2 NF NN	5

Table 10.1 Freedom House Scores for U.S. Press Freedom (2008–2017)[16]

Year	*Legal environment*	*Political environment*	*Economic environment*	*Total score*	*Freedom status*
2008	5	8	4	17	Free
2009	5	8	5	18	Free
2010	5	8	5	18	Free
2011	4	8	5	17	Free
2012	3	10	5	18	Free
2013	3	10	5	18	Free
2014	6	10	5	21	Free
2015	6	11	5	22	Free
2016	6	10	5	21	Free
2017	6	10	7	23	Free

Table 10.2 Freedom House Scores for China's Press Freedom (2008–2017)[17]

Year	*Legal environment*	*Political environment*	*Economic environment*	*Total score*	*Freedom status*
2008	28	35	22	85	Not free
2009	28	34	22	84	Not free
2010	28	34	22	84	Not free
2011	29	34	22	85	Not free
2012	29	34	22	85	Not free
2013	29	32	22	83	Not free
2014	29	33	22	84	Not free
2015	30	34	22	86	Not free
2016	30	35	22	87	Not free
2017	30	34	23	87	Not free

[16] The dataset in this table came from Refworld Global Law and Policy Database, a tool created and maintained by the United Nations High Commissioner for Refugees and is the leading source of information for making quality decisions about the status of asylum-seekers and refugees. *Freedom of the Press 2017—United States*, RefWorld, Geneva, Switzerland, *available at* https://www.refworld.org/reference/annualreport/freehou/2017/en/116626 (accessed between February 21, 2025 and March 31, 2025).

[17] The dataset in this table came from Refworld Global Law and Policy Database. *Freedom of the Press 2017—China*, RefWorld, Geneva, Switzerland, *available at* https://www.refworld.org/reference/annualreport/freehou/2017/en/118931 (accessed between February 21, 2025 and March 31, 2025).

Table 10.3 Freedom House Scores for North Korea's Press Freedom (2008-2017)[18]

Year	*Legal environment*	*Political environment*	*Economic environment*	*Total score*	*Freedom status*
2008	30	39	29	98	Not free
2009	30	40	29	99	Not free
2010	30	40	29	99	Not free
2011	30	38	29	97	Not free
2012	30	38	29	97	Not free
2013	30	37	29	96	Not free
2014	30	38	29	97	Not free
2015	30	38	29	97	Not free
2016	30	38	29	97	Not free
2017	30	39	29	98	Not free

Table 10.4 Freedom House Scores for Cuba's Press Freedom (2008–2017)[19]

Year	*Legal environment*	*Political environment*	*Economic environment*	*Total score*	*Freedom status*
2008	30	36	28	94	Not free
2009	30	35	28	93	Not free
2010	30	35	28	93	Not free
2011	30	34	28	92	Not free
2012	29	34	28	92	Not free
2013	29	35	28	92	Not free
2014	28	34	28	90	Not free
2015	28	35	28	91	Not free
2016	28	35	28	91	Not free
2017	28	35	28	91	Not free

[18] The dataset in this table came from Refworld Global Law and Policy Database. *Freedom of the Press 2017—North Korea*, RefWorld, Geneva, Switzerland, *available at* https://www.refworld.org/reference/annualreport/freehou/2017/en/119039 (accessed between February 21, 2025 and March 31, 2025).

[19] The dataset in this table came from Refworld Global Law and Policy Database. *Freedom of the Press 2017—Cuba*, RefWorld, Geneva, Switzerland, *available at* https://www.refworld.org/reference/annualreport/freehou/2017/en/118928 (accessed between February 21, 2025 and March 31, 2025).

Table 10.5 Freedom House Scores for Nondemocratic Countries with FOI Laws[20]

Country	*Legal environment*	*Political influences*	*Economic pressure*	*Total score*	*Press freedom status*
China (2007)	28	34	22	84	Not free
Angola (2002)	21	33	25	79	Not free
Zimbabwe (2002)	26	34	23	83	Not free
Russia (2009)	23	33	24	80	Not free
Uzbekistan (1997)	N/A	N/A	N/A	N/A	N/A
Azerbaijan (2005)	23	27	22	72	Not free
Tajikistan (2002)	29	27	24	80	Not free
Iran (2009)	30	36	24	90	Not free
Jordan (2007)	21	22	18	61	Not free
Kazakhstan (2015)	29	33	23	85	Not free
Guinea (2010)	24	30	17	71	Not free
Vietnam (2016)	30	33	22	85	Not free
Afghanistan (2014)	20	27	19	66	Not free
Rwanda (2013)	24	32	24	80	Not free
Kyrgyzstan (2007)	22	25	20	67	Not free
Liberia (2010)	17	23	21	61	Not free
Sri Lanka (2016)	19	26	19	64	Not free

(continued)

[20] The dataset in this table came from Freedom House's annual freedom in the world rankings. The years in the table indicates when the FOI laws were enacted. *Comparative and Historical Data*, Freedom in the World, Freedom House, Washington, DC, *available at* https://freedomhouse.org/reports/publication-archives (accessed between February 21, 2025, and March 31, 2025).

Table 10.5 (continued)

Country	*Legal environment*	*Political influences*	*Economic pressure*	*Total score*	*Press freedom status*
Tunisia (2011)	27	33	25	85	Not free
Ethiopia (2008)	27	30	19	76	Not free
Bangladesh (2009)	20	27	16	63	Not free
Yemen (2012)	27	33	23	83	Not free
Armenia (2003)	23	26	16	65	Not free

Codes for Disclosure and Non-Disclosure Decisions in Table 7.9 **and** Table 8.1**:**

1. Approved, in whole, disclosure of the requested information.
2. Denied, in whole, disclosure of the requested information.
3. Approved partial disclosure of the requested information and denied disclosure of other information sought.
4. The applicant did apply for information disclosure or ask for support of information disclosure via this entity, but the entity neither approved nor denied disclosure of the requested information. The entity received the petition and didn't do anything about it. The entity received the petition and returned it to the applicant. The entity received the petition and forwarded it to another entity. The entity didn't receive the petition.
5. The applicant neither applied for information disclosure nor asked for support of information disclosure via this entity.
6. The entity was ordered by an oversight organization or court to review the application and determine if the information should be released.
7. Any other scenarios not listed above.

Codes for Disclosure Rationales in Table 7.9 **and** Table 8.1:

DA: The organization is a public enterprise or institution explicitly provided in the OGI Regulations and relevant laws.

DB: The organization is a public enterprise or institution implied by the OGI Regulations and relevant laws.

DC: The organization is an administrative agency or empowered organization authorized by an administrative agency to handle relevant work.

DD: The organization is neither an administrative agency nor an empowered organization, but it is still subject to administrative reconsideration.

DE: The organization is neither an administrative agency nor an empowered organization, but it is still subject to administrative litigation.

DF: Requested information is of legitimate public concern.

DG: Requested information is not exempt from disclosure and should be disclosed according to the OGI Regulations and/or relevant laws.

DH: Requested information is in the hands of the organization.

DI: Requested information is relevant to the applicant's special needs.

DJ: Requested information should be disclosed because of the organization's desire to meet the service needs of its customers, not because of the legal requirements of the OGI Regulations.

DK: The organization failed to fulfill its legal obligation of reviewing the information request, deciding laws to apply and what decision to make, and notifying the applicant of the decision. The organization failed to cite proper laws when making the non-disclosure determination.

DL: When reviewing a request for records, the organization engaged in a blanket denial of access to records. It is wrong. The organization should divide the records into different portions and disclose portions that warrant disclosure.

DM: Any other rationales not listed above.

DN: No rationales for disclosure were given.

Codes for Non-Disclosure Rationales in Table 7.9 **and** Table 8.1:

NA: Requested information is exempt from disclosure under the OGI Regulations and relevant laws.

NB: Requested information is not created by the organization in the process of performing its duties involving public interests.

NC: Requested information appears in internal documents.

ND: Requested information is internal management information or procedural information.

NE: Requested information needs summarization, assembly, reproduction or statistical analysis.

NF: Requested information is irrelevant to the applicant's special needs.

NG: Requested information does not exist. Requested information cannot be found.

NH: Requested information is not in the possession of the organization which received the request and the applicant should look for the information elsewhere.

NI: Request is ambiguous and fails to conform to required application format/channel. Request is in essence consulting or filing petitions, accusations or complaints in disguise of applying for governmental information via OGI Regulations. Request contains too many applications. There is no proof of request being sent by the applicant and/or being received by the entity. Some required application information is missing. The applicant is asking for information that is hard to share for whatever reason, therefore, the applicant should examine the information in person at a designated government facility.

NJ: Requested information is not official information.

NK: Requested information has been transferred to archival institutions.

NL: Requested information is the subject of repeated requests, or the sought information is already proactively disclosed. The applicant intends to overwhelm courts by producing a massive number of OGI lawsuits.

NM: The organization is not a public enterprise or institution, thus not subject to the OGI Regulations and relevant laws. The organization is not a public enterprise or institution, thus not subject to administrative reconsideration and administrative litigation.

NN: The organization is a public enterprise or institution that should disclose information with reference to the OGI Regulations, but one of the situations listed below applies: The information sought has already been disclosed upon request (either verbally or in writing). The petitioner has failed to prove that the information sought is held or produced by the organization. The organization has not received the application. The organization has already replied to the information request. The information does not exist. The information needs summarization, assembly, reproduction or statistical analysis. The information is internal and has nothing to do with public service. The information sought does not qualify as disclosable governmental information defined in the OGI Regulations and implementation measures. The information sought is irrelevant to the applicant's special needs. Whether the public enterprise/institution should disclose the requested information or not should be determined by itself, not by courts. The organization does not have the sought information, and it should be obtained from elsewhere. The organization does not know how to disclose the requested information due to lack of implementation measures by the oversight agency in the State Council. The applicant should have appealed to an oversight organization for information instead of bringing the public enterprise/institution to court. The oversight agency in the State Council has not created binding rules regarding disclosure of information held by the subordinate public enterprise/institution.

NO: The organization is neither an administrative agency nor empowered organization, thus not subject to administrative reconsideration.

NP: The organization is neither an administrative agency nor an empowered organization, thus not subject to administrative litigation.

NQ: The organization is neither an administrative agency nor empowered organization, thus not subject to the OGI Regulations.

NR: Any other rationales not listed above.

NS: No rationales for non-disclosure were given.

Bibliography

Secondary Sources

Books

A Source Book in Chinese Philosophy. Translated and compiled by Wing-tsit Chan. Princeton, NJ: Princeton University Press, 1963.

Allport, Gordon W., and Leo J. Postman. *The Psychology of Rumor*. New York, NY: Henry Holt, 1947.

Altschull, J. Herbert. *Agents of Power: The Media and Public Policy*. White Plains, NY: Longman, 1995.

Anthony, Carol K., and Hanna Moog. *I Ching: The Oracle of the Cosmic Way*. Stow, MA: Anthony Publishing Company, 2002.

Bailey, Paul John. *China in the Twentieth Century*. Hoboken, NJ: Wiley-Blackwell, 2001.

Balkin, Jack M. *The Laws of Change: I Ching and the Philosophy of Life*. New York, NY: Schocken Books, 2002.

Ban, Gu. *Book of Han*[汉书]. Annotated by Shigu Yan. Beijing, China: Zhonghua Press, 2000.

Bandurski, David, and Martin Hala, eds. *Investigative Journalism in China: Eight Cases in Chinese Watchdog Journalism*. Hong Kong, China: Hong Kong University Press, 2010.

Barron, Jerome A. *Freedom of the Press for Whom? The Right of Access to Mass Media*. Bloomington, IN: Indiana University Press, 1973.

Baum, Richard. *Burying Mao: Chinese Politics in the Age of Deng Xiaoping*. Princeton, NJ: Princeton University Press, 1996.

Y. Tang, *Freedom of Information Law in China*,
https://doi.org/10.1007/978-981-96-7842-6

Berger, Charles R., and Steven H. Chaffee, eds. *Handbook of Communication Science*. Newbury Park, CA: Sage. 1989.
Birkinshaw, Patrick. *Freedom of Information: The Law, the Practice and the Ideal*. Cambridge, UK: Cambridge University Press, 2010.
Boden, Jeanne. *The Wall Behind China's Open Door: Towards Efficient Intercultural Management in China*. Brussels, Belgium: ASP-VUB Press, 2008.
Borgwardt, Elizabeth. *A New Deal for the World: America's Vision for Human Rights*. Cambridge, MA: Belknap Press of Harvard University Press, 2005.
Brady, Anne-Marie. *Marketing Dictatorship: Propaganda and Thought Work in Contemporary China*. Lanham, MD: Rowman & Littlefield, 2008.
Brooks, Taeko. *The Original Analects: Sayings of Confucius and His Successors*. New York, NY: Columbia University Press, 1998.
Brucker, Herbert. *Freedom of Information*. New York, NY: Macmillan, 1949.
Brugger, Bill. *China Since the "Gang of Four."* London, UK: Croom Helm, 1980.
Burgh, Huge de, ed. *Making Journalists: Diverse Models, Global Issues*. London, UK: Routledge, 2005.
Busha, Charles H., and Stephen P. Harter. *Research Methods in Librarianship: Techniques and Interpretations*. Waltham, MA: Academic Press, 1980.
Cantor, Norman F. *The Civilization of the Middle Ages: A Completely Revised and Expanded Edition of Medieval History*. New York, NY: Harper Perennial, 1994.
Carson, Rachel. *Silent Spring*. Boston, MA: Houghton Mifflin, 1962.
Chai, Chu. *The Sacred Books of Confucius, and Other Confucian Classics*. New Hyde Park, NY: University Books, 1965.
Cheek, Timothy. *Propaganda and Culture in Mao's China: Deng Tuo and the Intelligentsia*. Oxford, UK: Clarendon Press, 1997.
Ch'ien, Tuan-shêng. *The Government & Politics of China 1912-1949*. Stanford, CA: Stanford University Press, 1970.
Chong, Woei Lien. Chi*na's Great Proletarian Cultural Revolution: Master Narratives and Post-Mao Counternarratives*. Lanham, MD: Rowman & Littlefield Publishers, 2002.
Christians, Clifford G., Theodore Glasser, and Denis McQuail. *Normative Theories of the Media: Journalism in Democratic Societies*. Chicago, IL: University of Illinois Press, 2009.
Chung, Jae Ho, ed. *Charting China's Future: Political, Social, and International Dimensions*. Lanham, MD: Roman and Littlefield, 2006.
Confucius. *The Analects*. Translated by David Hinton. Berkeley, CA: Counterpoint Press, 1998.
Cook, Fred James. *The Muckrakers*. New York, NY: Doubleday, 1972.
Cooper, Kent. T*he Right to Know: An Exposition of the Evils of News Suppression and Propaganda*. New York, NY: Farrar, Straus and Cudahy, 1956.

Coronel, Sheila S. ed. *The Right to Know: Access to Information in Southeast Asia*. Manila, Philippines: Philippine Center for Investigative Journalism and Southeast Asian Press Alliance, 2003.

Crone, Tom. *Law and the Media*. Edited by Philip Alberstat, Tom Cassels and Estelle- Overs. Oxford, UK: Focus Press, 2002.

Cross, Harold L. The *People's Right to Know: Legal Access to Public Records and Proceedings*. New York, NY: Columbia University Press, 1953.

Curran, James, and Myung-jin Park, eds. *De-Westernizing Media Studies*. London, UK: Routledge, 2000.

Currier, Edwar. *The Political Text Book*. Charleston, SC: Nabu Press, 2010.

Dai, Huang. *Yaobang Hu and Re-examination of Cases Involving Unjust, False or Wrong Charges* [胡耀邦与平反冤假错案]. Beijing, China: China Workers Publishing House, 2004.

Darch, Colin, and Peter G. Underwood. *Freedom of Information and the Developing World: The Citizen, the State and Models of Openness*. Oxford, UK: Chandos Publishing, 2009.

Declercq, Dominik. Wri*ting against the State: Political Rhetorics in Third & Fourth Century*. Boston, MA: Brill Academic Publishers, 1998.

Denecke, Wiebke. T*he Dynamics of Masters Literature: Early Chinese Thought from Confucius Han Feizi*. Cambridge, MA: Harvard University Asia Center, 2011.

Deng, Xiaoping. *Selected Works of Deng Xiaoping* [邓小平文选第三卷]. Vol.3. Beijing, China: People's Press, 1994.

Deng, Xiaoping. *Selected Works of Deng Xiaoping* [邓小平文选第二卷]. Vol.2. Beijing, China: People's Press, 1994.

Donsbach, Wolfgang, ed. *International Encyclopedia of Communication*. Hoboken, NJ: Wiley-Blackwell, 2008.

Downing, John. *Radical Media: Rebellious Communication and Social Movements*. Thousand Oaks, CA: Sage Publications, 2001.

Emerson, Thomas I. *The System of Freedom of Expression*. New York, NY: Random House, 1970.

Fan, Ye. *Book of Later Han* [后汉书]. Hangzhou, China: Zhejiang Ancient Books Publishing House, 2000.

Fang, Hanqi, ed. *A History of Chinese Journalism* [中国新闻事业通史]. Vol.1. Beijing, China: Renmin University of China Press, 1992.

Finkelstein, David M., and Kristen Gunness, eds. *Civil-Military Relations in Today's China: Swimming in a New Sea*. Armonk, NY: M.E. Sharpe, 2006.

Florini, Ann, and Joseph E. Stiglitz, eds. *The Right to Know: Transparency for an Open World*. New York, NY: Columbia University Press, 2007.

Foerstel, Herbert N. *Freedom of Information and the Right to Know: The Origins and Applications of the Freedom of Information Act*. Westport, CT: Greenwood Press, 1999.

Folsom, Ralph H., John H. Minan, and Lee Ann Otto. *Law and Politics in the People's Republic of China in a Nutshell*. Eagan, MN: West Group, 1992.

Forges, Roger V. Des, Ning Luo, and Yen-bo Wu, eds. *Chinese Democracy and the Crisis of 1989: Chinese and American Reflections*. Albany, NY: State University of New York Press, 1993.

Fryer, John. *Oriental Studies: The Philosophies and Religions of China*. Hong Kong, China: Kelly &Walsh, 1900.

Fu, Zhengyuan. *China's Legalists: the Earliest Totalitarians and Their Art of Ruling*. Armonk, NY: M. E. Sharpe, 1996.

Gallagher, Aileen. *Muckrakers: American Journalism during the Age of Reform*. New York, NY: Rosen Classroom, 2006.

Gao, Wenqian. *Zhou Enlai: The Last Perfect Revolutionary*. New York, NY: PublicAffairs Books, 2008.

Geddes, Barbara. *Paradigms and Sand Castles: Theory Building and Research Design in Comparative Politics*. Ann Arbor, MI: University of Michigan Press, 2003.

General Office of the Chinese Communist Party Central Commission for Discipline Inspection, ed. *Openness in Governmental Affairs* [政务公开]. Beijing, China: Fangzheng Press, 2004.

Gernet, Jacques. *A History of Chinese Civilization*. Translated by J. R. Foster and Charles Hartman. Cambridge, UK: Cambridge University Press, 1996.

Gittings, John. *The Changing Face of China: From Mao to Market*. New York, NY: Oxford University Press, 2006.

Goodman, David S. G. *Deng Xiaoping and the Chinese Revolution: A Political Biography*. New York, NY: Psychology Press, 1994.

Gross, Peter. *Entangled Evolutions: Media and Democratization in Eastern Europe*. Baltimore, MD: Johns Hopkins University Press, 2002.

Guo, Xiaoqin. *State and Society in China's Democratic Transition: Confucianism, Leninism, and Economic Development*. New York, NY: Psychology Press, 2003.

Hachten, William A. Th*e World News Prism: Changing Media of International Communication*. Ames, IA: Iowa State University Press, 1999.

Hachten, William A., and Harva Hachten. The *World News Prism: Changing Media, Clashing Ideologies*. Ames, IA: Iowa State University Press, 1987.

Hallin, Daniel C., and Paolo Mancini. Comp*aring Media Systems: Three Models of Media and Politics*. Cambridge, UK: Cambridge University Press, 2004.

Hamrin, Carol Lee, and Suisheng Zhao, eds. *Decision-Making in Deng's China: Perspectives from Insiders*. 2nd ed. Armonk, NY: M.E. Sharpe, 1995.

Han, Fei Tzu. *Han Fei Tzu: Basic Writings*. Translated by Burton Watson. New York, NY: Columbia University Press, 1964.

Hoffman, Daniel N. *Government Secrecy and the Founding Fathers: A Study in Constitutional*. Westport, CT: Greenwood Press, 1981.

Hong, Junhao. *The Internationalization of Television in China: the Evolution of Ideology, Society and Media since the Reform*. Westport, CT: Praeger, 1998.

Hsiao, Ching-chang, and Timothy Cheek. *"Open and Closed Media: External and Internal Newspapers in the Propaganda System."* In *Decision-making in Deng's China: Perspectives from Insiders*, edited by Carol Lee Hamrin and Suisheng Zhao. Armonk, NY: M.E. Sharpe, 1995.

Hsü, Leonard Shihlien. *The Political Philosophy of Confucianism: An Interpretation of the Social and Political Ideas of Confucius, His Forerunners, and His Early Disciples*. New York, NY: Curzon Press, 1975.

Hucker, Charles O. *China's Imperial Past: An Introduction to Chinese History and Culture*. Stanford, CA: Stanford University Press, 1995.

Huntington, Samuel P. *The Third Wave: Democratization in the late Twentieth Century*. Norman, OK: University of Oklahoma Press, 1991.

Huxley, Thomas Henry. *Evolution and Ethics and Other Essays*. New York, NY: D. Appleton, 1896.

Ingelhart, Louis Edward, ed. *Press and Speech Freedom in America, 1619–1995: A Chronology*. Westport, CT: Greenwood Press 1997.

Jacobstein, J. Myron, and Roy M. Mersky. *Fundamentals of Legal Research*. 8th ed. New York, NY: Foundation Press, 2002.

Keng, Lu. "*Press Control in 'New China' and 'Old China.'*" In *Media's China, China's Media*, edited by Chin-Chuan Lee, 147-62. Boulder, CO: Westview Press, 1994.s

Kennedy, David M., and Thomas A. Bailey. T*he American Spirit: United States History as Seen by Contemporaries: to 1877*. Stamford, CA: 2009.

Kirkland, Russell. *Taoism: the Enduring Tradition*. New York, NY: Psychology Press, 2004.

Kishlansky, Mark A. *Sources of World History*. Vol.2. New York, NY: HarperCollins, 1995.

Klosek, Jacqueline. The *Right to Know: Your Guide to Using and Defending Freedom of Information Law in the United States*. Westport, CT: Praeger, 2009.

Kuhn, Philip A. *Soulstealers: The Chinese Sorcery Scare of 1768*. Cambridge, MA: Harvard University Press, 1990.

Kunz, Christina L., Deborah A. Schmedemann, Ann L. Bateson, Matthew P. Downs, and Mehmet Konar-Steenber. *The Process of Legal Research*. 7th ed. New York, NY: Aspen Publishers, 2008.

Lampton, David M., ed. *The Making of Chinese Foreign and Security Policy in the Era of Reform, 1978-2000*. Stanford, CA: Stanford University Press, 2001.

Lawrance, Alan. *China since 1919: Revolution and Reform: A Sourcebook*. London, UK: Routledge, 2004.

Lawson, Chappell H. *Building the Fourth Estate: Democratization and the Rise of a Free Press Mexico*. Berkeley, CA: University of California Press, 2002.

Lee, Chin-Chuan. *Money, Power and Media: Communication Patterns and Bureaucratic Control in Cultural China*. Evanston, IL: Northwestern University Press, 2000.

Lee, Hong Yung. *The Politics of the Chinese Cultural Revolution: A Case Study*. Berkeley, CA: University of California Press, 1978.

Leese, Daniel. *Mao Cult: Rhetoric and Ritual in China's Cultural Revolution*. Cambridge, UK: Cambridge University, 2011.

Leng, Shao-Chuan, and Hungdah Chiu. *Criminal justice in Post-Mao China: Analysis and Documents*. Albany, NY: State University of New York Press, 1985.

Lenin, Vladimir. *Lenin Collected Works*. Vol. 5.Moscow, Russia: Foreign Language Publishing House, 1961.

Leonard, Thomas C. *The Power of the Press: The Birth of American Political Reporting*. New York, NY: Oxford University Press, 1986.

Levy, Leonard W. *Emergence of a Free Press*. New York, NY: Oxford University Press, 1985.

Levy, Leonard. *Original Intent and the Framers Constitution*. New York, NY: Macmillan, 1988.

Li, Cheng. *Chinese Politics in the Xi Jinping Era: Reassessing Collective Leadership*. Washington, DC: Brookings Institution Press, 2016.

Li, Gucheng. *A Glossary of Political Terms of the People's Republic of China*. Hong Kong, China: Chinese University Press, 1995.

Li, Mo. *Gu Shu Pou Tan* [孤树裒谈]. Shanghai, China: Shanghai Ancient Books Publishing House, 2002.

Lieberthal, Kenneth. *Governing China: from Revolution through Reform*. New York, NY: W. W. Norton & Company, 2004.

Lin, Aijun. *Legal Protection for the Right to Know* [知情权的法律保障]. Shanghai, China: Fudan University Press, 2010.

Lin, Yutang. *A History of the Press and Public Opinion in China*. Chicago, IL: The University of Chicago Press, 1936.

Ling, George Fusun. *China Developing: Cultural Identity of Emerging Societies*. Singapore, Singapore: World Scientific, 2008.

Littlejohn, Ronnie. *Confucianism: An Introduction*. New York, NY: Palgrave Macmillan, 2011.

Liu, Alan P. L. *Communications and National Integration in Communist China*. Berkeley, CA: University of California Press, 1971.

Liu, Fangtong, Songjie Huang, and George F. McLean. *Philosophy and Modernization in China*. Washington, D.C.: The Council for Research in Values and Philosophy, 1997.

Liu, Hen. *Government Information Disclosure Systems* [政府信息公开制度]. Beijing, China: China Social Sciences Press, 2004.

Liu, Jie. *Right to Know and Freedom of Information Law* [知情权与信息公开法]. Beijing, China: Tsinghua University Press, 2005.

Liu, Yandong, and Zhihao Lou. *Choice of the People: Chinese Communist Party and Future of China* [人民的选择: 中国共产党与中国的前途]. Beijing, China: China Youth Publishing House, 1991.

Lockard, Craig A. *Societies, Networks, and Transitions: A Global History*. 2nd ed. Belmont, CA: Wadsworth Publishing, 2010.

Locke, John. *The Two Treatises of Government*. London, UK: C. and J. Rivington, 1824.

Locke, John. *Two Treatises of Government (1690)*. New York: NY: Hafner Press, 1947.

Locke, John. *Second Treatise of Government*. Raleigh, NC: Hayes Barton Press, 1952.

Loewe, Michael, and Edward L. Shaughnessy, eds. *The Cambridge History of Ancient China: from the Origins of Civilization to 221 B.C.*. Cambridge, UK: Cambridge University Press, 1999.

Lu, Xing. *Rhetoric in Ancient China, Fifth to Third Century, B.C.E.: A Comparison with Classical Greek Rhetoric*. Columbia, SC: University of South Carolina Press, 1998.

Lu, Xing. *Rhetoric of the Chinese Cultural Revolution: The Impact on Chinese Thought, Culture and Communication*. Columbia, SC: University of South Carolina Press, 2004.

Lv, Buwei, ed. *Lv's Commentaries of History*[吕氏春秋]. Beijing, China: Foreign Languages Press, 2010.

Lynch, Daniel C. *After the Propaganda State: Media, Politics, and "Thought Work" in Reformed China*. Stanford, CA: Stanford University Press, 1999.

Mao, Zedong. *Collected Works of Mao Zedong* [毛泽东选集第四卷]. Vol.4. Beijing, China: People's Press, 1961.

Mao, Zedong. *Selected Works of Mao Zedong on Journalism* [毛泽东新闻工作文选]. Beijing, China: Xinhua Publishing House, 1983.

Marsh, Norman, ed. *Public Access to Government-Held Information: A Comparative Symposium*. London, UK: Stevens & Sons, 1987.

Martin, John Leslie, and Arju Grover Chaudhary. *Comparative Mass Media Systems*. New York, NY: Longman, 1983.

Martin, Shannon E. *Freedom of Information: The News the Media Use*. Bern, Switzerland: Peter Lang, 2008.

Marx, Karl, and Friedrich Engels. *Collected Works: 1870–71*.Vol. 22. London, UK: Lawrence & Wishart, 1986.

McGrath, Alistair E. His*torical Theology: An Introduction to the History of Christian Thought*. Eugene, OR: Wipf & Stock Publishers, 1998.

McQuail, Denis. *Mass Communication Theory: An Introduction*. Thousand Oaks, CA: Sage Publications, 1987.

Meiklejohn, Alexander. *Free Speech and Its Relation to Self-Government*. New York, NY: Harper and Brothers, 1948. Reprinted 2001 by The Lawbook Exchange, Ltd.

Meiklejohn, Alexander. *Political Freedom: the Constitutional Powers of the People*. New York, NY: Harper and Brothers, 1960. Reprinted 1979 by Greenwood Press.

Mendel, Toby. *Freedom of Information: A Comparative Legal Survey*. Paris, France: United Nations Educational Scientific and Cultural Organization (UNESCO), 2008.

Merrill, John C. *The Imperative of Freedom: A Philosophy of Journalistic Autonomy*. New York, NY: Hastings House, 1974.

Merrill, John C., and S. Jack Odell. *Philosophy and Journalism*. New York, NY: Longman, 1983.

Merrill, John C., and Ralph L. Lowenstein. *Media Messages & Men: New Perspectives in Communication*. New York, NY: David McKay Company, 1971.

Mill, John Stuart. *On Liberty*. London, UK: J. W. Parker &Son, 1859.

Mill, John Stuart. *On Liberty*. Paris, France: F. Alcan, 1899.

Milton, John. *Milton's Areopagitica; a Speech for the Liberty of Unlicensed Printing*. New York, NY: Palgrave Macmillan, 1915.

Mittler, Barbara. *A Newspaper for China? Power, Identity, and Change in Shanghai's News Media 1872-1912*. Cambridge, MA: Harvard University Asia Center, 2004.

Montesquie, Charles de Secondat. *The Spirit of the Laws*. Edited by David Wallace Carrithers. Berkeley, CA: University of California Press, 1977.

Moore, Jennifer Oldstone. *Taoism: Origins, Beliefs, Practices, Holy Texts, Sacred Places*. New York, NY: Oxford University Press, 2003.

Mosco, Vincent. *The Political Economy of Communications*. Thousand Oaks, CA: Sage Publications, 1996.

Moynihan, Daniel Patrick. *Secrecy: The American Experience*. New Haven, CT: Yale University Press, 1998.

Nerone, John C., ed. *Last Rights: Revisiting Four Theories of the Press*. Urbana IL: University of Illinois Press, 1995.

New Media for a New China. Edited by James F. Scotton and William A. Hachten. Hoboken, NJ: Wiley-Blackwell, 2010.

O'Brien, David M. *The Public's Right to Know: The Supreme Court and the First Amendment*. Westport, CT: Praeger, 1981.

O'Reilly, James T. *Federal Information Disclosure: Procedures, Forms and the Law*. Colorado Springs, CO: Shepard's/McGraw-Hill, 1994.

Old Book of Tang [旧唐书]. Edited and compiled by Liu Xu. Beijing, China: Zhonghua Press, 2002.

Overholser, Geneva, and Kathleen Hall Jamieson, eds. *The Institutions of American Democracy: The Press*. New York, NY: Oxford University Press, 2005.

Paine, Thomas. *Common Sense*. New York, NY: Penguin, 1986.

Party Propaganda Work Documents 1949–1993 Volume One. Edited by Chinese Communist

Party Central Propaganda Department Office. Beijing, China: Chinese Communist Party School Publishing House, 1994.

Peerenboom, Randall. *China's Long March toward Rule of Law*. Cambridge, UK: Cambridge University Press, 2002.

Pember, Don R., and Clay Calvert. *Mass Media Law*. New York, NY: McGraw-Hill, 2013.

Pember, Don R., and Clay Calvert. *Mass Media Law*. New York, NY: McGraw-Hill, 2009–2010.

Picard, Robert G. *The Press and the Decline of Democracy: The Democratic Socialist Response in Public Policy*. Westport, CN: Greenwood Press, 1985.

Plato. *The Republic: The Statesman of Plato*. Translated by Henry Davis and George Burges. Princeton, NJ: M.W.Dunne, 1901.

Polumbau, Judy. "*Professionalism in China's Press Corps*." In *Chinese Democracy and the Crisis of 1989: Chinese and American Reflections,* edited by Roger V. Des Forges, Ning Luo and Yen-bo Wu. Albany, NY: State University of New York Press, 1993.

Popper, Karl R. *The Open Society and Its Enemies*. Princeton, NJ: Princeton University Press, 1971.

Przeworski, Adam, Michael E. Alvarez, Jose Antonio Cheibub, and Fernando Limongi. *Democracy and Development: Political Institutions and Well-Being in the World, 1950–1990*. Cambridge, United Kingdom: Cambridge University Press, 2000.

Qing, Christine Zhen-Wei. *China's Information Revolution: Managing the Economic and Social Transformation*. Washington, DC: World Bank Publications, 2007.

Raaflaub, Kurt A., Josiah Ober, Robert Wallace, Paul Cartledge, and Cynthia Farrar. *Origins of Democracy in Ancient Greece*. Berkeley, CA: University of California Press, 2007.

Randal, Marlin. *Propaganda and the Ethics of Persuasion*. Peterborough, Canada: Broadview Press, 2002.

Randall, Vicky, ed. *Democratization and the Media*. London, UK: Frank Cass, 1998.

Rawski, Evelyn Sakakida. *The Last Emperors: A Social History of Qing Imperial Institutions* Berkeley, CA: University of California Press, 2001.

Rites of Zhou [周礼]. Translated and annotated by Xuan Qian, Xingqi Qian, Huabao Wang and Binghong Xie. Changsha, China: Yuelu Publishing House, 2001.

Rivers, William L., and Wilbur Schramm. *Responsibility in Mass Communication*. New York, NY: Harper & Row, 1969.

Roberts, Alasdair. *Blacked Out: Government Secrecy in the Information A*ge. New York, NY: Cambridge University Press, 2006.

Robinet, Isabelle, and Phyllis Brooks. *Taoism: Growth of a Religion*. Stanford, CA: Stanford University Press, 1997.

Rudolph, Jörg. *Cankao-Xiaoxi: Foreign News in the Propaganda System of the People's Republic of China*. Baltimore, MD: Maryland Series in Contemporary Asian Studies, 1984.

Saich, Tony, and Benjamin Yang. *The Rise to Power of the Chinese Communist Party Documents and Analysis*. Armonk, NY: M.E. Sharpe, 1996.

Sanders, Karen. *Ethics and Journalism*. Thousand Oaks, CA: Sage Publications, 2003.

Shambaugh, David. *China's Communist Party: Atrophy and Adaptation*. Washington, DC: Woodrow Wilson Center Press, 2008.

Shang, Yang. *The Book of Lord Shang: A Classic of the Chinese School of Law*. Clark, NJ: The Lawbook Exchange, 2003.

Shirk, Susan L., ed. *Changing Media, Changing China*. New York, NY: Oxford University Press, 2010.

Shrivastava, K.M. *The Right to Information: A Global Perspective*. Frankfort, IL: Lancer, 2009.

Siebert, Fred S., Theodore Peterson and Wilbur Schramm. Fou*r Theories of the Press: The Authoritarian, Libertarian, Social Responsibility and Soviet Communist Concepts of What the Press Should Be and Do*. Urbana, IL: University of Illinois Press, 1956.

Sima, Qian. *Records of the Grand Historian: Han Dynasty*. Translated by Burto Watson. New York, NY: Columbia University Press, 1993.

Sima, Qian. *Records of the Grand Historian: Qin Dynasty*. Translated by Burton Watson. New York, NY: Columbia University Press, 1993.

Sima, Qian. *Records of the Grand Historian: Shang Yang*. Translated by Burton Watson. New York, NY: Columbia University Press, 1993.

Sima, Qian. *The First Emperor: Selections from the Historical Records*. Edited by K. E. Brashier and translated by Raymond Dawson. New York, NY: Oxford University Press, 2007.

Smith, Adam. *An Inquiry into the Nature and Causes of the Wealth of Nations*. Edited by Edwin Cannan. Chicago, IL: University Of Chicago Press, 1977.

Spencer, Herbert. The *Study of Sociology*. London, UK: H. S. King, 1873.

Stefanick, Lorna. *Controlling Knowledge: Freedom of Information and Privacy Protection in networked World*. Vancouver, Canada: University of British Columbia Press, 2011.

Sullivan, Lawrence. *Historical Dictionary of the Chinese Communist Party*. Lanham, MD: Scarecrow Press, 2011.

Sutton, Francis X. *A World to Make: Development in Perspective*. Piscataway, NJ: Transaction Publishers, 1990.

Swados, Harvey, ed. Years *of Conscience: The Muckrakers: An Anthology of Reform Journalism*. New York, NY: Meridian Books, 1962.

The China Reader: The Reform Era. Edited by Orville Schell and David Shambaugh. New York, NY: Vintage Books, 1998.

The Party Leads All: The Evolving Role of The Chinese Communist Party. Edited by Jacques Delisle and Guobin Yang. Washington, DC: Brookings Institution Press, 2022.

The Tang Code: General Principles. Vol. 1. Translated by Wallace Johnson. Princeton, NJ: Princeton University, 1979.

Tao, Baichuan. *The Chinese Ombudsman and Control System*. Queens, NY: Center of Asian Studies, St. John's University, 1971.

Taylor, Jay. *The Generalissimo: Chiang Kai-shek and the Struggle for Modern China*. Cambridge, MA: Harvard University Press, 2009.

Teiwes, Frederick C., and Warren Sun. *The End of the Maoist Era: Chinese Politics During the Twilight of the Cultural Revolution, 1972–1976*. Armonk, NY: M.E. Sharpe, 2008.

Theroux, Paul. *Riding the Iron Rooster: By Train Through China*. Boston, MA: Houghton Mifflin Harcourt, 2006.

Tournu, Christophe, and Neil Forsyth. *Milton, Rights and Liberties*. Bern, Switzerland: Peter Lang, 2007.

Tung, William L. *The Political Institutions of Modern China*. New York, NY: Springer, 1968.

Twitchett, Denis Crispin, Michael Loewe and John King Fairbank, eds. *The Cambridge History of China: The Ch'in and Han Empires, 221 B.C.-A.D. 220*. Vol. 1. Cambridge, UK: Cambridge University Press, 1986.

Tzu, Chuang. *The Complete Works of Chuang Tzu*. Translated by Burton Watson. New York, NY: Columbia University Press, 1968.

Tzu, Sun. *The Art of War.* Translated and annotated by Lionel Giles, edited by James H. Ford and Shawn Conners. El Paso, TX: El Paso Norte Press: Special Edition Books, 2009.

Tzu., Mo. *Mo Tzu: Basic Writings*. Translated by Burto Watson. New York, NY: Columbia University Press, 1963.

Villanueva, Ernesto. Derecho de acceso a la Información Pública en Latinoamérica: Estudio Introductioria Y Compilacion [Right of Access to Public Information in Latin America: Introductory Studies and Compilations]. Mexico

City, Mexico: Institute for Legal Research, National Autonomous University of Mexico [Instituto de Investigaciones Jurídicas, Universidad Nacional Autónoma de México], 2003.

Wang, Mingqing. *Waving the Duster* [挥麈录]. Shanghai, China: Shanghai Bookstore Publishing House, 2009.

Webster, Mary E. *The Federalist Papers: In Modern Language Indexed for Today's Political Issues*. Bellevue, WA: Merril Press, 1999.

Wei, Yongzheng, and Lina Zhou. *The Law of Journalism and Mass Communication in China* [新闻传播法教程], Beijing, China: China Renmin University Press, 2022 (7th Edition).

Welch, Holmes. *Taoism: the Parting of the Way*. Boston, MA: Beacon Press, 1966.

Wesson, Robert G. *The Imperial Order*. Berkeley, CA: University of California Press, 1967.

Williams, Kevin. *Read All about It! A History of the British Newspaper*. New York, NY: Taylor & Francis Group, 2010.

Williams, S. Wells. *The Middle Kingdom: A Survey of the Geography, Government, Literature, Life, Arts and History of the Chinese Empire and its Inhabitants*. Vol.2. New York, NY: Charles Scribner's Sons, 1883.

Wong, Yiu-chung. *From Deng Xiaoping to Jiang Zemin: Two Decades of Political Reform in the People's Republic of China*. Lanham, MD: University Press Of America, 2005.

Wu, Silas H.L. *Communication and Imperial Control in China: Evolution of the Palace Memorial System, 1693–1735*. Cambridge, MA: Harvard University Press, 1970.

Xi, Jinping. *Xi Jinping: The Governance of China*. Beijing, China: Foreign Languages Press, 2022.

Xiao, Weibing. *Freedom of Information Reform in China: Information Flow Analysis*. New York, NY: Taylor & Francis Group, 2011.

Yan, Jiaqi, and Gao Gao. *Turbulent Decade: A History of the Cultural Revolution*. Honolulu, HI: University of Hawaii Press, 1996.

Yang, Xiping. *New Inspirations from Mohism* [墨学新悟]. Beijing, China: Sino-Culture Press, 2012.

Yao, Xinzhong. *An Introduction to Confucianism*. Cambridge, UK: Cambridge University, 2000.

Yu, Haiqing. *Media and Cultural Transformation in China*. London, UK: Taylor & Francis, 2009.

Zelezny, John D. *Communications Law: Liberties, Restraints, and the Modern Media*. Boston, MA: Wadsworth Publishing Company, 2010.

Zhang, Jiayu. "Whistleblowers and Proper Functioning of Society" [吹哨人与社会良性运转], in *Spicy World-A Note of Social Observation by a Young Man from Mainland China* [麻辣人世间-一个大陆青年的社会观察笔记]. Taibei, Taiwan: Xiuwei Publishing House[秀威出版], 2011.

Zhang, Mingjie. *Open Government: Research on OGI Laws* [开放的政府—政府信息公开法律制度研究]. Beijing, China: China Law Press, 2003.

Zhao, Yuezhi. *Media, Market, and Democracy in China: Between the Party Line and the Bottom Line*. Urbana, IL: University of Illinois Press, 1998.

Zhao, Yuezhi. *Communication in China: Political Economy, Power, and Conflict*. Lanham, MD: Rowman & Littlefield Publishers, 2008.

Zhou, Enlai. *Selected Works of Enlai Zhou* [周恩来选集].Vol. 1.Beijing, China: People's Press, 1980.

Zhou, Enlai. *Selected Works of Enlai Zhou* [周恩来选集].Vol.2.Beijing, China: People's Press, 1984.

Zhou, Hanhua, ed. *Academic Draft of OGI Regulations: Draft, Explanation, Rationale and Legislative Examples* [政府信息公开条例专家建议稿—草案、说明、理由、立法例]. Beijing, China: Chinese Legal Publishing House, 2003.

Zhou, Hanhua. *Comparison of Foreign Freedom of Information Systems* [外国政府信息公开制度比较]. Beijing, China: China Legal Publishing House, 2003.

Zhou, Hanhua. My *Country's Experience with and Consideration of Open Governmental Affairs* [我国政府公开的实践与探索]. Beijing, China: China Law Publishers, 2003.

Zhou, Hanhua. *Government Governance and Administrative Law*. [政府监管与行政法].Beijing, China: Beijing University Press, 2007.

Zuckman, Harvey L., Robert L. Corn-Revere, Robert M. Frieden, and Charles H. Kennedy. *Modern Communications Law*. Vol. 2. Eagan, MN: West Group, 1999.

Zuo, Qiuming. *The Tso Chuan: Selections from China's Oldest Narrative History*. Translated by Burton Watson. New York, NY: Columbia University Press, 1989.

Zuo, Qiuming. *The Chronicle of Zuo*. Compiled and annotated by Dongrun Zhu. Shanghai, China: Shanghai Ancient Books Publishing House, 2007.

Law Reviews and Legal Journals

Ackerman, John M., and Irma E. Sandoval-Ballesteros. "The Global Explosion of Freedom of Information Laws." *Administrative Law Review* 58 (2006): 90.

Barry, Wm. Theodore DE. *"The 'Constitutional Tradition' in China."* *The Journal of Chinese Law* 9 (1995): 7.

Blasi, Vincent. "The Checking Value in First Amendment Theory." *American Bar Foundation Research Journal* 3 (1977): 521.

Bunker, Matthew D., Sigman L Splichal, Bill F. Chamberlin and Linda M. Perry. "Access to Government-Held Information in the Computer Age: Applying Legal Doctrine to Emerging Technology." *Florida State University Law Review* 20 (1992–1993): 543.

Chafee, Zechariah, Jr. "Legal Problems of Freedom of Information in the United Nations." *Law and Contemporary Problems* 14 (1949): 545.

Cheung, Anne S. Y. "Public Opinion Supervision: A Case Study of Media Freedom in China." *Columbia Journal of Asian Law* 20 (2006–2007): 357.

Cooper, Phillip J. "The Supreme Court, the First Amendment, and Freedom of Information." *Public Administration Review* 46 (1986): 622.

Cox, Archibald. "Executive Privilege." *University of Pennsylvania Law Review* 122 (1974): 1383.

Deva, Surya. "Corporate Complicity in Internet Censorship in China: Who Cares for the Global Compact or the Global Online Freedom Act." *George Washington International Law Review* 39 (2007): 255.

Eisen, Joel B. "The New Energy Geopolitics?: China, Renewable Energy, and the 'Greentech Race.'" *Chicago-Kent Law Review* 86 (2011): 9.

Emerson, Thomas I. "Legal Foundations of the Right to Know." *Washington University Law Quarterly* 1976, no.1 (1976): 1.

Erik, Ugland. "Demarcating a Right to Gather News: A Sequential Interpretation of the First Amendment. "*Duke Journal of Constitutional Law & Public Policy* 3 (2008): 113.

Feng, Jiang. "Party Regulations and State Laws in China: A Disappearing Boundary and Growing Tensions." *Chinese Law & Government* 51 (5-6) (2019): 260.

Feng, Yujun. "Legal Culture in China: A Comparison to Western Law." *NZACL* [New Zealand Association for Comparative Law] *Yearbook* 15 (2009).

Foster, Frances H. "American Trust Law in a Chinese Mirror." *Minnesota Law Review* 94 (2010): 602.

Freedman, Eric. "Freedom of Information and the First Amendment in a Bureaucratic Age." *Brooklyn Law Review* 49 (1983): 835.

Freeman, Robert. "Thirty Years of FOIL." *Government, Law and Policy Journal* 11 (1) (2009): 4.

Gordon, David. "American Influences on Sun Yat-sen." *Education about Asia* 16 (2) (fall 2011) (special issue: US, Asia, and the World, 1620–1914).

Griswold, Erwin. "Government in Ignorance of the Law: A Plea for Better Publication of Executive Legislation." *Harvard Law Review* 48 (1934): 198.

Guthrie, Doug. "The Quiet Revolution: The Emergence of Capitalism." *Harvard International Review* 25 (2) (2003): 48.

Halstuk, Martin E. "Holding the Spymasters Accountable after 9/11: A Proposed Model for CIA Disclosure Requirements under the Freedom of

Information Act." *Hastings Communications and Entertainment Law Journal* 27 (1) (2004–2005): 80.

Halstuk, Martin E. "Policy of Secrecy-Pattern of Deception: What Federalist Leaders Thought about a Public Right to Know, 1794–98." *Communication Law and Policy* 7 (1) (2002): 51.

Halstuk, Martin E. "When is an Invasion of Privacy Unwarranted under the FOIA? An Analysis of the Supreme Court's 'Sufficient Reason' and 'Presumption of Legitimacy' Standards." *University of Florida Journal of Law and Public Policy* 16 (3) (2005): 361.

Halstuk, Martin E. "When Secrecy Trumps Transparency: Why the Open Government Act of 2007 Falls Short." *CommLaw Conspectus: Journal of Communications Law and Policy* 16 (2) (2007–2008): 427.

Halstuk, Martin E., and Bill F. Chamberlin. "The Freedom of Information Act 1966-2006: A Retrospective on the Rise of Privacy Protection over the Public Interest." *Communication Law and Policy* 11 (4) (2006): 511.

Halstuk, Martin E., and Eric B. Easton. "Of Secrets and Spies: Strengthening the Public's Right to Know about the CIA." *Stanford Law and Policy Review* 17 (2) (2006): 353.

He, Shili. "Some Thoughts on Typical Exemptions for Government Information Disclosure." [关于政府信息免予公开典型条款的几点思考] *Politics Science and Law* 3 (2009): 37.

Hubbard, Paula, and Weibing Xiao. "Open Government Information in Chinese State-owned Enterprises." *I/S: A Journal of Law and Policy for the Information Society* 22 (2017): 57.

Janofsky, Leonard S. "A.B.A. Attacks Delay and the High Cost of Litigation." *American Bar Association Journal* 65 (1979): 1323.

Keller, Perry. "Privilege and Punishment: Press Governance in China." *Cardozo Arts & Entertainment Law Journal* 21 (2003): 87.

Kohlmeier, Louis M. "The Journalist's Viewpoint." *Administrative Law Review* 23 (1970–1971): 143.

Kutner, Luis. "Freedom of Information: Due Process of the Right to Know." *Catholic Lawyer* 18 (1972): 50.

Lamble, Stephen. "Freedom of Information, a Finnish Clergyman's Gift to Democracy." *Freedom of Information Review* 97 (2002): 2.

Lamble, Stephen. "United States FOI Laws Are a Poor Model for Statutes in Other Countries." *Freedom of Information Review* 106 (2003): 51.

Lewis, Anthony. "Public Right to Know about Public Institutions: The First Amendment as Sword." *The Supreme Court Review* 1980 (1980): 1.

Lewis, Anthony. "The Right to Scrutinize Government: Toward a First Amendment Theory of Accountability." *University of Miami Law Review* 34 (1980): 793.

Lidberg, Johan, Gail Phillips, and Stephen Tanner. "The Freedom of Information Index: Measuring the Gap Between the Promise and Practice of Information Legislation." *Freedom of Information Review* 108 (2003): 88.

Liebman, Benjamin L. "The Media and the Courts: Towards Competitive Supervision?" 834 *The China Quarterly* 208 (2011): 833.

Liebman, Benjamin L. "Watchdog or Demagogue? The Media in the Chinese Legal System." *105 Columbia Law Review* 1 (2005): 1.

Liu, Hua. "On Several Legal Issues Concerning Government Information Disclosure." [论政府信息公开的若干法律问题] *Politics Science and Law* 6 (2008): 66.

Liu, Wenjing. "Approaching Democracy through Transparency: A Comparative Law Study on Chinese Open Government Information." *American University International Law Review* 26 (2011): 983.

Meiklejohn, Alexander. "The First Amendment Is an Absolute." *The Supreme Court Review* 1961 (1961): 245.

Melcher, Lauren. "The Fog of War?" *News Media & the Law* 31 (2007): 12.

Minzner, Carl F. "Riots and Cover-ups: Counterproductive Control of Local Agents in China." *University of Pennsylvania Journal of International Law* 31 (2009–2010): 115.

Note. "The First Amendment Right to Gather State-Held Information." *Yale Law Journal* 89 (1980): 923.

O'Connor, Stephen. "Global Internet Freedom Act: Can a Proactive United States' Internet Freedom Law Forestall China's One Internet, Two System Policy." *International Journal of Civic Society Law* 2 (2004): 30.

Ou, Yangwu, and Yanbin Lv. "Governmental Information Publicity System and Legislation of Governmental Information Publicity in China." [政府信息公开制度与我国的政府信息公开立法] *Journal of Guangxi Administrative Cadre Institute of Politics and Law* 21 (2006): 19.

Peled, Roy, and Yoram Rabin. "The Constitutional Right to Information." *Columbia Human Rights Law Review* 42 (2011): 357.

Peng, Chun. "Beyond Government Transparency in China? The Challenges to Open Public Enterprises and Institutions." *University of Pennsylvania Asian Law Review* 16 (2021): 214.

Piotrowski, Suzanne J., Yahong Zhang, Wenxuan Yu, and Weiwei Lin. "Key Issues for Implementation of the Chinese Open Government Information Regulations." *Public Administration Review* 69 (2009): S129.

Relly, Jeannine E. "Freedom of Information Laws and Global Diffusion: Testing Rogers's Model." *Journalism & Mass Communication Quarterly* 89 (2012): 431.

Roberts, Alasdair. "Structural Pluralism and the Right to Information." *University of Toronto Law Journal* 51 (2001): 262.

Saba, Roberto. "An Individual's Right to Access Information in the Hands of the Government." [El derecho De la Persona a Acceder a la Informacion en Poder del Gobierno] *Comparative Media Law Journal* [Derecho Comparado De La Informacion] 3 (Jan-June 2004): 45.

Seppanen, Samuli. "Interrogating Illiberalism Through Chinese Communist Party Regulations." *Cornell International Law Journal* 52 (2) (2019): 267.

Sheng, Hua. "Perspective on Free Speech in China: Big Character Posters in China: A Historical Survey." *Journal of Asia Law* 4 (2) (1990): 234.

Snell, Rick. "Administrative Compliance-Evaluating the Effectiveness of Freedom of Information." *Freedom of Information Review* no. 93 (2001): 26.

Stevenson, Christopher. "Breaching the Great Firewall: China's Internet Censorship and the Quest for Freedom of Expression in a Connected World." *Boston College International Comparative Law Review* 30 (2007): 531.

Tang, Yong. "Merely Window Dressing or Substantial Authoritarian Transparency? Twelve Years of Enforcing China's Version of Freedom of Information Law." *Journal of Media Law and Ethics* 8 (2) (Fall/Winter 2020): 68–97.

Tang, Yong. "Defaming Officials and Celebrities: Evolution of Libel Law and the Sullivan Impact in China." *Journal of Media Law and Ethics* 7 ½ (Spring 2019): 41–67.

Tang, Yong. "For Whose Eyes Only? China's Journalistic Internal Reference System and Its Legal and Political Implications," *Journal of Information Policy* 7 (2017): 1-37.

Tang, Yong. "'Laws Are A Big Bell…It Will Never Ring Itself!' Journalistic Role in China's First Freedom of Information Law." *Journal of Media Law and Ethics* 5 (3-4) (2016): 77-105

Tang, Yong. "Feeling for Rocks while Crossing the River": Analysis of the Statutory Language of China's First Freedom of Information Law," *Journal of Information Policy*, 4: 342-376 (2014).

Wei, Li. "Comment: Judicial Interpretation in China." *Willamette Journal of International Law and Dispute Resolution* 5 (1997): 87.

Weiner, Rebecca. "Chinese Justice: The Fiction, The Facts, The Favoritism." *Journal of Law and the Humanities* 14 (2002): 225.

Winfield, Betty H., Takeya Mizuno, and Christopher E Beaudion. "Confucianism, Collectivism and Constitutions: Press Systems in China and Japan." *Communication Law and Policy* 5 (2000): 323.

Wu, Changhua. "Improving the Legal and Policy Foundation for Public Access to Environmental Information in China." *Temple Journal of Science, Technology & Environmental Law* 24 (2005): 291.

Wu, Weiguang. "The Rationale of China's Media Regulation Policy in the Process of the Institutional Transformation." *Notre Dame Journal of International & Comparative Law* 7 (1) (2017): 64.

Wu, Xiaofeng. "Understanding of Criminal Reconciliation in Ancient China." *Frontiers of Law in China* 5 (1) (2010): 91-114.

Xiao, Ming. "Analysis of State of Operation of Chinese OGI System According to 245 Annual OGI Work Reports from 2008 to 2010." [政府信息公开制度运行状态考察:基于2008 年至2010年245份政府信息公开工作年度报告] *Law Science Monthly* 10 (2011): 78.

Xie, Donghui. "Justice Reform in Republic of China and Its Implications on Today [民国时期的司法改革及其当下启示]." *China Law Review* 3 [中国法律评论] (2016).

Yin, Ping. "Chinese Government Information Disclosure and Rule of Law: From SARS to Bird Flu." [信息公开与法治政府—从"非典"到"禽流感"的启示] *Journal of Hebei Law Science* 11 (2004): 146.

Youm, Kyu Ho, and Amy Kristin Sanders. "International and Comparative Law as a Reverse Perspective on Communication Law." *Communication Law & Policy* 25 (2) (2020): 103–112.

Zhou, Hanhua. "Basic Considerations in Drafting of Regulations on Openness of Government Information (Academic Draft)." [起草《政府信息公开条例》(专家建议稿)的基本考虑], *Chinese Journal of Law* 6 (2002):57.

Zhou, Hanhua. "Some Problems and Policy Suggestions Concerning Implementation of *OGI Regulations*." [政府信息公开条例》实施的问题与对策探讨] *Chinese Public Administration* 7 (2009): 11.

Zhu, Guobin. "*Constitutional Review in China: An Unaccomplished Project or a Mirage?*" *Suffolk University Law Review* 43 (3) (May 2010): 625.

Zhu, Yingping. "Analysis of Disclosure of Internal and Preparatory Government Information." [行政机关内部准备性行为的信息公开问题探析] *Studies in Law and Business* 3 (2010): 69.

Other Academic Journals

Becker, Jonathan. "Lessons from Russia: A Neo-Authoritarian Media System." *European Journal of Communication* 19 (2004): 139.

Betty, Winfield, and Peng Zengjun. "Marketplace or Party Controls? Chinese Media in Transition." *Gazette* 67 (2005): 255.

Binder, Carroll. "Freedom of Information and the United Nations." *International Organization* 6 (1952): 210.

Blanton, Thomas S. "Openness Revolution: The Rise of a Global Movement for Freedom of Information." *Development Dialogue* 1 (2002): 16.

Bloom, Terry Adams, and Johanna Cleary. "Staking a Claim for Social Responsibility: An Argument for Dual Responsibility Model." *The International Journal on Media Management* 11 (2009): 1.

Bovens, Mark. "Information Rights: Citizenship in the Information Society." *Journal of Political Philosophy* 10 (2002): 317.

Canham, Erwin D. "International Freedom of Information." *Law and Contemporary Problems* 14 (1949): 584.

Cao, Lei, and Xiu Su. "Mysterious Internal Movies during the Cultural Revolution." [文革中神秘的"内参片"] *Journal of Memories and Archives* 8 (2010): 18.

Chen, Dong. "An Introduction of Jungians in Ancient China." [中国古代经筵概论] *Qilu Journal* 202 (1) (2008): 52.

Cheng, Qiuping, and Jian Peng. "Communication Analysis of Internal Reference." *Press Outpost* 6 (2005): 41.

Chen, Lidan. "Open Information System and Crisis Communication in China." *Chinese Journal of Communication* 1 (2008): 38.

Chen, Linda, and Junín Chen." On Impediments to Information Flow during Crisis of Songhuajiang River Contamination." [松花江水污染事件中信息流障碍分析] *Journal of Press Circles* 6 (2005): 21.

Chien, Sharon. "Historical Development of Library Education in China." *The Journal of Library History (1974–1987)* 20 (1985): 368.

Chou, Yangsun, and Andrew J. Nathan. "Democratizing Transition in Taiwan." *Asian Survey* 27 (1987): 277.

Colin, Keith Ronald, and Zhiqiu Lin. "Judicial Interpretation of China's Supreme People's Court as 'Secondary Law' with Special Reference to Criminal law." *China Information* 23 (2) (2009): 223.

Cutler, David M, and Lawrence H Summers. "The COVID-19 Pandemic and the $16 Trillion Virus." *The Journal of The American Medical Association* 324 (15) (2020): 1495–1496.

Deng, Jiwen. "Information Dissemination of Former Soviet Union from Point of View of Media: A Brief History." [传媒视野下前苏联的信息发布:一个简史] *Journal of Central South University of Forestry and Technology (Social Sciences Edition)* 5 (2) (2011): 11.

Deng, Quanshi. "A Big Case Alarming Deng Xiaoping." [惊动邓小平的一桩大案] *Yan-Huang Historical Review* 12 (2004): 14.

Diamond, Larry, and Leonardo Morlino. "The Quality of Democracy: An Overview." *Journal of Democracy* 15 (2004): 21.

Dong, Li. "News Censorship in Song Dynasty." [浅析宋代新闻管制] *Journal of Magnificent Writing* 10 (2010): 7.

Duan, Hongqing. "How Chinese Media Shall Push Forward Open Government Information." [中国媒体如何推进信息公开] *China Reform* 9 (2011) (captured by Internet Archive Wayback Machine on October 11, 2011), retrieved from https://web.archive.org/web/20111011013413/http://article.chinalawinfo.com/Article_Detail.asp?ArticleID=63344 (accessed between February 21, 2025 and March 31, 2025).

Dun, Feng, and Ting Zhao. "Wartime Management of Foreign Journalists by Chongqing Nationalist Government During War Against Japanese Aggression." [抗战时期重庆国民政府对外国记者的管理刍议] *Southeast Communication* 10 (2010): 83.

Fan, Ruxia. "Historical Characteristics of Archiving in Ancient China." [我国古代档案工作的历史特点] *Journal of Fujian Normal University (Social Science Edition)*] 1 (2000): 125.

Feng, Guodu. "Archival Institutions in Ancient China." [我国古代档案馆] *Journal of Zhongzhou Today & Yesterday* 3(1997): 19.

Fruehauf, Heiner. "The Science of Symbols Exploring a Forgotten Gateway to Chinese Medicine. "*Journal of Chinese Medicine* 69 (2002): 23.

Fung, Edmund S. K. "The Idea of Freedom in Modern China Revisited: Plural Conceptions and Dual Responsibilities." *Modern China* 32 (2006): 453.

Gasiorowski, Mark J. "An Overview of the Political Regime Change Dataset." *Comparative Political Studies* 29 (1996): 469.

Gasiorowski, Mark J., and Timothy J. Power. "The Structural Determinants of Democratic Consolidation: Evidence from the Third World." *Comparative Political Studies* 31 (1998): 740.

Gauthier, Candance Cummins. "Right to Know, Press Freedom, Public Discourse." *Journal of Mass Media Ethics* 14 (1999): 197.

Gong, Qingxin. "Research on Origins of Chinese Government and University-Owned Archives." [中国档案、中国高校档案源流研究] *Journal of Guanzi* 4 (2006): 113.

Grant, Jennifer. "Internal Reporting by Investigative Journalists in China and Its Influence on Government Policy." *International Communication Gazette* 41 (1988): 53.

Gu, Haibing. "There Should Be Disclosure of Party Affairs." [应当有党务信息公开] *Journal of Cultural Criticism* 5 (2007): 76.

Gu, Mai'nan. "Looking for Mathematician Jinrun Chen." [寻访数学家陈景润] *Yan-Huang Historical Review* 8 (2007): 58.

Halstuk, Martin E., and Bill F. Chamberlin. "Open Government in the Digital Age: The Legislative History of How Congress Established a Right of Public Access to Electronic Information Held by Federal Agencies." *Journalism and Mass Communication Quarterly* 78 (1) (2001): 45.

Harrison, Henrietta. "Newspapers and Nationalism in Rural China, 1890-1929." *Past & Present* 166 (2000): 181.

Hassid, Jonathan. "Controlling the Chinese Media: An Uncertain Business." *Asian Survey* 8 (2008): 414.

Hazell, Robert, and Ben Worthy. "Assessing the Performance of Freedom of Information." *Government Information Quarterly* 27 (2010): 352.

Hood, Steven J. "The Myths of Asian-Style Democracy." *Asian Survey* 38 (1998): 853.

Houn, Franklin W. "Chinese Communist Control of the Press." *The Public Opinion Quarterly* 22 (1958–1959): 438.

Hu, Cang-ze. "Change of Supervisory System of Tang Dynasty." [唐代监察体制的变革] *Journal of Fujian Teachers University (Philosophy and Social Sciences Edition)* 112 (3) (2001).

Huang, Chengju. "Transitional Media v. Normative Theories: Schramm, Altschull and China." *Journal of Communication* 53 (3) (2003): 444.

Huang, Chunping. "Information Dissemination Methods in Han Dynasty." [汉代信息发布手段探析] *Journal of Zhejiang Institute of Media and Communications* 18 (2011): 9.

Huang, Chunping. "Release of News in Han Dynasty-Looked from Aspect of Material of Bamboo Slips." [从出土简牍看汉帝国中央的信息发布] *Journal of Journalism &Communication* [新闻与传播研究] 4 (2006): 2.

Hubbard, Paul. "China's Regulations on Open Government Information: Challenges of Nationwide Policy Implementation." *Open Government: A Journal on Freedom of Information* 4 (1) (April 2008).

Hucker, Charles O. "The Traditional Chinese Censorate and the New Peking Regime." *The American Political Science Review* XLV (1951): 1041.

Hung, Chin-fu. "The Politics of Cyber Participation in the PRC: The Implications of Contingency for the Awareness of Citizens' Rights." *Issues & Studies* 42 (2006): 137.

Janofsky, Leonard S. "Facing the Crises of Court Costs and Delay-Initiatives for the Bar." *Leader* 7B (1981–1982): 22.

Jha, Prabhat, Patrick E Brown, and Rashid Ansumana. "Counting the Global COVID-19 Dead." *The Lancet* 399 (2022): 10339.

Jia, Bingshen. "Truth-Seeking Warrior: Note on Famous Xinhua Journalist Senling Feng." [追求真理的战士（下）-记新华社著名记者冯森龄] *Journal of Journalism Knowledge* 2 (1998).

Jiang, Fang, and Yanhui Gao. "Freedom of information Act in the United States: A Comparison with Government Information Public Regulation in China." [美国"情报自由法"浅析—兼与中国《政府信息公开条例》比较] *Journal of Xi'an University of Electronics and Technology (Social Science Edition)* 3 (2008): 133.

Jiang, Min. "Internet Companies in China: Dancing between the Party Line and the Bottom Line." *Asie.Visions* 47 (2012).

Jin, Feng. "My Experience of Writing *Neican* as a *People's Daily Journalist*." [我在《人民日报》写内参的经历] *Yan-Huang Historical Review* 10 (2005).

Jing, Bifeng, and Zhishuang Su. "Revisiting Party Directive that Party Papers Shall Not Criticize Same-Level Party Committees." ["党报不得批评同级党委"再认识] *Journal of Youth Journalist* 7 (2011).

Jing, Ming. "Origins of Party Directive 'Party Papers shall Not Criticize Same-Level Party Committees.'" ["党报不得批评同级党委"指示的来历] *Yan-Huang Historical Review* 7 (2008).

Kang, Jian, and Ling Fu. "An Exploration of Legal Protection of Citizens' Right to Know." [公民知情权法律保障之探析] *Journal of Liaoning University (Philosophy and Social Sciences Edition)* 32 (6) (2004): 124.

King, Gary, Jennifer Pan, and Margaret Roberts. "How Censorship in China Allows Government Criticism but Silences Collective Expression." *American Political Science Review* 107 (May 2013): 326-43, https://doi.org/10.1017/S0003055413000014.

Kluver, Randolph. "The Architecture of Control: a Chinese Strategy for E-Governance." *Journal of Public Policy* 25 (2005): 75.

Lai, Maosheng, and Hui Yan. "Survey on Public Awareness of OGI Regulations." [我国《政府信息公开条例》的"公众认知度"调查] *Digital Library Forum* 5 (10–13) (2008): 42.

Lam, Willy. "The Maoist Revival and the Conservative Turn in Chinese Politics." *China Perspectives*, no. 2012/2 (2012): 5–15.

Lan, Ling. "Open Government and Transparency Policy: China's Experience with SARS." *International Public Management Review* 6 (2005): 63.

Leeper, Roy V. "Richmond Newspapers, Inc. v. Virginia and the Emerging Right of Access." *Journalism Quarterly* 61 (1984): 615.

Levitsky, Steven, and Lucan A. Way. "The Rise of Competitive Authoritarianism." *Journal of Democracy* 13 (2002): 51

Li, Bo. "What Is Constitutionalism?" *Perspectives* 1 (6) (2000).

Li, Chonghua. "How did Nationalist Government Treat Foreign Journalists in Temporary Capital?" [国民政府对陪都外国记者的态度] J*ournal of Zhejiang Normal University (Social Sciences)* 2 (2006): 77.

Li, Mingde. "Commentary on Research of Press Spokespersons System." [新闻发言人制度研究述评] *Shanghai Journalism Review* 5 (2006).

Li, Shaozhang. "Questioning Party Directive that Party Papers Shall Not Criticize Same-Level Party Committees." ["党报不得批评同级党委"质疑] *Baokan Yewu Tansuo* 9 (2009).

Li, Xianggang. "China's Constitution Shall Explicitly Include Right to Know." [我国宪法应明确规定知情权] *Seek Truth from Facts* 2 (2006): 67.

Liao, Jitian. "Is Dibao Ancient Newspaper?: Reexamination of Evolution of Ancient Chinese Newspapers." [邸报是古代报纸吗? 中国古代报纸发展线索再梳理], *Journal of Journalism & Communication* 1 (2010): 12.

Liao, Yuan, and Zhenzhen Yi. "Examine Power of Emergency Information Disclosure from Perspective of Wenchuan Earthquake." [由汶川地震看突发事件信息公开的力量] *View* 8 (2008): 76.

Lidberg, Johan. "The International Freedom of Information Index: A Watchdog of Transparency in Practice." *Nordicom Review* 30 (2009): 167.

Lin, Chia-ju."A Textual Analysis of the Coverage of SARS and the Image of China." *Asian Social Science* 8 (2012): 49.

Lin, Yu, and Jun Guo. "Examination of Coverage by *Southern Weekend* on OGI Matters." [《南方周末》政府信息公开问题报道分析] *Journal of Youth Journalist* 16 (2010): 77.

Liu, Haiming. "Misunderstanding of Wilbur Lang Schramm's Soviet Communism Theory of Newspapers." [施拉姆在"报刊的苏联共产主义理论"论述中的误读] *Journal of Hunan Mass Media Vocational Technical College* 5 (2005): 26.

Liu, Lizi. "Study of *Dibao* and Government Information Dissemination in Ancient China." [浅谈邸报与我国古代政务信息的公布] *The World of Lantai* 7(2009): 49.

Liu, Wenying. "An Evaluation of History of Chinese Archives." [中国档案事业发展史探析] *Journal of Sichuan Cultural Relic* 1 (2002): 66.

Lu, Pengcheng. "Historical Review of Concept of Freedom of Speech, Freedom of the Press and Freedom of Information in Modern China." [言论自由、出版自由与新闻自由概念传入中国的历史考察] *China Media Report Overseas* 6 (2010): 20.

Lv, Yanbin. "Review Third Anniversary of Implementation of *OGI Regulations*." [政府信息公开条例实施三周年检讨] *China Reform* 5 (2011).

Lyer, Venkat. "Freedom of Information: Principles for Legislation." *Media Asia* 28 (1) (2016): 17.

Maciejewski, Jeffrey J., and David T. Ozar. "Natural Law and the Right to Know in a Democracy." *Journal of Mass Media Ethics* 20 (2005): 121.

Mackinnon, Stephen R. "Toward a History of the Chinese Press in the Republican Period." *Modern China* 23 (1997): 3.

Martin, Shannon E. , and Kamilla Benko. "Forming FOIA: The Influence of Editors and Publishers on the Freedom of Information Act." *Media History Monographs* 14 (1) (2011–2012):1–33.

McClure, Charles R, and John Carlo Bertot. "The Chief Information Officer (CIO): Assessing Its Impact." *Government Information Quarterly* 17 (2000): 7.

McCombs, Maxwell E. , and Donald L. Shaw. "The Agenda-Setting Function of Mass Media." *Public Opinion Quarterly* 36 (1972): 2.

Merrill, John, and John Nerone. "The Four Theories of the Press Four and a Half Decades Later: A Retrospective." *Journalism Studies* 3 (2002): 133.

Meyers, Christopher. "Justifying Journalistic Harms: Right to Know vs. Interest in Knowing." *Journal of Mass Media Ethics* 8 (1993): 133.

Moss, William W. "Dang'an: Contemporary Chinese Archives." *The China Quarterly* 145 (1996): 112.

Mulvenon, James. "So Crooked They Have to Screw Their Pants On: New Trends in Chinese Military Corruption." *China Leadership Monitor* 19 (2006): 1.

Nahon, Karine Barzilai. "Gatekeeping: A Critical Review." *Annual Review of Information Science and Technology* 43 (2009): 433

Ognianova, Ekaterina. "The Transitional Media System of Post-Communist Bulgaria." *Journalism and Mass Communication Monographs* 162 (1997): 1.

Ostini, Jennifer, and Anthony Y.H. Fung. "Beyond the Four Theories of the Press: A New Model of National Media Systems." *Mass Communication & Society* 5 (2002): 41.

Pan, Zhongdang, and Joseph Man Chan. "Shifting Journalistic Paradigms: How China's Journalists Assess 'Media Exemplars." *Communication Research* 30 (2003): 649.

Peng, Ke. "*Study on Chinese Ancient Confidentiality Laws*" [中国古代保密法律制度初探] *Journal of Liaoning Police Academy* 1 (2011): 20.

Peterson, Warren A. , and Noel P. Gist. "Rumor and Public Opinion." *The American Journal of Sociology* 57 (2) (1951): 159.

Pfafman, Tessa M., Christopher J. Carpenter, and Yong Tang. "The Politics of Racism: Constructions of African Immigrants in China on ChinaSMACK." *Communication, Culture and Critique* 8 (4) (2015): 540.

Pope, James S. "The Cult of Secrecy." *Nieman Reports* (October 1951): 9.

Popkin, James. "Running the New 'Improved' FOIA Obstacle Course." *Columbia Journalism Review* 28(1989): 45.

Qiao, Mu. "Communication Effects and Political Impact of SMS Messages." [手机短信的传播效果与政治影响] *Journal of Contemporary Communications* 4 (2008): 76.

Richardson, Brian. "The Public's Right to Know: A Dangerous Notion." *Journal of Mass Media Ethics* 19 (2004): 46.

Sanft, Charles. "Law and Communication in Qin and Western Han China." *Journal of the Economic and Social History of the Orient* 53 (2010): 679.

Schedler, Andreas. "What is Democratic Consolidation?" *Journal of Democracy* 9 (1998): 91.

Sen, Amartya. "Development: Which Way Now?" *The Economic Journal* 93 (1983): 745.

Sen, Amartya. "Ingredients of Famine Analysis: Availability and Entitlements." *Quarterly Journal of Economics* 96 (1981): 433.

Shambaugh, David. "China's Propaganda System: Institutions, Processes and Efficacy." *The China Journal* 57 (2007): 25.

Snell, Rick, and Weibing Xiao. "Freedom of Information Returns to China." *Public Administration Today* 10 (2007):44.

Su, Yun. "Internal Reports on Shenzhen Residents Fleeing to Hong Kong in 1960s." [六十年代深圳大逃亡期间一份用生命写出的内参] *Century* 5 (1994).

Sun, Qian. "Characteristics of China's Procuratorial System." *Qiushi* 2, no.2 (April 2010).

Sun, Shulei. "Study of Official Documents in Qing Dynasty." [清代公文制度考略] *Journal of Qinghai Normal University (Philosophy and Social Science Edition)* 120, No.1 (2007): 58.

Sun, Xiangyuan. "Information Disclosure: Double-Edged Sword, Taking SARS Coverage As Example [从SARS 报道看信息公开的"双刃剑"作用] Journ*al of Hunan University of Arts and Science (Social Science Edition)* 29, no.5 (2004): 50.

Sun, Xupei. "Reflections on 30-Year-Long Legislative History of Press Law." [三十年新闻立法历程与思考] *Yan-Huang Historical Review* 2 (2012).

Sun, Yunchuan, and Liubing Gao. "Environmental Management Research on Government Online Information Resources." [政府网上信息资源环境管理研究] *Journal of Library Science* 11 (1999):13.

Tan, Yeling. "Transparency Without Democracy: The Unexpected Effects of China's Environmental Disclosure Policy." *Governance: An International Journal of Policy, Administration, and Institutions* 27 (2014): 23.

Tang, Xiaotian. "New Thoughts on Party Directive that Party Papers Shall Not Criticize Same-Level Party Committees ["党报不得批评同级党委"规定之新认识] *Journal of Youth Journalist* 15 (2009): 63.

Tang, Yong. "Journalistic Right in the 'First Rough Draft of History': A Comparative Study of News Copyright in the United States and the People's Republic of China." *Chinese Journal of Communication*, 6 (1) (2013): 24-44.

Tang, Yong, Xue Dou, and Mary Beth Oliver. " 'Harmonious Middle Kingdom and Dangerous Beautiful Country?' Exploring Cultivation Effects of Domestic and U.S.-Made TV Programs on Chinese College Students." *International Journal of Communication* 12 (2018): 4421–4442.

Tanner, Murray Scot. "China Rethinks Unrest." *The Washington Quarterly* 27 (2004): 138.

Tong, Jingrong, and Colin Sparks. "Investigative Journalism in China Today." 10 *Journalism Studies* 3 (2009): 337.

Trevaskes, Susan. "A Law Unto Itself: Chinese Communist Party Leadership and *Yifa zhiguo* in the Xi Era." *Modern China* 44 (4) (2018) : 347.

Uhm, Kiyul. "The Founders and Revolutionary Underpinning of the Concept of the Right to Know." *Journalism & Mass Communication Quarterly* 85 (2008): 393.

Volz, Yong Z., and Chin-Chuan Lee. "American Pragmatism and Chinese Modernization: Importing the Missouri Model of Journalism Education to Modern China." *Media Culture & Society* 31 (5) (2009):711.

Wanyan, Shaoyuan. "Neican in Ancient Chinese Governments." [古代官府的"内参"] *Digest* 1 (2007).

Wang, Haiyan, and Francis L. F. Lee. "Research on Chinese Investigative Journalism, 1978–2013: A Critical Review." *China Review* 14 (2) (Special Issue: Doing Sinology in Former Socialist States) (Fall 2014): 215.

Wang, Jinyu."Research on Central Archive of Southern Song Dynasty." [南宋六部架阁库研究] *Journal of Archives and Construction* 6 (2001): 13.

Wang, Lili. "Chinese Think Tanks Affiliated with Media Organizations: Positioning and Growth Paths." [中国媒体智库的定位与发展路径] *The Press* 2 [新闻战线] (2018).

Wang, L. Sophia. "The Independent Press and Authoritarian Regimes: The Case of the Dagong bao in Republican China." *Pacific Affairs* 67 (1994): 216.

Wang, Lingying. "Examination of Internal Reference Orientation in Internet Age." [网络时代的内参取向探析] *Shanghai Journalism Review* 9 (2010): 81.

Wang, Robin R. "Dong Zhongshu's Transformation of 'Yin-Yang' Theory and Contesting of Gender Identity." *Philosophy East and West* 55 (2005): 209.

Wang, Shuya. "Evolution of Writing Style of Official Documents from Pre-Qin to Han Dynasty." [试论先秦到汉代的公文文气演变] *Journal of Data of Culture and Education* 2 (2010): 223.

Weerdt, Hilde De." 'Court Gazettes' and 'Short Reports': Official Views and Unofficial Readings of Court News." *Journal of Chinese Studies* 27(2): (2009): 167.

Wen, Jiabao. "Let Power Be Exercised in Sunshine." [让权力在阳光下运行] *Qiushi* 8(2012).

White, David Manning. "The 'Gate Keeper': A Case Study in the Selection of News." *Journalism Quarterly* 27 (1950): 383.

Wu, Tingjun, and Changyong Xia. "History and Status Quo of Crisis Communication in China." [我国公共危机传播的历史回顾与现状分析] *Journal of Modern Communication* 6 (2010): 32.

Xia, Gongran, and Xiaomei Xia. "Cultural Revolution Transformed Me." ["文革"对我的洗礼] *Journal of Observation and Reflection* 4 (2002).

Xia, Gongran, and Xiaomei Xia. "How Neican Covers Farmer Household Responsibility System." [内参反映"包产到户"的前前后后] *Journal of Observation and Reflection* 1 (2002).

Xia, Junsheng. "How Zhongguancun Came into Birth." [中关村高新技术产业区的由来] *Yan-Huang Historical Review* 7 (2009).

Xia, Yan. "Government Secret Leaking and Protection in Ancient China." [古代官场的泄密与保密] *Journal of Reporter's Notes* 1 (2011).

Xiao, Weibing. "China's Limited Push Model of FOI Legislation." *Government Information Quarterly* 27 (2010): 346.

Xiao, Weibing. "The Improved Information Environment as a Key Rationale for Freedom of Information Reform in China." *Journal of Information Polity* 15 (3) (2010): 177.

Xiao, Zhao. "Kangxi Emperor Used Secret Spies to Investigate Public Opinion." [康熙借密探察民情] *Happiness* 2 (2009).

Xie, Dan, Xiaotong Qi, and Qingling Xiao. "Short Reports in Ancient China." [浅析中国古代小报] *Journal of Media Studies* 2 (2008).

Xu, Shiping. "An Overview of Ancient Preservation Technology Used for Chinese Archives." [中国古代档案保护技术概览] *Journal of Archives Science Study Supplement* A08 (1996): 20.

Xu, Xunlei. "Baimiao Township Government Seeks Self-Defeat?" [白庙乡孤独求败?] *West China* 7 (2010): 27.

Xu, Xunlei. "Review on *Bid Farewell to Hunger*." [读《告别饥饿] *Yan-Huang Historical Review* 11 (2009).

Yan, Huai, and Suisheng Zhao. "Notes on China's Confidential Documents." *Journal of Contemporary China* 2 (1993): 75.

Yan, Zhenguo. "Review Comments in Memory of Bo Lao." [重温批示追忆薄老] *Hundred Year Tide* 9 (2009): 63.

Yang, Fan. "The Role of CPC Regulations in Chinese Judicial Decisions." *China Review* 19 (2) (May 2019): 69-98.

Yang, Shusen. "Secrets Guarding in Ancient China and Official Seal Management." [中国古代保密工作和印玺管理] *Journal of Office Administration* 3 (2007).

Yang, Zhenquan. "Behind-the-Scene Story about Public Broadcasting Mao Zedong's Death." [毛泽东主席逝世公开广播的背后] *International Communications* 8/9 (2006).

Yi, Xudong. "Account on Haideng v. Yongxiang Jing." [舌剑唇枪辩海灯-范应莲诉敬永祥"侵害海灯法师名誉权"一案始末(续)] *Journalism Review* 10 (1993).

Yin, Jiafei. "Beyond the Four Theories of the Press: A New Model for the Asian and the World Press." *Journalism & Communication Monographs* 10 (2008): 4.

You, Biao. "Written Language Delivery Between Government and Locality of Song Dynasty." [宋代朝廷与地方之间的"文字"传递—围绕邸报及其相关问题而展开] *Journal of Hebei University (Philosophy and Social Science Edition)* 28 (3) (2003): 11.

Yu, Huanchun. "One Nei*can* Article Repudiates "Two Estimations." [一份内参推翻"两个估计"] *Yan-Huang Historical Review* 8 (2004).

Yu, Xiaoli. "Anti-Communication or Obscurantism? Study on Taoist Concept of Communication." [反传播还是愚民政策? 试论道家的传播观] *Journal of Fuyang Teachers College (Social Science Edition)* 97 (1) (2004): 107.

Yuan, Zhuo. "Confidentiality of Ancient Chinese Official Documents." [管窥古代公文的保密制度] *Journal of Lantai World* 02x (2007): 57.

Yun, Guoqiang, and Pin Lv. “Relationship Between Media and Government: Taking Example of SARS Incident.” [以SARS疫情为例看传媒与政府的关系] *21st Century* 14 (2003).

Zhang, Chi. “Preliminary Analysis of Legalist Communication Thought in Pre-Qin Period.” [先秦法家传播思想述论] *Journal of Anqing Teachers College (Social Science Edition)* 21 (3) (2002): 18.

Zhang, Junchang. “Evolution of Chinese Policies, Laws and Regulations on News Coverage of Emergency Incidents.” [中国媒体报道突发事件政策法律法规之变迁] *TV Research* 5 (2009): 33.

Zhang, Xiaoling. “Seeking Effective Public Space: Chinese Media at the Local Level.” *China: An International Journal* 5 (2007): 55.

Zhao, Fen. “Comparing Official Gazettes with Short Reports in Ancient China.” [中国古代官报与小报的比较] *Journal of Youth Journalist* 2 (2010): 74.

Zhao, Hailin. “Tianfu: National Archival Institution at Zhou Dynasty.” [周朝的国家档案馆——天府] *Journal of Archives* 5 (1985).

Zhao, Zhengqun. “Discussion of Anti-Corruption through Openness in Government Affairs.”[以政务公开反腐败论要] *Theory and Modernization* 6 (2001): 54.

Zheng, Shengfeng. “Inspirations from Exposing Nandan Coal Disaster Concealment.” [南丹矿难的成功揭露留给人们的启示] *Journalistic Front* 9 (2003).

Zheng, Silin. “Comparing U.S. Information Disclosure Laws with Its Chinese and Canadian Counterparts.”[我国信息公开法与美国、加拿大关于信息公开条款的比较] *Archives of Hubei* 7 (2007): 14.

Zhou, Hanhua. “Legislative History of *OGI Regulations* in China.” [《政府信息公开条例》出台始末] *E-Government* 7 (2008): 15.

Zhu, Huaxin, Jiangchun Hu, and Wentao Sun. “Analysis Report on Public Opinions on the Internet in China in 2007.” [2007中国互联网舆情分析报告] *Journal of Today’s Mass Media* 2 (2008): 31.

Zhu, Songyan. “Analysis of and Thoughts on the Current Situation of FOI in China.” *Journal of Expanding Horizons* 3 (2003): 31.

Zhu, Wei, and Yanpin Teng. “From Concept to Fundamental Constitutional Rights: Several Legal Principles on Right to Know.” [从观念到宪法基本权利—知情权的一般法理] *Journal of Hangzhou Teachers College(Social Sciences Edition)* 1 (2005): 103.

Zhu, Wei. “Government Information Publicity: Legislative Model and System Coordination.” [政府信息公开:立法模式及制度协调] *Journal of Hangzhou Teachers College(Social Sciences Edition)* 1 (2004):110.

Zhu, Ying, and Yi Liu. “From SARS to H1N1 Flu: Evolution of China’s Government Information Disclosure.” [从“非典”到“甲型H1N1 流感”—中国政府信息公开的变迁] *Southeast Communication* 61 (9) (2009): 66.

Zou, Ying. “Postal System and Communication in Ancient China.” [中国古代邮驿制度与传播] *Journal of Xianning College* 23 (4) (2003): 99.

Dissertations and Theses

Bishop, Cheryl Ann. "Internationalizing the Right to Know: Conceptualizations of Access to Information in Human Rights Law." PhD Diss., The University of North Carolina at Chapel Hill, 2009.

Chen, Xi. "The Dynamics of Chinese Media Practices and Regulation: Explanations and Interpretations." PhD. diss., Virginia Polytechnic Institute and State University, 2007.

Cramer, Benjamin W. "Freedom of Environmental Information in America." PhD diss., The Pennsylvania State University, 2009.

Fattah, Geoffrey. "'Strangers' in the Courtroom: An Examination of Access Theory and the Public's Right to Open Courts from *Depasquale* to *Richmond*." Master's thesis, The University of Utah, 2011.

Halstuk, Martin E. "Exploring the Future of Open Government in the Digital Age: A Reevaluation of the Significance of the Electronic Freedom of Information Act of 1996." PhD diss., University of Florida, 1999.

Hampton, Ellen M. "Freedom of Information in Post-Communist Countries: Case Studies of the Czech Republic, Croatia and Bosnia and Herzegovina." Master's thesis, The University of North Carolina at Chapel Hill, 2007.

Hoch, Katrina. "Judicial Transparency: Communication, Democracy and the United States Federal Judiciary." PhD diss., University of California, San Diego, 2009.

Jiang, Min. "Civic Interactions with Chinese Government Networks: Information Technology, Institutions, and Agency." PhD diss., Purdue University, 2007.

Lebovic, Samuel Martin. "Fighting for Free Information: American Democracy and the Problem of Press Freedom in a Totalitarian Age, 1920-1950." PhD diss., The University of Chicago, 2011.

Li, Qinglin. "The Constitution and Narrative of Imperial Autocracy-on Discourse and Mode of Communication in Period of Imperialism of China."[皇权专制的建构和叙事] PhD diss., Communication University of China, 2006.

Lidberg, Johan. "Keeping the Bastards Honest-The Promise and Practice of Freedom of Information Legislation." PhD diss., Murdoch University, 2006.

Lin, Aijun. "Legal Protection for Right to Know: Insight of Journalism and Communication." [论知情权的法律保障:新闻传播学的视角] PhD diss., Fudan University, 2007.

Ngeow, Chow Bing. "Democratic Development in China's Urban Communities." PhD diss., Northeastern University, 2010.

Reinertsen, Jens. F. "Assessing Access to Information in China-Legal Development and International Standards." Master's thesis, China University of Political Science and Law, 2009.

Robinson, Laura. "Freedom of Speech in the Roman Republic." PhD diss., Johns Hopkins University, 1940.

Shang, Jie. "Research on Mechanism of China's Journalistic Internal Reference." [中国新闻内参机制分析] Master's thesis, Henan University, 2008.
Silver, Derigan A. "National Security and Transparency: The Legal Frameworks and Factors Federal Courts Use to Balance Competing Democratic Values." PhD diss., The University of North Carolina at Chapel Hill, 2009.
Tang, Yong. "Chinese Freedom of Information: An Evaluation of the Legislative History, Rationales, Significance and Efficacy of Regulations of the People's Republic of China on Open Government Information." PhD diss., The Pennsylvania State University at University Park, 2012.
Wang, Huayu. "A Study on Emperors' Information Channels in Song Dynasty." [宋朝君主的信息渠道研究] PhD. diss., Peking University, 2008.
Wang, Xiaoru. "Behind the Great Firewall: The Internet and Democratization in China." PhD diss., The University of Michigan, 2009.
Wang, Yong. "Analysis of Open Government Information."[政府信息公开论] PhD diss., China University of Political Science and Law, 2005.
Xiao, Dongmei. "Research on Public Access to Information Resources." [信息资源公共获取制度研究] PhD diss., Wuhan University, 2007.
Yi, Xiaoyang. "Research on Legislation of Government Information Publicity." [政府信息公开的立法研究] Master's thesis, Xiangtan University, 2003.
Zhang, Yanjie. "Research on Legal System of Open Government Information from Perspective of Information Exemption." [政府信息公开法律制度研究 — 从豁免公开的角度] Master's thesis, China University of Political Science and Law, 2007.
Zhou, Jiandong. "The Studies on Open Government Information from View of Public Field." [公共性视野下的政府信息公开研究] PhD diss., Shandong University, 2007.

Conference Proceedings and Working Papers

Azubuike, Abraham A. "Accessibility of Government Information as a Determinant of Inward Foreign Direct Investment in Africa." Paper presented at the 72nd IFLA (Internal Federation of Library Associations and Institutions) General Conference and Council, Seoul, South Korea, August 20–24, 2006.
Banisar, David. "Freedom of Information International Trends and National Security." Paper presented at the Workshop on "Democratic and Parliamentary Oversight of Intelligence Services," held in Geneva 3rd-5th October 2002, organized by the Working Group on the Parliamentary Control of Armed Forces (PCAF) and the Working Group on Democratic Control of Internal Security Services (DCOIS) of the Geneva Center for the Democratic Control of Armed Forces.

Bernstein, Thomas. "Unrest in Rural China: A 2003 Assessment." Center for the Study of Democracy (CSD) Working Papers, Center for the Study of Democracy, University of California, Irvine, August 1, 2004.

Bishop, Cheryl Ann. "The United Nations and Access to Information as a Human Right." Paper presented at the annual meeting of the International Communication Association, Montreal, Quebec, Canada, May 22–26, 2008.

Blevins, Katie. "The Constitutional Right-to-Information on the Individual Level: As Suggested by First Amendment Precedent in the Supreme Court." Paper presented at the annual convention of the Association for Education in Journalism and Mass Communication, Denver, Colorado, August 4–7, 2010.

Byrne, Alex. "Freedom of Access to Information and Freedom of Expression in a Pluralistic World." Paper invited for The New Norcia Library Lecture, New Norcia, Western Australia, September 17, 1998.

Choldin, Marianna Tax. "Beginning a Conversation on Access to Information and Freedom of Expression." Paper prepared for the 62nd IFLA (The International Federation of Library Associations and Institutions) General Conference, Beijing, China, August 25–31, 1996.

Geddes, Barbara. "Authoritarian Breakdown: Empirical Test of a Game Theoretic Argument." Paper prepared for presentation at the annual meeting of the American Political Science Association, Atlanta, Georgia, September 2–5, 1999.

Keidel, Albert. "The Economic Basis for Social Unrest in China." Paper presented for The Third European-American Dialogue on China, The George Washington University, Washington, D.C., May 26-27, 2005.

Li, Baoling. "On the Barriers to the Development of e-Government in China." Paper published in proceedings of the 7th International Conference on Electronic Commerce, Xi'an, China, August 15–17, 2005.

Lidberg, Johan. "Beyond the Freedom of Information Index: An Audit of FOI Reform." Paper presented at the Media and Global Divides Conference in Stockholm, Sweden, July 20–25, 2008.

Lorentzen, Peter, Pierre Landry, and John Yasuda. "Transparent Authoritarianism? An Analysis of Political and Economic Barriers to Greater Government Transparency in China." Paper presented at the American Political Science Association annual meeting, Washington, D.C., September 4, 2010.

McMillan, John. "Freedom of Information and Whistleblower Legislation: An Australian Perspective." Paper delivered to the 9th Asian Ombudsman Association Conference, Hong Kong, China, November 28-December 1, 2005.

Pan, Zhongdang, and Joseph Man Chan. "Assessing Media Exemplars and Shifting Journalistic Paradigms: A Survey Study of China's Journalists." Paper presented at the annual meeting of International Communication Association, San Diego, California, May 23–27, 2003.

Popescu, Bogdan G. "Press Freedom in Non-Democratic Regimes." Paper prepared for delivery at the ECPR (European Consortium for Political Research) Graduate Conference, Dublin City University, Dublin, Ireland, August 30-September 1, 2010.

Roberts, Alasdair. "Access to Government Information: An Overview of Issues." First written for the Carter Center's Transparency for Growth Conference, Atlanta, Georgia, May 1999 and later compiled as a chapter in working paper Access to Information: A Key to Democracy (edited by Laura Neuman, November 2002), the Carter Center, Alanta, Georgia, available at http://www.cartercenter.org/documents/1272.pdf (accessed between February 21, 2025 and March 31, 2025).

Tang, Yong, and Martin E. Halstuk. "Flying Dragon Seeking Freedom of Information: A Critique of Chinese Open Government Information Regulations." Paper presented at the annual AEJMC (Association for Education in Journalism and Mass Communication) convention, St. Louis, Missouri, August 10–13, 2011.

Tang, Yong, Xue Dou, and Mary Beth Oliver. "Harmonious Middle Kingdom and Dangerous Beautiful Country? Exploring Cultivation Effects of CCTV and US Television Programs on Chinese Viewers." Paper presented at the annual NCA (National Communication Association) convention, Chicago, Illinois, November 20–23, 2014.

Tang, Yong. "An Enforcement 'Black Hole'-The Chinese Communist Party and Its Own Freedom of Information Law." Paper presented at the annual NCA (National Communication Association) convention, New Orleans, Louisiana, November 21–24, 2024.

Tang, Yong. "Transparency of Public Enterprises and Institutions in China: A Freedom of Information Law Perspective." Paper presented at the annual AEJMC (Association for Education in Journalism and Mass Communication) convention, Philadelphia, Pennsylvania, August 8–11, 2024.

Tang, Yong. "Defaming Officials and Celebrities: Evolution of Libel Law and the Sullivan Impact in China." Paper presented at the annual ICA (International Communication Association) convention, San Diego, California, May 25–29, 2017.

Tang, Yong. "Merely Window Dressing? Accomplishments and Challenges in Enforcing China's First Freedom of Information Law." Paper presented at the annual ICA (International Communication Association) convention, Fukuoka, Japan, June 9–13, 2016.

Tang, Yong. "Journalistic Role in Chinese Freedom of Information." Paper presented at the annual ICA (International Communication Association) convention, London, United Kingdom, June 17–21, 2013.

Tang, Yong. "Journalistic Internal Reference: Exemption from China's Freedom of Information Law." Paper presented at the AEJMC (Association for

Education in Journalism and Mass Communication) Southeast Colloquium, University of South Florida, Tampa, Florida, February 28-March 2, 2013.
Tang, Yong. " 'Feeling for Rocks while Crossing the River': Analysis of The Statutory Language of China's First Freedom of Information Law." Paper presented at the AEJMC (Association for Education in Journalism and Mass Communication) Southeast Colloquium, University of South Florida, Tampa, Florida, February 28-March 2, 2013.
Tang, Yong. "Secrecy and Transparency of the Chinese Government: A Historical Perspective." Paper presented at the annual AEJMC (Association for Education in Journalism and Mass Communication) convention, Chicago, Illinois, August 9–12, 2012.
Tang, Yong. "Who Owns the 'First Rough Draft of History'? -A Comparative Study of News Copyright in the United States and the People's Republic of China." Paper presented at the annual ICA (International Communication Association) convention, Boston, Massachusetts, May 26–30, 2011.
Wong, Dennis Sing-Wing. "Restorative Justice for Juveniles in Hong Kong: Reflections of a Practitioner." Paper presented at the IIRP (International Institute for Restorative Practices)'s Sixth International Conference on Conferencing, Circles and other Restorative Practices, Penrith, New South Wales, Australia, March 3–5, 2005.
Xiao, Weibing. "Democratization as a Rationale for Freedom of Information Reform in China." Working paper series of School of Economic Law, Shanghai University of Political Science and Law, available at the Social Science Research Network (SSRN) website, November 9, 2010.
Zheng, Lei. "Enacting and Implementing Open Government Information Regulations in China: Motivations and Barriers." Paper published in proceedings of the 1st International Conference on Theory and Practice of Electronic Governance, Macao, China, December 10–13, 2007.

Newspapers and Magazines (Print and Online)

An, Kulei. "Skills of Jinsong Hao." [郝劲松的技术活] *Southern People Weekly* 20 (2008): 64.
"A Leader with Unmatched Wisdom-Deng Xiaoping in the Eye of Oriana Fallaci." *China Daily*, July 29, 2021, https://www.chinadaily.com.cn/a/202107/29/WS615c4c8ea310cdd39bc6d299.html (accessed between February 21, 2025 and March 31, 2025).
"Auditing Reports to Be Opened." *People's Daily Online*, July 05, 2003, http://english.peopledaily.com.cn/200307/05/eng20030705_119503.shtml (accessed between February 21, 2025 and March 31, 2025).
Bai, Jianfeng. "Disclosure of Government Information Is the Principle While Nondisclosure Is an Exception." [政府信息公开是原则,不公开是例外]

People's Daily, April 30, 2008 (captured by Internet Archive Wayback Machine on May 11, 2008), retrieved from https://web.archive.org/web/20080511072252/http://opinion.people.com.cn/GB/7182797.html (accessed between February 21, 2025 and March 31, 2025).

Bao, Jian. "Shanghai Leads China: 400 OGI Cases Filed Within Four Years." [上海:四年400起政府信息公开"民告官" 居全国首位] *People's Daily*, republished by *China News Service*, November 12, 2008, http://www.chinanews.com.cn/gn/news/2008/11-12/1446373.shtml (accessed between February 21, 2025 and March 31, 2025).

Barboza, David. "Most Dangerous in China: An Editor." *The New York Times*, April 18, 2005, http://www.nytimes.com/2005/04/17/business/worldbusiness/17iht-caijing.html (accessed between February 21, 2025 and March 31, 2025).

Barboza, David. "Liu Binyan, a Fierce Insider Critic of China, Dies at 80." *The New York Times*, December 6, 2005, http://www.nytimes.com/2005/12/06/international/asia/06liu.html?_r=1 (accessed between February 21, 2025 and March 31, 2025).

Barboza, David. "Chinese Regulators Caution TV Talent Shows." *The New York Times*, March 21, 2006, http://www.nytimes.com/2006/03/21/technology/21iht-hunan.html (accessed between February 21, 2025 and March 31, 2025).

Barboza, David. "China Passes Japan as Second-Largest Economy." *The New York Times*, August 15, 2010, http://www.nytimes.com/2010/08/16/business/global/16yuan.html (accessed between February 21, 2025 and March 31, 2025).

Barboza, David. "Obtaining Financial Records in China." *The New York Times*, October 26, 2012, http://www.nytimes.com/2012/10/27/business/global/obtaining-financial-records-in-china.html?ref=world&_r=0 (accessed between February 21, 2025 and March 31, 2025).

Barstow, David. "Behind TV Analysts, Pentagon's Hidden Hand." *The New York Times*, April 20, 2008, http://www.nytimes.com/2008/04/20/us/20generals.html?pagewanted=1&_r=1 (accessed between February 21, 2025 and March 31, 2025).

Becker, Jasper. "Comrade Jiang Zemin Does Indeed Seem a Proper Choice." *London Review of Books* 23 (10), May 24, 2001, available at http://www.lrb.co.uk/v23/n10/jasper-becker/comrade-jiang-zemin-does-indeed-seem-a-proper-choice (accessed between February 21, 2025 and March 31, 2025).

Becker, Jo. "U.S. Approved Business With Blacklisted Nations." *The New York Times*, December 23, 2010, http://www.nytimes.com/2010/12/24/world/24sanctions.html?pagewanted=all (accessed between February 21, 2025 and March 31, 2025).

Bernstein, Nina. "Officials Hid Truth of Immigrant Deaths in Jail." *The New York Times*, January 9, 2010, http://www.nytimes.com/2010/01/10/us/10detain.html (accessed between February 21, 2025 and March 31, 2025).

Boehler, Patrick. "China's Foreign Ministry Curtails Access to Declassified Historic Archives." *South China Morning Post*, August 9, 2013, https://www.scmp.com/news/china-insider/article/1295456/chinas-diplomats-curtail-access-their-historic-archives (accessed between February 21, 2025 and March 31, 2025).

Branigan, Tania. "Televised Confessions on State-Run TV Consolidate China's Social Control." *The Guardian*, August 11, 2014, https://www.theguardian.com/world/2014/aug/11/televised-confessions-state-tv-china-social-control (accessed between February 21, 2025 and March 31, 2025).

Branigan, Tania. "Chinese Anger over Alleged Cover-up of High-Speed Rail Crash: Authorities Accused of Muzzling Media Coverage after Crash in Zhejiang Province Kills at least 38 People and Injures 192." *The Guardian*, July 25, 2011, http://www.guardian.co.uk/world/2011/jul/25/chinese-rail-crash-cover-up-claims (accessed between February 21, 2025 and March 31, 2025).

Campbell, Charlie, and Amy Gunia. "China Says It's Beating Coronavirus. But Can We Believe Its Numbers?" *Time*, April 1, 2020, https://time.com/5813628/china-coronavirus-statistics-wuhan/ (accessed between February 21, 2025 and March 31, 2025).

Chen, Baocheng. "Judicial Interpretation on OGI Regulations Deleted 'Three Security and One Stability.' " [最高法公布《关于审理政府信息公开行政案件若干问题的规定》,"三安全一稳定信息不公开"被删] *Southern Metropolis Daily*, August 15, 2011, republished by Aoyi News [奥一新闻] (captured by Internet Archive Wayback Machine on September 23, 2011), retrieved from https://web.archive.org/web/20110923120823/http://gcontent.oeeee.com/0/3f/03f5446139179452/Blog/ea0/4e2a0b.html (accessed between February 21, 2025 and March 31, 2025).

Chen, Baocheng. "Ministry of Human Resources and Social Security Publishes Same Annual OGI Work Reports in Two Years." [人社部官网信息公开年报被指两年一字不差] *Southern Metropolis Daily*, March 29, 2011, republished by Sina News, http://news.sina.com.cn/c/p/2011-03-29/062622198498.shtml (accessed between February 21, 2025 and March 31, 2025).

Chen, Baocheng. "Only 20 Percent of Agencies under State Council Get Passing Grade in Transparency." [国务院机构仅二成透明度及格] *Southern Metropolis Daily*, September 29, 2011 (captured by Internet Archive Wayback Machine on October 1, 2011), retrieved from https://web.archive.org/web/20111001200910/http://gcontent.oeeee.com/0/3f/03f5446139179452/Blog/8f0/20cf31.html (accessed between February 21, 2025 and March 31, 2025).

Chen, Bo. "Officials Respond to Allegations of "Bargaining for Reduced Fines Levied against Unlicensed Cabs." [官方回应"黑车罚款还价"] *The Beijing News*, republished by *Sina News*, August 5, 2010, https://news.sina.com.cn/o/2010-08-05/090317917524s.shtml (accessed between February 21, 2025 and March 31, 2025).

Chen, Liang. "Beijing Summons Thousands of County-Level Officials to Learn the Art of Ruling." *Global Times*, January 26, 2015, https://www.globaltimes.cn/content/904046.shtml (accessed between February 21, 2025 and March 31, 2025).

Chen, Limin. "Internet Users Hit 384 Million." *China Daily*, January 16, 2010, https://www.chinadaily.com.cn/bizchina/////2010-01/16/content_9330234.htm#:~:text=Updated:%202010%2D01%2D16,Internet%20only%20through%20mobile%20phones (accessed between February 21, 2025 and March 31).

Chen, Mo. "Key of *OGI Regulations* Is to Make OGI Legal Obligation of Government." [条例的要害是把信息公开变成政府的法定义务] *21st Century Business Herald*, republished by *Sina Finance*, April 26, 2007, http://finance.sina.com.cn/g/20070426/09223543933.shtml (accessed between February 21, 2025 and March 31, 2025).

Chen, Weihua. "Dongguan Statistics Bureau Publishes Almost Duplicate Annual OGI Work Reports in Three Years." [东莞统计局信息公开工作报告 三年几乎一字未改] *Beijing Times*, April 3, 2011, at AA03, republished by CNTV, http://news.cntv.cn/map/20110403/100240.shtml (accessed between February 21, 2025 and March 31, 2025).

Chen, Yanhui. "Demystify Neican." [内参揭秘] *Phoenix Weekly* 14 (2005): 35–39.

Cheng, Zhongyuan, Zhenghua Li, and Jincai Zhang. "Elimination of 'Two Estimations' and Resumption of National College Entrance Exam." [推倒"两个估计"与恢复高考] *China Reading Weekly*, June 21, 2017, http://epaper.gmw.cn/zhdsb/html/2017-06/21/nw.D110000zhdsb_20170621_1-05.htm (accessed between February 21, 2025 and March 31, 2025).

Chien, Amy Chang, and Chang Che. "Memes, Puns and Blank Sheets of Paper: China's Creative Acts of Protest." *The New York Times*, November 28, 2022, https://www.nytimes.com/2022/11/28/world/asia/china-protests-blank-sheets.html (accessed between February 21, 2025 and March 31, 2025).

"China Adopts Law on Cyber Security." *People's Daily*, November 7, 2016, http://en.people.cn/n3/2016/1107/c90000-9138132.html (accessed between February 21, 2025 and March 31, 2025).

"China Adopts National Security Law." *China Daily*, July 1, 2015, http://www.chinadaily.com.cn/china/2015-07/01/content_21150783.htm (accessed between February 21, 2025 and March 31, 2025).

"China further Declassifies Diplomatic Files." *People's Daily Online*, May 13, 2006 (captured by Internet Archive Wayback Machine on November 5, 2007), retrieved from https://web.archive.org/web/20071105100800/http://english.peopledaily.com.cn/200605/13/eng20060513_265380.html (accessed between February 21, 2025 and March 31, 2025).

"China's Road of Free Information Flow Cautious but Resolute." *People's Daily Online*, November 8, 2007 (captured by Internet Archive Wayback Machine on June 29, 2018), retrieved from https://web.archive.org/web/20180629050930/http://en.people.cn/90001/90782/6299198.html (accessed between February 21, 2025 and March 31, 2025).

"China's Mobile Phone Users Hit 1b." *China Daily*, May 24, 2012, http://www.chinadaily.com.cn/business/2012-05/24/content_15374280.htm (accessed between February 21, 2025 and March 31, 2025).

"China's Strongman Rule Sets a Test for the West: President Xi Challenges Notion that Prosperity Leads to Liberalism." *Financial Times*, October 30, 2016, https://www.ft.com/content/76c27ac6-9c5b-11e6-a6e4-8b8e77dd083a (accessed between February 21, 2025 and March 31, 2025)

"Chinese City Freezes Plans for Chemical Plant after Barrage of Complaints." *The New York Times*, May 30, 2007, http://www.nytimes.com/2007/05/30/world/asia/30iht-pollution.1.5924588.html (accessed between February 21, 2025 and March 31, 2025).

"Chinese Whispers: Not Believing What They Read in the Papers, China's Leaders Commission Their Own." *The Economist,* June 17, 2010, https://www.economist.com/asia/2010/06/17/chinese-whispers (accessed between February 21, 2025 and March 31, 2025).

Cody, Edward. "China Growing More Wary over Rash of Protests: Cell Phones, Internet Spread the Word, Magnify Fallout." *The Washington Post*, August 10, 2005, https://www.washingtonpost.com/archive/politics/2005/08/10/china-grows-more-wary-over-rash-of-protests/7e21a4f4-45e3-4a6f-928b-9294c98339f4/ (accessed between February 21, 2025 and March 31, 2025).

Cody, Edward. "China Uses Heavy Hand Even with Its Gadflies." *The Washington Post*, April 9, 2008, http://www.washingtonpost.com/wp-dyn/content/article/2008/04/08/AR2008040803274.html?sid=ST2008040801507 (accessed between February 21, 2025 and March 31, 2025).

Coy, Peter. "Xi Jinping is the Second Coming of Mao Zedong." *The New York Times*, October 7, 2022, https://www.nytimes.com/2022/10/07/opinion/xi-jinping-mao-zedong.html (accessed between February 21, 2025 and March 31, 2025).

"CPC Plenum to Discuss Social Harmony." *China Daily*, October 8, 2006, ttp://www.chinadaily.com.cn/china/2006-10/08/content_703052.htm (accessed between February 21, 2025 and March 31, 2025).

"CPC Unveils Regulation to Promote Transparency in Party Affairs." *China Daily*, December 25, 2017, http://global.chinadaily.com.cn/a/201712/25/WS5a410271a31008cf16da35a0.html (accessed between February 21, 2025 and March 31, 2025).

Dai, Zhiyong. "Government Facilities Should Not be Off-Limits to Public." [政府机关不是高墙深院] *Southern Weekend*, April 20, 2012, http://www.infzm.com/content/74411 (accessed between February 21, 2025 and March 31, 2025).

Dalmer, Bert. "Creating 'Terrorism' out of Misdemeanors." *The Des Moines Register*, May 16, 2005.

Dalmer, Bert. "Many of Bush Administration's Claimed 'Terrorism' Arrests Are Misleading." *The Des Moines Register*, July 18, 2004.

Davidson, Lee. "Sailors Exposed to Deadly Agents: Pentagon finally Concedes Dangers from 1960s Tests." *Desert News*, May 24, 2002, https://www.deseret.com/2002/5/24/19656838/sailors-exposed-to-deadly-agents/ (accessed between February 21, 2025 and March 31, 2025).

"Democratic Elections, Democratic Decision-Making, Democratic Management, and Democratic Supervision." [民主选举、民主决策、民主管理、民主监督] *People's Daily Online*, June 5, 2013, http://qzlx.people.com.cn/n/2013/0605/c364582-21742507.html (accessed between February 21, 2025 and March 31, 2025).

Deng, He. "How Did Lawyer Enchong Zheng Divulge State Secrets? " [律师郑恩宠是如何泄露国家秘密的?] *Bund Pictorial*, republished by *People's Daily Online*, November 6, 2003 (captured by Internet Archive Wayback Machine on January 6, 2004), retrieved from https://web.archive.org/web/20040106195750/http://unn.people.com.cn/GB/14748/2172850.html (accessed between February 21, 2025 and March 31, 2025).

Ding, Dong. "Shunxing Huang, a Scientist Who Does Not Yield to Political Pressure Easily." [水土不服的黄顺兴] *History Reference* [文史资料选辑] 163 (22) (2010), excerpted by *People's Daily Online*, April 14, 2011 (captured by Internet Archive Wayback Machine on March 4, 2016), retrieved from https://web.archive.org/web/20160304090638/http://history.people.com.cn/GB/198819/207809/14391587.html (accessed between February 21, 2025 and March 31, 2025).

"Expert Says that External Pressure from WTO Compelled China to Reform Internally." [专家谈入世十年:外部压力倒逼国内改革] *Yangcheng Evening News*, republished by *China News Service*, December 5, 2011, https://www.chinanews.com.cn/cj/2011/12-05/3509402.shtml (accessed between February 21, 2025 and March 31, 2025).

Fei, Weiwei. "Citizen-Based Approach Shall Be Adopted to Deal with Well-Being Issues." [抓民生,"群众主体是关键"] *People's Daily*, republished by *Haixinews.com.cn*, March 7, 2012 (captured by Internet Archive Wayback

Machine on November 3, 2013), retrieved from https://web.archive.org/web/20131103083431/http://www.haixinews.com.cn/html/2012/zhongyangmeitikanhaixi_0307/3059.html (accessed between February 21, 2025 and March 31, 2025).

Feuer, Alan. "Battle Over the Bailout." *The New York Times*, February 12, 2010,http://www.nytimes.com/2010/02/14/nyregion/14fed.html?pagewanted=all (accessed between February 21, 2025 and March 31, 2025).

"Fortune Global 500." *Fortune Magazine*, https://fortune.com/ranking/global500/ (accessed between February 21, 2025 and March 31, 2025).

Fowler, Geoffrey A., and Juying Qin. "China Pushes Openness: First Order: Unveil Rules Dictating Transparency." *The Wall Street Journal*, February 28, 2007, http://online.wsj.com/article/SB117260663002921026.html (accessed between February 21, 2025 and March 31, 2025).

Gan, Nectar. "What Do We Actually Know about China's Mysterious Spy Agency?" *South China Morning Post*, December 22, 2018, https://www.scmp.com/news/china/politics/article/2179179/what-do-we-actually-know-about-chinas-mysterious-spy-agency (accessed between February 21, 2025 and March 31, 2025).

Gong, Jingqi. "A Whistle Giver." [发哨子的人] *PEOPLE*, republished by Independent Chinese PEN Center, March 10, 2020, https://www.chinesepen.org/blog/archives/145003 (accessed between February 21, 2025 and March 31, 2025).

Gui Jie. "Press Release System Pushes Public Governance to Greater Transparency." [新闻发布 制度推动公共治理走向透明] *China Youth Daily*, September 15, 2012, https://zqb.cyol.com/html/2012-09/15/nw.D110000zgqnb_20120915_4-03.htm (accessed between February 21, 2025 and March 31, 2025).

Gui, Jie. "Reporters Should Go Wherever Tough Places: Inside Information about Premier Zhu Writing Inscription for CCTV Focus Report." [希望记者越是艰难的地方越要去—-朱镕基破例为《焦点访谈》题词内幕] *China Youth Daily*, September 22, 2011, https://zqb.cyol.com/html/2011-09/22/nw.D110000zgqnb_20110922_2-11.htm (accessed between February 21, 2025 and March 31, 2025).

Guo, Jianguang. "He Stays at Northwestern Corner of China Forever: Famous Journalist Fan Changjiang's Last Days of His Life in Luzhuang." [永远的"西北角"——新闻巨擘范长江在芦庄的最后岁月] *The Paper*, March 30, 2021, https://m.thepaper.cn/baijiahao_11960039 (accessed between February 21, 2025 and March 31, 2025).

Guo, Kai. "China Decides to Accept PM2.5." *Global Times*, December 23, 2011, http://www.globaltimes.cn/NEWS/tabid/99/ID/689657/China-decides-to-accept-PM25.aspx (accessed between February 21, 2025 and March 31, 2025).

Guo, Shaofeng. "NPC Standing Committee Member Xu Xianming: Right to Know and Right to Supervise Shall Be Written into Constitution." [全国人大常委会委员徐显明:知情权监督权应入宪] *Beijing News*, republished by *Phoenix News*, December 11, 2008, https://news.ifeng.com/mainland/200812/1211_17_916562.shtml (accessed between February 21, 2025 and March 31, 2025).

He, Zongzhi, Sijing Wang, and Ran Huang. "FOI Still Has a Long Way to Go." [政府信息公开:还有一段路要走] *21st Century Business Herald*, republished by *Sina Finance*, July 8, 2008, http://finance.sina.com.cn/china/hgjj/20080708/02595065285.shtml (accessed between February 21, 2025 and March 31, 2025).

Hua, Qing. "Speed up Work on Legislation of Press Law according to Scientific Principle of Rule of Law and Effective Management." [科学、依法、有效管理加快新闻领域立法工作] *People's Daily*, November 3, 2008, republished by *Sohu News*, November 4, 2008, https://news.sohu.com/20081104/n260419205.shtml (accessed between February 21, 2025 and March 31, 2025).

Hua, Yu. "Fear of Dragons." *The New York Times*, October 7, 2011, http://www.nytimes.com/2011/10/08/opinion/08iht-edyu08.html (accessed between February 21, 2025 and March 31, 2025).

Huang, He. "Genetically Modified Rice: Fujian Province Suspends Ban on GMR." [转基因大米:福建"叫停通知"被叫停] *Southern Weekend*, republished by *QQ News*, December 20, 2010 (captured by Internet Archive Wayback Machine on December 8, 2022), retrieved from https://web.archive.org/web/20221208051823/http://news.qq.com/a/20101220/001341.htm (accessed between February 21, 2025 and March 31, 2025).

Huang, Xinghang, Wenbin Fei, and Jian Huang. "Former Nandan County Party Secretary Ruizhong Wan Blames Himself as Disloyal and Unfilial before Being Executed." [南丹原县委书记万瑞忠临行刑前自责"不忠不孝"] *People's Court Daily*, February 21, 2004, republished by *China News Service*, February 23, 2004, https://www.chinanews.com.cn/n/2004-02-23/26/405057.html (accessed between February 21, 2025 and March 31, 2025.

Jacobs, Andrew. "Chinese Chemical Plant Site Moves after Outcry." *The New York Times*, January 14, 2009, http://www.nytimes.com/2009/01/15/world/asia/15fujian.html?scp=4&sq=px%20xiamen&st=cse (accessed between February 21, 2025 and March 31, 2025).

Jacobs, Andrew. "In Leaked Lecture, Details of China's News Cleanups." *New York Times*, June 3, 2010, http://www.nytimes.com/2010/06/04/world/asia/04china.html (accessed between February 21, 2025 and March 31, 2025).

Jakes, Susan. "Beijing's SARS Attack." *Time*, April 8, 2003, https://content.time.com/time/subscriber/article/0,33009,441615,00.html (accessed between February 21, 2025 and March 31, 2025).

Jakes, Susan. “The Time Magazine Office of Letters and Visits.” *Time*, January 23, 2007, http://china.blogs.time.com/2007/01/23/the_time_magazine_office_of_le/ (accessed between February 21, 2025 and March 31, 2025).

Jia, Qingjun. “Li Hongzhang’s Chinese Political Experience Helps Russian Officials Escape Penalty for Crowd Crush.” [李鸿章的“经验介绍”和沙俄朝臣的“啥事没有”], *Guangming Daily Online*, June 7, 2004, https://www.gmw.cn/02blqs/2004-06/07/content_76836.htm (accessed between February 21, 2025 and March 31, 2025).

Jiang, Cunyung. “Do well Matters of Primary Importance Which Allows 900 Million Peasants to Become Masters of Their Own Affairs.” [把村民自治这件让九亿农民当家作主的大事办好], *People’s Daily*, republished by *Govopendata.com*, March 3, 1999, https://cn.govopendata.com/renminribao/1999/3/3/10/#1146306 (accessed between February 21, 2025 and March 31, 2025).

Jin, Weixin, and Xudong Zhou. “Deputy Mayor Xiangdong Ma’s Wife Buys over Officials and Journalists.” [马向东老婆贿倒官员记者] *Beijing Youth Daily*, republished by *People’s Daily Online*, March 26, 2002 (captured by Internet Archive Wayback Machine on April 14, 2002), retrieved from https://web.archive.org/web/20020414005701/http://www.people.com.cn/GB/shizheng/19/20020326/694898.html (accessed between February 21, 2025 and March 31, 2025).

Johnson, Ian. “Train Wreck in China Heightens Unease on Safety Standards.” *New York Times*, July 24, 2011, http://www.nytimes.com/2011/07/25/world/asia/25train.html (accessed between February 21, 2025 and March 31, 2025).

Kahn, Joseph. “China’s State Secrets Agency Will Guard One Less: Death Tolls.” *The New York Times*, September 13, 2005, http://www.nytimes.com/2005/09/13/international/asia/13china.html (accessed between February 21, 2025 and March 31, 2025).

Kahn, Joseph. “Pace and Scope of Protest in China Accelerated in ’05.” *New York Times*, January 20, 2006, http://www.nytimes.com/2006/01/20/international/asia/20china.html?_r=0 (accessed between February 21, 2025 and March 31, 2025).

Kaiman, Jonathan. “China Airs ‘Confession’” by Swedish Rights Worker; Critics Charge Coercion, *The Los Angeles Times*, January 20, 2016, http://www.latimes.com/world/asia/la-chinese-held-swedish-rights-activist-20160120-story.html (accessed between February 21, 2025 and March 31, 2025).

Keane, John. “The China Labyrinth.” *The New York Times*, February 14, 2012, http://www.nytimes.com/2012/02/15/opinion/the-china-labyrinth.html?ref=china (accessed between February 21, 2025 and March 31, 2025).

Kristof, Nicholas D. “The Real News in China Comes out in Restricted Periodicals.” *The New York Times*, September 24, 1991, http://www.nytimes.com/1991/09/24/world/the-real-news-in-china-comes-out-in-restricted-periodicals.html (accessed between February 21, 2025 and March 31, 2025).

Kristof, Nicholas D. "What's the Law in China? It's No Secret (Finally)." *The New York Times*, November 20, 1988, http://www.nytimes.com/1988/11/20/world/what-s-the-law-in-china-it-s-no-secret-finally.html (accessed between February 21, 2025 and March 31, 2025).

Lei, Yi. "Three Earthquakes during the Cultural Revolution." ["文革"中的三次地震] *Economic Observer Online*, June 10, 2008, https://www.eeo.com.cn/observer/special/2008/06/10/102682.shtml (accessed between February 21, 2025 and March 31, 2025).

Leonard, Jonathan Norton. "Rachel Carson Dies of Cancer; 'Silent Spring' Author Was 56." *The New York Times*, April 15, 1964, https://archive.nytimes.com/www.nytimes.com/books/97/10/05/reviews/carson-obit.html?_r=1 (accessed between February 21, 2025 and March 31, 2025).

"Li on American Hatred." *The New York Times*, September 3, 1896, https://www.nytimes.com/1896/09/03/archives/li-on-american-hatred-chinese-laborers-he-says-have-higher-virtues.html (accessed between February 21, 2025 and March 31, 2025).

Li, Hujun. "State Earthquake Administration Officially Releases Wenchuan Earthquake Intensity Distribution Map." [中国地震局正式公布汶川地震烈度分布图] *Caixin*, September 1, 2008, https://china.caixin.com/2008-09-01/100059432.html (accessed between February 21, 2025 and March 31, 2025).

Li, Hujun. "Tsinghua Academic Requests Information on Seismic Intensity Distribution." [清华学者申请公开汶川地震烈度信息] *Caijing*, June 13, 2008, https://china.caixin.com/2008-06-13/100059101.html (accessed between February 21, 2025 and March 31, 2025).

Li, Shuming, and Weihong Lv. "Three Professors from Beijing University Watched Closely on Tolls of Beijing Airport Expressway." [北大三教授"盯上"首都机场高速路] *Procuratorial Daily*, republished by Xinhua News Agency, June 18, 2008 (captured by Internet Archive Wayback Machine on June 21, 2008), retrieved from https://web.archive.org/web/20080621223627/http://news.xinhuanet.com/legal/2008-06/18/content_8389725.htm (accessed between February 21, 2025 and March 31, 2025).

Li, Shuming. "Shanghai Resident Questions Fairness of Being Beaten Without Compensation." [上海市民追问"打了白打"] *Procuratorial Daily*, November 3, 2010 (captured by Internet Archive Wayback Machine on April 13, 2021), retrieved from https://web.archive.org/web/20210413034001/http://news.jcrb.com/jxsw/201011/t20101103_461426.html (accessed between February 21, 2025 and March 31, 2025).

Liang, Ruoqiao. "For Whose Eyes Only?" *Global Times*, August 24, 2010, https://www.globaltimes.cn/content/566822.shtml_ (accessed between February 21, 2025 and March 31, 2025).

Liao, Zhuobin, and Xiaozhen Cheng. "Focus on Legislative Proposals of the Chinese People's Political Consultative Conference and the National People's Congres: Citizens can Sue Government Agencies for Non-Disclosure of Information." [聚焦两会之提案议案 信息不公开市民可起诉] *Information Times*, March 4, 2003, at A3, republished by *China.com.cn* (captured by Internet Archive Wayback Machine on June 24, 2003), retrieved from https://web.archive.org/web/20030624004653/http://www.china.com.cn/chinese/law/285943.htm (accessed between February 21, 2025 and March 31, 2025).

Lin, Jie, and Xiangyang Sun. "Twenty-Six Guangzhou Citizens Bring Guangzhou Labor Bureau to Court." [26名市民状告广州市劳保局] *China Youth Daily*, January 7, 2008, http://zqb.cyol.com/content/2008-01/07/content_2022076.htm (accessed between February 21, 2025 and March 31, 2025).

Lin, Yunshi. "China Plans to Specify Nine Kinds of State Secrets." [中国拟明确界定国家秘密的九种类型] *Caixin*, May 15, 2012, http://china.caixin.com/2012-05-15/100390469.html (accessed between February 21, 2025 and March 31, 2025).

Link, Perry. "China: The Anaconda in the Chandelier." *New York Review of Books*, April 11, 2002, http://www.nybooks.com/articles/15258 (accessed between February 21, 2025 and March 31, 2025).

Liu, Xiang. "Guangzhou Daily Newspaper Group Becomes Second Chinese Media Group Going for Initial Public Offering." [广州日报社成第二家整体上市报业集团] *Economic Weekly*, republished by *Sina News*, April 10, 2012, http://news.sina.com.cn/m/2012-04-10/104124247401.shtml (accessed between February 21, 2025 and March 31, 2025).

Lynch, Russell. "A Chinese Journalist Has Appeared on State Television 'Confessing' to Causing the Stock Market Chaos: Journalist and Brokers Admit Trading Abuses After Two-Month Share Slump, *The Independent*, August 31, 2015, http://www.independent.co.uk/news/business/news/a-chinese-journalist-has-appeared-on-state-television-confessing-to-causing-the-stock-market-chaos-10480041.html (accessed between February 21, 2025 and March 31, 2025).

Ma, Hui. "Food Safety Inspection Team Served Tainted Fruit. NPC Member Recommends Whistleblowing Protection." [食品安全检查组遇问题水果招待委员建议监督放权于民] *21st Century Business Herald*, June 30, 2011.

Magnier, Mark. "China's Leaders Take Aim at Military Corruption." *The Los Angeles Times*, January 17, 2007, https://www.latimes.com/archives/la-xpm-2007-jan-17-fg-china17-story.html (accessed between February 21, 2025 and March 31, 2025).

Magnier, Mark. "Rosy Reports from Underlings Leave Chinese Leaders in the Dark: Workers are Conditioned to Give Bosses only Good News, Letting

Problems such as SARS Get out of Control." *The Los Angeles Times*, February 16, 2004, http://articles.latimes.com/2004/feb/16/world/fg-info16 (accessed between February 21, 2025 and March 31, 2025).

McCraw, David E. "How I Got the Story: The Lawsuit behind The New York Times's Pulitzer-Winning Military Analyst Story." *Columbia Journalism Review*, April 29, 2009, http://www.cjr.org/campaign_desk/how_i_got_the_story_david_mccr.php?page=all (accessed between February 21, 2025 and March 31, 2025).

Meng, Ziyi and Yuan Ye. "China's Think Tanks: One Hundred Schools of Thought Contend, at Least Seemly" [中国智库:看上去的百家争鸣?] *Financial Times Chinese*, September 24, 2015, http://www.ftchinese.com/story/001063806?full=y (accessed between February 21, 2025 and March 31, 2025).

Mi, Aini. "Annual Watch Says County-Level Government Agencies Are Weakest in Opening Government Information." [报告称县级政府信息公开最薄弱] *Oriental Outlook Weekly*, republished by *Sina News*, November 21, 2011, http://news.sina.com.cn/c/sd/2011-11-21/140623499862.shtml (accessed between February 21, 2025 and March 31, 2025).

Min, Dahong. "Chinese Internet amid SARS Crisis." ["非典"(SARS)危机中的中国互联网] *People's Daily Online*, November 22, 2004 (captured by Internet Archive Wayback Machine on January 18, 2005) , retrieved from https://web.archive.org/web/20050118080030/http://www.people.com.cn/GB/14677/40628/3003430.html (accessed between February 21, 2025 and March 31, 2025).

Newman, Richard J., Doug Podolsky, and Penny Loeb. "Bad Blood." *U.S. News and World Report*, June 27, 1994.

Niu, Huiqing. "Review of Current Problems of China's Government Press Secretaries." [中国政府新闻发言人现存问题剖析] *People's Daily Online*, May 25, 2007 (captured by Internet Archive Wayback Machine on June 18, 2013), retrieved from https://web.archive.org/web/20130618135256/http://media.people.com.cn/GB/22114/84301/84308/5778820.html (accessed between February 21, 2025 and March 31, 2025).

"Open Party Affairs to Ensure Proper Exercise of Power, Official from General Office of CCP Answers Reporters' Questions about OPA Regulations." [推进党务公开 让权力在阳光下运行 ——中央办公厅有关负责人就《中国共产党党务公开条例(试行)》答记者问]. *Xinhua News Agency*, December 25, 2017, http://www.xinhuanet.com/politics/2017-12/25/c_1122164925.htm (accessed between February 21, 2025 and March 31, 2025).

Osnos, Evan. "Mo Yan and China's 'Nobel Complex.'" *New Yorker*, October 11, 2012, http://www.newyorker.com/online/blogs/books/2012/10/mo-yan-and-chinas-nobel-complex.html (accessed between February 21, 2025 and March 31, 2025).

Osnos, Evan. "The Forbidden Zone: How Far can a Provocative Editor Go?" *New Yorker*, July 20, 2009, http://www.newyorker.com/reporting/2009/07/20/090720fa_fact_osnos (accessed between February 21, 2025 and March 31, 2025).

"Print Media Reform Stops Mandatory Subscription." *People Daily,* November 28, 2003, http://english.peopledaily.com.cn/200311/28/eng20031128_129230.shtml (accessed between February 21, 2025 and March 31, 2025).

Qiang, Xiao. "Xia Lin, Xinhua Deputy Chief Editor, Reveals Secret Details of Old News Stories." *China Digital Times*, June 1, 2010, http://chinadigitaltimes.net/2010/06/xia-lin-夏林-xinhua-deputy-chief-editor-reveals-secret-details-of-old-news-stories (accessed between February 21, 2025 and March 31, 2025).

Qin, Xudong. "Anhui Provincial People's Government Is Tried at an Administrative Court for Possible Violations of OGI Regulations." [信息公开行政诉讼案开庭 安徽省政府成被告] *Caijing*, October 9, 2008 (captured by Internet Archive Wayback Machine on October 10, 2008), retrieved from https://web.archive.org/web/20081010211853/http://www.caijing.com.cn/2008-10-09/110018705.html (accessed between February 21, 2025 and March 31, 2025).

Qu, Changrong. "From Zero to 60 Percent: Citizen Zhengjun Zhao's Journey to Protect His Right to Know." [从0到60%:公民赵正军的"公开"维权路] *People's Daily*, May 5, 2009.

"Redefining Public Institutions." *Beijing Review*, republished by China.org.cn, May 23, 2012, available at http://www.china.org.cn/opinion/2012-05/23/content_25450895.htm (accessed between February 21, 2025 and March 31, 2025).

Rosenthal, Elisabeth. "Under Pressure, Chinese Newspaper Pulls Exposé on a Charity." *The New York Times*, March 24, 2002, http://www.nytimes.com/2002/03/24/world/under-pressure-chinese-newspaper-pulls-expose-on-a-charity.html (accessed between February 21, 2025 and March 31, 2025).

Rudd, Kevin. "The Return of Red China: Xi Jinping Brings Back Marxism." *Foreign Affairs*, November 9, 2022, https://www.foreignaffairs.com/china/return-red-china (accessed between February 21, 2025 and March 31, 2025).

Selsky, Andrew. "Pentagon Releases Gitmo Detainees' Names." *The Washington Post*, May 15, 2006.

Shang, Shaoxiang. "Reform of Press and Publication Industry and Ensuing Challenges." [新闻出版业改革及面临的问题] *People's Daily Online*, January 21, 2009 (captured by Internet Archive Wayback Machine on November 16, 2009), retrieved from https://web.archive.org/web/20091116083155/http://media.people.com.cn/GB/22114/52789/143863/8709400.html (accessed between February 21, 2025 and March 31, 2025).

Shen, Hong. "Sun Xupei: China Is Missing Best Opportunity to Enact Press Law." [中国错过了 新闻法出台的最佳时机] *The New York Times Chinese*, June 28, 2013, https://cn.nytimes.com/china/20130628/cc28pressfreedom/ (accessed between February 21, 2025 and March 31, 2025).

Shen, Hong. "Sun Xupei: Telling the Truth is Harder than Finding the Truth in China." [在中国 表达真理比发现真理还难] The New York Times Chinese, June 29, 2013, https://cn.nytimes.com/china/20130629/cc29pressfreedom/ (accessed between February 21, 2025 and March 31, 2025).

Shen, Liang, and Yunzi Wu. "People's Daily Editorials and Commentaries: Behind the Scene Stories." [探秘人民日报评论台前幕后] *Southern Weekend*, November 13, 2010, republished by *Guancha.cn* [观察者], July 26, 2013, available at https://www.guancha.cn/politics/2013_07_26_161344.shtml?web (accessed between February 21, 2025 and March 31, 2025).

Sheng, Dalin. "It Is Encouraging to Find that Government Is No Longer Covering up Sensitive Events." [喜见敏感事件不再捂盖子] *Qilu Evening News*, republished by *Phoenix TV*, November 19, 2008, https://news.ifeng.com/opinion/200811/1119_23_884599.shtml (accessed between February 21, 2025 and March 31, 2025).

Shi, Yan, Xiaojia Zhu, Xiaohan Shi and Shu Wang. "Behind-the-Scene Story about CBS Journalist Wallace's Interview with Jiang Zemin." [华莱士采访江泽民内幕] *Southern Metropolis Daily*, republished by Wenxuecity on April 13, 2012, available at https://www.wenxuecity.com/news/2012/04/13/1723950.html (accessed between February 21, 2025 and March 31, 2025).

Shi, Yan. "Valuable Experiment in Orderly Political Participation." [有序政治参与的有益尝试] *People's Daily*, republished on the website of the National People's Congress, May 12, 2010, http://www.npc.gov.cn/zgrdw/npc///xinwen/rdlt/rdjs/2010-05/12/content_1572611.htm (accessed between February 21, 2025 and March 31, 2025).

Shobert, Benjamin A. "US Inches a BIT Closer to China." *Asia Times*, May 5, 2010 (captured by Internet Archive Wayback Machine on May 8, 2010), retrieved from https://web.archive.org/web/20100508203418/http://www.atimes.com/atimes/China_Business/LE05Cb01.html (accessed between February 21, 2025 and March 31, 2025).

Shuang, Rui. "Henan Provincial People's Congress Standing Committee Holds Meeting Live Broadcast by Internet." [河南省第十一届人大常委会会议首次实现网络直播], *Xinhua News Agency*, republished on the central Chinese government's official web portal, March 29, 2012, https://www.gov.cn/jrzg/2012-03/29/content_2102689.htm (accessed between February 21, 2025 and March 31, 2025).

Snell, Rick. "Opening up the Mindset Is Key to Change." *Canberra Times*, November 4, 2008, sec. 10–11.

Song, Xiaowei. "Research on Legislative History of Chinese Press Shall Value Tradition." [新闻立法史研究须重传统] *Chinese Social Sciences Today*, May 30, 2012.

"State Council of China Talks about Whistleblower Law for the First Time, Proposing High Rewards and Rigorous Protections for Whistleblowers." [国务院首提企业"吹哨人"制度:重奖、严格保护内部"告密者"] *The Paper* [澎湃新闻], September 23, 2019, https://m.thepaper.cn/baijiahao_4503267 (accessed between February 21, 2025 and March 31, 2025).

Su, Ling. "Reporter Personally Experiences Non-Disclosure of Government Information." [记者亲历"信息不公开"] *Southern Weekend*, July 10, 2008, http://www.infzm.com/content/14380 (accessed between February 21, 2025 and March 31, 2025).

Su, Yongtong, and Jing Ju. "Press Secretaries of Party Committees Share Party Information with Citizens." [党委新闻发言人:与人民共享"党务信息"] *Southern Weekend*, January 14, 2010, http://www.infzm.com/content/40253 (accessed between February 21, 2025 and March 31, 2025).

Su, Yongtong, and Muzi Cai. "Initial Enforcement of *OGI Regulations* Faces Obstacles [实施信息
公开新法遭遇开头难], *Southern Weekend*, July 10, 2008, http://www.infzm.com/content/14378 (accessed between February 21, 2025 and March 31, 2025).

Su, Yongtong. "Exclusive: Zhangzhou PX Environmental Impact Assessment Approval Document." [独家披露:漳州PX环评批复书] *Southern Weekend*, February 22, 2009, http://www.infzm.com/content/24173 (accessed between February 21, 2025 and March 31, 2025).

"Sun-Sentinel Investigation: FEMA." *Sun Sentinel*, https://www.sun-sentinel.com/2004/11/23/sun-sentinel-investigation-fema/ (accessed between February 21, 2025 and March 31, 2025).

Sun, Xuyang. "First OGI Lawsuit Stalled in Chenzhou."[政府信息公开第一案僵持郴州] *Beijing News*, republished by *Sina Finance*, May 13, 2008, https://finance.sina.cn/sa/2008-05-13/detail-ikftpnny1555957.d.html?from=wap (accessed between February 21, 2025 and March 31, 2025).

"The Party Committee of Heilongjiang Province Publishes Its OPA Implementation Rules." [黑龙江省贯彻《中国共产党党务公开条例(试行)》实施细则] *Heilongjiang Daily*, April 16, 2018, http://epaper.hljnews.cn/hljrb/20180416/347421.html (accessed between February 21, 2025 and March 31, 2025).

"The Party Committee of Jiangsu Province Publishes Its OPA Implementation Rules." [中共江苏省委关于贯彻《中国共产党党务公开条例(试行)》实施细则] *Xinhua Daily*, republished by *People's Daily Online*, July

31, 2018, http://cpc.people.com.cn/n1/2018/0731/c64387-30180003.html (accessed between February 21, 2025 and March 31, 2025).

Toppo, Greg. "Education Dept. Paid Commentator to Promote Law." *USA Today*, January 7, 2005 (captured by Internet Archive Wayback Machine on April 8, 2005), retrieved from https://web.archive.org/web/20050408073305/http://www.usatoday.com/news/washington/2005-01-06-williams-whitehouse_x.htm (accessed between February 21, 2025 and March 31, 2025).

Tu, Ming. "Behind-the-Scene Proponent of *OGI Regulations*." [政府信息公开条例的背后推手] *Phoenix TV*, republished by Reformdata.org, March 21, 2007, http://www.reformdata.org/2007/0321/15413.shtml (accessed between February 21, 2025 and March 31, 2025).

"Vigorously Fight Against Unhealthy Practices of Reporting Good News Only." [坚决纠正报喜不报忧的不良风气] *People's Daily*, September 10, 2001 (captured by Internet Archive Wayback Machine on December 15, 2002), retrieved from https://web.archive.org/web/20021215170730/http://www.people.com.cn/GB/guandian/26/20010910/555626.html (accessed between February 21, 2025 and March 31, 2025).

Wall Street Journal China Real Time Report. "How Does the World See Xi Jinping? Pew Offers a Report Card." *The Wall Street Journal*, July 15, 2014, http://blogs.wsj.com/chinarealtime/2014/07/15/pew-report-finds-many-worried-about-war-unimpressed-by-xi-jinping/ (accessed between February 21, 2025 and March 31, 2025).

Wang, Chen. "Vigorously Push Forward Construction of System of Party Committee Press Secretaries." [积极推进党委新闻发言人制度建设] *Qiushi*, October 16, 2010 (captured by Internet Archive Wayback Machine on October 20, 2010), retrieved from https://web.archive.org/web/20101020221143/http://www.qstheory.cn/zxdk/2010/201020/201010/t20101012_52116.htm (accessed between February 21, 2025 and March 31, 2025).

Wang, Duan. "Tainted Milk Victims Take Fight to Hong Kong." *Caixin*, May 6, 2010, https://www.caixinglobal.com/2010-05-06/tainted-milk-victims-take-fight-to-hong-kong-101018319.html (accessed between February 21, 2025 and March 31, 2025).

Wang, Jiaxin, and Man Liu. "National Health Commission Denies a Lawyer's OGI Request for Daily Coronavirus Test Results on the Grounds of the Deliberative Privilege Exemption." [卫健委回复律师信息公开申请:疫情检测日报属过程性信息暂不公开] *Southern Metropolis Daily*, republished by *Sohu News*, March 28, 2020, https://www.sohu.com/a/383868171_161795 (accessed between February 21, 2025 and March 31, 2025).

Wang, Junxiu, and Pengjie Zhang. "Supreme Court Official: Half of OGI-Related Lawsuits Are Dismissed." [官员称:半数信息公开诉讼案被法院拒之门外] *China Youth Daily*, republished by *Global Times*, November 27,

2011, https://china.huanqiu.com/article/9CaKrnJthcb (accessed between February 21, 2025 and March 31, 2025).

Wang, Junxiu. " Sixty-Eight Villagers of Yu Yao, Zhejiang Province Successfully Force Municipal Government to Change Its Original Non-Disclosure OGI Decision." [浙江余姚68名村民信息公开案告赢市政府] *China Youth Daily*, republished by *China News Service*, October 10, 2008, http://www.chinanews.com.cn/sh/news/2008/10-10/1407244.shtml (accessed between February 21, 2025 and March 31, 2025).

Wang, Junxiu. "Lawyer Discusses Various Strange Phenomena regarding FOI." [一律师披露政府信息公开之怪现状] *China Youth Daily*, May 10, 2008, http://zqb.cyol.com/content/2008-05/10/content_2175261.htm (accessed between February 21, 2025 and March 31, 2025).

Wang, Min. "Analysis of China's Government-Run Blogs." [我国政府博客现状分析] *People's Daily Online*, May 10, 2007 (captured by Internet Archive Wayback Machine on May 13, 2007), retrieved from https://web.archive.org/web/20070513051417/http://media.people.com.cn/GB/22114/44110/75857/5714324.html (accessed between February 21, 2025 and March 31, 2025).

Wang, Peng. "Military Spokespersons Show off Chinese Military's Openness and Confidence." [军事新闻发言人制度展示我军开放与自信] *China Youth Daily*, November 29, 2013, http://zqb.cyol.com/html/2013-11/29/nw.D110000zgqnb_20131129_2-10.htm (accessed between February 21, 2025 and March 31, 2025).

Wang, Shaozhe. "*Op-ed: Accusations Saying China Will Tighten Media Control Are Groundless*." *People's Daily Online*, February 24, 2016, http://en.people.cn/n3/2016/0224/c98649-9020663.html (accessed between February 21, 2025 and March 31, 2025).

Wang, Xin. "Journalistic OGI Applications for PM2.5 Data Yield 32% of Response Rate." [记者申请PM2.5信息公开 31省区市10个答复] *Southern Metropolis Daily*, republished by ChinaTransparency.org, January 11, 2012 (captured by Internet Archive Wayback Machine on February 19, 2022), retrieved from https://web.archive.org/web/20220219172530/http://www.ogichina.org/article/180/12880.html (accessed between February 21, 2025 and March 31, 2025).

Wang, Yijun. "Chinese Academy of Social Sciences Survey Finds that More Than Half of Chinese City Government Websites Substandard." [社科院调研发现逾半数城市政府网站"不及格"] *China Youth Daily*, republished by *China News Service*, February 22, 2010, http://www.chinanews.com.cn/gn/news/2010/02-22/2130014.shtml (accessed between February 21, 2025 and March 31, 2025).

Wang, Yijun. "State Secrets Become Excuse for Nondisclosure?" [拒绝公开信息,"国家秘密"成挡箭牌?] *China Youth Daily*, December 12,

2009, http://article.cyol.com/home/zqb/content/2009-12/02/content_2963336.htm (accessed between February 21, 2025 and March 31, 2025).

Wei, Mingyan, and Shaofeng Guo. "OGI Regulations Still Encounter Implementation Bottlenecks Four Years After Its Enactment." [信息公开条例实施4年仍遭执行难] *Beijing News*, May 15, 2012, http://www.bjnews.com.cn/news/2012/05/15/199113.html (accessed between February 21, 2025 and March 31, 2025).

Wen, Jiabao. "Seriously Adhere to the Spirits of the 17th National Congress of the CPC to Promote Vigorously the Work of Incorruptibility Construction and Anti-Corruption." [认真贯彻党的十七大精神大力推进廉政建设和反腐败工作] 9 *QIUSHI* [求是] 9 (6) (2008):5–10.

Wen, Jiabao. "Speech delivered at National Meeting on Law-Based Administration)." [温家宝在全国依法行政工作会议上的讲话] *People's Daily*, September 20, 2010 (captured by Internet Archive Wayback Machine on September 23, 2010), retrieved from https://web.archive.org/web/20100923193404/http://politics.people.com.cn/GB/101380/12772650.html (accessed between February 21, 2025 and March 31, 2025).

Wu, Nan. "Chinese Bloggers on the History and Influence of the 'Fifty Cent Party.'" *The Digital Times*, May 15, 2008, http://chinadigitaltimes.net/2008/05/chinese-bloggers-on-the-history-and-influence-of-the-fifty-cent-party/ (accessed between February 21, 2025 and March 31, 2025).

Wu, Nengxi. "Starting from Assessment of Stalin." [从评价斯大林说起] *People's Daily Online*, August 25, 2010 (captured by Internet Archive Wayback Machine on June 7, 2011), retrieved from https://web.archive.org/web/20110607235409/http://media.people.com.cn/GB/192301/192377/192680/201060/201062/12533386.html (accessed between February 21, 2025 and March 31, 2025).

Wu, Yu. "Citizens Are Calling for Special Investigation into 723 Train Crash." [民间呼吁启动"7·23动车事故"特别调查] *DW News*, July 26, 2011, https://www.dw.com/zh/%E6%B0%91%E9%97%B4%E5%91%BC%E5%90%81%E5%90%AF%E5%8A%A8723%E5%8A%A8%E8%BD%A6%E4%BA%8B%E6%95%85%E7%89%B9%E5%88%AB%E8%B0%83%E6%9F%A5/a-15265997 (accessed between February 21, 2025 and March 31, 2025).

Xiao, Hui, Zhiming Bao, and Yuwu Gao. "Zhongnan Hospital of Wuhan University in COVID-19 Pandemic: Doctors Fight from Beginning to End" [武汉疫情中的中南医院:他们打满全场], *Caixin*, republished by *Matters*, May 3, 2020, https://matters.town/a/vh2mam7fb4ic (accessed between February 21, 2025 and March 31, 2025).

Xie, Haitao, Ning Yu, Xin He, Jieqi Luo, Kaixi Huang, and Duan Wang. "Zhou Family Legacy: Thick Blood, Fat Profits." *Caixin*, August 22, 2014, http://english.caixin.com/2014-08-22/100720251.html (accessed between February 21, 2025 and March 31, 2025).

"Xinhua Neican Exposes Black Whistle in Chinese Football." [新华社内参捅破中国足坛的黑哨坚冰] *New Daily* [每日新报], January 8, 2002, republished by China.com (captured by Internet Archive Wayback Machine on November 9, 2002), retrieved from https://web.archive.org/web/20021109210646/http://www.china.com.cn/chinese/SPORT-c/94580.htm (accessed between February 21, 2025 and March 31, 2025).

Xinhua. "New Rules Issued to Require Government Transparency." *China Daily*, April 24, 2007, http://www.chinadaily.com.cn/china/2007-04/24/content_858745.htm (accessed between February 21, 2025 and March 31, 2025).

Xinhua. "Landmark Decree to Encourage Government Transparency." *China Daily*, April 24, 2007, http://www.chinadaily.com.cn/china/2007-04/24/content_857930.htm (accessed between February 21, 2025 and March 31, 2025).

Xu, Xuejiang. "Death Toll of Tangshan Earthquake: More Than 240,000." [唐山地震死亡24万多人] *People's Daily*, November 23, 1979.

Yang, Dali. "Wuhan Officials Tried to Cover up Covid-19—and Sent It Careening Outward." *Washington Post*, March 10, 2020, https://www.washingtonpost.com/politics/2020/03/10/wuhan-officials-tried-cover-up-covid-19-sent-it-careening-outward/ (accessed between February 21, 2025 and March 31, 2025).

Ye, Doudou. "Ministry of Railways, How Hard Is Open Government Information? [铁道部,信息公开有多难?] *Caixin*, September 29, 2011, http://china.caixin.com/2011-09-29/100310845.html (accessed between February 21, 2025 and March 31, 2025).

Yuan, Duanduan, and Nan Xu. "Why Is Disclosure of Environmental Information So Hard? Story of 29 OGI Request Forms." [环境信息公开咋这么难 29份信息公开申请表的遭遇] *Southern Weekend*, June 23, 2010, https://www.infzm.com/contents/46698 (accessed between February 21, 2025 and March 31, 2025).

Yuan, Yue. "Xiamen PX Incident." [厦门PX事件] *Sanlian Life Weekly*, republished by *Sina News*, September 27, 2007, http://news.sina.com.cn/c/2007-09-27/165713986641.shtml (accessed between February 21, 2025 and March 31, 2025).

Zhang, Tailing. "Fake Newsrooms Write Fake Journalistic Internal Reference for Desperate Petitioners." [假编辑部收千元为上访者写内参] *Beijing News*, republished by *Sina Finance*, August 2, 2010, https://finance.sina.cn/sa/2010-08-02/detail-ikftpnny0176483.d.html?from=wap (accessed between February 21, 2025 and March 31, 2025).

Zhang, Wei. "Initial Purpose of OGI Legislation: Create Mechanism to Push Reform: View of CASS Scholar Zhou Hanhua on *OGI Regulations*." [立法初衷就是要建立一种改革倒逼机制：中国社科院研究员周汉华谈政府信

息公开条例] *Legal Daily*, republished by Sohu News, May 3, 2011, http://news.sohu.com/20110503/n280474900.shtml (accessed between February 21, 2025 and March 31, 2025).

Zhang, Xianming. "Supreme Court of China Issues Judicial Interpretation of *OGI Regulations*, Providing Courts with Guidance on OGI-Related Lawsuits." [最高人民法院颁布司法解释 全面规范审理政府信息公开行政案件有关问题], PEOPLE'S COURT DAILY, republished by the Supreme Court of China website, August 15, 2011 (captured by Internet Archive Wayback Machine on February 19, 2022), retrieved from https://web.archive.org/web/20220219074628/https://www.court.gov.cn/zixun-xiangqing-3024.html (accessed between February 21, 2025 and March 31, 2025).

Zhang, Xianming. " *Cancao Xiaoxi*: from Internal Report to Newspaper Accessible to All."《参考消息》:从"内部刊物"到公开发行] *Phoenix TV*, November 15, 2007, https://news.ifeng.com/history/3/200710/1019_337_264646.shtml (accessed between February 21, 2025 and March 31, 2025).

Zhang, Xiaosong, and Zhengguang Luo. "Code of Civil Law Draft Rules See 126 Revisions and Anyone Who Defames Communist Heroes And Revolutionary Martyrs will Face Civil Liability." [民法总则草案作126处修改 抹黑英雄烈士将被追责] *Global Times*, March 13, 2017, http://lianghui.huanqiu.com/2017/roll/2017-03/10298234.html (accessed between February 21, 2025 and March 31, 2025).

Zhang, Yang, and Changchun Cai. "Administrative Reconsideration Committees Are Established across 108 Government Agencies in 19 Provinces to Ensure Impartiality." [19省份108单位设行政复议委员会 杜绝官官相护] *People's Daily*, republished by *China News Service*, March 28, 2012, http://www.chinanews.com/fz/2012/03-28/3779138.shtml (accessed between February 21, 2025 and March 31, 2025).

Zhang, Yannong. "Full Text of People's Daily Publisher Yannong Zhang's Speech to Kick off His Paper's College Campus Tour." [人民日报校园行活动启动 社长张研农演讲全文] *People's Daily Online*, November 23, 2009 (captured by Internet Archive Wayback Machine on November 27, 2009), retrieved from https://web.archive.org/web/20091127204920/http://media.people.com.cn/GB/120837/10433201.html (accessed between February 21, 2025 and March 31, 2025).

Zhao, Jin. "Why Is Press Freedom Law Still a Dream in China?" [《新闻法》为何至今悬而未立?] *The Youth Journalist*, republished by *People's Daily Online*, February 12, 2009 (captured by Internet Archive Wayback Machine on February 19, 2009), retrieved from https://web.archive.org/web/20090219221025/http://media.people.com.cn/GB/22114/42328/145310/8792516.html (accessed between February 21, 2025 and March 31, 2025).

Zhao, Lei, and Yongtong Su. "Many Doubts about Government Information Disclosure." [政府信息疑点仍多] *Southern Weekend*, May 8, 2008, http://www.infzm.com/content/11911/ (accessed between February 21, 2025 and March 31, 2025).

Zhao, Wenming. "First OGI Lawsuit: Retired Workers Take Government to Court for Its Failure to Disclose Information." [政府信息公开条例第一案:退休职工告政府信息不公开] *Legal Daily*, republished by *Xinhua News Agency*, May 6, 2008 (captured by Internet Archive Wayback Machine on May 9, 2008), retrieved from https://web.archive.org/web/20080509015423/http://news.xinhuanet.com/legal/2008-05/06/content_8112790.htm (accessed between February 21, 2025 and March 31, 2025).

Zheng, Jie. "All Branches of Chinese Military Train First Team of Experts in Foreign Publicity." [中国军队培训首批外宣团队 覆盖全军各军兵种] *Oriental Morning Post*, republished by *Sina News*, March 23, 2009, http://mil.news.sina.com.cn/2009-03-23/0825546181.html (accessed between February 21, 2025 and March 31, 2025).

Zheng, Tingying. "Declassified Diplomatic Documents Show that Dalai Lama Stole and Sold Gold, Silver and Jewelry when Exiled from Tibet." [中国外交部解密档案显示达赖流亡时盗卖金银财宝] *Youth Reference News*, republished by *Sina News*, January 13, 2009, http://news.sina.com.cn/c/2009-01-13/145817035599.shtml (accessed between February 21, 2025 and March 31, 2025).

Zhu, Dequan. "Unanswered Questions about First OGI Litigation Involving a Journalist." ["政府侵犯新闻采访权第一案"悬疑] *Dazhong Newspaper Group Online*, August 23, 2006 (captured by Internet Archive Wayback Machine on January 5, 2011), retrieved from https://web.archive.org/web/20110105051846/http://qnjz.dzwww.com/zk/200608/t20060801_1680429.htm (accessed between February 21, 2025 and March 31, 2025).

Zhu, Sibei. "Officials Should Not Be Considered Freak When They Become Disclosure Friendly" [应剔除"一公开就异类"思维] *Xinmin Evening News*, republished by *Economic Daily Online*, February 29, 2012, http://views.ce.cn/view/ent/201202/29/t20120229_23113736.shtml (accessed between February 21, 2025 and March 31, 2025).

News Services, Radio and TV Stations

"Administrative Reconsideration Law of the People's Republic of China ." [中华人民共和国行\政复议法] *Xinhua News Agency*, republished by web portal of the State Council, September 1, 2023, https://www.gov.cn/yaowen/liebiao/202309/content_6901584.htm (accessed between February 21, 2025 and March 31, 2025).

"Biography of Lin Xia." [夏林简介] *Xinhua News Agency,* 2000–2003 (captured by Internet Archive Wayback Machine on February 14, 2003), retrieved from https://web.archive.org/web/20030214211854/http://www.xinhuanet.com/xhsjj/ling_xl.htm (accessed between February 21, 2025 and March 31, 2025).

Bristow, Michael. "China's Internet Spin Doctors." *BBC News*, December 16, 2008, http://news.bbc.co.uk/2/hi/asia-pacific/7783640.stm (accessed between February 21, 2025 and March 31, 2025).

Chen, Wei. "WTO Official Exclaims WTO Has Made China More Transparent and Foreign Trade Statistics Are No Longer State Secrets." [WTO官员叹中国入世后政策透明:此前外贸数字都是机密] *Xinhua News Agency*, republished by *Phoenix TV*, November 20, 2011 (captured by Internet Archive Wayback Machine on November 23, 2011), retrieved from https://web.archive.org/web/20111123041456/http://finance.ifeng.com/news/macro/20111120/5101852.shtml (accessed between February 21, 2025 and March 31, 2025).

"China Announces New Measures to Promote Openness." *Voice of America*, April 24, 2007, https://www.voanews.com/a/a-13-2007-04-24-voa9/337433.html (accessed between February 21, 2025 and March 31, 2025).

"China Cover-up Official Executed." *BBC News*, February 20, 2004, http://news.bbc.co.uk/2/hi/asia-pacific/3507067.stm (accessed between February 21, 2025 and March 31, 2025).

"China Didn't Warn Public of Likely Pandemic for 6 Key Days." *Associated Press*, April 15, 2020, https://apnews.com/article/virus-outbreak-health-ap-top-news-international-news-china-clamps-down-68a9e1b91de4ffc166acd6012d82c2f9 (accessed between February 21, 2025 and March 31, 2025).

"China Lawmakers Add Defaming Party Heroes to Civil Code Offences." *Reuters*, March 12, 2017, https://www.reuters.com/article/world/china-lawmakers-add-defaming-party-heroes-to-civil-code-offences-idUSKBN16K0AF/ (accessed between February 21, 2025 and March 31, 2025).

"China's Bo Xilai Implicated in Wife's Crime-State Media." *BBC*, September 19, 2012, http://www.bbc.co.uk/news/world-asia-china-19645314 (accessed between February 21, 2025 and March 31, 2025).

"China's Xi Underscores CPC's Leadership in News Reporting." *Xinhua News Agency*, February 19, 2016 (captured by Internet Archive Wayback Machine on February 20, 2016), retrieved from https://web.archive.org/web/20160220102128/http://news.xinhuanet.com/english/2016-02/19/c_135114305.htm (accessed between February 21, 2025 and March 31, 2025).

"China to Merge State Media Broadcasting Giants." *China Global Television Network*, March 21, 2018, https://america.cgtn.com/2018/03/21/china-to-merge-state-media-broadcasting-giants (accessed between February 21, 2025 and March 31, 2025).

"Chinese Communist Party New Politburo Members Study Constitution together and Hu Jintao Delivers Speech." [新一届中共中央政治局集体学习胡锦涛发表讲话] *China News Service*, December 26, 2002 https://www.chinanews.com.cn/2002-12-26/26/257773.html (accessed between February 21, 2025 and March 31, 2025).

"Chinese Football Fans Riot over Penalty." *BBC News*, March 25, 2002, http://news.bbc.co.uk/2/hi/asia-pacific/1892421.stm (accessed between February 21, 2025 and March 31, 2025).

"Chinese Government Launches Anti-Corruption Mobile App." *China Global Television Network*, January 1, 2015, https://america.cgtn.com/2015/01/01/chinese-government-launches-anti-corruption-mobile-app (accessed between February 21, 2025 and March 31, 2025).

"Chongqing Vice Mayor Wang Lijun Is Receiving Vacation-Style Treatment." [重庆市副市长王立军正接受休假式治疗] *Xinhua News Agency*, February 8, 2012 (captured by Internet Archive Wayback Machine on February 11, 2012), retrieved from https://web.archive.org/web/20120211005933/http://news.xinhuanet.com/local/2012-02/08/c_122672681.htm (accessed between February 21, 2025 and March 31, 2025).

Dakss, Brian. "Birth Control Patch Users Warned, FDA: It Puts Women at Higher Risk for Clots than Pill Does." *CBS/AP*, November 11, 2005 (captured by Internet Archive Wayback Machine on November 24, 2005), retrieved from https://web.archive.org/web/20051124020740/http://www.cbsnews.com/stories/2005/11/11/earlyshow/health/health_news/main1037611.shtml (accessed between February 21, 2025 and March 31, 2025).

Feng, Xiaofang. "OGI Regulations Listed on Legislative Plan and Could Be Adopted by End of 2006." [《政府信息公开条例》入立法计划有望年内出台] *Xinhua News Agency*, republished by the official website of the State Council of the People's Republic of China, March 17, 2006, http://www.gov.cn/jrzg/200603/17/content_229647.htm (accessed between February 21, 2025 and March 31, 2025).

Gan, Nectar. "Xi Jinping Tells China's National Security Chiefs to Prepare for 'Worst Case' Scenarios." *CNN*, June 1, 2023, https://www.cnn.com/2023/05/31/china/china-xi-national-security-meeting-intl-hnk/index.html (accessed between February 21, 2025 and March 31, 2025).

"Garbage Collectors Take away Two-Million-Yuan Deposit Book Mistakenly Abandoned by Corrupt Official's Wife." [男子收废品收走纪委书记巨款存折] *China Weekly*, republished by *Phoenix TV*, May 6, 2009, https://news.ifeng.com/society/1/200905/0506_343_1142568.shtml (accessed between February 21, 2025 and March 31, 2025).

"History and Development of Xinhua News Agency Heilongjiang Bureau." [新华通讯社在黑龙江省的分支机构的沿革和发展] *Xinhua News Agency*,

January 10, 2013 (captured by Internet Archive Wayback Machine on March 21, 2015), retrieved from https://web.archive.org/web/20150510041641/http://hlj.xinhuanet.com/hljfs/2013-01/10/c_132092257.htm (accessed between February 21, 2025 and March 31, 2025).

Huo, Xiaoguang, and Bin Li. "General Secretary Xi Jinping Chairs News and Public Opinion Work Conference and Visits People's Daily, Xinhua News Agency and China Central Television" [习近平总书记主持召开党的新闻舆论工作座谈会并到人民日报社、新华社、中央电视台调研侧记] *Xinhua News Agency*, February 20, 2016, http://news.xinhuanet.com/politics/2016-02/20/c_1118106530.htm (accessed between February 21, 2025 and March 31, 2025).

Ivry, Bob. "Fed Loses Bid For Review Of Bailout Disclosure Ruling." *Bloomberg News*, August 23, 2010, http://www.bloomberg.com/news/2010-08-23/u-s-appeals-court-refuses-to-review-disclosure-ruling-on-fed-bailouts.html. (accessed between February 21, 2025 and March 31, 2025).

Ivry, Bob. "Mark Pittman's Fed Legacy: 'Maybe Tomorrow the Dog Will Talk.'" *Bloomberg News*, November 27, 2011, http://www.bloomberg.com/news/2011-11-28/mark-pittman-s-fed-legacy-maybe-tomorrow-the-dog-will-talk-.html (accessed between February 21, 2025 and March 31, 2025).

Jiang, Steven. "Trial by Media? Confessions Go Prime Time in China." *CNN*, January 26, 2016, http://www.cnn.com/2016/01/26/asia/china-television-confessions/ (accessed between February 21, 2025 and March 31, 2025).

Kang, Dake. "In Xi's China, even Internal Reports Fall Prey to Censorship." *Associated Press*, October 31, 2022, https://apnews.com/article/health-china-beijing-covid-wuhan3c199e3f1a084013da18fc9e6061e775 (accessed between February 21, 2025 and March 31, 2025).

King, Gary. "China's 'Internet Police' Targets Collective Action." *National Public Radio*, August 8, 2012, http://www.npr.org/2012/08/08/158448847/chinas-internet-police-targets-collective-action (accessed between February 21, 2025 and March 31, 2025).

Kuhn, Anthony. "China Moves Toward Release of Classified Data." *National Public Radio*, http://www.npr.org/templates/story/story.php?storyId=9803236 (accessed between February 21, 2025 and March 31, 2025).

Li, Huizi, and Zhuo Cheng. "China Narrows Definition of 'State Secrets' to Boost Government Transparency." *Xinhua News Agency*, April 29, 2010 (captured by Internet Archive Wayback Machine on May 3, 2010), retrieved from https://web.archive.org/web/20100503144515/http://news.xinhuanet.com/english2010/china/2010-04/29/c_13272939.htm (accessed between February 21, 2025 and March 31, 2025).

Li, Yajie, and Qin Zhang. "Thirty-One Provincial Governments Adopts Rules on Openness in Governmental Affairs." [目前全国31个省(自治区、直辖

市)政府建立政务公开管理制度] *Xinhua News Agency*, December 10, 2006 (captured by Internet Archive Wayback Machine on December 12, 2006), retrieved from https://web.archive.org/web/20061212054433/http://news.xinhuanet.com/politics/2006-12/10/content_5463416.htm (accessed between February 21, 2025 and March 31, 2025).

Liao, Yi. "National Library of China Creates Nation's First Coordinated Platform for Distributing Government Information." [国家图书馆建立我国首个"政府信息整合服务平台"] *Xinhua News Agency*, republished by Gov.cn, April 30, 2009, https://www.gov.cn/jrzg/2009-04/30/content_1301142.htm (accessed between February 21, 2025 and March 31, 2025).

Liu, Wenjie. "Five Doctoral Candidates from Hunan's Xiangtan University Sue Government for Refusing to Release Information about Administrative Fees." [湖南湘潭大学五博士状告政府 要求公开收费信息] *Xinhua News Agency*, June 6, 2008 (captured by Internet Archive Wayback Machine on June 8, 2008), retrieved from https://web.archive.org/web/20080608093817/http://news.xinhuanet.com/legal/2008-06/06/content_8319893.htm (accessed between February 21, 2025 and March 31, 2025).

Mendoza, Martha, and Christopher Sullivan. "Billions in Penalties for Wrongdoing Uncollected." *Associated Press*, republished by *NBC News*, March 19, 2006, https://www.nbcnews.com/id/wbna11877818 (accessed between February 21, 2025 and March 31, 2025).

Mendoza, Martha. "AP Review Finds Federal Government Missing Deadlines and Time Limits." *Associated Press*, March 13, 2006 (captured by Internet Archive Wayback Machine on May 15, 2006), retrieved from https://web.archive.org/web/20060515043200/http://www.ap.org/foi/foi_031306b.html (accessed between February 21, 2025 and March 31, 2025).

"Operation of Chinese Central Government Website Draws Worldwide Attention." [中国政府网开通吸引世界目光] *Xinhua News Agency*, January 4, 2006 (captured by Internet Archive Wayback Machine on January 12, 2006), retrieved from https://web.archive.org/web/20060112022617/http://news.xinhuanet.com/politics/2006-01/04/content_4005174.htm (accessed between February 21, 2025 and March 31, 2025).

Roberts, Dexter. "Xi Jinping Is the World's Most Popular Leader, Says Survey." *Bloomberg News*, December 18, 2014, http://www.bloomberg.com/bw/articles/2014-12-18/xi-jinping-wins-the-popularity-conest (accessed between February 21, 2025 and March 31, 2025).

"Shijiazhuang City Government Spokesperson: We Have Undeniable Responsibility for Sanlu Milk Contamination Incident." [石家庄政府新闻发言人:三鹿奶粉事件我们有不可推卸的责任] *China Central Television*, September 30, 2008, http://news.cctv.com/xwlb/20080930/101980.shtml (accessed between February 21, 2025 and March 31, 2025).

"State Council Legislative Affairs Office Deputy Director Meets the Press." [国务院法制办副主任就《政府信息公开条例》答记者问] *Xinhua News Agency*, republished by *Phoenix TV*, April 24, 2007, https://news.ifeng.com/mainland/200704/0424_17_108239.shtml (accessed between February 21, 2025 and March 31, 2025).

Walsh, Nick Paton. "The Wuhan Files." *CNN*, December 1, 2020, https://www.cnn.com/2020/11/30/asia/wuhan-china-covid-intl/index.html (accessed between February 21, 2025 and March 31, 2025).

Wang, Dake. "In Xi's China, even Internal Reports Fall Prey to Censorship." *Associated Press*, October 31, 2022, https://apnews.com/article/health-china-beijing-covid-wuhan-3c199e3f1a084013da18fc9e6061e775 (accessed between February 21, 2025 and March 31, 2025).

Wang, Li. "People's Daily Publisher Says that 'Microblog Queen' Yao Chen Is Our Competitor." [人民日报社长:"微博女王"姚晨是我们的"对手"] *Phoenix TV*, April 29, 2012, http://culture.ifeng.com/1/detail_2012_04/29/14235106_0.shtml (accessed between February 21, 2025 and March 31, 2025).

Wang, Tianyu. "Explainer: Why Does China Have So Many State-Owned Enterprises." *China Global Television Network*, June 14, 2021, https://news.cgtn.com/news/2021-06-14/Explainer-Why-China-has-so-many-state-owned-enterprises-115vt8ntcZ2/index.html (accessed between February 21, 2025 and March 31, 2025).

Wu, Zijing. "Party-Controlled China Site Raises $222 Million In Enlarged IPO." *Bloomberg News*, April 19, 2012, http://www.bloomberg.com/news/2012-04-18/china-s-party-website-people-cn-seeks-18-ipo-premium.html (accessed between February 21, 2025 and March 31, 2025).

Yang, Weihan. "Supreme Court Research Institute Director Talks about Enhancing Justice Fairness and Credibility." [最高人民法院研究室主任谈加强公正司法提高公信力] *Xinhua News Agency*, republished by *Sina News*, October 28, 2013, available at http://news.sina.com.cn/o/2013-10-28/215028554335.shtml accessed between February 21, 2025 and March 31, 2025).

Internet-Only Sources

"A Century of Serving the Library Community." HeinOnline, Buffalo, New York, available at https://home.heinonline.org/about-us/ (accessed between February 21, 2025 and March 31, 2025).

"Access to Congress." The Citizen Media Law Project (currently the Digital Media Law Project), the Berkman Klein Center for Internet & Society at Harvard University, Cambridge, Massachusetts, available at http://www.citmedialaw.org/legal-guide/access-congress (accessed between February 21, 2025 and March 31, 2025).

"Administrative Division." State Council of the People's Republic of China, Beijing, China, August 26, 2014, available at http://english.www.gov.cn/archive/china_abc/2014/08/27/content_281474983873401.htm (accessed between February 21, 2025 and March 31, 2025).

Alvarez, Mike, Jose Antonio Cheibub, Fernando Limongi, and Adam Przeworski. "ACLP Political and Economic Database Codebook." Pompeu Fabra University, Barcelona, Spain, December 1999, available at https://econ.upf.edu/~satorra/dades/ACLP_Codebook.PDF (accessed between February 21, 2025 and March 31, 2025).

Amy, Sim Kok Eng, and Jing Hu. "Access to Environmental Information in China: Evaluation of Local Compliance." Article 19, London, United Kingdom, December 2010, available at https://www.article19.org/data/files/pdfs/reports/access-to-environmental-information-in-china-evaluation-of-local-compliance.pdf (accessed between February 21, 2025 and March 31, 2025).

"A Model Freedom of Information Law." Article 19, London, United Kingdom, available at http://www.article19.org/data/files/pdfs/standards/modelfoilaw.pdf (accessed between February 21, 2025 and March 31, 2025).

"Annual OGI Work Report of the Ministry of Foreign Affairs (2011)." [外交部2011年政府信息公开工作年度报告] the Ministry of Foreign Affairs, Beijing, China, March 30, 2012, available at https://www.mfa.gov.cn/web/wjb_673085/zfxxgk_674865/zfxxgknb/201203/t20120330_9277415.shtml (accessed between February 21, 2025 and March 31, 2025).

Bandurski, David. "History of High-Speed Propaganda Tells All." China Media Project at the University of Hong Kong, Hong Kong, China, July 25, 2011 (captured by Internet Archive Wayback Machine on August 27, 2011), retrieved from https://web.archive.org/web/20110827052438/http://cmp.hku.hk/2011/07/25/14036/ (accessed between February 21, 2025 and March 31, 2025).

Bandurski, David. "The Marxist View of Journalism (马克思主义新闻观)." China Media Project, the University of Hong Kong, Hong Kong, China, July 5, 2007, available at https://chinamediaproject.org/2007/07/05/the-marxist-view-of-journalism-%E9%A9%AC%E5%85%8B%E6%80%9D%E4%B8%BB%E4%B9%89%E6%96%B0%E9%97%BB%E8%A7%82/ (accessed between February 21, 2025 and March 31, 2025).

Banisar, David. "Effective Open Government: Improving Public Access to Government Information." Report for Organization for Economic Co-operation and Development, Paris, France, May 29, 2012, available at https://papers.ssrn.com/sol3/papers.cfm?abstract_id=2069870 (accessed between February 21, 2025 and March 31, 2025).

Banisar, David. "Freedom of Information around the World 2006: A Global Survey of Access to Government Information Laws." Report for Privacy

International, London, United Kingdom, July 2006, available at http://www.freedominfo.org/documents/global_survey2006.pdf (accessed between February 21, 2025 and March 31, 2025).

Baughman, James L. "The Fall and Rise of Partisan Journalism." Center for Journalism Ethics, School of Journalism & Mass Communication, University of Wisconsin-Madison, Madison, Wisconsin, April 20, 2011, available at http://ethics.journalism.wisc.edu/2011/04/20/the-fall-and-rise-of-partisan-journalism/ (accessed between February 21, 2025 and March 31, 2025).

Bennett, Steven C. "Litigation in China: Ten Things You Must Know." Corporate Counsel Business Journal, Darien, Connecticut, October 1, 2008, available at https://ccbjournal.com/articles/litigation-china-ten-things-you-must-know (accessed between February 21, 2025 and March 31, 2025).

Bertoni, Eduardo. "Freedom of Information, Three Harmless Words? The Role of the Media and Access to Information Laws." Originally published in Spanish by the World Bank Institute, republished by Center for Studies on Freedom of Expression and Access to Information at Palermo University School of Law, Buenos Aires, Argentina, available at http://www.palermo.edu/cele/pdf/ATIandMedia.pdf (accessed between February 21, 2025 and March 31, 2025).

Brechner Center for Freedom of Information. "Florida's Government in the Sunshine: A Citizen's Guide." The University of Florida, Gainesville, Florida, 2006, available at https://original-ufdc.uflib.ufl.edu/UF00088828/00001/5x (accessed between February 21, 2025 and March 31, 2025).

"By Country." Global Right to Information Rating (produced by Access Info Europe and Centre for Law and Democracy), Madrid, Spain, available at http://www.rti-rating.org/country-data/ (accessed between February 21, 2025 and March 31, 2025).

Chan, Alan. "Laozi." Stanford Encyclopedia of Philosophy, Stanford University, Stanford, California, first published on December 15, 2001, substantive revision on Jun 27, 2012, available at http://plato.stanford.edu/entries/laozi/ (accessed between February 21, 2025 and March 31, 2025).

Chen, Lidan. "The 17th Party Congress Report Supports an Open Information Policy." [十七大报告展现开放的信息政策], Changzhou Zugong, Changzhou CCP Committee Organization Department, Changzhou, China, December 14, 2007, https://zg.changzhou.gov.cn/content/suitable/show?id=4772&catid=2206 (accessed between February 21, 2025 and March 31, 2025).

Cheng, Quan. "General Administration of Quality Supervision, Inspection and Quarantine Is Embroiled in OGI Scandal." [质检总局深陷信息公开门], Sina Finance, Beijing, China, November 5, 2008, https://m.cj.sina.cn/page/aHR0cDovL2ZpbmFuY2Uuc2luYS5jb20uY24vZy8yMDA4MTEwNS8wNTI0NTQ2ODgxNC5zaHRtbA?from=redirect (accessed between February 21, 2025 and March 31, 2025).

"China Core Newspapers Full-text Database." Part of the China National Knowledge Infrastructure (CNKI) database, Beijing, China, available at https://oversea.cnki.net/kns?dbcode=CCND (accessed between February 21, 2025 and March 31, 2025).
"China Judgements Online." [中国裁判文书网]. Supreme Court of the People's Republic of China, Beijing, China, available at https://wenshu.court.gov.cn (accessed between February 21, 2025 and March 31, 2025).
"China's Massive Web Audience Turns to Social, Mobile, Video." Emarketer, New York, New York, March 6, 2012 (captured by Internet Archive Wayback Machine on March 8, 2012), retrieved from https://web.archive.org/web/20120308210132/http://www.emarketer.com/Article.aspx?R=1008882 (accessed between February 21, 2025 and March 31, 2025).
"Chinese Law and Policy on Open Government Information." Open Government Information in China, Yale University Law School Paul Tsai China Center, New Haven, Connecticut, available at https://law.yale.edu/china-center/resources/open-government-information-china (accessed between February 21, 2025 and March 31, 2025).
"Collection of Media Reports on Wang Lijun Incident." [媒体报道王立军薄熙来事件始末] 21cn.com, Guangzhou, China, May 22, 2012 (captured by Internet Archive Wayback Machine on May 25, 2012), retrieved from https://web.archive.org/web/20120525121116/http://news.21cn.com/today/topic/2012/05/22/11937242.shtml (accessed between February 21, 2025 and March 31, 2025).
"Constitution of the People's Republic of China [1954]." Cornell University, Ithaca, New York, available at https://ecommons.cornell.edu/server/api/core/bitstreams/f7bbb8b4-822c-467e-b51c-430e44430e4d/content (accessed between February 21, 2025 and March 31, 2025).
"Constitution of the People's Republic of China [1975]." University of Southern California, Los Angels, California, available at https://china.usc.edu/sites/default/files/article/attachments/peoples-republic-of-china-constitution-1975.pdf (accessed between February 21, 2025 and March 31, 2025).
"Constitution of the People's Republic of China [1978]." University of Southern California, Los Angels, California, available at https://china.usc.edu/sites/default/files/article/attachments/peoples-republic-of-china-constitution-1978.pdf (accessed between February 21, 2025 and March 31, 2025).
"Constitution of the People's Republic of China, 1982." University of Southern California, Los Angels, California, available at https://china.usc.edu/node/20328 (accessed between February 21, 2025 and March 31, 2025).
"Coronavirus Resources Center." Johns Hopkins University, Baltimore, Maryland (JHU has stopped collecting data as of March 10, 2023), available at https://coronavirus.jhu.edu (accessed between February 21, 2025 and March 31, 2025).

"Corruption Perceptions Index." Transparency International, Berlin, Germany, available at http://www.transparency.org/research/cpi/overview (accessed between February 21, 2025 and March 31, 2025).

"Council of Europe Convention on Access to Official Documents." Council of Europe Treaty Series No. 205, Council of Europe, Strasbourg Cedex, France, available at http://conventions.coe.int/Treaty/en/Treaties/html/205.htm (accessed between February 21, 2025 and March 31, 2025).

"Court Sides with Clinics on Freedom of Information Act Exemptions." Yale University Law School, New Haven, Connecticut, August 24, 2022, available at https://law.yale.edu/yls-today/news/court-sides-clinics-freedom-information-act-exemptions (accessed between February 21, 2025 and March 31, 2025).

"CPC Central Committee Pays High Attention to Qinrong Gao's Suffering, Causing His Surprising Retrial Likely." [打假记者高勤荣案重大转折:中央高度关注,或将迎来再审] Jingpingtai [鲸平台], Shanghai, China, April 18, 2023, available at https://www.jingpt.com/article/c7141726-bfcf-4998-8b05-d31ce8978dfb (accessed between February 21, 2025 and March 31, 2025).

Curry, Jane Leftwich. "The Media and Intra-Elite Communication in Poland: The Role of 'Special Bulletins'." Rand Report (December 1980, N-1514/4), Rand Corporation, Santa Monica, California, available at https://www.rand.org/pubs/notes/N1514z4.html (accessed between February 21, 2025 and March 31, 2025).

Darbishire, Helen. "Proactive Transparency: The Future of the Right to Information? A Review of Standards, Challenges, and Opportunities." Paper for Access to Information Program, World Bank Institute Governance Working Paper Series, World Bank, Washington DC, 2010, available at https://documents1.worldbank.org/curated/en/100521468339595607/pdf/565980WP0Box351roactiveTransparency.pdf (accessed between February 21, 2025 and March 31, 2025).

"Digital Media Law Project." The Berkman Klein Center for Internet & Society, Harvard University, Cambridge, Massachusetts, available at https://cyber.harvard.edu/research/dmlp (accessed between February 21, 2025 and March 31, 2025).

Dong, Dong. "General Administration of Quality Supervision, Inspection and Quarantine Accepts First OGI Request for Information Concerning Toyota Recall Incident." [国家质检总局受理第一例丰田召回信息公开申请] Netease Auto, Guangzhou, China, March 9, 2010 (captured by Internet Archive Wayback Machine on March 15, 2010), retrieved from https://web.archive.org/web/20100315042928/http://auto.163.com/10/0309/13/61BC5KAL000816HJ.html (accessed between February 21, 2025 and March 31, 2025).

Drinhausen, Katja and Helena Legarda. " 'Comprehensive National Security' Unleashed: How Xi's Approach Shapes China's Policies at Home and Abroad." The Mercator Institute for China Studies (MERICS), Berlin, Germany, September 15, 2022, available at https://www.merics.org/en/report/comprehensive-national-security-unleashed-how-xis-approach-shapes-chinas-policies-home-and (accessed between February 21, 2025 and March 31, 2025).

Du, Hongmei. "After Two Consecutive Victories in Administrative Reconsideration, House Demolition Documents Are Finally Released." [行政复议两连胜,拆迁文件终获公开] Wqsheng.com, Beijing Shengyun Law Firm, Beijing, China, June 1, 2012, https://web.archive.org/web/20220219110320/http://www.wqsheng.com/template/T_Content/wapindex.aspx?nodeid=23&itemid=1293 (accessed between February 21, 2025 and March 31, 2025).

Duan, Hongqing. "Pin Ma: One Single Person Fights Lonely and Publicly Against Government Violations of OGI Regulations." [马骋:一个人的信息公开战争] Caixin blog, April 24, 2015, available at https://duanhongqing.blog.caixin.com/archives/84413?originReferrer=caixinsearch_pc (accessed between February 21, 2025 and March 31, 2025).

Dzirkals, Lilita, Thane Gustafson and A. Ross Johnson. "The Media and Intra-Elite Communication in the USSR." Rand Report (September 1982, R.2869). Rand Corporation, Santa Monica, California, available at https://www.rand.org/pubs/reports/R2869.html (accessed between February 21, 2025 and March 31, 2025).

"European Enlightenment." Britannica Online Encyclopedia, Chicago, Illinois, available at http://www.britannica.com/EBchecked/topic/188441/Enlightenment (accessed between February 21, 2025 and March 31, 2025).

"Explore CPJ's Database of Attacks on the Press." Committee to Protect Journalists, New York, available at https://cpj.org/data/location/ (accessed between February 21, 2025 and March 31, 2025).

"Famous Lawyer Jinsong Hao Requests Information Disclosure On Jia Yang Case." [知名律师郝劲松申请杨佳案信息公开] HSW.cn [华商网], Xi'an, China, October 20, 2008 (captured by Internet Archive Wayback Machine on March 15, 2016), retrieved from https://web.archive.org/web/20160315202433/http://news.jcrb.com/lvshi/200810/t20081020_84260.html (accessed between February 21, 2025 and March 31, 2025).

"FAQ#29." About the Right-to-Know Law, Commonwealth of Pennsylvania Office of Open Records, Harrisburg, Pennsylvania, available at https://www.openrecords.pa.gov/rtkl/about.cfm (accessed between February 21, 2025 and March 31, 2025).

"FOIA Survey: FDA's Slow Response Means Stories Go Unpublished." Association of Health Care Journalists, Columbia, Missouri, April 10, 2008, available at https://healthjournalism.org/blog/2008/04/foia-survey-fdas-slow-response-means-stories-go-unpublished/ (accessed between February 21, 2025 and March 31, 2025).

"For Your Services." China State Railway Group Corporation, Beijing, China, available at http://www.china-railway.com.cn/wnfw/ (accessed between February 21, 2025 and March 31, 2025).

"Freedom in the World Comparative and Historical Data." Freedom House, Washington, DC, available at http://www.freedomhouse.org/report-types/freedom-world (accessed between February 21, 2025 and March 31, 2025) or https://freedomhouse.org/reports/publication-archives (accessed between February 21, 2025 and March 31, 2025).

"Freedom in the World Research Methodology." Freedom House, Washington, DC, available at https://freedomhouse.org/reports/freedom-world/freedom-world-research-methodology (accessed between February 21, 2025 and March 31, 2025).

"Freedom of the Press 2017 – China." RefWorld, Geneva, Switzerland, available at https://www.refworld.org/reference/annualreport/freehou/2017/en/118931 (accessed between February 21, 2025 and March 31, 2025).

"Freedom of the Press 2017 – Cuba." RefWorld, Geneva, Switzerland, available at https://www.refworld.org/reference/annualreport/freehou/2017/en/118928 (accessed between February 21, 2025 and March 31, 2025).

"Freedom of the Press 2017 - North Korea." RefWorld, Geneva, Switzerland, available at https://www.refworld.org/reference/annualreport/freehou/2017/en/119039 (accessed between February 21, 2025 and March 31, 2025).

"Freedom of the Press 2017 - United States." RefWorld, Geneva, Switzerland, available at https://www.refworld.org/reference/annualreport/freehou/2017/en/116626 (accessed between February 21, 2025 and March 31, 2025).

"Freedom of the Press, Publication Archives." Freedom House, Washington, DC, available at https://freedomhouse.org/reports/publication-archives (accessed between February 21, 2025 and March 31, 2025).

"Freedom of the Press Research Methodology." Freedom House, Washington, DC, available at https://freedomhouse.org/freedom-press-research-methodology (accessed between February 21, 2025 and March 31, 2025).

"Frequent Questions." Area Designations for the 2012 Annual Fine Particle (PM2.5) Standard, United States Environmental Protection Agency, Washington, DC, available at https://www3.epa.gov/pmdesignations/2012standards/faq.htm (accessed between February 21, 2025 and March 31, 2025).

"Full-Text Database Communication & Mass Media Complete." EBSCO, Ipswich, MA, available at https://www.ebsco.com/products/research-databases/communication-mass-media-complete (accessed between February 21, 2025 and March 31, 2025).

"Full-Text Database Legal Source." EBSCO, Ipswich, MA, available at https://www.ebsco.com/products/research-databases/legal-source (accessed between February 21, 2025 and March 31, 2025).

"Full Text of Constitution of Communist Party of China." The State Council of the People's Republic of China, Beijing, China, available at http://english.www.gov.cn/news/topnews/202210/26/content_WS635921cdc6d0a757729e1cd4.html (accessed between February 21, 2025 and March 31, 2025).

"Gazettes." The State Council of the People's Republic of China, Beijing, China, available at https://english.www.gov.cn/archive/statecouncilgazette/ (accessed between February 21, 2025 and March 31, 2025).

"Global Right to Information Rating." Launched by AccessInfo Europe (AIE) and Centre for Law and Democracy, Madrid, Spain, available at http://www.rti-rating.org/index.php (accessed between February 21, 2025 and March 31, 2025).

Goldberg, David. "Promoting Practical Access to Democracy: A Survey of Freedom of Information in Central and Eastern Europe." Edited by Sara Buchanan and Pauline Donaldson. Report researched and written for Article 19, London, United Kingdom, October 2002, available at http://www.article19.org/data/files/pdfs/publications/freedom-of-information-survey-of-central-and-e.pdf (accessed between February 21, 2025 and March 31, 2025).

Han, Mei. "Interpretation and Applicability of Answers of the Supreme People's Court about Several Issues Concerning Reputation-Related Lawsuits." [《最高人民法院关于审理名誉权案件若干问题的解答》的理解与适用], posted on the website of the National People's Congress, Beijing, China, available at http://www.npc.gov.cn/zgrdw/huiyi/lfzt/qqzrfca/2008-12/21/content_1462861.htm (accessed between February 21, 2025 and March 31, 2025).

"Highlights of Development of Chinese E-Government: From September 2002 to September 2003." [2002.9–2003.9中国电子政务大事记] China.com.cn, the State Council Information Office, Beijing, China, February 6, 2004 (captured by Internet Archive Wayback Machine on May 12, 2004), retrieved from https://web.archive.org/web/20040512225649/http://www.china.com.cn/chinese/zhuanti/dzzwbg/492027.htm (accessed between February 21, 2025 and March 31, 2025).

"Historical Data on Country RTI Rating Scores." Global Right to Information Rating, a joint project by AccessInfo Europe and the Centre for Law and Democracy, available at https://www.rti-rating.org/historical/ (accessed between February 21, 2025 and March 31, 2025).

Hong, Bing. "A Newspaperman Who Never Feels Anxious: Interview with Fang Zuo, Founding Editor of *Southern Weekend*." [从容不迫的办报人:南方周末创始人左方访谈] Sohu Media, Beijing, China, October 31, 2003, https://media.news.sohu.com/74/76/news215027674.shtml (accessed between February 21, 2025 and March 31, 2025).

Horsley, Jamie P. "China Adopts First Nationwide Open Government Information Regulations." Freedominfo.org, Washington, DC, May 9, 2007, available at http://www.freedominfo.org/2007/05/china-adopts-first-nationwide-open-government-information-regulations/ (accessed between February 21, 2025 and March 31, 2025).

Horsley, Jamie P. "The Chinese Communist Party's Experiment with Transparency." Brookings Institution, Washington, DC, February 8, 2018, available at https://www.brookings.edu/articles/the-chinese-communist-partys-experiment-with-transparency/ (accessed between February 21, 2025 and March 31, 2025).

Horsley, Jamie P. "The Chinese Communist Party's Experiment with Transparency: Unpacking the CCP's New Regulations on 'Open Party Affairs.'" The Diplomat, Diplomatic Media, Arlington, Virginia, February 1, 2018, available at https://thediplomat.com/2018/02/the-chinese-communist-partys-experiment-with-transparency/ (accessed between February 21, 2025 and March 31, 2025).

Horsley, Jamie P. "Open Government Developments in China: Implications for US Businesses." China Business Review, republished by US-China Business Council, Washington, DC, July 1, 2019, available at https://www.chinabusinessreview.com/open-government-developments-in-china-implications-for-us-businesses/ (accessed between February 21, 2025 and March 31, 2025).

Horsley, Jamie P. "Regulations of the Communist Party of China on Open Party Affairs (For Trial Implementation)." Translation by Jamie P. Horsley, China Center at Yale University Law School, New Haven, Connecticut, available at https://law.yale.edu/sites/default/files/china-law-documents/horsley_eng._open_party_affairs_regulations.pdf (accessed between February 21, 2025 and March 31, 2025).

Horsley, Jamie P. "Rule of Law in China: Incremental Progress." Paper for incorporation in C. Fred Bergsten, N. Lardy, B. Gill & D. Mitchell, *The China Balance Sheet in 2007 and Beyond*. A joint project by the Center for Strategic and International Studies and the Peterson Institute for International Economics, Washington, DC, April 2007, available at https://www.csis.org/programs/freeman-chair-china-studies/past-projects/china-balance-sheet/papers (accessed between February 21, 2025 and March 31, 2025).

Horsley, Jamie P. "Shanghai Advances the Cause of Open Government Information in China." Freedominfo.org, Washington, DC, April 20, 2004, available at http://www.freedominfo.org/2004/04/shanghai-advances-the-cause-of-open-government-information-in-china/ (accessed between February 21, 2025 and March 31, 2025).

Horsley, Jamie P. "Update on China's Open Government Information Regulations: Surprising Public Demand Yielding Some Positive Results." Freedominfo.org, Washington, DC, April 23, 2010, available at http://www.freedominfo.org/2010/04/update-on-china-open-government-information-regulations/ (accessed between February 21, 2025 and March 31, 2025).

Hu, Jiwei. "Hardships and Misfortunes in Formulation of First Press Law in People's Republic of China (1–8)." [制定中国第一部新闻法的艰辛与厄运1–8], Xys.org [新语丝], available at http://www.xys.org/xys/ebooks/others/history/contemporary/hujiwei/ (accessed between February 21, 2025 and March 31, 2025).

Huang, Huan. "Memories of Yang Mu on Writing Ne*ican* to Repudiate "Two Estimations." [穆扬回忆高考恢复:写内参揭发"两个估计"] China.com.cn, Beijing, China, republished by Reformdata.org, May 29, 2007, available at http://www.reformdata.org/2007/0529/13908.shtml (accessed between February 21, 2025 and March 31, 2025).

"Human Rights Expert Highlights Significance of China's Signing 21 International Human Rights Covenants." [人权专家:中国加入21个国际人权公约的意义], Sohu, April 9, 2004, http://news.sohu.com/2004/04/09/87/news219788774.shtml (accessed between February 21, 2025 and March 31, 2025).

"Hundred Schools of Thought." [诸子百家].Chinese Text Project, available at http://ctext.org/ (accessed between February 21, 2025 and March 31, 2025).

"Internet Filtering in China in 2004–2005: A Country Study." OpenNet Initiative, Harvard University, Cambridge, Massachusetts, April 13, 2005, available at http://cyber.law.harvard.edu/publications/2005/Internet_Filtering_in_China_in_2004_2005 (accessed between February 21, 2025 and March 31, 2025).

Jiao, Zhuwang. "Shanghai Police Authority Responds to Jinsong Hao who Requested Information Disclosure on Jia Yang Case." [上海警方对郝劲松就杨佳案申请信息公开进行答复] HSW.cn [华商网], Xi'an, China, November 13, 2008 (captured by Internet Archive Wayback Machine on May 22, 2009), retrieved from https://web.archive.org/web/20090522212730/http://www.hsw.cn/news/2008-11/13/content_10403312.htm (accessed between February 21, 2025 and March 31, 2025).

"Joint Statement on Freedom of Expression as a Driver of All Other Human Rights on the Occasion of the World Press Freedom Day 2023." United Nations Educational, Scientific and Cultural Organization, Paris, France, May 2, 2023, available at https://www.unesco.org/en/days/press-freedom-2023/joint-statement#:~:text=At%20its%20very%20first%20session,the%20United%20Nations%20is%20consecrated.%E2%80%9D (accessed between February 21, 2025 and March 31, 2025).

Lang, Xianping. "Campaigns Do Not Work for Managing Economy." [治理经济不能靠"运动"] JRJ.com [金融界], Beijing, China, May 16, 2012 (captured by Internet Archive Wayback Machine on May 19, 2012), retrieved from https://web.archive.org/web/20120519092855/http://finance.jrj.com.cn/opinion/2012/05/16091613139548-1.shtml (accessed between February 21, 2025 and March 31, 2025).

Law, Angharad. "Freedom of information in Hong Kong." Journalism and Media Studies Centre, the University of Hong Kong, Hong Kong, China, March 24, 2010, available at http://jmsc.hku.hk/2010/03/freedom-of-information-in-hong-kong/ (accessed between February 21, 2025 and March 31, 2025).

Li, Guangyu. "Deputy Director of Supreme Court Administrative Tribunal Guangyu Li Talks about Stories Behind Judicial Interpretation of *OGI Regulations* at 48th Rule of Law Forum." [最高人民法院行政审判庭副庭长李广宇做客第四十八期法治政府论坛 政府信息公开司法解释的台前幕后] Institute of Rule of Law, China University of Political Science and Law, Beijing, China, November 23, 2011, available at http://fzzfyjy.cupl.edu.cn/info/1223/4323.htm (accessed between February 21, 2025 and March 31, 2025).

Li, Lei. "Changing Functions of Local Governments and Lessons from Sanlu Tainted Milk Scandal." [地方政府职能转变与三鹿奶粉事件的教训] Sina Finance, Beijing, China, January 12, 2009, available at http://finance.sina.com.cn/china/hgjj/20090112/17335750186.shtml (accessed between February 21, 2025 and March 31, 2025).

"Madison Debates." The Avalon Project at Yale Law School, Yale University, New Haven, Connecticut, available at http://avalon.law.yale.edu/18th_century/debates_811.asp (accessed between February 21, 2025 and March 31, 2025).

Martin, Michael F. "Understanding China's Political System." U.S. Congressional Research Service, Washington, DC, April 14, 2010, available at http://www.fas.org/sgp/crs/row/R41007.pdf (accessed between February 21, 2025 and March 31, 2025).

"Media Freedom and Information Access Clinic." Law School, Yale University, New Haven, Connecticut, available at https://law.yale.edu/studying-law-yale/clinical-and-experiential-learning/our-clinics/media-freedom-and-information-access-clinic (accessed between February 21, 2025 and March 31, 2025).

"Media Sustainability Index: Archived Reports." International Research and Exchanges Board, Washington, DC, available at https://www.irex.org/media-sustainability-index-archived-reports (accessed between February 21, 2025 and March 31, 2025).

"Media Sustainability Index (MSI)." International Research and Exchanges Board, Washington, DC, available at https://www.mediasustainabilityindex.org/ (accessed between February 21, 2025 and March 31, 2025).

Mendel, Toby. "Freedom of Information as an Internationally Protected Human Right." Article 19, London, United Kingdom, available at http://www.article19.org/data/files/pdfs/publications/foi-as-an-international-right.pdf (accessed between February 21, 2025 and March 31, 2025).

Mendel, Toby. "Freedom of Information: A Comparative Legal Survey." United Nations Educational Scientific and Cultural Organization, Paris, France, 2008, available at https://law.yale.edu/sites/default/files/documents/pdf/Intellectual_Life/CL-OGI_Toby_Mendel_book_%28Eng%29.pdf (accessed between February 21, 2025 and March 31, 2025).

"Methodology." Global Right to Information Rating, available at https://www.rti-rating.org/methodology/ (accessed between February 21, 2025 and March 31, 2025).

"MFIA and New York Times Win FOIA Case; Ruling Clarifies Law Surrounding Personal Privacy Exemption." Yale University Law School, New Haven, Connecticut, November 11, 2010 (captured by Internet Archive Wayback Machine on November 25, 2011), retrieved from https://web.archive.org/web/20111125063954/http://www.law.yale.edu/news/12466.htm (accessed between February 21, 2025 and March 31, 2025).

Minzner, Carl. "Social Instability in China: Causes, Consequences, and Implications." Report of Center for Strategic and International Studies, Washington, DC, June 12, 2005 (captured by Internet Archive Wayback Machine on September 10, 2009), retrieved from https://web.archive.org/web/20090910132629/http://csis.org/files/media/csis/events/061205_mizner_abstract.pdf (accessed between February 21, 2025 and March 31, 2025).

"National Bureau of Statistics: Health Institutions Nationwide Admit 8.4 Billion Patients in 2022." [国家统计局:2022年医疗卫生机构总诊疗人次数达84亿人次], Sohu, Beijing, China, March 2, 2023, https://www.sohu.com/a/648495618_121118853 (accessed between February 21, 2025 and March 31, 2025).

Neill, Andrea. "Liberating Information Shifting from Reactive to Proactive Disclosure." Office of the Information Commissioner of Canada, Quebec, Canada, April 20, 2010 (captured by Internet Archive Wayback Machine on May 13, 2013), retrieved from https://web.archive.org/web/20130513211539/http://www.oic-ci.gc.ca/eng/med-roo-sal-med_speeches-discours_2010_3.aspx (accessed between February 21, 2025 and March 31, 2025).

"Note on Publication of the OPA Implementation Rules by the Party Committee of Peking University." [关于印发《北京大学党务公开实施办法》的通知], Peking University, Beijing, China, May 18, 2021, available at https://xxgk.pku.edu.cn/docs/20210518152610022473.pdf (accessed between February 21, 2025 and March 31, 2025).

"OGI Website." Beijing Capital Group Corporation, Beijing, China, available at https://www.bjcapital.com/html1/folder/2112/4503-1.htm (accessed between February 21, 2025 and March 31, 2025).

"OGI Website." Beijing Public Transport Corporation, Beijing, China, available at https://www.bjbus.com/home/fun_information.php?uSec=00000186&uSub=00000186 (accessed between February 21, 2025 and March 31, 2025).

"OGI Website." China Datang Corporation, Beijing, China, available at https://www.china-cdt.com/dtwz/xxgk/jbxx/A024006001Gone1.html (accessed between February 21, 2025 and March 31, 2025).

"OGI Website." China Everbright Environment Corporation, Hong Kong, China, available at https://www.cebenvironment.com/sc/env_man/infodisclosure.php (accessed between February 21, 2025 and March 31, 2025).

"OGI Website." Nanjing Water Group Corporation, Nanjing, China, available at https://www.jlwater.com/portalSection/10000165 (accessed between February 21, 2025 and March 31, 2025).

"OGI Website." Peking Union Medical College Hospital, Beijing, China, available at http://www.cams.ac.cn/xxgk/xxgkzd/index.htm (accessed between February 21, 2025 and March 31, 2025).

"OGI Website." Peking University, Beijing, China, available at https://xxgk.pku.edu.cn/ (accessed between February 21, 2025 and March 31, 2025).

"OGI Website." Shenyang Water Group Corporation, Shenyang, China, available at https://www.syswgw.com/swgk?id=39 (accessed between February 21, 2025 and March 31, 2025).

"OGI Website." State Grid Corporation of China Beijing Branch, Beijing, China, available at http://www.bj.sgcc.com.cn (accessed between February 21, 2025 and March 31, 2025).

"OGI Website." Tsinghua University, Beijing, China, available at https://www.tsinghua.edu.cn/zjqh/xxgk1.htm (accessed between February 21, 2025 and March 31, 2025).

"OGI Website." West China Hospital of Sichuan University, Chengdu, China, available at https://www.wchscu.cn/xxgk.htm (accessed between February 21, 2025 and March 31, 2025).

"Organizational Structure of the State Council." The State Council of the People's Republic of China, Beijing, China, available at https://english.www.gov.cn/archive/chinaabc/201911/22/content_WS5ed77233c6d0b3f0e9499854.html (accessed between February 21, 2025 and March 31, 2025) and https://www.gov.cn/gwyzzjg/zuzhi/ (accessed between February 21, 2025 and March 31, 2025).

Panzardi, Roberto, Carlos Calcopietro, and Enrique Fanta Ivanovic. "New-Economy Sector Study: Electronic Government and Governance: Lessons from Argentina." The World Bank, Washington, DC, July 2002, available at http://documents.worldbank.org/curated/en/527061468769894044 (accessed between February 21, 2025 and March 31, 2025).

"Polity IV Project: Political Regime Characteristics and Transitions, 1800–2010." Center for Systemic Peace (CSP), Vienna, Virgina, available at http://www.systemicpeace.org/polity/polity4.htm (accessed between February 21, 2025 and March 31, 2025).

"Public Access to Information and Secrecy: The Legislation in Brief." The Ministry of Justice, Government Offices of Sweden, Stockholm, Sweden, available at https://www.government.se/contentassets/2ca7601373824c8395fc1f38516e6e03/public-access-to-information-and-secrecy.pdf (accessed between February 21, 2025 and March 31, 2025).

Puddephatt, Andrew. "Exploring the Role of Civil Society in the Formulation and Adoption of Access to Information Laws: The Cases of Bulgaria, India, Mexico, South Africa, and the United Kingdom." Access to Information Working Paper Series for World Bank Institute, 2009, World Bank, Washington, DC, available at https://documents.worldbank.org/en/publication/documents-reports/documentdetail/302751468044082294/pdf (accessed between February 21, 2025 and March 31, 2025).

"Reference News." China Media Guide, Danwei.org, August 9, 2008 (captured by Internet Archive Wayback Machine on May 6, 2009), retrieved from https://web.archive.org/web/20090506073529/http://www.danwei.org/media_guide/newspapers/reference_news.php (accessed between February 21, 2025 and March 31, 2025).

"Regulations of the People's Republic of China on Open Government Information." Revised April 3, 2019, and effective May 15, 2019. Yale University Law School China Center, New Haven, Connecticut, available at https://law.yale.edu/sites/default/files/area/center/china/2022-9-5_jph_rev_ogir.pdf (English translation) (accessed between February 21, 2025 and March 31, 2025).

"Regulations of the People's Republic of China on Open Government Information." Revised April 3, 2019, and effective May 15, 2019. Yale University Law School China Center, New Haven, Connecticut, available at https://law.yale.edu/sites/default/files/area/center/china/2019-4_ch_revsd_ogi_regulations.pdf (Chinese version) (accessed between February 21, 2025 and March 31, 2025).

"Report of the Working Group on Transparency and Accountability." International Monetary Fund, Washington, D.C., October 1998, available at http://www.imf.org/external/np/g22/taarep.pdf (accessed between February 21, 2025 and March 31, 2025).

Ronaghan, Stephen A. “Benchmarking E-government: A Global Perspective-Assessing the United Nations Member States.” Report for United Nations Division for Public Economics and Public Administration, and American Society for Public Administration. New York, New York, May 2002, available at https://digitallibrary.un.org/record/3868821?ln=en&v=pdf (accessed between February 21, 2025 and March 31, 2025).

Rosenhause, Sharon. “FEMA’s Stumbles, Katrina Controversy Lead the Sun-Sentinel on Dedicated Watchdog Campaign.” Poynter, St. Petersburg, Florida, May 17, 2006, available at https://www.poynter.org/archive/2006/femas-stumbles-katrina-controversy-lead-the-sun-sentinel-on-dedicated-watchdog-campaign/ (accessed between February 21, 2025 and March 31, 2025).

“Roster of Editors and Reporters at People’s Daily.” [人民日报采编部门人员名单], People’s Daily Online, Beijing China, February 16, 2007 (captured by Internet Archive Wayback Machine on February 24, 2007), retrieved from https://web.archive.org/web/20070224143536/http://media.people.com.cn/GB/5406002.html (accessed between February 21, 2025 and March 31, 2025).

“State FOIA Laws: A Guide to Protecting Sensitive Water Security Information.” Association of Metropolitan Water Agencies, Washington, DC, July 2002, available at http://www.awwaneb.org/pdfs/securityprivacy.pdf (accessed between February 21, 2025 and March 31, 2025).

“Statement by European RTI Community on the world’s First Official Access to Information Day.” Access Info Europe, Madrid, Spain, September 28, 2016, available at https://www.access-info.org/2016-09-28/statement-by-european-rti-community-on-the-worlds-first-official-access-to-information-day/ (accessed between February 21, 2025 and March 31, 2025).

Stiglitz, Joseph E. “On Liberty, the Right to Know, and Public Discourse: The Role of Transparency in Public Life.” Oxford Amnesty Lecture, Oxford, United Kingdom., January 27,1999, available at http://documents.worldbank.org/curated/en/436941546609601734 (accessed between February 21, 2025 and March 31, 2025).

“Study on Ways and Means of Promoting Transparency in International Transfers of Conventional Arms: Report of the Secretary-General.” United Nations Experts Group, UN Document A/46/301, New York, New York, September 1991, available at https://front.un-arm.org/wp-content/uploads/assets/HomePage/ODAPublications/DisarmamentStudySeries/PDF/SS-24.pdf (accessed between February 21, 2025 and March 31, 2025).

Sun, Liping. “Precise Assessment of Social Conflicts in China.” [准确定位社会矛盾] EEO [经济观察网], Beijing, China, December 17, 2007, available at http://www.eeo.com.cn/observer/special/2007/12/17/89477.shtml (accessed between February 21, 2025 and March 31, 2025).

"Task Force Suggestions." Carnegie Media Law for Journalism Schools, available at https://jschoollegal.wordpress.com/task-force-suggestions/ (accessed between February 21, 2025 and March 31, 2025).

"Traditional Chinese Studies." [国学]. Guoxuewang [国学网], Beijing, China, available at http://www.guoxue.com/ (accessed between February 21, 2025 and March 31, 2025).

"Transparency of Government Policymaking, 1–7 (Best)." World Bank, Washington, DC, available at https://prosperitydata360.worldbank.org/en/indicator/WEF+GCIHH+EOSQ049 (accessed between February 21, 2025 and March 31, 2025).

"Transparency & Silence: A Survey of Access to Information Laws and Practices in 14 Countries." Open Society Justice Initiative, Justice in Action Series, New York, New York, September 2006, available at https://www.justiceinitiative.org/uploads/016719b6-115e-40b8-ad00-00d24b1e3f71/transparency_20060928.pdf (accessed between February 21, 2025 and March 31, 2025).

"The Chongqing Municipal Party Committee Publishes Its OPA Implementation Rules." [中共重庆市委印发《重庆市实施〈中国共产党党务公开条例(试行)〉办法》] Hualongwang [华龙网], Chongqing, China, May 7, 2018, available at http://cq.cqnews.net/html/2018-05/07/content_44265299.htm (accessed between February 21, 2025 and March 31, 2025).

"The CPI Explained." Transparency International, Berlin, Germany, available at https://www.transparency.org/en/cpi/2024 (accessed between February 21, 2025 and March 31, 2025).

"The Ministry of National Defense." Beijing, China, available at http://eng.mod.gov.cn/ (accessed between February 21, 2025 and March 31, 2025).

"The National Radio and Television Administration." Beijing, China, available at https://www.nrta.gov.cn/ (accessed between February 21, 2025 and March 31, 2025).

"The Public's Right to Know: Principles on Right to Information Legislation." Article 19, London, United Kingdom, 2006, available at http://www.article19.org/data/files/pdfs/standards/righttoknow.pdf(accessed between February 21, 2025 and March 31, 2025).

"The Right to Information: Good Law and Practice." Right2info.org (captured by Internet Archive Wayback Machine on October 21, 2008), retrieved from https://web.archive.org/web/20081021053124/http://www.right2info.org/ (accessed between February 21, 2025 and March 31, 2025).

"The 54 Statistical Report on China's Internet Development." China Internet Network Information Center, Beijing, China, available at https://www.cnnic.com.cn/IDR/ReportDownloads/202411/P020241101318428715781.pdf (accessed between February 21, 2025 and March 31, 2025).

"UJRC Convenes Three Training Workshops on Access to Information." Al Urdun Al Jadid Research Center, Amman, Jordan, March 2009, available at http://freedominfo.org/documents/Information%20is%20Right%20for%20all%20-%20Eng%202.pdf (accessed between February 21, 2025 and March 31, 2025).

"Vanhanen Polyarchy Dataset." Vanhanen measures of democracy, 1800–2018, available at https://xmarquez.github.io/democracyData/reference/vanhanen.html (accessed between February 21, 2025 and March 31, 2025).

"Vanhanen's Index of Democracy." The Peace Research Institute Oslo (PRIO), Oslo, Norway, available at https://www.prio.org/data/20 (accessed between February 21, 2025 and March 31, 2025).

Wang, Xing. "Is It Hard to Interview Government Officials? Much Easier If You Don't Say You Are a Reporter." [采访政府难?别说你是记者就容易了], Guancha.cn [观察者], Shanghai, China, July 12, 2014, available at https://www.guancha.cn/WangXing?web (accessed between February 21, 2025 and March 31, 2025).

Wei, Jing. "Journalist Sues Wei County Civil Affairs Bureau in Hebei Province for Non-Compliance of *OIG Regulations*." [媒体人诉河北蔚县民政局不公开低保名单], ChinaTransparency.org, Beijing, China, May 17, 2012 (captured by Internet Archive Wayback Machine on February 19, 2022), retrieved from https://web.archive.org/web/20220219074641/http://www.ogichina.org/article/180/13954.html (accessed between February 21, 2025 and March 31, 2025).

Wei, Wang. "Jiang Ping: Rule of Law Progressing in China." China.org.cn [中国网], Beijing, China, October 31, 2008, available at http://www.china.org.cn/china/reform-opening-up/2008-10/31/content_16697241.htm (accessed between February 21, 2025 and March 31, 2025).

"Wen Jiabao: Advance Open Government Information and Create Conditions for Citizens to Hold Government Accountable." [温家宝:推进政务公开 创造条件让群众监督政府], Gov.cn, the State Council of the People's Republic of China, Beijing, China, March 26, 2012, https://www.gov.cn/ldhd/2012-03/26/content_2100430.htm (accessed between February 21, 2025 and March 31, 2025).

"What Is Corruption?" Transparency International, Berlin, Germany, available at https://www.transparency.org/en/what-is-corruption (accessed between February 21, 2025 and March 31, 2025).

"What We Do." The Centre for Law and Democracy, Halifax, Nova Scotia, Canada (captured by Internet Archive Wayback Machine on October 16, 2010), retrieved from https://web.archive.org/web/20110125175850/http://www.law-democracy.org/?page_id=110 (accessed between February 21, 2025 and March 31, 2025).

"Whistleblower Protection Act: An Overview." U.S. Congressional Research Service, Washington, DC, March 12, 2007, available at http://www.fas.org/sgp/crs/natsec/RL33918.pdf (accessed between February 21, 2025 and March 31, 2025).

"World Press Freedom Index." Reporters Without Borders, Paris, France, available at https://rsf.org/en/index (accessed between February 21, 2025 and March 31, 2025).

"Worldwide Governance Indicators." World Bank Group, Washington, DC, available at https://www.worldbank.org/en/publication/worldwide-governance-indicators (accessed between February 21, 2025 and March 31, 2025).

Xu, Jianguo. "Enact China's Own Whistleblower Protection Law: Inspirations from European Union's Legislative Experience." [徐国建:制定一部中国的"吹哨人"保护法-欧盟立法的启示], Shanghai University of Political Science and Law, Shanghai, China, February 10, 2020, available at https://www.shupl.edu.cn/2020/0217/c1170a73457/page.htm (accessed between February 21, 2025 and March 31, 2025).

Yefengchui [野风吹]. "Lack of Aggressive Media Outlets Leads to Prevalence of Fake Reporters." [假记者猖獗背后是真媒体缺位], Sohu, Beijing, China, December 15, 2006, available at https://star.news.sohu.com/20061215/n247060757.shtml (accessed between February 21, 2025 and March 31, 2025).

Yi, Ruichi. "Most Comprehensive Survey: Revenues of 198 Publicly-Traded Environmental Protection Companies in 2020." [最全盘点!涉198家!环保上市公司2020年业绩大榜] China Shuiwang [中国水网], Beijing, China, May 31, 2021, available at https://www.h2o-china.com/news/324142.html (accessed between February 21, 2025 and March 31, 2025).

Yihailongmoshiniandeng [衣海弄墨十年灯]. "Internal Reference Materials Written by Reporters from Xinhua News Agency Shall Be Disclosed as Open Government Information." [新华社内参也应属于公开的政府信息之列] Tianya Forum [天涯论坛], Haikou, China, July 23, 2009, available at https://tianya.my/thread/0/12504535/1.html (accessed between February 21, 2025 and March 31, 2025).

Yu, Jianrong. "Use Constitution to Hold Bottom Line of Social Stability." [让宪法守住社会稳定的底线] Speech delivered at the Beijing Lawyers Association, Falvjie [法律界], Beijing, China, February 21, 2010 (captured by Internet Archive Wayback Machine on March 2, 2010), retrieved from https://web.archive.org/web/20100302202616/http://news.mylegist.com/1607/2010-02-21/21030.html (accessed between February 21, 2025 and March 31, 2025).

Yu, Keping. "Democracy in China: Challenge or Opportunity?" Harvard University, Cambridge, Massachusetts, available at http://www.ash.harvard.edu/extension/ash/docs/democracyinchina.pdf (accessed between February 21, 2025 and March 31, 2025).

Yuan, Shawn. "Inside the Early Days of China's Coronavirus Cover-Up: The Dawn of a Pandemic—As Seen Through the News and Social Media Posts that Vanished from China's Internet." Wired, San Francisco, California, May 1, 2020, available at https://www.wired.com/story/inside-the-early-days-of-chinas-coronavirus-coverup/ (accessed between February 21, 2025 and March 31, 2025).

Zhang, Laney. "China: Open Government Regulations Revised." Library of Congress, Washington, DC, September 10, 2019, available at https://www.loc.gov/item/global-legal-monitor/2019-09-10/china-open-government-regulations-revised/ (accessed between February 21, 2025 and March 31, 2025).

Zhang, Qun. "Development of Secrets Protection Laws in Late Qing Dynasty and Republic of China." [清末和民国时期保密法律发展概略] Baomi.org, Beijing, China, January 29, 2012 (captured by Internet Archive Wayback Machine on October 31, 2012), retrieved from https://web.archive.org/web/20121031191752/http://www.baomi.org/bmyw_info.php?optionid=31&auto_id=1256 (accessed between February 21, 2025 and March 31, 2025).

Primary Sources

Constitution, Statutes, Regulations, Party and Government Directives and Reports

Administrative Punishments Law of the People's Republic of China [中华人民共和国行政处罚法] effective March 1996, amended August 2009, September 2017 and January 2021.

Administrative Supervision Law of the People's Republic of China [中华人民共和国行政监察法] effective May 1997, amended June 2010.

Archives Law of the People's Republic of China [中华人民共和国档案法] effective January 1988, amended July 1996.

Civil Servants Law of the People's Republic of China [中华人民共和国公务员法] effective January 2006, amended December 2018.

Constitution of the People's Republic of China [中华人民共和国宪法] effective December 1982, amended April 1988, March 1993, March 1999, March 2004 and March 2018.

Constitution of the Chinese Communist Party [中国共产党章程] revised and adopted October 2022

Cyber Security Law of People's Republic of China [中华人民共和国网络安全法] effective November 7, 2016.

Decision by the Central Committee of the Chinese Communist Party on Strengthening the Construction of Party Governance Capability [中共中央关于加强党的执政能力建设的决定] adopted September 2004.

Decision of the Supreme Procuratorate on Enforcing Transparency at All Levels of Procuratorates [最高人民检察院关于在全国检察机关实行《检务公开》的决定] effective October 1998.

Decisions of the Chinese Communist Party Central Committee on Some Major Issues in Agricultural and Rural Work [中共中央关于农业和农村工作若干重大问题的决定] adopted October 1998.

Disciplinary Regulations of the Chinese Communist Party [中国共产党纪律处分条例] effective December 2003, amended in December 2015, December 2018 and December 2023.

Eleventh Five-Year Plan Outline of the People's Republic of China for National Economy and Social Development [中华人民共和国国民经济和社会发展第十一个五年规划纲要] published March 2006.

Emergency Response Law of the People's Republic of China [中华人民共和国突发事件应对法] effective November 2007.

Explanation Memorandum of State Council Informatization Office for Drafting OGI Regulations [政府信息公开条例(草案)起草说明] 2002.

Explanation of the State Council Legislative Affairs Office on OGI Regulations (Draft)[国务院法制办关于《中华人民共和国政府信息公开条例(草案)》的说明] distributed 2006.

Explanation of the Supreme Court on Several Questions Related to the Implementation of the Administrative Litigation Law [《最高人民法院关于执行〈中华人民共和国行政诉讼法〉若干问题的解释》] effective March 2000.

General Office of the State Council on Promoting Openness in Government Affairs around All Government Agencies at Township Level [中共中央办公厅、国务院办公厅关于在全国乡镇政权机关全面推行政务公开制度的通知]issued December 2000.

Guide on Disclosure of Information Held by Xuzhou Municipal Political Consultative Conference [江苏省徐州市政协信息公开指南] issued July 2007.

Guidelines Regarding Information Disclosure of China Securities Regulatory Commission [中国证监会政府信息公开指南], China Securities Regulatory Commission, Beijing, China.

Guiding Opinions on Open Information Work of Public Enterprises and Institutions in the Transportation Sector [《交通运输公共企事业单位信息公开指导意见》] effective October 2008.

Health and Physical Education in 2022 [2022年卫生健康和体育], The National Bureau of Statistics, Beijing, China, available at https://www.gov.cn/guoqing/2023-03/10/content_5745876.htm (accessed between February 21, 2025 and March 31, 2025).

Hu, Jintao. "Report to the 17th National Party Congress." Beijing, October 2007.

Hu, Jintao. "Report to the 18th National Party Congress." Beijing, November 2012.

Hu, Yaobang. "Report to the 12th National Party Congress." Beijing, September 1982.

Implementation Measures for Archives Law of the People's Republic of China [中华人民共和国档案法实施办法] effective November 1990, amended June 1999.

Implementation Measures for Law of the People's Republic of China on Guarding State Secrets [中华人民共和国保守国家秘密法实施办法] effective May 1990, amended May 2012 as Regulations for Implementation of Law of the People's Republic of China on Guarding State Secrets (Exposure Draft) [中华人民共和国保守国家秘密法实施条例(征求意见稿)].

Implementation Measures of the Ministry of Ecology and Environment on Disclosure of Information Held by Public Environmental Protection Institutions [生态环境部《环境保护公共事业单位信息公开实施办法(试行)] effective on October 1, 2010.

Implementation Measures of the Ministry of Education on Disclosure of Information Held by Universities and Colleges [教育部《高等学校信息公开办法》] effective September 1, 2010.

Implementation Measures of the Ministry of Environmental Protection on Disclosure of Information Held by Environmental Protection Enterprises and Institutions [环境保护部《企业事业单位环境信息公开办法》] effective on January 1, 2015.

Implementation Measures of the Ministry of Health on Disclosure of Information Held by Hospitals and Other Medical Care Institutions [卫生部《医疗卫生服务单位信息公开管理办法》(试行)] effective on August 1, 2010.

Implementation Measures of the Ministry of Housing and Urban-Rural Development on Disclosure of Information Held By Water Supply, Gas Supply and Heating Supply Companies [住房和城乡建设部《供水、供气、供热等公共企事业单位信息公开实施办法》] effective on February 1, 2022.

Implementation Measures of the Ministry of Transport on Disclosure of Information Held by Public Transportation Enterprises [交通运输部《公共交通企业信息公开规定》] effective April 1, 2022.

Implementation Measures of the National Energy Administration on Disclosure of Information Held By Electricity Supply Companies [国家能源局《供电企业信息公开实施办法》] effective on November 23, 2021.

Implementation Measures of the National Health Commission, the National Administration of Traditional Chinese Medicine and the National Administration of Disease Control and Prevention on Disclosure of Information Held by Hospitals and Other Health Care Providers [国家卫生健康委、国家中医药局和国家疾控局《医疗卫生机构信息公开管理办法》] effective on February 1, 2022.

Implementation Measures of the National Population and Family Planning Commission on Disclosure of Information (for Trial Implementation) [人口计生委《政府信息公开规定(试行)] effective on May 20, 2008.
Implementation Measures of the National Population and Family Planning Commission on Disclosure of Information Held by Population and Family Planning Service Providers (for Trial Implementation) [国家人口计生委《人口和计划生育技术服务机构信息公开办法》](试行)effective on February 3, 2009.
Implementation Measures of the State Council for Formulating Information Disclosure Provision Regarding Public Enterprises and Institutions [国务院办公厅《公共企事业单位信息公开规定制定办法》] effective January 1, 2021.
Implementation Measures of the State Environmental Protection Administration on Disclosure of Environmental Information [国家环境保护总局《环境信息公开办法》(试行)] effective on May 1, 2008.
Implementation Rules of the Chongqing Municipal Party Committee on CCP Open Party Affairs Regulations (for Trial Implementation) [《中共重庆市委发布〈中国共产党党务公开条例(试行)〉办法》] effective April 27, 2018.
Implementation Rules of Disclosure of Information Held by Sinan County Political Consultative Conference 2012[贵州省思南县政协2012年度政务公开实施方案] issued June 2012.
Implementation Rules of the National Railway Administration on Open Government Information [国家铁路局政府信息公开实施办法] effective May 15, 2019.
Implementation Rules of the Party Committee of Heilongjiang Province on CCP Open Party Affairs Regulations (for Trial Implementation) [中共黑龙江省省委发布《中国共产党党务公开条例(试行)》实施细则] effective April 2, 2018.
Implementation Rules of the Party Committee of Jiangsu Province on CCP Open Party Affairs Regulations (for Trial Implementation) [中共江苏省委发布《中国共产党党务公开条例(试行)》实施细则] promulgated July 6, 2018.
Implementation Rules of the Party Committee of Peking University on CCP Open Party Affairs Regualtions (for Trial Implementation) [中共北京大学委员会印发《北京大学党务公开实施办法》] effective October 16, 2012.
Information Disclosure Implementation Rules for Public Utilities Institutions Such As Water, Gas, Heating Supply Companies [供水、供气、供热等公用事业单位信息公开实施办法] effective October 2008.
Information Disclosure Implementation Rules of Colleges and Universities [高等学校信息公开办法] effective September 2010.
Information Disclosure Implementation Rules of the Ministry of Housing and Urban-Rural Construction [住房和城乡建设部政府信息公开实施办法] effective August 2009.
Information Disclosure Rules of Health Institutions (Exposure Draft) [医疗卫生机构信息公开实施办法(征求意见稿)] issued August 2009.

Interim Measures of the Ministry of Commerce for Making Administrative Affairs.

Interim Rules of Information Disclosure Implementation for Public Institutions on Environmental Protection [《环境保护公共事业单位信息公开实施办法(试行)》] effective October 2010.

Interim Rules of the State Council Legislative Affairs Office on Publicizing Drafts of Laws and Regulations for Public Comment[国务院法制办公室法律法规草案公开征求意见暂行办法] effective March 2007.

Interpretation of Supreme People's Court and Supreme People's Procuratorate on Several Issues Regarding Applicable Law in Cases of Using Information Networks to Commit Defamation and Other Such Crimes [最高人民法院、最高人民检察院关于办理利用信息网络实施诽谤等刑事案件适用法律若干问题的解释], Beijing, China [issued on September 6, 2013 and took effect on September 10, 2013.

Jiang, Zemin. "Report to the 14th National Party Congress." Beijing, October 1992.

Jiang, Zemin. "Report to the 15th National Party Congress." Beijing, September 1997.

Jiang, Zemin. "Report to the 16th National Party Congress." Beijing, November 2002.

Known to the Public [商务部政务公开暂行办法] issued November 2003.

Law of the People's Republic of China on Guarding State Secrets [中华人民共和国保守国家秘密法] effective May 1989, amended April 2010 and February 2024.

Legislation Law of the People's Republic of China [中华人民共和国立法法] effective July 2000, amended March 2015 and March 2023.

Measures for the Administration of Release of News and Information in China by Foreign News Agencies [外国通讯社在中国境内发布新闻信息管理办法] effective September 2006.

National Security Law of People's Republic of China [中华人民共和国国家安全法] effective July 1, 2015 (repealed 1993 National Security Law).

Notice of the Chinese Communist Party Central Propaganda Department and the State Administration of Press and Publication on Prohibiting Regular Open Publications from Citing Xinhua Internal Reference Materials [关于不得在出版物上公开引用发表新华社内参涉密信息的通知] issued April 1998.

Notice of the Fujian Provincial People's Government on Printing and Distributing the Fujian Province's Working Plan to Handle Challlenges Related to Accession into World Trade Organization [福建省人民政府关于印发福建省应对加入世贸组织行动计划纲要的通知] issued by the Fujian Provincial People's Government [Gazette of Fujian Provincial People's Government, minzheng 2001, No. 175], available at http://zfgb.fj.gov.cn/929 (accessed between February 21, 2025 and March 31, 2025).

Notice of the General Administration of Press and Publication on Protecting Journalists' Lawful Interviewing Rights [新闻出版总署关于保障新闻采编人员合法采访权利的通知] issued October 31, 2007.
Notice of the General Office of State Council and the General Office of the Chinese Communist Party Central Committee on Universalizing System of Open VillageAffairs and Democratic Administration in Rural Areas [中共中央办公厅、国务院、公厅关于在农村普遍实行村务公开和民主管理制度的通知] issued April 1998.
Notice of the General Office of the Chinese Communist Party Central Committee and the General Office of the State Council on Forwarding LGNI Guidance on the Establishment of E-Government [中办国办关于转发《国家信息化领导小组关于我国电子政务建设指导意见》的通知]issued August 2002
Notice of the General Office of the Chinese Communist Party Central Committee on Enhancing the Construction of Grassroots Organizations in the Rural Areas[中共中央办公厅关于加强农村基层组织建设的通知] issued October 1994.
Notice of the General Office of the Chinese Communist Party Central Committee and
Notice of the General Office of the State Council on Preparing Well for Implementing Regulations of the People's Republic of China on Open Government Information [国务院办公厅关于做好施行《中华人民共和国政府信息公开条例》准备工作的通知]issued August 2007.
Notice of the General Office of the State Council on Printing and Distributing Key Work Arrangements for 2012 OGI [国务院办公厅关于印发2012年政府信息公开重点工作安排的通知] issued April 2012.
Notice of the General Office of the State Council on Reaffirming Provisions on Formulation and Publication of Nationally Applicable Foreign Trade and Investment-Related Laws, Regulations, and Policies [国务院办公厅关于重申制定、发布全国性对外经贸法规、政策有关规定的通知] issued March 1992.
Notice of the Legislative Affairs Office of the State Council on the Pilot Project for Developing the Administrative Reconsideration Committees in Several Provinces and Special Municipalities [国务院法制办公室关于在部分省、直辖市开展行政复议委员会试点工作的通知] issued September 2008.
Notice of the Ministry of Commerce on Issuing the "Interim Measures of the Ministry of Commerce for Making Administrative Affairs Known to the Public" [商务部关于印发《商务部政务公开暂行办法》的通知] No.444 (2003).
Notice of the Ministry of Finance and the National Development and Reform Commission on Fees Collected for Providing Open Government Information and Other Relevant Issues [财政部国家发展改革委关于提供政府公开信息收取费用等有关问题的通知] issued June 2008.

Notice of the Ministry of Transportation on Printing the Interim Rules on Openness in Government Affairs [《关于印发《交通部机关政务公开规定(试行)》的通知》] No. 58 (2004).
Notice of the Organization Department and the State Commission Office for Public Sector Reform of the Chinese Communist Party Central Committee on Standardizing the Number of Assistants and Deputy Secretary-Generals at the Local Level [中组部、中央编办关于规范地方政府助理和副秘书长配备问题的通知] issued January 2009.
Notice of the Supreme Court on Printing and Distributing Six Provisions on Transparent Judiciary and Several Provisions on Media Supervision of the Courts [最高人民法院印发《关于司法公开的六项规定》和《关于人民法院接受新闻媒体舆论监督的若干规定》的通知] issued December 2009.
Notice of the Supreme Procuratorate on Printing and Distributing the Opinion on Further Deepening the Disclosure of Procuratorate Information [最高人民检察院关于印发《关于进一步深化人民检察院"检务公开"的意见》的通知] issued June 26, 2006.
Opinion of the General Office of the Chinese Communist Party Central Committee on Information Disclosure of Grassroots Party Organizations [关于党的基层组织实行党务公开的意见] issued September 2010.
Opinion of the General Office of the State Council on Implementation Outline for Pushing Forward Administration by Law in an All-Round Way [国务院办公厅关于贯彻落实全面推进依法行政实施纲要的实施意见] issued March 2004.
Opinions of the General Office of the Chinese Communist Party Central Committee and the General Office of the State Council on Further Promoting Openness in Government Affairs [《中共中央办公厅国务院办公厅关于进一步推行政务公开的意见》] issued March 2005.
Opinions of the General Office of the Chinese Communist Party Central Committee and the General Office of the State Council on Deepening Open Government Affairs and Strengthening Government Service [关于深化政务公开加强政务服务的意见] issued August 2011.
Opinions of the General Office of the Chinese Communist Party Central Committee and the General Office of the State Council on Perfecting and Improving System of Openness and Democratic Administration of Village Affairs [中共中央办公厅、国务院办公厅关于健全和完善村务公开和民主管理制度的意见] issued June 2004.
Opinions of the General Office of the State Council on Improving the Work of Disclosing Government Information Upon Request [国务院办公厅关于做好政府信息依申请公开工作的意见] issued January 2010.
Opinions of the General Office of the State Council on Several Issues Concerning the Enforcement of Regulations of the People's Republic of China on Open

Government Information [国务院办公厅关于施行《中华人民共和国政府信息公开条例》若干问题的意见] issued April 2008.
Organic Law of the Villager Committees of the People's Republic of China [中华人民共和国村民委员会组织法] effective November 1998, amended October 2010.
Personal Information Protection Law of the People's Republic of China [中华人民共和国个人信息保护法] adopted August 20, 2021, effective November 1, 2021.
Provisions of Guangzhou Municipality on Open Government Information [广州市政府信息公开规定] effective January 2003.
Provisions of *Shanghai* Municipality on Open Government *Information* [上海市政府信息公开规定] effective May 2008, amended December 2010.
Provisions of the Supreme People's Court on Issues concerning Trying Administrative Cases of Government Information Disclosure (Exposure Draft) [最高人民法院关于审理政府信息公开行政案件若干问题的规定(征求意见稿)] issued November 2009.
Provisions of the Supreme People's Court on Issues concerning Trying Administrative Cases of Government Information Disclosure [最高人民法院关于审理政府信息公开行政案件若干问题的规定] effective August 2011.
Provisions of the Supreme People's Court on Judicial Transparency [最高人民法院关于司法公开的六项规定] effective December 2009.
Provisions of the Supreme People's Court on Media Supervision [最高人民法院关于接受新闻媒体舆论监督的若干规定] effective December 2009.
Regulations of the People's Republic of China on Open Government Information [中华人民共和国政府信息公开条例] effective May 2008.
Regulations of the People's Republic of China on Open Government Information [中华人民共和国政府信息公开条例] effective May 2019.
"Report in 2022 on National Development in Education." [2022年全国教育事业发展统计公报] , the Ministry of Education, Beijing, China, available at http://www.moe.gov.cn/jyb_sjzl/sjzl_fztjgb/202307/t20230705_1067278.html (accessed between February 21, 2025 and March 31, 2025).
Report on the Review Results of the Proposals from the Deputies of the Second Plenary Session of the 10th National People's Congress by the Internal and Judicial Affairs Committee of the National People's Congress [全国人大内务司法委员会关于第四届全国人民代表大会第二次会议主席团交付审议的代表提出的议案审议结果的报告] adopted October 2004.
Several Provisions of The Supreme Court on Vigorously Enforcing the System of Public Trials [最高人民法院关于严格执行公开审判制度的若干规定] issued March 1999.
Tentative Regulations of the Chinese Communist Party on Open Party Affairs [中国共产党党务公开条例(试行)] effective December 2017.
U.S. Administrative Procedure Act of 1946, 5 U.S. C. §1002 (1946).

U.S. Freedom of Information Act, 5 U.S.C. § 552 (1994).
U.S. Government in the Sunshine Act of 1976, 5 U.S.C. § 552 (1976).
U.S. House and Senate Reports on freedom of information legislation (1966–2007).
U.S. Housekeeping Statute, 5 U.S.C. § 301(1789).
Wen, Jiabao. "Annual Report on the Work of the Government to the National People's Congress." March 2004-March 2012.
White Paper on China's Efforts and Achievements in Promoting Rule of Law [《中国的法治建设》白皮书] published February 2008.
White Paper on Socialist System of Laws with Chinese Characteristics [中国特色社会主义法律体系白皮书] published October 2011.
White Paper on the Progress of Human Rights Cause in 2003 [2003年中国人权事业的进展] published March 2004.
Zhao, Ziyang. "Report to the 13th National Party Congress." Beijing, China, October 1987.

Bilateral and International Treaties and Documents

Article 19, The Universal Declaration of Human Rights, adopted by the General Assembly of the United Nations, New York, December 1948.
China's trade agreements with the World Trade Organization, signed November 2001.
International Covenant on Civil and Political Rights, adopted by the General Assembly of the United Nations, New York, December 1966.
Memorandum of Understanding Between the Government of the United States of America and the Government of People's Republic of China Concerning Market Access [中华人民共和国政府和美利坚合众国政府关于市场准入的谅解备忘录] signed October 1992.
Treaty of Amsterdam, Amsterdam, the Netherlands, October 1997, available at https://www.cvce.eu/content/publication/1999/1/1/578ebb8e-d641-4650-b1e3-3b3a795e01c9/publishable_en.pdf (accessed between February 21, 2025 and March 31, 2025).
The United Nations Economic Commission for Europe (UNECE) Convention on Access to Information, Public Participation in Decision-Making and Access to Justice in Environmental Matters, adopted June 1998, entered into force on October 2001.
Universal Declaration of Human Rights, United Nations, New York, available at https://www.un.org/en/about-us/universal-declaration-of-human-rights#:~:text=Article%2019,media%20and%20regardless%20of%20frontiers (accessed between February 21, 2025 and March 31, 2025).

Interviews

Email and telephone interviews with a Beijing lawyer who wants to remain anonymous because of the sensitivity of the topic (February 2012).

Email and telephone interviews with journalists from a wide variety of leading and local news organizations in China. They want to remain anonymous because of the sensitivity of the topic (June 2012 to November 2012).

Email interview with Jun Wang, a professor of mass media law at the Communication University of China (March 2010).

Email interview with Yanbin Lv, a legal scholar at China Academy of Social Sciences Institute of Law (March 2010).

Interviews/conversations with party, government, university and media officials who want to remain anonymous due to the sensitivity of the topic (2009-2025).

Telephone interview with Gang He, managing editor of Caijing, a prestigious financial publication known for investigative journalism (September 2011).

WeChat interviews with Yongzheng Wei, one of the most recognized media law scholars in China (June 2020 and December 2024).

WeChat interview with Zejin Yao, a professor of media law studies at China University of Political Science and Law (December 2024).

Sample Interview Questions about Journalistic Use of OGI Regulations

(1) 您以及您所在的新闻单位在促进政府信息公开的立法方面做过哪些方面的工作 ? (What have you and/or your news organization done to help with the legislation of *OGI Regulations*?)

(2)您以及您所在的新闻单位在政府信息公开条例出台后做过哪些方面的宣传报道工作,以促进公众和新闻记者对该法律的了解 ?(What have you and/or your news organization done to help promote the public and journalists' familiarity with the law after *the OGI Regulations*' enactment in 2007 and its enforcement in 2008?)

(3)自政府信息公开条例实施以来,您以及您所在的新闻单位是否利用该法向政府部门申请过信息公开?(Have you or your news organization ever applied for governmental information via filing OGI requests to any government agencies since the implementation of *OGI Regulations*?)

(4)如果申请过,一共有多少起这样的申请?多少次申请成功?多少次申请失败?有没有相关的统计数据?(If yes, can you tell me how many OGI applications have you and/or your news organizations made? Out of those applications, how many resulted in disclosure of information and how many resulted in non-disclosure? Any numbers or statistics to share with me?)

(5) 您以及您所在的新闻单位有没有因为申请失败而向上级部门提起行政复议的情况?如果有,行政复议的结局一般是怎么样?(Have you and/or your news

organization ever appealed to superior agencies for administrative reconsideration? If yes, what is the general outcome?)

(6)您以及您所在的新闻单位有没有因为申请失败而向法院提起诉讼的情况?(If your OGI applications encounter dismissals, rejections or denials, have you and/or your news organization ever sued agencies for judicial relief? If yes, what is the general outcome?)

(7)对申请到的政府信息,您以及您所在的新闻单位一般怎么处理?(How do you and/or your news organization handle the information obtained via OGI requests?)

(8)如果您觉得您不掌握太多的信息,您以及您所在的新闻单位是否愿意推荐一两位申请过政府信息公开的记者与我做更深入的访谈?(Is it possible for you and/or your news organization to recommend me one or two journalists who are familiar with *OGI Regulations* if you feel you don't know much about this topic?)

(9)您以及您所在的新闻单位是否愿意向其他编辑记者转发我的这份调查表?(Can you and/or your news organization forward this questionnaire to other people in the newsroom?)

(10)不同性质和类型的新闻媒体在申请政府信息公开方面有什么不同的特点?(As far as you know, how are media entities different when it comes to applying for governmental information via OGI requests?

(11)您以及您所在的新闻单位认为政府信息公开法律今后应该如何改进,才能更好地为新闻报道服务?(How should *OGI Regulations* be revised to better serve journalists and news organizations?)

(12)您以及您所在的新闻单位认为今后应该做哪些方面的工作,才能让《中华人民共和国政府信息公开条例》成为新闻记者更有效的工具(更有力的武器)?(What should be done in the future to make *OGI Regulations* a more effective tool for newsgathering and news reporting?

(13)国外的信息自由法,您知道多少?(How much do you know about freedom of information laws in foreign countries?)

(14)就新闻记者与政府信息公开条例而言,您还有别的想和我分享的吗?(For journalistic use of *OGI Regulations*, what else do you want to share with me?)

OGI-Related Court Cases Compiled from China Judgements Online

Bao Guoqing v. Guangzhou No. 1 Bus Company [包国庆诉广州市第一巴士有限公司信息公开案](Guangdong Province Guangzhou City Intermediate Court, June 23, 2015). https://wenshu.court.gov.cn/ (registration needed for access) (accessed between February 21, 2025 and March 31, 2025).

Chen Daxue and Wu Changling v. Rui'an City Office for Immigrant Resettlement [陈大学与吴昌令诉浙江瑞安市移民安置办公室信息公开案] (Zhejiang

Province Wenzhou City Intermediate Court, September 6, 2017). https://wenshu.court.gov.cn/ (registration needed for access) (accessed between February 21, 2025 and March 31, 2025).

Chen Yuejun v. Tianjin Bus Company [陈跃军诉天津巴士实业有限公司信息公开案] (Tianjin City Beichen District Trial Court, November 29, 2018). https://wenshu.court.gov.cn/ (registration needed for access) (accessed between February 21, 2025 and March 31, 2025).

Chenhong v. Jiangsu Changshu Sino French Water Company [陈鸿诉江苏常熟中法水务有限公司信息公开案] (Jiangsu Province Suzhou City Intermediate Court, March 10, 2017). https://wenshu.court.gov.cn/ (registration needed for access) (accessed between February 21, 2025 and March 31, 2025).

Chenhong v. State Grid Changshu City Electricity Supply Company [陈鸿诉国网江苏省电力公司常熟市供电公司信息公开案] (Jiangsu Province Suzhou City Intermediate Court, February 28, 2017). https://wenshu.court.gov.cn/ (registration needed for access) (accessed between February 21, 2025 and March 31, 2025).

Ding Ruibing v. Haimen City Radio and TV Station [丁锐兵诉江苏省海门市广播电视台信息公开案] (Jiangsu Province Nantong City Intermediate Court, October 27, 2017). https://wenshu.court.gov.cn/ (registration needed for access) (accessed between February 21, 2025 and March 31, 2025).

Ding Zipeng v. State Grid Shandong Zaozhuang Power Supply Company [丁自鹏诉国网山东省电力公司枣庄供电公司] (Shandong Province Zaozhuang City Xuecheng District Trial Court, May 7, 2019). https://wenshu.court.gov.cn/ (registration needed for access) (accessed between February 21, 2025 and March 31, 2025).

Fang Jinhua v. China Telecom Suqian Branch [方金华诉中国电信股份有限公司宿迁分公司 信息公开案] (Jiangsu Province Suqian City Intermediate Court, May 16, 2014). https://wenshu.court.gov.cn/ (registration needed for access) (accessed between February 21, 2025 and March 31, 2025).

Feng Genqing v. Taizhou City Jiaojiang District Bureau for Housing, Urban-Rural Development [冯根青诉台州市椒江区住房和城乡建设局信息公开案] (Zhejiang Province Taizhou City Jiaojiang District Trial Court, May 6, 2019). https://wenshu.court.gov.cn/ (registration needed for access) (accessed between February 21, 2025 and March 31, 2025).

Han Suhua v. Zhenzhou Orphanage [韩素华诉河南郑州市儿童福利院信息公开案] (Henan Province High Court, October 23, 2020). https://wenshu.court.gov.cn/ (registration needed for access) (accessed between February 21, 2025 and March 31, 2025).

Liu Aijun v. Beijing No. 6 Hospital [刘爱军诉北京市第六医院信息公开案] (Beijing City No.2 Intermediate Court, March 31, 2016). https://wenshu.court.gov.cn/ (registration needed for access) (accessed between February 21, 2025 and March 31, 2025).

Liu Aijun v. Zhengzhou Preschool Education College [刘爱军诉郑州幼儿师范高等专科学校信息公开案] (Henan Province Zhengzhou City Intermediate Court, December 12, 2016). https://wenshu.court.gov.cn/ (registration needed for access) (accessed between February 21, 2025 and March 31, 2025).

Liu Hong v. Beijing Dongcheng District No. 1 Center for Public Housing and Land Management [刘红诉北京市东城区房屋土地经营管理一中心信息公开案] (Beijing City No.2 Intermediate Court, April 8, 20140). https://wenshu.court.gov.cn/ (registration needed for access) (accessed between February 21, 2025 and March 31, 2025).

Liu Shuping v. China Post Zhongmou County Branch [刘书平诉中国邮政集团公司河南省中牟县分公司信息公开案] (Henan Province Zhengzhou City Intermediate Court, November 15, 2017). https://wenshu.court.gov.cn/ (registration needed for access) (accessed between February 21, 2025 and March 31, 2025).

Liu Shuping v. China Post Zhongmou County Branch [刘书平诉中国邮政集团公司河南省中牟县分公司信息公开案] (Henan Province Zhengzhou City Intermediate Court, November February 27, 2018). https://wenshu.court.gov.cn/ (registration needed for access) (accessed between February 21, 2025 and March 31, 2025).

Liu Shuping v. State Grid Zhongmou County Branch [刘书平诉国网河南省电力公司中牟县供电公司信息公开案] (Henan Province Zhengzhou City Intermediate Court, December 19, 2016). https://wenshu.court.gov.cn/ (registration needed for access) (accessed between February 21, 2025 and March 31, 2025).

Luo Siwen v. Guizhou Power Grid Guiyang Station [罗嗣文诉贵州电网有限责任公司贵阳供电局信息公开案] (Guizhou Province Guiyang City Nanming District Trial Court, December 12, 2017). https://wenshu.court.gov.cn/ (registration needed for access) (accessed between February 21, 2025 and March 31, 2025).

Qiu Ailing v. Fuzhou City Water Supply Company [邱爱玲诉福建福州市自来水有限公司信息公开案](Fujian Province Fuzhou City Gulou District Trial Court, July 1, 2021). https://wenshu.court.gov.cn/ (registration needed for access) (accessed between February 21, 2025 and March 31, 2025).

Residents' Committee of Jiuduyangguang Community v. Zhaozhou Electric Power Supply Company [九度阳光小区业主委员会诉黑龙江省大庆市肇州县电业局信息公开案] (Heilongjiang Province Daqing City Intermediate Court, August 20, 2018). https://wenshu.court.gov.cn/ (registration needed for access) (accessed between February 21, 2025 and March 31, 2025).

Shao Mingliang v. State Grid Jiangsu Changshu Power Supply Company [邵明亮诉国网江苏省电力公司常熟市供电公司信息公开案] (Jiangsu Province Suzhou City Intermediate Court, February 28, 2017). https://wenshu.court.gov.cn/ (registration needed for access) (accessed between February 21, 2025 and March 31, 2025).

Sun Yangbing v. China Mobile Shenzhen Branch [孙阳兵诉中国移动通信集团广东有限公司深圳分公司信息公开案] (Guangdong Province Shenzhen City Intermediate Court, December 5, 2014). https://wenshu.court.gov.cn/ (registration needed for access) (accessed between February 21, 2025 and March 31, 2025).

Xing Wenyuan v. State Grid Beijing Electric Power Company [邢文元诉国网北京市电力公司信息公开案] (Beijing City High Court, March 18, 2020). https://wenshu.court.gov.cn/ (registration needed for access) (accessed between February 21, 2025 and March 31, 2025).

Xing Wenyuan v. State Grid Beijing Electric Power Company [邢文元诉国网北京市电力公司信息公开案] (Beijing No. 2 Intermediate Court, June 28, 2018). https://wenshu.court.gov.cn/ (registration needed for access) (accessed between February 21, 2025 and March 31, 2025).

Yan Hongjun v. China Mobile Dongguan Branch [闫红军诉中国移动通信集团广东有限公司东莞分公司信息公开案] (Guangdong Province Dongguan City Intermediate Court, December 21, 2017). https://wenshu.court.gov.cn/ (registration needed for access) (accessed between February 21, 2025 and March 31, 2025).

Yongfa Security Equipment Factory v. Changzhou City Institute for Product Quality Supervision and Testing [平湖市永发保安设备厂诉江苏常州市产品质量监督检验所信息公开案] (Jiangsu Province High Court, October 31, 2019). https://wenshu.court.gov.cn/ (registration needed for access) (accessed between February 21, 2025 and March 31, 2025).

You Hanrui v. Beijing Drainage Group[尤瀚睿诉北京城市排水集团有限责任公司信息公开案](Beijing City No. 2 Intermediate Court, May 14, 2018). https://wenshu.court.gov.cn/ (registration needed for access) (accessed between February 21, 2025 and March 31, 2025).

Zhong Weixi v. Juye County Service Center for Coal Industry [仲伟洗诉山东省巨野县煤炭工业服务中心信息公开案] (Shandong Province Heze City Intermediate Court, August 31, 2020). https://wenshu.court.gov.cn/ (registration needed for access) (accessed between February 21, 2025 and March 31, 2025).

Zhuo Liangbing v. Taizhou City Jiaojiang District Bureau for Housing and Urban-Rural Development [卓良兵诉台州市椒江区住房和城乡建设局信息公开案](Zhejiang Province Taizhou City Jiaojiang District Trial Court, May 6, 2019). https://wenshu.court.gov.cn/ (registration needed for access) (accessed between February 21, 2025 and March 31, 2025).

Homeowner Association of Nanjing Fengshang International Apartment v. State Grid

Bai Guangming v. Urumqi City Saybagh District People's Government [白光明诉乌鲁木齐市沙依巴克区人民政府信息公开案] (Xinjiang Automonous Region Urumqi City Intermediate Court, July 4, 2018) https://wenshu.court.gov.cn/ (registration needed for access) (accessed between February 21, 2025 and March 31, 2025).

Bai Jintao v. Shanxi Provincial People's Government [白锦涛诉山西省人民政府信息公开案] (Shanxi Province High Court, June 28, 2017) https://wenshu.court.gov.cn/ (registration needed for access) (accessed between February 21, 2025 and March 31, 2025).

Bai Yan v. Gansu Provincial Department of Public Security and Gansu Provincial People's Government [白燕诉甘肃省公安厅与甘肃省人民政府信息公开案] (Gansu Province High Court, March 12, 2020) https://wenshu.court.gov.cn/ (registration needed for access) (accessed between February 21, 2025 and March 31, 2025).

Bai Yan v. National Education Examinations Authority [白燕诉教育部考试中心信息公开案] (Beijing City No.1 Intermediate Court, September 25, 2018). https://wenshu.court.gov.cn/ (registration needed for access) (accessed between February 21, 2025 and March 31, 2025).

Bai Yan v. Renmin University of China [白燕诉中国人民大学信息公开案] (Beijing City Haidian District Trial Court, June 22, 2018). https://wenshu.court.gov.cn/ (registration needed for access) (accessed between February 21, 2025 and March 31, 2025).

Bi Yanhai v. Gu County People's Government [毕研海诉古县人民政府信息公开案] (Shanxi Province High Court, April 26, 2016) https://wenshu.court.gov.cn/ (registration needed for access) (accessed between February 21, 2025 and March 31, 2025).

Bi Yongyuan v. Jiangsu Changshu Sino French Water Company [毕永元诉常熟中法水务有限公司信息公开案] (Jiangsu Province Suzhou City Intermediate Court, March 10, 2017). https://wenshu.court.gov.cn/ (registration needed for access) (accessed between February 21, 2025 and March 31, 2025).

Bi Yongyuan v. State Grid Changshu City Electricity Supply Company [毕永元诉国网江苏省电力公司常熟市供电公司信息公开案] (Jiangsu Province Suzhou City Intermediate Court, February 28, 2017). https://wenshu.court.gov.cn/ (registration needed for access) (accessed between February 21, 2025 and March 31, 2025).

Cai Xiaoming v. China Mobile Changsha Branch [蔡晓明诉中国移动通信集团湖南有限公司长沙分公司信息公开案] (Hunan Province Changsha City Tianxin District Trial Court, March 26, 2014). https://wenshu.court.gov.cn/ (registration needed for access) (accessed between February 21, 2025 and March 31, 2025).

Cao Linlin v. Anhui Provincial Bureau of Finance and China Ministry of Finance [曹琳琳诉安徽省财政厅与中华人民共和国财政部信息公开案] (Anhui Province Hefei City Luyang District Trial Court, March 31, 2020) https://wenshu.court.gov.cn/ (registration needed for access) (accessed between February 21, 2025 and March 31, 2025).

Cao Lishu v. Chongqing City Rongchang District People's Government [曹礼淑诉重庆市荣昌区人民政府信息公开案] (Chongqing City No. 5 Intermediate Court, December 19, 2017) https://wenshu.court.gov.cn/ (registration needed for access) (accessed between February 21, 2025 and March 31, 2025).

Chao Chunfu v. Tianjin City Baodi District People's Government [晁春富诉天津市宝坻区人民政府信息公开案] (Tianjin City No.1 Intermediate Court, May 10, 2019) https://wenshu.court.gov.cn/ (registration needed for access) (accessed between February 21, 2025 and March 31, 2025).

Chen Qingguo , et al. v. Yiwu Municipal People's Government [陈清国等诉义乌市人民政府信息公开案] (Zhejiang Province Yiwu City Trial Court, December 19, 2017) https://wenshu.court.gov.cn/ (registration needed for access) (accessed between February 21, 2025 and March 31, 2025).

Chen Ce and Chen Ruidi v. Wenzhou City Lucheng District Center for Urban Village Redevelopment [陈策与陈瑞弟诉温州市鹿城区城中村改造建设中心信息公开案] (Zhejiang Province Wenzhou City Intermediate Court, December 1, 2020). https://wenshu.court.gov.cn/ (registration needed for access) (accessed between February 21, 2025 and March 31, 2025).

Chen Chuanbing v. Fujian Provincial People's Government and Fuzhou Municipal People's Government [陈传兵诉福建省人民政府与福州市人民政府信息公开案] (Fujian Province Fuzhou City Intermediate Court, February 27, 2017) https://wenshu.court.gov.cn/ (registration needed for access) (accessed between February 21, 2025 and March 31, 2025).

Chen Fagao v. Feidong County Bureau of Finance [陈发高诉肥东县财政局信息公开案] (Anhui Province Feidong County Trial Court, 2017) (date and month of verdict unknown) https://wenshu.court.gov.cn/ (registration needed for access) (accessed between February 21, 2025 and March 31, 2025).

Chen Fengjiao v. Xingyang Municipal People's Government [陈凤娇诉荥阳市人民政府信息公开案] (Henan Province Zhengzhou City Intermediate Court, February 5, 2018) https://wenshu.court.gov.cn/ (registration needed for access) (accessed between February 21, 2025 and March 31, 2025).

Chen Hua v. Nanjing University of Information Science and Technology [陈华诉南京信息工程大学信息公开案] (Jiangsu Province Nanjing City Intermediate Court, January 29, 2021). https://wenshu.court.gov.cn/ (registration needed for access) (accessed between February 21, 2025 and March 31, 2025).

Chen Huagang v. Yichang City Xiling District People's Government and Yichang Municipal People's Government [陈华刚诉宜昌市西陵区人民政府与宜昌市人民政府信息公开案] (Hubei Province Yichang City Intermediate Court, November 16, 2020) https://wenshu.court.gov.cn/ (registration needed for access) (accessed between February 21, 2025 and March 31, 2025).

Chen Jiafa, et al. v. Dafang County People's Government [陈家发等诉大方县人民政府信息公开案] (Guizhou Province Bijie City Intermediate Court, June 7, 2018) https://wenshu.court.gov.cn/ (registration needed for access) (accessed between February 21, 2025 and March 31, 2025).

Chen Jianguo, et al. v. Fuzhou City Jin'an District People's Government and Fuzhou Municipal People's Government [陈建国等诉福州市晋安区人民政府与福州市人民政府信息公开案] (Fujian Province High Court, May 30, 2016) https://wenshu.court.gov.cn/ (registration needed for access) (accessed between February 21, 2025 and March 31, 2025).

Chen Jiaonan v. Changzhou City Benniu Township People's Government [陈校南诉常州市奔牛镇人民政府信息公开案] (Jiangsu Province Changzhou City Xinbei District Trial Court, February 28, 2019) https://wenshu.court.gov.cn/ (registration needed for access) (accessed between February 21, 2025 and March 31, 2025).

Chen Kaiquan and Gao Longxiang v. Meishan City Dongpo District Chongli Township People's Government [陈凯全与高龙香诉眉山市东坡区崇礼镇人民政府信息公开案] (Sichuan Province Meishan City Pengshan District Trial Court, April 3, 2018) https://wenshu.court.gov.cn/ (registration needed for access) (accessed between February 21, 2025 and March 31, 2025).

Chen Lin v. Jianghan University [陈琳诉江汉大学信息公开案] (Hubei Province High Court, September 28, 2020). https://wenshu.court.gov.cn/ (registration needed for access) (accessed between February 21, 2025 and March 31, 2025).

Chen Qiwu v. Beijing City Chaoyang District People's Government [陈启武诉北京市朝阳区人民政府信息公开案] (Beijing City Chaoyang District Trial Court, July 30, 2019) https://wenshu.court.gov.cn/ (registration needed for access) (accessed between February 21, 2025 and March 31, 2025).

Chen Qiyu v. Shangrao County People's Government and Shangrao Municipal People's Government [陈其俞诉上饶县人民政府与上饶市人民政府信息公开案] (Jiangxi Province Shangrao City Intermediate Court, November 30, 2018) https://wenshu.court.gov.cn/ (registration needed for access) (accessed between February 21, 2025 and March 31, 2025).

Chen Shiqing v. Fujian Province Party School [陈世清诉中共福建省委党校信息公开案] (Fujian Province Fuzhou City Intermediate Court, April 7, 2015). https://wenshu.court.gov.cn/ (registration needed for access) (accessed between February 21, 2025 and March 31, 2025).

Chen Shiqing v. Gutian County Party School [陈世清诉中共古田县委党校信息公开案] (Fujian Province Ningde City Intermediate Court, February 15, 2016). https://wenshu.court.gov.cn/ (registration needed for access) (accessed between February 21, 2025 and March 31, 2025).

Chen Weizhi v. Henan Provincial Administration of Culture and Tourism [陈维智诉河南省文化和旅游厅信息公开案] (Henan Province Zhengzhou National High and New Technology Industries Development Zone Trial Court, June 26, 2020) https://wenshu.court.gov.cn/ (registration needed for access) (accessed between February 21, 2025 and March 31, 2025).

Chen Xinrong v. Ningdu County People's Government [陈新荣诉宁都县人民政府信息公开案](Jiangxi Province Ganzhou City Intermediate Court, March 23, 2020) https://wenshu.court.gov.cn/ (registration needed for access) (accessed between February 21, 2025 and March 31, 2025).

Chen Yudan v. Shanghai City Chongming District Urban Planning and Natural Resources Bureau [陈玉丹诉上海市崇明区规划和自然资源局信息公开案] (Shanghai City No.1 Intermediate Court, September 24, 2019) https://wenshu.court.gov.cn/ (registration needed for access) (accessed between February 21, 2025 and March 31, 2025).

Chen Yuejun v. China United Network Communication Group [陈跃军诉中国联合网络通信有限公司信息公开案] (Beijing City No.2 Intermediate Court, March 30, 2016). https://wenshu.court.gov.cn/ (registration needed for access) (accessed between February 21, 2025 and March 31, 2025).

Chen Yuejun v. Tianjin Metro [陈跃军诉天津市地下铁道运营有限公司信息公开案] (Tianjin City No.2 Intermediate Court, November 3, 2015). https://wenshu.court.gov.cn/ (registration needed for access) (accessed between February 21, 2025 and March 31, 2025).

Chen Zhenbang v. Changsha City Furong District People's Government [陈振邦诉长沙市芙蓉区人民政府信息公开案] (Hunan Province High Court, February 6, 2017) https://wenshu.court.gov.cn/ (registration needed for access) (accessed between February 21, 2025 and March 31, 2025).

Chen Zhong v. Qidong Municipal People's Government [陈忠诉启东市人民政府信息公开案] (Jiangsu Province Nantong City Intermediate Court, May 14, 2018) https://wenshu.court.gov.cn/ (registration needed for access) (accessed between February 21, 2025 and March 31, 2025).

Cheng Ansheng v. Shenqiu County People's Government [程安生诉沈丘县人民政府信息公开案] (Henan Province Zhoukou City Intermediate Court, March 20, 2019) https://wenshu.court.gov.cn/ (registration needed for access) (accessed between February 21, 2025 and March 31, 2025).

Cheng Wenyi v. China Mobile Ezhou Branch [程文艺诉中国移动通信集团湖北有限公司鄂州分公司信息公开案] (Hubei Province Ezhou City Intermediate Court, April 28, 2017). https://wenshu.court.gov.cn/ (registration needed for access) (accessed between February 21, 2025 and March 31, 2025).

Cheng Xinwu v. Xuyong County People's Government [成信伍诉叙永县人民政府信息公开案] (Sichuan Province Luzhou City Intermediate Court, September 29, 2020) https://wenshu.court.gov.cn/ (registration needed for access) (accessed between February 21, 2025 and March 31, 2025).

Cheng Yuejun v. China Mobile Communications Corporation [程跃军诉中国移动通信集团公司信息公开案] (Beijing City No.2 Intermediate Court, March 30, 2016). https://wenshu.court.gov.cn/ (registration needed for access) (accessed between February 21, 2025 and March 31, 2025).

CITIC Land Corporation v. Shangli County Bureau of Natural Resources and Planning [中信置业有限公司诉上栗县自然资源和规划局信息公开案] (Jiangxi Province Pingxiang City Anyuan District Trial Court, March 10, 2020) https://wenshu.court.gov.cn/ (registration needed for access) (accessed between February 21, 2025 and March 31, 2025).

Cui Dongmei v. Zhengzhou City Huiji District People's Government [崔东梅诉郑州市惠济区人民政府信息公开案] (Henan Province Zhengzhou City Railway Transport Intermediate Court, September 18, 2017) https://wenshu.court.gov.cn/ (registration needed for access) (accessed between February 21, 2025 and March 31, 2025).

Cui Xunzhang v. Ji'nan City Huaiyin District People's Government [崔勋章诉济南市槐荫区人民政府信息公开案] (Shandong Province High Court, December 29, 2017) https://wenshu.court.gov.cn/ (registration needed for access) (accessed between February 21, 2025 and March 31, 2025).

Cui Xunzhang v. Jinan City Huaiyin District Bureau for Housing Security and Property Management [崔勋章诉济南市槐荫区住房保障和房产管理局信息公开案] (Shandong Province Jinan City Intermediate Court, May 13, 2019). https://wenshu.court.gov.cn/ (registration needed for access) (accessed between February 21, 2025 and March 31, 2025).

Dai Wei v. Ji'nan City Huaiyin District Housing Acquisition Service Center [戴伟诉济南市槐荫区房屋征收服务中心信息公开案] (Shandong Province High Court, April 28, 2019). https://wenshu.court.gov.cn/ (registration needed for access) (accessed between February 21, 2025 and March 31, 2025).

Dai Zongming v. Yichang Municipal People's Government and Hubei Provincial People's Government [代宗明诉宜昌市人民政府与湖北省人民政府信息公开案] (Hubei Province Yichang City Intermediate Court, November 25, 2019) https://wenshu.court.gov.cn/ (registration needed for access) (accessed between February 21, 2025 and March 31, 2025).

Dang Xiulan, et al. v. Liulin County People's Government [党秀兰等诉柳林县人民政府信息公开案] (Shanxi Province Jinzhong City Intermediate Court, July 24, 2020) https://wenshu.court.gov.cn/ (registration needed for access) (accessed between February 21, 2025 and March 31, 2025).

Deng Xiulan v. Chengdu Municipal People's Government [邓秀兰诉成都市人民政府信息公开案] (Sichuan Province High Court, August 20, 2014) https://wenshu.court.gov.cn/ (registration needed for access) (accessed between February 21, 2025 and March 31, 2025).

Ding Shujuan v. Nanchang City Xihu District People's Government [丁淑娟诉南昌市西湖区人民政府信息公开案] (Jiangxi Province High Court, March 22, 2016) https://wenshu.court.gov.cn/ (registration needed for access) (accessed between February 21, 2025 and March 31, 2025).

Dong Jianshe v. Qingzhou Municipal People's Government [董建设诉青州市人民政府信息公开案] (Shandong Province Weifang City Intermediate Court, May 22, 2019) https://wenshu.court.gov.cn/ (registration needed for access) (accessed between February 21, 2025 and March 31, 2025).

Du Laixing v. Nan'an Municipal Bureau of Public Security and Quanzhou Municipal Bureau of Public Security [杜来兴诉南安市公安局与泉州市公安局信息公开案] (Fujian Province Quanzhou City Licheng District Trial Court, December 20, 2017) https://wenshu.court.gov.cn/ (registration needed for access) (accessed between February 21, 2025 and March 31, 2025).

Du Yongzhong v. Wensu County People's Government [杜永忠诉温宿县人民政府信息公开案](Xinjiang Autonomous Region Aksu Prefecture Intermediate Court, February 22, 2021) https://wenshu.court.gov.cn/ (registration needed for access) (accessed between February 21, 2025 and March 31, 2025).

E Yanping v. Benxi City Pingshan District People's Government and Benxi Municipal People's Government [鄂彦平诉本溪市平山区人民政府与本溪市人民政府信息公开案] (Liaoning Province Benxi City Intermediate Court, November 2, 2016) https://wenshu.court.gov.cn/ (registration needed for access) (accessed between February 21, 2025 and March 31, 2025).

Fan Qigang v. Haining Municipal People's Government [范其刚诉海宁市人民政府信息公开案] (Zhejiang Province Jiaxing City Intermediate Court, August 24, 2020) https://wenshu.court.gov.cn/ (registration needed for access) (accessed between February 21, 2025 and March 31, 2025).

Fan Renyuan v. Changzhou Municipal Archival Institution and Changzhou Municipal People's Government [范人媛诉常州市档案局与常州市人民政府信息公开案] (Jiangsu Province Changzhou City Xinbei District Trial Court, March 25, 2020) https://wenshu.court.gov.cn/ (registration needed for access) (accessed between February 21, 2025 and March 31, 2025).

Fang Jifeng v. Beijing City Xicheng District People's Government [房际凤诉北京市西城区人民政府信息公开案] (Beijing City No. 4 Intermediate Court, November 15, 2019) https://wenshu.court.gov.cn/ (registration needed for access) (accessed between February 21, 2025 and March 31, 2025).

Fang Hong v. Nan'ning City Qingxiu District People's Government [方闳诉南宁市青秀区人民政府信息公开案] (Guangxi Zhuang Autonomous Region Nan'ning City Intermediate Court, November 3, 2017) https://wenshu.court.gov.cn/ (registration needed for access) (accessed between February 21, 2025 and March 31, 2025).

Fang Shumei v. Yantai City Fushan District People's Government [房树梅诉烟台市福山区人民政府信息公开案] (Shandong Province Yantai City Intermediate Court, September 16, 2019) https://wenshu.court.gov.cn/ (registration needed for access) (accessed between February 21, 2025 and March 31, 2025).

Fang Wei v. Wuchang Municipal People's Government [房威诉五常市人民政府信息公开案] (Heilongjiang Province Harbin City Intermediate Court, October 18, 2018) https://wenshu.court.gov.cn/ (registration needed for access) (accessed between February 21, 2025 and March 31, 2025).

Fang Wenping v. Shanghai City Jiading District Bureau of Affordable Housing and Shanghai Municipal Bureau of Affordable Housing [方文平诉上海市嘉定区住房保障和房屋管理局与上海市房屋 管理局信息公开案] (Shanghai City Jing'an District Trial Court, June 24, 2020) https://wenshu.court.gov.cn/ (registration needed for access) (accessed between February 21, 2025 and March 31, 2025).

Fang Yuzhen v. Yichang Municipal People's Government [方玉贞诉宜昌市人民政府信息公开案] (Hubei Province Yichang City Intermediate Court, March 18, 2019) https://wenshu.court.gov.cn/ (registration needed for access) (accessed between February 21, 2025 and March 31, 2025).

Feng Haijun v. Changsha City Wangcheng District People's Government and Changsha Municipal People's Government [冯海军诉长沙市望城区人民政府与长沙市人民政府政府信息公开案] (Hunan Province High Court, April 9, 2019) https://wenshu.court.gov.cn/ (registration needed for access) (accessed between February 21, 2025 and March 31, 2025).

Feng Huina v. Sichuan Provincial People's Government [冯惠娜诉四川省人民政府信息公开案](Sichuan Province Chengdu City Intermediate Court, May 31, 2019) https://wenshu.court.gov.cn/ (registration needed for access) (accessed between February 21, 2025 and March 31, 2025).

Feng Ruiyang v. Zhongxiang Municipal People's Government [冯睿洋诉钟祥市人民政府信息公开案] (Hubei Province Jingmen City Intermediate Court, June 15, 2018) https://wenshu.court.gov.cn/ (registration needed for access) (accessed between February 21, 2025 and March 31, 2025).

Feng Wen v. Beijing City Xicheng District People's Government [冯雯诉北京市西城区人民政府信息公开案] (Beijing City No. 4 Intermediate Court, November 4, 2019) https://wenshu.court.gov.cn/ (registration needed for access) (accessed between February 21, 2025 and March 31, 2025).

Feng Yan v. Mianyang Municipal Bureau of Public Security [冯琰诉绵阳市公安局信息公开案](Sichuan Province Mianyang City Intermediate Court, March 22, 2021) https://wenshu.court.gov.cn/ (registration needed for access) (accessed between February 21, 2025 and March 31, 2025).

Feng Yongjun v. Shantai County Development and Reform Bureau [冯勇军诉三台县发展和改革局信息公开案] (Sichuan Province Mianyang City Intermediate Court, January 19, 2021) https://wenshu.court.gov.cn/ (registration needed for access) (accessed between February 21, 2025 and March 31, 2025).

Fu Ailian v. Beijing Municipal Commission of Planning and Natural Resources [付爱廉诉北京市规划和自然资源委员会信息公开案] (Beijing City Tongzhou District Trial Court, April 23, 2020) https://wenshu.court.gov.cn/ (registration needed for access) (accessed between February 21, 2025 and March 31, 2025).

Fu Guangyi v. Beihai City Haicheng District People's Government [符广艺诉北海市海城区人民政府信息公开案] (Guangxi Zhuang Autonomous Region Beihai City Intermediate Court, June 29, 2017) https://wenshu.court.gov.cn/ (registration needed for access) (accessed between February 21, 2025 and March 31, 2025).

Fu Shuqing v. Chongqing City Changshou District Public Security Bureau [傅淑清诉重庆市长寿区公安局信息公开案] (Chongqing City Changshou District Trial Court, April 17, 2019)https://wenshu.court.gov.cn/ (registration needed for access) (accessed between February 21, 2025 and March 31, 2025).

Fu Tianxi, et al. v. Honghu Municipal People's Government [付天喜等诉洪湖市人民政府信息公开案] (Hubei Province Jingzhou City Intermediate Court, October 23, 2018). https://wenshu.court.gov.cn/ (registration needed for access) (accessed between February 21, 2025 and March 31, 2025).

Fu Wenrong v. State Grid Yiwu Electricity Supply Company [傅文荣诉国网浙江义乌市供电公司信息公开案](Zhejiang Province Jinhua City Intermediate Court, September 18, 2017). https://wenshu.court.gov.cn/ (registration needed for access) (accessed between February 21, 2025 and March 31, 2025).

Gao Fuyun and Yun Zhonghe v. Inner Mongolia Autonomous Region People's Government [高福云与云中和诉内蒙古自治区人民政府信息公开案] (Inner Mongolia Autonomous Region Hohhot City Intermediate Court, April 2, 2018) https://wenshu.court.gov.cn/ (registration needed for access) (accessed between February 21, 2025 and March 31, 2025).

Gao Lichun v. Suzhou City National High-Tech Industrial Development Zone Development and Reform Commission and Suzhou City Huqiu District People's Government [高利春诉苏州国家高新技术产业开发区经济发展和改革局并苏州市虎丘区人民政府信息公开案] (Jiangsu Province Suzhou City Huqiu District Trial Court, February 8, 2018) https://wenshu.court.gov.cn/ (registration needed for access) (accessed between February 21, 2025 and March 31, 2025).

Gao Yanhua v. Beijing City Xicheng District People's Government [高艳华诉北京市西城区人民政府信息公开案] (Beijing City No. 4 Intermediate Court, October 21, 2019) https://wenshu.court.gov.cn/ (registration needed for access) (accessed between February 21, 2025 and March 31, 2025).

Gao Yongchen v. Tangshan Municipal People's Government [高永臣诉唐山市人民政府信息公开案] (Hebei Province Tangshan City Intermediate Court, June 15, 2018) https://wenshu.court.gov.cn/ (registration needed for access) (accessed between February 21, 2025 and March 31, 2025).

Geng Chaochao v. Hangzhou Xiaoshan Environment Group Company [耿超超诉杭州萧山环境集团有限公司信息公开案] (Zhejiang Province Hangzhou City Intermediate Court, December 29, 2020). https://wenshu.court.gov.cn/ (registration needed for access) (accessed between February 21, 2025 and March 31, 2025).

Geng Jiafeng v. Huantai County People's Government [耿家峰诉桓台县人民政府信息公开案] (China Supreme Court, December 23, 2019) https://wenshu.court.gov.cn/ (registration needed for access) (accessed between February 21, 2025 and March 31, 2025).

Geng Liping v. Tangshan City Center for Municipal Engineering and Environmental Sanitation [耿丽萍诉唐山市市政工程环境卫生事务中心信息公开案] (Hebei Province Tangshan City Intermediate Court, September 24, 2020). https://wenshu.court.gov.cn/ (registration needed for access) (accessed between February 21, 2025 and March 31, 2025).

Gong Chengyuan v. Urumqi Municipal People's Government [龚成元诉乌鲁木齐市人民政府信息公开案] (Xinjiang Autonomous Region Urumqi City Intermediate Court, April 6, 2021) https://wenshu.court.gov.cn/ (registration needed for access) (accessed between February 21, 2025 and March 31, 2025).

Gu Fengxiao v. Beijing Xingchuang Investment Company [谷凤孝诉北京兴创投资有限公司信息公开案] (Beijing City No.2 Intermediate Court, September 18, 2015). https://wenshu.court.gov.cn/ (registration needed for access) (accessed between February 21, 2025 and March 31, 2025).

Gu Hongru v. Wen County People's Government [顾鸿茹诉温县人民政府信息公开案] (Henan Province Jiaozuo City Intermediate Court, March 18, 2019) https://wenshu.court.gov.cn/ (registration needed for access) (accessed between February 21, 2025 and March 31, 2025).

Gu Ming v. China Mobile Suqian Branch [顾明诉中国移动通信集团江苏有限公司宿迁分公司信息公开案] (Jiangsu Province Xuqian City Intermediate Court, December 29, 2020). https://wenshu.court.gov.cn/ (registration needed for access) (accessed between February 21, 2025 and March 31, 2025).

Guangzhou Famous Store Management Company v. Guangdong Airport Authority [广州市睿杰名店管理有限公司诉广东省机场管理集团有限公司信息公开案] (Guangdong Province High Court, November 20, 2017). https://wenshu.court.gov.cn/ (registration needed for access) (accessed between February 21, 2025 and March 31, 2025).

Gui Kangjie v. Hubei Province Xiaochang County People's Government [桂康杰诉湖北省孝昌县人民政府信息公开案] (Hubei Province Xiaogan City Intermediate Court, December 24, 2019) https://wenshu.court.gov.cn/ (registration needed for access) (accessed between February 21, 2025 and March 31, 2025).

Guo Bing v. China State Railway Group Company [郭兵诉中国铁路总公司信息公开案] (Beijing City High Court, November 12, 2019). https://wenshu.court.gov.cn/ (registration needed for access) (accessed between February 21, 2025 and March 31, 2025).

Guo Junmei v. Shenzhen City Management Center for Public hospitals [郭俊梅诉深圳市公立医院管理中心信息公开案] (Guangdong Province Shenzhen City Intermediate Court, October 8, 2015). https://wenshu.court.gov.cn/ (registration needed for access) (accessed between February 21, 2025 and March 31, 2025).

Guo Junmei v. Shenzhen Public Hospital Management Center [郭俊梅诉深圳市公立医院管理中心信息公开案] (Guangdong Province Shenzhen City Intermediate Court, October 8, 2015), https://wenshu.court.gov.cn/ (registration needed for access) (accessed between February 21, 2025 and March 31, 2025).

Guo Meirong v. Xuchang Municipal People's Government [郭美荣诉许昌市人民政府信息公开案] (Henan Province Xuchang City Intermediate Court, November 18, 2020) https://wenshu.court.gov.cn/ (registration needed for access) (accessed between February 21, 2025 and March 31, 2025).

Guo Wenchun v. Ningxia Hui Autonomous Region Commission for Health and Family Planning [郭文春诉宁夏回族自治区卫生和计划生育委员会信息公开案] (Ningxia Hui Autonomous Region Yinchuan City Xingqing District Trial Court, March 22, 2018) https://wenshu.court.gov.cn/ (registration needed for access) (accessed between February 21, 2025 and March 31, 2025).

Guo Zheng v. Cangzhou Sports Management Center [郭正诉沧州体育管理中心信息公开案] (Hebei Province Cangzhou City Intermediate Court, October 10, 2020). https://wenshu.court.gov.cn/ (registration needed for access) (accessed between February 21, 2025 and March 31, 2025).

Guo Zijun, et al. v. Shandong Provincial People's Government [郭自军等诉山东省人民政府信息公开案] (Shandong Province High Court, September 20, 2016) https://wenshu.court.gov.cn/ (registration needed for access) (accessed between February 21, 2025 and March 31, 2025).

Han Junxue v. Linzhou Municipal Bureau of Public Security [韩俊学诉林州市公安局信息公开案] (Henan Province High Court, September 13, 2018) https://wenshu.court.gov.cn/ (registration needed for access) (accessed between February 21, 2025 and March 31, 2025).

Han Linghua v. Xuchang Municipal People's Government [韩玲花诉许昌市人民政府信息公开案] (Henan Province Xuchang City Intermediate Court, November 18, 2020) https://wenshu.court.gov.cn/ (registration needed for access) (accessed between February 21, 2025 and March 31, 2025).

Han Xiangjun, et al. v. Gushi County People's Government [韩祥军等诉固始县人民政府信息公开案] (Henan Province Xinyang City Intermediate Court, July 10, 2020) https://wenshu.court.gov.cn/ (registration needed for access) (accessed between February 21, 2025 and March 31, 2025).

Hangzhou Huayuan Hotel v. Hangzhou City Xiacheng District People's Government [杭州华园宾馆有限公司诉杭州市下城区人民政府信息公开案] (Zhejiang Province Hangzhou City Intermediate Court, September 28, 2020) https://wenshu.court.gov.cn/ (registration needed for access) (accessed between February 21, 2025 and March 31, 2025).

He Dan v. Ningxia Hui Autonomous Region Health and Family Planning Commission [何丹诉宁夏回族自治区卫生和计划生育委员会信息公开案] (Ningxia Hui Autonomous Region Yinchuan City Xingqing District Trial Court, March 22, 2018) https://wenshu.court.gov.cn/ (registration needed for access) (accessed between February 21, 2025 and March 31, 2025).

He Gailan v. Xi'an Municipal People's Government and Shaanxi Provincial People's Government [何改兰诉西安市人民政府与陕西省人民政府信息公开案] (Shaanxi Province Xi'an Railway Transport Intermediate Court, November 19, 2019). https://wenshu.court.gov.cn/ (registration needed for access) (accessed between February 21, 2025 and March 31, 2025).

He Xiuqing v. Nanchong Municipal People's Government and Sichuan Provincial People's Government [何秀清诉南充市人民政府与四川省人民政府信息公开案] (Sichuan Province Nanchong City Intermediate Court, October 10, 2019) https://wenshu.court.gov.cn/ (registration needed for access) (accessed between February 21, 2025 and March 31, 2025).

He Yufu v. Jilin City Fengman District People's Government [何玉馥诉吉林市丰满区人民政府信息公开案] (Jilin Province Jilin City Intermediate Court, August 1, 2018). https://wenshu.court.gov.cn/ (registration needed for access) (accessed between February 21, 2025 and March 31, 2025).

He Yurui v. Nanyang City Wolong District People's Government [何玉蕊诉南阳市卧龙区人民政府信息公开案] (Henan Province Nanyang City Intermediate Court, January 26, 2021) https://wenshu.court.gov.cn/ (registration needed for access) (accessed between February 21, 2025 and March 31, 2025).

Hengfeng County Xuhai Renewable Resources Company v. State Grid Hengfeng County Electricity Supply Company [横峰县徐海再生资源有限公司诉国网江西省电力有限公司横峰县供电分公司信息公开案] (Jiangxi Province High Court, December 17, 2020). https://wenshu.court.gov.cn/ (registration needed for access) (accessed between February 21, 2025 and March 31, 2025).

Hongyilong Investment Management Company v. China Securities Regulatory Commission Xiamen Branch [宏亿隆投资管理有限公司诉中国证券监督管理委员会厦门监管局信息公开案] (Fujian Province Xiamen City Siming District Trial Court, December 13, 2017) https://wenshu.court.gov.cn/ (registration needed for access) (accessed between February 21, 2025 and March 31, 2025).

Hongyilong Investment Management Company v. National Small and Medium Enterprise Stock Transfer System [宏亿隆投资管理有限公司诉全国中小企业股份转让系统有限责任公司信息公开案] (Beijing City High Court, December 7, 2018). https://wenshu.court.gov.cn/ (registration needed for access) (accessed between February 21, 2025 and March 31, 2025).

Hu Dongsheng v. Beijing Municipal Department of Public Security [胡东升诉北京市公安局信息公开案] (Beijing City Dongcheng District Trial Court, April 29 2019) https://wenshu.court.gov.cn/ (registration needed for access) (accessed between February 21, 2025 and March 31, 2025).

Hu Guiqin v. Chongqing City Yubei District People's Government and Chongqing Municipal People's Government [胡贵琴诉重庆市渝北区人民政府与重庆市人民政府信息公开案] (Chongqing High Court, April 12, 2018) https://wenshu.court.gov.cn/ (registration needed for access) (accessed between February 21, 2025 and March 31, 2025).

Hu Weijuan v. Jiangxi Provincial People's Government [胡微娟诉江西省人民政府信息公开案](Jiangxi Province Nanchang Railway Transport Intermediate Court, June 25, 2018) https://wenshu.court.gov.cn/ (registration needed for access) (accessed between February 21, 2025 and March 31, 2025).

Hu Xiuhua v. Beijing City Fengtai District Bureau of Public Security [胡秀华诉北京市公安局丰台分局信息公开案] (Beijing City Fengtai District Trial Court, February 23, 2021) https://wenshu.court.gov.cn/ (registration needed for access) (accessed between February 21, 2025 and March 31, 2025).

Hu Yukun v. Peking University [胡玉坤诉北京大学信息公开案] (Beijing City No.1 Intermediate Court, April 24, 2019). https://wenshu.court.gov.cn/ (registration needed for access) (accessed between February 21, 2025 and March 31, 2025).

Hu Zhengli v. Guizhou Provincial People's Government [胡正礼诉贵州省人民政府信息公开案] (Guizhou Province Guiyang City Intermediate Court, December 4, 2019) https://wenshu.court.gov.cn/ (registration needed for access) (accessed between February 21, 2025 and March 31, 2025).

Hu Zhengqun v. Guizhou Provincial People's Government [胡正群诉贵州省人民政府信息公开案] (Guizhou Province Guiyang City Intermediate Court, December 4, 2019) https://wenshu.court.gov.cn/ (registration needed for access) (accessed between February 21, 2025 and March 31, 2025).

Hua Wenmao v. Beijing City Tongzhou District People's Government [花文茂诉北京市通州区人民政府信息公开案] (Beijing City No. 3 Intermediate

Court, April 18, 2014) https://wenshu.court.gov.cn/ (registration needed for access) (accessed between February 21, 2025 and March 31, 2025).

Huang Jinlan v. Jiangsu Province Nanjing Municipal Bureau of Public Security Gulou Branch [黄金兰诉江苏省南京市公安局鼓楼分局信息公开案] (Jiangsu Province High Court, December 16, 2019) https://wenshu.court.gov.cn/ (registration needed for access) (accessed between February 21, 2025 and March 31, 2025).

Huang Longyuan v. Zunyi County People's Government [黄龙远诉遵义县人民政府信息公开案] (Guizhou Province High Court, June 24, 2016) https://wenshu.court.gov.cn/ (registration needed for access) (accessed between February 21, 2025 and March 31, 2025).

Huang Qunlin v. Miluo Municipal People's Government [黄群琳诉汨罗市人民政府信息公开案] (Hunan Province Yueyang City Intermediate Court, November 20, 2020) https://wenshu.court.gov.cn/ (registration needed for access) (accessed between February 21, 2025 and March 31, 2025).

Huang Shengkun v. Liancheng County People's Government [黄盛坤诉连城县人民政府信息公开案] (Fujian Province Longyan City Intermediate Court, May 30, 2019) https://wenshu.court.gov.cn/ (registration needed for access) (accessed between February 21, 2025 and March 31, 2025).

Huang Wanbi v. Chongqing City Ba'nan District People's Government [黄万碧诉重庆市巴南区人民政府信息公开案] (Chongqing City No.5 Intermediate Court, December 16, 2019) https://wenshu.court.gov.cn/ (registration needed for access) (accessed between February 21, 2025 and March 31, 2025).

Huang Yu v. Changsha Municipal People's Government [黄宇诉长沙市人民政府信息公开案] (Hunan Province High Court, December 9, 2014) https://wenshu.court.gov.cn/ (registration needed for access) (accessed between February 21, 2025 and March 31, 2025).

Huang Zhengfeng and Liu Xiaodi v. Nanjing City Traffic Transport Bureau [黄正峰与刘小弟诉南京市交通运输局信息公开案] (Nanjing Railway Transport Court, April 14, 2017) https://wenshu.court.gov.cn/ (registration needed for access) (accessed between February 21, 2025 and March 31, 2025).

Huo Weidi v. Jimsar County People's Government [霍惟迪诉吉木萨尔县人民政府信息公开案] (Xinjiang Autonomous Region Changji Hui Autonomous Prefecture Intermediate Court, May 10, 2021) https://wenshu.court.gov.cn/ (registration needed for access) (accessed between February 21, 2025 and March 31, 2025).

Jia Longzhou v. Xi'an City Lintong District People's Government [贾龙洲诉西安市临潼区人民政府信息公开案] (Shaanxi Province Xi'an Railway Transport Intermediate Court, April 17, 2018) https://wenshu.court.gov.cn/ (registration needed for access) (accessed between February 21, 2025 and March 31, 2025).

Jia Youbao v. Beijing Mass Transit Railway Operation Corporation[贾友宝诉北京京港地铁公司有限公司信息公开案] (Beijing City No.2 Intermediate Court, June 14, 2019). https://wenshu.court.gov.cn/ (registration needed for access) (accessed between February 21, 2025 and March 31, 2025).

Jia Youbao v. Beijing Municipal Administration & Communication Car Company [贾友宝诉北京市政交通一卡通有限公司信息公开案] (Beijing City No. 1 Intermediate Court, June 9, 2020). https://wenshu.court.gov.cn/ (registration needed for access) (accessed between February 21, 2025 and March 31, 2025).

Jia Youbao v. Beijing Public Transport Corporation [贾友宝诉北京公共交通控股集团有限公司信息公开案] (Beijing City Fengtai District Trial Court, January 15, 2019). https://wenshu.court.gov.cn/ (registration needed for access) (accessed between February 21, 2025 and March 31, 2025).

Jia Youbao v. Beijing Xianglong Bus Passenger Transport Company [贾友宝诉北京祥龙公交客运有限公司信息公开案] (Beijing City No.1 Intermediate Court, December 10, 2019). https://wenshu.court.gov.cn/ (registration needed for access) (accessed between February 21, 2025 and March 31, 2025).

Jia Youbao v. Beijing Xiaoju Technology Company [贾友宝诉北京小桔科技有限公司信息公开案] (Beijing City High Court, February 25, 2020). https://wenshu.court.gov.cn/ (registration needed for access) (accessed between February 21, 2025 and March 31, 2025).

Jia Youbao v. China Mobile Qingdao Branch [贾友宝诉中国移动通信集团山东有限公司青 岛分公司信息公开案] (Shandong Province High Court, January 31, 2019). https://wenshu.court.gov.cn/ (registration needed for access) (accessed between February 21, 2025 and March 31, 2025).

Jia Youbao v. China Postal Express & Logistics Corporation [贾友宝诉中国邮政速递物流股份有限公司信息公开案] (Beijing City No.2 Intermediate Court, January 29, 2019). https://wenshu.court.gov.cn/ (registration needed for access) (accessed between February 21, 2025 and March 31, 2025).

Jia Youbao v. China State Railway Group Company [贾友宝诉中国铁路总公司信息公开案] (Beijing City High Court, April 23, 2019). https://wenshu.court.gov.cn/ (registration needed for access) (accessed between February 21, 2025 and March 31, 2025).

Jia Youbao v. China Telecommunications Corporation Beijing Branch [贾友宝诉中国电信股份有限公司北京分公司信息公开案] (Beijing City High Court, December 5, 2018). https://wenshu.court.gov.cn/ (registration needed for access) (accessed between February 21, 2025 and March 31, 2025).

Jia Youbao v. China United Network Communication Group Beijing Branch [贾友宝诉中国联合网络通信有限公司北京市分公司信息公开案] (Beijing City No.2 Intermediate Court, November 23, 2018). https://wenshu.court.gov.cn/ (registration needed for access) (accessed between February 21, 2025 and March 31, 2025).

Jia Youbao v. China United Network Communication Group Qingdao Branch [贾友宝诉中国联合网络通信有限公司青岛市分公司信息公开案] (Shandong Province High Court, January 31, 2019). https://wenshu.court.gov.cn/ (registration needed for access) (accessed between February 21, 2025 and March 31, 2025).

Jia Youbao v. Communication University of China [贾友宝诉中国传媒大学信息公开案] (Beijing City Chaoyang District Trial Court, February 13, 2018). https://wenshu.court.gov.cn/ (registration needed for access) (accessed between February 21, 2025 and March 31, 2025).

Jia Youbao v. Great Wall Broadband Network Service Corporation Qingdao Branch [贾友宝诉长城宽网络服务有限公司青岛分公司信息公开案] (Shandong Province Qingdao City Intermediate Court, March 22, 2018). https://wenshu.court.gov.cn/ (registration needed for access) (accessed between February 21, 2025 and March 31, 2025).

Jia Youbao v. Shandong Broadcast & TV Network Company [贾友宝诉山东广电网络有限公司信息公开案] (Shandong Province High Court, November 20, 2018). https://wenshu.court.gov.cn/ (registration needed for access) (accessed between February 21, 2025 and March 31, 2025).

Jiang Aiming, et al. v. State Grid Corporation of China [姜爱明等诉国家电网信息公开案] (Beijing City High Court, July 6, 2017). https://wenshu.court.gov.cn/ (registration needed for access) (accessed between February 21, 2025 and March 31, 2025).

Jiang Xinqiao v. Mohe Municipal People's Government [蒋新巧诉漠河市人民政府信息公开案] (Heilongjiang Province Da Hinggan Ling Prefecture Intermediate Court, April 25, 2018) https://wenshu.court.gov.cn/ (registration needed for access) (accessed between February 21, 2025 and March 31, 2025).

Jiang Yifei, et al. v. Guilin Municipal Bureau of Ecological and Environmental Protection [蒋以飞等诉桂林市生态环境局信息公开案] (Guangxi Zhuang Autonomous Region High Court, December 31, 2020) https://wenshu.court.gov.cn/ (registration needed for access) (accessed between February 21, 2025 and March 31, 2025).

Jiang Yuelin v. Shulan Municipal People's Government [姜跃林诉舒兰市人民政府信息公开案](Jilin Province Jilin City Intermediate Court, May 29, 2019) https://wenshu.court.gov.cn/ (registration needed for access) (accessed between February 21, 2025 and March 31, 2025).

Jiang Yumin v. Changzhou City Zhonglou District People's Government [姜毓敏诉常州市钟楼区人民政府信息公开案] (Jiangsu Province Changzhou City Intermediate Court, January 15, 2014) https://wenshu.court.gov.cn/ (registration needed for access) (accessed between February 21, 2025 and March 31, 2025).

Jiangsu Yongda Pharmaceutical Company v. Yancheng Municipal People's Government [江苏永大药业有限公司诉盐城市人民政府信息公开案] (Jiangsu Province Yancheng City Intermediate Court, June 28, 2019) https://wenshu.court.gov.cn/ (registration needed for access) (accessed between February 21, 2025 and March 31, 2025).

Jiangxi Haojing Rice Industry Limited Company v. Suichuan County People's Government and Ji'an Municipal People's Government [江西好景米业有限公司诉遂川县人民政府与吉安市人民政府信息公开案] (Jiangxi Province Ji'an City Intermediate Court, October 28, 2018) https://wenshu.court.gov.cn/ (registration needed for access) (accessed between February 21, 2025 and March 31, 2025).

Jiao Qihong v. Hefei High-tech Industrial Development Zone Management Council for Baiyan Science and Technology Park [焦其红诉合肥高新技术产业开发区柏堰科技园管理委员会信息公开案] (Anhui Province Feixi County Trial Court, December 20, 2018). https://wenshu.court.gov.cn/ (registration needed for access) (accessed between February 21, 2025 and March 31, 2025).

Jin Min v. Xingyi Municipal People's Government [金敏诉兴义市人民政府信息公开案] (Guizhou Province High Court, August 30, 2020) https://wenshu.court.gov.cn/ (registration needed for access) (accessed between February 21, 2025 and March 31, 2025).

Ju Bangyu v. Harbin City Pingfang District Bureau of Economic Development [鞠帮宇诉哈尔滨市平房区经济发展局信息公开案] (Heilongjiang Province Harbin City Pingfang District Trial Court, December 25, 2018) https://wenshu.court.gov.cn/ (registration needed for access) (accessed between February 21, 2025 and March 31, 2025).

Ju Hongqin v. Weihai Municipal People's Government [鞠红芹诉威海市人民政府信息公开案] (Shandong Province Weihai City Intermediate Court, December 15, 2017) https://wenshu.court.gov.cn/ (registration needed for access) (accessed between February 21, 2025 and March 31, 2025).

Ju Xianying, et al. v. Pei County People's Government [居宪营等诉沛县人民政府信息公开案] (Jiangsu Province Xuzhou City Intermediate Court, May 31, 2019) https://wenshu.court.gov.cn/ (registration needed for access) (accessed between February 21, 2025 and March 31, 2025).

Ke Yuehui v. China Telecom Guangdong Branch [柯跃辉诉中国电信股份有限公司广东分公司信息公开案] (Guangdong Province Guangzhou City Intermediate Court, October 13, 2015). https://wenshu.court.gov.cn/ (registration needed for access) (accessed between February 21, 2025 and March 31, 2025).

Kong Lingjie v. Zhengzhou City Jinshui District People's Government [孔令杰诉郑州市金水区人民政府信息公开案] (Zhengzhou Railway Transport Intermediate Court, October 27, 2016)https://wenshu.court.gov.cn/ (registration

needed for access) (accessed between February 21, 2025 and March 31, 2025).

Kuang Meimei v. Anyang Municipal Bureau of Public Security Yindu Branch [匡海梅诉安阳市公安局殷都分局信息公开案] (Henan Province Anyang City Beiguan District Trial Court, September 26, 2017) https://wenshu.court.gov.cn/ (registration needed for access) (accessed between February 21, 2025 and March 31, 2025).

Kuang Tianfang v. Suining Municipal People's Government [旷天放诉遂宁市人民政府信息公开案] (Sichuan Province Suining City Intermediate Court, November 30, 2018) https://wenshu.court.gov.cn/ (registration needed for access) (accessed between February 21, 2025 and March 31, 2025).

Lei Xiangda v. Shuicheng County People's Government [雷祥达诉水城县人民政府信息公开案] (Guizhou Province Liupanshui City Intermediate Court, July 16, 2018) https://wenshu.court.gov.cn/ (registration needed for access) (accessed between February 21, 2025 and March 31, 2025).

Lei Yingsu v. Chongqing Municipal People's Government [雷应素诉重庆市人民政府信息公开案] (Chongqing City No.5 Intermediate Court, August 21, 2018) https://wenshu.court.gov.cn/ (registration needed for access) (accessed between February 21, 2025 and March 31, 2025).

Li Anlin v. Henan Provincial Health Commission and Henan Provincial People's Government [李安林诉河南省卫生健康委员会与河南省人民政府信息公开案] (Henan Province Zhengzhou National High and New Technology Industries Development Zone Trial Court, October 26, 2020) https://wenshu.court.gov.cn/ (registration needed for access) (accessed between February 21, 2025 and March 31, 2025).

Li Bangjun v. China Ministry of Public Security [李帮君诉中华人民共和国公安部信息公开案] (Beijing City No. 2 Intermediate Court, December 8, 2020) https://wenshu.court.gov.cn/ (registration needed for access) (accessed between February 21, 2025 and March 31, 2025).

Li Buyun v. Yancheng City Tinghu District People's Government and Yancheng Municipal People's Government [李步云诉盐城市亭湖区人民政府与盐城市人民政府信息公开案] (Jiangsu Province Yancheng City Intermediate Court, August 10, 2020) https://wenshu.court.gov.cn/ (registration needed for access) (accessed between February 21, 2025 and March 31, 2025).

Li Chengbao v. Beijing Municipal People's Government [李成宝诉北京市人民政府信息公开案](Beijing City No.2 Intermediate Court, December 27, 2018) https://wenshu.court.gov.cn/ (registration needed for access) (accessed between February 21, 2025 and March 31, 2025).

Li Fengping v. Mohe Municipal People's Government [李凤苹诉漠河市人民政府信息公开案] (Heilongjiang Province Daxing'anling Prefecture Intermediate Court, March 30, 2021) https://wenshu.court.gov.cn/ (registration needed for access) (accessed between February 21, 2025 and March 31, 2025).

Li Guoli v. Tangshan Municipal People's Government [李国利诉唐山市人民政府信息公开案] (Hebei Province Tangshan City Intermediate Court, December 16, 2019) https://wenshu.court.gov.cn/ (registration needed for access) (accessed between February 21, 2025 and March 31, 2025).

Li Hanhe v. Hunan Province Information Center for Land and Resources [李汉和诉湖南省国土资源信息中心信息公开案] (Hunan Province Changsha City Intermediate Court, August 15, 2018). https://wenshu.court.gov.cn/ (registration needed for access) (accessed between February 21, 2025 and March 31, 2025).

Li Hong v. Anhui Provincial People's Government [李红诉安徽省人民政府政府信息公开案] (Anhui Province High Court, October 9, 2014) https://wenshu.court.gov.cn/ (registration needed for access) (accessed between February 21, 2025 and March 31, 2025).

Li Hong v. Zhengzhou City Zhongyuan District People's Government [李宏诉郑州市中原区人民政府信息公开案] (Henan Province High Court, May 23, 2016) https://wenshu.court.gov.cn/ (registration needed for access) (accessed between February 21, 2025 and March 31, 2025).

Li Jinghai v. Wafangdian City Public Housing Management Office [李景海诉瓦房店市房屋管理办公室信息公开案] (Liaoning Province Dalian City Intermediate Court, February 15, 2019). https://wenshu.court.gov.cn/ (registration needed for access) (accessed between February 21, 2025 and March 31, 2025).

Li Jinghai v. Wafangdian City Social Security Center for Government Agencies and Institutions [李景海诉瓦房店市机关事业单位社会保险中心信息公开案] (Liaoning Province Zhuanghe City Trial Court, May 29, 2018). https://wenshu.court.gov.cn/ (registration needed for access) (accessed between February 21, 2025 and March 31, 2025).

Li Juan v. Anshan Municipal People's Government [李娟诉鞍山市人民政府信息公开案] (Liaoning Province Anshan City Intermediate Court, June 8, 2020) https://wenshu.court.gov.cn/ (registration needed for access) (accessed between February 21, 2025 and March 31, 2025).

Li Junkun v. Zhejiang University [李俊昆诉浙江大学信息公开案] (Zhejiang Province Hangzhou City Xihu District Trial Court, August 28, 2017). https://wenshu.court.gov.cn/ (registration needed for access) (accessed between February 21, 2025 and March 31, 2025).

Li Kangnian v. Guangzhou Medical University [李抗念诉广州医科大学信息公开案](Guangdong Province Guangzhou City Intermediate Court, November 6, 2015), https://wenshu.court.gov.cn/ (registration needed for access) (accessed between February 21, 2025 and March 31, 2025).

Li Kangnian v. Guangzhou Medical University [李抗念诉广州医科大学信息公开案](Guangdong Province High Court, June 27, 2017), https://wenshu.court.gov.cn/ (registration needed for access) (accessed between February 21, 2025 and March 31, 2025).

Li Kangnian v. Guangzhou Medical University [李抗念诉广州医科大学信息公开案](Guangdong Province Guangzhou Railway Transport Intermediate Court, September 21, 2018), https://wenshu.court.gov.cn/ (registration needed for access) (accessed between February 21, 2025 and March 31, 2025).

Li Kunming v. Chongqing City Ba'nan District People's Government [李坤明诉重庆市巴南区人民政府信息公开案] (Chongqing City No.5 Intermediate Court, May 9, 2020) https://wenshu.court.gov.cn/ (registration needed for access) (accessed between February 21, 2025 and March 31, 2025).

Li Mingbo v. Nanjing City Jiang Bei New District Taxation Department, Jiangsu Provincial Tax Service, State Taxation Administration [李明柏诉国家税务总局南京江北新区税务局信息公开案] (Jiangsu Province Nanjing Railway Transport Court, July 17, 2019) https://wenshu.court.gov.cn/ (registration needed for access) (accessed between February 21, 2025 and March 31, 2025).

Li Mingliang v. Shandong Normal University [李明亮诉山东师范大学信息公开案] (Shandong Province Ji'nan City Intermediate Court, March 29, 2019). https://wenshu.court.gov.cn/ (registration needed for access) (accessed between February 21, 2025 and March 31, 2025).

Li Ruiling v. Xingyang Municipal People's Government [李瑞玲诉荥阳市人民政府信息公开案] (Henan Province Zhengzhou City Intermediate Court, August 28, 2020) https://wenshu.court.gov.cn/ (registration needed for access) (accessed between February 21, 2025 and March 31, 2025).

Li Shu'an v. Henan Provincial Administration for Market Regulation and China State Administration for Market Regulation [李树安诉河南省市场监督管理局与国家市场监督管理总局信息公开案] (Henan Province Zhengzhou National High and New Technology Industries Development Zone Trial Court, January 21, 2020) https://wenshu.court.gov.cn/ (registration needed for access) (accessed between February 21, 2025 and March 31, 2025).

Li Shuai v. Tianjin City Xiqing District People's Government [李帅诉天津市西青区人民政府信息公开案] (Tianjin City No.1 Intermediate Court, January 30, 2018) https://wenshu.court.gov.cn/ (registration needed for access) (accessed between February 21, 2025 and March 31, 2025).

Li Shuanglin v. China Railway Beijing Group Company [李双林诉北京铁路局信息公开案] (Beijing City No. 1 Intermediate Court, April 24, 2017). https://wenshu.court.gov.cn/ (registration needed for access) (accessed between February 21, 2025 and March 31, 2025).

Li Shuhua and Peng Shujun v. Zigong City Ziliujing District People's Government and Zigong Municipal People's Government [李淑华与彭术君诉自贡市自流井区人民政府与自贡市人 民政府信息公开案] (Sichuan Province Zigong City Intermediate Court, October 27, 2020) https://wenshu.court.gov.cn/ (registration needed for access) (accessed between February 21, 2025 and March 31, 2025).

Li Sihua v. Jiangxi Provincial People's Government [李思华诉江西省人民政府信息公开案] (Jiangxi Province Nanchang Railway Transport Intermediate Court, August 28, 2019) https://wenshu.court.gov.cn/ (registration needed for access) (accessed between February 21, 2025 and March 31, 2025).

Li Sihua v. Xinyu Municipal People's Government [李思华诉新余市人民政府信息公开案] (Jiangxi Province Nanchang Railway Transport Intermediate Court, September 10, 2019) https://wenshu.court.gov.cn/ (registration needed for access) (accessed between February 21, 2025 and March 31, 2025).

Li Simo v. Chongqing City Shapingba District People's Government [李思模诉重庆市沙坪坝区人民政府信息公开案] (Chongqing City No. 1 Intermediate Court, March 4, 2020) https://wenshu.court.gov.cn/ (registration needed for access) (accessed between February 21, 2025 and March 31, 2025).

Li Suzhen, et al. v. Henan Province Luoyang Municipal People's Government [李素珍等诉河南省洛阳市人民政府信息公开案] (China Supreme Court, December 19, 2019) https://wenshu.court.gov.cn/ (registration needed for access) (accessed between February 21, 2025 and March 31, 2025).

Li Wanzheng v. Zunhua Municipal People's Government [李万正诉遵化市人民政府信息公开案] (Hebei Province Tangshan City Intermediate Court, August 9, 2019) https://wenshu.court.gov.cn/ (registration needed for access) (accessed between February 21, 2025 and March 31, 2025).

Li Weiping v. Chongqing City Yongchuan District People's Government [李维平诉重庆市永川区人民政府信息公开案] (Chongqing City No.5 Intermediate Court, October 28, 2019) https://wenshu.court.gov.cn/ (registration needed for access) (accessed between February 21, 2025 and March 31, 2025).

Li Wenwen v. Guizhou Provincial People's Government [李文文诉贵州省人民政府信息公开案] (Guizhou Province Guiyang City Intermediate Court, September 6, 2018) https://wenshu.court.gov.cn/ (registration needed for access) (accessed between February 21, 2025 and March 31, 2025).

Li Wuguo v. Linxiang Municipal People's Government [李武国诉临湘市人民政府信息公开案](Hunan Province Yueyang City Intermediate Court, July 29, 2020) https://wenshu.court.gov.cn/ (registration needed for access) (accessed between February 21, 2025 and March 31, 2025).

Li Xiaoxia v. Hukou County Public Security Bureau [李小霞诉湖口县公安局信息公开案] (Jiangxi Province Jiujiang City Intermediate Court, December 7, 2020) https://wenshu.court.gov.cn/ (registration needed for access) (accessed between February 21, 2025 and March 31, 2025).

Li Xiuzhen v. Beijing Xuanfang Investment Management Group Company [李秀珍诉北京宣房投资管理集团有限公司信息公开案] (Beijing City No.2 Intermediate Court, August 13, 2020). https://wenshu.court.gov.cn/ (registration needed for access) (accessed between February 21, 2025 and March 31, 2025).

Li Xueyu v. Guiyang County People's Government [李雪玉诉桂阳县人民政府信息公开案] (Hunan Province Chenzhou City Intermediate Court, April 27, 2020) https://wenshu.court.gov.cn/ (registration needed for access) (accessed between February 21, 2025 and March 31, 2025).

Li You v. Chongqing City Ba'nan District People's Government [李游诉重庆市巴南区人民政府信息公开案] (Chongqing City No.5 Intermediate Court, November 2, 2020) https://wenshu.court.gov.cn/ (registration needed for access) (accessed between February 21, 2025 and March 31, 2025).

Li Yunping v. Kunming City Xishan District People's Government [李云萍诉昆明市西山区人民政府信息公开案] (Yunnan Province High Court, July 23, 2015) https://wenshu.court.gov.cn/ (registration needed for access) (accessed between February 21, 2025 and March 31, 2025).

Li Yuzhen v. Guizhou Provincial People's Government [李玉珍诉贵州省人民政府信息公开案] (Guizhou Province Guiyang City Intermediate Court, December 4, 2019) https://wenshu.court.gov.cn/ (registration needed for access) (accessed between February 21, 2025 and March 31, 2025).

Li Yuzhen v. Qiannan Buyi and Miao Autonomous Prefecture Municipal People's Government [李玉珍诉黔南布依族苗族自治州人民政府信息公开案] (Guizhou Province High Court, October 8, 2019) https://wenshu.court.gov.cn/ (registration needed for access) (accessed between February 21, 2025 and March 31, 2025).

Li Zhengxiang v. Taihe County Shayinghe National Wetland Park Management Bureau [李正祥诉太和县沙颍河国家湿地公园管理局信息公开案] (Anhui Province Taihe County Trial Court, November 30, 2018). https://wenshu.court.gov.cn/ (registration needed for access) (accessed between February 21, 2025 and March 31, 2025).

Li Zhiguo v. Changsha City Furong District Office for Land Acquisition and Property Demolition [李治国诉长沙市国土资源局芙蓉区分局征地拆迁事务所信息公开案] (Hunan Province Changsha City Intermediate Court, November 21, 2019). https://wenshu.court.gov.cn/ (registration needed for access) (accessed between February 21, 2025 and March 31, 2025).

Li Zhongmin v. Xinhua County People's Government [李中民诉新化县人民政府信息公开案] (Hunan Province Loudi City Intermediate Court, June 27, 2019) https://wenshu.court.gov.cn/ (registration needed for access) (accessed between February 21, 2025 and March 31, 2025).

Li Zhongwen v. Fujian Provincial People's Government [李忠文诉福建省人民政府信息公开案] (Fujian Province Fuzhou City Intermediate Court, October

26, 2019) https://wenshu.court.gov.cn/ (registration needed for access) (accessed between February 21, 2025 and March 31, 2025).

Liang Chaotang v. State Grid Liaocheng City Electricity Supply Company [梁朝堂诉国网山东省电力公司聊城供电公司信息公开案] (Shandong Province Liaocheng City Intermediate Court, December 12, 2020). https://wenshu.court.gov.cn/ (registration needed for access) (accessed between February 21, 2025 and March 31, 2025).

Liang Chaotang v. State Grid Shandong Province Electric Power Company [梁朝堂诉国网山东省电力公司信息公开案] (Shandong Province Jinan City Shizhong District Trial Court, March 29, 2021). https://wenshu.court.gov.cn/ (registration needed for access) (accessed between February 21, 2025 and March 31, 2025).

Liao Chuanshang v. Hongjiang City Center for Tourism Development Affairs [廖传上诉洪江市旅游发展事务中心信息公开案] (Hunan Province Huaihua Railway Transport Trial Court, October 30, 2019). https://wenshu.court.gov.cn/ (registration needed for access) (accessed between February 21, 2025 and March 31, 2025).

Liao Guoqing v.Huainan City Construction Investment Corporation [廖国庆诉淮南市城市建设投资有限责任公司信息公开案] (Anhui Province Huainan City Intermediate Court, June 23, 2017). https://wenshu.court.gov.cn/ (registration needed for access) (accessed between February 21, 2025 and March 31, 2025).

Liao Haijun v. Anhua County People's Government and Yiyang Municipal People's Government [廖海军诉安化县人民政府与益阳市人民政府信息公开案] (Hunan Province Yiyang City Intermediate Court, May 21, 2019) https://wenshu.court.gov.cn/ (registration needed for access) (accessed between February 21, 2025 and March 31, 2025).

Liao Xingguo v. Chongqing City Ba'nan District People's Government [廖兴国诉重庆市巴南区人民政府信息公开案] (Chongqing City No. 5 Intermediate Court, October 29, 2019) https://wenshu.court.gov.cn/ (registration needed for access) (accessed between February 21, 2025 and March 31, 2025).

Lin Fei v. China United Network Communication Group Yanbian Branch [林飞诉中国联合网络通信有限公司延边州分公司信息公开案] (Jilin Province Yanbian Korean Autonomous Prefecture Intermedia Court, September 2, 2014). https://wenshu.court.gov.cn/ (registration needed for access) (accessed between February 21, 2025 and March 31, 2025).

Lin Lan v. Chengdu City Jinjiang District People's Government [林岚诉成都市锦江区人民政府信息公开案] (Sichuan Province High Court, July 28, 2016) https://wenshu.court.gov.cn/ (registration needed for access) (accessed between February 21, 2025 and March 31, 2025).

Lin Ming v. Chongqing City Ba'nan District People's Government [林明诉重庆市巴南区人民政府信息公开案] (Chongqing City No.5 Intermediate Court, February 27, 2019) https://wenshu.court.gov.cn/ (registration needed for access) (accessed between February 21, 2025 and March 31, 2025).

Liu Chunhua v. Ordos Municipal Bureau of Supervision [刘春华诉鄂尔多斯市监察局信息公开案] (Inner Mongolia Autonomous Region Ordos City Dongsheng District Trial Court, November 20, 2017) https://wenshu.court.gov.cn/ (registration needed for access) (accessed between February 21, 2025 and March 31, 2025).

Liu Cuihua v. Renshou County Public Security Bureau [刘翠花诉仁寿县公安局信息公开案] (Sichuan Province Meishan City Dongpo District Trial Court, March 27, 2019) https://wenshu.court.gov.cn/ (registration needed for access) (accessed between February 21, 2025 and March 31, 2025).

Liu Daiqiang v. Chongqing Municipal People's Government [刘代强诉重庆市人民政府信息公开案] (Chongqing City High Court, October 31, 2016) https://wenshu.court.gov.cn/ (registration needed for access) (accessed between February 21, 2025 and March 31, 2025).

Liu Defa v. Ye County Bureau of Civil Affairs [刘德法诉叶县民政局信息公开案] (Henan Province Wugang City Trial Court, August 12, 2019) https://wenshu.court.gov.cn/ (registration needed for access) (accessed between February 21, 2025 and March 31, 2025).

Liu Dejun v. Shifang Municipal People's Government [刘德均诉什邡市人民政府信息公开案] (Sichuan Province High Court, November 28, 2019) https://wenshu.court.gov.cn/ (registration needed for access) (accessed between February 21, 2025 and March 31, 2025).

Liu Huiqing v. Dongtai Municipal People's Government [刘惠情诉东台市人民政府信息公开案] (Jiangsu Province Yancheng City Intermediate Court, April 24, 2020) https://wenshu.court.gov.cn/ (registration needed for access) (accessed between February 21, 2025 and March 31, 2025).

Liu Jiang v.The Ministry of Public Security [刘江诉中华人民共和国公安部信息公开案] (Beijing City No. 2 Intermediate Court, January 12, 2021) https://wenshu.court.gov.cn/ (registration needed for access) (accessed between February 21, 2025 and March 31, 2025).

Liu Jiankun v. Emeishan Municipal People's Government [刘建坤诉峨眉山市人民政府信息公开案] (Sichuan Province Leshan City Intermediate Court, October 14, 2020) https://wenshu.court.gov.cn/ (registration needed for access) (accessed between February 21, 2025 and March 31, 2025).

Liu Kaizhen v. Ministry of Natural Resources [刘开珍诉自然资源部信息公开案] (Beijing City No.1 Intermediate Court, April 25, 2019) https://wenshu.court.gov.cn/ (registration needed for access) (accessed between February 21, 2025 and March 31, 2025).

Liu Minying, et al. v. Chengdu Municipal People's Government [刘敏英等诉成都市人民政府信息公开案] (Sichuan Province High Court, June 30, 2014) https://wenshu.court.gov.cn/ (registration needed for access) (accessed between February 21, 2025 and March 31, 2025).

Liu Peng v. Shayang County People's Government [刘鹏诉沙洋县人民政府信息公开案] (Hubei Province Jingmen City Intermediate Court, July 26, 2018) https://wenshu.court.gov.cn/ (registration needed for access) (accessed between February 21, 2025 and March 31, 2025).

Liu Ping v. Tsinghua University [刘平诉清华大学信息公开案](Beijing City No.1 Intermediate Court, September 17, 2018). https://wenshu.court.gov.cn/ (registration needed for access) (accessed between February 21, 2025 and March 31, 2025).

Liu Qinfeng and Yao Baohua v. Changzhou City Zhonglou District People's Government [刘勤凤与姚宝华诉常州市钟楼区人民政府信息公开案] (Jiangsu Province Changzhou City Intermediate Court, December 18, 2017) https://wenshu.court.gov.cn/ (registration needed for access) (accessed between February 21, 2025 and March 31, 2025).

Liu Rongmei v. Yuan'an County People's Government [刘荣梅诉远安县人民政府信息公开案](Hubei Province Yichang City Intermediate Court, September 30, 2018) https://wenshu.court.gov.cn/ (registration needed for access) (accessed between February 21, 2025 and March 31, 2025).

Liu Shuiping v. State Grid Zhongmou County Electricity Supply Company [刘书平诉国网河南省电力公司中牟县供电公司信息公开案] (Henan Province High Court, September 21, 2018). https://wenshu.court.gov.cn/ (registration needed for access) (accessed between February 21, 2025 and March 31, 2025).

Liu Shuping v. Henan Province Zhengzhou City Zhengdong New District People's Government [刘书平诉河南省郑州市郑东新区管理委员会信息公开案] (China Supreme Court, January 21, 2020) https://wenshu.court.gov.cn/ (registration needed for access) (accessed between February 21, 2025 and March 31, 2025).

Liu Shuxiang v. Dalian City Emergency Medical Service [刘淑香诉大连市急救中心信息公开案] (Liaoning Province Dalian City Intermediate Court, June 17, 2019). https://wenshu.court.gov.cn/ (registration needed for access) (accessed between February 21, 2025 and March 31, 2025).

Liu Xian v. Shanghai City Hongkou District Bureau of Housing Security and Management [刘弦诉上海市虹口区住房保障和房屋管理局信息公开案] (Shanghai City No. 3 Intermediate Court, November 29, 2019) https://wenshu.court.gov.cn/ (registration needed for access) (accessed between February 21, 2025 and March 31, 2025).

Liu Xianguang v. Nanzhao County People's Government [刘献广诉南召县人民政府信息公开案] (Henan Province High Court, September 6, 2019) https://wenshu.court.gov.cn/ (registration needed for access) (accessed between February 21, 2025 and March 31, 2025).

Liu Xiaoyun v. Xinyu Municipal People's Government [刘晓云诉新余市人民政府信息公开案](Jiangxi Province Nanchang Railway Transport Intermediate Court, September 10, 2019) https://wenshu.court.gov.cn/ (registration needed for access) (accessed between February 21, 2025 and March 31, 2025).

Liu Xingyuan v. Tangshan Municipal People's Government [刘兴远诉唐山市人民政府信息公开案] (Hebei Province Tangshan City Intermediate Court, September 20, 2018) https://wenshu.court.gov.cn/ (registration needed for access) (accessed between February 21, 2025 and March 31, 2025).

Liu Yanmei v. Baoqing County People's Government [刘艳梅诉宝清县人民政府信息公开案] (Heilongjiang Province Shuangyashan City Intermediate Court, August 11, 2017) https://wenshu.court.gov.cn/ (registration needed for access) (accessed between February 21, 2025 and March 31, 2025).

Liu Yonghong, et al. v. Chongqing City Shapingba District People's Government [刘永红等诉重庆市沙坪坝区人民政府信息公开案] (Chongqing City No. 1 Intermediate Court, May 14, 2020) https://wenshu.court.gov.cn/ (registration needed for access) (accessed between February 21, 2025 and March 31, 2025).

Liu Yun, et al. v. Anshan Municipal People's Government [刘云等诉鞍山市人民政府信息公开案] (Liaoning Province Anshan City Intermediate Court, November 5, 2019) https://wenshu.court.gov.cn/ (registration needed for access) (accessed between February 21, 2025 and March 31, 2025).

Liu Yuxin v. Harbin Municipal People's Government [刘玉欣诉哈尔滨市人民政府信息公开案] (Heilongjiang Province Daqing City Intermediate Court, December 17, 2018) https://wenshu.court.gov.cn/ (registration needed for access) (accessed between February 21, 2025 and March 31, 2025).

Liu Zhenghua v. Yanjin County People's Government and Zhaotong Municipal People's Government [刘正华诉盐津县人民政府与昭通市人民政府信息公开案] (Yunnan Province Zhaotong City Intermediate Court, October 12, 2019) https://wenshu.court.gov.cn/ (registration needed for access) (accessed between February 21, 2025 and March 31, 2025).

Liu Zhongfeng v. Tsinghua University [刘中锋诉清华大学信息公开案] (Beijing City No.1 Intermediate Court, June 15, 2017). https://wenshu.court.gov.cn/ (registration needed for access) (accessed between February 21, 2025 and March 31, 2025).

Long Derui v. Yunnan Province Baoshan Municipal People's Government and Yunnan Provincial People's Government [龙德蕊诉云南省保山市人民政府与云南省人民政府信息公开案] (Yunnan Province Baoshan City Intermediate Court, January 22, 2021) https://wenshu.court.gov.cn/ (registration needed for access) (accessed between February 21, 2025 and March 31, 2025).

Long Taiping v. State Grid Yuanjiang Electricity Supply Company[龙太平诉国网湖南省电力公司沅江市供电分公司信息公开案](Hunan Province Yiyang City

Intermediate Court, July 27, 2017). https://wenshu.court.gov.cn/ (registration needed for access) (accessed between February 21, 2025 and March 31, 2025).

Lu Jing v. Taizhou City Jiaojiang District Bureau for Housing and Urban-Rural Development [卢京诉台州市椒江区住房和城乡建设局信息公开案](Zhejiang Province Taizhou City Jiaojiang District Trial Court, May 6, 2019). https://wenshu.court.gov.cn/ (registration needed for access) (accessed between February 21, 2025 and March 31, 2025).

Lu Lanfa v. Shanghai City Pudong New Area Bureau of Planning and Natural Resources and Shanghai Municipal Bureau of Planning and Natural Resources [陆兰法诉上海市浦东新区规划和自然资源局与上海市规划和 自然资源局信息公开案] (Shanghai City Jing'an District Trial Court, February 25, 2020) https://wenshu.court.gov.cn/ (registration needed for access) (accessed between February 21, 2025 and March 31, 2025).

Lu Xiuzhen v. Hui'an County People's Government [卢秀珍诉惠安县人民政府信息公开案] (Fujian Province Xiamen City Intermediate Court, July 23, 2019) https://wenshu.court.gov.cn/ (registration needed for access) (accessed between February 21, 2025 and March 31, 2025).

Lu Zhiming v. Yueyang City Yunxi District People's Government [卢志明诉岳阳市云溪区人民政府信息公开案] (Hunan Province Yueyang City Intermediate Court, March 1, 2021) https://wenshu.court.gov.cn/ (registration needed for access) (accessed between February 21, 2025 and March 31, 2025).

Lu Zuoyu v. Beijing City Chaoyang District Bureau of Public Security [陆祚钰诉北京市公安局朝阳分局信息公开案] (Beijing City Chaoyang District Trial Court, November 13, 2019) https://wenshu.court.gov.cn/ (registration needed for access) (accessed between February 21, 2025 and March 31, 2025).

Lujiang County Jufulou Restaurant v. China Mobile Lujiang Branch and China Mobile Anhui Branch [庐江县矾山镇聚福楼饭店诉中国移动通信集团安徽有限公司庐江县分公司与中国移动通信集团安徽有限公司信息公开案] (Anhui Province Hefei City Intermediate Court, November 14, 2019). https://wenshu.court.gov.cn/ (registration needed for access) (accessed between February 21, 2025 and March 31, 2025).

Luo Jinju v. Guizhou Provincial People's Government [罗金菊诉贵州省人民政府信息公开案] (Guizhou Province Guiyang City Intermediate Court, November 22, 2019) https://wenshu.court.gov.cn/ (registration needed for access) (accessed between February 21, 2025 and March 31, 2025).

Luo Shuqiang and Luo Shuli v. Hebei Provincial People's Government [罗术强与罗术立诉河北省人民政府信息公开案] (Hebei Province Shijiazhuang City Intermediate Court, July 25, 2019) https://wenshu.court.gov.cn/ (registration needed for access) (accessed between February 21, 2025 and March 31, 2025).

Luo Sujun v. Zhengzhou City Guancheng Hui Ethnicity District People's Government [罗素君诉郑州市管城回族区人民政府信息公开案] (Henan Province Zhengzhou City Intermediate Court, December 8, 2020) https://wenshu.court.gov.cn/ (registration needed for access) (accessed between February 21, 2025 and March 31, 2025).

Luo Wenbin v. Chengdu City Jinjiang District People's Government and Chengdu Municipal People's Government [罗文斌诉成都市锦江区人民政府与成都市人民政府信息公开案] (Sichuan Province Chengdu City Intermediate Court, March 9, 2020) https://wenshu.court.gov.cn/ (registration needed for access) (accessed between February 21, 2025 and March 31, 2025).

Luo Zhanghua v. Chengdu City Jinjiang District People's Government and Chengdu Municipal People's Government [罗章华诉成都市锦江区人民政府与成都市人民政府信息公开案] (Sichuan Province Chengdu City Intermediate Court, March 12, 2020) https://wenshu.court.gov.cn/ (registration needed for access) (accessed between February 21, 2025 and March 31, 2025).

Luo Zhongjing v. Guizhou Provincial People's Government [罗忠敬诉贵州省人民政府信息公开案] (Guizhou Province Guiyang City Intermediate Court, January 18, 2018) https://wenshu.court.gov.cn/ (registration needed for access) (accessed between February 21, 2025 and March 31, 2025).

Lv Haili v. China United Network Communication Group Jiyuan Branch [吕海利诉中国联合网络通信有限公司济源市分公司信息公开案] (Henan Province Mengzhou City Trial Court, July 30, 2018). https://wenshu.court.gov.cn/ (registration needed for access) (accessed between February 21, 2025 and March 31, 2025).

Lv Yanqin v. Gaoyi County People's Government [吕彦芹诉高邑县人民政府信息公开案] (Hebei Province Shijiazhuang City Intermediate Court, June 28, 2020) https://wenshu.court.gov.cn/ (registration needed for access) (accessed between February 21, 2025 and March 31, 2025).

Ma Juncai v. Xi'an Daxing District Commission for Comprehensive Urban Redevelopment and Management [马均才诉西安大兴新区(土门地区)综合改造管理委员会信息公开案](Shaanxi Province Xi'an Railway Transport Trial Court, June 26, 2018). https://wenshu.court.gov.cn/ (registration needed for access) (accessed between February 21, 2025 and March 31, 2025).

Ma Junling v. Harbin City Hulan District People's Government [马峻岭诉哈尔滨市呼兰区人民政府] (Heilongjiang Province Harbin City Intermediate Court, October 30, 2020) https://wenshu.court.gov.cn/ (registration needed for access) (accessed between February 21, 2025 and March 31, 2025).

Ma Junliu v. Beijing City Haidian District Bureau of Public Security [马君榴诉北京市公安局海淀分局信息公开案] (Beijing City Haidian District Trial Court,

September 2, 2020) https://wenshu.court.gov.cn/ (registration needed for access) (accessed between February 21, 2025 and March 31, 2025).

Ma Li v. Fuwai Huazhong Cardiovascular Hospital [马丽诉阜外华中心血管病医院信息公开案] (Henan Province Zhengzhou City Hi-tech Industrial Development Zone Trial Court, November 30, 2020). https://wenshu.court.gov.cn/ (registration needed for access) (accessed between February 21, 2025 and March 31, 2025).

Ma Yunqing , et al. v. China Ministry of Public Security [马云轻等诉中华人民共和国公安部信息公开案] (Beijing City No. 2 Intermediate Court, March 22, 2019) https://wenshu.court.gov.cn/ (registration needed for access) (accessed between February 21, 2025 and March 31, 2025).

Ma Zhenjun v. Xichuan County Dashiqiao Township Elementary and Junior High School [马振军诉淅川县大石桥乡中心学校信息公开案] (Henan Province Nanyang City Intermediate Court, July 20, 2017). https://wenshu.court.gov.cn/ (registration needed for access) (accessed between February 21, 2025 and March 31, 2025).

Man Guipeng v. Linghai City Service Center for Urban and Rural Development [满桂彭诉临海市城乡建设服务中心信息公开案] (Liaoning Province Jinzhou City Intermediate Court, May 22, 2020). https://wenshu.court.gov.cn/ (registration needed for access) (accessed between February 21, 2025 and March 31, 2025).

Mao Zhifan v. Changchun City Kuancheng District People's Government and Changchun Municipal People's Government [毛志范诉长春市宽城区人民政府与长春市人民政府信息公开案] (Jilin Province Changchun City Intermediate Court, July 14, 2020) https://wenshu.court.gov.cn/ (registration needed for access) (accessed between February 21, 2025 and March 31, 2025).

Mei Guiying v. Changzhou Municipal People's Government and Jiangsu Provincial People's Government [梅桂英诉常州市人民政府与江苏省人民政府信息公开案] (Jiangsu Province Nanjing City Intermediate Court, June 24, 2020) https://wenshu.court.gov.cn/ (registration needed for access) (accessed between February 21, 2025 and March 31, 2025).

Meng Haixia v. Jiangsu Provincial Department of Public Security [孟海霞诉江苏省公安厅信息公开案] (Jiangsu Province Nanjing City Intermediate Court, February 10, 2015) https://wenshu.court.gov.cn/ (registration needed for access) (accessed between February 21, 2025 and March 31, 2025).

Mengzi Hongfeng Chemical Company v. Mengzi Municipal Bureau of Education [蒙自红丰化工有限公司诉蒙自市教育局信息公开案] (Yunnan Province Mengzi City Trial Court, March 11, 2019) https://wenshu.court.gov.cn/ (registration needed for access) (accessed between February 21, 2025 and March 31, 2025).

Ming Jing and Lin Ming v. Chongqing Municipal People's Government [明静与林明诉重庆市人民政府信息公开案] (Chongqing City No. 5 Intermediate Court, December 16, 2019) https://wenshu.court.gov.cn/ (registration needed for access) (accessed between February 21, 2025 and March 31, 2025).

Mo Congxiang v. Buyi and Miao Autonomous Prefecture of QianNan Municipal People's Government [莫从香诉黔南布依族苗族自治州人民政府信息公开案] (Guizhou Province High Court, August 26, 2019) https://wenshu.court.gov.cn/ (registration needed for access) (accessed between February 21, 2025 and March 31, 2025).

Mo Congxiang v. Duyun Municipal People's Government [莫从香诉都匀市人民政府信息公开案] (Guizhou Province Qiannan Buyi and Miao Autonomous Prefecture Intermediate Court, November 23, 2020) https://wenshu.court.gov.cn/ (registration needed for access) (accessed between February 21, 2025 and March 31, 2025).

Mo Congxiang v. Guizhou Provincial People's Government [莫从香诉贵州省人民政府信息公开案] (Guizhou Province Guiyang City Intermediate Court, December 4, 2019) https://wenshu.court.gov.cn/ (registration needed for access) (accessed between February 21, 2025 and March 31, 2025).

Nan Zhongxi, et al. v. Huangling County People's Government and Yan'an Municipal People's Government [南忠喜等诉黄陵县人民政府与延安市人 民政府信息公开案] (Shaanxi Province Tongchuan City Intermediate Court, March 27, 2018) https://wenshu.court.gov.cn/ (registration needed for access) (accessed between February 21, 2025 and March 31, 2025).

Nanjing Power Supply Company [南京市锋尚国际公寓住宅小区业主委员会诉国网江苏省电力公司南京供电公司信息公开案] (Jiangsu Province Nanjing Railway Transport Trial Court, July 27, 2016). https://wenshu.court.gov.cn/ (registration needed for access) (accessed between February 21, 2025 and March 31, 2025).

Nanjing Taishan Educational Service Management Company v. Nanjing Municipal People's Government [南京泰山教育产业服务管理有限公司诉南京市人民政府信息公开案] (Jiangsu Province Nanjing City Intermediate Court, June 18, 2020) https://wenshu.court.gov.cn/ (registration needed for access) (accessed between February 21, 2025 and March 31, 2025).

Nanjing Zhang Gangning Piano Manufacturing Company v. Nanjing City Yuhuatai District People's Government [南京张钢宁钢琴制作有限公司诉南京市雨花台区人民政府信息公开案] (Jiangsu Province Nanjing City Intermediate Court, December 18, 2017) https://wenshu.court.gov.cn/ (registration needed for access) (accessed between February 21, 2025 and March 31, 2025).

Nanyang Zhenghe Information Consulting Company v. Xichuan County Dashiqiao Township Elementary and Junior High School [南阳正和信息咨询

有限公司诉淅川县大石桥乡中心学校信息公开案] (Henan Province Nanyang City Intermediate Court, November 15, 2017). https://wenshu.court.gov.cn/ (registration needed for access) (accessed between February 21, 2025 and March 31, 2025).

Ni Jinke v. Yuyao City Association for Science and Technology [倪进科诉余姚市科学技术协会信息公开案] (Zhejiang Province Ningbo City Intermediate Court, September 30, 2015). https://wenshu.court.gov.cn/ (registration needed for access) (accessed between February 21, 2025 and March 31, 2025).

Ni Yulan v. Beijing Xicheng District Center for Public Housing and Land Management [倪玉兰诉北京市西城区房屋土地经营管理中心信息公开案] (Beijing City No.2 Intermediate Court, November 25, 2019). https://wenshu.court.gov.cn/ (registration needed for access) (accessed between February 21, 2025 and March 31, 2025).

Nie Cheng'an v. Chuxiong Municipal People's Government [聂成安诉楚雄市人民政府信息公开案] (Yunnan Province High Court, June 13, 2016) https://wenshu.court.gov.cn/ (registration needed for access) (accessed between February 21, 2025 and March 31, 2025).

Niu Congquan v. Zhengzhou City Zhongyuan District People's Government [牛从泉诉郑州市中原区人民政府信息公开案] (Henan Province High Court, December 26, 2019) https://wenshu.court.gov.cn/ (registration needed for access) (accessed between February 21, 2025 and March 31, 2025).

Ou Hongyu and Li Fei v. Xichong County People's Government [欧洪玉与李飞诉西充县人民政府信息公开案] (Sichuan Province Nanchong City Intermediate Court, September 20, 2019) https://wenshu.court.gov.cn/ (registration needed for access) (accessed between February 21, 2025 and March 31, 2025).

Pan Gangju v. Guizhou Provincial Department of Natural Resources [潘刚菊诉贵州省自然资源厅信息公开案] (Guizhou Province High Court, July 13, 2020) https://wenshu.court.gov.cn/ (registration needed for access) (accessed between February 21, 2025 and March 31, 2025).

Pan Guomin, et al. v. Chengde City Shuangfengsi Reservoir Construction Management Bureau [潘国民等诉承德市双峰寺水库工程建设管理局信息公开案] (Hebei Province Chengde City Intermediate Court, June 15, 2017). https://wenshu.court.gov.cn/ (registration needed for access) (accessed between February 21, 2025 and March 31, 2025).

Pan Jun v. Yichang Municipal People's Government [潘俊诉宜昌市人民政府信息公开案] (Hubei Province Yichang City Intermediate Court, December 5, 2017) https://wenshu.court.gov.cn/ (registration needed for access) (accessed between February 21, 2025 and March 31, 2025).

Pan Xiaoling v. Tonglu County People's Government [潘晓凌诉桐庐县人民政府信息公开案] (Zhejiang Province Hangzhou City Intermediate Court, April

19, 2019) https://wenshu.court.gov.cn/ (registration needed for access) (accessed between February 21, 2025 and March 31, 2025).

Peng Houchang v. Chengdu City Wenjiang District Bureau of Public Security [彭厚昌诉成都市公安局温江区分局信息公开案] (Sichuan Province Chengdu City Intermediate Court, April 11, 2018) https://wenshu.court.gov.cn/ (registration needed for access) (accessed between February 21, 2025 and March 31, 2025).

Peng Longmei v. Guizhou Province Suiyang County People's Government [彭龙美诉贵州省绥阳县人民政府信息公开案] (Guizhou Province High Court, July 25, 2017) https://wenshu.court.gov.cn/ (registration needed for access) (accessed between February 21, 2025 and March 31, 2025).

Peng Xiongli v. Chengdu Municipal Bureau of Local Taxation and Sichuan Provincial Bureau of Local Taxation [彭雄丽诉成都市地方税务局与四川省地方税务局信息公开案] (Sichuan Province Chengdu City Intermediate Court, September 21, 2018) https://wenshu.court.gov.cn/ (registration needed for access) (accessed between February 21, 2025 and March 31, 2025).

Peng Xiongli v. State Taxation Administration Chongzhou Municipal Branch and State Taxation Administration Chengdu Municipal Branch [彭雄丽诉国家税务总局崇州市税务局与国家税务总局成都市税务局信息公开案] (Sichuan Province Chengdu City Intermediate Court, September 13, 2018) https://wenshu.court.gov.cn/ (registration needed for access) (accessed between February 21, 2025 and March 31, 2025).

Peng Yihe v. Guiyang Municipal People's Government and Guizhou Provincial People's Government [彭译河诉贵阳市人民政府与贵州省人民政府信息公开案] (Guizhou Province Guiyang City Intermediate Court, December 8, 2020) https://wenshu.court.gov.cn/ (registration needed for access) (accessed between February 21, 2025 and March 31, 2025).

Pu Qingrong v. Chengdu City Wuhou District Municipal People's Government [蒲清蓉诉成都市武侯区人民政府] (Sichuan Province High Court, December 9, 2019) https://wenshu.court.gov.cn/ (registration needed for access) (accessed between February 21, 2025 and March 31, 2025).

Qi De'an v. Xi'an City Baqiao District People's Government [戚德安诉西安市灞桥区人民政府信息公开案] (Shaanxi Province Xi'an Railway Transport Intermediate Court, November 12, 2020) https://wenshu.court.gov.cn/ (registration needed for access) (accessed between February 21, 2025 and March 31, 2025).

Qian Cuoliang v. Dongyang City Geshan Township People's Government [搴撮良诉东阳市歌山镇人民政府信息公开案] (Zhejiang Province Dongyang City Trial Court, August 27, 2018) https://wenshu.court.gov.cn/ (registration needed for access) (accessed between February 21, 2025 and March 31, 2025).

Qian Meiying v. Changzhou Municipal Commission for Development and Reform [钱美英诉常州市发展和改革委员会信息公开案] (Jiangsu Province Changzhou City Xinbei District Trial Court, June 17, 2019) https://wenshu.court.gov.cn/ (registration needed for access) (accessed between February 21, 2025 and March 31, 2025).

Qin Dayou v. Jianshi County People's Government [秦大由诉建始县人民政府信息公开案] (Hubei Province Enshi Tujia and Miao Automonous Prefecture Intermediate Court, November 12, 2019) https://wenshu.court.gov.cn/ (registration needed for access) (accessed between February 21, 2025 and March 31, 2025).

Qin Mingkang v. Gaoyou Municipal Bureau of Public Security [秦明康诉高邮市公安局信息公开案] (Jiangsu Province Yangzhou City Jiangdu District Trial Court, June 9, 2020) https://wenshu.court.gov.cn/ (registration needed for access) (accessed between February 21, 2025 and March 31, 2025).

Qin Yun'e v. Qidong Municipal Bureau of Affordable Housing and Urban-Rural Development [衾允娥诉启东市住房和城乡建设局信息公开案] (Jiangsu Province Nantong Economic and Technological Development Zone Trial Court, October 19, 2020) https://wenshu.court.gov.cn/ (registration needed for access) (accessed between February 21, 2025 and March 31, 2025).

Qiu Haifeng v. Haikou City Qiongshan District People's Government [邱海峰诉海口市琼山区人 民政府信息公开案] (Hainan Province High Court, December 6, 2019) https://wenshu.court.gov.cn/ (registration needed for access) (accessed between February 21, 2025 and March 31, 2025).

Qu Wenheng v. Shenyang Office of Work Capacity Evaluations and Rehabilitation Management [曲文衡诉沈阳市劳动鉴定康复管理办公室信息公开案] (Liaoning Province Shenyang City Huanggu District Trial Court, June 26, 2018). https://wenshu.court.gov.cn/ (registration needed for access) (accessed between February 21, 2025 and March 31, 2025).

Qu Zhe v. Shenyang Office of Work Capacity Evaluations and Rehabilitation Management [曲哲诉沈阳市劳动鉴定康复管理办公室信息公开案] (Liaoning Province Shenyang City Huanggu District Trial Court, June 26, 2018). https://wenshu.court.gov.cn/ (registration needed for access) (accessed between February 21, 2025 and March 31, 2025).

Ran Shufang v. Fengjie County People's Government and Chongqing Municipal People's Government [冉术芳诉奉节县人民政府与重庆市人民政府信息公开案] (Chongqing City No. 5 Intermediate Court, December 14, 2018) https://wenshu.court.gov.cn/ (registration needed for access) (accessed between February 21, 2025 and March 31, 2025).

Rao Sixia v. China State Railway Group Company [饶思霞诉中国铁路总公司信息公开案] (Beijing City No.1 Intermediate Court, April 23, 2018). https://wenshu.court.gov.cn/ (registration needed for access) (accessed between February 21, 2025 and March 31, 2025).

Rao Sixia v. Chongqing City Construction Investment Group Corporation [饶思霞诉重庆市城市建设投资(集团)有限责任公司信息公开案] (Chongqing City No.5 Intermediate Court, August 7, 2018). https://wenshu.court.gov.cn/ (registration needed for access) (accessed between February 21, 2025 and March 31, 2025).

Rao Sixia v. Chongqing-Guiyang Railway Company [饶思霞诉渝黔铁路有限责任公司信息公开案] (Chongqing City No.5 Intermediate Court, August 7, 2018). https://wenshu.court.gov.cn/ (registration needed for access) (accessed between February 21, 2025 and March 31, 2025).

Ren Heguo v. Chongqing Municipal People's Government [任和国诉重庆市人民政府信息公开案] (Chongqing City No. 5 Intermediate Court, February 3, 2021) https://wenshu.court.gov.cn/ (registration needed for access) (accessed between February 21, 2025 and March 31, 2025).

Ren Yuanyuan v. Qingjian County People's Government [任园园诉清涧县人民政府信息公开案] (Shaanxi Province Yulin City Intermediate Court, September 29, 2019) https://wenshu.court.gov.cn/ (registration needed for access) (accessed between February 21, 2025 and March 31, 2025).

Ruan Chengjun v. Fenggang County People's Government and Zunyi Municipal People's Government [阮成军诉凤冈县人民政府与遵义市人民政府信息公开案] (Guizhou Province Zunyi City Intermediate Court, April 28, 2019) https://wenshu.court.gov.cn/ (registration needed for access) (accessed between February 21, 2025 and March 31, 2025).

Sanhe Tongxin Cement Products Company v. State Grid Jibei Electric Power Company [三河市同心水泥制品有限公司诉国网冀北电力有限公司信息公开案] (Beijing City No.2 Intermediate Court, September 29, 2019). https://wenshu.court.gov.cn/ (registration needed for access) (accessed between February 21, 2025 and March 31, 2025).

Shaanxi Dazheng Electric Group Company v. Xi'an City Yanta District People's Government [陕西大正电气集团有限公司诉西安市雁塔区人民政府信息公开案] (Shaanxi Province High Court, October 25, 2016) https://wenshu.court.gov.cn/ (registration needed for access) (accessed between February 21, 2025 and March 31, 2025).

Shanghai New Wenhui Law Firm v. Zhejiang Province Monitoring Center for Press, Publication, Radio and Television [上海市新文汇律师事务所诉浙江省新闻出版广播电视监测中心信息公开案] (Zhejiang Province Hangzhou City Xihu District Trial Court, March 26, 2018). https://wenshu.court.gov.cn/ (registration needed for access) (accessed between February 21, 2025 and March 31, 2025).

Shanghai Tairui Property Development Corporation v. Shanghai City Jing'an District People's Government and Shanghai Municipal People's Government [上海泰瑞物业发展公司诉上海市静安区人民政府与上海市人 民政府信息公开案] (Shanghai City No.3 Intermediate Court, September 19, 2017) https://wenshu.court.gov.cn/ (registration needed for access) (accessed between February 21, 2025 and March 31, 2025).

Shao Mingliang v. Jiangsu Changshu Sino French Water Company [邵明亮诉常熟中法水务有限公司信息公开案] (Jiangsu Province Suzhou City Intermediate Court, March 10, 2017). https://wenshu.court.gov.cn/ (registration needed for access) (accessed between February 21, 2025 and March 31, 2025).

Shen Fengqing v. Yangzhou Municipal Health Commission [沈凤琴诉扬州市卫生健康委员会信息公开案] (Jiangsu Province High Court, July 21, 2020) https://wenshu.court.gov.cn/ (registration needed for access) (accessed between February 21, 2025 and March 31, 2025).

Shen Gongming v. Shanghai Municipal People's Government [沈公明诉上海市人民政府信息公开案] (Shanghai City No. 3 Intermediate Court, July 20, 2020)上海市第三中级人民法院二〇二〇年七月二十日 https://wenshu.court.gov.cn/ (registration needed for access) (accessed between February 21, 2025 and March 31, 2025).

Shi Chunlin v. Yilan County People's Government [史春林诉依兰县人民政府信息公开案] (Heilongjiang Province Ha'erbin City Intermediate Court, March 15, 2021) https://wenshu.court.gov.cn/ (registration needed for access) (accessed between February 21, 2025 and March 31, 2025).

Shi Huifeng v. Zhejiang University [史慧锋诉浙江大学信息公开案] (Zhejiang Province Hangzhou City Intermediate Court, April 7, 2020). https://wenshu.court.gov.cn/ (registration needed for access) (accessed between February 21, 2025 and March 31, 2025).

Shi Huiqing v. Fuzhou Municipal People's Government [施惠卿诉福州市人民政府信息公开案] (Fujian Province Fuzhou City Railway Transport Court, November 23, 2020) https://wenshu.court.gov.cn/ (registration needed for access) (accessed between February 21, 2025 and March 31, 2025).

Shi Lianyou, et al. v. Jilin Province Dunhua Municipal People's Government [师连友等诉吉林省敦化市人民政府信息公开案] (China Supreme Court, January 31, 2018) https://wenshu.court.gov.cn/ (registration needed for access) (accessed between February 21, 2025 and March 31, 2025).

Shi Weiyue v. Guizhou Provincial People's Government [石维月诉贵州省人民政府信息公开案] (Guizhou Province Guiyang City Intermediate Court, December 6, 2018) https://wenshu.court.gov.cn/ (registration needed for access) (accessed between February 21, 2025 and March 31, 2025).

Song Chunyou v. Beijing City Haidian District People's Government [宋春有诉北京市海淀区人民政府信息公开案] (Beijing City No. 4 Intermediate Court, September 18, 2015) https://wenshu.court.gov.cn/ (registration needed for access) (accessed between February 21, 2025 and March 31, 2025).

Song Kuihua v. Shenyang City Yuhong District People's Government [宋奎华诉沈阳市于洪区人民政府信息公开案] (Liaoning Province Shenyang City Intermediate Court, August 6, 2018) https://wenshu.court.gov.cn/ (registration needed for access) (accessed between February 21, 2025 and March 31, 2025).

Song Qichen v. Shandong Province Tai'an City Daiyue Notary Office [宋其臣诉山东省泰安市岱岳公证处信息公开案] (Shandong Province Tai'an City Intermediate Court, September 10, 2018). https://wenshu.court.gov.cn/ (registration needed for access) (accessed between February 21, 2025 and March 31, 2025).

Song Shuping v. Beijing City Xicheng District People's Government [宋淑萍诉北京市西城区人民政府信息公开案] (Beijing City No.4 Intermediate Court, November 4, 2019) https://wenshu.court.gov.cn/ (registration needed for access) (accessed between February 21, 2025 and March 31, 2025).

Song Weizhong v. Beijing Municipal Department of Public Security Changping Branch [宋维忠诉北京市公安局昌平分局信息公开案] (Beijing City Changping District Trial Court, June 28, 2020) https://wenshu.court.gov.cn/ (registration needed for access) (accessed between February 21, 2025 and March 31, 2025).

Song Wenchao v.Changsha Kaifu District Public Works Bureau [宋稳朝诉湖南省长沙市开福区工务局信息公开案] (Hunan Province Changsha City Kaifu District Trial Court, August 6, 2018). https://wenshu.court.gov.cn/ (registration needed for access) (accessed between February 21, 2025 and March 31, 2025).

Sun Baomei v. Beijing Xicheng District Center for Public Housing and Land Management [孙宝妹诉北京市西城区房屋土地经营管理中心信息公开案] (Beijing City No.2 Intermediate Court, October 27, 2017). https://wenshu.court.gov.cn/ (registration needed for access) (accessed between February 21, 2025 and March 31, 2025).

Sun Jiayang v. Shenyang Municipal People's Government [孙嘉阳诉沈阳市人民政府信息公开案] (Liaoning Province Shenyang City Intermediate Court, November 28, 2017) https://wenshu.court.gov.cn/ (registration needed for access) (accessed between February 21, 2025 and March 31, 2025).

Sun Jinya v. Yancheng Municipal People's Government [孙金亚诉盐城市人民政府信息公开案] (Jiangsu Province Yancheng City Intermediate Court, January 3, 2019) https://wenshu.court.gov.cn/ (registration needed for access) (accessed between February 21, 2025 and March 31, 2025).

Sun Lan v. Yancheng Municipal People's Government [孙兰诉盐城市人民政府信息公开案] (Jiangsu Province Yancheng City Intermediate Court, December 24, 2019) https://wenshu.court.gov.cn/ (registration needed for access) (accessed between February 21, 2025 and March 31, 2025).

Sun Longxiang v. Beijing Xingchuang Investment Company [孙龙祥诉北京兴创投资有限公司信息公开案] (Beijing City No.2 Intermediate Court, September 18, 2015). https://wenshu.court.gov.cn/ (registration needed for access) (accessed between February 21, 2025 and March 31, 2025).

Sun Qingjun v. Jiangsu Province Zhenjiang City Transportation Management Office [孙庆君诉江苏省镇江市运输管理处信息公开案] (Jiangsu Province Zhenjiang City Intermediate Court, December 10, 2019). https://wenshu.court.gov.cn/ (registration needed for access) (accessed between February 21, 2025 and March 31, 2025).

Sun Qingjun v. State Grid Zhenjiang Electricity Supply Company [孙庆君诉国网江苏省电力公司镇江供电公司信息公开案] (Jiangsu Province High Court, November 17, 2016). https://wenshu.court.gov.cn/ (registration needed for access) (accessed between February 21, 2025 and March 31, 2025).

Sun Yangbing v. China Mobile Anhui Branch [孙阳兵诉中国移动通信集团安徽有限公司信息公开案] (Anhui Province Hefei City Shushan District Trial Court, June 26, 2018). https://wenshu.court.gov.cn/ (registration needed for access) (accessed between February 21, 2025 and March 31, 2025).

Sun Yangbing v. China Mobile Anhui Branch[孙阳兵诉中国移动通信集团安徽有限公司信息公开案] (Anhui Province Hefei City Intermediate Court, December 18, 2019). https://wenshu.court.gov.cn/ (registration needed for access) (accessed between February 21, 2025 and March 31, 2025).

Sun Yangbing v. China Mobile Shenzhen Branch [孙阳兵诉中国移动通信集团广东有限公司深圳分公司信息公开案] (Guangdong Province Shenzhen City Intermediate Court, August 23, 2016). https://wenshu.court.gov.cn/ (registration needed for access) (accessed between February 21, 2025 and March 31, 2025).

Sun Yujian v. China Ministry of Justice [孙宇剑诉中华人民共和国司法部信息公开案] (Beijing City No. 3 Intermediate Court, April 2, 2014) https://wenshu.court.gov.cn/ (registration needed for access) (accessed between February 21, 2025 and March 31, 2025).

Sun Yujian v. Dalian Municipal People's Government [孙宇剑诉大连市人民政府信息公开案] (Liaoning Province Dalian City Intermediate Court, February 27, 2018) https://wenshu.court.gov.cn/ (registration needed for access) (accessed between February 21, 2025 and March 31, 2025).

Tang Jinghua, et al. v. Fuzhou Land Development Center [汤景华等诉福州市土地发展中心信息公开案] (Fujian Province Fuzhou City Gulou District Trial Court, April 14, 2015). https://wenshu.court.gov.cn/ (registration needed for access) (accessed between February 21, 2025 and March 31, 2025).

Tang Liangwei , et al. v. Fuzhou Municipal Land Development Center [汤俩伟等诉福州市土地发展中心信息公开案] (Fujian Province High Court, February 27, 2019) https://wenshu.court.gov.cn/ (registration needed for access) (accessed between February 21, 2025 and March 31, 2025).

Tang Libo v. Jiangsu Changshu Sino French Water Company[唐立波诉江苏常熟中法水务有限公司信息公开案] (Jiangsu Province Suzhou City Intermediate Court, March 10, 2017). https://wenshu.court.gov.cn/ (registration needed for access) (accessed between February 21, 2025 and March 31, 2025).

Tang Lizhen v. Health Commission of Guilin Municipal People's Government [唐丽珍诉桂林市卫生健康委员会信息公开案] (Guangxi Zhuang Autonomous Region Guilin City Intermediate Court, March 25, 2020) https://wenshu.court.gov.cn/ (registration needed for access) (accessed between February 21, 2025 and March 31, 2025).

Tang Moumou v. Changsha City Furong District Bureau of Urban Management and Law Enforcement and Changsha City Furong District People's Government [唐某某诉长沙市芙蓉区城市管理和行政执法局并长沙市芙蓉区人民政府信息公开案] (Hunan Province Changsha City Furong District Trial Court, January 8, 2018) https://wenshu.court.gov.cn/ (registration needed for access) (accessed between February 21, 2025 and March 31, 2025).

Tang Yanjun v. Beijing City Dongcheng District Center for Public Security and Forensic Science Services [唐延军诉北京市东城区公安司法鉴定中心信息公开案] (Beijing City Dongcheng District Trial Court, August 24, 2015). https://wenshu.court.gov.cn/ (registration needed for access) (accessed between February 21, 2025 and March 31, 2025).

Tao Wei v. Fu'ning County People's Government and Yancheng Municipal People's Government [陶卫诉阜宁县人民政府与盐城市人民政府信息公开案] (Jiangsu Province Yancheng City Intermediate Court, November 25, 2020) https://wenshu.court.gov.cn/ (registration needed for access) (accessed between February 21, 2025 and March 31, 2025).

Tian Ning v. Xi'an City Weiyang District People's Government [田宁诉西安市未央区人民政府信息公开案] (Shaanxi Province Xi'an Railway Transport Intermediate Court, May 29, 2018) https://wenshu.court.gov.cn/ (registration needed for access) (accessed between February 21, 2025 and March 31, 2025).

Tian Shuwu v. Tianjin City Jinghai District Bureau of Public Security Firefighting Unit [田树武诉天津市静海区公安消防支队信息公开案] (Tianjin City Jinghai District Trial Court, October 15, 2018)https://wenshu.court.gov.cn/ (registration needed for access) (accessed between February 21, 2025 and March 31, 2025).

Tian Xiaohua and Luo Mingfang v. Anyue County People's Government and Ziyang Municipal People's Government [田小华与罗明芳诉安岳县人民政府与资阳市人民政府信息公开案] (Sichuan Province Ziyang City Intermediate Court, April 20, 2018) https://wenshu.court.gov.cn/ (registration needed for access) (accessed between February 21, 2025 and March 31, 2025).

Tian Ye v. Liaoning Provincial Commission for Development and Reform [田冶诉辽宁省发展和改革委员会信息公开案] (Liaoning Province Shenyang

City Heping District Trial Court, January 29, 2018) https://wenshu.court.gov.cn/ (registration needed for access) (accessed between February 21, 2025 and March 31, 2025).

Tianjin Changtian Law Firm v. Tianjin City Hedong District Department of Taxation [天津长天律师事务所诉国家税务总局天津市河东区税务局信息公开案] (Tianjin City Hedong District Trial Court, December 31, 2019) https://wenshu.court.gov.cn/ (registration needed for access) (accessed between February 21, 2025 and March 31, 2025).

Tong Lihui v. Development and Reform Commission of Hunan Province [佟立辉诉湖南省发展和改革委员会信息公开案] (Hunan Province Changsha Railway Transport Trial Court, June 16, 2019) https://wenshu.court.gov.cn/ (registration needed for access) (accessed between February 21, 2025 and March 31, 2025).

Ürümqi Haida Breeding Company v. Ürümqi City Tianshan District People's Government [乌鲁木齐海达养殖有限责任公司诉乌鲁木齐市天山区人民政府信息公开案] (Xinjiang Autonomous Region Ürümqi City Intermediate Court, December 29, 2017). https://wenshu.court.gov.cn/ (registration needed for access) (accessed between February 21, 2025 and March 31, 2025).

Wan Yun v. Jiangxi Provincial People's Government [万赟诉江西省人民政府信息公开案] (Jiangxi Province Nanchang Railway Transport Intermediate Court, May 18, 2020). https://wenshu.court.gov.cn/ (registration needed for access) (accessed between February 21, 2025 and March 31, 2025).

Wang Daohong v. Hefei City Shushan District People's Government [汪道宏诉合肥市蜀山区人民政府信息公开案] (Anhui Province Hefei City Intermediate Court, April 10, 2018) https://wenshu.court.gov.cn/ (registration needed for access) (accessed between February 21, 2025 and March 31, 2025).

Wang Dejun v. China Mobile Hai'an Branch [王德军诉中国移动通信集团江苏有限公司海安分公司信息公开案] (Jiangsu Province Nantong City Intermediate Court, March 4, 2016). https://wenshu.court.gov.cn/ (registration needed for access) (accessed between February 21, 2025 and March 31, 2025).

Wang Guohai, Zhang Chunxiang and Wang Lin v. Hangzhou Land Banking Center [王国海、张春香与王林诉杭州市土地储备中心信息公开案] (Zhejiang Province Hangzhou City Xihu District Trial Court, March 1, 2016). https://wenshu.court.gov.cn/ (registration needed for access) (accessed between February 21, 2025 and March 31, 2025).

Wang Guoji v. Baoji City Jintai District People's Government [王国基诉宝鸡市金台区人民政府信息公开案] (Shaanxi Province Baoji City Intermediate Court, April 14, 2021) https://wenshu.court.gov.cn/ (registration needed for access) (accessed between February 21, 2025 and March 31, 2025).

Wang Huizhong v. Dongtai Municipal People's Government and Yancheng Municipal People's Government [王惠忠诉东台市人民政府与盐城市人民政

府信息公开案] (Jiangsu Province Yancheng City Intermediate Court, May 10, 2019) https://wenshu.court.gov.cn/ (registration needed for access) (accessed between February 21, 2025 and March 31, 2025).

Wang Jiangli v. Beijing Xingchuang Investment Company [王江力诉北京兴创投资有限公司信息公开案] (Beijing City No.2 Intermediate Court, September 18, 2015). https://wenshu.court.gov.cn/ (registration needed for access) (accessed between February 21, 2025 and March 31, 2025).

Wang Jiaxin, et al. v. Qingdao-Jinan High-Speed Railway Company [王家信等诉胶济铁路客运专线有限责任公司信息公开案] (Shandong Province Ji'nan City Intermediate Court, September 14, 2017). https://wenshu.court.gov.cn/ (registration needed for access) (accessed between February 21, 2025 and March 31, 2025).

Wang Jinyang v. Yancheng Xinyang Economic Zone Administration Committee [王金洋诉盐城市新洋经济区管理委员会信息公开案] (Jiangsu Province Yancheng City Intermediate Court, November 9, 2015). https://wenshu.court.gov.cn/ (registration needed for access) (accessed between February 21, 2025 and March 31, 2025).

Wang Juan v. Beijing Municipal Bureau of Public Security [王娟诉北京市公安局信息公开案] (Beijing City Dongcheng District Trial Court, October 27, 2017) https://wenshu.court.gov.cn/ (registration needed for access) (accessed between February 21, 2025 and March 31, 2025).

Wang Juan v. Xi'an Municipal People's Government [王娟诉西安市人民政府信息公开案] (Shaanxi Province Xi'an Railway Transport Intermediate Court, August 11, 2020) https://wenshu.court.gov.cn/ (registration needed for access) (accessed between February 21, 2025 and March 31, 2025).

Wang Leying v. Yichang Municipal People's Government [王乐英诉宜昌市人民政府信息公开案] (Hubei Province Yichang City Intermediate Court, March 18, 2019) https://wenshu.court.gov.cn/ (registration needed for access) (accessed between February 21, 2025 and March 31, 2025).

Wang Minghui v. Jilin Provincial Prison for Women and Jilin Provincial Prison Administration Agency [王明辉诉吉林省女子监狱与吉林省监狱管理局信息公开案] (Jilin Province Changchun City Intermediate Court, December 22, 2020) https://wenshu.court.gov.cn/ (registration needed for access) (accessed between February 21, 2025 and March 31, 2025).

Wang Mufa v. Huian County People's Government [王木法诉惠安县人民政府信息公开案] (Fujian Province Xiamen City Intermediate Court, December 3, 2019) https://wenshu.court.gov.cn/ (registration needed for access) (accessed between February 21, 2025 and March 31, 2025).

Wang Qiang v. Wenzhou Daily Media Group[王强诉温州日报报业集团信息公开案] (Zhejiang Province Wenzhou City Intermediate Court, March 31, 2020). https://wenshu.court.gov.cn/ (registration needed for access) (accessed between February 21, 2025 and March 31, 2025).

Wang Qingdou, et al. v. Weng'an County People's Government [王青斗等诉瓮安县人民政府信息公开案] (Guizhou Province High Court, November 14, 2018) https://wenshu.court.gov.cn/ (registration needed for access) (accessed between February 21, 2025 and March 31, 2025).

Wang Qingning v. Xianning Municipal People's Government and Hubei Provincial People's Government [王庆宁诉咸宁市人民政府与湖北省人民政府信息公开案] (Hubei Province Xianning City Intermediate Court, June 12, 2020) https://wenshu.court.gov.cn/ (registration needed for access) (accessed between February 21, 2025 and March 31, 2025).

Wang Ran v. Beijing Municipal People's Government [王然诉北京市人民政府信息公开案] (Beijing City No.2 Intermediate Court, October 25, 2018) https://wenshu.court.gov.cn/ (registration needed for access) (accessed between February 21, 2025 and March 31, 2025).

Wang Ronghua v. Feidong County No.4 People's Hospital [王荣华诉肥东县店埠镇中心卫生院信息公开案] (Anhui Province Hefei City Intermediate Court, June 11, 2020). https://wenshu.court.gov.cn/ (registration needed for access) (accessed between February 21, 2025 and March 31, 2025).

Wang Shicui v. Duyun Municipal People's Government [王时翠诉都匀市人民政府信息公开案] (Guizhou Province Qiannan Buyei and Miao Autonomous Prefecture Intermediate Court, May 10, 2018) https://wenshu.court.gov.cn/ (registration needed for access) (accessed between February 21, 2025 and March 31, 2025).

Wang Shuai v. Wenshui County Xicheng Township People's Government [王帅诉文水县西城乡人民政府信息公开案] (Shanxi Province Fenyang City Trial Court, August 24, 2020) https://wenshu.court.gov.cn/ (registration needed for access) (accessed between February 21, 2025 and March 31, 2025).

Wang Shuhua v. Zunhua Municipal People's Government [王树华诉遵化市人民政府信息公开案] (Hebei Province Tangshan City Intermediate Court, May 11, 2020) https://wenshu.court.gov.cn/ (registration needed for access) (accessed between February 21, 2025 and March 31, 2025).

Wang Wei v. China Mobile Shaanxi Branch [王伟诉中国移动通信集团陕西有限公司信息公开案] (Xi'an City Yanta District Trial Court, October 22, 2015). https://wenshu.court.gov.cn/ (registration needed for access) (accessed between February 21, 2025 and March 31, 2025).

Wang Wensheng v. Xiamen Municipal Bureau of Market Supervision [王文生诉厦门市市场监督管理局信息公开案] (Fujian Province Xiamen City Siming District Trial Court, August 13, 2019) https://wenshu.court.gov.cn/ (registration needed for access) (accessed between February 21, 2025 and March 31, 2025).

Wang Wujun v. China Mobile Tangyin Branch [王武军诉中国移动通信集团河南有限公司安阳市汤阴分公司信息公开案] (Henan Province Anyang City Intermediate Court, July 4, 2018). https://wenshu.court.gov.cn/ (registration

needed for access) (accessed between February 21, 2025 and March 31, 2025).
Wang Xiang and Li Liqiong v. Maguan County People's Government [王祥与李丽琼诉马关县人民政府信息公开案] (Yunnan Province Wenshan Zhuang and Miao Autonomous Prefecture Intermediate Court, October 30, 2019) https://wenshu.court.gov.cn/ (registration needed for access) (accessed between February 21, 2025 and March 31, 2025).
Wang Xinmei v. Yueyang Municipal People's Government [王新美诉岳阳市人民政府信息公开案] (Hunan Province Yueyang City Intermediate Court, December 15, 2020) https://wenshu.court.gov.cn/ (registration needed for access) (accessed between February 21, 2025 and March 31, 2025).
Wang Yan and Hu Jianying v. Anyue County People's Government [王燕与胡建英诉安岳县人民政府信息公开案] (Sichuan Province Ziyang City Intermediate Court, June 12, 2018) https://wenshu.court.gov.cn/ (registration needed for access) (accessed between February 21, 2025 and March 31, 2025).
Wang Yanling v. Xinxiang Municipal Bureau of Finance [王燕岭诉新乡市财政局信息公开案] (Henan Province Xinxiang City Hongqi District Trial Court, June 4, 2020) https://wenshu.court.gov.cn/ (registration needed for access) (accessed between February 21, 2025 and March 31, 2025).
Wang Yonghua v. Tianquan County People's Government [王永华诉天全县人民政府信息公开案] (Sichuan Province High Court, June 11, 2019) https://wenshu.court.gov.cn/ (registration needed for access) (accessed between February 21, 2025 and March 31, 2025).
Wang Yongjie v. Zhengzhou City Zhongyuan District People's Government [王永杰诉郑州市中原区人民政府信息公开案] (Henan Province Zhengzhou City Intermediate Court, October 28, 2019) https://wenshu.court.gov.cn/ (registration needed for access) (accessed between February 21, 2025 and March 31, 2025).
Wang Yuting v. Shanghai Municipal People's Government [王玉亭诉上海市人民政府信息公开案] (Shanghai City High Court, January 8, 2019) https://wenshu.court.gov.cn/ (registration needed for access) (accessed between February 21, 2025 and March 31, 2025).
Wang Zheliang v. Jiangsu Changshu Sino French Water Company [王哲良诉常熟中法水务有限公司信息公开案] (Jiangsu Province Suzhou City Intermediate Court, March 10, 2017). https://wenshu.court.gov.cn/ (registration needed for access) (accessed between February 21, 2025 and March 31, 2025).
Wang Zheliang v. State Grid Changshu City Electricity Supply Company [王哲良诉国网江苏省电力公司常熟市供电公司信息公开案] (Jiangsu Province Suzhou City Intermediate Court, February 28, 2017). https://wenshu.court.gov.cn/ (registration needed for access) (accessed between February 21, 2025 and March 31, 2025).

Wang Zhenbao v. State Grid Shandong Province Electric Power Company [王振宝诉国网山东省电力公司信息公开案] (Shandong Province Ji'nan City Intermediate Court, March 8, 2016). https://wenshu.court.gov.cn/ (registration needed for access) (accessed between February 21, 2025 and March 31, 2025).

Wang Zhenbao v. State Grid Shandong Province Electric Power Company [王振宝诉国网山东省电力公司信息公开案] (Shandong Province Ji'nan City Intermediate Court, February 20, 2017). https://wenshu.court.gov.cn/ (registration needed for access) (accessed between February 21, 2025 and March 31, 2025).

Wang Zhenbao v. State Grid Shandong Province Electric Power Company [王振宝诉国网山东省电力公司信息公开案] (Shandong Province Ji'nan City Intermediate Court, May 7, 2019). https://wenshu.court.gov.cn/ (registration needed for access) (accessed between February 21, 2025 and March 31, 2025).

Wang Zhongxiang v. TianjinTaida Cogeneration Company [王忠祥诉天津泰达热电公司信息公开案] (Tianjin No.2 Intermediate Court, November 1, 2017). https://wenshu.court.gov.cn/ (registration needed for access) (accessed between February 21, 2025 and March 31, 2025).

Wang Zuyu v. Guizhou Provincial People's Government [王祖玉诉贵州省人民政府信息公开案] (Guizhou Province Guiyang City Intermediate Court, November 28, 2017) https://wenshu.court.gov.cn/ (registration needed for access) (accessed between February 21, 2025 and March 31, 2025).

Wei Mingxian v. Guizhou Provincial People's Government [韦明先诉贵州省人民政府信息公开案] (Guizhou Province Guiyang City Intermediate Court, December 26, 2019) https://wenshu.court.gov.cn/ (registration needed for access) (accessed between February 21, 2025 and March 31, 2025).

Wei Shaolin v. Henan Provincial People's Government [魏少林诉河南省人民政府信息公开案] (Henan Province Zhengzhou City Intermediate Court, December 26, 2017) https://wenshu.court.gov.cn/ (registration needed for access) (accessed between February 21, 2025 and March 31, 2025).

Wei Taifang v. Chengdu Municipal Bureau of Public Security and Sichuan Provincial Bureau of Public Security [魏太芳诉成都市公安局与四川省公安厅信息公开案] (Sichuan Province Chengdu City Intermediate Court, April 18, 2019) https://wenshu.court.gov.cn/ (registration needed for access) (accessed between February 21, 2025 and March 31, 2025).

Wen Hao, et al. v. Sanya Municipal People's Government [文豪等诉三亚市人民政府信息公开案] (Hainan Province Haikou Maritime Court, November 23, 2020) https://wenshu.court.gov.cn/ (registration needed for access) (accessed between February 21, 2025 and March 31, 2025).

Wen Hongjun and Fan Lingling v. Zhengzhou City Huiji District Financial Development Corporation [温红军与范玲玲诉郑州市惠济区财务开发公司信

息公开案] (Henan Province Zhengzhou City Intermediate Court, December 4, 2020). https://wenshu.court.gov.cn/ (registration needed for access) (accessed between February 21, 2025 and March 31, 2025).

Wenda Kindergarten v. Heilongjiang Center for Disease Control and Prevention [闻达幼儿园诉黑龙江省疾病预防控制中心信息公开案] (Heilongjiang Province Harbin City Xiangfang District Trial Court, January 9, 2019). https://wenshu.court.gov.cn/ (registration needed for access) (accessed between February 21, 2025 and March 31, 2025).

Wu Baoshan v. Yongqing County People's Government [武宝山诉永清县人民政府信息公开案] (Hebei Province Langfang City Intermediate Court, October 31, 2018) https://wenshu.court.gov.cn/ (registration needed for access) (accessed between February 21, 2025 and March 31, 2025).

Wu Guoxing v. Kaili Municipal People's Government [吴国兴诉凯里市人民政府信息公开案] (Guizhou Province High Court, June 27, 2018) https://wenshu.court.gov.cn/ (registration needed for access) (accessed between February 21, 2025 and March 31, 2025).

Wu Hefa v. Qiannan Buyi and Miao Autonomous Prefecture People's Government [吴和发诉黔南布依族苗族自治州人民政府信息公开案] (Guizhou Province High Court, November 4, 2019) https://wenshu.court.gov.cn/ (registration needed for access) (accessed between February 21, 2025 and March 31, 2025).

Wu Sijuan, et al. v. Zhejiang Provincial People's Government [吴四娟等诉浙江省人民政府信息公开案] (Zhejiang Province Hangzhou City Intermediate Court, October 14, 2020) https://wenshu.court.gov.cn/ (registration needed for access) (accessed between February 21, 2025 and March 31, 2025).

Wu Wengui v. Chengdu Municipal People's Government and Sichuan Provincial People's Government [吴文桂诉成都市人民政府与四川省人民政府信息公开案] (Sichuan Province Chengdu City Intermediate Court, January 22, 2019) https://wenshu.court.gov.cn/ (registration needed for access) (accessed between February 21, 2025 and March 31, 2025).

Wu Yuankai v. Guizhou Provincial People's Government [吴元开诉贵州省人民政府信息公开案] (Guizhou Province Guiyang City Intermediate Court, December 26, 2019) https://wenshu.court.gov.cn/ (registration needed for access) (accessed between February 21, 2025 and March 31, 2025).

Wu Yuda v. Ministry of Transport [巫宇达诉中华人民共和国交通运输部信息公开案] (Beijing City No.2 Intermediate Court, July 1, 2019) https://wenshu.court.gov.cn/ (registration needed for access) (accessed between February 21, 2025 and March 31, 2025).

Wu Zaimei v. Pingxiang Hospital of Traditional Chinese Medicine [邬再梅诉萍乡市中医院信息公开案] (Jiangxi Province Pingxiang City Intermediate Court,

August 21, 2017). https://wenshu.court.gov.cn/ (registration needed for access) (accessed between February 21, 2025 and March 31, 2025).

Wu Zhongren v. Zhijin County People's Government [伍中仁诉织金县人民政府信息公开案] (Guizhou Province Bijie City Intermediate Court, October 23, 2020). https://wenshu.court.gov.cn/ (registration needed for access) (accessed between February 21, 2025 and March 31, 2025).

Wu Zhou v. Yancheng City Tinghu District People's Government and Yancheng Municipal People's Government [吴洲诉盐城市亭湖区人民政府与盐城市人民政府信息公开案] (Jiangsu Province Yancheng City Intermediate Court, November 25, 2020) https://wenshu.court.gov.cn/ (registration needed for access) (accessed between February 21, 2025 and March 31, 2025).

Wulian County Bus Company v. Wulian County People's Government [五莲县公共汽车有限责任公司诉五莲县人民政府信息公开案] (Shandong Province Rizhao City Intermediate Court, August 12, 2020) https://wenshu.court.gov.cn/ (registration needed for access) (accessed between February 21, 2025 and March 31, 2025).

Xia Guixian v. Jiangxi Provincial People's Government [夏桂县诉江西省人民政府信息公开案] (Jiangxi Province Nanchang Railway Transport Intermediate Court, April 1, 2019) https://wenshu.court.gov.cn/ (registration needed for access) (accessed between February 21, 2025 and March 31, 2025).

Xia Maogen v. Jiangxi Provincial People's Government [夏毛根诉江西省人民政府信息公开案](Jiangxi Province Nanchang Railway Transport Intermediate Court, August 28, 2019) https://wenshu.court.gov.cn/ (registration needed for access) (accessed between February 21, 2025 and March 31, 2025).

Xia Xin v. Peking Union Medical College Hospital [夏欣诉中国医学科学院北京协和医院信息公开案] (Beijing City No.2 Intermediate Court, December 25, 2015). https://wenshu.court.gov.cn/ (registration needed for access) (accessed between February 21, 2025 and March 31, 2025).

Xia Xin v. Peking Union Medical College Hospital [夏欣诉中国医学科学院北京协和医院信息公开案] (Beijing City No.2 Intermediate Court, May 18, 2015). https://wenshu.court.gov.cn/ (registration needed for access) (accessed between February 21, 2025 and March 31, 2025).

Xianyang Taixi Chemical Fertilizer Company v. Xianyang Municipal Department of Finance [咸阳太西化肥有限公司诉咸阳市财政局信息公开案] (Shaanxi Province Xianyang City Qindu District Trial Court, September 20, 2017) https://wenshu.court.gov.cn/ (registration needed for access) (accessed between February 21, 2025 and March 31, 2025).

Xiao Gui v. Huarong County People's Government [肖瑰诉华容县人民政府信息公开案] (Hunan Province Yueyang City Intermediate Court, October 9, 2020) https://wenshu.court.gov.cn/ (registration needed for access) (accessed between February 21, 2025 and March 31, 2025).

Xiao Xianhuai, et al. v. Shangyou County People's Government [肖显槐等诉上犹县人民政府信息公开案] (Jiangxi Province Ganzhou City Intermediate Court, December 17, 2019) https://wenshu.court.gov.cn/ (registration needed for access) (accessed between February 21, 2025 and March 31, 2025).

Xie Changlin v. Guiyang Municipal People's Government [谢长林诉贵阳市人民政府信息公开案] (Guizhou Province High Court, December 8, 2016) https://wenshu.court.gov.cn/ (registration needed for access) (accessed between February 21, 2025 and March 31, 2025).

Xie Meimei v. Guiyang Municipal People's Government [谢梅梅诉贵阳市人民政府信息公开案] (Guizhou Province High Court, December 8, 2016) https://wenshu.court.gov.cn/ (registration needed for access) (accessed between February 21, 2025 and March 31, 2025).

Xie Qing v. Guiyang Municipal People's Government [谢清诉贵阳市人民政府信息公开案] (Guizhou Province High Court, December 8, 2016) https://wenshu.court.gov.cn/ (registration needed for access) (accessed between February 21, 2025 and March 31, 2025).

Xie Rujing, et al. v. Zhuhai City Jinwan District People's Government [谢汝敬等诉珠海市金湾区人民政府信息公开案] (Guangdong Province Zhuhai City Intermediate Court, June 11, 2018) https://wenshu.court.gov.cn/ (registration needed for access) (accessed between February 21, 2025 and March 31, 2025).

Xie Xiaofeng v. Harbin City Xiangfang District People's Government [谢笑峰诉哈尔滨市香坊区人民政府信息公开案] (Heilongjiang Province Harbin City Intermediate Court, July 14, 2016) https://wenshu.court.gov.cn/ (registration needed for access) (accessed between February 21, 2025 and March 31, 2025).

Xie Zhaohui v. Chongqing Municipal People's Government [谢照惠诉重庆市人民政府信息公开案] (Chongqing City No.5 Intermediate Court, November 30, 2020) https://wenshu.court.gov.cn/ (registration needed for access) (accessed between February 21, 2025 and March 31, 2025).

Xie Zhi v. Guiyang Municipal People's Government [谢志诉贵阳市人民政府信息公开案] (Guizhou Province High Court, December 8, 2016) https://wenshu.court.gov.cn/ (registration needed for access) (accessed between February 21, 2025 and March 31, 2025).

Xing Chunming v. Rongcheng Municipal Bureau of Public Security [邢春明诉荣成市公安局信息公开案] (Shandong Province Rongcheng City Trial Court, March 20, 2019) https://wenshu.court.gov.cn/ (registration needed for access) (accessed between February 21, 2025 and March 31, 2025).

Xiong Shiwei, et al. v. Chongqing City Shapingba District People's Government [熊仕伟等诉重庆市沙坪坝区人民政府信息公开案] (Chongqing City No.1

Intermediate Court, March 4, 2020) https://wenshu.court.gov.cn/ (registration needed for access) (accessed between February 21, 2025 and March 31, 2025).

Xu Baoyuan v. China Ministry of Commerce [许保元诉中华人民共和国商务部信息公开案] (Beijing City No.2 Intermediate Court, May 20, 2019) https://wenshu.court.gov.cn/ (registration needed for access) (accessed between February 21, 2025 and March 31, 2025).

Xu Bin v. Tianjin Binhai New Area Xiangluowan Public Utilities Company [徐宾诉天津滨海新区响螺湾公共事业发展有限公 司信息公开案] (Tianjin City High Court, December 28, 2017). https://wenshu.court.gov.cn/ (registration needed for access) (accessed between February 21, 2025 and March 31, 2025).

Xu Chunmiao v. State Grid Zhoushan City Electricity Supply Company [徐春苗诉国网浙江省电力有限公司舟山供电公司信息公开案] (Zhejiang Province Zhoushan City Intermediate Court, February 11, 2019). https://wenshu.court.gov.cn/ (registration needed for access) (accessed between February 21, 2025 and March 31, 2025).

Xu Congdong v. China Ministry of Public Security [徐从东诉中华人民共和国公安部信息公开案] (Beijing City No. 2 Intermediate Court, October 31, 2018) https://wenshu.court.gov.cn/ (registration needed for access) (accessed between February 21, 2025 and March 31, 2025).

Xu Gen v. Chongqing City Jiulongpo District People's Government [徐根诉重庆市九龙坡区人民政府信息公开案] (Chongqing City No.5 Intermediate Court, June 29, 2020) https://wenshu.court.gov.cn/ (registration needed for access) (accessed between February 21, 2025 and March 31, 2025).

Xu Guangyue v. Chongqing City Nan'an District People's Government [徐光月诉重庆市南岸区人民政府信息公开案] (Chongqing City No.5 Intermediate Court, November 27, 2019) https://wenshu.court.gov.cn/ (registration needed for access) (accessed between February 21, 2025 and March 31, 2025).

Xu Hongyuan v. Chengdu City Shuangliu District People's Government and Chengdu Municipal People's Government [徐洪元诉成都市双流区人民政府与成都市人民政府信息公开案] (Sichuan Province High Court, July 26, 2016) https://wenshu.court.gov.cn/ (registration needed for access) (accessed between February 21, 2025 and March 31, 2025).

Xu Jiaxiu v. Guiyang Municipal People's Government [徐家秀诉贵阳市人民政府信息公开案] (Guizhou Province High Court, December 8, 2016) https://wenshu.court.gov.cn/ (registration needed for access) (accessed between February 21, 2025 and March 31, 2025).

Xu Liya v. Henan Provincial Bureau of Natural Resources [许丽亚诉河南省自然资源厅信息公开案] (Henan Province Zhengzhou National High and New Technology Industries Development Zone Trial Court, June 26, 2020) https://wenshu.court.gov.cn/ (registration needed for access) (accessed between February 21, 2025 and March 31, 2025).

Xu Qipeng, et al. v. Qingdao Municipal Bureau of Public Security Traffic Police Unit [徐启鹏等诉青岛市公安局交通警察支队信息公开案] (Qingdao City Shinan District Trial Court, June 28, 2018) https://wenshu.court.gov.cn/ (registration needed for access) (accessed between February 21, 2025 and March 31, 2025).

Xu Shanlang v. Nanjing Medical University [徐善朗诉南京医科大学信息公开案] (Jiangsu Province Nanjing City Intermediate Court, August 10, 2020). https://wenshu.court.gov.cn/ (registration needed for access) (accessed between February 21, 2025 and March 31, 2025).

Xu Shuang v. Liaoyang City Baita District Bureau of Public Security [徐爽诉辽阳市公安局白塔公安分局信息公开案] (Liaoning Province Dengta City Trial Court, May 16, 2018)辽宁省灯塔市人民法院 https://wenshu.court.gov.cn/ (registration needed for access) (accessed between February 21, 2025 and March 31, 2025).

Xu Wenyan v. Sheyang County Bureau of Planning [徐文艳诉射阳县规划局信息公开案] (Jiangsu Province Jianhu County Trial Court, September 8, 2018) https://wenshu.court.gov.cn/ (registration needed for access) (accessed between February 21, 2025 and March 31, 2025).

Xu Xianliu, et al. v. Taizhou City Gaogang District People's Government [徐先刘等诉泰州市高港区人民政府信息公开案] (Jiangsu Province Taizhou City Intermediate Court, January 28, 2021) https://wenshu.court.gov.cn/ (registration needed for access) (accessed between February 21, 2025 and March 31, 2025).

Xu Xiuwen v. Hanshan County People's Government [徐秀雯诉含山县人民政府信息公开案] (Anhui Province Maanshan City Intermediate Court, June 25, 2018) https://wenshu.court.gov.cn/ (registration needed for access) (accessed between February 21, 2025 and March 31, 2025).

Xu Yunxiang v. Xuchang Municipal People's Government [徐运祥诉许昌市人民政府信息公开案] (Henan Province Xuchang City Intermediate Court, November 18, 2020) https://wenshu.court.gov.cn/ (registration needed for access) (accessed between February 21, 2025 and March 31, 2025).

Xu Zehui v. Yuan'an County People's Government [徐泽惠诉远安县人民政府信息公开案] (Hubei Province Yichang City Intermediate Court, August 28, 2019) https://wenshu.court.gov.cn/ (registration needed for access) (accessed between February 21, 2025 and March 31, 2025).

Xu Zhuoyun v. Jiangxi Provincial People's Government [许卓云诉江西省人民政府信息公开案] (Jiangxi Province Nanchang Railway Transport Intermediate Court, July 25, 2018) https://wenshu.court.gov.cn/ (registration needed for access) (accessed between February 21, 2025 and March 31, 2025).

Xu Zhuoyun v. Nanchang Municipal Bureau of Urban and Rural Planning [许卓云诉南昌市城乡规划局信息公开案] (Jiangxi Province Nanchang City Railway Transport Trial Court, August 21, 2018) https://wenshu.court.gov.cn/ (registration needed for access) (accessed between February 21, 2025 and March 31, 2025).

Xu Zhuoyun v. Nanchang Municipal People's Government [许卓云诉南昌市人民政府信息公开案] (Jiangxi Province Nanchang Railway Transport Intermediate Court, April 12, 2019) https://wenshu.court.gov.cn/ (registration needed for access) (accessed between February 21, 2025 and March 31, 2025).

Xue Mingyuan v. Sichuan Provincial Bureau of Land and Resources and China Ministry of Land and Resources [薛明远诉四川省国土资源厅与中华人民共和国国土资源部信息公开案] (Sichuan Province Chengdu City Intermediate Court, August 17, 2017) https://wenshu.court.gov.cn/ (registration needed for access) (accessed between February 21, 2025 and March 31, 2025).

Xue Zhaohui v. Jiangsu Provincial Department of Public Security and China Ministry of Public Security [薛朝辉诉江苏省公安厅与中华人民共和国公安部信息公开案] [Beijing City Dongcheng District Trial Court, April 23, 2019] https://wenshu.court.gov.cn/ (registration needed for access) (accessed between February 21, 2025 and March 31, 2025).

Yan Qiaoying v. Taiyuan Municipal People's Government [阎巧英诉太原市人民政府信息公开案] (Shaanxi Province High Court, August 21, 2017) https://wenshu.court.gov.cn/ (registration needed for access) (accessed between February 21, 2025 and March 31, 2025).

Yan Weiguo v. Shandong Provincial People's Government [颜卫国诉山东省人民政府信息公开案] (Shandong Province Ji'nan City Intermediate Court, October 28, 2019) https://wenshu.court.gov.cn/ (registration needed for access) (accessed between February 21, 2025 and March 31, 2025).

Yan Xiantong v. Wenzhou Port Group Corporation [颜贤童诉温州港集团有限公司信息公开案] (Zhejiang Province Wenzhou City Intermediate Court, March 14, 2017). https://wenshu.court.gov.cn/ (registration needed for access) (accessed between February 21, 2025 and March 31, 2025).

Yang Chaogui v. Guizhou Provincial People's Government [杨朝贵诉贵州省人民政府信息公开案] (Guizhou Province Guiyang City Intermediate Court, December 4, 2019) https://wenshu.court.gov.cn/ (registration needed for access) (accessed between February 21, 2025 and March 31, 2025).

Yang Dehai v. Qiannan Buyi and Miao Autonomous Prefecture Municipal People's Government [杨德海诉黔南布依族苗族自治州人民政府信息公开案] (Guizhou Province High Court, August 26, 2019) https://wenshu.court.gov.cn/ (registration needed for access) (accessed between February 21, 2025 and March 31, 2025).

Yang Dezhi v. Guizhou Provincial People's Government [杨德芝诉贵州省人民政府信息公开案] (Guizhou Province Guiyang City Intermediate Court,

December 4, 2019) https://wenshu.court.gov.cn/ (registration needed for access) (accessed between February 21, 2025 and March 31, 2025).

Yang Dezhi v. Qiannan Buyi and Miao Autonomous Prefecture Municipal People's Government [杨德芝诉黔南布依族苗族自治州人民政府信息公开案] (Guizhou Province High Court, November 29, 2019) https://wenshu.court.gov.cn/ (registration needed for access) (accessed between February 21, 2025 and March 31, 2025).

Yang Enwen v. Guizhou Provincial People's Government [杨恩文诉贵州省人民政府信息公开案] (Guizhou Province Guiyang City Intermediate Court, December 6, 2018) https://wenshu.court.gov.cn/ (registration needed for access) (accessed between February 21, 2025 and March 31, 2025).

Yang Guoan v. Xiangcheng Municipal People's Government [杨国安诉项城市人民政府信息公开案] (Henan Province Zhoukou City Intermediate Court, July 26, 2018) https://wenshu.court.gov.cn/ (registration needed for access) (accessed between February 21, 2025 and March 31, 2025).

Yang Jiandong v. Jiangsu Changshu Sino French Water Company [杨建东诉常熟中法水务有限公司信息公开案] (Jiangsu Province Suzhou City Intermediate Court, March 10, 2017). https://wenshu.court.gov.cn/ (registration needed for access) (accessed between February 21, 2025 and March 31, 2025).

Yang Jiandong v. State Grid Changshu City Electricity Supply Company [杨建东诉国网江苏省电力公司常熟市供电公司信息公开案] (Jiangsu Province Suzhou City Intermediate Court, February 28, 2017). https://wenshu.court.gov.cn/ (registration needed for access) (accessed between February 21, 2025 and March 31, 2025).

Yang Jianping v. China Mobile Huizhou Branch [杨建平诉中国移动通信集团广东有限公司惠州分公司信息公开案] (Guangdong Province Huizhou City Intermediate Court, December 22, 2017). https://wenshu.court.gov.cn/ (registration needed for access) (accessed between February 21, 2025 and March 31, 2025).

Yang Jin v. Chongqing City Yuzhong District Bureau of Public Security [杨进诉重庆市公安局渝中区分局信息公开案] (Chongqing City No.5 Intermediate Court, January 5, 2021) https://wenshu.court.gov.cn/ (registration needed for access) (accessed between February 21, 2025 and March 31, 2025).

Yang Jinzhu v. China State Railway Group Company [杨金柱诉中国铁路总公司信息公开案] (Beijing City No.1 Intermediate Court, March 28, 2017). https://wenshu.court.gov.cn/ (registration needed for access) (accessed between February 21, 2025 and March 31, 2025).

Yang Jinzhu v. Wuxi City Liangxi District People's Government and Wuxi Municipal People's Government [杨金柱诉无锡市梁溪区人民政府与无锡市人民政府信息公开案] (Jiangsu Province Wuxi City Intermediate Court, July 1, 2020) https://wenshu.court.gov.cn/ (registration needed for access) (accessed between February 21, 2025 and March 31, 2025).

Yang Jinzhu v. Yancheng Municipal People's Government and Jiangsu Provincial People's Government [杨金柱诉盐城市人民政府与江苏省人民政府信息公开案] (Jiangsu Province Yancheng City Intermediate Court, July 14, 2020) https://wenshu.court.gov.cn/ (registration needed for access) (accessed between February 21, 2025 and March 31, 2025).

Yang Jun v. Tu Autonomous County of Huzhu People's Government [杨军诉互助土族自治县人民政府信息公开案] (Qinghai Province High Court, March 29, 2021) https://wenshu.court.gov.cn/ (registration needed for access) (accessed between February 21, 2025 and March 31, 2025).

Yang Lianzhao v. Wuyang County People's Government [杨连召诉舞阳县人民政府信息公开案] (Henan Province Luohe City Intermediate Court, June 25, 2019) https://wenshu.court.gov.cn/ (registration needed for access) (accessed between February 21, 2025 and March 31, 2025).

Yang Maohe v. Guizhou Provincial People's Government [杨茂和诉贵州省人民政府信息公开案] (Guizhou Province Guiyang City Intermediate Court, November 22, 2019) https://wenshu.court.gov.cn/ (registration needed for access) (accessed between February 21, 2025 and March 31, 2025).

Yang Moumou v. Guangzhou City Huadu District People's Government and Guangzhou Municipal People's Government [杨某某诉广州市花都区人民政府与广州市人民政府信息公开案] (Guangdong Province Guangzhou City Railway Transport Intermediate Court, September 25, 2018) https://wenshu.court.gov.cn/ (registration needed for access) (accessed between February 21, 2025 and March 31, 2025).

Yang Ou v. Suzhou Lawyers Association [杨鸥诉苏州市律师协会信息公开案] (Jiangsu Province Suzhou City Intermediate Court, December 30, 2019). https://wenshu.court.gov.cn/ (registration needed for access) (accessed between February 21, 2025 and March 31, 2025).

Yang Shifeng v. Guangxi Working Fitness Assessment Committee [阳世凤诉广西壮族自治区劳动能力鉴定委员会信息公开案] (Guangxi Autonomous Region Nanning Railway Transport Intermediate Court, June 24, 2019). https://wenshu.court.gov.cn/ (registration needed for access) (accessed between February 21, 2025 and March 31, 2025).

Yang Wei v. Xiangtan Municipal Bureau of Public Security [杨威诉湘潭市公安局信息公开案] (Hunan Province Xiangtan City Yuetang District Trial Court, December 21, 2020) https://wenshu.court.gov.cn/ (registration needed for access) (accessed between February 21, 2025 and March 31, 2025).

Yang Xianhua v. China Telecom Changsha Branch [杨先华诉中国电信股份有限公司长沙 分公司信息公开案] (Hunan Province Changsha City Intermediate Court, August 14, 2018). https://wenshu.court.gov.cn/ (registration needed for access) (accessed between February 21, 2025 and March 31, 2025).

Yang Xiaochun v. Dongtai Municipal People's Government [杨小春诉东台市人民政府信息公开案] (Jiangsu Province Yancheng City Intermediate Court,

September 26, 2019) https://wenshu.court.gov.cn/ (registration needed for access) (accessed between February 21, 2025 and March 31, 2025).

Yang Yang v. Zhuzhou City Public Transportation Company [杨阳诉株洲市公共交通有限责任公司信息公开案] (Hunan Province Zhuzhou City Tianyuan District Trial Court, December 24, 2018). https://wenshu.court.gov.cn/ (registration needed for access) (accessed between February 21, 2025 and March 31, 2025).

Yang Yaquan v. Wuchuan Municipal People's Government [杨亚权诉吴川市人民政府信息公开案] (Guangdong Province Zhanjiang City Intermediate Court, June 20, 2018) https://wenshu.court.gov.cn/ (registration needed for access) (accessed between February 21, 2025 and March 31, 2025).

Yang Zaiyun v. Guizhou Provincial People's Government [杨再云诉贵州省人民政府信息公开案] (Guizhou Province Guiyang City Intermediate Court, December 4, 2019) https://wenshu.court.gov.cn/ (registration needed for access) (accessed between February 21, 2025 and March 31, 2025).

Yang Zhengquan v. State Grid Shandong Electric Power Company and State Grid Feicheng City Electricity Supply Company [杨政权诉国网山东省电力公司和国网山东省电力公司肥城市供电公司信息公开案](Shandong Province Tai'an City Intermediate Court, April 24, 2017). https://wenshu.court.gov.cn/ (registration needed for access) (accessed between February 21, 2025 and March 31, 2025).

Yao Baohua v. Changzhou City Housing and Urban-Rural Development Bureau [姚宝华诉常州市住房和城乡建设局信息公开案] (Jiangsu Province Changzhou City Xinbei District Trial Court, September 4, 2019)https://wenshu.court.gov.cn/ (registration needed for access) (accessed between February 21, 2025 and March 31, 2025).

Yao Tushan v. Quzhou Land Banking Center [姚土山诉衢州市土地储备中心信息公开案](Zhejiang Province Quzhou City Intermediate Court, October 28, 2016). https://wenshu.court.gov.cn/ (registration needed for access) (accessed between February 21, 2025 and March 31, 2025).

Ye Lijuan v. Jiande Municipal People's Government [叶丽娟诉建德市人民政府信息公开案] (Zhejiang Province Hangzhou City Intermediate Court, April 2, 2019) https://wenshu.court.gov.cn/ (registration needed for access) (accessed between February 21, 2025 and March 31, 2025).

Ye Lijuan v. Zhejiang Province Jiande City Notary Office [叶丽娟诉浙江省建德市公证处信息公开案] (Zhejiang Province Jiande City Trial Court, December 5, 2018). https://wenshu.court.gov.cn/ (registration needed for access) (accessed between February 21, 2025 and March 31, 2025).

Yin Yanting v. China University of Political Science and Law [尹艳婷诉中国政法大学信息公开案] (Beijing City No.1 Intermediate Court, July 22, 2020). https://wenshu.court.gov.cn/ (registration needed for access) (accessed between February 21, 2025 and March 31, 2025).

Yu Hongli v. Chongqing City Jiulongpo District People's Government [余红丽诉重庆市九龙坡区人民政府信息公开案] (Chongqing City No. 5 Intermediate Court, March 1, 2018) https://wenshu.court.gov.cn/ (registration needed for access) (accessed between February 21, 2025 and March 31, 2025).

Yu Ping v. Nanjing City Liuhe District People's Government and Nanjing Municipal People's Government [郁平诉南京市六合区人民政府与南京市人民政府信息公开案] (Jiangsu Province Nanjing City Intermediate Court, July 31, 2020) https://wenshu.court.gov.cn/ (registration needed for access) (accessed between February 21, 2025 and March 31, 2025).

Yu Shaoli v. Beijing City Yanqing District Heating Supply Station [于少丽诉北京市延庆区市政供暖所信息公开案] (Beijing City No.1 Intermediate Court, February 24, 2018). https://wenshu.court.gov.cn/ (registration needed for access) (accessed between February 21, 2025 and March 31, 2025).\

Yu Wufang v. Wuhan Land Consolidation and Banking Center [喻五仿诉武汉市土地整理储备中心信息公开案] (Hubei Province Wuhan City Intermediate Court, February 2, 2015). https://wenshu.court.gov.cn/ (registration needed for access) (accessed between February 21, 2025 and March 31, 2025).

Yu Yi v. Henan Province Zhengzhou City Erqi District People's Government [余沂诉河南省郑州市二七区人民政府信息公开案] (China Supreme Court, March 30, 2020) https://wenshu.court.gov.cn/ (registration needed for access) (accessed between February 21, 2025 and March 31, 2025).

Yuan Fujiao v. Beijing City Xicheng District Bureau of Public Security and Beijing City Xicheng District People's Government [袁富姣诉北京市公安局西城分局与北京市西城区人民政府信息公开案] (Beijing City Xicheng District Trial Court, November 7, 2019) https://wenshu.court.gov.cn/ (registration needed for access) (accessed between February 21, 2025 and March 31, 2025).

Yuan Tie v. Capital Iron and Steel Corporation [袁铁诉首钢总公司信息公开案] (Beijing City Shijingshan District Trial Court, June 24, 2016). https://wenshu.court.gov.cn/ (registration needed for access) (accessed between February 21, 2025 and March 31, 2025).

Yuan Wubing v. Qidong Municipal Bureau of Civil Affairs [袁武兵诉启东市民政局信息公开案] (Jiangsu Province Haimen City Trial Court, December 4, 2017) https://wenshu.court.gov.cn/ (registration needed for access) (accessed between February 21, 2025 and March 31, 2025).

Yue Zhiqiang v. Tieling Municipal Bureau of Public Security [岳志强诉铁岭市公安局信息公开案] (Liaoning Province Changtu County Trial Court, September 12, 2019) https://wenshu.court.gov.cn/ (registration needed for access) (accessed between February 21, 2025 and March 31, 2025).

Zeng Huiyuan v. Guiyang City Yunyan District People's Government [曾惠袁诉贵阳市云岩区人民政府信息公开案] (Guizhou Province High Court, August

30, 2017) https://wenshu.court.gov.cn/ (registration needed for access) (accessed between February 21, 2025 and March 31, 2025).

Zeng Lingxin v. China Telecom Yancheng Branch [曾令鑫诉中国电信股份有限公司盐城分公司信息公开案] (Jiangsu Province Yancheng City Intermediate Court, March 29, 2018). https://wenshu.court.gov.cn/ (registration needed for access) (accessed between February 21, 2025 and March 31, 2025).

Zeng Qinghua v. China Mobile Jiangxi Branch [曾清华诉中国移动通信集团江西有限公司信息公开案] (Jiangxi Province High Court, April 26, 2019). https://wenshu.court.gov.cn/ (registration needed for access) (accessed between February 21, 2025 and March 31, 2025).

Zeng Qinghua v. China Mobile Shenzhen Branch [曾清华诉中国移动通信集团广东有限公司深圳分公司信息公开案] (Guangdong Province Shenzhen City Intermediate Court, October 19, 2018). https://wenshu.court.gov.cn/ (registration needed for access) (accessed between February 21, 2025 and March 31, 2025).

Zeng Xianru v. Xinjiang Uygur Autonomous Region People's Government[曾宪茹诉新疆维吾尔自治区人民政府信息公开案] (Xinjiang Uygur Autonomous Region Urumqi City Intermediate Court, September 29, 2019) https://wenshu.court.gov.cn/ (registration needed for access) (accessed between February 21, 2025 and March 31, 2025).

Zeng Yuzhong v. Jintang County Bureau of Development and Reform and Chengdu Municipal Commission for Development and Reform [曾玉忠诉金堂县发展和改革局与成都市发展和改革委员会信息公开案] (Sichuan Province Pengzhou City Trial Court, June 12, 2018) https://wenshu.court.gov.cn/ (registration needed for access) (accessed between February 21, 2025 and March 31, 2025).

Zhang Aihong and Kang Yuqiu v. Hengshui Municipal Center of Land Banking [张爱红与康玉秋诉衡水市土地储备中心信息公开案] (Hebei Province Hengshui City Intermediate Court, December 26, 2019) https://wenshu.court.gov.cn/ (registration needed for access) (accessed between February 21, 2025 and March 31, 2025).

Zhang Baozhen, et al. v. Luoyang National High and New Technology Industries Development Zone Management Commission [张保珍等诉洛阳高新技术产业开发区管理委员会信息公开案] (Henan Province High Court, November 23, 2020) https://wenshu.court.gov.cn/ (registration needed for access) (accessed between February 21, 2025 and March 31, 2025).

Zhang Daxue v. Shijiazhuang City Qiaoxi District People's Government [张大雪诉石家庄市桥西区人民政府信息公开案] (Hebei Province Shijiazhuang City Qiaoxi District Trial Court, March 28, 2018) https://wenshu.court.gov.cn/ (registration needed for access) (accessed between February 21, 2025 and March 31, 2025).

Zhang Guoping v. Shanghai City Minxin District Commission for Development and Reform [张国平诉上海市闵行区发展与改革委员会信息公开案] (Shanghai City No. 1 Intermediate Court, March 13, 2018) https://wenshu.court.gov.cn/ (registration needed for access) (accessed between February 21, 2025 and March 31, 2025).

Zhang Guoshun v. Queshan County People's Government [张国顺诉确山县人民政府信息公开案] (Henan Province Zhumadian City Intermediate Court, November 28, 2018) https://wenshu.court.gov.cn/ (registration needed for access) (accessed between February 21, 2025 and March 31, 2025).

Zhang Hongxin v. Shandong Province Laixi Municipal People's Government and Shandong Province Qingdao Municipal People's Government [张红信诉山东省莱西市人民政府与山东省青岛市人民政府信息公开案] (China Supreme Court, March 25, 2020) https://wenshu.court.gov.cn/ (registration needed for access) (accessed between February 21, 2025 and March 31, 2025).

Zhang Hua v. Hunan Provincial People's Government [张华诉湖南省人民政府信息公开案] (Hunan Province High Court, April 11, 2016) https://wenshu.court.gov.cn/ (registration needed for access) (accessed between February 21, 2025 and March 31, 2025).

Zhang Jianguo v. Stage Grid Zhuzhou Power Supply Company [张建国诉国网湖南省电力有限公司株洲供电分公司信息公开案] (Hunan Province Zhuzhou City Hetang District Trial Court, April 28, 2018). https://wenshu.court.gov.cn/ (registration needed for access) (accessed between February 21, 2025 and March 31, 2025).

Zhang Jinfeng v. Huinan County Fumin Zhen People's Government [张金凤诉辉南县抚民镇人民政府信息公开案] (Jili Province Huinan County Trial Court, April 24, 2018) https://wenshu.court.gov.cn/ (registration needed for access) (accessed between February 21, 2025 and March 31, 2025).

Zhang Jinzhu v. Beijing Shijingshan District Environmental Sanitation Service Center [张金柱诉北京市石景山区环境卫生服务中心信息公开案] (Beijing City No.1 Intermediate Court, May 25, 2018). https://wenshu.court.gov.cn/ (registration needed for access) (accessed between February 21, 2025 and March 31, 2025).

Zhang Jiying v. Tianjin City Xiqing District People's Government [张季英诉天津市西青区人民政府信息公开案] (Tianjin City No. 1 Intermediate Court, May 31, 2018) https://wenshu.court.gov.cn/ (registration needed for access) (accessed between February 21, 2025 and March 31, 2025).

Zhang Lilei v. Langfang City Qingquan Water Supply Company [张立雷诉廊坊市清泉供水有限责任公司信息公开案] (Hebei Province Langfang City Guangyang District Trial Court, December 17, 2018). https://wenshu.court.gov.cn/ (registration needed for access) (accessed between February 21, 2025 and March 31, 2025).

Zhang Meixiang v. Haiyang Municipal People's Government [张梅香诉海阳市人民政府信息公开案] (Shandong Province Yantai City Intermediate Court, November 6, 2019) https://wenshu.court.gov.cn/ (registration needed for access) (accessed between February 21, 2025 and March 31, 2025).

Zhang Mingwang v. Guangshan County People's Government [张明旺诉光山县人民政府信息公开案] (Henan Province Xinyang City Intermediate Court, September 14, 2020) https://wenshu.court.gov.cn/ (registration needed for access) (accessed between February 21, 2025 and March 31, 2025).

Zhang Qiang v. South China University of Technology [张强诉华南理工大学信息公开案] (Guangdong Province Guangzhou Railway Transport No.1 Court, July 14, 2017). https://wenshu.court.gov.cn/ (registration needed for access) (accessed between February 21, 2025 and March 31, 2025).

Zhang Shiyan v. Suzhou University [张世炎诉苏州大学信息公开案] (Jiangsu Province High Court, July 30, 2017). https://wenshu.court.gov.cn/ (registration needed for access) (accessed between February 21, 2025 and March 31, 2025).

Zhang Shuanjun v. Mianchi County People's Government [张拴军诉渑池县人民政府信息公开案] (Henan Province Sanmenxia City Intermediate Court, May 23, 2018) https://wenshu.court.gov.cn/ (registration needed for access) (accessed between February 21, 2025 and March 31, 2025).

Zhang Tao v. Fujian Provincial People's Government [张涛诉福建省人民政府信息公开案] (Fujian Province Fuzhou City Intermediate Court, November 17, 2015) https://wenshu.court.gov.cn/ (registration needed for access) (accessed between February 21, 2025 and March 31, 2025).

Zhang Weiyan v. Liaoyuan Municipal People's Government [张维艳诉辽源市人民政府信息公开案] (Jilin Province Liaoyuan City Intermediate Court, September 19, 2019) https://wenshu.court.gov.cn/ (registration needed for access) (accessed between February 21, 2025 and March 31, 2025).

Zhang Xihua v. Tangshan City Lu'nan District People's Government [张锡华诉唐山市路南区人民政府信息公开案] (Hebei Province Tangshan City Lu'nan District Trial Court, December 11, 2017) https://wenshu.court.gov.cn/ (registration needed for access) (accessed between February 21, 2025 and March 31, 2025).

Zhang Xiongwei v. Shanghai City Hongkou District People's Government [张雄伟诉上海市虹口区人民政府信息公开案] (Shanghai City No.2 Intermediate Court, November 8, 2017) https://wenshu.court.gov.cn/ (registration needed for access) (accessed between February 21, 2025 and March 31, 2025).

Zhang Xiuchun v. Mianyang City Anzhou District People's Government and Mianyang Municipal People's Government [张秀春诉绵阳市安州区人民政府与绵阳市人民政府信息公开案] (Sichuan Province Mianyang City Intermediate Court, December 28, 2017) https://wenshu.court.gov.cn/ (registration

needed for access) (accessed between February 21, 2025 and March 31, 2025).

Zhang Xujiang v. Hanzhong City Nanzheng District People's Government [张旭江诉汉中市南郑区人民政府信息公开案] (Shaanxi Province Hanzhong City Intermediate Court, January 28, 2021) https://wenshu.court.gov.cn/ (registration needed for access) (accessed between February 21, 2025 and March 31, 2025).

Zhang Yicai v. Beijing City Miyun District Bureau of Public Security and Beijing Municipal Bureau of Public Security [张益才诉北京市公安局密云分局与北京市公安局信息公开案] (Beijing City Dongcheng District Trial Court, June 18, 2019) https://wenshu.court.gov.cn/ (registration needed for access) (accessed between February 21, 2025 and March 31, 2025).

Zhang Yuangui v. Chongqing City Yongchuan District People's Government [张元贵诉重庆市永川区人民政府信息公开案] (Chongqing City No.5 Intermediate Court, May 9, 2020) https://wenshu.court.gov.cn/ (registration needed for access) (accessed between February 21, 2025 and March 31, 2025).

Zhang Yuxiang v. Changsha City Yuelu District People's Government and Changsha Municipal People's Government [张宇香诉长沙市岳麓区人民政府与长沙市人民政府信息公开案] (Hunan Province High Court, June 6, 2017] https://wenshu.court.gov.cn/ (registration needed for access) (accessed between February 21, 2025 and March 31, 2025).

Zhang Zheng v. Mian County People's Government [张政诉勉县人民政府信息公开案] (Shaanxi Province Hanzhong City Intermediate Court, May 24, 2018) https://wenshu.court.gov.cn/ (registration needed for access) (accessed between February 21, 2025 and March 31, 2025).

Zhang Zhicheng v. Tianjian City Heping District Bureau of Public Security and Tianjin Municipal Bureau of Public Security [张志成诉天津市公安局和平分局与天津市公安局信息公开案] (Tianjin City Heping District Trial Court, April 8, 2018) https://wenshu.court.gov.cn/ (registration needed for access) (accessed between February 21, 2025 and March 31, 2025).

Zhang Zhihua v. Shifang Municipal People's Government [张志华诉什邡市人民政府信息公开案] (Sichuan Province High Court, December 9, 2019) https://wenshu.court.gov.cn/ (registration needed for access) (accessed between February 21, 2025 and March 31, 2025).

Zhang Zhiyun v. Jiangsu Province Department of Natural Resources and Jiangsu Provincial People's Government [张志云诉江苏省自然资源厅与江苏省人民政府信息公开案] (Jiangsu Province Nanjing City Intermediate Court, December 10, 2020) https://wenshu.court.gov.cn/ (registration needed for access) (accessed between February 21, 2025 and March 31, 2025).

Zhang Zongfa v. Jiangsu Changshu Sino French Water Company [张宗法诉常熟中法水务有限公司信息公开案](Jiangsu Province Suzhou City Intermediate

Court, March 10, 2017). https://wenshu.court.gov.cn/ (registration needed for access) (accessed between February 21, 2025 and March 31, 2025).

Zhang Zongfa v. State Grid Changshu City Electricity Supply Company [张宗法诉国网江苏省电力公司常熟市供电公司信息公开案] (Jiangsu Province Suzhou City Intermediate Court, February 28, 2017). https://wenshu.court.gov.cn/ (registration needed for access) (accessed between February 21, 2025 and March 31, 2025).

Zhang Zongqing v. Tianjin City Xiqing District People's Government [张宗清诉天津市西青区人民政府信息公开案] (Tianjin City No.1 Intermediate Court, January 30, 2018) https://wenshu.court.gov.cn/ (registration needed for access) (accessed between February 21, 2025 and March 31, 2025).

Zhao Donghua v. Yibin Municipal People's Government [赵东华诉宜宾市人民政府信息公开案] (Sichuan Province Yibin City Intermediate Court, April 22, 2019) https://wenshu.court.gov.cn/ (registration needed for access) (accessed between February 21, 2025 and March 31, 2025).

Zhao Fuqian and Zhao Longsheng v. Xiuwen County People's Government [赵福黔与赵龙生诉修文县人民政府信息公开案] (Guizhou Province High Court, December 15, 2014) https://wenshu.court.gov.cn/ (registration needed for access) (accessed between February 21, 2025 and March 31, 2025).

Zhao Guanghai v. Chongqing Municipal People's Government [赵光海诉重庆市人民政府信息公开案] (Chongqing City No. 5 Intermediate Court, April 21, 2017) https://wenshu.court.gov.cn/ (registration needed for access) (accessed between February 21, 2025 and March 31, 2025).

Zhao Jihua v. Shanghai City Jing'an District Bureau of Affordable Housing and Shanghai City Jing'an District People's Government [赵继华诉上海市静安区住房保障和房屋管理局与上海市静安区人民政府信息公开案] (Shanghai City Railway Transport Trial Court, October 30, 2017) https://wenshu.court.gov.cn/ (registration needed for access) (accessed between February 21, 2025 and March 31, 2025).

Zhao Jihua v. Shanghai City Jing'an District People's Government [赵继华诉上海市静安区人民政府信息公开案] (Shanghai City No.2 Intermediate Court, December 20, 2017) https://wenshu.court.gov.cn/ (registration needed for access) (accessed between February 21, 2025 and March 31, 2025).

Zhao Liang v. Hunan Provincial Department of Environmental Protection [赵亮诉湖南省环境保护厅信息公开案] (Hunan Province Changsha City Intermediate Court, January 21, 2016) https://wenshu.court.gov.cn/ (registration needed for access) (accessed between February 21, 2025 and March 31, 2025).

Zhao Lichun v. Xiamen Municipal Bureau of Public Security [赵利春诉厦门市公安局信息公开案] (Fujian Province Xiamen City Intermediate Court, January 8, 2019) https://wenshu.court.gov.cn/ (registration needed for access) (accessed between February 21, 2025 and March 31, 2025).

Zhao Rui v. Hanzhong City Hantai District Bureau of Transportation [赵蕊诉汉中市汉台区交通运输局信息公开案] (Shaanxi Province Hanzhong City Hantai District Trial Court, September 5, 2018) https://wenshu.court.gov.cn/ (registration needed for access) (accessed between February 21, 2025 and March 31, 2025).

Zhao Shuiyun and Shi Pengwen v. Quwo County People's Government and Linfen Municipal People's Government [赵水云与石朋文诉曲沃县人民政府与临汾市人民政府信息公开案] (Shanxi Province Yuncheng City Intermediate Court, November 9, 2018) https://wenshu.court.gov.cn/ (registration needed for access) (accessed between February 21, 2025 and March 31, 2025).

Zheng Guoyong v. Longyan Municipal People's Government [郑国勇诉龙岩市人民政府信息公开案] (Fujian Province Sanming City Intermediate Court, December 26, 2017) https://wenshu.court.gov.cn/ (registration needed for access) (accessed between February 21, 2025 and March 31, 2025).

Zheng Junhai v. Pingdingshan Municipal People's Government [郑军海诉平顶山市人民政府信息公开案] (Henan Province Luohe City Intermediate Court, December 3, 2018) https://wenshu.court.gov.cn/ (registration needed for access) (accessed between February 21, 2025 and March 31, 2025).

Zheng Mingjie v. China Internet Network Information Center [郑敏杰诉中国互联网络信息中心信息公开案] (Beijing City No.1 Intermediate Court, March 22, 2019). https://wenshu.court.gov.cn/ (registration needed for access) (accessed between February 21, 2025 and March 31, 2025).

Zheng Wangjie v. Xinzheng Municipal People's Government [郑王杰诉新郑市人民政府信息公开案] (Henan Province High Court, September 22, 2017) https://wenshu.court.gov.cn/ (registration needed for access) (accessed between February 21, 2025 and March 31, 2025).

Zheng Xinming, et al. v. Fuzhou Municipal Bureau of Natural Resources and Planning and Fuzhou Municipal People's Government [郑新明等诉福州市自然资源和规划局与福州市人民政府信息公开案] (Fujian Province Fuzhou City Cangshan District Trial Court, June 18, 2020) https://wenshu.court.gov.cn/ (registration needed for access) (accessed between February 21, 2025 and March 31, 2025).

Zheng Yuexiang v. Xiamen Municipal People's Government [郑月香诉厦门市人民政府信息公开案] (Fujian Province Zhangzhou City Intermediate Court, May 31, 2017) https://wenshu.court.gov.cn/ (registration needed for access) (accessed between February 21, 2025 and March 31, 2025).

Zhong Jiazi v. Jiangsu Provincial Department of Civil Affairs and Ministry of Civil Affairs [钟家梓诉江苏省民政厅与中华人民共和国民政部信息公开案] (Jiangsu Province Nanjing City Intermediate Court, August 12, 2020) https://wenshu.court.gov.cn/ (registration needed for access) (accessed between February 21, 2025 and March 31, 2025).

Zhou Jianguo v. Jiangsu Changshu Sino French Water Company [周建国诉江苏常熟中法水务有限公司信息公开案] (Jiangsu Province Suzhou City Intermediate Court, March 10, 2017). https://wenshu.court.gov.cn/ (registration needed for access) (accessed between February 21, 2025 and March 31, 2025).

Zhou Jianguo v. State Grid Changshu Power Supply Company [周建国诉国网江苏省电力公司常熟市供电公司信息公开案] (Jiangsu Province Suzhou City Intermediate Court, February 28, 2017). https://wenshu.court.gov.cn/ (registration needed for access) (accessed between February 21, 2025 and March 31, 2025).

Zhou Xin'ai v. Beijing Municipal People's Government [周新爱诉北京市人民政府信息公开案] (Beijing City No. 2 Intermediate Court, December 28, 2018) https://wenshu.court.gov.cn/ (registration needed for access) (accessed between February 21, 2025 and March 31, 2025).

Zhou Yang v. Wuhan City Jiang'an District People's Government and Wuhan Municipal People's Government [周洋诉武汉市江岸区人民政府与武汉市人民政府信息公开案] (Wuhan City Railway Intermediate Court, October 31, 2018) https://wenshu.court.gov.cn/ (registration needed for access) (accessed between February 21, 2025 and March 31, 2025).

Zhou Yong v. The First Affiliated Hospital of Zhengzhou University [周勇诉郑州大学第一附属医院信息公开案] (Henan Province Zhengzhou City Zhongyuan District Trial Court, June 20, 2018). https://wenshu.court.gov.cn/ (registration needed for access) (accessed between February 21, 2025 and March 31, 2025).

Zhu Guohong v. Wuxi Municipal Bureau of Land and Resources [朱国洪诉无锡市国土资源局信息公开案] (Jiangsu Province Wuxi City Liangxi District Trial Court, July 2, 2018) https://wenshu.court.gov.cn/ (registration needed for access) (accessed between February 21, 2025 and March 31, 2025).

Zhu Pingguo v. Yichang City Xiling District People's Government and Yichang Municipal People's Government [朱平国诉宜昌市西陵区人民政府与宜昌市人民政府信息公开案] (Hubei Province Yichang City Intermediate Court, December 2, 2020) https://wenshu.court.gov.cn/ (registration needed for access) (accessed between February 21, 2025 and March 31, 2025).

Zhu Yanli v. Tenchong Municipal People's Government and Baoshan Municipal People's Government [朱艳丽诉腾冲市人民政府与保山市人民政府信息公开案] (Yunnan Province Baoshan City Intermediate Court, December 24, 2019) https://wenshu.court.gov.cn/ (registration needed for access) (accessed between February 21, 2025 and March 31, 2025).

Zhu Yanli v. Tengchong Municipal People's Government [朱艳丽诉腾冲市人民政府信息公开案] (Yunnan Province Baoshan City Intermediate Court, June 12, 2020) https://wenshu.court.gov.cn/ (registration needed for access) (accessed between February 21, 2025 and March 31, 2025).

Zhu Yanli v. Tengchong Municipal Public Security Bureau[朱艳丽诉腾冲市公安局政府信息公开案] (Yunnan Province Baoshan City Intermediate Court, June 5, 2019) https://wenshu.court.gov.cn/ (registration needed for access) (accessed between February 21, 2025 and March 31, 2025).

Zhu Yuangang v. Guangyuan City Lizhou District People's Government [朱元刚诉广元市利州区人民政府信息公开案] (Sichuan Province Guangyuan City Intermediate Court, December 4, 2017) https://wenshu.court.gov.cn/ (registration needed for access) (accessed between February 21, 2025 and March 31, 2025).

Zhuhai Special Economic Zone White Lotus Industrial Development Corporation v. Zhuhai Municipal Bureau of Land and Resources [珠海经济特区白莲实业发展总公司诉珠海市国土资源局信息公开案] (Guangdong Province Zhuhai City Intermediate Court, June 19, 2017) https://wenshu.court.gov.cn/ (registration needed for access) (accessed between February 21, 2025 and March 31, 2025).

Zou Huinan v.State-Owned Assets Supervision and Administration Commission of the State Council [邹慧楠诉国务院国有资产监督管理委员会信息公开案] (Beijing City No.1 Intermediate Court, December 28, 2015) https://wenshu.court.gov.cn/ (registration needed for access) (accessed between February 21, 2025 and March 31, 2025).

Zuo Dengfeng v. Tongling City Yi'an District Bureau of Natural Resources and Planning [左登峰诉铜陵市自然资源和规划局义安区分局信息公开案] (Anhui Province Tongling City Yi'an District Trial Court, May 26, 2023) https://wenshu.court.gov.cn/ (registration needed for access) (accessed between February 21, 2025 and March 31, 2025).

Zuo Qizhong v. Chongqing City Changshou District Bureau of Public Security [左其中诉重庆市长寿区公安局政府信息公开案] (Chongqing City Changshou District Trial Court, August 30, 2017) https://wenshu.court.gov.cn/ (registration needed for access) (accessed between February 21, 2025 and March 31, 2025).

OGI-Related Court Cases Compiled from Beida Fabao and Other Sources

Baltimore Sun Co. v. Ehrlich, 437 F.3d 410 (4th Cir. Feb. 15, 2006).

Bao v. Shanghai Yangpu District Bureau of Housing (Shanghai, 2010).

Bingting Wang v. Shanghai Hongkou District People's Government (Shanghai, 2009).

Department of Air Force v. Rose, 425 U.S. 352 (1976).

Houchins v. KQED, 438 U.S. 1 (1978).

Jia Lei v. Shanghai Jing'an District People's Government (Shanghai, 2010).

Jianguo Xu v. Huangzhou District Transportation Bureau (Huanggang, Hubei Province, 2008).

Jianqiu Zhang, et al. v. Chaling County Bureau of Finance (Chaling, Hunan Province, 2008).

Kai Li v. Sichuan Provincial Bureau of Education (Chengdu, Sichuan Province, 2009).

Lan Xie v. Tangshan Lunan District Development and Reform Bureau (Tangshan, Hebei Province, 2012).

Lan Xie v. Tangshan Municipal Land and Resources Bureau (Tangshan, Hebei Province, 2012).

Lee v. Minner, 458 F. 3d 194 (3d Cir.2006).

Lianmian Kang, et al. v. Guangzhou Municipal Bureau of Labor and Social Security (Guangzhou, Guangdong Province, 2007).

Milner v. Department of the Navy, 131 S. Ct. 1259 (2011).

NARA v. Favish, 541 U.S. 157 (2004).

Pell v. Procunier, 417 U.S. 817 (1974).

Press-Enterprise v. Riverside Superior Court, 478 U.S. 1 (1986).

Qiuqin Xu v. Shanghai Pudong District Construction and Transportation Commission (Shanghai, 2009).

Richmond Newspapers v. Virginia, 448 U.S. 555 (1980).

Ronghua Zhang, et al. v. Zhengzhou Huiji District Human Resources and Social Security Bureau (Zhengzhou, Henan Province, 2010).

Saxbe v. Washington Post, 417 U.S. 843 (1974).

Shanghai Shitou Dyestuff Company v. Shanghai Municipal Science and Technology Commission (Shanghai, 2008).

Wang v. Shanghai Municipal Bureau of Human Resources and Social Security (Shanghai, 2011).

Xiangtan University Law Professors v. Xiangtan Municipal People's Government (Xiangtan, Hunan Province, 2008).

Yan Li v. Jiyuan Municipal Bureau of Housing and Urban-Rural Construction (Jiyuan, Hunan Province, 2010).

Yaofang Xu, et al. v. Yuyao Municipal People's Government (Yuyao, Zhejiang Province, 2008).

Youjian Huang, et al. v Rucheng Municipal People's Government (Rucheng, Hunan Province, 2008).

Yousheng Lu v. Shanghai Municipal Bureau of Industry and Commerce (Shanghai, 2009).

Yulai Yuan v. Anhui Provincial People's Government (2008).

Zhang, et al. v. Shanghai Bureau of Planning, Land and Resources (Shanghai, 2010).

Kolibri 360 GmbH
Ferdinand-Jühlke-Straße 7
99095 Erfurt, Deutschland
produktsicherheit@kolibri360.de